Gabbys

WORDSPELLER ESL

Spanish to English Dictionary

2-Color First Condensed Edition

- Spell your word by the way it sounds using Spanish or English letters

- Escriba mal su palabra en Español o Inglés para encontrar la palabra correcta en Inglés

- Cross-references your word with other words which may sound the same or are spelled similar (is it petal or pedal or peddle?)

- Provides all potential suffix endings associated with your word

- Gabbys es una herramienta de recursos de aprendizaje en la que cada palabra raíz en inglés que encuentres proporcionará homófonos, palabras confusas, sufijos y prefijos

- Provides prefixes with definitions that can be associated with your word

Diane M. Frank

Search for your misspelled word using either Spanish or English alphabet letters. Over 100,000 entries of commonly used American English words are housed within this dictionary with multiple misspellings per word based upon their phonetic sound. Brief definitions allow for quick referral to the proper word you wish to use allowing you access to a standard dictionary for further definition. Extensive cross-referencing allows for words that are either similar in meaning, spelling or sound. Is it 'petal' or 'pedal' or 'peddle'? Spanish letters are cross-interpreted with American English spellings as well. Spanish words such as 'jiubili, yubili, llubili' sound like 'jubilee' in English. Asian vowel sounds such as 'lau, low or loh' closely resemble the word, 'law' in English. Many vowel sound combinations are associated with many other languages and also transposed onto English misspelled words to simplify location of a correctly spelled word.

2-color editions have misspelled words printed in a second color to allow differentiation between a properly spelled word and a misspelled word for those challenged with searching in dictionaries. All available prefixes are defined. Each correctly spelled word lists all potential suffix endings as well. Use this resource learning tool as a bridge to go from the sound of your word to a standard dictionary if further comprehension is necessary. Proper nouns are listed only if common to everyday communication and if they are cross referenced with another homophone or confusable word. Free tutorial: www.gabbyswordspeller.com/tutorial.php

NOTE: There are over 500 ways to misspell the word 'physician'. To avoid overpopulating the print edition, only 84 misspellings are entered. If you require a larger database to locate your misspelled word, the publisher recommends you try using the Apps available on all platforms.

Notice of Rights

All rights reserved. No part of this book may be reproduced, digitized, stored in a retrieval system or transmitted in any form or by any means, without the prior written permission of the publisher.

Notice of Liability

The author and publisher have made every effort to ensure the accuracy of the information herein. However, the information contained in this book is sold without warranty, either expressed or implied. Neither the author, co-author, publisher, dealers or distributors will be held liable for any mistakes.

Authored by Diane Frank
Co-Authored by Gabrielle M. Purcell
Publisher i.m.Press
Copyright © Jan, 2020 by i.m. Press Publishers
PO Box 412, Rainier, Washington 98576, USA

Library of Congress Cataloging-in-Publication Data
Library of Congress Control Number: 2020901663

Gabbys Wordspeller ESL; Spanish to English Dictionary   2-color, First Edition

Summary: Search for you misspelled word using either Spanish or English alphabet letters. Over 100,000 entries of commonly used American English words with multiple misspellings per word based upon their phonetic sound. Brief definitions allow for quick referral to the proper word you wish to use allowing you to access to a standard dictionary for further definition. Extensive cross-referencing allows for words that are either similar in meaning/sound/spelling. Is it 'petal' or 'pedal' or 'peddle'? Spanish letters are cross-interpreted with American English spellings as well. Spanish words such as 'jiubili, yubili, llubili' sound like 'jubilee' in American English. Asian vowel sounds such as 'lau, low or loh' closely resemble the word, 'law' in English. Defined Prefixes as well as all available Suffix endings for base words are easily located. Use this reference tool as a bridge to go from the sound of your word to a standard dictionary. Satisfies all common core standards. Most proper nouns are not listed unless employed in everyday use (i.e. months, days, animals, legal, medical). Dictionary is printed in a horizontal position to allow smaller hands (elementary grades 3-6) to quickly peruse this reference book.

For a vertical (standard layout) use "Wordspeller ESL; Phonetic Dictionary", ISBN 978-0-9830381-5-3. To contact the publisher please visit www.impresspublishers.com / www.word-speller.com / www.gabbyswordspeller.com
Keywords: wordspeller,word speller,ESL,ESL dictionary,wordspeller ESL,phonetic dictionary,spanish dictionary,spanish english,EFL dictionary,EFOL dictionary,ESOL dictionary,language,spanish language,elementary dictionary,spelling dictionary

ISBN 978-0-9801025-3-6
Manufactured in the United States of America
1st Edition

Table of Contents

Author's Word	iv - v
Foreword	vi
Introduction	vii
Traduccion	viii
Methodology	ix
Legend	1
Dictionary	2-551

AUTHOR'S WORD

Correspondence between the Author of "Gabbys Wordspeller ESL Dictionary", Diane Frank and a Lexicographer who was a world traveled speaker on 'Dictionaries'.

In 2008, Diane Frank presented a copy of the first edition of "Gabbys Wordspeller & Phonetic Dictionary" to a local school district in Yelm, WA. This is her experience...

The Yelm Curriculum Director denied acceptance of Gabbys for the Yelm School District based upon the fact that they interpreted the dictionary as not being a dictionary at all. As well, A Professional Trade Committee Review turned down my book as inappropriate for bookstores because it didn't reflect any of the standardized requirements for acceptance. In my frustration at being compared to standard books when my book is anything but standard, I contacted Lexicographer, Professor Lynch, of Rutgers University for professional evaluation as to whether my phonetic dictionary should be classified as a dictionary. Lynch is world traveled giving lectures concerning 'dictionary firsts' predominately in the 18th century. He enlightens as to the 'first' dictionaries and controversy surrounding a 'first' of any reference tool that could be classified as a dictionary. Professor Lynch provided numerous responses, one of which is listed below;

> _Diane_: "I have published the first known Phonetic Dictionary. I was just crucified by a Tradebook Review committee and I'm challenged in educating people as to what a phonetic dictionary is."
>
> _Jack_: "Well, I'm not sure what I can do from here, though you should note that the phrase "phonetic dictionary" has been in use for more than 150 years. In 1855, for instance, there appeared The American Phonetic Dictionary of the English Language."
>
> _Diane_: "This book has been accused of not being a REAL dictionary (by a few)."
>
> _Jack_: "Then you should let them know that "dictionary" has had a wide range of applications over the centuries. Since 1631, the word "dictionary" has been used with this meaning:
>
>> By extension: A book of information or reference on any subject or branch of knowledge, the items of which are arranged in alphabetical order; an alphabetical encyclopædia: as a Dictionary of Architecture, Biography, Geography, of the Bible, of Christian Antiquities, of Dates, etc.
>> ~~~
>> There are all sorts of reference works we'd be likely to call other things -- encyclopedias, gazetteers, and so on -- that have been called dictionaries by their makers. In these cases, the essential sense 'word-book' is supplanted by the accidental one of 'reference book in alphabetical order' arising out of the alphabetical arrangement used in modern word-books.
>
> (Both quotations come from the Oxford English Dictionary) So good luck in your squabbles with the critics, and don't let narrow-minded criticisms get you down."

Author Personal Story

My daughter and I shared a height of inspiration one night which ran contrary to what was happening in our lives at the time. Because of this night I have come to thank my bicycle accident which I experienced when riding home from college where I was finishing my degree. If not for this accident, which herniated discs in my back and left me nearly debilitated for 1.5 years, this book would not exist today.

During this time of debilitation, I watched my life fall apart and my career come to a screeching halt. It was in this span of time that my daughter, Gabby (who had been diagnosed at 8 with dyslexia) had my full attention one night when she became verbally irate at having to write a two paragraph report for her high school class.

I observed helplessly from my bed as she slumped over in my office chair literally crying so hard it was as if her self-esteem had suffered its last straw and was flowing out with her tears. She cried that this task would take her all night and that she had so much other homework still to accomplish. This was her first month as a freshman in high school. And she was right, we had been going through this hell since she started kindergarten and her reading skills were still below a fifth grade level.

Never had I felt so strongly the brutality of feeling so hopeless and powerless all at the same time in my entire life. I was a single mother and my two children meant everything in the world to me. And there we found ourselves, that evening in September 1997, at the lowest point in our lives, all hopes that we would be successful at anything…EVER…was drained…gone! It was in this moment of quiet, as the two of us sat and wept, exhausted with the thoughts of this helplessness in resolving our dilemmas, that Gabby suddenly burst out with the only possible intelligent solution. "Mom! Why don't you write me a dictionary that spells the words the way I hear them so that I can write?" I was stunned, such a sudden change in attitude. So swift the change that I was taken aback and could only exuberantly and decidedly reply, "Okay, I will".

And that's what I did fulltime while laid up in my bed watching the rest of the world go by at the peak of my life. A kindred soul thought my endeavor worthy enough to purchase me Macintosh's first powerbook so I could write in a reclined posture. I kept up the "good" work and managed finally to finish the first dictionary eleven years later.

I wish to thank…of course, my children, Gabby and Will who were forced to deal with our poverty as I maniacally typed away the days which turned into years.

My further inspiration came in 2008 after finally publishing the first "Gabbys Wordspeller Phonetic Dictionary". I had traveled to Mexico to rest for a few weeks and visit a friend. I was approached by the Club de Lioness (Lions Club) in Manzanillo, Mexico to purchase dictionaries for those in need. Soon thereafter a professor who taught at the Universidad de Colima took my dictionary to show to the publication office which printed/distributed textbooks. After a mere 5 days they phoned us up to come to meet them in Colima. Upon my arrival the publication officer was adamant in wishing to lease rights to print the book for distribution to their universities in over 30 Latin countries.

While awaiting to hear back from the university, I had made an observation within those 5 days of over 40 Latino adults and children who had explored the dictionary at the ESL school and witnessed them struggling to transpose the sounds of their letters from Spanish to English which appeared just short of burdensome. But by their being so enthralled with the dictionary I decided to get back to work and write another dictionary. My intention was to make all those transformations for them as well as include Spanish words to replace English words.

This dictionary you are holding in your hands now is the result of that work. All the Wordspeller Dictionaries were built letter by letter without a methodology to work with. All methodologies considered would reveal too many choices and for those who are swimming in a sea of letters, the most relevant results are absolutely essential. If you cannot find your word, please keep in mind there are 500 ways to spell the word 'physician' and this dictionary only allowed 84 misspellings. Gabbys Wordspeller is now celebrating her 12th birthday as of February, 2020 and she's proud to be in over 100 countries and over 900 school districts. She has grown so big that she was turned into an App on all Smartphone and Tablet devices in 2010.

Thank you to everyone who supported the belief that this unique resource tool could be helpful in bridging the communication divide that results from using a language that has the most shallow orthography in the world!

This dictionary does have a larger database housed in an App for digital devices.
Contact the publisher for more information or visit:
word-speller.com / gabbyswordspeller.com
A free version is available at phoneticdictionary.com

FOREWORD

The literal meaning of the word *dyslexia* – from its Greek roots is – "difficulty with words"

Dr. Maryanne Wolfe, author of *Proust and the Squid: The Story and Science of the Reading Brain*, explains, "the more you know about a word, the faster you can read it." Dr. Virginia Berninger, of the University of Washington, has demonstrated that reading fluency is enhanced for dyslexic students through instruction that focuses on the interrelation between the three "forms" shared by each word: the meaning of the word, its visual appearance, and its sound.

And here is where dyslexics encounter their biggest barrier: spelling. The most persistent and pervasive symptom of dyslexia is an orthographic barrier; they have difficulty remembering the conventional spelling of phonetically irregular words. Many educators focus on intensive teaching of phonics, as this provides one avenue for decoding many of the simpler words encountered by beginning readers. English is not a phonetic language, but rather a polyglot and amalgam of words drawn from different languages, often retaining spellings that reflect histories and pronunciations long forgotten.

If you can't spell a word, you cannot find it in a dictionary.

Through brain scans, Dr. Sally Shaywitz of Yale University has shown that dyslexic readers typically underutilize the "visual word form area" of the brain – the part of the visual cortex believed to be involved in instantaneous recognition of whole words. This is the part of the brain that probably stores a picture of the right letters arranged in the right order, the part that is engaged when you choose the correct spelling because it just *looks* right to you.

It isn't that dyslexic writers are unable to spell a word; with their creative problem-solving strengths, they can easily spell the same word half a dozen different ways. As Andrew Jackson once said, "its a damn poor mind that can think of only one way to spell a word." The problem is in figuring out which spelling is the one that everyone else will use and understand.

This is where the most powerful tool – the dictionary – is also the most inaccessible. Because if we err in guessing the first 2 or 3 letters of the word, we will never find it.

And here is where *Gabbys Wordspeller* becomes indispensible – it provides the key to the door that opens the dictionary. It is where all those phonetic decoding skills emphasized by well-meaning primary school teachers can finally be brought to fruition: *krecher* may not be a word, but it *is* a spelling, albeit an incorrect one. In a regular dictionary, it leads us to the Kremlin, which is not where we wanted to go. But Gabbys phonetic dictionary gives us the answer in exactly the place we have gone to find it: "creature."

Suname leads to tsunami. *Fanomanen* takes us to phenomenon. *Ekselerate* turns into accelerate. And pretty soon, the world of words is ours for the taking. If we already know the meaning of the word, that is all that is needed. The correct spelling is there, in a form that we can copy and use. If our trip to the dictionary is also a search for meaning, or etymology, or information as to usage, or a set of synonyms, then *Gabbys* has opened the door for us. By providing the spelling we need, we can access the larger dictionary or thesaurus which can provide us with whatever information we seek.

This reference book should be in every school library, in every classroom, and at home on every student's desk. It is the key to independence for every learner.

-Abigail Marshall, Author of *The Everything Parent's Guide to Children with Dyslexia* and *When Your Child Has ... Dyslexia*
She also manages the Dyslexia the Gift site for Davis Dyslexia Association Int'l

Introduction

If you do not know the first 2-3 letters your word starts with how can you find it in a dictionary?

Over 100,000 entries of commonly used American English words are housed within this dictionary with multiple misspellings per word based upon their phonetic sound. Find your word using Spanish or English misspellings and transposed Asian vowel sounds. Brief definitions allow you to quickly see which word you wish to use; is it 'pedal', 'peddle' or 'petal'? You will then be able to access to a standard dictionary for further definition.

- Extensive cross-referencing allows for words that are either similar in meaning, spelling or sound.
- Homophones and confusable words listed with each root word (if similar in sound or spelling).
- Spanish letters are transposed with American English letter sounds.
- Spanish letters such as 'jiubili, yubili, llubili' sound like 'jubilee'.
- Asian vowel sounds such as 'lau, low or loh' closely resemble the word, 'law'.
- Many vowel sound combinations are associated with many other languages and are transposed into English misspelled words to simplify location of a correctly spelled word.
- Satisfies all common core standards
- All available prefixes are defined
- All potential suffix endings are listed with each root word.
- Use this learning resource tool as a 'bridge' to go from the sound of your word to a definition.

2-color editions show misspelled words in a second color to quickly locate a correctly spelled word allowing for those challenged with searching in dictionaries (e.g. lau, law).

Gabbys Wordspeller Dictionaries are currently being used:

> - In ALL school grade levels (primarily useful in 3rd-5th grades) in many countries
> - By challenged spellers who have Dyslexia or other spelling challenge
> - In ESL adult learning centers
> - By those new to spelling the English language (e.g. ESL, EFOL, ESOL, EFL)
> - By poets and those who have simply 'lost' the spelling of a word

Proper nouns are listed only if common to everyday communication and if they are cross referenced with another homophone or confusable word. Free tutorial is available to fully utilize this dictionary at: **www.gabbyswordspeller.com/tutorial.php**

NOTE: There are over 500 ways to misspell the word 'physician'. To avoid overpopulating the print edition, only 84 misspellings are entered. If you require a larger database to locate your misspelled word, the publisher recommends you try using the Apps available on all platforms. "Wordspeller ESL Dictionary" and "American Wordspeller ESL" Apps.

To contact the publisher - www.impresspublishers.com / www.word-speller.com / www.gabbyswordspeller.com

Traducción

al español

Si no conoces las primeras 2-3 letras una palabra comienza con cómo la encuentras en un diccionario?

Busca tu palabra mal escrita "por la forma en que suena" usando letras en español o inglés.

Gabbys Wordspeller© Dictionary te invita a escribir mal tu palabra en Español o Inglés para localizar rápidamente más de 100,000 palabras correctamente escritas. Gabbys es una herramienta de recursos de aprendizaje en la que cada palabra raíz en inglés que encuentres proporcionará homófonos, palabras confusas, sufijos y prefijos. Los editons de 2 colores enumeran palabras mal escritas en color burdeos para permitir una búsqueda más rápida (e.g. llaket, jacket).

       Localice su palabra con la ortografía española, como:
- Ais o aiz = ice/eye(s)
- Llaquet o yaket o yaquet o llaket = jacket
- Leit = late

Palabras en español como 'jiubili, yubili, llubili' suena como la palabra inglesa 'jubilee'.

Este libro se imprime en una posición horizontal para permitir que las manos más pequeñas (niños grados 3-6) naveguen más rápidamente.

Para un diseño vertical (estándar), localice **Wordspeller ESL Phonetic Dictionary**.

Esta edición está listada con la mayoría de los distribuidores de libros o se pone en contacto con el editor **wordspeller.net/contact.php**.

Este diccionario es también una aplicación que tiene una base de datos mucho más grande.
Wordspeller ESL Dictionary - App for Apple
American Wordspeller ESL - App for Android, for all digital devices.

Gabbys Methodology

Gabbys Wordspeller ESL Dictionary is a learning resource tool. An appropriate definition would be; any tool that helps teachers teach and students learn. Gabbys teaches without teaching. When you are searching for a word, your vocabulary will expand as you witness that a misspelled word can mean many other words if spelled incorrectly. And as you misspell one word after another, you learn more words because this dictionary performs:

Cross-referencing... Which word do you truly want to use?
- *emigrant* or *immigrant*?
- *gym* or *gem*?
- *marry* or *merry*?
- *scene* or *seen* or *seine*?
- *pedal* or *petal* or *peddle*?
- *carrot* or *karat* or *caret* or *carat*?

Learn how to spell the word correctly the first time you hear it!

korts, sounds like...	*bol*, sounds like it...
cords	ball
quartz	bowl
courts	bawl
quarts	bull
chords	baul

Tens of thousands of words are cross-referenced extensively throughout this dictionary.

Misspellings often involve transposing letters which are most commonly misinterpreted when listening. Some people do not annunciate their letters or may speak with an accent.

t	with	*d*	*au*	with	*ow*
b	with	*p*	*ch*	with	*sh*
ph	with	*f*	*ou*	with	*ow*
kn	with	*n*	*th*	with	*f*
qu	with	*kw*	*c*	with	*s*

Need help with adding suffixes or prefixes to the words in the dictionary?
Go to the website which has a free tutorial that shows you step-by-step.
www.gabbyswordspeller.com/tutorial.php

The tutorial on the website can be downloaded as a PowerPoint or PDF

Or, use the LEGEND on the following page!

LEGEND

love, *, ed, ving, vable, vableness, vably, vability, er, eless, ely,
A SPECIAL/ DEEP AFFECTION FOR
(or see lovely) "prefixes: un"

SUFFIXES

		ed	ving	vable	vableness	vably	vability	er	eless	ely
	Add S									
love	*									
love	loves	loved	loving	lovable	lovableness	lovably	lovability	lover	loveless	lovely

PREFIXES

love										
un + love	unloved	unloving	unlovable		unlovably	unlovability			unlovely

"prefixes: un"

funny, nnies, nnier, nniest, nniness, CREATES SMILE/ LAUGHTER, HUMOR
"prefixes: un"

	Add S		gged	gging
funny	*			
funny	lugs	lugged	lugging

After a word = add an 'S'

* = S

luceng, look(ing) / lug(gging) | look | looking | / | lug | lugging

Sometimes letters are doubled at the end when adding a suffix

a, PREFIX INDICATING "TO/ TOWARDS/ AT" MOST OFTEN MODIFIES THE WORD
absilut, absolute
ab, PREFIX INDICATING "FROM/ AWAY FROM" MOST OFTEN MODIFIES THE WORD
aback, SURPRISED
abaid, abide
abak, aback
abal, able
abalishen, abolition
abalone, A MOLLUSK
abanden, abandon
abandon,*, ned, ning, nment, LEFT ALL ALONE
abaration, aberration
abart, apart
abate,*, ed, ting, table, ement, ements, SUBSIDE/ REDUCE/ DECREASE
abatizing, appetizing
abaut, about
abawt, about
abazet, opposite
abbey,*, A MONASTERY
abbreveashen, abbreviate(tion)
abbreviate,*, ed, ting, tion, tor, tory, SHORTEN/ CONDENSE
abcent, absent
abcerd, absurd
abcint, absent
abcurd, absurd
abdicate,*, ed, ting, tion, tor, able, RELINQUISH
abdikate, abdicate
abdikeit, abdicate
abdiman, abdomen
abdomen, minal, minally, STOMACH AREA
abducate, abdicate
abduct,*, ted, ting, tee, tion, tor, KIDNAP
abdukate, abdicate
abdukt, abduct
abdumen, abdomen
abe, abbey
abed, abet
abedeinse, obedience
abedeint, obedient

abedience, obedience
abel, able / apple / appeal
abelete, ability
abelishen, abolition
abelone, abalone
abeluty, ability
aberant, aberrant
aberegine, aborigine
aberigine, aborigine
aberition, aberration
aberrant, tly, nce, ncy, DEVIATE/ STRAY AWAY FROM
aberration,*, nal, DEVIATE FROM THE STANDARD/ NORM
abes, abyss
abet,*, ted, tting, tment, BACK UP/ ENCOURAGE/ APPROVE
abetchuery, obituary
abeting, abet(tting)
abezit, opposite
abide,*, ed, er, ding, dingly, dance, STAY, WITHSTAND
abidid, abide(d)
abil, able / apple
ability, ties, CAPACITY "prefixes: dis/ in"
abilone, abalone
abirant, aberrant
abirition, aberration
abis, abyss
abitchuery, obituary
abituary, obituary
abl, able / apple
abitchuery, obituary
abituary, obituary
abius, abuse
able, ly, bility, CAPABLE "prefixes: dis/ en/ un"
ableb, ad-lib
ablederate, obliterate
ableveus, oblivious
ablib, ad-lib
abliveon, oblivion
abliveus, oblivious
abnakshus, obnoxious
abnormal, lly, lity, NOT TYPICAL/ NATURAL
abnokios, obnoxious

aboard, ONTO SOMETHING SUCH AS VESSEL/ TRAIN/ ORGANIZATION (or see about)
abof, above
abol, able / apple
abolesh, abolish
abolish, hes, hed, hing, her, hment, hable, ition, END, TERMINATE
abolishon, abolition
abolition, nist, DESIRE TO END/ TERMINATE SOMETHING
abomanable, abominable
abominable, ly, eness, HORRID
abominuble, abominable
aborant, aberrant
aborchen, abortion
aborchun, abortion
abord, aboard / abort
aboregini, aborigine
aboreginul, aborigine(nal)
aborigine,*, nal, INDIGINEOUS, NATIVE
aborijinul, aborigine(nal)
aborilleny, aborigine
aborilinal, aborigine(nal)
aborshun, abortion
abort,*, ted, ting, tion, STOP/ QUIT ACTION (or see aboard)
abortion,*, CANCEL PROJECT/ PREGNANCY
about, APPROXIMATELY
above, OVER
abowt, about
aproppeate, appropriate
aproximat, approximate
aprruval, approve(val)
abral, april january
abrasive, ely, eness, ROUGH, SCOURING
abredg, abridge
abreg, abridge
abrehenshun, apprehension
abrel, april
abreveashen, abbreviate(tion)
abreveat, abbreviate
abreveation, abbreviate(tion)
abreviate, abbreviate

abridge, *, ed, ging, er, SHORTEN LENGTH BY CONDENSING/ REWRITING
abrig, abridge
abrihenshun, apprehension
abrikot, apricot
abril, april
abrilld, abridge(ed)
abrillt, abridge(ed)
abrivicishon, abbreviate(tion)
abrivieit, abbreviate
abroad, LEFT HOME TO GO OVERSEAS
abrod, abroad
abrol, april
abropt, abrupt
abrowtch, approach
abruhensev, apprehensive
abruhenshun, apprehension
abrul, april
abrupt, tly, tness, SUDDEN
abscess, sses, ssed, ssing, ssion, INFECTION IN THE BONE
absence, *, NOT PRESENT, UNAVAILABLE (or see absent(s))
absens, absence / absent(s)
absent, tly, tee, teeism, INTENTIONALLY UNAVAILABLE (or see absence)
abserd, absurd
abserdity, absurd(ity)
abserdly, absurd(ly)
abses, abscess
absilute, absolute
absilutly, absolute(ly)
absins, absence / absent(s)
absint, absent
absintee, absent(ee)
absird, absurd
absirdety, absurd(ity)
absirdly, absurd(ly)
absolute, tely, tion, tism, DEFINITELY
absolve, *, ed, ving, vable, er, lution, FORGIVEN, RELEASED
absorb, *, bed, bing, bingly, bable, ber, bance, bent, rption, rptive, rptivity, COLLECT/ GATHER "prefixes: non"
absorbshen, absorption
absorbtef, absorptive

absorbtion, absorption
absorption, ACCUMULATE/ HOLD/ GATHER
absorptive, vity, ion, ACCUMULATES/ HOLDS/ GATHERS
absorshen, absorption
absortef, absorptive
absortion, absorption
absortive, absorptive
abstain, *, ned, ning, nment, ner, tinence, DENY, REFRAIN
abstane, abstain
abstein, abstain
abstinent, nce, tly, VOLUNTARILY DENY/ REFRAIN
abstract, *, ted, ting, tedly, tedness, tion, tionist, APART FROM, THEORETICAL
abstrakt, abstract
abstruct, obstruct
abstunent, abstinent
absulootly, absolute(ly)
absulution, absolve(lution)
absunt, absent
absurd, dly, dity, dities, dness, CRAZY
absurdety, absurd(ity)
abtetude, aptitude
abtitude, aptitude
abtumin, abdomen
abuf, above
abul, able
abulishen, abolition
abulone, abalone
abundance, *, nt, ntly, PLENTY
abundince, abundance
abundint, abundance(nt)
aburant, aberrant
aburation, aberration
aburegene, aborigine
aburijene, aborigine
aburition, aberration
abuse, *, sed, sing, sive, siveness, TREAT WRONGLY "prefixes: dis"
abusef, abuse(sive)
abusif, abuse(sive)
abutizing, appetizing
abuve, above
abuze, abuse

abuzet, opposite
aby, abbey
abyss, smal, smally, ssal, CHASM, GREAT DEPTH EITHER PHYSICAL/ EMOTIONAL
abzaulv, absolve
abzdanent, abstinent
abzent, absent
abzilute, absolute
abzint, absent
abzolv, absolve
abzorb, absorb
abzuloot, absolute
abzulute, absolute
abzulution, absolve(lution)
ac, PREFIX INDICATING "TO/ TOWARDS/ AT" MOST OFTEN MODIFIES THE WORD
academic, *, mism, micism, mia, mician, mical, mically, SCHOOLING
academy, mies, SPECIAL SCHOOL
acadume, academy
acamadasions, accomodations
acampany, accompany
acadintul, accident(al)
accedental, accident(al)
accel, *, lled, lerate, ABBREVIATION OF 'ACCELERATE' (or see excel)
accelarate, accelerate
accelerate, *, ed, ting, tion, tor, QUICKEN, FORCE TO GO/ MOVE, GAS PEDAL
accelirate, accelerate
accent, *, TONES IN SPEECH, HIGHLIGHTS
accentuate, *, ted, ting, tion, TO EMPHASIZE
accepshen, except(ion)
accept, *, ted, ting, tingly, tance, table, tably, tability, tation, APPROVE (or see except) "prefixes: un"
acceptinse, accept(ance)
acceshen, accession
accesorize, accessory(rize)
access, sses, ssed, ssing, ssible, ssibility, ssion, ENTER "prefixes: in"
accession, *, ned, ning, ENTER "prefixes: de"
accessory, ries, rize, rizing, ADDITIONAL
accident, *, tal, tally, INVOLUNTARILY

acclaim, amatory, amation, LOUD APPROVAL/ APPLAUSE (or see acclaimate)
acclimate, *, ed, ting, tion, tize, tized, tizing, tization, BECOME ACCUSTOMED TO (or see acclaim(ation))
accomadate, accommodate
accomadation, accommodate(tion)
accomedate, accommodate
accomedashen, accommodate
accomidation, accommodate(tion)
accommodate, *, ting, tion, tive, ASSIST "prefixes: un"
accomodation, accommodate(tion)
accompany, nies, nied, nying, niment, nist, GOES ALONG WITH "prefixes: un"
accompeny, accompany
accomplice, *, PARTICIPATED IN A CRIME
accomplish, hes, hed, hing, hmert, hable, her, GOAL/ IDEA ACHIEVED
accomudation, accommodate(tion)
accord, *, ded, ding, dingly, dance, dant, dantly, GIVE, GRANT TO, IN HARMONY WITH "prefixes: dis"
account, *, ted, ting, tant, tancy, table, tability, RESPONSIBLE/ LIABLE FOR "prefixes: un"
accredit, *, ted, ting, table, tation, tive, RESPONSIBLE/ LIABLE FOR "prefixes: un"
accrue, *, ual, ed, uing, TO STORE/ SAVE UP "prefixes: non/ un"
accuate, acuate
acudental, accidental(al)
accuiesent, acquiesce(nt)
accumulate, *, ted, ting, tion, t've, tively, tor, GAT-HER/ GROW "prefixes: bio"
accupuncture, acupuncture
accurate, ely, eness, acy, CORRECT "prefixes: in"
accuse, *, ed, sing, singly, satory, satorial, satorially, sative, sation, er, CHARGE OR IMPLY
accustom, med, FAMILIAR, HABITUAL "prefixes: un"
ace, *, ed, A SCORE IN GAME, ON DIE(DICE), TO WIN
acebt, except / accept
acedik, acetic / acidic / ascetic
acempany, accompany
acer, acre
acerens, occur(rence)
aceshun, accession

acetic, tous, PROPERTIES OF VINEGAR, SOUR (or see ascetic/ acidic)
acetify, fies, fied, fying, fier, fication, OF ACETIC, CONVERT TO ACID/ VINEGAR (or see acidify)
acewmulate, accumulate
ache, *, ed, hing, hy, hiness, HURT
acheeve, achieve
achenda, agenda
acheve, achieve
achieve, *, ed, ving, vment, vable, vably, vability, GAIN "prefixes: over/ un/ under"
achin, action
achiteit, agitate
achol, agile
achual, actual
acid, *, dic, dity, dly, dulate, dulated, dulating, dulation, dulent, dulous, dulously, CHEMICAL COMPOUND
acidemic, academic
acidental, accident(al)
acidic, CHEMICAL BALANCE, OF ACID (or see acetic/ ascetic)
acidify, fies, fied, fying, fiable, fication, fier, CONVERT TO ACID (or see acetify) "prefixes: de"
aciuponcsher, acupuncture
ack, ache
ackawnt, account
acklimation, acclimate(tion) / acclaim(amation)
acknowledge, *, ed, ging, ement, gable, er, RECOGNIZE
ackomplish, accomplish
ackord, accord
ackownt, account
ackraget, aggregate
ackred, acrid
ackret, acrid
acks, ax / ache(s) / ask
acksderminate, exterminate
ackseal, axis(ial)
ackses, access / ax(es) / axis
ackseshen, accession
acksesory, accessory
acksglood, exclude
acksul, axil / axle
ackuiesent, acquiesce(nt)

ackumulate, accumulate
ackustumed, accustom(ed)
aclemate, acclimate
aclimate, acclimate
aclimation, acclimate(tion) / acclaim(amation)
acne, AFFLICTION OF THE SKIN
acnolege, acknowledge
acomadashen, accommodate(tion)
acomblesh, accomplish
acomadate, accommodate
acomidate, accommodate
acomidation, accommodate(tion)
acompany, accompany
acompined, accompany(nied)
acomplise, accomplice
acomplish, accomplish
acompuny, accompany
acomudashen, accommodate(tion)
acomudate, accommodate
acord, accord
acordant, accord(ant)
acostum, accustom
acount, account
acoustic, *, cal, cally, OF SOUND
acquaint, *, ted, ting, tance, ASSOCIATE WITH "prefixes: un"
acquaintance, *, eship, FAMILIAR
acquiesce, *, ed, cing, ence, ent, ently, AGREE/ ALLOW IN A HUMBLE/ PASSIVE WAY
acquire, *, red, ring, rement, rable, er, OBTAIN
acquisition, *, ned, ning, nist, ACQUIRED
acquisitive, ely, eness, READILY ACQUIRES
acquit, *, tted, tting, ttal, ttance, ttances, tter, ABSOLVES, FREED
acquittal, *, ABSOLVES, FREE OF JUDGMENT
acqwaentense, acquaintance
acqwantinse, acquaintance
acrabats, acrobat(s)
acrad, acrid
acraget, aggregate
acravat, aggravate
acre, *, eage, AMOUNT OF LAND
acred, acrid

acreget, **aggregate**
acrevat, **aggravate**
acrid, dity, dliy, BITTER/ CAUSTIC SMELL "prefixes: sub"
acriget, **aggregate**
acrit, acrid
acrivat, **aggravate**
acro, PREFIX INDICATING 'END/ BEGINNING/ HEIGHT' MOST OFTEN MODIFIES THE WORD
acrobat, *, tic, tics, INVOLVES VARIOUS CONFIGURATIONS
acroget, **aggregate**
acronym, *, INITIALS, FIRST LETTER OF WORDS
across, OVER
acrovat, **aggravate**
acruget, **aggregate**
acruvat, **aggravate**
acseal, axis(ial)
acsebt, except / accept
acsecute, execute
acsel, excel / accel / axle
acselurashen, accelerate(tion)
acsent, accent
acsentric, eccentric
acsepshen, except(ion)
acsept, accept / except
acses, access / excess
acsesurize, accessory(rize)
acshan, action
acshen, action
acshin, action
acshooul, actual
acshual, actual
acshuated, actuate(d)
acshun, action
acsis, access / ax(es) / axis
acsisory, accessory
acsite, excite
acsiul, axis(ial)
acskershin, excursion
acspereanse, experience
act, *, ted, ting, tor, ACTION "prefixes: over/ re/ retro/ under"
actaf, active
actapus, octopus

actef, active
actein, octane
actevate, activate
acteve, active
actin, action
action, *, nable, nably, DOING, MOVEMENT "prefixes: in/ re"
activate, *, ed, ting, tion, START "prefixes: de/ in"
active, ely, vity, veness, vate, vation, tor, vist, vism, MOVING, CAUSE TO ACT "prefixes: bio/ in/ over/ pro/ re/ retro"
actouber, october
actovate, activate
actseed, exceed
actual, lly, lity, lization, lize, REAL
actuate, *, ted, ting, tion, INITIATE/ BEGIN ACTIVITY "prefixes: de/ un"
actule, actual
actuvate, activate
actuve, active
acudemic, academic
acuemulate, accumulate
acuesativ, acquisitive
acuiesant, acquiesce(nt)
acuisativ, acquisitive
acuital, acquittal
acult, occult
acumpany, accompany
acumpened, accompany(nied)
acumulate, accumulate
acupansy, occupancy
acupuncture, *, rist, TREATMENT FOR HEALING BODY
acurate, accurate
acurens, occur(rrence)
acurit, accurate
acuse, accuse
acustic, acoustic
acustumed, accustom(ed)
acute, ely, eness, SHARP
acwatic, aquatic
acwaynt, acquaint
acwayntense, acquaintance
acwazition, acquisition

acweesent, acquiesce(nt)
acwifalent, equivalent
acwire, acquire
acwit, acquit
acwuzeshun, acquisition
acwyre, acquire
ad, PREFIX INDICATING 'TO/ TOWARDS' MOST OFTEN MODIFIES THE WORD, SHORT FOR ADVERTISEMENT (or see at/ add/ aid)
adacity, audacity
adakit, etiquette
adalesint, adolescent
adam, atom
adamant, tly, tine, RELENTLESS, NOT PENETRABLE, A METAL
adamently, adamant(ly)
adamize, atom(ize)
adapt, *, ted, ting, tive, tively, tation, table, tableness, tability, ter, tor, ADJUST (or see adept) "prefixes: pre/ retro"
adasity, audacity
adatif, additive
add, *, dded, dding, ddable, dditive, ddition, dditional, dditionally, ddendum, INCREASE, PLUS, MORE THAN BEFORE
addendum, *, SOMETHING ADDED
addict, *, ted, ting, tion, tive, HABITUAL/ OBSESSIVE USE
additive, *, MORE, AN INCREASE, ADDITIONALLY
address, sses, ssed, ssing, ssee, ROUTE/ LOCATION OF "prefixes: re"
adebt, adapt / adept
adec, attic / addict
adecuasi, adequacy
adecuat, adequate
adek, attic / addict
adekt, addict
adekuasi, adequacy
adekuat, adequate
adelesinse, adolescence
ademant, adamant
ademant, adamant
ademize, atom(ize)
ademunt, adamant

adenaficashun, identification
adendum, addendum
adept, tly, tness, SKILLFUL (or see adapt)
adequace, adequacy
adequacy, cies, ABILITY
adequate, ely, eness, SUFFICIENT "prefixes: in"
adequise, adequacy
adequot, adequate
ader, adhere
adeshen, edition / add(ition)
adetif, additive
adetion, edition / add(ition)
adetude, attitude
adewlation, adulate(tion)
adegate, agitate
adgitate, agitate
adgrenalin, adrenaline
adgudekashen, adjudicate(tion)
adgunct, adjunct
adgust, adjust
adhear, adhere
adhere, *, ed, ring, ent, ently, erce, esion, esive, STICKS TO
adhesion, STICKS TO
adhesive, *, eness, STICKS TO
adible, audible
adic, attic / addict
adict, addict
adicuasi, adequacy
adieu, * GOOD-BYE
adik, attic / addict
adikit, etiquette
adikshen, addict(ion)
adikt, addict
adimant, adamant
adimdum, addendum
adimunt, adamant
adindum, addendum
adinefecashin, identification
adiquacy, adequacy
adiquase, adequacy
adiquit, adequate
adiquot, adequate
adishen, edition / add(ition)

aditev, additive
adition, edition / add(ition)
aditiv, additive
aditude, attitude
adiu, adieu
adjacent, tly, NEAR "prefixes: non"
adjasent, adjacent
adjasint, adjacent
adje, etch / edge
adjective, *, val, vally, WORD THAT MODIFIES A NOUN
adjewdikashen, adjudicate(tion)
adjewlation, adulate(tion)
adjishon, adhesion
adjisiv, adhesive
adjitate, agitate
adjoin, *, ned, ning, nt, nts, TO JOIN/ UNITE
adjost, adjust
adjourn, *, ned, ning, nment, DELAY
adjudicate, *, ed, ting, tion, tor, tive, JUDGE
adjudikashen, adjudicate(tion)
adjulation, adulate(tion)
adjunct, *, tive, tly, tion, JOINS/ ACCOMPANIES
adjust, *, ted, ting, table, tment, CHANGE TO NEW CIRCUMSTANCE
adleb, ad-lib
adlesense, adolescence
adlesinse, adolescence
ad-lib, *, bbed, bbing, SPONTANEOUS PREPARATION
adlleisent, adjacent
adllost, adjust
adllukeit, adjudicate
adllurn, adjourn
admayer, admire
admenaster, administer
admenastrashen, administrate(tion)
admenester, administer
admenister, administer
admenistration, administrate(tion)
admenustrashen, administrate(tion)
admeshun, admission
admet, admit
admichin, admission
admichun, admission

admided, admit(tted)
adminaster, administer
administer, *, red, ring, SUPERVISE, DISPENSE
administrate, *, ed, ting, tion, tive, tively, tor, ONE WHO SUPERVISES
admire, *, er, ring, rable, rably, ration, CHERISH
admisable, admissible
admisef, admission(ive)
admishun, admission
admisible, admissible
admissible, ly, bility, ALLOWABLE, ALSO SPELLED "ADMISSABLE" "prefixes: in"
admission, *, ive, ENTRANCE, ADMIT TO
admisuf, admission(ive)
admit, *, tted, tting, ttance, ttedly, ALLOW "prefixes: non"
admited, admit(tted)
admizable, admissible
admizible, admissible
admonish, hes, hed, hing, her, hment, ition, itions, itory, WARN/ ADVISE/ DIRECT AGAINST
admyre, admire
ado, adieu
adobiografe, autobiography
adobt, adopt
adobyografy, autobiography
adograf, autograph
adolecense, adolescence
adolescence, nt, OF YOUTH
adolescent, *, YOUTH
adolesense, adolescence
adolesinse, adolescence
adolesint, adolescent
adolt, adult
adom, atom
adomadik, automatic
adoment, adamant
adometer, odometer
adomider, odometer
adomint, adamant
adomize, atom(ize)
adomobil, automobile
adoo, adieu
adoor, adore

adopt,*,ted,ting,tion,tive,table,ACQUIRE "prefixes: un"
adore,*,ed,ring,ringly,rable,rably,rability,rableness,ration,WORSHIP
adorn,*,ned,ning,nment,ENHANCE
adranalin,adrenaline
adrenaline,HORMONE
adrenulen,adrenaline
adress,address
adrift,MOVE/ FLOAT WITHOUT DIRECTION
adroit,tly,tness,NIMBLE,SKILLFUL
adsedura,etcetera
adsetera,etcetera
adshe,etch / edge
adt,eight / ate
adu,adieu
adukit,etiquette
adulate,*,ed,ting,tor,tory,tion,EXCESSIVE PRAISE/ COMPLIMENT
adulesinse,adolescence
adulesint,adolescent
adult,*,FULLY MATURE PHYSICALLY
adulterate,*,ed,ting,tion,ant,tor,DEBASE OR ALTER "prefixes: un"
adultery,rous,rously,rer,SEX WITH OTHERS WHEN MARRIED
adum,atom
adumant,adamant
adumint,adamant
adumize,atom(ize)
aduquacy,adequacy
adutif,additive
adutude,attitude
advais,advice / advise
advance,*,ed,cing,ement,PROGRESS "prefixes: dis"
advans,advance
advanse,advance
advantage,*,ed,ging,eous,eously,BENEFIT, BETTER CHANCE "prefixes: dis"
advantech,advantage
advantig,advantage
advantuge,advantage
advecate,advocate
advekate,advocate

advencher,adventure
advent,*,EXPECTED/ IMPORTANT ARRIVAL
adventure,*,er,rous,rously,esome,ess,EXPLORATION "prefixes: mis"
adverb,*,bial,OF VERBS
advercity,adverse(sity)
advers,adverse
adversarie,adversary
adversary,ries,rial,OPPONENT
adverse,ely,eness,sity,sities,sary,saries,sarial,sative,satively,OPPOSE (or see averse)
adversly,adverse(ly)
advert,*,ted,ting,tence,CHANGE DIRECTION/ ATTENTION TOWARDS (or see avert) "prefixes: in"
advertise,*,ed,sing,ement,DECLARE
advertize,advertise
advicate,advocate
advice,RECOMMEND (or see advise)
advikete,advocate
advincher,adventure
advinture,adventure
advirb,adverb
advirsare,adversary
advirse,adverse
advirsere,adversary
advise,*,ed,sing,edly,edness,ement,sor,ser,sory,sable,sably,sability,INFORM (or see advice) "prefixes: in/ un"
advize,advise / advice
advizuble,advise(sable)
advocate,*,ed,ting,tory,acy,tion,tor,SUPPORTER
advukate,advocate
advurb,adverb
advurcity,adverse(sity)
advurs,adverse
advursary,adversary
advursle,adverse(ly)
advursudy,adverse(sity)
advurtise,advertise
adyetiv,adjective
adyewlation,adulate(tion)
adyeycent,adjacent
adyukeit,adjudicate

adyurn,adjourn
ael,ail
aem,aim
aemeable,amiable
aenckshes,anxious
aengwish,anguish
aenjul,angel
aenkre,angry
aenkshes,anxious
aent,aunt / ant
aenus,anus
aenxiatee,anxiety
aepaloge,apology
aerial,BY AIRCRAFT
aero,PREFIX INDICATING 'AIR' MOST OFTEN MODIFIES THE WORD
aerobic,*,OXYGEN EXERCISE
aerodynamic,*,cal,cally,AIR MOTION
aerosol,*,COMPRESSED CONTENTS IN A CAN
aesthetic,*,cal,cally,PLEASING TO THE EYES
aet,eight / ate
af,PREFIX INDICATING 'TO/ TOWARDS' MOST OFTEN MODIFIES THE WORD
afadavit,affidavit
afair,affair
afale,avail
afare,affair
afder,after
afeador,aviator
afeator,aviator
afect,effect / affect
afectation,affect(ation)
afection,affection
afed,aphid
afedavit,affidavit
afekshen,affection
afekshin,affection
afekt,effect / affect
afektashin,affect(ation)
afektation,affect(ation)
afektion,affection
afeleat,affiliate
afemanit,effeminate

afend,offend
afenity,affinity
afens,offense
afensef,offense(sive)
afensif,offense(sive)
afer,affair / ever
afermative,affirm(ative)
afes,office
afeser,office(r)
afeshent,efficient
afeshul,official
afet,aphid
afeus,effuse
afews,effuse
affadavit,affidavit
affair,*,INTERACTION/ BUSINESS
affare,affair
affecient,efficient
affect,*,ted,ting,ter,tation,tive,CAUSE SOMETHING TO HAPPEN, TRYING TO IMPRESS, PRETENTIOUS (or see effect) "prefixes: dis/ un"
affection,*,nate,nately,nateness,TO EXPRESS FONDNESS
affenity,affinity
affidavit,*,LEGALLY BINDING STATEMENT
affiliate,*,ed,ting,tion,ASSOCIATED WITH "prefixes: dis/ un"
affinity,tive,ATTRACTION
affirm,*,med,ming,mative,mation,SUPPORT WITH APPROVAL "prefixes: dis/ un"
afflict,*,ted,tion,ter,tively,DISTRESS
affluence,*,nt,ntly,ABUNDANCE
affluent,tly,ABUNDANCE
afford,*,ded,dable,dability,dance,SPARE "prefixes: un"
affront,*,ted,ting,CONFRONT
affus,effuse
afid,aphid
afileat,affiliate
afimanit,effeminate
afinity,affinity
afinse,offense
afinsef,offense(sive)
afirm,affirm

afis,office
afiser,office(r)
afishal,official
afishensy,efficiency
afishent,efficient
afishinsy,efficiency
afishul,official
afishuly,official(lly)
afit,aphid
aflict,afflict
aflikt,afflict
afloat,FLOATING
aflot,afloat
afluense,affluence
afluent,affluent
afluinse,affluence
afoot,ABOUT TO HAPPEN, IN PROGRESS
aford,afford
afordable,afford(able)
afore,PREFIX INDICATING 'BEFORE' MOST OFTEN MODIFIES THE WORD
afortuble,afford(able)
afot,afoot / aphid
afraid,FEARFUL
afrayed,afraid
afrebaudy,every(body)
afrewar,every(where)
afront,affront
afrunt,affront
aften,often
after,PREFIX INDICATING 'AFTER' MOST OFTEN MODIFIES THE WORD FOLLOWING
aftur,after
afud,aphid
afudavit,affidavit
afurmative,affirm(ative)
afus,office / effuse
afuser,office(r)
afut,afoot
ag,PREFIX INDICATING 'SOIL/ FIELD' MOST OFTEN MODIFIES THE WORD
again,REPEAT
against,TOWARD, FACING, OPPOSITE OF FLOW

agany,agony
agasent,adjacent
agasint,adjacent
agd,age(d)
age,*,ed,ging,eless,MEASURE OF TIME "prefixes: over/ under"
agen,again / age(ging)
agency,cies,OF BUSINESS, OPERATION OF POWER
agenda,*,SCHEDULE/ FORMAT/ PLAN
agene,agony
agenst,against
agent,*,ncy,ncies,CATALYST, INTRODUCED TO PERFORM A TASK "prefixes: re"
agenta,agenda
ageny,agony
agern,adjourn
agetat,agitate
agetiv,adjective
agewdicate,adjudicate
aggravate,*,ed,ting,tingly,tion,AGITATE
aggravation,AGITATE
aggregate,*,ed,ting,ely,tion,tive,tor,FORM TOGETHER, UNITE "prefixes: dis"
aggresef,aggressive
aggresefly,aggressive(ly)
aggreshen,aggression
aggresive,aggressive
aggression,*,OFFENSIVE/ ROUGH/ FORCEFUL
aggressive,ely,eness,ssor,AGGRAVATE/ AGITATE "prefixes: un"
aggressor,*,ONE WHO AGGRAVATES/ AGITATES
aggretion,aggression
agile,lity,eness,LIMBER, FLEXIBLE
aginda,agenda
aginst,against
aginsy,agency
agint,agent
aginy,agony
agirn,adjourn
agitate,*,ed,ting,tor,tion,tive,edly,AROUSE, AGGRAVATE, AGGRESSIVE STIMULATION
ago,PAST
agony,nies,nize,nized,nizing,SUFFER

agorn,adjourn
agrabat,acrobat
agravashen,aggravation
agravate,**aggravate**
agravation,aggravation
agrecultsher,agriculture
agree,*,eed,eeing,eement,eeable,eeably,CONSENT TO "prefixes: dis"
agregate,aggregate
agrekulcher,agriculture
agrenalin,adrenaline
agresef,aggressive
agreshen,aggression
agresif,aggressive
agresifle,aggressive(ly)
agresion,aggression
agresiv,aggressive
agresor,aggressor
agression,aggression
agressive,aggressive
agretion,aggression
agrevat,aggravate
agri,agree
agribat,acrobat / aggravate
agricultcher,agriculture
agriculture,*,ral,rist,ralist,ralism,ralization,FARMING
agriget,aggregate
agrikulcher,agriculture
agrivate,acrobat / aggravate
agrobat,acrobat / aggravate
agrovat,acrobat / aggravate
agrubat,acrobat / aggravate
agruget,aggregate
agruvashen,aggravation
agruvat,aggravate / acrobat
agruvation,aggravation
agsberament,experiment
agsblane,explain
agsebt,except / accept
agsecutive,executive
agseed,exceed
agsept,except / accept
agsersize,exercise / exorcise

agsert,exert
agspel,expel
agsplan,explain
agsplisit,explicit
agsrem,extreme
agstend,extend
agstenshen,extension
agstenuate,extenuate
agstereor,exterior
agsternal,external
agstinkt,extinct
agstradite,extradite
agstrakt,extract
agstreem,extreme
agstrordenair,extraordinaire
agstrordinery,extraordinary
agsturnal,external
agucolture,agriculture
agudecate,adjudicate
agudikate,adjudicate
agul,agile
agunct,adjunct
agune,agony
agunt,agent
aguny,agony
agust,august
agustible,adjust(able)
agutate,agitate
agutev,adjective
agzemt,exempt
ahead,COMING UP
ahed,ahead
ahod,ahold
ahold,TAKE NOTICE,MAKE CONTACT,GAIN CONTROL
ahpotment,appointment
ai,eye / ice
aian,ion
aib,I've
aibory,ivory
aibrau,eyebrow
aicon,icon
aid,*,ded,ding,HELP
aidem,item

aidentical,identical
aidentifaj,identify
aidentifikeshon,identification
aidentifiqueichon,identification
aidentiti,identity
aidia,idea
aidio,ideo
aidol,idle / idol
aifi,ivy
ail,*,led,ling,lment,SICK/ NOT WELL (or see ale/ aisle)
ail,oil
ailach,eyelash
ailand,island
aile,aisle
ailend,island
aim,*,med,ming,mless,mlessly,mlessness,FOCUS ON A POINT,DIRECT ATTENTION
ainches,anxious
ainckshes,anxious
ainkshus,anxious
aiodain,iodine
aion,ion
aionesfir,ionosphere
aionusfir,ionosphere
aiorn,iron
air,*,red,ring,rless,SPACE,A GAS/ AURA (or see are/ heir/ err) "prefixes: un"
airate,irate
airborne,OFF THE GROUND
airea,area
aireni,irony
airis,iris
airloom,heirloom
airobic,aerobic
airodynamic,aerodynamic
airoganse,arrogance
aironic,ironic
airport,*,AIRCRAFT BASE
ais,ice / eye(s)
aisi,icy
aisicol,icicle
aising,icing
aisle,*,ed,PASSAGEWAY

aisoleit, isolate
ait, eight / ate
aitalic, italic
aitem, item
aiuris, iris
aiurn, iron
aiurny, irony
aivi, ivy
aivori, ivory
aiz, eye(s) / ice
aj, age / edge
ajar, WHEN A DOOR IS NOT CLOSED ALL THE WAY
ajasent, adjacent
ajasint, adjacent
ajative, adjective
ajaur, ajar
aje, age
ajed, ahead
ajenda, agenda
ajensy, agency
ajent, agent
ajern, adjourn
ajetate, agitate
ajewdicat, adjudicate
ajewdikashen, adjudicate(tion)
ajil, agile
ajilety, agile(lity)
ajinda, agenda
ajinsy, agency
ajint, agent
ajitate, agitate
ajodikate, adjudicate
ajor, ajar
ajorn, adjourn
ajost, adjust
ajourn, adjourn
ajrenalin, adrenaline
ajudikate, adjudicate
ajul, agile
ajunct, adjunct
ajunt, agent
ajurn, adjourn
ajust, adjust

ajustible, adjust(able)
ajutev, adjective
ak, ache
akademe, academy
akademic, academic
akadume, academy
akamidate, accommodate
akashenul, occasion(al)
akaumplish, accomplish
akawnt, account
akcelaration, accelerate(tion)
akchen, action
akchuel, actual
akchun, action
akedemik, academic
akeishon, occasion
aker, acre
akerens, occur(rrence)
akewmulate, accumulate
akewpunksher, acupuncture
akews, accuse
akewsashen, accuse(sation)
akidemic, academic
akiuponcsher, acupuncture
akiut, acquit
aklemate, acclimate
aklimation, acclimate(tion) / acclaim(amation)
aklumate, acclimate
aknaulig, acknowledge
akne, acne
aknolege, acknowledge
akod, echo(ed)
akomedashen, accommodate
akomidate, accommodate
akomidation, accommodate(tion)
akomodate, accommodate
akompaned, accompany(nied)
akompeny, accompany
akomplis, accomplice
akomplish, accomplish
akomudate, accommodate
akonume, economy
akord, accord

akordant, accord(ant)
akorinse, occur(rrence)
akount, account
akr, acre
akrabat, acrobat
akrabatek, acrobat(ic)
akrad, acrid
akragate, aggregate
akranem, acronym
akrat, acrid
akrebat, acrobat
akred, acrid
akree, agree
akregate, aggregate
akrenem, acronym
akret, acrid
akrevat, aggravate
akribat, acrobat
akrid, acrid
akrigate, aggregate
akrinem, acronym
akrit, acrid
akrivat, aggravate
akrobat, acrobat
akrogate, aggregate
akronem, acronym
akross, across
akrovat, aggravate
akrubat, acrobat
akrugat, aggregate
akruget, aggregate
akrunem, acronym
akruvat, aggravate
aks, ax / ache(s) / ask / ask(ed) / ax(ed)
aksald, excel(lled) / accel(lled)
akschange, exchange
aksd, ax(ed) / ask(ed)
aksderminate, exterminate
aksdurminate, exterminate
akseal, axis(ial)
aksedent, accident
akseed, exceed
aksel, excel / accel / axle

akselarashen, accelerate(tion)
akselarate, accelerate
akselaratur, accelerate(tor)
akseld, excel(lled) / accel(lled)
akselerate, accelerate
akselirashen, accelerate(tion)
akseluratur, accelerate(tor)
aksent, accent
aksentric, eccentric
aksentuate, accentuate
aksepshen, except(ion)
aksept, accept / except
akseptense, accept(ance)
akseptid, accept(ed)
akseptinse, accept(ance)
akses, access / ax(es) / axis / ask(s)
aksesares, accessory(ries)
aksesarize, accessory(rize)
aksesd, access(ed)
aksesible, access(ible)
aksesirize, accessory(rize)
aksesory, accessory
aksesuble, access(ible)
aksesurize, accessory(rize)
aksglude, exclude
aksglute, exclude
akshen, action
akshin, action
akshual, actual
akshuat, actuate
akshuated, acuate(d)
akshuel, actual
akshun, action
aksident, accident
aksidentul, accident(al)
aksil, axle
aksint, accent
aksintuate, accentuate
aksis, ax(es) / axis / access
aksisory, accessory
aksite, excite
aksitment, excite(ment)
akskeus, excuse

akskusis, excuse(s)
aksle, axil / axle
aksol, axil / axle
aksorsize, exercise / exorcise
akspensif, expense(sive)
akspinsif, expense(sive)
aksplan, explain
aksplisit, explicit
akspres, express
akspreshen, express(ion)
aksquse, excuse
akst, ax(ed) / ask(ed)
akstereor, exterior
akstinkt, extinct
aksturnal, external
aksudentul, accident(al)
aksul, axil / axle
aksulens, excel(lled) / accel(lled)
aksus, axis / ax(es)
akt, act / ache(d)
akter, act(or)
aktevate, activate
akteve, active
aktir, act(or)
aktivate, activate
aktive, active
aktober, october
aktovate, activate
aktuate, actuate
aktur, act(or)
aktuvate, activate
aktuve, active
akuazition, acquisition
akudemic, academic
akuiesent, acquiesce(nt)
akult, occult
akumpany, accompany
akumulate, accumulate
akupansy, occupancy
akupunksher, acupuncture
akur, occur / acre
akurense, occur(rrence)
akuret, accurate

akurints, occur(rrence)
akusashen, accuse(sation)
akuse, accuse
akustik, acoustic
akustumed, accustom(ed)
akute, acute
akwa, aqua
akwaent, acquaint
akwantense, acquaintance
akwashin, equation
akwasition, acquisition
akwate, equate
akwater, equator
akwatic, aquatic
akwaynt, acquaint
akwayntinse, acquaintance
akwazeshin, acquisition
akwefer, aquifer
akwesishun, acquisition
akwet, acquit
akwezishun, acquisition
akwinox, equinox
akwipment, equipment
akwire, acquire
akwit, acquit
akwitment, equipment
akwivulense, equivalent(ncy)
akwivulint, equivalent
akwoduct, aqueduct
akwufir, aquifer
akwuzishen, acquisition
akyerit, accurate
akzamen, examine
akzenshuate, accentuate
akzent, accent
akzinshuate, accentuate
akzint, accent
al, PREFIX INDICATING 'TO/ TOWARDS' MOST OFTEN MODIFIES THE WORD (or see ail/ ale/ all/ awl)
alabai, alibi
alabi, alibi
alactrishun, electrician
alagator, alligator

alagible, eligible
alaik, alike
alain, align
alaiv, alive
alakwens, eloquence
alakwent, eloquent
alaquens, eloquence
alarm, *, med, ming, mingly, mist, ALERT
alasteck, elastic
alastick, elastic
alastreus, illustrious
alau, allow
alauans, allowance
alaven, eleven
alayans, alliance
albem, album
albow, elbow
album, *, MEDIA COLLECTION
alchi, algae
alcohol, lic, lism, CHEMICAL
alcove, *, NOOK
alder, *, A TREE (or see altar/ alter)
aldir, alder / altar / alter
aldur, alder / altar / alter
ale, *, A BREWED DRINK (or see ail/ all/ alley/ awl)
alean, alien
aleas, alias
alebi, alibi
aleby, alibi
alecate, allocate
alech, allege
alechens, allegiance
aleckt, elect
alecktrek, electric
alederite, illiterate
aledge, allege
alee, alley
alef, olive
aleg, allege
alegal, illegal
alegatur, alligator
alege, allege
alegeidor, alligator

alegens, allegiance / elegance
alegins, allegiance
alein, alien
aleinashen, alien(ation)
aleinate, alien(ate)
alej, allege
alejanse, allegiance
alejens, allegiance
alejins, allegiance
alekate, allocate
alekshen, elect(ion)
alekt, elect
alektrician, electrician
alektrik, electric
alektrishen, electrician
alekwens, eloquence
alekwent, eloquent
alemenade, eliminate
alemony, alimony
aleon, alien
alequence, eloquence
alequent, eloquent
alerche, allergy
alerchic, allergic
alerge, allergy
alerges, allergy(gies)
alergic, allergic
alerllic, allergic
alert, *, ted, ting, tness, NOTIFY, SHARPLY AWARE
alesit, elicit / illicit
alet, elite
aletist, elite(tist)
aleun, alien
aleunashen, alien(ation)
aleunate, alien(ate)
aleus, alias
alev, olive
aleveate, alleviate
aleven, eleven
aleviate, alleviate
alevieit, alleviate
alevin, eleven
alevinth, eleven(th)

alevon, eleven
aley, alley
alf, elf
alfabedikul, alphabet(ical)
alfabet, alphabet
alfibetize, alphabet(ize)
alfubedikul, alphabet(ical)
alfubutize, alphabet(ize)
algae, WATER ORGANISM
algebra, aic, aically, TYPE OF MATH
algubra, algebra
ali, ally / alley
alians, alliance
alias, ses, ANOTHER NAME
alibi, *, EXCUSE
alicate, allocate
alid, ally(lied)
aliderate, illiterate
alien, *, nate, nation, nable, FOREIGNER (or see alliance)
 "prefixes: in/ un"
alienashen, alien(ation)
alif, olive
aligater, alligator
algeidor, alligator
align, *, ned, ning, nment, STRAIGHTEN "prefixes: re"
alikate, allocate
alike, SIMILAR
alikwens, eloquence
alikwent, eloquent
alillens, allegiance
alimenate, eliminate
alimony, MONETARY ALLOWANCE AFTER DIVORCE
alimpic, olympic
aline, align
alinment, align(ment)
aliquence, eloquence
aliquent, eloquent
alirt, alert
alis, ally(lies)
alisit, elicit / illicit
aliterate, illiterate
alitest, elite(tist)
aliunate, alien(ate)

alive, NOT DEAD, HAS SPIRIT
alivieit, alleviate
alja, algae
aljebra, algebra
aljibra, algebra
alk, elk
alkali, ine, inity, loid, CHEMICAL BALANCE
alkohol, alcohol
alkove, alcove
alkuhol, alcohol
all, EVERYTHING (or see ail/ ale/ awl) "prefixes: over"
allege, *, ed, ging, edly, ASSERT
allegiance, *, nt, LOYALTY
allelo, PREFIX INDICATING 'OTHER/ ALTERNATE' MOST OFTEN MODIFIES THE WORD
allenda, agenda
allergic, SENSITIVE/ REACTION TO
allergy, gies, genic, gic, SENSITIVE/ REACTION TO
alletiv, adjective
alleviate, *, ed, ting, tion, tive, tory, RELIEVE
alley, *, yway, PASSAGEWAY (or see ally)
alli, ally / alley
alliance, *, cing, JOIN "prefixes: mis/ pro"
alligator, *, LARGE REPTILE
alliteit, agitate
alli, algae
allocate, *, ed, ting, tion, table, tor, ASSIGN
allol, agile
allow, *, wed, wing, wable, wance, PERMIT "prefixes: dis/ un"
allowance, *, PERMITTED, ALLOTTED
alloy, *, METALS TOGETHER
alltogether, altogether
allude, *, ed, ding, usion, usive, CASUALLY MAKE REFERENCE TO (or see elude)
allure, *, ed, ring, ement, ringly, TEMPT
allusion, *, ive, TO MENTION INDIRECTLY/ CASUALLY (or see illusion)
allusive, TO MENTION INDIRECTLY/ CASUALLY (or see elusive/ illusive)
ally, llies, llied, llying, lliance, UNITED (or see alley)
almanac, *, BOOK WITH INFORMATION AS IT RELATES TO SPACE/ STARS

alminak, almanac
almonak, almanac
almost, CLOSE, COULD BE BUT IS NOT
almozt, almost
almunak, almanac
alof, aloof
alogeidor, alligator
alokate, allocate
alokeit, allocate
alone, NO ONE, NOTHING ELSE
aloof, fly, fness, RESERVED/ DISINTERESTED COMPOSURE
aloore, allure
aloosuf, allusive / elusive / illusive
alop, elope
aloqeit, allocate
aloquence, eloquence
aloquent, eloquent
alosiv, allusive / elusive/ illusive
aloun, alone
alow, allow
alowins, allowance
alowy, alloy
aloy, alloy
alphabet, *, tic, tical, tize, tizes, tized, tizing, tization, tizer, SET OF SYMBOLS/ LETTERS TO FORM WORDS
alphebetical, alphabet(ical)
alphubedikul, alphabet(ical)
already, BY THIS TIME
also, INCLUDED, ALONG WITH
alt, PREFIX INDICATING 'HIGH' MOST OFTEN MODIFIES THE WORD
altamatum, ultimatum
altar, *, PLATFORM FOR WORSHIP (or see alter/ alder)
altematum, ultimatum
alter, *, red, ring, ration, SLIGHTLY CHANGE/ MODIFY (or see alder/ altar) "prefixes: in"
alterashen, alter(ation)
alternate, *, ed, ting, ely, tely, tion, tive, tively, TO GO BACK AND FORTH BETWEEN, ROTATE "prefixes: sub"
alternative, *, ely, CHOICES/ OPTIONS
alternutiv, alternative
altetude, altitude
although, EVEN THOUGH

alti, PREFIX INDICATING 'HIGH' MOST OFTEN MODIFIES THE WORD
altimatum, ultimatum
altir, alder / altar / alter
altirashen, alter(ation)
altiration, alter(ation)
altird, alter(ed)
altirnetly, alternate(ly)
altirnitef, alternative
altirnutiv, alternative
altitude, *, HEIGHT
alto, PREFIX INDICATING 'HIGH' MOST OFTEN MODIFIES THE WORD
altogether, IN ONE PLACE
altumatum, ultimatum
altur, alder / altar / alter
alturashen, alter(ation)
alturation, alter(ation)
alturd, alter(ed)
alturnetly, alternate(ly)
alturnutiv, alternative
altwogether, altogether
aluby, alibi
alucate, allocate
alude, elude
aluf, aloof
alufent, elephant
alugable, eligible
alujen, illusion / allusion
alukate, allocate
alukwens, eloquence
alukwent, eloquent
alumenum, aluminum
aluminate, illuminate
aluminum, A METAL
alumony, alimony
alumunum, aluminum
aluquence, eloquence
aluquent, eloquent
alure, allure
alurgik, allergic
alurjik, allergic
alurt, alert

alusif, allusive / elusive / illusive
alusion, allusion / illusion
alusov, allusive / elusive / illusive
alustrious, illustrious
aluv, olive
always, FOREVER (or see aim)
alwaz, always
alweis, always
aly, ally
alyan, alien
alyke, alike
am, PRESENT TENSE OF "BE/ BEING" (or see aim)
amachur, amateur
amaculet, immaculate
amagen, imagine
amagenation, imagine(nation)
amakewlit, immaculate
amakulit, immaculate
amasher, amateur
amateur, *, rish, rishly, NONPROFESSIONAL
amatur, amateur
amaunt, amount
amawntuble, amount(able)
amaze, *, ed, edly, zing, zingly, ement, IMPRESS
ambaquety, ambiguity
ambechis, ambitious
ambegedy, ambiguity
ambegues, ambiguous
ambekyues, ambiguous
ambeshun, ambition
ambeshushnes, ambitious(ness)
ambetious, ambitious
ambi, PREFIX INDICATING 'BOTH/ AROUND' MOST OFTEN MODIFIES THE WORD
ambichen, ambition
ambiches, ambitious
ambiguity, ties, TWO OR MORE WAYS AN EXPRESSION COULD BE INTERPRETED
ambiguous, sly, sness, TWO OR MORE WAYS AN EXPRESSION COULD BE INTERPRETED "prefixes: un"
ambiquety, ambiguity
ambishisnes, ambitious(ness)
ambishun, ambition

ambishus, ambitious
ambishushnes, ambitious(ness)
ambition, *, DESIRE TO ACHIEVE A GOAL
ambitious, sly, sness, STRIVING DILIGENTLY TOWARDS A GOAL
ambiulans, ambulance
amblanse, ambulance
amblins, ambulance
ambolanse, ambulance
amboosh, ambush
amboshd, ambush(ed)
ambuguedy, ambiguity
ambulance, *, atory, atories, RESCUE VEHICLE
ambulence, ambulance
ambush, hes, hed, her, ENTRAP
ambushd, ambush(ed)
ambutashen, amputate(tion)
ame, aim
ameable, amiable
ameba, amoeba
amechur, amateur
amedeat, immediate
ameds, emit / omit
ameible, amiable(ly)
ameis, amaze
ameiz, amaze
amekibul, amicable
amekuble, amicable
amend, *, ded, ding, dment, dable, datory, REPAIR
amense, immense
amensurabl, immensurable
amenus, ominous
amepa, amoeba
amerchen, immerse(sion)
amergensee, emergency
amerse, immerse / emersed
amershen, immerse(sion)
amertize, amortize
ameshen, omission / emission
ameteut, immediate
amethist, amethyst
amethyst, *, PURPLE QUARTZ
ameuble, amiable / amiable(ly)

amewsd, amuse(d)
amewsmint, amuse(ment)
amiable, eness, ly, bility, GOOD-NATURED
amicable, ly, bility, FRIENDLY
amichur, amateur
amikable, amicable
amikuble, amicable
amind, amend
amindment, amend(ment)
aminse, immense
aminsurable, immensurable
aminus, ominous
amirchen, immerse(sion)
amirse, immerse / emersed
amirshen, immerse(sion)
amishen, omission / emission
amit, emit / omit
amithist, amethyst
amitz, emit / omit
amiuble, amiable(ly)
amius, amuse
ammonea, ammonia
ammonia, aic, A GAS
ammurshen, immerse(sion)
amne, omni
amnevore, omnivore
amnivore, omnivore
amochure, amateur
amoeba, *, bic, ANIMAL
among, gst, IN THE MIDST OF, WITH OTHERS
amonia, ammonia
amonkst, among(st)
amonya, ammonia
amortize, *, zable, tization, IN LOAN CALCULATION
amount, *, ted, ting, SUM
amownt, amount
ampakuety, ambiguity
ampegues, ambiguous
ampekuedy, ambiguity
ampel, ample
ampetate, amputate
ampeutashen, amputate(tion)
ampewtation, amputate(tion)

amphi, PREFIX INDICATING 'BOTH/ AROUND' MOST OFTEN MODIFIES THE WORD
ampigewus, ambiguous
ampil, ample
ampition, ambition
ampiuteit, amputate
amplafikashen, amplify(fication)
ample, er, est, eness, ENOUGH, PLENTY
amplefy, amplify
amplifucation, amplify(fication)
amplify, fies, fied, fier, ying, fiable, fication, MAGNIFY SOUND "prefixes: pre"
amplufikashen, amplify(fication)
amplufy, amplify
ampol, ample
amportant, important
ampukuety, ambiguity
ampul, ample
amputashen, amputate(tion)
amputate, *, ed, ting, tion, tee, REMOVE LIMB FROM MAIN TORSO
amrold, emerald
amruld, emerald
amune, immune
amunety, immune(nity)
amung, among
amunity, immune(nity)
amunkst, among(st)
amunxt, among(st)
amurchen, immerse(sion)
amurgensee, emergency
amurse, immerse / emersed
amurshen, immerse(sion)
amuse, *, ed, sing, ement, ENTERTAIN
amuthist, amethyst
amuze, amuse
amuzment, amuse(ment)
amythest, amethyst
an, PREFIX INDICATING 'TO/ TOWARDS' MOST OFTEN MODIFIES THE WORD
ana, PREFIX INDICATING 'UP/ BACK/ AGAIN' MOST OFTEN MODIFIES THE WORD
anadot, anecdote

anagma, enigma / enema
anal, lly, NEAR/ INVOLVING THE ANUS (or see annul)
analesis, analysis
analidek, analytic
analigy, analogy
analitek, analytic
analize, analyze
analog, gous, gously, TYPE OF WAVE/ SOUND
analogy, gies, gous, gously, LIKENESS
analysis, ses, BREAKDOWN TO STUDY
analyst, *, PERSON WHO STUDIES DETAILS
analytic, *, cal, cally, PERSON WHO STUDIES DETAILS
analyze, *, ed, zing, er, zable, zation, STRICT EXAMINATION/ STUDY "prefixes: un"
anamashen, animate(tion)
anamation, animate(tion)
anamulistik, animal(istic)
anarchy, hies, hism, hist, histic, hic, hical, hically, NO GOVERNMENT/ CAPITALISM
anarkey, anarchy
anasthesia, anesthesia
anatomy, mic, mical, mically, COMPLETE STRUCTURE OF A BODY
anaumely, anomaly
anauns, announce
anayaleit, annihilate
anbroder, embroider
ancestor, *, ry, tral, trally, LINEAGE
anchor, *, red, ring, rage, rages, STABILITY, BOAT HOLD
ancient, *, tness, tly, OLD, GREAT IN AGE
anckshes, anxious
ancorij, encourage / anchor(age)
ancsayeti, anxiety
anches, anxious
ancsiuty, anxiety
and, WORD USED AS A CONJUNCTION, THIS PLUS THAT, ALSO, INCLUDING (or see ant/ aunt/ end)
andanger, endanger
andefir, endeavor
andevur, endeavor
andlis, endless
andure, endure
ane, any

anebody, anybody
anebreated, inebriate(d)
anecdote, *, tal, STORY (or see antidote)
anedot, anecdote / antidote
anedotul, anecdote(tal)
anegma, enigma / enema
anekdote, anecdote
anekwitable, inequitable
anel, anal / annul
anelidek, analytic
anelog, analog
anelyze, analyze
anemal, animal
anemashen, animate(tion)
anemate, animate
anemation, animate(tion)
aneme, enemy
anemea, anemia
anemek, anemic
anemia, BLOOD HAS A DEFICIENCY/ NEED (or see enema/ enigma)
anemic, cally, BLOOD HAS A DEFICIENCY/ NEED
anemul, animal
anemulestik, animal(istic)
anequitable, inequitable
aneresm, aneurysm
anerism, aneurysm
anerjetek, energetic
anes, anus
aneshil, initial
anesthesia, iologist, iology, AN ANESTHETIC
anesthetic, *, cally, ist, ize, PAIN KILLER
anesthetist, *, ONE WHO ADMINISTERS ANESTHESIA
anesthetize, *, ed, zing, zation, TO DULL PAIN WITH DRUG
anesthezia, anesthesia
anesthutize, anesthetize
aneurysm, *, WEAK BLOOD VESSEL WALL AT BASE OF BRAIN
anew, FRESH/ NEW START
anewity, annuity
anewol, annual
anezthetic, anesthetic
anforse, enforce

angaje,engage
angchus,anxious
angchus,anxious
angel,*,lic,lical,lically,SPIRITUAL BEING (or see angle)
angelek,angel(ic)
anger,*,red,ring,gry,grily,MAD
angil,angel / angle
angir,anger
angle,*,ed,ling,er,SLANT/ TILT/ PERSPECTIVE IN DEGREES (or see angel)
angrafe,engrave
angrave,engrave
angre,angry
angrele,angrily
angreust,angry(riest)
angri,angry
angrily,OF ANGER
angry,rier,riest,EMOTION OF IRRITATED DISAPPOINTMENT
angryest,angry(riest)
angshes,anxious
angshus,anxious
angsiute,anxiety
anguish,hed,hing,SORROW
angul,angle / angel
angwish,anguish
angziute,anxiety
anialate,annihilate
anibreated,inebriate(d)
anidot,anecdote / antidote
anidotul,anecdote(tal)
anikdote,anecdote / antidote
anil,anal / annul
anilate,annihilate
anilidek,analytic
anilize,analyze
anilog,analog
anilyze,analyze
animal,*,listic,lise,lism,list,lity,NOT HUMAN
animashen,animate(tion)
animate,*,ed,ting,tion,tic,to,LIVELY,AS IF REAL
"prefixes: in"
animea,anemia / enema

animec,anemic
animic,anemic
animul,animal
animulistek,animal(istic)
aniresm,aneurysm
anis,anus
anishal,initial
anisthedek,anesthetic
anisthetic,anesthetic
anisthezia,anesthesia
anitiate,initiate
aniu,anew
aniual,annual
aniulate,annihilate
anjekshen,inject(ion)
anjel,angel
anjelik,angel(ic)
anjil,angel
anjoiment,enjoy(ment)
anjul,angel
ankches,anxious
ankchus,anxious
anker,anchor
ankor,anchor
ankoreg,encourage / anchor(age)
ankreust,angry(riest)
ankry,angry
ankshis,anxious
ankshus,anxious
anksiuty,anxiety
ankulent,inoculate(ant)
ankureg,anchor(age)
ankurig,encourage / anchor(age)
anlarje,enlarge
anliten,enlighten
anmal,animal
annihilate,*,ed,ting,tion,tor,DESTROY
announce,*,ed,cing,ement,er,DECLARE
annoy,*,yed,ying,yance,IRRITATE
annoyents,annoy(ance)
annual,*,lly,lize,YEARLY "prefixes: bi/ semi"
annuely,annual(lly)
annuity,ties,ANNUAL STIPEND/ PAYMENT

annul,lment,VOID,REVOKE (or see anal)
annunciate,*,ed,ting,tion,tor,tory,ANNOUNCE (or see enunciate/ pronounciate)
anoed,annoy(ed)
anoent,anoint
anof,enough
anogreashen,inaugurate(tion)
anogreation,inaugurate(tion)
anoint,*,ted,ting,tment,TO SELECT/ CONSECRATE
anolidek,analytic
anomale,anomaly
anomaly,lies,lous,lously,listic,NOT NORMAL, IRREGULAR
anomile,anomaly
anomulus,anomaly(lous)
anonemous,anonymous
anonemusly,anonymous(ly)
anonimous,anonymous
anonimusly,anonymous(ly)
anonseate,enunciate/ annunciate
anonymity,REMAINS UNKNOWN
anonymous,sly,sness,mity,NOT KNOWN
anoqulent,inoculate(ant)
anoresm,aneurysm
anorgee,energy
anorgetek,energetic
anorkey,anarchy
anormus,enormous
another,ADDITIONAL
anothir,another
anough,enough
anounse,announce
anowe,annoy
anownse,announce
anoy,annoy
anoyance,annoy(ance)
anoyd,annoy(ed)
anportant,important
anrich,enrich
anrol,enroll
anrold,enroll(ed)
anser,answer
anseruble,answer(able)

ansestor,ancestor
anshent,ancient
anshunt,ancient
ansiklopedea,encyclopedia
ansir,answer
ansistor,ancestor
ansur,answer
ansuruble,answer(able)
answer,*,red,ring,rable,rably,SOLUTION "prefixes: un"
ant,*,SMALL SIX-LEGGED INSECT (or see and/ ante/ anti/ aunt)
antagonize,*,ed,ist,istic,istically,ENEMY/ OPPOSITION
antai,anti / ante
antay,anti / ante
ante,PREFIX INDICATING 'BEFORE/ PRECEDING' MOST OFTEN MODIFIES THE WORD, POKER EXPRESSION, TO PRECEDE/ COME BEFORE (or see anti/ aunt(ie))
antebiotik,antibiotic
antecepate,anticipate
antefreeze,antifreeze
antehistamene,antihistamine
anteke,antique
antekwedy,antique(uity)
antekwity,antique(uity)
antelope,*,MAMMAL
antena,antenna
antenna,DEVICE TO ATTRACT SIGNALS/ FREQUENCY
anterior,*,rity,rly,BEFORE, IN FRONT OF, TOWARDS THE FRONT (or see interior)
antesapashen,anticipate(tion)
antesepate,anticipate
antesupation,anticipate(tion)
anthem,*,SONG
anthim,anthem
anthrapology,anthropology
anthripology,anthropology
anthropology,*gical,STUDY OF HUMANITY
anti,OPPOSE/ DISAGREE, PREFIX INDICATING 'AGAINST' MOST OFTEN MODIFIES THE WORD (or see aunt(ie)/ ante)
antibiotic,*,cally,MANMADE CHEMICAL
anticepate,anticipate
anticipate,*,ed,ting,tion,tive,tory,EXPECT

antidote,*,tal,USED TO REVERSE EFFECTS OF POISON (or see anecdote)
antifreeze,SUBSTANCE TO PREVENT FREEZING
antihistamine,INACTIVATES HISTAMINE
antikwedy,antique(uity)
antilope,antelope
antina,antenna
antique,*,ed,ely,uity,uate,uated,ANCIENT
antiquedy,antique(uity)
antireor,anterior / interior
antisapashen,anticipate(tion)
antisupation,anticipate(tion)
antonym,*,mic,mous,WORDS WITH OPPOSITE MEANINGS
antorse,endorse / indoor(s)
antser,answer
antulope,antelope
anu,anew
anual,annual
anuale,annual(lly)
anudot,anecdote
anuel,annual
anuety,annuity
anuile,annual(lly)
anuity,annuity
anul,annul
anulidek,analytic
anulise,analyze
anulyze,analyze
anumashen,animate(tion)
anumate,animate
anumation,animate(tion)
anumel,animal
anumilestik,animal(istic)
anunseate,enunciate/ annunciate
anuresm,aneurysm
anurgee,energy
anurjetek,energetic
anus,LOWER ORIFICE
anustheshu,anesthesia
anusthetik,anesthetic
anuther,another
anuzthetek,anesthetic

anvilope,envelope
anvirunmint,environment
anvy,envy
anwritch,enrich
anxaieti,anxiety
anxiety,ties,ious,iously,iousness,UNEASINESS
anxious,iously,iousness,UNEASINESS
any,ybody,yhow,ymore,yone,ything,yway,ywhere, ytime,SOME AT RANDOM, A PORTION OF
anybody,y's,ANY PERSON
anyerism,aneurysm
anyual,annual
anyurism,aneurysm
aoch,ouch
ap,PREFIX INDICATING 'TO/ TOWARDS' MOST OFTEN MODIFIES THE WORD (or see up)
apacalips,apocalypse
apacalyps,apocalypse
apademic,epidemic
apakalips,apocalypse
apal,apple / appall
apaloge,apology
aparatus,apparatus
apareshun,apparition
aparint,apparent
aparition,apparition
apart,MAKE INTO SEPARATE PIECES
apartment,*,ROOMS IN DWELLING
apartmint,apartment
apasenter,epicenter
apasom,opossum
apathetic,cal,cally,INDIFFERENT, NO EMOTION
apathy,hetic,INDIFFERENT, NO EMOTION
apatight,appetite
apatit,appetite
apatizer,appetizer
apatizing,appetizing
apaucalips,apocalypse
apaukalips,apocalypse
apaukalyps,apocalypse
apauled,appall(lled)
apaustrufe,apostrophe
apdoman,abdomen

apdukt, abduct
apduman, abdomen
apeal, appeal
apearance, appearance
apecal, apical
apecl, apical
apeel, appeal
apekal, apical
apel, apple / appeal / appall
apendektumy, appendectomy
apenyun, opinion
apera, opera
aperal, apparel
aperant, apparent
aperatus, apparatus
apereit, operate
apereshen, apparition
aperil, apparel
aperint, apparent
aperishen, apparition
aperition, apparition
apertiun, opportune
aperul, apparel
aperunt, apparent
apesode, episode
apetait, appetite
apethetik, apathetic
apetight, appetite
apetit, appetite
apetizer, appetizer
aphed, aphid
aphid, *, INSECT
apical, lly, APEX, TIP/ TOP OF "prefixes: sub"
apidemic, epidemic
apikal, apical
apil, apple / able / appeal
apindectemy, appendectomy
apineun, opinion
apinion, opinion
apinyun, opinion
apiol, appeal
apirans, appearance
apirens, appearance

apiretion, apparition
apithetik, apathetic
apitite, appetite
apitizer, appetizer
aplakashen, application
aplaud, applaud
aplauz, applause
aple, apple
aplecable, applicable
aplecant, applicant
aplecation, application
aplecator, applicator
aplefeus, oblivious
aplekant, applicant
aplekashen, application
aplekator, applicator
aplekuble, applicable
apli, apply
aplianse, appliance
aplicable, applicable
aplicant, applicant
aplicator, applicator
aplid, apply(lied)
apliderate, obliterate
aplifeus, oblivious
aplikashen, application
aplikation, application
aplikator, applicator
aplikuble, applicable
apliveon, oblivion
aplod, applaud
aplos, applause
aplukant, applicant
aplukashen, application
aplukation, application
aplukator, applicator
aply, apply
apocalypse, ptic, ptical, ptically, pticism, AN EXPRESSION STARTED BY RELIGION NOW BEING COMMONLY USED TO MEAN DESTRUCTION/ END OF EVERYTHING WE KNOW
apodimic, epidemic
apoent, appoint

apoentment, appointment
apoint, appoint
apointment, appointment
apokolypse, apocalypse
apokulypse, apocalypse
apol, apple / able / appall
apold, appall(lled)
apolegize, apology(gize)
apoligize, apology(gize)
apology, gies, gize, gizes, gized, gizing, getic, getically, ASK FORGIVENESS
apolstery, upholstery
apoluge, apology
apolugize, apology(gize)
aponent, opponent
aponit, opponent
apose, oppose
apostrophe, *, SYMBOL IN ENGLISH LANGUAGE
aposum, opossum
apotizing, appetizing
apotment, appointment
apounent, opponent
apous, oppose
apoynt, appoint
apoze, oppose
appal, apple / appall
appall, *, lled, lling, llingly, DISMAYED, SHOCKED, HORRIFIED
apparatus, ses, EQUIPMENT
apparel, CLOTHING
apparent, tly, tness, CLEAR
apparition, *, SPIRIT
appatite, appetite
appatizer, appetizer
appeal, *, led, ling, lingly, lable, CALL FOR MERCY, VIEW FAVORABLY "prefixes: un"
appear, *, red, ring, rance, BECOME VISIBLE "prefixes: dis"
appearance, *, BECOME VISIBLE
appel, appeal / apple
appendectomy, mies, REMOVE APPENDIX FROM BODY
apper, appear
apperal, apparel
apperent, apparent

Column 1 (definitions)

appetite, *, tive,izing,izer, DESIRE, A HUNGER, A FOOD
appetizer, *, FOOD BEFORE A MEAL
appetizing,gly,zer, DESIRE, A HUNGER, A FOOD
applaud, *, ded,ding,use, USE HANDS TO CLAP
applause, ACCLAIM, USE HANDS TO CLAP
apple, *, FRUIT
appliance, *, SPECIALIZED TOOL/ MACHINE TO PERFORM SPECIFIC TASKS
applicable, eness,ly, RELEVANT, USEFUL "prefixes: in"
applicant, *, CANDIDATE FOR EMPLOYMENT
applicate, *, ed,ting,tion,tor,ant, PUT TO USE, APPLY
application, *, FORM TO APPLY FOR WORK "prefixes: dis"
applicator, *, ting, USED TO APPLY SOMETHING
apply, lies, lied, lying, lier, liable, liableness, licate, lication, licator, lictory, licative, licatively, licable, licably, licability, PUT ON, RELEVANT TO "prefixes: mis/ pre/ un"
appoint, *, ted,ting,tee,tment, ASSIGN, DESIGNATE "prefixes: dis"
appointment, *, AN ASSIGNED TIME "prefixes: dis"
apprahenshun, apprehension
appraisal, *, ser, sement, EVALUATION
appraise, *, ed,sing,sable, ement,er,sal, EVALUATION
apprapo, apropos
appreciate, *, ed, ting,tion,tory, tive,able, GRATEFUL "prefixes: in/ un"
apprehend, *, ded, ding,nsive, nsively, nsiveness,nsion, nsible, TO SEIZE, BE CAUTIOUS "prefixes: mis"
apprehension, *, CAUTIOUS, HESITANT "prefixes: mis"
apprehensive, ely, eness, ion, ible, CAUTIOUS "prefixes: mis"
apprentice, *, ed, cing, eship, LEARNER/ IN TRAINING
appresif, oppress(ive)
appripo, apropos
approach, hes, hed, hing, hable, hability, hableness, hably, ADVANCE TOWARDS, NEARING "prefixes: in/ un"
appropo, apropos
appropriate, *, ted, ting, ely, eness, PROPER TO, BELONGS ALONG WITH, IN CHARACTER WITH "prefixes: in/ mis/ non"
approve, *, ed, ving, val,vable, vingly, ACCEPTANCE/ COMMENDATION "prefixes: dis"

approximate, ed, ely, ting,tion, AROUND/ SOMEWHAT
apprupo, apropos
apra, opera
apracot, apricot
aprahenshun, apprehension
apraisal, appraisal
apraise, appraise
apral, april
aprapo, apropos
aprase, appraise
aprased, appraise(d)
aprasing, appraise(sing)
aprazul, appraisal
apreciate, appreciate
aprehend, apprehend
aprehenshun, apprehension
aprehensive, apprehensive
aprehind, apprehend
aprekot, apricot
aprel, april
apren, apron
aprentis, apprentice
apres, oppress
apresheate, appreciate
apreshen, oppress(ion)
apresif, oppress(ive)
aprhenshun, apprehension
apricot, *, FRUIT
aprikot, apricot
april, A MONTH OF THE YEAR (ENGLISH)
aprin, apron
aprintise, apprentice
apripo, apropos
aproach, approach
aproch, approach
aprol, april
apron, *, CLOTHING PROTECTOR
apropos, SUITABLE IN A PARTICULAR SITUATION/ TIME
apropreate, appropriate
apropriate, appropriate
aproprieit, appropriate
aprotch, approach
aproval, approve(val)

aproxemat, approximate
aproxemation, approximate(tion)
aproximate, approximate
aproximeit, approximate
aproxumation, approximate(tion)
apruful, approve(val)
apruhensev, apprehensive
aprul, april
aprupo, apropos
apruvel, approve(val)
apsalutly, absolute(ly)
apsens, absence / absent(s)
apsent, absent
apsentee, absent(ee)
apserd, absurd
apserdle, absurd(ly)
apshen, option
apsiloot, absolute
apsins, absence / absent(s)
apsintee, absent(ee)
apsird, absurd
apsoloot, absolute
apsolute, absolute
apsolution, absolve(lution)
apsolv, absolve
apsorb, absorb
apstane, abstain
apstinent, abstinent
apstract, abstract
apstrukshen, abstract(ion) / obstruct(ion)
apstunent, abstinent
apsulootly, absolute(ly)
apsulute, absolute
apsululy, absolute(ly)
apsurd, absurd
apsurdly, absurd(ly)
aptemais, optimize
aptetood, aptitude
aptetude, aptitude
aptikate, abdicate
aptimen, abdomen
aptitewd, aptitude
aptitude, *, TENDENCY TOWARDS, AFFINITY FOR

aptomen,abdomen
aptumen,abdomen
apul,apple
aputhetik,apathetic
aputit,appetite
aputizer,appetizer
apuzit,opposite
apzaulv,absolve
apzolv,absolve
apzorb,absorb
aqaint,acquaint
aqefir,aquifer
aqire,acquire
aqiumuleit,accumulate
aqiuponcsher,acupuncture
aqiut,acquit
aqua,atic,atics,ueous,WATER, TO DO WITH WATER, A COLOR "prefixes: non/ sub"
aquaduct,aqueduct
aquaent,acquaint
aquafer,aquifer
aquaier,aquire
aquaint,acquaint
aquareum,aquarium
aquarium,*,FISH CONTAINER
aquatic,*,IN WATER "prefixes: non/ semi/ sub"
aqueduct,*,rous,PROVIDES WATER
aquefer,aquifer
aquiesent,acquiesce(nt)
aquifer,*,rous,PROVIDES WATER
aquintonce,acquaintance
aquipid,equip(pped)
aquisishon,acquisition
aquiureit,accurate
aquius,accuse
aquivalint,equivalent
aqute,acute
aqwazitun,acquisition
aqwiesent,acquiesce(nt)
aqwire,acquire
aqwit,acquit
aqwuzishen,acquisition
ar,are / heir / air / our / hour

ara,array / aura
arachnid,*,noid,WINGLESS ANTHROPODS
aradekate,eradicate
aradic,erratic / erotic
aradikashen,eradicate(tion)
aradikate,eradicate
araign,arraign
araignment,arraign(ment)
arainment,arraign(ment)
arakned,arachnid
arangment,arrange(ment)
aranj,arrange
aranment,arraign(ment)
arase,erase
araser,eraser
arashinal,irrational
aratic,erratic
araudik,erotic
aray,array
arayn,arraign
araze,erase
arazer,eraser
arbeder,arbiter
arbeter,arbiter
arbetrate,arbitrate
arbiter,*,tral,ONE WHO MAKES DETERMINATION
arbitrary,rily,riness,RANDOM DETERMINATION
arbitrate,*,ed,ting,tion,tor,TO DETERMINE
arborne,airborne
arbutrashen,arbitrate(tion)
arbutrate,arbitrate
arc,*,PART OF A CURVE (or see ark/ arch)
arcade,*,dia,OF GAMES OR ARCHED PASSAGEWAY
arcaek,archaic
arch,hes,hed,hing,A CURVED BEND, PREFIX INDICATING 'CHIEF/ BEGINNING' MOST OFTEN MODIFIES THE WORD (or see ark/ arc) "prefixes: over"
archaek,archaic
archaic,OLD-FASHIONED, ANCIENT
archeology,gist,gical,STUDY OF PEOPLE
archer,*,ry,ONE WHO USES BOWS AND ARROWS
archetekt,architect
archir,archer

architect,*,ture,tural,BUILDER
archive,*,ed,ving,val,vist,PLACE OF PUBLIC RECORDS "prefixes: un"
archur,archer
archure,archer
arckiology,archeology
arctic,NORTH POLE "prefixes: sub"
ardefishal,artificial
ardekle,article
ardent,tly,PASSIONATE
ardery,artery
ardest,artist
ardewous,arduous
ardgewus,arduous
ardifishul,artificial
ardikle,article
ardint,ardent
ardiry,artery
ardist,artist
ardjewous,arduous
ardufishul,artificial
ardukle,article
arduous,sly,sness,DIFFICULT
ardury,artery
are,TO BE,IS (or see air/ heir/ hour/ our)
area,*,al,RANGE OF CONCEPT/ EVENT/ OPERATION
arear,arrear
ared,arid
aregate,irrigate
aregenashen,originate(tion)
aregeno,oregano
aregenul,origin(al)
arejenul,origin(al)
arekshin,erect(ion)
arekt,erect
aren't,CONTRACTION OF THE WORDS "ARE NOT"
arena,*,ENCLOSED SPACE
arend,errand
areplasible,irreplaceable
areprochible,irreproachable
arer,error / arrear
arest,arrest
arestokrat,aristocrat

arethmatic, arithmetic
areu, area
areul, aerial
arezt, arrest
argeumint, argument
argew, argue
argkeumint, argument
argue, *, ed, uing, uable, uably, DEBATE, DISCUSS "prefixes: in/ un"
argument, *, tation, tative, tum, DEBATE, DISCUSS
arguous, arduous
arguwus, arduous
aria, area
arid, dity, PARCHED "prefixes: semi"
arie, awry
arife, arrive
ariful, arrival
arigate, irrigate
arigenashen, originate(tion)
ariginul, origin(al)
arijinul, origin(al)
arind, errand
arint, aren't
ariplasible, irreplaceable
arir, error
arisol, aerosol
aristocrat, *, tic, acy, WEALTHY UPPER CLASS
arithmetic, cal, cally, cian, MATH
arivd, arrive(d)
arive, arrive
arivul, arrival
arjuwus, arduous
ark, *, BOX/ CHEST/ CUPBOARD/ BOAT (or see arc/ arch)
arkade, arcade
arkaek, archaic
arkaik, archaic
arkeoligy, archeology
arketekt, architect
arkeu, argue
arkiology, archeology
arkitect, architect
arkiteksher, architect(ure)
arkive, archive

arktic, arctic
arku, argue
arkumint, argument
arkutekshur, architect(ure)
arkyve, archive
arloom, heirloom
arm, *, med, ming, mament, APPENDAGE ON UPPER TORSO, TO TAKE UP WEAPONS "prefixes: dis/ un/ under"
armature, *, tation, tative, tum, DEVICE OR STRUCTURE/ SUPPORT
arme, army
armes, army(mies)
armicher, armature
armonica, harmonica
armor, red, ry, ries, rer, BODY PROTECTION, COVERING, MILITARY/ WEAPONS "prefixes: un"
armucher, armature
armur, armor
army, mies, MANY BODIES
arn, iron
arnamint, ornament
arnge, orange
arnje, orange
arnt, aren't
arnument, ornament
aro, arrow
aroara, aurora
arobek, aerobic
arobik, aerobic
arochun, erosion
arode, erode
arodik, erotic
arodynamic, aerodynamic
aroganse, arrogance
arogate, irrigate
arogent, arrogance(nt)
arogint, arrogance(nt)
aroma, *, atic, atize, ODOR, SMELL
aromadek, aroma(tic)
arond, errand
aronic, ironic
aror, error
arora, aurora

arosef, erosive
aroshin, erosion
arosive, erosive
around, HERE AND THERE
arouse, *, ed, sing, sal, AWAKEN/ STIMULATE/ ACTIVATE
arouzel, arouse(sal)
arow, arrow
arownd, around
arowsul, arouse(sal)
arowze, arouse
arport, airport
arraign, *, ned, ning, nment, ANSWER INDICTMENT
arrange, *, ed, ging, ement, er, ADJUST, SITUATE "prefixes: dis/ un"
arranment, arraign(ment)
array, *, yed, ORDER "prefixes: dis"
arrear, *, rage, PAST DUE
arrest, *, ted, ting, tingly, SUSPEND, CAPTURE
arrival, *, BE AT DESTINATION
arrive, *, ed, ving, val, PRESENT AT DESTINATION
arrogance, nt, ntly, OVERLY SELF-IMPORTANT
arrow, *, SHAFT WITH POINT
arrowgance, arrogance
arsen, arson
arson, *, nist, MALICIOUS/ INTENTIONAL BURNING
arsunest, arson(ist)
art, *, tist, tistry, tsy, ty, tistic, tistical, tistically, tisan, tful, tfully, tfulness, tless, tlessly, tlessness, tiness, METHOD OF EXPRESSION "prefixes: in/ non"
arteculate, articulate
artefishel, artificial
artekewlate, articulate
artekulashen, articulate(tion)
artekulate, articulate
artelury, artillery
artereal, arterial
arterial, *, PATH FOR FLOW
artery, ries, ric, CHANNEL FOR TRANSPORTATION
artesdik, artist(ic)
artest, artist
artestek, artist(ic)
arthridek, arthritis(ic)
arthridis, arthritis

arthritis,ic,INFLAMMATION
arthudox,orthodox
article,*,PART,ONE OF SEVERAL
articulate,*,ed,ting,tion,tely,eness,INTEGRATE, SPECIFIC "prefixes: dis/ in"
artificial,lly,SIMULATED,NOT REA_
artifishul,artificial
artik,arctic
artikel,article
artikewlate,articulate
artikulashen,articulate(tion)
artikulate,articulate
artillery,FOR WEAPONS
artireal,arterial
artiry,artery
artisdik,artist(ic)
artist,*,tistic,tistically,SKILLED "prefixes: in/ un"
artistek,artist(ic)
artsh,arch
artsher,archer
artucle,article
artufishul,artificial
artury,artery
arubshen,erupt(ion) / irrupt(ion)
arubt,erupt / irrupt
arubtif,erupt(ive) / irrupt(ive)
arugate,irrigate
arupshen,erupt(ion) / irrupt(ion)
arupt,erupt / irrupt
aruptif,erupt(ive) / irrupt(ive)
aruption,erupt(ion) / irrupt(ion)
arye,awry
aryve,arrive
as,WORD USED TO COMPARE, PREFIX INDICATING 'TO/ TOWARDS' MOST OFTEN MODIFIES THE WORD (or see ace)
asaeal,assail
asaee,essay
asail,assail
asalt,assault
asasen,assassin
asault,assault
asay,essay

asbekt,aspect
asberashun,aspirate(tion)
asberegus,asparagus
asbeshulee,especially
asbestos,TYPE OF FIBER
asbir,aspire
asburin,aspirin
ascape,escape
ascend,*,ded,ding,dable,dance,dancy,dant,der, nsion,nsional,DOMINANT,RISING ABOVE,GO UP (or see assent/ ascent)
ascendant,*,nce,DOMINANT,RISE ABOVE OTHERS
ascension,*,nal,TO GO UP
ascent,*,nsion,MOTION UPWARDS (or see assent/ ascend)
ascertain,*,ned,ning,nable,nably,ner,nment,MAKE SURE "prefixes: un"
ascetic,cal,cally,cism,STRICT,SEVERE,EXCESSIVE (or see acetic/ acidic)
ascind,ascend / ascent / assent
ascrow,escrow
asd,ask(ed) / ax(ed) / ace(d) / acid
asdeem,esteem
asdonesh,astonish
ased,ask(ed) / ax(ed) / acid / ace(d)
asedek,acetic / acidic / ascetic
asemble,assemble / assemble(ly)
asemetric,asymmetric
asemewlate,assimilate
asemulate,assimilate
asend,ascend / ascent / assent
asendent,ascendant
asense,essence
asenshil,essential
asent,ascend / ascent / assent
asential,essential
asershen,assert(ion)
asert,assert
asertane,ascertain
asertif,assert(ive)
asertion,assert(ion)
ases,assess / access / ace(s)
aseshun,accession

asesible,access(ible)
asesment,assessment
asest,assist
asesuble,access(ible)
aset,acid / asset
asetic,acetic / acidic / ascetic
asexual,NOT SEXUAL
asfalt,asphalt
asfault,asphalt
asfikseate,asphyxiate
asfixiate,asphyxiate
asfolt,asphalt
ashamed,dly,TOUCHED BY SHAME,NOT PROUD "prefixes: un"
ashamt,ashamed
asheeve,achieve
asher,assure
ashirense,assure(rance)
ashtarik,asterisk
ashuranse,assure(rance)
asid,acid / aside
aside,SEPARATE FROM
asidic,acetic / acidic / ascetic
asiduous,assiduous
asign,assign
asignment,assignment
asijuous,assiduous
asilum,asylum
asim,awesome
asimble,assemble
asimetric,asymmetric
asimetry,asymmetry
asimilate,assimilate
asimulate,assimilate
asind,ascend
asindent,ascendant
asine,assign
asinment,assignment
asinse,essence
asinshul,essential
asint,ascend / ascent / assent
asirshen,assert(ion)
asirt,assert

asirtane,ascertain
asirtev,assert(ive)
asist,assist
asitic,acetic / acidic / ascetic
ask,* ,ked,king,DORMANT STATE "prefixes: un"
askalador,escalator
askalater,escalator
askap,escape
askort,escort
askrow,escrow
askt,ask(ed) / ax(ed)
askulader,escalator
asleep,DORMANT STATE
asmu,asthma
asocheate,associate
associate,associate
asolt,assault
asorded,assorted
asordment,assortment
asorted,assorted
asortment,assortment
asosheate,associate
asoshiate,associate
asparagus,VEGETABLE
aspect,* ,OUTLOOK
aspekt,aspect
asperagus,asparagus
asperashun,aspirate(tion)
asperation,aspirate(tion)
asperen,aspirin
asperugus,asparagus
aspeshilee,especially
aspeshulee,especially
aspestus,asbestos
asphalt,MINERAL PITCH
asphixiate,asphyxiate
asphyxiate,* ,ed,ting,tion,OF BREATHING
aspirashun,aspirate(tion)
aspiration,aspirate(tion)
aspirate,* ,ed,ting,tor,tion,tional,AMBITION, OF BREATHING "prefixes: un"
aspire,* ,ed,ring,er,rate,rant,ration,GOAL,DESIRE "prefixes: un"
aspirin,* ,PAIN RELIEVER

asprashun,aspirate(tion)
aspren,aspirin
aspurashun,aspirate(tion)
aspuration,aspirate(tion)
aspuren,aspirin
assail,lable,lant,IMPACT UPON "prefixes: un"
assasin,assassin
assassin,* ,nate,nation,TO MURDER,A MURDERER
assault,* ,ted,ting,ATTACK WITH INTENT TO HARM
assemble,* ,ed,ling,lage,ly,PUT TOGETHER "prefixes: dis/ un"
assent,* ,ted,ting,ter,tor,tingly,tive,tively,tiveness, AGREEMENT (or see ascent)
assert,* ,ted,ting,tion,table,ter,tive,tively,tiveness, INSIST
assess,sses,ssed,ssing,ssment,ssable,EXAMINE, EVALUATE "prefixes: non"
assessment,* ,APPRAISAL,EVALUATION
asset,* ,POSSESS SOMETHING VALUABLE
assiduous,sly,DILIGENT
assign,* ,ned,ning,nment,APPORTION
assignment,* ,ASSIGNED WORK
assimetric,asymmetric
assimilate,* ,ed,ting,tion,MAKE INTO, BECOME LIKE
assint,assent
assist,* ,ted,ting,tant,tance,HELP
associate,* ,ed,ting,tion,tive,CONNECTION TO "prefixes: dis/ non"
assorted,ting,tment,VARIOUS TYPES
assortment,VARIOUS TYPES
assume,* ,ed,ming,mingly,mer,mable,mption,mptive, SUPPOSE A FACT "prefixes: un"
assumption,* ,ive,TAKE FOR GRANTED
assure,* ,ed,rance,rances,CERTAINTY "prefixes: re"
assymetric,asymmetric
ast,ask / ask(ed) / ax(ed)
asteem,esteem
astemate,estimate
asterik,asterisk
asterisk,LITTLE TEXT STAR
asteroed,asteroid
asteroid,* ,PERTAINING TO STAR
asthetik,aesthetic

asthma,atic,atical,atically,DIFFICULTY BREATHING
asthmu,asthma
astimate,estimate
astonesh,astonish
astonish,hes,hed,hing,hment,SURPRISE/ IMPRESS
astragen,estrogen
astral,ly,STELLAR "prefixes: sub"
astrawneme,astronomy
astrek,asterisk
astrengent,astringent
astrenjint,astringent
astrenot,astronaut
astres,estrus
astrik,asterisk
astringent,* ,ncy,tly,ACRID "prefixes: sub"
astrinot,astronaut
astris,estrus
astroed,asteroid
astrol,astral
astrolegy,astrology
astrology,ger,gic,gical,gically,gist,PREDICT THE FUTURE WITH THE STARS
astronaut,* ,PERSON OF SPACE FLIGHT
astroneme,astronomy
astronomic,mical,mically,NUMEROUS/ GREAT PROPORTION
astronomy,mer,mers,OBSERVE CELESTIAL BODIES "prefixes: bio"
astronot,astronaut
astronume,astronomy
astroyd,asteroid
astrugen,estrogen
astrul,astral
astrunot,astronaut
astumate,estimate
astural,astral
asturik,asterisk
asturisk,asterisk
asum,awesome / assume
asumetric,asymmetric
asumpshen,assumption
asumption,assumption
asumshen,assumption

asunse, essence
asurans, assure(rance)
asurants, assure(rance)
asurshen, assert(ion)
asurtif, assert(ive)
asylom, asylum
asylum, REFUGE FOR DESTITUTE
asymetric, asymmetric
asymmetric, cal, ry, ries, OFF-BALANCE
asymmetry, ries, OFF-BALANCE
at, A PREPOSITION EXPRESSING LOCATION OR SOMETHING IN PARTICULAR, PREFIX INDICATING 'TO/ TOWARDS' MOST OFTEN MODIFIES THE WORD (or see ate/ eight/ add)
atach, attach
atack, attack
ataen, attain
atain, attain
atak, attack
atament, adamant
atamint, adamant
atane, attain
atatch, attach
atcheeve, achieve
ate, PAST TENSE FOR THE WORD 'EAT' (or see ate/ eight/ add) "prefixes: over"
atec, attic / addict
ated, add(ed)
atek, attic / addict
atekwase, adequacy
atembt, attempt
atemobel, automobile
atempt, attempt
atemt, attempt
atenchin, attention
atend, attend
atendens, attend(ance)
atendent, attend(ant)
atenshin, attention
atentef, attentive
atention, attention
atentive, attentive
atequasy, adequacy

ateqwit, adequate
aternal, eternal
aterney, attorney
atest, attest
atesy, odyssey
atetif, additive
atetude, attitude
atgasent, adjacent
atgasint, adjacent
atgern, adjourn
atgewdikate, adjudicate
atgust, adjust
athear, adhere
atheist, ism, tic, tical, tically, DISBELIEF IN A GOD
athek, ethic
athere, adhere
athesif, adhesive
athic, ethic
athiest, atheist
athik, ethic
athleat, athlete
athlete, *, tic, tics, tically, SPORTS TRAINED, ATHLETE "prefixes: deca"
athletic, *, tically, SPORTS TRAINED, ATHLETE
athnek, ethnic
athnuk, ethnic
athorety, authority
athrek, ether(ic)
athuk, ethic
atic, attic / addict
atid, add(ed)
atikit, etiquette
atikwit, adequate
atikwuse, adequacy
atimant, adamant
atimint, adamant
atimt, attempt
atinchon, attention
atind, attend
atinshun, attention
atipecle, atypical
atipikul, atypical
atiquit, adequate

atiquot, adequate
atire, attire
atisum, autism
atitif, additive
atitude, attitude
atmechen, admission
atmedid, admit(tted)
atmenester, administer
atmenustrashen, administrate(tion)
atmeshen, admission
atmesphere, atmosphere
atmichen, admission
atmided, admit(tted)
atminaster, administer
atminastrashin, administrate(tion)
atminuster, administer
atminustrashen, administrate(tion)
atmird, admire(d)
atmire, admire
atmisef, admission(ive)
atmisfeer, atmosphere
atmishun, admission
atmisphere, atmosphere
atmisuble, admissible
atmit, admit
atmonish, admonish
atmosfear, atmosphere
atmosphere, ric, rical, rically, AROUND A PLANET "prefixes: sub"
atmusfeer, atmosphere
atmusphere, atmosphere
atmyre, admire
atobiografy, autobiography
atograf, autograph
atolesense, adolescence
atolesint, adolescent
atom, *, mic, mically, mize, mizer, PARTICLES OF ELEMENT "prefixes: non/ sub"
atomadik, automatic
atomatik, automatic
atomobel, automobile
atonal, *, lity, listic, lly, CANNOT HEAR TRUE TONES
atone, *, eable, nable, ement, MAKE UP FOR, AMEND

atonime, autonomy
atonome, autonomy
atorney, attorney
atracshun, attraction
atract, attract
atraction, attraction
atrakshun, attraction
atrakt, attract
atraktif, attract(ive)
atrebute, attribute
atrefee, atrophy
atrenulen, adrenaline
atress, address
atreum, atrium
atribute, attribute
atriem, atrium
atrifee, atrophy
atriss, address
atrium,* , GLASS ROOM
atrocious, sly, sness, OUTRAGEOUS
atrocity, ties, OUTRAGEOUS
atrocius, atrocious
atrofee, atrophy
atrophy, hies, hied, hic, DEGENERATE
atrosety, atrocity
atroshus, atrocious
atrufee, atrophy
atsetera, etcetera
atsheve, achieve
attach, hes, hed, hing, hment, FASTEN "prefixes: un"
attack,* , ked, king, ker, ASSAIL
attain,* , ned, ning, nability, nable, nableness, nment, GAIN "prefixes: un"
attempt,* , ted, ting, TRY TO ACCOMPLISH
attemt, attempt
attenchon, attention
attend,* , ded, ding, dingly, dance, dant, der, ACCOMPANY, GO TO "prefixes: in"
attention, ive, FOCUS ON "prefixes: in"
attentive, ively, eness, FOCUS ON "prefixes: in"
attest,* , ted, ting, tation, tations, BEAR WITNESS TO THE TRUTH, CAN BE CERTIFIED TO BE CORRECT
attic,* , IN THE ROOF (or see addict)

attichon, attention
attinchon, attention
attire,* , ed, ring, APPAREL
attitude,* , dinal, MENTAL POSTURE
attorney,* , REPRESENTATIVE OF LAW
attotode, attitude
attract,* , ted, ting, tive, tively, TO DRAW TOWARDS "prefixes: un"
attraction,* , DRAWN TOWARDS
attribute,* , ed, ting, tion, TO CREDIT "prefixes: de"
atukit, etiquette
atulesense, adolescence
atum, atom / autumn
atument, adamant
aturnal, eternal
aturney, attorney
atutif, additive
atutode, attitude
atvacate, advocate
atvanse, advance
atvantech, advantage
atvanteg, advantage
atvantuge, advantage
atvencher, adventure
atvenshure, adventure
atvirb, adverb
atvirsary, adversary
atvirse, adverse
atverse, adverse
atversery, adversary
atvertize, advertise
atvincher, adventure
atvinsher, adventure
atvirb, adverb
atvirsary, adversary
atvirse, adverse
atvise, advice / advise
atvisuble, advise(sable)
atvize, advise / advice
atvokate, advocate
atvukate, advocate
atvurb, adverb
atvurcity, adverse(sity)
atvursle, adverse(ly)
atvurtize, advertise

atypical, IRREGULAR
aubazit, opposite
auader, outer
aubligate, obligate
aubozit, opposite
aubrebul, operable
aubtemal, optimal
aubuzit, opposite
aucalate, osculate / oscillate
auch, ouch
aucilate, osculate / oscillate
aucsedashin, oxidate(tion)
aucsedate, oxidate
aucshen, auction
auction,* , ning, neer, neering, SELL BY BID
aud, odd / ought / out
audacity, WILLING/ DARING TO DEAL WITH DIFFICULT ISSUE/ SITUATION
audamate, automate
audamotive, automotive
audasity, audacity
audeance, audience
audeble, audible
audej, outage
audem, autumn
audeo, audio
auder, otter / outer / odd(er)
audesh, outage
audeshun, audition
audet, audit
audetorium, auditorium
audety, odd(ity)
audfit, outfit
audgo, outgo
audiance, audience
audible, ly, bility, eness, WELL HEARD "prefixes: in/ sub"
audience,* , GROUP WHO OBSERVES
audimotive, automotive
auding, outing
audio, HEAR
audir, otter / outer
audishun, audition
audit,* , ted, ting, tor, tory, UNDER EXAMINATION

audition,*,ned,ning,SUBMIT TO EXAMINATION "prefixes: sub"
auditorium,*,FOR PUBLIC AUDIENCE
audity,odd(ity)
audlau,outlaw
audle,odd(ly)
audlieng,outlying
audline,outline
audlook,outlook
audobiography,autobiography
audomotive,automotive
audpost,outpost
audraje,outrage
audrit,outright
audside,outside
audskirt,outskirt
audsmart,outsmart
audstanding,outstand(ing)
audwerd,outward
audwet,outwit
auel,owl
auer,our / hour / oar
auful,awful
auger,*,TOOL TO BORE SOMETHING
augir,auger
augment,*,ted,ting,tation,INCREASE SIZE "prefixes: bio"
augre,auger
august,A MONTH OF THE YEAR (ENGLISH)
auil,owl
auksedashin,oxidate(tion)
auksedate,oxidate
aukshun,auction
auksidize,oxide(dize)
auktober,october
aukward,awkward
aul,owl / all / awl
auldir,alder / altar / alter
aulfubet,alphabet
aulso,also
autamatum,ultimatum
autematum,ultimatum
auter,alter / altar

aulternate,alternate
aultirnetly,alternate(ly)
autogethur,altogether
aultumatum,ultimatum
aulturnate,alternate
aulways,always
auneng,awning
auns,ounce / own(s)
aunt,*,tie,SISTER OF MOTHER/ FATHER (or see ant)
auntefrese,antifreeze
aupaset,opposite
auperuble,operable
aupewlent,opulent
aupiruble,operable
aupizit,opposite
aupoyntmint,appointment
aupshen,option
auptemal,optimal
auptimize,optimize
auptumistic,optimist(ic)
aupulent,opulent
aupuset,opposite
aur,hour / our / oar
aura,*,al,ric,LIGHT FIELD
aurajin,origin
aurekel,auricle / oracle
auri,awry
aurickle,auricle / oracle
auricle,*,cular,OF THE EAR (or see oracle)
aurikel,auricle / oracle
aurk,arc / ark
aurle,hour(ly)
aurmer,armor
auroara,aurora
aurora,*,al,RADIANT EMISSION
aurthodox,orthodox
ausalate,osculate / oscillate
auselate,osculate / oscillate
ausem,awesome
ausilate,osculate / oscillate
ausim,awesome
auspicious,sly,sness,FAVORABLE "prefixes: in"
auspishus,auspicious

auspitious,auspicious
austere,ely,HARSH
ausulate,osculate / oscillate
ausum,awesome
aut,out / ought
autall,outage
autej,outage
autem,autumn
automate,automate
automobel,automobile
auteo,audio
auter,otter / outer
autfit,outfit
autgo,outgo
authentic,cally,city,cate,cation,cator,VALID,NOT FICTITIOUS OR FAKE "prefixes: in"
auther,author
authintik,authentic
authir,author
author,*,red,ring,CREATOR/ ORIGINATOR
authoretarian,authoritarian
authoritarian,DICTATORIAL
authority,ties,tative,tatively,EXERCISES COMMAND
autim,autumn
autimate,automate
autimotive,automotive
auting,outing
autio,audio
autir,otter / outer
autism,stic,BRAIN FIRING MALADY
autlain,outline
autlaiiin,outlying
autlaw,outlaw
autlet,outlet
autlieng,outlying
autline,outline
autlook,outlook
autluk,outlook
autly,odd((ly)
auto,PREFIX INDICATING 'OF OR BY ONESELF' MOST OFTEN MODIFIES THE WORD
autobiografy,autobiography

Word	Forms / Definition
autobiography, hies, her, hical, hically, WRITTEN BY ONESELF "prefixes: semi"	
autobyografy, autobiography	
autograf, autograph	
autograph, *, hed, hing, her, hic, hics, hical, hically, AUTHOR'S SIGNATURE	
automadik, automatic	
automate, *, ed, ting, ticity, tion, tism, SELF-CONTROLLING, PERFORMS THRU PROGRAMMING	
automatic, *, cally, SELF-CONTROLLING, PERFORMS THRU PROGRAMMING "prefixes: semi"	
automobel, automobile	
automobile, *, PERSONAL TRANSPORTATION	
automotive, ASSOCIATED WITH VEHICLES	
autoname, autonomy	
autonime, autonomy	
autonomy, mous, mist, INDEPENDENCE "prefixes: semi"	
autopsy, *, POST-MORTEM EXAMINATION	
autpost, outpost	
autput, output	
autragus, outrage(ous)	
autrait, outright	
autraje, outrage	
autreill, outrage	
autrite, outright	
autsaid, outside	
autscurt, outskirt	
autset, outset	
autside, outside	
autskert, outskirt	
autskurt, outskirt	
autsmart, outsmart	
autstand, outstand	
autstanding, outstand(ing)	
autumate, automate	
autumn, FALL SEASON	
autwerd, outward	
autwet, outwit	
autwid, outwit	
autwit, outwit	
autwurd, outward	
auxilery, auxiliary	
auxiliary, ries, HELP OR AID	

Word	Forms / Definition
avacado, avocado	
avacodo, avocado	
avacuate, evacuate	
avade, evade	
avaeleble, available	
avail, *, led, ling, lable, READY TO USE/ HELP "prefixes: un"	
available, bly, bility, READY TO USE/ HELP "prefixes: bio/ un"	
avaire, aviary	
avakuate, evacuate	
avalable, available	
avalanche, *, ed, COME DOWN/ DESCEND WITH GREAT ACCUMULATION	
avale, avail	
avalible, available	
avaluade, evaluate	
avaluashen, evaluate(tion)	
avaluate, evaluate	
avanew, avenue	
avantig, advantage	
avantij, advantage	
avaperation, evaporate(tion)	
avaporashen, evaporate(tion)	
avarage, average	
avaredge, average	
avasef, evasive	
avashen, evasion	
avashun, aviation	
avasive, evasive	
avate, evade	
avau, avow	
aveador, aviator	
aveashin, aviation	
aveation, aviation	
avecado, avocado	
avedent, evident	
aveere, aviary	
avekado, avocado	
avekshin, evict(ion)	
avekt, evict	
avelanch, avalanche	
avenchur, adventure	
avendful, eventful	

Word	Forms / Definition
avenew, avenue	
avenge, *, ed, ging, er, INFLICT PAIN/ HARM IN RETALIATION	
avenje, avenge	
avenshuale, event(ually)	
avent, event	
aventful, eventful	
aventshur, adventure	
avenue, *, WAY TO PERFORM, STREET/ ROAD IN BETWEEN	
aver, ever	
average, *, ed, ging, IN BETWEEN	
averb, adverb	
avere, aviary	
averege, average	
averije, average	
aversarie, adversary	
averse, ely, eness, sion, sions, sive, sively, siveness, rsion, rsive, GO OFF COURSE, AGAINST/ OPPOSE (or see adverse)	
avert, *, ted, ting, table, tible, rsion, rsive, GO OFF COURSE, CHANGE DIRECTION/ ATTENTION AWAY FROM (or see advert/ overt)	
avertise, advertise	
averyen, ovary(rian)	
aviador, aviator	
aviary, ries, PLACE TO KEEP BIRDS	
aviashun, aviation	
aviation, tor, FLYING TRANSPORTATION	
aviator, *, ONE WHO PILOTS AIR SHIPS	
avicado, avocado	
avicate, advocate	
avidens, evidence	
avident, evident	
aviere, aviary	
avikado, avocado	
avikd, evict	
avikshen, evict(ion)	
avikt, evict	
avikted, evict(ed)	
avilanch, avalanche	
avincher, adventure	
avindful, eventful	
avinew, avenue	
avinge, avenge	

avinje,avenge
avint,event
avintful,eventful
avinu,avenue
avirage,average
avirej,average
avirse,averse / adverse
avirsere,adversary
avirtize,advertise
avocado,*,EDIBLE FRUIT
avocate,advocate
avoed,avoid
avoid,*,ded,ding,dance,dable,dably,STAY CLEAR OF, PURPOSELY STAY AWAY FROM "prefixes: un"
avokodo,avocado
avolve,evolve
avow,*,wed,wing,wable,wably,wedly,STATE THAT IT'S TRUTH "prefixes: dis"
avoyd,avoid
avrag,average
avrebaudy,every(body)
avrebode,every(body)
avree,every
avrege,average
avridge,average
avrige,average
avriviashen,abbreviate(tion)
avucate,advocate
avukodo,avocado
avulanch,avalanche
avundful,eventful
avurb,adverb
avurij,average
avurse,averse / adverse
avurt,avert / advert / overt
avurtize,advertise
awa,away
await,*,ted,ting,TO EXPECT
awake,*,en,ening,king,FROM SLEEP
award,*,ded,ding,A PRIZE
aware,eness,CAUTIOUS,ALERT "prefixes: un"
awate,await
away,SOMEWHERE ELSE

awayt,await
awbuzit,opposite
awcshen,auction
awd,odd / ought / out
awdacity,audacity
awdamate,automate
awdamotive,automotive
awdasety,audacity
awdeanse,audience
awdeble,audible
awdege,outage
awdeje,outage
awdeo,audio
awder,outer / otter
awdet,audit
awdete,odd(ity)
awdetoreum,auditorium
awdfet,outfit
awdgo,outgo
awdible,audible
awdij,outage
awdimotive,automotive
awding,outing
awdir,outer / otter
awdishun,audition
awdit,audit
awdition,audition
awditorium,auditorium
awdity,odd(ity)
awdlet,outlet
awdlieng,outlying
awdline,outline
awdlook,outlook
awdrit,outright
awdside,outside
awdskirt,outskirt
awdsmart,outsmart
awdstanding,outstand(ing)
awdur,outer / otter
awdwet,outwit
awdwurd,outward
awe,*,ed,wing,TAKEN ABACK,STUNNED
aweic,awake

awel,owl
awer,our / hour
awesome,ely,eness,IMPRESSIVE
awfil,awful
awful,lly,lness,DREADFUL
awger,auger
awgest,august
awgir,auger
awgist,august
awgment,augment
awgmint,augment
awgre,auger
awgur,auger
awgus,august
awgust,august
awhile,FOR SOME TIME NOW
awil,awhile
awkewpie,occupy
awksedize,oxide(dize)
awksegin,oxygen
awkshun,auction
awkupy,occupy
awkward,dly,dness,BUNGLING OR EMBARRASSING
awl,*,TOOL FOR SEWING LEATHER (or see owl/ all)
awlso,also
awning,*,ROOF OVERHANG
aword,award
awpazit,opposite
awperuble,operable
awpozit,opposite
awpuzit,opposite
awr,our / hour
awreginal,origin(al)
awrekt,erect
awrickle,auricle
awrie,awry
awrikle,auricle
awroara,aurora
awrode,erode
awrora,aurora
awru,aura
awry,OFF COURSE
awselate,osculate / oscillate

axint, accent
axis, xes, ial, ially, A PIVOTAL POINT ON WHICH SOMETHING IS CENTERED (or see ax(es)) "prefixes: bi"
axkerjen, excursion
axklude, exclude
axkuze, excuse
axle, *, ROD WITH TWO WHEELS ATTACHED (or see axil)
axol, axil / axle
axplan, explain
axsedintal, accident(al)
axseed, exceed
axselense, excellent
axseluratur, accelerate(tor)
axsenshuate, accentuate
axsent, accent
axsentuate, accentuate
axsept, accept / except
axseptense, accept(ance)
axseptinse, accept(ance)
axses, access / ax(es) / axis
axsesares, accessory(ries)
axsesori, accessory
axsesurize, accessory(rize)
axshule, actual
axshun, action
axsident, accident
axsidental, accident(al)
axsidint, accident
axsint, accent
axsintuate, accentuate
axst, ax(ed) / ask(ed)
axsudentul, accident(al)
axterminate, exterminate
axturminate, exterminate
axturnal, external
axual, actual
axuated, acuate(d)
axukute, execute
axul, axil / axle
axule, actual
ayenda, agenda
ayol, aisle

awtraje, outrage
awtreich, outrage
awtrite, outright
awtsaid, outside
awtscurt, outskirt
awtset, outset
awtside, outside
awtskurt, outskirt
awtsmart, outsmart
awtstanding, outstand(ing)
awtum, autumn
awtur, outer / otter
awtvard, outward
awtward, outward
awtwerd, outward
awtwit, outwit
awtwurd, outward
awul, owl
awur, our / hour
ax, xes, xed, xing, TOOL WITH A SHARP BLADE FOR CHOPPING WOOD (or see ache(s)/ axis/ ask)
axcebt, except / accept
axcedent, accident
axceed, exceed
axcelerate, accelerate
axchange, exchange
axchoole, actual
axcident, accident
axclude, exclude
axcurshin, excursion
axderminate, exterminate
axdurminate, exterminate
axebt, except / accept
axecutive, executive
axent, accent
axepshen, except(ion)
axeptinse, accept(ance)
axesory, accessory
axess, access
axeul, axis(ial)
axglood, exclude
axicute, execute
axil, *, ANGLE BETWEEN STEM/ BRANCH (or see axle)

awsem, awesome
awsilate, osculate / oscillate
awsome, awesome
awspeshus, auspicious
awspitious, auspicious
awstear, austere
awsteer, austere
awsulate, osculate / oscillate
awsum, awesome
awt, out / ought
awtamobil, automobile
awtem, autumn
awter, otter / outer
awtesm, autism
awtfit, outfit
awtgo, outgo
awthentik, authentic
awthintik, authentic
awthir, author
awthority, authority
awtim, autumn
awting, outing
awtir, otter / outer
awtism, autism
awtitorium, auditorium
awtizm, autism
awtlain, outline
awtlaing, outlying
awtlaw, outlaw
awtlet, outlet
awtlieng, outlying
awtline, outline
awtlo, outlaw
awtlook, outlook
awtluk, outlook
awtlying, outlying
awtobiografy, autobiography
awtopse, autopsy
awtpost, outpost
awtput, output
awtrage, outrage
awtragus, outrage(ous)
awtrait, outright

ayris,iris
ayurn,iron
ayvori,ivory
azbekt,aspect
azberigus,asparagus
azbestus,asbestos
azburashun,aspirate(tion)
azdragen,estrogen
azemulate,assimilate
azendent,ascendant
azertane,ascertain
azfalt,asphalt
azfault,asphalt
azfikseate,asphyxiate
azfolt,asphalt
azhr,azure
azide,aside
azilum,asylum
azinment,assignment
azinshul,essential
azma,asthma
azmu,asthma
azpekt,aspect
azpir,aspire
azpren,aspirin
azspect,aspect
azteem,esteem
azthma,asthma
aztonesh,astonish
aztral,astral
aztranaut,astronaut
aztrawneme,astronomy
aztrengent,astringent
aztringent,astringent
aztroid,asteroid
aztrol,astral
aztrolegy,astrology
aztronume,astronomy
aztrul,astral
aztrunot,astronaut
azumshin,assumption
azurtane,ascertain
b, be / bee

ba,bay
babby,baby
babe,TERM OF ENDEARMENT
babesit, babysit
baby,bies, bied, bying,CHILD UNDER THE AGE OF ONE YEAR
babysit, *, tter, tting, sat,WATCH OTHERS CHILDREN
bacen,bacon / bake(king) / basin
bacet,basset
bach,back / batch / badge / bash / bake / bog / balk / baulk
bachelor, *, UNMARRIED MAN
bacher,badger
bachful,bashful
bachiler,bachelor
bachin,back(ing) / bake(king) / batch(ing) / bacon
bachuler,bachelor
bacin,bacon
back, *, ked, king, ker,GO TO THE PREVIOUS/ PAST, IN THE REAR OF (or see bake) "prefixes: un"
backward, *, dness,IN REVERSE
backwurd,backward
bacon,SALTED HOG MEAT/ FAT
bacos,because
bacteri,PREFIX INDICATING 'BACTERIA' MOST OFTEN MODIFIES THE WORD
bacteria,al, ium,MICROSCOPIC ORGANISM "prefixes: non"
bactirea,bacteria
bactireul,bacteria(l)
bactiria,bacteria
bacuerd,backward
bad,dly, dness,NOT GOOD (or see bat/ bade)
badare,battery
badchelor,bachelor
badder,batter
bade,PAST TENSE FOR THE WORD 'BID' (or see bat/ bad)
badel,battle
bader,batter
badery,battery
badge, *,INSIGNIA (or see batch)
badger, *, red, ring,TO HECKLE SOMEONE, AN ANIMAL
badiry,battery

badje,badge
badjur,badger
badle,battle
badol,battle
badore,battery
badre,battery
badshelor,bachelor
badul,battle
baduly,body(dily)
badur,batter
badury,battery
bae,bay
baege,beige
baej,beige
bael,bail / bale
baenkwit,banquet
baet,bait / bate
bafal,befall
bafileon,pavilion
bafol,befall
bag, *, gged, gging, gger, ggy, ggier, ggiest,A CONTAINER TO HOLD ITEMS (or see back/ beige/ batch/ badge)
bagage,baggage
bagall,baggage
bagd,bag(gged) / back(ed)
bage,badge / beige / baggy
baged,bag(gged) / back(ed)
bagege,baggage
bageje,baggage
bagel, *, ROLL WITH A HOLE
bagener,begin(nner)
bager,bag(gger) / badger
baggage,LUGGAGE
baggy,ggies, gily, giness,LOOSE, SAGGY
bagige,baggage
bagil,bagel
baginer,begin(nner)
bagir,badger / bag(gger)
bagle,bagel
baguj,baggage
bagul,bagel
bagur,bag(gger) / badger
bahaf,behave

bahaver, behavior
bahavior, behavior
bahind, behind
bai, buy / by / bye
baianual, biannual
baias, bias
baicentenial, bicentennial
baid, bide
baienial, biennial
baifoucals, bifocals
baige, beige
baije, beige
baik, bike
bail, *, led, ler, LIBERATE, REMOVE FROM (or see bale/ bowel)
bailaderal, bilateral
bailateral, bilateral
bailef, bailiff
bailif, bailiff
bailiff, *, CIVIL OFFICER OR FUNCTIONARY
bailingual, bilingual
bailiniar, bilinear
baind, bind
baineri, binary
bainokiular, binocular
bainomial, binomial
bainquet, banquet
baiofisics, biophysics
baiografy, biography
baiol, bile
baiolochi, biology
baiolollii, biology
baiopsi, biopsy
baioritem, biorhythm
baiosaid, biocide
baiosfir, biosphere
baiou, bio
baiourithem, biorhythm
baipartisan, bipartisan
bair, bear / bare
baisentenial, bicentennial
baiseps, biceps
baisicol, bicycle

bait, *, ted, ting, LURING TO CATCH (or see bate/ bite)
baiu, bayou
baj, badge / beige / batch
bajer, badger
bak, back / bake / balk / baulk
bakd, bake(d) / back(ed)
bake, *, ed, king, er, COOK FOOD IN AN OVEN (or see back) "prefixes: un"
bakeeny, bikini
baken, bacon
bakene, bikini
bakery, ries, WHERE PASTRIES ARE BAKED
bakini, bacon
bakini, bikini
bakiry, bakery
bakose, because
bakry, bakery
bakt, bake(d) / back(ed)
bakterea, bacteria
baktereul, bacteria(l)
baktirea, bacteria
bakuerd, backward
bakuj, baggage
bakwerd, backward
bakwurd, backward
bal, ball / bale / bail / bawl
bala, ballet
balad, ballad / ballade
balarena, ballerina
balat, ballot / ballad / ballade
balay, ballet
balcene, balcony
balcony, nies, PORCH ABOVE THE FIRST STORY ON A BUILDING
balcuny, balcony
bald, ding, dness, LOOSING HAIR (or see bold/ ball(ed)/ bale(d)/ bail(ed))
bale, *, ed, ling, er, TO BUNDLE (or see bail)
baled, bale(d) / bail(ed) / ballad / ballade
baleef, belief
baleeve, believe

balef, bailiff
baleger, beleaguer
balens, balance
balerena, ballerina
balestic, ballistic
balet, ballet / ballot / ballad / ballade
baleve, believe
balevuble, believe(vable)
balid, ballad / ballade
balif, bailiff
balins, balance
balirena, ballerina
balit, ballot / ballet
balk, *, ked, king, ker, kingly, ALSO 'BAULK', EXPRESS UNWILLINGNESS TO DO SOMETHING, HINDER/ PREVENT (or see bulk/ baulk) "prefixes: un"
balkeny, balcony
balkune, balcony
ball, *, lled, lling, ROUND OBJECT FOR THROWING/ SPORTS, A FORMAL DANCE STYLE (or see bawl/ bail/ bale)
ballad, *, dic, dist, dry, SIMPLE SONG/ POEM (or see ballade)
ballade, *, SPECIFIC STYLE OF POEM/ MUSICAL PIECE (or see ballad)
balled, ballad / ballade / ball(ed)
baller, badger
ballerena, ballerina
ballerina, *, FEMALE DANCER
ballet, *, CLASSICAL DANCE (or see ballot)
ballid, ballad / ballade
ballistic, *, PROJECTILE IN AIR
balloon, *, ned, ning, FULL OF AIR
ballot, *, ted, ting, ter, OF VOTING
balm, *, OINTMENT FROM PLANTS
balme, balmy
balmy, mier, miest, mily, miness, OF WARM/ MILD CLIMATE
balo, below / bellow / billow
balonee, bologna / baloney
baloney, NONSENSE, MEAT (or see bologna)
balong, belong
baloom, bloom

baloon,balloon
balot,ballot / ballet
balow,below / billow / bellow
bals,bowel(s) / ball(s) / bale(s) / bail(s)
baluf,bailiff
balume,bloom
balune,balloon
balunse,balance
balurena,ballerina
banana,*,EDIBLE FRUIT
band,*,ded,ding,COLLECTION OF PERFORMING MUSICIANS,TO BE GROUPED/ BOUND TOGETHER "prefixes: contra/ multi"
bandage,*,ed,ging,FOR REPAIRING WOUNDS
bandry,boundary
baneeth,beneath
baner,banner
banesh,banish
banevulense,benevolence
banign,benign
banine,benign
banir,banner
banish,hes,hed,hing,hment,CONDEMNED TO EXILE
bank,*,ked,king,ker,BUSINESS THAT STORES GOODS/ CASH, SMALL BERM/ HILL "prefixes: under"
bankrupt,tcy,tcies,BROKE TO THE BANK,CAN'T PAY
bankrupsee,bankrupt(cy)
bankwit,banquet
banner,*,TYPE OF SIGN
banquet,*,FEAST WITH FRIENDS
banquit,banquet
bantry,boundary / pantry
banur,banner
baptesm,baptism
baptism,*,mal,ize,REBIRTHING RITUAL
baptize,*,ed,zing,REBIRTHING RITUAL
baptizm,baptism
bar,*,rred,rring,LONG/ FLAT SECTION/ COUNTER (or see bare/ bear)
bara,barrette / beret
barack,barrack
barbarian,*,ic,UNCIVILIZED PERSON
barbecue,*,ed,uing,GRILLED MEAT

barbekew,barbecue
barbeku,barbecue
barber,*,CUTS HAIR
barberean,barbarian
barberian,barbarian
barbetchuet,barbiturate
barbichuit,barbiturate
barbique,barbecue
barbir,barber
barbitchuet,barbiturate
barbiturate,*,SEDATIVE DRUG "prefixes: non"
barbur,barber
barc,bark
barch,barge
barder,barter
bardur,barter
bare,*,ed,ring,rren,WITHOUT COVER (or see bear/ berry/ bury)
bareave,bereave
barech,barrage
bareck,barrack
bareeve,bereave
bareft,bereft
barel,barrel
barell,barrage
baren,barren
bareng,bearing / bar(rring) / bare(ring)
barestur,barrister
baret,barrette / beret
baretone,baritone
bareur,barrier
bargain,*,ned,ning,AFFORDABLE DEAL
barge,*,ed,ging,FLAT-BOTTOM BOAT,BEHAVE LIKE A BOAT
bargen,bargain
bargun,bargain
bargund,bargain(ed)
baricade,barricade
barier,barrier
barikade,barricade
baril,barrel
barin,barren
baring,bearing / bare(ring) / bar(rring)

barister,barrister
barit,barrette / beret
baritone,*,DEEP TONE
barje,barge
bark,*,ked,king,ker,SOUND FROM A DOG,COVER ON TREES "prefixes: de"
baril,barge
barn,*,LARGE STRUCTURE FOR FARM ANIMALS (or see born/ barren)
baro,PREFIX INDICATING 'PRESSURE/ WEIGHT' MOST OFTEN MODIFIES THE WORD (or see barrow/ borrow)
baroge,barrage
baroje,barrage
barol,barrel
barometer,*,tric,INSTRUMENT MEASURING PRESSURE
baromiter,barometer
baron,barren
baroque,TYPE OF MUSIC, WILD, UNUSUAL
barou,barrow
barow,borrow / burrow / borough
barrack,*,LODGE FOR MANY PEOPLE
barrage,*,ed,ging,ALL AT ONCE
barrel,*,led,ling,DRUM OR GREAT SPEED
barren,nly,nness,UNFERTILE
barrette,*,CLASP (or see beret)
barricade,*,ded,ding,BLOCK AGAINST
barrier,*,OBSTRUCTION
barring,EXCEPTING, REFUSAL (or see bear(ing)/ bar(ing))
barrister,*,LAWYER
barrow,CASTRATED HOG (or see borrow)
bartender,*,TENDS BAR
barter,*,red,ring,TRADE
bartinder,bartender
bartur,barter
baruton,baritone
bary,berry / bury
bas,base / bass
basball,baseball
basboll,baseball
base,*,ed,sing,eless,A FOUNDATION,FORM IN BASEBALL (or see bass/ vase) "prefixes: de"
baseach,beseech

baseball, SPORT
baseech, beseech
basek, basic
basekly, basic(ally)
basel, basil
basement, *, UNDER HOUSE
basen, basin
baserd, buzzard
bases, basis / base(s)
baset, basset
bash, hes, hed, hing, A PARTY, TO SMASH/ DESTROY SOMETHING, INSULT SOMEONE
bashfel, bashful
bashful, SHY
basi, PREFIX INDICATING 'BOTTOM/ BASE' MOST OFTEN MODIFIES THE WORD
basic, *, cally, FUNDAMENTAL
baside, beside
basik, basic
basikly, basic(ally)
basil, HERB
basin, *, SHAPED LIKE BOWL
basis, ON WHICH IT STANDS (or see base(s))
basit, basset
basket, *, WOVEN CONTAINER
baskit, basket
baskut, basket
basmant, basement
basmint, basement
baso, PREFIX INDICATING 'BOTTOM/ BASE' MOST OFTEN MODIFIES THE WORD
basoon, bassoon
basquet, basket
bass, sses, ssist, A FISH, STRINGED INSTRUMENT, LEVEL OF SOUND TONE/ FREQUENCY (or see base)
basset, DOG, HOUND
bassoon, HORN
basuk, basic
basul, basil
basun, basin / bassoon
basurk, berserk
basus, basis / base(s)
basut, basset

bat, *, tted, tting, tter, STUFFING, TOOL USED IN BASEBALL, TO HIT (or see bate/ bait)
batch, hes, hed, hing, INCREMENTS/ CERTAIN AMOUNTS OF SOMETHING AT A TIME (or see badge/ botch)
batcheler, bachelor
batchuler, bachelor
bate, *, ed, ting, DECREASE, HOLD BACK (or see bait)
batel, battle
baten, batten
batenshul, potential
bater, batter
batery, battery
bath, *, hroom, A PLACE TO WASH, TO IMMERSE IN LIQUID (or see bathe)
bathe, *, ed, hing, ers, TO WASH UP, IMMERSE IN LIQUID (or see bath)
batil, bottle / battle
batin, batten
batinshul, potential
batiry, battery
batle, battle
batn, baton / batten
batom, bottom
baton, *, WAND
batore, battery
batre, battery
batrothed, betrothed
batshelor, bachelor
batshiler, bachelor
batten, SECURE/ STRENGTHEN, WOOD STRIPS (or see bat(tting))
batter, *, red, ring, FRYING MIXTURE, BASEBALL PLAYER, TO BE ATTACKED
battery, ries, APPLIES TO MILITARY, MECHANICAL, ELECTRICAL, BASEBALL
battle, *, ed, ling, FIGHT BETWEEN TWO FORCES
batul, battle
batur, batter
batury, battery
batwen, between
bauch, botch
bauchulism, botulism
baul, ball / bawl / bail / bale / bowel

baulk, *, ked, king, ker, kingly, ALSO 'BALK', EXPRESS UNWILLINGNESS TO DO SOMETHING, HINDER/ PREVENT (or see bulk/ balk) "prefixes: un"
baulm, balm
baulme, balmy
bauls, bowel(s) / bawl(s) / ball(s)
baund, bound
baundri, boundary
bauns, bounce / bound(s)
baunse, bounce(cy) / buoyant(ncy)
baunti, bounty
bauntiful, bountiful
bauntre, boundary
baurk, bark
baush, botch
baut, bought / bout
bautel, bottle
bavileon, pavilion
bawdil, bottle
bawildre, bewilder
bawl, *, led, ling, ler, WEEP, SHOUT AT (or see ball)
bawls, bawl(s) / bowel(s) / ball(s)
bawnd, bound
bawnse, bounce / bound(s)
bawntee, bounty
bawntiful, bountiful
bay, *, RELATES TO WINDOW, BARN, DOG HOWLING, SHIP HOSPITAL, AIRCRAFT, SHRUB, OCEAN INLET
bayas, bias
bayeniaol, biennial
bayle, bail / bale
bayol, bile
bayond, beyond
bayou, OUTLET OF WATER
bayu, bayou
bazaar, *, SALE OF ARTICLES (or see bizarre)
bazel, basil
bazen, basin
bazil, basil
bazin, basin
bazul, basil
bazurk, berserk
bazzar, bizarre / bazaar

be, A VERB EXPRESSING PRESENT TENSE, A PREFIX INDICATING 'COMPLETELY/ INTENSELY' MOST OFTEN MODIFIES THE WORD (or see bee)
beach, hes, hed, hing, SHORELINE (or see beech)
beacon,*, SIGNAL (or see beckon)
bead,*, ded, ding, ROUNDED FORM/ OBJECT (or see beat/ beef)
beafy, beef
beagle,*, DOG
beagul, beagle
beak,*, BIRD BILL
beaker,*, VESSEL
beam,*, med, ming, TO SHINE, LINEAR SUPPORT
bean,*, VEGETABLE, TO HURT (or see been/ bin)
bear,*, ring, rish, rishly, ANIMAL, PUT PRESSURE ON/ AGAINST (or see bare/ beer/ bearing)" prefixes: over"
bearable, TOLERABLE "prefixes: un"
beard,*, ded, MALE FACIAL HAIR
bearing,*, SUPPORTS, PRESSURE, MACHINE PART, HEADING (or see bare(ring))
beast,*, tly, tliness, ANIMA
beat,*, ting, ten, ter, THRASH/ STRIKE/ HIT (or see beet) "prefixes: un/ up"
beau,*, BOYFRIEND (or see bow/ bough)
beauru, bureau
beautician,*, HAIRDRESSER
beautiful, lly, EYE PLEASER
beautishun, beautician
beauty, ties, tify, tiful, tifully, tifous, teously, teousness, tification, PLEASING TO THE SENSES, GMP
beaver,*, ANIMAL
bebleografy, bibliography
became, PAST TENSE FOR THE WORD 'BECOME'
because, THE REASON FOR
becin, beckon, beacon / bacon
becken, beckon / beacon / bacon
beckon,*, ned, ning, TO SUMMON/ CALL FORTH, ENTICE TO COME (or see beacon/ bacon)
beckun, beckon/ beacon/ bacon
become,*, ming, came, GOING TO BE (or see became) "prefixes: un"
becon, beckon / beacon / bacon

becos, because
becum, become
becun, beckon / beacon / bacon
becus, because
becuz, because
bed,*, ded, dding, SOMETHING TO SLEEP/ LIE DOWN UPON (or see bead/ bet/ bit/ beat)
beded, bet(tted) / bed(dded) / bead(ed)
beder, better / bid(dder) / bitter / bet(ttor)
bedid, bet(tted) / bed(dded)
bedil, beetle
bedir, better / bid(dder) / bitter / bet(ttor)
bedol, beetle
bedraggled, MUSSED UP
bedragled, bedraggled
bedraguled, bedraggled
bedridden, CONFINED TO BED
bedriden, bedridden
bedritin, bedridden
bedrothed, betrothed
bedspread,*, BED COVER
bedspred, bedspread
bedud, bet(tted) / bed(dded)
bedul, beetle
bedur, better / bid(dder) / bitter / bet(ttor)
bedwritin, bedridden
bee,*, FURRY INSECT (or see be)
beech, TREE (or see beach)
beedil, beetle
beedul, beetle
beef, fy, finess, fed, fing, FLESHY, MEAT FROM BOVINE, TO COMPLAIN
beek, beak
beeker, beaker
beekin, beacon
beem, beam
been, PAST TENSE FOR THE WORD 'BE' (or see bean)
beeng, being
beer,*, FERMENTED BREW (or see bear)
beerd, beard
beest, beast
beestro, bistro
beet,*, A VEGETABLE (or see beat)

beetle,*, BUG
beetul, beetle
beever, beaver
befall, OCCUR
befol, befall
before, PREVIOUS
befour, before
befrend, befriend
befriend,*, ded, MAKE FRIENDS WITH
befrind, befriend
beg,*, gged, gging, PLEAD (or see big/ beach)
began, PAST TENSE FOR THE WORD 'BEGIN'
begar, beggar
begen, begin
begenir, begin(nner)
beger, beggar
beggar,*, ry, rly, rliness, ONE WHO BEGS
beggir, beggar
beggur, beggar
begil, beagle / bagel
begin,*, nner, nning, gan, TO START
beginer, begin(nner)
begir, beggar
begle, beagle / bagel
begot, bigot
begul, beagle / bagel
begur, beggar
begut, bigot
begutre, bigot(ry)
behaf, behalf
behalf, ON THE PART OF
behave,*, ed, ving, vior, ACT IN A PARTICULAR WAY "prefixes: mis"
behaveor, behavior
behavior,*, ral, rism, rist, ristic, MANNERISMS, ATTITUDE
behavyur, behavior
behind, TO THE BACK
behoof, behoove
behoove,*, ed, ving, TO BE PROPER
behufe, behoove
behuve, behoove
bei, bay
beibi, baby

beibisit, babysit
beibisat, babysat
beic, bake
beich, beige
beicon, bacon
beid, bade
beige, COLOR
beigol, bagel
beik, bake
beikeri, bakery
beikon, bacon
beikri, bakery
beil, bail / bale / bawl
beilif, bailiff
being,*, EXISTS
beis, bass / base / vase
beisbal, baseball
beisic, basic
beisin, basin
beisis, basis
beisment, basement
beisol, basil
beit, bait / bate
beith, bathe
bejaind, behind
bekame, became
beken, beckon / beacon / bacon
beker, beaker
bekin, beckon / beacon / bacon /vegan
bekit, bigot
bekom, become
bekon, beckon / beacon / bacon /vegan
bekos, because
bekum, become
bekur, beaker
bekus, because
bekut, bigot
bekuz, because
beladed, belated
beladid, belated
belated, dly, OVERDUE
belatide, belated
beld, build / bill(ed) / built

bele, belly
beleaguer, BLOCK, SIEGE
belegarant, belligerent
beleger, beleaguer
beleon, billion
belerds, billiards
belevuble, believe(vable)
beli, belly
belicherent, belligerent
belief,*, FAITH, HOPE "prefixes: dis/ mis/ un"
believe,*, ed,ving,vable, vably,vability, FAITH, HOPE "prefixes: dis/ mis/ un"
believeable, believe(vable)
beligerent, belligerent
belillerent, belligerent
belise, police
belittle,*, ed,ling,ement, TO INSULT
belle, belly
belligerent, tly,nce,ncy, WAR-LIKE AGGRESSIVENESS
bellow,*, wed,wing, DEEP ROAR, INSTRUMENT (or see below/ billow)
belly, llies, ABDOMEN "prefixes: under"
belo, bellow / below / billow
belonee, bologna / baloney
belong,*, ging,gings, HAVE RIGHTS TO
beloon, balloon
belou, bellow
below, BENEATH, LOWER (or see bellow/ billow)
belt,*, ted,ting, STRAP TO WEAR AROUND THE WAIST, PUNCH/ HIT SOMETHING (or see built) "prefixes: un"
belurds, billiards
belyon, billion
belyunar, billion(aire)
bemt, beam(ed)
ben, been / bin / bean
benafactor, benefactor
benaficial, beneficial
benaficiary, beneficiary
benafishiary, beneficiary
benafishul, beneficial
benafit, benefit
benansa, bonanza

benanu, banana
bench, hes,hed, hing, RELATES TO LAW, GEOLOGY, SPORTS "prefixes: un"
bend,*, ding,nt, CROOK/ ANGLE (or see bent/ bind) "prefixes: un"
bended, bent
bendid, bent
bene, PREFIX INDICATING 'GOOD/ WELL' MOST OFTEN MODIFIES THE WORD
beneath, UNDER, LOWER
beneeth, beneath
benefactor,*, tion, CONTRIBUTOR
beneficial, lly, HELPFUL "prefixes: un"
beneficiary, ries, ONE WHO BENEFITS FROM
benefishiery, beneficiary
benefishul, beneficial
benefit,*, ted,ting, TO SERVE "prefixes: dis"
benevolance, benevolence
benevolence, nt, BIG HEARTED, KIND
benevolent, ntly, BIG HEARTED, KIND
benevulense, benevolence
benge, binge
benifactor, benefactor
benificial, beneficial
benifisheary, beneficiary
benifishul, beneficial
benifit, benefit
benign, nity, nities, nly, KINDLY
benine, benign
benje, binge
benll, bench
bent, PAST TENSE FOR THE WORD" BEND" "prefixes: un"
bented, bent
benufactor, benefactor
benuficial, beneficial
benuficiary, beneficiary
benufisheary, beneficiary
benufishul, beneficial
benufit, benefit
beond, beyond
ber, burr / bear / bare / beer
berbin, bourbon
berch, birch

berd, bird / beard
berden, burden
berdinsum, burden(some)
bere, berry / bury / bare / bear
bereave, *, ed, ving, ement, ANGUISH OVER LOSS
bereble, bearable
berecade, barricade
bereft, LACKING/ LOSS/ DEPRIVED
berek, barrack
berekade, barricade
berel, barrel
beren, barren
bereng, bearing / bare(ring)
berer, bear(er) / barrier
berestur, barrister
beret, *, CLOTH CAP (or see barrette)
beretone, baritone
bereul, burial
bereur, barrier
bergendy, burgundy
bergler, burglar
bergundy, burgundy
beri, bury / berry
berial, burial
berible, bearable
bericade, barricade
berick, barrack
berier, barrier
berikade, barricade
berikeid, barricade
beril, barrel
berin, barren
bering, bearing / bar(ing) / bar(rring)
beriqueid, barricade
berister, barrister
beristir, barrister
beritone, baritone
beriv, bereave
berkler, burglar
berlap, burlap
berlesk, burlesque
berly, burly
berm, *, med, SLOPED SOIL

bern, burn
bernt, burnt
bero, barrow / burrow / burro / borough
berog, barrage
beroj, barrage
berol, barrel
beron, barren
berow, barrow / borrow
berp, burp
berry, rries, FRUIT (or see bury)
bersaverense, persevere(rance)
bersd, burst
bersding, burst(ing)
berserk, VIOLENT FRENZY
berst, burst
berth, *, PLACE TO SETTLE INTO/ SLEEP (or see birth)
berthday, birthday
berthdei, birthday
bertoun, baritone
beruble, bearable
berubul, bearable
berukad, barricade
berul, barrel
beruton, baritone
bery, berry / bury
berzd, burst
berzding, burst(ing)
bes, bee(s) / best
besanes, business
besar, bizarre / bazaar
besd, best / beast
bese, busy
beseach, beseech
beseech, her, hingly, IMPLORE
besely, busy(sily)
besenes, business
beserk, berserk
besi, busy
beside, *, ALONGSIDE, AS WELL AS
besines, business
besirk, berserk
besk, bisque
besket, biscuit

besque, bisque
best, PAST TENSE FOR THE WORD 'BETTER' (or see beast)
bestro, bistro
besurk, berserk
besy, busy
bet, *, tted, tting, ttor, PLACE A WAGER WITH HOPE OF WINNING SOMETHING (or see beet/ beat/ bed)
beted, bet(tted) / bed(dded)
beter, better / bid(dder) / bitter / bet(ttor)
betid, bet(tted) / bed(dded)
betir, better / bid(dder) / bitter / bet(ttor)
beton, baton
betor, better / bid(dder) / bitter / bet(ttor)
betray, *, yal, yer, VIOLATION OF TRUST
betrothed, ENGAGEMENT TO SOMEONE
better, red, ring, rment, MORE SUPERIOR (or see bet(ttor))
betud, bet(tted) / bed(dded)
between, IN THE MIDDLE OF HERE AND THERE
beudeful, beautiful
beudiful, beautiful
beudy, beauty
beugl, bugle
beurd, beard
beuro, bureau
beurocrasy, bureaucracy
beurocrat, bureaucrat
beut, butte
beuteshun, beautician
beutiful, beautiful
beuty, beauty
bevarige, beverage
bevel, *, led, ling, INCLINED SURFACE
beverage, *, FLAVORED LIQUID TO DRINK
bevil, bevel
bevir, beaver
bevirage, beverage
bevle, bevel
bevol, bevel
bevrag, beverage
bevrech, beverage
bevrig, beverage

bevul,bevel
bevur,beaver
beware,CAUTION
bewere,beware
bewhere,beware
bewhove,behoove
bewilder,*,red,ring,ringly,rment,CONFUSE
bewt,butte
bewte,beauty
bewteful,beautiful
bewteshin,beautician
bewyon,bouillon
beyeng,being
beyond,OUT OF REACH
beyut,butte
bezar,bizarre / bazaar
bezd,best / beast
beze,busy
bezenes,business
bezerk,berserk
bezi,busy
beznes,business
bezt,best / beast
bezunes,business
bezzar,bizarre / bazaar / buzz(er)
bi, PREFIX INDICATING 'TWO/ TWICE' MOST OFTEN MODIFIES THE WORD (or see by/ bye/ bee)
biadic, biotic
biagrafik,biography(hic)
bialegy,biology
bianeal,biennial / biannual
bianel,biennial / biannual
biannual,TWICE A YEAR (or see biennial)
bianuel,biannual
bianyual,biannual
bias, PREFERENCE TOWARDS/ FOR "prefixes: un"
biatic, biotic
biaudec, biotic
biagrafe, biography
biaulugy,biology
biautec, biotic
bibleografy,bibliography
bibleogrufy,bibliography

biblio,PREFIX INDICATING 'BOOK' MOST OFTEN MODIFIES THE WORD
bibliography,hies,hic,hical,LIST OF PRINTED MATERIAL
bic,bike / beak
bicame,became
bicas,because
bicentenial,bicentennial
bicentennial,*,,TWO HUNDRED YEAR MARK
biceps,MUSCLES
bich,beech / beach
bicker,*,red,ring,ARGUE (or see bike(r)
bicom,become
bicon,beacon / beckon
bicos,because
bicus,because
bicycle,*,,ed,ling,list,TWO-WHEEL TRANSPORTATION
bid,*,,dder,dding,TO TELL, BE TOLD, BID FAREWELL, WAGER SOMETHING TO GAIN SOMETHING ELSE (or see bite(r)/ bitter/ bit/ bed/ bide/ bead) "prefixes: over/ under"
bidder, bitter / bid(der) / bite(r)
bide, *,,ed,,ding,WAIT, WITHSTAND (or see bid/ bite) "prefixes: un"
bider, bite(r) / bid(dder) / bitter
bidol, beetle
bidrageld, bedraggled
bidraguled, bedraggled
bidtrothed, betrothed
bieng, buy(ing)
bienial, biennial / biannual
biennial,TWO YEARS (or see biannual)
bif,beef
bifal,befall
bifocals,TWO-PART LENS
bifocul,bifocals
bifokul,bifocals
bifol,befall
bifor,before
bifour,before
bifrend,befriend
big,gger,ggest,ggy,LARGE (or see beg)
bigan,began / begin
bigetry,bigot(ry)

bigin,begin
bigol,beagle
bigot,ted,try,NARROW-MINDED "prefixes: un"
bigutry,bigot(ry)
bihaf,behave / behalf
bihalf,behave / behalf
bihav,behave / behalf
bihind,behind
bijaf,behalf
bijeivior,behavior
bijuv,behoove
bikame,became
bike,*,,ed,king,er,WHEEL TRANSPORTATION "prefixes: retro"
bikeeny,bikini
bikeim,became
biker,*,,RIDES MOTORCYCLE (or see bicker/ beaker)
bikini,*,,TWO-PIECE BATHING SUIT
bikose,because
bikum,become
bikur,bicker / biker
bikus,because
bikut,bigot
bilak,black
bilanear,bilinear
bilards,billiards
bilateral,BOTH SIDES
bilatirul,bilateral
bild,build / bill(ed) / built
bile,FLUID MADE BY THE LIVER (or see bill)
biled,build / bill(ed) / built
bilenear,bilinear
bileef,belief
bileeve,believe
bileger,beleaguer
bileided,belated
bileited,belated
bilengual,bilingual
bilengwul,bilingual
bileon,billion
bilerds,billiards
bileve,believe
bilevuble,believe(vable)

billiards,billiards
bilif,belief
bilinear,TWO LINES
bilingual,SPEAKS TWO LANGUAGES
bilingwal,bilingual
bilion,billion
bilitol,belittle
biliv,believe
bill,*,lled,lling,TOTAL COSTS (or see bile) "prefixes: over/ pre"
billiards,POOL GAME
billion,*,nth,naire,ONE THOUSAND MILLION
billow,*,wed,wing,OF WINE (or see below/ bellow)
bilo,billow / below / bellow
bilonee,baloney / bologna
bilong,belong
bilow,below / billow / bellow
bilt,built / build
biurds,billiards
bilyon,billion
bilyunar,billion(aire)
bim,beam
bimonthly,TWICE A MONTH
bimunthly,bimonthly
bin,*,nned,nning,COMPARTMENT FOR STORAGE, PREFIX INDICATING 'TWO/ TWICE' MOST OFTEN MODIFIES THE WORD (or see been/ bean)
binanu,banana
binanzu,bonanza
binary,ries,UNITS OF TWO
binch,binge / bench
bind,*,bound,ding,dingly,der,HOLD THINGS TOGETHER "prefixes: multi/ un"
bineeth,beneath
binefacter,benefactor
binery,binary
binevilance,benevolence
binevulense,benevolence
bing,being / binge
binge,*,ed,ging,SPREE
binid,beneath
binign,benign
binine,benign

binith,beneath
binje,binge
binll,binge / bench
binocular,*,DEVICE THAT MAGNIFIES FOR BOTH EYES
binokuler,binocular
binomeal,binomial
binomial,*,HAS TWO NAMES/ TERMS
binoquler,binocular
bint,bent
binufakter,benefactor
binufishal,beneficial
binufishary,beneficiary
binufit,benefit
binury,binary
bio,PREFIX INDICATING 'LIFE' MOST OFTEN MODIFIES THE WORD
biocide,dal,CIVILIZATION CHOKING OFF IT'S OWN LIFE SUPPLY
biodagradable,biodegradable
biodegradable,ELEMENTS EASILY BREAKS DOWN
biodec,biotic
biofisics,biophysics
biofizecs,biophysics
biografee,biography
biography,hies,hic,hical,STORY OF PEOPLE'S HISTORY "prefixes: auto"
biogrufee,biography
biology,gical,gically,gist,STUDY OF LIFE "prefixes: exo/ pre"
bion,beyond
biond,beyond
biophisics,biophysics
biophysics,STUDY OF LIFE
biopsy,sies,STUDY OF TISSUE
biorethum,biorhythm
biorhythm,BIOLOGICAL RHYTHM
biorithum,biorhythm
biorythm,biorhythm
bios,bias
biosfeare,biosphere
bioside,biocide
biosphere,ALL THAT SUPPORTS LIFE ON EARTH

biotic,*,ABOUT LIVE ORGANISMS "prefixes: pre/ pro/ sym"
bipadle,bipedal
bipardesan,bipartisan
bipardisan,bipartisan
bipartisan,TWO SIDES SHARING SAME PURPOSE
bipedal,ANIMAL THAT USES TWO LEGS/ ARMS
bipedle,bipedal
bipedul,bipedal
bipetle,bipedal
biqueim,became
biquini,bikini
bir,burr / beer
birben,bourbon
birch,A TREE
bird,*,ANIMAL WITH WINGS/ FEATHERS (or see beard)
birden,burden
birdensum,burden(some)
birdinsum,burden(some)
biret,barrette / beret
birglur,burglar
birgundy,burgundy
birkler,burglar
birlesk,burlesque
birlup,burlap
birm,berm
birn,burn
birnt,burnt
biro,burro / burrow / borough
birometer,barometer
birp,burp
birsd,burst
birsding,burst(ing)
birst,burst
birth,*,hed,hing,PHYSICAL BODY BECOMES VISIBLE (or see berth) "prefixes: re"
birthday,*,DATE OF BIRTH
birzd,burst
birzding,burst(ing)
bis,PREFIX INDICATING 'TWO/ TWICE' MOST OFTEN MODIFIES THE WORD
bisaid,beside
bisar,bizarre / bazaar

biscuit,*,NORMALLY GOES WITH GRAVY, A SOFT ROLL
biscut,biscuit
bise,busy
biseach,beseech
biseech,beseech
bisekul,bicycle
bisenteneal,bicentennial
biseps,biceps
bisi,busy
bisich,beseech
bisicle,bicycle
biside,beside
bisikul,bicycle
bisintineal,bicentennial
bisk,bisque
biskit,biscuit
biskut,biscuit
bisness,business
bisnis,business
bisnus,business
bisque,OF SPORTS, A SOUP
bisquet,biscuit
bist,beast
bistro,NIGHTCLUB
bisurk,berserk
bisy,busy
bit,*,TINY INCREMENTS OF SOMETHING, TOOL FOR DRILLING, PAST TENSE FOR THE WORD 'BITE' (or see bite/ bid/ bead/ beat/ beet)
bite,*,ting,ter, USE OF MOUTH AS A TOOL(or see bit) "prefixes: non/ over/ under"
biter,bitter / bid(dder) / bite(r)
bitol,beetle
biton,baton
bitray,betray
bitrei,betray
bitriey,betray
bitrothed,betrothed
bitter,*,rer,rest,red,ring,rly,rness, UNPLEASANT/ HARSH, ALCOHOLIC BREW (or see bid(dder)/ bite(r))
bituin,between
bitur,bitter / bid(dder) / bite(r)
between,between

biuer,beware
biugol,bugle
bius,bias
biusfere,biosphere
biusphere,biosphere
biut,butte
biutj,beauty
biutifol,beautiful
biutishan,beautician
biutres,buttress
biver,beaver
biwar,beware
biwelder,bewilder
biwilder,bewilder
biyopse,biopsy
biyorethum,biorhythm
biyou,bayou
biyu,bayou
biyus,bias
bizar,bizarre / bazaar
bizarre,ely,eness, PECULIAR (or see bazaar)
bizee,busy
bizenes,business
bizerk,berserk
biznes,business
bizurk,berserk
bizzar,bizarre / bazaar
black,*,ken,kened,ker,kest, COLOR
bladder,HOLDS URINE/ LIQUIDS
blade,*, USED TO SLICE/ CUT
bladur,bladder
blaenkit,blanket
blaind,blind
blair,blare
blait,blight
blak,black
blam,blame
blame,*,ed,ming,mable,eful,eless,elessly,eness, WHAT/ WHO IS RESPONSIBLE
bland,der,dest,dly,dness, EXPRESSIVELY FLAT
blank,NOTHING
blanket,*,ted,ting, COVER
blankit,blanket

blanquet,blanket
blare,*,ed,ring,SOUND LOUDLY
blasa,plaza
blase,blaze
blasem,blossom
blasfemus,blasphemy(mous)
blasfemy,blasphemy
blasma,plasma
blasphemy,mous, SPEAK BADLY OF SOMEONE
blast,*,ted,ting, BURSTING FORCE/ RUSH, PREFIX INDICATING "GERM/ BUD" MOST OFTEN MODIFIES THE WORD, BURSTING FORCE/ RUSH
blastek,plastic
blastik,plastic
blasto,PREFIX INDICATING "GERM/ BUD" MOST OFTEN MODIFIES THE WORD, BURSTING FORCE/ RUSH
blatebus,platypus
blater,bladder
blatibus,platypus
blaus,blouse
blawse,blouse
blaze,*,ed,zing,er, FLAME, HORSE MARK, PROCLAIM, SPORT COAT
blazu,plaza
blea,plea
bleach,es,hed,hing, TO MAKE WHITE "prefixes: un"
bleachers,SEATS FOR SPECTATORS
bleak,kish,kly,kness, PALLID, DESOLATE, STARK
bled,PAST TENSE FOR THE WORD 'BLEED'
bleech,bleach
bleechers,bleachers
bleed,*,der,ding, LOOSE BLOOD, ALLOW RELEASE OF FLUID
bleef,belief
bleek,bleak
bleid,blade
bleim,blame
bleinket,blanket
bleis,blaze
blek,bleak
blemish,hes,hed,hing,her, DEFECT ON A SURFACE
blemp,blimp
blend,*,ded,ding,der, MIX

blenk,blink
bler,blur / blare
blerb,blurb
bles,bless / bliss
bless,ssess,ssed,ssing,FAVOR UPON (or see bliss) "prefixes: un"
blester,blister
blew,TO DO WITH AIR,PAST TENSE FOR THE WORD 'BLOW' (or see blue)
blezurd,blizzard
blich,bleach
blichers,bleachers
blid,bleed
blight,*,DESTROYED BY ORGANISM (or see plight)
blik,bleak
blimp,*,HELIUM BALLOON
blind,*,ded,ding,ders,WITHOUT SIGHT,WINDOW COVERING (or see blend)
blink,*,ked,king,ker,TO OPEN/ CLOSE/ OPEN ' prefixes: un"
blinker,*,TURN INDICATORS ON VEHICLES
blir,blur
blirb,blurb
blire,blur(rry)
blis,bliss
blisful,bliss(ful)
bliss,ssful,ssfully,ssfulness,EXTREMELY HAPPY (or see bless)
blister,*,red,ring,SORE
blisurd,blizzard
bite,blight
blizzard,*,VIOLENT STORM
blo,blow / below
bloan,blown
bloat,*,ted,ting,SWELL (or see blot)
block,*,ked,king,kage,IN PATHWAY "prefixes: un"
blockade,*,ed,ding,OBSTRUCT JCT TRAVEL
blod,blood / bloat / blown
blog,*,gged,gging,gger,COMPUTER INTERNET TERM (or see block)
blok,block / blog
blokade,blockade
blokeid,blockade

blon,blown / blonde
blonde,*,A COLOR
blone,blown / blonde
blont,blonde / blown
blood,*,ded,dy,dily,dless,diness,BODY FLUID CARRYING NUTRIENTS
blooish,blue(uish)
bloom,*,med,ming,OPEN UP
bloqueid,blockade
blosim,blossom
blossom,*,med,ming,FLOURISH
blosum,blossom
blot,*,tted,tting,tter,SPOT,STAIN (or see bloat/ blood)
blouse,es,WOMAN'S SHIRT
blout,bloat
blouze,blouse
blow,*,wing,lew,wn,FORCEFUL AIR CURRENT (or see below)
blown,TO DO WITH AIR,PAST TENSE FOR THE WORD "BLOW" "prefixes: over"
blowse,blouse
blowt,bloat
blu,blue / blew
blubber,*,red,ring,ry,rer,WHALE FAT,SOBBING
blubur,blubber
blud,blood
blue,*,uish,uing,COLOR (or see blew)
bluesh,blue(uish)
bluff,*,ffed,ffing,ffer,A CLIFF,TO PRETEND/ FAKE
blume,bloom
blunder,*,red,ring,BUNGLES
blunt,*,tly,tness,DULL
bluper,blubber
blupir,blubber
blur,*,rred,rring,rry,INDISTINCT/ FUZZY
blurb,*,bed,bing,SHORT DESCRIPTION
blush,hes,hed,hing,PHYSICAL RESPONSE IN THE CHEEKS,TYPE OF WINE "prefixes: un"
blut,blood
bluty,blood
bo,bough / bow / beau
boar,*,SWINE,PIG (or see bore)

board,*,ded,ding,MILLED WOOD,FURNISH WITH FOOD (or see bore(d)) "prefixes: over/ pre"
boast,*,ted,ting,tful,tfully,TO BRAG,COMPLIMENT
boat,*,ting,ter,VESSEL IN WATER
bob,*,bbed,bbing,TO MOVE UP AND DOWN (or see bobbin/ bop)
bobbin,*,SEWING TOOL (or see bop(pping))
bobd,bop(pped) / bob(bbed)
boben,bobbin / bob(bbing)
bobin,bobbin / bob(bbing)
bobt,bop(pped) / bob(bbed)
boc,buck / box / bog
boch,budge / bull
bochet,budget
bochulism,botulism
bock,box / bog
bocks,box
bocs,box
bodchulism,botulism
boddle,bottle
bode,*,PAST TENSE FOR THE WORD 'BIDE',TO WAIT (or see body/ bought)
bodeese,bodice / body
bodel,bottle
bodely,body(dily)
bodem,bottom
bodes,body(dies) / bodice
bodice,WOMAN'S GARMENT FOR UPPER TORSO
bodim,bottom
bodis,body(dies) / bodice
bodjulism,botulism
bodle,bottle
bodul,bottle
bodulism,botulism
bodum,bottom
body,dies,dily,THE PHYSICAL FORM WHICH HOUSES A SPIRIT/ LIFE (or see bodice) "prefixes: under"
boe,boy / buoy
boee,boy / buoy
boel,boil
boence,bounce(cy) / buoyant(ncy)
boensy,buoyant(ncy)
boent,buoyant

boes, boy(s)
boesdrus, boisterous
boestures, boisterous
boeul, boil
boeunse, buoyant(ncy)
bofalou, buffalo
bofer, buffer
bog, *, gged, gging, ggy, gginess, SOGGY/ SPONGY/ WET SOIL AREA/ GROUND, SLOW DOWN, A LAVATORY (or see balk/ baulk)
boj, boy / buoy
boiant, buoyant
boient, buoyant
boil, *, led, ling, ler, BRING LIQUID TO STEAM TEMPERATURE
boince, buoyant(ncy)
boiol, boil
boischeros, boisterous
boisdrus, boisterous
boishuazi, bourgeois(ie)
boisterous, sly, sness, ROWDY
boiunse, buoyant(ncy)
boiunt, buoyant
bojwaze, bourgeois(ie)
bok, book / poke / bog / baulk / balk
boka, bouquet
bokei, bouquet/ bucket
bokol, buckle
boks, box
bol, ball / bowl / bawl / bull
bolb, bulb
bolbus, bulb(ous)
bolch, bulge
bold, der, dest, dly, dness, BRAVE, STANDS OUT (or see bolt) "prefixes: semi"
bolder, boulder / bold(er)
bole, bowl / ball / bawl / bully
bolef, belief
boletin, bulletin
boletle, belittle
boleve, believe
bolidel, belittle
boligerant, belligerent

bolion, bouillon
bolistic, ballistic
bolit, bullet
boliten, bulletin
bolivard, boulevard
bolk, bulk / baulk / balk
boll, bowl / ball / bawl
bollet, budget
bollion, bullion / bouillon
bolm, balm
bolme, balmy
bolmy, balmy
bologna, MIXTURE OF MEAT TYPES (or see baloney)
bolonee, baloney / bologna
bolster, *, red, ring, SUPPORT
bolt, *, ted, ting, SECURES, THREADED ROD WITH HEAD (or see bold) "prefixes: un"
bolter, boulder / bold(er)
bolyon, bullion / bouillon
bom, balm / bomb
bomb, *, bed, bing, ber, EXPLOSIVE DEVICE
bomirang, boomerang
bon, bone
bona fide, GENUINE
bonafide, SPELLED AS TWO WORDS "BONA FIDE", GENUINE
bonanza, BONUS DEAL
bond, *, ded, ding, dage, dable, der, TO JOIN/ ATTACH TO, TIE UP "prefixes: non"
bondry, boundary
bone, *, ed, ning, ny, nier, niest, niness, SKELETAL
bonefide, bona fide
boneon, bunyon / bunion
bones, bone(s) / bunny(nnies) / bonus
bonifide, bona fide
bonion, bunyon / bunion
bonis, bonus / bunny(nnies)
bonsy, bounce(cy) / buoyant(ncy)
bonufide, bona fide
bonus, ses, EXTRA, ADDITIONAL, MORE
bony, bone
bonyen, bunyon / bunion
bonyon, bunion / bunyon

book, *, ked, king, kish, kishly, kishness, kie, BOUND PAPER WITH A COVER, TO RESERVE A PLACE "prefixes: over"
bookie, *, BOOKS BETS
booky, bookie
boomerang, *, ged, ging, ARTICLE FOR SPORT
boomurang, boomerang
boose, booze / buzz
boost, *, ted, ting, ter, TO LIFT (or see boast/ bust)
boosum, bosom
boot, *, OVER ANKLE SHOE (or see butte) "prefixes: re"
booteek, boutique
booth, *, PRIVATE STALL/ AREA
bootshur, butcher
booy, buoy
booyon, bouillon / bullion
booze, HARD LIQUOR (or see buzz)
bop, *, pped, pping, pper, TO HIT/ WHACK (or see bob)
boped, bop(pped) / bob(bbed)
bopt, bop(pped) / bob(bbed)
boqol, buckle
boquet, bouquet / bucket
bor, boar / bore / bar
borbon, bourbon
borc, bark
bord, board / bore(d)
bordem, boredom
border, *, red, ring, TO LIMIT
bordim, boredom
bordor, boredom
bordum, boredom
bordur, border
bore, *, ed, ring, ringly, PIERCE/ PUNCTURE/ DRILL, LACKS INTEREST, PAST TENSE FOR THE WORD 'BEAR' (or see boar) "prefixes: re"
boredom, DOLDRUMS, LACK OF INTEREST
boren, borne / born
boret, barrette / beret
borin, borne / born
borlap, burlap
born, BROUGHT INTO EXISTENCE (or see borne/ barn) "prefixes: in/ re/ un"

borne, SUFFIX MEANING TO BE CARRIED/ MOVED BY A PARTICULAR THING (or see born/ barn)

bornt, burnt

boro, PREFIX INDICATING 'BORON' MOST OFTEN MODIFIES THE WORD (or see borrow/ borough)

borot, borrow(ed)

borough, *, SELF-GOVERNING TOWN (or see burrow/ burro/ borrow)

borow, borrow/ burrow/ borough

borrow, *, wed, wing, wer, LOAN (or see burrow)

borst, burst

bort, bore(d) / board

borter, border

bortur, border

bos, boss / bus

bose, bough(s) / bow(s) / bossy

bosed, boss(ed)

boseness, boss(iness)

boserd, buzzard

boshel, bushel

bosiness, boss(iness)

bosom, *, med, my, mier, miest, WOMEN'S BREASTS

boss, sses, ssed, ssing, ssy, ssily, ssiness, COMMAND/ ORDER SOMEONE TO DO SOMETHING, ONE IN CHARGE "prefixes: under"

bossom, bosom

bossy, siness, DOMINEERING

bost, boast / boss(ed) / boost

bosy, bossy

bot, but / butt / boat / bought

botany, nic, nical, nist, OF PLANTS

botch, hes, hed, hing, MESS SOMETHING UP, SLANG WORD IN WRESTLING, A BAND

botcher, butcher

botchulism, botulism

bote, boat / bought

boteek, boutique

botel, bottle

botem, bottom

boter, butter

botes, body(dies) / bodice

both, TWO TOGETHER (or see booth)

bother, *, red, ring, rsome, ANNOY "prefixes: un"

botil, bottle

botim, bottom

botiney, botany

botle, bottle

botler, butler / bottle(r)

botn, button

botney, botany

botni, botany

botok, buttock

botom, bottom

boton, button

botshulism, botulism

bottle, *, ed, ling, er, GLASS CONTAINER

bottom, *, med, ming, mless, mlessness, BASE

botul, bottle

botulism, FOOD POISONING

botum, bottom

boty, body

bou, beau / bow

boudis, bodice

bough, *, BUNCHED FLOWERS, TREE BRANCHES, PART OF A SHIP (or see bow/ beau)

bought, PURCHASED, PAST TENSE FOR THE WORD 'BUY' (or see bout) "prefixes: over"

bouillon, BROTH (or see bullion)

boulder, *, LARGE ROCK (or see bold)

boulevard, *, AVENUE

boulion, bouillon / bullion

bouls, bowel(s) / bowl(s)

bounce, *, ed, cing, cy, er, REBOUND, UP/ DOWN ACTION (or see buoyant(nce))

bound, *, ded, ding, dless, dlessly, dlessness, TO HOLD, JUMP, DESTINY "prefixes: in/ out/ re/ un"

boundary, ries, A LIMIT/ BORDERLINE

bounse, bounce / buoyant(ncy)

bounsy, bounce

bountiful, lly, lness, PLENTIFUL

bounty, ties, tiful, tifully, tifulness, teous, teously, teousness, PAYMENT/ REWARD FOR CAPTURE, PLENTY, ABUNDANCE

bouquet, BUNCH OF FLOWERS

bourbon, WHISKEY

bourgeois, sis, PROPERTY-OWNING UPPER MIDDLE CLASS

bout, *, A SPELL OF, TEMPORARY EXPERIENCE (or see boat)

bouth, both

boutique, *, WOMEN'S CLOTHING

bouwls, bowel(s)

bouyant, buoyant

bouynce, buoyant(ncy)

bow, *, wed, wing, BEND, HAIR ORNAMENT, TOOL USED WITH INSTRUMENT/ ARROW (or see bough/ beau) "prefixes: un"

bowel, *, INTESTINES OF ANYTHING

bowkay, bouquet

bowl, *, led, ling, ler, ROUND VESSEL, GAME OF BALLS WITH PINS (or see ball/ bawl)

bowlder, boulder / bold(er)

bownce, bounce / bounce(cy)

bownd, bound

bowndee, bounty

bowndeful, bountiful

bowndery, boundary

bowndury, boundary

bowndy, bounty

bownse, bounce / bound(s)

bownsee, bounce(cy)

bowntee, bounty

bownteful, bountiful

bownts, bounce / bound(s)

bowt, bout

bowteek, boutique

box, xes, xed, xing, xer, xy, SQUARE SHAPED CONTAINER, SPORT "prefixes: un"

boy, *, yish, yishly, YOUNG MALE (or see buoy)

boyanse, buoyant(ncy)

boyant, buoyant

boyent, buoyant

boyint, buoyant

boyle, boil

boyol, boil

boysdrus, boisterous

boysterus, boisterous

boyunse, buoyant(ncy)

boyunt, buoyant
bozard, buzzard
bra,*, WOMEN'S UNDERGARMENT
brace,*, ced, cing, SUPPORT (or see brass/ braise) "prefixes: un"
bracelet,*, WRIST ORNAMENT
bracket,*, ting, FIXTURE TO ATTACH TO, TO ENCLOSE WITHIN
bracoli, broccoli
brad,*, VERY SMALL NAILS (or see brat/ braid)
brael, brail / braille
braen, brain
braes, brace / braise
braf, brave
brag,*, gged, gging, ggart, TO BOAST/ PRAISE
bragert, braggart
braggart,*, ONE WHO BOASTS
bragirt, braggart
braid,*, ded, ding, TO INTERTWINE TOGETHER
brail, OF BOATS, BIRD, FISH (or see braille)
braille, TEXT FOR THE BLIND (or see brail)
brain,*, nless, nlessly, nlessness, ny, THINKING PART/ MASS IN THE SKULL
braise,*, ed, sing, TO BROWN MEAT THEN COVER TO COOK (or see brace)
brakale, broccoli
brake,*, ed, king, er, TO STOP, HOLD BACK (or see break)
braket, bracket
brakible, breakable
brakit, bracket
brakle, broccoli
brakoli, broccoli
brakuble, breakable
bral, brail / braille / brawl
bran,*, A GRAIN YOU EAT (or see brain/ brawn/ brown/ brand)
brand,*, ded, ding, A NAME THAT SIGNIFIES OWNERSHIP "prefixes: mis/ un"
brane, brain
brankeal, bronchial
braquet, bracket
bras, brace / brass / braise / bra(s)
braslet, bracelet

brass, ssy, ssier, ssiest, ssily, ssiness, METAL, MILITARY OFFICERS (or see brace/ braise)
brat,*, tty, ttish, SOMEONE WHO IS AGGRAVATING/ IRRITATING (or see braid/ brad)
brathren, brethren
brau, bra / brow
braud, broad
braukali, broccoli
braukle, broccoli
braun, brown / brawn
braus, browse / brow(s)
braut, broad / brought
brave,*, ed, ving, er, ely, est, ery, eness, COURAGEOUS
braw, bra
brawkley, broccoli
brawl,*, LOUD FIGHT
brawn, MUSCLES (or see brown)
brawnkeul, bronchial
brawnkitis, bronchitis
brawnze, bronze
brayed, braid
brayel, brail / braille
braz, braise / brace / bra(s)
breach, hes, hed, hing, BREAK CONTRACT/ AGREEMENT
bread, ded, ding, dth, BAKED DOUGH (or see bred/ breed)
breadth, THE EXTENT/ DISTANCE/ BROADNESS (or see breath)
break,*, king, kage, ker, roke, COME APART (or see brake)
breakable, CAN COME APART "prefixes: un"
breakuble, breakable
breast,*, ted, BOSOM
breath, hes, hed, hing, hless, hlessly, her, INHALE, EXHALE AIR (or see breadth)
brec, brick
brech, breach
bred, PASTE TENSE OF "BREED", HAVING MATED (or see bread/ breed/ barrette) "prefixes: in/ under"
breed,*, ding, der, red, TO MATE FOR PROCREATION, A CLASSIFICATION/ TYPE (or see bred/ bread) "prefixes: in/ un"
breef, brief
breeng, bring
breenk, brink

breeth, breath
breeve, bereave
breeze,*, ed, zing, zily, zy, GENTLE WIND
bref, brief
brege, bridge
breid, braid
breif, brief
breik, brake
breil, braille
brein, brain
breiq, brake
breis, brace / braise
breislet, bracelet
breiv, brave
brej, bridge
brek, brick / break
brel, brail / braille
breluns, brilliance
brelyans, brilliance
brem, brim
breng, bring
brenk, brink
brese, breeze
brest, breast
bret, barrette / beret / breed / bread / bred
breth, breath / breadth
brethless, breath(less)
brethlis, breath(less)
brethren, PLURAL FOR BROTHER
brethrin, brethren
brew,*, wed, wing, A DRINK CONCOCTION
breze, breeze
bribe,*, ed, bing, ery, REWARD FOR CORRUPTION
brich, breach
brick,*, ked, king, CLAY BLOCK
brid, bride / bright / bread
bride,*, dal, FEMALE GETTING MARRIED
bridegroom,*, MALE GETTING MARRIED
bridesmaid,*, ATTENDS BRIDE
bridge,*, ed, ging, eable, eless, LINK FOR TRAVEL "prefixes: under"
bridgroom, bridegroom
bridgrum, bridegroom

bridle, *, ed, ling, FOR RESTRAINT (or see brittle) "prefixes: un"
bridmade, bridesmaid
bridol, bridle / brittle
bridsmaid, bridesmaid
bridul, bridle / brittle
brief, *, fed, fing, SHORT/ SWEET/ TO THE POINT, UNDERWEAR
brig, bridge
bright, *, ter, test, tly, tness, STRONG LIGHT ENERGY
brij, bridge
brik, brick
brileans, brilliance
briliance, brilliance
brilliance, nt, INTENSE LIGHT ENERGY
brilliant, ntly, INTENSE LIGHT ENERGY
brim, *, mmed, mming, THE EDGE/ RIM OF SOMETHING
bring, *, ging, rought, BEAR FORTH "prefixes: up"
brink, NEAR THE EDGE
brit, bright / bride
britesmade, bridesmaid
britle, bridle / brittle
brittle, eness, CRISP (or see bridle)
britul, bridle / brittle
brn, burn / barn
bro, *, SHORT FOR BROTHER (or see bra)
broad, *, dly, den, dness, AS IN WIDTH OR BREADTH
broadcast, *, ted, ting, ter, ANNOUNCE, SCATTER
broccoli, VEGETABLE (same as brocoli)
brochere, brochure
brochure, *, PAMPHLET
brocoli, VEGETABLE (same as broccoli)
brocolli, broccoli
brod, broad / brought / brood
brodkast, broadcast
broeel, broil
broel, broil
broil, *, led, ling, ler, WAY TO COOK
brok, broke
brokali, broccoli
broke, en, PAST TENSE FOR THE WORD 'BREAK', NO MONEY "prefixes: un"
brokle, broccoli

brokley, broccoli
brokule, broccoli
brol, brawl
bron, brawn / brown
brona, prana / piranha
bronceal, bronchial
bronch, PREFIX INDICATING 'BRONCHIAL' MOST OFTEN MODIFIES THE WORD
broncheul, bronchial
bronchi, PREFIX INDICATING 'BRONCHIAL' MOST OFTEN MODIFIES THE WORD
bronchial, lly, OF THE AIR/ BREATHING PASSAGES
bronchitis, BREATHING PROBLEM
broncho, PREFIX INDICATING 'BRONCHIAL' MOST OFTEN MODIFIES THE WORD
bronckial, bronchial
bronkaidis, bronchitis
bronkeul, bronchial
bronkites, bronchitis
bronquial, bronchial
bronse, bronze
bronze, ed, zing, METALLIC
brood, *, ding, dingly, CONCERNING OFFSPRING IN A GROUP, TO GRIEVE, BIRD SITTING ON EGGS
broodel, brutal
brook, *, STREAM
broom, *, FOR SWEEPING
broonet, brunet
brootal, brutal
brootle, brutal
bropane, propane
brosh, brush
brosher, brochure
broshur, brochure
brot, brought / broad
broth, SOUP
brother, *, rly, MALE SIBLING
brought, PAST TENSE FOR THE WORD 'BRING'
broun, brown / brawn
brow, *, ABOVE EYES (or see browse)
browl, brawl
brown, *, ned, ning, ner, nest, COLOR (or see brawn)

browse, *, ed, sing, er, GLANCE/ PERUSE/ CASUALLY GO THROUGH (or see brow(s))
broyl, broil
brud, brood
brudel, brutal
brue, brew
bruise, *, ed, sing, er, A BLOW TO, DAMAGED TISSUE
bruke, brook
brume, broom
brunet, DARK COLOR
brunkitis, bronchitis
brunnet, brunet
bruro, bureau
bruse, bruise
brush, hes, hed, hing, ENCOUNTER, HAIR TOOL, BUSHES "prefixes: under"
brutal, lly, lize, lization, lity, SAVAGE
bruther, brother
brutil, brutal
bruz, bruise
brydgroom, bridegroom
brydle, bridle / brittle
brydsmade, bridesmaid
bryt, bright
buanse, bounce(cy)
bubble, *, ed, ling, er, ly, AIR, GAS GLOBULES
bubil, bubble
buble, bubble
bucame, became
buch, budge / bull
bucher, butcher
buchur, butcher
buck, *, ked, king, UNSEAT RIDER, MALE DEER, DOLLAR
bucket, *, A CONTAINER
buckil, buckle
buckit, bucket
buckle, *, ed, ling, TOOL TO SECURE SOMETHING, TO FOLD UNDER PRESSURE
bud, *, dded, dding, READY TO OPEN, FULL OF FUTURE POTENTIAL (or see butt/ butte/ but) "prefixes: de/ dis"
budder, butter

buddy,ddies,ddied,ddying,SOMEONE YOU BEFRIEND, TRAVEL ALONGSIDE (or see beauty)
bude,buddy / beauty
budeful,beautiful
buden,button
buder,butter
budge,*,ed,ging,TO MOVE
budget,*,ted,ting,ter,tary,RATION A SPECIFIC AMOUNT FOR EXPENDITURES
budi,buddy / beauty
budiful,beautiful
budin,button
budj,budge
budler,butler
budok,buttock
budres,buttress
budris,buttress
budrothed,betrothed
buduk,buttock
budy,buddy / beauty
buee,buoy
bufa,buffet
bufal,befall
bufalo,buffalo
bufei,buffet
bufer,buffer
buff,*,ffed,ffing,ffer,A COLOR,NUDE,MASCULINE/ MUSCULAR,TO POLISH WITH CLOTH "prefixes: re"
buffalo,*,ANIMAL
buffer,*,red,ring,ABSORBS SHOCK,POLISHES
buffet,*,SELF-SERVE RESTAURANT
bufilo,buffalo
bufir,buffer
bufol,befall
bufrend,befriend
bufulo,buffalo
bufur,buffer
bug,*,gged,gging,ggy,ggier,ggiest,gginess,gger,ERROR IN DEVICE,AN INSECT,TO IRRITATE SOMEONE/SOMETHING,SPY DEVICE (or see budge) "prefixes: de"
buge,budge / buggy
bugel,bugle

bugener,begin(nner)
buget,budget
buggy,ggies,LIGHTWEIGHT CARRIAGE FOR MANY PURPOSES
bugil,bugle
bugin,begin
bugit,budget
bugle,*,INSTRUMENT
bugul,bugle
bugwazee,bourgeois(ie)
bugy,buggy
buhaf,behave
buhind,behind
build,*,der,ding,dable,lt,CONSTRUCT (or see built) "prefixes: over/ re/ up"
built,PAST TENSE FOR THE WORD 'BUILD'
buj,budge
bujet,budget
bujit,budget
bujwau,bourgeois
bujwazee,bourgeois(ie)
buk,buck / book / bug
bukame,became
bukaus,because
buke,bookie
bukel,buckle
bukene,bikini
buket,bucket
bukie,bookie
bukil,buckle
bukit,bucket
bukos,because
bul,bull
bulated,belated
bulaten,bulletin
bulatide,belated
bulavard,boulevard
bulb,*,bous,OF PLANTS,GLASS GLOBES WITH FILAMENTS
bulbus,bulb(ous)
bulch,bulge
bulck,bulk
bule,bully

buledul,belittle
buleef,belief
buleeve,believe
bulef,belief
buleger,beleaguer
bulegirant,belligerent
buleon,bullion / bouillon
bulese,police
bulet,bullet
buletin,bulletin
bulevard,boulevard
buleve,believe
bulevuble,believe(vable)
bulge,*,ed,ging,SWELL OUT
bulian,bouillon
buligerant,belligerent
bulijurent,belligerent
bulion,bullion / bouillon
bulistic,ballistic
bulit,bullet
bulitel,belittle
buliten,bulletin
bulivard,boulevard
bulje,bulge
bulk,ky,kiness,kier,kiest,MASS OF SOMETHING
bull,*,MALE ANIMAL (or see budge)
bullet,*,PROJECTILE
bulletin,*,DOCUMENT
bullion,OF GOLD (or see bouillon)
bully,llies,llied,llying,INTIMIDATOR
bullyon,bouillon / bullion
bulo,blow / below
bulonee,baloney / bologna
bulong,belong
buloon,balloon
bulow,below / bellow / billow
bulp,bulb
bulune,balloon
buluvard,boulevard
buly,bully
bulyon,bullion / bouillon
bumbelbee,bumblebee
bumblebee,*,BIG BEE

bumer, bummer
bumerang, boomerang
bumir, bummer
bummer, OF QUARRY, NOT HAPPY
bumur, bummer
bumurang, boomerang
bunana, banana
bunansa, bonanza
bunch, hes, hed, hing, MORE THAN A FEW IN THE GROUP
bundle,*,ed,ling,er, TO GROUP/ BIND TOGETHER "prefixes: un"
bune, bunny
buneeth, beneath
buneon, bunion / bunyon
bunes, bunny(nnies) / bonus
buneun, bunyon / bunion
bunevilance, benevolence
bungil, bungle
bungle,*,ed,ling,ler, MESS UP, SPOIL, WRECK
bunie, bunny
bunine, benign
bunion,*, SWELLING ON BIG TOE, ALSO SPELLED "BUNYON"
bunis, bunny(nnies)
bunny, nies, RABBIT
bunsh, bunch
buny, bunny
bunyon,*, SWELLING ON BIG TOE, ALSO SPELLED "BUNION"
bunyun, bunion / bunyon
buond, beyond
buorgeoise, bourgeois(ie)
buownse, bounce(cy)
buoy,*, FLOATING DEVICE
buoyant, ncy, TO FLOAT
buquet, bouquet / bucket
bur, burr
bura, barrette / beret
buracracy, bureaucracy
buracrat, bureaucrat
burakracy, bureaucracy
burau, bureau
buraukracy, bureaucracy

burave, brave
burbon, bourbon
burch, birch
burd, bird
burden,*,ned,ning,nsome, HEAVY LOAD "prefixes: dis/ over/ un"
burdensum, burden(some)
burdin, burden
burdinsum, burden(some)
burdon, burden
bureal, burial
bureau,*, A DRESSER, GOVERNMENT DEPARTMENT
bureaucracy, cies, at, GOVERNMENT ADMINISTRATION
bureaucrat,*, AGENTS OF GOVERNMENT ADMINISTRATION
bureeve, bereave
bureft, bereft
buret, barrette / beret
bureve, bereave
burgendy, burgundy
burgeois, bourgeois
burglar,*, ry, ries, rize, rizes, rized, rizing, ROBBER/ THIEF
burglir, burglar
burgundy, A COLOR, A WINE
burial,*, BURYING DECEASED
burileans, brilliance
buring, bring
burite, bright
burkler, burglar
burlap, WOVEN HEMP/ JUTE
burlee, burly
burlesk, burlesque
burlesque, er, MOCKERY
burlip, burlap
burlluasi, bourgeois(ie)
burly, BIG MUSCULAR BODY
burm, berm
burn,*,ned,ning,nable,nt, SCORCH "prefixes: un"
burnt, BEEN BURNED, PAST TENSE FOR THE WORD 'BURN'
buro, burro / burrow / borough / bureau
burocrasy, bureaucracy
burocrat, bureaucrat

burog, barrage
burokracy, bureaucracy
burokrat, bureaucrat
buromiter, barometer
burow, burro / burrow / borough / bureau
burp,*,,ped,ping, BELCH
burr,*,,rred,rring, PRICKLY SEED, ROUGH EDGES, EXPRESSION FOR BEING COLD "prefixes: de"
burro,*, DONKEY (or see burrow/ borough)
burrow,*,,wed,wing, LODGE INTO HOLE (or see burro/ borough)
bursd, burst
burst,*,,ting,ter, ERUPT
burth, berth / birth
burthday, birthday
bury, ries, ried, rying, PUT IN GROUND (or see berry) "prefixes: un"
bus, sses, ssed, ssing, LARGE VEHICLE TO TRANSPORT MANY PASSENGERS, CARRIER OF INFORMATION
busar, bizarre / bazaar
busd, bust / boost / bus(ssed)
busdid, bust(ed) / burst
busech, beseech
buseech, beseech
busel, bustle
busem, bosom
buserd, buzzard
buses, bus(sses)
bushel,*, MEASUREMENT OF AMOUNT
bushil, bushel
bushwaze, bourgeois(ie)
busi, busy
buside, beside
busil, bustle
busim, bosom
business, sses, A SERVICE
busle, bustle
business, business
busniss, business
bust,*,,ted,ting,ty, tier, tiest, HEAD AND SHOULDERS, WOMEN'S BREASTS, CAUGHT RED-HANDED (or see boost/ burst/ bus(ssed))
busted, burst / bust(ed)

bustle, *, ed, ling, HURRIES ABOUT, FOR SKIRTS
busul, bustle
busum, bosom
busurk, berserk
busy, sies, sier, siest, ENGROSSED
but, A PREPOSITION MEANING "EXCEPT/ ONLY/ DIFFERENCE" (or see but/ butte/ bud/ boot)
butcher, *, red, ring, CUT UP
bute, boot / but / butt / butte
buted, butt(ed) / bud(dded)
buteek, boutique
buteful, beautiful
buten, button
butenchul, potential
buter, butter
buth, booth
buti, buddy / beauty
butid, butt(ed) / bud(dded)
butiful, beautiful
butike, boutique
butin, button
butinchul, potential
butir, butter
butishun, beautician
butler, *, MALE SERVANT
butlur, butler
butok, buttock
buton, baton / button
butra, betray
butres, buttress
butris, buttress
butrothed, betrothed
buts, butt(s) / bud(s) / boot(s)
butsher, butcher
butshir, butcher
butt, *, tted, tting, REAR END/ BOTTOM OF SOMETHING, FORCE UPON (or see bud/ but/ butte)
butte, *, HILL/ MOUNTAIN WITH FLAT TOP (or see but/ butt)
butter, red, ring, ry, CHURNED FROM MILK
buttock, *, RUMP
button, *, ned, ning, FIXTURE FOR CLOTHING "prefixes: un"

buttress, TO STRENGTHEN
butuk, buttock
between, between
buty, buddy / beauty
buvileon, pavilion
buware, beware
buwee, buoy
buwelder, bewilder
buwildre, bewilder
buwro, bureau
buwte, beauty
buy, *, ying, yer, bought, TO PURCHASE (or see bye/ by/ bi)
buyent, buoyant
buyint, buoyant
buyond, beyond
bazar, bizarre / bazaar / buzz(er)
buzd, buzz(ed) / bust / bus(ssed)
buzded, bust(ed)
buze, booze / buzz
buzer, buzz(er) / bizarre / bazaar
buzerd, buzzard
buzerk, berserk
buzir, buzz(er) / bizarre / bazaar
buzor, buzz(er) / bizarre / bazaar
buzted, bust(ed) / burst
buzum, bosom
buzurk, berserk
buzz, zzes, zzed, zzing, zzer, A SOUND, DEVICE WHICH MAKES SOUND
buzzar, bizarre / bazaar / buzz(er)
buzzard, *, CARNIVOROUS BIRD
buzzer, buzz(er) / bizarre / bazaar
by, ALONGSIDE, PREFIX INDICATING 'NEAR/ SECONDARY' MOST OFTEN MODIFIES THE WORD(or see bye/ bi/ buy)
bye, AS IN GOOD-BYE (or see by/ bi/ buy)
byeneul, biennial / biannual
byker, bike(r)
bysenteneal, bicentennial
byu, bayou
c, see / sea
ca, say / saw

cabach, cabbage
cabage, cabbage
cabarei, cabaret
cabaret, TYPE OF MUSICAL SHOW
cabbage, *, VEGETABLE
cabdive, captive
cabduve, captive
cabech, cabbage
cabel, cable
caben, cabin
caberay, cabaret
cabich, cabbage
cabichulate, capitulate
cabige, cabbage
cabin, *, RUSTIC STRUCTURE
cabinet, *, try, STORAGE WITH DOORS, POLITICAL ADVISORY
cabiret, cabaret
cabitate, capitate
cabitch, cabbage
cable, *, ed, ling, WIRE ROPE, CONNECTION
cabnet, cabinet
cabnit, cabinet
caboose, LAST CAR ON A TRAIN
cabsel, capsule
cabshure, capture
cabten, captain
cabture, capture
cabtuve, captive
cabul, cable
cabus, caboose
cac, PREFIX INDICATING 'HARSH/ BAD' MOST OFTEN MODIFIES THE WORD (or see cake/ caulk/ cock)
cach, catch / cache / cash
cache, *, ed, hing, PLACE TO HIDE ITEMS IN (or see cash/ catch)
cacher, catcher / cashier
cachup, ketchup / catsup
cachwul, casual
cackle, *, ed, ling, SHRILL SOUND/ LAUGH
caco, PREFIX INDICATING 'HARSH/ BAD' MOST OFTEN MODIFIES THE WORD
cacol, cackle

cacoon, cocoon
cactis, cactus
cactus, ses, ti, DESERT PLANT
cacun, cocoon
cadagory, category
cadal, cattle
cadaver, *, ric, LIFELESS BODY
caddie, caddy
caddy, ddie, ddies, PERSON WHO CARRIES CLUBS IN GOLF, BOX
cadech, cottage
cadecism, catechism
cadee, caddy
cadegerize, categorize
cadegory, category
cadekism, catechism
cadil, cattle
cadilist, catalyst
cadilog, catalog
cadinse, cadence
cadl, cattle
cadle, cattle
cadol, cattle
cadugorize, categorize
cadugory, category
cadul, cattle
cadulist, catalyst
cadulize, catalyst(yze)
cadulog, catalog
cadur, cater
caduract, cataract
caf, calf / cave / cough
cafa, cafe
cafanated, caffeine(nated)
cafe, *, SMALL RESTAURANT (or see coffee/ calf)

cafeene, caffeine
cafene, caffeine
cafeteria, *, SELF-SERVE RESTAURANT
caffeine, nate, nated, nation, nism, ALSO SPELLED "CAFFEIN", STIMULANT, DIURETIC "prefixes: de/ under"
cafin, caffeine
cafiteria, cafeteria
cafs, calves / cave(s)
cafunated, caffeine(nated)
cafutirea, cafeteria
cage, *, ed, ging, FOR CONFINEMENT
cagwal, casual
cahoot, *, IN PARTNERSHIP
cahute, cahoot
cainker, canker / chancre
cairfree, carefree
cairful, careful
caje, cage
cajewul, casual
cajole, *, ed, ling, COAX
cajuol, casual
cajut, cahoot
cajwul, casual
cak, caulk / calk / cake / cock
cakd, cake(d)
cake, *, ed, king, ey, BAKED SWEET DOUGH, RESEMBLES CAKE
cakel, cackle
cakt, cake(d)
caktis, cactus
caktus, cactus
caky, khaki
cal, call / cowl / kale
calaberate, collaborate
calabrate, calibrate
caladeral, collateral
calag, collage / college
calametous, calamity(tous)
calamity, ties, tous, tously, DISASTER
calander, calendar / calender / colander
calanize, colony(nize)
calany, colony

calapse, collapse
calas, callous / callus
calasthenics, calisthenics
calastomy, colostomy
calasul, colossal
calateral, collateral
calaug, collage
calcefy, calcify
calcify, fies, fied, fying, fication, fier, BECOME RIGID, LIME/ CALCIUM DEPOSIT "prefixes: de"
calcilate, calculate
calcilus, calculus
calcium, ELEMENT ON EARTH
calcufy, calcify
calculate, *, ed, ting, tingly, tion, tor, TO MENTALLY/ MATHEMATICALLY ESTIMATE/ FIGURE "prefixes: in/ mis/ un"
calculus, li, ses, REFERENCE TO MATH, ORGAN STONE "prefixes: pre"
cale, kale
calebrate, calibrate
calech, college
caleflower, cauliflower
caleg, colleague / college
calegen, collision
caleget, collegiate
calek, colic
calendar, *, red, ring, rize, dric, drical, REGISTER OF MONTHS/ DAYS OF THE YEAR (or see calender/ colander)
calender, *, red, ring, rer, PRESS/ ROLLER FOR PAPER/ CLOTH (or see calendar/ colander)
calendula, MEDICINAL FLOWER
caler, collar / call(er)
cales, callous / callus
calesthenics, calisthenics
calf, lves, lved, lving, YOUNG BOVINE, BIRTHING OF BOVINE, LOWER PORTION OF LEG
caliber, *, bre, OF MEASUREMENT, DIAMETER (or see caliper) "prefixes: sub"
calibrate, *, ed, ting, tion, tor, SET/ DETERMINE MEASUREMENT/ SIZE
calibre, caliber

calide,collide
calidiscope,kaleidoscope
califlower,cauliflower
calig,college
caligen,collision
caligent,collegiate
calinder,calendar / calender / colander
calindula,calendula
caliper,*,lliper,INSTRUMENT FOR MEASURING (or see caliber)
calire,calorie
calis,callous / callus
calision,collision
calisthenics,EXERCISES
calk,DEVICE FOR SHOES (or see caulk)
calkilate,calculate
calkulus,calculus
call,*,lled,lling,ller,ATTEMPT TO CONTACT/ INVITE SOMEONE TO ANSWER/ RESPOND (or see cowl) "prefixes: mis"
callan,cayenne
calleague,colleague
callous,llus,ses,sed,sly,sness,HARDENED/ ROUGH AREA ON SKIN/ PLANT,INSENSITIVE BEHAVIOR, ALSO SPELLED "CALLUS"
callus,ses,sed,sing,sity,llose,HARDENED/ ROUGH AREA ON SKIN/ PLANT,INSENSITIVE BEHAVIOR, ALSO SPELLED "CALLOUS"
calm,mes,med,ming,mly,mative,mness,TO SOOTHE (or see come)
calobrate,calibrate
calokweul,colloquial
caloquial,colloquial
calorie,*,ric,rically,rific,UNIT OF MEASUREMENT FOR FOOD
calorize,*,ed,zing,PROCESS USED IN METALLURGY
calos,callous / callus
calostemy,colostomy
calosthenics,calisthenics
calous,callous / callus
calsefy,calcify
calseum,calcium
caluber,caliber

calubrate,calibrate
calunder,colander
caluper,caliper
calur,collar / call(er)
calury,calorie
calus,callous / callus
calusthenics,calisthenics
calves,ed,ving,PLURAL FOR THE WORD 'CALF', YOUNG BOVINE, BIRTHING BOVINE
camb,camp
came,PAST TENSE FOR THE WORD 'COME', CHANNEL USED FOR MANUFACTURING "prefixes: over"
camel,*,ANIMAL
camend,commend
camendible,commendable
camenduble,commendable
camera,*,TAKES PHOTOS
camfor,camphor
camind,commend
caminduble,commendable
camins,commence
camitee,committee
camofloje,camouflage
camouflage,*,,ed,ging,DISGUISED
camp,*,ped,ping,per,STAY OVERNIGHT/ OUTDOORS IN WILDERNESS "prefixes: en"
campaign,,ned,ning,ner,ACTION TO INFLUENCE
campane,campaign
campein,campaign
camphor,ric,FROM TREES, MEDICINAL
campis,campus
campus,ses,SCHOOL GROUNDS
camra,camera
camuflodge,camouflage
camul,camel
camune,commune
camunicate,communicate
camunity,community
camute,commute
can't,CONTRACTION OF THE WORDS 'CAN NOT' (or see cane)
can,*,nned,nning,nner,nnery,ABLE TO, TIN VESSEL (or see can) cent/ sand/ can(nned)/ con(nned))

canabis,cannabis
canabol,cannibal
canabus,cannabis
canal,*,WHERE FLUIDS FLOW
canalop,cantaloupe
canan,canon / canyon
canapi,canopy
canare,cannery / canary
canary,ries,A YELLOW BIRD (or see cannery)
cancel,*,led,ling,lable,ler,llation,DELETE,RENDER NULL/ VOID
cancellation,*,DELETE, ELIMINATE, INVALIDATE
cancer,rous,DISEASE
cancl,cancel
cancr,cancer
cancur,chancre / canker
candedate,candidate
candid,dly,dness,TO BE FRANK/ TRUTHFUL
candidate,*,acy,acies,SEEKS OFFICE
candle,*,ed,ling,WAX WITH WICK
candudite,candidate
candul,candle
candy,dies,died,WEET TREAT
cane,*,ned,STICK OF WOOD/ SUGAR
canebulize,cannibal(ize)
canelop,cantaloupe
caneon,canyon
canere,cannery / canary
canery,cannery / canary
canesis,kinesis
cangaroo,kangaroo
cangruis,congruous
canibal,cannibal
canibis,cannabis
canikcanik,kinnikinnick
canin,cannon / canine
canine,*,DOG
canion,canyon
canipe,canopy
caniry,cannery / canary
canister,*,CONTAINER
canker,*,rous,DISEASE, SORE (or see chancre)
cannabis,A USEFUL PLANT

cannery, ries, PLACE WHICH CANS FOOD (or see canary)
cannery

cannibal, *, lism, listic, lize, EATS FLESH OF ITS OWN SPECIES
cannibal

cannon, *, WEAPON
canon, cannon

canopy, pies, pied, ying, COVERING FOR SHELTER
canosieur, connoisseur
canseld, cancel(lled)
canser, cancer
cansil, cancel
cansilashen, cancellation
cansir, cancer
cansl, cancel
cansr, cancer
cansul, cancel
cansulation, cancellation
cansuld, cancel(lled)

cantaloupe, *, pe, pes, EDIBLE FRUIT

cantankerous, sly, sness, RESISTANT, DIFFICULT
canted, candid

canteen, *, CONTAINER FOR LIQUIDS
cantelope, cantaloupe
cantena, cantina

canter, *, SPEED OF HORSE
cantidit, candidate
cantiguis, contiguous
cantilope, cantaloupe
cantin, canteen

cantina, *, SALOON, BAG FOR SADDLE
cantul, candle
cantulope, cantaloupe
cantur, canter
canty, candy
canubelize, cannibal(ize)
canubil, cannibal
canubis, cannabis
canulop, cantaloupe
canupe, canopy
canuster, canister

canvas, ses, WOVEN HEMP/ NATURAL FIBERS (or see canvass)

canvass, sser, TO SOLICIT (or see canvas)
canves, canvas / canvass
canvis, canvas / canvass
canvus, canvass / canvas

canyon, *, DEEP VALLEY

cap, *, pped, pping, pful, TOP, HAT, TO LIMIT (or see cape) "prefixes: re/ un"

capability, ties, CAPACITY, ABILITY, SKILL

capable, eness, ly, bility, bilities, CAPACITY, ABILITY, SKILL "prefixes: in"

capacity, ties, STATUS OF, AMOUNT "prefixes: over"
capadol, capital / capitol
capalery, capillary
capasety, capacity
capatol, capital / capitol
capatulism, capitalism
capcher, capture
capchun, caption
capchur, capture
capdivate, captivate
capdof, captive
capduvate, captivate

cape, *, ped, CLOAK, GARMENT, LAND FORM (or see cap)
capebilety, capability
capechulate, capitulate
capedal, capital
capedalism, capitalism
capedul, capital / capitol
capedulism, capitalism
capelary, capillary
capetate, capitate
capetul, capital / capitol
capetulate, capitulate
capetulesm, capitalism
capichulate, capitulate
capidal, capital
capidalism, capitalism

capillary, ries, OF THE BODY

capital, *, list, lists, lististically, lize, lizable, lizes, lized, lizing, lization, llly, llism, LARGE, MAIN, TOP (or see capitol) "prefixes: under"

capitalism, PRIVATE/ FREE ENTERPRISE

capitate, *, ed, ting, tion, tions, tive, COUNTING/ TAXING BY HEADS, HEAD OF SOMETHING

capitol, CENTER OF GOVERNMENT (or see capital)

capitulate, *, ed, ting, ant, tion, tions, tor, tory, CONSENT/ GIVE IN/ YIELD "prefixes: re"
capol, couple
capsais, capsize
capshun, caption
capshur, capture
capsile, capsule

capsize, *, ed, zing, OVERTURN A BOAT

capsulate, *, ed, ting, tion, tor, MATERIAL BEING CONTAINED "prefixes: de/ en/ in"

capsule, *, ed, ling, lar, late, lize, lizing, CONTAINED MATERIAL, COMPACT FORM WITH PROTECTIVE EXTERIOR

captain, *, ONE WHO COMMANDS
captin, captain

caption, *, ned, nless, HEADING OR TITLE

captivate, *, ed, ting, CHARMED, HELD UNWILLFULLY

captive, vity, vation, vator, CONTROLLED/ HELD AGAINST ONE'S WILL
captun, captain

capture, *, ed, ring, er, TAKE BY FORCE "prefixes: re"
captuvate, captivate
captuve, captive
capubility, capability
capuble, capable
capudul, capital / capitol
capudulesm, capitalism
capulary, capillary
caput, kaput
caputate, capitate
caqui, khaki

car, *, rful, AUTOMOBILE (or see care)
caracter, character
carakter, character

caramel, *, lize, lizes, lized, lizing, lization, CANDY, HEAT PROCESS
caraoke, karaoke

carat, *, MILLIGRAMS (or see caret/ carrot/ karat)
carate, karate
carauti, karate

caravan, *, ned, ning, ner, GROUP OF VEHICLES/ TRAVELERS
carbarator, carburetor

carbender,carpenter
carberator,carburetor
carbin,carbon
carbinete,carbonate
carbirater,carburetor
carbon,*,,nize,nator,FORMS ORGANIC COMPOUNDS
carbonate,*,,ed,ting,tion,SALT OR GAS "prefixes: bi/ de"
carbunete,carbonate
carbureitor,carburetor
carburetor,*,HEART OF COMBUSTIBLE ENGINE
carcass,sses,EXTERNAL REMAINS OF ANYTHING
carcenoullen,carcinogen
carcino,PREFIX INDICATING 'CANCER' MOST OFTEN MODIFIES THE WORD
carcinogen,*,nic,nicity,nesis,CANCER CAUSING
carcinoullen,carcinogen
carcus,carcass
card,*,,ded,ding,STIFF PAPER,ASKED FOR I.D. (or see cart)
cardboard,THICK PAPER
cardeac,cardiac
cardenul,cardinal
cardi,PREFIX INDICATING 'HEART' MOST OFTEN MODIFIES THE WORD
cardiac,OF THE HEART
cardilege,cartilage
cardin,carton
cardinal,*,A BIRD,RANK IN CATHOLIC CHURCH
cardio,PREFIX INDICATING 'HEART' MOST OFTEN MODIFIES THE WORD
cardulege,cartilage
care,*,,ed,ring,ringly,eful,efully,efulness,eless, elessness,CONCERN OVER (or see carry) "prefixes: multi/ un"
careboo,caribou
carebral,cerebral
carebrul,cerebral
carech,carriage
carecter,character
caredge,carriage
caredor,corridor
careen,*,,ned,ning,LEAN TO ONE SIDE
career,*,PROFESSION

carefree,WITHOUT CARE
careful,lly,lness,WITH CARE
carege,carriage
carekter,character
careless,ssly,ssness,NOT WITH CARE
caremel,caramel
careoki,karaoke
carer,career
cares,care(s) / caress
caress,sses,ssed,ssing,ssingly,ssive,ssively,PET/ STROKE SMOOTHLY/ GENTLY
caret,*,PROOFREADING MARK (or see carrot/ carat/ karat)
careur,carrier
carful,careful
cargo,oes,os,FREIGHT ON VESSEL
cariage,carriage
carib,carob
caribou,reindeer
caricature,*,,ed,,ring,rist,EXAGGERATED IMITATION
carich,carriage
caricter,character
carie,carry
carier,carrier
carige,carriage
carikter,character
carioke,karaoke
carii,career
carisma,charisma
carit,carat / caret / carrot / karat
carivan,caravan
carkis,carcass
carkus,carcass
carlis,careless
carma,karma
carmel,caramel
carmil,caramel
carmu,karma
carmul,caramel
carnashun,carnation
carnation,*,FLOWER
carneishon,carnation

carnival,*,TRAVELING AMUSEMENT SHOW
carnivore,*,,rous,EATS FLESH
carnuvil,carnival
carnuvore,carnivore
carob,LOCUST BEAN RESEMBLING CHOCOLATE
caroberate,corroborate
carode,corrode
carogan,corrode(osion)
carogate,corrugate(d)
carojen,corrode(osion)
carojin,corrode(osion)
caroke,karaoke
carol,*,,led,,ling,SONGS
caroner,coroner
carosef,corrode(osive)
carosel,carousel
carosene,kerosene
caroshen,corrode(osion)
carot,carat / caret / carrot / karat
caroty,karate
carouse,*,,ed,sing,UNDESIRABLE DRUNKEN BEHAVIOR
carousel,*,MERRY-GO-ROUND
carowsel,carousel
carpenter,*,,try,BUILDS WITH WOOD
carpet,*,,ted,ting,SOFT FLOOR COVERING
carpinder,carpenter
carpinter,carpenter
carpit,carpet
carriage,*,PULLED FOUR-WHEELED CART,OF CARRYING "prefixes: mis/ under"
carrier,*,ONE WHO TRANSPORTS (or see career)
carrot,*,VEGETABLE (or see carat/ caret/ karat)
carry,rries,rried,rrying,rrier,rriage,TO TRANSPORT "prefixes: mis"
carsenagen,carcinogen
carsinoullen,carcinogen
carsinugen,carcinogen
cart,*,,ted,ting,VEHICLE FOR TRANSPORT
cartilage,SOFT BONE IN THE BODY "prefixes: sub"
cartin,carton
cartleg,cartilage
cartn,carton

cartnul,cardinal
carton,*,PAPER BOX
cartoon,*,ning,nist,ANIMATED CARICATURES
cartrege,cartridge
cartridge,*,REFILLABLE/ REPLACEABLE CONTAINER
cartrige,cartridge
cartulige,cartilage
cartun,carton / cartoon
carubtion,corrupt(ion)
carubu,caribou
carudge,carriage
carupd,corrupt
carupshen,corrupt(ion)
carupt,corrupt
carusel,carousel
carusen,kerosene
carut,carat / caret / carrot / karat
carve,*,ed,ving,er,TO SHAPE WITH KNIFE
cary,carry
casadilla,quesadilla
casal,castle / cause(sal)
casc,cask
cascade,*,ed,ding,LIKE A WATERFALL
cascara,TREE
case,*,ed,sing,CERTAIN NUMBER OF ITEMS CONTAINED TOGETHER (too many definitions, please see standard dictionary) "prefixes: en/ upper"
casedilla,quesadilla
caseng,casing
caseno,casino
caserole,casserole
casete,cassette
cash,hed,hing,MONETARY/ MONEY (or see cache)
cashei,cache
cashere,cashier
cashew,*,NUT
cashier,*,HANDLES MONEY
cashmere,GOAT WOOL
cashon,caution
cashos,cautious
cashu,cashew
cashual,casual
cashuol,casual

cashwul,casual
casil,castle
casing,*,COVERING OR SUPPORT
casino,*,FOR GAMBLING
casirole,casserole
casiroll,casserole
cask,*,KEG FOR LIQUIDS
caskade,cascade
caskeid,cascade
caskera,cascara
casket,*,COFFIN
caskit,casket
casmic,cosmic
casol,castle
casserole,*,MIXTURE OF FOOD INTO ONE DISH
cassette,*,AUDIO CARTRIDGE
cast,*,ting,ter,TO THROW AWAY FROM (or see caste) "prefixes: mis/ over/ re/ up"
caste,*,A SOCIAL CLASS OF PEOPLE (or see cast)
caster,*,ON/ FOR FURNITURE, FISHING, MOLD MAKER, CONDIMENT STAND
castle,*,ed,FORTRESS
castrate,*,ed,ting,tion,REMOVE REPRODUCTIVE ORGANS
castreit,castrate
castum,costume
casual,lly,lness,BY CHANCE, RELAXED
casudilla,quesadilla
casul,castle
caswal,casual
cat,*,ANIMAL,PREFIX INDICATING "APART/ DOWN" MOST OFTEN MODIFIES THE WORD
cata,PREFIX INDICATING "APART/ DOWN" MOST OFTEN MODIFIES THE WORD
catal,cattle
catalog,*,ged,ging,LIST IN ORDER
catalyst,*,ysis,ytic,yze,yzes,yzed,yzing,yzer,STIMULUS "prefixes: bio"
catapult,*,ted,ting,TO BE HURLED
cataract,*,EYE DISEASE OR WATERFALL
catastrophe,*,hic,DISASTER, A SUDDEN TURN, ALSO AMERICAN SPELLED 'CATASTROPHY'

catastrophy,hies,hic,DISASTER, A SUDDEN TURN, ALSO BRITISH SPELLED 'CATASTROPHE'
catch,hes,hing,her,aught,CAPTURE (or see cache)
catcher,*,BASEBALL FIELD POSITION
catchup,ketchup / catsup
catech,cottage
catechism,TEACHING OF CHRISTIAN PRINCIPLES
catecism,catechism
categorize,*,ed,zing,zable,zation,ASSIGN TO SPECIFIC AREA/ RANGE "prefixes: un/ mis"
category,ries,ric,rical,rically,ricalness,rize,rizes,rized, rizing,rizable,rization,SPECIFIC AREA/ RANGE "prefixes: mis/ un"
catekisom,catechism
catelog,catalog
catepiler,caterpillar
catepult,catapult
cater,*,red,ring,PROVIDE FOR
cateract,cataract
caterpillar,*,WORM
cath,PREFIX INDICATING 'APART/ DOWN' MOST OFTEN MODIFIES THE WORD
catichisom,catechism
catigorize,categorize
catigory,category
catikisom,catechism
catilist,catalyst
catilog,catalog
catl,cattle
catle,cattle
catol,cattle
catsup,ketchup
cattle,DOMESTIC BEEF, BOVINE
catugorize,categorize
catugory,category
catukism,catechism
catulist,catalyst
catulize,catalyst(yze)
catulog,catalog
catupiler,caterpillar
catupult,catapult
caturact,cataract
cau,cow

cauc,caulk
cauch,couch
cauchis,cautious / caucus
caucus,ses,NOMINATION PARTY
caught,PAST TENSE FOR THE WORD 'CATCH',OBTAINED (or see cot)
caul,call / cowl
caulagen,collision / collagen
caulam,column
cauliflower,VEGETABLE
caulk,*,ked,king,FILL SEAMS/ JOINTS (or see calk)
caulm,calm
caulom,column
caum,calm / come
caumpatency,competence(cy)
caumpetence,competence
caumpitence,competence
caumputency,competence(cy)
council,council
caunsel,council
caunt,count
caunter,counter
caunti,county
caunvex,convex
cause,*,ed,sing,sal,sality,salities,sation,BRING ABOUT "prefixes: retro"
caushes,cautious
caushesly,cautious(ly)
caushus,cautious
causmic,cosmic
caustic,cal,cally,city,CORROSIVE CHEMICAL "prefixes: en"
caut,caught / cot
caution,*,ned,ning,nary,ous,BEWARE, BE CAREFUL "prefixes: pre"
cautious,sly,sness,PREPARED FOR DANGER "prefixes: in"
cava,kava
cavalry,ries,MOUNTED SOLDIERS
cave,*,ed,ving,HOLE IN THE EARTH
cavern,*,nous,HOLLOW IN EARTH
cavety,cavity
cavilry,cavalry

cavirn,cavern
cavitate,*,ed,ting,tion,HOLLOWED OUT AREAS/ BUBBLES
cavity,ties,tate,tation,tational,HOLLOWED OUT AREA, DECAYED TOOTH
cavs,calves / cave(s)
cavu,kava
cavulry,cavalry
cavurn,cavern
cawcus,caucus
cawl,call / cowl
cawshesly,cautious(ly)
cawshis,cautious
cawshun,caution
cawt,caught / cot
cawtion,caution
cayan,cayenne
cayenne,HOT PEPPER
cayning,canine
cazual,casual
ce,see / sea
cease,ses,ed,sing,eless,elessly,STOP (or see sea(s)/ seize/ see(s)) "prefixes: sur/ un"
cebrabol,separable
cechup,ketchup / catsup
cecoia,sequoia
cecs,sex
cecshual,sexual
cecstaiol,sextile
cecstant,sextant
cecstet,sextet
cecstilion,sextillion
cecstuplet,sextuplet
cecstupol,sextuple
cecuin,sequin
cediment,sediment
cedol,settle
ceel,keel
cefal,civil
cefalezation,civil(ization)
cegar,cigar
cegrageit,segregate
ceibel,sable

ceiber,saber
ceibol,sable
ceiling,*,OVERHEAD IN ROOM (or see seal)
ceip,cape
ceis,case
ceivant,savant
ceivor,savior
cel,cell / seal / sell
celabent,celibate
celabet,celibate
celafane,cellophane
celar,cellar / sell(er) / seal(er)
celary,celery
celebrate,*,ed,ting,tion,tive,tory,ant,REJOICE
celebreit,celebrate
celebrity,ties,PERSON WELL EXPOSED TO THE PUBLIC
celer,cellar / sell(er) / seal(er)
celery,VEGETABLE
celeschial,celestial
celestial,*,lly,SPIRITUAL, NOT PHYSICAL ON THIS PLANE "prefixes: sub"
celf,self
celfish,selfish
celibate,acy,tarian,ABSENT FROM SEXUAL ACTIVITY "prefixes: un"
celibet,celibate
celibrate,celebrate
celibriti,celebrity
celiliqui,soliloquy
celinder,cylinder
celious,cellulose
celing,ceiling / seal(ing)
celir,cellar / sell(er) / seal(er)
celistial,celestial
celulait,cellulite
celular,cellular
cellous,cellulose
cell,*,llular,llularly,llularity,OF STRUCTURES/ SCIENCE (or see sell/ sail/ keel) "prefixes: intra/ multi/ sub/ uni"
cellafane,cellophane
cellar,*,STORAGE UNDERGROUND (or see sell)
cellophane,PLASTIC WRAP

cellular, rly, rity, OF COMMUNICATIONS OR SCIENCE "prefixes: intra/ multi/ non/ sub/ uni"
cellulite, FAT POCKETS IN THE BODY
cellulose, sic, CARBOHYDRATE "prefixes: non"
celofane, cellophane
celofein, cellophane
celophane, cellophane
celseus, celsius
celsius, METHOD OF REPORTING TEMPERATURE
celt, *, tic, TOOL, GROUP OF PEOPLE, LANGUAGE
celubasy, celibate(acy)
celubet, celibate
celubit, celibate
celubrate, celebrate
celular, cellular
celulite, cellulite
celulose, cellulose
celur, cellar / sell(er) / seal(er)
cem, seem / seam
cemai, semi
cematari, cemetery
cement, ted, ter, tum, tation, tatory, tless, COMBINATION OF MATERIALS WHICH HARDENS, CONCRETE
cemest, chemist
cemester, semester
cemetery, ries, tarial, GRAVEYARD
cemi, semi
ceminal, seminal
ceminor, seminar
cemist, chemist
cemiteri, cemetery
cempothe, sympathy
cems, seem(s) / seam(s)
cemutary, cemetery
cenador, senator
cenameter, centimeter
cenator, senator
cendral, central
cendrulize, centralize
cenet, senate
cenik, cynic
cenikal, cynical
cenima, cinema

cens, sense
cense, since / sense / cent(s) / scent(s)
censeer, sincere
censeishon, sensation
censhual, sensual
censhury, century
censibol, sensible
censitive, sensitive
censor, *, red, ring, rship, rable, rious, riously, riousness, sure, CONTROL INFORMATION (or see sensor/ censure) "prefixes: pre"
censure, rable, er, SEVERE/ OFFICIAL CRITICISM/ STATEMENT (or see censor/ sensor)
census, SURVEY (or see sense(s))
cent, *, PREFIX INDICATING 'HUNDRED/ HUNDREDTH' MOST OFTEN MODIFIES THE WORD, MONETARY (or see scent/ sent)
centans, sentence
centennial, *, lly, HUNDREDTH YEAR ANNIVERSARY "prefixes: bi"
center, *, red, ring, THE MIDDLE "prefixes: con/ re"
centi, PREFIX INDICATING 'HUNDRED/ HUNDREDTH' MOST OFTEN MODIFIES THE WORD
centigrade, *, WAY OF REPORTING TEMPERATURE
centiment, sentiment
centimeter, *, MORE THAN 0.39 OF AN INCH
centinial, centennial
centipede, *, POISONOUS BUG
central, lly, lity, lism, lize, FOCUS BETWEEN TWO OR MORE "prefixes: non"
centralize, *, ed, zing, zation, LOCATE CONVENIENTLY IN THE CENTER/ MIDDLE "prefixes: de/ non"
centri, PREFIX INDICATING 'CENTER' MOST OFTEN MODIFIES THE WORD (or see sentry)
centric, cal, cally, city, AT OR NEAR CENTER "prefixes: exo"
centro, PREFIX INDICATING 'CENTER' MOST OFTEN MODIFIES THE WORD
centrul, central
centry, sentry / centri
centugrade, centigrade
centumeter, centimeter
centupede, centipede

century, ries, YEAR MARK
cenverdable, convertible
cepareit, separate
cepareitor, separator
ceparit, separate
ceprabal, separable
ceprator, separator
ceptember, september
ceptic, septic
cepurator, separator
cer, care
ceramic, *, CLAY-FIRING METHOD
cerashen, serrate(tion)
cerat, carat / caret / carrot / karat / serrate
ceration, serrate(tion)
cerb, curb
cerc, church
cercimscribe, circumscribe
cercle, circle
cercol, circle
cerculate, circulate
cercumcise, circumcise
cercumfurens, circumference
cercumsais, circumcise
cercumscribe, circumscribe
cercumstance, circumstance
cerdafy, certify
cerden, certain
cerdenle, certain(ly)
cerdenly, certain(ly)
cerdifai, certify
cerdify, certify
cerdle, curdle
cerdufy, certify
cere, care / carry
cereal, EDIBLE GRAIN (or see surreal)
cerebr, PREFIX INDICATING 'BRAIN' MOST OFTEN MODIFIES THE WORD
cerebral, lly, IN/ OF THE BRAIN "prefixes: intra"
cerebro, PREFIX INDICATING 'BRAIN' MOST OFTEN MODIFIES THE WORD
cereit, serrate

ceremony,nies,nial,nially,nious,FORMAL GROUP GATHERING "prefixes: un"
cerendipiti,serendipity
cereneid,serenade
ceret,carat / caret / carrot / karat
cereul,cereal / surreal
cereur,carrier
cerf,curve / surf
cerfew,curfew
cerfue,curfew
ceri,carry
cerial,cereal / serial
cericewlum,curriculum
cericuture,caricature
cerikachur,caricature
cerikulum,curriculum
cerimony,ceremony
cerin,serene
cerisel,carousel
cerit,carat / caret / carrot / karat
ceriul,cereal / serial
cerivan,caravan
cerkemscribe,circumscribe
cerklar,circular
cerkle,circle
cerkomferinse,circumference
cerkul,circle
cerkumsize,circumcise
cerkus,circus
cerl,curl
cermon,sermon
cernal,colonel
cernil,colonel / kernel
cerogun,corrode(osion)
cerol,carol
cerosene,kerosene
cerot,carat / caret / carrot / karat
cerpent,serpent
cerpentin,serpentine
cerqiular,circular
cerqiuleit,circulate
cerques,circus
cerquet,circuit

cersanthemum,chrysanthemum
cerse,curse
cersif,cursive
cersog,corsage
certain,nly,nty,nties,nness,KNOW FOR SURE "prefixes: un"
certale,curtail
certan,curtain
certatude,certitude
certefai,certify
certeficashen,certificate(tion)
certeficate,certificate
certeil,curtail
certen,certain
certifi,certify
certificasion,certificate(tion)
certificate,*,ed,ting,tion,VALIDATION FOR LEARNING
certifiquet,certificate
certify,fies,fied,fying,fier,fiable,fiably,ficated,fication, MAKE CERTAIN,A LEGAL DOCUMENT "prefixes: de/re"
certin,certain
certinly,certain(ly)
certitude,*,FEELING THAT SOMETHING IS CERTAIN "prefixes: in"
certsy,curtsy
certufi,certify
certul,curdle
certunle,certain(ly)
certunly,certain(ly)
certutude,certitude
cerunsy,currency
cerunt,currant / current
cerus,cirrus / scirrhus
cerusel,carousel
cerut,carat / caret / carrot / karat
ceruvan,caravan
cerv,curve / serve
cervant,servant
cervis,service
cervitud,servitude
cervix,xes,ical,OF THE NECK
cervuchure,curvature

cery,curry / carry
ces,see(s) / sea(s) / seize / cease
cesami,sesame
ceshel,seashell
ceshon,session
cest,cyst / zest
cesta,siesta
cetol,settle
cesturn,cistern
ceval,civil
cevalezation,civil(ization)
cevant,seventh
ceven,seven
cevendi,seventy
ceventieth,seventieth
ceventin,seventeen
ceventy,seventy
cever,sever
cevil,civil
cevin,seven
cevilezation,civil(ization)
cevir,severe
cevol,civil
cevolezation,civil(ization)
cevon,seven
cevontin,seventeen
cevral,several
cevrans,severance
cevul,civil
cevulization,civil(ization)
cevulezation,civil(ization)
cevun,seven
cew,cue
cewth,couth
cextant,sextant
cez,see(s) / sea(s) / seize / cease
cfood,seafood
cfud,seafood
chacra,chakra
chader,chatter
chado,shadow
chaf,chafe / chaff
chafd,shaft / chafe(d) / chaff(ed)

chafe, *, ed,fing,ANNOYED/ IRRITATED, RUBBED UNTIL SORE (or see chaff/ chaff)
chaff, *, ffed,ffing,ffer,ffy,TO TEASE/ JOKE WITH SOMEONE (or see chafe)
chafs,chafe(s) / chaff(s)
chaft,shaft / chafe(d) / chaff(ed)
chain, *, ned,ning,LINKS PUT/ HOOKED TOGETHER "prefixes: en/ un"
chair, *, red, ring, FURNITURE, HEAD OF MEETINGS/ ORGANIZATION
chak,chalk / choke / shock / chock
chakra, , CENTERS IN BODY
chalenge,challenge
chalenll,challenge
chalinge,challenge
chalk, , ked, king, ky, LIMESTONE
challenge, *, ed,ging,gable, er, TEST OF SKILLS
champagne, EFFERVESCENT WINE
champane,champagne
champeon,champion
champion, *, ned, ning, nship, WINS CONTEST OF SKILL
chanal,channel
chance, *, ed , A GAMBLE
chancre, *, rous, ULCERATION ON THE SKIN (or see canker)
chandelier, *, LAMP WITH MANY ARMS FOR BULBS
chandulere,chandelier
chane,chain
chanel,channel
change, *, ed,ging,gable, TRANSFORM "prefixes: un"
chanil,channel
channel, *, led, ling,ler, lize, AVENUE TO RECEIVE "prefixes: re"
channelize, *, zed,zing,zation,TO CHANNEL/ DIRECT "prefixes: de/ re"
chanse,chance / chant(s)
chant, *, ted,ting,tingly, RECITE/ REPEAT WORDS IN VERBAL RHYTHM (or see chain(ed))
chanul,channel
chaos,otic, APPEARS TO US TO BE DISORGANIZED
chap, *, pped,pping, DRY/ ROUGH SKIN, LEATHER PART
chapel, *, FOR RITUALS
chaplain, *, PERFORMS RITUAL SERVICES

chaplan,chaplain
chapter, *, SECTION OF PRINT, COLLEGE OR SCHOOL
chapul,chapel
char, *, rred,rring, TO BURN/ BLACKEN, CHORES (or see chair/ chore/ share)
character, *, ristic,ristically,rize,rization, PERSONALITY/ QUALITIES
charade, *, PANTOMIME GAME
charch,charge
charcoal, *, led, ORGANIC SUBSTANCE IN EARTH
charder,charter
chare,chair / cherry / sherry / share
charecter,character
charge, *, ed,er,ging, eable, APPLY TOWARDS CREDIT, CREATE POWER, ENERGIZE, APPLY FORCE "prefixes: dis/ over/ re/ sur/ under"
charguble,charge(able)
chari,cherry / sherry
charidy,charity
charisma,atic, INSPIRATIONAL QUALITY
charitable,ly, GIVING
charity,ties,table, GIVING UNCONDITIONALLY
charj,charge
charjuble,charge(able)
charjure,charge(r)
charkol,charcoal
charm, *, med,ming,mingly,mer, ALLUREMENT, LUCKY OBJECT
chart, *, ted,ting, PLOT OUT "prefixes: un"
charter, *, red, ring, CONTRACT, OUTLINE "prefixes: un"
charutable,charitable
chary,cherry / sherry
chas,chase / chaste
chasd,chaste / chase(d)
chase, , ed,sing,er, PURSUE TO CAPTURE (or see chaste)
chasem,chasm
chasim,chasm
chasm, *, mic, DEEP VOID
chassis, FRAME OF VEHICLE
chaste,er, est, ely, eness, SIMPLE, PLAIN, FAITHFUL (or see chase(d))
chasum,chasm
chasy,chassis

chater,chatter / shatter
chatter, *, red, ring, TALK TOO MUCH ABOUT UNINTERESTING TOPICS
chauffeur, *, DESIGNATED DRIVER
chauk,chalk / choke / shock / chock
chaukra,chakra
chaumein,chowmein
chaurkol,charcoal
chauvinist, *, tic, tically,sm, TERM FOR MEN WHO ARE UNREASONABLE AND AGGRESSIVE, BELIEVE THEY ARE SUPERIOR
chayold,child
chayos,chaos
chazm,chasm
chazum,chasm
cheap,per,pest, ply, pens, LOW COST (or see chip)
cheat, *, ted,ting, ter, DISHONEST ACQUISITION
check, *, ked,king,ker, kers,kered, BANK DRAFT, A MARK, TO MAKE CERTAIN, A GAME "prefixes: re/ un"
cheef,chief
cheep,cheap
cheer, *, red, ring, ringly, rer, rful, rfully, rfulness, ry, rily, riness,rless, HAPPY/ JOYFUL/ ENCOURAGEMENT/ SHOUTING/ TOASTING
cheese, CURDLED MILK
cheet,cheat
chef, , HEAD COOK (or see sheaf)
chein,chain
cheinch,change
cheis,chase
cheist,chaste
chek,check / cheek
chekan,chicken
chekurs,check(ers)
cheldren,children
chelenge,challenge
chelren,children
chemest,chemist
chemical, *, OF CHEMISTRY "prefixes: bio"
chemist, *, SCIENTIST WHO STUDIES PROPERTIES OF MATTER "prefixes: bio"
chemistry, MOTHER OF SCIENCE, STUDY OF MATTER "prefixes: bio"

chemney,chimney
chemotherapy,RADIATION TREATMENT
chemucal,chemical
chemustry,chemistry
chen,chin
cheep,cheap / sheep
chepd,chip(pped) / ship(pped)
cheped,chip(pped) / ship(pped)
cher,share / chair / cheer
cherch,church
chere,cherry / sherry / cheer
cheretable,charitable
cherety,charity
cheridy,charity
cheritable,charitable
cherity,charity
cherle,sure(ly)
chern,churn
cherry,rries,LITTLE RED FRUIT (or see sherry)
chery,cherry / sherry
chese,cheese
chest,schist
chevolry,chivalry
chevulry,chivalry
chew,*,wed,wing,wable,GRIND WITH TEETH
chewt,shute / chute
cheys,chase
cheyst,chaste
chic,STYLISH
chick,*,YOUNG BIRD,GIRL
chicken,*,FOWL,BIRD
chicory,HERB
chief,*,tain,HIGHEST AUTHORITY
chif,chief
chik,chick
chiken,chicken
chikury,chicory
child,*,,dren,dish,dishly,dishness,dly,dlike,PERSON UNDER AGE 18
children,PEOPLE UNDER AGE 18
chilostomy,colostomy
chilren,children
chimest,chemist

chimist,chemist
chimney,*,,SMOKE STACK
chimotherapy,chemotherapy
chimukul,chemical
chin,*,,POINT OF JAW (or see shin/ shine)
chip,*,,pped,pping,pper,THIN SLICE/ WEDGE OF SOMETHING (or see ship/ cheap) "prefixes: bio"
chiped,chip(pped) / ship(pped)
chiquen,chicken
chirch,church
chirle,sure(ly)
chiro,PREFIX INDICATING "HAND" MOST OFTEN MODIFIES THE WORD
chiropractor,tic,REALIGNS BONES OF BODY FOR HEALTH
chirtch,church
chis,cheese
chisel,*,,led,ling,TOOL FOR FORMING SHAPES
chist,schist
chit,cheat
chivalry,rous,COURTEOUS AND HELPFUL GENTLEMAN
chizt,schist
chizul,chisel
chlor,PREFIX INDICATING 'GREEN/ CHLORINE' MOST OFTEN MODIFIES THE WORD
chlorene,chlorine
chlorine,nate,idize,CHEMICAL IRRITANT
chloro,PREFIX INDICATING 'GREEN/ CHLORINE' MOST OFTEN MODIFIES THE WORD
chock,*,,ked,king,TO BLOCK/ SECURE/ BRACE (or see choke/ chalk/ shock)
chocklat,chocolate
choclat,chocolate
chocolate,*,,ty,tier,tiest,FROM CACAO NUT
choice,*,,SELECTION "prefixes: pro–"
choir,*,,SINGING GROUP
chok,chalk / choke / shock / chock
choke,*,,ed,king,kingly,er,RESTRICTED SUPPLY OF AIR/ MOVEMENT(or see chalk/ shock/ chock)
choklat,chocolate
choklut,chocolate
chokra,chakra

chol,PREFIX INDICATING 'BILE/ GALLBLADDER' MOST OFTEN MODIFIES THE WORD
chole,PREFIX INDICATING 'BILE/ GALLBLADDER' MOST OFTEN MODIFIES THE WORD
cholesterol,NATURALLY PRESENT IN THE BODY
cholk,chalk
cholostemy,colostomy
choo,chew / shoe
choose,*,,sing,er,sy,sier,siest,sily,siness,hose,PICK ONE OVER THE OTHER (or see chew(s)/ chose)
chop,*,,pped,pping,pper,ppy,ppier,pppiest,ppily,ppiness,HACK/ CUT INTO PIECES, SUDDEN CHANGE IN DIRECTION (or see shop)
chopeng,chop(pping) / shop(pping)
chor,chore / shore / char
choral,OF A CHOIR (or see coral/ corral/ chorale)
chorale,A HYMN OF SIMPLE TUNE (or see choral/ corral/ coral)
chorcol,charcoal
chord,*,,OF MUSICAL NOTES (or see cord/ short)
chore,*,,SMALL TASKS (or see shore)
chorkol,charcoal
chorn,shorn
chorus,A UNION OF PERFORMERS (or see course)
chorz,chore(s) / shard(s)
chose,en,HAVING SELECTED,PAST TENSE FOR THE WORD 'CHOOSE' (or see choose)
chouc,choke / chock / chalk
chovanism,chauvinism
chovanist,chauvinist
chovenism,chauvinism
chovenist,chauvinist
chovinism,chauvinism
chovinist,chauvinist
chovunism,chauvinism
chovunist,chauvinist
chow main,chow mein
chow mein,CHINESE FOOD
choyse,choice
chrapnul,shrapnel
chremendos,tremendous
christmas,A RELIGIOUS HOLIDAY

chrom, PREFIX INDICATING 'COLOR/ CHROMIUM' MOST OFTEN MODIFIES THE WORD (or see chrome)
chrome, ed,ming, METALLIC
chromizone,chromosome
chromo, PREFIX INDICATING 'COLOR/ CHROMIUM' MOST OFTEN MODIFIES THE WORD
chromosome,*, DNA STRAND
chronalogical, chronology(gical)
chronic, cally, city, CONTINUOUS
chronicle,*, ed,ling, LIST OF FACTS
chronk,shrunk
chrono, PREFIX INDICATING 'TIME' MOST OFTEN MODIFIES THE WORD
chronology,gical,lgically, ORGANIZE BY DATES
chronulogical, chronology(gical)
chrud,shrewd / truth
chrunk,shrunk
chrys, PREFIX INDICATING 'GOLD' MOST OFTEN MODIFIES THE WORD
chrysanthemum,*, FLOWER
chryso, PREFIX INDICATING 'GOLD' MOST OFTEN MODIFIES THE WORD
chu,chew
chue,chew
chugar,sugar
chugur,sugar
churade,charade
chural,choral / coral / corral / chorale
church,hes,hy, FOR RELIGIOUS PURPOSES
churle,sure(ly)
churn,*,ned,ning, FAT, MILK SEPARATION
chus,chew(s) / choose / shoe(s)
chuse,chew(s) / choose / choose(sy) / shoe(s)
chute,*,ed,ting, RAPID/ STEEP DESCENT (or see shoot/ shut)
ci,sigh / key
cianide,cyanide
cibra,zebra
ciburnetiks,cybernetics
ciclist,cyclist
cicual,sequel
cicuens,sequence
cid,kid / kite

cidecen,citizen
cider,STRONG JUICE
cidur,cider
cig,zyg
cigar,*, ROLLED TOBACCO
cigarette,*, OF TOBACCO
cilinder,cylinder
cilinoid,solenoid
cilion,zillion
cilosal,colossal
cimbeosis,symbiosis
cimbol,cymbal / symbol
cimen,semen
ciment,cement
cimist,chemist
cimpathetic,sympathetic
cimpathy,sympathy
cinail,senile
cinc,zinc
cinch,hes, hed, hing, FIRM GRIP ON, EASILY ACHIEVED, FOR CERTAIN (or see singe)
cinda,kind of
cinder,*, CHARRED SUBSTANCE (or see send)
cinduf,kind of
cine, PREFIX INDICATING 'MOTION PICTURE' MOST OFTEN MODIFIES THE WORD
cinema,*, atic, MOTION PICTURE
cinery,canary / cannery
cineth,zenith
cing,zing / sing
cinia,zinnia
cinima,cinema
cinior,senior
cinnamon,SPICE FROM TREE BARK
cinsestently,consistent(ly
cinsistency,consistence(cy)
cinspirusy,conspiracy
cinstrucshen,construction
cint,can't / cent / scent / sent
cintential,centennial
cinverdable,convertible
cip,zip / sip
cipol,sepal

circle,*,ed,ling, ROUND FIGURE/ SHAPE "prefixes: semi"
circomphrence,circumference
circuit,*,try, MAKES THE ROUNDS, GOES AROUND, NETWORK
circular,*, GOES AROUND IN THE SHAPE OF A CIRCLE "prefixes: semi"
circulate,*,ed,ting,tion, FLOWING/ MOVING "prefixes: un"
circum, PREFIX INDICATING 'AROUND' MOST OFTEN MODIFIES THE WORD
circumcise,*, ed,sing,sion,er, REMOVAL OF FORESKIN ON PENIS "prefixes: un"
circumference, DISTANCE/ LINE AROUND A CIRCLE
circumscribe,*, ed, bing, bable, er, SET NARROW LIMITS, ENCIRCLE "prefixes: un"
circumstance,*,ntial,ntially,ncality,calism,ntiate, INCIDENT
circus,ses, ENTERTAINING PERFORMANCE IN TENTS
cireol,cereal / serial
cirial,cereal / serial
cirios,serious
ciris,series
cirius,serious
cirkemscribe,circumscribe
cirkumscribe,circumscribe
cirkumsize,circumcise
cirnel,colonel / kernel
ciroberate,corroborate
cirogun,corrode(osion)
cirom,serum
cirou,zero
cirqiuler,circular
cirrus, CLOUD TYPE/ SHAPE (or see scirrhus)
cirsanthemum,chrysanthemum
cirten,certain
cirteus,courteous
cirus, cirrus / scirrhus
cirvature,curvature
cis, PREFIX INDICATING 'ON THIS SIDE' MOST OFTEN MODIFIES THE WORD
cist, COFFIN OF THE STONE AGE (or see cyst/ kiss(ed))
citashun,citation
citation,*, A SUMMONS

cite,*,ed,ting,tation,tations,OFFICIALLY CALL FORTH (or see site)	**clap**,*,pped,pping,pt,SOUND,GONORRHEA	cleen,clean
cistern,*,nal,CONTAINER/ COLLECTOR FOR LIQUID/ WATER	clarical,clerical	cleer,clear
citizen,*,nry,nship,MEMBER OF, WITH PRIVILEGES	**clarify**,fies,GIVE SPECIFIC MEANING TO	cleerance,clearance
citres,citrus	**clarity**,MAKE CLEAR	cleff,cliff
citric,ACID FROM FRUIT	clarvoyants,clairvoyance	cleim,claim
citrus,FRUIT	claset,closet	clek,click / clique
citusin,citizen	**clash**,hes,hed,hing,COLLIDE, LOUD SOUND	clen,clean
city,ties,METROPOLIS	clasha,cliche	**clench**,hes,hed,hing,TO HOLD/ GRASP TIGHTLY (or see clinch)
ciu,cue	clasic,classic	cleng,cling
ciunide,cyanide	clasifay,classify	clenik,clinic
ciupon,coupon	clasify,classify	clens,cleanse / clean(s)
civic, CITIZENSHIP	**clasp**,*,,ped,ping,HOLD "prefixes: en/ un"	clenser,cleanser
ciyen,cayenne	**class**,sses,ssed,ssing,ssy,GROUPED TOGETHER DUE TO SIMILARITIES "prefixes: un/ under"	clenzr,cleanser
civil,lly,lize,lizes,lized,lizing,lization,lizations,OF STATE OR COMMUNITY "prefixes: in/ un"	**classic**,*,,cal,cally,WITHSTOOD TEST OF TIME "prefixes: neo/ semi"	clep,clip
civilean,civilian	**classify**,fies,fied,fying,fication,fiable,ABLE TO PLACE INTO A GROUP "prefixes: de/ non/ un"	cleptomaniac, kleptomania(c
civilian,*, NOT MILITARY CITIZENS	clastrefoubia,claustrophobia	clepur,clipper
civul,civil	clastrefoubic,claustrophobic	clerady,clarity
civulization,civil(ization)	clasuc,classic	clerchi,clergy
cla,claw	clauc,clock / cloak	cler,clear
clad,*, ding, WEARING ON BODY, COVERED WITH "prefixes: un"	claud,cloud	clerd,clear(ed)
clae,clay	clauged,clog(gged) / cloak / clock(ed)	cleredy,clarity
claient,client	**clause**,*, ,sal,STIPULATION (or see claw(s)	clereng,clear(ing)
claim,*,,med,ming,mer,mant,mable,ASSERT POSSESSION OF (or see clamor/ climb) "prefixes: re/ de"	**claustrophobia**,FEAR OF COZY/ TIGHT PLACES	clerense,clearance
	claustrophobic,FEAR OF COZY/ TIGHT PLACES	clerety,clarity
claimant,*, TAKE POSSESSION OF	**claw**,*, ,wed,wing,HOOKED,FINGERLIKE (or see clause)	**clergy**,gies, ORDAINED BY CHRISTIANS
claimax,climax	clawn,clown	**clerical**,OFFICE WORKER
claimet,climate	clawsit,closet	cleridi,clarity
clairvoyance,nt, THOSE WHO CHANNEL INFORMATION	clawzet,closet	clering,clear(ing)
clam,*,,mmed,mming,SHELLFISH (or see claim)	**clay**, SOIL FROM EARTH	clerity,clarity
clamable,claim(able)	clayent,client	**clerk**,*, ,kly,PERFORMS GENERAL DUTIES
clament,claimant	**clean**,*, ,ned,ning,ner,nly,liness,UNSOILED "prefixes: un"	clerle,clear(ly)
clamor,*, ,red,ring,rer,SUDDEN/ LOUD/ INSISTENT NOISE (or see claim(er)	**cleanse**,*, ,sed,sing,er,MAKE CLEAN	clerlli,clergy
clamp,*,,ped,ping,PINCH TOGETHER	**cleanser**,CHEMICALS USED TO CLEAN	clert,clear(ed)
clams,claim(s) / clam(s)	**clear**,*,red,ring,rance, FREE OF OBSTRUCTION	clert,clear(ed)
clan, BODIES OF LIKE-MINDED INDIVIDUALS	**clearance**,*, TO CLEAR OF	clarvoyanse,clairvoyance
clandestine,ely, eness, WITH DECEPTION IN MIND	**cleat**,*, FOR TRACTION,STRENGTH	clesha,cliche
clandustine,clandestine	clebtomaniac,kleptomania(c	clet,cleat
	clecha,cliche	cletoras,clitoris
	cleche,cliche	**clever**,rly,rness,INGENIOUS
	cleck,click / clique	clew,clue
		cliant,client

clibtomaniac, kleptomania(c)
cliche,*,,STEREOTYPICAL PHRASE
click,*,ked,king,ker,SNAPPING NOISE, FIT WELL TOGETHER (or see clique)
clics,click(s) / clique(s)
client,*,tele, CUSTOMER
cliff,*,,STEEP ROCK FACE
clik,click / clique
clim,climb
climate,*,tic,tize,tized,tizing,tization,WEATHER OR ATMOSPHERIC CONDITION "prefixes: ac/ bio"
climax,xes,xed,xing,actic, GREATEST HEIGHT
climb,*,bed,bing,bable,MOMENTUM UPWARDS, GO UP (or see claim)
clims,climb(s)
climute,climate
clin,clean
clinch,hes,hed,hing,her, TO RESOLVE, FASTEN,' HOLD (or see clench)
cling,*,clung,ging,gy,gingly,ger, ATTACH TIGHTLY TO
clinic,*,cal,cally, PLACE FOR EXAMINATION "prefixes: sub"
clinser, cleanser
cirans, clearance
cirge, clergy
clirk, clerk
clisha, cliche
clishe, cliche
clit, cleat
clitoris,ral,POINT FOR FEMININE AROUSAL
cloak,*,ked,king,A GARMET, TO CONCEAL/ DISGUISE (or see clock) "prefixes: un"
clob, club
clobber,*,red,ring, TO BEAT UP
clober, clobber
cloc, cloak / clock
cloch, clutch / clock

clock,*,ked,king,KEEP TIME (or see cloak)
cloder, clutter
clodur, clutter
clofe, clove
clofur, clover
clog,*,gged,gging,STOPPED/ BACKED UP (or see cloak/ clock(ed)) "prefixes: un"
cloger, closure
cloister,*,red,ring,OF BUILDINGS,TO ENCLOSE
clojer, closure
clok, clock / cloak
cloked, clog(gged) / cloak / clock(ed)
clomp, clump
clomsi, clumsy
clone,*,ed,ning, REPLICAS (or see clown/ cologne)
clos,clothes / claw(s) / close / clause
closder, cluster
close,*,ed,sing,ely,er,est,SHUT DOWN, NEAR TO (or see clause/ clothes) "prefixes: en/ ex/ re/ un"
closet,*,ted,ting,SMALL PRIVATE SPACE
closher, closure
closir,close(r) / closure
closlain, clothesline
closline, clothesline
closter, cluster
closturfobeu, claustrophobia
closur, close(r) / closure
closure,*, CONCEAL, SHUT DOWN (or see close(r))
clot,*,tted,tting,LUMP, MASS OF MATTER
cloted, clot(tted)
cloter, clutter
cloth,*,he,hes,hed,hing,WOVEN FIBERS INTO MATERIAL, USED FOR CLOTHING (or see close)
clothes,OUTER/ UNDER GARMENTS FOR THE BODY (or see close/ cloth(es)) "prefixes: under"
clothesline,*, LINE FOR HANGING GARMENTS/ CLOTHES ON
cloths,clothes / cloth(es)
clothsline, clothesline
clotur, clutter
clouc, cloak
cloud,*,dy,ded,ding,diness,SMOKE, WATER PARTICLES, OBSCURES VISION "prefixes: over"

cloun,clown / clone / cologne
clous,close / clothes / cloth(es)
clouslain, clothesline
clout,INFLUENCE, TO STRIKE (or see cloud)
clouv, clove
clove,*, OF A PLANT, FORM OF MEASUREMENT
clover,*,, HERBAL PLANT
clow, claw
clowd, cloud
clown,*,ned,ning,nish,FUNNY, GOOFY, NOT NORMAL, SOMETIMES RIDICULOUS / OBNOXIOUS
clows,clothes / claw(s) / close / clause
clowsit, closet
clowt, clout
cloyster, cloister
cloz,clothes / claw(s) / close / clause
clozer, close(r) / closure
clozir, close(r) / closure
clozline, clothesline
clozur, close(r) / closure
club,*, bbed, bbing, GROUP MEMBERSHIP, AN INSTRUMENT USED AS A WEAPON
cluch, clutch
cluder, clutter
clue,*,ed,eless, elessness, HINT
clump,*,ped,ping,py, COLLECTION OF/ INTO A MASS
clumsy,sily,siness, AWKWARDLY DONE
clumze, clumsy
clurgy, clergy
cluster,*,red,ring,ry,GROUPINGS TOGETHER "prefixes: non"
clutch,hes,hed,hing,USED TO CHANGE GEARS IN TRANSMISSION, GRASP FIRMLY, GROUP OF EGGS "prefixes: de"
cluter, clutter
clutorus, clitoris
clutter,CONFUSING SIGHT OR NOISE "prefixes: un"
co,PREFIX INDICATING 'WITH/ TOGETHER' MOST OFTEN MODIFIES THE WORD (or see so/ sew)
co-op,COMMUNITY-OWNED BUSINESS, A COOPERATIVE (or see coop/ coup)
coach,hes,hed,hing,TO GUIDE OTHERS (or see couch)
coagiuleit, coagulate

coagulate, *, ed, ting, tion, TO THICKEN, FORM CLOTS
coal, *, ORGANIC SUBSTANCE IN THE EARTH
coalition, *, nal, nist, VOLUNTARY GATHERING OF PEOPLE FOR A CAUSE
coar, core / corp
coarse, er, est, ely, eness, HARSH, ABRASIVE, ROUGH (or see course)
coast, *, ted, ting, BETWEEN LAND AND WATER, TO BE MOVING WITHOUT PROPULSION (or see cost) "prefixes: bi/ intra"
coaster, *, TO SET DRINKS ON
coat, *, ted, ting, OUTER GARMENT FOR WARMTH "prefixes: over/ sur/ under"
coax, xes, xed, xing, TO PERSUADE/ INFLUENCE
cob, *, TUBULAR IN SHAPE
cobalt, CHEMICAL, BLUE COLORING
cobi, cubby
cobolt, cobalt
cobra, *, SNAKE
cobweb, *, SPIDER'S WEB
coc, caulk / cock
cocaine, NARCOTIC DRUG
cocane, cocaine
coch, coach
cocher, kosher
coches, cautious
cochus, cautious
cock, *, ky, A ROOSTER, OF MASCULINE SUGGESTION (or see cook)
cockroach, hes, INFESTATING INSECT/ BUG
cocktail, *, ALCOHOLIC BEVERAGES
cocoa, FROM THE CACAO SEED
coconut, *, FRUIT
cocoon, *, HOME SPUN BY LARVAE
cocroch, cockroach
coctale, cocktail
cocun, cocoon
cocunut, coconut
cocus, caucus
cod, *, FISH, A POD, A PENINSULA (or see code/ caught/ could/ cold)
code, *, ded, ding, LANGUAGE "prefixes: en"
codeine, DRUG FROM OPIUM

coden, cotton / codeine
codich, cottage
codien, codeine
codin, cotton / codeine
codol, cuddle
coduge, cottage
coed, *, BOTH SEXES
coel, coil
coelate, collate
coen, coin
coencident, coincident
coenside, coincide
coensident, coincident
coerce, *, ed, cing, cible, cion, cive, civeness, cively, FORCE INTO COMPLIANCE "prefixes: in/ non"
coersment, coerce(ment)
cof, cough / cuff
cofe, cove / coffee / cough
cofen, coffin / cough(ing)
cofert, covert / cover(ed)
coffee, BEVERAGE (or see cove)
coffin, *, BOX FOR TRANSPORT, CASKET
cofi, coffee
cofin, coffin / cough(ing)
cofy, coffee
cognative, cognitive
cogneshun, cognition
cognezant, cognizant
cognisant, cognizant
cognition, nal, ive, PERCEPTIVE/ AWARE (or see cognizant) "prefixes: pre/ retro"
cognitive, ely, vism, ion, COME TO KNOW THROUGH PERCEPTION/ REASONING "prefixes: pre/ retro"
cognizant, nce, able, ably, nce, ition, PERCEPTIVE/ AWARE
cognutev, cognitive
cohabitate, *, ed, ting, tion, DWELL/ LIVE TOGETHER
cohabutate, cohabitate
coherent, nce, ncy, WORKS CONSISTENTLY/ PREDICTABLY "prefixes: in/ non"
coherse, coerce
cohersive, coerce(cive)
cohersment, coerce(ment)
cohesive, ely, eness, ion, BONDS TOGETHER

cohesuf, cohesive
cohort, *, CO-PARTNER
cohurse, coerce
cohursive, coerce(cive)
coil, *, led, ling, SPIRAL SHAPE "prefixes: un"
coin, *, ned, nage, METAL USED FOR MONEY
coincide, *, ed, ding, ence, ent, TO HAPPEN/ OCCUPY AT SAME TIME
coincident, nce, tal, tally, CHANCE HAPPENING "prefixes: un"
coiol, coil
coircment, coerce(ment)
cok, cook / cock
cokane, cocaine
cokes, coax
cokie, cookie
cokroch, cockroach
coktale, cocktail
col, PREFIX INDICATING 'INTESTINES' MOST OFTEN MODIFIES THE WORD (or see call/ cowl/ coal)
colabereit, collaborate
colaborate, collaborate
colach, collage
coladerul, collateral
colage, collage
colaid, collide
colamedy, calamity
colanais, colonize
colander, *, STRAINER
colani, colony
colanize, colony(nize)
colanoid, solenoid
colaps, collapse
colapse, collapse
colapsuble, collapse(sible)
colar, color / collar / call(er)
colard, collard greens
colash, collage / college
colastomy, colostomy
colasul, colossal
colate, collate
colcher, culture
cold, der, dest, dly, OPPOSITE OF HOT (or see colt)

coldesak, cul-de-sac
coldslaw, coleslaw
cole, coal / call
coleage, colleague
colech, college
colechat, collegiate
colecshon, collection
colect, collect
colection, collection
colector, collect(or)
coleg, colleague / college
colegen, collision / collagen
coleget, collegiate
colegiate, collegiate
coleit, collate
colekshin, collection
colem, column
colen, colon
colenise, colonize
colenoid, solenoid
coleny, colony
coler, color / cooler / collar
colerdgrins, collard greens
colesh, college
coleshon, collision / coalition
coleshun, collision / coalition
coleslaw, CABBAGE SALAD
colic, PAIN CAUSED BY ACID IN THE INTESTINES
colich, college
colide, collide
coliflower, cauliflower
colig, colleague / college
coligen, collision / collagen
colijin, collision
colillet, collegiate
colim, column
colinary, culinary
colinoid, solenoid
coliny, colony
coliyet, collegiate
colk, calk / caulk
collaborate, *, ed, ting, tion, tive, tively, COOPERATE
collage, *, MIXED MEDIA ART

---

collagen, *, nic, nous, FIBROUS PROTEIN FOUND IN BONE/ TISSUE
collander, colander
collapsable, collapse(sible)
collapse, *, ed, sing, sable, BREAK DOWN
collar, *, red, rless, RIM ON SHIRT, BELT FOR NECK
collard greens, VEGETABLE
collate, *, ed, ting, tion, MERGE, COMPARE
collateral, lly, lize, USED TO GUARANTEE/ SECURE A LOAN
colleague, *, ASSOCIATE
collect, *, ted, ting, tion, tive, tor, GATHER "prefixes: non/ re"
collection, *, ACT OF GATHERING THINGS "prefixes: re"
college, *, HIGHER EDUCATION
collegiate, OF COLLEGE AND/ OR STUDENTS
collide, *, ed, ding, ision, RUN INTO
collision, *, ACT OF RUNNING INTO
colloquia, al, PLURAL FOR COLLOQUIUM, STYLE/ ADVENT OF WRITING OR SPEAKING
colloquial, lity, lly, lness, lism, ium, iums, STYLE/ ADVENT OF WRITING OR SPEAKING
colloquium, *, MEETING/ CONFERENCE OF SPEAKERS ON SPECIFIC TOPIC
colm, calm
colmenate, culminate
colminate, culminate
colo, PREFIX INDICATING 'INTESTINES' MOST OFTEN MODIFIES THE WORD
coloch, collage / college
colog, collage / college
cologne, *, TOILET WATER (or see colon)
colokweul, colloquial
colon, INTESTINES, PUNCTUATION IN TEXT (or see cologne)" prefixes: semi"
colonais, colonize
coloneal, colonial
colonel, * , U.S. MILITARY OFFICER (or see kernel)
colonial, list, lism, FIRST EUROPEANS TO AMERICA "prefixes: neo"
colonize, *, ed, zing, zation, FIRST SETTLERS "prefixes: de"
colony, nies, nize, ACCUMULATION OF SIMILAR PEOPLES

---

color, *, red, ring, rful, rless, rlessly, rlessness, ration, rant, rize, rizes, rized, rizing, rization, HUES OF LIGHT SPECTRUM "prefixes: bi/ de/ un/ uni"
colossal, GREAT MAGNITUDE
colostomy, mies, INVOLVES INTESTINES/ ANUS
coloun, cologne / colon
colpret, culprit
colsla, coleslaw
colt, *, THE YOUNG OF SOME IN ANIMAL KINGDOM (or see cold)
coltevate, culminate
cultivate, cultivate
coltsfoot, USEFUL HERB
coltuvate, cultivate
coluge, college
column, *, ned, nar, nist, VERTICAL PILLARS OR ROWS, WRITTEN ARTICLE
colun, colon
colunise, colonize
coluny, colony
colurd, collard greens
colvert, culvert
com, PREFIX INDICATING 'WITH/ TOGETHER' MOST OFTEN MODIFIES THE WORD (or see come/ comb)
coma, *, atose, UNCONSCIOUSNESS (or see comma) "prefixes: semi"
comand, command
comander, commander
comasery, commissary
comb, *, bed, bing, TOOL FOR HAIR (or see come)
combain, combine
combat, *, ted, ting, tant, tive, OPPOSE
combensashen, compensation
comber, cumber
combersome, cumber(some)
combination, *, tive, able, UNIFY "prefixes: re"
combine, *, ed, ning, nation, BRING TOGETHER, FARM MACHINE
combineishon, combination
comboshtion, combustion
combrahensiv, comprehensive
combunashen, combination
combunation, combination

commander,*,DOMINANCE, MILITARY

commemorate,*,ed,ting,tion,tive,HONORING SOMEONE OR SOMETHING OF THE PAST "prefixes: re"

commence,*,ed,cing,ement,TO BEGIN "prefixes: re"

commend,*,ded,ding,dable,dation,SERIES OF CIRCLES WITH SAME CENTER POINT "prefixes: re"

commendable,*,eness,ly,ation,PRAISEWORTHY

commendation,*,PRAISE "prefixes: re"

commensurable,bility,bly,ate,SHARE THE SAME MEASURABLE QUALITIES "prefixes: in"

commensurate,ely,tion,able,EQUAL/ CORRESPONDS TO "prefixes: in"

comment,*,ted,ting,tate,tary,taries,tative,tation,tator, MAKE REMARKS, GIVE OPINION

commentate,*,ed,ting,tion,tive,tor,ary,aries,TO COMMENT UPON

commentator,*,tate,ONE WHO GIVES OPINIONS/ REMARKS

commerce,EXCHANGING WARES OR GOODS

commercial,*,lize,lization,ADVERTISEMENTS, ABOUT TRADE "prefixes: non/ un"

comisary, commissary

comision, commission

commissary,ries,MILITARY STORE

commission,*,ned,ning,ALOTED SUM/ PERCENT, DELEGATE "prefixes: de"

commissioner,*,POSITION OF AUTHORITY

commit,*,tted,ttedly,tting,tment,ttable,tter,RELEGATE, ENTRUST "prefixes: non/ over/ un"

committee, committee

commitment,*,OBLIGATED, ENTRUSTED TO SOMEONE OR SOMETHING

committee,*,SELECTED GROUP TO DO WORK "prefixes: sub"

commodity,ties,OBJECT FOR TRADE

commodore,*,MILITARY OFFICER

common,*,nly,ner,nest,nness,FAMILIAR "prefixes: un"

communal,*,OF COMMUNITY

commune,*,COLLECTION OF PEOPLE WITH SIMILAR IDEAS/ VALUES

communicable,PASSED ON, ABLE TO COMMUNICATE "prefixes: in"

---

comfurter, comfort(er)

comic,*,cal,cally,cality,calness,FUNNY, HUMOROUS

comidian, comedian

comidore, commodore

comidy, comedy

comimurate, commemorate

comin, common

comind, commend

comindation, commendation

cominduble, commendable

comins, commence

cominsirate, commensurate

comint, comment

comintative, commentate(tive)

comintator, commentator

comirse, commerce

comirshul, commercial

comisary, commissary

comishen, commission

comishener, commissioner

comisioner, commissioner

comissary, commissary

comission, commission

comit, comet / commit

comitee, committee

comition, commission

comitioner, commissioner

comitment, commitment

comittee, committee

comity, comedy

comiun, commune

comiunal, communal

comiunicabol, communicable

comiunikeit, communicate

comiunion, communion

comiuniquet, communicate

comiunisom, communism

comiunist, communist

comiuniti, community

comiut, commute

comloda, cum laude

comma,*,PUNCTUATION (or see coma)

command,*,ded,ding,der,DOMINATING, DIRECTING

---

combustchen, combustion

combustible,*,bility,eness,ion,ive,POTENTIAL TO IGNITE INTO FLAMES

combustion,ive,CHEMICAL REACTION, FIRE/ OXYGEN

come,*,ming,came,RESPOND, GO TOWARDS (or see comb/ cum) "prefixes: over/ up"

comec, comic

comedeun, comedian

comedian,*,AMUSING ENTERTAINER

comedy,dies,dic,HUMOROUS ACCOUNTS

comemorate, commemorate

comence, commence

comend, commend

comendable, commendable

comendation, commendation

comendeishon, commendable

comenduble, commendable

comens, commence

comensirate, commensurate

comensurate, commensurate

coment, comment

comentative, commentate(tive)

comentator, commentator

coments, commence / comment(s)

comerbund, cummerbund

comerce, commerce

comercial, commercial

comerse, commerce

comershul, commercial

comesary, commissary

comeshen, commission

comeshener, commissioner

comet,*,SPACE MATTER AND ICE AT HIGH SPEED (or see commit)

comete, committee

cometion, commission

cometioner, commissioner

cometment, commitment

comewn, commune

comfert, comfort

comfort,*,ted,ting,ter,RELIEF, CALM, PLEASANT "prefixes: dis"

comfortable,ly,RELIEF, CALM, PLEASANT "prefixes: un"

communicate, *, ed, ting, tion, tive, tion, tively, tiveness, able, EXCHANGE INFORMATION "prefixes: ex/ in/ non/ un"

communion, *, CHRISTIAN RITUAL

communism, TYPE OF GOVERNMENT

communist, *, tic, ADVOCATE OF COMMUNISM

community, ties, ASSOCIATION OF SIMILAR PEOPLES

commute, *, ed, ting, table, INTERCHANGE, DISTANCE TRAVEL, MATHEMATICAL EXPRESSION, REDUCE/ REPLACE "prefixes: in/ non"

comodity, commodity

comodore, commodore

comon, common

compact, *, ted, ting, tion, SMALLEST DIMENSION POSSIBLE "prefixes: sub"

compaiol, compile

compalshen, compulsion

compaltion, compulsion

companeon, companion

companion, *, nship, MATE/ PARTNER

company, nies, ASSOCIATION OF INDIVIDUALS "prefixes: intra"

comparable, ly, eness, bility, SIMILAR, ALIKE "prefixes: in"

compare, *, ed, ring, arative, aratively, rable, rably, rison, PARALLEL EXAMINATION "prefixes: in"

comparetive, compare(rative)

comparison, *, ENGAGING EXAMINATION

compartment, *, tal, tally, talize, talized, talizing, SECTIONED SEPARATELY "prefixes: non"

compasinet, compassionate

compasionate, compassionate

compass, ses, DIRECTION FINDER "prefixes: en"

compassion, nate, nless, TAKE PITY ON

compassionate, ely, eness, TAKE PITY ON

competency, competence(cy)

competens, competence

compatible, bility, bilities, AGREEABLE "prefixes: bio/ in/ non"

compayol, compile

compedidor, competitor

compeditor, competitor

compel, lled, lling, llingly, llingness, DRIVEN TO, AN URGING/ DESIRE

compelation, compellation / compilation

compeleishon, compilation / compellation

compeleition, compilation

compellation, *, NAME, DENOMINATION (or see compilation)

compensate, *, ed, ting, tion, tory, MAKE UP FOR "prefixes: over"

compensation, MAKE UP FOR "prefixes: de"

compenseit, compensate

compeny, company

comper, compare

comperable, comparable

comperative, compare(rative)

compereson, comparison

comperison, comparison

compersome, cumber(some)

comperuble, comparable

compes, compass

compete, *, ed, ting, tition, titive, titively, titiveness, titor, BE BETTER THAN

competence, cy, cies, ABLE TO PERFORM WITH SKILL/ KNOWLEDGE "prefixes: in"

competent, nce, ncy, BEING ADEQUATE "prefixes: in"

competincy, competence(cy)

competishen, competition

competition, *, MATCH FOR SKILL TESTING

competitor, *, ONE WHO COMPETES

compilashun, compellation / compilation

compilation, *, BRING/ PUT TOGETHER, COMBINE, A COLLECTION (or see compellation)

compile, *, ed, ling, lation, BRING/ PUT TOGETHER, COMBINE

compinsate, compensate

compit, compete

compitance, competence

compitence, competence

compitency, competence(cy)

compiut, compute

compiuteishon, computation

compiuter, computer

compizishen, composition

complacence, cy, cies, nt, ntly, HAPPY WITH SELF (or see complaisance)

complai, comply

complain, *, ned, ning, nt, ner, FIND FAULT

complaisance, nt, DESIRE TO PLEASE, CIVIL (or see complacence)

complakeishon, complication

complasens, complacence / complaisance

complein, complain

complekate, complicate

compleks, complex

complekshin, complexion

complement, *, tal, tary, tarily, tarity, tarities, tation, WHEN ADDED MAKES COMPLETE (or see compliment)

compleshin, completion

complete, *, ed, ting, tly, CONCLUDE, FINISH "prefixes: in"

completion, CONCLUDE/ FINISH

complex, xes, xity, COMBINATION OF INTERCONNECTED PARTS

complexion, *, ned, SKIN PHYSICAL CHARACTERISTIC

compli, comply

compliant; tly, nce, ncy, CONFORM/ AGREE TO "prefixes: in/ non"

complicashin, complication

complicate, *, ed, ting, tion, MORE TO CONSIDER "prefixes: un"

complication, * ADDITIONAL INVOLVEMENT/ CONSIDERATION

complient, compliant

complikashun, complication

complikat, complicate

compliment, *, ted, ting, tary, PRAISE, EXPRESS ADMIRATION (or see complement)

complishon, completion

complit, complete

complokeit, complicate

comploqueit, complicate

complucashun, complication

complukate, complicate

complument, complement / compliment

comply, lies, ying, liance, liant, CONFORM

compolshon, compulsion

compoition, compulsion

component, *, PHASE/ PART OF SOMETHING "prefixes: sub"
compose, *, ed,sing,er, TO FORM "prefixes: de/ dis/ re"
composite, *, PARTS OF THE WHOLE
composition, *, nal,nally, IDENTIFY/ ARRANGE PARTS OF THE WHOLE
compost, *, ted,ting, RECYCLING ORGANIC MATTER
composure, CENTERED STATE OF MIND
compound, *, ded,ding, ADDITIONAL PARTS, TO ADD TO THE WHOLE
compounent, component
compownd, compound
compoze, compose
comprable, comparable
compramais, compromise
compramise, compromise
compreble, comparable
comprehend, *, ded,ding,nsion,nsive, nsible, GRASP, UNDERSTAND "prefixes: in"
comprehenshun, comprehension
comprehensible, bility, eness, ABLE TO GRASP/ UNDERSTAND "prefixes: in"
comprehension, ive, ible, UNDERSTAND/ GRASP "prefixes: in"
comprehensive, ely, UNDERSTAND/ GRASP "prefixes: in"
comprehinsive, comprehensive
comprejenshon, comprehension
compreshun, compression
compress, ses, sed, sing, sible, sibility, ssive, ssion, COMPACT, CONDENSE "prefixes: de/ in"
compression, nal, REDUCING VOLUME
compressor, *, MACHINE THAT CONDENSES/ REDUCES
compretion, compression
comprijend, comprehend
compromise, *, ed, sing, OUTCOME IMPERFECT, AGREE FOR THE SAKE OF BEING AGREEABLE "prefixes: un"
compruble, comparable
compruhensive, comprehensive
comprumize, compromise
comptroller, *, CONTROLLER OF FINANCES
compuder, computer
compulashun, compellation / compilation
compulsary, compulsory

compulsev, compulsive
compulshun, compulsion
compulsion, *, ive, IRRESISTIBLE URGE TO ACT
compulsive, ely, eness, ion,sory, GIVEN TO ACT ON URGES
compulsory, rily, REINFORCED FACT
compultion, compulsion
compusition, composition
computashun, computation
computation, *, nal, ive, ively, TO RECKON/ ESTIMATE
compute, *, ed, ting, table, FIGURE DATA, ESTIMATE
computency, competence(cy)
computer, *, rize, rized, rization, ELECTRONIC DATA PROCESSOR "prefixes: bio"
computince, competence
computishen, competition
compuzishen, composition
comrade, *, ely, ery, eship, CLOSE ASSOCIATES
comtroler, comptroller
comudoor, commodore
comunal, communal
comune, commune / common
comunecuble, communicable
comunete, community
comunicable, communicable
comunicate, communicate
comunion, communion
comunism, communism
comunist, communist
comunity, community
comurse, commerce
comurshal, commercial
comusery, commissary
comutable, commute(table)
comute, commute
con, *, nned, nning, TO TRICK, PREFIX INDICATING 'WITH/ TOGETHER' MOST OFTEN MODIFIES THE WORD (or see cone)
conaseur, connoisseur
conasure, connoisseur
conc, conch / konk
concaf, concave
concaquently, consequently(ly)

concarge, concierge
concave, *, ed,ving, ely, eness, vity, vities, OF INWARD CURVES "prefixes: bi"
conceairg, concierge
conceal, *, led, ling, lment, TO HIDE FROM SIGHT
concede, *, ed, ding, YIELD (or see conceit)
conceit, ted, VAIN (or see concede)
conceivable, bility, eness, ly, ABILITY TO UNDERSTAND, IMAGINE "prefixes: in"
conceive, *, ed, ving, vable, vably, vability, vableness, A THOUGHT WHICH BECOMES "prefixes: mis"
concent, consent
concentrate, *, ed, ting, tion, FOCUS, CONDENSE "prefixes: de"
concentric, cally, city, SERIES OF CIRCLES WITH SAME CENTER POINT
concept, *, tive, tively, IDEA/ PLAN
conception, nal, MOMENT OF CREATION "prefixes: mis/ pre"
conceptual, lism, lize, lly, lization, lizer, THOUGHTS BECOMING
concequence, consequence
concequens, consequence
concerg, concierge
concern, *, ned, ning, nment, WORRIED ABOUT NEGATIVE OUTCOME, INTEREST IN "prefixes: non/ un"
concert, *, ted, ting, PLAN/ WORK/ ACT TOGETHER IN MUSIC/ THEATER "prefixes: pre"
concervashon, conservation
conceshon, concession
concesion, concession
concession, *, TO PART WITH SOME CONTROL, SELL UNDER AUTHORITY
conch, hes, A SHELL, OF DOME
conchas, conscious
concheinchus, conscientious
conches, conscious / conch(es)
conchis, conscious / conch(es)
conchos, conscious / conch(es)
conchus, conscious / conch(es)
concierge, OVERSEES GATES/ ENTRYWAYS
concint, consent
concise, ely, eness, TO THE POINT WITH FEW WORDS

consistensy,consistent(ncy)
consistent,consistent
conclewsive,conclusive
conclude,*,ed,ding,usion,usive,WRAP-UP, SUMMARIZED ENDING
conclugen,conclusion
conclusion,*,FINALIZE,END
conclusive,ely,eness,FINALIZE,END "prefixes: in"
conclution,conclusion
concoct,*,ted,ting,PUTTING TOGETHER IDEAS
concrete,ely,eness,HARDENED GRAVEL MIXTURE
concussion,*,ssive,INJURY FROM IMPACT
concution,concussion
condemn,*,ned,ning,nation,STEP TOWARDS ELIMINATION
condensashen,condensation
condensation,*,GAS REDUCED TO LIQUID
condense,*,ed,er,sing,sable,sation,REDUCE
condescend,ding,dingly,TALK DOWN TO SOMEONE, TREAT AS AN INFERIOR
condesend,condescend
condewit,conduit
condimeneum,condominium
condiment,*,SPICES,SAUCES
condinsashen,condensation
condinsation,condensation
condisend,condescend
condishen,condition
condition,*,ned,ning,nal,TO FORCE INTO ANOTHER FORM, RESTRUCTURE "prefixes: bi/ de/ pre/ un"
condolence,*,SYMPATHY FOR SOMEONE'S PAIN
condom,*,COVER FOR PENIS
condomeneum,condominium
condominium,*,FORM OF APARTMENTS
condone,*,ed,ning,FORGIVE
conduct,*,ted,ting,tion,tive,tor,ESCORT,TRANSPORT, BEHAVIOR "prefixes: mis"
conductor,*,rial,rship,TRANSMITS,LEADS,GUIDES "prefixes: semi"
conduit,CHANNEL FOR ENERGY,FLUIDS, ETC.
condukter,conductor
condum,condom
condument,condiment

condunsation,condensation
cone,*,GEOMETRIC SHAPE OF MANY THINGS
conect,connect
conekshen,connection
conesur,connoisseur
conexshon,connection
confadant,confidant / confident
confaid,confide
confain,confine
confainment,confinement
confection,*,nary,nery,ner,A DESSERT
confedant,confidant / confident
confederate,*,acy,tion,UNITED ALLIANCE
confedont,confidant
confeduret,confederate
confedy,confetti
confekshen,confection
conference,*,MEETING FOR DISCUSSION
confermation,confirmation
confermeishon,confirmation
confesion,confession
confess,sses,ssed,ssing,ssion,ssor,DISCLOSE INFORMATION,ADMIT FACTS
confession,*,nal,ADMIT INVOLVEMENT
confetion,confession
confetti,PARTY MATERIAL
confety,confetti
confidant,*,TRUSTED PERSON (or see confident)
confide,*,ed,ding,SHARE THOUGHTS WITH SOMEONE
confidence,nt,ntial,TRUST
confidenshul,confidential
confident,tly,tial,TRUST
confidential,lly,lity,lness,PRIVATE/ SECRET
confidont,confidant
configerashun,configuration
configuration,*,ARRANGEMENT OF PARTS
confine,*,ed,ning,nment,RESTRICTED,IMPRISONED "prefixes: un"
confinement,BEING RESTRICTED,IMPRISONED
confinment,confinement
confirents,conference
confirm,*,med,ming,mation,mative,TO VALIDATE "prefixes: dis"

confirmation,*,ive,ACT OF VALIDATION
confirmeishon,confirmation
confius,confuse
confiushon,confusion
conflict,*,ted,ting,GOES AGAINST
conform,*,med,ming,mer,mist,mity,mism,mance,TO TAKE ON ANOTHER FORM "prefixes: dis/ non/ un"
confrens,conference
confrins,conference
confront,*,ted,ting,tation,tational,FACE, ENCOUNTER
confudant,confidant / confident
confudense,confidence
confujen,confusion
confuranse,conference
confurmashun,confirmation
confuse,*,ed,sing,DISORDER,OFF-CENTER
confusion,STATE OF DISORDER, OFF-CENTER
congectivitis,conjunction(ivitis)
conger,conjure
congest,*,ed,ting,tible,tive,tion,TOO MUCH WITHIN A SMALL SPACE/ PLACE "prefixes: de"
congestun,congest(ion)
conglomerate,*,ed,ting,tion,GATHERED INTO MASS
congradulashen,congratulation
congraduleishon,congratulation
congraduleit,congratulate
congrageishon,congregation
congrageit,congregate
congratulate,*,ed,ting,tion,WISH ONE WELL, COMPLIMENT
congratulation,*,EXPRESS WISHING ONE WELL, COMPLIMENT
congregate,*,ed,ting,tion,GATHERING,ASSEMBLY
congregation,*,nal,TO GATHER,ASSEMBLY
congress,ssional,ssionally,LEGISLATIVE ASSEMBLY TO PROMOTE A GROUPS INTERESTS
congrewedy,congruent(uity)
congrewes,congruous
congrewint,congruent
congrewity,congruent(uity)
congrigate,congregate
congris,congress
congruedy,congruent(uity)

congruent, nce, ncy, ntly, uity, uties, AGREEMENT, CONSISTENCE(CY) "prefixes: in/ non"
congrugashun, congregation
congrugate, congregate
congruous, sly, sness, AGREEMENT, CONSISTENCE(CY) "prefixes: in"
conifer, *, TREE GROUP
coning, cunning / con(nning)
conjesten, congest(ion)
conjoncshon, conjunction
conjugal, lity, lly, RELATION WITH PARTNER/ MATE
conjugate, *, ed, ting, tion, tive, RELATION WITH PARTNER/ MATE
conjunctavitis, conjunction(ivitis)
conjunction, *, nal, nally, ivitis, UNIFICATION, BRING TOGETHER
conjunkshen, conjunction
conjure, *, ed, ring, CREATE/ CONSPIRE
conkaf, concave
conkafety, concave(vity)
conkavudy, concave(vity)
conker, conquer
conklude, conclude
conkrete, concrete
conkur, conquer
conkushen, concussion
conkwest, conquest
conllonchshon, conjunction
conllugal, conjugal
conllur, conjure
conasure, connoisseur
connect, *, ted, ting, tive, tivity, tion, BOND, ASSOCIATE, BRING TOGETHER "prefixes: dis/ un"
connection, *, ACT OF BRINGING TOGETHER, LINK, BOND
conniseur, connoisseur
conisieur, connoisseur
connoisseur, *, SPECIALIZES, TRAINED, WELL-VERSED IN SOMETHING SUCH AS THE FINE ARTS
conoseur, connoisseur
conosieur, connoisseur
conosure, connoisseur
conphert, comfort
conqer, conquer
conquer, *, red, ring, OBTAIN BY FORCE

conquest, *, WIN BY WILL
consacrashen, consecrate(tion)
consacrate, consecrate
consacration, consecrate(tion)
consainment, consignment
consais, concise
consait, conceit
consalidate, consolidate
consaquently, consequent(ly)
conscientious, sly, sness, WITH UNSELFISH MOTIVES
conscious, sly, sness, AWARE OF PHYSICAL REALITY "prefixes: non/ semi/ sub/ un"
consdatute, constitute
conseal, conceal
consecrate, *, ed, ting, tive, tor, tory, tion, tive, MAKE SACRED/ HOLY "prefixes: de"
consecutive, ely, eness, DIRECTLY FOLLOWING ANOTHER "prefixes: in"
consedarashen, considerate(tion)
conseduration, considerate(tion)
conseed, conceit / concede
conseevable, conceivable
conseeve, conceive
conseinshus, conscientious
conseintious, conscientious
consekcutive, consecutive
consekiutiv, consecutive
consekwential, consequent(ial)
consekwently, consequent(ly)
consel, conceal / council / counsel
consemate, consummate
consensus, ual, ually, AGREEMENT, MUTUAL CONSENT
consent, *, ted, ting, YIELD OR COMPLY
consentrate, concentrate
consentric, concentric
consepshun, conception
consept, concept
conseption, conception
conseptual, conceptual
consejiutiv, consecutive
consequence, *, nt, REACTION TO AN ACTION "prefixes: in"

consequent, *, tly, ntial, ntially, ntiality, ntialness, ntialist, ntialism, REACTION TO AN ACTION "prefixes: in"
consern, concern
consert, concert
conservation, nist, nism, TO PRESERVE/ PROTECT
conservative, *, ely, eness, vism, PRACTICES RESTRAINT "prefixes: neo/ semi"
conservator, *, ry, ries, rial, rship, PROTECTOR/ GUARDIAN
conservatory, ries, A SCHOOL OF MUSIC, GREENHOUSE
conserve, *, ed, ving, vatist, vative, vator, vatize, vation, TO PRESERVE/ PROTECT/ RESTRAIN
conseshun, concession
consestintly, consistent(ly)
conset, conceit / concede
consetion, concession
consev, conceive
consevable, conceivable
conseve, conceive
consid, concede
conshas, conscious
conshes, conscious
conshus, conscious
consider, *, red, ring, rable, rate, ENGAGE IN THOUGHT "prefixes: in/ un"
considerate, ely, eness, ation, ENGAGE IN THOUGHT "prefixes: in"
consierge, concierge
consif, conceive
consignment, *, GIVING SOMEONE A PERCENT FOR SELLING YOUR WARES
consikwense, consequence
consil, conceal / council
consilation, consolation
consimate, consummate
consinent, consonant
consinment, consignment
consintrate, concentrate
consintric, concentric
consiquence, consequence
consirvation, conservation
consirvator, conservator
consirvatory, conservatory
consirve, conserve
consise, concise

consist,*,ted,ting,tence,tent,COMPOSED OF
consistence,cy,cies,HOW FLUID,VISCOUS "prefixes: in"
consistency, consistence(cy)
consistent,tly,COMPOSED OF "prefixes: in"
consivabol, conceivable
consolation,*,TO OFFER SOLACE/ SUPPORT FOR EFFORT (or see constellation)
console,*,ed,ling,lable,latory,er,lingly,SOOTHE, OFFER SUPPORT, CABINET FOR ELECTRONICS (or see counsel/ council) "prefixes: dis/ in"
consolidate,*,ed,ting,tion,PUT ALL TOGETHER
consonant,*,LETTERS IN ENGLISH WORDS THAT AREN'T VOWELS
consoom, consume
conspearusy, conspiracy
conspicuous,sly,sness,OBVIOUS,STRIKING "prefixes: in"
conspikuos, conspicuous
conspikyous, conspicuous
conspiracy,cies,A GROUP OF PEOPLE PLOTTING AN EVENT TO UPSET STATUS QUO
constancy, DILIGENT/ REPEATEDLY CONSISTENT
constant,*,tly,ncy,UNIFORM, UNCHANGING "prefixes: in"
constatushen, constitution
constatute, constitute
constellation,*,NAME FOR GROUPED CELESTIAL STARS (or see consolation)
constense, constancy
constetute, constitute
constilashen, constellation
constilation, constellation
constint, constant
constipashen, constipation
constipation, RESTRICTED BOWEL MOVEMENT
constitushen, constitution
constitute,*,ed,ting,tion,SET-UP/ CREATE/ ESTABLISH "prefix: re"
constitution,*,nal,WRITTEN RULES/ PRINCIPLES/ REGULATIONS "prefixes: un"
constrict,*,ted,ting,tion,tive,PREVENT FROM PROPER MOVEMENT
construct,*,ted,ting,tion,tive,tional,ticnally, MOLD/ FORM/ CREATE "prefixes: de/ re"

construction,nal,nally,BUILDING/ FORMING "prefixes: mis/ re"
constulashen, constellation
constulation, constellation
constupashen, constipation
consucrat, consecrate
consukwenshul, consequent(ial)
consukwently, consequent(ly)
consukwinse, consequence
consulashen, consolation
consulation, consolation
consult,*,ted,ting,tant,tation,table,tative,tatively,ter, COMMUNICATE WITH SOMEONE WHO IS SEEKING ADVICE
consultashen, consult(ation)
consumate, consummate
consume,*,ed,er,erism,ming,mable,mption,mptive, DECOMPOSE OR DESTROY, INGEST, MAKE USE OF
consumeit, consummate
consummate,*,ed,ting,COMPLETE, FULFILL
consumpshen, consumption
consumption,ive,USED, DIGESTED, DECOMPOSED
consumshen, consumption
consunent, consonant
consuquential, consequent(ial)
consurt, concert
consuration, conservation
consurvator, conservator
consurvatory, conservatory
consurve, conserve
contact,*,ted,ting,TOUCHING, ASSOCIATION WITH
contagious,sly,sness,SPREAD TO OTHERS
contain,*,ned,ning,ner,nment,HOLD WITHIN
contaminate,*,ed,ting,ant,tion,SOMETHING INCLUDED WHICH DOESN'T BELONG AT ALL "prefixes: de"
conteguis, contiguous
conteichos, contagious
conteillos, contagious
contein, contain
contemplate,*,ed,ting,tion,tive,tively,tiveness,TO OBSERVE THOROUGHLY
contemporary,ries,riness,REFLECTIVE OF CURRENT TIMES "prefixes: non"

contempt,tible,tibleness,tibly,tuous,tuously,THE STATE OF BEING DISHONORED/ DISRESPECTED
contend,*,ded,ding,der,CHOOSE OR FORCED TO DEAL WITH, FACE OFF
content,*,ted,tedly,tedness,tment,THAT WHICH IS CONTAINED WITHIN, SATISFIED "prefixes: dis"
contenual, continue(ual)
contenuense, continuance
contenuisly, continue(uously)
contenule, continue(ual)
contest,*,ted,DISPUTE, FOR SUPERIORITY "prefixes: in"
context,ture,INTERWOVEN MEANING IN TEXT
contiguis, contiguous
contiguous,sly,sness,NEIGHBORING/ SHARING A BORDER
contimplate, contemplate
contimporary, contemporary
continent,*,tal,LAND MASS "prefixes: intra/ sub"
continet, continent
contingent,*,nce,ncy,ncies,MAY HAPPEN IF...
continiu, continue
continiuans, continuance
continllent, contingent
contint, content
continuance,POSTPONEMENT TO CONTINUE AT A FUTURE DATE
continuants, continuance
continue,*,ed,uing,ual,ually,uation,uouse,uously, uousness,uity,KEEP GOING "prefixes: dis"
continyent, contingent
contorshenist, contortionist
contortionist,*,FLEXIBLE ACTS WITH THE BODY
contour,*,red,ring,THE SHAPE/ FORM OF OUTLINE
contra,PREFIX INDICATING 'AGAINST' MOST OFTEN MODIFIES THE WORD
contrabersi, controversy
contraception,ive,FOR PREVENTION OF PREGNANCY
contract,*,ted,ting,tor,tual,tive,tion,tionary, WRITTEN OBLIGATION OF SERVICE "prefixes: non/ sub"
contraction,*,nal,nary,MUSCLES TIGHTENING, COMBINATION OF WORDS

contradict,*,ted,ting,tion,tory,CONTRARY/ OPPOSE/ DENY
contrak,contract
contrakshen,contraction
contrary,ries,rily,riness,rian,riety,rieties,PROVE OPPOSITE, DENY "prefixes: sub"
contrast,*,ted,ting,tingly,tive,tively,tiveness,table, tably, COMPARING DIFFERENCES
contraversy,controversy
contravert,controvert
contravertible,controvert(ible)
contrebiut,contribute
contrebute,contribute
contrery,contrary
contribiut,contribute
contribute,*,ed,ting,tion,tive,tory,GIVE, LEND
contrition,AMENDING SIN WITH PRAYER
contro,PREFIX INDICATING 'AGAINST' MOST OFTEN MODIFIES THE WORD
controbersi,controversy
control,*,lled,lling,ller,llable,llably,llability,ATTEMPT TO GAIN ORDER "prefixes: bio/ in/ sub/ un"
controversy,sies,sial,DIFFERENCE IN OPINION, DEBATE
controvert,*,ted,ting,ter,tible,tibly,DEBATE STRONGLY AGAINST "prefixes: in"
contrudik,contradict
contrusepshun,contraception
contumplate,contemplate
contunent,continent
conture,contour
conufir,conifer
conva,convey
convalescence,nt,RECOVERING HEALTH
convay,convey
convayer,convey(or)
convelesents,convalescence
convene,*,ed,ning,CALL TO APPEAR, MEET
convenient,nce,nces,EASE OF FACILITIES, COMFORT "prefixes: in"
convense,convince
convention,*,nal,PEOPLE GATHERING, AN ASSEMBLY "prefixes: non/ un"
convenyant,convenient

convenyut,convenient
conversashen,conversation
conversation,*,nal,nally,nalist,COMMUNICATING THOUGHTS
converse,es,sing,sant,EXCHANGE INFORMATION, MADE OPPOSITE/ REVERSE
converseishon,conversation
conversion,*,CHANGED IN ONE FORM OR ANOTHER "prefixes: bio"
convert,*,ted,ting,ter,rsion,OF CHANGE, TRANSFORM "prefixes: in"
convertible,bility,CHANGE FROM ONE FORM TO ANOTHER, VEHICLE WITH REMOVABLE ROOF
convex,xes,xed,xedly,xedness,xing,xly,xity,xities, CURVING OUTWARD "prefixes: bi/ sub"
convey,*,yed,ying,yable,yance,yances,yancing,yor, TRANSFER OF PEOPLE/ ITEMS/ MEANING/ EXPRESSION "prefix: re"
convicshen,convict(ion)
convict,*,ted,ting,tion,HAVING BEEN FOUND GUILTY/ AT FAULT
convilesense,convalescence
convin,convene
convince,*,ed,cing,TO PERSUADE SOMEONE TO YOUR OPINION "prefixes: in"
convinient,convenient
convinshon,convention
convintion,convention
conviration,conversation
convirse,converse
convirt,convert
convulesense,convalescence
convulesent,convalescent
convulgin,convulsion
convulshen,convulsion
convulsion,*,sive,sively,INTENSE MUSCLE CONTRACTION
convurgin,conversion
convursashen,conversation
convursation,conversation
convurtable,convertible
coocoo,cuckoo
cood,could

coodent,couldn't
cooger,cougar
cook,*,ked,king,PREPARE FOOD "prefixes: pre"
cookie,*,SWEET CAKE TREAT
cool,*,led,ling,lingly,lly,lness,ler,BETWEEN WARM/ COLD TEMPERATURE, EXPRESSION OF APPRECIATION "prefixes: pre/ sub/ un/ under"
cooler,*,COLD CONTAINER FOR FOOD
coom lada,cum laude
coop,*,ped,SMALL CAGE FOR SMALL ANIMALS (or see co-op/ coup)
cooperate,*,ed,ting,tion,tive,UNITE TO PRODUCE
coordinate,*,ed,ting,ely,eness,tive,tion,tor,ORGANIZE FOR DESIRED RESULTS, LINE SYSTEM "prefixes: in/ un"
cooth,couth
cop,*,pped,pping,pper,SLANG FOR "POLICE", RUN OUT OF ENERGY (or see co-op/ coup/ coop/ cope/ copy)
copbord,cupboard
cope,*,ed,ping,TO DEAL WITH STRESS, SHAPE/ MATCH (or see co-op/ coup/ coop/ copy)
coper,copper
copeur,copy(pier)
copi,copy
copitchulate,capitulate
copiuleit,copulate
copkeic,cupcake
copler,coupler
copol,couple
copper,*,ry,METAL
copulate,*,ed,ted,tion,PHYSICAL SEXUAL UNITY
copur,copper
coputr,computer
coputer,computer
copy,pies,pied,ying,TO REPRODUCE
copyuter,computer
cor,TO TRICK, PREFIX INDICATING 'WITH/ TOGETHER' MOST OFTEN MODIFIES THE WORD (or see core/ car)
coraborate,corroborate
coragated,corrugate(d)
coral,OCEAN REEF ANIMALS
corc,cork
corchal,cordial

cord, *, STRANDS WOVEN/ TWISTED TOGETHER (or see chord/ quart(s)/ quartz)
cordaroy, corduroy
cordial, ity, lness, lly, GRACIOUS, KIND, A LIQUEUR
cordinate, coordinate
cordunate, coordinate
corduroy, RIBBED MATERIAL
core, *, ed, ring, THE CENTER OF (or see corp)
corect, correct
coredor, corridor
corelate, correlate
coreleit, correlate
cores, core(s) / chorus / caress
corespond, correspond
corgul, cordial
coridor, corridor
corigate, corrugate
corilate, correlate
coriner, coroner
corinery, coronary
coris, chorus / course
corispond, correspond
corjil, cordial
cork, *, ked, BARK FROM A TREE (or see quark) "prefixes: un"
corllal, cordial
corn, *, GRAIN, ON TOE
cornacopia, cornucopia
cornea, al, PART OF EYE
corneishon, carnation
corner, *, red, ring, WHERE WALLS OR LINES MEET, NO WAY OUT
cornia, cornea
cornikopea, cornucopia
cornol, colonel
cornucopia, HORN OF PLENTY
coroborate, corroborate
corode, corrode
corogan, corrode(osion)
corogin, corrode(osion)
corojin, corrode(osion)
coronary, ries, HEART ARTERIES
coroner, *, , INVESTIGATES SUSPICIOUS DEATHS

coropt, corrupt
corosef, corrode(osive)
coroud, corrode
corp, *, , NUMBER OF PEOPLE WORKING TOGETHER (or see core)
corparul, corporal
corpirate, corporate
corporal, OF THE PHYSICAL BODY
corporate, tion, ely, UNITE MANY INTO ONE "prefixes: in/ non"
corpret, corporate
corpse, *, , DEAD BODY
corpural, corporal
corpurate, corporate
corral, *, , FENCED ENCLOSURE FOR ANIMALS (or see coral)
correct, *, ted, ting, tly, tion, tional, table, tible, tness, tor, TO SET RIGHT/ STRAIGHT "prefixes: in/ over"
correlate, *, , ed, ting, tion, IF ONE... THEN THE OTHER
correspond, *, , ded, ding, dence, SIMILAR/ RELATED TO, COMMUNICATE WITH
corridor, *, , NARROW PASSAGE
corroborate, *, , ed, ting, tion, tive, tively, tor, tory, CAN BACK UP THE TRUTH WITH EVIDENCE
corrode, , ed, ding, osion, osive, dant, dible, dibility, CHEMICAL EROSION, EATEN AWAY
corrugate, *, , ed, ting, ALTERNATING BENDS, FORMS
corrupt, *, , ted, ting, tion, tible, tibly, tibility, tibleness, tness, TO NEGATIVELY STEER OFF COURSE "prefixes: in"
cors, course / coarse / core(s)
corsage, *, , FLOWERS TO WEAR, BODICE
corse, course / coarse / core(s)
corsog, corsage
corsoge, corsage
cort, cord / court / quart
cort-marshul, court-martial
corteks, cortex
cortex, xes, tices, tical, tically, INTERNAL ORGAN'S PROTECTIVE LAYER "prefixes: sub"
corts, cord(s) / court(s) / quart(s)
corudoor, corridor
corugate, corrugate
corugeit, corrugate

corul, choral / coral / corral / chorale
corulate, correlate
corunary, coronary
coruner, coroner
corupt, corrupt
coruspond, correspond
cos, cause / cuss
cosdodian, custodian
cosdum, costume
cosee, cozy
coshen, caution
cosher, kosher
coshis, cautious
coshun, caution
cosin, cousin
cosmic, cally, NOT OF THIS PHYSICAL PLANE
cosmopolitan, BELONGS TO THE WORLD, NO ATTACHMENT
cosmos, UNIVERSAL HARMONY
cosp, cusp
cospid, cuspid
cost, *, , ting, tly, EXPENSE (or see coast/ cause(d))
costard, custard
costem, custom
coster, coaster
costic, caustic
costodian, custodian
costom, custom / costume
costomer, customer
costomize, custom(ize)
costoom, costume
costume, *, , GARMENTS TO SUIT A CHARACTER TYPE
cosy, cozy
cot, *, , FOLDING BED (or see caught/ coat/ cut)
cotage, cottage
cotej, cottage
coten, cotton
cotleri, cutlery
cotn, cotton
coton, cotton
cottage, *, , SMALL DWELLING
cotton, PLANT WHICH CLOTH IS PRODUCED FROM
cotuge, cottage

coualishon,coalition
coubalt,cobalt
coubra,cobra
couc,caulk
couch,hes,hed,hing,FURNITURE,PUT-DOWN (or see coach)
coucnot,coconut
coucoa,cocoa
couconot,coconut
coud,code / could
coudin,codeine
coued,coed
couers,coerce
couf,cough / cove
cougar,*,ANIMAL
cough,*,hed,hing,FORCEFULLY EXPEL AIR FROM LUNGS
cought,caught / cot / cough(ed)
couinsaid,coincide
couinsedent,coincident
coujabiteit,cohabitate
coujerent,coherent
coujirent,coherent
coujisev,cohesive
coujort,cohort
coukein,cocaine
coul,coal
couladeral,collateral
coulateral,collateral
could,PAST TENSE FOR THE WORD 'CAN'
could've,CONTRACTION OF THE WORDS 'COULD HAVE'
couldn't,CONTRACTION OF THE WORDS 'COULD NOT'
coulishun,coalition
coulon,cologne / colon
couloniol,colonial
coulouniol,colonial
coulsla,coleslaw
coum,comb
coun,cone
council,*,A GROUP MEETING TO DISCUSS/ MAKE DECISIONS (or see counsel/ console)
counsel,*,led,ling,lor,GIVES ADVISE, PROVIDES INFORMATION (or see console/ council)
counside,coincide

count,*,ted,ting,table,tless,ADD THE NUMBER OF THINGS "prefixes: dis/ mis/ re-/ un "
counter,*,red,ring,ract,PREFIX INDICATING "AGAINST" MOST OFTEN MODIFIES THE WORD,SURFACE FOR SERVING, SOMETHING THAT COUNTS, OPPOSING MOVE "prefixes: en"
country,ries,OUT OF THE CITY, COLLECTION OF STATES, NATION OF PEOPLE "prefixes: up"
county,ties,A GEOGRAPHICAL AREA
coup,QUICK/ SUCCESSFUL MOVE (or see coop)
couple,*,ed,ling,er,PARTNERS, BRING TWO TOGETHER "prefixes: un"
coupler,*,ling,DEVICE FOR CONNECTING
coupon,*,REDEEM FOR CASH VALUE
coupurate,cooperate
couquein,cocaine
courage,eous,eously,eousness,BRAVE IN FACING DANGER "prefixes: dis/ en"
courier,*,MESSENGER
cours,course / coerce
course,*,PATH, IDEA, CONCEPT TO FOLLOW (or see coarse) "prefixes: dis/ re"
coursive,coerce(cive)
coursment,coerce(ment)
court,*,ted,ting,ENCLOSED AREA, HALL/ CHAMBER FOR SPORTS/ CIVIC ACTIVITIES FOLLOW (or see quart)
court-martial,led,ling,MILITARY TRIAL
courteous,sly,sness,POLITE
courtesy,sies,POLITE BEHAVIOR "prefixes: dis"
cousi,cozy
cousin,*,KINSHIP, RELATIVE
coust,coast
couster,coaster
cout,caught / cot / coat
couth,SOPHISTICATED "prefixes: un"
coux,coax
cova,kava
cove,*,ed,ving,NOOK, CAVE (or see coffee)
covenant,*,AGREEMENT, CONTRACT TO KEEP PROMISE "prefixes: un"
cover,*,red,ring,rage,TO HIDE/ PROTECT "prefixes: dis/ re/ un/ under"
coverage,ACT OF HIDING OR BEING PROTECTED

covert,tly,tness,UNDER COVER, DISGUISED, SHELTERED
covet,DESIRE WITHOUT REGARDS TO CONSEQUENCE
covrach,coverage
covunent,covenant
covurt,covert
cow,*,THE FEMININE OF VARIOUS SPECIES, BOVINE
coward,*,dly,dliness,dice,CANNOT BRAVELY FACE DANGER
cowch,couch
cowculus,calculus
cowerd,coward
cowkulate,calculate
cowl,*,ling,A HOOD (or see call)
cownder,counter
cownsul,council / counsel / console
cownt,count
cowntur,counter
cownty,county
cowurd,coward
coxs,coax
coyol,coil
coz,cause
cozmic,cosmic
cozmopoletin,cosmopolitan
cozmos,cosmos
cozy,zies,zily,ziness,COMFORTABLE, CONTENT, SNUG
crab,*,CRUSTACEAN, HARD SHELLED OCEAN ANIMAL
crachin,creation / crash(ing)
crack,*,ked,king,TO SPLIT APART, SLANG FOR A SERIOUSLY ADDICTIVE DRUG, A SOUND
cracker,*,YEASTLESS BISCUIT, FIREWORKS
crackle,*,ed,ling,SOUND, GLAZE ON POTTERY
cracol,crackle
crader,crater / creator
cradible,credible
cradle,*,ed,ling,ter,tily,tiness,KILL USING HANDS, BED FOR INFANT, HOLD IN ARMS, TOOL
cradul,cradle
crafe,crave
craft,*,ted,ting,ter,tily,tiness,KILL USING HANDS, VESSEL FOR TRAVEL
craj,cry
craid,cried
craim,crime

crain,crane
crank,crank
crais,cries
craises,crisis
krak,crack
crakel,crackle
craker,cracker
cral,crawl
cram,*,mmed,mming,FORCE INTO A SPACE
cramp,*,ped,ping,CONFINES,MUSCLE CONTRACTIONS
crampt,cramp(ed)
cranberry,ries,EDIBLE BERRY
crane,*,ed,ning,A MACHINE,TO STRETCH OUT
craneum,cranium
crani,PREFIX INDICATING 'SKULL' MOST OFTEN MODIFIES THE WORD
cranio,PREFIX INDICATING "SKULL" MOST OFTEN MODIFIES THE WORD
cranium, *, ia, ial,SKULL "prefixes: endo/ intra'
crank,*,ked,king,ky,TOOL,SOMEONE IRRITABLE
cranny,nies,CREVICE, NOOK, CRACK
crany,cranny
craon,crayon
crap,*,pped,pping,ppy,GAME OF DICE,TIRED OUT (or see creator)
crape,crepe / crap(ppy)
craquer,cracker
crase,crazy
crash,hes,hed,hing,SOUND,TO RUN INTO,OFF OF SOMETHING
crass,sness,COARSE,THICK,DENSE
crate, *, ed, ting, BOX, BOX UP
crater, *,red,ring, BOWL-SHAPED DEPRESSION, CONCAVE (or see creator)
crauch,crouch
craud,crowd
craul,crawl
craun,crown
craunec,chronic
craunekl,chronicle
crave, *, ed, ving, TO YEARN, DESIRE HEAVILY
crawl, *, led, ling, ON HANDS AND KNEES, MOVE SLOWLY, CROUCHED POSITION

cray,cry
crayon, *, WAX PENCIL
crazy,zier, zziest,zily,ziness,INSANE,INFATUATED
creachin,creation
creader,creator
creak, *, ked, king, NOISE (or see creek)
creal,creel
cream,my,mily,miness,FROM MILK,TO WHIP ON SOMEONE (or see creme)
creap,creep
creapy,creep
crease, *, ed, sing, MAKE FOLDED LINES, MARK IN "prefixes: in"
creashun,creation
creasul,creosol
create, *, ed, ting, tive, tively, tiveness, tion, tivity,TO TURN THOUGHT INTO REALITY "prefixes: mis/ pro/ re"
createf,creative
creation, *, nist,ACT OF CREATING
creative,ely, eness,ion, vity,IMAGINE/ CREATE SOMETHING UNUSUAL "prefixes: un"
creator, *, ONE WHO TURNS THOUGHT INTO PHYSICAL REALITY
creature, *, ely,SOMETHING OTHER THAN HUMAN, ANIMATE, INANIMATE
creb,crib
crebeg,cribbage
crec,creek / creak
crecher,creature
crechor,creature
credable,credible
credeer,creditor
credenchol,credential
credential, *, led,TO VALIDATE CONFIDENCE,ASSURE OF AUTHENTICITY "prefixes: un"
creder,critter
credible,ly, bility, eness,WORTHY/ BELIEVABLE "prefixes: in"
credibul,credible
credider,creditor
credinshul,credential
credisize,criticize

credit, *, ted,ting,table,tor, RECORD OF HANDLING OTHER'S MONEY/ SPENDING/ EARNINGS,ACCOUNT TO BORROW AGAINST "prefixes: ac/ dis/ un"
creditor, *, ONE WHOM MONEY IS OWED TO
creduble,credible
creducal,critical
creecher,creature
creek, *, SMALL STREAM/ TRIBUTARY (or see creak)
creel,FISH BASKET, OF SEWING MACHINES
creen,careen
creenkul,crinkle
creep, *, rept,ping,py,per, SOMETHING WHICH CAUSES FEARFUL SENSATION,TO SNEAK UP
creider,crater
creidol,cradle
creif,crave
crein,crane
creion,crayon
creisote,creosote
creit,crate
creitor,crater
creiv,crave
creke,creak / creek
crekit,cricket
cremate, *, ed,ting,tion,tor,torium,BURN A BODY TO ASH
creme,LIKE CREAM (or see cream)
cremenul,criminal
cremson,crimson
creng,cringe
crenium,cranium
crenj,cringe
crenkle,crinkle
creosol,BLACK,FROM TAR AND RESIN (or see creosote)
creosote,FROM WOOD TAR USED FOR PRESERVATIVE/ ANTISEPTIC (or see creosol)
crep,creep / crepe
crepe, *, THIN PAPER,FABRIC (or see creep)
creple,cripple
crept,PAST TENSE FOR THE WORD 'CREEP'
creptic,cryptic
crepy,creep
crescendo, *, di,GRADUAL/ GROWING/ INCREASING

crescent, *, SHAPE OF QUARTER MOON
crescross, crisscross
crese, crease
cresendo, crescendo
cresent, crescent / croissant
cresmas, christmas
cresmus, christmas
crest, *, ted, ting, TOP/ CROWN/ PEAK
cresunt, crescent / croissant
cretable, credible
creteek, critique
creteke, critique
cretible, credible
cretik, critic
cretir, critter / creator
cretisize, criticize
creusol, creosol
creusote, creosote
crevasse, *, ed, sing, FISSURE OF GLACIER/ RIVER (or see crevice)
crevice, *, CRACK/ FISSURE (or see crevasse)
crevus, crevasse crevice
crew, *, GANG/ BODY OF PEOPLE (or see cruise)
 "prefixes: un"
crewd, crude
crews, cruise / crew(s)
crewsade, crusade
crewshul, crucial
crewsufix, crucifix
crewton, crouton
creyniom, cranium
creyon, crayon
creysi, crazy
criasol, creosol
criasot, creosote
crib, *, bbed, bbing, bbage, ENCLOSURE/ CONTAINER, CHEAT SHEET
cribach, cribbage
cribage, cribbage
cribbage, GAME, CARDS
cribd, crib(bbed)
cribeg, cribbage
cric, creek / creak

crichor, creature
crichur, creature
cricket, *, INSECT
crid, cried
cridenshols, credential(s)
credentials, credential(s)
crider, critter
cridik, critic
cridual, critical
cridusize, criticize
cried, PAST TENSE FOR THE WORD 'CRY'
creitor, creator
cries, PAST TENSE FOR THE WORD 'CRY'
criet, create
crieydor, creator
crik, creek / creak
criket, cricket
cril, creel
crim, crime / cream / creme
crime, *, ACT AGAINST MAN'S LAWS
crimeit, cremate
crimenal, criminal
criminal, *, lly, ONE WHO VIOLATED MAN'S LAWS
crimson, COLOR
cringe, *, ed, ging, RECOIL IN POSTURE, RETRACT
crinj, cringe
crinkle, *, ed, ling, NOISE, CRUMPLE
crip, creep
criple, cripple
cripol, cripple
cripple, *, ed, ling, ler, LAME, DISABLE
criptic, cryptic
criquet, cricket / croquet
cris, crease
crisanthemom, chrysanthemum
criscross, crisscross
crisis, ses, TURNING POINT IN LIFE
crismas, christmas
crismus, christmas
crisont, croissant
crisp, ply, piness, py, BRITTLE, FRESH
crisscross, sses, ssed, ssing, TWO LINES THAT INTERSECT TO FORM AN "X"

cristal, crystal
cristashen, crustacean
cristl, crystal
cristolize, crystal(ize)
critasais, criticize
criter, critter
critic, *, cal, cize, cism, ique, ONE WHO PASSES JUDGMENT
critical, cally, calness, BEING JUDGMENTAL "prefixes: sub/ un"
criticize, *, ed, zing, ism, TO PROVIDE PERSONAL JUDGMENT
critique, *, ed, uing, PROVIDE WRITTEN OPINION
critirr, critter
critter, *, NON-HUMAN CREATURE
crivis, crevice
criz, cries
croak, *, ked, king, FROG SOUND, TO DIE
croan, crone
croch, crutch
crochet, *, ted, ting, KNIT WITH NEEDLE
crock, *, kery, KETTLE, POT, DEROGATORY RESPONSE (or see croak)
crocodile, *, LARGE BROWN REPTILE
crocus, FLOWER
croissant, *, FRENCH PASTRY
crok, crock / croak
crokedile, crocodile
croket, croquet / croquette
crokudile, crocodile
crol, crawl
crom, crumb
crombl, crumble
crompl, crumple
cronalogical, chronology(gical)
cronch, crunch
crone, *, AGED WOMAN WITH WISDOM
cronec, chronic
cronecal, chronicle
cronological, chronology(gical)
cronucl, chronic
cronucl, chronicle
crony, nies, FRIENDS, BUDDIES

crook, *, ked,kedly,kedness,kery,DISHONORABLE PERSON, A BEND/ HOOK (or see croak)
croose,cruise / crew(s)
crop, *, pped,pping,YIELD IN FIELD, SUDDEN APPEARANCE "prefixes: over"
croquet, GAME (or see croquette)
croquette, PREPARED FOOD (or see croquet)
cros,cross / crow(s)
crosant,croissant
croshay,crochet
cross,sses,ssed,ssing,TWO LINES PERFORMING INTERSECTION "prefixes: un"
crost,cross(ed) / crust
crostashen,crustacean
crotch,hless,WHERE LEGS MEET THE TORSO,FORK OF SOMETHING
crou,crow
crouch,hes,hed,hing,HUDDLE,SQUAT,CRINGE
croud,crowd
croukej,croquette / croquet
croum,chrome
croumosoum,chromosome
croumou,chromo
croun,crown / crone
crouquei,croquette / croquet
croushey,crochet
crouton, SMALL TOAST
crow, *, wed,wing,BOAST,ROOSTER SOUND
crowch,crouch
crowd, *, ded,ding,BODIES CLOSE TOGETHER "prefixes: over"
crowkus,crocus
crown, *, ned,ning,PEAK,CREST,TOP, HEAD ADORNMENT "prefixes: un"
crowshay,crochet
crowtch,crouch
cru,crew
cruc,crook
cruch,crutch
crucial, UPMOST IMPORTANCE
crucifix,xion,PERTAINING TO CHRISTIAN CROSS
crucs,crux
crude,er,est,ely,eness,NEED FURTHER DEVELOPMENT

crudenshul,credential
crudinshuls,credential(s)
crue,crew
cruise, *, ed,sing,er,MOVE ABOUT IN CAR/ BOAT FOR PLEASURE (or see crew)
cruke,crook
cruks,crux
crumb, *, ble,TINY BITS OF SOMETHING
crumble, *, ed,ling,ly,FALL APART IN PIECES
crumple, *, ed,ling,WRINKLE,SQUEEZE OR FORM CREASES
crunch,hes,hed,hing,hy,hiness,TO BREAK, WRINKLE
crupt,corrupt
crusade, *, ed,ding,er,MOVEMENT WITH ASSERTIVE INTENT
cruse,cruise / crew(s)
cruseid,crusade
crusendo,crescendo
crush,hes,hed,hing,her,hable,TO SMASH
crushul,crucial
crust, *, ty,ted,tal,tless,PASTRY LINING,PLANETARY GEOLOGY "prefixes: en"
crustacean, *, eous,WATER ANIMAL,ANTHROPOD
crutch,hes,TOOL FOR SUPPORT
cruteek,critique
cruteke,critique
cruton,crouton
crux,xes,TROUBLE, CROSS
cry,ries,ried,ying,VERBAL SOUND, EMOTIONAL RELEASE
cryptic,cally,calness,CODES TO CONCEAL OR HIDE
crysis,crisis
crystal,*, ,llize,llized,llizing,llizability,llizable,llization, llizer,lline,llinity,llite,OF OR LIKE CLEAR QUARTZ ROCK
cshel,seashell
cu,cue
cuadrent,quadrant
cuagiuleit,coagulate
cuagmayer,quagmire
cuaier,choir
cuaint,quaint
cuak,quake
cual,quail

cualify,qualify
cuality,quality
cuam,qualm
cuandry,quandary
cuantify,quantify
cuantity,quantity
cuarel,quarrel
cuarentin,quarantine
cuark,quake
cuasar,quasar
cuasi,quasi
cuayer,choir
cuazar,quasar
cubby,bies,SMALL, SNUG SPACE
cube, *, ed,bic,bicle,bicles,SHAPE WHERE ALL SIDES ARE THE SAME,MATHEMATICAL EXPRESSION (or see cubby)
cubek,cubic
cubekle,cubicle
cubic,OF A CUBE,MATHEMATICAL EXPRESSION
cubicle, *, AREA SECTIONED OFF, SMALL SPACE
cubird,cupboard
cuburd,cupboard
cubuse,caboose
cuc,cook
cuce,cook / kook / cookie
cuci,kook / cookie
cuckoo, *, oed,oing,BIRD, CRAZY
cucu,cuckoo
cucumber,*, ,VEGETABLE
cucune,cocoon
cud,WHAT A COW CHEWS (or see could/ cue(d)/ cute)
cudaver,cadaver
cuddle, *, ed,ling,er,ly,HOLD SNUGGLY
cudent,couldn't
cudet,cadet
cudev,could've
cudint,couldn't
cudle,cuddle
cudov,could've
cudy,could've
cue, *, ed,uing,SIGNAL/ SIGN, SOMETHING WHICH DISTINGUISHES "prefixes: mis"

cueic,quake / quick
cueint,quaint
cueisar,quasar
cueizar,quasar
cuek,quake
cuel,quail
cuen,queen
cuepon,coupon
cuerc,quirk
cueshten,question
cuf,cuff
cufer,cover
cuferege,coverage
cuff,*,fed,fing,FIST BLOW,ON SLEEVES, ON CREDIT, RESTRAINT FOR WRISTS/ ANKLES
cuger,cougar
cugole,cajole
cuil,quill
cuilt,quilt
cuin,queen
cuintuplet,quintuplet
cuir,queer
cuirk,quirk
cuisine,FINE COOKING
cuit,quit / quite
cuiver,quiver
cuk,cook / cock / kook
cuke,cook / cookie /kook
cuki,kook / cookie
cukoon,cocoon
cuku,cuckoo
cukumber,cucumber
cul,cool
cul-de-sac,*,BULB SHAPE AT END OF STREET WITH EXIT/ ENTRANCE BEING THE SAME
culagen,collision / collagen
culamity,calamity
culander,colander
culapse,collapse
culejet,collegiate
culekshun,collection
culekt,collect
culektur,collect(or)

culenary,culinary
culendjula,calendula
culer,color / cooler
culide,collide
culidescope,kaleidoscope
culigen,collision
culinary,ART OF FOOD PREPARATION
culindula,calendula
culishun,collision
cultion,collision
culmenate,culminate
culminate,*,ed,ting,tion,CLIMAX/ GREAT HEIGHT
cull,*,lled,lling,ller,TO SEPARATE OUT FROM OTHERS, CHOOSE, GLEAN (or see cool)
culoge,collage
culokweul,colloquial
culone,cologne / colon
culoneul,colonial
culoquial,colloquial
culor,color
culostimy,colostomy
culosul,colossal
culprit,*,ONE WHO COMMITTED AN OFFENSE
culsher,culture
cult,GROUP OF PEOPLE WITH FIRM RELIGIOUS BELIEFS
cultavashen,cultivate(tion)
cultivashen,cultivate(tion)
cultivate,*,ed,ting,tion,DEVELOP/ FACILITATE GROWTH OF SOMETHING
cultsher,culture
culture,*,ral,rally,ESSENCE OF A GROUP/ SOCIETY, NURTURING "prefixes: ac/ bi/ en/ sub"
culvert,*,A DRAIN
cum,WITH/ TOGETHER,A SECRETION (or see come)
cum laude,METHOD OF COMPARING GRADUATES AGAINST ONE ANOTHER
cumaletive,cumulative
cumand,command
cumander,commander
cumber,*,red,ring,rsome,rsomely,rsomeness, CHALLENGING DUE TO WEIGHT/SIZE/STRUCTURE "prefixes: en"
cumberbun,cummerbun

cumbersome,elyeness,CHALLENGING DUE TO WEIGHT/SIZE/STRUCTURE "prefixes: en"
cumbine,combine
cumbuschen,combustion
cumbustible,combustible
cumedean,comedian
cumemorate,commemorate
cumenduble,commendable
cumenserite,commensurate
cuments,commence
cumerbund,cummerbund
cumershal,commercial
cumewtable,commute(table)
cumfert,comfort
cumfertible,comfortable
cuminduble,commendable
cumishen,commission
cumishioner,commissioner
cumitee,committee
cumitment,commitment
cumlota,cum laude
cummerbund,*,BAND FOR WAIST WORN WITH FORMALS
cumnee,company
cumodity,commodity
cumpartment,compartment
cumpashun,compassion
cumpashunet,compassionate
cumpass,compass
cumpatuble,compatible
cumpedidor,competitor
cumpel,compel
cumpeny,company
cumperible,comparable
cumperison,comparison
cumpersome,cumber(some)
cumpete,compete
cumpetitor,competitor
cumpient,compliant
cumpile,compile
cumplane,complain
cumplasens,complacence / complaisance
cumplecshun,complexion

cumpleks,complex	cunfetion,confetion	cunsise,concise
cumpleshun,completion	cunfetty,confetti	cunsist,consist
cumplete,complete	cunfide,confide	cunsistency,consistence(cy)
cumplians,compliant(nce)	configuration,configuration	cunsiter,consider
cumply,comply	cunfine,confine	cunsole,console
component,component	cunfinment,confinement	cunsoludate,consolidate
cumpose,compose	cunfirm,confirm	cunsoom,consume
cumposier,composure	cunflict,conflict	cunsoul,console
cumposit,composite	cunform,conform	cunspikuos,conspicuous
cumpownd,compound	cunfront,confront	cunstrict,constrict
cumpreshun,compression	cunfugin,confusion	cunstrucshen,construction
cumpresor,compressor	cunfuse,confuse	cunstruct,construct
cumpress,compress	cunfusion,confusion	cunsult,consult
cumpuder,computer	cunglomurete,conglomerate	cunsurn,concern
cumpulsery,compulsory	cungradulashen,congratulation	cuntamunate,contaminate
cumpulshun,compulsion	cungratshulate,congratulate	cuntane,contain
cumpulsuve,compulsive	cungruint,congruent	cunteguis,contiguous
cumpute,compute	cungunctavitis,conjunction(ivitis)	cuntemporary,contemporary
cumputer,computer	cuning,cunning	cuntemt,contempt
cumulative, ely, eness, ACCUMULATION/ COLLECTS	cunjest,congest	cuntend,contend
cumunal,communal	cunjested,congest(ed)	content,content
cumunikable,communicable	cunjestion,congest(ion)	cuntenuense,continuance
cumunyon,communion	cunjunctivitis,conjunction(ivitis)	cuntest,contest
cumutable,commute(table)	cunjunkshen,conjunction	cuntiguis,contiguous
cunal,canal	cunklusev,conclusive	cuntrakshen,contraction
cunclude,conclude	cunklusion,conclusion	cuntree,country
cunclusive,conclusive	cunkokt,concoct	cuntrery,contrary
cunclution,conclusion	cunkushun,concussion	cuntrishen,contrition
cuncoct,concoct	**cunning**,gly,gness, CRAFTY, SKILLFUL	cuntrol,control
cundem,condemn	cunsederashen,considerate(tion)	cunvay,convey
cundense,condense	cunseed,concede	cunvekt,convict
cundinse,condense	cunseel,conceal	cunvence,convince
cundishen,condition	cunseet,conceit	cunvene,convene
condition,condition	cunseeve,conceive	cunvenshen,convention
cundolense,condolence	cunseevuble,conceivable	cunvenyent,convenient
cundone,condone	cunsent,consent	cunverdable,convertible
cundukt,conduct	cunsentric,concentric	cunvergin,conversion
cunekshen,connection	cunsepshual,conceptual	cunvershen,conversion
cunekt,connect	cunsepshun,conception	cunvert,convert
cunfecshin,confection	cunseption,conception	cunvertable,convertible
cunferm,confirm	cunservutive,conservative	cunvulgin,convulsion
cunfeshun,confession	cunsiduration,considerate(tion)	cunvulshen,convulsion
cunfess,confess	cunsinment,consignment	cuoda,quota

cuonative,quantitative
cuorum,quorum
cuoshent,quotient
cuot,quote
cuota,quota
cuouda,quota
cuoushent,quotient
cuout,quote
cuouta,quota
cup,*,pped,pping,VESSEL/ SHAPE LIKE SMALL BOWL (or see coop/ coup/)
cupal,couple
cupasity,capacity
cupboard,*,CABINET IN KITCHEN
cupcake,*,SMALL CAKE
cupe,coop
cupil,couple
cupitchulate,capitulate
cupler,coupler
cupon,coupon
cupqueic,cupcake
cupul,couple
cupyuter,computer
cuqui,cookie
curabirate,corroborate
curable,bility,eness,ly,CAN BE CURED "prefixes: in"
curach,courage
curader,curator
curage,courage
cural,corral
curamic,ceramic
currant,currant / current
curator,*,APPOINTED BY COURT, OVERSEER "prefixes: pro"
curb,*,bed,bing,FOR RESTRAINT, TO PROTECT SOMETHING
curcle,circle
curcumsize,circumcise
curd,*,USED TO MAKE CHEESE (or see cure(d))
curdesy,courtesy
curdeus,courteous
curdisy,courtesy
curdle,*,ed,ling,COAGULATING

cure,*,ed,ring,rative,rable,GET BACK TO EQUILIBRIUM/ HEALTHY STATE (or see curry)
cureen,careen
cureer,career
curege,courage
curekt,correct
curekulum,curriculum
curency,currency
curensy,currency
curent,currant / current
cureosedy,curiosity
cureosity,curiosity
cures,cure(s) / care(s) / caress
curess,caress
cureur,courier
cureus,curious
cureusol,creosol
curf,curve
curfew,*,A TIME TO BE OFF THE STREETS
curfu,curfew
curi,curry
curiculum,curriculum
curier,courier
curige,courage
curiosity,ties,ACT OF BEING CURIOUS
curious,sly,sness,INQUISITIVE, QUESTIONING "prefixes: in"
curiqiulum,curriculum
curl,*,led,ling,ler,ly,A TWIST, LOOP, RINGLET "prefixes: un"
curnol,colonel / kernel
curnul,colonel / kernel
curoberate,corroborate
curoborate,corroborate
curode,corrode
curogen,corrode(osion)
curogun,corrode(osion)
curojin,corrode(osion)
curosef,corrode(osive)
curoshen,corrode(osion)
curotion,corrode(osion)
curoty,karate
curowse,carouse

currant,FRUIT, BERRY (or see current)
currency,cies,MONEY
current,*,tly,tness,AS OF NOW IN TIME, FLOWING, HOW WATER/ AIR CARRIES ITSELF (or see currant) "prefixes: in/ re/ under"
curriculum,*,lar,LEARNING COURSES
curry,rried,rric,SPICE
cursash,corsage
curse,ed,sing,edness,SWEAR
cursive,ely,FLOWING HAND WRITING
curtail,lment,SHORTEN
curtain,*,TEMPORARY DIVIDER, CLOTH PROTECTION
curtale,curtail
curten,curtain
curtesy,courtesy
curteus,courteous
curtsy,sies,sied,ying,FEMALE BOW TO AUDIENCE
curtul,curdle
curuge,courage
curvature,*,PROFILE OF SHAPE
curve,*,ed,ving,vature,BEND WITH NO ANGLES "prefixes: in/ up/ re"
curvechure,curvature
cury,curry
cus,cuss
cusen,cousin
cuset,cassette
cushen,cushion
cushion,*,ned,ning,PADDING TO SOFTEN, FORM OF PROTECTION
cusin,cousin
cusp,*,pid,pidate,pidated,pidation,INTERSECTION OF TWO ARCS/ CURVES/ POINTS
cuspid,*,dal,dated,TOOTH "prefixes: bi"
cuss,sses,ssed,ssing,ssedly,ssedness,sser,TO CURSE
custard,*,DESSERTS
custedy,custody
custodian,*,al,nship,GUARDIAN
custody,dies,dial,dian,UNDER CARE OF GUARDIAN, IMPRISONED
custom,*,mable,mize,TRADITION, HABIT "prefixes: ac"
customary,ries,rily,riness,ROUTINE, TRADITIONALLY
customer,*,CLIENT, PURCHASER

customize, *, ed, zing, zation. INDIVIDUAL SHAPE/ DESIGN FOR DESIRED RESULTS
cut, *, tter, tting, CAUSE SEPARATION (or see cud/ cute) "prefixes: in/ over/ un/ under/ upper"
catastrufe, catastrophe
cute, er, test, tie, APPEALING TO THE EYE, SHREWD
cutev, could've
cuth, couth
cuticle, *, AROUND NAILS AND CELLS
cutlary, cutlery
cutlery, CUTTING TOOL, KNIVES
cutov, could've
cutukle, cuticle
cutv, could've
cuvenent, covenant
cuver, cover
cuvit, covet
cuvridge, coverage
cuwiat, quiet
cuzen, cousin
cuzn, cousin
cwuzene, cuisine
cyanide, ELEMENT FOR POISON/ EXTRACTING GOLD
cybernetics, STUDY OF COMMUNICATIONS SYSTEMS
cyborg, *, HUMAN MODIFIED INTO PARTIAL ROBOT
cycle, *, ed, ling, REPEATING INTERVALS, A COURSE OF EVENTS, REVOLUTIONS "prefixes: bi/ en/ re"
cyclist, *, THOSE WHO RIDE TWO-WHEELED BIKES
cyclone, *, nic, nal, nically, CONICAL SHAPED WIND STORM
cylanoid, solenoid
cylinder, *, dric, drical, drically, drically, GEOMETRIC SHAPE WHICH MAY BE MOBILE OR STATIONERY
cymbal, *, list, MUSICAL INSTRUMENT (or see symbol)
cympathetic, sympathetic
cympathy, sympathy
cynic, *, cal, cally, calness, cism, DISBELIEVER
cynical, lly, lness, BEING A DISBELIEVER
cyst, tic, SACK OF FLUID "prefixes: en"
cyt, PREFIX INDICATING 'CELL' MOST OFTEN MODIFIES THE WORD
cyto, PREFIX INDICATING 'CELL' MOST OFTEN MODIFIES THE WORD

czar, *, RULER OF PEOPLE
da, day / they
dab, *, bbed, bbing, bber, BLOT/ DIP/ BARELY TOUCH
dabate, debate
dabble, *, ed, ling, er, PARTICIPATE WITHOUT SERIOUS COMMITMENT
dabekable, despicable
dabelatate, debilitate
dabilutate, debilitate
dable, dabble
dabre, debris
dacend, descend / dissent / descent / decent
daciduous, deciduous
dacind, descend / dissent / descent / decent
daclare, declare
dacree, decree
dacrepit, decrepit
dacury, daiquiri
dad, *, ddy, ddies, TERM FOR 'FATHER' (or see that/ date/ they'd)
dada, data
dadu, data
dadukt, deduct
dadur, daughter
daduse, deduce
dae, day
daedy, deity
dafalt, default
dafeet, defeat
dafenative, definitive
dafensable, defensible
dafense, defense
dafeshansy, deficiency
daffy, ffily, ffiness, BEING SILLY
dafiants, defiance
dafide, divide
dafie, defy / daffy
dafiense, defiance
dafinative, definitive
dafindant, defendant
dafine, define
dafinse, defense
dafinsible, defensible

dafisable, divisible
dafishantsy, deficiency
dafishensy, deficiency
dafishent, deficient
dafisubilety, divisible(bility)
dafoleate, defoliate
daform, deform
dafraust, defrost
dafray, defray
dafrod, defraud
dafumation, defamation
dafunkt, defunct
dafur, defer
dafuze, diffuse
dafy, defy / daffy
dagavoo, deja vu
dager, dagger
dagger, *, SHARP INSTRUMENT
dagree, degree
dai, die / day / dye
daiabetic, diabetic
daiabitis, diabetes
daiabolical, diabolical
daiafram, diaphragm
daiagram, diagram
daialect, dialect
daialog, dialogue
daiameder, diameter
daiari, diary
daiaria, diarrhea
daic, dyke
daidy, deity
daiegnous, diagnose
daiegnousis, diagnosis
daier, dire
daigres, digress
daijeschon, digestion
daijest, digest
dail, dial
daileit, dilate
dailleschon, digestion
daillest, digest
dailut, dilute

daily, lies, EVERY DAY (or see dally/ dale)
daim, dime
daimend, diamond
daimond, diamond
dain, dine
dainamic, dynamic
dainasti, dynasty
dainet, dinette
dainosor, dinosaur
dainoumait, dynamite
dainty, tily, tiness, FRAGILE, DELICATE
daiol, dial
daiper, diaper
daiquiri, *, MIXED RUM DRINK
dair, dare
dairy, ries, WHERE MILK IS
dairyar, derriere
dais, dice
daisect, dissect
daisy, sies, A FLOWER
daity, deity
daiv, dive
daivershon, diversion
daiversiti, diversity
daivert, divert
daiyestion, digestion
dajavu, deja vu
dakary, daiquiri
daklare, declare
dakline, decline
dakorate, decorate(tion)
dakrate, decorate(tion)
dakree, decree
dakrepit, decrepit
dakury, daiquiri
dal, dale / dowel / doll / dole / they'll
dalar, dollar
dalay, delay
dale,*, VALLEY (or see daily/ dalles/ dell/ dolly)
daleburite, deliberate
dalectable, delectable
dalema, dilemma
dalenkwent, delinquent

dalenquent, delinquent
daler, dollar
dalereus, delirious
daleshus, delicious
dalete, delete
dalfan, dolphin
dali, dolly
daliberate, deliberate
dalima, dilemma
dalinquent, delinquent
dalishus, delicious
dalite, delight / daylight
daliver, deliver
dalles, SHALLOW RIVER ROCK BOTTOM WITH RAPIDS (or see dowel/ doll)
dally, llies, llied, llying, TO DABBLE IN, NOT SERIOUS (or see dale/ daily/ dolly)
daloot, dilute
dalugen, delusion / dilute(tion)
daluks, deluxe
dalushen, delusion / dilute(tion)
dalute, dilute
daluxe, deluxe
daly, daily / dally / dale
dam,*, mmed, mming, BARRIER AGAINST WATER (or see damn)
damage,*, ed, ging, TO HARM/ ALTER NEGATIVELY
damall, damage
damand, demand
dameg, damage
damenish, diminish
dameno, domino
damenor, demeanor
damenshen, dimension
damented, demented
damention, dimension
damenyen, dominion
damestic, domestic
damig, damage
daminish, diminish
damino, domino
daminyun, dominion
damize, demise

damn, ned, ning, nable, nation, EXPRESSION OF FRUSTRATION (or see dam)
damolish, demolish
damonik, demon(ic)
damp, per, pest, MOIST "prefixes: un"
dampen,*, ned, ning, ner, TO MOISTEN
damper,*, CONTROLS FLOW
dampin, dampen
dampun, dampen
dampur, damper
damsel,*, YOUNG WOMAN
damsul, damsel
damug, damage
damzul, damsel
dan, then / than
danc, dank
dance,*, ed, cing, er, TO BODILY MOVE TO MUSIC
dancher, danger
dandreff, dandruff
dandruff, FLAKEY SKIN ON SCALP
danger,*, rous, rously, rousness, BEWARE OF IMMINENT HARM "prefixes: en"
dangle,*, er, ling, ly, TO SWING FREELY
dangul, dangle
danjur, danger
dank, kly, kness, UNPLEASANTLY DAMP
danller, danger
danominashun, denomination
danote, denote
danse, dance
dante, dainty
danty, dainty
danyer, danger
daoderant, deoderant
daoderize, deoderize
daparsher, departure
dapart, depart
dapartment, department
daparture, departure
dapend, depend
dapikt, depict
dapind, depend
dapindant, dependant / dependent

dapindence, dependence
dapleshin, depletion
daplete, deplete
daploma, diploma
daplomacy, diplomacy
daplorable, deplorable
daplore, deplore
daport, deport
dapose, depose
daposit, deposit
dapresheate, depreciate
dapreshen, depression
dapress, depress
daprive, deprive
darbe, darby
darbies, HANDCUFFS
darby, bies, PLASTERER'S TOOL
darc, dark
dare, *, ed, ring, ringly, ringness, HAVE COURAGE TO CHALLENGE (or see dairy)
dareair, derriere
darear, derriere
darect, direct
darection, direction
darectory, directory
darekshun, direction
darektory, directory
darelik, derelict
darevutive, derivative
darier, derriere
darivadev, derivative
darivative, derivative
darive, derive
dark, *, ker, kest, ken, kened, kness, OPPOSITE OF LIGHT "prefixes: semi"
darling, *, gly, gness, SOMEONE ENDEARING/ BELOVED
darn, TO SEW, SHORT FOR "OH, TOO BAD..."
dart, *, ted, ting, OF SPORT, MOVE WITH QUICK SPEED
darulik, derelict
dary, dairy
das, day(s) / daze / that(s)
dasal, dazzle
dasbikable, despicable

dasbite, despite
dasblay, display
dasburse, disperse / disburse
dascrepshun, description
dasdrakt, distract
dasdruction, destruction
dasdrust, distrust
dase, daisy / daze
dasease, decease / disease
daseet, deceit
daseeve, deceive
dasegin, decision
dasel, dazzle
dasember, december
dasenagrate, disintegrate
dasend, descend / dissent / descent / decent
dasendent, descendant
dasenshen, dissension / descension
dasent, dissent / descent / decent / descend
dasentugrate, disintegrate
daservise, disservice
dasesd, decease(d) / disease(d)
dasese, decease / disease
daset, deceit
dasetful, deceit(ful)
daseve, deceive
dash, hes, hed, hing, SMALL AMOUNT OF, QUICKLY IN SHORT TIME, TEXT TYPE
dasidewus, deciduous
dasifur, decipher
dasigen, decision
dasijen, decision
dasile, docile
dasimbur, december
dasinagrate, disintegrate
dasind, descend / dissent / descent / decent
dasinshen, dissension / descension
dasinshent, dissent(ient)
dasint, dissent / descent / decent / descend
dasipher, decipher
dasiple, disciple
daskreptef, descriptive
daskripshen, description

daskwalefy, disqualify
dasmiss, dismiss
dasosheate, dissociate
daspare, despair
daspekable, despicable
daspense, dispense
daspensible, dispensable
dasperse, disperse / disburse
daspikable, despicable
daspite, despite
daspize, despise
dasplay, display
daspondent, despondent
daspose, dispose
daspute, dispute
dasrebutuble, disreputable
dasrobe, disrobe
dastardly, dliness, COWARDLY
dasteengwish, distinguish
dastengwesh, distinguish
dastenkt, distinct
dastill, distill
dastingwish, distinguish
dastirdly, dastardly
dastort, distort
dastract, distract
dastress, distress
dastroy, destroy
dasturb, disturb
dasturdly, dastardly
dasul, dazzle
dasy, daisy
dat, date / that / dot
data, FACTS, INFORMATION
dataunt, detente
date, *, ed, ting, TIME REFERENCE, A SOCIAL OUTING WITH ANOTHER, A FRUIT "prefixes: up"
detective, detective
datekt, detect
datektif, detective
datektor, detector
datenshin, detention
dater, daughter

daterant,deterrent
datereate,deteriorate
daterent,deterrent
datereorate,deteriorate
datergent,detergent
determinent,determine(nt)
datont,detente
datu,data
daturgent,detergent
daturjent,detergent
daturmen,determine
daturmenashen,determination
daturmnent,determine(nt)
daubt,doubt
dauder,daughter
daug,dog
daughter,*,, FEMALE BORN/ LEGALLY ENDOWED TO MOTHER/ FATHER
daul,dowel / doll
daule,dolly
daulfen,dolphin
daulur,dollar
daun,don't / daunt / don(nned) / dawn(ed) / down
daunt,*,, ted,ting,ter,tingly,tless,tlessness,MAKE SOMEONE FEEL DISCOURAGED/UNSURE (or see don't/ don(nned)/ dawn(ed)) "prefixes: un"
daus,douse / dowse
dausand,thousand
dausil,docile
daut,doubt
dauter,daughter
dautful,doubt(ful)
dav,they've
davegen,division
davejin,division
davelop,develop
daversidy,diversity
daversudy,diversity
davert,divert
davesubility,divisible(bility)
davide,divide
davigen,division
davine,divine

davisable,divisible
davision,division
davize,device
davoid,devoid
davorse,divorce
davoshen,devotion
davout,devout
davurt,divert
davurzade,diversity
dawn,*,, ned,ning,MORNING DAYBREAK (or see don/ down)
dawrekt,direct
daws,douse / dowse
day,*, SUNRISE TO SUNRISE (or see daze)
dayabetic,diabetic
dayabitis,diabetes
dayabolicol,diabolical
dayagnous,diagnose
dayagnousis,diagnosis
dayagonal,diagonal
dayagram,diagram
dayagrom,diaphragm
dayalect,dialect
dayalog,dialogue
dayameter,diameter
dayari,diary
dayaria,diarrhea
dayede,deity
dayer,dire
daying,dying
dayity,deity
dayjavue,deja vu
daylight, LIGHT IN THE DAY
daynamic,dynamic
daynesti,dynasty
daynet,dinette
daynomait,dynamite
daynosor,dinosaur
dayol,dial
dayper,diaper
daytont,detente
daze,ed,NOT OF CLEAR THINKING, CONFUSED (or see daisy/ day(s))

dazeese,disease / daisy(s)
dazel,dazzle
dazzle,*,, ed,ling,INFLUENCE BY UNUSUAL MEASURES
dcline, decline
de,PREFIX INDICATING 'AWAY FROM/ DOWN FROM/ REVERSE/ NEGATIVE' MOST OFTEN MODIFIES THE WORD (or see the/ thee/ they)
deacon,*,, ness,nry,nries,OFFICIAL OF A CHURCH "prefixes: sub"
deactivate,*,, ed,ting,tion,tor,STOP ACTION, DISSOLVE
deactovate,deactivate
dead,dly,dlier,dliest,den,dens,dened,dening,dener, PAST TENSE FOR THE WORD 'DIE', NO LONGER ALIVE/ FUNCTIONAL (or see deed/ did) "prefixes: un"
deaden,*,, ner,ning,ner,TO SEEM DEAD, NUMB (or see did(n't)
deadleist,dead(liest)
deaf,fen,fening,feningly,fness,fly,LOSS OF THE ABILITY TO HEAR
deakon,deacon
deaktevat,deactivate
deaktuvate,deactivate
deal,*,, ler,ling,dealt,ARRANGEMENT BETWEEN PEOPLE, DO IN CARD GAME (or see dell/ dill)
dealed,dealt
dealt,PAST TENSE FOR THE WORD 'DEAL'
deam,deem
dean,*,, HEAD OF FORMAL GROUP (or see den)
deanky,dinky
deap,deep
dear,rly,rmess,rie,HEARTFELT (or see deer)
death,hless,hly,WHEN THE SPIRIT LEAVES THE BODY
debach,debauch
debasition,deposition
debate,*,, ed,ting,ARGUE FACTS
debauch,hes,hed,hing,hment,hery,heries,CORRUPT, CHANGED FROM ORIGINAL DIRECTION
debauchury,debauch(ery)
debazishen,deposition
debelatate,debilitate
debeit,debate
debelutat,debilitate

debenar, debonair
deber, deburr
debet, debit
debilitate, *, ed, ting, tion, tive, NOT UP TO PAR, WEAKEN
debinar, debonair
debir, deburr
debisition, deposition
debit, *, ted, ting, A DEBT OWING
debizeshen, deposition
debloma, diploma
deblomusy, diplomacy
debo, depot
deboch, debauch
debochury, debauch(ery)
debonair, CHARMING, LIKABLE, AIR OF CLASS
deboner, debonair
debosition, deposition
debotch, debauch
debozeshen, deposition
debozishen, deposition
debre, debris / deburr
debri, debris
debrief, *, fed, fing, fings, REPORT IN AFTER MISSION/ EVENT
debris, GARBAGE, RUBBISH
debry, debris
debt, *, tor, IN THE STATE OF OWING TO ANOTHER
debth, depth
debtor, ONE WHO OWES ANOTHER (or see detour/ deter)
debude, deputy
debunair, debonair
debunar, debonair
debunk, *, ked, king, ker, MAKE UNTRUE, PROVE FALSE
deburr, *, rred, rring, REMOVE BURRS/ ROUGH EDGES
debut, *, ted, ting, FIRST SHOWING TO THE PUBLIC (or see debit)
debutize, deputize
debuty, deputy
dec, PREFIX INDICATING 'TEN' MOST OFTEN MODIFIES THE WORD (or see deck)
deca, PREFIX INDICATING 'TEN' MOST OFTEN MODIFIES THE WORD (or see deck)

decade, *, TEN YEARS (or see decay(ed))
decadence, ncy, ON THE DECLINE/ DETERIORATE
decadent, tly, ON THE DECLINE/ DETERIORATE
decal, *, IMAGE OF PICTURE OR WORDS
decanter, *, VESSEL FOR STORAGE
decapitate, *, ed, ting, tion, tor, LOSS OF HEAD
decarate, decorate(tion)
decate, decade / decay(ed)
decay, *, yed, ying, DETERIORATE, CHANGE FROM ONE FORM TO ANOTHER
decease, *, ed, TO PASS AWAY, DEPART FROM THIS PHYSICAL REALITY (or see disease) "prefixes: pre"
decedent, *, PAST TENSE FOR THE WORD 'DECEASED' (or see decedent)
deceit, tful, tfully, tfulness, TO PURPOSELY MISLEAD
deceive, *, ed, ving, vingly, vable, vably, vableness, vability, TO PURPOSELY MISLEAD "prefixes: un"
decelerate, *, ed, ting, tion, tor, TO DECREASE SPEED
december, A MONTH OF THE YEAR (ENGLISH)
decency, cies, WHAT'S PROPER
decend, descend / decent
decension, descension
decent, tly, tness, RESPECTABLE (or see descent/ dissent)
decentralize, *, ed, zing, zation, TAKE FROM A FEW AND GIVE TO MANY, TO SHARE AROUND
deception, *, ive, ively, iveness, THE ACT OF PURPOSELY MISLEADING "prefixes: un"
deceptive, ely, eness, THE ACT OF PURPOSELY MISLEADING
decerate, decorate
dech, ditch
dechevled, dishevel(ed)
dechonary, dictionary
deci, PREFIX INDICATING 'TENTH' MOST OFTEN MODIFIES THE WORD
decibel, *, MEASUREMENT OF SOUND WAVES
decide, *, ed, ding, edly, er, ision, FORM A CONCLUSION, PICK AN OPTION "prefixes: un"
deciduous, SHEDS ITS LEAVES IN THE FALL "prefixes: in"
decifur, decipher
decimal, *, lize, lized, lizing, A POINT TO SEPARATE NUMBERS
decimate, *, ed, ting, TO DESTROY, KILL ONE IN TEN

decimber, december
decimeit, decimate
decind, descend / dissent / descent / decent
decint, descent / decent / dissent / descend
decintralize, decentralize
decipher, *, red, ring, rable, rer, rment, TO DECODE "prefixes: in"
decision, *, ive, ively, iveness, FINAL CONCLUSION "prefixes: in"
deck, *, ked, king, OUTDOOR FLOOR
deckorus, decorous
deckrotive, decorative
deckstarety, dexterity
decksterity, dexterity
deckstrus, dexterous
declaration, *, ive, tory, ANNOUNCEMENT, MAKE A STATEMENT
declare, *, ed, ring, rable, edly, ration, rations, rative, rator, ratory, ratorily, TO STATE/ ANNOUNCE "prefixes: un"
declaration, declaration
decline, *, ed, ning, nation, DOWNWARD BEND/ SLOPE
decode, *, ed, ding, dable, er, DECAY, TO TRANSFORM TO BASIC ELEMENTS
decompose, *, ed, sing, sition, DECAY, TO TRANSFORM TO BASIC ELEMENTS
decon, deacon
decorashun, decoration
decorate, *, ed, ting, tor, tion, tive, ADORN, ORNAMENTAL "prefixes: re"
decoration, ADORNMENT, ORNAMENTAL
decorative, ely, eness, ADORNMENT, ORNAMENTAL
decoreishon, decoration
decoreit, decorate
decorous, sly, sness, COMPATIBLE/ APPROPRIATE, DIGNIFIED "prefixes: in"
decorum, COMPATIBLE/ APPROPRIATE, MATCHES "prefixes: in"
decoy, *, A FAKE TO FOOL OR MISLEAD
decradive, decorative
decrative, decorative
decrease, *, ed, sing, BECOME LESS THAN THE ORIGINAL "prefixes: non"

decree,*,ed,eeing,eeable,JUDICIAL/ AUTHORITATIVE DECISION
decrepit,tly,tude,tate,tated,tating,tation,tness,WEAK/ WORN/ WASTED
decrese,decrease
decritive,decorative
decrous,decorous
decrutive,decorative
decsterity,dexterity
decteishon,dictation
decteit,dictate
decudens,decadence
decudent,decedent / decadent
decompose,decompose
decurate,decorate(tion)
ded,dead / deed / did
dedakashun,dedication
dedakate,dedicate
dedar,debtor
deden,didn't / den / deaden
dedicate,*,ed,ting,tion,tory,tive,APPROPRIATE,DEVOTE
dedication,*,nal,APPROPRIATE,DEVOTE
dedikeishon,dedication
dedikeit,dedicate
dedin,deaden
dedinate,detonate
dediqueishon,dedication
dediqueit,dedicate
dedir,debtor
dedle,dead(ly)
dedleist,dead(liest)
dedleur,dead(lier)
dedly,dead(ly)
dedlyest,dead(liest)
dednate,detonate
dedo,ditto
dedonate,detonate
dedor,debtor
dedriment,detriment
dedrument,detriment
deduce,*,ed,cing,DRAW CONCLUSION FROM EVIDENCE
deduct,*,ted,ting,tible,tibilty,tion,tive,SUBTRACT, TAKE AWAY "prefixes: non"

dedukashun,dedication
dedukate,dedicate
dedukn,deaden
deed,*,ded,AN ACT/ CONTRACT/ AGREEMENT (or see dead) "prefixes: mis"
deel,deal
deeled,dealt
deem,*,med,JUDGED/ BELIEVED/ THOUGHT
deen,dean / den
deenge,dinghy / dingy
deenky,dinky
deep,per,pest,ply,pen,penly,pened,pness,BEYOND THE SURFACE,GREAT IN DIMENSION
deer,ANIMAL (or see dear)
def,deaf / thief / thieve
deface,*,ed,cing,eable,ement,er,ALTER THE FACE/ FRONT OF
defain,define
defakate,defecate
defalt,default
defamation,tory,INTENT TO INJURE ANOTHER'S CHARACTER
defame,*,ed,ming,mation,matory,er,INTENT TO INJURE ANOTHER'S CHARACTER
defanishun,definition
defanit,definite
defasit,deficit
defastate,devastate
default,*,ted,ting,ter,LEGALLY FAILING TO ANSWER, FAIL AN AGREEMENT
defayans,defiance
defeat,*,ted,ting,tism,tist,OVERCOME, OVERTHROW
defecate,*,ed,ting,tion,tor,CLEAR THE BOWELS
defechant,deficient
defect,*,ted,ting,tion,tor,NOT USEFUL AS INTENDED,MARRED "prefixes: in"
defective,ely,eness,NOT USEFUL AS INTENDED
defector,*,ABANDON NATIVE STATE/ COUNTRY
defecult,difficult
defekate,defecate
defekeit,defecate
defekt,defect
defektive,defective

defektor,defector
defemation,defamation
defend,*,ded,ding,PROTECT
defendant,*,ONE WHO DEFENDS/ PROTECTS AGAINST
defenet,definite
defenetly,definite(ly)
defenishun,definition
defense,*,sive,eless,elessly,elessness,PROTECT AGAINST ATTACK
defensible,eness,bility,ly,ABLE TO DEFEND "prefixes: in"
defenutef,definitive
defequeit,defecate
defer,*,rred,rring,rrable,rence,rent,rrer,rential,rral, rment,DELAY,POST-PONE,YIELD TO ANOTHER (or see differ)
deferens,difference
deferensheate,differentiate
deferent,different
deferentiate,differentiate
defesit,deficit
defews,diffuse
defi,defy
defiance,nt,ntly,CHALLENGE,RESIST,OPPOSE
deficate,defecate
deficiency,cies,SHORT OF EXPECTATIONS/ NEEDS, NOT ENOUGH
deficient,tly,ncy,LESS THAN EXPECTED/ NEEDED
deficit,*,OWE MORE THAN WHAT'S AVAILABLE
deficult,difficult
defide,divide
defients,defiance
defikate,defecate
defimation,defamation
defind,defend
defindant,defendant
define,*,ed,ning,SET BOUNDARIES/ RULES/ BORDERS "prefixes: in/ re"
defineshun,definition
definet,definite
definetion,definition
definetly,definite(ly)
definite,ely,eness,tive,FOR SURE,ABSOLUTELY

definition,*,nal,STATEMENT DESCRIBING BOUNDARIES/ RULES/ BORDERS
definitive,ely,eness,FOR CERTAIN,FINAL
definute,definite
defir,defer / differ
defishant,deficient
defishantsy,deficiency
defisit,deficit
defistate,devastate
defius,diffuse
deflashun,deflate(tion)
deflate,*,ed,ting,tion,tionary,tionist,REMOVE VOLUME/ FULLNESS,REDUCE
deflect,*,ted,ting,tive,tor,tion,RICHOCHET OFF/ ALTER COURSE/ DIRECTION OF SOMETHING
defleit,deflate
defoleate,defoliate
defoliate,*,ed,ting,tion,tor,LOSS OF LEAVES FROM PLANT
deforestation,*,REMOVE TREES FROM FOREST
deforistashun,deforestatior
deform,*,med,ming,mation,medly,medness,mity,OF UNUSUAL/ ABNORMAL FORM
deforustashin,deforestatior
defostate,devastate
defoulieit,defoliate
defraud,*,ded,ding,der,dation,dment,ROB OF RIGHTS/ PROPERTY
defraust,defrost
defray,*,yed,ying,yer,yal,yment,yable,MONETARY COMPENSATION/ ARRANGEMENT
defrense,difference
defrent,different
defrint,different
defrod,defraud
defrost,*,ted,ting,ter,REMOVE FROST/ ICE
defruns,difference
defukate,defecate
defumashun,defamation
defunct,NO LONGER IN USE
defuneshun,definition
defunetle,definite(ly)
defunishun,definition

defunit,definite
defur,defer / differ
defurinse,difference
defurns,difference
defuse,diffuse
defusit,deficit
defustate,devastate
defuze,diffuse
defy,fies,fied,ying,fier,TO RESIST/ DARE/ CHALLENGE
deg,dig
degekt,deject
degenerate,*,ed,ting,tive,acy,ely,eness,BECOME LESS, OPPOSITE OF GETTING BETTER
degenerate,degenerate
degit,digit
degradashen,degrade(dation)
degrade,*,ed,ding,dable,dability,dation,LOWER/ BREAK DOWN IN RANK/ STANDARDS/ GRADE "prefixes: bio"
degree,*,MEASUREMENT OF STANDARD/ ANGLES, SUM OF
degression,ive,LOWERING, DECREASING (or see digress(ion))
degrudashen,degrade(dation)
dehidrate,dehydrate
dehumanize,*,ed,zing,zation,REMOVE HEALTHY HUMAN CHARACTERISTICS
dehumidify,fies,fied,fying,fier,fication,REMOVE MOISTURE FROM THE AIR
dehydrate,*,ed,ting,tion,tor,REMOVE MOISTURE FROM
dei,day
deici,dicey
deida,data
deif,they've
deili,daily
deillavu,deja vu
deinti,dainty
deis,daze
deishavu,deja vu
deisi,dicey
deit,date
deita,data

deity,ties,SUPREME BEING
deiv,they've
deja vu,TWO WORDS (deja vu),SEEN BEFORE
deject,*,ted,ting,tedly,tedness,tion,DISPIRIT, DISCOURAGE
dejenurate,degenerate
dejinurate,degenerate
dejit,digit
dek,deck
deka,PREFIX INDICATING 'TEN' MOST OFTEN MODIFIES THE WORD (or see deck)
dekad,decay(ed) / decade
dekadins,decadence
dekadint,decedent / decadent
dekal,decal
dekantur,decanter
dekaputate,decapitate
dekay,decay
dekeid,decade
deken,deacon
dekerashun,decoration
dekerate,decorate
dekin,deacon
deklare,declare
dekleration,declaration
dekline,decline
deklurashun,declaration
dekodable,decode(dable)
dekode,decode
dekompose,decompose
dekon,deacon
dekorashun,decoration
dekorate,decorate(tion) / decorate
dekorative,decorative
dekorus,decorous
dekoy,decoy
dekradashen,degrade(dation)
dekratev,decorate(tion) / decorative
dekrative,decorative
dekree,decree
dekrepit,decrepit
dekrese,decrease
dekrous,decorous

dekrudev, decorative
dekrus, decorous
dekrutive, decorative
deksderady, dexterity
deksdrus, dexterous
dekshunare, dictionary
deksterudy, dexterity
dekstrus, dexterous
dektion, diction
dekudens, decadence
dekudent, decedent / decadent
dekumpose, decompose
dekun, deacon
dekurashun, decoration
dekurater, decorate(tor)
del, deal / dell / dill
delacatesen, delicatessen
delacit, delicate
delacusy, delicacy
delagation, delegation
delait, delight
delakatesen, delicatessen
delaket, delicate
delay, *, yed, ying, yer, DETAIN, HINDER, PROLONG
deld, dealt
dele, deli
deleburant, deliberate
delecacy, delicacy
delectable, *, eness, bility, ly, HIGHLY PLEASURABLE
deled, dealt
delegate, *, ed, ting, tion, tor, ee, able, APPOINT AS REPRESENTATIVE, ENTRUST "prefixes: non"
delegation, *, TO DELEGATE, ASSEMBLY OF PEOPLE "prefixes: non"
delegeishon, delegation
delekt, delict
delenkwent, delinquent
delenquent, delinquent
deler, deal(er)
delereus, delirious
delete, *, ed, ting, tion, REMOVE/ UNDO "prefixes: un"
deleverens, deliverance
delf, delve

deli, *, A DELICATESSEN, STORE WITH VARIETY OF PREPARED FOODS/ MEATS
deliberate, *, ed, ting, eness, ely, tion, PURPOSEFUL, CAREFULLY THOUGHT OUT "prefixes: un"
deliburate, deliberate
delicacy, cies, OF REFINED QUALITY IN TASTE "prefixes: in"
delicate, *, ely, eness, FRAGILE, FINE QUALITY, CHOICE "prefixes: in"
delicatessen, *, STORE WITH VARIETY OF PREPARED FOODS/ MEATS
delicious, sly, sness, EXQUISITE TASTE, HAPPY TO TASTE BUDS
deligation, delegation
delight, *, ted, ting, tful, tedly, tfully, tfulness, PROVIDE GREAT SATISFACTION (or see daylight)
delikatesen, delicatessen
deliket, delicate
delinquent, tly, ncy, ncies, FAILURE TO SATISFY AGREEMENT ON TIME
deliquet, delicate
delir, deal(er)
delirious, sly, sness, IRRATIONAL BEHAVIOR
delishus, delicious
delite, delight / daylight
deliver, *, red, ring, ry, rable, rability, rer, rance, TO SEND/ PRESENT ITEMS SUCH AS GOODS/ THOUGHTS/ ARTICLES
deliverance, *, TO BE RESCUED, AN ANNOUNCEMENT
dell, A HOLLOW/ VALLEY (or see deal/ dill)
deloot, dilute
delor, deal(er)
delt, dealt
delugashun, delegation
delugen, delusion / dilute(tion)
delukatesen, delicatessen
delukit, delicate
deluks, deluxe
delukusy, delicacy
delur, deal(er)
delusion, nal, PAST TENSE FOR THE WORD 'DELUDE', BEING MISLED, HAVING FALSE IMPRESSION
delute, dilute

deluxe, FINEST QUALITY
delve, *, ed, ving, TO BURY/ DIG INTO
dem, deem / dim / them / they
demacrasy, democracy
demacrat, democrat
demagogue, *, guery, gic, gical, LEADER WHO USES POPULAR EMOTIONS
demagrafy, demography
demakratic, democratic
demalishun, demolition
demand, *, ded, ding, COMMAND/ INSIST ON FULFILLMENT OF DESIRES "prefixes: un"
demarcation, *, SETTING BOUNDARIES, ESTABLISHING GUIDELINES
demarkashun, demarcation
demble, dimple
demean, *, ned, ning, HUMILIATE
demeanor, CONCERNING BEHAVIOR/ CONDUCT "prefixes: mis"
demenor, demeanor
demented, CRAZY, UNPOPULAR BEHAVIOR/ THOUGHTS
demer, dimmer
demestek, domestic
demi, PREFIX INDICATING 'HALF/ PARTLY' MOST OFTEN MODIFIES THE WORD
demigog, demagogue
demikrat, democrat
demilaturise, demilitarize
demilitarize, *, ed, zing, zation, REMOVE MILITARY
demiluturise, demilitarize
demin, demon
deminstrate, demonstrate
demir, dimmer
demise, ed, sing, TRANSFER, PASSED FROM THIS REALITY
demobilize, *, ed, zing, zation, DISARM, DISBAND
democracy, cies, BY AND FOR ALL PEOPLE
democrat, *, ONE IN PARTY WHO WORKS FOR SOCIAL EQUALITY FOR ALL
democratic, ize, ization, PROCESS OF WORKING TOWARDS SOCIAL EQUALITY FOR ALL "prefixes: un"
demography, hic, hical, hically, STATISTICS/ RECORDS OF PUBLIC VITAL INFORMATION
demokrasy, democracy

demokrat,democrat
demokratic,democratic
demokruse,democracy
demolish,hes,hed,hing,ition,DESTROY, RUIN
demolition,*,nist,ACT OF DESTROYING/ RUINING
demon,*,nic,niac,nically,nization,nize,nizes,nized,nizing,nization,nism,MAKE OR APPEAR EVIL
demonek,demon(ic)
demonstrate,*,ed,ting,tion,tive,HOW TO, EXPLAIN CLEARLY/ DELIBERATELY "prefixes: in/ un"
demple,dimple
demugog,demagogue
demuleshin,demolition
demun,demon
demunstrashen,demonstrate(tion)
demunstrate,demonstrate
demur,dimmer
den,*,CONCEALED HIDEOUT, COZY/ TUCKED AWAY PLACE (or see then)
denacher,denature
denaiol,denial
denaturalize,es,ed,zing,zation,REMOVE CITIZENSHIP OR NATURE OF
denature,*,ed,ring,rant,rat on,ROB OF NATURAL COMPOSURE
dencher,denture
dendr,PREFIX INDICATING "TREE" MOST OFTEN MODIFIES THE WORD
dendrait,dendrite
dendri,PREFIX INDICATING "TREE" MOST OFTEN MODIFIES THE WORD
dendrite,*,PATHWAYS OF NEURONS CARRYING IMPULSES IN THE BRAIN
deneichor,denature
deng,ding
denge,dingy / dinghy
dengle,dangle
deni,deny
deniable,lity,ly,REFUSE AS TRUTH, DISAVOW
denial,*,REFUSE, DENY
denil,denial
denim,*,HEAVY COTTON FABRIC
denir,dinner

deniul,denial
denje,dingy
denky,dinky
denomenator,denominator
denomination,*,nal,nally,nalism,ive,tor,SPECIES OF THE WHOLE, SEPARATE BUT SAME
denominator,*,OF FRACTIONS
denote,*,ed,ting,tive,table,tation,tive,tative, DESIGNATED, SYMBOLIZES
dense,er,est,ely,eness,sity,THICK/ COMPACT, CLOSE TOGETHER
density,ties,DEGREE OF MASS/ CONCENTRATION
dent,*,AN IMPRESSION OR HOLLOW, PREFIX INDICATING 'TOOTH' MOST OFTEN MODIFIES THE WORD (or see didn't)
dental,*,OF TEETH
denti,PREFIX INDICATING 'TOOTH' MOST OFTEN MODIFIES THE WORD
dentist,*,try,DOCTOR FOR TEETH
denture,*,rist,ARTIFICIAL TEETH
denum,denim
denur,dinner
deny,nies,nied,ying,nial,NOT ADMIT, WON'T CLAIM "prefixes: un"
deoderant,deodorant
deoderint,deodorant
deoderize,deodorize
deodorant,HIDES ODOR/ SMELLS
deodorize,*,ed,zing,zation,er,REMOVE ODOR/ SMELL
deoksidize,deoxidize
deoksudize,deoxidize
deoxidize,*,ed,zing,REMOVE OXYGEN
dep,deep / dip
deparcher,depart(ure)
deparjur,depart(ure)
deparsher,depart(ure)
depart,*,ted,ting,ture,GO AWAY FROM
departer,depart(ure)
department,*,tal,talize,talizes,talized,talizing,SECTIONS OF THE WHOLE, A SUBSET
departure,*,TO GO AWAY FROM, LEAVE
depazeshen,deposition
depazishen,deposition

depend,*,ded,ding,dable,dably,dability,dant,dent,dence,RELY ON "prefixes: in/ un"
dependant,*,RELATIONSHIP TO OTHER THINGS (or see dependent) "prefixes: in"
dependence,cy,cies,TO NEED/ RELY UPON "prefixes: in"
dependent,*,tly,nce,SUPPORTED BY OTHERS "prefixes: in"
deper,dipper
depewtise,deputize
depict,*,ted,ting,tion,SHAPE/ FORM/ CREATE IMAGE
depir,dipper
depiuti,deputy
deplete,*,ed,ting,tive,table,tability,tion,USE TO THE END, RUNNING OUT OF
depletion,THE ACT OF RUNNING OUT OF
deploma,diploma
deplomacy,diplomacy
deplomat,diplomat
deplorable,ly,bility,eness,LAMENT
deplore,*,ed,ring,ringly,rable,LAMENT
deploy,*,yed,ying,yable,yer,yment,PREPARE TO BE USED/ MAKE USE OF "prefixes: re"
depo,depot
depoortashen,deportation
depor,deep(er)
deporcher,depart(ure)
deport,*,ted,ting,tment,tation,tee,table,BE EXPELLED, SENT FROM COUNTRY
deportation,ACT OF SENDING FROM THE COUNTRY
deportee,*,ONE WHO WAS DEPORTED FROM COUNTRY
depose,*,ed,sing,sal,er,sable,sition,WRITE OR SPEAK UNDER OATH
deposit,*,ted,ting,tor,tories,PLACE SOMETHING OF VALUE INTO SAFEKEEPING "prefixes: non"
deposition,*,STATEMENT UNDER OATH
depot,*,LOADING/ UNLOADING STATION FOR TRANSPORT
depravashen,deprivation
depravation,deprivation
depreciate,*,ed,ting,able,tion,tive,tingly,ESTIMATE OF LOWER VALUE
depresheate,depreciate
depreshen,depression

depresion, depression	derik, derrick	desalinate, *, ed, ting, tion, tor, nize, nizes, nized, nizing, nization, REMOVE SALT FROM
depress, sses, ssed, ssing, ssion, LOWER IN ELEVATION, LOW IN HOPE/ FAITH	derilect, derelict	desalow, disallow
depression, * , A LOW POINT	dering, during / dare(ring)	desalugen, disillusion
deprivation, LACK OF ACCESS TO	**derivative**, *, ely, ion, ional, ROOT/ ORIGIN OF	desalunate, desalinate
deprive, *, ed, ving, vable, val, vation, er, PREVENT FROM HAVING ACCESS TO	**derive**, *, ed, ving, vable, vative, vatively, vation, vational, FROM THE ORIGINAL, DESCENDED FROM	desapashen, dissipate(tion)
depruvashen, deprivation	**derma**, PREFIX INDICATING "SKIN" MOST OFTEN MODIFIES THE WORD	desapate, dissipate
depth, *, A MEASURE DOWNWARDS OR INTO	**dermal**, atitis, mis, CONCERNS THE SKIN "prefixes: endo/ intra/ sub"	desaplen, discipline
depude, deputy	**dermat**, PREFIX INDICATING "SKIN" MOST OFTEN MODIFIES THE WORD	desapoint, disappoint
depudize, deputize	**dermato**, PREFIX INDICATING "SKIN" MOST OFTEN MODIFIES THE WORD	desaprove, disapprove
depur, dipper		desaray, disarray
depusishen, deposition	dermes, dermal(mis)	desarm, disarm
deputize, *, ed, zing, APPOINT AS DEPUTY	dermititus, dermal(atitis)	desarmament, disarmament
deputy, ties, tize, tizes, tized, tizing, AGENT OF THE LAW	dermle, dermal	desaster, disaster
depuzishen, deposition	dermotidus, dermal(atitis)	desatisfaction, dissatisfy(faction)
dequeid, decade	dermul, dermal	desavantage, disadvantage
der, dear / deer / dare / there / they're	dermus, dermal(mis)	desbaleef, disbelief / disbelieve
derable, durable	dermutidis, dermal(atitis)	desband, disband
deracenate, deracinate	derof, thereof	desbar, disbar / despair
deracinate, * , ed, ting, tion, UPROOT, REMOVE FROM NATIVE LAND/ CULTURE/ ENVIRONMENT	**derrick**, *, TOWERLIKE EQUIPMENT WITH A CENTRAL POST	desbaret, desperate
deralik, derelict	**derriere**, *, REAR END, GLUTEUS MAXIMUS MUSCLES	desbatch, dispatch
derapi, therapy	dert, dirt	desbekable, despicable
derasenate, deracinate	derty, dirty	desberit, desperate
derashen, duration	deruble, durable	desbicable, despicable
derasinate, deracinate	derulik, derelict	desbikable, despicable
deration, duration	dery, dairy	desbiret, desperate
derbai, thereby	des, this / these / ditch	desbite, despite
derdee, dirty	desabellity, disability	desblay, display
dere, dairy	desable, disable	desbondent, despondent
derear, derriere	desacord, disaccord	desboret, desperate
derekshen, direction	desacrate, desecrate	desbot, despot
derektury, directory	desadisfacshen, dissatisfy(faction)	desbozul, disposal
derelict, * tion, SOMEONE/ SOMETHING LEFT WITHOUT A GUIDE	desadvantage, disadvantage	desbute, dispute
deress, duress	desafect, disaffect	desbuzishun, disposition
derevative, derivative	desagre, disagree	desc, desk / disk / disc
derfor, therefore / therefor	desaid, decide	descard, discard
deri, dairy	desain, design	descaunt, discount
derible, durable	desainer, designer	**descend**, *, ded, ding, dible, dable, nt, nsion, STEP DOWN FROM, DOWNWARD (or see descent/ decent) "prefixes: con/ un"
deric, derrick	desakord, disaccord	
derier, derriere		

descendant,*,dent,PREVIOUS/ PRIOR TO THE CURRENT GENERATION,IN RELAT ON TO
descension,nal,GO DOWN/ INTO,SINK/ FALL (or see dissension)
descent,*,nsion,PAST TENSE FOR THE WORD "DESCEND",A STEP DOWN (or see decent/ descend)
descerech, discourage
descharge, discharge
descleim, disclaim
desclose, disclose
descontenue, discontinue
descord, discord
descors, discourse
descotek, discotheque
descover, discover
descredit, discredit
descremenate, discriminate
descrepensy, discrepancy
descrete, discreet / discrete
descretion, discretion
describe,*,ed,bing,bable,er,iptively,iptiveness,iptivist,iptivism,EXPLAIN DETAILS OF SOMETHING
descripshen, description
description,*,ive,PROVIDE DETAILS,EXPLAIN
descriptive,*,ely,eness,vist,vism,PROVIDE DETAILS, EXPLAIN
descumfert, discomfort
descurech, discourage
descushen, discussion
descust, disgust
descuver, discover
desdanation, destination
desdane, disdain
desdany, destiny
desdaste, distaste
desdein, disdain
desdent, distant
desdeny, destiny
desdination, destination
desdinduble, distend(sible)
desdindubleshen, distend(nsion)
desdindubletion, distend(nsion)
desdint, distant

desdiny, destiny
desditute, destitute
desdort, distort
desdrabute, distribute
desdrakt, distract
desdrot, distraught
desdruckshen, destruction
desdruktion, destruction
desdrust, distrust
desdunashun, destination
desduny, destiny
desdurb, disturb
desdutute, destitute
desease, disease
deseble, decibel
desecragate, desegregate
desecragation, desegregate(tion)
desecrate,*,ed,ting,er,tor,tion,TO TREAT WHAT'S SACRED TO OTHERS AS UNSACRED
desecrogate, desegregate
desecrogation, desegregate(tion)
desee, dizzy
deseese, decease / disease
deseet, deceit
desefect, disaffect
desegon, decision
desegregate,*,ed,ting,tion,tionist,UNDO RACIAL SEGREGATION
desegrigate, desegregate
desegrugate, desegregate
deselarate, decelerate
deselurate, decelerate
desemate, decimate
desember, december
desemul, decimal
desencion, descension
desend, descend / descent / dissent / decent
desendent, descendant
desenherit, disinherit
desensee, decency
desent, decent / descent
desenter, dissent(er)
desentient, dissent(ient)

desentralise, decentralize
deseepshun, deception
deseption, deception
deseptive, deceptive
desern, discern
desert,*,ted,ting,ter,tification,tion,LAND LACKING LUSH VEGETATION,TO LEAVE WITHOUT PERMISSION (or see dessert) "prefixes: non/ semi/ un"
deserter,*,SOMEONE WHO LEAVES/ ABANDONS WITHOUT PERMISSION
deserve,*,ed,ving,edly,er,REWARD/ PUNISHMENT FOR ACT/ THOUGHT/ DEED "prefixes: un"
deservise, disservice
desesd, decease(d) / disease(d)
deset, deceit
desetful, deceit(ful)
deseve, deceive
desfegure, disfigure
desfigure, disfigure
desfunction, dysfunction
desfunkshen, dysfunction
desgais, disguise
desgard, discard
desgarge, discharge
desgise, disguise
desgoint, disjoint
desgrase, disgrace
desgrechun, discretion
desgretion, discretion
desgruntle, disgruntle
desgruntled, disgruntle(d)
desgurag, discourage
desgus, discus / discuss
desgust, disgust / discuss(ed)
desguys, disguise
desh, dish
desharden, dishearten
desharten, dishearten
deshevel, dishevel
desheveld, dishevel(ed)
deshonest, dishonest
deshonor, dishonor

deshonorable, dishonorable
desibal, decibel
desible, decibel
desicrate, desecrate
desid, decide
desidewus, deciduous
desifer, decipher
design, *, ned, ning, nable, nedly, ner, CREATION OF A MODEL, OUTLINE/ PLAN FOR SOMETHING "prefixes: re/ un"
designate, *, ed, ting, tion, tive, tory, tor, TO ASSIGN/ APPOINT "prefixes: re"
designer, *, ONE WHO CREATES DESIGNS
desijien, decision
desijues, deciduous
desil, diesel
desilat, desolate
desimal, decimal
desimanate, disseminate
desimate, decimate
desimbark, disembark
desimber, december
desincy, decency
desind, descend
desine, design
desiner, designer
desinfect, disinfect
desingage, disengage
desinsee, decency
desinshen, dissension / descension
desint, decent / descent
desintary, dysentery
desintegrate, disintegrate
desinter, dissent(er) / dissent
desintient, dissent(ient)
desintion, dissension / descension
desintralise, decentralize
desinugrate, disintegrate
desipher, decipher
desipul, disciple
desirable, *, bility, eness, ly, LIKE TO HAVE

desire, *, ed, ring, rous, rously, rousness, rable, rability, rableness, rably, A WISH/ WANT/ COMPULSION FOR "prefixes: un"
desirtashen, dissertation
desiruble, desirable
desis, disease / decease
desisd, disease(d) / decease(d)
desisev, decision(ive)
desjoint, disjoint
desk, *, FURNITURE (or see disc/ disk)
deskard, discard
deskerdeus, discourteous
deskerege, discourage
desklame, disclaim
deskonekt, disconnect
deskontenue, discontinue
deskord, discord
deskordeus, discourteous
deskors, discourse
deskover, discover
deskredit, discredit
deskremenate, discriminate
deskrepdef, descriptive
deskrepincy, discrepancy
deskribe, describe
deskripshen, description
deskunekt, disconnect
deskurdeus, discourteous
deskurege, discourage
deskus, discus / discuss
deskushun, discussion
deskust, disgust / discuss(ed)
deskuver, discover
deskwalefy, disqualify
desl, diesel
desleksea, dyslexia
deslexia, dyslexia
deslocate, dislocate
desloch, dislodge
deslodge, dislodge
deslog, dislodge
deslokate, dislocate
desmantul, dismantle

desmanul, dismantle
desmay, dismay
desmei, dismay
desmember, dismember
desmimbur, dismember
desmiss, dismiss
desmount, dismount
desmownt, dismount
desmul, dismal
desobay, disobey
desobedeanse, disobedience
desocheate, dissociate
desociate, dissociate
desolate, ed, ely, eness, tion, er, DESERTED, EMPTY OF
desolenate, desalinate
desolushen, dissolute(tion)
desolute, dissolute
desolve, dissolve
deson, disown
desonent, dissonant
desoner, dishonor
desonerible, dishonorable
desonest, dishonest
desonins, dissonant(nce)
desont, decent / descent
desorder, disorder
desorderly, disorderly
desoreint, disorient
desosheate, dissociate
desoubei, disobey
desoubidience, disobedience
desown, disown
despair, *, red, ring, ringly, DEEPLY TROUBLED, HOPELESS
despais, despise
desparashin, desperation
despare, despair
desparedy, disparity
despatch, dispatch
despense, dispense
despensible, dispensable
desperashun, desperation
desperate, ely, eness, ado, tion, OF FEELING FRANTIC, GIVEN TO HOPELESSNESS

desperation, BEYOND REGARD FOR HOPE
desperit, desperate
desperity, disparity
desperse, disperse / disburse
despicable, eness,ly,bility, BEING WORTHLESS/ NO GOOD
despikable, despicable
despinse, dispense
despinsuble, dispensable
despise, *, ed, sing, sing, sal, sable, sableness, edness, ement, er, VERY LOW OPINION OF, STRONG DISLIKE "prefixes: un"
despit, despite
despite, ed,ting,eful,efully,eous,eously,IN SPITE OF, INSULT, MALICE, ILL INTENT
despiut, dispute
desplas, displace
desplased, displaced(d)
desplay, display
despleis, displace
desplejur, displease(sure)
desplesed, displeased(d)
desplesher, displease(sure)
desplis, displease
despond, *, ded, ding, dingly, dency, dent, SEVERELY DISPIRITED/ DEPRESSED/ HOPELESS
despondent,ncy,tly, SEVERELY DISPIRITED/ DEPRESSED
desposal, disposal
desposeshun, disposition
desposition, disposition
despositive, dispositive
desposuble, disposable
despot, *, tic, tical, tically, tism, ABUSIVE/ TYRANNICAL USE OF POWER
despraporshen, disproporticn
desproportion, disproportion
despurashin, desperation
despurit, desperate
despusishun, disposition
despute, dispute
desputuble, dispute(table)
despuzition, disposition
desqualify, disqualify

desqwalefy, disqualify
desregard, disregard
desrepare, disrepair
desreputable, disreputable
desrespect, disrespect
desrespkt, disrespect
desrigard, disregard
desriper, disrepair
desrobe, disrobe
desrobt, disrupt
desropt, disrupt
desrubshen, disruption
desrubt, disrupt
desrupshen, disruption
desrupt, disrupt
desruption, disruption
dessapate, dissipate
dessapation, dissipate(tion)
dessatisfaction, dissatisfy(faction)
dessemble, dissemble
dessenter, dissent(er)
dessert, *, A TASTY SWEET DISH FOLLOWING MAIN COURSE (or see desert)
dessertation, dissertation
dessimble, dissemble
dessinter, dissent(er)
dessirtashen, dissertation
dessociate, dissociate
dessolute, dissolute
dessolution, dissolute(tion)
destanashin, destination
destanation, destination
destance, distance
destane, disdain
destany, destiny
destaste, distaste
destemper, distemper
desten, distend / destine
destenation, destination
desteni, destiny
destenkt, distinct
destense, distance
destenshen, distend(nsion)

destent, distant
destention, distend(nsion)
desterb, disturb
destill, distill
destimper, distemper
destinachen, destination
destination, *, ARRIVAL POINT "prefixes: pre"
destinct, distinct
destinduble, distend(sible)
destine, *, ned,ning,ny, nation, FATE, PREORDAINED, SPECIFIC OUTCOME (or see destiny) "prefixes: pre"
destint, distant
destiny, nies, FATE, OVERALL ARRIVAL POINT
destitute, *, eness, tion, WITHOUT POSSESSION OF, HOMELESS
destort, distort
destrabute, distribute
destract, distract
destraught, distraught
destrekt, district
destrikt, district
destrot, distraught
destroy, *, yed, ying, yable, yer, OBLITERATE/ RUIN/ DEMOLISH
destruct, *, ted, ting, tible, tibility, tion, tive, tor, DESTROY A MISSILE AFTER LAUNCH "prefixes: in/ non"
destruction, ACT OF RUINING/ DEMOLISHING
destructive, ely, eness, vity, OBLITERATE/ RUIN/ DEMOLISH
destrukshen, destruction
destruktive, destructive
destruktof, destructive
destrust, distrust
destulashen, distill(ation)
destunashin, destination
destuny, destiny
destutute, destitute
desuade, dissuade
desubel, decibel
desubilety, disability
desucrate, desecrate
desufect, disaffect
desugree, disagree

desukrate, desecrate
desul, diesel
desulit, desolate
desulooshen, dissolute(tion)
desuloot, dissolve
desulow, disallow
desumal, decimal
desumate, decimate
desumbark, disembark
desunt, decent / descent
desupashen, dissipate(tion)
desupate, dissipate
desupeer, disappear
desupoent, disappoint
desuprove, disapprove
desurn, discern
desurt, desert / dessert
desurtashen, dissertation
desurve, deserve
deswade, dissuade
det, debt
detach, hes, hed, hedly, hedness, hing, ment, hable, hably, her, PULL AWAY FROM, SEPARATE "prefixes: semi"
detachment, *, DISCONNECTED, SEPARATE FROM THE WHOLE
detail, *, led, ling, ler, EXACT PARTICULARS
detain, *, ned, ning, nable, nment, nee, TO KEEP FROM GOING, HOLD BACK, DELAY
detakashun, dedication
detakate, dedicate
detale, detail
detane, detain
detauks, detox
detch, ditch
detect, *, ted, ting, table, tably, tability, tion, tor, UNCOVER, SENSE, DISCOVER
detective, *, ONE WHO UNCOVERS FACTS, DISCOVERS
detector, *, A DEVICE WHICH SENSES/ DISCOVERS
deteil, detail
detekt, detect
detektif, detective
detektur, detector
deten, deaden

detenate, detonate
detenshen, detention
detente, *, CEASE-FIRE, LESSENING OF TENSIONS BETWEEN WARRING PEOPLE
detention, *, FORCED CONFINEMENT
deter, *, rred, rring, rrable, rrability, rment, rent, rrence, ATTEMPT TO RESTRAIN FROM (or see detour/debtor)
deterant, deterrent
detereate, deteriorate
deterent, deterrent
detergent, *, CHEMICAL CLEANSER
deteriorate, *, ed, ting, tion, tive, LOOSE FORM/ FUNCTION
determenent, determine(nt)
determination, *, DECIDED, DECISION, STRONG DESIRE FOR ACCOMPLISHMENT
determine, *, ed, ning, nism, nist, nistic, nistically, nedly, nedness, ner, nant, nate, nation, native, natively, nable, THINK OUT, PLAN A COURSE OF ACTION "prefixes: in/ non/ pre"
deterrent, nce, PAST TENSE FOR "DETER", USED TO PREVENT/ RESTRAIN
detest, *, ted, ting, table, tably, tability, tableness, tation, ter, EXTREME DISLIKE, DISAGREE WITH
deteur, detour / debtor / deter
deth, death
deticashun, dedication
deticate, dedicate
detikashun, dedication
detikate, dedicate
detin, deaden
detinate, detonate
detinshun, detention
detir, debtor / detour / deter
detirmenedly, determine(dly)
detirmenent, determine(nt)
detly, dead(ly)
detnate, detonate
deto, ditto
detoks, detox
detoksefy, detoxify
detoksuficashen, detoxify(fication)

detonate, *, ed, ting, table, tion, tive, tor, CAUSE TO EXPLODE
detont, detente
detor, debtor / detour / deter
detour, *, red, ring, STEER FROM PRIMARY PATH/ ROAD
detox, xes, xed, xing, xify, xicate, xication, xicant, SLANG FOR "DETOXIFY", ELIMINATE CHEMICALS FROM THE BODY
detoxicate, *, ed, ting, tion, DETOXIFY, REMOVE IMPURITIES
detoxify, fies, fied, fying, fication, REMOVE IMPURITIES FROM BODY
detract, *, ted, ting, tion, tive, tively, tor, TAKES AWAY FROM
detrament, detriment
detriment, *, tal, tally, COULD HARM, NEGATIVE INPUT
detrument, detriment
dets, debt(s)
detukashun, dedication
detukate, dedicate
detunate, detonate
detur, deter / detour / debtor
deture, detour / debtor / deter
deturgent, detergent
deturmen, determine
deturmenashen, determination
deturmenent, determine(nt)
deturmenism, determine(nism)
deturminent, determine(nt)
deuce, *, ed, edly, TWO DOTS ON DICE, GAMBLING EXPRESSION (or see duce)
deva, ENTITY OF GOOD SPIRITS (or see diva)
devadend, dividend
devain, divine
devastate, *, ed, ting, tive, tion, tor, TOTAL DISARRAY/ CHAOTIC ARRANGEMENT, UNRECOGNIZABLE
devaulv, devolve
deveanse, deviance
deveant, deviant
deveashen, deviation
deveat, deviate
deveation, deviation
deveents, deviance

devegen, division
devel, devil
develop, *, ed, ping, pment, pmental, pmentally, per, GATHERING OF THOUGHTS AND PLANS TOGETHER INTO ON "prefixes: re/ under"
deverse, diverse
devershen, diversion
devestate, devastate
deveunse, deviance
deveunt, deviant
deviance, cy, UNACCEPTABLE BEHAVIOR
deviant, *, ate, THOSE WHO DISPLAY UNACCEPTABLE BEHAVIOR
deviate, *, ed, ting, tingly, tion, ance, ant, TO STEER OFF THE PATH "prefixes: un"
deviation, *, nism, nist, TO DEVIATE, BE DEVIANT
device, SOMETHING DESIGNED TO BE USED AS A TOOL/ AID (or see devise)
devide, divide
devidend, dividend
devil, *, led, ling, lish, lishness, lishly, lment, lry, FOOD PROCESS, MAN'S CREATION OF A BEING TO BE FEARED
devine, divine
devious, sly, sness, NOT TRUTHFUL, EVASIVE IN TRUTH/ DIRECTION
devise, *, ed, sing, sable, er, O= WILLS/ PROPERTY, TO CREATE (or see device)
devisible, divisible
devistate, devastate
devize, devise / device
devoid, dness, ABSENCE OF, EMPTY
devol, devil
devolve, *, ed, ving, ement, lution, lutionist, DOWNWARD, DEGENERATE, DETERIORATE
devorse, divorce
devoshen, devotion
devostate, devastate
devote, *, ed, edly, edness, ting, tion, tional, tee. DEDICATED, LOYAL COMMITMENT
devotion, *, nal, nally, DEDICATED, LOYAL
devour, *, red, ring, ringly, rer, EARNEST TO RELIGION
devout, tly, tness, DEEPLY DEVOTED

devoyd, devoid
devu, deva / diva
devudend, dividend
devul, devil
devulg, divulge
devulution, devolve(lution)
devursity, diversity
devurt, divert
devustate, devastate
dew, *, wed, wing, wless, wy, wier, wiest, MOISTURE THAT COLLECTS INTO DROPS (or see do/ due/ doe) "prefixes: un"
dewal, dual / duel
dewdle, doodle
dewet, duet
dewing, doing
dewl, duel / dual
dewo, duo
dewplecity, duplicity
dewplekate, duplicate
dewplex, duplex
dewse, duce / deuce / due(s)
dewsh, douche
dex, deck(s) / dig(s)
dexshen, diction
dexshunery, dictionary
dexsteridy, dexterity
dexterity, ties, SHARP/ QUICK MENTAL/ PHYSICAL SKILL MODIFIES THE WORD
dextero, PREFIX INDICATING "RIGHT" MOST OFTEN MODIFIES THE WORD
dexterous, sly, sness, OF DEXTERITY
dextr, PREFIX INDICATING "RIGHT" MOST OFTEN MODIFIES THE WORD
dextro, PREFIX INDICATING "RIGHT" MOST OFTEN MODIFIES THE WORD
dextrus, dexterous
deyli, daily
dez, these
dezal, diesel
dezapashen, dissipate(tion)
dezapate, dissipate
dezapeer, disappear
dezaster, disaster

dezbot, despot
deze, dizzy
dezeez, disease
dezenteant, dissent(ient)
dezert, desert / dessert
dezerve, deserve
dezignate, designate
dezine, design
deziner, designer
dezinteant, dissent(ient)
dezirable, desirable
dezire, desire
dezklose, disclose
dezl, diesel
dezmay, dismay
dezmul, dismal
dezolve, dissolve
dezordurly, disorderly
dezposuble, disposable
dezrepare, disrepair
dezugnate, designate
dezul, diesel
dezurt, desert / dessert
dezurtashen, dissertation
dezurve, deserve
dfraust, defrost
dfrost, defrost
dfroust, defrost
ddukt, deduct
di, PREFIX INDICATING "FROM/ AWAY/ NEGATIVE" MOST OFTEN MODIFIES THE WORD
dia, PREFIX INDICATING "ACROSS/ THROUGH" MOST OFTEN MODIFIES THE WORD
diabalekle, diabolical
diabedik, diabetic
diabetes, IMBALANCE IN GLUCOSE LEVELS
diabetic, SOMEONE WITH GLUCOSE IMBALANCE
diabolic, cal, ize, izes, ized, izing, ism, OF BEING/ SEEMING EVIL/ CRUEL, OF THE DEVIL
diabolical, lly, lness, OF BEING DIABOLIC, EVIL
diacdavate, deactivate
diactevate, deactivate
diafram, diaphragm

diagenul, diagonal
diagnose, *, ed, sing, sable, sis, stically, stician, TO STUDY THE NATURE OF A PROBLEM
diagnosis, OPINION ON THE NATURE OF A PROBLEM
diagnul, diagonal
diagnule, diagonal(lly)
diagonal, lly, OPPOSITE/ CATTY CORNER FROM
diagram, *, mmed, mming, mmatic, mmatical, mmatically, mmable, DRAWING "prefixes: mis/ un"
diahrea, diarrhea
dial, *, led, ling, ler, FACE OF WATCH, PLACE A PHONE CALL "prefixes: mis/ re"
dialasis, dialysis
dialect, *, tal, tally, tic, tician, ticism, tical, tically, THE WAY THE LANGUAGE IS SPOKEN
dialogue, *, ed, uing, gist, gistic, gize, gizes, gized, gizing, VERBAL COMMUNICATION BETWEEN ENTITIES
dialysis, ytic, ytically, lyze, lyzes, lyzed, lyzing, lyzable, lyzability, lyzation, CLEANSE THE BLOOD OF WASTES, SEPARATE SUBSTANCES BY DIFFUSION
diameter, *, ric, rical, trically, tral, STRAIGHT LINE THROUGH THE CENTER OF A CIRCULAR SHAPE LEAVING EQUAL PARTS "prefixes: semi"
diamider, diameter
diamond, *, CUT STONE INTO GEM/ SHAPE/ PATTERN
diaper, *, red, ABSORBENT PANTS FOR FLUIDS
diaphragm, *, matic, matically, A DIVISION BETWEEN TWO THINGS, CONTRACEPTIVE DEVICE
diarea, diarrhea
diaretik, diuretic
diarrhea, al, hoea, hoeic, VERY LIQUID FECAL EXCREMENT
diary, ries, rist, rize, rizes, rized, rizing, LOG/ JOURNAL OF THOUGHTS EACH DAY
diatery, dietary
dibach, debauch
dibais, device / devise
dibate, debate
dibauch, debauch
dibeit, debate
dibelutate, debilitate
diber, dipper / diaper
dibiletate, debilitate
diblomu, diploma

diblomusy, diplomacy
dibochury, debauch(ery)
diborc, divorce
dibs, SLANG FOR LAYING A CLAIM, SMALL MONETARY PARTICIPATION
dibur, dipper / diaper
dic, thick / dike / dyke
dical, decal
dicanter, decanter
dicapitate, decapitate
dicaudame, dichotomy
dicay, decay
dice, *, ed, cing, ey, PLURAL FOR "DIE", TWO CUBES WITH VARIETY OF DOTS, TO CHOP UP (or see dicey)
dicelerate, decelerate
dicember, december
dicenci, decency
dicensy, decency
dicentrolize, decentralize
dicet, deceit
diceve, deceive
dicey, cier, eist, IFFY/ RISKY WITH ELEMENT OF DANGER
dich, ditch / dish
dichenereit, degenerate
diches, ditch(es)
dicheveled, disheveled(ed)
dichotomy, mies, mic, mous, mously, mize, mizes, mized, mizing, mization, SEPARATION/ DIVISION INTO TWO PARTS
dichroic, cism, DIFFERENT COLORS FROM DIFFERENT ANGLES
dicker, *, red, ring, RALLY TO STRIKE A DEAL
diclain, decline
dicler, declare
dicompos, decompose
dicon, deacon
dicotomy, dichotomy
dicoy, decoy
dicreped, decrepit
dicrepit, decrepit
dicroek, dichroic
dicshen, diction
dicshunairy, dictionary

dictate, *, ed, ting, tor, tory, torial, COMMAND/ RULE/ GIVE ORDERS
dictation, TO WRITE OR TYPE WHAT SOMEONE IS SAYING
dictatorial, lly, lness, OPPRESSIVE, AUTHORITARIAN
dicteishon, dictation
dicteit, dictate
diction, A WAY OF SPEAKING, ENUNCIATION "prefixes: retro"
dictionary, ries, WORDS WITH DEFINITIONS ARRANGED ALPHABETICALLY
did, does, PAST TENSE FOR THE WORD "DO" (or see dead/ died) "prefixes: un"
diden, didn't / deaden
dident, didn't
didn't, CONTRACTION OF THE WORDS "DID NOT " (or see dent/ deaden)
dido, ditto
didoct, deduct
didukt, deduct
diduse, deduce
die, *, ed, dying, dead, TO BE DEAD/ CEASE TO BE ALIVE, AN ENGRAVED STAMP, A PUNCHED OUT TEMPLATE, CUBE USED FOR GAMING (or see dye)
died, PAST TENSE FOR THE WORD "DIE" (or see dye(d))
diegnosus, diagnosis
dielekt, dialect
diere, diary
dierrhea, diarrhea
diesel, *, led, ling, TYPE OF ENGINE/ FUEL "prefixes: bio"
diet, *, ted, ting, tary, taries, tetic, tetically, tician, SPECIFIC FOOD/ BEVERAGE
dietary, ries, A SYSTEM OF FOOD FOR TYPES OF PEOPLE
dieti, deity
dif, PREFIX INDICATING "FROM/ AWAY/ NEGATIVE" MOST OFTEN MODIFIES THE WORD (or see thief/ thieve)
dif, thief/ thieve
difadend, dividend
difai, defy
difain, define
difalt, default
difase, deface

difault,default
difayans,defiance
dife,dive
difechant,deficient
difechensj,deficiency
difeet,defeat
difeis,deface
difekult,difficult
difend,defend
definitive,definitive
defense,defense
defensible,defensible
defensive,defense(sive)
difer,defer / differ
diferens,difference
diferense,difference
diferensheate,differentiate
diferent,different
diferentiate,differentiate
diferently,different(ly)
diferintiate,differentiate
difeshensy,deficiency
difet,defeat
difews,diffuse
differ,*,red,ring,rent,rence,rential,TO NOT BE ALIKE
differantly,different(ly)
difference,*,QUALITIES NOT ALIKE "prefixes: in"
different,tly,tness,tial,NOT THE SAME "prefixes: in"
differential,*,RATE DIFFERENCE/ VARIANCE
differentiate,*,ed,ting,tion,TO OUTLINE DIFFERENCES, BIOLOGY TERM "prefixes: un"
difficult,ty,ties,NOT EASY TO PERFORM
diffuse,*,ed,sing,ely,eness,er,sive,sible,sibility, ELIMINATE FOCUS BY SPREADING OUT, TO END PRESSURE
difichant,deficient
difichensy,deficiency
dificult,difficult
difiense,defiance
difikult,difficult
difine,define
difir,defer / differ
difishant,deficient

difishensy,deficiency
difit,defeat
difius,diffuse
diflact,deflect
diflate,deflate
difleit,deflate
difoleate,defoliate
difor,differ / defer
diforensheate,differentiate
diforent,different
diform,deform
diformed,deform(ed)
diformeishon,deformation
difraud,defraud
difraust,defrost
difray,defray
difrense,difference
difrent,different
difrod,defraud
difrost,defrost
difucult,difficult
difukult,difficult
difunkt,defunct
difur,defer / differ
difurense,difference
difurensheate,differentiate
difurent,different
difurently,different(ly)
difurinsheate,differentiate
difurintly,different(ly)
difuse,diffuse
dify,defy
dig,*,dug,gging,gger,TO GO BELOW/ BEYOND THE SURFACE
digesgen,digestion
digest,*,ted,ting,tible,tibility,tibleness,tive,tively, tiveness,tion,CONSUME,PROCESS, SUMMARIZATIONS "prefixes: pre/ un"
digestev,digest(tive)
digestif,digest(tive)
digestion,CONSUME AND PROCESS
digestuf,digest(tive)
digestyon,digestion

diget,digit
digit,*,tize,tization,tal,tally,talize,talization,COUNTING/ MEASURING
dignafid,dignified
dignafied,dignified
dignified,STATELY IN FIGURE OR FORM, HONORABLE
dignify,fies,fied,fying,EXPRESS HONOR FOR
dignity,ties,tary,WORTHY OF RESPECT,HONOR "prefixes: in"
dignosis,diagnosis
dignufied,dignified
digrade,degrade
digree,degree
digreid,degrade
digress,sses,ssed,ssing,ssion,ssional,ssionary,ssive, ssively,ssiveness,WANDER AWAY FROM, DEPART FROM MAIN TOPIC/ SUBJECT (or see degression)
dijaidreit,dehydrate
dijest,digest
dijestev,digest(tive)
dijeston,digestion
dijet,digit
dijit,digit
dika,decay
dikad,decay(ed)
dikanter,decanter
dikautumy,dichotomy
dikdutoreal,dictatorial
dike,*,ed,king,er,ALSO SPELLED "DYKE", A BARRIER/ CAUSEWAY/ PASSAGE
diker,dicker
diklar,declare
diklin,decline
dikotumy,dichotomy
dikrepit,decrepit
dikroic,dichroic
dikshen,diction
dikshenare,dictionary
dikshun,diction
dikshunare,dictionary
diksterity,dexterity
diktashen,dictation
diktate,dictate

diktater, dictate(tor)
diktation, dictation
diktatur, dictate(tor)
diktion, diction
diktionery, dictionary
diktutoreal, dictatorial
dil, dial / dill / deal
dialgense, diligence
dialit, delight
diajense, diligence
dilate, *, ed, ting, tion, tability, table, tably, tingly, tive, EXPAND/ SWELL/ BROADEN
diatont, dilettante
diiay, delay
diectable, delectable
diedaly, dillydally
diiei, delay
diieit, dilate
diiekt, dialect
diiema, dilemma
dilemma, *, atic, NOT A SITUATION OF CHOICE
dilenkwent, delinquent
dilenquent, delinquent
diiereus, delirious
dileshos, delicious
dilete, delete
diletont, dilettante
dilettante, *, tish, tism, A DABBLER FOR AMUSEMENT
dilidaly, dillydally
diligence, nt, ntly, STEADY PERSEVERANCE, CONSTANT
dilikt, dialect
dilillens, diligence
dilincuent, delinquent
dilinquent, delinquent
dilirious, delirious
dilishos, delicious
dilit, delete
diliver, deliver
diliyens, diligence
dill, AN HERB (or see dial/ deal)
dillect, deject
dilledaly, dillydally
dillenereit, degenerate

dillit, digit
dillydally, llies, yied, ying, SHOULD BE SEPARATED INTO 2 WORDS "DILLY DALLY", TO WASTE TIME
diloot, dilute
diluchen, delusion / dilute(tion)
dilucs, deluxe
dilugen, delusion / dilute(tion)
dilugense, diligence
dilugent, diligence(nt)
dilujents, deluxe
diluks, deluxe
dilur, deal(er)
dilushen, delusion / dilute(tion)
dilute, *, ed, ting, eness, tion, tive, er, WEAKEN THE STRENGTH OF
dilutont, dilettante
diluxe, deluxe
dim, *, mmed, mming, mly, mness, mmer, mmest, BETWEEN BRIGHT AND DARK, NOT CLEAR/ BRIGHT (or see dime)
dimagog, demagogue
dimais, demise
dimand, demand
dimaugraphy, demography
dimaulesh, demolish
dimble, dimple
dime, *, A COIN (or see dim)
dimean, demean
dimeanor, demeanor
dimen, demean
dimend, diamond
dimenor, demeanor
dimension, *, nless, nal, nally, nality, nless, MORE THAN ONE LAYER "prefixes: multi"
dimentchen, dimension
dimented, demented
dimer, dimmer
dimestek, domestic
diminish, hes, hed, hing, hingly, hment, TO LESSEN/ MAKE SMALLER
dimis, demise
dimize, demise
dimmer, *, LESSEN BRIGHTNESS

dimobalize, demobilize
dimocrat, democrat
dimografy, demography
dimokresy, democracy
dimolish, demolish
dimolishin, demolition
dimon, demon / diamond
dimond, diamond
dimonek, demon(ic)
dimoubilais, demobilize
dimple, *, ed, ling, ly, A DEPRESSION INTO SURFACE, INDENTATION
dimukratic, democratic
dimulishun, demolition
dimunstrate, demonstrate
dimur, dimmer
din, den / dine / dean / didn't
dinaiol, denial
dinamek, dynamic
dinamic, dynamic
dinamination, denomination
dinamite, dynamite
dinasor, dinosaur
dinasty, dynasty
dinaumenation, denomination
dincher, denture
dindrite, dendrite
dine, *, ed, ning, er, TO EAT
dineichor, denature
diner, *, PLACE TO EAT (or see dinner)
dinesor, dinosaur
dinet, dinette
dinette, DINING ROOM/ PLACE NEAR KITCHEN TO EAT
ding, *, ged, ging, BELL SOUNDS, INDENTATIONS/ MARKS
dingee, dinghy / dingy
dinger, *, HOME RUN BASEBALL
dinghy, hies, SMALL BOAT/ VESSEL ON WATER (or see dingy)
dingy, gier, giest, giness, gily, DIM/ MURKY, NOT VIBRANT (or see dinghy/ dinky)
dinial, denial
dinie, deny
dinil, denial

dinisor,dinosaur
dinje,dingy
dinky,kier,kiest,SMALL/ TINY
dinlli,dingy
dinner,*,EVENING MEAL (or see diner)
dinomenashin,denomination
dinomenator,denominator
dinominashan,denomination
dinominator,denominator
dinomite,dynamite
dinosaur,*,PREHISTORIC CREATURES
dinostea,dynasty
dinote,denote
dinse,dense
dinsity,density
dint,dent / didn't / dine(d)
dintal,dental
dintist,dentist
dinture,denture
dinumite,dynamite
dinur,diner / dinner
dinusor,dinosaur
dinusty,dynasty
diocsidais,deoxidize
dioderant,deodorant
diodorais,deodorize
dioreu,diarrhea
dioshieit,dissociate
dioudorant,deodorant
dioudrvais,deodorize
diowdorant,deodorant
dioxidais,deoxidize
dipendence,dependence
dip,*,pper,pped,pping,SLIGHTLY IMMERSE/ DECLINE/ GO INTO
diparcher,departure
diparsher,departure
dipart,depart
dipartment,department
diparture,departure
dipect,depict
dipend,depend
dipendant,dependant / dependent

diper,diaper / dipper
diplechen,depletion
dipleshin,depletion
diplete,deplete
diploma,*,DOCUMENT FOR COMPLETION OF COURSE/ SCHOOL
diplomacy,SKILLFUL NEGOTIATIONS
diplomat,*,tic,tics,tically,acy,tist,PERSON WHO PERFORMS TACTFUL NEGOTIATIONS "prefixes: non/ un"
diplorable,deplorable
diplore,deplore
dipo,depot
diporcher,depart(ure)
diport,deport
diportashon,deportation
diportee,deportee
dipose,depose
diposeshon,deposition
diposit,deposit
dipous,depose
dipozishen,deposition
dipper,*,SPOON WITH HANDLE,A BIRD (or see diaper)
dipres,depress
dipresheate,depreciate
dipreshen,depression
dipresion,depression
diprive,deprive
dipur,diaper / dipper
diquej,decay
diquer,dicker
dirashen,duration
dirdee,dirty
dire,ely,eness,EXTREME, DISASTROUS
direct,*,ted,ting,tly,tness,tor,tion,tive,torate,torship, tory,AIM FOR/ WITH, OF COMMANDS "prefixes: in/ mis/ multi/ non/ re/ sub/ un"
direction,*,nal,nality,nless,WAVE/ SIGNALS IN SPACE "prefixes: in/ multi/ non/ uni"
directive,*,eness,A DIRECTION/ INDICATOR/ GUIDE
directory,ries,BOOK WITH ALPHABETICAL LISTINGS "prefixes: sub"
direkshen,direction

direktory,directory
direng,during
diress,duress
dirivative,derivative
dirive,derive
dirmal,dermal
dirmas,dermal(mis)
dirmatites,dermal(atitis)
dirmle,dermal
dirmul,dermal
dirmus,dermal(mis)
dirmutidus,dermal(atitis)
dirmutitis,dermal(atitis)
dirt,ty,ties,tied,tying,tier,tiest,tily,tiness,SOILED, SOIL (earth)
dirty,tied,tier,tiest,ying,tily,tiness, UNCLEAN
dis,PREFIX INDICATING "NOT/ OPPOSITE/ LACK OF" MOST OFTEN MODIFIES THE WORD (or see this/ dice/ die(s)/ dye(s))
disability,disability
disability,ties,UNABLE TO PERFORM AT NECESSARY CAPACITY
disable,*,ed,ling,ement,bility, UNABLE TO PERFORM, DISCONNECT
disaccord,*,ded,ding,NOT IN HARMONY/ AGREEMENT
disadisfaction,dissatisfy(faction)
disadvantage,*,ed,ging,eous,eously,eousness,A DIFFICULTY/ CHALLENGE IN ACCOMPLISHING SUCCESS/ GOAL
disaffect,*,ted,ting,tedly,tion,NEGATIVELY AFFECT SOMEONE CONCERNING ANOTHER
disagree,*,eed,eeing,eement,eeable,eeably,eeability, eeableness,NOT AGREE WITH
disaid,decide
disaier,desire
disaifer,decipher
disaipol,disciple
disairabol,desirable
disait,deceit
disakree,disagree
disalanate,desalinate
disalau,disallow
disallow,*,wed,wing,wance,wable,NOT ALLOWED

disalow, disallow
disalugen, disillusion
disalusion, disillusion
disalute, dissolute
disalution, dissolute(tion)
disambiguate, *, ed, ting, tion, EXPRESSION OPEN TO MISINTERPRETATION, CONFUSING
disanens, dissonant(nce)
disanent, dissonant
disapate, dissipate
disapation, dissipate(tion)
disaper, disappear
disaplen, discipline
disappear, *, red, ring, rance, VANISH FROM SIGHT
disappoint, *, ted, tedly, ting, tingly, tment, HOPES NOT REALIZED
disapprove, *, ed, ving, vingly, val, DOESN'T CARE FOR/ APPROVE OF
disaray, disarray
disarm, *, med, ming, mament, mer, REMOVE POWER/ WEAPONS
disarmament, *, ACT OF DISARMING
disarray, *, yed, ying, DISORDERED/ JUMBLED
disassociate, dissociate
disaster, *, rous, rously, rousness, MISFORTUNE, CALAMITY, EXTENSIVE DAMAGE
disatation, dissertation
disatisfaction, dissatisfy(faction)
disavantage, disadvantage
disayer, desire
disayerabol, desirable
disbaleef, disbelief / disbelieve
disband, *, ded, ding, dment, DISMISSED FROM GROUP OR MILITARY
disbar, rred, rring, REMOVED FROM LEGAL COURT OR PRACTICE (or see despair)
disbatch, dispatch
disbecable, despicable
disbekable, despicable
disbelief, *, eve, DOESN'T BELIEVE TO BE TRUE
disbelieve, *, ed, ving, vingly, er, DOESN'T BELIEVE TO BE TRUE
disberse, disperse / disburse

disbicable, despicable
disbikable, despicable
disbileef, disbelief / disbelieve
disbite, despite
disblay, display
disblese, displease
disbolef, disbelief / disbelieve
disbondent, despondent
disbose, dispose
disbozishun, disposition
disbozul, disposal
disbraporshen, disproportion
disbuleef, disbelief / disbelieve
disburse, *, ed, sing, sable, ement, er, FUND, PAY OUT MONEY (or see disperse)
disbusishun, disposition
disbute, dispute
disbuzishun, disposition
disc, *, COMPUTER/ MUSIC STORAGE DEVICES, SECTIONS IN THE SPINE, BRAKE PARTS (or see disk)
discard, *, ded, ding, TO RID OF/ THROW AWAY
discaunt, discount
discension, dissension / descension
discerach, discourage
discern, *, ned, ning, nible, nibleness, nibly, nment, PERCEIVE ONE FROM ANOTHER, SEE A DIFFERENCE "prefixes: in"
discharge, *, ed, ging, eable, er, TO RELEASE FROM
discinshen, dissension / descension
disciple, *, ONE WHO FOLLOWS A TEACHER
discipline, *, ed, ning, nable, nary, narian, er, nal, CONTROL/ TRAIN TO PERFORM SPECIFICALLY "prefixes: in"
disclaim, *, med, ming, mer, NOT LAY CLAIM TO, DISOWN/ DENY RESPONSIBILITY OF
disclem, disclaim
disclose, *, ed, sing, sure, ser, REVEAL/ MAKE KNOWN "prefixes: un"
discombobulate, *, ed, ting, tion, DISTURB, PERPLEX
discomfort, *, ted, ting, tingly, table, UNCOMFORTABLE, UNHAPPY
disconnect, *, ted, ting, tion, tedly, tedness, BE REMOVED FROM CONNECTION WITH

discontinue, *, ed, uing, uation, uity, uities, uance, uous, uously, uousness, uity, unities, er, ABANDON, CEASE, STOP THE USE OF
discord, dance, dancy, dancies, dant, dantly, NOT IN HARMONY WITH, DISAGREE WITH
discotek, discotheque
discotheque, *, NIGHTCLUB WITH MUSIC
discount, *, ted, ting, MAKE LESS, REDUCE PRICE OF
discourage, *, ed, ging, ement, gingly, er, LESSEN HOPES OF ACCOMPLISHING
discourse, *, ed, sing, er, REVEAL/ MAKE KNOWN
discourteous, sies, sly, sness, NOT POLITE/ COURTEOUS
discover, *, red, ring, rer, ry, ries, rable, TO FIND, REALIZE "prefixes: un"
discownt, discount
discraib, describe
discredit, *, ted, ting, table, tably, tor, GIVE NO CREDIT TO, DISBELIEF
discreet, tly, tness, GUARDED, CAREFUL, SUBTLE (or see discrete) "prefixes: in"
discremenate, discriminate
discrepancy, cies, nt, ntly, DIFFERENCE BETWEEN
discrepant, ntly, ncy, DIFFERENCE BETWEEN THINGS
discrepchen, description
discreptef, descriptive
discreption, description
discrete, ely, eness, tion, SEPARATE PARTS, DISTINCT/ FINITE (or see discreet) "prefixes: in"
discretion, nary, narily, MAKE YOUR OWN DECISION/ JUDGMENT, BEING DISCREET "prefixes: in"
discribe, describe
discriminate, *, ed, ting, nation, nable, nably, nability, nant, nately, native, nator, natory, natorily, USING DIFFERENCE AGAINST, CHOOSE ONE OVER ANOTHER "prefixes: in"
discripchen, description
discripshen, description
discumbobulate, discombobulate
discumfert, discomfort
discunect, disconnect
discuntenue, discontinue
discurach, discourage
discurage, discourage

discurech, discourage
discus, ses, USED FOR THROWING (or see discuss)
discuss, sses, ssed, ssing, ssable, ssant, sser, ssion, CONVERSATION TO EXAMINE SUBJECT (or see discus)
discussion, *, ACT OF CONVERSATION TO EXAMINE SUBJECT
discust, disgust
discuver, discover
disdain, *, ned, ning, nful, nfully, nfulness, SCORN, CONTEMPT FOR, REJECT
disdein, disdain
disdend, distend
disdendible, distend(sible)
disdendshen, distend(nsion)
disdendtion, distend(nsion)
disdent, distant
disderb, disturb
disdinduble, distend(sible)
disdort, distort
disdrabushen, distribute(tion)
disdrabute, distribute
disdrakt, distract
disdrebute, distribute
disdress, distress
disdrot, distraught
disdrubute, distribute
disdruckshen, destruction
disdruktion, destruction
disdrust, distrust
disdulashen, distill(ation)
disdurb, disturb
dise, dice / dizzy / dicey
disease, *, ed, sing, BLOCK OF ENERGY ALLOWING TISSUE BREAKDOWN VIA MINUTE ORGANISMS
disecragate, desegregate
disecragation, desegregate(tion)
disecrogate, desegregate
disecrogation, desegregate(tion)
disect, dissect
disease, decease / disease
diseet, deceit
diseeve, deceive

disefect, disaffect
disefectant, disinfect(ant)
diseragate, desegregate
diseragation, desegregate(tion)
diserigeichen, desegregate(tion)
disegrigeit, desegregate
disegrogate, desegregate
disegrogation, desegregate(tion)
diseibol, disable
disekt, dissect
diselarate, decelerate
diselooshen, dissolute(tion)
diseloot, dissolute
disembar, december
disembark, *, ked, king, kation, kment, MOVE FROM SHIP TO SHORE
disemble, dissemble
disembowel, *, led, ling, lment, REMOVE ORGANS/ INTESTINES
disembur, december
diseminate, disseminate
disenagrate, disintegrate
disenchan, descension / dissension
disend, descend / decent / descent / dissent
disendant, descendant
disenfect, disinfect
disengage, *, ed, ging, ement, SET FREE FROM BEING ATTACHED
disenherit, disinherit
disenshent, dissent(ient)
disenshin, dissension / descension
disenshun, dissension / descension
disent, dissent / decent / descend / descent
disentagrate, disintegrate
disentary, dysentery
disenter, dissent(er)
disentient, dissent(ient)
disention, dissension / descension
disentralize, decentralize
disepchen, deception
diseplen, discipline
disepoint, disappoint
diseption, deception

diseray, disarray
disern, discern
disert, dessert / desert
disertation, dissertation
diserv, deserve
diservice, disservice
disesd, decease(d) / disease(d)
diset, deceit
disetful, deceit(ful)
diseve, deceive
disfigure, *, ed, ring, ration, ement, CAUSING UNSIGHTLY APPEARANCE
disfoncshon, disfunction
disfonction, dysfunction
disfunkshon, dysfunction
disgais, disguise
disgarge, discharge
disgise, disguise
disgoint, disjoint
disgrace, *, ed, cing, eful, efully, efulness, er, SHAME, DISHONOR
disgrechen, discretion
disgretion, discretion
disgrundeld, disgruntle(d)
disgruntle, *, ed, ling, ement, NOT CONTENTED, UNGRATIFIED
disguise, *, ed, sing, sable, er, MASK TRUE IDENTITY "prefixes: un"
disgurag, discourage
disgus, discuss / discus
disgust, *, ted, ting, tingly, tingness, REPUGNANT, AWFUL (or see discuss(ed))
dish, hes, hed, hing, SHALLOW PLATE/ BOWL/ VESSEL, TO SERVE IT UP (or see ditch)
disharten, dishearten
dishaveled, dishevel(ed)
dishearten, *, ned, ning, nment, LOOSE SPIRIT/ HOPE/ COURAGE
dishevel, *, led, ling, lment, MESSED UP, UNTIDY
dishonest, ty, tly, ties, BEING DECEITFUL, NOT HONEST
dishonor, *, red, ring, rable, rably, rableness, NOT TREATED RESPECTFULLY, SHAMEFUL

dishonorable, ly, eness, UNRESPECTABLE, NOT HONORABLE
disi, dizzy
disidvantage, disadvantage
disifer, decipher
disillusion, ned, nment, ive, NO LONGER UNDER ILLUSION, KNOWING
disilushen, disillusion
disimanate, disseminate
disimbark, disembark
disimbul, dissemble
disimbur, december
disin, design
disiner, designer
disinfect, *, ted, ting, tant, tion, tor, CLEANSE AWAY UNWANTED MICROORGANISMS
disingage, disengage
disinherit, *, ted, ting, tance, REMOVED FROM A WRITTEN WILL
disint, descend / decent
disintegrate, *, ed, ting, tion, tor, able, tive, TO FALL APART
disintery, dysentery
disintient, dissent(ient)
disiplen, discipline
disipul, disciple
disir, desire
disirable, desirable
disis, decease / disease
disisev, decision(ive)
disiv, deceive
disjoint, *, ted, ting, tedly, tedness, DISLOCATE, ALTER UNITY/ MOVEMENT
disk, *, FLAT/ CIRCULAR, FLOWER HEAD, STEEL BLADE (or see disc/ desk)
diskard, discard
diskeruge, discourage
disklame, disclaim
disklose, disclose
diskomfurt, discomfort
diskonect, disconnect
diskontenue, discontinue
diskord, discord
diskors, discourse

diskotek, discotheque
diskover, discover
diskownt, discount
diskredit, discredit
diskrepincy, discrepancy
diskreshun, discretion
diskrete, discreet / discrete
diskribe, describe
diskripshen, description
diskumbobulate, discombobulate
diskumfert, discomfort
diskunekt, disconnect
diskuntenue, discontinue
diskurdeus, discourteous
diskurege, discourage
diskus, discus / discuss
diskust, disgust / discuss(ed)
diskuver, discover
diskwalefy, disqualify
diskwolify, disqualify
dislecsea, dyslexia
disleksea, dyslexia
dislexia, dyslexia
dislocate, *, ed, ting, tion, MOVE FROM ORIGINAL PLACE
disloch, dislodge
dislodge, *, ed, ging, gment, MOVE FROM FIXED POSITION
dislog, dislodge
dismal, lly, llness, DEPRESSING/ GLOOMY
dismanle, dismantle
dismantle, *, ed, ling, ement, er, REMOVE, TAKE APART
dismanul, dismantle
dismay, *, yed, ying, yingly, DISTRESS, DREAD, DISILLUSIONED
dismbark, disembark
dismej, dismay
dismember, *, red, ring, rment, DESTROY/ REMOVE ALL PARTS OF THE WHOLE
dismiss, sses, ssed, ssing, ssal, ssion, ssive, ssively, ssiveness, ssible, PERMIT TO LEAVE, REMOVE, DISCHARGE "prefixes: non/ pre/ re"
dismount, *, ted, ting, table, REMOVE FROM POSITION
dismownt, dismount
dismul, dismal

disoba, disobey
disobdeinse, disobedience
disobedience, nt, ntly, REFUSE TO BE CONTROLLED
disobey, *, yed, ying, edient, ediently, edience, BEYOND CONTROL
disociate, dissociate
disolfe, dissolve
disolve, dissolve
dison, disown
disonance, dissonant(nce)
disonent, dissonant
disoner, dishonor
disonerible, dishonorable
disoninse, dissonant(nce)
disonist, dishonest
disonurable, dishonorable
disorder, *, red, ring, rly, redness, NOT ORGANIZED
disorderly, liness, NOT PROPER ORDER
disoreint, disorient
disorient, *, ted, ting, tate, tates, tated, tating, tation, LOSS OF PERCEPTION, CONFUSED
disosheate, dissociate
disoubei, disobey
disoubidiens, disobedience
disown, *, ned, ning, RELEASE OWNERSHIP OF
dispair, despair
dispais, despise
dispar, despair
disparity, ties, GAP BETWEEN, INEQUALITY
disparody, disparity
disparty, disparity
dispatch, hes, hed, hing, her, SEND SOMEONE OUT
dispekable, despicable
dispensable, bility, eness, CAN BE DISCARDED "prefixes: in"
dispense, *, ed, sing, er, sable, sability, sableness, sary, TO DISTRIBUTE "prefixes: un"
disper, despair
disperse, *, ed, sing, sion, sive, sively, siveness, er, sal, SCATTER INTO VARIOUS DIRECTIONS (or see disburse)
disperudy, disparity
dispeutible, dispute(table)

dispewt, dispute
dispikuble, despicable
dispinsable, dispensable
dispite, despite
dispiut, dispute
dispize, despise
displace, *, ed, cing, eable, ement, er, NOT IN PLACE OR POSITION NORMALLY FOUND
display, *, yed, ying, ON SHOW, EXHIBITION
displease, *, ed, sing, sure, NOT TO SOMEONE'S SATISFACTION
displeis, displace
displejur, displease(sure)
displese, displease
displesher, displease(sure)
displis, displease
dispondent, despondent
disposable, *, bility, eness, CAN DISCARD/ THROW AWAY
disposal, able, PLACE/ WAY TO DISCARD ITEMS
dispose, *, ed, sing, sal, sable, er, TO RID OF, ORGANIZE "prefixes: in/ pre/ un"
disposition, nal, ATTITUDE, INCLINATION "prefixes: in"
dispositive, FINAL SETTLEMENT OF COURT CASE
disposual, disposal
dispraporshen, disproportion
disproportion, nal, nate, nately, nally, nateness, nation, NOT IN RELATION TO ITSELF OR ITS SURROUNDINGS
disput, dispute
dispute, *, ed, ting, table, tably, tability, tableness, tant, DEBATE "prefixes: in/ un"
disputible, dispute(table)
disqard, discard
disqualify, fies, fied, ying, fication, fiable, fier, DISBAR, REMOVE FROM COMPETITION
disregard, *, ded, ding, PAY NO NOTICE OF OR ATTENTION TO
disrepair, NEED TO BE FIXED
disreputable, eness, bility, y, OF POOR REPUTATION/ CHARACTER
disrespect, *, ted, ting, table, tful, tfully, tfulness, SHOW NO HONOR/ RESPECT
disrigard, disregard
disriper, disrepair

disripiutabol, disreputable
disrobe, *, ed, bing, UNDRESS, REMOVE GARMENTS
disropt, disrupt
disrupt, *, ted, ting, tion, tive, tiveness, tively, INTERRUPT, CAUSE CHAOS
disruption, INTERRUPT, CAUSE CHAOS
dissalute, dissolute
dissalution, dissolute(tion)
dissanence, dissonant(nce)
dissanent, dissonant
dissapate, dissipate
dissapation, dissipate(tion)
dissatation, dissertation
dissatisfy, fies, fied, fying, faction, factory, UNHAPPY WITH OUTCOME
dissect, *, ted, ting, tion, tible, tor, CRITICALLY EXAMINE, TAKE APART
dissemble, *, ed, ling, lingly, lance, HIDING TRUE FEELINGS/ FACTS
disseminate, *, ed, ting, tion, tive, tor, TO PASS ON, SPREAD
dissend, descend / descent / dissent
dissension, *, INTENSE DIFFERENCE/ DISAGREEMENT IN OPINION (or see descension)
dissent, *, ted, ting, ter, tience, tiency, tient, tiently, nsion, WILL NOT BEND TOWARDS MAJOR AUTHORITY (or see descent)
dissertation, *, nal, nist, WRITTEN/ FORMAL PAPER FOR DEGREE
disservice, UNWANTED SERVICE
dissipate, *, ed, edly, edness, ting, tive, tor, tion, DISAPPEARS, GOES AWAY
dissociate, *, ed, ting, tion, able, tive, STOP ASSOCIATING WITH "prefixes: un"
dissolute, ely, eness, tion, DISMEMBER, DISINTEGRATE, TERMINATE
dissolve, *, ed, ving, vable, ent, er, luble, lubility, lubleness, BREAK AWAY TO NOTHING, DISAPPEAR
dissonance, dissonant(nce)
dissonant, tly, nce, ncies, LACK OF COMPLETION/ CONSISTENCY
dissosheate, dissociate

dissuade, *, ed, ding, dable, er, asion, sive, sively, siveness, SWAY SOMEONE AWAY FROM INTENDED IDEA/ PATH
distalashen, distill(ation)
distance, *, ed, cing, nt, TIME/ SPACE IN BETWEEN
distane, disdain
distanst, distance(d)
distant, tly, REMOVED IN MIND OR BODY FROM THIS PLACE OR TIME
distaste, eful, efully, efulness, DOESN'T LIKE THE WAY IT APPEALS TO THE SENSES
disteengwish, distinguish
disteist, distaste
distemper, CONTAGIOUS DISEASE IN ANIMALS, OF PAINTING
distence, distance
distend, *, ded, ding, nsibility, sible, nsion, SWELLING FROM INTERNAL PRESSURE
distengwish, distinguish
distenkt, distinct
distent, distant
disterb, disturb
distill, *, lled, lling, llation, llate, llable, llatory, ller, llery, lleries, SEPARATION, CONDENSATION OF LIQUID
distimper, distemper
distinct, tly, tness, tion, tive, tively, tiveness, CONTRAST, DISTINGUISHED, DIFFERENT "prefixes: in"
distinguish, hed, hes, hing, hable, hably, her, DIFFERENCE/ UNIQUENESS "prefixes: contra/ in/ un"
distort, *, ted, ting, tion, tional/ tnary, tive, ter, WARP/ TWIST/ CONFUSE FROM NATURAL/ PROPER FORM
distrabushen, distribute(tion)
distrabute, distribute
distract, *, ted, ting, tingly, tion, tive, tibility, tible, tor, DEVIATE FROM ORIGINAL FOCUS/ INTENT
distrat, distraught
distraught, tly, EXTREME STRESS
distrekt, district
distress, sses, ssed, ssing, ssingly, ssful, GREAT NEED, PAIN OR GRIEF
distribute, *, ed, ting, tion, tional, tive, tively, tal, tor, TO SPREAD AROUND, PASS ALONG "prefixes: re/ un"

district,*,,SPECIFIC AREA OF TERRITORY/ LAND "prefixes: re/ sub"
distrocshen,destruction
distroct,destruct
distroctive,destructive
distrot,distraught
distroy,destroy
distruction,destruction
distructive,destructive
distrukshen,destruction
distruktof,destructive
distrust,*,,ted,ting,tful,NOT TRUST OR HAVE CONFIDENCE IN
distulashen,distill(ation)
distunst,distance(d)
disturb,*,,bed,bing,bingly,bance,bances,ber,TO MAKE IRREGULAR, INTERRUPT "prefixes: un"
disuade,dissuade
disubility,disability
disueid,dissuade
disufectant,disinfect(ant)
disugre,disagree
disugree,disagree
disulow,disallow
disulugen,disillusion
disulushen,dissolute(tion)
disulute,dissolute
disumbark,disembark
disuneins,dissonant(nce)
disunent,dissonant
disupate,dissipate
disupation,dissipate(tion)
disupeer,disappear
disuplen,discipline
disupoint,disappoint
disuprove,disapprove
disuray,disarray
disurn,discern
disurvuse,disservice
diswade,dissuade
dit,died / diet / dye(d) / did
ditach,detach
ditan,detain

ditch,hes,hed,hing,A GULLEY IN THE EARTH,SKIP OUT OF SCHOOL,LEAVE SOMEONE
ditect,detect
ditective,detective
ditector,detector
ditein,detain
ditekt,detect
ditektur,detector
ditel,detail
ditenshon,detention
diterent,deterrent
ditereorate,deteriorate
diteriorate,deteriorate
diterllent,detergent
ditermenint,determine(nt)
ditermin,determine
ditermination,determination
diteryent,detergent
ditest,detest
dito,ditto
ditocs,detox
ditocsikeit,detoxicate
ditox,detox
ditoxiqueit,detoxicate
ditrakt,detract
ditto,*,COPY,DUPLICATE,SAME BACK TO YOU
ditur,deter
diturgent,detergent
diturmenism,determine(nism)
diubolikul,diabolical
diufram,diaphragm
diugnose,diagnose
diugram,diagram
diul,dial
diulekt,dialect
diulog,dialogue
diure,diary
diurea,diarrhea
diuretek,diuretic
diuretic,*,,INCREASES THE ELIMINATION OF LIQUID
diureuh,diarrhea
diutery,dietary
diva,GODDESS (or see deva)

divadend,dividend
divaid,divide
divain,divine
divaiz,devise/ device
divaulv,devolve
divaut,devout / devote
dive,*,,ving,er,dove,TO PLUNGE HEAD-FIRST INTO ANYTHING
divelop,develop
diverse,ely,sify,sifies,sified,sifying,sifability,sifable, sification,sion,eness,sifier,rt,sity,A VARIETY, OTHER THAN THE NORM
diversion,*,,nal,nary,nist,CHANGE COURSE/ DIRECTION "prefixes: bio"
diversity,ties,TO BE DIFFERENT "prefixes: sub"
divert,*,,ted,ting,tingly,rse,rsion,rsity,CHANGE COURSE/ DIRECTION
divians,deviance
divide,*,,ed,ding,ision,isive,er,isor,SEPARATE,CREATE PARTS "prefixes: sub"
dividend,*,,A NUMBER THAT CAN BE DIVIDED BY ANOTHER NUMBER
divieishon,deviation
divieit,deviate
divient,deviant
divine,ely,eness,nity,OF A HIGH DEGREE, SUPREME, ABOVE AVERAGE (or see define) "prefixes: semi"
divise,device / devise
divisible,bility,ly,CAN BE DIVIDED "prefixes: in/ multi"
division,*,,nal,SEPARATE PARTS WITHIN THE WHOLE "prefixes: multi/ sub"
divize,devise
divoed,devoid
divoid,devoid
divolve,devolve
divorce,*,,ed,cing,eable,ee,FORMAL DIVISION/ SEPARATION FROM
divoshen,devotion
divout,devout
divoution,devotion
divu,diva / deva
divudend,dividend
divulge,*,,ed,ging,ence,REVEAL A SECRET/ FACT
divurse,diverse

dofisable,divisible
dofol,duffle
dog, *, ggy,ggies,IN CANIS ANIMAL FAMILY (or see dodge) "prefixes: under"
doge,dodge / dog
dogma, *, atize,atizes,atized,atizing,atism,atist,atic, atically,PRINCIPLES/ TRUTHS DECIDED BY AUTHORITY
dogmadek,dogmatic
dogmatic, *, cally, BELIEVE YOUR PRINCIPLES ARE THE TRUTH
dogmutized,dogma(tized)
doil,duel / dual
doing, one, CURRENTLY IN THE ACT OF
doje,dodge
dok,dock
dokewment,document
dokma,dogma
dokter,doctor
doktren,doctrine
dokument,document
dol,doll/ dole / dual / duel / dull
dolar,dollar
dolcimer,dulcimer
dole, *, ed,ling,eful,DEAL/ HAND/ GIVE OUT PORTIONS OF SOMETHING (or see dolly)
doler,dollar
dolfen,dolphin
dolfin,dolphin
dolir,dollar
doll, *,lled,lling,lly,llish,llishly,llishness,A TOY,CUTE LOOKING, GET DRESSED UP (or see dole/ dodge)
dollar, *, U.S. MONEY/ BILL
dolly,lies,OBJECT WITH WHEELS FOR MOVING THINGS, TOOL FOR VARIOUS TRADES,A DOLL
dolphin, *, LIVES IN WATER, CETACEAN
dolsemer,dulcimer
dolsumer,dulcimer
dom,dome / doom / dumb
domain, *,anial,TERRITORY/ PROPERTY WITH BOUNDARIES "prefixes: sub"
domane,domain
domanet,dominant

---

doc,dock / duck / dose
docd,dock(ed) / duct / duck(ed)
docenchen,descension / dissension
docend,descend / dissent / decent
docent,descend / dissent / descent / decent
doch,dodge
docile,ely,lity,OF RECEPTIVE/ ACCEPTABLE ATTITUDE, ABLE TO CONFORM
docinchen,descension / dissension
docind,descend / dissent / descent / decent
docint,descend / dissent / descent / decent
dock, *, ked,king,ker, TYPE OF HERB BEHAVIOR, LOADING PLATFORM FOR VESSELS, TO REMOVE "prefixes: un"
docma,dogma
docmadek,dogmatic
doct,dock(ed) / duct / duck(ed)
doctor, *, red,ring,rly,ral,rate,ONE WHO REPAIRS BODILY INJURY "prefixes: pre"
doctrenul,doctrine(nal)
doctrine, *, nal,nality,nally,naire, DOGMATIC TEACHING OF BELIEFS/ VALUES "prefixes: in"
document, *, ted,ting,tary,tation,tal,talist,table,ter, PAPERS WHICH STATE EVIDENCE
documentary,ries,rily,FACTS FOR PUBLIC VIEWING "prefixes: semi"
dodad,doodad
dodch,dodge
doder,daughter
doderize,deodorize
dodge, *, ed,ging,er,MOVES ASIDE,SHIFTS FROM PREDICTED POSITION (or see dog)
dodil,doodle
dodul,doodle
dodurent,deoderant
doe, *, FEMALE OF SHEEP/ GOAT/ DEER/ RABBIT/ ANTELOPE (or see do/ dough)
doel,duel / dual
doeng,doing
does,A TENSE OF THE WORD 'DO', DOING CURRENTLY (or see due(s)/ doe(s)/ dose/ douse)
doesn't,CONTRACTION OF THE WORDS "DOES NOT"
doet,duet
dofesubelity,divisible(bility)

---

divurshen,diversion
divursity,diversity
divurt,divert
dixtarety,dexterity
diyect,deject
diyul,dial
dizalujen,disillusion
dizapashen,dissipate(tion)
dizapate,dissipate
dizastur,disaster
dizatation,dissertation
dizayrabol,desirable
dizbondent,despondent
dize,dizzy
dizeez,disease
dizembark,disembark
dizemunate,disseminate
dizenteant,dissent(ient)
dizi,dizzy
dizinfect,disinfect
dizmantul,dismantle
dizmul,dismal
dizobay,disobey
dizolve,dissolve
dizorder,disorder
dizordurly,disorderly
dizposuble,disposable
dizrepare,disrepair
dizrespekt,disrespect
dizumbark,disembark
dizupashe,dissipate(tion)
dizupate,dissipate
dizuray,disarray
dizzy,zier,ziest,zily,zied,zying,FUZZY,DISORIENTED, UNFOCUSED
do,oing,oes,one,oable,did, THE ACT OF (or see dew/ due/ doe/ dough) "prefixes: over/ un/ under"
doal,dual / duel
dob,dub
dobal,double
dobil,double
dobl,double
dobul,double

domasile,domicile
dome,* ,ed,ming,HALF CIRCLE/ 1800 (or see dumb/ doom) "prefixes: semi"
domein,domain
domenate,dominate
domeneer,domineer
domeneit,dominate
domenint,dominant
domenio,dominion
domenyen,dominion
domestic,* ,cally,cate,cated,cating,cation,cator,cable, city,cities,cize,FORCED TO CONFORM TO HUMAN USE "prefixes: semi"
domi,dummy
domicile,* ,ed,ling,liary,liate,liation,HOME/ RESIDENCE
**dominance,cy,AUTHORITY, RULE "prefixes: pre"
**dominant,tly,nce,AUTHORITY, RULE "prefixes: pre"
dominate,* ,ed,ting,tion,tive,tor,ant,POWER OVER, OVERRULER "prefixes: pre/ sub"
domineer,* ,red,ring,ringly,EXCESSIVE RULE OVER OTHERS
domineit,dominate
dominion,* ,ium,CONTROL OVER TERRITORY, OWNERSHIP OF
dominish,diminish
domino,oes,MASQUERADE COSTUME, GAME
domnate,dominate
domonent,dominant
domosile,domicile
domplin,dumpling
domunate,dominate
domunet,dominant
domusile,domicile
don,* ,nned,nning,TO PUT ON,ADDED TO NAME (or see dawn/ done)
don't,CONTRACTION FOR WORDS "DO NOT" (or see daunt/ don(nned)/ dawn(ed))
donate,* ,ed,ting,tion,tor,tive,A GIFT, PERHAPS WITH STRINGS ATTACHED
donc,dunk
dond,don't / daunt / don(nned) / dawn(ed)

done,PAST TENSE FOR THE WORD "DO", TASK/ JOB COMPLETED "prefixes: re/ under"
doner,donor
dong,dung
dongari,dungaree
dongen,dungeon
dongeri,dungaree
donjen,dungeon
donk,dunk
donkey,* ,AN ANIMAL
donor,* , ,rship,SOMEONE WHO GIVES SOMETHING AWAY
donqui,donkey
dont,don't / daunt / don(nned) / dawn(ed)
donur,donor
donut,doughnut
dooal,duel / dual
dood,dude
doodad,* , ,GADGET, DECORATION
doode,duty
doodle,* ,ed,ling,er,IDLY SKETCH, DRAW
doom,* ,med,ming,msday,THE END OF
doon,dune
doop,dupe
dooplicity,duplicity
door,* ,rless,OBJECT WHICH SEPARATES TWO SIDES WHEN CLOSED
doose,duce / deuce / due(s)
doosh,douche
doote,duty
dooz,due(s)
dope,* ,ed,ping,er,ey,SLANG FOR DRUGS,NOT SMART
doplex,duplex
doplicate,duplicate
doplicity,duplicity
doqiument,document
doqiumentary,documentary
dor,door
doreishon,duration
dorivative,derive(vative)
dorive,derive
dormant,ncy,ASLEEP
dormatory,dormitory

dormet,dormant
dormetory,dormitory
dormit,dormant
dormitory,ries,A LARGE PLACE WITH MANY ROOMS FOR SLEEPING/ LIVING
dormut,dormant
dormutory,dormitory
dorsal,lly,ON THE BACK
dorsil,dorsal
dorsul,dorsal
dos,does / doze / doe(s) / dose / due(s) / dowse / those
dosable,disable
dosach,dosage
dosage,* ,AMOUNT OF DRUG
dosbekable,despicable
dosberse,disperse / disburse
dosbikable,despicable
dosblased,displace(d)
dosblay,display
dosbose,dispose
doscremenate,discriminate
doscrete,discreet / discrete
dosderb,disturb
dosdrakt,distract
dosdrebute,distribute
dosdress,distress
dosdrust,distrust
dosdurb,disturb
dose,* ,ed,sing,sage, sages,SPECIFIC AMOUNT OF SOMETHING (or see doze/ due(s)) "prefixes: over"
dosech,dosage
dosege,dosage
dosej,dosage
dosemanate,disseminate
dosembar,december
dosend,descend / dissent / descent / decent
dosent,doesn't / descend / dissent / descent / decent
dosenugrate,disintegrate
doser,dozer
dosfigyer,disfigure
dosgreshun,discretion
dosgruntle,disgruntle
dosh,douche

dosich,dosage
dosige,dosage
dosij,dosage
dosil,docile
dosimbur,december
dosimer,dulcimer
dosin,dozen
dosind,descend / dissent / descent / decent
dosint,descend / dissent / descent / decent
dosk,dusk
doskrete,discreet / discrete
dospinse,dispense
dosplaced,displace(d)
dosplay,display
dosplease,displease
dospose,dispose
dosposuble,disposable
dospozul,disposal
dosputuble,dispute(table)
dosqualify,disqualify
dosreputuble,disreputable
dosrupshen,disruption
dosrupt,disrupt
dost,dust
dostengwish,distinguish
dosterb,disturb
dostingwish,distinguish
dostract,distract
dostress,distress
dostrust,distrust
dosuj,dosage
dosul,docile
dot,* ,tted,tting,ROUND SPOTS (or see dote)
dote,* ,ed,ting,tingly,TO WATCH OVER, OVERSEE CLOSELY (or see dot/ coubt)
doted,dot(tted) / dote(d)
doter,daughter
dotir,daughter
dotur,daughter
dou,doe / dough
double,* ,ed,ling,eness,ly,er,TWICE AS MANY AS THE ORIGINAL "prefixes: re"

doubt,* ,ted,ting,table,tingly,tful,tfully,tless,tlessly,NOT COMPLETELY BELIEVABLE "prefixes: re/ un"
douche,* ,ed,hing,INTRODUCING FLUID INTO CAVITY OF BODY
dough,hy,hier,hiest,hiness,PASTY / TACKY MIXTURE, MONEY
doughnut,* ,ROUND PASTRY WITH HOLE
doul,dual / duel / dowel / dole
douls,dowel(s)
doum,dome
doumein,domain
doumenion,dominion
doumestic,domestic
douminion,dominion
doumisaiol,domicile
doun,down
douneit,donate
douner,donor / down(er)
doup,dope
dous,dose / douse / those / thus
dousand,thousand
douse,* ,ed,sing,er,SMOTHER,PUT OUT, EXTINGUISH, SEEKS WATER,ALSO SPELLED 'DOUSE' (or see dowse)
dousech,dosage
dousej,dosage
dousell,dosage
douser,dozer
dout,doubt / dote
dove,* ,PAST TENSE FOR THE WORD "DIVE", A BIRD
dovegin,division
dovesubelity,divisible(bility)
dovesubl,divisible
dovine,divine
dovisability,divisible(bility)
dovorse,divorce
dow,dough / doe
dowel,* ,led,ling,USED LIKE A NAIL/ PIN/ SCREW
dowen,doing
dowl,dowel
down,OPPOSITE OF UP, FEATHERS OF A FOWL
downut,doughnut
dows,douse / dowse / dowel(s)

dowse,* ,ed,sing,er, SMOTHER,PUT OUT, EXTINGUISH, SEEKS WATER,ALSO SPELLED 'DOUSE' (or see douse)
dowt,doubt
dowtful,doubt(full)
dowzer,dozer
doz,doze / does / dose
doze,* ,ed,zing,er,zy,zily,ziness,SLEEP LIGHTLY (or see dose)
dozen,TWELVE OF SOMETHING
dozent,doesn't
dozer,*,HEAVY EQUIPMENT WHICH MOVES EARTHEN MATERIAL
drad,dread
draft,*,ted,ting,ter,tier,tiest,ty,tily,tiness,A LIGHT BREEZE,TO PULL/ DRAW FROM "prefixes: in/ over/ up"
drag,*,gged,gging,ggingly,SLIDE/ PULL WITH DIFFICULTY, PULLING WITHOUT LIFTING, MEN IN WOMEN'S CLOTHING
dragen,dragon
dragenfly,dragonfly
dragin,dragon
draginfly,dragonfly
dragon,*,nish,MYTHICAL ANIMAL
dragonfly,lies,INSECT
draj,dry
draid,dried
draier,drier
draiest,driest
draif,drive
draik,drake
drain,*,ned,ning,nage,FLUID/ ENERGY FLOWING AWAY FROM, OUTLET "prefixes: under"
draiv,drive
drake,*,INSECT FOR BAIT, MALE IN DUCK FAMILY
drama,*,atic,atical,atically,atize,aturgy,atist,GIVEN TO THEATER/ PLAYS/ CHARACTER ROLES "prefixes: over/ melo"
dramatize,*,ed,zing,zation,GIVEN TO THEATER/ PLAYS/ CHARACTER ROLES "prefixes: over"
dran,drawn / drain
drank,PASTE TENSE FOR THE WORD "DRINK"
draot,drought

drape, *, ed, ping, ery, eries, HANGING CLOTH USED TO VEIL SOMETHING FROM SIGHT OR TO ENHANCE
drapir, dropper
drapur, dropper
dras, dress
drastic, cally, SEVERELY
drau, draw
draught, U.K. WORD FOR DRAFT (or see drought)
draul, droll / drawl
draun, drawn / drown
drauper, dropper
drause, drowsy
draut, drought
draw, *, wing, wn, rew, wable, TO BRING FORTH FROM OUT OF SIGHT, BRING TOWARDS "prefixes: over/ un"
drawin, drawn
drawl, *, led, ling, ler, lingly, TO DRAG VOWELS OUT SLOWLY IN SPEAKING (or see droll)
drawn, PAST TENSE FOR THE WORD "DRAW" (or see drown) "prefixes: in/ over"
drawnd, drown(ed)
drawpur, dropper
drawt, drought
dread, *, ded, ding, dful, dfully, dfulness, COMPLETE APPREHENSION IN FACING A SITUATION
dream, *, med, ming, mless, mlessly, mlessness, mful, mfully, mfulness, mily, my, mt, IMAGINE, THINK, ENVISION "prefixes: un"
dreary, rily, riness, GLOOMY
drebul, dribble
drebuld, dribble(d)
drech, dredge
dred, dread
dredge, *, ed, ging, er, TO GATHER OBJECTS UP FROM THE BOTTOM OF A BODY OF WATER WITH TOOLS/ MACHINERY
dreem, dream
dreft, drift
dreg, dredge
dreid, dried
dreik, drake
drein, drain
dreip, drape
drej, dredge
drel, drill
drell, dredge
drem, dream
drench, hes, hed, hing, her, SOAKING WET
drenk, drink
drenker, drinker
drep, drip
drere, dreary
drery, dreary
dres, dress
dreser, dresser
dress, sses, sser, ssing, ssage, TO PUT ON CLOTHING "prefixes: re/ un/ under"
dresser, ONE WHO HELPS OTHERS DRESS IN COSTUMES, A CABINET WITH DRAWERS
dresur, dresser
drew, PAST TENSE FOR THE WORD "DRAW" "prefixes: over"
drewl, drool
drewp, droop
drezur, dresser
dri, dry
dribble, *, ed, ling, er, SMALL OR SHORT AMOUNT OF ANYTHING
dribul, dribble
drid, dried
dried, PAST TENSE FOR THE WORD "DRY"
drier, MORE DRY
driest, MOST" DRY
drift, *, ted, ting, tingly, tless, ty, ter, AMBLES ABOUT/ AROUND/ AWAY WITH EASE
drill, *, lled, lling, llable, ller, TO BORE, MAKE OPENINGS
drim, dream
drinch, drench
drink, *, king, rank, ker, kable, kability, runk, TO TAKE IN LIQUIDS
drinker, *, ONE WHO OVER INDULGES IN ALCOHOL
drip, *, pped, pping, ppy, pless, FALLING DROPS OF FLUID
drire, dreary
dris, dry(ries)
driur, drier / dryer

drive, *, ving, en, rove, er, TO MOVE/ PUSH/ RIDE SOMETHING ALONG "prefixes: over"
drizzle, *, ed, ling, ly, VARIETY OF RAINFALL
dro, draw
drofe, drove
drog, drug
drol, drawl / droll
droll, ller, llest, llness, lly, ODDLY HUMOROUS (or see drawl)
droma, drama
dron, drone/ drawn / drown
dronc, drunk
drone, *, ed, ning, ningly, er, SINGLE TONE SOUND, A BEE, INCAPABLE OF FREE WILL/ THOUGHT, REMOTE COMBAT VEHICLE
drool, *, led, ling, lingly, ler, SALIVA COMING FROM MOUTH
droop, *, ped, ping, pingly, py, TO LAY FORWARD LAZILY, SLUMP
drop, *, pped, pping, ppings, pper, LIQUID FALLING IN BLOBS, LET SOMETHING GO
droper, dropper
dropir, dropper
dropper, *, rful, AN INSTRUMENT WHICH ALLOWS A DROP AT A TIME
dropur, dropper
drouf, drove
drought, *, ty, LONG PERIODS OF TIME WITHOUT WATER (or see draught)
droun, drone / drown
drouse, drowsy
drout, drought
drouv, drove
drouze, drowsy
drove, *, PAST TENSE FOR THE WORD "DRIVE", MANY OF SOMETHING
drow, draw
drown, *, ned, ning, INTAKE OF WATER WHICH MAY KILL (or see drawn)
drowsy, sily, siness, NEARING SLEEP
drowt, drought
droz, draw(s)
dru, drew / true

druch, drudge
druchary, drudge(ry)
drudge, *, ed, ging, ery, eries, gingly, MENIAL/ DULL WORK
druel, drool
drug, *, gged, gging, ggy, CHEMICALS (or see drudge)
drugd, drug(gged) / drudge(d)
druge, drudge / drug
druj, drudge
drujary, drudge(ry)
druk, drug
drul, drool
drum, *, mmed, mming, mmer, PERCUSSION INSTRUMENT, A LURING SOUND OR ACTION
drumd, drum(mmed)
drumer, drum(mmer)
drunk, *, ken, ker, kest, kard, PAST TENSE FOR THE WORD "DRINK", SOMEONE WHO DRINKS TOO MUCH ALCOHOL
drupe, droop
drus, dress
dry, ries, ried, ying, yable, yer, yest, iest, yable, yness, yly, TO REMOVE MOISTURE "prefixes: semi"
dryd, dried
dryer, APPLIANCE THAT DRIES CLOTHES (or see drier)
dryest, driest
dryur, drier / dryer
du, dew / due/ do
duable, do(able) / due(able)
dual, lity, lly, lism, TWO WORKING THE SAME, DOUBLE (or see duel) "prefixes: no"
duarf, dwarf
duarfs, dwarf(rves)
duat, duet
dub, *, bbed, bbing, bber, TITLE/ NAME BESTOWED ON YOU BY ANOTHER, SOUND RECORDING
dubal, double
dubate, debate
dubilutate, debilitate
duble, double
dublikate, duplicate
dubol, double
dubry, debris
dubul, double

ducanter, decanter
duce, *, TWO, PEACE, LEAVING, LATER, STREET GANG (or see deuce)
ducenchen, descension / dissension
ducend, descend / dissent / descent / decent
ducent, dissent / descent / decent / descend
duch, douche
ducinchen, descension / dissension
ducind, descend / dissent / descent / decent
ducint, dissent / descent / decent / descend
duck, *, ked, king, ker, ky, TO STOOP/ TUCK/ DIVE, FOWL/ BIRD (or see duct)
ducline, decline
duct, *, ted, ting, tless, tal, CABLE/ CHANNEL FOR VARIOUS THINGS, TAPE (or see duck(ed))
dud, *, DOESN'T WORK, CLOTHES (or see dude)
dudad, doodad
dude, *, TOURIST ON A RANCH, INFORMAL REFERENCE TO ANOTHER PERSON (or see duty)
duded out, DRESSED SNAZZY
dudi, duty
dudil, doodle
dudol, doodle
dudy, duty
due, *, OUTSTANDING DEBT, DATE IT IS PAYABLE UPON (or see dew/ do) "prefixes: en/ over/ un"
dueble, do(able) / due(able)
duel, *, ling, list, ler, DISPUTE/ FIGHT BETWEEN TWO PEOPLE/ FACTIONS (or see dual/ dwell)
duen, doing
dueng, doing
duet, *, tist, TWO VOICES/ INSTRUMENTS PERFORMING TOGETHER
duf, dove
dufalt, default
dufase, deface
dufeet, defeat
dufel, duffel
dufenative, definitive
dufendant, defendant
dufense, defense
dufensible, defensible
duffel, CANVAS/ WOOL MATERIAL

duffil, duffel
duffle, duffel
dufianse, defiance
dufide, divide
dufil, duffel
dufinative, definitive
dufine, define
dufishant, deficient
dufishensy, deficiency
dufle, duffel
dufol, duffel
dufray, defray
duful, duffel
dufunkt, defunct
dufy, defy
dugrade, degrade
dugree, degree
duible, do(able) / due(able)
duil, dual / duel
duin, doing
duing, doing
duk, duck / duke / duct
duka, decay
dukanter, decanter
dukd, duck(ed) / duct / duke(d)
duke, *, edom, FISTS, POSITION UNDER THAT OF PRINCE (or see duck/ duct)
dukline, decline
dukrepit, decrepit
dukt, duck(ed) / duct / duke(d)
dul, dual / duel / dull
dulay, delay
dulcimer, *, STRINGED INSTRUMENT
dulectable, delectable
dulema, dilemma
dulereus, delirious
dulete, delete
dulever, deliver
duliburate, deliberate
dulicacy, delicacy
dulimu, dilemma
dulishus, delicious
dulite, delight / daylight

duliver, deliver
dull,*, lled, lling, ller, llest, llish, llness, lly, llard, WITHOUT SHINE/ ATTRACTIVENESS, BORING (or see duel/ dual)
dulsemur, dulcimer
dulsimer, dulcimer
dulujen, delusion / dilute(tion)
duluxe, deluxe
dum, doom / dumb
dumand, demand
dumb,*, ber, best, bing, bly, bness, mmy, CANNOT SPEAK, NOT TOO BRIGHT, MANNEQUIN
dumbling, dumpling
dume, dummy / doom
dumean, demean
dumeener, demeanor
dumenish, diminish
dumenshen, dimension
dumention, dimension
dumenyen, dominion
dumer, dumb(er)
dumes, dummy(mies)
dumesdek, domestic
dumest, dumb(est)
dumestic, domestic
dumie, dummy
duminish, diminish
duminted, demented
dumir, dumb(er)
dumist, dumb(est)
dumize, demise
dummy, mmies, mmied, mmying, ONE BEING MANIPULATED INTO ACTION/ MOTION, A MANNEQUIN/ PUPPET
dumonik, demon(ic)
dumor, dumb(er)
dump,*, ped, ping, per, py, pily, piness, pier, piest, TO HEAVILY FALL, BE DROPPED
dumpling,*, DOUGHBALLS COOKED IN SAUCE
dumur, dumb(er)
dumy, dummy
dun, done / dune
dunce,*, DEROGATORY TERM FOR SLOW LEARNER
dune,*, MOUND/ HILL OF SAND

dung,*, ged, ging, gy, MANURE (or see dunk)
dungaree,*, HEAVY COTTON CLOTHING
dungeon,*, PRISON CELL, CASTLE BASEMENT
dungeree, dungaree
dunguree, dungaree
dunie, deny
dunjen, dungeon
dunk,*, ked, king, TO DIP INTO (or see dung)
dunomenator, denominator
dunomunashin, denomination
dunote, denote
duns, dunce / dune(s)
duo, uet, A PAIR
duol, dual / duel
duorf, dwarf
duorfs, dwarf(rves)
duparsher, departure
dupart, depart
dupartment, department
duparture, departure
dupe,*, ed, ping, TO TRICK/ DECEIVE
dupend, depend
dupendant, dependant / dependent
dupendence, dependence
dupikt, depict
dupind, depend
duplacate, duplicate
duplaqueit, duplication
duplequeit, duplication
dupleshin, depletion
duplete, deplete
duplex, xes, xity, TWO WORKING IDENTICALLY, SIDE-BY-SIDE
duplicate,*, ed, ting, tion, tor, able, ability, tely, tive, COPY OF THE ORIGINAL "prefixes: in/ re"
duplicity, tous, TWO-FACED, MISLEADING
dupliqueit, duplication
duplokate, duplicate
duploma, diploma
duplomusy, diplomacy
duplorable, deplorable
duplore, deplore
dupose, depose

dupozishen, deposition
dupozit, deposit
dupresheate, depreciate
duprive, deprive
durable,*, bility, eness, ly, USEFUL MANY TIMES "prefixes: non"
durachon, duration
durashen, duration
duration, FROM NOW UNTIL...
durdee, dirty
durebul, durable
durect, direct
durection, direction
durectory, directory
dureishon, duration
durekshun, duration
durekt, direct
durektory, directory
dureng, during
dureshon, duration
duress, UNDER STRESS, RESTRAINED FROM FREEDOM
duretion, duration
durible, durable
during, AT THE SAME TIME
durivadive, derivative
durivative, derivative
durive, derive
durmatites, dermal(atitis)
durt, dirt
durty, dirty
dus, does / due(s) / deuce
dusabiludy, disability
dusable, disable
dusaster, disaster
dusbite, despite
dusblay, display
dusbose, dispose
dusbute, dispute
duscrete, discreet / discrete
duscretion, discretion
discuss, discuss
dusdane, disdain
dusdent, distend

dusdention, distend(nsion)
dusdentshen, distend(nsion)
dusderb, disturb
dusdort, distort
dusdrakt, distract
dusdrebute, distribute
duse, does / due(s) / deuce
duseese, decease / disease
duseft, deceive(d)
dusember, december
dusemble, dissemble
dusembul, dissemble
dusemunate, disseminate
dusenagrate, disintegrate
dusenchen, descension / dissension
dusend, descend / dissent / cescent / decent
dusendent, descendant
dusenshen, dissension / descension
dusent, dissent / descent / decent / descend
duses, decease / disease / deuce(s)
dusest, decease(d) / disease'(d)
duset, deceit
dusetful, deceit(ful)
dusev, deceive
dusevd, deceive(d)
duseze, disease
dusfegure, disfigure
dusgard, discard
dusgise, disguise
dusgrase, disgrace
dush, douche
dushevul, dishevel
dusidewus, deciduous
dusimanate, disseminate
dusimbul, dissemble
dusimbur, december
dusin, dozen
dusinagrate, disintegrate
dusindent, descendant
dusinshun, dissension / descension
dusint, doesn't
dusipul, disciple
dusk, ky, kily, kiness, END OF DAY BEFORE NIGHTFALL

duskremanate, discriminate
duskrepensy, discrepancy
duskrete, discreet / discrete
duskribe, describe
duskripshen, description
duskust, disgust
duskuver, discover
duskwolify, disqualify
duslocate, dislocate
dusloge, dislodge
dusmanul, dismantle
dusmay, dismay
dusmiss, dismiss
dusmownt, dismount
dusolfe, dissolve
dusoreant, disorient
duspensible, dispensable
duspeut, dispute
duspinse, dispense
duspite, despite
dusplay, display
dusplease, displease
duspose, dispose
dusposil, disposal
dusposuble, disposable
dusregard, disregard
dusrobe, disrobe
dust, *, ted, ting, ty, tless, tily, tiness, ter, TINY PARTICLES
OF MATTER
dustane, disdain
duste, dust
dusteengwish, distinguish
dustendible, distend(sible)
dustenkt, distinct
dusterb, disturb
dustill, distill
dustingwish, distinguish
dustintible, distend(sible)
dustort, distort
dustract, distract
dustress, distress
dustroy, destroy
dustrukshen, destruction

duswrubshen, disruption
duswrubt, disrupt
dute, duty
dutektur, detector
dutenshin, detention
dutereate, deteriorate
dutereorate, deteriorate
duterint, deterrent
dutermin, determine
duterminashen, determination
duti, duty
duturgent, detergent
duty, ties, tiful, tifully, tifulness, teous, OBLIGATION,
RESPONSIBILITY, NECESSARY "prefixes: un"
duv, dove
duvejin, division
duvelup, develop
duversity, diversity
duvesubelity, divisible(bility)
duvide, divide
duvigen, division
duvigin, division
duvijen, division
duvine, divine
duvise, device
duvisubil, divisible
duvize, device
duvoid, devoid
duvorse, divorce
duvoshen, devotion
duvursedy, diversity
duwen, doing
dux, duck(s) / duct / duke(s)
duz, due(s) / does
duzaster, disaster
duzen, dozen
duzent, doesn't
duzeze, disease
duzin, dozen
duzint, doesn't
duzolve, dissolve
duzoreint, disorient

dwarf,*,fed,fing,fish,fishly,fishness,fism,rves,STUNTED FROM FULL GROWTH "prefixes: semi"
dwarves,MORE THAN ONE DWARF (or see dwarf)
dwell,lled,lling,ller,lt,DELAY,LINGER
dwendle,dwindle
dwindle,*,ed,ling,er,SHRINK,DEGENERATE,SHRIVEL
dworf,dwarf
dyagnol,diagonal
dyagnose,diagnose
dyalekt,dialect
dyameter,diameter
dyatery,dietary
dye,*,ed,eing,er,yable,STAIN/ COLOR/ PIGMENTS TO APPLY (or see die/ dii) "prefixes: over"
dyet,diet
dyetery,dietary
dyignose,diagnose
dying,TOWARDS DEATH, TRANSFORMATION "prefixes: un"
dyke,*,MASCULINE LESBIAN (or see dike)
dylate,dilate
dynamic,*,ism,ist,istic,cal,cally,MOTION OF HIGH ENERGY "prefixes: bio"
dynamite,tic,er,EXPLOSIVES
dynasty,ties,STRING OF HEREDITARY RULERS
dypur,diaper / dipper
dyre,dire
dys,PREFIX INDICATING "BAD" MOST OFTEN MODIFIES THE WORD (or see die(s)/ dice)
dysekt,dissect
dysentery,ric,INFECTIOUS DISEASE
dysfunction,*,nal,NOT ACTING WITHIN IDEAL LIMITS
dyslexia,ic,TIMING IN CORPUS CALLOSUM NEURON SIGNALS WHICH AFFECTS COMMUNICATION BETWEEN BRAIN HEMISPHERES
dyufram,diaphragm
dyul,dial
dyulog,dialogue
dyureuh,diarrhea
each,ONE APIECE, TREATED INDIVIDUALLY
eager,rly,rness,MOTIVATED, VERY INTERESTED
eagle,*,BIRD
ear,*,GROWTH ON HEAD TO HEAR WITH

earing,earring
early,lier,liest,liness,PRIOR TO ORIGINAL TIME
earn,*,ned,ning,ner,REWARD FOR SERVICE/ LABOR (or see urn) "prefixes: non/ un"
earnest,*,tly,tness,SINCERE FEELINGS, EFFORT, MONEY TRANSACTION TO HOLD CONTRACT
earring,*,EAR ADORNMENT
earth,*,hed,hing,hen,hly,hlier,hliest,OUR PLANET "prefixes: un"
ease,*,ed,sing,eful,efully,efulness,sy,ABLE TO PERFORM WITHOUT STRAIN/ EFFORT (or see easy) "prefixes: dis/ un"
easel,*,TRIPOD TO HOLD WORKBOARDS, ETC.
easement,*,LEGAL USE/ RIGHTS TO SOMETHING, TO HELP MAKE EASIER
easily,NO DIFFICULTY
east,tern,ternly,tward,terly,terlies,terner,ting,tings, COMPASS DIRECTION
easy,sier,siest,silly,siness,NOT DIFFICULT/ HARD (or see ease) "prefixes: un"
eat,*,ting,ten,tery,table,tables,ter,edible,TO INGEST "prefixes: over"
eaves,OVERHANG OF A BUILDING
eaze,ease / easy
eb,ebb
ebademik,epidemic
ebasode,episode
ebb,,bbed,bbing,TO FALL/ SINK/ RECEDE
ebdikate,abdicate
ebdumin,abdomen
ebedemek,epidemic
eberigenie,aborigine
ebide,abide
ebirijeny,aborigine
ebiss,abyss
ebnormul,abnormal
ebolish,abolish
ebomenable,abominable
ebominable,abominable
ebony,BLACK WOOD
ebord,aboard / abort
ebort,abort / aboard
ebowt,about

ebreveate,abbreviate
ebrod,abroad
ebsolv,absolve
ebstain,abstain
ebundinse,abundance
ebune,ebony
ebuve,above
academic,academic
eccentric,*,cally,city,cities,ODD, NOT OF THE NORM
ecema,eczema
ech,each / etch / edge / itch
echd,itch(ed) / etch(ed)
echo,oes,oed,oing,oingly,REPETITIVE SOUNDS BOUNCING BACK TOWARDS ORIGINATOR "prefixes: re"
echu,issue
echud,issue(d)
eckbrest,express(ed)
eckdravert,extrovert
ecksdensible,extensible
ecksderminate,exterminate
ecksdreem,extreme
eckspedeant,expedient
ecksplikuble,explicable
ecksploit,exploit
eckstensev,extensive
eckstensibly,extensible(ly)
ecksterminate,exterminate
ecksturminate,exterminate
eckuivocal,equivocal
eckwalibreum,equilibrium
eckwunimity,equanimity
eclectic,cally,cism,COMPILATION OF OTHERS WORK/ VARIOUS SOURCES
eclektic,eclectic
eclepse,eclipse
eclipse,*,ed,sing,ptic,SHADOW CAST BY PLANETARY BODIES BLOCKING ANOTHER PLANETARY BODY
ecnolege,acknowledge
eco,PREFIX INDICATING "ECOLOGY" MOST OFTEN MODIFIES THE WORD (or see echo)
ecoli,A BACTERIA, PROPERLY SPELLED "E COLI"

ecology, gical, gically, gist, SCIENCE ON ORGANISMS IN THE ENVIRONMENT
ecology, ecology
economy, mies, mic, mics, mical, mically, mize, mism, mist, GOODS AND MONEY "prefixes: dis/ non/ un"
economy, economy
ecosfere, ecosphere
ecosfir, ecosphere
ecosistem, ecosystem
ecosphere, BREATHABLE AREA FOR LIFE
ecosystem, *, ORGANISMS INTERACTING TO CREATE ENVIRONMENT
ecquit, acquit
ecsallereit, exaggerate
ecsamin, examine
ecsampol, example
ecsaspereit, exasperate
ecscaveit, excavate
ecsclimashin, exclamation
ecsebt, except / accept
ecselerate, accelerate
ecsempt, exempt
ecsepshen, except(ion)
ecsibit, exhibit
ecsid, exceed
ecsite, excite
ecsklumashen, exclamation
ecspedishon, expedition
ecspekt, expect
ecspirians, experience
ecspos, expose
ecstasy, sies, atic, atically, JUBILANT, IN BLISS
ecsteengwish, extinguish
ecstradite, extradite
ecstrakt, extract
ecstuse, ecstasy
ecto, PREFIX INDICATING "OUTSIDE" MOST OFTEN MODIFIES THE WORD
ecuivalent, equivalent
ecute, acute
ecwanemity, equanimity
ecwashin, equation
ecwatic, aquatic

ecwilebreum, equilibrium
eczema, atous, SKIN IRRITATION FROM BACTERIA
eczima, eczema
ed, eat / eight / ate
edable, edible
edabt, adapt
edakit, etiquette
edapd, adapt
edapt, adapt
edatur, editor
edch, etch / edge / itch
eddy, ddies, ddied, ying, CIRCULAR MOVING CURRENT IN WATER/ AIR
ede, eddy
edel, it'll
edelescense, adolescence
edelt, adult
edendum, addendum
edeology, ideology
edeosy, idiocy
edept, adept
edeshen, edition / add(ition)
edet, edit
edetur, editor
edeusy, idiocy
edeut, idiot
edge, *, ed, ging, gy, gier, giest, giness, er, POINT OF ANGLE WHERE ONE ANGLE DROPS OFF AT
edgust, adjust
edhere, adhere
edi, eddy
edible, *, lity, eness, CAN BE SAFELY EATEN "prefixes: in"
edibol, edible
edikit, etiquette
edikshen, addict(ion)
edil, it'll
edindum, addendum
ediosy, idiocy
edishen, edition / add(ition)
edit, *, ted, ting, tor, tion, MAKE READY FOR PUBLICATION "prefixes: in/ un"
edition, *, ONE OUT OF A SET OF A PUBLISHED VOLUME (or see add(ition))

editor, *, rial, rially, rialist, rialize, rializes, rialized, rializing, DIRECTOR/ PREPARER OF WRITTEN MATERIAL
editur, editor
ediukeit, educate
edj, etch / edge / itch
edjust, adjust
edmechen, admission
edmichen, admission
edmire, admire
edmishun, admission
edmit, admit
edmonish, admonish
edobt, adopt
edolt, adult
edoo, adieu
edopt, adopt
edore, adore
edorn, adorn
edrenulin, adrenaline
edres, address
edroit, adroit
edsedura, etcetera
edself, itself
edsh, etch / edge / itch
edu, adieu
eduble, edible
educate, *, ed, ting, tion, tional, tive, tor, INSTRUCT "prefixes: in/ un"
edukit, etiquette
edul, it'll
edulescense, adolescence
edult, adult
edut, edit
edvantij, advantage
edverse, adverse
edvirse, adverse
edvise, advise / advice
edvurse, adverse
edy, eddy
edzetera, etcetera
eel, *, OCEAN FISH
eet, eat / yet
ef, if / eve

efact, effect / affect
efadent, evident
efaire, affair
efakt, effect / affect
efal, evil
efalushin, evolution
efan, even
efar, ever
efare, affair
efect, effect / affect
efegy, effigy
efekt, effect / affect
efektive, effect(ive) / affect(ive)
efeminate, effeminate
efeminit, effeminate
efen, even
efening, evening
efenity, affinity
efer, ever / affair
efert, effort
eferves, effervesce
efervesant, effervescent
efervescent, effervescent
efeus, effuse
efews, effuse

effect, *, ted, ting, tive, tively, tiveness, tual, tually, tualness, tuate, tuation, RESULT, FULFILLMENT ACCOMPLISHMENT (or see affect) "prefixes: in"
effeminate, acy, acies, ely, eness, OF FEMININE PERSUASION
effervesce, *, ed, cing, ence, ent, ently, GASEOUS BUBBLES, HAPPY FEELINGS
effervescent, tly, nce, GASEOUS BUBBLES, STRONG FEELINGS
efficacy, city, cious, ciously, ciousness, TO BE EFFECTIVE "prefixes: in"
efficiency, cies, nt, PRODUCE WELL IN SHORT PERIOD OF TIME, TYPE OF LIVING QUARTERS
efficient, tly, ncy, PRODUCE EFFECTIVELY IN SHORT PERIOD OF TIME "prefixes: in"
effigy, gies, SOMETHING CONSTRUCTED IN HUMAN LIKENESS

effort, *, tless, tlessly, tlessness, ATTEMPT TO PRODUCE, SHOW SKILLS/ TALENTS
effuse, *, ed, sing, sion, sive, sively, siveness, EXPRESS/ FLOW/ SPREAD FREELY

efichent, efficient
eficiency, efficiency
efident, evident
efigy, effigy
efil, evil
efilli, effigy
efilushen, evolution
efin, even
efinity, affinity
efir, ever
efirves, effervesce
efirvesant, effervescent
efishensy, efficiency
efishent, efficient
efishiensi, efficiency
efisiancy, efficiency
efl, evil
eflikt, afflict
eflot, afloat
efluinse, affluence
efning, evening
efodent, evident
efogy, effigy
efol, evil
efolushin, evolution
efolve, evolve
efon, even
efoot, afoot
efor, ever
eford, afford
efort, effort
efrad, afraid
efrebote, every(body)
efreda, every(day)
efree, every
efrething, every(thing)
efrewer, every(where)
efrewun, every(one)
efriwun, every(one)

efront, affront
efrunt, affront
efryday, every(day)
efudent, evident
efugy, effigy
eful, evil
efulushun, evolution
efur, ever
efurt, effort
efurves, effervesce
efurvesent, effervescent
efuse, effuse
efut, afoot
eg, edge / egg / etch / itch
egajurate, exaggerate
egalatarian, egalitarian
egalitarian, *, nism, EQUALITY OF ALL PEOPLES
egalutarean, egalitarian
egekt, eject
egemplify, exemplify
egenst, against
eger, eager
egern, adjourn
egg, *, gged, gging, ggy, PRODUCED BY FOWL / BIRD / REPTILES
eginst, against
egle, eagle
egneranse, ignorant(nce)
egneshin, ignition
egneus, igneous
egnide, ignite
egnishin, ignition
egnite, ignite
egnor, ignore
egnorants, ignorant(nce)
egnurant, ignorant
ego, *, oism, oist, otistic, oistical, oistically, otist, otism, ocentric, PART OF US THAT IS SELF-SERVING/ FEARFUL (or see echo)
egotist, tic, tical, tically, CENTERED ON SELF
egotistic, cal, cally, CENTERED ON ONESELF
egre, agree
egresiv, aggressive

egsabishen, exhibit(ion)	egsept, except / accept	egsplod, explode
egsadera, etcetera	egsersize, exercise / exorcise	egsplor, explore
egsagurate, exaggerate	egsert, exert	egsplorashen, explore(ration)
egsajurate, exaggerate	egsesif, excess(ive) / access(ive)	egsploratory, explore(ratory)
egsakt, exact	egsest, exist	egsploshen, explosion
egsam, exam	egsetara, etcetera	egsplosive, explosive
egsample, example	egsglumashen, exclamation	egsplunashen, explanation
egsaspurate, exasperate	egshale, exhale	egsport, export
egsastshin, exhaust(ion)	egsibeshen, exhibit(ion)	egsportashen, export(ation)
egsbarenshal, experiential	egsibit, exhibit	egspos, expose
egsbereanse, experience	egsilarate, exhilarate / accelerate	egspres, express
egsberenshal, experiential	egsile, exile	egspurashen, expire(ration)
egsberimentashen, experiment(ation)	egsima, eczema	egspurt, expert
egsbire, expire	egsimplify, exemplify	egsqwizit, exquisite
egsblan, explain	egsimt, exempt	egstend, extend
egsblekuble, explicable	egsist, exist	egstengwish, extinguish
egsblod, explode	egsistens, exist(ence)	egstenkt, extinct
egsblor, explore	egsit, exit	egstensev, extensive
egsbloshen, explosion	egskershun, excursion	egstenshen, extension
egsbort, export	egskurshen, excursion	egstenuate, extenuate
egsboz, expose	egskuvate, excavate	egstereor, exterior
egsbres, express	egsorsize, exercise / exorcise	egsternul, external
egsburenshal, experiential	egsost, exhaust	egstinkt, extinct
egsburt, expert	egsostshen, exhaust(ion)	egstinsev, extensive
egscavate, excavate	egsotic, exotic	egstra, extra
egsclusive, exclusive	egspadishen, expedition	egstradite, extradite
egsdensible, extensible	egspand, expand	egstrakt, extract
egsdra, extra	egspans, expanse / expense	egstravert, extrovert
egsdradite, extradite	egspect, expect	egstrem, extreme
egsdrakt, extract	egspedient, expedient	egstremly, extreme(ly)
egsdreem, extreme	egspeedeint, expedient	egsrordinare, extraordinaire
egsdrordinary, extraordina re	egspel, expel	egsrordinary, extraordinary
egsdrordinary, extraordina y	egspense, expense	egsturnal, external
egsduse, ecstasy	egsperament, experiment	egsubishen, exhibit(ion)
egsebit, exhibit	egspereanse, experience	egsulent, excellent
egsebt, except / accept	egspinse, expense	egsurshen, exert(ion)
egsecutive, executive	egspirashen, expire(ration)	egsurt, exert
egsedira, etcetera	egspire, expire	egszemt, exempt
egseed, exceed	egsplanashen, explanation	egukate, educate
egsemplify, exemplify	egsplanatory, explanatory	egul, eagle
egsempt, exempt	egsplane, explain	egur, eager
egsemshen, exempt(ion)	egsplecable, explicable	egzajurate, exaggerate
egsepshen, except(ion)	egsplesit, explicit	egzakt, exact

egzam, exam	einol, anal	ekosistem, ecosystem
egzample, example	einos, anus	ekosphere, ecosphere
egzema, eczema	einus, anus	eksadra, etcetera
egzershin, exert(ion)	eipril, April	eksagerashen, exaggerate(tion)
egzile, exile	eir, air / heir / err	etsail, exile
egzilurate, exhilarate / accelerate	eirborn, airborne	eksajurashen, exaggerate(tion)
egzima, eczema	eirlum, heirloom	eksakute, execute
egzimpt, exempt	eirport, airport	eksalant, excellent
egzimt, exempt	eis, ace	eksalins, excel(llence)
egzist, exist	eit, eight / ate	eksallereit, exaggerate
egzit, exit	ej, edge / etch / itch	eksam, exam
egzotek, exotic	ejakt, eject	eksamen, examine
egzurshen, exert(ion)	**eject,** * , ted, ting, tion, table, tive, tor, tors, FORCED TO LEAVE/ BE EXPELLED	eksamenashen, examine(nation)
egzursize, exercise / exorcise		eksamin, examine
egzurtion, exert(ion)	ejekt, eject	eksaminashen, examine(nation)
ehed, ahead	ejenda, agenda	eksample, example
eibol, able	ejern, adjourn	eksampol, example
eice, ace	ejorn, adjourn	eksapurashen, exasperate(tion)
eich, age	ejrenalin, adrenaline	eksaqute, execute
eick, ache	ejukate, educate	ekspereit, exasperate
eicur, acre	ejusduble, adjust(able)	eksated, exit(ed)
eid, aid	ejust, adjust	eksbarenshal, experiential
eight, * , teen, teenth, tieth, ty, ENGLISH NUMBER (or see ate)	ekademe, academy	eksbedeant, expedient
	ekadume, academy	eksberament, experiment
eighteen, nth, nths, ENGLISH NUMBER	ekallereit, exaggerate	eksberenshal, experiential
eik, ache	ekaunemity, equanimity	eksbire, expire
eikr, acre	except, accept / except	eksbirenshal, experiential
eil, ail / ale / aisle	ekcesori, accessory	eksblan, explain
eilias, alias	ekchange, exchange	eksblanashen, explanation
eilien, alien	eklektic, eclectic	eksblanatory, explanatory
eill, age	eklipse, eclipse	eksbleckable, explicable
eillent, agent	ekliptik, eclipse(ptic)	eksblinashen, explanation
eim, aim	eknolege, acknowledge	eksblod, explode
eimiabol, amiable	eknor, ignore	eksblor, explore
einal, anal	eknurint, ignorant	eksblorashen, explore(ration)
einchent, ancient	eko, echo / ego	eksbloshen, explosion
eincor, anchor	ekod, echo(ed)	eksbloytashen, exploit(ation)
einger, anger	ekology, ecology	eksbortashen, export(ation)
eingol, angle	ekolugy, ecology	eksbos, expose
eingri, angry	ekonimy, economy	eksbres, express
eingrili, angrily	ekonume, economy	eksburashen, expire(ration)
einguish, anguish	ekosestum, ecosystem	eksburenshal, experiential
einklos, enclose	ekosfere, ecosphere	eksburt, expert

ekscalate, escalate / escalade	eksesif, excess(ive) / access(ive)	ekspektashen, expect(tation)
ekscaveit, excavate	eksesis, excess(es) / access(es)	ekspektent, expect(ant)
ekscerjen, excursion	eksesori, accessory	ekspel, expel
ekschange, exchange	eksetera, etcetera	ekspend, expend
eksclemashin, exclamation	eksfoleate, exfoliate	ekspense, expense
eksclusive, exclusive	eksglud, exclude	ekspensef, expense(sive)
ekscurshin, excursion	eksglumashen, exclamation	eksperament, experiment
ekscuse, excuse	eksglut, exclude	ekspereanse, experience
eksdansev, extensive	ekshale, exhale	eksperenshal, experiential
eksdensible, extensible	eksibishen, exhibit(ion)	ekspert, expert
eksderminate, exterminate	eksibit, exhibit	ekspinse, expense
eksdra, extra	eksid, exceed	ekspire, expire
eksdradite, extradite	eksilarat, exhilarate / accelerate	ekspirenshal, experiential
eksdrakt, extract	eksile, exile	eksplan, explain
eksdravert, extrovert	eksilens, excel(llence)	eksplanashen, explanation
eksdreem, extreme	eksimplify, exemplify	eksplanatory, explanatory
eksdrem, extreme	eksimpt, exempt	eksplecable, explicable
eksdremly, extreme(ly)	eksimshen, exempt(ion)	eksplicit, explicit
eksdrivurt, extrovert	eksinshuate, accentuate	eksplisit, explicit
eksdrordinare, extraordinaire / extraordinary	eksintrik, eccentric	eksplisitly, explicit(ly)
eksdurminate, exterminate	eksirpt, excerpt	eksplod, explode
eksebit, exhibit	eksistens, exist(ence)	eksploet, exploit
eksebt, except / accept	eksit, exit / excite	eksploit, exploit
eksecutive, executive	eksitment, excite(ment)	eksplor, explore
eksedra, etcetera	eksjibit, exhibit	eksplorashen, explore(ration)
eksekute, execute	ekskalate, escalate / escalade	eksploratory, explore(ratory)
eksel, excel / accel	eksklumashen, exclamation	eksploshen, explosion
ekselarashen, accelerate(tion)	ekskurshen, excursion	eksplosive, explosive
ekseld, excel(lled) / accel(lled)	ekskuse, excuse	eksployt, exploit
ekselense, excellent	ekskuvaded, excavate(d)	eksplunashen, explanation
ekselerashen, accelerate(tion)	ekskuvashen, excavate(tion)	eksport, export
ekselerate, accelerate	ekskuvate, excavate	eksportashen, export(ation)
ekselurashen, accelerate(tion)	ekskwisit, exquisite	ekspos, expose
ekseluratur, accelerate(tor)	ekslusef, exclusive	eksprenshal, experiential
eksemplify, exemplify	eksolent, excellent	ekspres, express
eksentrek, eccentric	eksorbeint, exorbitant	ekspurenshal, experiential
eksentric, eccentric	eksorbident, exorbitant	eksqus, excuse
eksentrik, eccentric	eksorsize, exercise / exorcise	ekstaci, ecstasy
eksepshen, except(ion)	ekspadishen, expedition	ekstacy, ecstasy
ekseptense, accept(ance)	ekspand, expand	ekstansive, extensive
ekserpt, excerpt	ekspans, expanse / expense	ekstend, extend
eksert, exert	ekspedishen, expedition	ekstengwish, extinguish
ekses, excess / access	ekspekt, expect	ekstensebly, extensible(ly)

elastic, *, cally, city, cize, cizes, cized, cizing, STRETCHES OUT/ SHRINKS BACK "prefixes: in"
elastrate, illustrate
elate, *, ed, ting, tion, RAISED MOOD/ SPIRIT
elavashen, elevate(tion)
elavater, elevate(r)
elbow, *, wed, wing, JOINT IN THE ARM
elbum, album
elchuhol, alcohol
elder, *, est, rly, liness, rship, ONE WHO HAS LIVED MORE YEARS THAN OTHERS (or see alder)
eldur, elder
ele, alley
elect, *, ted, ting, tion, tions, table, tive, tively, tiveness, tor, toral, torally, torate, tioneer, tioneers, tioneered, tioneering, TO MAKE A CHOICE "prefixes: un"
elective, *, ely, eness, OPTION TO CHOOSE
elector, *, ral, rally, rate, VOTERS
electric, cal, cals, cally, city, ify, ro, cian, FREQUENCY/ ENERGY EXISTING IN ALL PARTICLES "prefixes: bio"
electrician, *, PEOPLE WHO WORK WITH WIRES/ ELECTRICITY
electrishun, electrician
electro, PREFIX INDICATING "ELECTRIC" MOST OFTEN MODIFIES THE WORD
electron, *, nic, nics, nically, A CHARGED PARTICLE
eledge, allege
elefant, elephant
elefint, elephant
elegable, eligible
elegance, BEAUTIFUL/ CLASSY "prefixes: in"
eleganse, allegiance / elegance
elegant, tly, nce, BEAUTIFUL/ CLASSY "prefixes: in"
elege, allege
elegible, eligible
elegul, illegal
elejense, allegiance / elegance
elekt, elect
elektev, elective
elektric, electric
elektrishen, electrician
elekul, illegal

ekstensev, extensive
ekstenshen, extension
ekstenuate, extenuate
ekstenzable, extensible
ekstereur, exterior
ekstind, extend
ekstinkt, extinct
ekstinsebly, extensible(ly)
ekstinsev, extensive
ekstra, extra
ekstradite, extradite
ekstrakt, extract
ekstravert, extrovert
ekstrem, extreme
ekstremly, extreme(ly)
ekstrivurt, extrovert
ekstrordinare, extraordinaire
ekstrordinary, extraordinary
ekstruvert, extrovert
eksturnal, external
ekstuse, ecstasy
eksubishen, exhibit(ion)
eksulant, excellent
eksulashen, exhale(lation)
eksulins, excellent(nce)
eksuqushen, execute(tion)
eksurpt, excerpt
eksurshen, exert(ion)
eksursize, exercise / exorcise
eksurt, exert
eksuvashen, excavate(tion)
ekto, ecto
ekuate, equate
ekute, acute
ekwabil, equable
ekwable, equable
ekwade, equity
ekwader, equator
ekwal, equal
ekwalebreum, equilibrium
ekwalete, equality
ekwaliz, equal(ize)
ekwanimety, equanimity

ekwanimity, equanimity
ekwashun, equation
ekwate, equate / equity
ekwatur, equator
ekwaul, equal
ekwauzition, acquisition
ekwebul, equable
ekwel, equal
ekwelebreum, equilibrium
ekwenox, equinox
ekwevalent, equivalent
ekwevokul, equivocal
ekwil, equal
ekwinoks, equinox
ekwip, equip
ekwipment, equipment
ekwit, acquit
ekwity, equity
ekwivokate, equivocate
ekwivulent, equivalent
ekwolity, equality
ekwoliz, equal(ize)
ekwotek, aquatic
ekwuble, equable
ekwude, equity
ekwul, equal
ekwulebrium, equilibrium
ekwuliz, equal(ize)
ekwunimity, equanimity
ekwunox, equinox
ekwuzition, acquisition
ekzema, eczema
el, eel / ail / ill / ale
elagint, elegant
elakwens, eloquence
elakwense, eloquence
elakwent, eloquent
elamentary, elementary
elaquence, eloquence
elaquens, eloquence
elaquent, eloquent
elarm, alarm

elekwens, eloquence
elekwent, eloquent
elemanate, eliminate
element, *, tal, tally, tary, BASIC, FUNDAMENTAL "prefixes: retro"
elementary, rily, riness, FIRST AND BASIC
elephant, *, AN ANIMAL
eleptic, elliptic
elere, allure
elergik, allergic
elert, alert
elet, elite
eletist, elite(tist)
elevashen, elevate(tion)
elevate, *, ed, ting, tion, tional, tor, RAISE HORIZONTAL LEVEL
eleveate, alleviate
eleveit, elevate
eleven, nth, nths, AN ENGLISH NUMBER
elevin, eleven
elevinth, eleven(th)
elf, elves, fin, fish, IMAGINARY ENTITIES
elfs, elf(lves)
elgebra, algebra
elianse, alliance
elicit, *, ted, ting, tation, tor, PROVOKE/ DRAW RESPONSE (or see illicit)
eliderate, illiterate
elifent, elephant
eligable, eligible
eligent, elegant
eligible, *, bly, bility, bilities, POTENTIAL TO BE CHOSEN "prefixes: in"
elijibol, eligible
elikwens, eloquence
elikwent, eloquent
elimenate, eliminate
eliminate, *, ed, ting, tion, tive, tor, tory, GET RID OF, DISPOSE
elimineit, eliminate
elimony, alimony
eline, align
elipse, ellipse

elipsus, ellipsis
eliptic, elliptic
eliquence, eloquence
eliquent, eloquent
eliset, elicit / illicit
elisit, elicit / illicit
elistrate, illustrate
elite, *, tist, tism, GROUP OF THOSE WHO BELIEVE THEY ARE THE BEST OF THEIR KIND/ CATEGORY
eliturate, illiterate
elivashen, elevate(tion)
elive, alive
elk, IN THE DEER FAMILY
ellipse, sis, GEOMETRIC SHAPE
ellipsis, SYMBOL USED IN PLACE OF A WORD (...)
elliptic, cal, cally, city, cities, OVAL SHAPE, TO BE CONCISE "prefixes: semi"
ellisit, elicit / illicit
elliterate, illiterate
ellustrious, illustrious
elnes, ill(ness)
elogekul, illogical
elogicul, illogical
elongate, *, ed, ting, tion, TO LENGTHEN, MAKE LONGER
elood, elude
eloor, allure
eloosuf, allusive / elusive / illusive
eloot, elude
elope, *, ed, ping, GO AWAY TO BE WED WITHOUT NOTIFICATION
eloquence, *, TASTEFULLY/ PERSUASIVELY COMMUNICATED
eloquent, tly, tness, nce, STRIKING/ MOVING EXPRESSION "prefixes: in"
elorm, alarm
elostrious, illustrious
elovate, elevate
eloy, alloy
else, *, NOT WHO/ WHAT/ WHERE INTENDED OR EXPECTED
elsewhere, SOMEWHERE OTHER THAN WHERE EXPECTED TO BE
elso, also

eletude, altitude
elitude, altitude
elucidate, *, ed, ting, tion, tive, tor, tory, useness, usion, MAKE CLEAR/ UNDERSTANDABLE, EXPLAIN
elude, *, ed, ding, usive, usion, GET AWAY, NOT BE PERCEIVED/ DEFINED (or see allude)
elufint, elephant
elugable, eligible
elugant, elegant
elugens, elegant(nce) / elegance
elugent, elegant
elugint, elegant
elukwens, eloquence
elukwent, eloquent
elumenade, illuminate
elumentary, elementary
elumenum, aluminum
eluminate, illuminate
elumintry, elementary
eluminum, aluminum
elumony, alimony
eluquence, eloquence
eluquent, eloquent
elure, allure
elurgik, allergic
elurjik, allergic
elurt, alert
elushun, illusion / allusion
elusive, ely, eness, sory, GET AWAY, NOT BE PERCEIVED (or see allusive/ illusive)
elustrate, illustrate
elustrious, illustrious
eluud, elude
eluvashen, elevate(tion)
eluvate, elevate
em, PREFIX INDICATING "INTO/ ON/ PUT INTO" MOST OFTEN MODIFIES THE WORD (or see am/ them)
emachure, amateur
emaculet, immaculate
emage, image
emagenashen, imagine(ation)
emagrant, immigrant / emigrant
emagrashen, immigrate(tion)

emagrate, immigrate
emagrunt, immigrant / emigrant
emagunashen, imagine(ation)
emaj, image
emajinashen, imagine(nation)
emakewlit, immaculate
emakulit, immaculate
emanate, *, ed, ting, tion, tional, tionist, tive, EMITS, GIVES OFF, SENDS OUT
emancipate, *, ed, ting, tion, FREE FROM BONDAGE
emanens, eminence / imminence / immanence
emanent, eminent / imminent / immanent
emanit, eminent / imminent / immanent
emansepade, emancipate
emansipate, emancipate
ematashin, imitate(tion)
ematate, imitate
emation, imitate(tion)
emeterial, immaterial
emature, immature
embankment, *, A BURM/ MOUND
embargo, oes, RESTRICT FROM PORTS
embaris, embarrass
embark, *, ked, king, PREPARING TO TAKE A JOURNEY "prefixes: dis"
embarrass, sses, ssed, ssing, ssingly, ssment, UNDESIRABLY EXPOSED "prefixes: dis"
embassy, sies, SAFE PLACE WITHIN ANOTHER COUNTRY
embaudes, embody(dies)
embed, *, dded, dding, SINK INTO UNTIL FLUSH
ember, *, SPARK/ COAL FROM FIREWOOD
emberis, embarrass
embiluki, umbilical
embishun, ambition
emblem, *, A SYMBOL OR FIGURE
emblie, imply
emblum, emblem
embody, dies, died, dying, diment, diments, OF A VISIBLE FORM, TANGIBLE, PARTS INTO A WHOLE "prefixes: dis"
emboss, sses, ssed, ssing, sser, ssment, IMPRINT INTO
embostur, imposter
emboudes, embody(dies)

embrace, *, ed, cing, eable, ement, er, TO HOLD DEAR
embrase, embrace
embreis, embrace
embreo, embryo
embroeder, embroider
embroider, *, red, ring, rer, ry, ries, STITCH WITH NEEDLE/ THREAD
embrufe, improve
embrufment, improve(ment)
embryo, *, onic, onical, onically, ology, ologist, otic, SOMETHING GROWING INSIDE BEFORE IT EMERGES "prefixes: pre"
embtee, empty
embulense, ambulance
embur, ember
embush, ambush
embuzishun, impose(sition)
emcompruble, incomparable
emcumblete, incomplete
emeable, amiable
emedeat, immediate
emej, image
emenate, emanate
emend, amend
emense, immense
emensurable, immensurable
emerald, A COLOR, A GEMSTONE
emerchen, immerse(sion)
emerge, *, ed, ging, ence, ent, ency, encies, COME FROM WITHIN, ERUPT, COME INTO BEING
emergency, cies, TO BE DEALT WITH IMMEDIATELY
emerjensee, emergency
emers, emersed / immerse
emersable, immersible
emersed, STANDING OUT OR RISING ABOVE A SURFACE, PARTS ABOVE WATER (or see immerse(d))
emershen, immerse(sion)
emeshen, emission / omission
emeterial, immaterial
emfadek, emphatic
emfasis, emphasis / emphasize
emfusis, emphasis / emphasize
emidiet, immediate

emigrant, *, FOREIGNER FROM ANOTHER COUNTRY (or see immigrant)
emigrate, *, ed, ting, tion, LEAVE A COUNTRY TO GO TO ANOTHER (or see immigrate)
emigreit, emigrate
emigrunt, immigrant / emigrant
emij, image
eminate, emanate
emind, amend
eminence, cy, FORMAL RANK/ POSITION (or see imminence/ immanence)
eminens, eminence / imminence / immanence
eminent, tly, nce, SOMEONE WHO ACHIEVES BEYOND OTHERS (or see eminence/ imminence/ immanence) "prefixes: pre"
eminse, immense
eminsurable, immensurable
emirchen, immerse(sion)
emirge, emerge
emirs, emersed / immerse
emirsable, immersible
emirshen, immerse(sion)
emission, *, SOMETHING DISCHARGED, PUT INTO CIRCULATION (or see omission)
emit, *, tted, tting, tter, DISCHARGE, PUT OUT A FREQUENCY (or see omit)
emitate, imitate
emitation, imitate(tion)
emiterial, immaterial
emiuleit, emulate
emmagrate, immigrate / emigrate
emmensurable, immensurable
emmershen, immerse(sion)
emminsurable, immensurable
emmirsible, immersible
emmobile, immobile
emmpresion, impression
emmpressive, impressive
emmurshen, immerse(sion)
emobile, immobile
emochun, emotion
emograte, immigrate / emigrate
emonate, emanate

emonens,eminence / imminence / immanence
emonent,eminent / imminent / immanent
emonia,ammonia
emople,immobile
emoral,immoral
emordul,immoral
emortal,immortal
emortalety,immortal(ity)
emorul,immoral
emoshin,emotion
emoterial,immaterial
emotion,*,nal,nally,nality,nless,nalize,nalizes,nalized, nalizing,ive,ivism,REACTION CAUSED BY CHEMICALS RELEASED BY WHAT WE ARE THINKING "prefixes: non/ un"
emownt,amount
empachuis,impetuous
empact,impact
empairm,empower
empar,empower
emparasist,empirical(cist)
empare,impair
emparetive,imperative
emparical,empirical
emparment,empower(ment)
emparor,emperor
empathy,ABILITY TO UNDERSTAND/ FEEL ANOTHER PERSON'S EXPERIENCE, FEELINGS
empaurment,empower(ment)
empayer,empire
empeach,impeach
empecable,impeccable
empechuis,impetuous
empede,impede
empeed,impede
empeishent,impatient
empekuble,impeccable
emperative,imperative
emperfect,imperfect
emperor,*,RULER OF PEOPLE/ LAND
empersenate,impersonate
empersonal,impersonal
empersonashen,impersonate(tion)

empersonate,impersonate
empetchuis,impetuous
emphasis,ize,PLACE GREAT IMPORTANCE IN/ UPON "prefixes: de-/ over"
emphasize,*,ed,zing,is,PLACE GREAT IMPORTANCE IN/ UPON "prefixes: de-/ over"
emphatic,cally,PLACE GREAT IMPORTANCE IN/ UPON
emphisis,emphasis / emphasize
empire,*,REGION OF PEOPLE/ LAND RULED BY AN EMPEROR
empirer,emperor
empirfect,imperfect
empirical,lly,cism,cist,cists,rics,RELIES ONLY ON OBSERVATION/ EXPERIMENT
empirsonal,impersonal
emplai,imply
emplament,implement
emplant,implant
emplicate,implicate
emplication,implicate(tion)
emploe,employee / employ
emploer,employer
emplolli,employee
employ,*,yed,ying,yable,yability,yer,yee,yeement,USE SOMETHING/ SOMEONE TO COMPLETE A TASK WHICH MAY/ MAY NOT INVOLVE MONEY (or see employee) "prefixes: sub/ un"
employee,*,SOMEONE WHO IS LEGALLY HIRED AND WORKS FOR PAY (or see employ) "prefixes: non/ under"
employer,*,SOMEONE WHO PAYS SOMEONE ELSE TO WORK "prefixes: non"
employment,*,BEING HIRED TO WORK "prefixes: un"
emplucashen,implicate(tion)
emplucate,implicate
emplument,implement
emply,imply
empofuresh,impoverish
empolite,impolite
empolse,impulse
emport,import
emportant,important
emportashen,import(ation)

emportins,important(nce)
empose,impose
emposible,impossible
emposter,imposter
emposuble,impossible
empound,impound
empour,empower
empourtens,important(nce)
empourtent,important
empoverish,impoverish
empower,*,red,ring,ment,TEACH/ PROVIDE SOMEONE WITH ABILITY TO DO THINGS FOR THEMSELVES "prefixes: dis"
empoze,impose
empraktecul,impractical
emprapuble,improbable
emprasev,impressive
emprashen,impression
emprasise,imprecise
empravize,improvise
emprechen,impression
emprecise,imprecise
empregnable,impregnable
empregnate,impregnate
empregnuble,impregnable
emprent,imprint
empres,empress / impress
empresef,impressive
empreshen,impression
empresif,impressive
empresise,imprecise
empresive,impressive
empresont,imprison(ed)
empress,sses,FEMALE RULER OF EMPIRE (or see impress)
empretion,impression
emprint,imprint
emprison,imprison
emprobable,improbable
emprobais,improvise
emprof,improve
empromptu,impromptu
empromtu,impromptu

empropable, improbable
emproper, improper
emprovais, improvise
emprove, improve
emprovement, improve(ment)
emprovisation, improvise(sation)
emprovize, improvise
emprovusashen, improvise(sation)
emprufe, improve
emprus, empress / impress
empruve, improve
empruvize, improvise
emptee, empty
empty, ties, tied, tying, tier, tiest, tily, tiness, REMOVE CONTENTS FROM SOMETHING "prefixes: non"
empulite, impolite
empuls, impulse
empulse, impulse
empulsef, impulse(sive)
empulsive, impulse(sive)
empurfect, imperfect
empurfekt, imperfect
empuror, emperor
empursenate, impersonate
empursonal, impersonal
emput, input
emputate, amputate
empuzishen, impose(sition)
emruld, emerald
emte, empty
emug, image
emugrant, immigrant / emigrant
emugrashen, immigrate(tion) / emigrate(tion)
emugrate, immigrate
emuj, image
emulate, *, ed, ting, tion, tive, tively, tor, lous, lously, lousness, STRIVE TO LIVE UP TO
emune, immune
emunens, eminence / imminence / immanence
emunety, immune(nity)
emunezashen, immunize(zation)
emunise, immunize
emurg, emerge

emurgensee, emergency
emursable, immersible
emurse, immerse / emersed
emutashin, imitate(tion)
emutate, imitate
emuterial, immaterial
emuze, amuse
en, PREFIX INDICATING "INTO/ ON/ PUT INTO" MOST OFTEN MODIFIES THE WORD (or see prefix in/ un/ inn)
en-lau, in-law
enabiledy, inability
enability, inability
enabishen, inhibit(ion)
enable, *, ed, ling, ement, er, EMPOWER/ AID SOMEONE/ SOMETHING TO PERFORM MORE EFFICIENTLY (or see unable) "prefixes: dis"
enabul, enable / unable
enaccessible, inaccessible
enact, *, ted, ting, tment, table, tor, tive, TO PERFORM/ MAKE INTO (or see inactive)
enaction, inaction
enacuracy, inaccurate(acy)
enacurate, inaccurate
enadekwit, inadequate
enadequate, inadequate
enadikwit, inadequate
enadmisible, inadmissible
enadukwit, inadequate
enadvaisable, inadvisable
enadverbent, inadvertent
enadverdent, inadvertent
enadvirdent, inadvertent
enadvisable, inadvisable
enagerashen, inaugurate(tion)
enagiureit, inaugurate
enaksesible, inaccessible
enakshen, inaction
enakt, enact
enaktif, inactive / enact(ive)
enakurite, inaccurate
enalegy, analogy
enalegy, analogy
enalesis, analysis

enaleuble, inalienable
enalienable, inalienable
enaligy, analogy
enaliuble, inalienable
enalugy, analogy
enamament, inanimate
enamel, *, led, ling, ler, list, PAINT, A PROTECTIVE COATING
enamoly, anomaly
enanemit, inanimate
enanimate, inanimate
enanomint, inanimate
enapal, enable / unable
enappreciative, inappreciative
enapproachable, inapproachable
enappropriate, inappropriate
enapresative, inappreciative
enaprochible, inapproachable
enapropieit, inappropriate
enapropriate, inappropriate
enapul, enable / unable
enaquerisy, inaccurate(acy)
enaquiret, inaccurate
enaqulashen, inoculate(tion)
enaqulate, inoculate
enaqurite, inaccurate
enarferins, interfere(nce)
enarkey, anarchy
enarup, interrupt
enasinse, innocence
enate, innate
enatequit, inadequate
enatible, inaudible
enatmisable, inadmissible
enatvirdent, inadvertent
enatvisable, inadvisable
enatvurtent, inadvertent
enaudible, inaudible
enauf, enough
enaugurate, inaugurate
enaukulate, inoculate
enaumily, anomaly
enauperable, inoperable

enauperate, inoperate
enauperative, inoperate(tive)
enautibol, inaudible
enavadif, innovate(tive)
enbalid, invalid
enbankment, embankment
enbark, embark
enbasee, embassy
enbed, embed
enbeishon, invasion
enbent, invent
enberis, embarrass
enbert, invert
enbertebrait, invertebrate
enbest, invest
enbigareit, invigorate
enbinsuble, invincible
enblem, emblem
enboard, inboard
enbois, invoice
enbord, inboard
enboss, emboss
enbrase, embrace
enbroder, embroider
enburt, invert
enbutashen, invitation
encamp, *, ped, ping, pment. BE IN/ OF A CAM?
encandeashen, incandescent
encantashen, incantation
encantation, incantation
encapable, incapable
encapacitate, incapacitate
encapacity, incapacity
encapsulate, *, ed, ting, tion, SURROUND, ENCLOSE
encapuble, incapable
encarnate, incarnate
encarneit, incarnate
encarsereit, incarcerate
encarsurate, incarcerate
encase, *, ed, sing, ement, ENCLOSE/ SURROUND WITH A COVER
encast, encase(d)
encendiary, incendiary

encenerate, incinerate
encensibal, insensible
encentive, incentive
enception, incept(ion)
encereg, encourage / anchor(age)
encesant, incessant
enceshon, incision
encesint, incessant
encesunt, incessant
ench, inch
enchant, *, ted, ting, tment, DELIGHT, FASCINATE
"prefixes: dis"
enchenyewus, ingenuous
enchor, anchor
enchur, ensure / insure
encindeary, incendiary
encinereit, incinerate
encinsir, insincere
encircle, *, ed, ling, ement, SURROUND WITH A CIRCLE
encishon, incision
encisor, incise(sor)
encite, incite / inside
encitment, incite(ment)
encityus, insidious
encize, incise
enclanation, incline(nation)
encline, incline
enclood, include
enclose, *, ed, sing, sable, sure, SURROUND/ KEEP IN
encloser, enclose(sure)
enclosment, enclose(ment)
enclude, include
encluesef, inclusive
enclueshen, inclusion
enclunashen, incline(nation)
enclusef, inclusive
enclusion, inclusion
encogneto, incognito
encoherent, incoherent
encojerent, incoherent
encokneto, incognito
encombatent, incompetent
encomber, encumber

encome, income
encommodious, incommode(dious)
encomode, incommode
encomodious, incommode(dious)
encomoteous, incommode(dious)
encomparable, incomparable
encompass, sses, ssed, ssing, ITEMS WITHIN A CIRCLE
encompatent, incompetent
encompatible, incompatible
encompetent, incompetent
encomplete, incomplete
encomplit, incomplete
encompruble, incomparable
enconclusef, inconclusive
enconclusive, inconclusive
enconsiderate, inconsiderate
enconsistent, inconsistent
enconvenient, inconvenient
encorach, encourage
encoragable, incorrigible
encore, *, ed, ring, ASKED TO PERFORM MORE BY AN AUDIENCE
encorect, incorrect
encorellable, incorrigible
encorij, encourage / anchor(age)
encorporate, incorporate
encorrect, incorrect
encounter, *, red, ring, TO EMBARK UPON SOMETHING/ SOMEONE
encourage, *, ed, ging, gingly, ement, INSTILL FAITH/ HOPE
encrease, increase
encredible, incredible
encremenate, incriminate
encrement, increment
encremineit, incriminate
encriminate, incriminate
encrimineit, incriminate
encris, increase
encroach, hes, hed, hing, hingly, hment, her, NEARLY TRESPASSING
encrust, *, ted, ting, tation, FORM A THICK COVER/ EXTERIOR
encualler, inquire

encubate, incubate
encusisishon, inquisition
encusitiv, inquisitive
encumbent, incumbent
encumber, *, red, ring, brance, brances, brancer, TO BE A WEIGHT/ BURDEN, TO HAMPER
encumode, incommode
encumpatable, incompatible
encumplete, incomplete
encunklusif, inconclusive
encunsestant, inconsistent
encunveneunt, inconvenient
encupasitate, incapacitate
encupasity, incapacitate
encur, incur
encurable, incurable
encuragable, incorrigible
encurej, encourage / anchor(age)
encurekt, incorrect
encurig, encourage / anchor(age)
encyclopedia, *, REFERENCE SOURCE THAT DEFINES/ EXPLAINS THINGS THAT ARE NOUNS
encyst, *, ted, ting, tation, tment, WITHIN A CYST (or see insist)
end, *, ded, ding, NO MORE, OVER (or see and) "prefixes: un/ up"
endait, indict
endakashen, indicate(tion)
endaluble, indelible
endanger, *, red, ring, rment, IN HARM'S WAY, NEEDS PROTECTION
endangurment, endanger(ment)
endanjer, endanger
endapendense, independent, independent(nce)
endasishen, indecision
endastrial, industrial
endau, endow
endaument, endow(ment)
endavigual, individual
endear, *, red, ring, ringly, rment, VERY FOND OF
endeavor, *, red, ring, rer, SET ABOUT THE TASK TO DO SOMETHING
endebted, indebted

endecashen, indicate(tion)
endecision, indecision
endecisive, indecisive
endecks, index
ended, indebted
endeed, indeed
endefanete, indefinite
endefinite, indefinite
endefir, endeavor
endefur, endeavor
endefurent, indifferent
endego, indigo
endeinyer, endanger
endelible, indelible
endelluble, indelible
endemafy, indemnify
endemic, *, cally, city, ism, CONFINED/ LIVING IN ONE GROUP/ AREA
endemnafy, indemnify
endent, indent
endentashen, indent(ation)
endependense, independent(nce)
endependent, independent
ender, inter / enter
enderfere, interfere
endermetant, intermittent
endesent, indecent
endeted, indebted
endever, endeavor
endevillual, individual
endex, index
endicashen, indicate(tion)
endicate, indicate
endid, indeed
endifrent, indifferent
endigo, indigo
endikeit, indicate
endir, endear
endirmedent, intermittent
endirmetant, intermittent
endisisuf, indecisive
endite, indict
endivor, endeavor

endjur, endure
endless, ssly, ssness, WILL NEVER STOP
endlis, endless
endo, PREFIX INDICATING "INSIDE" MOST OFTEN MODIFIES THE WORD
endocrain, endocrine
endocrine, nology, nologic, nological, nologist, OF THE GLANDS IN THE BODY
endoctineit, indoctrinate
endoer, endure
endolch, indulge
endoose, induce
endormetant, intermittent
endors, indoor(s)
endorse, *, ed, sing, ement, TO SUPPORT/ AFFIRM IN WRITING (or see indoor(s))
endostry, industry
endoument, endow(ment)
endow, *, wed, wing, wment, PROVIDE SOMEONE SOMETHING THEY WANT/ NEED "prefixes: dis"
endrukit, intricate
endruspect, introspect
enduce, induce
enduckshen, induct(ion)
enducktor, induct(or)
enduction, induct(ion)
endukren, endocrine
endukshen, induct(ion)
endukt, induct
enduktor, induct(or)
endulge, indulge
endulgense, indulge(nce)
endupendent, independent
endur, inter / enter / endure
endure, *, ed, ring, rance, rable, rably, PUT UP WITH/ TOLERATE "prefixes: un"
endurmedeate, intermediate
enduse, induce
enduseshin, indecision
endustreul, industrial
endustry, industry
enduztreal, industrial
ene, any

enebody,anybody
eneckwitable,inequitable
eneduble,inedible
enefitabol,inevitable
eneg,inning
enegma,enigma / enema
enegreit,integrate
eneibol,unable / enable
eneilienable,inalienable
eneit,innate
enekwetable,inequitable
enekwity,inequity
enema, *, RECTAL CLEANSING (or see anemia/ enigma)
enemik,anemic
enemut,intimate
enemy,mies,A FOE, NOT FRIENDS WITH
eneng,inning
eneproachable,inapproachable
enept,inept
enequitable,inequitable
enequity,inequity
ener,inner
eneract,interact
enerchange,interchange
enercom,intercom
enerconnect,interconnect
enercors,intercourse
enerelate,interrelate
energetic,cally,TO HAVE LOTS OF ENERGY "prefixes: bio"
energy,gies,gize,gizes,gizing,gizer,gization,getic, getically,HAVING ENOUGH POWER TO DO SOMETHING "prefixes: de-"
enerject,interject
enerjetek,energetic
enerjetic,energetic
enerkorse,intercourse
enerllect,interject
enerllectic,energetic
enerlude,interlude
enermedeary,intermediary
enermingle,intermingle
enermission,intermission

enermost,innermost
enernashenul,international
enernet,internet
enersculastic,interscholastic
enersect,intersect
enersection,intersection
enersekshen,intersection
enersept,intercept
enersperse,intersperse
enerstate,interstate
enersteit,interstate
enert,inert
enervene,intervene
enervu,interview
enervul,interval
enerwoven,interwoven
enescapable,inescapable
enesense,innocence
enesheation,initiate(tion)
eneskeipabol,inescapable
enesqueipabol,inescapable
enesthezia,anesthesia
enevidible,inevitable
enevitable,inevitable
enexpensive,inexpensive
enexperience,inexperience
enfachuashen,infatuate(tion)
enfachuate,infatuate
enfachueit,infatuate
enfadik,emphatic
enfallible,infallible
enfaltrate,infiltrate
enfaluble,infallible
enfansy,infant(ncy)
enfant,infant
enfantry,infantry
enfasiz,emphasis / emphasize
enfatchuashen,infatuate(tion)
enfatik,emphatic
enfatuate,infatuate
enfecshus,infect(ious)
enfect,infect
enfekshen,infect(ion)

enfekt,infect
enfeltrate,infiltrate
enfenativly,infinite(tively)
enfentre,infantry
enfereorety,inferior(ity)
enferior,inferior
enfermashen,information
enfermation,information
enfesiz,emphasis / emphasize
enfestructure,infrastructure
enfeureate,infuriate
enfiltrate,infiltrate
enfinetly,infinite(ly)
enfinite,infinite
enfirmary,infirmary
enfirmashen,information
enfirmation,inform(ation)
enfisiz,emphasis / emphasize
enfistructure,infrastructure
enfite,invite
enfitengly,invite(ingly)
enfiurieit,infuriate
enfius,infuse
enflagingly,unflagging(ly)
enflame,inflame
enflamitory,inflame(mmatory)
enflamation,inflammation
enflamatory,inflame(mmatory)
enflamutory,inflame(mmatory)
enflapable,unflappable
enflarmeichon,inflammation
enflashen,inflate(tion)
enflate,inflate
enflection,inflection
enfleit,inflate
enfleksuble,inflexible
enflemashen,inflammation
enflewanse,influence
enflexchen,inflection
enflexible,inflexible
enflextion,inflection
enflicked,inflict
enflict,inflict

enfilimation, inflammation
enfluanse, influence
enfluence, influence
enfluensable, influence(able)
enflumation, inflammation
enforce, *, ed, cing, ement, eable, cability, er, SUPPORT, TO BACK "prefixes: un"
enform, inform
enformal, informal
enformant, informant
enformation, inform(ation)
enfraction, infraction
enfrakshen, infraction
enfrared, infrared
enfrastructure, infrastructure
enfrekwent, infrequent
enfrenj, infringe
enfrequent, infrequent
enfringe, infringe
enfriquent, infrequent
enfrured, infrared
enfugen, infuse(sion)
enfujen, infuse(sion)
enfultrate, infiltrate
enfunsy, infant(ncy)
enfunt, infant
enfuntre, infantry
enfuriate, infuriate
enfurmashen, inform(ation)
enfurmery, infirmary
enfuse, infuse
enfushen, infuse(sion)
enfusiz, emphasis / emphasize
enfustrukture, infrastructure
engage, *, ed, ging, gingly, ement, er, TO PUT INTO MOTION, DIRECT ATTENTION "prefixes: dis"
enganly, ungainly
enge, inch
engect, inject
engection, inject(ion)
engeill, engage
engekshen, inject(ion)
engelate, ungulate

engen, engine
engeneer, engineer
engenious, ingenious
engenuity, ingenuity
engenuous, ingenuous
engenyus, ingenious
enger, injure / anger
engerent, inherent
engest, ingest
enget, ingot
engilate, ungulate
engine, *, MACHINE/ DEVICE USED FOR POWER/ PROPELLING
engineer, *, red, ring, PUT ITEMS TOGETHER TO BECOME SOMETHING ELSE "prefixes: bio"
enginuety, ingenuity
engoement, enjoy(ment)
engoeuble, enjoy(able)
engoiment, enjoy(ment)
engolf, engulf
engot, ingot
engoy, enjoy
engoyuble, enjoy(able)
engrain, ingrain
engrave, *, ed, ving, er, TO MARK/ CARVE TEXT/ SYMBOLS INTO SOMETHING
engredient, ingredient
engrein, ingrain
engreiv, engrave
engridant, ingredient
enguish, anguish
engulate, ungulate
engulf, *, fed, fing, TAKE IN, OVERCOME
engun, engine
enguneer, engineer
engury, injure(ry)
engustes, injustice
engut, ingot
enhabetent, inhabit(ant)
enhabit, inhabit
enhabitency, inhabit(ancy)
enhalant, inhalant
enhalation, inhale(lation)

enhale, inhale
enhance, *, ed, cing, ement, cive, er, MAKE MORE APPEALING
enharent, inherent
enharet, inherit
enharitance, inherit(ance)
enharmonic, *, ed, cing, ement, cive, er, MUSICAL NOTATION/ FREQUENCY (or see inharmonic)
enhebit, inhibit
enhelashen, inhale(lation)
enherent, inherent
enherit, inherit
enheritance, inherit(ance)
enhewmane, inhumane
enhibishen, inhibit(ion)
enhibit, inhibit
enhormonic, inharmonic / enharmonic
enhosbatalety, inhospitable(ality)
enhosbitable, inhospitable
enhubishen, inhibit(ion)
enhulashen, inhale(lation)
enhumane, inhumane
eni, any
enialate, annihilate
enibishen, inhibit(ion)
enibode, anybody
enicuality, inequality
enielate, annihilate
enig, inning
enigma, *, atic, atical, atically, NOT EXPLAINABLE, NOT UNDERSTOOD (or see enema/ anemia)
enigrate, integrate
enima, enema / anemia
enime, enemy
enimut, intimate
enindashen, inundate(tion)
enindate, inundate
ening, inning
enipropreut, inappropriate
eniquality, inequality
enir, inner / inter
enircom, intercom
enircors, intercourse

enirelate, interrelate
enirgetek, energetic
enirgy, energy
enirlude, interlude
enirmission, intermission
enirnet, internet
enirsculastic, interscholastic
enirsection, intersection
enirtwine, intertwine
enirupt, interrupt
enirvene, intervene
enirview, interview
enirvue, interview
enishiashen, initiate(tion)
enishieit, initiate
enishul, initial
enisial, initial
enisthezia, anesthesia
enitial, initial
enitiate, initiate
enitiation, initiate(tion)
eniulate, annihilate
enjabit, inhabit
enjarmonic, inharmonic / enharmonic
enje, inch
enjecshen, inject(ion)
enjekt, inject
enjelate, ungulate
enjen, engine
enjeneer, engineer
enjenuedy, ingenuity
enjenuity, ingenuity
enjenuous, ingenuous
enjenyewus, ingenuous
enjeret, inherent
enjerest, inherit
enjest, ingest
enjibit, inhibit
enjin, engine
enjineer, engineer
enjumein, inhumane
enjoement, enjoy(ment)
enjospitable, inhospitable

enjostis, injustice
enjoy,*,yed,ying,yment,yable,yably,yableness,
 APPRECIATE "prefixes: pre"
enjoyuble, enjoy(able)
enjulate, ungulate
enjuner, engineer
enjure, injure
enjustice, injustice
enk, ink
enkabuble, incapable
enkamped, encamp(ed)
enkampment, encamp(ment)
enkapacity, incapacity
enkapasitate, incapacitate
enkapasity, incapacity
enkapuble, incapable
enkarserade, incarcerate
enkase, encase
enkeipabol, incapable
enker, anchor / incur
enkerej, encourage / anchor(age)
enkewbate, incubate
enkipacity, incapacity
enkiur, incur
enklin, incline
enkling, inkling
enklood, include
enklose, enclose
enkloshur, enclose(sure)
enkloze, enclose
enklud, include
enklunashen, incline(nation)
enklusef, inclusive
enklusev, inclusive
enklushen, inclusion
enkogneto, incognito
enkomber, encumber
enkomodeus, incommode(dious)
enkompus, encompass
enkomputent, incompetent
enkonsistent, inconsistent
enkore, encore
enkoreg, encourage / anchor(age)

enkoreguble, incorrigible
enkorpurate, incorporate
enkownter, encounter
enkreduble, incredible
enkredulus, incredulous
enkreese, increase
enkremunate, incriminate
enkroch, encroach
enkrument, increment
enkrust, encrust
enkubeit, incubate
enkum, income
enkumbent, incumbent
enkumber, encumber
enkumodeus, incommode(dious)
enkumpatuble, incompatible
enkumpus, encompass
enkunsiduret, inconsiderate
enkunsistent, inconsistent
enkunvenyunt, inconvenient
enkupacity, incapacity
enkupasedy, incapacity
enkupasitate, incapacitate
enkurable, incurable
enkurekt, incorrect
enkwesishun, inquisition
enkwire, inquire / inquire(ry)
enkwisative, inquisitive
enkwisition, inquisition
enlaiteu, enlighten
enland, inland
enlarge,*,ed,ging,ement,er,MAKE BIGGER/ GREATER
enlargment, enlarge(ment)
enlarje, enlarge
enlaw, in-law
enles, unless
enlest, enlist
enlet, inlet
enlighten,*,,ned,ning,nment,ACHIEVE GREATER
 KNOWLEDGE
enlist,*,,ted,ting,tment,ter,SIGN-UP,JOIN SOMETHING
enliten, enlighten
enllect, inject

enllinir, engineer	enpresidented, (un)precedent(ed)
enlloi, enjoy	enpresise, imprecise
enlund, inland	enpresive, impressive
enmachure, immature	enpreson, imprison
enmade, inmate	enpressed, impress(sed)
enmate, inmate	enprint, imprint
enmature, immature	enprison, imprison
enmeit, inmate	enprobuble, improbable
ennacurate, inaccurate	enpromptu, impromptu
enner, inner	enpromtu, impromptu
ennuendo, innuendo	enpropable, improbable
enoardinent, inordinate	enproper, improper
enoberable, inoperable	enprove, improve
enoberative, inoperate(ative)	enprovement, improve(ment)
enocence, innocence	enprovisation, improvise(sation)
enocreate, inaugurate	enprovise, improvise
enoculate, inoculate	enprovusashen, improvise(sation)
enoculation, inoculate(tion)	enprufe, improve
enodible, inaudible	enpruve, improve
enof, enough	enpruvize, improvise
enogreashen, inaugurate(tion)	enpulite, impolite
enograte, inaugurate	enpulse, impulse
enogurate, inaugurate	enpulsef, impulse(sive)
enokewlate, inoculate	enpulsive, impulse(sive)
enokulation, inoculate(tion)	enput, input
enomoly, anomaly	enquaier, inquire
enonimus, anonymous	enqubate, incubate
enonseade, enunciate/ annunciate	enqueipable, incapable
enoparchun, inopportune	enquesidev, inquisitive
enoperable, inoperable	enquirable, incurable
enoperate, inoperate	enquire, SEE WORD "INQUIRE"
enoperative, inoperate(tive)	enquisadev, inquisitive
enopertune, inopportune	enquisition, inquisition
enopurative, inoperate(ative)	enquisitive, inquisitive
enopurtunity, inopportune(nity)	enquizeshen, inquisition
enoqulent, inoculate(ant)	**enrage**, *, ed, ging, ement, GREAT ANGER/ RAGE
enorcors, intercourse	enraj, enrage
enordenate, inordinate	enrech, enrich
enordunet, inordinate	**enrich**, hes, hed, hing, hment, MAKE BETTER/ FINER
enorgetek, energetic	enrjekshen, interject(ion)
enorgy, energy	enrol, enroll
enormis, enormous	**enroll**, *, led, ling, lment, llee, JOIN, ENLIST
enormous, sly, sness, GIGANTIC/ BIGGEST	enrolment, enroll(ment)

enormus, enormous	
enorpherans, interfere(nce)	
enorsect, intersect	
enorvul, interval	
enosent, innocence(nt)	
enotable, inaudible	
enotibol, inaudible	
enouf, enough	
enough, TIME TO STOP	
enovadef, innovate(tive)	
enovate, innovate	
enovative, innovate(tive)	
enoveit, innovate	
enowe, annoy	
enownse, announce	
enoy, annoy	
enoyens, annoy(ance)	
enpare, impair	
enpatient, inpatient	
enpecable, impeccable	
enpech, impeach	
enpeishant, inpatient/ impatient	
enpersonate, impersonate	
enpli, imply	
enpolite, impolite	
enpolse, impulse	
enportant, important	
enpose, impose	
enposibul, impossible	
enposter, imposter	
enposuble, impossible	
enpound, impound	
enpoverish, impoverish	
enpownd, impound	
enpractical, impractical	
enprasise, imprecise	
enpration, impression	
enpravize, improvise	
enprecise, imprecise	
enpregnable, impregnable	
enpregnate, impregnate	
enpres, impress	
enpreshen, impression	

enroot, enroute
enroute, OR "EN ROUTE", IN THE PROCESS OF TRAVELING TO/ TOWARDS
enrut, enroute
ensabordinate, insubordinate
ensadent, incident
ensafishent, insufficient
ensaiclopidia, encyclopedia
ensaid, inside
ensain, ensign
ensait, insight
ensakure, insecure
ensakuredy, insecure(rity)
ensakurity, insecure(rity)
ensalate, insulate
ensane, insane
ensanetashen, insanitary(ation)
ensaneteri, insanitary
ensanety, insane(nity)
ensanidy, insane(nity)
ensanitary, insanitary
ensanitashen, insanitary(ation)
ensasheat, insatiate
ensasheuble, insatiable
ensatiable, insatiable
ensatiate, insatiate
ensaulvent, insolvent
ensbarashen, inspire(ration)
ensbekable, unspeakable
ensboken, unspoken
enscraib, inscribe
enscribe, inscribe
enscription, inscription
enseam, inseam
ensebordinate, insubordinate
ensect, insect
ensecticide, insecticide
ensecure, insecure
ensedent, incident
ensedius, insidious
ensegnea, insignia
ensegnifukent, insignificant
ensejen, incision

ensekt, insect
ensektaside, insecticide
enselashen, insulate(tion)
ensem, inseam
ensemanation, inseminate(tion)
enseminate, inseminate
ensemineit, inseminate
ensen, ensign
ensenarate, incinerate
ensendiary, incendiary
ensense, incense
ensenseer, insincere
ensensible, insensible
ensensitive, insensitive
ensentive, incentive
ensentuf, incentive
ensenuashen, insinuate(tion)
ensenuate, insinuate
ensepshen, incept(ion)
ensept, incept
ensequir, insecure
enserekshen, insurrection
ensermowntible, insurmountable
ensershen, insert(ion)
ensert, insert
ensesint, incessant
ensest, incest / insist / encyst
ensh, inch
ensher, ensure / insure
enshiranse, insure(rance)
enshree, entry / entree
enshure, insure
enshurence, insure(rance)
enside, inside / insight / incite
ensident, incident
ensidious, insidious
ensidnea, insignia
ensigen, incision
ensight, insight / incite / inside
ensightation, incite(tation)
ensightment, incite(ment)
ensign, *, MILITARY RANK
ensignia, insignia

ensignificant, insignificant
ensiklopedia, encyclopedia
ensikure, insecure
ensikuredy, insecure(rity)
ensilate, insulate
ensilin, insulin
ensim, enzyme / inseam
ensimanashen, inseminate(tion)
ensimanate, inseminate
ensin, ensign
ensinarate, incinerate
ensincere, insincere
ensinereit, incinerate
ensinsative, insensitive
ensinse, incense
ensinsuble, insensible
ensinuashen, insinuate(tion)
ensinuate, insinuate
ensircol, encircle
ensirection, insurrection
ensishen, incision
ensisor, incise(sor)
ensist, insist
ensistent, insist(ent)
ensitation, incite(tation)
ensite, inside / insight / incite
ensiteful, insight(ful)
ensitement, incite(ment)
ensiteus, insidious
ensition, incision
ensiur, ensure
ensize, incise
enskribe, inscribe
enskripshen, inscription
ensolt, insult
ensoluble, insoluble
ensolvable, insolvable
ensolvent, insolvent
ensomnia, insomnia
ensovent, insolvent
ensoyuble, insoluble
ensparashen, inspire(ration)
enspecshen, inspect(ion)

enspect,inspect
enspection,inspect(ion)
enspekable,unspeakable
enspekshen,inspect(ion)
enspekt,inspect
enspire,inspire
enspoken,unspoken
enspuration,inspire(ration)
enstall,install
enstalment,install(ment)
enstance,instance
enstant,instant
enstanteneous,instantaneous
enstanteinius,instantaneous
enstatute,institute
enstatution,institute(tion)
enstaulment,install(ment)
ensted,instead
enstenked,instinct
enstense,instance
enstetushen,institute(tion)
enstigate,instigate
enstigeit,instigate
enstill,instill
enstinct,instinct
enstinse,instance
enstintaneusly,instantaneous(ly)
enstitute,institute
enstol,install
enstolashen,install(ation)
enstolment,install(ment)
enstrament,instrument
enstriment,instrument
enstrucshen,instruct(ion)
enstruct,instruct
enstruction,instruct(ion)
enstrukt,instruct
enstrument,instrument
enstrumental,instrument(al)
enstugate,instigate
enstunt,instant
enstuntly,instant(ly)
ensubordinate,insubordinate

ensucure,insecure
ensue,*,ed,uing,CLOSELY FOLLOW
ensufishent,insufficient
ensugnifakent,insignificant
ensulate,insulate
ensulation,insulate(tion)
ensulin,insulin
ensult,insult
ensunseer,insincere
ensure,*,ed,ring,GUARANTEE/ PROMISE (or see insure)
ensurkle,encircle
ensurmauntabol,insurmountable
ensurmountable,insurmountable
ensurrection,insurrection
ensurshen,insert(ion)
ensurt,insert
ensyklopedia,encyclopedia
ensym,enzyme
ent,end / and
entacate,indicate
entact,intact
entaferance,interfere(rance)
entager,integer
entagral,integral
entagrate,integrate
entail,*,led,ling,lment,RESTRICTIONS TO OWNERSHIP "prefixes: dis"
entais,entice
entaitol,entitle
entak,intact / intake
entale,entail
entalect,intellect
entalectual,intellect(ual)
entamet,intimate
entangible,intangible
entangle,*,ed,ling,ement,GET MIXED UP IN "prefixes: dis/ un"
entangol,entangle
entanjuble,intangible
entareor,anterior / interior
entarmedeate,intermediate
entate,entity
enteger,integer

entegral,integral
entegrate,integrate
entegreit,integrate
entegrity,integrity
entegrude,integrity
enteik,intake
enteingol,entangle
entekashen,indicate(tion)
entelagents,intelligent(nce)
entelijuble,intelligible
entelillent,intelligent
enteliyent,intelligent
entellect,intellect
entelugeble,intelligible
entelugint,intelligent
entenation,intonate(tion)
entend,intend
entense,intense
entenshin,intent(ion)
entensity,intense(sity)
entensuve,intense(sive)
entent,intent
enter,*,red,ring,rable,rance,GO INTO,PREFIX INDICATING "INTESTINE" MOST OFTEN MODIFIES THE WORD "prefixes: re"
enteract,interact
entercede,intercede
entercept,intercept
enterchange,interchange
entercom,intercom
enterconnect,interconnect
entercourse,intercourse
enterd,enter(ed)
entereor,anterior / interior
entereleit,interrelate
enterferans,interfere(nce)
enterfere,interfere
enterference,interfere(rance)
entergekshen,interject(ion)
enterim,interim
enterior,anterior / interior
enterject,interject
enterllect,interject

enterlock, interlock
enterlude, interlude
entermediary, intermediary
entermediate, intermediate
entermetant, intermittent
entermingle, intermingle
entermission, intermission
entern, intern
enternal, internal
enternational, international
enternet, internet
entero, PREFIX INDICATING "INTESTINE" MOST OFTEN MODIFIES THE WORD
enterog, entourage
enterogate, interrogate
enterogeit, interrogate
enterpreneur, entrepreneur
enterpret, interpret
enterpretation, interpretation
enterprise, *, sing, singly, USE AMBITION TO TAKE ON RISKS
enterrelate, interrelate
enterrogate, interrogate
enterrupt, interrupt
enterscholastic, interscholastic
entersept, intercept
entersid, interceded
entersperse, intersperse
enterstate, interstate
entertain, *, ned, ning, nment, ner, AMUSE/ ENGAGE SOMEONE
entertaner, entertain(er)
entertainment, entertain(ment)
entertwine, intertwine
enterupt, interrupt
enterval, interval
entervene, intervene
enterview, interview
enterwoven, interwoven
entestine, intestine
entety, entity
entever, endeavor
enthooseastik, enthuse(siastic)

enthrall, *, led, ling, OVERWHELMED WITH AWE
enthrol, enthrall
enthuse, ed, siasm, siastic, siastically, HAVE INTEREST/ ENERGY FOR "prefixes: over/ un"
enthuseastek, enthuse(siastic)
enthuziazm, enthuse(siasm)
entice, *, ed, cing, ement, er, APPEAL TO, ALLURE, SUCCUMB TO
entid, end(ed)
entidle, entitle
entiger, integer
entigo, indigo
entigral, integral
entigration, integrate(tion)
entil, until
entilect, intellect
entimadate, intimidate
entimadeit, intimidate
entimate, intimate
entimidate, intimidate
entina, antenna
entinse, intense
entinsive, intense(sive)
entint, intent
entintion, intent(ion)
entire, ely, ety, COMPLETE, THE WHOLE THING
entireleit, interrelate
entirest, interest
entirferans, interfere(nce)
entirle, entire(ly)
entirmediate, intermediate
entirmitant, intermittent
entirnet, internet
entirpreneur, entrepreneur
entirprize, enterprise
entirprutashen, interpretation
entirty, entire(ty)
entisepate, anticipate
entitle, *, ed, ling, ement, RIGHTS, AUTHORITY TO
entity, ties, A BEING WITH HUMAN FORM "prefixes: non"
entlis, endless
ento, into

entoishen, intuit(ion)
entolerable, intolerable
entolrabol, intolerable
entonate, intonate
entoneit, intonate
entor, enter
entouet, intuit(ive)
entourage, *, GROUP WHO TRAVELS WITH IMPORTANT/ FAMOUS PEOPLE
entowment, endow(ment)
entoxicate, intoxicate
entra, entree
entrabert, introvert
entraduction, introduce(ction)
entraduse, introduce
entrakit, intricate
entral, enthrall
entramural, intramural
entrance, ed, cing, PLACE/ WAY TO GET IN
entranet, intranet
entrapreneur, entrepreneur
entraspect, introspect
entravenous, intravenous
entray, entree
entree, *, A MEAL, FOOD SERVING (or see entry)
entrege, intrigue
entrense, entrance
entrensic, intrinsic
entrepreneur, *, rial, rialism, rism, rship, ONE WHO RISKS FINANCING A NEW BUSINESS/ ENTERPRISE
entres, entry(ries) / entree(s)
entrest, interest
entri, entry / entree
entricate, intricate
entrigue, intrigue
entrinsic, intrinsic
entroduce, introduce
entrodus, introduce
entrospect, introspect
entrost, interest / entrust
entrovert, introvert
entrude, intrude
entrudukshen, introduce(ction)

entruduse, introduce
entrugen, intrusion
entrumural, intramural
entrunse, entrance
entrupreneur, entrepreneur
entrupt, interrupt
entrusef, intrusive
entrushen, intrusion
entrusib, intrusive
entrust, *, ted, ting, LEAVE THE CARE OF SOMETHING/ SOMEONE TO ANOTHER (or see interest)
entry, ries, rant, OPENING GOING IN, ENTER INTO (or see entree) "prefixes: re/ sub"
entuative, intuit(ive)
entueshen, intuit(ion)
entuetion, intuit(ion)
entufere, interfere
entuger, integer
entugrate, integrate
entuishen, intuit(ion)
entuit, intuit(ive) / intuit
entuition, intuit(ion)
entunate, intonate
entur, enter
enuract, interact
enurauj, entourage
enurem, interim
enurlock, interlock
enurmediate, intermediate
enurmetant, intermittent
enturn, intern
enturnal, internal
enturnalize, internal(ize)
enturpreit, interpret
enturpreitashon, interpretation
enturpreneur, entrepreneur
enturpret, interpret
enturprise, enterprise
entursept, intercept
enturtane, entertain
enturtaner, entertain(er)
enturtanment, entertain(ment)
entus, enthuse

entutes, entity(ties)
entwoishen, intuit(ion)
entwoit, intuit(ive)
entyre, entire
enubelidy, inability
enubishen, inhibit(ion)
enuendo, innuendo
enuf, enough
enuindo, innuendo
enume, enemy
enunciate, *, ed, ting, tion, tions, tive, tively, tor, SPEAK CLEARLY/ SPECIFICALLY (or see annunciate)
enundate, inundate
enundeit, inundate
enunseate, enunciate/ annunciate
enupresheative, inappreciative
enuprochible, inapproachable
enupropreut, inappropriate
enur, inner
enuract, interact
enurcom, intercom
enurelate, interrelate
enurferins, interfere(nce)
enurgee, energy
enurgekshen, interject(ion)
enurim, interim
enurjetek, energetic
enurlude, interlude
enurmediary, intermediary
enurmingle, intermingle
enurmission, intermission
enurmost, innermost
enurnet, internet
enursculastic, interscholastic
enursecshen, intersection
enursperse, intersperse
enurt, inert
enurupt, interrupt
enurval, interval
enurvene, intervene
enurview, interview
enurvue, interview
enurwoven, interwoven

enuscapubIe, inescapable
enusense, innocence
enusent, innocence(nt)
enuther, another
enuvate, innovate
envachinate, invaginate
envade, invade
envaginate, invaginate
envagination, invaginate(tion)
envaiabol, enviable
envaiorment, environment
envajunate, invaginate
envalid, invalid
envalope, envelope
envaluable, invaluable
envasef, invasive
envashen, invasion
envashenation, invaginate(tion)
envasion, invasion
envatashen, invitation
envate, invade
envaulve, involve
enve, envy
enved, envy(vied)
eneid, invade
envelope, *, ed, ping, ement, ENCLOSE/ WRAP TO PROTECT SOMETHING
envensable, invincible
envenshen, invent(ion)
envent, invent
enventory, inventory
enverdebrae, invertebrate
envereably, invariable(ly)
enverse, inverse
enversion, inversion
enversive, inverse(sive)
envert, invert
envertebrate, invertebrate
enves, envy(vies)
envest, invest
envestagashen, investigate(tion)
envestigate, investigate
envestmant, invest(ment)

envetashen, invitation
enveuble, enviable
enveus, envious
enviable, ly, SOMEONE WISHING THEY HAD
enviding, invite(ingly)
envigorate, invigorate
envilope, envelope
envincible, invincible
envintory, inventory
enviornmental, environment(al)
envios, envious
envious, sly, sness, BEING JEALOUS
envirdebrate, invertebrate
environment, *, tal, tally, talist, =alism, EXTERIOR SURROUNDINGS
envirs, inverse
envirsion, inversion
envirsive, inverse(sive)
envirtebrate, invertebrate
envisability, invisible(bility)
envisible, invisible
envitashen, invitation
envitation, invitation
enviteishon, invitation
envitingly, invite(ingly)
envizable, invisible
envoice, invoice
envoluntary, involuntary
envolve, involve
envoyse, invoice
envuiid, invalid
envurdabrae, invertebrate
envurt, invert
envuteishon, invitation
envy, vies, vied, vying, vyingly, vious, viously, viousness, viable, WANT SOMETHING THAT SOMEONE ELSE HAS "prefixes: un"
enward, inward
enword, inward
enwrech, enrich
enwrich, enrich
enwroll, enroll
eny, any

enybody, anybody
enyect, inject
enzerkle, encircle
enzide, inside
enzyme, *, matic, mic, mically, mology, CHEMICAL ACTION CREATED BY CELLS "prefixes: endo/ exo/ non/ pro"
ep, PREFIX INDICATING "OVER/ NEAR" MOST OFTEN MODIFIES THE WORD
epacalypse, apocalypse
epacolypse, apocalypse
epaculypse, apocalypse
epademic, epidemic
epareshin, apparition
eparition, apparition
epart, apart
epartmint, apartment
epasenter, epicenter
epasode, episode
epauculypse, apocalypse
epazode, episode
epeal, appeal
epeel, appeal
eperatus, apparatus
eperinse, appearance
eperint, apparent
eperul, apparel
epi, PREFIX INDICATING "OVER/ NEAR" MOST OFTEN MODIFIES THE WORD
epicenter, *, CENTRAL SPOT OF EARTHQUAKE
epidemic, *, MANY LIVES AT RISK IN AN AREA
episode, *, PARTS OF AN ONGOING SHOW
episoud, episode
epizode, episode
epliense, appliance
eplod, applaud
eply, apply
epodemec, epidemic
epoint, appoint
epointment, appointment
epocalypse, apocalypse
epocolypse, apocalypse
epoculypse, apocalypse
epokalypse, apocalypse

epokelypse, apocalypse
epokilypse, apocalypse
epokolypse, apocalypse
epokulypse, apocalypse
epoynt, appoint
epoyntment, appointment
eprasal, appraisal
epreciate, appreciate
eprentis, apprentice
epresheate, appreciate
eprintise, apprentice
epruvel, approve(val)
epsolv, absolve
epsorb, absorb
epstane, abstain
epsurd, absurd
eptikate, abdicate
epusode, episode
epzolv, absolve
epzorb, absorb
epzurd, absurd
eqaul, equal
eqaulity, equality
eqaunimity, equanimity
eqauzition, acquisition
eqivocate, equivocate
equable, ly, bility, eness, IS EQUAL TO, SAME IN VALUE, UNIFORM "prefixes: in"
equal, *, led, ling, lly, able, lize, lizes, lized, lizing, lizer, lization, SAME AS, EQUIVALENT, UNIFORM "prefixes: un"
equalibrium, equilibrium
equality, ties, tarian, tarianism, OF BEING THE SAME, EQUIVALENT "prefixes: in"
equanemity, equanimity
equanimity, ties, mous, OF EVEN TEMPERAMENT
equate, *, ed, ting, tion, table, tability, COMPARE/ BALANCE/ MAKE UNIFORM "prefixes: un"
equation, *, nal, nally, BALANCE OF BOTH SIDES
equator, *, rial, rially, ONE OF TWO HALVES OF A PLANET/ STAR "prefixes: sub"
equel, equal
equelebreum, equilibrium

Word/Prefix	Definition	Examples
equevocal,equivocal		
equi, PREFIX INDICATING "EQUAL" MOST OFTEN MODIFIES THE WORD		
equifocal, equivocal		
equifocate, equivocate		
equil, equal		
equilibrium, * , BALANCE, STABILITY "prefixes: dis/ non"		
equinox, xes, WHEN DAY/ NIGHT ARE IN EQUAL PARTS		
equip, * , pped, pping, pper, pment, TO MAKE READY FOR A TASK, EVENT		
equipment, ARTICLES/ IMPLEMENTS TO PERFORM WORK		
equity, ties, tize, tizes, tized, tizing, tization, HOW MUCH YOU OWN, JUSTICE/ RIGHTS "prefixes: in"		
equivalent, tly, nce, ncy, THE SAME AS, EQUAL "prefixes: non"		
equivilense, equivalent(ncy)		
equivocal, lity, lly, lness, ate, EQUAL ENOUGH TO LEAD TO MISINTERPRETATION, SUSPICION, DOUBT "prefixes: un"		
equivocate, * , ed, ting, tingly, tor, tory, tion, tions, EQUAL ENOUGH TO LEAD TO MISINTERPRETATION, SUSPICION, DOUBT		
erabrochuble, irreproachable		
eracer, eraser		
eradable, irritable		
eradeate, irradiate		
eradesent, iridescent		
eradiate, irradiate		
eradic, erratic / erotic		
eradicate, * , ed, ting, tion, tive, able, ably, tor, ELIMINATE, DISPOSE "prefixes: in/ un"		
eradukashen, eradicate(tion)		
eragardles, irregardless		
eragashen, irrigate(tion)		
eragate, irrigate		
eragation, irrigate(tion)		
eraguardless, irregardless		
erain, arraign		
erakned, arachnid		
eran, arraign		
erand, errand		
erange, arrange		
erangment, arrange(ment)		
eranment, arraign(ment)		
erant, errant		
eraplasible, irreplaceable		
eraprochuble, irreproachable		
erapt, irrupt		
erasbonsuble, irresponsible		
erasbonzible, irresponsible		
erase, * , ed, sing, er, sable, ELIMINATE COMPLETELY		
eraser, * , RUBBER/ FELT PAD FOR REMOVING INK		
erashinul, irrational		
erashunal, irrational		
erasistible, irresistible		
erasol, aerosol		
eraspective, irrespective		
eraspektif, irrespective		
erasponsuble, irresponsible		
erasponzuble, irresponsible		
eratant, irritant		
eratashen, irritate(tion)		
eratate, irritate		
eratible, irritable		
eratic, erratic / erotic		
erational, irrational		
eratrevible, irretrievable		
eraudik, erotic		
eravokable, irrevocable		
eray, array		
erayn, arraign		
erazestuble, irresistible		
erazistuble, irresistible		
erb, herb		
erbal, herb(al)		
erbashis, herb(aceous)		
erbel, herb(al)		
erbivore, herbivore		
erborne, airborne		
erbul, herb(al)		
erbulism, herb(alism)		
erbulist, herb(alist)		
erc, irk		
erch, urge		
erchen, urchin		
erchin, urchin		
erea, area		
erebrochuble, irreproachable		
erect, * , ted, ting, tion, tile, table, tly, tness, tor, SET STRAIGHT UP, RAISE		
ered, arid		
eredable, irritable		
eredesent, iridescent		
ereer, arrear		
eregardles, irregardless		
eregashen, irrigate(tion)		
eregate, irrigate		
eregation, irrigate(tion)		
eregeno, oregano		
eregewler, irregular		
eregler, irregular		
erekshen, erect(ion)		
erelavense, irrelevant(nce)		
erelavent, irrelevant		
erelebant, irrelevant		
ereluvense, irrelevant(nce)		
ereluvint, irrelevant		
erena, arena		
ereng, earring		
erent, errant		
ereperuble, irreparable		
erepirable, irreparable		
ereplacabol, irreplaceable		
ereprochible, irreproachable		
erepruble, irreparable		
erepurable, irreparable		
erer, error		
eresistible, irresistible		
erespective, irrespective		

erest,arrest
erestokrat,aristocrat
eretable, irritable
eretant,irritant
eretashen,irritate(tion)
eretat,irritate
eretibul,irritable
eretrevible,irretrievable
eretrievable,irretrievable
ereu,area
ereul,aerial
erevocable,irrevocable
erg,urge
ergense,urge(ncy)
ergent,urge(nt)
erginsy,urge(ncy)
ergint,urge(nt)
eri,awry
eribrochuble,irreproachable
erid,arid
eridable, irritable
eridesent,iridescent
erift,arrive(d)
eriful,arrival
erigardles,irregardless
erigashen,irrigate(tion)
erigate,irrigate
erigation,irrigate(tion)
erigeit,irrigate
eriguardless,irregardless
erind,errand
ering, earring / err(ing)
eriplasible,irreplaceable
eriproachable,irreproachable
erir,error
erisbonsuble,irresponsible
erisistible,irresistible
erisol,aerosol
erispective,irrespective
erispektif,irrespective
erisponsuble,irresponsible
eristocrat,aristocrat
eritable, irritable

eritant,irritant
eritate,irritate
erithmatic,arithmetic
eritrevuble,irretrievable
erive,arrive
erivokuble,irrevocable
erivul,arrival
erizisduble,irresistible
erj,urge
erjense,urge(nce) / urge(ncy)
erjinse,urge(nce) / urge(ncy)
erjint,urge(nt)
erk,irk
erle,early
erli,early
erll,urge
erloom,heirloom
erly,early
ern,earn / urn
ernest,earnest
ero,arrow
erobik,aerobic
erochun,erosion
erode, *, ed,ding,osion,osive,dible,dibility,osible, WEAR, WASH AWAY "prefixes: non/ un"
erodik,erotic
eroduble, irritable
erodynamic, aerodynamic
eroganse,arrogance
erogate,irrigate
erogint,arrogance(nt)
eroma,aroma
eromadek,aroma(tic)
erond,errand
eronic,ironic
eror,error
erosbonsuble,irresponsible
erosef,erosive
erosion,nal,nally, WEARING, WASHING AWAY
erosive,eness,vity, WEARS/ WASHES AWAY
erosponsuble,irresponsible
erote,erode

erotic,ca,cally,cize,cism,tology,tological,tologist, SEXUAL AROUSAL/ SENSATION
erotuble, irritable
erport,airport
err, *,rred,rring,rrancy,SHORT FOR ERROR,TO MAKE A MISTAKE (or see ear/ air/ heir) "prefixes: un"
erradiate,irradiate
errand, *, TRAVEL TO PERFORM A TASK
errant,tly, try, TO WANDER "prefixes: in"
erratate,irritate
erratic,cally, cism, SUDDEN/ UNPREDICTABLE MOVEMENTS OR THOUGHTS
errogate,irrigate
error, *, NOT CORRECT
ershen,urchin
ertearial, arterial
erth, earth
erubt, erupt / irrupt
erubtif, erupt(ive) / irrupt(ive)
erubtion, erupt(ion) / irrupt(ion)
erudeble, irritable
erugardles, irregardless
erugashen,irrigate(tion)
erugate, irrigate
erugation,irrigate(tion)
eruguardless, irregardless
erunt, errant
eruplasuble,irreplaceable
eruprochuble,irreproachable
erupshen,erupt(ion) / irrupt(ion)
erupt, *, ted, ting, tion, tive, tible, FORMING BULGE WHICH OPENS/ BURSTS (or see irrupt)
eruptif, erupt(ive) / irrupt(ive)
erur,error
erusbonsuble,irresponsible
erusistible, irresistible
erusol, aerosol
eruspective,irrespective
eruspektif,irrespective
erusponsuble,irresponsible
erutant,irritant
erutashen,irritate(tion)
erutate, irritate

eruteble, irritable
erutible, irritable
erutrevible, irretrievable
erutuble, irritable
eruvokuble, irrevocable
eruzistuble, irresistible
es, is / ease
esa, essay
esael, assail
esail, assail
esalt, assault
esans, essence
esanse, essence
esasen, assassin
esault, assault
esay, essay
esbeshulee, especially
escalade, * , er, TO SCALE WALL WITH LADDERS (or see escalator)
escalate, * , ed, ting, tor, tory, tion, TO RISE (or see escalade) "prefixes: de-"
escaleit, escalate
escalator, * , A CONVEYOR WHICH CARRIES/ MOVES ITEMS/ PEOPLE
escapade, * , AN ADVENTURE WITHOUT PERMISSION
escape, * , ed, ping, pable, er, pist, pism, pee, pees, pology, pologist, TO GET AWAY FROM WITHOUT PERMISSION "prefixes: in"
escort, * , ted, ting, SOMEONE WHO ACCOMPANIES TO ASSIST
escrow, * , wed, wing, MONEY RETAINED BY THIRD PARTY
escuisit, exquisite
esculator, escalator
esdeem, esteem
ese, ease / easy
esedik, acetic / acidic / ascetic
esei, essay
esemble, assemble
esemulate, assimilate
esence, essence
esend, ascend / isn't
esenshul, essential
esent, ascend / ascent / assent / isn't

esential, essential
esert, assert
esesmint, assessment
esfikseat, asphyxiate
esfixeat, asphyxiate
eshamed, ashamed
esherance, assure(rance)
eshew, issue
eshu, issue
eshurance, assure(rance)
eside, aside
esidik, acetic / acidic / ascetic
esidjewus, assiduous
esiguous, assiduous
esil, easel
esilum, asylum
esily, easily
esimble, assemble
esimelate, assimilate
esimetric, asymmetric
esind, ascend
esindant, ascendant
esine, assign
esinment, assignment
esinse, essence
esinshul, essential
esint, ascend / ascent / assent / isn't
esirt, assert
esist, assist
eskapade, escapade
eskape, escape
eskeip, escape
eskort, escort
eskplinashen, explanation
eskrow, escrow
eskulate, escalate / escalade
eskulater, escalator
eskupade, escapade
esm, ism
esment, easement
esmint, easement
esnt, ascend / ascent / assent / isn't
esofigus, esophagus

esolt, assault
esophagus, gi, geal, TUBE IN THE THROAT
esordment, assortment
esorted, assorted
esortment, assortment
esosheate, associate
esoshiate, associate
esoteric, ca, cally, cism, KNOWLEDGE GAINED BY A FEW
especially, PARTICULARLY, MOST CERTAINLY
esperugus, asparagus
espeshaly, especially
espeshulee, especially
espir, aspire
esploushon, explosion
espos, expose
espous, expose
espres, express
esqueip, escape
essay, * , yed, ying, yist, yistic, WRITE ABOUT A SPECIFIC POINT/THING
essence, * , THE AMBIANCE OR BASIC SENSE OF THE OVERALL
essential, * , lly, tiality, tialness, MUST HAVE, MOST IMPORTANT "prefixes: in/ non/ un"
est, east
estableshment, establish(ment)
establish, es, ed, hing, hment, her, hmentarian, TO CREATE A BASIS, BEGINNING "prefixes: dis/ non"
estamashen, estimate(tion)
esteem, * , med, ming, BEST REGARDS FOR, ADMIRE "prefixes: dis"
esteengwish, extinguish
estem, esteem
estemut, estimate
estern, east(ern)
estim, esteem
estimashen, estimate(tion)
estimate, * , ed, ting, tion, able, ably, ableness, tive, tor, TO APPROXIMATE BASED ON KNOWLEDGE "prefixes: in/ over/ under"
estimeit, estimate
estirle, east(erly)
estonesh, astonish

estragen, estrogen
estrawlegy, astrology
estrengent, astringent
estringent, astringent
estris, estrus
estrogen, A HORMONE CREATED BY FEMALES BEGINNING AT PUBERTY
estrollen, estrogen
estrolugy, astrology
estronume, astronomy
estrugen, estrogen
estrus, rum, ual, WHEN CONCEP"ION IS POSSIBLE
estumashen, estimate(tion)
estumit, estimate
esturle, east(erly)
esue, issue
esuense, issue(uance)
esuinse, issue(uance)
esul, easel
esume, assume
esunse, essence
esunt, ascend / ascent / assent / isn't
esylum, asylum
et, eat / eight / ate
etable, edible
etach, attach
etack, attack
etaen, attain
etak, attack
etalek, italic
etane, attain
etatch, attach
etcetera, MORE OF THE SAME
etch, hes, hed, hing, her, CARVE INTO (or see edge/ itch)
ete, eddy
etempt, attempt
etemt, attempt
etenchin, attention
etend, attend
etenshin, attention
etenshun, attention
eternal, lly, nity, nities, lity, lize, lizes, lized, lizirg, FOREVER
eteusy, idiocy

eteut, idiot
ether, ric, ALL THINGS AROUND AND BEYOND THE EARTH
ethic, *, cal, cally, cality, calness, cist, JUDGMENT OF CONDUCT/ BEHAVIOR "prefixes: bio/ un"
ethnac, ethnic
ethnic, *, cally, city, cities, nology, nologist, nologic, nologically, GROUP OF PEOPLE WITH THE SAME LANGUAGE, TRAITS
ethnuk, ethnic
ethrik, ether(ic)
ethuk, ethic
etikit, etiquette
etimt, attempt
etinchon, attention
etinshun, attention
etiquette, RULES OF PROPER BEHAVIOR
etire, attire
etmonish, admonish
etrakshun, attraction
etrakt, attract
etroshus, atrocious
ets, it's / eat(s)
etself, itself
etsetara, etcetera
etsulf, itself
eturnal, eternal
eturney, attorney
eu, PREFIX INDICATING "GOOD" MOST OFTEN MODIFIES THE WORD
eucalyptus, A TREE
euchoi, enjoy
euforia, euphoria
eul, eel
eullin, engine
eunaform, uniform
euphoria, ant, ic, ically, FEELS JOYFUL/ UNREAL
euraneum, uranium
eurinery, urinary
euterprais, enterprise
eutopea, utopia
evacuate, *, ed, ting, tion, tive, tor, TO EMPTY FROM A PLACE

evade, *, ed, ding, asion, evasive, er, TO NOT BE/ THINK/ BEHAVE AS EXPECTED
evadins, evidence
evakuashen, evacuate(tion)
evakuate, evacuate
evale, evil(lly)
evaluashen, evaluate(tion)
evaluate, *, ed, ting, tion, tive, TO STUDY/ REVIEW FOR FINAL OPINION/ JUDGMENT
evalushen, evolution
evalutionery, evolution(ary)
evan, even
evanly, even(ly)
evaperate, evaporate
evaperation, evaporate(tion)
evaporate, *, ed, ting, tion, LIQUID/ SOLID CONVERTED INTO GAS
evapurashen, evaporate(tion)
evapurate, evaporate
evaquiveit, evacuate
evarewer, every(where)
evasef, evasive
evashen, evasive
evasion, TO NOT BE/ THINK/ BEHAVE AS EXPECTED
evasive, ely, eness, TO NOT BE/ THINK/ BEHAVE AS EXPECTED
evate, evade
eve, THE EVENING, A PERIOD OF TIME BEFORE AN EVENT
evedins, evidence
evekshin, evict(ion)
evekt, evict
even, *, ed, ning, nly, nness, LEVEL WITH "prefixes: un"
evendful, eventful
evening, *, AFTER 6 O'CLOCK P.M.
evenshuele, event(ually)
event, *, tual, tually, tful, tfully, tfullness, SOMETHING OUT OF THE ORDINARY, WILL HAPPEN IN THE FUTURE "prefixes: un"
eventful, lly, lness, SOMETHING OUT OF THE ORDINARY
eventualy, event(ually)
ever, rmore, AT ANY TIME "prefixes: for"
everewar, every(where)
everves, effervesce

everesent, effervescent	evrry, every	exaustshen, exhaust(ion)
every,*,ybody,yday,yone,ything,ywhere, ALL	evryday, every(day)	exbarenshal, experiential
eves, eaves	evrywere, every(where)	exbedeant, expedient
evict,*,ted,ting,tion,tee, TO FORCIBLY REMOVE	evs, eaves	exberenshal, experiential
evidence,*,ed,cing,nt, PROOF OF TRUTH "prefixes: in"	evudens, evidence	exbirenshal, experiential
evidens, evidence	evudins, evidence	exblanashen, explanation
evident,tly,tial,tiality,tiary,tialism,nce, PROOF OF BEING SEEN, UNDERSTOOD, TRUTH "prefixes: in"	evudintly, evident(ly)	exblanatory, explanatory
evikshen, evict(ion)	evul, evil	exblikuble, explicable
eviktion, evict(ion)	evule, evil(lly)	exblode, explode
evil,*,lly,lness, OPPOSITE OF LOVE, THREATENING	evulushin, evolution	exbloetashen, exploit(ation)
evilutionary, evolution(ary)	evuneng, evening	exblor, explore
evin, even	evunle, even(ly)	exbloshen, explosion
evindful, eventful	ew, ewe / you / yew	exbloshun, explosion
evinly, even(ly)	eway, away	exblosive, explosive
evinshuale, event(ually)	**ewe**,*, FEMALE SHEEP (or see you/yew)	exblunashen, explanation
evint, event	ewrekt, erect	exborashen, expire(ration)
evintualy, event(ually)	**ex**, PREFIX INDICATING "FORMER/ OUTSIDE/ EXTERNAL" MOST OFTEN MODIFIES THE WORD	exbort, export
evir, ever	**exact**,ted,ting,tingly,tingness,tly,tness,table,tor, SPECIFIC "prefixes: in"	exbortashen, export(ation)
evl, evil	exagerate, exaggerate	exbos, expose
evneng, evening	exageration, exaggerate(tion)	exbress, express
evning, evening	**exaggerate**,*,ted,tedly,ting,tingly,tive,tion,tor, STRETCH/ ELONGATE THE TRUE FORM	exburashen, expire(ration)
evoke,*,ed,king,ocable,ocator,er, MAKE HAPPEN, CREATE REACTION	exail, exile	exburenshal, experiential
evol, evil	exajurashen, exaggerate(tion)	excalate, escalate / escalade
evolucion, evolution	exakude, execute	**excavate**,*,ed,ting,tion,tor, DIG FOR SOMETHING "prefixes: un"
evolushenary, evolution(ary)	exakushen, execute(tion)	**exceed**,*,ded,ding,dingly,dance, EXCEL, DO MORE THAN EXPECTED
evolution,*,nal,nally,nary,narily,nist,nism, THE ACT OF EVOLVING	exale, exhale	**excel**,*,lled,lling,llence,llency,llent, PERFORM BETTER THAN NORMAL/ AVERAGE (or see accel) "prefixes: un"
evolvd, evolve(d)	**exam**,*,mine, A TEST/ EVALUATION	excelaration, accelerate(tion)
evolve,*,ed,ving,lution, ADAPT, GAIN WISDOM, TRANSFORM	examenashen, examine(nation)	**excellent**,tly, OUTSTANDING
evon, even	**examine**,*,ed,ning,nation,nable,ee,er, CLOSELY CAREFULLY OBSERVE	excelurashen, accelerate(tion)
evoneng, evening	**example**,*,ed,ling, SIMILAR TO, USED TO DESCRIBE "prefixes: un"	exceluration, accelerate(tion)
evor, ever	exampul, example	excenshuate, accentuate
evow, avow	examunashen, examine(nation)	excentuate, accentuate
evre, every	exaqushen, execute(tion)	excepshen, except(ion)
evrebode, every(body)	**exasperate**,*,ed,edly,ting,tingly,tion, GREATLY ANNOY/ IRRITATE	**except**,*,ted,ting,tion,tional,tionalism,tionality, tionalness, tionalness, tionable, tive, THIS BUT NOT THAT, EXTRACT FROM (or see accept) "prefixes: un"
evreda, every(day)	exaspereit, exasperate	**excerpt**,*,ted,ting,tible,tion,tor, A SMALL PART OF THE WRITTEN WHOLE
evretheng, every(thing)	exaspiration, exasperate(tion)	excesorize, accessory(rize)
evrewer, every(where)	exaspurate, exasperate	
evrewun, every(one)		
evriwun, every(one)		

excesory, accessory
excess, sses,ssive,ssively,ssiveness, MORE THAN ENOUGH (or see access)
exchange, *, ed,ging,eable,eability,er, TO TRADE
excinshuate, accentuate
excite, *, ed,ting,ement,table,tability,tableness, AROUSE, FEEL TINGLY INSIDE "prefixes: un"
excksbedeant, expedient
exclamation, *, nal, DISPLAY OF FORCE/ ENTHUSIASM/ WILLFULNESS, PUNCTUATION, EXCLAMATION POINT
exclameichon, exclamation
exclameishon, exclamation
excloot, exclude
exclude, *, ded,ding,usive,usively,usiveness, usivity, usion,usions,usionary, NOT INCLUDED AS PART OF SOMETHING OR GROUP
exclusive, ely, eness, SPECIAL, UNLIKE ANY OTHER
excursion, *, nist,ive,ively,iver.ess, A SHORT TRIP, CHEAP FARE
excuse, *, ed,sing,sable,sably,sableness,er, REASONS FOR A PROBLEM BEING "prefixes: in/ un"
excuvashen, excavate(tion)
excuvation, excavate(tion)
exdansev, extensive
exdensible, extensible
exdensive, extensive
exdensubly, extensible(ly)
exderminate, exterminate
exdinsev, extensive
exdravert, extrovert
exdruvirt, extrovert
exdurminate, exterminate
execute, *, ed,ting,tion,tor, CARRY OUT/ ENFORCE/ ENACT A PLAN, TO KILL FOR RELIGIOUS/ POLITICAL REASONS
executive, *, ely, PERSON WITH POSITION/ POWER TO CREATE/ ENACT WITHIN AN ORGANIZATION
exekiut, execute
exelarate, exhilarate / accelerate
exema, eczema

exemplify, fies,fied,fying,fiable,fication,fier, MAKE CLEAR OR CONVINCING
exempt, ted,ting,tion,tible, SET FREE, EXCUSE FROM DUTY/ TAXES/ RULES/ LEGAL HOLDINGS
exemshen, exempt(ion)
exepshen, except(ion)
exequtef, executive
exercise, *, ed,sing,sable, er, MENTAL/ PHYSICAL ACTIVITY FOR IMPROVEMENT (or see exorcise)
exert, *, ted,ting,tion, PUT FORTH POWER/ ENERGY
exest, exist
exfoliate, *, ed,ting,tion,tive,ant,tor, LAYERS LIFTING OFF
exglusef, exclusive
exhale, *, ed,ling,lation, TO BREATH OUT
exhaust, *, ted,ting,tion,tive,tively,tiveness,ter,tible, tibility, RUN OUT OF, DISCHARGE, FUMES FROM A MOTOR "prefixes: in"
exhaustein, exhaust(ion)
exhibit, *, ted,ting,tion,tioner,tory,tor,tive,tively, tionist, tionism, ON SHOW
exhilarate, *, ed,ting,tingly,tion,tive,tor, REFRESHING, EXCITING (or see accelerate)
exhilation, exhale(lation)
exhostion, exhaust(ion)
exhostshen, exhaust(ion)
exhulation, exhale(lation)
exibit, exhibit
exicute, execute
exicution, execute(tion)
exikude, execute
exikushen, execute(tion)
exikut, execute
exile, *, ed,ling,lic, TO REMOVE/ BE REMOVED FROM YOUR COUNTRY
exilurate, exhilarate
exima, eczema
eximplify, exemplify
exirsize, exercise / exorcise
exirtion, exert(ion)
exist, *, ted,ting,tence,tent,tential,tentially,tialism, OF FORM, AN ENTITY "prefixes: in/ pre"
exit, *, ted,ting, TO LEAVE FROM

exitment, excite(ment)
exjaust, exhaust
exjeil, exhale
exjibit, exhibit
exjilueit, exhilarate
exkalate, escalate / escalade
exkergen, excursion
exkerjen, excursion
exkeus, excuse
exkius, excuse
exklumashen, exclamation
exkro, escrow
exkulate, escalate / escalade
exkurgen, excursion
exkurshun, excursion
exkuze, excuse
exlant, excellent
exo, PREFIX INDICATING "OUTSIDE/ EXTERNAL" MOST OFTEN MODIFIES THE WORD
exorbeant, exorbitant
exorbetant, exorbitant
exorbiant, exorbitant
exorbitant, tly, WAY TOO MUCH, RIDICULOUS AMOUNT
exorcise, *, ed,sing,ism,ist, BANISH/ EXPEL SPIRITS (or see exercise)
exost, exhaust
exostshen, exhaust(ion)
exotic, *, cally, MYSTERIOUS/ DIFFERENT/ STRANGE
expadishen, expedition
expadition, expedition
expand, *, ded,ding,der,dable,dability,nse, TO EXTEND BEYOND WHAT IS
expanse, *, sive,sively,siveness,sivity,sion,sionary,sible, sionism, EXTEND BEYOND WHAT IS (or see expense)
exparential, experiential
expayer, expire
expect, *, ted,tedly,ting,tation,tant,tantly,table,tably, tedness,tancy,tancies, WANT/ WISH SOMETHING TO HAPPEN "prefixes: un"
expedient, *, tly,ncy,ncies, HASTEN THE PROCESS BUT MAY COMPROMISE INTEGRITY "prefixes: in"
expedition, *, nary,ous,ously,ousness, JOURNEY TO GATHER INFORMATION

expel,*,,lled,lling,llable,llant,llee,ller,FORCE OUT/ AWAY FROM

expend,*,,ded,ding,dable,dability,diture,PAY OUT

expense,*,,ed,sing,sive,sively,siveness,REQUIRES TIME AND/ OR MONEY (or see expanse) "prefixes: in"

experiential, experiential

experience,*,,ed,cing,ntial,ntially,SKILL/ KNOWLEDGE ABOUT "prefixes: in/ un"

experiential,lly,GAIN KNOWLEDGE/ WISDOM THROUGH EXPERIENCE

experiment,*,,ted,ting,tation,tal,tally,talism,ter,TRY SOMETHING NEW

expert,*,,tly,tness,tise,SPECIALIZES IN, GREAT DEAL OF EXPERIENCE "prefixes: in"

expire,*,,ed,ring,ration,ratory,ry,DETERIORATE, RUN OUT OF TIME

expirential, experiential

expirians, experience

explain,*,,ned,ning,anation,nable,ner,anatory,anatorily, LIST THE FACTS ABOUT SOMETHING

explanation,PROVIDE DETAILS/ REASONS FOR/ ABOUT

explanatory,rily, AIDS/ SERVES TO EXPLAIN SOMETHING "prefixes: un"

explein, explain

explenashen, explanation

expleneishon, explanation

explicable,ly, CAN BE EXPLAINED "prefixes: in"

explicit,*,,tly,tness,SPECIFIC,EXACT,FACTUAL "prefixes: in"

explikable, explicable

explinashen, explanation

explode,*,,ed,ding,osion,osive,SUDDEN POWERFUL FORCE OUT "prefixes: un"

exploit,*,,ted,ting,tate,tation,tative,TAKE UNFAIR ADVANTAGE OF FOR SELFISH GAIN "prefixes: non/ under"

explore,*,,ed,ring,ration,ratory,SEARCH BEYOND WHAT IS KNOWN

explosion,INTENSE FORCE/ BLAST

explosive,ely,eness,INTENSIVE ACTION/ REACTION "prefixes: un"

exploud, explode

exploushon, explosion

---

exploytation, exploit(ation)

explunashen, explanation

expodeshen, expedition

exporashen, expire(ration)

export,*,,ted,ting,tation,table,tability,ter,SHIP GOODS OUT OF THE COUNTRY "prefixes: re"

expose,*,,ed,sing,sure,sal,sition,sitive,sitory,sition,sitor, er, LET IT OUT/ BE SEEN "prefixes: non/ over/ under"

exposhur, expose(sure)

expous, expose

expres, express

expreshun, express(ion)

express,sses,ssed,ssing,ssion,ssional,ssionless,ssible, ssive,ssively,ssiveness,ssivity,ssionism,sser, TO VERBALIZE/ ACT OUT WHAT ONE THINKS, GET THERE FASTER "prefixes: in/ un"

expurashen, expire(ration)

expuration, expire(ration)

expurential, experiential

exquisite,ely,eness,PERFECTLY BEAUTIFUL

exqwisit, exquisite

exsalins, excel(llence)

exsdensive, extensive

exseed, exceed

exsel, excel / accel

exselarashen, accelerate(tion)

exselaratur, accelerate(tor)

exseld, excel(lled) / accel(lled)

exselens, excel(llence)

exselent, excellent

exselerashen, accelerate(tion)

exselurashen, accelerate(tion)

exselurate, accelerate

exseluratur, accelerate(tor)

exsenshuate, accentuate

exsentrik, eccentric

exserpd, excerpt

exsersize, exercise / exorcise

exses, excess / access

exsesif, excess(ive) / access(ive)

exsesis, excess(es) / access(es)

exsesory, accessory

exshange, exchange

---

exsibition, exhibit(ion)

exsid, exceed

exsilent, excellent

exsilurate, exhilarate / accelerate

exsintrik, eccentric

exsirped, excerpt

exsistens, exist(ence)

exsitment, excite(ment)

exskalate, escalate / escalade

exskavate, excavate

exskuvashen, excavate(tion)

exsost, exhaust

expedient, expedient

exspektashen, expect(ation)

exspektent, expect(ant)

exspel, expel

exspense, expense

exsplod, explode

exsploshen, explosion

exsplosive, explosive

exstase, ecstasy

exstend, extend

exstengwish, extinguish

exstenshen, extension

exstinsibly, extensible(ly)

extract, extract

extradite, extradite

extrakt, extract

extravert, extrovert

extrem, extreme

extremly, extreme(ly)

extrivurt, extrovert

extrordenary, extraordinary

extusee, ecstasy

exsubishen, exhibit(ion)

exsulens, excel(llence)

exsulent, excellent

exsuqushen, execute(tion)

exsurpt, excerpt

exsursais, exercise

exteenkt, extinct

extend,*,ded,ding,dsion,nsive,nsively,nsiveness,:table, dability,dible,nsible,STRETCH/ ADD BEYOND WHAT EXISTS "prefixes: over/ pre"
extenquish, extinguish
extensible,bility,bly,ABLE TO STRETCH BEYOND WHAT EXISTS "prefixes: in"
extension,*,ive,STRETCH/ ADD BEYOND WHAT EXISTS
extensive,ely,eness,ible,STRETCH/ ADD BEYOND WHAT EXISTS
extenuate,*,ed,ting,tingly,tion,tive,tor,tory,LESSEN A MISTAKE BY PROVIDING GOOD EXCUSE
exterior,*,rity,rize,rizes,rized,rizing,rization,OUTSIDE LAYER
exterminate,*,ed,ting,tion,tive,tor,tory,able, COMPLETELY GET RID OF
external,lly,lism,lity,lize,lizes,lized,lizing,lization, OUTSIDE OF SOMETHING OR SOMEONE
extinct,tion,tive, DOES NOT EXIST ANY LONGER
extinguish,hes,hed,hing,hable,hment,her,TO PUT OUT, END "prefixes: in"
extra,*, PREFIX INDICATING "OUTSIDE/ BEYOND" MOST OFTEN MODIFIES THE WORD, MORE OF THE SAME
extract,*,ted,ting,tion,table,tive,tively,tor,TAKE/ DRAW FROM
extradite,*,ed,ting,tion,RELEASE FROM ONE LEGAL AUTHORITY TO ANOTHER
extraneous,sly,sness,EXTRA, FROM OUTSIDE OF, NOT NECESSARY
extraordinaire,*,ry,OVER AND ABOVE, EXCELLENT
extraordinary,rily,riness,OVER AND ABOVE, EXCELLENT
extravurt, extrovert
extreme,*,ely,eness,mity,rnities,mism, OF THE GREATEST/MOST
extrim, extreme
extro,PREFIX INDICATING "OUTSIDE/ BEYOND" MOST OFTEN MODIFIES THE WORD
extrovert,*,ted,tly,OUTGOING, GREGARIOUS
exterminate, exterminate
exuated, acuate(d)
exukushen, execute(tion)
exuqushen, execute(tion)
exuqute, execute
exursize, exercise / exorcise

exurt, exert
exurtion, exert(ion)
exzamen, examine
exzema, eczema
eychent, agent
eycur, acre
eye,*,ed,ying,ORGAN OF SIGHT (or see I)
eyebrow,*, HAIR AROUND TOP OF EYES
eyelash,hes,HAIR ON EYELIDS
eylias, alias
eylien, alien
eymiabol, amiable
eynol, anal
eynos, anus
eyquer, acre
ez, ease / easy
eza, essay
ezal, easel
ezale, easily
ezali, easily
ezaly, easily
ezay, essay
ezbeshulee, especially
ezdragen, estrogen
eze, easy / ease
ezel, easel
ezele, easily
ezil, easel
ezile, easily
ezinshil, essential
ezkort, escort
ezle, easily
ezli, easily
ezly, easily
ezment, easement
ezol, easel
ezole, easily
ezoli, easily
ezoly, easily
ezoteric, esoteric
ezperagus, asparagus
ezsperugus, asparagus
eztablush, establish

ezteem, esteem
eztem, esteem
eztim, esteem
eztimate, estimate
eztonish, astonish
eztrawlegy, astrology
eztrogin, estrogen
eztrus, estrus
ezul, easel
ezule, easily
ezuli, easily
ezuly, easily
fabal, fable
fabalus, fabulous
fabel, fable
fabelus, fabulous
fabewlus, fabulous
fabewlusly, fabulous(ly)
fabil, fable
fabilus, fabulous
fable,*, MYTH/ LEGEND/ STORY
fabol, fable
fabrecation, fabricate(tion)
fabrek, fabric
fabrekashin, fabricate(tion)
fabrekate, fabricate
fabric,*,cate,cation,cator,THREADS WOVEN TOGETHER "prefixes: bio"
fabricate,*,ed,ting,tion,tor,TO CREATE, CHANGE FROM ONE MATERIAL FORM TO ANOTHER "prefixes: pre"
fabrukashen, fabricate(tion)
fabrukate, fabricate
fabuare, february
fabul, fable
fabules, fabulous / fable(s)
fabulis, fabulous
fabulous,sly,sness,EXCELLENT, WONDERFUL
fabulus, fabulous
fabululsly, fabulous(ly)
fac, face / fake / phase / faze
facade,*, FALSE FRONT, PHONY
facalty, faculty

face,*, ed, cing, cial, cially, cable, eable, EXTERIOR FRONT, ON FRONT OF HEAD (or see phase) "prefixes: re/ sur"
facechus, facetious
facelity, facility
facelty, faculty
facen, fasten / face(cing) / fake(king)
faceshus, facetious
facest, fascist
facet,*, tious, ONE PLANE/FACE/SIDE AMONG MANY (or see faucet) "prefixes: multi"
facetious, sly, sness, NOT SERIOUS, BEING AMUSING
facha, fascia
fachel, facial
fachen, fashion
fachest, fascist
fachinuble, fashion(able)
fachism, fascism
fachist, fascist
fachul, facial
fachun, fashion
fachunible, fashion(able)
facial,*, lly, list, HAVING TO DO WITH THE FACE
facilitate,*, ed, ting, tion, tive, tor, HELP/ ENABLE SUCCESS
facility, ties, PLACE PROVIDING SERVICES
facin, fasten / face(cing) / fake(king)
facinate, fascinate
facishus, facetious
facism, fascism
facit, facet / faucet
facitious, facetious
facshun, faction
fact,*, tual, tuality, tuality, tualness, tualism, FOR REAL, TRUE (or see fake(d)/ fax/ face(d)) "prefixes: contra"
faction,*, nal, nally, nalism, OF MATH, PART OF A LARGER GROUP
faculty, ties, tative, tatively, SKILL OR ABILITY, TEACHING STAFF
fad,*, CURRENT STYLE (or see fade/ fate)
fadam, fathom
fadar, father / fodder
fadaret, federate

fade,*, ed, cing, ding, eless, LOSS OF COLOR/ MEMORY/ SUBSTANCE (or see fate) "prefixes: pre"
fadel, fatal
fadelity, fidelity
fadom, fathom
fadul, fatal
faen, feign
faer, fair / fire
faes, phase
fafret, favorite
fag,*, gged, ggot, ggoting, BUNDLE OF STICKS, CIGARETTE, DEROGATORY REMARK
fagism, fascism
fahrenheit, OF THERMOMETERS/ TEMPERATURE
faiber, fiber
faier, fire
fail,*, led, ling, lingly, lure, NOT SUCCEED (or see fall) "prefixes: un"
failo, philo
failou, philo
fain, feign / vain / vein / vane / fine
fainans, finance
faind, find
fainol, final
faint,*, ted, ting, tly, tness, ter, LOOSE OXYGEN TO BRAIN CAUSING COLLAPSE, NOT CLEAR
fair,*, red, ring, rly, rness, PLACE OF ACTIVITY, IN BETWEEN GOOD AND BAD (or see fare / fire) "prefixes: un"
fairenhite, fahrenheit
fairwel, farewell
fairy, ries, TINY ENTITIES WITH WINGS SEEN ONLY TO A FEW (or see ferry)
fais, phase
fait, fight
faith,*, hful, hfully, hless, hlessly, hlessness, HAVING A BELIEF OR HOPE "prefixes: multi/ un"
faiv, five
faiz, phase
fajism, fascism
fak, fake
fakchinul, faction(al)
fakd, fact / fake(d)

fake,*, ed, king, er, PHONY OR ILLUSION
fakelty, faculty
fakilty, faculty
fakshen, faction
fakshunil, faction(al)
fakt, fact / fake(d)
faktionul, faction(al)
fakulty, faculty
fal, fail / fall / fowl / foul
falacy, fallacy
falanthropist, philanthropy(pist)
fald, fault / fail(ed)
falek, phalli(c)
falese, fallacy
falfill, fulfill
fali, phalli
falic, phalli(c)
falicity, felicity
falise, fallacy
fall,*, llen, lling, fell, A SEASON, COME DOWN (or see fail)
fallacy, cies, NOT TRUE, UNFOUNDED
fallow, wness, AGRICULTURE EXPRESSION, NOT ACTIVE (or see follow)
fallsefy, falsify
fallsify, falsify
falo, follow / fallow
faloer, follow(er)
falose, fallacy
falosify, philosophy
falou, follow / fallow
falow, follow / fallow
falowir, follow(er)
false, ely, eness, sies, sify, sity, sifier, shood, NOT TRUE
falsify, fies, fied, fying, fiable, fiability, fication, fier, PRETEND/ FEIGN TO BE TRUTHFUL
falt, fault / fail(ed)
falter,*, red, ring, ringly, rer, LOOSE FOOTING/ CONFIDENCE (or see fault) "prefixes: un"
faluse, fallacy
faly, folly
fam, fame
famas, famous
famaslee, famous(ly)

famblee,family
fame,*,ed,ming,mous,REKNOWN,RECOGNIZED,PUBLIC REPUTATION "prefixes: de/ in"
famelur,familiar
famen,famine
fames,famous
fameslee,famous(ly)
familiar,rly,rity,EXPERIENCE WITH,A KNOWING "prefixes: over/ un"
family,lies,lial,GROUP OF PEOPLE RELATED IN SOME WAY "prefixes: multi/ sub"
famine,*,ish,SEVERE LACK OF FOOD OVER TIME
famis,famous
famislee,famous(ly)
famlee,family
famous,sly,sness,WIDELY KNOWN "prefixes: in"
famus,famous
famuslee,famous(ly)
fan,*,nned,nning,nner,nny,MOTION TO CREATE BREEZE/LIFT, SPREAD OUT (or see feign)
fana,fauna
fanadek,phonetic / fanatic
fanatic,*,cal,cally,cism,EXTREME/ IRRATIONAL ENTHUSIASM,HIGHLY MOTIVATED IN BELIEF/ BEHAVIOR (or see phonetic)
fancy,cier,ciest,ciful,cifully,cifulness,DECORATIVE, PLAYFUL, LIGHT
fane,feign / fan(ny)
fanedik,phonetic / fanatic
fanesh,finish
fanetic,phonetic / fanatic
fang,*,ged,ging,TOOTH IN SNAKE/ CANINE/ SPIDER "prefixes: de"
fangeprint,fingerprint
fangernail,fingernail
fangur,finger
fanic,phonic
fanomanen,phenomenon
fanomena,phenomenon
fanomenul,phenomenal
fanominul,phenomenal
fansee,fancy
fant,faint

fantaja,fantasy(sia)
fantastic,cal,cally,cality,calness,ABSOLUTELY GREAT
fantastikul,fantastic(al)
fantasy,sies,sia,size,sizes,sized,sizing,sist,DREAMY IDEA OF A FUTURE EVENT
fantem,phantom
fantesy,fantasy
fantisy,fantasy
fantum,phantom
fantusy,fantasy
faond,found
faprecate,fabricate
faprek,fabric
faprekashin,fabricate(tion)
faprukashen,fabricate(tion)
fapulus,fabulous
far,rther,rthest,QUITE A DISTANCE AWAY (or see for/ fare/ fair/ fire)
farce,SATIRE,NON-FACTUAL, COMICAL
farder,farther
fare,*,ed,ring,COST FOR TRANSPORTATION, PRESENT CONDITION (or see fair/ fire/ fairy)
farenhite,fahrenheit
fares,ferry(ries) / fairy(ries)
farest,far(thest)
farewell,*,GOOD-BYE
farit,ferret
farm,*,med,ming,mable,mer,LAND WHERE ANIMALS/ CROPS ARE RAISED/ GROWN "prefixes: un"
farmaceutical,pharmaceutic(al)
farmasist,pharmacist
farmasutical,pharmaceutic(al)
farmir,farm(er)
farmisist,pharmacist
farmosutekul,pharmaceutic(al)
farmusutekul,pharmaceutic(al)
faro,pharoah
farotious,ferocious
fars,farce / fair(s)
farsighted,dness,ABLE TO SEE FARTHER AWAY BETTER THAN CLOSE UP
farsited,farsighted

farther,hest,rmost,EXCEEDS CURRENT PHYSICAL DIMENSION/ DEPTH (or see further)
farthist,farther(hist)
farthur,farther
faruel,farewell
farwell,farewell
fary,ferry / fairy
fas,phase / face / faze
fasa,fascia
fascanate,fascinate
fascia,ae,as,al,ROOFLINE ADDENDUM, BIOLOGY / ANATOMY TERM
fascinate,*,ed,edly,ting,tingly,tion,tor,CAPTIVATES INTEREST/ ATTENTION
fascism,st,stic,CENTRALIZED OPPRESSIVE CONTROL
fascist,*,tic,sm,PERSON WHO SUPPORTS OPPRESSIVE/ AUTHORITARIAN CONTROL
fasd,face(d) / fast / phase(d) / faze(d)
fasechan,physician
fasea,fascia
fasechis,facetious
fasechus,facetious
fasecian,physician
fased,face(d) / fast / phase(d)
fasek,physique / physic
fasel,fossil
faselisd,fossil(ized)
faselitashen,facilitate(tion)
faselitation,facilitate(tion)
faselity,facility
faselutate,facilitate
fasen,fasten / face(cing)
fasenate,fascinate
fasener,fastener
faseque,physique
faseshan,physician
faseshis,facetious
faseshus,facetious
fasesm,fascism
faset,facet / faucet
fasetious,facetious
fasfate,phosphate
fasha,fascia

fashel, facial
fashen, fashion
fashenuble, fashion(able)
fashest, fascist
fashil, facial
fashin, fashion
fashinuble, fashion(able)
fashion, *, ned, ning, nable, nably, nability, nableness, ner, CLOTHING STYLES WITHIN A CERTAIN TIMEFRAME "prefixes: un"
fashism, fascism
fashist, fascist
fashul, facial
fashun, fashion
fashunebul, fashion(able)
fasia, fascia
fasichon, physician
fasichus, facetious
fasician, physician
fasik, physic / physique
fasil, fossil
fasilatashen, facilitate(tion)
fasilatat, facilitate
fasilatation, facilitate(tion)
fasilety, facility
fasilitate, facilitate
fasility, facility
fasin, fasten / face(cing)
fasinate, fascinate
fasiner, fastener
fasing, face(cing) / phase(ing)
fasique, physique
fasishus, facetious
fasism, fascism
fasit, facet / faucet
fasition, physician
fasitious, facetious
fasner, fastener
fasnir, fastener
fasnor, fastener
fasnur, fastener
fast, *, ted, ting, ter, test, tness, tnesses, RATE OF SPEED, TO NOT EAT FOOD, REMAIN FIXED/ SECURE

fasten, *, ned, ning, ner, ADHERE, CLOSE, SECURE "prefixes: un"
fastener, *, , BUTTONS, ZIPPERS, SNAPS, CLOSURE
fasul, fossil
fasunate, fascinate
fat, *, tter, ttest, tten, ttening, tteningly, tty, tness, tso, LAYER OF FOOD STORE IN MOST LIVING THINGS (or see fad/ fade/ fate/ fought) "prefixes: non"
fatal, *, lly, lity, lities, list, lism, LIFE THREATENING
fate, *, ed, eful, efully, efulness, THE BELIEF THAT EVENTS ARE PRE-PLANNED
fateg, fatigue
fatek, fatigue
fath, faith
father, *, MALE PARENT, NAME FOR A PRIEST
fathom, *, med, ming, mless, mable, MEASUREMENT FOR THE OCEAN DEPTH, DEEP TO UNDERSTAND "prefixes: un"
fathur, feather / father
fatia, fascia
fatig, fatigue
fatigue, *, ed, uing, gable, EXHAUSTION, WEARY, MILITARY CLOTHING "prefixes: inde"
faucet, *, , PLUMBING DEVICE FOR WATER/ LIQUIDS
fauculize, focal(ize)
faukalize, focal(ize)
faul, foul / fowl / fall
faulsefy, falsify
faulsify, falsify
fault, *, ted, ting, tier, tiest, ty, tless, tlessly, tily, tiness, SOMETHING/ SOMEONE TO BLAME, A PROBLEM, TECTONIC EXPRESSION (or see falter)
faulter, falter
faun, *, HALF GOAT HALF HUMAN (or see fawn)
fauna, ANIMALS OF A REGION
faund, found
faundashen, foundation
faundation, foundation
faundry, foundry
faunic, phonic
faunt, found
fauntry, foundry
fausefy, falsify

fausel, fossil
fausfate, phosphate
fausify, falsify
fausit, faucet
fausphate, phosphate
fauster, foster
fausul, fossil
faut, fought
faux, FALSE/ IMITATION/ FAKE/ ARTIFICIAL
fauxpas, ALSO FAUX PAS, A BLUNDER
faveret, favorite
favor, *, red, ring, rable, rably, rableness, rite, rer, PREFERENCE FOR "prefixes: dis/ un"
favorite, *, tism, PREFERENCE FOR
fawcet, faucet
fawdur, fodder
fawel, foul / fowl
fawl, foul / fowl
fawlust, foul(est)
fawn, *, BABY DEER (or see faun)
fawnd, fond / found
fawndashen, foundation
fawnt, font / found
fawntry, foundry
fawsefy, falsify
fawsel, fossil
fawsify, falsify
fawsilized, fossil(ized)
fawsul, fossil
fawt, fought
fawul, foul / fowl
fax, xes, xed, xing, SEND A LETTER BY PHONE (or see fact(s))
fayer, fire
fayol, file
faze, *, ed, zing, SEND A LETTER BY PHONE (or see phase)
fazechen, physician
fazek, physique
fazeshan, physician
fazichen, physician
fe, fee
feable, feeble

fear,*,red,ring,rful,rfully,rfulness,rless,rlessly,-lessness, rsome,rsomely,rsomeness,AFRAID,POWERLESS
feasent,pheasant
feasible,eness,ly,bility,QUESTION/ STUDY ABILITY TO ACCOMPLISH/ ACHIEVE "prefixes: de/ inde/ un"
feast,*,ted,ting,GREAT AMOUNT OF FOOD
feasta,fiesta
feasubilety,feasible(bility)
feasuble,feasible
feat,*, PERFORM WITH UNUSUAL ABILITY (or see feet)
feather,*,red,ring,ry,BIRD CLOTHES,A DECORATIVE EFFECT
feature,*, ed,ring,eless, SPECIAL "prefixes: dis/ multi/ un"
feb,fib
febal,feeble
febiueri,February
february,A MONTH OF THE YEAR (ENGLISH)
febuare,february
febul,feeble
febwuare,february
fecechus,facetious
fecer,figure
feces,EXCREMENT, WASTE PRODUCT, BODILY DISCHARGE (or see face(s))
feceshan, physician
feceshis,facetious
fecetious,facetious
fech,fetch
fecher,feature
fechet,fidget
fecichan, physician
fecility,facility
feckle,fickle
fecsher,fixture
fecster,fixture
fed,PAST TENSE FOR THE WORD "FEED"
fedality,fidelity
fedar,fetter / feed(er) / feather
fedarashen,federation
fedaration,federation
fedarul,federal
fedder,fetter / feed(er)

fede,fifty
feder,fetter / feed(er) / feather
federal,*,Ily, list,lize,lizes,lized,lizing,lism,ation,ative, NATIONAL GOVERNMENT "prefixes: con"
federate,*, ed,ting,tion,tive, GROUPS JOINED UNDER ONE UNIT/ UMBRELLA
federation,*,ive, GROUP OF PEOPLE FORMING IN UNION, UNITED
federeishon,federation
fedir,fetter / feed(er) / feather
fedirate,federate
fediration,federation
fedish,fetish
fedle,fiddle
fedler,fiddle(r)
fedral,federal
fedrol,federal
fedul,fiddle
fedulize,fertile(lize)
fedur,fetter / feed(er) / feather
fedurashen,federation
fedurate,federate
fedy,fifty
fee,*, COST FOR/ TO DO SOMETHING
feeble,er, est, eness, ly, WEAK, LACKS STRENGTH "prefixes: en"
feebul,feeble
feecher,feature
feed,*, ding,der,fed, GIVE FOOD TO (or see feet) "prefixes: under"
feel,*, ling,lings,felt,ler, USE OF TOUCH/ EMOTIONS TO SENSE ENVIRONMENT "prefixes: un"
feeld,field
feer,fear
feest,feast
feesta,fiesta
feet,MORE THAN ONE FOOT (or see feat)
fefer,fever
feferish,fever(ish)
fefir,fever
fefiresh,fever(ish)
fefor,fever
feftee,fifty

fefteen,fifteen
feften,fifteen
fefth,fifth
feftinth,fifteen(th)
feftis,fifty(ties)
fefty,fifty
fefur,fever
fefurish,fever(ish)
feg,fig
fegen,fission / fusion
feger,figure
fegit,fidget
fegmint,figment
feianse,fiance'
feibol,fable
feibor,favor
feic,fake / face / phase
feidol,fatal
feign,*,ned,ning,TO PRETEND/ COPY
feild,field
feimos,famous
fein,feign
feirou,pharoah
feis,phase / face
feit,fate
feitol,fatal
feiver,favor
feiz,phase
fejin,fission / fusion
fejit,fidget
fejon,fission / fusion
fekle,fickle
fekment,figment
feks,fix
feksher,fixture
fekshun,fiction
fekst,fix(ed)
fekster,fixture
feksus,fix(es)
fekul,fickle
fekur,figure
fel,feel / fell / fill / full
felade,fillet

feladendron, philodendron
felanthrepy, philanthropy
felanthropist, philanthropy(pist)
felay, fillet
feld, felt / field / fill(ed) / fell(ed)
feldration, filtrate(ion)
feldur, filter / field(er)
fele, fillet / filly
felicity, ties, tous, tously, tousness, tate, tates, tated, tation, tator, HAPPINES WITH PERFECTION "prefixes: in"
feline, *, ely, eness, nity, OF CATS
fell, lled, lling, ller, PAST TENSE FOR THE WORD "FALL", CUT DOWN TREE (or see fill/ feel)
felm, film
felosofy, philosophy
felt, PAST TENSE FOR THE WORD "FEEL", CRUSHED WOOL/ COTTON (or see field)
felter, filter
felth, filth
felthe, filthy
feltration, filtrate(ion)
feludindron, philodendron
felurmonek, philharmonic
female, *, eness, THE FEMININE, LIFE GIVER
femanen, feminine
femanist, feminist
femelear, familiar
feminine, nity, ely, eness, nism, ist, ize, izes, ized, izing, ization, mme, THE COMPLIMENT OF MASCULINE "prefixes: de"
feminist, *, tic, A PERSON WHO SUPPORTS WOMEN'S EQUALITY WITH MEN
femunin, feminine
femunist, feminist
fen, fin
fence, *, ed, cing, eless, er, OUTSIDE BARRIER/ WALL, A SPORT
fench, finch
fender, *, PART OF A BICYCLE/ VEHICLE, A SCREEN, A GUITAR
fenedic, phonetic / fanatic
fenesh, finish
fenetick, phonetic / fanatic

fenger, finger
fengernail, fingernail
fengerprint, fingerprint
fengur, finger
fenish, finish
fenker, finger
fenkerprint, fingerprint
fenkur, finger
fennel, EDIBLE HERB
fenomanen, phenomenon
fenomena, phenomenon
fenominul, phenomenal
fense, fence
fensh, finch
fentur, fender
feonsa, fiance'
fepel, feeble
fepol, feeble
fepuary, february
fepul, feeble
fepuwary, february
fer, fear / for / fir / fur / far / fair / fare
ferbed, forbid
ferbedin, forbid(dden)
ferbid, forbid
ferdelize, fertile(lize)
ferdul, fertile
ferdulizashen, fertile(lization)
fere, ferry / fairy / furry
ferefur, forever
ferenhite, fahrenheit
feres, ferry(ries) / fairy(ries)
feret, ferret
ferever, forever
fergave, forgave
fergetful, forget(ful)
fergif, forgive
fergifness, forgive(ness)
fergit, forget
fergitful, forget(ful)
fergive, forgive
fergivnes, forgive(ness)
fergot, forgot

fergoten, forgot(tten)
feriner, foreign(er)
ferius, furious
ferkets, forget(s)
ferkiv, forgive
ferlough, furlough
ferlow, furlough
ferm, firm
fermaledy, formal(ity)
fermality, formal(ity)
fermashen, formation
fermation, formation
ferment, *, ted, ting, table, tability, tation, tative, MOVING TOWARDS FERMENTATION
fermentation, nal, ENZYMATIC/ CELLULAR REACTION
fermenteishon, fermentation
fern, *, A PLANT
fernachur, furniture
fernecher, furniture
fernes, furnace
fernis, furnace
fernish, furnish
ferniture, furniture
fernus, furnace
fernush, furnish
fero, pharoah / furrow
ferochusle, ferocious(ly)
ferocious, sly, sness, FIERCE, INTENSE
feroshusle, ferocious(ly)
ferotious, ferocious
feroushos, ferocious
ferow, furrow / pharoah
ferr, PREFIX INDICATING "IRON" MOST OFTEN MODIFIES THE WORD
ferret, *, MEMBER OF THE WEASEL FAMILY
ferri, PREFIX INDICATING "IRON" MOST OFTEN MODIFIES THE WORD
ferro, PREFIX INDICATING "IRON" MOST OFTEN MODIFIES THE WORD
ferroso, PREFIX INDICATING "IRON" MOST OFTEN MODIFIES THE WORD
ferry, rries, rried, rrying, BOAT THAT CROSSES WATER CARRYING THINGS (or see fairy/ furry)

fers, fierce / fear(s) / first
fersake, forsake
fersakin, forsake(n)
fersd, first
ferse, fierce
fersest, fierce(st)
fersly, fierce(ly)
fersnis, fierce(ness)
ferst, first
ferther, farther / further
ferthur, farther / further
fertile, lity, ely, eness, lize, ABLE/ READY TO PRODUCE, PREPARE FOR PRODUCTION "prefixes: in/ inter" PRODUCTION
fertilize, *, ed, er, zing, zation, USED TO ENHANCE PRODUCTION
fertulize, fertilize
feruel, farewell
ferut, ferret
ferwal, farewell
ferwel, farewell
fery, ferry / fairy / furry
ferys, ferry(ries) / fairy(ries)
ferzd, first
ferzt, first
fesabilety, feasible(bility)
fesable, feasible
fesasist, physicist
fescal, fiscal
fesdev, festive
feseble, feasible
fesechus, facetious
fesekl, physical
fesekly, physical(lly)
feseks, physics
fesent, pheasant
feseologe, physiology
feseshan, physician
feseshus, facetious
fesetion, physician
fesetious, facetious
fesh, fish
feshen, fission / fusion
fesible, feasible

fesical, physical
fesichus, facetious
fesics, physics
fesik, physique
fesikle, physical
fesiatashen, facilitate(tion)
fesilaty, facility
fesint, pheasant
fesiologe, physiology
fesiology, physiology
fesishen, physician
fesishus, facetious
fesition, physician
fesitious, facetious
feskal, fiscal
fesode, facade
fest, fist
festaful, festive(val)
festive, ely, eness, val, vity, vities, A CELEBRATION
festofil, festive(val)
fesubility, feasible(bility)
fesuble, feasible
fesunt, pheasant
fesusist, physics(cist)
fet, feet / feat / feed / fed
fetarashen, federation
fetaration, federation
fetch, hes, hed, hing, TO GET AND BRING BACK
feteg, fatigue
feter, fetter / feed(er)
feth, fifth
fethar, feather
fethur, feather
fetir, fetter / feed(er)
fetirashen, federation
fetish, hes, hism, hist, OBSESSION FOR SOMETHING
fetler, fiddle(r)
fetter,*, red, ring, TO SHACKLE/ RESTRAIN "prefixes: un"
feturation, federation
feture, feature
feu, few
feucher, future

feud, *, ding, dal, dalism, dality, dalize, datory, A LONGSTANDING QUARREL/ FIGHT
feugen, fusion / fission
feul, fuel
feuld, field
feum, fume
feumegat, fumigate
feumigate, fumigate
feumugation, fumigate(tion)
feuree, fury / furry
feurius, furious
feus, fuse
feushen, fusion / fission
feut, feud
fever, *, red, ring, rish, BODY TEMPERATURE TOO HIGH
fevir, fever
fevirish, fever(ish)
fevur, fever
fevurish, fever(ish)
few, MORE THAN TWO
fewchur, future
fewd, feud
fewgen, fusion / fission
fewgitive, fugitive
fewmigashen, fumigate(tion)
fewmigate, fumigate
fewmigation, fumigate(tion)
fewnarul, funeral
fewreus, furious
fews, fuse
fewton, futon
fewul, fuel
fex, fix
fext, fix(ed)
feyuree, fury
fezability, feasible(bility)
fezable, feasible
fezacul, physical
fezakle, physical
fezakul, physical
fezalogical, physiology(gical)
fezasest, physics(cist)
fezek, physique

fiction, nal, nalize, nalizes, nalized, nalizing, nalization, tious, tiously, tiousness, ive, ively, STORIES/ BOOKS ABOUT MADE UP CHARACTERS "prefixes: non"
fid, *, A BLUNT TOOL MADE OF WOOD OR METAL (or see feed/fit)
fidde, fifty
fiddle, *, er, ling, AN INSTRUMENT
fiddy, fifty
fide, fifty
fidelity, FAITHFUL "prefixes: in"
fider, fight(er) / fit(tter)
fidget, *, ted, ting, tingly, ty, tiness, AN INSTRUMENT
fidir, fight(er) / fit(tter)
fidle, fiddle
fidlur, fiddle(r)
fidol, fiddle
fidor, fight(er) / fit(tter)
fidul, fiddle
fidur, fight(er) / fit(tter)
fidy, fifty
field, *, der, ding, LAND WITH FEW IF NO TREES "prefixes: in/ sub/ up"
fierce, er, est, ely, eness, DANGEROUS, THREATENING
fiesta, *, CELEBRATION
fif, fifth
fife, five
fifth, filth
fift, fifth
fifteen, nth, NUMBER
fiftees, fifty(ties)
fifteith, fifty(tieth)
fiften, fifteen
fiftenth, fifteen(th)
fiftes, fifty(ties)
fifth, *, ONE-FIFTH OF FIVE PARTS
fiftin, fifteen
fifty, ties, tieth, A NUMBER
fig, *, A FRUIT
figen, fission
figer, figure
figerene, figurine
figet, fidget

fight, *, ter, ting, fought, STRUGGLE, BATTLE BETWEEN "prefixes: in"
figit, fidget
figiur, figure
figiurin, figurine
figment, *, IMAGINARY
figure, *, ed, ring, ral, rant, ration, rative, ratively, rativeness, rine, SHAPE/ FORM OF SOMETHING, NUMBERS "prefixes: con/ dis/ pre"
figurine, *, SHAPE/ FORM OF SOMETHING
fijen, fission / fusion
fijet, fidget
fijon, fission / fusion
fikchen, fiction
fiker, figure
fikle, fickle
fikment, figment
fiks, fix / fig(s)
fikshin, fiction
fikshur, fixture
fikster, fixture
fiksus, fix(es)
fikt, fix(ed)
fikul, fickle
fikur, figure
fil, fill / fell / file / feel
fila, fillet
filadendron, philodendron
filanthrepy, philanthropy
filanthropist, philanthropy(pist)
filarmonek, philharmonic
filasofical, philosophy(hical)
fild, file(d) / field / fill(ed)
fildration, filtrate(ion)
fildur, filter
file, *, ed, ling, er, TO ORGANIZE, TOOL TO GRIND, FORM A LINE (or see fill/ fillet/ filly) "prefixes: inter/ pre"
filermonek, philharmonic
filet, fillet
filey, fillet
filhermonic, philharmonic
filings, file(lings) / feel(ings)
filjarmonic, philharmonic

fezekle, physical
fezeks, physics
fezent, pheasant
fezeology, physiology
fezeshan, physician
fezik, physique
fezikol, physical
feziks, physics
fezint, pheasant
fezubelity, feasible(bility)
fezuble, feasible
fezucul, physical
fezuks, physics
fezukul, physical
fezulogically, physiology(gically)
fezunt, pheasant
fezusist, physics(cist)
fi, fee
fiance', HUMAN TO BE MARRIED
fiar, fire
fib, *, bber, bbing, TO TELL A LIE
fiber, *, brous, PLANT MATERIAL (or see fib(bber) / fever) "prefixes: multi"
fibre, fiber
fibrous, sly, sness, TEXTURE IS THREAD-LIKE "prefixes: multi"
fibur, fiber
ficeshan, physician
fichar, feature
fichen, fish(ing) / fusion / fission
ficher, feature
fichet, fidget
fichur, feature
ficichen, physician
fiction, physician
fickle, er, est, eness, WILL LIKELY CHANGE PERSPECTIVE/ PREFERENCE
ficshan, fiction
ficshen, fiction
ficsher, fixture
ficshon, fiction
ficster, fixture

fill, *, lled, lling, ller, MAKE OPPOSITE OF EMPTY (or see file/fell)
fillet, *, ted, ting, ALSO FILET, BONES REMOVED FROM FISH/ ANIMALS
filly, llies, YOUNG FEMALE HORSE
film, *, med, ming, mation, my, mily, miness, mer, A COATING, A MOVING PICTURE "prefixes: bio"
filodendron, philodendron
filosofy, philosophy
filosophy, philosophy
filt, file(d) / field / fill(ed)
filter, *, red, ring, rless, rable, trable, trate, rer, USED TO SEPARATE / SORT "prefixes: bio"
filth, hy, DIRTIEST OF THE DIRTY, NASTY
filthy, hier, hiest, DIRTIEST OF THE DIRTY, NASTY
filtrate, *, ed, ting, tation, TO SEPARATE / STRAIN
filudendron, philodendron
filurmonic, philharmonic
fily, filly
fimanist, feminist
fimel, female
fimilear, familiar
fin, *, nned, nning, EXTRUSION FOR WEAVING THROUGH AIR/ WATER (or see fine)
final, *, lly, le, list, lize, lizes, lized, lizing, lization, lizer, THE END, THE LAST "prefixes: semi"
finance, *, ed, cing, cial, cials, cially, ceable, cier, ABOUT MONEY
finants, finance
finch, hes, A BIRD
find, *, der, ding, found, REVEAL THE UNSEEN/ UNKNOWN
findur, fender / find(er)
fine, *, er, est, ed, ning, ely, eness, THIN, VERY NICE, MONETARY PUNISHMENT (or see fin)
finedik, phonetic / fanatic
finel, final / fennel
finely, fine(ly) / final(lly)
fines, finesse / fine(s) / fine(st)
finesh, finish
finesse, *, HANDLE WITH SKILL/ CONTROL/ DELICATELY (or see fine(st))
finetic, phonetic / fanatic

finger, *, red, ring, ON THE HAND, USE THE HAND, EXTRUSION
fingernail, *, ON THE FINGER
fingerprint, *, ted, ting, ON THE FINGER
finight, finite
finish, es, hed, hing, her, TO COMPLETE "prefixes: semi/ un"
finite, ely, eness, LIMITED
finker, finger
finkerprint, fingerprint
finle, final / fennel
finol, final / fennel
finomanen, phenomenon
finomena, phenomenon
finominul, phenomenal
finse, fence
finsh, finch
fintur, fender
finul, final / fennel
finuly, final(lly)
fionsa, fiance'
fiper, fiber
fipur, fiber
fir, *, AN EVERGREEN TREE (or see fire/ fur/ for/ fear)
firbed, forbid
firbedin, forbid(dden)
firbiten, forbid(dden)
firdul, fertile
firdulize, fertilize
fire, *, ed, ring, er, CHEMICAL REACTION THAT BURNS, TAKE JOB AWAY, EMOTIONAL (or see far/ furry) "prefixes: mis/ retro"
firefur, forever
firevur, forever
firgave, forgave
firgefnis, forgive(ness)
firget, forget
firgetful, forget(ful)
firgitful, forget(ful)
firgive, forgive
firgot, forgot
firgoten, forgot(tten)
firketing, forget(tting)

firkets, forget(s)
firkiteng, forget(tting)
firkiv, forgive
firlow, furlough
firm, *, med, ming, mly, mness, mer, mest, BETWEEN SOFT/ HARD, CAPITALIST GROUP
firmaledy, formal(ity)
firmality, formal(ity)
firmashen, formation
firmation, formation
firment, ferment
firn, fern
firnus, furnace
firochusle, ferocious(ly)
firoshis, ferocious
firoshusle, ferocious(ly)
firow, furrow
firs, fir(s) / fire(s) / first / fierce
firsaken, forsake(n)
first, *, tly, BEFORE ALL
firtalize, fertilize
firtul, fertile
firy, furry
firzd, first
fis, fizz
fisasist, physicist
fiscal, lly, REFERRING TO MONEY
fisealugist, physiology(gist)
fisecal, physical
fisek, physic / physique
fiseks, physics
fiselity, facility
fiseolagekul, physiology(gical)
fiseolochi, physiology
fiseologist, physiology(gist)
fiseology, physiology
fiseshan, physician
fiseshen, physician
fisesist, physicist
fish, hed, hing, hy, her, hery, heries, VERTEBRATE IN WATER, CATCH FISH IN WATER
fishun, fission / fish(ing) / fusion
fisi, physi

fisic, physic / physique
fisical, physical
fisician, physician
fisics, physics
fisicul, physical
fisik, physique
fisiolochi, physiology
fisiologest, physiology(gist)
fisiololli, physiology
fision, fission / fusion
fisique, physique
fisisest, physicist
fisishan, physician
fisishen, physician
fisition, physician
fiskul, fiscal
fisode, facade
fisokul, physical
fisiologically, physiology(gically)
fisots, facade(s)
fission, nable, USE HEAT TO SPLIT AN ATOMS NUCLEUS (or see fusion)
fist,*, ted, ting, CLOSED HAND, AN EXPRESSION (or see feast)
fit,*, tted, tting, ttingly, ttingness, tter, ttest, tful, tfully, tfulness, tness, SOMETHING THAT WEARS WELL, EMOTIONAL OUTBURST (or see fight/ feat/ feet) "prefixes: mis/ retro/ un"
fite, fight / fifty
fiteg, fatigue
fiter, fight(er) / fit(tter)
fith, fifth
fitlur, fiddle(r)
fitur, fight(er) / fit(tter) / feature
fity, fifty
fiu, few
fiucher, future
fiuchitiv, fugitive
fiuchor, future
fiud, feud
fiul, fuel
fiullitiv, fugitive
fium, fume

fiumigeit, fumigate
fiuneral, funeral
fius, fuse
five,*, er, AN ENGLISH NUMBER
fiver, fever
fix, xes, xed, xer, xing, xate, xates, xated, xating, xation, xative, xatives, xable, INTENSE FOCUS, TO REPAIR "prefixes: un"
fixture,*, PERMANENTLY FASTENED
fizalogical, physiology(gical)
fizasist, physicist
fizek, physique
fizeolagekul, physiology(gical)
fizeologist, physiology(gist)
fizeology, physiology(gical)
fizeology, physiology
fizeshan, physician
fizesist, physicist
fizicol, physical
fizik, physique
fiziks, physics
fiziologest, physiology(gist)
fiziological, physiology(gical)
fizisest, physics(cist)
fizocol, physical
fizological, physiology(gical)
fizukle, physical
fizulogically, physiology(gically)
fizz, zes, zed, zing, zy, A CHEMICAL ACTION
flabides, phlebitis
flabites, phlebitis
flabodumy, phlebotomy
flabotimest, phlebotomy(mist)
flack, flake
flader, flatter / fillet
fladery, flatter
flafur, flavor
flag,*, gged, gging, gger, MATERIAL WITH A SYMBOL, TO WAVE SOMEONE OVER, TAG SOMEONE "prefixes: re"
flai, fly
flaier, flier

flail,*, led, ling, THRASH ABOUT, A TOOL FOR THRASHING GRAIN
flain, flat(tten)
flair,*, APTITUDE/ KNACK FOR, DEMEANOR(or see flare)
flait, flight
flake,*, ed, king, er, ky, kier, kiest, kily, kiness, THIN LAYER, NOT RELIABLE
flal, flail
flamable, flammable
flame,*, ed, ming, mer, TIP OF FIRE, SUDDEN ERUPTION
flamingo,*, A BIRD, DANCE
flammable,*, bility, CAN CATCH ON FIRE "prefixes: in"
flanel, flannel
flank,*, ked, king, ker, THE REAR, SIDES
flannel,*, COTTON MATERIAL
flap,*, pped, pping, pper, ppy, WAVE ABOUT, REMOVABLE COVER
flare,*, ed, ring, SHOOTING LIGHT, TO SPREAD OUT (or see flair)
flash, hes, hed, hing, her, LIGHTS FOR A BRIEF MOMENT, TATTOO LINGO
flat,*, tten, tter, tters, ttest, ttens, ttened, ttening, ttener, THIN, HORIZONTAL, OFF KEY
flatter,*, ry, PRAISE THAT'S NOT SINCERE/ SERIOUS "prefixes: un"
flatur, flat(tter) / flatter
flau, flaw / flow
flauder, flounder
flaur, flower / flour / floor
flaus, floss / flaw(s)
flavor,*, red, ring, rful, rless, PERCEIVED BY TASTEBUDS ON THE TONGUE
flaw,*, wed, wless, wlessly, wlessness, NOT RIGHT (or see flow)
flawer, flour / flower
flawnder, flounder
flayer, flier
fle, flea / flee
flea,*, A TINY BUG (or see flee)
flebaidis, phlebitis
flebant, flippant
flebidis, phlebitis
flebitis, phlebitis

flebodumy, phlebotomy
fleck,*,ked,king,BITS/ PIECES/ FLAKES OF SOMETHING (or see flex)
flecks,fleck(s) / flex
flecs,flex / fleck(s)
fled,PAST TENSE FOR THE WORD "FLEE" (or see fleet/ flee(d))
flee,*,eed,eeing,led,eer,RUN AWAY (or see flea)
fleece,es,ed,cing,cy,er,SHEEP COAT,COAT MATERIAL
fleet,*,ted,ter,ting,tingly,ter,test,tingness,tly,tness, GROUP OF BOATS,MOVE SWIFTLY,QUICK-Y
flegm, phlegm
fleim, flame
fleimabol, flammable
fleivor, flavor
fleks, flex / fleck(s)
flem, phlegm
flemingo, flamingo
flemsy, flimsy
flench, flinch
fleng, fling
flent, flint
fleol, flail
flep, flip
flepant, flippant
fleper, flipper
fler, flare / flair
flert, flirt
flery, flurry
flese, fleece / flea(s)
flesh,hy,hier,hiest,hiness,hly,hlier,hliest,hliress,SOFT/ FIRM PARTS OF FRUIT/ ANIMALS
flete, fleet
flew,PAST TENSE FOR THE WORD "FLY" (or see flu/ flue) "prefixes: over"
flewent, fluent
flewid, fluid
flex,xes,xed,xing,xible,xibly,xibility,xibleness,TO BEND, TEMPORARILY BEND (or see fleck(s)) "prefixes: re/ retro"
fli, fly / flea / flee
fliar, flier / fly(er)
flibent, flippant

flibidis, phlebitis
flibitis, phlebitis
flibodumy, phlebotomy
flibotimest, phlebotomy(mist)
flick,*,ker,king,kered,kering,keringly,SNAP, CANDLE FLAME ACTION
flid, flew / flight
flier,*,A PIECE OF PAPER WITH INFORMATION TO BE CIRCULATED (or see fly(er)
flight,*,ty,tless,TO TRAVEL THROUGH THE AIR "prefixes: over"
flik, flick
flim, phlegm
flimengo, flamingo
flimsy,sier,siest,siness,LIGHTWEIGHT, DELICATE
flinch,hes,hed,hing,hingly,her,TO JERK "prefixes: un"
fling,*,ging,lung,ger,THROW/ CAST AWAY,A CAREFREE TIME
flint,*,ty,tiness,USED TO START FIRE
flip,*,pped,pping,pper,ALTERNATING SIDES WHILE IN THE AIR
fliper, flipper
flippant,tly, tness,NOT TREAT SERIOUSLY
flipper,*,MOVEABLE EXTRUSION ON ANIMALS FOR MOVEMENT, MANMADE FOOT PADDLES
flirt,*,ted,ting,tation,tatios,tatiousness,ty, tier, tiest, tily, tiness, TEASING/ TOYING WITH
flis, fleece
flit,*,tted,tting,tter,tters,ttered,ttering,DART IN/ OUT (or see flight/ fleet)
fliur, flier / fly(er)
flo, flow
float,*,ted,ting,ter,table,tability,STAYS ON TOP OF LIQUID/ AIR, BUOYANT
flock,*,ked,king,GROUP TOGETHER
flocshueit, fluctuate
floctiueit, fluctuate
flod, flood / float
floder, flutter / float(er)
floent, fluent
flof, fluff
flok, flock
flone, flown

flong, flung
flood,*,ded,ding,dable,der,TOO MUCH WATER
flooint, fluent
flook, fluke
floor,*,red,ring,rage,A SURFACE TO WALK ON "prefixes: sub/ under"
flooride, fluoride
floot, flute
flop,*,pped,pping,ppy,ppier,ppiest,ppily,ppiness,FALL FLAT DOWN, LOOSE
flor, floor / flour / flower
floral,*,lly, FLOWERS
florescent,nce, FLOWERING (or see fluorescent) "prefixes: in"
floresh, flourish
florid, fluoride
florish, flourish
florist,*, WORKS WITH FLOWERS
flosh, flush
floss,sses,ssed,ssing,sser,WAY TO CLEAN BETWEEN TEETH
floster, fluster
flot, float / flood
floter, flutter / float(er)
flounder,*,red,ring,FISH,STRUGGLE FOR PROPER STANCE
flour,red,ring,ry,rier,riest,GRINDING GRAIN TO POWDER (or see flower)
flourescent, fluorescent / florescent
flouride, fluoride
flourish,hes, hed, hing, GROW HEALTHY AND STRONG
flout, float
flow,*,wed,wing,wingly,STEADILY MOVING ALONG, MOVEMENT "prefixes: in/ over/ under"
flower,*,red,ring,ry,rer,orescent,orescence,PLANT, PART OF PLANT WHICH PREPARES THE SEED (or see flour) "prefixes: de"
flown,PAST TENSE FOR THE WORD "FLY"
flownder, flounder
flu,A VIRUS (or see flew/ flue)
flubotemist, phlebotomy(mist)
flubotemy, phlebotomy
fluc, fluke

Word	Forms / Definition
flucks, flux	
flucshuate, fluctuate	
fluctuate, *, ed, ting, tion, ant, MOVE BACK AND FORTH IN DEGREES	
flud, flood	
fludder, flutter	
fluder, flutter	
flue, *, CHIMNEY PIPE (or see flew/ flu)	
flued, fluid	
fluent, tly, ncy, CONSISTENTLY CORRECT	
fluff, *, fed, fing, fy, ffier, ffiest, ffily, ffiness, LIGHTEN UP BY SHAKING	
fluid, *, dal, dally, dity, dly, dness, dic, dize, dizes, dized, dizing, dization, dizer, LIQUID STATE "prefixes: semi"	
fluke, *, ky, kily, kiness, UNUSUAL OCCURRENCE, PART OF A FISH, PART OF ANCHOR	
fluks, flux	
flumengo, flamingo	
flung, PAST TENSE FOR THE WORD "FLING" (or see flunk)	
flunk, *, ked, king, ker, TO FAIL	
flunt, fluent	
fluo, PREFIX INDICATING "FLUORINE" MOST OFTEN MODIFIES THE WORD	
fluor, PREFIX INDICATING "FLUORINE" MOST OFTEN MODIFIES THE WORD	
fluorescent, nce, ILLUMINATING LIGHT (or see florescent)	
fluoride, date, dates, dated, dating, dation, GAS, CHEMICAL ADDED TO WATER CONSIDERED POISONOUS	
fluoro, PREFIX INDICATING "FLUORINE" MOST OFTEN MODIFIES THE WORD	
flur, flour	
fluraid, fluoride	
fluresent, florescent / fluorescent	
fluresh, flourish	
flurid, flouride	
flurish, flourish	
flurry, rries, rried, rrying, SPORADIC, FAST SNOW/ BEHAVIOR	
flurt, flirt	
flury, flurry	
flush, hes, hed, hing, hable, her, RID OF SOMETHING	
fluster, *, ed, ting, red, ring, CONFUSED, NERVOUS	
flute, *, ed, ting, tist, AN INSTRUMENT/ DESIGN	
fluter, flutter	
flutter, *, red, ring, BACK AND FORTH OR UP AND DOWN VIGOROUSLY	
flux, xes, xed, xing, xion, OF/ PROMOTES FLUIDITY/ FLOW "prefixes: re"	
fly, lies, lew, ying, yer, AIRBORNE, INSECT (or see flier) "prefixes: over"	
fo, foe / faux / for / four	
foal, *, led, ling, YOUNG ANIMAL	
foalt, foal(ed)	
foam, *, med, ming, my, ENCASED POCKETS OF AIR	
fobea, phobia	
fobia, phobia	
focal, lly, lize, lizes, lized, lizing, lization, KEEP ON FOCUS WITH EYES/ MENTALLY/ EMOTIONALLY "prefixes: bi"	
focechen, physician	
foceshan, physician	
foceshis, facetious	
focetion, physician	
foch, fudge	
focichen, physician	
focis, focus	
focishen, physician	
focition, physician	
focks, fox	
focle, focal	
foculize, focal(ize) / focal	
focus, ses, sed, sing, sable, ser, CONCENTRATE ONLY ON ONE THING OR THOUGHT, HAVE NO THOUGHTS "prefixes: re/ un"	
fod, food	
fodagraf, photo(graph)	
fodar, fodder	
fodasenthesis, photosynthesis	
fodasinthesis, photosynthesis	
fodch, fudge	
fodder, *, FOOD FOR CATTLE	
fodegraf, photo(graph)	
foder, fodder	
fodigraf, photo(graph)	
fodir, fodder	
fodisinthasis, photosynthesis	
fodo, photo	
fodograf, photo(graph)	
fodon, photon / futon	
fodosinethsis, photosynthesis	
fodugraf, photo(graph)	
fodur, fodder	
fodusinthesis, photosynthesis	
foe, *, AN ADVERSARY (or see faux)	
foel, foil / foal	
foeul, foil	
fog, *, gged, gger, gging, ggy, A MISTY CLOUD "prefixes: de"	
foil, *, led, ling, ler, THIN SHEETS OF METAL, TRICKED	
fok, folk / fog	
fokes, focus	
fokis, focus	
fokle, focal	
foklize, focal(ize)	
foks, folk(s) / fox	
fokul, focal	
fokulize, focal(ize)	
fokus, focus	
fol, foal / fool / full / fall	
folanthrapy, philanthropy	
fold, *, ded, der, ding, dable, BEND/ CREASE OVER (or see foal(ed)/ fool(ed)/ fault) "prefixes: en/ inter/ over/ multi/ un"	
folder, *, FOLDED SHEET TO HOLD PAPERS	
foldur, folder	
foleashun, foliate(tion)	
foleate, foliate	
folecity, felicity	
foleg, foliage	
folesee, fallacy	
folesh, fool(ish)	
folfill, fulfill	
foliage, ed, aceous, ate, ation, ABOUT PLANTS	
foliate, *, ed, ting, tion, THIN SHEETS, CONCERNS LEAVES "prefixes: bi/ de/ multi/ uni"	
folicity, felicity	
folig, foliage	
folish, fool(ish)

folk,* ,ksy,STYLE OF MUSIC,THE PARENTS/ PEOPLE
folksee,folk(sy)
follow,* ,wed,wing,wer,ONE BEHIND ANOTHER (or see fallow)
folly,llies,FOOLISH
folo,follow / fallow
foloer,follow(er)
folowir,follow(er)
fols,false / foal(s) / fall(s)
folsefy,falsify
folsify,falsify
folt,foal(ed) / fold
folter,folder
foltur,folder
foly,folly
folze,false
fombal,fumble
fombl,fumble
fombul,fumble
fome,foam / foam
fomileur,familiar
fomy,foam
fon,fun / phone / fawn / faun
fona,fauna
fonadik,phonetic / fanatic
fonagraf,phonograph
fonatek,phonetic / fanatic
foncshin,function
fond,der,dest,dly,ness,ATTRACTED TO (or see font/ phone(dl))
fondamental,fundamental
fondle,* ,ed,ling,AFFECTIONATE TOUCHING WITH HANDS
fondumentle,fundamental
fone,phone / funny / phony
fonec,phonic
fonedik,phonetic / fanatic
fonegraf,phonograph
fonek,phonic
fonel,funnel
fonemic,phoneme(mic)
fonetic,phonetic / fanatic
fongas,fungus

fongus,fungus
foni,funny / phony
fonic,phonic
fonigraf,phonograph
fonik,phonic
fonil,funnel
fonimic,phoneme(mic)
fonkshen,function
font,* ,tal,SIZE/ STYLE OF LETTERS, BASIN (or see fond)
fontementul,fundamental
fonugraf,phonograph
fonul,funnel
food,* ,WHAT IS CHEWED/ SWALLOWED FOR SUSTENANCE
fool,* ,led,ling,lingly,lish,lishly,lishness,lery,DOESN'T COMPREHEND THE SITUATION
foome,fume
foonrul,funeral
foot,ting,tings,tage,tless,tling,ter,ATTACHED TO LEG, FIRM SPOT, U.S. MEASUREMENT OF LENGTH "prefixes: under"
footon,futon
fophade,phosphate
for,PREFIX INDICATING "AWAY/ OFF/ EXTREMELY" MOST OFTEN MODIFIES THE WORD,ALSO MEANS, GIVE TOWARDS, BELONGS TO (or see fore/ four/ far)
forach,forage
forage,* ,ed,ging,er,TO SEARCH FOR
foram,forum
foran,foreign
foraner,foreign(er)
forasdry,forest(ry)
forast,forest
forastir,forest(er)
forbedin,forbid(dden)
forbet,forbid
forbetin,forbid(dden)
forbid,* ,dden,dding,ddingly,ddingness,ddance,dder, bade,NOT ALLOWED
forbiten,forbid(dden)
force,* ,ed,cing,celess,eful,efully,efulness,cible,cibly, cibility,cibleness,er,A PUSH OR PULL WITH INTENSE ENERGY "prefixes: en/ un"

forceps,MEDICAL INSTRUMENT
forchanet,fortunate
forchen,fortune
forchun,fortune
forchunet,fortunate
forchunitly,fortunate(ly)
fordafid,fortify(fied)
forde,forty
fordeath,fortieth
fordeen,fourteen
fordefication,fortification
fordefid,fortify(fied)
fordefy,fortify
fordeith,forty(tieth)
forder,farther
fordi,forty
fordifid,fortify(fied)
fordify,fortify
fordle,fertile
fordufecashen,fortification
fordufid,fortify(fied)
fordufy,fortify
fordulizashen,fertilize(zation)
fordulize,fertilize
fordyeth,fortieth
fore,PREFIX INDICATING "BEFORE/ IN FRONT" MOST OFTEN MODIFIES THE WORD, FRONT OF A VESSEL (or see four/ for)
foreg,forage
forego,es,one,oing,oer,PRECEDE, GO BEFORE
foregone,PAST TENSE FOR THE WORD "FOREGO"
foreign,ner,ners,NOT FAMILIAR, FROM ANOTHER PLACE
forein,foreign
forem,forum
foren,foreign
forenir,foreign(er)
foresaw,PAST TENSE FOR THE WORD WORD 'FORESEE'
foresdashen,forest(ation)
foresdry,forest(ry)
foresee,* ,saw,een,eeing,eeable,eeably,eer,TO KNOW BEFORE IT HAPPENS/ YOU SEE IT
foresent,florescent / fluorescent

foreside, LAND ALONG THE OCEAN, THE FRONT OR UPPER PART OF SOMETHING (or see foresight)
foresight, *, ted, tedly, tedness, KNOW/ THINK BEFOREHAND (or see farsighted)
foresite, foresight
forest, *, ted, tal, tial, tation, ter, try, LAND MADE UP OF WILD ANIMALS/ PLANTS, LARGE/ HEAVILY WOODED/ TREED AREA "prefixes: dis/ re"
forestashen, forest(ation)
foresteul, forest(ial)
forestur, forest(er)
foretuety, fortuity
forever, ON AND ON WITHOUT END
foreword, *, INTRODUCTORY WRITING (or see forward)
forfat, forfeit
forfeit, *, ted, ting, ture, FORCED TO LET GO OF
forfut, forfeit
forg, fork / forge / forage
forgave, PAST TENSE FOR THE WORD "FORGIVE"
forge, *, ed, ging, eable, eability, er, ery, eries, FAKE COPY, SOFTEN METAL BY FIRE (or see forage)
forgeiv, forgave
forget, *, tting, got, gotten, tter, tful, tfully, tfulness, ttable, CHOOSE TO OR CANNOT REMEMBER "prefixes: un"
forgifnes, forgive(ness)
forgit, forget
forgitful, forget(ful)
forgive, *, en, ving, eness, gave, vable, vably, er, GIVEN MERCY, PARDON, EXCUSED "prefixes: un"
forgo, forego / foregone
forgon, foregone
forgot, tten, PAST TENSE FOR THE WORD "FORGET"
forgoten, forgot(tten)
forige, forage / forge
forim, forum
foreign, foreign
foriner, foreign(er)
forisdashen, forest(ation)
forisdry, forest(ry)
forist, forest
foristation, forest(ation)
foristir, forest(er)
foristry, forest(ry)

forjie, forge / forage
fork, *, ked, king, TOOL FOR EATING/ WORKING, SPLIT IN THE PATH
forketing, forget(tting)
forkit, forget
forkiv, forgive
forlow, furlough
form, *, med, ming, mation, mational, mative, matively, mable, mless, mer, SHAPED BY FORCE OR INTENT "prefixes: con/ multi/ pre/ re/ -re/ un"
formad, format
formaded, format(tted)
formader, format(tter)
formal, *, lly, lity, lities, lize, lization, lizer, PROPER, DONE WITH CERTAIN RULES, DRESS-UP OCCASION "prefixes: in/ semi"
formalesation, formal(ization)
formalidy, formal(ity)
formalise, formal(ize)
formaluzashen, formal(ization)
formaly, formal(lly) / former(ly)
formashen, formation
format, *, tted, tting, tter, tion, tive, tively, SPECIFIC PROTOCOL/ DESIGN/ SHAPE/ STRUCTURE MOST OFTEN USED "prefixes: un"
formated, format(tted)
formatef, format(ive)
formater, format(tter)
formatif, format(ive)
formation, *, nal, MADE/ ENCOURAGED INTO A SHAPE "prefixes: re"
formativly, format(ively)
formd, form(ed)
formeishon, formation
formel, formal
formelize, formal(ize)
formely, formal(lly)
former, *, rly, PREVIOUSLY, USED TO BE
formetive, format(ive)
formewla, formula
formewlashen, formula(tion)
formil, formal
formily, formal(lly) / former(ly)

formir, former
formirly, former(ly) / formal(lly)
formitevly, format(ively)
formitive, format(ive)
formiula, formula
formle, formal
formolezashen, formal(ization)
formolize, formal(ize)
formotev, format(ive)
formotivly, format(ively)
formt, form(ed)
formul, formal
formula, *, ate, ates, ated, ating, ation, aic, aically, arize, arizes, arized, arizing, arizer, lism, SPECIFIC MIXTURE OF MOLECULES
formulashen, formula(tion)
formule, formal(lly)
formulisashen, formal(ization)
formulise, formal(ize)
formulu, formula
formuluzashen, formal(ization)
formuly, formal(lly)
formur, former
formurly, former(ly)
formutef, format(ive)
formutivly, format(ively)
forogt, forage(d)
foroshus, ferocious
fors, force / four(s) / farce
forsaid, foreside / foresight
forsaided, farsighted
forsait, foreside / foresight
forsaited, farsighted
forsake, *, en, king, sook, ABANDON, QUIT
forsakin, forsake(n)
forsau, foresaw
forsaw, foresaw
forseable, foresee(able)
forsee, foresee
forseik, forsake
forseps, forceps
forseuble, foresee(able)
forshen, fortune

forside, foreside / foresight
forsite, foresight / foreside
fort, * , tify, tress, A STRUCTURE OR AREA TO BE PROTECTED
fortafid, fortify(fied)
fortchunetly, fortunate(ly)
forte, forty
forteen, fourteen
forteenth, fourteenth
forteeth, forty(tieth)
forteficashen, fortification
fortefid, fortify(fied)
fortefy, fortify
fortens, fourteen(s)
forteuth, forty(tieth)
fortewnit, fortunate
forth, hright, MOVEMENT FORWARD (or see fourth)
fortieth, * , AN ENGLISH NUMBER
fortifai, fortify
fortification, * , PROTECTING AN AREA/ STRUCTURE, TO STRENGTHEN/ IMPROVE UPON
fortifid, fortify(fied)
fortifiqueishon, fortification
fortify, fies, fied, fying, fyingly, fiable, fier, ficat on, STRENGTHEN / ADD / IMPROVE UPON "prefixes: un"
fortifyed, fortify(fied)
fortinth, fourteenth
fortith, fortieth
fortoety, fortuity
fortufecation, fortification
fortufid, fortify(fied)
fortufy, fortify
fortuity, ties, tous, tously, tousness, SELF-CREATED OPPORTUNITY
fortunate, ely, eness, SELF-CREATED OPPORTUNITY
fortune, * , GREAT WEALTH "prefixes: mis"
fortunetly, fortunate(ly)
fortunit, fortunate
fortunitly, fortunate(ly)
forty, ties, tieth, tyish, AN ENGLISH NUMBER
fortyeth, forty(tieth)
foruge, forage
forujt, forage(d)

forum, * , GROUP OF PEOPLE IN DISCUSSION
forun, foreign
foruner, foreign(er)
forusdashen, forest(ation)
forusdry, forest(ry)
forust, forest
forustashen, forest(ation)
foruster, forest(er)
forustre, forest(ry)
forward, * , ded, ding, dly, dness, GO AHEAD, BE FRANK (or see foreword)
forwurd, forward / foreword
fos, foe(s) / faux / fuss
fosal, fossil
fosder, foster
fosdur, foster
fosechus, facetious
0fosefy, falsify
fosel, fossil
foselisd, fossil(ized)
foseshan, physician
foset, faucet
fosetion, physician
fosfade, phosphate
fosfate, phosphate0
fosfeit, phosphate
fosiches, facetious
fosify, falsify
fosil, fossil
fosilisd, fossil(ized)
fosishen, physician
fosition, physician
fosphate, phosphate
fossil, * , lize, lized, lizing, lizable, lization, ssorial, CARBON MATTER TURNED TO STONE "prefixes: sub"
foster, * , red, ring, rage, PLACEBO PARENT
fosul, fossil
fosulisd, fossil(ized)
fosulzd, fossil(ized)
fosut, faucet
fot, foot / food / fought
fotagraf, photo(graph)
fotar, fodder

fotasinthesis, photosynthesis
fotegraf, photo(graph)
foter, fodder
fother, father
fotigraf, photo(graph)
fotigue, fatigue
fotir, fodder
foto, photo
fotograf, photo(graph)
foton, photon / futon
fotosinthesis, photosynthesis
fotugraf, photo(graph)
fotur, fodder
fotusinthesis, photosynthesis
fou, foe
foubia, phobia
foucos, focus
foucus, focus
fought, PAST TENSE FOR THE WORD "FIGHT"
foul, * , led, ling, ler, lest, lly, lness, OFFENSIVE, OUTSIDE OF THE RULES (or see fowl)
fouli, folly
foum, foam
foun, phone
founagraf, phonograph
found, ded, der, ding, PAST TENSE FOR THE WORD "FIND", ONE WHO DISCOVERED/ LOCATED FIRST, INITIAL DATE OF DISCOVERY "prefixes: un"
foundashen, foundation
foundation, * , nal, nally, nalist, nalism, BASE/ BASIS FOR A BUILDING/ CORPORATION/ BUSINESS/ FRIENDSHIP
foundry, ries, WHERE METAL IS MELTED
founou, phono
founougraf, phonograph
fountain, * , STATUE OR STRUCTURE SHOOTING WATER
fountin, fountain
four, * , rth, rteen, AN ENGLISH NUMBER (or see fore/ for)
fourest, forest
fourever, forever
fourfit, forfeit
fourgave, forgave
fourget, forget
fourgive, forgive

fourgot,forgot
fourmadur,format(tter)
fourmalize,formal(ize)
fourmashin,formation
fourmer,former
fourmul,formal
fours,force / four(s)
foursau,foresaw
foursaw,foresaw
fourseable,foresee(able)
foursee,foresee
fourteen,*,nth,AN ENGLISH NUMBER
fourteenth,*,AN ENGLISH NUMBER, ONE OF 14
fourth,*,hly,AN ENGLISH NUMBER, ONE TO FOUR PARTS (or see forth)
fourtinth,fourteenth
fourtuety,fortuity
fourwurd,forward
fouton,photon
foutou,photo
foutousinthesis, photosynthesis
fow,foe / faux
fowel,foul / fowl
fowks,fox
fowl,*,ler,ling, WILD BIRD (or see foul/ foal)
fowlest,foul(est)
fowlust,foul(est)
fownd,found
fowndashun,foundation
fowndation,foundation
fowndre,foundry
fownt,found
fowntin,fountain
fowt,fought
fowul,foul / fowl
fox,xes,xed,xing,xy,xier,xiest,xiness,A FURRY ANIMAL
foyel,foil
foyl,foil
foz,fuzz / foe(s)
fozdur,foster
fozel,fossil
fozter,foster
fra,fray

fracshan,fraction
fracshenal,fraction(al)
fracsher,fracture
fracshun,fraction
fracshur,fracture
fraction,*,nal,nally,nalize,nalizes,nalized,nalizing, nalization,nary,nate,nates,nated,nating,nation, nator,nary,PART OF THE WHOLE (or see friction/ fracture)
fractioneal,fraction(al)
fracture,*,ed,ring,rable,A BREAK, BROKEN (or see fraction)
frad,afraid / fray(ed) / freight / fraud
fraded,freight(ed)
frader,freighter
fradewlent,fraud(ulent)
fradewlently,fraud(ulently)
frael,frail
fraeltee,frail(ty)
fragelidy,fragile(lity)
fraghted,freight(ed)
fragile,ely,lity,DELICATE
fragise,franchise
fragment,*,ted,ting,tal,tary,tarily,tize,tizes,tized,tizing, tation,PIECE OF THE WHOLE
fragmint,fragment
fragmintashen,fragment(ation)
fragmintul,fragment(al)
fragrance,*,cy,nt,A SMELL, AROMA
fragrant,*,tly,nce,nces,A SMELL, AROMA
fragrinse,fragrance
fragrint,fragrant
fragul,fragile
frai,fry
fraid,fried
fraidei,Friday
fraight,freight
fraighter,freighter
frail,ler,lest,lty,lties,VERY DELICATE
frailtee,frail(ty)
frais,fries
frait,freight
frailety,fragile(lity)

frajiludy,fragile(lity)
frajul,fragile
frakchen,fraction
frakment,fragment
frakmentashen,fragment(ation)
frakmentul,fragment(al)
frakmint,fragment
frakmintul,fragment(al)
frakshenul,fraction(al)
frakshin,fraction
frakshur,fracture
fraktionul,fraction(al)
frakul,freckle
frale,frail
fralest,frail(est)
fralic,frolic
fralill,fragile
fraluc,frolic
frame,*,ed,ming,mable,er,STRUCTURE TO ENCASE SOMETHING, CRIMINAL ACT "prefixes: sub/ under"
framur,frame(r)
franc,*,FRENCH MONEY (or see frank)
franchise,*,ee,ement,er,MEMBERSHIP OF SPORTS TEAMS/ BUSINESS "prefixes: disen/ en"
frandikly,frantic(ally)
frank,*,ker,kest,kly,kness,HONEST, OPEN EXPRESSION, HOT DOGS (or see franc)
frankist,frank(est)
frankle,frank(ly)
franshise,franchise
frantek,frantic
frantekly,frantic(ally)
frantic,cally,ANXIOUS, DISORDER, WILDLY RUNNING ABOUT
frantikly,frantic(ally)
frash,fresh
frate,freight / fray(ed)
frater,freighter
fraternal,*,lly,lism,BROTHERS, MALE FRIENDSHIP
fraternity,ties,MEN'S SOCIAL/ SOCIETY "prefixes: con"
fraternize,*,ed,zing,zation,er,INAPPROPRIATE RELATIONSHIP "prefixes: non"
fratid,freight(ed)

fraud, *, dly, dulent, dulen=ly, dulence, TRICK NG/ CHEATING
fraul, frail
fraulec, frolic
fraulek, frolic
frauler, frail(er)
fraulic, frolic
fraulik, frolic
fraulist, frail(est)
fraultee, frail(ty)
fraun, frown
frauns, frown(s)
frawd, fraud
frawdly, fraud(ly)
frawn, frown
fraxshen, fraction
fre, free / fray
fray, *, yed, ying, MATERIAL THAT UNRAVELS, A BRAWL, SITUATION THAT IS STRESSFUL OR EXCITING
freak, *, ked, king, ky, kier, kiest, kily, kiness, kish, SHOCKING/ ODD, UNUSUAL
freaze, freeze
frech, fridge
freched, fridge
frechen, fresh(en)
frecher, fresh(er)
frechnur, fresh(ener)
frechun, fresh(en)
freckle, *, ed, ling, ly, BEAUTY SPOT ON SKIN
frecol, freckle
frection, friction
fred, free(d) / fret / afraid
fredom, freedom
fredum, freedom
free, *, eed, eeing, eer, eest, eely, eeness, eedom, LIBERTY
freedom, *, TO HAVE LIBERTY
freedum, freedom
freekwensee, frequency
freekwint, frequent
freekwintly, frequent(ly)
freeky, freak
freese, freeze
freetim, freedom

freeze, *, roze, zing, er, zable, LIQUID TO SOLID, WATER AT 32° F, 0° C "prefixes: re/ sub/ un"
freg, fridge
freged, frigid
freghted, freight(ed)
fregit, frigid
freight, *, ted, ting, ter, GOODS BEING TRANSPORTED
freighter, *, SHIP CARRYING CARGO
freigrans, fragrance
freigrant, fragrant
freigter, freighter
freiht, freight
freim, frame
freit, freight / fright
freitor, freight
frej, fridge
frejid, frigid
frek, freak
frekal, freckle
frekol, freckle
frekqint, frequent
frekqintly, frequent(ly)
frekshen, friction
frekul, freckle
frekwensee, frequency
frekwent, frequent
frekwently, frequent(ly)
freky, freak
frel, frail
frely, free(ly)
fren, french / fringe
french, A NATIONALITY (or see fringe)
frend, friend
frendle, friend(ly)
frendleist, friend(liest)
frendlenes, friend(liness)
frendleur, friend(lier)
frenge, french / fringe
frense, frenzy
frent, friend
frentleist, friend(liest)
frentleur, friend(lier)
frently, friend(ly)

frenzy, zies, zied, CHAOTIC EXCITEMENT
frequency, cies, nt, DISTANCE/ NUMBER OF TIMES BETWEEN WAVE PEAKS, NUMBER OF OCCURRENCES
frequent, *, ted, ting, tly, tness, ntation, ter, ncy, HOW OFTEN "prefixes: un"
freqwensee, frequency
freqwint, frequent
freqwintly, frequent(ly)
fres, freeze / free(s) / frizz
frese, freeze / frizz
fresh, her, hest, hen, hens, hened, hening, hener, hly, hness, PEAK CONDITION "prefixes: re"
freshenur, fresh(ener)
freshin, fresh(en)
freshir, fresh(er)
freshnur, fresh(ener)
freshon, fresh(en)
freshur, fresh(er)
frestrate, frustrate
fret, *, tted, tting, tless, PART OF A CLOCK/ STRINGED INSTRUMENT, TO WORRY, BE ERODED/ CORRODED (or see afraid/ free(d))
fretem, freedom
freter, freighter
fretum, freedom
frevalus, frivolous
frevolus, frivolous
frewgul, frugal
frewktose, fructose
frez, freeze / frizz / free(s)
freze, frizz / freeze / free(s)
fri, fry / free
fric, freak
frich, fridge
friched, frigid
frichid, frigid
fricshen, friction
fricshon, friction
friction, nal, nless, RESISTANCE BETWEEN TWO THINGS (or see fraction)
fricuensi, frequency
fricuent, frequent
frid, fried / fright

frida,friday
friday,*,,A DAY OF THE WEEK (ENGLISH)
friden,frighten
fridgarator,refrigerate(tor)
fridge,*,SLANG FOR REFRIGERATOR
fridom,freedom
fridy,friday
fried,PAST TENSE FOR THE WORD "FRY",COOK IN SKILLET "prefixes: re"
friend,*,,dly,dlier,dliest,dliness,FRIENDSHIP,MUTUAL INTEREST/ ADMIRATION "prefixes: un"
frier,fry(er)
fries,ed,COOK IN SKILLET,GET TOO HOT,POTATOES DEEP FRIED
frig,fridge
frigarador,refrigerate(tor)
friged,frigid
frigerator,refrigerate(tor)
friget,frigid
fright,*,,ned,ning,TO SUDDENLY SCARE SOMEONE
frighten,*,ten,tener,tens,tened,tening,tful,tfully,tfulness, SUDDEN FEAR
frigid,dly,dness,dity,STIFF/ COLD
frigirator,refrigerate(tor)
frigit,frigid
frij,fridge
frijik,frigid
frik,freak
frikshen,friction
frikshenles,friction(less)
frikshenul,friction(al)
friktion,friction
friktional,friction(al)
frillid,frigid
frin,friend
finch,french / fringe
frind,friend
frindleist,friend(liest)
frindlenes,friend(liness)
frindleur,friend(lier)
frindly,friend(ly)
fringe,*,,ed,ging,DECORATIVE EDGE, ON THE OUTSIDE EDGE (or see french)

frinsy,frenzy
frint,friend
frintleist,friend(liest)
frintleur,friend(lier)
frintly,friend(ly)
frinzy,frenzy
fris,fries / frizz / first / freeze
frisy,frizz
frit,fried / fright
friten,frighten
frivalus,frivolous
frivolous,sly,sness,lity,SILLY,NOT SERIOUS
frivulus,frivolous
friz,frizz / freeze / fries
frize,frizz / fries
frizy,frizz
frizz,zzes,zzed,zzing,zzier,zziest,zzy,zziness,zzily, zziness,zzle,KINKY/ WAVY (or see freeze/ fries)
frock,frog
frod,fraud
frodewlint,fraud(ulent)
frodewlintly,fraud(ulently)
frodth,froth
frodulent,fraud(ulent)
frodulently,fraud(ulently)
frog,*,,gged,ggy,AN AMPHIBIAN
frogle,frugal
frogy,frog(ggy)
frojewlint,fraud(ulent)
frojewlintly,fraud(ulently)
frojiledy,fragile(lity)
frojulent,fraud(ulent)
frojulently,fraud(ulently)
frok,frog
frolek,frolic
frolec,frolic
frolic,*,,cked,cking,PLAY LIGHTHEARTED, ROMP HAPPILY
frolik,frolic
froluc,frolic
from,WHERE IT WAS BEFORE
frond,front
frondeer,frontier
front,*,,ted,ting,OUTSIDE FACING, GIVE IN ADVANCE

frontal,lly,IN/ AT THE FRONT OF "prefix: pre"
fronteer,frontier
frontid,front(ed)
frontier,*,FRINGE OR EDGE OF A PLACE OR IN INFORMATION
frontle,frontal
froogle,frugal
frooishen,fruition
froot,fruit
fros,froze
frosd,frost / froze
frosdee,frost
frosen,froze(n)
frosin,froze(n)
frost,*,,ted,ting,ty,tier,tiest,tless,tily,tiness,COATING OF SOMETHING ON OBJECT,ICE,ICING ON CAKES (or see froze)
froth,*,,hed,hing,hy,hier,hiest,hily,hiness,FOAM
frous,froze
frousen,frozen
frouzen,frozen
frowd,fraud
frown,*,,ned,ning,ningly,ner,MOUTH TURNED DOWN, DOESN'T APPROVE
frozd,frost / froze
froze,en,PAST TENSE FOR THE WORD "FREEZE"
frozen,PAST TENSE FOR THE WORD "FREEZE" prefixes: un"
fructose,NATURAL SUGAR
frude,fruit
frueshin,fruition
frugle,frugal
fruishin,fruition
frugal,lly,lity,lities,lness,VERY LITTLE WASTE
frugelidy,fragile(lity)
frugiledy,fragile(lity)
frugle,frugal
fruit,*,,ted,ting,ty,tiness,tful,tfully,tfulness,tless, SEED BEARING PART PRODUCED BY FEMALE PLANTS "prefixes: un"
fruition,A REALIZATION/ REWARD FOR EFFORT/ ACCOMPLISHMENT
frujilety,fragile(lity)

frujiludy, fragile(lity)
fruktose, fructose
frum, from
frund, front
frundeer, frontier
frundle, frontal
frunt, front
frunteer, frontier
fruntle, frontal
frushtrate, frustrate
frustrate,*,ed,ting,tingly,ter,tion,tive, SHAKEN BY LACK OF KNOWLEDGE OR INFORMATION "prefixes: re"
frustreit, frustrate
frut, fruit
frute, fruit
fry,ries,ried,ying,yer, COOK IN SKILLET, GET TOO HOT, GET IN TROUBLE
fryd, friday / fried
fryday, friday
fu, few
fucechan, physician
fuceshan, physician
fuceshes, facetious
fuch, fudge
fucher, future
fucichan, physician
fucishan, physician
fucishas, facetious
fucition, physician
fud, feud / food / foot
fudaledy, fidelity
fudch, fudge
fudelity, fidelity
fudge,*,ed,ging, CHOCOLATE DESSERT, EXAGGERATE THE TRUTH
fudon, futon
fued, feud
fuel,*,led,ling,ler, USED TO POWER THINGS "prefixes: bio/ re"
fug, fudge
fugative, fugitive
fugitive,*, RUNAWAY, ROAMS
fugt, fudge(d)

fuil, fuel
fuj, fudge
fujative, fugitive
ful, fool / full / fuel
fula, fillet
fulanthrapist, philanthropy(pist)
fulanthrapy, philanthropy
fulate, fillet
fulay, fillet
fuld, fool(ed) / fuel(ed)
fule, fuel / fool / full / full(lly)
fuled, fool(ed) / fuel(ed)
fuler, full(er)
fulesh, fool(ish)
fulesity, felicity
fulest, full(est)
fulfill,*,lled,lling,llment,ller, CONTENT, HAVE WHAT WAS WANTED "prefixes: un"
fulir, full(er)
fulish, fool(ish)
fulisity, felicity
fulist, full(est)
full,ler, lest, lly, llness, HOLDING THE MOST IT CAN HOLD
fulor, full(er)
fulosofy, philosophy
fulur, full(er)
fulust, full(est)
fuly, full
fum, fume
fumbel, fumble
fumbil, fumble
fumble,*, ed,ling,er, DROP SOMETHING ACCIDENTALLY, DROP A BALL DURING PLAY
fumbol, fumble
fume,*, ed,ming,mingly,my,migate, EMIT STEAM/ GAS/ SMOKE, SMELL
fumegashen, fumigate(tion)
fumegate, fumigate
fumegation, fumigate(tion)
fumelear, familiar
fumigashen, fumigate(tion)
fumigate,*, ed,ting,tion,ant, TO FLOOD/ OVERWHELM WITH SMOKE/ GAS

fumpl, fumble
fumugation, fumigate(tion)
fun,nny,nnier,nniest, HAPPINESS, PLAYFUL (or see fund(s))
funal, funnel
funarul, funeral
funcshenul, function(al)
funcshin, function
function,*, ned,ning,nal,nally,nalist, nality, nalities, nalism,nary,nalize,nalizes,nalization, SERVE, HAVE OPERATIONAL, PERFORM "prefixes: inter/ multi/ neo/ over/ pre"
functionul, function(al)
functshen, function
fund,*, ded, ding, der, PUT MONEY TOWARDS, HOLDS MONEY FOR PURPOSE "prefixes: re/ un"
fundamental,*, lly, lism, NECESSARY
fundemintol, fundamental
fundumintel, fundamental
fundur, fund(er)
fune, funny
funedic, phonetic / fanatic
funeir, fun(nnier)
funeist, fun(nniest)
funel, funnel
funeor, fun(nnier)
funeral,*, EVENT HONORING THE DEAD
funes, finesse / fun(nnies)
funetic, phonetic / fanatic
funeur, fun(nnier)
fungis, fungus
fungus, NOT A PLANT BUT IS LIVING AND GROWS
funie, funny
funies, fun(nnies)
funiest, fun(nniest)
funil, funnel
funior, fun(nnier)
funiral, funeral
funkshenul, function(al)
funkshin, function
funkshunal, function(al)
funkus, fungus
funle, funnel

funnel, *, led, ling, CONE SHAPE WITH HOLE IN MIDDLE
funnil, funnel
funny, nnies, nnier, nniest, nniness, CREATES SMILE/ LAUGHTER, HUMOR "prefixes: un"
funol, funnel
funomenal, phenomenal
funominul, phenomenal
funrul, funeral
funs, fund(s)
funt, fund
funtamental, fundamental
funy, funny
funyer, fun(nnier)
funyest, fun(nniest)
funyur, fun(nnier)
fuor, four
fur, *, rred, rring, rry, rless, HAIR ON ANIMAL (or see for/ fury) "prefixes: under"
furbed, forbid
furbedin, forbid(dden)
furbet, forbid
furbid, forbid
furbiten, forbid(dden)
furdal, fertile
furdalize, fertilize
furdil, fertile
furdulizashen, fertilize(zation)
furdulize, fertilize
fure, fury / furry
furefir, forever
furefur, forever
furesteul, forest(ial)
fureus, furious
furever, forever
furgave, forgave
furgefnis, forgive(ness)
furget, forget
furgetful, forget(ful)
furgitful, forget(ful)
furgive, forgive
furgivnes, forgive(ness)
furgot, forgot
furgotin, forgot(tten)

furious, sly, sness, BEYOND ANGRY
furket, forget
furketing, forget(tting)
furkiv, forgive
furlough, *, A LEAVE OF ABSENCE
furlow, furlough
furm, firm
furmaledy, formal(ity)
furmality, formal(ity)
furmashen, formation
furment, ferment
furn, fern
furnace, *, HEATER
furnacher, furniture
furnature, furniture
furnish, hes, hed, hing, hings, PLACE FURNITURE INTO A ROOM "prefixes: un"
furniture, OBJECTS/ ARTICLES PLACED IN A ROOM FOR COMFORT
furnusher, furniture
furochusle, ferocious(ly)
furod, furrow(ed)
furoshus, ferocious
furoshusle, ferocious(ly)
furot, furrow(ed)
furotious, ferocious
furou, furrow
furow, furrow
furrow, *, wed, wing, A TRENCH IN THE SOIL, WRINKLE IN BROW
furry, rrier, rriest, HAIRY (or see fury)
fursake, forsake
fursaken, forsake(n)
furst, first
furtal, fertile
further, red, ring, est, MORE THAN FAR (or see farther)
furtile, fertile
furtulize, fertile(lize)
fury, ries, rious, RAGE (or see furry)
furzd, first
fuse, *, ed, sing, sible, ITEM WHICH PROTECTS FROM FIRE HAZARD, USED TO IGNITE EXPLOSIVES, MELT ITEMS TOGETHER (or see fuss/ fuzz) "prefixes: inter"

fusechus, facetious
fuseir, fuss(ier) / fuzz(ier)
fuseist, fuss(iest) / fuzz(iest)
fusek, physique
fuselitate, facilitate
fuselitation, facilitate(tion)
fuselity, facility
fuseshen, physician
fuseur, fuss(ier) / fuzz(ier)
fushen, fusion / fission
fusher, future
fusiches, facetious
fusilatate, facilitate
fusilatation, facilitate(tion)
fusines, fuss(iness) / fuzz(iness)
fusion, nism, BLEND/ COMBINE, SCIENTIFIC TERM (or see fission) "prefixes: in"
fusishen, physician
fusition, physician
fusod, facade
fuss, sses, ssed, ssing, ssy, ssily, ssiness, TO FOCUS ON MINOR DETAILS (or see fuse/ fuzz)
fusy, fuss / fuzz
fut, food / foot / feud
futaledy, fidelity
futch, fudge
futeg, fatigue
futon, *, A CUSHION/ MATTRESS WITH HEAVY COTTON BATTING (or see photon)
futsher, future
future, *, rity, ristic, ristically, rless, rlessness, rism, A TIME AFTER NOW
fuz, fuzz / fuse / fuss
fuzd, fuse(d) / fuss(ed)
fuze, fuse / fuss / fuzz
fuzed, fuse(d) / fuss(ed)
fuzeir, fuss(ier) / fuzz(ier)
fuzek, physique
fuzines, fuss(iness) / fuzz(iness)
fuzt, fuse(d) / fuss(ed)
fuzyest, fuss(iest) / fuzz(iest)
fuzynes, fuss(iness) / fuzz(iness)

Word	Related
fuzz,*,zzy,zzes,zzed,zzing,zzies,zzier,zziest,zziness,FUR/ OTHER MATERIAL, BLURRY TO THE EYES (or see fuse/fuss)	
fuzzyness,fuss(ines) / fuzz(iness)	
fynite,finite	
ga,gay	
gab,*,bbed,bbing,bby,bbier,bbiest,TALKING JUST TO BE TALKING (or see jab)	
gabe,gab(bby) / have	
gaber,jabber	
gach,gauge / hatch / hash	
gack,jack / hack	
gad,jade / gate / had / hate	
gader,gather / gaiter	
gadget,*,AN ITEM USED AS A TOOL	
gadyet,gadget	
gaend,gain(ed)	
gaf,golf / gave	
gafel,gavel	
gaful,gavel	
gag,*,gged,gging,NEARLY CHOKE, TO KEEP SOMEONE FROM SPEAKING (or see gauge/ jag/ hag)	
gagd,gag(gged) / gauge(d) / jag(gged)	
gagels,goggles	
gaget,gadget	
gaid,guide	
gaidens,guidance	
gail,jail / gale	
gain,*,ned,ning,nful,nfully,BENEFIT, IMPROVE	
gair,hair / hare	
gait,*,DISTANCE BETWEEN FOOTSTEPS (or see gate/hate)	
gaiter,*,WRAP FOR LEGS BELOW THE KNEE, SLANG FOR ALLIGATOR	
gaje,gauge	
gajit,gadget / hatchet	
gak,jack	
gakass,jackass	
gakd,jack(ed) / hack(ed)	
gal,*,REFERENCE TO A FEMALE (or see gall/ gale/jail)	
galactic,cally,THE MILKY WAY, GALAXY "prefixes: inter"	
galan,gallon	
galant,gallant	

Word	Related
galari,gallery	
galashes,galoshes	
galaxy,xies,PLANETS/ STARS WITHIN A SYSTEM	
gale,*,STRONG WINDS (or see gal/ galley/ jail)	
galeksy,galaxy	
galen,gallon	
galent,gallant	
galep,gallop	
galeri,gallery	
galery,gallery	
galexy,galaxy	
galey,galley / jelly	
galf,golf	
gali,galley / jelly	
galin,gallon	
galip,gallop	
galiry,gallery	
gall,*,lled,lling,TO UNNERVE/ IRRITATE/ ANNOY/ RUB SOMEONE/ SOMETHING THE WRONG WAY, A GROWTH (or see gal)	
gallant,*,ted,ting,tly,try,COURAGEOUS, STATELY, AMOROUS, IN REFERENCE TO MALES	
gallen,gallon	
gallery,ries,ria,SHOWPLACE FOR ART	
gallet,gadget	
galley,*,KITCHEN IN A VESSEL, ANCIENT BOAT	
gallon,*,U.S. MEASURE FOR LIQUID	
gallop,*,ped,ping,GAIT OF A HORSE OR ANIMAL BEING RIDDEN	
gallows,STRUCTURE FROM WHICH PEOPLE WERE HUNG TO DEATH	
gallun,gallon	
galon,gallon	
galop,gallop	
galory,gallery	
galous,gallows	
galows,gallows	
galoshes,RUBBER BOOTS	
galre,gallery	
galun,gallon	
galup,gallop	
galury,gallery	
galy,july / jelly	

Word	Related
gam,jam / jamb / game	
gamble,*,ed,ling,er,BET MONEY ON NUMBERS	
game,*,ming,er,COMPETITION TO WIN	
gamet,gamut	
gamut,FULL SCALE OF MUSICAL NOTES, THE WHOLE RANGE OF THINGS	
gander,*,MALE GOOSE	
gane,gain	
ganedic,genetic	
ganeuary,may	
gang,*,ged,ging,GROUP OF PEOPLE/ THINGS WITH COMMONALITY	
ganitor,janitor	
gant,gain(ed) / chant	
gantlet,gauntlet	
ganuary,january	
gap,*,pped,pping,ppy,pper,A SPACE, BREAK IN CONTINUITY (or see gape)	
gape,ped,ping,pingly,NORMALLY CONCERNS THE MOUTH OPENING WIDE (or see gap/gob)	
gar,jar	
garach,garage	
garage,*,ed,ging,STRUCTURE INTENDED FOR VEHICLES	
garantee,guarantee	
garanti,guarantee	
garbach,garbage	
garbage,TRASH	
gard,guard	
garden,*,ned,ning,ner,GROWING PLANTS	
gardeun,guardian	
gardian,guardian	
garela,gorilla / guerrilla	
garentee,guarantee	
gargen,jargon	
gargle,*,ed,ling,RINSE THE THROAT WITH LIQUID	
gargoele,gargoyle	
gargoiol,gargoyle	
gargoyle,*,CARVED GOTHIC FIGURES	
garila,gorilla / guerrilla	
garland,*,PLANT ITEMS WOVEN TOGETHER	
garlic,cky,EDIBLE BULB FROM PLANT	
garment,*,"CLOTHING ""prefixes: under"""	
garner,*,red,ring,nish,GATHER/ GAIN SOMETHING	

garnish, hes, hed, hing, hment, hee, iture, DECORATION FOR FOOD/ DRINK, TO PORTION OUT
gart, guard
garteun, guardian
gas, ses, ssed, ssing, seous, seousness, sify, sifies, sified, sifying, sification, NOT LIQUID OR SOLID, PETROLEUM PRODUCT
gasoline, USED TO POWER MOTORS
gasp, *, ped, ping, STRUGGLE FOR AIR
gastr, PREFIX INDICATING "STOMACH" MOST OFTEN MODIFIES THE WORD
gastro, PREFIX INDICATING "STOMACH" MOST OFTEN MODIFIES THE WORD
gasture, gesture
gasuntite, gesundheit
gate, *, ted, ting, CLOSURE TO MONITOR EXIT/ ENTRANCE
gater, alligator / gaiter
gather, *, red, ring, COLLECT TOGETHER
gator, alligator / gaiter
gaudy, dier, diest, dily, diness, OUTRAGEOUS STYLE NAMED AFTER FAMOUS ARCHITECT IN BARCELONA
gaug, gauge / gouge
gauge, *, ed, ging, eable, eably, er, INSTRUMENT FOR MEASURING THINGS SUCH AS PRESSURE "prefixes: en/ mis/ multi/ re" (or see gouge)
gaul, gal
gauly, jolly / golly
gaun, gown
gaunt, tly, tness, HAGGARD/ THIN, LACKING AVERAGE VOLUME/ SIZE (or see jaunt)
gauntlet, *, CHALLENGE
gaurantee, guarantee
gaus, gauze
gauze, zily, zy, CLOTH FOR BANDAGES
gava, java
gave, PAST TENSE FOR THE WORD "GIVE"
gavel, *, WOODEN HAMMER USED IN COURTROOMS
gaw, jaw
gawalk, jaywalk
gawn, gown
gawok, jaywalk
gawul, jowl
gay, *, yly, BRIGHT, HAPPY, HOMOSEXUAL (or see guy)

gayet, gadget
gaywalk, jaywalk
gaywok, jaywalk
gaz, jazz / gaze / gauze
gaze, *, ed, zing, er, A LONG LOOK AT (or see gauze)
gazuntite, gesundheit
ge, PREFIX INDICATING "EARTH" MOST OFTEN MODIFIES THE WORD
geagrafee, geography
gear, *, red, ring, INTERLOCKING NOTCHED RINGS WHICH DRIVE MACHINES
geburish, gibber(ish)
ged, get / head
gedo, ghetto
geeneol, genial
geens, jean(s) / gene(s)
geese, MORE THAN ONE GOOSE
gef, give
geffy, jiffy
geft, gift
geg, gig / jig
gegle, giggle / jiggle
gei, gay
geib, gave
geich, gauge
geill, gauge
gein, gain
geip, gape
geipvain, grapevine
geis, gaze
geit, gait / gate
geiter, gaiter
geiv, gave
geiz, gaze
gel, *, lled, lling, llable, SEMI-SOFT/ FIRM SUBSTANCE (or see jello/ jail/ gal)
gelatin, *, nous, LIKE JELLO
geld, guild / guilt / jell(ed)
gele, jelly
geletin, gelatin
geli, july / jelly
gelt, guilt / jilt / jell(ed) / guild
gelty, guilt

gelus, jealous
gelutin, gelatin
gely, july / jelly
gem, *, STONE, JEWEL (or see gym)
gemek, gimmick
gemik, gimmick
gemmy, jimmy
gemnaseum, gymnasium
gemnast, gymnast
gen, gene / jean
genacide, genocide
genarate, generate
genaration, generation
genarulize, general(ize)
genarus, generous
genasis, genesis
gender, *, rless, CLASSIFICATION BY SEX "prefixes: en"
gendr, gender
gene, *, STRING OF CHROMOSOMES (or see jean)
genedic, genetic
genepig, guinea pig
general, *, lly, lity, lities, lize, lizes, lized, lizing, lizable, lizability, lization, ENCOMPASSES MANY THINGS, A MILITARY OFFICER "prefixes: over"
generate, *, ed, ting, tion, tively, tiveness, tor, CREATE, PRODUCE
generation, *, nal, PEOPLE BORN IN GROUPS AT SAME TIME "prefixes: inter/ multi"
generator, *, MACHINE THAT CREATES AC ENERGY
genereit, generate
generic, *, cally, GENERAL NAME BRAND/ CLASSIFICATION
generous, sly, sness, osity, osities, GIVE AWAY WHAT CAN BE SPARED "prefixes: multi"
genesis, BEGINNING OF TIME/ EVENT "prefixes: bio"
genetic, *, cal, cally, cist, trix, STUDY OF GENES AND ASSOCIATED PARTICLES "prefixes: bio"
geneul, genial
geneus, genius
genial, lly, lity, lness, WELCOMING, DOESN'T APPEAR JUDGMENTAL
genie, *, MAGIC ENTITY IN A BOTTLE
geniral, general

genirus,genirous
genises,genesis
genital,*,lia,lly,EXTERNAL REPRODUCTIVE ORGANS
genius,ses,sness,CAPABLE OF DEEP THINKING
genjur,ginger
genle,gentle
genocide,dal,dally,KILLING CERTAIN PEOPLES SYSTEMATICALLY
genome,*,mic,STUDY OF HUMAN GENES AND ALL ASSOCIATED INTERACTIONS
genre',*,DIFFERENT STYLES/ MEDIUM, EXPRESSION FOR ART, MUSIC "prefixes: sub"
genrul,general
gentle,er,est,tility,eness,KIND IN BEHAVIOR/ DISPOSITION, NON-THREATENING
gentul,gentle
genucide,genocide
genuine,ely,eness,TRUTHFUL,REAL
genurul,general
genurus,generous
genus,nera,METHOD TO ORGANIZE PLANTS AND ANIMALS "prefixes: sub"
genyus,genius
geo, PREFIX INDICATING "EARTH" MOST OFTEN MODIFIES THE WORD
geography,hies,hic,hical,hically,ophysicist,THE STUDY OF EVERYTHING ON THE SURFACE OF THE EARTH "prefixes: bio"
geology,gies,gic,gical,gist,ophysicist,STUDY OF THE EARTH'S CRUST
geometry,ries,ric,rical,rically,rize,rizes,rized,rizing,rization,rician,VARIOUS SHAPES/ SYMBOLS/ LINES/ ANGLES
gep,gyp
gepardy,jeopardy
gepsee,gypsy
gepsum,gypsum
gerantee,guarantee
gerbil,*,A SMALL RODENT
gere,gear / jury
geresdikshen,jurisdiction
gergul,gurgle
gerila,gorilla / guerrilla

gerk,jerk
gerky,jerky
gerl,girl
gerlfrend,girlfriend
germ,*,minate,BACTERIA
germinate,*,ed,ting,tion,tive,tor,SEED BEGINNING TO GROW
gernal,journal
gernalist,journal(ist)
gerne,journey / gurney
gernulest,journal(ist)
gerny,gurney / journey
gert,girth
gerter,girder
gerth,girth
gerunte,guarantee
gerur,juror
gery,jury
gesd,guest / guess(ed) / jest
gese,geese / guess
gesoontite,gesundheit
gess,guess
gest,jest / just / guest / guess(ed)
gesture,*,ed,ring,BODILY MOTIONS
gesundheit, WISHING GOOD HEALTH TO SOMEONE WHO SNEEZED (German)
gesundjait,gesundheit
gesuntite,gesundheit
get,*,got,tta,tten,tter,tting,TO TAKE IN, HAVE IT (or see jet)
gete,jetty
geter,jitter
geto,ghetto
getsam,jetsam
gety,jetty
gev,give
gewdeshal,judicial
gewdishes,judicious
gewel,jewel
gewly,july
gewn,june / goon
gews,juice

geyser,*,WATER WHICH SHOOTS UP FROM A HOLE IN THE EARTH
ghetto,*,A SECTION OF LAND WHERE OVERCROWDING IS A RESULT OF DISCRIMINATION
ghost,*,tly,SPIRITS WHICH PROVE TO EXIST BUT ARE INVISIBLE TO US
gi,guy
giant,*,HUGE,ENORMOUS
gib,jib / jibe
gibber,*,red,ring,rish,rer,LANGUAGE/ WORDS THAT DO NOT MAKE SENSE (or see jibe)
gibe,*,ed,bing,bingly,COMMENT MADE TO PROVOKE NEGATIVE FEELINGS IN ANOTHER (or see jibe)
giberish,gibber(ish)
gid,get / guide
giddy,ddier,ddiest,ddily,ddiness,JOYFUL, EXTREMELY EXCITED,FRIVOLOUS (or see jibe)
gide,guide
gidense,guidance
gif,give
giffy,jiffy
gift,*,ted,ting,TO GIVE SOMETHING WITHOUT EXPECTATIONS OF RETURN
gig,* ARRANGEMENT FOR MUSICAL PERFORMANCE (or see jig)
giga, PREFIX INDICATING "ONE BILLIONTH" MOST OFTEN MODIFIES THE WORD
gigantic,cally,ism,INCREDIBLY HUGE, ENORMOUS
gigger,jigger
giggle,*,ed,ling,lly,er,STYLE OF LAUGHING (or see jiggle)
gigle,giggle
gigol,giggle
gigsaw,jigsaw
gilatnus,gelatin(ous)
gild,guild / guilt / jell(ed)
gildy,guilt
giloshes,galoshes
gilt,guild / guilt / jell(ed)
gilty,guilt
gily,july / jelly
gim,gem / gym
gimic,gimmick

gimik,gimmick
gimmick,*,ky,TRICK,ATTENTION GETTER
gimmy,jimmy
gimnaseum,gymnasium
gimnast,gymnast
ginacologist,gynecology(gist)
ginarashin,generation
ginarate,generate
ginarator,generator
ginarulize,general(ize)
ginarus,generous
ginasis,genesis
gindur,gender
gine pig,guinea pig
ginecologist,gynecology(gist)
ginerik,generic
ginetic,genetic(s)
ginger,*,red,ring,ry,rly,EDIBLE PLANT,TO BE CAUTIOUS
gingle,jingle
ginks,jinx
ginokologist,gynecology(gist)
ginrul,general
ginter,gender
ginucalugist,gynecology(gist)
ginucide,genocide
ginucologist,gynecology(gist)
ginuen,genuine
ginul,gentle
ginurulize,general(ize)
ginus,genus
ginuses,genesis
giologee,geology
giometry,geometry
gip,gyp
gipsee,gypsy
gipsum,gypsum
gir,gear
girate,gyrate
girble,gerbil
gird,*,ded,ding,der,PHYSICALLY PROTECT YOURSELF, PHYSICAL PROTECTION BY GIRDLE/ BELT/ STRAPS "prefixes: under"

girder,*,BEAM USED FOR HORIZONTAL BRACING IN BUILDINGS
girgul,gurgle
girl,*,ly,YOUNG FEMALE PERSON
girlfriend,*,A GIRL WHO IS ALSO A FRIEND
girm,germ
girmanate,germinate
girnalist,journal(ist)
girney,gurney / journey
girnul,journal
girth,*,WIDTH OF SOMETHING ACROSS, CIRCUMFERENCE
giry,jury
gis,geese
giser,geyser
gisuntite,gesundheit
git,get
gito,ghetto
gitter,jitter
give,*,ving,gave,en,PROVIDE/ GIFT/ PRESENT SOMETHING (or see jive) "prefixes: mis"
gizer,geyser
gizuntite,gesundheit
glachal,glacial
glachel,glacial
glachil,glacial
glachol,glacial
glacial,*,ally,ate,ates,ated,ating,ation,ICE,FROZEN WATER,FROM THE WORD 'GLACIER' "prefixes: en/ inter/ sub"
glacier,*,red,ial,ICE,FROZEN WATER AROUND MOUNTAIN
glad,dder,ddest,dly,PLEASED
glaico,glyco
glaid,glide
glair,glare
glamour,rous,rously,rousness,orize,orizes,orized, orizing,orization,orizer,ALLURING, BEWITCHING
glance,*,ed,cing,A QUICK LOOK
gland,*,dule,dular,dulous,dulously,dless,ORGANS IN THE BODY "prefixes: multi"
glans,glance

glare,*,ed,ring,ringly,ringness,A SHARP LOOK WITH THE EYES,INTENSE LIGHT
glas,glass / glaze
glaser,glacier / glaze(r)
glashal,glacial
glashel,glacial
glasher,glacier
glashil,glacial
glashol,glacial
glass,sses,ssed,ssy,ssful,ssier,ssiest,ssily,ssiness,HARD/ FLAT/ FRAGILE SUBSTANCE MADE WITH MIXTURE OF MINERALS/ CHEMICALS
glaze,*,ed,zing,er,A COATING OF SUBSTANCE ON SOMETHING "prefixes: multi/ over/ under"
glazr,glaze(r)
gleam,*,med,ming,my,mier,miest,A BRIEF MOMENT IN APPEARANCE
glech,glitch
gleder,glitter
gledur,glitter
glee,*,eful,efully,efulness,WITH JOY, EXUBERANCE "prefixes: un"
gleful,glee(ful)
gleis,glaze
gleisur,glacier
gleiz,glaze
glemmer,glimmer
glempse,glimpse
glent,glint
glesen,glisten
glesten,glisten
gletch,glitch
gleu,glue
glew,glue
gli,glee
glich,glitch
glide,*,ed,ding,er,TO MOVE SMOOTHLY WITHOUT RESISTANCE
glider,glide(r) / glitter
glim,gleam
glimer,glimmer
glimmer,*,red,ring,A DIM LIGHT
glimpse,*,ed,sing,SLIGHT GLANCE,SEE BRIEFLY

glint,*,ted,ting,A TWINKLE, SPARKLE
glisen,glisten
glisten,*,ned,ning,TO REFLECT LIGHT, SHINY
glitch,hes,hy,MONKEYWRENCH IN THE PLANS, PROBLEM IN THE OPERATION OF
glite,glide
gliter,glitter / glide(r)
glitter,*,red,ring,ringly,ry,SHINY SPECKS, FLECKS OF LIGHT (or see glider)
gliture,glitter / glide(r)
glo,glow
gloat,*,ted,ting,tingly,ter,OVERLY PROUD OF AN ACCOMPLISHMENT
global,lly,lize,lizes,lized,lizing,lization,lism,l zer, INCORPORATES THE GLOBE, INCLUDES THE WORLD
globe,*,ed,bing,boid,THE SHAPE AND PICTURE OF THE WORLD
globel,global
globul,global
glof,glove
glofs,glove(s)
glomp,*,ped,ping,MANY THINGS WHICH GRAB / STICK, AFFECTIONATE POUNCE/ HUG
gloo,glue
gloom,*,med,ming,my,mily,miness,DULL SENSE OF FEAR
glorifai,glorify
glorify,fies,fied,fying,fication,fier,ious,WORSHIP
glorufy,glorify
glory,ries,rify,rious,riously,riousness,IN HONOR, PRAISE "prefixes: in"
glosery,glossary
gloss,sses,ssed,ssing,ssy,ssier,ssiest,ssily,ssiness,SHINE UP "prefixes: semi"
glossary,ries,AREA IN SOME BOOKS WITH DEFINITIONS
glot,gloat
glote,gloat / glow(ed)
glou,glow
glove,*,ed,ving,eless,COVERING FOR HANDS
glow,*,wed,wing,wingly,wer,TO BE LITE FROM WITHIN, INTERNAL LIGHT
gluco,PREFIX INDICATING "SUGAR" MOST OFTEN MODIFIES THE WORD

glucose,SUGAR, SYRUP
glucous,glucose
glue,*,ed,uing,ey,uily,uiness,TYPE OF LIQUID USED TO STICK THINGS TOGETHER, STUCK TO SOMETHING "prefixes: un"
gluecose,glucose
glufs,glove(s)
glukose,glucose
glum,mly,mness,mmer,mmest,DISAPPOINT, NEGATIVE PERSPECTIVE, APPEARS TO BE NO SOLUTION, SULLEN (or see gloom)
glumy,glum(mmy) / gloom
glutinous,sly,STICKS TOGETHER, LIKE GLUE
gluvs,glove(s)
glyco,PREFIX INDICATING "SUGAR" MOST OFTEN MODIFIES THE WORD
gnat,*,tty,tier,tiest,TINY FLY
gnaw,*,wed,wing,MOUTH OR CHEW ON SOMETHING GENTLY
gnome,*,A SMALL HUMAN ENTITY WHICH ONLY SOME PEOPLE CAN SEE
go,oes,oing,one,READY, SET, MOVE/ MOBILIZE TO ANOTHER PLACE "prefixes: in/ under"
goad,*,ded,ding,TO PROD/ POKE/ FORCE SOMETHING/ SOMEONE TO REACT (or see goat)
goal,*,lie,SOMETHING TO ACHIEVE/ GO FOR, ATTEMPT TO REACH
goalie,*,SOMEONE WHO DEFENDS AGAINST SOMEONE WHO WANTS TO MAKE POINTS IN A GAME
goat,*,AN ANIMAL
goatee,*,A BEARD SHAVED TO A POINT
gob,*,ed, A CLUMP/LUMP OF WAY TOO MUCH OF SOMETHING
gobble,*,ed,ling,er,TO EAT VERY QUICKLY
goble,gobble
goblet,*,A DRINKING VESSEL
goblin,*,AN ENTITY ONLY SOME PEOPLE CAN SEE
gobul,gobble
god,*,REFERENCE TO A SUPREME BEING (or see good/ got/ goad/ goth) "prefixes: un"
goddess,sses,FEMALE ENTITY WHO CO-CREATES
gode,gaudy
goden,gotten

goen,join
goent,joint / join(ed)
goes,FORM OF "GO", IS MOVING TO ANOTHER SPACE/ ATTITUDE/ LEVEL
goest,joist
gof,golf
gofener,governor
gofer,gopher / golf(er)
gofeul,jovial
gofur,gopher
gog,jog
gogels,goggles
goger,jog(gger)
goggles,SAFETY EYE PROTECTION
gogils,goggles
gogir,jog(gger)
goguls,goggles
gogur,jog(gger)
goin,join
goint,joint / join(ed)
goke,joke / jockey
goky,jockey
gol,goal
golaktik,galactic
gold,den,A PRECIOUS METAL
golden,nly,nness,THE COLOR OF GOLD
goldun,golden
gole,goal / goalie / golly / jolly
golf,*,fed,fing,fer,A SPORT
golie,goal / goalie / golly / jolly
golly,VERBAL EXPRESSION OF SURPRISE (or see goalie/ jolly)
goloshes,galoshes
golt,jolt / gold
golten,golden
goly,jolly / golly / jolly / goalie
gon,gone / join / going
gondes,jaundice
gone,er,PAST TENSE FOR THE WORD "GO", ALREADY LEFT
goner,*,SOMEONE WHO IS GONE OR IN TROUBLE
gong,*,A MUSICAL INSTRUMENT
gonir,gone(r)

gont, jaunt, gaunt / join(ed)
gontlet, gauntlet
gonur, gone(r)
good, *, dly, dly, dness, ACCEPTABLE
good-bye, *, FAREWELL EXPRESSION FOR LEAVING
goods, STUFF, STUFF FOR SALE
gooly, july
goon, *, THUG, A DEROGATORY NAME FOR SOMEONE
goose, geese, A FEMALE BIRD, SQUEEZE SOMEONE (or see juice)
goot, jute
gopher, *, A RODENT, SOMEONE WHO GOES TO PICK UP SOMETHING
gor, jar / gore
gorch, gorge
gord, gourd / guard
gore, *, ed, PIERCED BY A HORN, BLOOD FROM INJURY
gorela, gorilla / guerrilla
gorge, *, ed, ging, er, TO STUFF, GEOLOGICAL FORMATION "prefixes: dis/ en"
gorgeous, sly, sness, SOMETHING VERY ATTRACTIVE
gorgis, gorgeous
gorgus, gorgeous
gorilla, *, A MAMMAL (or see guerrilla)
gorillus, gorgeous
gorj, gorge
gorjus, gorgeous
gorlend, garland
gorlic, garlic
gorma, gourmet
gorment, garment
gorner, garner
gornish, garnish
gos, goes / gauze
gosep, gossip
gosepd, gossip(ed)
gosip, gossip
gospel, *, PARTS OF THE BIBLE
gossip, *, ped, ping, per, pry, py, WORDS SAID ABOUT SOMEONE WHO ISN'T AROUND TO HEAR
gost, ghost
gosup, gossip

got, tten, PAST TENSE FOR THE WORD "GET", ACQUIRE SOMETHING YOU DIDN'T HAVE BEFORE (or see goat/ god/ jot)
gote, goat / goatee / gaudy
goten, gotten
goter, gutter
goth, hic, hically, hicism, DARK FORM OF SELF EXPRESSION, MEDIEVAL THEME
gothec, goth(ic)
gotin, gotten
gotten, PAST TENSE FOR THE WORD "GET/ GOT"
goty, gaudy
gouge, *, ed, ging, MAKE HOLES OR GROOVES INTO
goun, gown
gourd, *, FRUIT FROM A PLANT
gourmet, *, ONE WHO UNDERSTANDS FINE FOODS
gous, goes
gout, goat
gouti, goatee
goverment, government
govern, *, ned, ning, nable, nance, ness, nment, nor, CONTROLLING ENTITIES WHO UPHOLD, CREATE RULES "prefixes: un"
government, *, tal, tally, talize, GROUP OF PEOPLE WHO RULE, UPHOLDS RULES FOR A PEOPLE "prefixes: inter"
governor, *, ness, rate, STATE ELECTED POLITICIAN
goveul, jovial
govirment, government
govnur, governor
gowge, gouge
gown, *, FULL LENGTH DRESS/ROBE
gownse, jounce
gowul, jowl
goy, joy
goyful, joy(ful)
goyn, join
goynd, joint / join(ed)
goynt, joint / join(ed)
goyus, joy(us)
goz, goes / gauze / jaw(s)
gra, gray

grab, *, bbed, bbing, bby, bbable, bber, TAKE ROUGHLY/ QUICKLY
grabel, gravel / grapple
grabetate, gravitate
grable, grapple / gravel
grabuling, gravel(ing) / grapple(ling)
grace, *, ed, cing, eful, efully, efulness, cious, ciously, ciousness, ELEGANCE (or see graze) "prefixes: dis/ un"
grachuashen, graduate(tion)
grachus, gracious
gracious, sly, sness, PERFORM ELEGANTLY "prefixes: un"
grad, *, SHORT FOR 'GRADUATE' (or see grade/ grate/ great) "prefixes: under"
grade, *, ed, ding, er, dient, LEVEL IN LEARNING, DEGREES, STEPS (or see grate/ great/ grad) "prefixes: de/ inter/ multi/ retro/ sub/ up"
gradeant, grade(dient)
gradetude, gratitude
gradful, grateful
gradguashen, graduate(tion)
gradiant, grade(dient)
gradify, gratify
graditude, gratitude
gradjual, gradual
gradjuate, graduate
gradle, great(ly)
gradly, great(ly)
gradual, lly, lness, lism, MOVEMENT A BIT AT A TIME
graduate, *, ed, ting, tion, CEREMONY CELEBRATING COMPLETION, MOVE UP TO THE NEXT LEVEL "prefixes: under"
graf, graph
grafait, graphite
grafe, grave
grafek, graphic
graffiti, to, PICTURES/ WORDS PLACED/ PAINTED IN PUBLIC PLACES WITHOUT PERMISSION
grafic, graphic
grafite, graphite / graffiti / gravity
grafity, gravity / graffiti
graft, *, ted, ting, ter, TO ATTACH PART OF A LIVE THING TO PART OF ANOTHER LIVE THING "prefixes: en"

grafudy,gravity
grafux,graphic
gragereus,gregarious
graguashen,graduate(tion)
graguate,graduate
graim,grime / grim
graimi,grimy
grain, *, ned, ner, nless, ny, anul, EDIBLE PLANT/ SEED, WOOD TEXTURE, BASIC CHARACTERISTIC "prefixes: en/ multi"
graind,grind
grainery,granary
grainual,granule
graip,gripe
grajeashen,graduate(tion)
grajual,gradual
grajuashen,graduate(tion)
grajuate,graduate
gram, *, MEASURE OF WEIGHT "prefixes: deca"
gramatical,grammatical
grammar, *, atical, rian, atology, WORDS AND THE WAY THEY ARE USED BY PEOPLE
grammatical,lly, lity, lness, WORDS AND THE WAY THEY ARE USED BY PEOPLE "prefixes: un"
gran,grain
granary,ries, GRAIN STOREHOUSE
granait,granite
grand,der, dest, dly, dness, deur, diose, OF GREAT STATURE, IMMENSE, BEST THERE IS (or see grant)
grandeos,grandiose
grandiose,ely, eness, sity, IMPRESSIVE STATURE
grandure,grand(eur) / grand(er)
granery,granary
granet,granite
granite,IGNEOUS ROCK
granola,DRIED GRAIN AND FRUIT MIXED TOGETHER
grant, *, ted, ting, tee, tor, GIVE WHAT WAS ASKED FOR
granual,granule
granule, *, lar, larity, larly, late, lates, lated, lating, lation, lative, lator, VERY SMALL MASS OF SOMETHING "prefixes: multi"
granut,granite
grape, *, FRUIT OF THE VINE

grapefruit, *, CITRUS FRUIT
grapevine, *, VINE OF A FRUIT
grapfruit,grapefruit
grapfrut,grapefruit
graph, *, hed, hing, her, hic, TO PLOT ON, SHOWS CHANGES IN NUMBERS
graphic, *, cal, cally, cness, cacy, VISUAL ART BY PEOPLE OR COMPUTER
graphite, TYPE OF ROCK
grapple, *, ed, ling, er, TO STRUGGLE/ WRESTLE WITH
grapul,grapple / gravel
grapvine,grapevine
grase,grace / graze
grashis,gracious
grasp, *, ped, ping, pable, GET A FIRM HOLD OF SOMETHING "prefixes: un"
grass, sses, ssed, ssing, ssy, ssier, ssiest, ssiness, PLANT
grat,great / grate / grade
grate, *, ed, ting, er, FABRICATED METAL/ STEEL, KITCHEN DEVICE, SOMETHING IRRITATING (or see great/ grade)
grateant,grade(dient)
grateful,lly, llness, APPRECIATE "prefixes: un"
gratetude,gratitude
gratiant,grade(dient)
gratifai,gratify
gratify,fies, fied, fying, fication, itude, tuity, FULFILLING, PLEASURABLE
gratitude, *, APPRECIATION "prefixes: in"
gratle,great(ly)
gratly,great(ly)
gratshuation,graduate(tion)
gratuate,graduate
gratuity,ties, tous, tously, tousness, TIP/ MONEY FOR SERVICE
grauch,grouch
graul,growl
graund,ground
graus,grouse
grave, *, er, est, ely, eness, en, WHERE SOMETHING IS BURIED, SERIOUS SITUATION
gravedy,gravity
gravel, *, led, ling, lly, SMALL ROCKS

gravitate, *, ed, ting, tive, tion, BEING DRAWN BY A FORCE
gravitation, nal, nally, THE ACT OF BEING AFFECTED BY GRAVITY
gravity, tate, tative, tation, POWERFUL FORCE KEEPING THINGS FROM FLOATING INTO SPACE
gravul,gravel
gravy, vies, THICK SAUCE
grawl,growl
grawnd,ground
gray, *, yer, ying, COLOR, FROM AGING
graze, *, ed, zing, er, HOW HERD ANIMALS EAT (or see grace)
grease, *, ed, sing, er, sy, sier, siest, eless, sily, siness, FROM ANIMAL FAT, LUBRICANT FOR MOVING MACHINE PARTS
great, *, ter, test, tly, tness, HIGH ON THE SCALE OF IMPRESSIVE (or see grate)
greater,great(er) / grate(r)
greatful,grateful
gred,grid / greed
gredy,grit(tty) / greed
greed,dy, dier, diest, dily, diness, TAKE MORE THAN NEED
greef,grief
green, *, ner, nest, COLOR, PLANTS
greese,grease
greet, *, ted, ting, TO WELCOME
greeve,grieve
greeze,grease
grefiti,graffiti
gregarious,sly, sness, PREFERS TO LIVE IN SOCIAL ENVIRONMENT WITH LIKE KIND
greid,grade
greif,grave
greip,grape
greipfruit,grapefruit
greis,grace / graze
greishos,gracious
greit,grate / great
greiuy,gravy
greiv,grave
greiz,graze
grell,grill
grem,grim / grime

grematical,grammatical
gren,grin / green
grenola,granola
grep,grip
greshus,gracious
gret,grit / greet / greed
grety,grit(tty) / greed
grew,PAST TENSE FOR THE WORD "GROW"
grewsome,gruesome
grey,gray
greze,grease
grid,*,PERPENDICULAR LINES (or see greed)
griddle,*,ed,ling,er,FLAT COOKING UTENSIL
gride,grit(tty)
gridul,griddle
grief,eve,DEEP SADNESS (or see grieve)
grieve,*,ed,ving,vant,vance,vances,gous,gously,gousness,MOURNING A LOSS
grif,grief
grifete,graffiti
grigarious,gregarious
grill,,lled,lling,ller,COOK ON METAL GRID OVER COALS
grim,mmer,mmest,mly,mness,STUBBORN, VIRTUALLY UNCHANGABLE (or see grime)
grime,,ed,ming,my,DIRT/ GREASE/ SOOT (or see grimy)
grimy,mier,miest,mily,miness,DIRT/ GREASE/ SOOT
grin,,,ned,ning,SMILE BROADLY (or see green)
grind,*,ded,ding,round,der,TO MILL/ CHOP/ SMASH/ PULVERIZE (or see grin(nned))
grinola,granola
grip,*,pped,pping,pper,FIRMLY GRASP, HAND HOLD (or see gripe)
gripe,*,ed,ping,er,VERBALLY COMPLAINING TO SOME OTHER THAN THE INTENDED RECIPIENT (or see grip)
gris,grease
grit,*,tted,tting,tty,ttier,ttiest,ttily,ttiness,GRANULES OF VARIETY OF MATERIAL, GROUND CORN (or see greet)
grit,greet
grital,griddle
gritle,griddle
grity,grit(tty)

gro,grow
groan,*,,ned,ning,MOAN FROM PAIN
grocery,ries,FOOD, NON-FOODS BOUGHT FROM STORE
grof,gruff / grove
groggy,gier,giest,ggily,gginess,NOT QUITE AWAKE, STUPOR
grombol,grumble
grone,groan
groof,groove
groom,*,,med,ming,mer,MALE GETTING MARRIED, TO CLEAN THE BODY
groove,*,,ed,ving,vv,vier,viest,vily,viness,LONG INDENTATION IN SOMETHING, GET IN-STEP TO BE COOL
grope,*,,ed,ping,per,TO AIMLESSLY ATTEMPT TO GRASP WITH HAND (or see group)
grosery,grocery
grosry,grocery
gross,sses,ssed,ssing,sser,ssest,ssly,ssness,SUM BEFORE EXPENDITURES, MEASUREMENT OF WEIGHT,DISTASTEFUL, REPULSIVE "prefixes: en"
grotesk,grotesque
grotesque,ely,eness,UGLY, DESPICABLE
groth,growth
grou,grow
grouch,hes,hy,hier,hiest,hy,hily,hiness,UNREASONABLY IRRITATED
grouf,grove
groul,growl
groun,groan / grown
ground,*,,ded,ding,der,dless,dlessly,dlessness,THE EARTH, FEET PLANTED SOLIDLY, BE ON THE EARTH'S SURFACE "prefixes: over/ under"
group,*,,ped,ping,per,pable,pie,TO PUT SIMILAR OBJECT, THINGS, PEOPLE TOGETHER "prefixes: re/ semi/ sub/ un"
grouse,*,GAME BIRD (or see gross)
grout,*,,ted,ting,ter,MORTAR FOR TILE/ STONE (or see growth)
grove,*,A FIELD WHERE TREES WITH EDIBLE FRUIT IS GROWN
grow,*,,wing,rew,wn,wth,GET BIGGER/ TALLER "prefixes: in/ over/ under"

growch,grouch
growl,*,,led,ling,ler,VERBAL WARNING COMING FROM DEEP IN THE THROAT
grown,PAST TENSE FOR THE WORD "GROW" (or see groan) "prefixes: in/ over/ under"
grownd,ground
grows,grow(s) / grouse / gross
growth,*,COMPARE SIZE OR AMOUNT OF SOMETHING GROWING "prefixes: in/ inter/ over/ up"
groz,gross / grow(s) / grouse
grub,*,bbed,bbing,bber,bby,bbier,bbiest,bbily,bbiness,SLANG FOR FOOD, DIRTY AND MESSY
grudch,grudge
grudge,*,,ed,ging,gingly,eless,er,WILL NOT FORGIVESOMEONE "prefixes: un"
gruel,*,,ling,RUNNY/ SLOPPY BOWL OF FOOD
grueling,gly,HARD AND TEDIOUS
gruesome,ely,eness,AWFUL
gruf,groove
grufete,graffiti
gruff,ffer,ffest,ffly,ffiness,RUDE AND ROUGH
grufiti,graffiti
grug,grudge
grugarious,gregarious
gruj,grudge
grumatical,grammatical
grumble,*,,ed,ling,LOW/ IRRITABLE MUMBLING, STOMACH SOUNDS WHEN HUNGRY
grundled,grunt(led)
grunola,granola
grunt,*,,ted,ting,tingly,tled,ANNOYED VERBAL RESPONSE, LOW-RANK WORKER "prefixes: dis"
grupe,group
grusome,gruesome
guady,gaudy
guage,gauge
guantlet,gauntlet
guarantee,*,,eed,eeing,tor,BACK UP A CLAIM, WITHOUT A DOUBT
guard,*,,ded,ding,dian,PROTECT AGAINST INVADER "prefixes: un"
guardian,*,,nship,PROTECTOR
guaze,gauze

gubalee,jubilee
gubelashen,jubilant(atior)
gubilation,jubilant(ation)
gud,good / gut
gud-by,good-bye
guder,gutter
guderal,guttural
gudge,judge
gudishal,judicial
gudishes,judicious
gudjment, judge(gment)
gudjmint, judge(gment)
gudo,judo
guds,goods / gut(s)
guel,jewel
guerrilla,*,PEOPLE WHO HIDE WHEN FIGHTING (or see gorilla)
guess,sses,ssed,ssing,sser,TAKE A GAMBLE AT THE PROPER ANSWER, DON'T KNOW ANSWER
guest,*,STAYING TEMPORARILY AT A PLACE THAT IS NOT YOURS (or see guess(ed))
gufener,governor
gufner,governor
gug,jug / judge
guggle,juggle
gugment, judge(gment)
gugmental, judge(gmental)
gugmint, judge(gment)
gugmintal, judge(gmental)
gugul,juggle
guidance,RECEIVE DIRECTION
guide,*,ded,ding,dance,SHOW THE WAY "prefixes: mis"
guil,jewel
guild,*, COOPERATIVE GROUP OF PEOPLE WITH A PARTICULAR INTEREST
guilt,ty,tier,tiest,tily, tiness, BEING OR FEELING RESPONSIBLE FOR AN ACTION
guineapig,*,TWO WORDS "GUINEA PIG", A RODENT
gujment, judge(gment)
gujmental, judge(gmental)
gujmint, judge(gment)
gujmintal, judge(gmental)
gul,gull / jewel / joule

gulactic,galactic
gulaktek,galactic
gulatnus,gelatin(ous)
guleble,gull(ible)
gull,*,llery,lled,lling,llible,llibility,llibly,TYPE OF BIRD,TO BE TRICKED/ DECEIVED
guloshes,galoshes
gulp,*,ped,ping,pingly,per,TAKE IN A LARGE MOUTHFUL
guly,july
gum,*,mmed,mming,my,mmier,mmiest,mmily,miness, SOMETHING CHEWABLE, RUBBERY, FROM A TREE
gumble,jumble
gump,jump
gun,*,nned,nning,nner,A FIRING WEAPON, TO STEP ON THE ACCELERATOR, TO SHOOT SOMEONE (or see goon/ june)
gune,june / goon
gungle,jungle
gungul,jungle
guniur,junior
gunk,junk
gunker,junk(er)
gunkie,junkie
gunkshen,junction
gunksher,juncture
gunyer,junior
guppy,ppies,FISH
gurbel,gerbil
gurd,gourd
gurder,girder
gure,jury
gurer,juror
guresdiction,jurisdiction
gurgle,*, ed,ling,SOUNDS COMING FROM THE THROAT, BUBBLING SOUND
guri,jury
gorilla,guerrilla / gorilla
gurk,jerk
gurl,girl
gurlfrend,girlfriend
gurm,germ
gurmenate,germinate

gurmet,gourmet
gurnelist,journal(ist)
gurney,*,A COT/ STRETCHER TO CARRY BODIES (or see journey)
gurnol,journal
gurter,girder
gurth,girth
gus,goose / juice
gusd,gust / just
gusdefecation,justify(fication)
gusdefiable,justifiable
gusdes,justice
gusdify,justify
guse,goose / juice
gusee,juicy
gush,hes,hed,hing,SPEW FORTH IN SUDDEN BURST
gusle,guzzle
gust,*, ted,ting,ty, tier, tiest, tily, tiness, BIG BLOWS IN BURSTS, ERRATIC / HIGH WINDS (or see just)
gustefy,justify
gustes,justice
gustification,justify(fication)
gut,*, tted, tting,INSIDES OF LIVING THINGS, TO REMOVE INSIDES (or see good/ jewt/ jut)
gute,jute
gutir,gutter
guto,judo
gutter,*,red,ring,ral,ALONG ROOFS FOR RAIN COLLECTION
guttural,*,lly, lity, lism, lness, lizes, lized, lizing, lization, TYPE OF SOUND MADE IN THE THROAT
guvernment,government
guviner,governor
guvinile,juvenile
guy,*, MALES, WIRE OR ROPE USED TO SUPPORT OR STEADY SOMETHING
guynacologist,gynecology(gist)
guzzle,*, ed,ling,er, RAPIDLY DRINK
gy,guy / eye / ice
gybrau,eyebrow
gym,*, mnast, mnasium,A PLACE TO WORK-OUT (or see gem) "prefixes: multi"

gymnasium, *, A BUILDING WHERE PEOPLE DO PHYSICAL ACTIVITIES
gymnast, *, tics, ONE WHO PRACTICES THE ART OF MANIPULATING THEIR BODIES
gyn, PREFIX INDICATING "FEMALE" MOST OFTEN MODIFIES THE WORD
gyne, PREFIX INDICATING "FEMALE" MOST OFTEN MODIFIES THE WORD
gynecology, gical, gist, THE SCIENCE OF, ONE WHO STUDIES WOMEN'S ORGANS
gyno, PREFIX INDICATING "FEMALE" MOST OFTEN MODIFIES THE WORD
gyp, *, ped, ping, TO CHEAT/ STEAL
gypsum, CHALKY ROCK
gypsy, sies, PEOPLE WHO CHOOSE TO BE ON THE FRINGE OF SOCIETY FOR WHATEVER REASON
gyrate, *, ed, ting, tion, TO SPIRAL "prefixes: multi"
ha, hay / hey
habachi, hibachi
habe, happy
haben, happen
habin, happen
habit, *, ted, ting, table, tability, tableness, tably, tant, tat, tation, tual, tuate, tuates, tuated, tuating, tuation, tude, tudinal, tus, DOING THE SAME THING OVER AND OVER
habitat, *, tation, tational, tor, NATURAL HOME FOR LIVING THINGS "prefixes: inter/ non"
habitual, *, lly, lness, ate, SOMEONE WHO DEALS WITH MANY HABITS
habochi, hibachi
haby, happy
hach, hatch / hash / hack
hachet, hatchet
hachit, hatchet
hack, *, ked, king, kies, ker, ktivate, ktivism, ktivist, TO ILLEGALLY ACCESS PRIVATE DATA ON COMPUTERS, CHOP AT
hactare, hectare
had, PAST TENSE FOR THE WORD "HAVE" (or see hat)
hade, hate
haden't, hadn't
hadint, hadn't

hadn't, CONTRACTION OF THE WORDS "HAD NOT"
hadur, hot(tter)
hael, howl
haf, half / have / halve
hafen, haven / heaven
hafhasert, haphazard
hafhazard, haphazard
hafhazurdle, haphazard(ly)
hafint, haven't
hafnt, haven't
hafun, haven / heaven / have(ving)
hagerd, haggard
haggard, *, dly, dness, ROUGH, WORN
haggle, *, ed, ling, er, DEBATING OVER PRICE/ CONTRACT
hagio, PREFIX INDICATING "HOLY " MOST OFTEN MODIFIES THE WORD
hagurd, haggard
haiku, *, FORM OF JAPANESE POETRY
hail, *, led, ling, ler, RAIN IN THE FORM OF ICE, LOUD VOCAL WELCOME (or see hale)
hainger, hanger
hainkerchef, handkerchief
hair, ry, rier, riest, riness, STRANDS OF WHICH GROW FROM THE SKIN (or see hare / heir/ harry)
hak, hawk / hack
hakd, hack(ed)
haker, hack(er)
haktare, hectare'
hal, PREFIX INDICATING "SALT/ HALOGEN" MOST OFTEN MODIFIES THE WORD (or see hall/ hale/ haul/ haul/ howl)
halagen, halogen
halagenic, halogen(ic)
halareus, hilarious
hale, *, ed, ling, er, est, eness, TO COMPLY, PULL/ DRAG SOMEONE/ SOMETHING (or see hall/ haul/ haul/ holly)
halegram, hologram
halekopter, helicopter
haleluya, hallelujah
half, lve, lves, WHOLE MADE INTO TWO PARTS (or see have / halve)
halfhasard, haphazard

halfhasurdly, haphazard(ly)
halibut, A FISH
haligen, halogen
haligenic, halogen(ic)
hall, *, NARROW CORRIDOR WITH DOORS INSIDE A BUILDING (or see hale/ haul/ hail/ hail)
hallelujah, *, REJOICE
halloween, *, A HOLIDAY
halm, helm
halo, *, lation, REFLECTS LITE COMING FROM WITHIN SOMEONE, PREFIX INDICATING "SALT/ HALOGEN" MOST OFTEN MODIFIES THE WORD (or see hollow/ hello)
halogen, *, nate, nates, nating, nation, nic, NONMETALLIC/ REACTIVE CHEMICALS, TYPE OF LIGHT SOURCE
halokost, holocaust
halow, hollow / halo
halowen, halloween
halp, help
halpful, helpful
halt, *, ted, ting, ter, STOP NOW (or see haul(ed))
halter, *, GEAR FOR A HORSE, A SHIRT
halubet, halibut
halugram, hologram
halve, *, ed, ving, TO SEPARATE ONE INTO TWO PARTS (or see have)
haly, holly
ham, *, mmed, mming, PORK, TO BE GOOFY
hamak, hammock
hambergur, hamburger
hamburger, *, BEEF GROUND UP
hamer, hammer
hamileate, humiliate
hammer, *, red, ring, rer, FORCE SOMETHING IN, HAND TOOL
hammock, *, WOVEN FABRIC STRETCHED BETWEEN TWO POINTS TO SIT OR LIE IN
homogenize, homogenize
hamper, *, red, ring, PUT CLOTHES INTO, GET IN THE WAY OF PROGRESS
hamster, *, A RODENT
hamuk, hammock
hamur, hammer

hand, *, ded, ding, dful, dy, AT THE END OF THE ARM WITH FINGERS ON IT "prefixes: over/ ur/ under"
hande, handy
handeist, handy(diest)
handel, handle
handeur, handy(dier)
handicap, *, pped, pping, pper, UNABLE TO FUNCTION AT FULL CAPACITY, CHALLENGED "prefixes: multi"
handil, handle
handkerchief, *, SQUARE CLOTH
handle, *, ed, ling, er, FOR HANDS OR WITH HANDS "prefixes: mis"
handmade, MADE BY HAND NOT BY MACHINE
handout, *, GIVE SOMETHING TO SOMEONE IN NEED
handsome, ely, eness, GOOD LOOKING, SIZABLE AMOUNT/ BENEFITS
handul, handle
handy, dier, diest, SOMETHING EASILY AVAILABLE
hang, *, ged, ging, ger, SECURE SOMETHING ABOVE THE FLOOR ALLOWING FOR A VERTICAL POSITION "prefixes: over"
hangar, *, PLACE FOR LARGE TRANSPORTATION VESSELS (or see hanger)
hanger, *, FOR SUSPENSION OFF THE GROUND (or see hangar)
hank, hang
hankerchief, handkerchief
hansome, handsome
hant, hand
hantecap, handicap
hantel, handle
hantil, handle
hantmade, handmade
hantowt, handout
hantul, handle
hanty, handy
haord, horde / hoard
hapale, happy(pily)
hape, happy
hapeir, happy(pier)
hapeist, happy(piest)
hapele, happy(pily)
hapen, happen

hapenes, happy(piness)
hapeur, happy(pier)
haphazard, dly, dness, dous, dously, DO THINGS UNSAFELY, DISORGANIZED
hapie, happy
hapile, happy(pily)
hapin, happen
hapines, happy(piness)
happen, *, ned, ning, AN EVENT THAT HAS OCCURRED
happy, ppier, ppiest, ppily, ppiness, BEING JOYFUL IN LIFE "prefixes: un"
hapule, happy(pily)
hapun, happen
hapy, happy
hapyer, happy(pier)
hapyest, happy(piest)
hapynes, happy(piness)
har, hair / heir / hare
harass, sses, ssed, ssing, ssment, AGGRAVATE BEYOND NORMAL
haray, hurrah
harbor, *, red, ring, rer, rless, rage, WHERE BOATS DOCK, HOLD ONTO
hard, der, dest, den, dener, dy, CHALLENGING, DENSE, SOLID (or see heart) "prefixes: semi"
hardily, heart(ily)
hardin, hard(en)
hardles, heartless
hardly, BARELY, NOT QUITE
hardship, *, TOUGH TIMES
hardware, *, TOOLS, USE TO BUILD WITH, REPAIR MATERIAL
hardy, dier, diest, dily, diness, STRONG AND CAPABLE
hardyness, hardy(diness)
hare, *, A WILD RABBIT (or see hair/ harry/ here)
haredetary, hereditary
haredity, heredity
harefy, horrify
harendus, horrendous
harer, horror
haretitary, hereditary
haretity, heredity
hareur, hair(ier)

hareust, hair(iest)
harfest, harvest
harfik, horrify(fic)
harindus, horrendous
harison, horizon
harm, *, med, ming, mful, mfully, mfulness, mless, mlessly, mlessness, TO INJURE "prefixes: un"
harmeny, harmony
harmfel, harm(ful)
harmlis, harm(less)
harmonica, *, MUSICAL INSTRUMENT
harmonize, *, ed, zing, er, zation, SYNCHRONIZE SOUNDS
harmony, nies, nic, nically, nious, niously, niousness, nist, nium, nize, nizes, nized, nizing, nizable, nization, nizer, VARIETY OF DIFFERENT SOUNDS VIBRATING AT A COMPATIBLE FREQUENCY "prefixes: dis/ en/ in/ re/ sub/ un"
harmuny, harmony
harness, sses, ssed, ssing, sser, HOLD ONTO "prefixes: un"
haroen, heroin / hero(ine)
haroik, hero(ic)
haroin, heroin / hero(ine)
haron, heron / heroin / hero(ine)
harp, *, ped, ping, per, pist, MUSICAL INSTRUMENT, TO NAG
harpoon, *, ned, ning, ner, TO STAB WITH A LONG METAL POLE WITH BARB ON THE END
harpsichord, *, A MUSICAL INSTRUMENT
harry, rries, rried, rrying, WAR PILLAGE/ RAID, STRESS/ DISTRESS (or see hair/ hare)
harsh, her, hest, hly, hness, STERN AND ROUGH
hart, *, MALE DEER (or see hard/ heart)
harteist, heart(iest) / hard(iest)
harteur, heart(ier) / hard(ier)
harth, hearth
hartily, heart(ily)
hartiness, hardy(diness)
hartles, heartless
hartly, hardly
hartship, hardship
hartware, hardware
harty, heart / hardy

haruble,horrible
harvest,*,ed,ting,ter,BRING IN RIPENED FOOD
harwer,hardware
hary,hair / harry
has,ACQUIRED (or see have)
hasard,hazard
hase,haze / haze
hasel,hassle / hazel
hasen,hasten
hash,hes,hed,hing,hish,A FOOD,TO TALK IT OVER
hasil,hassle
hasn't,CONTRACTION OF THE WORDS "HAS NOT"
haspitality,hospitality
hassle,*,ed,ling,TO AGITATE
haste,*,ed,ting,en,ened,ening,ty,tier,tiest,tily,tiness,DO IT QUICKLY
hasten,ned,ning,TO SPEED UP
hasul,hassle / hazel
hat,*,COVERING FOR HEAD (or see had/ hate)
hatch,hes,hed,hing,hling,COVER OF STORAGE AREA, LIVE THINGS COMING FROM EGGS
hatchet,*,SMALL AX
hate,*,ed,ting,eful,efully,efulness,eable,er,tred,MOST OPPOSITE FROM LOVE (or see haughty/ hot)
haud,hod / hot / haul(ed)
haude,hod(ddie) / haughty / hood / hot(ttie)
hauder,hot(tter)
hauefur,however
haughty,tier,tiest,tily,tiness,ACTING AS IF BETTER THAN OTHERS
hauk,hawk / hock
haul,*,led,ling,ler,lage,TRANSPORT A LOAD (or see hall) "prefixes: in/ over"
hauleluea,hallelujah
haulo,hollow / wallow
haulter,halter / alter
haultur,halter
haunch,hes,hed,hless,REAR LEGS ON ANIMALS,ARCH
haund,hound
haunt,*,ted,ting,tingly,ter,TO SPOOK
haups,hops
haured,horrid
haurur,horror

haus,house
hausd,house(d)
hauspus,hospice
haustej,hostage
haustel,hostel / hostile
haustig,hostage
haut,hot / hod
haute,haughty / hod(ddie) / hood / hot(ttie)
hauty,haughty / hod(ddie) / hood / hot(ttie)
hauvel,hovel
hauztul,hostel / hostile
hav,halve / have / half
havd,halve(d)
have,TO POSSESS,ACQUIRE (or see half/ halve)
haven,*,A SAFE PLACE (or see heaven/ have(ving))
haven't,CONTRACTION OF THE WORDS "HAVE NOT"
havin,haven / heaven
havint,haven't
havs,halve(s)
havun,haven / heaven
haw,how
hawever,however
hawk,*,A BIRD (or see hock)
hawl,howl / haul
hawle,holly
hawnd,hound
hawnt,hound
hawvul,hovel
hay,*,yed,ying,DRY GRASS,ALFALFA,WORKING WITH HAY (or see hey)
haz,has / haze
hazard,*,ded,ding,dous,dously,dousness,DANGEROUS "prefixes: bio"
haze,*,ed,zing,zy,zier,ziest,zily,ziness,SMOKE,MIST, DUST,BLURRY
hazel,A PLANT,A COLOR (or see hassle)
haznt,hasn't
hazurd,hazard
he,A MALE
he'd,CONTRACTION OF THE WORDS "HE COULD, HE SHOULD,HE WOULD, HE HAD"
he'll,CONTRACTION OF THE WORDS "HE WILL" (or see hell/ heal/ heel)

he's,CONTRACTION OF THE WORDS "HE IS"
head,*,ded,ding,der,dy,dsier,diest,dily,diness,BODY PART ON TOP OF SHOULDERS,ON TOP OF,LEADING "prefixes: multi/ over/ sub"
heal,*,led,ling,ler,lable,TO CURE,SOMEONE WHO CURES,MEND (or see heel/ he'll)
health,hy,hier,hiest,hily,hiness,hful,hfully,hfulness,OF SOUND BODY/ MIND "prefixes: un"
heap,*,ped,ping,TO MOUND UP
hear,*,ring,rd,SOUND IN EARS (or see here) "prefixes: over"
heard,PAST TENSE FOR "HEAR" (or see herd) "prefixes: un"
hearsay,GOSSIP
hearse,A VEHICLE FOR MOVING CASKETS
hearst,hearse
heart,*,ty,tier,tiest,tily,tiness,tless,tlessly,tlessness,AN ORGAN IN A BODY (or see hard) "prefixes: dis"
hearth,*,SURROUNDING A FIREPLACE "prefixes: multi"
heartless,ssly,ssness,CRUEL
heat,*,ted,tedly,tedness,ting,er,tless,WARM,FOR MAKING WARM (or see heed/ he'd) "prefixes: over/ un"
heave,*,ed,ving,TO THRUST SOMETHING HEAVY USING FORCE
heaven,*,nly,nlier,nliest,nliness,A EUPHORIC STATE OF MIND,DIVINE
heavy,vier,viest,vily,viness,OF GREAT WEIGHT
hebachi,hibachi
hebapotamus,hippopotamus
hebnutize,hypnotize
heckle,*,ed,ling,er,ANNOYING NOISES/ WORDS AIMED AT A SPEAKER
hecksugon,hexagon
heckup,hiccup
hectare,*,METRIC MEASUREMENT,2.5 ACRES
hectic,cally,CONFUSING RUSH
hecto,PREFIX INDICATING "ONE HUNDRED" MOST OFTEN MODIFIES THE WORD
hed,head / hit / he'd / heat / heed
hedch,hitch / hedge
hedeus,hideous
hedge,*,ed,ging,BUSHES,TO TRIM BY CUTTING

hedid, heed(ed) / head(ed) / head(ed)
hedud, heed(ed) / head(ed) / head(ed)
heed,*,,ded,ding,PAY ATTENTION,TAKE NOTICE OF (or see heat/ he'd/ heat) "prefixes: un"
heef, heave
heel,*,,led,ling,PART OF THE FOOT (or see heal/ he'll)
heep, heap
heet, heat
hefen, heaven
hefer, heifer
hefon, heaven
hefur, heifer
hefy, heavy
heg, hedge
heifer,*,,IMMATURE COW
height,*,,ten,tens,tened,tening,tener,MEASURE TOP TO BOTTOM,MAKE TALLER
heigth, height
heimlek, heimlich
heimlich,A MANEUVER WHICH CLEARS WINDPIPE FOR BREATHING
heir,*,,rless,rship,ress,ONE WHO RECEIVES MONEY/ PROPERTY BEQUEATHED TO THEM UPON SOMEONES DEATH (or see hair/ air/ err)
heirarchy, hierarch
heirloom,*,,SOMETHING PRECIOUS HANDED DOWN TO FOLLOWING GENERATIONS
heiroglyph, hieroglyph
heis, haze / haste / guess
heist,*,,ted,ting,ter,THEFT,ROBBERY (or see haste)
heiten, height(en)
heith, height
heithen, height(en)
hej, hedge
heks, hex
heksigon, hexagon
heksugon, hexagon
hektare, hectare'
hektik, hectic
hekul, heckle
hekup, hiccup
hel, heel / hell / heal / he'll / hill
helakopter, helicopter

helareus, hilarious
held,PAST TENSE FOR THE WORD "HOLD"
heleom, helium
helicopter,*,,FLYING MACHINE
helio,PREFIX INDICATING "SUN" MOST OFTEN MODIFIES THE WORD
helium,A GAS
hell,*,,lled,lling,llish,llishly,llishness,llion,AN IMAGINARY PLACE OF GREAT DISCOMFORT (or see he'll/ heal/ heel)
hello,*,,AMERICAN GREETING
helm,*,,STEERING PART OF A BOAT
helmet,*,,ted,A PROTECTIVE COVER FOR THE HEAD
helo, hello
help,*,,ped,ping,pings,pful,per,pless,SOMEONE/ SOMETHING BEING AIDED
helpd, help(ed)
helpful,lly,lness,THOSE WHO AID OTHERS "prefixes: un"
helpfulnes, helpful(ness)
helpless,ssly,ssness,UNABLE TO AID ONESELF
helpt, help(ed)
helt, held / hilt
helth, health
hem,*,,mmed,mming,HAVING TO DO WITH BORDERS ON THINGS (or see him/ hymn)
hema,PREFIX INDICATING "BLOOD" MOST OFTEN MODIFIES THE WORD
hemarag, hemorrhage
hemaroid, hemorrhoids
hemat,PREFIX INDICATING "BLOOD" MOST OFTEN MODIFIES THE WORD
hemato,PREFIX INDICATING "BLOOD" MOST OFTEN MODIFIES THE WORD
hemerag, hemorrhage
hemeroid, hemorrhoids
hemi,BRAND NAME,PREFIX INDICATING "HALF" MOST OFTEN MODIFIES THE WORD
hemirag, hemorrhage
hemisphere,*,,ric,rical,rically,ONE HALF OF EARTH
hemmaroid, hemorrhoids
hemmoroid, hemorrhoids
hemo,PREFIX INDICATING "BLOOD" MOST OFTEN MODIFIES THE WORD

hemorag, hemorrhage
hemoroid, hemorrhoids
hemorrhage,*,,ed,ging,gic,VALUABLE/ UNCONTROLLABLE LOSS
hemorrhoids,dal,dectomy,VARICOSE VEINS IN ANUS
hemosfere, hemisphere
hemp,*,,A PLANT USEFUL FOR CLOTHING/ MATERIAL/ ROPE/ PAPER
hemself, himself
hemurag, hemorrhage
hemuroid, hemorrhoids
hen,*,,FEMALE CHICKEN
hena, henna
hence,*,,THEREFORE,AND SO
hender, hinder
hendrance, hindrance
henge, hinge
henje, hinge
henna,PLANT FOR DYING HAIR/ FABRIC,FOR TEMPORARY TATTOOS
hens, hen(s) / hence
hent, hint
hep, heap / hip
hepabotamus, hippopotamus
hepacrite, hypocrite
hepakrete, hypocrite
hepatitis,ILLNESS CAUSED BY VIRUS
hepnosis, hypnosis
hepnutize, hypnotize
hepobotamus, hippopotamus
hepokrite, hypocrite
hepopotamus, hippopotamus
hepothesis, hypothesis
hept,PREFIX INDICATING "SEVEN" MOST OFTEN MODIFIES THE WORD
hepta,PREFIX INDICATING "SEVEN" MOST OFTEN MODIFIES THE WORD
hepy, hip(py)
her,*,,IN REFERRING TO A FEMALE (or see hear/ here/ hair/ hare/ heir)
heracane, hurricane
herass, harass

herb, *, bed, bal, balism, balist, baceous, baceously, bage, bivore, PLANTS FOR HEALING/ COOKING WITH (THE "JUDGMENTAL" IS SILENT)
herbavor, herbivore
herbivore, *, rous, PLANT EATING ANIMAL (THE "JUDGMENTAL" IS SILENT)
herbulist, herb(alist)
herd, *, ded, ding, der, ANIMALS GATHERED INTO A GROUP FOR MOVING (or see heard/ hurt)
herdle, hurdle / hurtle
herdul, hurdle / hurtle
here, *, IN THIS VICINITY, WHERE YOU ARE (or see hear/ hair/ hare/ harry)
hered, hurry(ried)
hereditary, rily, riness, ABLE TO BE PASSED ON FROM ONE GENERATION TO ANOTHER
heredity, table, tability, tament, tarian, tarianism, tary, tarily, tariness, PASSED DOWN THROUGH GENERATIONS
hereist, hair(iest)
herendus, horrendous
heresay, hearsay
hereur, hair(ier)
hericane, hurricane
herison, horizon
herizun, horizon
herl, hurle
hermetic, cal, cally, PROTECTED/ AIRTIGHT ENVIRONMENT
hermit, *, tic, tical, tically, A RECLUSE, CRUSTACEAN
hernia, *, al, ABDOMINAL MUSCLE PROBLEM
hero, oes, oic, oics, oical, oically, oicalness, oine, oines, oism, BRAVE ACT TO SAVE SOMETHING FROM PERIL OR DEATH
heroek, hero(ic)
heroin, MANMADE DRUG TO EASE PAIN, ADDICTIVE (or see hero(ine))
heron, *, A BIRD (or see heroin/ hero(ine))
hers, hearse / her(s) / here(s) / hear(s)
herself, SHE ALONE, FEMALE SELF
herst, hearse
hert, hurt / heard / herd
hertful, hurt(ful)

herth, hearth
hertle, hurdle / hurtle
hertul, hurdle / hurtle
hery, hair / hurry / harry
herz, hearse / her(s) / here(s) / hear(s)
hes, his / hiss / he's
hesatashen, hesitate(tion)
hesatation, hesitate(tion)
hesderical, hysterical
hesdorean, historian
hesdorik, historic
hesdory, history
hesdurekteme, hysterectomy
hesetashen, hesitate(tion)
hesetation, hesitate(tion)
hesitant, tly, nce, ncy, tate, tation, PAUSE TO CONSIDER BEFORE CONTINUING, CONSIDERING BEFORE STARTING
hesitashen, hesitate(tion)
hesitate, *, ted, ting, tingly, tant, tantly, tation, tive, er, TAKE A PAUSE BEFORE CONTINUING "prefixes: un"
hesterektomy, hysterectomy
hesterical, hysterical
hestorian, historian
hestorical, historic(al)
hestorik, historic
hestory, history
hesutashen, hesitate(tion)
hesutation, hesitate(tion)
het, head / hit / he'd / heat / heed
hetch, hitch
hetero, PREFIX INDICATING "OTHER/ DIFFERENT" MOST OFTEN MODIFIES THE WORD
heteus, hideous
hetid, heed(ed) / heat(ed) / head(ed)
hetud, heed(ed) / heat(ed) / head(ed)
heu, hue / who
heug, huge
heuj, huge
heumen, human
heve, heave / heavy
hevin, heaven
hevy, heavy

hew, hue / who
hewman, human / humane
hewmer, humor
hewmid, humid
hewmileate, humiliate
hex, xes, xed, xing, xer, xagon, CURSE, A COMPUTATION, PREFIX INDICATING "SIX" MOST OFTEN MODIFIES THE WORD
hexagon, *, nal, SIX-SIDED FIGURE/ SHAPE
hey, AN EXCLAMATION FOR GREETING/ FOR SURPRISE, WAY OF GREETING (or see hay)
hezetante, hesitant
hezitate, hesitate
hezutashen, hesitate(tion)
hi, A WELCOME GREETING (or see high)
hiarchy, hierarch
hibachi, *, ROUND COOKING GRILL
hiberacteve, hyperactive
hibernate, *, ed, ting, tion, tor, SLEEP OVER THE WINTER
hibochi, hibachi
hibopotamus, hippopotamus
hibred, hybrid
hibrud, hybrid
hiccup, *, pped, pping, THROAT MUSCLE IN TEMPORARY SPASM
hid, dden, IN HIDING, PAST TENSE FOR THE WORD "HIDE", STORED FROM EYESIGHT (or see hide/ height/ hit)
hidch, hitch / hedge
hide, *, ding, TO STORE FROM EYESIGHT, SKIN OFF OF ANIMAL (or see hid/ height/ hit)
hiden, hid(dden)
hideous, sly, sness, FRIGHTFULLY UGLY
hideout, *, WHERE SOMEONE GOES TO HIDE
hidout, hideout
hidrant, hydrant
hidrashen, hydrate(tion)
hidrat, hydrate
hidration, hydrate(tion)
hidrent, hydrant
hidroelectric, hydroelectric
hidrophonic, hydroponic
hidroponic, hydroponic

hidrugen,hydrogen
hierarch,*,hy,hies,hic,hical,hically,hize,hizes,hized,hizing,hization,OF FORMAL RANK
hieroglyph,*,hic,CARVED,PAINTED SYMBOLS FROM PAST PEOPLES
hiest,heist
hif,hive
hifen,hyphen
hifenate,hyphen(ate)
hifer,heifer
hifin,hyphen
higene,hygiene
higenist,hygiene(nist)
high,*,her,hest,hly,hness,ALTITUDE BETWEEN THE GROUND AND SPACE, A EUPHORIC SENSE UNDER THE INFLUENCE OF A HALLUCINOGEN (or see hi)
hight,height
hijack,*,ked,king,ker,TAKE VEHICLE/ VESSEL BY FORCE
hijene,hygiene
hike,*,ked,king,ker,TO WALK ON ROUGH/ NATURAL TERRAIN
hikoo,haiku
hiku,haiku
hikup,hiccup
hilarious,sly,sness,ity,ABSOLUTELY FUNNY
hill,*,lled,lling,ller,lly,MOUNDS ON THE EARTH (or see he'll) "prefixes: up"
hilt,*,SWORD OR DAGGER HANDLE, COMPLETELY AND ABSOLUTELY
him,REFERENCE TO MALE OVER THERE, MALE/ THIRD PERSON (or see hem/ hymn)
himarag,hemorrhage
himaroid,hemorrhoids
hime,hemi
himeroid,hemorrhoids
himesfere,hemisphere
himesphere,hemisphere
himiroid,hemorrhoids
himlek,heimlich
himluk,heimlich
himoroid,hemorrhoids
himp,hemp
himself,HIS OWN SELF

himuroid,hemorrhoids
hin,hen
hince,hence
hinch,hinge
hind,THE REAR PORTION OF AN ANIMAL
hinder,*,red,ring,rer,drance,IN THE WAY OF PROGRESS OR SUCCESS "prefixes: un"
hindrance,*,IN THE WAY OF PROGRESS/ SUCCESS
hinge,*,ed,ging,eless,SWINGS BY WAY OF A PIN ENCASED IN A HINGE "prefixes: un"
hinje,hinge
hinse,hence
hint,*,ted,ting,tingly,TINY PORTION OF THE FULL FACT
hip,*,pper,ppest,pply,pness,ppy,ppier,ppiest,THE PELVIC AREA ON PEOPLE/ ANIMALS, TO BE COOL/ INDIFFERENT TO SOCIAL PRESSURE
hipadrete,hypocrite
hipapotamus,hippopotamus
hipatidus,hepatitis
hipauthusis,hypothesis
hipawthusis,hypothesis
hipe,hype / hip
hiperactive,hyperactive
hiperactuve,hyperactive
hipernate,hibernate
hipnosis,hypnosis
hipnosus,hypnosis
hipnutise,hypnotize
hipocrite,hypocrite
hipokrit,hypocrite
hipopotamus,hippopotamus
hipotenuse,hypotenuse
hipothurmeu,hypothermia
hipothusis,hypothesis
hippopotamus,*,LARGE/ HEAVY HERBIVORE
hir,her / hire / here
hiracane,hurricane
hirarchy,hierarch
hirass,harass
hird,heard / herd / hurt / hire(d)
hirdul,hurdle / hurtle
hire,*,ed,ring,rable,er,PAID TO WORK (or see high(er))
hirison,horizon

hirl,hurle
hirmet,hermit
hirmetic,hermetic
hiro,hero
hiroek,hero(ic)
hiroglif,hieroglyph
hiroin,hero(ine) / heroin
hirs,hearse / her(s) / hire(s)
hirself,herself
hirst,hearse
hirt,hurt / heard / herd
hirtul,hurdle / hurtle
hirz,her(s) / hearse / hire(s)
his,BELONGS TO HIM (or see hiss)
hisdarecal,hysterical
hisderektomy,hysterectomy
hisdorean,historian
hisdoric,historic
hisdurekteme,hysterectomy
hiself,himself
hiss,sses,ssed,ssing,ssy,sser,SOUND A SNAKE/ STEAM MAKES (or see his)
hisself,himself
hist,PREFIX INDICATING "LIVING TISSUE" MOST OFTEN MODIFIES THE WORD
histare,history
histarical,hysterical
histere,history
histerical,hysterical
histo,PREFIX INDICATING "LIVING TISSUE" MOST OFTEN MODIFIES THE WORD
historian,*,PEOPLE WELL STUDIED IN HISTORY
historic,cal,calness,cally,city,cize,cizes,cized,cizing,ize,izes,ized,izing,izingly,ry,izedly,iographer,ization,iography,EVENT ABOUT THE PAST "prefixes: pre"
history,ries,ric,ricism,rize,ricization,riography,ABOUT THE PAST "prefixes: pre"
histrektomy,hysterectomy
histure,history
histurektemy,hysterectomy
hit,*,tting,ttable,tter,STRIKE A BLOW (or see height/ hid/ hide) "prefixes: over"

hitch, hes, hed, hing, JOIN TWO THINGS TOGETHER BY WAY OF (or see hedge) "prefixes: un"
hite, height / hide
hiten, height(en) / hid(dden)
hiteout, hideout
hiteus, hideous
hith, height
hithen, height(en)
hitout, hideout
hitrashen, hydrate(tion)
hitrate, hydrate
hitun, height(en)
hive, *, BUMPS ON A PERSON, HOME OF BEES OR WASPS
ho, hoe / who / hue
hoard, *, ded, ding, der, TO STOCKPILE MORE GOODS THAN NECESSARY (or see horde)
hoarse, er, rest, ely, eness, en, ens, ened, ening, VOICE/ THROAT IS RASPY/ ROUGH (or see horse)
hoax, xes, A TRICK IN DECEPTION
hob, gob
hobble, *, ed, ling, WALK WITH A LIMP
hobby, bies, A PASTTIME
hobe, hope / hobby
hobful, hope(ful)
hobil, hobble
hobless, hope(less)
hobt, hop(pped) / hope(d)
hobul, hobble
hoby, hobby
hock, *, ked, king, CUT OF MEAT/ LEG, TO PAWN ITEMS (or see hawk/ hog/ hokey)
hockey, A SKATING SPORT (or see hokey)
hocky, hokey / hockey
hod, *, ddie, HOLDER FOR MORTAR (or see hot/ hold/ hood)
hode, haughty / hod(ddie) / hood
hodel, hotel
hoder, hot(tter)
hodir, hot(tter)
hody, haughty
hoe, *, ed, oing, A HAND TOOL (or see whole/ whore)
hoest, hoist
hof, huff

hofel, hovel
hofer, hover
hoful, hovel
hofur, hover
hog, *, gged, gging, A PIG, SOMEONE WHO EATS LIKE A PIG
hoist, *, ted, ting, LIFT OR RAISE UP
hok, hawk / hock / hog
hokey, kier, kiest, yness, kily, CORNY, NOT REALISTIC (or see hockey)
hoks, hoax / hock(s)
hoky, hockey / hokey
hol, hole / whole / haul / hall
hold, *, ding, dings, held, der, KEEP FROM MOVING/ FALLING, TO GRASP, KEEP STILL (or see haul(ed)) "prefixes: in/ up"
holder, *, SOMETHING THAT HOLDS THINGS
hole, *, ed, ling, AN OPENING/ SPACE/ ORIFICE/ GAP (or see holy/ holly/ whole/ wholly)
holegram, hologram
holeist, holy(liest)
holer, holler / haul(er) / hollow
holeur, holy(lier)
holey, wholly / whole / holy
holi, holy / holly / whole / wholly
holiday, *, A DAY OF REMEMBRANCE/ HONORING SOMEONE/ EVENT
holigram, hologram
holl, hall / haul / whole / hole
holler, *, red, ring, YELLING/ CALLING LOUDLY
hollow, *, wed, wing, wly, wness, TO DIG/ CARVE OUT SO INSIDE IS EMPTY (or see halo/ haul(er))
holly, lies, PLANT (or see holy/ hole/ whole/ wholly)
holo, PREFIX INDICATING "WHOLE" MOST OFTEN MODIFIES THE WORD (or see hollow/ hello)
holocaust, *, DEVASTATING DESTRUCTION OF PEOPLE/ PLACES
hologram, *, A THREE DIMENSIONAL ILLUSION, VISUAL REFLECTED BY LASERS
holow, hollow
holoween, halloween
holsal, wholesale
holsel, wholesale

holsem, wholesome
holsome, wholesome
holster, *, HOLDER FOR A PISTOL
holsum, wholesome
holt, hold / halt / haul(ed)
holter, halter / hold(er)
holuday, holiday
hologram, hologram
holur, holler
holy, lier, liest, liness, lism, listic, listically, SACRED (or see hole/ holly/ wholly/ hole/ whole) "prefixes: un"
hom, whom / home
homade, homemade
home, *, ey, ely, elier, eliest, eliness, eless, elessness, STRUCTURE WHERE SOMEONE LIVES
homeless, ssness, HAVING NO HOME
homely, PERSON WHO IS WITHDRAWN/ SHY
homemade, NOT MADE BY A MACHINE IN A FACTORY
homeny, hominy
homeo, PREFIX INDICATING "THE SAME" MOST OFTEN MODIFIES THE WORD
homer, *, HOME RUN IN BASEBALL
homevur, whomever
homey, HOME BOY
hominy, GROUND CORN
homir, homer
homless, homeless
homly, homely
homo, PREFIX INDICATING "THE SAME" MOST OFTEN MODIFIES THE WORD
homogenize, *, ed, zing, zation, er, CREAM/ MILK MIXED TOGETHER
homogenous, sly, sness, SIMILAR/ UNIFORM TO, THE SAME AS
homur, homer
homy, homey
honch, haunch / hunch
hond, hone(d) / haunt / hound
hondred, hundred
hone, *, ed, ning, er, TO SHARPEN (or see honey)
honemoon, honeymoon
honemun, honeymoon
honer, honor

honerary, honorary
honest, ty, ties, tly, tness, TRUTHFUL ("JUDGMENTAL" IS SILENT) "prefixes: dis"
honet, hundred
honey, *, ed, ying, A LIQUID FROM NECTAR MADE BY BEES
honeymoon, *, ned, ning, ners, WHAT A COUPLE HAS AFTER THEIR WEDDING
honimoon, honeymoon
honimun, honeymoon
honist, honest
honit, hundred
honk, *, ked, king, A HORN SOUND, SOUND A GOOSE MAKES
honker, hunk(er) / honk
honor, *, red, ring, rer, rless. rable, rably, rableness, rarium, rary, ree, rific, RESPECT. STRONG MORAL INTEGRITY "prefixes: dis/ re"
honorary, AWARD OF HONOR
hont, haunt / hone(d) / hunt
hontred, hundred
honur, honor
honymoon, honeymoon
hoo, hue / who
hood, *, ded, ding, dless, dly, JACKET / HAT COMBINATION, ENGINE COVER ON CAR, IN THE NEIGHBORHOOD (or see hoot/ who'd)
hooever, whomever
hoof, *, fed, fing, fer, oves, oved, FEET OF SOME ANIMALS
hook, *, ked, king, A CURVED TOOL WITH SHARP TIP FOR GRABBING "prefixes: un"
hoomever, whomever
hoop, *, ped, ping, THINGS THAT ARE A CIRCLE USED AS A TOOL/ TOY (or see hop)
hooray, hurrah
hoos, who's / whose / hue(s)
hoot, *, ted, ting, ter, SOUND OWL MAKES, FOND EXPRESSION TOWARDS SOMEONE (or see hood/ who'd)
hoove, *, ed, MORE THAN ONE HOOF
hop, *, pped, pping, ppy, JUMP UP AND DOWN LIKE A RABBIT, A PLANT (or see hope)
hopd, hop(pped) / hope(d)

hope, *, ed, ping, er, eful, efully, efulness, eless, elessly, elessness, WISH FOR SOMETHING (or see hop/ hops/ hobby)
hopful, hope(ful)
hopless, hope(less)
hops, A PLANT (or see hope(s))
hopscotch, GAME
hopskoch, hopscotch
hor, hour / horror / whore
horable, horrible
horafid, horrify(fied)
horascope, horoscope
hord, hoard / hard / horde / horrid
horde, *, ed, ding, MANY THINGS/ PEOPLE ALL TOGETHER AT ONCE, SWARMS OF (or see hoard/ hard/ hardy/ horrid)
hordervs, hors d'oevres
hordurves, hors d'oevres
horeble, horrible
hored, hoard / horrid / horde
horefik, horrify(fic)
horefy, horrify
horendous, horrendous
horer, horror
horescope, horoscope
horir, horror
horiscope, horoscope
horizon, *, nal, ntal, WHERE THE SUN/ MOON RISES/ SETS
horizontal, *, lly, lness, lity, POSITION SITUATED LINEAR WITH THE HORIZON
hormeny, harmony
hormful, harm(ful)
hormles, harm(less)
hormone, *, nal, nally, HEMICALS MANUFACTURED BY THE BODY (pineal gland) "prefixes: pro"
hormuny, harmony
horn, *, ned, ning, ny, INSTRUMENT PLAYED BY BLOWING, USED FOR SOUND ON VEHICLES AND VESSELS
horne, horny

hornet, *, LARGE VOLATILE WASP
horny, MADE OF HORN, SLANG FOR CERTAIN DESIRES
horoscope, *, pic, USING THE STARS TO GUESS THE FUTURE
horrendous, sness, sly, TERRIBLE, DREADFUL
horrible, ly, eness, AWFUL, UGLY, HORRENDOUS
horrid, dly, dness, HORROR, DREADFUL, OFFENSIVE
horrify, fies, fied, fying, fyingly, fication, fic, ror, VERY FRIGHTENING, BEYOND SCARY
horror, *, OVERPOWERING/ UNIMAGINABLE FEAR
horsd'oevres, TWO WORDS 'hors d'oevres', APPETIZERS
horse, *, ed, sing, ANIMAL(or see hoarse/ horror) "prefixes: un"
hort, horde / hard
horte, horde / hardy
horuble, horrible
horufid, horrify(fied)
horufy, horrify
horur, horror
horuscope, horoscope
horusontel, horizontal
hos, hoe(s) / hose / who's / hue(s) / whose
hosbedul, hospital
hosbetality, hospitality
hosbidul, hospital
hosbitality, hospitality
hosbituble, hospitable
hosbitul, hospital
hosdege, hostage
hosdej, hostage
hosdel, hostel / hostile
hosdij, hostage
hosdul, hostel / hostile
hose, *, ed, sing, RUBBER TUBE(or see whose/ who's)
hospetable, hospitable
hospetality, hospitality
hospetul, hospital
hospice, *, LODGING FOR TRAVELERS, PROGRAM FOR PATIENTS
hospitable, ly, leness, KIND/ FRIENDLY TO GUESTS
hospital, *, lize, lized, lizing, lization, PLACE FOR SICK/ INJURED PEOPLE "prefixes: multi/ post"
hospitality, ties, KINDNESS TO GUESTS

host,*,ted,ting,tess,TO SPONSOR,ONE WHO ENTERTAINS/ IS IN CHARGE	
hostage,*,PERSON HELD AGAINST THEIR WILL	
hostel,*,ler,ling,lry,SHELTERS AROUND THE WORLD WHERE TRAVELING PEOPLE MAY STAY CHEAPLY (or see hostile)	
hoster,holster	
hostes,host(ess)	
hostige,hostage	
hostile,lity,lities,ACTS AGGRESSIVE/ ANGRY (or see hostel)	
hostis,host(ess)	
hostle,hostile / hostel	
hostul,hostel / hostile	
hostus,host(ess)	
hot,tter,ttest,ttie,CAN BURN, WARMER THAN WARM,IN REFERENCE TO SOMEONE VERY ATTRACTIVE (or see hod/ hold/ hood/ hoot/ who'd)	
hote,haughty / hod(ddie) / hold / hood / hot(ttie)	
hotel,*,BUILDINGS WITH ROOMS FOR TRAVELERS TO STAY THE NIGHT	
hoter,hot(tter)	
hotur,hot(tter)	
hoty,haughty / hod(ddie) / hood / hot(ttie)	
houefur,however	
houl,howl / haul	
hound,*,ded,ding,TO AGITATE SOMEONE, BE PERSISTENT LIKE A HOUND DOG ON A SCENT, A DOG	
hour,*,rly,SECONDS (or see our)	
house,*,ed,sing,STRUCTURE/ DWELLING TO LIVE IN	
hovel,*,A TINY DWELLING, SMALL OPEN STRUCTURE	
hover,*,red,ring,TO FLOAT ABOVE FOR A PERIOD OF TIME WITHOUT MOVING, TO FLOAT ABOVE	
hovil,hovel	
hovul,hovel	
hovur,hover	
how,EXPLAIN THE WAY SOMETHING IS SAID OR DONE, QUESTION THE WAY SOMETHING HAPPENS	
however,IN ANY EVENT, ON THE OTHER HAND, STILL	
howl,*,led,ling,lingly,ler,SOUND DOG MAKES, A LOUD SOUND	
hownd,hound	
hownt,hound	
howse,house	
hox,hoax / hock(s)	
hoyster,oyster	
hoz,hose / hoe(s) / who's / whose	
hozbetuble,hospitable	
hozdul,hostel / hostile	
hozpetality,hospitality	
hozpitable,hospitable	
hozt,host	
hoztus,host(ess)	
hu,hue / who	
hub,*,THE CENTER OF SOMETHING WHICH HOLDS IT ALL TOGETHER, KEEPS IT MOVING	
hubcap,*,COVER FOR WHEELS, COVERS THE HUB	
huch,hutch / huge / hush	
huckleberry,ries,AN EDIBLE BERRY	
hud,hood / hoot / who'd / hut	
huddle,*,ed,ling,FORM/ HUNCH INTO A TIGHT GROUP	
hude,hood / hoot / who'd	
hudel,huddle	
hue,*,SHADES, DEGREES OF THE SAME COLOR (or see who) "prefixes: multi/ un"	
huever,whoever	
huf,hoof / huff / hoove	
hufd,huff(ed) / hoove(d)	
hufed,huff(ed) / hoove(d)	
huff,*,ffed,ffing,ffy,DEEP GASPS FOR AIR, DEEP BREATH OUT	
hug,*,gged,gging,ggable,ggably,gger,WRAP ARMS AROUND SOMEONE/ SOMETHING WITH GOOD INTENT (or see huge)	
hugable,hug(ggable)	
hugd,hug(gged)	
huge,er,est,eness,ely,ENORMOUS IN BULK, TAKES UP ALOT OF SPACE (or see hutch)	
hugible,hug(ggable)	
hugt,hug(gged)	
huguble,hug(ggable)	
huj,huge / hutch	
huk,hook / hug	
hukd,hug(gged)	
hukeble,hug(ggable)	
huklberry,huckleberry	
hukt,hook(ed) / hug(gged)	
hul,hull/ who'll	
hulareus,hilarious	
hull,*,MAINFRAME/ COVER (or see who'll) "prefixes: multi"	
hum,*,mmed,mming,mmer,A SOUND MADE WITH LIPS PURSED (or see whom)	
human,*,ne,nness,nism,nist,nistic,nistically,nitarian, nitarianism,nity,nities,nize,nizes,nized,nizing, nization,nly,HOMO SAPIEN BEING (or see humane) "prefixes: in/ neo/ sub"	
humane,ely,eness,BE FAIR, CIVILIZED, REFINED (or see human) "prefixes: in"	
humble,*,ed,ling,er,est,ly,eness,NOT SELF-RIGHTEOUS, ISN'T FLAGRANTLY PROUD OR OPINIONATED	
humbul,humble	
humdinger,OUTSTANDING	
humed,humid	
humeleate,humiliate	
humen,human	
humenbird,hummingbird	
humengbird,hummingbird	
humer,humor / hummer	
humerus,humor(ous)	
humes,hummus / humus	
humever,whomever	
humid,dity,difiy,difies,difed,difier,difying,dification,dly, MOISTURE IN THE AIR	
humiliate,*,ed,ting,tion,ity,BELITTLED, ATTACK ON SELF-ESTEEM, HARSH JUDGMENT	
humility,RESPECTFUL / MODEST	
humin,human	
huminbird,hummingbird	
humis,hummus / humus	
hummer,*,TYPE OF TRUCK	
hummingbird,*,TINY BIRD	
hummus,CHICKPEA, GARBONZO MIXTURE FOR AN EDIBLE SPREAD (or see humus)	
humongous,sly,HUGE, ENORMOUS	
humor,*,red,ring,rous,rously,rousness,rless,rlessly, rlessness,rist,resque,FUNNY (or see hummer)	
hump,*,ped,ping,A BUMP, WHAT A MALE DOG DOES	
humple,humble	

humud,humid
humur,humor / hummer
humus, ORGANIC RICH SOIL (or see hummus)
hunch,hes,hed,hing,BENT OVER,HAVE AN IDEA
hundred,*,dth,A NUMBER USED IN THE U.S.
hunemoon,honeymoon
hunet,hundred / hunt(ed)
hung,PAST TENSE FOR THE WORD "HANG" "prefixes: over"
hunger,*,red,ring,gry,grily,griness,TO NEED/ WANT SOMETHING DESPERATELY (or see hunger)
hungry,rier,riest,rily,riness, NEED FOOD
hunk,*,ker,ky,CHUNK OF SOMETHING (or see hung/ honk)
hunker,hunk(er)
hunnet,hundred / hunt(ed)
hunsh,hunch
hunt,*,ted,ting,ter,PURSUE TO LOCATE
huntch,hunch
huntret,hundred
huntrid,hundred
huntur,hunt(er)
huny,honey
hunymoon,honeymoon
hup,hoop / hub
hupcap,hubcap
hur,her
huracane,hurricane
hurass,harass
hurb,herb
hurbavore,herbivore
hurd,heard / herd / hurt
hurdid,herd(ed) / hurt(ed)
hurdle,*,ed,ling,er,JUMP OVER OBSTACLES (or see hurtle)
hure,hurry
huredetary,hereditary
hureditare,hereditary
huredity,heredity
huricane,hurricane
hurifek,horrify(fic)
hurisun,horizon
hurle,*,ed,ling,er,PITCH/ SWING SOMETHING

hurmetic,hermetic
hurmit,hermit
huroik,hero(ic)
hurrah,*, YELL FOR JOY
hurricane,*, HIGH WINDS FROM THE SEAS
hurried,hurry(ried)
hurry,ries,ried,rying,TO GO FASTER THAN NORMAL "prefixes: un"
hurs,hearse / her(s)
hurself,herself
hurst,hearse
hurt,*,ting,tful,tfully,tfulness,PAIN, CAUSES PAIN (or see herd/ heard) "prefixes: un"
hurtle,*,ed,ling,TO THROW/ FLING VIOLENTLY WITH GREAT FORCE (or see hurdle)
hury,hurry
hurz,her(s) / hearse
hus,hue(s) / who's / whose
husband,*,dman,ubby,PARTNER OF A WIFE, MARRIED TERM
husbend,husband
husbind,husband
husderical,hysterical
hush,hes,hed,hing,BEING TOLD TO BE QUIET WITH A SOUND, GET SILENT
husk,*,ked,king,ker,ky,PROTECTIVE SHELLS ON THE FRUIT FROM PLANTS, TO REMOVE HUSKS
husky,kies,kier,kiest,kily,kiness,A DOG, SOMEONE WHO IS LARGER IN SIZE AND MUSCLE THAN PEERS
husle,hustle
husler,hustle(r)
huspend,husband
hustle,*, ed,ling,er, GET A MOVE ON IT, SOMEONE WHO GAMBLES AT POOL
hut,*, RAMSHACKLE STRUCTURE, WORD USED IN FOOTBALL (or see hoot)
hutch,hes, CAGE FOR ANIMALS, TO HOLD DISHES
hutel,huddle
hutul,huddle
huv,hoove
huz,who's / whose / hue(s)
huzbend,husband
huze,hue(s) / who's / whose

huzpend,husband
hwich,witch / which
hybernate,hibernate
hybred,hybrid
hy,hi / high

hybrid,*,dism,dist,dity,dize,dizes,dized,dizing,dizable, dization,dizer,OFFSPRING FROM TWO ANIMALS OR PLANTS
hydr,PREFIX INDICATING "WATER/ LIQUID" MOST OFTEN MODIFIES THE WORD
hydrant,*, CAP FOR ACCESS TO STORED WATER
hydrate,*,ed,ting,tion,tor,ADD WATER "prefixes: de/ re"
hydraulic,*, USE OF LIQUID UNDER PRESSURE TO MAKE PARTS MOVE
hydrint,hydrant
hydro,PREFIX INDICATING "WATER/ LIQUID" MOST OFTEN MODIFIES THE WORD
hydroelectric,cal,cally, USED TO RUN MACHINES VIA WATER PRESSURE THROUGH GENERATORS
hydrogen,nate,nates, nated,nating,nation,nator,nize, nizes,nized,nizing,nization,nous, eology,graphy, A COMMON/ PLENTIFUL GAS
hydroponic,*, cally, cist, ist, USE OF WATER WITH ADDED VITAMINS/ MINERALS TO FEED ROOT PLANTS INSTEAD OF SOIL
hyfen,hyphen
hygene, hygiene
hygiene, nist, nics, nics, nically, CARE FOR THE EXTERIOR OF THE BODY "prefixes: un"
hygro, PREFIX INDICATING "MOISTURE" MOST OFTEN MODIFIES THE WORD
hyjack,hijack
hyke, hike
hymn,*, ned,ning,nal,nist,RELIGIOUS SONG (or see him/ hem)
hymorag,hemorrhage
hypawthusis, hypothesis
hype, EXAGGERATING (or see hip)
hyper, PREFIX INDICATING "ABOVE/ OVER" MOST OFTEN MODIFIES THE WORD
hyperactive,vity,UNFOCUSED ENERGY

hypernate, hibernate
hyperthermia, hypothermia
hypethermia, hypothermia
hyphen, *, nate, nates, nated, nating, nation, A MARK WHICH SHOWS CONNECTION BETWEEN TWO WORDS
hyphenate, hyphen(ate)
hypnosis, SLIP TO A PLACE IN THE SUBCONSCIOUS MIND
hypnotic, cally, ize, ism, PUT INTO A SUBCONSCIOUS STATE OF MIND, MAGNETICALLY DRAWN TO SOMETHING
hypnotize, *, ed, zing, osis, ism, TALKED INTO A SUBCONSCIOUS STATE OF MIND
hypo, PREFIX INDICATING "BELOW/ UNDER" MOST OFTEN MODIFIES THE WORD
hypocrite, *, tical, tically, isy, isies, SOMEONE WHO SAYS ONE THING BUT DOES ANOTHER, LYING
hypotenuse, LONGEST SIDE OF TRIANGLE, USUALLY THE BASE
hypothermia, BODY BELOW NORMAL TEMPERATURE
hypothesis, ses, A THEORY FORMED DUE TO LACK OF INFORMATION OR TIME
hypothusis, hypothesis
hysdurekteme, hysterectomy
hysterectomy, mies, REMOVAL OF FEMALE ORGANS/ UTERUS
hysterical, lly, lness, EXTREME EMOTION
hytrashen, hydrate(tion)
hytrat, hydrate
I, REFERS TO SELF (or see eye)
I'd, CONTRACTION OF THE WORDS "I WOULD, I COULD, I SHOULD, I HAD'
I'll, CONTRACTION OF THE WORDS 'I WILL' (or see ill)
I'm, CONTRACTION OF THE WORDS 'I AM'
I've, CONTRACTION OF THE WORDS hy I HAVE'
ia, yaw
iaju, yahoo
ial, aisle / y'all / I'll
iam, yam
ian, yawn
ianc, yank
iarn, yarn
iarou, yarrow

iat, yacht
iaun, yawn
ibrau, eyebrow
ibreveate, abbreviate
ibreviate, abbreviate
ibrow, eyebrow
ice, *, ed, cing, cy, cily, FROZEN WATER
ich, itch / each
ichu, issue
ichuense, issue(uance)
ichuinse, issue(uance)
icicle, *, FROZEN ICE SHAPED LIKE DAGGERS
icing, TOPPING FOR BAKED GOODS
ickstensev, extensive
icoli, ecoli
icon, *, nic, nical, nically, noclasm, noclast, noclastic, noclastically, nography, nographer, nographic, nographical, nolater, nology, nological, nologist, nomatic, nomaticism, SYMBOLS OR IMAGES THEY REPRESENT, PREFIX INDICATING "IMAGE" MOST OFTEN MODIFIES THE WORD
icono, PREFIX INDICATING "IMAGE" MOST OFTEN MODIFIES THE WORD
iconomi, economy
icosestem, ecosystem
icosfir, ecosphere
icselerate, accelerate
icuabol, equable
icueit, equate
icuinox, equinox
icuip, equip
icuiti, equity
icy, cier, ciest, cily, FROZEN WATER
id, BASED ON FREUD'S EGO THEORY (or see eye(d)/ I'd)
idalegy, ideology
idapt, adapt
idch, itch
idea, *, al, ally, alism, alist, alistic, alistically, ality, alize, alizes, alized, alizing, alizer, ally, ate, ates, ated, ating, ation, ational, ationally, ative, THE FORM/ THOUGHT OF SOMETHING "prefixes: un"
idel, it'll / idle / idol
ideological, ideological

idem, item
idemize, item(ize)
idenify, identify
idenity, identity
identical, lly, lness, EXACTLY THE SAME
identification, *, PICTURE/ LEGAL DOCUMENT PROVING WHO A PERSON IS (I.D.)
identify, fies, fied, fying, fication, fier, fiable, fiably, fiability, ity, TO RECOGNIZE "prefixes: un"
identity, ties, A CHARACTERISTIC WHICH IDENTIFIES ONE FROM ANOTHER
idenufi, identify
ideo, PREFIX INDICATING "IDEA" MOST OFTEN MODIFIES THE WORD (or see idio)
ideology, gic, gical, OF IDEAS/ THOUGHTS "prefixes: un"
ideosy, idiocy
ideut, idiot
idilogical, ideological
idim, item
idimise, item(ize)
idinefy, identify
idinety, identity
idinteku, identical
idintufecation, identification
idio, PREFIX INDICATING "PRIVATE/ INDIVIDUAL/ PROPER" MOST OFTEN MODIFIES THE WORD (or see ideo)
idiocy, cies, LACKS INTELLIGENCE
idiology, ideology
idiot, *, tic, tically, tness, ACTS LIKE A FOOL
idl, it'll / idle
idle, *, er, ling, RUN IN NEUTRAL, SITTING WITHOUT MOVING (or see idol/ it'll)
idmire, admire
idmit, admit
idmyre, admire
idol, *, lator, latry, latrous, lize, lizes, lized, lizing, lization, ADMIRED, WORSHIPPED (or see idle)
idolegy, ideology
idological, ideological
idoly, ideology
idolt, adult
idoo, adieu

idself, itself	iglu, igloo	igsplisit, explicit
idsetura, etcetera	ignait, ignite	igsplod, explode
idsulf, itself	ignarent, ignorant	igsplorashen, explore(ration)
idu, adieu	**igneous**, OLD ROCK FORMED BY HIGH HEAT	igsploshen, explosion
idul, idol / idle / it'll	ignerants, ignorant(nce)	igsplosive, explosive
idult, adult	ignerent, ignorant	igspoz, expose
idum, item	igneus, igneous	igstend, extend
idvanse, advance	ignicion, ignition	igstensev, extensive
idvantige, advantage	ignide, ignite	igstenshen, extension
idvize, advise / advice	ignishin, ignition	igstenuate, extenuate
ie, eye	**ignite**, *, ed, ting, tion, ter, SPARK TO MAKE IT START, START A FIRE "prefixes: pre"	igstereur, exterior
iea, yeah		igstinkt, extinct
iel, I'll / yell	**ignition**, *, ELECTRICAL SPARK TO START AN ENGINE "prefixes: pre"	igstrakt, extract
ielou, yellow		igsturnel, external
ielp, yelp	ignor, ignore	igsurt, exert
ieng, eye(ying)	**ignorant**, ntly, ance, LACKING INFORMATION	igueit, equate
ier, ear	**ignore**, *, ed, ring, rant, PURPOSELY NOT PAY ATTENTION	iguer, eager
iesterdei, yesterday	ignurent, ignorant	igul, eagle
iet, yet	igol, eagle	igzajerate, exaggerate
if, THEN THIS IF NOT THAT, IT COULD BE THIS OR THAT BASED ON WHETHER	igree, agree	igzakt, exact
	igsajurate, exaggerate	igzample, example
ife, ivy / iffy	igsakt, exact	igzasperate, exasperate
ifect, effect	igsample, example	igzile, exile
ifekt, effect / affect	igsberament, experiment	igzist, exist
iffy, fier, fiest, finess, PROBABILITY IT WILL/ WILL NOT HAPPEN	igsblanatory, explanatory	igzost, exhaust
	igsblod, explode	igzurt, exert
ifi, iffy	igsbozishen, expose(sition)	iil, eel
ifning, evening	igsebshen, except(ion)	iis, ease
ifol, evil	igsebt, except / accept	ijusduble, adjust(able)
ifre, ivory	igsecutive, executive	iknauleg, acknowledge
ifree, every	igsempt, exempt	iknolege, acknowledge
ifry, ivory	igsept, except / accept	iknor, ignore
ifs, eaves	igsert, exert	iknurent, ignorant
ify, ivy / iffy	igsglude, exclude	ikon, icon
ig, PREFIX INDICATING "NOT" MOST OFTEN MODIFIES THE WORD	igsilarate, exhilarate / accelerate	iksagerashen, exaggerate(tion)
	igsklute, exclude	iksajerashen, exaggerate(tion)
igalatarian, egalitarian	igsotik, exotic	iksam, exam
igaliterian, egalitarian	igspand, expand	iksamen, examine
igalutarean, egalitarian	igspans, expanse / expense	iksamenashen, examine(nation)
igect, eject	igspect, expect	iksampl, example
igel, eagle	igsperument, experiment	iksamunashen, examine(nation)
iger, eager	igspir, expire	iksblan, explain
igloo, *, DOME DWELLING BUILT OF ICE BLOCKS	igsplan, explain	iksblod, explode

iksblor,explore	ikstrem,extreme	ilend,island
iksbloshen,explosion	ikstrordenair,extraordinaire	ilent,island
iksblosive,explosive	ikstrordinery,extraordinary	ileptic,elliptic
iksboz,expose	iksturmenate,exterminate	ilesit,elicit / illicit
ikschange,exchange	ikuabol,equable	ilestrate,illustrate
ikscuse,excuse	ikuate,equate	ileterate,illiterate
iksebt,except / accept	ikueit,equate	iletest,elite(tist)
ikselirate,accelerate	ikuip,equip	ileven,eleven
ikseluratur,accelerate(tor)	ikwalibreum,equilibrium	ieventh,eleven(th)
iksepshen,except(ion)	ikwalite,equality	ieviate,alleviate
iksept,except / accept	ikwanimity,equanimity	ilicit,elicit / illicit
iksert,exert	ikwashun,equation	iiderate,illiterate
iksglud,exclude	ikwate,equate	iiderit,illiterate
iksit,excite	ikwater,equator	iigel,illegal
iksitment,excite(ment)	ikwaunimity,equanimity	iiiptical,elliptic(al)
ikskwisit,exquisite	ikwefalent,equivalent	iiktrishen,electrician
iksost,exhaust	ikwelbreum,equilibrium	iiind,island
ikspans,expanse / expense	ikwenox,equinox	ilipsus,ellipsis
ikspant,expand	ikwip,equip	ilisit,elicit / illicit
ikspektent,expect(ant)	ikwivalent,equivalent	iliterate,illiterate
ikspensef,expense(sive)	ikwunimity,equanimity	ilive,alive
ikspereanse,experience	ikzam,exam	**ill,Iness,NOT WELL**
iksperement,experiment	ikzamen,examine	illect,eject
ikspire,expire	**il, PREFIX INDICATING "NOT IN/ INTO/ ON" MOST OFTEN MODIFIES THE WORD (or see ill/ aisle/ i'll/ eel)**	**illegal**,lly,lity,lities,lize,lizes,lized,lizing,lization,AGAINST THE LAW,NOT LEGAL
iksplan,explain	iland,island	illeterate,illiterate
iksplanatory,explanatory	ilarm,alarm	**illicit**,tly,tness,PROHIBITED BY LAW,NOT ALLOWED (or see elicit)
iksplisity,explicit(ly)	ilash,eyelash	illiptic,elliptic
iksplod,explode	ilasteck,elastic	illisit,elicit / illicit
iksplor,explore	ilastic,elastic	**illiterate**,HARDLY ABLE TO READ AND WRITE,NOT EDUCATED
iksplorutory,explore(ratory)	ilastick,elastic	**illogical**,lly,lity,lities,NOT LOGICAL,NOT REALISTIC
iksploshen,explosion	ilastrate,illustrate	**illuminate**,*,ed,ting,tingly,tion,ance,ant,OF BEING ENLIGHTENED/ INFORMED "prefixes: retro"
iksplosive,explosive	ilaven,eleven	
ikspoz,expose	ilbow,elbow	illipic,elliptic
ikspreshen,express(ion)	ie,i'll	illisit,elicit / illicit
ikspress,express	ilect,elect	**illumine**,*,ed,ning,nance,nant,nate,nism,OF BEING ENLIGHTENED/ INFORMED
ikstend,extend	ilectiv,elective	
ikstengwish,extinguish	ilectrician,electrician	**illusion**,*,nal,nary,nist,nism,SENSE SOMETHING AS IF IT WERE PHYSICAL/ REAL (or see allusion) "prefixes: dis"
ikstensev,extensive	iledaret,illiterate	
ikstenshen,extension	ilegal,illegal	
ikstenuate,extenuate	ileganse,allegiance	**illusive**,ely,eness,SENSE SOMETHING AS IF IT WERE PHYSICAL/ REAL (or see allusive)
ikstereor,exterior	ilegul,illegal	
iksternul,external	ilekul,Illegal	
ikstradite,extradite		

illustrate, *, ed, ting, tive, tively, tion, tional, tor, DRAW A PICTURE, ONE WHO DRAWS
illustrious, sly, sness, FAMOUS FOR ACHIEVEMENT
ilness, ill(ness)
ilnus, ill(ness)
ilogikul, illogical
ilollical, illogical
ilongate, elongate
ilongeit, elongate
ilop, elope
ilorm, alarm
ilostrious, illustrious
ilud, elude
ilujen, illusion / allusion
ilumenade, illuminate
ilumeneit, illuminate
iluminate, illuminate
ilumineit, illuminate
ilund, island
ilur, allure
ilusdreus, illustrious
ilushen, illusion / allusion
ilusion, illusion / allusion
ilusiv, elusive
ilusive, illusive / allusive / e usive
ilustrate, illustrate
ilustreit, illustrate
ilustrious, illustrious
ilute, elude
im, PREFIX INDICATING "NOT/ IN/ INTO/ ON" MOST OFTEN MODIFIES THE WORD (or see them/ him/ I'm)
imaculet, immaculate
image, *, ed, ery, er, ging, gine, gism, A PICTURE REAL OR IN THE MIND
imagenashen, imagine(nation)
imaginashen, imagine(nation)
imagine, *, ed, ning, nable, ary, native, nativeness, natively, nation, A PICTURE/ THOUGHT IN THE MIND "prefixes: un"
imagrant, immigrant / emigrant
imagrate, immigrate / emigrate
imagrent, emigrant / immigrant

imagrints, emigrant(s) / immigrant(s)
imagrits, emigrant(s) / immigrant(s)
imagunashen, imagine(nation)
imaj, image
imajenashen, imagine(nation)
imanate, emanate
imancipate, emancipate
imanens, eminence / imminence / immanence
imanint, eminent / imminent / immanent
imanserable, immensurable
imansopate, emancipate
imatashin, imitate(tion)
imatate, imitate
imateit, imitate
imaterial, immaterial
imature, immature
imbankment, embankment
imbargo, embargo
imbark, embark
imbasee, embassy
imbaudes, embody(dies)
imbeded, embed(dded)
imbelikul, umbilical
imberis, embarrass
imbet, embed
imbilakul, umbilical
imblim, emblem
imbodys, embody(dies)
imboss, emboss
imbotys, embody(dies)
imboudes, embody(dies)
imbrase, embrace
imbreo, embryo
imbrorder, embroider
imbrufment, improve(ment)
imbtee, empty
imbur, ember
imbuse, embassy
imediate, immediate
imeduetly, immediate(lly)
imenate, emanate
imenent, eminent / imminent / immanent
imense, immense

imensurable, immensurable
imerch, emerge
imerchensi, emergency
imerg, emerge
imergency, emergency
imergensi, emergency
imerj, emerge
imersable, immersible
imerse, immerse / emersed
imersion, immerse(sion)
imertality, immortal(ity)
imetashen, imitate(tion)
imeterial, immaterial
imeteut, immediate
imfasis, emphasis / emphasize
imfusis, emphasis / emphasize
imicion, emission
imidiet, immediate
imigrant, immigrant / emigrant
imigrashen, immigrate(tion) / emigrate(tion)
imigrate, immigrate / emigrate
imigration, immigrate(tion) / emigrate(tion)
imigreit, immigrate
imigrunt, immigrant / emigrant
iminate, emanate
iminens, eminence / imminence / immanence
iminent, eminent / imminent / immanent
iminse, immense
iminsurable, immensurable
imirsable, immersible
imirsed, immerse(d) / emersed
imirshen, immerse(sion)
imirsion, immerse(sion)
imitate, *, ed, ting, tion, tional, tive, tively, tiveness, COPIES/ REPRODUCTIONS OF THE REAL THING
imiteit, imitate
imiterial, immaterial
imiun, immune
imiunais, immunize
inkombutent, incompetent
immaculate, ely, eness, NO SPOTS/ STAINS/ MARS/ FLAWS
immagrate, immigrate / emigrate

immanence, cy, nt, WITHIN, INTRINSIC (or see eminence/ imminence)

immanent, tly, WITHIN, INTRINSIC (or see eminent/ imminent)

immaterial, lly, lity, lism, lize, lizes, lized, lizing, NO IMPORTANT/ USEFUL FOR THE SITUATION

immature, ely, eness, rity, NOT OLD ENOUGH/ MATURE/ GROWN, FOOLISH

immeasurable, ly, bility, NOT ABLE TO MEASURE

immediate, ely, eness, RIGHT NOW

immense, ely, eness, GREAT IN SIZE, HUGE, VAST

immensurable, bly, bility, eness, IMPOSSIBLE TO MEASURE HOW VAST IT IS

immerchen, immerse(sion)

immerse, es, ed, sing, sion, sionist, sionism, sible, SINK INTO LIQUID/ THOUGHT/ ACTIVITY (or see emerse(d))

immershen, immerse(sion)

immersible, CAN BE SUBMERGED INTO LIQUID

immeterial, immaterial

immigrant, *, LEFT YOUR COUNTRY PERMANENTLY TO LIVE IN ANOTHER COUNTRY (or see emigrant) "prefixes: non"

immigrate, *, ed, ting, ant, tion, tioner, GOING TO ANOTHER COUNTRY (or see emigrate)

imminence, cy, nt, ntly, COULD POTENTIALLY HAPPEN (or see eminence/ immanence)

imminent, tly, ncy, IT WILL HAPPEN NO MATTER HOW LONG IT TAKES, INEVITABLE (or see eminent/ immanent)

immobile, lize, lizes, lized, lizing, lization, lizer, lity, lism, NOT ABLE TO MOVE/ BE MOVED

immoral, lly, lity, lities, list, NOT PROPER/ MORAL/ DECENT

immortal, lly, lity, lize, lizes, lized, lizing, lization, EXISTS FROM NOW ON, NEVER ENDING

immpresion, impression

immpresive, impressive

immune, nity, nities, nize, nize, FREE FROM, EXEMPT, HEALTHY

immunize, *, ed, zing, er, zation, PHARMACEUTICALS INTRODUCED INTO THE BODY TO FIGHT MICRO ORGANISMS WHICH MAY/ MAY NOT INVADE BODY

immurshen, immerse(sion)

---

immursion, immerse(sion)
imobile, immobile
imochen, emotion
imochun, emotion
imonate, emanate
imople, immobile
imoral, immoral
imorchen, immerse(sion)
imordle, immortal
imorshen, immerse(sion)
imortaledy, immortal(ity)
imortality, immortal(ity)
imorul, immoral
imoshon, emotion
imoterial, immaterial
imownt, amount

impact, *, ted, ting, tion, tive, TWO BODIES OF MASS COLLIDING INTO ONE ANOTHER, SIZABLE EFFECT

impair, *, red, ring, rer, rment, MAKE WORSE "prefixes: un"

impar, empower
imparer, emperor
imparical, empirical
imparment, empower(ment)
imparutev, imperative
impashent, impatient

impatient, tly, nce, NOT PATIENT, UNABLE TO RELAX

impaurment, empower(ment)

impeach, hes, hed, hing, her, hable, hment, CHARGE WITH CRIME/ MISDEMEANOR "prefixes: un"

impeachuis, impetuous

impeccable, ly, bility, NO FLAWS/ MISTAKES

impech, impeach

impechuous, impetuous

impede, *, ed, ding, er, DELAY/ OBSTRUCT "prefixes: un"

impeed, impede

impeishent, impatient

imper, impair

imperative, *, val, ely, eness, ABSOLUTELY ESSENTIAL, NECESSARY

imperfect, tly, tness, tion, tive, tiveness, NOT AS GOOD AS COULD BE

imperor, emperor

---

impersonal, lly, lity, lize, lizes, lized, lizing, ate, NOT ATTACHED IN A PERSONAL WAY, ABSENCE OF PERSONAL FEELINGS

impersonate, *, ed, ting, tion, tor, al, ACT/ BEHAVE LIKE SOMEONE ELSE

impetuous, sly, sness, osity, osities, ACT/ BEHAVE ON THE SPUR OF THE MOMENT

imphasis, emphasis / emphasize
impire, empire
impirical, empirical
implai, imply
implamint, implement

implant, *, ted, ting, tation, TO INSTILL IDEAS OR THOUGHTS, REPLACE BODY ORGAN WITH ANOTHER ONE

implecate, implicate

implement, *, ted, ting, tal, ter, tation, SOMETHING USED AS A TOOL, TO INCORPORATE INTO

implicate, *, ed, ting, tion, tional, tive, tively, BE TANGLED/ INVOLVED IN, SUSPECTED PARTICIPATION

imploe, employee / employ
imploer, employer
imploy, employ / employee
imployer, employer
implucate, implicate
implucation, implicate(tion)
implument, implement

imply, lies, lied, ying, lication, SUGGEST SOMETHING/ SOMEONE IS RESPONSIBLE

impolait, impolite

impolite, ely, eness, RUDE/ FRANK/ IMPERSONAL/ HONEST

impols, impulse

impolsive, impulse(sive)

import, *, ted, ting, tation, table, tability, BRING INTO THE COUNTRY FROM ANOTHER COUNTRY

important, tly, nce, PRIORITY, MUST BE TENDED TO "prefixes: un"

impose, *, ed, sing, sition, TO INTERRUPT, SUGGESTED REFERENCE, UNWELCOME INCLUSION

imposbul, impossible

impossible, ly, bility, NOT POSSIBLE, COULD NEVER HAPPEN
imposter, *, UNWELCOME INCLUSION, BE WHERE ONE IS NOT WANTED, ILLEGITIMATE
impound, *, ded, ding, TAKE AWAY/ CONFISCATE/ HOLD LAWFULLY
impour, empower
impourment, empower(ment)
impourtens, important(nce)
impourtent, important
impous, impose
impoverish, hed, her, hment, MARGINALIZED, UNABLE TO ADEQUATELY SUPPORT ONESELF
impraktecle, impractical
imprasev, impressive
imprashen, impression
imprechen, impression
imprecise, ely, eness, sion, NOT PRECISE/ FACTUAL
impregnable, bility, ly, NOT ABLE TO PENETRATE/ GET INTO MOVE
impregnate, *, ed, ting, tion, tor, able, TO INTRODUCE/ INJECT INTO, MAKE PREGNANT, INFUSE
impregneit, impregnate
impregnuble, impregnable
imprent, imprint
impresais, imprecise
impresef, impressive
impreshen, impression
impresif, impressive
impresion, impression
impress, sses, ssed, ssing, ssion, ssive, ssivley, ssible, ssibly, ssibility, ssibilities, ssibleness, ssment, FAVORABLY AFFECTED "prefixes: over/ un"
impression, *, nable, nability, nableness, nist, nistic, nism, ive, FAVORABLY AFFECTED, PRESSED/ MO-DED/ EMBOSSED INTO "prefixes: re/ un"
impressive, ely, eness, FAVORABLY AFFECTED "prefixes: re/ un"

impretion, impression
imprint, *, ted, ting, ter, PRINT/ STAMP INTO, TO LODGE/ INSTILL INTO MEMORY
imprison, *, ned, ning, nment, PLACE INTO PRISON, CONFINE, INCARCERATE
improbable, ly, bility, HIGHLY UNLIKELY, NOT NORMALLY POSSIBLE, MOST LIKELY NOT
improbabol, improbable
improf, improve
improgais, improvise
impromptu, OFF THE TOP OF YOUR HEAD, SPUR OF THE MOMENT IDEA
impropar, improper
improper, rly, rness, NOT PROPER/ ACCEPTABLE
impropuble, improbable
improvais, improvise
improve, *, ed, ving, er, ement, vable, vability, MAKE BETTER THAN BEFORE, TOWARDS PERFECTION "prefixes: over/ un"
improvise, *, ed, sing, er, sation, sational, sator, satorial, MAKE IT UP AS YOU GO, IMPROMPTU
improvusashen, improvise(sation)
impruf, improve
impte, empty
impulite, impolite
impuls, impulse
impulse, *, sion, sive, sively, siveness, SUDDEN ACT/ MOVEMENT WITHOUT APPARENT THOUGHT
impurer, emperor
impurfekt, imperfect
impursenate, impersonate
impursonal, impersonal
impursonation, impersonate(tion)
impuseshen, impose(sition)
input, input
imruld, emerald
imte, empty
imug, image
imigrant, immigrant / emigrant
imgrashen, immigrate(tion) / emigrate(tion)
imigrate, immigrate
imigrent, immigrant / emigrant
imuj, image

imun, immune
imunais, immunize
imunent, eminent / imminent / immanent
imunezashen, immunize(zation)
imunezation, immunize(zation)
imunise, immunize
imunity, immune(nity)
imunize, immunize
imurchen, immerse(sion)
imurgency, emergency
imursable, immersible
imurse, immerse / emersed
imurshen, immerse(sion)
imurtalety, immortal(ity)
imutashin, imitate(tion)
imutation, imitate(tion)
imuterial, immaterial
in, CONTAINED/ BELONGS WITHIN, CONFINED, ENTER, PREFIX INDICATING "NOT" MOST OFTEN MODIFIES THE WORD (or see inn/ en)
in-lau, in-law
in-law, *, PEOPLE RELATED BY MARRIAGE
inabel, enable / unable
inability, ties, UNABLE, NOT ABLE TO, WITHOUT CAPACITY TO
inabishen, inhibit(ion)
inable, enable / unable
inabler, enable(r)
inabul, enable / unable
inaccessible, bility, eness, ly, CANNOT BE OBTAINED, UNREACHABLE, NO ACCESS
inaccurate, ely, eness, acy, acies, NOT CORRECT/ FACTUAL/ ACCURATE
inacsesable, inaccessible
inacsesibol, inaccessible
inacshon, inaction
inact, enact
inaction, *, NO ACTION, IDLE
inactive, ely, eness, vity, vate, NO ACTION, IDLE (or see enact(ive))
inaculation, inoculate(tion)
inacurate, inaccurate
inadberdent, inadvertent

inadecuet, inadequate
inadequate, ely, eness, acy, acies, NOT ENOUGH, INADEQUATE, LACKING
inadmissible, bility, bly, NOT ALLOWED TO ENTER, NOT ADMISSIBLE/ ADMISSABLE
inadvaisable, inadvisable
inadverdent, inadvertent
inadvertent, tly, nce, ncy, ncies, NOT PAYING ATTENTION, NOT DIRECT/ STRAIGHTFORWARD
inadvisable, bility, ADVISE/ RECOMMEND AGAINST, BEST NOT TO DO/ SAY SOMETHING
inagiureit, inaugurate
inakd, enact
inakioret, inaccurate
inakshen, inaction
inaktif, enact(ive) / inactive
inakulation, inoculate(tion)
inaleable, inalienable
inaleuble, inalienable
inalienable, ly, bility, CANNOT TAKE AWAY
inalisis, analysis
inamal, enamel
inamel, enamel
inamet, intimate
inamul, enamel
inanimate, ely, eness, NOT ANIMATE, USUALLY AN OBJECT WHICH DOESN'T ACT/ MOVE
inaperable, inoperable
inaperate, inoperate
inaperative, inoperate(tive)
inaple, enable / unable
inappreciative, ely, eness, able, ably, NOT APPRECIATED/ GRATEFUL, ACTIONS NOT REGARDED AS USEFUL/ NECESSARY (also unappreciative)
inapproachable, NOT ACCESSIBLE/ APPROACHABLE, UNREACHABLE
inappropriate, ely, eness, NOT PROPER/ APPROPRIATE/ ACCEPTABLE AT THE MOMENT
inapul, enable / unable
inaquerit, inaccurate
inaquiuret, inaccurate
inaqulate, inoculate
inaqurite, inaccurate

inaferins, interfere(nce)
inasinse, innocence
inate, innate
inatequit, inadequate
inatible, inaudible
inatly, innate(ly)
inatmisable, inadmissible
inatvertense, inadvertent
inatvizable, inadvisable
inatvurtent, inadvertent
inaudible, ly, bility, NOT ABLE TO HEAR, NOT AUDIBLE, CAN'T BE HEARD
inaugurate, *, ed, ting, tion, tor, al, FORMALLY INSTALL/ BEGIN, ADDRESS TO THE PUBLIC
inaukulate, inoculate
inauperable, inoperable
inauperate, inoperate
inauperative, inoperate(tive)
inbade, invade
inbalid, invalid
inbankment, embankment
inbaris, embarrass
inbark, embark
inbasee, embassy
inbed, embed
inbeid, invade
inbeishon, invasion
inbent, invent
inberis, embarrass
inbert, invert
inberbrait, invertebrate
inbest, invest
inbet, embed
inbigareit, invigorate
inbinsuble, invincible
inblem, emblem
inblum, emblem
inboard, *, BOAT WITH MOTOR/ ENGINE INSIDE
inbois, invoice
inbord, inboard
inbosd, emboss(ed)
inboss, emboss
inbrase, embrace

inbreo, embryo
inbrorder, embroider
inburt, invert
inbutashen, invitation
incadesent, incandescent
incamped, encamp(ed)
incampment, encamp(ment)
incandescent, tly, nce, A BULB TYPE WITH A FILAMENT THAT HEATS UP, BRIGHT/ SHINING LITE
incantashen, incantation
incantation, *, nal, tory, SPELLS/ CHANTS FOR MAGIC
incapable, ly, eness, bility, NOT CAPABLE/ ABLE TO, DON'T HAVE WHAT IT TAKES TO ACCOMPLISH
incapacitate, *, ed, ting, tion, OUT OF ORDER, UNABLE TO FUNCTION AS USUAL, LACKING POWER TO
incapacity, ties, NOT ABLE EITHER PHYSICALLY/ MENTALLY TO PERFORM TASKS WELL
incarcerate, *, ed, ting, tion, SENTENCED TO CONFINEMENT
incarnate, *, ed, ting, tion, TAKE ON PHYSICAL FORM "prefixes: re"
incarneit, incarnate
incarserate, incarcerate
incarsereit, incarcerate
incase, encase
incast, encase(d)
incendiary, ries, ABLE TO CREATE FIRE, CIVIL UNREST
incense, ed, sing, AROMATIC PRESSED POWDER FOR BURNING
incentive, *, vize, vizes, vized, vizing, A MOTIVATION FOR PERFORMING A TASK "prefixes: dis"
incenurate, incinerate
incepshen, incept(ion)
incept, tor, tion, tive, tively, FROM THE BEGINNING, MOMENT OF CREATION
incercl, encircle
incerense, insure(rance)
incerkl, encircle
incesant, incessant
inceshon, incision
incessant, ncy, tly, CONTINUE WITHOUT STOPPING
incest, tuous, tuously, tuousness, SEX AMONGST THE FAMILY IF RELATED BY BLOOD

inch, hes, hed, hing, A U.S. MEASUREMENT
inchant, enchant
inchantmint, enchant(ment)
incher, ensure / insure / injure
inchoy, enjoy
inchrud, intrude
inchur, ensure / insure / injure
incide, incite/ inside
incident, *, nce, ntal, ntally, HAPPENING ATTACHED TO A LARGER EVENT, DISTINCT BUT SEEMINGLY MINOR
incindiary, incendiary
incinerate, *, ed, ting, tor, tion, TO BURN, COCKS TO ASHES WITH FIRE
incinereit, incinerate
incinsir, insincere
incircle, encircle
incise, *, ed, sing, sor, sion, CUT/ CARVE INTO
incishon, incision
incision, *, nal, ned, MAKE A CUT INTO
incist, insist
incite, *, ed, ting, tation, ement, er, TO ROUSE, SPUR/ PROVOKE TO ACT/ REBEL (or see inside/ insight)
incityus, insidious
inclain, incline
incline, *, ed, ning, nation, A GRADUALLY ELEVATED PLANE, TO GO UP, MOST LIKELY TO "prefixes: dis"
inclineishan, incline(nation)
inclood, include
inclose, enclose
incloser, enclose(sure)
inclosment, enclose(ment)
inclous, enclose
inclozur, enclose(sure)
include, *, ed, ding, usion, usive, usively, usiveness, dible, dable, ADD/ INVOLVE SOMETHING INTO GROUP OF OTHER THINGS
incluesef, inclusive
inclueshen, inclusion
incluesive, inclusive
inclusef, inclusive
inclushen, include(usion)
inclusion, *, ive, ADD/ INVOLVE SOMETHING INTO GROUP OF OTHER THINGS

inclusive, ely, eness, ADD/ INVOLVE SOMETHING INTO GROUP OF OTHER THINGS
incognedo, incognito
incognito, *, DISGUISED TO BE UNRECOGNIZABLE
incoherent, tly, nce, ncy, ncies, UNABLE TO COMPREHEND UNDERSTAND, CANNOT COMMUNICATE LOGICALLY/ UNDERSTANDABLE
incojerent, incoherent
incokneto, incognito
incomber, encumber
incombutent, incompetent
income, *, ming, MONEY COMING IN
incommode, *, ed, ding, dious, diously, DISTURB SOMEONE BY HAVING THEM CATER TO YOUR NEEDS UNNECESSARILY
incomode, incommode
incomodious, incommode(dious)
incomparable, bility, bly, NOTHING TO COMPARE TO
incompas, encompass
incompatible, bility, eness, ly, NOT ABLE TO GET ALONG WITH, TOO MANY DIFFERENCES
incompetent, tly, nce, ncy, NOT ABLE TO COMPETE/ KEEP UP, LACKS QUALIFICATIONS
incomplete, *, ely, eness, etion, NOT COMPLETE, NEEDS MORE TO FINISH
incomplit, incomplete
incompruble, incomparable
inconclusive, ely, eness, NO FINAL RESULTS, NO CERTAIN ANSWERS
inconsiderate, ely, eness, tion, ably, ableness, NOT CONCERNED WITH SOMEONE'S EMOTIONAL REACTION OR WELL BEING
inconsistent, tly, ncy, ncies, DOESN'T PERFORM STEADILY/ PREDICTABLY
incontinent, nce, tly, NOT ABLE TO CONTAIN/ CONTROL ONESELF
inconvenient, tly, nce, ncy, ncies, DOESN'T FIT INTO THE PLAN CAUSING DELAY OF FINISHING, NOT ON THE WAY THERE, UNPLANNED
incorect, incorrect
incorellabel, incorrigible
incoriguble, incorrigible

incorporate, *, ed, ting, tion, tive, tor, able, TO INCLUDE INTO THE WORKINGS OF, BROUGHT INTO A LARGER BODY, UNITE, COMBINE "prefixes: dis/ un"
incorporeit, incorporate
incorrect, tly, tness, NOT EXACT/ FACTUAL/ SUITABLE
incorrigible, ly, bility, eness, NOT ABLE TO BE CORRECTED/ REFORMED TO MEET EXPECTED STANDARDS
incorugible, incorrigible
incounter, encounter
incownter, encounter
increase, *, ed, sing, singly, sable, TO MAKE MORE THAN THERE WAS, ADD MORE
incredible, ly, lity, eness, ASTONISHING, BEYOND EXPECTATION
incredulous, sly, sness, CROSS BETWEEN INCREDIBLE AND RIDICULOUS
incremenate, incriminate
increment, *, tal, tally, MOVE EXACT AMOUNT IN ONE DIRECTION, INCREASE
incrimeneit, incriminate
incriminate, *, ed, ting, tion, TO ACCUSE OR LEND SUSPICION, CHARGE WITH A CRIME
incris, increase
incroach, encroach
incrochment, encroach(ment)
incruments, increment(s)
incrust, encrust
incualler, inquire
incubate, *, ed, ting, tion, tional, tive, tor, TO PROTECT AN EGG IN PERFECT ENVIRONMENT FOR EMBRYO TO GROW INTO FULL FORM
incuisishon, inquisition
incumbent, *, ntly, ncy, ncies, FILL A POST OR OFFICE
incumber, encumber
incumode, incommode
incumpatuble, incompatible
incunklusef, inconclusive
incunsideret, inconsiderate
incunsistent, inconsistent
incupasitate, incapacitate
incur, *, rred, rring, rrable, LIABLE FOR, ADDED DEBT IN ORIGINAL LOAN

Word	Forms	Definition
incurable	ly, bility, eness	SEEMINGLY UNABLE TO CURE, EXTREMELY DIFFICULT TO HEAL
incurach	encourage	
incureg	encourage / anchor(age)	
incurekt	incorrect	
incurellabal	incorrigible	
incurig	encourage / anchor(age)	
ind	and / end	
indainger	endanger	
indait	indict	
indanger	endanger	
indangurment	endanger(ment)	
indanjer	endanger	
indapendense	independent(nce)	
indasishen	indecision	
indastrial	industrial	
indau	endow	
indaument	endow(ment)	
indaveguel	individual	
indavishual	individual	
indebted	dness	OWE SOMETHING TO SOMEONE
indeber	endeavor	
indecent	ncy, ncies, ntly	NOT ACCEPTABLE BY SOCIETY'S STANDARDS
indecision		NOT ABLE TO BE FIRM IN MAKING A CHOICE
indecisive	eness, ely	NOT ABLE TO MAKE A FIRM CHOICE
inded	end(ed)	
indeded	indebted	
indedud	indebted	
indeed		CERTAINLY, CONFIRMATION
indefer	endeavor	
indeferent	indifferent	
indefinite	ely, eness	WITH NO END OR FINAL GOAL, NOT DEFINED
indefur	endeavor	
indefurent	indifferent	
indego	indigo	
indekat	indicate	
indeks	index	
indeleble	indelible	
indelible	bility, ly	HARD TO REMOVE, NEARLY PERMANENT
indemafy	indemnify	
indemic	endemic	
indemnify	fies, fied, fying, fication, fier	COMPENSATE/ REIMBURSE FOR LOSS
indent	*, ted, ting, tation	A DENT IN SOMETHING, DIFFERENT DEPTH FROM REST OF THE SURFACE
independent	*, tly, nce, ncy, ncies	ABLE TO STAND PRIMARILY ON ITS OWN, NOT DEPENDENT
inder	inter / enter	
indermetant	intermittent	
indesaisit	indecisive	
indesent	indecent	
indesiaisive	indecisive	
indeted	indebted	
indever	endeavor	
index	xes, dices, xed, xing, xical	TO CATEGORIZE, DIVIDE INTO GROUPS, PROVIDE A NAME FOR EASY RETRIEVAL "prefixes: sub"
indicate	*, ed, ting, tion, tive, tively, tor, tory	GIVE A SIGN TOWARDS A DIRECTION, PROVIDES INFORMATION, HELPS IN FIGURING ANSWER "prefixes: contra"
indicater	indicate(tor)	
indict	*, ted, ting, table, ter, tor, tment	CHARGE WITH A CRIME ("C" IS SILENT)
indid	indeed	
indifferent	tly, nce	NOT PARTIAL OR CONCERNED WITH CHOICES/ ACT/ EVENT
indifrent	indifferent	
indigenous		ORIGINAL TO THE LAND, NATIVE
indigo	*,	DEEP BLUE COLOR, COLOR FROM A PLANT
indikate	indicate	
indikeit	indicate	
indimec	endemic	
indintashen	indent(ation)	
indiqueit	indicate	
indir	endear	
indirmetant	intermittent	
indisant	indecent	
indisent	indecent	
indite	indict	
individual	*, lly, lism, lity, lize, lities, ization, ate	ON ITS OWN, DOESN'T BELONG TO A GROUP
indivillal	individual	
indjur	endure	
indlis	endless	
indocrain	endocrine	
indoctrinate	*, ed, ting, tion, tor	FORCED TEACHING PRINCIPLES/ IDEOLOGY TO ELIMINATE CREATIVE THINKING
indoctrineit	indoctrinate	
indoer	endure	
indolch	indulge	
indoneit	intonate	
indoor	*,	INSIDE A STRUCTURE/ DWELLING
indoose	induce	
indor	endure / indoor	
indormetant	intermittent	
indorse	endorse / indoor(s)	
indorsment	endorse(ment)	
indostry	industry	
indou	endow	
indoument	endow(ment)	
indow	endow	
indowment	endow(ment)	
indrakit	intricate	
indruspect	introspect	
indubitable	ly, bility	BEYOND A DOUBT
inducate	indicate	
induce	*, ed, cing, ement, er, cible	BRING ON, START/ MAKE HAPPEN
induckshen	induct(ion)	
inducktor	induct(or)	
induct	*, ted, ting, tee, tance, tion, tional, tive, tively, tiveness, tor	ELECTRIC CURRENT CHANGE, BE ENLISTED, TERM IN PHYSICS/ MILITARY/ EMBRYOLOGY/ CHEMISTRY/ MATHEMATICS
indukshen	induct(ion)	
induktor	induct(or)	
indulge	*, ed, ging, gingly, ger, gence, gencies, gent, gently,	TO AFFORD ONESELF A DESIRE, SATISFY AN IMPULSE "prefixes: over"
indur	inter / enter / endure	
indurmitant	intermittent	
induseshin	indecision	
industrial	lly, list, lness, lism, lize, lized, lizing, lization,	PRODUCTIVE, MANUFACTURES "prefixes: re"

industry, ries, rious, riously, rial, MACHINE/ TECHNOLOGY/ MANUFACTURING "prefixes: re"
induvijual, individual
inebriate, *, ed, ting, tion, iety, DRUNK/ INTOXICATED
ineckwitable, inequitable
inecsipiriens, inexperience
inecspenssif, inexpensive
inecwity, inequity
inedible, ly, CANNOT OR SHOULD NOT EAT
inefitaebol, inevitable
inegma, enigma / enema
inegreit, integrate
ineilienabol, inalienable
ineit, innate
inekspensef, inexpensive
inekwality, inequality
inekwitable, inequitable
inekwity, inequity
inema, enema / anemia
inemut, intimate
inendashen, inundate(tion)
inendate, inundate
inengs, inning(s)
ineprisative, inappreciative
ineprochable, inapproachable
ineproprieit, inappropriate
inept, tly, tness, titude, UNABLE, INCOMPETENT
inequality, ties, NOT EQUAL, DIFFERENCES EXIST
inequitable, ly, ty, NOT EQUAL, DIFFERENCES EXIST
inequity, ties, NOT FAIR/ JUST/ EQUAL
iner, inner / inter / enter
ineract, interact
inerbal, interval
inerchange, interchange
inercom, intercom
inerconnect, interconnect
inercors, intercourse
inerem, interim
inerferins, interfere(nce)
inerge, energy
inergetek, energetic
inerileit, interrelate
inerject, interject

inerjetek, energetic
inerkorse, intercourse
inerllect, interject
inerlletic, energetic
inerlock, interlock
inerlude, interlude
inermedeary, intermediary
inermingle, intermingle
inermishen, intermission
inermission, intermission
inermost, innermost
inernashenul, international
inernational, international
inernet, internet
inerrelate, interrelate
inersculastic, interscholastic
inersect, intersect
inersection, intersection
inersekshen, intersection
inersept, intercept
inersperse, intersperse
inersteit, interstate
inert, tly, tness, VISIBLY INACTIVE, NO APPARENT ACTION/ MOVEMENT
inertwine, intertwine
inerupt, interrupt
inervene, intervene
inerview, interview
inerviu, interview
inervol, interval
inervue, interview
inervul, interval
inerwoven, interwoven
inescapable, ly, bility, bilities, CANNOT ESCAPE
inesent, innocence(nt)
inesheashen, initiate(tion)
ineshul, initial
inesince, innocence
ineskeipabol, inescapable
inesqueipabol, inescapable
inesthesia, anesthesia
inetiale, initial(lly)
inetuble, inedible

inetvizable, inadvisable
ineursept, intercept
inevitable, bility, eness, ly, CANNOT AVOID
inevitabol, inevitable
inexcesable, inaccessible
inexpensive, ely, eness, FAIR PRICE, NOT EXPENSIVE
inexperience, ed, DOESN'T HAVE SKILLS TO PERFORM
inexpiriance, inexperience
infachuashen, infatuate(tion)
infachuate, infatuate
infachueit, infatuate
infadek, emphatic
infallible, lity, eness, ly, FOR CERTAIN
infaluble, infallible
infant, *, ncy, ncies, thood, tike, BABIES UP TO ONE YEAR OLD
infantry, ries, ymen, FOOT SOLDIERS
infasis, emphasis / emphasize
infatashen, invitation
infatik, emphatic
infatuate, ed, tion, edly, INSTANTLY ATTRACTED FOR BRIEF PERIOD OF TIME
infect, *, ted, ting, tion, tive, tor, tious, TO POLLUTE AN AREA "prefixes: dis/ retro"
infekshus, infect(ious)
infenatively, infinite(tively)
infent, infant
infentry, infantry
inferior, rity, rly, rity, LESSER THAN ANOTHER, NOT SUPERIOR
infermashen, inform(ation)
infermation, information
infermury, infirmary
infest, *, ed, ting, tation, THREATENINGLY OVERWHELM "prefixes: re"
infeureate, infuriate
infiltrate, *, ed, ting, tion, tive, PASS BEYOND BORDERS OF A SPACE WHERE UNINVITED
infinite, ely, eness, tude, tive, tival, tively, ty, ties, GOES ON AND ON PERHAPS FOREVER
infirmary, ries, SITE FOR MEDICAL CARE
infirmashen, information
infistructure, infrastructure

infite, invite
infiureit, infuriate
infius, infuse
inflagingly, unflagging(ly)
inflame, *, ed, ming, er, mmable, mmability, mmation, mmatory, mmatorily, TO PROVOKE/ INTENSIFY ANGER/ STRONG EMOTIONS, SWOLLEN TISSUE
inflammation, *, SWOLLEN TISSUE
inflapable, unflappable
inflarmeishon, inflammation
inflashen, inflate(tion)
inflate, *, ed, ting, tion, tionism, tionist, table, TO AIR UP, RAISE, EXPAND/ INCREASE "prefixes: dis"
inflection, *, nal, nally, nless, CHANGE IN FORM/ SOUND/ SHAPE
infleit, inflate
inflekshen, inflection
inflexsuble, inflexible
inflemashen, inflammation
inflewance, influence
inflexible, bility, eness, ly, WON'T BEND, STUBBORN, NOT FLEXIBLE
inflextion, inflection
inflict, *, ted, ting, tion, tor, tive, TO CAUSE PAIN, TO BRING ABOUT PUNISHMENT
inflimation, inflammation
influanse, influence
influence, *, ed, cing, eable, er, ntial, ntially, TO IMPRESS/ EXERT UPON, ONE WHO IMPRESSES OTHERS, AUTHORITY, POSITION OF POWER
inform, *, med, ming, mation, mer, mative, matively, mativeness, matory, mant, OFFER ADVICE/ FACTS "prefixes: dis/ un"
informal, lly, lity, NOT FORMAL, RELAXED/ UNRESTRICTED
informant, *, SOMEONE WHO PROVIDES INFORMATION TO HIGHER AUTHORITY
information, nal, COLLECTION OF DATA "prefixes: dis/ mis"
inforse, enforce
infotation, invitation
infra, PREFIX INDICATING "BENEATH" MOST OFTEN MODIFIES THE WORD
infraction, *, BREAK A RULE/ LAW/ CONTRACT

infrared, A LASER TYPE, A LEVEL OF FREQUENCY NEAR THE COLOR RED
infrastructure, SKELETAL/ FOUNDATION OF
infrenge, infringe
infrenji, infringe
infrequent, tly, ncy, OCCASIONALLY
infricuent, infrequent
infringe, *, ed, ging, er, ement, UNLAWFULLY OCCUPY/ DISREGARD SOMEONE'S BOUNDARIES
infugen, infuse(sion)
infultrate, infiltrate
infunuently, infinite(ly)
infunit, infinite
infunsy, infant(ncy)
infunt, infant
infuntry, infantry
infuriate, *, ed, ting, tingly, tion, ely, ENRAGE, FURIOUSLY ANGRY
infurmation, inform(ation)
infurmery, infirmary
infuse, *, ed, sing, sibility, sible, sive, er, LIQUID INTRODUCED/ INJECTED INTO ANOTHER LIQUID
infustashen, infest(ation)
infustrukture, infrastructure
infutashen, invitation
ing, inch
ingage, engage
ingaje, engage
ingalate, ungulate
inganuity, ingenuity
ingection, inject(ion)
ingeil, inhale
ingeilant, inhalant
ingeill, engage
ingekt, inject
ingen, engine
ingeneer, engineer
ingenious, sly, sness, ESPECIALLY CREATIVE IN PERSPECTIVE/ IDEAS (or see ingenuous) "prefixes: dis"
ingenos, ingenious
ingenuity, ties, ABLE TO USE CREATIVE IMAGINATION "prefixes: dis"

ingenuous, sly, sness, GENUINELY HONEST/ DIRECT/ NAIVE/ TRUSTING (or see ingenious) "prefixes: dis"
inger, injure
ingerent, inherent
ingery, injure(ry)
ingest, *, ted, ting, tive, tion, TO SWALLOW, SWALLOWED THROUGH THE MOUTH
inginuity, ingenuity
ingoeuble, enjoy(able)
ingolf, engulf
ingot, *, MASS OR CHUNK OF METAL
ingoy, enjoy
ingrafe, engrave
ingrain, *, ned, ning, ROUTED INTO, CARVED INTO, DEEPLY IMPRESSED WITHIN, ALSO SPELLED "ENGRAIN"
ingrave, engrave
ingredient, *, VARIETY OF ELEMENTS COMBINED TO MAKE SOMETHING ELSE
ingrein, ingrain
ingreiv, engrave
ingridient, ingredient
ingulate, ungulate
ingulf, engulf
ingun, engine
inguneer, engineer
ingury, injure(ry)
ingustes, injustice
inhabetent, inhabit(ant)
inhabit, *, ted, ting, tation, table, tant, tancy, tancies, TO OCCUPY, LIVE IN "prefixes: un"
inhalant, *, A DEVICE FOR BREATHING IN MEDICINE
inhalashin, inhale(lation)
inhale, *, ed, ling, lation, lational, er, lator, BREATH IN
inhanse, enhance
inharent, inherent
inharet, inherit
inharitance, inherit(ance)
inharmonic, ious, iously, iousness, icity, icities, ny, TONES NOT PEAKING TOGETHER, FREQUENCY NOT SYNCHRONIZED (or see enharmonic)
inheil, inhale
inherent, tly, BELONGS AS PART OF THE WHOLE, INSEPARABLE

inherit, *, ted, ting, tor, tress, table, tability, tableness, tance, GOODS AND MONEY RECEIVED WHEN SOMEONE DIES "prefixes: dis"
inhewmane, inhumane
inhibit, *, ted, ting, tor, tory, tive, ter, tion, KEEP BACK/ RESTRAINED, TIMID/ SLOW TO ACT "prefixes: dis/ un"
inhormonic, inharmonic / enharmonic
inhiumein, inhumane
inhobitable, inhospitable
inhospitable, eness, ly, ality, alities, NOT TREATED WARMLY/ FRIENDLY/ GENEROUSLY
inhubeshen, inhibit(ion)
inhulashen, inhale(lation)
inhumane, ely, CRUEL
inicuality, inequality
ingma, enigma / enema
inima, enema / anemia
inime, enemy / enema
inimet, intimate
inimutle, intimate(ly)
ining, inning
iniquity, ties, tous, tously, tousness, COMPLETELY LACKS MORALITY/ JUSTICE/ FAIRNESS
inisheation, initiate(tion)
inishieit, initiate
inishul, initial
inisial, initial
inisieit, initiate
initial, *, led, ling, lly, lize, lizes, lized, lizing, lizer, lism, ORIGINALLY, THE BEGINNING, THE FIRST
initiate, *, ed, ting, tion, tive, tor, tory, BREAK INTO NEW KNOWLEDGE, BEGIN SOMETHING NEW "prefixes: un"
injabit, inhabit
injans, enhance
injarmonic, inharmonic / enharmonic
inje, inch
inject, *, ted, ting, tion, table, tive, tor, INSERT SOMETHING INTO SOMETHING ELSE
injeilent, inhalant
injekshen, inject(ion)
injel, inhale

injelate, ungulate
injen, engine
injeneer, engineer
injeneus, ingenious
injenuidy, ingenuity
injenuous, ingenuous
injenyus, ingenuous
injerent, inherent
injeret, inherit
injest, ingest
injibit, inhibit
injin, engine
injineer, engineer
injiomein, inhumane
injospitabal, inhospitable
injostis, injustice
injoy, enjoy
injoymint, enjoy(ment)
injoyuble, enjoy(able)
injulate, ungulate
injun, engine
injunction, *, , COURT ORDER TO ACT
injure, *, ed, ring, ry, rious, riously, riousness, rer, DAMAGE, OFFEND, VIOLATE ANOTHER'S RIGHTS "prefixes: un"
injustice, *, , NOT PLAYING FAIRLY, SOMEONE'S RIGHTS VIOLATED
ink, *, king, ky, kier, kiest, FLUID USED IN A PEN
inkabuble, incapable
inkadesent, incandescent
inkamped, encamp(ed)
inkampment, encamp(ment)
inkantashen, incantation
inkantation, incantation
inkarsurate, incarcerate
inkase, encase
inkast, encase(d)
inkeipabol, incapable
inker, incur
inkerej, encourage / anchor(age)
inkewbate, incubate
inkiubeit, incubate
inkiur, incur
inkline, incline

inkling, A FEELING/ HINT/ IDEA
inklood, include
inkloshur, enclose(sure)
inkloze, enclose
inklud, include
inklusev, inclusive
inkognito, incognito
inkomber, encumber
inkomodeus, incommode(dious)
inkompruble, incomparable
inkompus, encompass
inkonsistent, inconsistent
inkoreg, encourage / anchor(age)
inkoreguble, incorrigible
inkorpurate, incorporate
inkownter, encounter
inkreduble, incredible
inkredulus, incredulous
inkreese, increase
inkroach, encroach
inkrochment, encroach(ment)
inkrument, increment
inkrust, encrust
inkum, income
inkumbent, incumbent
inkumber, encumber
inkumblete, incomplete
inkumodeus, incommode(dious)
inkumpatuble, incompatible
inkumplete, incomplete
inkumpus, encompass
inkunsiduret, inconsiderate
inkunvenyunt, inconvenient
inkupacity, incapacity
inkurect, incorrect
inkwesishun, inquisition
inkwesutev, inquisitive
inkwire, inquire(ry)
inkwisative, inquisitive
inlaiten, enlighten
inland, der, AWAY FROM THE SEA
inlarch, enlarge
inlarge, enlarge

inlargmint, enlarge(ment)
inlarje, enlarge
inlarll, enlarge
inles, unless
inlest, enlist
inlet, *, ting, RECESS BETWEEN LAND/ WATER, INSERTED
inlist, enlist
inliten, enlighten
inllect, inject
inllenus, ingenious
inllest, ingest
inllin, engine
inllinios, ingenious
inllinir, engineer
inlliur, incur
inlliurabol, incurable
inlloi, enjoy
inllor, injure
inllustis, injustice
inlund, inland
inmachure, immature
inmate, *, ONE CONFINED TO PRISON/ JAIL
inmature, immature
inmeit, inmate
inmertaledy, immortal(ity)
inmortalidy, immortal(ity)
inn, *, A DWELLING TO SLEEP FOR THE NIGHT
innacurate, inaccurate
innate, ely, eness, BELONGS WITH THE BODY
inner, rly, TOWARDS THE CENTER (or see inter)
innerchange, interchange
innerlock, interlock
innerlude, interlude
innermingle, intermingle
innermission, intermission
innermost, DIRECTLY IN THE CENTER
innernational, international
innernet, internet
innerscolastic, interscholastic
innertwine, intertwine
innervene, intervene
inning, *, A SECTION OF PLAY IN A GAME OF SPORTS
innocence, cy, cies, nt, FREE FROM ULTERIOR MOTIVES
innocent, tly, FREE FROM ULTERIOR MOTIVES
innovate, tive, tion, tor, tory, IMPROVE SYSTEM WITH NEW CREATIVE IDEA INSTILLING CHANGE
innuendo, *, UNOBVIOUS / INDIRECT HINT OR MEANING
inoberable, inoperable
inoburatef, inoperable(ative)
inocent, innocence(nt)
inocreate, inaugurate
inoculate, *, ed, ting, able, ability, ation, ative, ator, lum, ant, TO INJECT A PATHOGEN
inodmisabol, inadmissible
inodule, inaudible
inof, enough
ingerashen, inaugurate(tion)
ingerate, inaugurate
ingeration, inaugurate(tion)
ingurate, inaugurate
inokewlate, inoculate
inokewlent, inoculate(ant)
inokulation, inoculate(tion)
inonemus, anonymous
inonseate, enunciate/ annunciate
inoparchun, inopportune
inoperable, bly, bility, bleness, ative, ativeness, WILL NOT OPERATE
inopertiun, inopportune
inopirable, inoperable
inopirate, inoperate
inopirative, inoperate(tive)
inopportune, ely, eness, nity, NOT THE BEST TIME TO ENSURE SUCCESS
inopurable, inoperable
inopurate, inoperate
inopurative, inoperate(tive)
inopurtune, inopportune
inoqulashen, inoculate(tion)
inoqulent, inoculate(ant)
inordinate, acy, ely, eness, EXCESSIVE WITHOUT RESTRAINT/ CONTROL
inordunet, inordinate
inorge, energy
inorgetek, energetic
inormis, enormous
inormus, enormous
inorsect, intersect
inosense, innocence
inotable, inaudible
inougeration, inaugurate(tion)
inovadef, innovate(tive)
inovative, innovate(tive)
inoveit, innovate
inownse, announce
inpar, impair
inpashent, impatient
inpatient, *, VISITS HOSPITAL FOR TREATMENT (or see impatient)
inpech, impeach
inpecuble, impeccable
inpeishant, inpatient / impatient
inperfect, imperfect
impersonashen, impersonate(tion)
impersonate, impersonate
inplie, imply
inpolite, impolite
inpolse, impulse
inport, import
important, important
inpose, impose
inposebul, impossible
inposition, impose(sition)
inpossible, impossible
inposter, imposter
inpound, impound
inpoverish, impoverish
inpownd, impound
inpractical, impractical
inpragnuble, impregnable
inprasise, imprecise
inpravize, improvise
inprecise, imprecise
inpregnable, impregnable
inpregnate, impregnate
inpregnuble, impregnable
inprent, imprint
inpres, impress / empress
inpresion, impression

inpresive,impressive
inpreson,imprison
inprint,imprint
inprison,imprison
inprobuble,improbable
inpromptu,impromptu
inpromtu,impromptu
inpropable,improbable
inproper,improper
inprove,improve
inprovement,improve(ment)
inprovisation,improvise(sation)
inprovise,improvise
inprufment,improve(ment)
inpruve,improve
inpruvize,improvise
inpulse,impulse
inpulsive,impulse(sive)
input,*,tted,tting,ADD TO EXISTING INFORMATION
inquaier,inquire
inquazishen,inquisition
inqubate,incubate
inqueipabol,incapable
inquibeit,incubate
inquire,*,ed,ring,ringly,ry.ries,er,TO ASK OF,SEEK FURTHER INFORMATION
inquisishon,inquisition
inquisition,nal,nist,tor,TAKE PEOPLE IN AGAINST THEIR WILL TO INTERROGATE THEM
inquisitive,ely,eness,tor,TO SEEK ANSWERS/ KNOWLEDGE
inquisitor,rial,rially,TO INTERROGATE
inquiur,incur
inquiurabol,incurable
inquizadive,inquisitive
inquizeshen,inquisition
inrage,enrage
inraj,enrage
inrech,enrich
inreill,enrage
inrich,enrich
inrol,enroll
inrolmint,enroll(ment)

inroot,enroute
inroute,enroute
inrut,enroute
insabordinate,insubordinate
insacure,insecure
insadent,incident
insafishent,insufficient
insaiclopedia,encyclopedia
insaid,inside
insait,insight
insakuredy,insecure(rity)
insalate,insulate
insalin,insulin
insane,ely,eness,nity,nities,THINK IN UNPOPULAR MODALITY,MENTAL HEALTH IN DOUBT
insanetation,insanitary(ation)
insanifekent,insignificant
insanitary,ation,UNCLEAN/ UNACCEPTABLE
insarektion,insurrection
insatiable,ly,bility,eness,ate,APPETITE FOR SOMETHING THAT CANNOT BE SATIATED/ SATISFIED
insatiate,ely,eness,APPETITE FOR SOMETHING THAT CANNOT BE SATIATED/ SATISFIED
insawyuble,insoluble
insayuble,insoluble
insbarashen,inspire(ration)
insbekable,unspeakable
insboken,unspoken
insburashen,inspire(ration)
inscraib,inscribe
inscribe,*,ed,bing,bable,ber,LEAVE A MARK BY ANY METHOD
inscription,*,nal,nless,ive,ively,LEAVING A MARK BY MANY METHODS
inseam,*,SEAM ON THE INSIDE OF PANT LEGS
insebordinate,insubordinate
insect,*,BUGS (or see incest)
insecticide,*,dal,CHEMICALS TO KILL BUGS
insecure,ely,rity,rities,eness,ILL AT EASE,NOT SECURE/ COMFORTABLE WITH ENVIRONMENT
insedent,incident
insedius,insidious
insefficient,insufficient

insegnea,insignia
insegnifakent,insignificant
insein,insane
insejen,incision
insekiur,insecure
insekt,insect
insektaside,insecticide
insekurety,insecure(rity)
inselate,insulate
inselation,insulate(tion)
inseminate,*,ed,ting,tion,INJECT SEMEN INTO
insen,ensign
insenarade,incinerate
insendiary,incendiary
insenea,insignia
insense,incense
insenseer,insincere
insensible,ly,eness,bility,bilities,NOT MAKING SENSE TO PERCEIVER,MISUNDERSTOOD
insensitive,eness,vity,ely,DOESN'T EASILY REACT TO SENSORY INPUT
insentive,incentive
insentuf,incentive
insenuashen,insinuate(tion)
insenuate,insinuate
inseparable,bility,bly,WILL NOT BE DISJOINTED OR TAKEN APART
insepshen,inception(ion)
insept,incept
inseption,incept(ion)
inseqiur,insecure
insercol,encircle
inserekshen,insurrection
inserkle,encircle
insermountable,insurmountable
insert,*,ted,ting,ter,tion,tional,PLACE INTO ALREADY EXISTING FORM OR METHODOLOGY
inseshun,incision
insest,insist / incest / encyst
insestent,insist(ent)
insh,inch
insher,ensure / insure
insherance,insure(rance)

inshree, entry / entree
inshurans, insure(rance)
inshure, insure
insice, incise
insicor, incise(sor)
insicure, insecure
inside, *, er, INTERIOR OF A FORM (or see insight/ incite)
insident, incident
insidious, sly, sness, ILL INTENT DETECTABLE, MANIPULATE TO HARM WITHOUT BEING PERCEIVED AS SO
insidnea, insignia
insificient, insufficient
insigen, incision
insight, *, tful, tfully, tfulness, ABILITY TO PERCEIVE FUTURE OUTCOMES OF CURRENT EVENT (or see inside/ incite)
insightation, incite(tation)
insightment, incite(ment)
insignia, *, BADGES/ MEDALS OF HONOR/ AUTHORITY IN MILITARY
insignificant, tly, nce, NOT SIGNIFICANT/ WORTHY TO CALCULATE IN, NOT IMPORTANT
insiklopedea, encyclopedia
insim, inseam
insinarate, incinerate
insinate, incinerate
insincere, ely, rity, rities, NOT SINCERE/ TRUTHFUL
insinereit, incinerate
insiniueit, insinuate
insinsative, insensitive
insinseer, insincere
insinsuble, insensible
insintuf, incentive
insinuate, *, ed, ting, tion, tive, tingly, tor, LEADING TOWARDS ACCUSATION, INDIRECTLY IMPLYING
insishen, incision
insisor, incise(sor)
insist, *, ted, ting, tingly, tent, tently, tence, tency, MUST HAVE/ BE, ABSOLUTE (or see encyst)
insitation, incite(tation)

insite, inside / insight / incite
insiteful, insight(ful)
insitement, incite(ment)
insiteus, insidious
insition, incision
insize, incise
inskribe, inscribe
inskripshen, inscription
insolbabal, insolvable
insoliubal, insoluble
insoluble, bility, eness, bly, WILL NOT DISSOLVE IN LIQUID
insolvable, NOT ABLE TO BE SOLVED, NO ANSWER
insolvent, *, ncy, NOT ENOUGH FLUID CAPITAL TO GET OUT OF DEBT, CANNOT BE LIQUIDATED
insomnia, ac, PROBLEM SLEEPING
insovable, insolvable
inspaier, inspire
insparation, inspire(ration)
inspect, *, ted, ting, tion, tive, tor, torate, toral, torial, torship, EXAMINE FOR FLAWS
inspekable, unspeakable
insperation, inspire(ration)
inspire, *, ed, ring, ringly, er, ration, rational, rator, EMPOWER, INSTILL FAITH/ HOPE "prefixes: un"
inspoken, unspoken
instagate, instigate
install, *, lled, lling, llation, ller, llment, PUT SOMETHING/ SOMEONE INTO A PLACE TO PERFORM A FUNCTION, MAKE A PAYMENT (or see instill) "prefixes: un"
instance, *, ed, cing, AN EXAMPLE/ MOMENT
instant, tly, taneous, IN A WINK, RIGHT AWAY
instantaneous, sly, sness, HAPPENED SO QUICKLY THAT TIME COULDN'T BE MEASURED
instatushen, institute(tion)
instatute, institute
instaul, install
instaulment, install(ment)
instead, IN PLACE OF, A SUBSTITUTE
instegate, instigate
instenked, instinct
instense, instance
instentaneusly, instantaneous(ly)
instetution, institute(tion)

instigate, *, ed, ting, tion, tive, tor, PROVOKE, STIR UP, INITIATE AN ACTION
instigeit, instigate
instill, *, lled, lling, llation, INTRODUCE GRADUALLY (or see install)
instinct, *, tual, tive, tively, tiveness, KNOWINGNESS WE'RE ALL BORN WITH
instinse, instance
instintaneusly, instantaneous(ly)
institute, *, ed, ting, er, tion, tive, ESTABLISH TO WORK AS A GROUP, FORMAL PLACE OF LEARNING
institution, *, nal, nalism, nalist, nally, nalize, nalizes, nalized, nalizing, nalization, FORMAL PLACE OF LEARNING
instol, install
instolashen, install(ation)
instolment, install(ment)
instrament, instrument
instriment, instrument
instruct, *, ted, ting, tor, tion, tional, tive, tively, tiveness, PROVIDE KNOWLEDGE TO/ FOR OTHERS "prefixes: un"
instrument, *, tal, tally, talist, talism, tality, tation, AN ITEM WHICH MEASURES OR FUNCTIONS AS A DEVICE TO HELP WITH WORK, MUSICAL DEVICE "prefixes: bio"
instugate, instigate
instulation, install(ation) / instill(ation)
instunle, instant(ly)
instunlty, instant(ly)
instunt, instant
insubordinate, *, ely, tion, DOESN'T SUBMIT TO AUTHORITY
insucure, insecure
insue, ensue
insufficient, tly, ncy, ncies, NOT SUFFICIENT, NOT ENOUGH
insugnifakent, insignificant
insukurety, insecure(rity)
insulate, *, ed, ting, tion, tor, LAYER/ COAT OF SOMETHING FOR PROTECTION/ BARRIER
insuleit, insulate

insulin, SECRETED BY A HORMONE IN THE BODY, A MANMADE CHEMICAL TO TREAT DIABETES "prefixes: pro"
insunseer, insincere
insurcle, encircle
insure,*,ed,ring,er,rable,rability,rance, PROTECT AGAINST MONETARY/ PROPERTY/ JOB LOSS (or see ensure/ assure) "prefixes: re/ un/ under"
insurekshen, insurrection
insurens, insure(rance)
insurkle, encircle
insurmauntabol, insurmountable
insurmountable,ly, CANNOT BE ACHIEVED/ OVERCOME
insurrection,nary,naries,nism,nal,nally, REVOLT AGAINST FIGURES OF AUTHORITY
insurshen, insert(ion)
insurt, insert
insyklopedia, encyclopedia
insyme, enzyme
intact,tness, NOT AFFECTED BY A POTENTIALLY DAMAGING EVENT
intaferance, interfere(rance)
integral, integral
integrate, integrate
integration, integrate(tion)
intail, entail
intak, intact / intake
intake, A TUBE/ DEVICE WHICH TAKES IN FLUID/ AIR FOR MECHANICS (or see intact)
intale, entail
intalect, intellect
intalectual, intellect(ual)
intamit, intimate
intangible,*,bility,eness,ly, NOT REAL/ PHYSICAL
intanllibol, intangible
intarier, interior / anterior
intatee, entity
intecate, indicate
integer,*, TERM IN MUSIC AND MATH
integral,*,lly,lity, IMPORTANT PART OF THE WHOLE

integrate,*,ed,ting,ability,tion,tionist,tive,tor, INCLUDE INTO THE WHOLE, MAKE A PART OF A WHOLE "prefixes: dis"
integreit, integrate
integrity,ties, SOUND PRINCIPLES, HONORABLE
inteik, intake
inteligible, intelligible
intellent, intelligent
inteliyent, intelligent
intellect,*,tion,tive,tual,tually,tuality,tualism,tualize, ABILITY FOR MENTAL COMPREHENSION
inteller, integer
intelligent,tly,nce,er, LEVEL OF ABILITY TO PERFORM COMPLEX REASONING "prefixes: un"
intelligible,bility,ly, NOT UNDERSTANDABLE "prefixes: un"
intelugeble, intelligible
intenation, intonate(tion)
intend,*,ded,ding,der,dment, APPARENT GOAL (or see intent)
intense,ely,eness,sity,sities,sive,sively,sify,sifier, sification, FIRM/ FORWARD/ KEEN/ VIGOROUS/ EXTREME
intenshin, intent(ion)
intent,*,tly,tness,tion,tional,tionally,tioned,tionality, THOUGHTFULLY PLAN COURSE OF ACTION "prefixes: un"
inter,*,rred,rring, TO BURY, PREFIX INDICATING "BETWEEN/ AMONG" MOST OFTEN MODIFIES THE WORD (or see enter/ intra)
interact,*,ted,ting,tion,tions,tional,tionism,tionist, tionists,tive,tively,tivity, EXCHANGE BETWEEN TWO/ MORE THINGS (or see enter)
interagate, interrogate
interbin, intervene
intercede,*,ed,ding,er, MEDIATE/ FACILITATE
intercept,*,ted,ting,ter,tion,tive, PASS BETWEEN/ THROUGH A LINE/ OBSTRUCT A LINEAR ACTION
interchange,*,ed,ging,eability,eable,eableness,eably, EXCHANGE/ ALTERNATE BETWEEN/ WITH
intercom, INTERCOMMUNICATION SYSTEM/ COMMUNICATE BY MICROPHONE

interconnect,*,ted,ting,tion,tedness,tible, TO CONNECT BETWEEN TWO SOURCES
intercourse, INTERCHANGE OF FEELINGS/ THOUGHTS, COPULATION
interdisciplinary,rity,rian, WHEN ALL FIELDS/ SYSTEMS ARE INTERCONNECTED/ COMMUNICATING
interest,*,ted,tedly,ting,tingly, ATTENTIVENESS TO LEARN SOMETHING NEW, LENDERS COLLECT THIS "prefixes: dis/ un"
interfere,*,ed,ring,ringly,er,ence,ential, TO INTERCEPT BETWEEN ONGOING EXCHANGE, PRESENCE OF SLOWS PROGRESS
interim, A TEMPORARY PAUSE IN AN ONGOING PROJECT
interior,*,rity,rly,rize,rizes,rized,rizing,rization, INSIDE A STRUCTURE (or see anterior)
interject,*,ted,ting,tion,tory,torily, INTERRUPT WITH INFORMATION
interlock,*,ked,king,ker, CHAINLIKE, ONE ENMESHED WITH ANOTHER, PART OF ONE MECHANISM EMBEDDED INTO THE OTHER
interlude,*,dial, PAUSE DURING A PERFORMANCE/ ACTIVITY
intermediary,ries, FACILITATOR/ AMBASSADOR/ AGENT WHO AIDS COMMUNICATION BETWEEN GROUPS
intermediate,*,ed,ting,tion,tor,ary, HELPS WITH COMMUNICATION BETWEEN PEOPLE/ GROUPS "prefixes: dis"
intermetant, intermittent
intermingle,*,ed,ling,ement, MINGLE TOGETHER, INTERTWINED
intermission,*,ive, A BREAK BETWEEN EVENTS/ ACTIVITY/ PERFORMANCE
intermittent,nce,tly, STOPPING/ STARTING WITH PAUSES IN BETWEEN
intern,*,nship,nist,nment, A STUDENT PRACTICING UNDER SUPERVISION, SOMETHING CONFINED DURING WAR
internal,lly,lize,lization,lity, INSIDE A FORM/ BODY
international,lity,lly,lism,list,lize,lization, OUTSIDE NATIONAL BOUNDARIES
internet, A COMPUTER WEB WHICH LINKS COMPUTERS ALL OVER THE WORLD
interogeit, interrogate

interogeyt, interrogate
interoj, entourage
interpherens, interfere(nce)
interpret,*,,ted,ting,tability,table,ter,tive,tively,tation, REVIEW FACTS FOR FURTHER CLARIFICATION, BRING ABOUT THE MEANING OF
interpretation, nal, ACT OF REVIEWING FACTS FOR FURTHER CLARIFICATION
interprise, enterprise
interrelate, tion, tionship, TO RELATE THINGS TOGETHER, SECURE COMMON GROUND BETWEEN TWO THINGS
interrogate,*,,ed,ting,tion,tional,tive,tively,tor,tory,tories, TRANSMIT A SIGNAL FOR SETTING OFF AN APPROPRIATE RESPONSE, INTENSE QUESTIONING BY AUTHORITIES
interrupt,*,,ted,ting,tion,ter,tive, HINDER THE PROGRESS OF MOMENTARILY "prefixes: un"
interscholastic,*, ACTIVITIES BETWEEN SCHOOLS
intersect,*,,ted,ting,tion,tive, POINT WHERE TWO LINE CRISSCROSS, PLACE WHERE OPPOSING LINES CROSS
intersection,*,,nal, POINT WHERE TWO LINE CRISSCROSS, PLACE WHERE OPPOSING LINES CROSS
intersid, intercede
intersperse,*,,ed,edly,sing,sion, TO SCATTER, BEING SCATTERED ABOUT
interstate,*,, HIWAYS BETWEEN STATES, ROADS CONNECTING STATES
intersteit, interstate
intertane, entertain
intertanment, entertain(ment)
intertwine,*,,ed,ning,ningly,ement, WEAVE TOGETHER
interrupt, interrupt
interval,*, A PAUSE OR GAP BETWEEN
intervene,*,,ed,ning,ner,ntion,ntionist,ntionism, TO INTERFERE, GET BETWEEN
interview,*,,wed,wing,wer,wee, QUESTIONING PERSON FOR QUALIFICATIONS OR ANSWERS
interwoven, INTERTWINED, BRAIDED TOGETHER
intestine,*,,nal,nally, ORGAN INSIDE BODY WHERE FOOD IS PROCESSED
intety, entity
intever, endeavor

inthooseastik, enthuse(siastic)
inthooziazm, enthuse(siasm)
inthrall, enthrall
inthroll, enthrall
inthuseastek, enthuse(siastic)
inthusiasm, enthuse(siasm)
inticate, indicate
intication, indicate(tion)
intidle, entitle
intiger, integer
intigo, indigo
intil, until
intimadate, intimidate
intimadeit, intimidate
intimate, ely, er, tion, CLOSE/ BONDING, MAKE KNOWN
intimidate,*,,ed,ting,tion,tor, ATTEMPT TO LOWER SOMEONE'S SELF ESTEEM/ CONFIDENCE BY APPEARING GREATER THAN THEM
intinse, intense
intinshen, intent(ion)
intire, entire
intirle, entire(ly)
intirlee, entire(ly)
intirmediate, intermediate
intirmitant, intermittent
intirsept, intercept
intirty, entire(ty)
intise, entice
intite, entity
intitle, entitle
intis, endless
into, ENTER TO THE INSIDE
intocsikeit, intoxicate
intoishen, intuit(ion)
intolerable, eness, ly, bility, ance, ant, antly, WILL NOT TOLERATE, NOT ABLE TO DEAL WITH
intolrabol, intolerable
intonate,*,,ed,ting,tion,tional,er, ACCENT ON CERTAIN WORDS WHICH AFFECT MEANING
intormident, intermittent
intorse, endorse / indoor(s)
intortane, entertain
intourage, entourage

intoxicate,*,,ed,edly,ting,tingly,ant,tion, DRUNK FROM ALCOHOL, INEBRIATED, HIGH WITH EXCITEMENT "prefixes: dis"
intoxikeit, intoxicate
intoxiquet, intoxicate
intra, PREFIX INDICATING "INSIDE/ WITHIN" MOST OFTEN MODIFIES THE WORD (or see inter)
intradukshen, introduce(ction)
intraduse, introduce
intrakit, intricate
intramural, lly, EVENTS HAPPENING WITHIN, SCHOOL SPORTS
intrance, entrance
intranet,*, A WEB OF NETWORKING WITHIN A CLOSED/ RESTRICTED COMPUTER SYSTEM
intraspect, introspect
intravenous, sly, INJECTING FLUID INTO VEINS
intrees, entry(ries) / entree
intrege, intrigue
intrense, entrance
intrensic, intrinsic
intres, entry(ries) / entree
intrest, interest / entrust
intricate, ely, eness, acy, acies, OF THE TINIEST DETAIL
intridukshen, introduce(ction)
intrigue,*,,ed,uing,uingly,er, DEEPLY INTERESTED, CAPTIVATED
intrikeit, intricate
intrinsic, cal, cally, calness, ABSOLUTELY IMPORTANT, ESSENTIAL, CANNOT DO WITHOUT IT
intro, PREFIX INDICATING "INSIDE/ WITHIN" MOST OFTEN MODIFIES THE WORD (or see inter)
introduce,*,,ed,cing,er,ction,ctory,ctive,ctorily, ACQUAINTING PEOPLE TOGETHER, PRESENT SOMETHING
introduse, introduce
introspect, tion, tional, tive, tively, tiveness, TO GO WITHIN FOR KNOWLEDGE AND ANSWERS
introst, interest / entrust
introvert,*,,ted,rsion, SOMEONE WHO SPENDS MOST OF THEIR TIME WITH THEMSELVES, DOESN'T SEEK THE OUTSIDE WORLD FOR ANSWERS

intrude,*,ed,ding,er,usion,usive, ENTER WITHOUT INVITATION, FISSURES FILLED WITH MO_TEN LAVA
intrukit, intricate
intramural, intramural
intrunse, entrance
intrusion, ENTER WITHOUT INVITATION, ROCK FORM
intrusive, ely, eness, ENTER WITHOUT INVITATION
intrust, entrust / interest
intry, entry / entree
intu, into
intuative, intuit(ive)
intueshen, intuit(ion)
intufer, interfere
intuger, integer
intugrate, integrate
intuishen, intuit(ion)
intuit, tion, tional, tionism, tionalism, tionist, tive, tively, tiveness, A KNOWINGNESS WE ARE ALL BORN WITH, CAN SEE OUR OWN FUTURE
intunate, intonate
intuneit, intonate
intur, enter / inter
inturage, entourage
inturauj, entourage
inturileit, interrelate
inturmedeate, intermediate
inturmetant, intermittent
inturn, intern
inturnalize, internal(ize)
inturnil, internal
inturoj, entourage
inturopt, interrupt
inturpreit, interpret
inturpret, interpret
inturpretation, interpretation
inturpreteishon, interpretation
inturprise, enterprise
intursede, intercede
intursept, intercept
inturtane, entertain
inturtaner, entertain(er)
inturtanment, entertain(ment)
intutes, entity(ties)

intwoet, intuit(ive)
intyre, entire
inubelidy, inability
inubishen, inhibit(tion)
inucent, innocence(nt)
inuendo, innuendo
inuf, enough
inuindo, innuendo
inume, enemy
inunciate, enunciate/ annunciate
inundate,*,ed,ting,tion, OVERWHELMED, OVERFLOWING, OVER ABUNDANCE
inundeit, inundate
inunseade, enunciate/ annunciate
inupresheative, inappreciative
inuprochible, inapproachable
inupropreut, inappropriate
inur, inner
inuract, interact
inurcom, intercom
inurelate, interrelate
inurem, interim
inurge, energy
inurjetek, energetic
inurlock, interlock
inurlude, interlude
inurmediary, intermediary
inurmingle, intermingle
inurmission, intermission
inurmost, innermost
inurnashenul, international
inurnet, internet
inursculastic, interscholastic
inursection, intersection
inursperse, intersperse
inurt, inert
inurtwine, intertwine
inurupt, interrupt
inurval, interval
inurvene, intervene
inurvue, interview
inurwoven, interwoven
inuscapable, inescapable

inusense, innocence
inuvate, innovate
invade,*,ed,ding,er,asion,asive, OVERWHELM A TERRITORY OR PEOPLES BY UNWELCOME OCCUPATION, ENEMY WHO ENTERS TO OCCUPY A SYSTEM
invaginate,*,ed,ting,tion,tions, MEDICAL TERM INVOLVING FOLDING
invajenation, invaginate(tion)
invalid, dly, dity, date, dation, dator, dism, NOT VALID/ LEGAL, VOIDED, A PERSON INCAPABLE OF FUNCTIONING NORMALLY
invalope, envelope
invaluable, ly, eness, WORTH MORE THAN CAN BE BOUGHT FOR, MOST VALUABLE
invariable, ly, bility, eness, CONSTANT, NEVER CHANGING
invashen, invasion
invashenate, invaginate
invasion,*, nary, ATTEMPT TO CONQUER IN A HOSTILE MANNER, HOSTILE OVERTHROW
invasive, ely, eness, HOSTILE TAKEOVER
invatation, invitation
invate, invade
inved, envy(vied)
invee, envy
invegorate, invigorate
inveich, enrage
invelop, envelope
invensable, invincible
invenshen, invent(ion)
invent,*, ted, ting, tion, tor, tible, tive, tively, tiveness, CREATION FROM THOUGHT "prefixes: dis/ re"
inventory, ries, ried, rying, A CATALOG/ LIST OF GOODS
inverdebrate, invertebrate
inveriably, invariable(ly)
inverse,*, ely, sion, sive, rt, SWITCH AROUND, MAKE OPPOSITE, INSIDE OUT
inversion,*, ive, SWITCH AROUND, MAKE OPPOSITE, INSIDE OUT
invert,*,ed,tibility,tible,ter,rsion,rsive,SWITCH AROUND, MAKE OPPOSITE, INSIDE OUT
invertebrate,*, HAS NO SPINE/ BACKBONE
inves, envy(vies)

Column 1	Column 2	Column 3
invesible, invisible	inwrech, enrich	ipaukalypse, apocalypse
invest, *, ted, ting, tment, PUT TIME/ MONEY INTO SOMETHING/ PROJECT "prefixes: dis/ re"	inwroll, enroll	ipaukolypse, apocalypse
investigate, *, ed, ting, tion, tive, tor, tory, SEARCH FOR CLUES/ ANSWERS/ SIGNS	inyect, inject	ipawkalypse, apocalypse
investmunt, invest(ment)	inyest, ingest	ipoculypse, apocalypse
invetation, invitation	inyor, injure	ipokalypse, apocalypse
inveuble, enviable	inyostice, injustice	ipokolypse, apocalypse
inveus, envious	inyur, injure	ipokulypse, apocalypse
invezible, invisible	inzyme, enzyme	iquabol, equable
invigorate, *, ed, ting, tingly, tion, tive, tively, ant, er, BRING EXCITEMENT TO, RENEW	**iodine**, A CHEMICAL ELEMENT	iqual, equal
invilope, envelope	iol, yowl	iquevocate, equivocate
invincible, eness, ly, bility, NOT ABLE TO CONQUER/ PENETRATE	iomp, jump / hump	iquip, equip
invintory, inventory	**ion**, *, nize, nizes, nized, nizing, nizer, nization, nizable, ATOM/ PARTICLE WITH A CHARGE "prefixes: inter"	iquiti, equity
invious, envious	ionait, unite	iquivocate, equivocate
invirenment, environment	ionder, yonder	iqwantense, acquaintance
invirunmental, environment(al)	ionesfer, ionosphere	**ir**, PREFIX INDICATING "NOT" MOST OFTEN MODIFIES THE WORD (or see ear / ire)
invisability, invisible(bility)	ionesphere, ionosphere	irabrochuble, irreproachable
invisible, ly, eness, bility, NOT PERCEIVABLE, CANNOT SEE/ FEEL	iong, young	iradebul, irritable
invitation, *, nal, ASKED TO COME TO AN EVENT, WELCOME TO VISIT	iongster, youngsters	iradek, erratic / erotic
invite, *, ed, ting, tingly, tingness, ee, tor, tation, tatory, ASKED TO COME TO AN EVENT, WELCOME TO VISIT, OFFER PLEASURE "prefixes: dis/ un"	ionic, unique	iradekate, eradicate
inviteishon, invitation	ionik, unique	iradesent, iridescent
invoice, *, ed, cing, A DETAILED BILL DUE AND OWING	ionisfere, ionosphere	iradiate, irradiate
involope, envelope	ionison, unison	iradic, erratic / erotic
involuntary, rily, riness, DID NOT VOLUNTEER	**ionosphere**, ric, A PROTECTIVE LAYER SURROUNDING THE EARTH ABOVE 43 MILES, HOLES MADE IN IT WITH ROCKETS CREATE OZONE DEPLETION	iradikeit, eradicate
involve, *, ed, ving, ement, er, BE CAUGHT UP IN, INTERACTING WITH, OBLIGATE TIME/ THOUGHT "prefixes: un"	ionster, youngsters	iradubel, irritable
invotashen, invitation	iorin, urine	iradukashen, eradicate(tion)
invoyce, invoice	iosurp, usurp	iragardles, irregardless
invulid, invalid	iouc, yoke	iragashen, irrigate(tion)
invurdabrae, invertebrate	ioudel, yodel	iragate, irrigate
invurt, invert	iouga, yoga	iraguardless, irregardless
invy, envy	iougi, yogi	iraknid, arachnid
inward, *, dly, dness, FACING TOWARDS THE INSIDE, ON IN SIDE	iougurt, yogurt	iranment, arraign(ment)
inword, inward	iouman, yeoman	irant, errant
	iouni, yoni	iraplasible, irreplaceable
	ioupan, yaupon	iraproachable, irreproachable
	ipacalypse, apocalypse	irapt, irrupt
	ipacolypse, apocalypse	irasbonsabol, irresponsible
	ipaculypse, apocalypse	irasbonsuble, irresponsible
	ipakalypse, apocalypse	irase, erase
	ipakulypse, apocalypse	iraser, eraser
	ipaucalypse, apocalypse	irashenul, irrational
		irasistible, irresistible
		iraspective, irrespective

iraspektif, irrespective
irasponsuble, irresponsible
iratable, irritable
iratible, irritable
iratant, irritant
iratashen, irritate(tion)
iratate, irritate
iratation, irritate(tion)
irate, ely, eness, ANGRY
iratent, irritant
iratic, erratic / erotic
irational, irrational
iratrevible, irretrievable
iratuble, irritable
iraudik, erratic / erotic
iravokuble, irrevocable
iraze, erase
irazer, eraser
irazistuble, irresistible
irchin, urchin
ire, eful, efully, efulness, WRATH, INTENSE ANGER
irebrochuble, irreproachable
irect, erect
iredescent, iridescent
iredesent, iridescent
iredibl, irritable
iredubl, irritable
iregardless, irregardless
iregashen, irrigate(tion)
iregate, irrigate
iregation, irrigate(tion)
iregeuler, irregular
iregeuleredy, irregular(ity)
iregewler, irregular
ireglur, irregular
ireguardless, irregardless
iregular, irregular
iregularedy, irregular(ity)
ireit, irate
irekshen, erect(ion)
irekt, erect
irelavense, irrelevant(nce)
irelebant, irrelevant

irelevant, irrelevant
irelevense, irrelevant(nce)
ireluvense, irrelevant(nce)
ireluvint, irrelevant
iren, iron
ireny, irony
ireperuble, irreparable
irepirable, irreparable
ireproachable, irreproachable
ireprochible, irreproachable
irepruble, irreparable
irepurable, irreparable
ires, iris
iresbonsuble, irresponsible
iresistible, irresistible
irespective, irrespective
irespektif, irrespective
iresponsuble, irresponsible
iretant, irritant
iretashen, irritate(tion)
iretate, irritate
iretibul, irritable
iretreavible, irretrievable
iretribable, irretrievable
iretrievable, irretrievable
iretrivable, irretrievable
irevocable, irrevocable
irg, urge
irgint, urge(nt)
iribrochuble, irreproachable
irid, PREFIX INDICATING "IRIS/ RAINBOW" MOST OFTEN MODIFIES THE WORD
iridable, irritable
iridescent, tly, nce, A LIGHT REFLECTION WITH RAINBOW COLORS, ALSO SPELLED "IRRIDESCENT"
iriduble, irritable
irifd, arrive(d)
iriful, arrive(val)
irigardles, irregardless
irigashen, irrigate(tion)
irigate, irrigate
irigation, irrigate(tion)
irigeit, irrigate

iring, earring
iriplasible, irreplaceable
iriplecabol, irreplaceable
iris, PART OF THE EYE, A FLOWER
irisbonsuble, irresponsible
irisistible, irresistible
irispective, irrespective
irispektif, irrespective
irisponsuble, irresponsible
iritable, irritable
iritashen, irritate(tion)
iritate, irritate
iritation, irritate(tion)
iriteit, irritate
iritrevible, irretrievable
irivokuble, irrevocable
irizisduble, irresistible
irj, urge
irk, *, ked, king, ANNOYING
irn, earn / urn / iron
irnd, earn(ed) / iron(ed)
irnest, earnest
irochun, erosion
irode, erode
irodinamic, aerodynamic
irodynamic, aerodynamic
irogate, irrigate
iron, *, ned, ning, A METAL, A TOOL FOR TAKING WRINKLES OUT OF CLOTHES/ TOOL FOR GOLF/ SMOOTH OUT WRINKLES
irone, irony
ironic, cal, cally, ny, calness, OPPOSITE TO WHAT YOU WOULD EXPECT
irony, nies, ODDLY COINCIDENTAL
iropt, irrupt
irosbonsuble, irresponsible
irosef, erosive
iroshin, erosion
irosif, erosive
irosponsuble, irresponsible
irote, erode
iroud, erode
irovokuble, irrevocable

irowze,arouse
irradescent,iridescent
irradiate,*,ed,ting,tion,tor,ant,ILLUMINATE, EXPOSE TO RADIATION
irragate,irrigate
irragation,irrigate(tion)
irrant,errant
irraplasible,irreplaceable
irraproachable,irreproachable
irratable,irritable
irratant,irritant
irratate,irritate
irrate,irate
irratic,erratic
irrational,lity,lness,lly,lism,list,listic,NOT RATIONAL, NOT ABLE TO PROVE RATIONALE
irredescent,iridescent
irregardless,NOT REGARDED,ASIDE FROM THAT
irregate,irrigate
irregation,irrigate(tion)
irregular,*,rly,rity,NOT REGULAR
irreis,erase
irrelavent,irrelevant
irrelevant,ntly,nce,ncy,NOT RELEVANT, DOES NOT PERTAIN TO
irrepairable,irreparable
irreparable,ly,eness,bility,CANNOT BE REPAIRED
irreplaceable,ly,eness,bility,NOT ABLE TO BE REPLACED
irreproachable,ly,eness,bility,NOT ABLE TO BE APPROACHED, UNBLEMISHED
irresistible,ly,eness,bility,NOT ABLE TO RESIST
irrespective,ely,NOT TO BE CONSIDERED IN THE EQUATION/ CIRCUMSTANCE/ EVENT
irresponsible,ly,eness,bility,NOT RESPONSIBLE
irretrievable,ly,eness,bility,NOT ABLE TO BE UNDONE/ CHANGED
irrevocable,ly,eness,bility,NOT REVERSIBLE, CANNOT BE UNDONE/ CHANGED
iridescent,iridescent
irrigate,*,ed,ting,tion,tional,tive,tor,METHOD OF PROVIDING WATER TO "prefixes: sub"
irriplasible,irreplaceable
irritable,ly,eness,bility,ANNOY/ AGGRAVATE/ STIMULATE, INFLAMED TISSUE

irritant,*,ncy,ncies,SOMETHING THAT IRRITATES
irritate,*,ed,ting,tion,tive,tingly,tor,ANNOY/ AGGRAVATE/ STIMULATE, INFLAMMED TISSUE
irrogate,irrigate
irrouchon,erosion
irrousion,erosion
irrugation,irrigate(tion)
irruplacable,irreplaceable
irrupt,*,ted,ting,tion,tive,tively,SUDDENLY/ FORCIBLY INVADE/ ENTER (or see erupt)
irrutable, irritable
irth,earth
irubshen,erupt(ion) / irrupt(ion)
irubt, erupt / irrupt
irubtif,erupt(ive) / irrupt(ive)
irudebul,irritable
irudibul,irritable
irugardles,irregardless
irugashen,irrigate(tion)
irugate, irrigate
irugation,irrigate(tion)
iruguardless,irregardless
irune,irony
iruplaseble,irreplaceable
iruprochuble,irreproachable
irupshen, erupt(ion) / irrupt(ion)
irupt, erupt / irrupt
iruptif, erupt(ive) / irrupt(ive)
iruption, erupt(ion) / irrupt(ion)
irus, iris
irusbonsuble, irresistible
irusistible, irresistible
iruspective, irrespective
iruspektif, irrespective
irusponsuble, irresponsible
irutable, irritable
irutashen, irritate(tion)
irutate,irritate
irutation,irritate(tion)
irutrevible,irretrievable
irutrievable, irretrievable
irutuble, irritable
iruvokuble, irrevocable

iruzistuble,irresistible
is,THIRD PERSON SINGULAR, PRESENT IN TIME, PREFIX INDICATING "EQUAL" MOST OFTEN MODIFIES THE WORD (or see ease/ eye(s))
isalashen,isolate(tion)
isalation, isolate(tion)
isay,essay
isbeshalee, especially
isbeshulee, especially
iscape, escape
isdeem, esteem
ise, ice / icy / eye(s)
isel, easel
iselate, isolate
iselation, isolate(tion)
isenchol, essential
isencial, essential
isense, essence
isenshil, essential
isent, isn't
isential, essential
ishew, issue
ishu, issue
ishuense, issue(uance)
isier, icy(cier)
isikle, icicle
isilate, isolate
isilation, isolate(tion)
ising, icing
isinshul, essential
isint, isn't
isisly, easily
iskape, escape
iskort, escort
island,*,der,BODY OF LAND SURROUNDED BY WATER, ONE WHO LIVES ON AN ISLAND "prefixes: inter"
ism,*,A SUFFIX WHICH MEANS A SYSTEM OF PRINCIPLES, A PRACTICE
isment, easement
isn't,CONTRACTION OF THE WORDS 'IS NOT'
iso,PREFIX INDICATING "EQUAL" MOST OFTEN MODIFIES THE WORD
isofigus, esophagus

isolashen,isolate(tion)
isolate, *,ed,ting,tion,tionism,tionist,TO PREVENT HAVING CONTACT WITH ANOTHER THING
isoleit,isolate
isoli,easily
isoteric,esoteric
ispeshalee,especially
ispeshulee,especially
issuanse,issue(uance)
issue, *,ed,uing,er,uance,uable,DISTRIBUTE/ HAND OUT INFORMATION,POINT OF MATTER "pre=ixes: un"
issuence,issue(uance)
ist,east
istablish,establish
istablush,establish
isteem,esteem
istrologe,astrology
istros,estrus
istrus,estrus
isu,issue
isuance,issue(uance)
isue,issue
isuinse,issue(uance)
isulashen,isolate(tion)
isulate,isolate
isulation,isolate(tion)
it, *,PRONOUN REFERRING TO PERSON/ PLACE/ THING/ TIME/ EVENT (or see eat/ ate/ eight)
it'll,CONTRACTION OF THE WORDS 'IT WILL'
it's,CONTRACTION OF THE WORDS 'IT IS'
itach,attach
itak,attack
italic, *,cize,cized,cizing,cization,SLANTED STYLE OF PRINT TO ATTRACT ATTENTION
italisize,italic(ize)
itch,hes,hed,hing,hy,hiness,DESIRE TO SCRATCH,A NEED TO SATISFY (or see etch)
item, *,mize,mizer,mization,ARTICLE/ UNIT IN A COLLECTION,AN OBJECT
itenarary,itinerary
itenerate,itinerate
iteosy,idiocy
iternul,eternal

iteut,idiot
itinerary,ries,ate,ation,LIST OF DETAILS PERTAINING TO A TRIP
itinerate, *,ed,ting,ration,ary,LIST OF DETAILS PERTAINING TO A TRIP
itl,it'll / idle / idol
its,it's
itself,ONE ON ITS OWN
itsetera,etcetera
itul,idol / idle / it'll
itum,item
itumize,item(ize)
iturnal,eternal
iu,ewe / you / yew
iud,you'd
iudine,iodine
iul,you'll / yule / I'll
iun,ion
iunaited,unite(d)
iune,uni
iunecorn,unicorn
iunefai,unity
iuneform,uniform
iunesaicol,unicycle
iuni,uni
iunicorn,unicorn
iunifai,unity
iuniform,uniform
iunion,union
iunisaicol,unicycle
iunit,unit
iunitary,unitary
iuniteri,unitary
iuniti,unity
iuniversal,universal
iuniversiti,university
iunizur,ion(izer)
iur,your / you're
iurainium,uranium
iurathein,urethane
iurenolochi,uranology
iuria,urea
iuric,uric

iurinal,urinal
iurinari,urinary
iurineit,urinate
iurinol,urinal
iuriter,ureter
iurithein,urethane
iurithra,urethra
iurn,iron
iurologi,urology
iurs,yours
iurself,yourself
iurt,yurt
ius,use
iuser,user
iuseri,usury
iusful,useful
iushual,usual
iusles,useless
iutensol,utensil
iuteros,uterus
iuterus,uterus
iuth,youth
iuthfol,youthful
iutilais,utilize
iutilaiz,utilize
iutiliterian,utilitarian
iutilit,utility
iutinsil,utensil
iutopia,utopia
iuv,you've
ivacuate,evacuate
ivade,evade
ivakuashen,evacuate(tion)
ivakuate,evacuate
ivalueit,evaluate
ivaluashen,evaluate(tion)
ivaluate,evaluate
ivant,event
ivaparate,evaporate
ivaporate,evaporate
ivaporeit,evaporate
ivaquiveit,evacuate
ive,ivy

iveicion, evasion	izteem, esteem	jaidro, hydro
iveid, evade	jab, *, bbed, bbing, TO POKE, PUNCH (or see gab)	jaidrochen, hydrogen
iveishon, evasion	jabber, *, red, ring, ry, TALKS VERY FAST	jaidroelectric, hydroelectric
iven, even	jaber, jabber	jaidrollen, hydrogen
ivent, event	jabil, hobble	jaidroponic, hydroponic
ivning, evening	jabit, habit	jaier, hire / high(er)
ivoke, evoke	jabitat, habitat	jaifen, hyphen
ivol, evil	jabitchual, habitual	jaigantic, gigantic
ivolushon, evolution	jabitual, habitual	jaigro, hygro
ivolution, evolution	jac, hack / jack	jaik, hike
ivolve, evolve	jach, hatch	jaiku, haiku
ivory, A BONE OR HORN FROM MAMMALS	jachet, hatchet	jail, *, A BUILDING WHERE PEOPLE WHO BREAK LAWS ARE CONFINED (or see hale/ hail)
ivow, avow	jack, *, ked, king, ker, TO STEAL, TO RAISE/ LIFT, A GAME , PREFIX INDICATING "MALE/ LARGE/ HEAVY" MOST OFTEN MODIFIES THE WORD	jaillak, hijack
ivry, ivory		jaimlic, Heimlich
ivs, eaves		jaind, hind
ivy, vies, vied, A PLANT	jackass, sses, MALE DONKEY	jainder, hinder
ixagerate, exaggerate	jacket, *, ted, tless, A COVERING, PROTECTIVE COAT	jainderens, hinder(ance)
ixajurate, exaggerate	jacks, ses, TOOLS FOR HOLDING UP CARS, A GAME FOR KIDS	jaindrens, hinder(ance)
ixamunashen, examine(nation)		jainecolollist, gynecologist
ixblanatory, explanatory	jad, had / jade	jainter, hinder
ixempt, exempt	jade, *, ed, edly, edness, LACK OF ENTHUSIASM/ INTEREST RESULTING FROM TOO MUCH OF SOMETHING, A PRECIOUS STONE	jaip, hype
ixemshen, exempt(ion)		jaiper, hyper
ixequtif, executive		jaiperactive, hyperactive
ixitment, excite(ment)	jadent, hadn't	jaipo, hypo
ixkershen, excursion	jaeiv, have	jaipothermia, hypothermia
ixklude, exclude	jael, jail	jaipothesis, hypothesis
ixklute, exclude	jaf, half	jaipotnus, hypotenuse
ixkurjen, excursion	jafent, haven't	jair, hair / hire / high(er)
ixkus, excuse	jag, *, gged, gging, gger, gless, UNEVEN CUTS, POKE/ STAB/ SPREE	jaireit, gyrate
ixost, exhaust		jairoglifs, hieroglyphs
ixperiense, experience	jafhazerd, haphazard	jaiser, geyser
ixpire, expire	jagard, haggard	jait, height
ixplanatory, explanatory	jai, hi / high	jaiv, hive / jive
ixplisitly, explicit(ly)	jaiant, giant	jak, jack / hack / hawk
ixploet, exploit	jaiberneit, hibernate	jaket, jacket
ixseluratur, accelerate(tor)	jaibrid, hybrid	jaks, jacks
izbeshulee, especially	jaichin, hygiene	jal, jail / hall / haul
izenshil, essential	jaicu, haiku	jale, jail / jelly
izkape, escape	jaidaut, hideout	jaleluya, hallelujah
izkort, escort	jaidout, hideout	jalf, half
izment, easement	jaidrant, hydrant	jalibot, halibut
izoteric, esoteric	jaidraulic, hydraulic	jalibut, halibut
iztablish, establish	jaidreit, hydrate	

jalou,halo / hollow
jalouin,Halloween
jalow,halo
jalowin,Halloween
jalter,halter
jalv,halve
jaly,july / jelly
jam,*,FRUIT SPREAD,BEING STUCK (or see jamb/ ham)
jamb,*,HOLDS A STABLE OPENING FOR A DOOR (or see jam)
jamburger,hamburger
jamer,hammer
jamok,hammock
jamper,hamper
jamster,hamster
janch,haunch
jand,hand
jandaut,handout
jandel,handle
jandi,handy
jandicap,handicap
jandkerchiv,handkerchief
janedics,genetic(s)
janewery,january
janitor,*,tial,A CUSTODIAN,SOMEONE WHO SEES TO CLEANING/ MAINTENANCE OF PUBLIC BUILDING
jankerchief,handkerchief
janmeid,handmade
jant,haunt
january,A MONTH OF THE YEAR (ENGLISH)
januery,january
januyery,january
japen,happen
japi,happy
jar,*,rred,rring,STARTLE SOMEONE,GLASS CONTAINER WITH A LID (or see hor·or)
jarbor,harbor
jard,hard
jardi,hardy
jardli,hardly
jardship,hardship
jardwar,hardware
jargon,*,A DIALECT,THE WAY A LANGUAGE IS SPOKEN

jarm,harm
jarmonais,harmonize
jarmoni,harmony
jarmonic,harmonic
jarnes,harness
jarp,harp
jarpsicord,harpsichord
jarpun,harpoon
jarras,harass
jarsh,harsh
jarship,hardship
jart,heart
jartles,heartless
jarvest,harvest
jas,jazz / has
jasard,hazard
jasel,hassle
jasent,hasn't
jash,hash
jasol,hassle
jasture,gesture
jat,hat
jau,jaw / how
jaudy,haughty
jauever,however
jauk,hawk
jaul,haul / howl
jault,halt / hold
jaunch,haunch
jaund,hound
jaundice,ed,AN UNHEALTHY BODY CONDITION
jauns,jounce
jaunt,*,SPONTANEOUS/ BRIEF JOURNEY (or see haunt)
jauntlit,gauntlet
jaurt,heart
jaus,house / jaw(s) / joust
jaust,joust
jauti,haughty
jav,halve / have
java,COMPUTER SOFTWARE,COFFEE BEVERAGE
javen,haven
javent,haven't
jaw,*,PART OF THE MOUTH (or see how)

jawalk,jaywalk
jawlt,halt / hold
jawolk,jaywalk
jayer,hair / hire / high(er)
jayfen,hyphen
jayllin,hygiene
jaywalk,*,ked,king,ker,CROSSING A STREET AT AN INAPPROPRIATE PLACE
jazz,zes,zed,zing,zy,TYPE OF MUSIC,TO MODERNIZE
jealous,sy,sness,sly,sies,EMOTION WHICH ERUPTS WHEN ONE IS INSECURE/ FEARFUL
jean,*,THICK FABRIC USED FOR PANTS (or see gene)
jeaneul,genial
jeauluge,geology
jeb,gibe / jib / jibe
jebalashen,jubilant(ation)
jebi,heavy
jeburish,gibber(ish)
jecal,heckle
jech,jig / gig
jecol,heckle
jecs,hex
jectari,hectare
jectic,hectic
jecto,hecto
jed,head
jedch,hedge
jeens,jean(s) / gene(s)
jeep,*,A STYLE OF VEHICLE (or see gyp)
jefe,jiffy
jefer,heifer
jegle,jiggle
jegsaw,jigsaw
jei,hay / hey
jeil,hail / hale
jeilow,halo
jeing,hang
jeingar,hangar
jeiol,hale
jeis,haze
jeisel,hazel
jeiser,geyser
jeisol,hazel

jeist, haste
jeisten, hasten
jeit, hate
jeivac, jaywalk
jeiven, heaven / haven
jeiz, haze
jel, jail / gel / jell / hell
jelatin, gelatin
jelatnus, gelatin(ous)
jeld, held
jele, jelly
jelful, helpful
jeli, july / jelly
jelicopter, helicopter
jelis, jealous
jeliten, gelatin
jell, *, led, ling, ly, lify, CONSISTENCY BETWEEN LIQUID AND SOLID, A GELATIN (or see gel)
jello, A BRAND NAME FOR 'GEL', A GELATIN
jelly, llies, llied, llying, llify, llifying, llified, FRUIT SPREAD, SEMI SOLID SUBSTANCE
jelm, helm
jelmet, helmet
jelo, hello / jello
jelos, jealous
jelow, hello / yellow
jelp, help
jelpfol, helpful
jelplei, helpless
jelt, health
jelth, health
jeluten, gelatin
jely, july / jelly / hill
jem, gem / gym / hem / hymn / jam
jemi, hemi
jemisfir, hemisphere
jemmy, jimmy
jemnaseum, gymnasium
jemnast, gymnast
jemp, hemp
jen, gene / jean / hen
jena, henna
jenarashin, generation

jenarate, generate
jenarator, generator
jenarus, generous
jenaside, genocide
jendur, gender
jene, genie
jeneal, genial
jeneol, genial
jenereit, generate
jenerik, generic
jenerul, general
jenerus, generous
jenetic, genetics
jeneus, genius
jengle, jingle
jengur, ginger
jenicide, genocide
jenks, jinx
jenome, genome
jenorashon, generation
jenrul, general
jens, jean(s) / gene(s) / hence
jenter, gender
jentul, gentle
jentur, gender
jenuen, genuine
jenul, gentle
jenurulize, general(ize)
jenus, genus
jenyus, genius
jeografy, geography
jeol, jail / gel / jell
jeological, geology(gical)
jeometry, geometry
jeopardy, dize, dizes, dized, dizing, GREAT RISK OF DANGER IF NOT SKILLFUL ENOUGH
jep, gyp / jeep
jepardy, jeopardy
jepataitis, hepatitis
jeperdize, jeopardy(dize)
jepsee, gypsy
jepsum, gypsum
jer, her

jerbul, gerbil
jerd, heard / herd
jereditari, hereditary
jeredity, heredity
jeresdikshen, jurisdiction
jerk, *, ked, king, kily, kiness, ky, QUICK MOTION/ JOLT
jerky, DRIED MEAT
jermanate, germinate
jermit, hermit
jernal, journal
jernalist, journal(ist)
jerney, journey
jeror, juror
jerouin, heroin
jerowin, heroin
jerself, herself
jerselv, herself
jery, jury
jesitant, hesitant
jest, ter, ting, tingly, IN FUN, TO MAKE LIGHT OF
jesture, gesture
jet, *, ted, ting, ty, A PLANE, A ROCK, TYPE OF STREAM ACTION (or see get)
jete, jetty
jetero, hetero
jeterow, hetero
jeti, jetty
jeto, ghetto
jetsam, WASTE/ ITEMS ELIMINATED FROM A JET
jetty, ties, PIER/ STRUCTURE AT AN OCEAN SHORE
jety, jetty
jeulogical, geology(gical)
jevi, heavy
jewbalee, jubilee
jewdeshul, judicial
jewdishes, judicious
jewel, *, lry, ler, DECORATIVE ORNAMENTS FOR THE BODY (or see joule)
jewly, july
jewn, june
jewse, juice
jewt, jute
jewvinile, juvenile

Word	Definition/Related
jex, hex	
jexagon, hexagon	
ji, he / hi / high	
jib, *, bed, bing, ber, SAIL OF A BOAT, ARM OF A CRANE (or see jibe/ gibe)	
jibachi, hibachi	
jibapadamos, hippopotamus	
jibe, *, ed, bing, SAILING TERM, CONFORM, SHIFT (or see gibe)	
jich, hitch	
jicop, hiccup	
jid, he'd / heed / hid	
jidious, hideous	
jidius, hideous	
jier, hear	
jierd, heard	
jif, heave	
jife, jiffy	
jiffy, DONE FAST	
jifi, jiffy	
jig, *, ged, ging, ger, A DANCE, FISHING/ TOOLING DEVICE, TEMPLATE (or see gig) "prefixes: re"	
gigantic, gigantic	
jigger, A TOOL, THING THAT DOESN'T HAVE A NAME "A THING AMA JIGGER", MEASURING DEVICE	
jiggle, *, ed, ling, ly, ACTION LIKE JELLO IN MOTION, DANCE MOVEMENT (or see giggle)	
jigsaw, *, wed, wing, A CUTTING TOOL, A PUZZLE	
jil, heel / heal / hill / he'll	
jilarios, hilarious	
jilatnus, gelatin(ous)	
jilio, helio	
jilium, helium	
jilt, *, ted, ting, ter, REJECT SOMEONE'S AFFECTION (or see hilt)	
jily, july / jelly	
jim, gem / gym / him / hymn	
jimic, gimmick	
jimmy, mies, mied, ying, FORCE A LOCK TO OPEN	
jimnaseum, gymnasium	
jimnast, gymnast	
jimneisium, gymnasium	
jimnest, gymnast	

Word	Definition/Related
jimself, himself	
jin, jean / hen	
jinarashin, generation	
jinarate, generate	
jinarator, generator	
jinarulize, general(ize)	
jinarus, generous	
jinch, hinge	
jind, hind / hint	
jinder, gender / hinder	
jinderens, hindrance	
jindrens, hindrance	
jindur, gender / hinder	
jinerik, generic	
jinetic, genetics	
jinger, ginger	
jingle, *, ed, ling, ly, BELL SOUNDS, BRIEF, CATCHY TUNE	
jinks, jinx	
jinocide, genocide	
jinrul, general	
jint, hint	
jinter, gender	
jintul, gentle	
jinuen, genuine	
jinurulize, general(ize)	
jinus, genus	
jinuside, genocide	
jinusist, genesis	
jinx, xes, xed, SOMETHING THAT CAUSES BAD LUCK	
jiol, heal / he'll / heel / hill	
jiolugee, geology	
jiometry, geometry	
jiost, just	
jiostis, justice	
jip, **gyp** / heap / hip	
jipapadamos, hippopotamus	
jipnosis, hypnosis	
jipnotic, hypnotic	
jipnotiz, hypnotize	
jipocrit, hypocrite	
jipse, gypsy	
jipsi, gypsy	
jipsom, gypsum	

Word	Definition/Related
jipsum, gypsum	
jiir, here / hear / her	
jirate, gyrate	
jirble, gerbil	
jirm, germ	
jirmanate, germinate	
jirney, journey	
jirnul, journal	
jirnulist, journal(ist)	
jirou, hero	
jirow, hero	
jirs, hearse	
jirsei, hearsay	
jirur, juror	
jiry, jury	
jis, he's / hiss / his	
jisdori, history	
jisdorian, historian	
jisdoric, historic	
jisterectomi, hysterectomy	
jisterical, hysterical	
jistori, history	
jistorian, historian	
jistoric, historic	
jit, heat / hit / he'd	
jitter, *, red, ring, ry, BRIEF BURSTS OF SHAKING OR JIGGLING, A DANCE, FEARFUL REACTION	
jiu, hue	
jiubili, jubilee	
jiuch, huge	
jiuman, human	
jiumer, humor / hummer	
jiumes, hummus	
jiumid, humid	
jiumiliachon, humiliate(tion)	
jiumiliate, humiliate	
jiumiliti, humility	
jiumor, humor / hummer	
jiumus, hummus / humus	
jiv, heave	
jive, *, ed, ving, A RHYTHM STYLE OF MUSIC AND ALL ASSOCIATED WITH IT, MISLEADING/ PHONY (or see hive)	

job, *, bless, blessness, WORKING CONSISTENTLY FOR INCOME
jobcap,hubcap
jobi,hobby
joc,hock / hawk
joch,judge / hutch
jochmint,judge(gment)
joci,hockey
jock, *, SOMEONE WHO FOCUSES PRIMARILY ON SPORTS IN SCHOOL
jockey, *, yed, ying, RIDER IN HORSE RACING, METAPHOR FOR GETTING INTO POSITION TO WIN
joclberi,huckleberri
jocolberi,huckleberry
jod,hod / hoe(d) / hold / hard
jodol,huddle
joe,joy / hoe
joen,join
joent,joint / join(ed) / jaunt
joest,joist / hoist
jof,huff / hoof
jofeul,jovial
jog, *, gged, gging, gger, TYPE OF RUNNING (or see hog/ hug)
jogur,jog(gger)
join, *, ned, ning, nable, ner, BRING TWO OR MORE INDEPENDENT THINGS/ GROUPS TOGETHER IN UNION "prefixes: con/ dis/ en/ re/ sub/ un"
joint, *, ted, ting, WHERE PARTS INTERSECT, JUNCTION "prefixes: con/ dis/ un"
joist, *, HORIZONTAL/ PARALLEL BOARDS IN A STRUCTURE/ FOUNDATION (or see hoist)
jok,jock / joke
joke, *, ed, king, kingly, er, ester, COMMENT/ STORY INTENDED TO GENERATE LAUGHTER (or see jock)
joki,hockey / hokey
joky,jockey
jol,joule / jewel / hall / whole / hole / haul
jold,hold
jolder,holder / halter
jole,jolly / hole / whole
joler,holler
jolidei,holiday

jolly, lier, liest, lity, MERRY, LIVELY, GAY
jolocost,holocaust
jologram,hologram
jolseil,wholesale
jolsel,wholesale
jolsom,wholesome
jolster,holster
jolt, *, ted, ting, ty, A SUDDEN HARSH ACTION
jolter,holder / halter
joly,jolly
jomallenos,homogenous
jombl,humble / jumble
jombol,humble / jumble
jomdinger,humdinger
jomer,hummer
jomi,homey
jomingbird,hummingbird
jomini,hominy
jomir,hummer
jomoyenos,homogenous
jomp,hump
jonc,junk / honk
jonch,hunch
jonci,junkie
jondis,jaundice
jondred,hundred
jong,hung
jongal,jungle
jonger,hunger
jongri,hungry
jongul,jungle
joni,honey
jonimoon,honeymoon
jonk,junk
jonke,junkie
jonki,junkie
jont,jaunt / join(ed) / joint / hunt
jontir,hunt(er)
jooly,july
joon,june
joot,jute
jop,job / hop
jops,hops / hope(s) / job(s)

jopscoch,hopscotch
joqui,hockey / hokey
jor,whore / jar
joraizon,horizon
jorascoup,horoscope
jord,hoard / horde
jore,jury
jorebol,horrible
jorefai,horrify
jorendos,horrendous
jori,jury
joribol,horrible
jorifai,horrify
jorindos,horrendous
joriscoup,horoscope
jorizontal,horizontal
jormon,hormone
jorn,horn
jornet,hornet
jorni,horny
jornul,journal
jorofai,horrify
joror,horror
joroscoup,horoscope
jorror,horror
jors,horse
josband,husband
josc,husk
josel,jostle
josh, hing, her, TEASING WITH GOOD HUMOR (or see gosh)
jositeit,hesitate
josk,husk
joski,husky
josol,hustle
jospitabol,hospitable
jospitaliti,hospitality
jospitol,hospital
jostach,hostage
jostayol,hostile / hostel
jostel,hostel / hostile

jostle, *, ed, ling, ement, er, TO PUSH/ JUMBLE/ SHOVE/ BUMP/ COLLIDE IN A CROWDED SITUATION (or see hostel/ hostile)
josul,jostle
jot, *, ted, ting, QUICKLY WRITE SOMETHING DOWN, WRITE A QUICK NOTE (or see hot/ hut)
jotel,hotel
jou,hoe / how
joucs,hoax
jouel,jowl / joule
jouks,hoax
joule, *, A METHOD OF MEASURING (or see jewel)
jouli,holly / holy
joum,home
joumeid,homemade
joumi,homey
joumles,homeless
joumli,homely
joun,hone
jounce, *, ed,cing, TO BOUNCE AROUND
joup,hope
journal,*, ize, lizes, lized, lizing, lizer, lism, lization, list, AN ITEMIZED ACCOUNT OF AN EVENT OR SPAN OF TIME
journalist, *, tic, tically, ize, ism, ONE WHO DOCUMENTS/ RECOUNTS AN EVENT OR SPAN OF TIME
journey, *, yed, ying, TO TRAVEL OR TAKE A TRIP
jous, hose / hoe(s)
joust, *, ted, ting, ter, MEDIEVAL COMBAT (or see host)
joutel, hotel
jovel, hovel
jover, hover
jovial,lity, lness, lly, JOLLY, GOOD CHEER/ HUMOR
jovol,hovel
jow, jaw / hoe / how
jowl, *, led, THE JAW, FISH HEAD (or see joule)
jownse,jounce
joy, yful, yfully, yfulness, yous, yously, yousness, A PLEASURABLE STATE OF BEING, HARMONIOUS "prefixes: en/ over"
joyes,joy(ous)
joyesly,joy(ously)
joyfil,joy(ful)

joyvis,joy(ous)
joyn,join
joynd,joint / join(ed)
joynt,joint / join(ed)
joyst,joist
joyusness,joy(ousness)
ju,who
jub,hub
jubalashen,jubilant(ation)
jubcap,hubcap
jubilant,tly,lance,lancy,ation,ate,atory,EXHULTANT/ TRIUMPHANT/ FESTIVE
jubilee, *, A ROWDY/ FESTIVE CELEBRATION NORMALLY HONORING A TIMESPAN
juc,hook / juice
juce,juice / juicy
jud,who'd / hood
judeshal,judicial
judeshus,judicious
judge, *, ed, ging,ment, gmental, gmentally, FORM OPINION/ DECISION BASED ON ATTITUDE/ INFORMATION "prefixes: mis/ pre"
judgemental, judge(gmental)
judgmintal, judge(gmental)
judicial,lly,ary, ACTS/ ADMINISTRATION OF JUDGING
judicious,sly,sness, BEHAVING IN A JUDGMENTAL FASHION
judo, SELF-DEFENSE SPORT
judol,huddle
juel,joule / jewel / wale / well
juerl,whorl
juever,whoever
juf,hoof
jug, *, gged,gging,gful,A LARGE CONTAINER FOR FLUIDS/ LIQUID (or see judge/ hug)
juge,jug / judge
juggle, *, ed, ling,er, KEEP OBJECTS AFLOAT IN THE AIR SIMULTANEOUSLY
jugil,juggle
jugment,judge(gment)
jugmint, judge(gment)
juice, *, ed, er, cy, cier, ciest, cieless, LIQUID FROM FRUIT
juicy,cier,ciest, EDIBLE FOOD LADEN WITH MOISTURE

juj,judge
jujment, judge(gment)
jujmental, judge(gmental)
jujmint, judge(gment)
jujmintal, judge(gmental)
jul,joule / jewel / hull / who'll
juli, wholly / July
july, A MONTH OF THE YEAR (ENGLISH)
jum,whom / hum
jumble, *, ed, ling, TO MIX TOGETHER WITHOUT ORDER
jumever,whomever
jump, *, ped, ping, py, piness, per, TO TAKE TO THE AIR FOR NANOSECONDS TO DEFY GRAVITY
junc,junk
juncer,junk(er)
junction, *, nal, PLACE WHERE THINGS MEET, TIME/ PLACE INTERCHANGE "prefixes: dis/ sub"
junctivitis, conjunction(ivitis)
juncture, *, ONE POINT WHERE THINGS OR THOUGHTS MEET, PLACE FOR EXCHANGE
jundmeid,handmade
june,A MONTH OF THE YEAR (ENGLISH)
jungle, *, led, ly, PLACE WHERE PLANTS/ ANIMALS ARE ABUNDANT/ FREE FROM HUMAN RESTRAINT
junior, *, A CLASS LEVEL IN SCHOOL, THE MALE OFFSPRING OF A FATHER
junk,ked,king,ky,ker,kie, OBJECTS CONSIDERED TO BE OF NO VALUE
junke,junkie
junkie, *, PERSON WITH HABITUAL DRUG PROBLEM
junkshen,junction
junksher,juncture
junky,junkie
junyer,junior
juol,jewel / joule
juometree,geometry
jup,hoop
jurasdiction,jurisdiction
jurbel,gerbil
jurdol, hurdle
jure,jury / hurry
juresdiction,jurisdiction
juri,jury / hurry

Root/Word	Definition/Related Words
jurisdiction, nal, nally	AN AREA/ RANGE CONTROLLED BY PARTICULAR ENTITIES
jurk	jerk
jurky	jerky
jurm	germ
jurmenate	germinate
jurnal	journal
jurney	journey
jurni	journey
jurikein	hurricane
jurnil	journal
jurnilist	journal(ist)
jurnul	journal
jurokein	hurricane
juror, *	MEMBER OF A GROUP WHO SITS IN COURT AND JUDGES A DEFENDANT
jurt	hurt
jurtol	hurtle
jurusdikshen	jurisdiction
jury, ries, ried, ror, rist	A GROUP WHO SIT IN COURT AND JUDGES A DEFENDANT
jus, who's	whose
jusd	just
jusdes	justice
jusdifiable	justifiable
jusdify	justify
jusdufecation	justify(fication)
juse, juice	juicy
juser, juice(r)	
just, tly, tness	WHAT IS RIGHT BY SOCIAL NORMS "prefixes: un"
justefiable	justifiable
justefication	justify(fication)
justes	justice
justice, *, eless, elike, ciable, ciability	ONE WHO IS EMPLOYED BY THE GOVERNMENT TO MAKE LAWFUL DECISIONS "prefixes: in"
justifiable, bility, bleness, ly	DEFENDS THAT THE ACTION REFLECTS THE CAUSE "prefixes: un"
justify, fies, fied, fying, fyingly, fier, fication, ficative, ficatory	DEFEND REACTIONS, ARGUE IN DEFENSE OF ACTION/ THOUGHT "prefixes: un"
jusy, juice(cy)	

Root/Word	Definition/Related Words
jut, *, tted, tting	STICKS OUT (or see jute/ hoot/ hut)
jute	PLANT FIBER FOR WEAVING AND BRAIDING
juto	judo
juv	hoove
juvenile, *, lism, lity	A YOUTH, IMMATURE
juxta	PREFIX INDICATING "NEAR/ CLOSE" MOST OFTEN MODIFIES THE WORD
kabduve	captive
kaben	cabin
kabenet	cabinet
kaberay	cabaret
kabich	cabbage
kabige	cabbage
kabin	cabin
kabinet	cabinet
kable	cable
kabnet	cabinet
kabnit	cabinet
kaboose	caboose
kabsher	capture
kabsul	capsule
kabten	captain
kabture	capture
kabul	cable
kabunet	cabinet
kabuse	caboose
kacdus	cactus
kach, catch	cache / cash
kacher, catcher	cashier
kackel	cackle
kacl	cackle
kactus	cactus
kadagore	category
kadagorize	categorize
kadagory	category
kadagurize	categorize
kadal	cattle
kadalize	catalyst(yze)
kadavir	cadaver
kade	caddy
kadecism	catechism
kadegore	category
kadegurize	categorize

Root/Word	Definition/Related Words
kadekism	catechism
kadence	cadence
kadet	cadet
kadigore	category
kadigurize	categorize
kadikism	catechism
kadil	cattle
kadilist	catalyst
kadilog	catalog
kadinse	cadence
kadl	cattle
kadugore	category
kadugorize	categorize
kadugory	category
kadugurize	categorize
kadul	cattle
kadulist	catalyst
kadulize	catalyst(yze)
kadulog	catalog
kadur	cater
kaduract	cataract
kady	caddy
kaf, calf	cave
kafa	cafe
kafanated	caffeine(nated)
kafatirea	cafeteria
kafe, cafe	coffee
kafene	caffeine
kafetirea	cafeteria
kafi	coffee
kafinated	caffeine(nated)
kafine	caffeine
kafiterea	cafeteria
kafiteria	cafeteria
kafs, calves	cave(s)
kafunated	caffeine(nated)
kage	cage
kagol	cajole
kahoot	cahoot
kahute	cahoot
kail	kale
kaind	kind
kaindjarded	kindhearted

kaindjarted,kindhearted
kainker,chancre / canker
kairful,careful
kairopracter,chiropractor
kairou,chiro
kairoupractor,chiropractor
kait,kite
kaje,cage
kajole,cajole
kajuol,casual
kajwul,casual
kak,caulk / calk / cake / cock
kakd,cake(d)
kake,cake / khaki
kakil,cackle
kakoon,cocoon
kakt,cake(d)
kaktis,cactus
kakul,cackle
kakulashun,calculate(tion)
kakulation,calculate(tion)
kakulus,calculus
kaky,khaki
kal,kale / call
kalaidascoup,kaleidoscope
kalamity,calamity
kalcefy,calcify
kalceum,calcium
kalculashun,calculate(tion)
kalculate,calculate
kalculus,calculus
kale, AN EDIBLE PLANT
kalebrate,calibrate
kaleidoscope,*, pic,pical,pically,COLORFUL VIEWING OBJECT
kalek,colic
kalender,calendar / calender / colander
kalentur,calendar / calender / colander
kalepur,caliper / caliber
kaler,collar / call(er)
kales,callous / callus
kalesdenics,calisthenics
kalesterol,cholesterol
kalesthenics,calisthenics

kaliber,caliber
kalibrate,calibrate
kalide,collide
kalidoscope,kaleidoscope
kaliflower,cauliflower
kalindula,calendula
kalindur,calendar / calender / colander
kalintur,calendar
kalipur,caliper
kalir,collar / call(er)
kalire,calorie
kalis,callous / callus
kalisdenics,calisthenics
kalisthenics,calisthenics
kalk,calk / caulk
kalkewlashun,calculate(tion)
kalkewlate,calculate
kalkewlus,calculus
kalkilate,calculate
kalkulate,calculate
kalkulus,calculus
kalobrate,calibrate
kalokweul,colloquial
kalon,cologne / colon
kaloneil,colonial
kaloquial,colloquial
kalore,calorie
kalostemy,colostomy
kalqulus,calculus
kalsafy,calcify
kalseum,calcium
kalsufy,calcify
kaluber,caliber
kalubrate,calibrate
kaluper,caliper
kalury,calorie
kalus,callous / callus
kalusdenics,calisthenics
kalusthinics,calisthenics
kalvs,calves
kam,came
kamb,camp
kamend,commend

kamenduble,commendable
kamfer,camphor
kamil,camel
kaminduble,commendable
kamofloje,camouflage
kamp,camp
kampane,campaign
kampus,campus
kamru,camera
kamu,comma
kamul,camel
kamunecate,communicate
kamunety,community
kamute,commute
kancer,cancer / chancre / canker
kanded,candid
kandidat,candidate
kandil,candle
kandy,candy
kane,cane
kanebul,cannibal
kanebulize,cannibal(ize)
kaneon,canyon
kanepy,canopy
kanery,canary / cannery
kanesiology,kinesis(iology)
kanesis,kinesis
kangaroo,*, LARGE MARSUPIAL ANIMAL
kangrues,congruous
kanibul,cannibal
kanibus,cannabis
kanikanik,kinnikinnick
kanin,cannon / canine
kaniry,cannery / canary
kanister,canister
kanker,chancre / canker
kanon,cannon
kanopy,canopy
kanselashin,cancellation
kanseld,cancel(lled)
kansilashun,cancellation
kansild,cancel(lled)
kansir,cancer

kansul,cancel	kaptin,captain	karf,carve
kansulashen,cancellation	kaption,caption	karfl,careful
kansult,cancel(lled)	kaptuf,captive	karfre,carefree
kant,can't	kaptun,captain	karful,careful
kantalope,cantaloupe	kaptuvate,captivate	kargo,cargo
kantankerus,cantankerous	kapubilety,capability	karib,carob
kanted,candid	kapubul,capable	kariboo,caribou
kanteen,canteen	kapulery,capillary	kariouki,karaoke
kantelope,cantaloupe	**kaput**, DIED, PASSED OUT, FELL OVER DEAD	karisma,charisma
kantiguis,contiguous	kaputate,capitate	karit,carat / caret / carrot / karat
kantina,cantina	kapzize,capsize	karkes,carcass
kantir,canter	kar,car	karkus,carcass
kantrovert,controvert	karacter,character	karlis,careless
kantulope,cantaloupe	**karaoke**,GAME WHERE SONGS WITHOUT WORDS ARE SUNG TO	**karma**,A BELIEF
kantur,canter		karmil,caramel
kanubelize,cannibal(ize)	**karat**,* , A MEASUREMENT FOR GEMS AND GOLD (or see karate/ carrot/ carat/ caret)	karmu,karma
kanubis,cannabis		karmul,caramel
kanuster,canister	**karate**, MARTIAL ART FORM (or see karat)	karnashun,carnation
kanves,canvas / canvass	karbin,carbon	karneishon,carnation
kanvus,canvas / canvass	karbinete,carbonate	karnevul,carnival
kanyun,canyon	karbon,carbon	karnivore,carnivore
kaos,chaos	karburator,carburetor	karob,carob
kap,cap / cape	kard,card / care(d) / cart	karoburate,corroborate
kapabul,capable	kardboard,cardboard	karode,corrode
kapasety,capacity	kardeac,cardiac	karogen,corrode(osion)
kapdivate,captivate	kardenul,cardinal	karoke,karaoke
kape,cap / cape	kardilege,cartilage	karosef,corrode(osive)
kapechulate,capitulate	kardnul,cardinal	karosene,kerosene
kapedul,capital / capitol	kare,carry / care	karote,karate
kapedulism,capitalism	karebu,caribou	karouse,carouse
kapelary,capillary	karecatshure,caricature	karows,carouse
kapetate,capitate	karecter,character	karpenter,carpenter
kapetul,capital / capitol	kareer,career	karpet,carpet
kapetulesm,capitalism	karefree,carefree	karpinder,carpenter
kapibilety,capability	karekteriz,character(ize)	karpit,carpet
kapibul,capable	kareless,careless	kars,care(s) / car(s)
kapilary,capillary	kareng,care(ring)	karsenugen,carcinogen
kapitulate,capitulate	kareoke,karaoke	karsinugin,carcinogen
kapoot,kaput	karer,career	kart,cart
kapshun,caption	kares,care(s) / caress	kartoon,cartoon
kapsil,capsule	karet,carat / caret / carrot / karat	kartreg,cartridge
kapsize,capsize	kareur,carrier	kartrig,cartridge
kapsul,capsule	karevan,caravan	kartuleg,cartilage

kartune,cartoon
karudge,carriage
karukter,character
karul,carol
karusen,kerosene
karv,carve
kary,carry
kasadilla,quesadilla
kascade,cascade
kase,case
kasedeya,quesadilla
kaseno,casino
kaset,cassette
kash,cash / cache
kashen,caution
kasher,cashier
kashes(ly),cautious(ly)
kashmer,cashmere
kashosly,cautious(ly)
kashu,cashew
kashual,casual
kasine,casino
kasing,casing
kasiroll,casserole
kask,cask
kaskera,cascara
kasket,casket
kast,cast / caste
kastrate,castrate
kasudilla,quesadilla
kasul,castle
kat,cat
kata,PREFIX INDICATING "APART/ DOWN" MOST OFTEN MODIFIES THE WORD
katagorize,categorize
katagory,category
katalize,catalyst(yze)
katch,cache / cash / catch
katecism,catechism
kategore,category
kategurize,categorize
katekisom,catechism
katel,cattle

katelog,catalog
katepiler,caterpillar
katepult,catapult
kater,cater
kateract,cataract
katigore,category
katigurize,categorize
katikism,catechism
katl,cattle
katugory,category
katukism,catechism
katul,cattle
katulist,catalyst
katulize,catalyst(yze)
katulog,catalog
katupiler,caterpillar
katupult,catapult
katurakt,cataract
kau,cow
kauchen,caution
kaudej,cottage
kaufe,coffee / cough
kaugorize,categorize
kauk,caulk / calk / cake / cock
kaul,call / cowl
kauleg,college
kaumpatency, competence(cy)
kaumpelation, compilation
kaumpetancy, competence(cy)
kaumpilation, compilation
kaumpotency, competence(cy)
kaumu,comma
kaunasure,connoisseur
kauncekwently,consequent(ly)
kaunsaquently,consequent(ly)
kaunsuquenshul,consequent(ial)
kaunvex,convex
kausd,cause(d) / cost
kaushas,cautious
kaushen,caution
kaushon,caution
kaushos,cautious
kaut,caught / cot

kav,cave
kava,BEVERAGE FROM PLANT
kavety,cavity
kavilry,cavalry
kavirn,cavern
kavity,cavity
kavs,calves / cave(s)
kavude,cavity
kavulree,cavalry
kavurn,cavern
kawcus,caucus
kawshun,caution
kawshus,cautious
kawt, caught / cot
kayak,*,ker,king,CANOE-LIKE BOAT
kayen, cayenne
kaynine, canine
kayos,chaos
kaysadilla, quesadilla
kazadilla, quesadilla
kazual,casual
kazudilla, quesadilla
ke,key
kech,catch
kechen,kitchen
kechup,ketchup / catsup
ked, key(ed) / kid
kednapur, kidnap(pper)
kedny,kidney
kedul,kettle
kedy,kitty
keel,*,led,ling,less,FALL OVER,STRUCTURAL PART OF A BOAT
keen, nly,nness,ner, SHARP IN SENSES, VERY AWARE
keep,*,per, ping,pable, HOLD ON TO, WITHHOLD FROM SOMEONE, POSSESS "prefixes: up"
keibol,cable
keich, cage
keidor, cater
kein, cane
keinain, canine
keingaru, kangaroo
keios,chaos

keipabilidi, capability
keipabol, capable
keis, case
keising, casing
keitor, cater
keitur, cater
keiv, cave
kek, kick
kel, kill / keel / kale
keld, kill(ed) / kelt
kell, kill
keln, kiln
kelo, kilo
kelokweul, colloquial
keloquial, colloquial
kelowatt, kilowatt
kelp, WATER PLANT
kelt, celt / kilt / kill(ed)
kelur, kill(er)
kemakol, chemical
kemecol, chemical
kemest, chemist
kemestri, chemistry
kemicol, chemical
kemist, chemist
kemistri, chemistry
kemokol, chemical
kemostry, chemistry
kemotherupy, chemotherapy
kemukol, chemical
kemustri, chemistry
ken, kin / keen / can
kendergarten, kindergarten
kendling, kindle(ling)
kendom, kingdom
kendred, kind(red)
kendul, kindle
kendurgarten, kindergarten
kenel, kennel
kenesiology, kinesis(iology)
kenesis, kinesis
keng, king / kink
kengdom, kingdom

kenikkanik, kinnikinnick
kenk, king / kink
kenly, keen(ly)
kennel, *, led, ling, FENCING/ HOUSING FOR ANIMALS
 "prefixes: un"
kenol, kennel
kensum, consume
kentend, contend
kentenual, continue(ual)
kentling, kindle(ling)
kentred, kind(red)
kenturgarden, kindergarten
kenul, kennel
keosk, kiosk
keper, kipper
kepsize, capsize
kepur, kipper
ker, care
kerab, carob
keracter, character
keral, choral / coral / corral / chorale
keramel, caramel
keraoky, karaoke
kerat, carat / caret / carrot / karat
keravan, caravan
kerb, curb
kerd, curd
kerdeus, courteous
kerdul, curdle
kere, care / carry
kereb, carob
kerekt, correct
kerekturiz, character(ize)
kereoke, karaoke
keret, carat / caret / carrot / karat
kerf, curve
kerfiu, curfew
kerfle, careful / careful(lly)
kerfri, carefree
kerfue, curfew
kerful, careful
kerfule, careful(lly)
keri, carry

kerib, carob
kericuture, caricature
kerier, carrier
kerige, carriage / courage
kerikulum, curriculum
kerioke, karaoke
kerisel, carousel
kerisen, kerosene
kerit, carat / caret / carrot / karat
kerivan, caravan
kerl, curl
kerles, careless
kernal, colonel / kernel
kernel, *, ly, SMALL BITS/ SECTIONS OF CORN COB/
 NUTS/ SEEDS (or see colonel)
kernul, colonel / kernel
kerob, carob
keroberate, corroborate
kerol, carol
kerosell, carousel
kerosene, TYPE OF FUEL
kerot, carat / caret / carrot / karat
keroty, karate
kerp, curb
kersanthimum, chrysanthemum
kersash, corsage
kerse, curse / care(s)
kersive, cursive
kersoch, corsage
kersoje, corsage
kersuf, cursive
kertale, curtail
kertin, curtain
kertsy, curtsy
kertul, curdle
keruge, courage
kerunsy, currency
kerunt, currant / current
kerupt, corrupt
kerusel, carousel
kerusen, kerosene
kerut, caret / carrot / karat
keruvan, caravan

kerve,curve
kervicher,curvature
kervuchure,curvature
kery,curry / carry
kes,kiss
kesng,kiss(ing)
kest,kiss(ed) / cist
ket,kid / kit / kite
ketal,kettle
ketch,catch
ketchen,kitchen
ketcher,catcher
ketchup,TOMATO BASED CONDIMENT (also catsup)
keten,kitten
ketny,kidney
kets,kid(s) / kit(s) / kite(s)
kettle, *, LARGE IRON POT, METAL VESSEL WITH ROUNDED BOTTOM AND WIDE TOP
ketul,kettle
kety,kitty
keurader,curator
kew,cue
kewdos,kudos
kewe,kiwi
kewk,cook
kewth,couth
key, *, yed,ying, TOOL TO UNLOCK SOMETHING, IMPORTANT INFORMATION TO UNLOCK A MYSTERY
keyas,chaos
keylo,kilo
keyosk,kiosk
keysadilla,quesadilla
keysudeya,quesadilla
khaki, *, A TYPE OF COTTON PANT, A COLOR
ki,key
kiak,kayak
kian,cayenne
kibuse,caboose
kic,kick
kichen,kitchen
kick, *, ked,king,ker, STRIKE SOMETHING WITH FRONT OF FOOT

kid, *, ddy,dder,dding,ddingly,ddishness,dlike,YOUNG CHILD/ ANIMAL,JOKING(or see kite/ kit)
kiddy,kitty
kiden,kitten
kidnap, *, pped,pping,pper, ONE WHO STEALS AWAY WITH SOMEONE
kidnaper,kidnap(pper)
kidney, *, ORGANS IN THE BODY
kidni,kidney
kidny,kidney
kidur,kid(dder)
kidy,kid(ddy) / kitty
kigole,cajole
kijole,cajole
kik,kick
kil,kill / keel
kild,kill(ed) / kilt / keel(ed)
kiler,kill(er)
kill, *, led,ler,ling, TAKE LIFE AWAY FROM "prefixes: over"
kiln, *, A SPECIAL OVEN WHICH EXCEEDS 1000°
kilo,PREFIX INDICATING "THOUSAND" MOST OFTEN MODIFIES THE WORD
kiloge,collage
kilokweul,colloquial
kiloneul,colonial
kiloquial,colloquial
kilor,kill(er)
kilosil,colossal
kilostomy,colostomy
kilouat,kilowatt
kilowatt,ELECTRICAL MEASUREMENT
kilt, *, SKIRT OF SCOTTISH DESCENT (or see kill(ed))
kilur,kill(er)
kimast,chemist
kimecul,chemical
kimest,chemist
kimestry,chemistry
kimist,chemist
kimoutherapi,chemotherapy
kimponent,component
kimustry,chemistry
kin, *, nsmen,nfolk, RELATIVES (or see can)

kinal,canal
kincdom,kingdom
kind,dred,dly,dest,dness,der,WHAT TYPE, BEING NICE WITHOUT ULTERIOR MOTIVES "prefixes: un"
kind of,SORT OF,SOMEWHAT
kinda,kind of
kindergarten,ner,A CLASS LEVEL IN SCHOOL
kindhearted,dly,dness,A GENTLE SPIRIT
kindle, *, ed,ling, MATERIAL USED AS A FIRE STARTER "prefixes: en/ re"
kindolense,condolence
kindom,kingdom
kinducter,conductor
kinduf,kind of
kindukt,conduct
kindurgarden,kindergarten
kinery,canary / cannery
kinesis,iology,STUDY OF HEALTH/ MUSCLES OF THE BODY,HEALING USING KINERGETIC STUDY
kinet,PREFIX INDICATING "MOTION" MOST OFTEN MODIFIES THE WORD
kinfedy,confetti
kinfes,confess
kinfeshun,confession
kinfetion,confession
king, *, gdom, RULER IN A MONARCH
kingdom, *, AREA RULED BY MONARCHY "prefixes: sub"
kingradulashun,congratulation
kinikkanik,kinnikinnick
kink, *, ked,king,ky, SOMETHING THAT KNOT'S UP, A BEND/ HOOK IN A LINEAR SYSTEM (or see king) "prefixes: un"
kinkdom,kingdom
kinnikinnick,A PLANT
kinol,kennel
kinsestincy,consistence(cy)
kinsist(ent)ly,consistent(ly
kinsole,console
kinspirusy,conspiracy
kinstrucshen,construction
kinstruct,construct
kinsult,consult
kinsumpshen,consumption

kint,kind / can't / couldn't
kinta,kind of
kintaminate,contaminate
kintergarden,kindergarten
kintred,kind(red)
kinul,kennel
kinverdable,convertible
kiosk,*,INFORMATION STATION
kip,keep
kiper,kipper
kipper,*,FISH AND RELATED
kiral,chora l/ coral / corra l/ chorale
kirnel,colonel / kernel
kiroberate,corroborate
kirogen,corrode(osion)
kiropraktor,chiropractor
kiroshen,corrode(osion)
kirote,karate
kirsanthemum,chrysanthemum
kirsoch,corsage
kirten,curtain
kirteus,courteous
kiruge,courage
kirupraktor,chiropractor
kirvucher,curvature
kis,kiss
kisd,kiss(ed)
kiset,cassette
kiss,sses,ssed,ssing,sser,ssable,TOUCH WITH THE LIPS
kist,cist / kiss(ed)
kit,*,ACCUMULATION OF ITEMS IN A CONTAINER TO USE FOR A SPECIFIC TASK (or see kite)
kitastrufy,catastrophy / catastrophe
kitchen,*,PLACE TO PREPARE FOOD
kite,*,FRAME WITH COVERING THAT SAILS IN THE WIND BY A STRING (or see kit)
kiten,kitten
kitny,kidney
kitten,*,IMMATURE CAT
kitty,tties,tten,IMMATURE CAT,GAMBLING TERM
kity,kitty
kiub,cube
kiubic,cubic

kiubicol,cubicle
kiucumber,cucumber
kiumiulative,cumulative
kiur,cure
kiurabol,curable
kiureider,curator
kiurios,curious
kiuriosity,curiosity
kiut,cute
kiuticol,cuticle
kiwi,*,FRUIT,BIRD
kiyak,kayak
kiyan,cayenne
kiyen,cayenne
klad,clad
klairvoyants,clairvoyance
klam,clam / claim
klamable,claim(able)
klament,claimant
klamp,clamp
klan,clan
klandistine,clandestine
klap,clap
klapse,collapse
klarecul,clerical
klaricul,clerical
klarity,clarity
klarvoyuns,clairvoyance
klaset,closet
klash,clash
klasha,cliche
klasic,classic
klasify,classify
klasp,clasp
klass,class
klasuc,classic
klasufy,classify
klauged,clog(gged) / cloak / clock(ed)
klaun,clown
klausterfobic,claustrophobic
klaw,claw
klawsit,closet
klawzet,closet

klay,clay
klebtomaniac,kleptomania(c)
klecter,collect(or)
kleerense,clearance
kleet,cleat
kleff,cliff
klen,clean
klench,clench / clinch
kleng,cling
klenik,clinic
klenikul,clinic(al)
klense,cleanse
klensh,clench / clinch
klenz,cleanse
klenzer,cleanser
klep,clip
kleptomania,ac,acs,acal,OBSESSION WITH STEALING
klepur,clipper
kler,clear
klerense,clearance
klerge,clergy
klerical,clerical
klerify,clarify
klerity,clarity
klerk,clerk
klervoyents,clairvoyance
klet,cleat
kletorus,clitoris
klevur,clever
klew,clue
kliant,client
klicha,cliche
klick,click / clique
kliff,cliff
klik,click / clique
klim,climb
klimax,climax
klimet,climate
klimut,climate
klinch,clench / clinch
kling,cling
klinik,clinic
klinsh,clench / clinch

klinzr,cleanser	klozline,clothesline	**knot**,*,tted,tting,tty,ROPE/ STRING TIED WITH LOOPING CONFIGURATION,SPOT WHERE LIMBS GREW FROM (or see not/ naught)
klip,clip	klu,clue	**know**,*,wing,wn,wable,wer,wledge,HAVE IT IN YOUR MEMORY,ACCESS BY MEMORY (or see noun) "prefixes: un"
klipur,clipper	klub,club	**knowledge**,gable,gableness,gably,HAVING A MEMORY BASE
klirk,clerk	kluch,clutch	**known**,*,PAST TENSE FOR THE WORD 'KNOW', INFORMED/ AWARE OF
klisha,cliche	kludch,clutch	**knuckle**,*,ed,ling,FINGER JOINT BONE, TO FIST UP HAND TO DISPLAY BONE JOINTS
klitorus,clitoris	kluder,clutter	koagewlate, coagulate
kliunt,client	klue,clue	koagulate, coagulate
kloak,cloak	klump,clump	koal,coal / cool
klober,clobber	klumze,clumsy	koalition, coalition
kloester,cloister	klurge,clergy	koap,co-op
klofe,clove	kluster,cluster	koar,core / corp
klofur,clover	klutch,clutch	koarse,course / coarse
kloger,closure	kluter,clutter	koaster,coaster
klojure,closure	klutorus,clitoris	koat,coat
klok,clock / cloak	**knack**,HAVE A NATURAL SKILL/ TALENT FOR	kob,cob
klokd,clog(gged) / cloak / dock(ed)	**knap**,*,pped,pping,pper,ppy,HAIR AFFECTATION	kobalt,cobalt
klon,clown / clone / cologne	**knead**,*,ded,ding,PREPARING DOUGH FOR BAKING (or see knee(d)/ need))	kobolt,cobalt
klorene,chlorine	kned,knee(d) / knead	kobra,cobra
klos,clothes / claw(s) / close / clause	**knee**,*,ed,eing,BENDABLE JOINT HALFWAY DOWN LEG (or see need/ knead)	kobweb,cobweb
kloser,close(r) / closure	**kneel**,*,led,ling,ler,TO SIT ON YOUR KNEES	kocane,cocaine
klosher,closure	knel,kneel / knell	koch,coach
klosir,close(r) / closure	**knell**,*,led,ling,SOUND OF A BELL NORMALLY HEARD AT FUNERALS, A SOLEMN SOUND (or see nick)	kochen,caution
klosline,clothesline	knes,knee(s) / niece	kocher,kosher
klosterfobic,claustrophobic	**knew**,PAST TENSE FOR THE WORD "KNOW" (or see new)	koches,cautious
klosturfobia,claustrophobia	knewmerable,numerable	kock,cook / cock
klosur,close(r) / closure	**knick knack**,*,SMALL COLLECTIBLES,TRINKETS (or see nick)	kockroach,cockroach
klot,clot	**knife**,ed,fing,ives,SHARP,METAL BLADE WITH HANDLE FOR CUTTING	kocroch,cockroach
kloth,cloth	**knight**,*,ted,ting,tly,MEDIEVAL SOLDIER	kod,cod / code / could / cold / caught
kloud,cloud	**knit**,*,tted,tting,tter,USING NEEDLES/ YARN "prefixes: inter/ un"	kodage,cottage
kloun,clown	knitch,niche	kode,code
klout,clout	**knob**,*,HANDLES FOR DOORS AND DRAWERS	kodej,cottage
klove,clove	**knock**,*,ked,king,ker,SOUND MADE ON DOOR WITH FIST, USING THE FIST	kodene,codeine
klovur,clover	**knoll**,*,SMALL ROUND HILL	kodin,cotton
klowd,cloud		kodo,kudos
klown,clown		koduge,cottage
klowsit,closet		koed,coed
klowt,clout		
klowth,cloth / cloth(e)		
klowz,clothes / claw(s) / close / clause		
kloyster,cloister		
kloz,clothes / claw(s) / close / clause		
klozer,close(r) / closure		
klozit,closet		

koel,coil	kolapsubl,collapse(sible)	koluge,college
koen,coin	kolasal,colossal	kolum,column
koenside,coincide	kolate,collate	kolun,colon
koensudent,coincident	kold,cold	kolundir,colander
koersment,coerce(ment)	koldsfoot,coltsfoot	kolune,colony
kof,cough	kole, coal / call	kolunise,colonize
kofe,cove / coffee / cough	koleage,colleague	kolur,cooler / color / collar / call(er)
kofen,coffin / cough(ing)	koleague,colleague	kolvurt,culvert
kofert,covert	kolecshin,collection	kom, calm/ come/ comb
kofin, coffin / cough(ing)	kolecter,collect(or)	koma,coma / comma
kofy,coffee	koledg,college	komand,command
kognativ,cognitive	koleg, college	komander,commander
kognisant,cognizant	kolegent, collegiate	kombat,combat
kognishun,cognition	kolekt,collect	kombenation,combination
kognition, cognition	kolem,column	komber,cumber
kognutiv,cognitive	kolen,colon	kombinashun,combination
kohabutate,cohabitate	kolenary,culinary	kombine,combine
kohearent,coherent	kolendur,colander	kombinsashen,compensation
koherent,coherent	koleng, call(ing) / cowl(ing)	kombrahensiv,comprehensive
kohersive,coerce(cive)	kolenize,colonize	kombunashen,combination
kohesuf,cohesive	koleny,colony	kombustible,combustible
kohesuve, cohesive	koler,collar / call(er) / cooler	kombustion,combustion
kohort, cohort	kolerd,collar(ed) / collard greens	komec,comic
kohurse, coerce	kolesterol, cholesterol	komedian,comedian
koil, coil	kolic, colic	komedy, comedy
koin, coin	kolid, collide	komemerate,commemorate
koinside, coincide	koliflower, cauliflower	komendable, commendable
koinsudent, coincident	kolige, college	komendation, commendation
kok,cock / cook	kolijin, collision	komenduble, commendable
kokain, cocaine	kolim, column	komense, commence
kokane, cocaine	koliny, colony	koment, comment
koke, kook	kolishen, coalition	komentatur, commentator
koko, cocoa	kolk, calk / caulk	koments, commence
kokonut, coconut	kolm, calm	komerse, commerce
kokroch, cockroach	kolmenate, culminate	komershul, commercial
koks, coax	koloj, collage	komet, commit / comet
koktale, cocktail	kolostemy, colostomy	komfert, comfort
kokunut, coconut	kolpret, culprit	komfertible, comfortable
kol, call / cowl	kolsla, coleslaw	komfurter, comfort(er)
koladerul, collateral	kolslow, coleslaw	komic, comic
kolamedy, calamity	kolt, cold / colt	komidy, comedy
kolander, colander	koltivate, cultivate	komimurate, commemorate
kolaps, collapse	koltsfoot, coltsfoot	komin, common

Misspelling	Correct spelling
komindation	commendation
kominduble	commendable
kominsurate	commensurate
komint	comment
komintator	commentator
komirse	commerce
komirshul	commercial
komisary	commissary
komishner	commissioner
komit	comet / commit
komitee	committee
komitment	commitment
komity	comedy
komloda	cum laude
komodety	commodity
kompact	compact
kompar	compare
komparebul	comparable
kompartment	compartment
kompashun	compassion
kompashunet	compassionate
kompass	compass
kompatency	competence(cy)
kompatens	competence
kompatibility	compatible(tility)
kompeditor	competitor
kompel	compel
kompelation	compilation
kompensashen	compensation
komper	compare
kompete	compete
kompetence	competence
kompetency	competence(cy)
kompetior	competitor
kompilation	compilation
kompile	compile
kompinsate	compensate
kompitance	competence
kompitency	competence(cy)
kompizishen	composition
komplane	complain
komplasins	complacence / complaisance
komplecshun	complexion
kompleks	complex
kompleshun	completion
komplete	complete
komplians	compliant(nce)
kompliant	compliant
komplukashun	complication
komplukate	complicate
komplumint	complement / compliment
komply	comply
kompolation	compilation
komponent	component
kompose	compose
komposier	composure
komposit	composite
kompost	compost
komposyer	composure
kompound	compound
kompownd	compound
komprahensive	comprehensive
kompramise	compromise
komprehend	comprehend
komprehenshun	comprehension
komprehinsef	comprehensive
kompreshun	compression
kompresor	compressor
kompress	compress
kompretion	compression
kompruble	comparable
komprumize	compromise
komptroler	comptroller
kompulation	compilation
kompulsery	compulsory
kompulshun	compulsion
kompulsuve	compulsive
kompultion	compulsion
komputashun	computation
kompute	compute
komputence	competence
komputency	competence(cy)
komputer	computer
komputishen	competition
kompuzishen	composition
komrad	comrade
komtroler	comptroller
komudoor	commodore
komun	common / commune
komune	commune
komunest	communist
komunety	community
komunicate	communicate
komunism	communism
komunul	communal
komutable	commute(table)
kon	con / cone
konasur	connoisseur
koncaf	concave
koncafety	concave(vity)
koncakwently	consequent(ly)
koncavity	concave(vity)
koncavudy	concave(vity)
koncesion	concession
konch	conch
koncheinchus	conscientious
konchuse	conscious
konclewsef	conclusive
konclude	conclude
konclujen	conclusion
konclusef	conclusive
konclusion	conclusion
koncucrat	consecrate
koncution	concussion
kondem	condemn
kondensashen	condensation
kondense	condense
kondesend	condescend
kondewit	conduit
kondimeneum	condominium
kondiment	condiment
kondinsashun	condensation
kondisend	condescend
kondishen	condition
kondition	condition
kondolense	condolence
kondomeneum	condominium
kondone	condone
konduct	conduct

konducter,conductor	konger,conjure	konsedarashen,considerate(tion)
konduit,conduit	kongested,congest(ed)	konseduration,considerate(tion)
kondukt,conduct	konglomurete,conglomerate	konseed,concede
kondum,condom	kongradulashun,congratulation	konseet,conceit
kondument,condiment	kongratshulate,congratulate	konseeve,conceive
kone,cone	kongregashun,congregation	konseevuble,conceivable
konekshen,connection	kongres,congress	konsekwently,consequent(ly)
konekt,connect	kongrewint,congruent	konsel,council / counsel / console
konesur,connoisseur	kongrewity,congruent(uity)	konsemate,consummate
konfederit,confederate	kongrigate,congregate	konsent,consent
konfedont,confidant	kongris,congress	konsentrate,concentrate
konfeduret,confederate	kongruedy,congruent(uity)	konsentric,concentric
konfedy,confetti	kongrues,congruous	konsepshual,conceptual
konfekshun,confection	kongrugate,congregate	konsepshun,conception
konferanse,conference	kongrugation,congregation	konsept,concept
konferm,confirm	kongruint,congruent	konsequenshal,consequent(ial)
konfermashun,confirmation	konjunctivitis,conjunction(ivitis)	konserge,concierge
konfes,confess	konifur,conifer	konsern,concern
konfeshun,confession	konisur,connoisseur	konservation,conservation
konfesion,confession	konjer,conjure	konservator,conservator
konfetty,confetti	konjest,congest	konservatory,conservatory
konfide,confide	konjestion,congest(ion)	konserve,conserve
konfidense,confidence	konjewgul,conjugal	konservutive,conservative
konfidenshul,confidential	konjugul,conjugal	konseshun,concession
konfidential,confidential	konjunction,conjunction	konsestenly,consistent(lty)
konfidont,confidant	konjunctivitis,conjunction(ivitis)	konsetion,concession
konfigurashun,configuration	konjunkshen,conjunction	konsevator,conservator
konfine,confine	konjure,conjure	konseve,conceive
konfinment,confinement	konk,conch	konshenshis,conscientious
konfirents,conference	konkaf,concave	konsider,consider
konfirm,confirm	konkavety,concave(vity)	konsierge,concierge
konfirmashun,confirmation	konker,conquer	konsikwense,consequence
konfirmation,confirmation	konklusive,conclusive	konsimate,consummate
konflict,conflict	konkokt,concoct	konsinet,consonant
konform,conform	konkrete,concrete	konsinment,consignment
konfrunt,confront	konkwest,conquest	konsintrate,concentrate
konfudense,confidence	konquest,conquest	konsiquence,consequence
konfudenshul,confidential	konsacrat,consecrate	konsirv,conserve
konfudont,confidant	konsalidate,consolidate	konsirvation,conservation
konfujen,confusion	konscientious,conscientious	konsirvator,conservator
konfuranse,conference	konsecrashen,consecrate(tion)	konsirvatory,conservatory
konfuse,confuse	konsecrat,consecrate	konsise,concise
konfusion,confusion	konsecutive,consecutive	konsist,consist

konsistency,consistence(cy)	kontakt,contact
konsiter,consider	kontamenate,contaminate
konsolashen,consolation	kontane,contain
konsole,console	konteguis,contiguous
konsolidate,consolidate	kontekst,context
konsoul,console	kontemporary,contemporary
konspearusy,conspiracy	kontemt,contempt
konspikuos,conspicuous	kontend,contend
konspikyewus,conspicuous	kontent,content
konspirusy,conspiracy	kontenuel,continue(ual)
konstancy,constancy	kontest,contest
konstant,constant	kontiguis,contiguous
konstatushen,constitution	kontimplate,contemplate
konstilashen,constellation	kontimporary,contemporary
konstinse,constancy	kontinet,continent
konstint,constant	konting,content
konstipashen,constipation	kontinuance,continuance
konstitushen,constitution	kontorshenist,contortionist
konstrict,constrict	kontradik,contradict
konstrucshen,construction	kontrak,contract
konstruct,construct	kontrasepshun,contraception
konstulashen,constellation	kontrast,contrast
konstupashen,constipation	kontraversy,controversy
konstutushen,constitution	kontravertible,controvert(ible)
konsucrat,consecrate	kontrebute,contribute
konsucrating,consecrate(ing)	kontrery,contrary
konsukration,consecrate(tion)	kontrishen,contrition
konsukwinse,consequence	kontrol,control
konsulashun,consolation	kontrovert,controvert
konsult,consult	kontrovertible,controvert(ible)
konsumate,consummate	kontrudik,contradict
konsume,consume	kontrusepshun,contraception
konsumshen,consumption	kontumplate,contemplate
konsunet,consonant	kontunent,continent
konsurt,concert	kontunture,contour
konsurvashen,conservation	konufir,conifer
konsuration,conservation	konusur,connoisseur
konsurvator,conservator	konusy,convey
konsurvatory,conservatory	konvayor,convey(or)
konsurve,conserve	konvene,convene
konsurvutive,conservative	konvenyut,convenient
kontagus,contagious	konversashen,conversation
kontain,contain	konvershen,conversion

	konvert,convert
	konvex,convex
	konvict,convict
	konvinse,convince
	konvinshen,convention
	konvulesents,convalescence
	konvulgin,convulsion
	konvulshen,convulsion
	konvursashen,conversation
	konvursation,conversation
	konvurtable,convertible
	kood,could
	koodos,kudos
	kooger,cougar
	kook, *, ky,kier,kiest,kily,kiness,NEW SNOWBOARDER, ODD/ ECCENTRIC BEHAVIOR
	kookoo,cuckoo
	kooky,cookie
	kool,cool
	koop,coop / co-op
	kooperate,cooperate
	kooshin,cushion
	kooth,couth
	kope,cope / copy
	kopeir,copy(pier)
	koper,copper
	kopier,copy(pier)
	kopulate,copulate
	kopur,copper
	kopy,copy
	kor,car
	koral,choral / coral / corral / chorale
	kord,cord / chord / court
	kordaroy,corduroy
	kordinate,coordinate
	kords,cord(s) / chord(s) / court(s) / quart(s) / quartz
	kordunate,coordinate
	korduroy,corduroy
	kore,core / corp
	korekt,correct
	kores,chorus / course / core(s) / caress
	korespond,correspond
	korgil,cordial

korgul,cordial	kosd,cause(d) / cost / coast /	kownsul,council / counsel / console
koridoor,corridor	kosee,cozy	kownt,count
korigate,corrugate	koshen,caution	kowntur,counter
korilate,correlate	**kosher,*,red,ring,RESTRICTION IN FOOD PREPARATION,**	kownty,county
koriner,coroner	**LEGITIMATE/ FIT FOR OCCASION**	kowurd,coward
korinery,coronary	koshes,cautious	kowursif,coerce(cive)
koris,chorus / course	koshin,caution	kowursment,coerce(ment)
korispond,correspond	koshus,cautious	koyel,coil
korjil,cordial	kosmik,cosmic	koyn,coin
kork,cork / quark	kosmopolutin,cosmopolitan	koz,cause
korn,corn	kosmos,cosmos	kozd,cause(d) / cost
korner,corner / coroner	kost,cost / cause(d) / coast	kozmik,cosmic
korneu,cornea	koster,coaster	kozmopoletin,cosmopolitan
kornikopea,cornucopia	kostic,caustic	kozmos,cosmos
kornukopea,cornucopia	kostum,costume	kozy,cozy
kornur,corner / coroner	kostyume,costume	krab,crab
korode,corrode	kosy,cozy	krader,crater / creator
koroshen,corrode(osion)	kot,caught / cot / coat	kradul,cradle
korparul,corporal	kotage,cottage	kradur,crater / creator
korpirate,corporate	kotch,coach	krafe,crave
korps,corpse	koten,cotton	kraft,craft
korpural,corporal	kotuge,cottage	krain,crane
korpurate,corporate	kouch,couch	kraink,crank
kors,course / coarse	koulishun,coalition	krak,crack
korsd,coarse(d)	kounsil,council / counsel / console	krakel,crackle
korsoge,corsage	kount,count	kraker,cracker
kort,cord / court / quart	koursif,coerce(cive)	kral,crawl / corral
kort-marshul,court-martial	koursment,coerce(ment)	kram,cram
korteks,cortex	kova,kava	kramp,cramp
kortex,cortex	kove,cove	kranbery,cranberry
korts,quartz / court(s) / quart(s) / cord(s) / chord(s) /	kovenant,covenant	krane,crane
car(ts)	kover,cover	kraneum,cranium
korudoor,corridor	kovit,covet	krank,crank
korugate,corrugate	kovu,kava	krany,cranny
korul,choral / coral / corral / chorale	kovurt,covert	kraon,crayon
korulate,correlate	kow,cow	krap,crap / crepe
koruner,coroner	kowch,couch	krape,crepe / crap(ppy)
korunery,coronary	kowculus,calculus	krasee,crazy
korupt,corrupt	kowerd,coward	krash,crash
korus,chorus / course	kowersev,coerce(cive)	krass,crass
koruspond,correspond	kowkulate,calculate	krate,crate
korve,carve	kowl,call / cowl	krater,crater / creator
kos,cause	kownder,counter	kraul,crawl

kraut, PICKLED CABBAGE	krel, creel	kriket, cricket
krave, crave	kremate, cremate	krime, crime
krawnik, chronic	kreme, cream / creme	krimenal, criminal
krayon, crayon	kremenul, criminal	krimson, crimson
krazy, crazy	kreminal, criminal	kring, cringe
kreader, creator	kremsun, crimson	krinj, cringe
kreal, creel	kreng, cringe	kriptic, cryptic
kream, cream / creme	krenj, cringe	kripul, cripple
kreap, creep	krenkle, crinkle	krisade, crusade
kreapy, creep	krep, creep / crepe	kriscross, crisscross
krease, crease	kreple, cripple	krisis, crisis
kreashun, creation	kreptic, cryptic	krismus, christmas
kreasul, creosol	krepy, creep	krisont, croissant
kreate, create	krescross, crisscross	krisp, crisp
kreatef, create(ive)	krese, crease	kristal, crystal
kreative, creative	kresendo, crescendo	kristashen, crustacean
kreator, creator	kresent, crescent	kritesize, criticize
kreb, crib	kresont, croissant	kritik, critic
krebd, crib(bbed)	kresp, crisp	kritur, critter
krebeg, cribbage	kress, caress	kriz, cries
krecher, creature	krest, crest	kroak, croak
kredable, credible	kretable, credible	kroan, crone
krededer, creditor	kreteek, critique	krok, crock / croak
kreder, critter	kretik, critic	krokedile, crocodile
kredet, credit	kretikul, critical	kroket, croquet / croquette
kredible, credible	kreusol, creosol	krokudile, crocodile
kredibul, credible	kreusote, creosote	krokus, crocus
kredider, creditor	krevas, crevasse / crevice	krol, crawl
kredik, critic	krevus, crevasse / crevice	krom, chrome / crumb
kredisize, criticize	krew, crew	kromizone, chromosome
kredit, credit	krewd, crude	kronac, chronic
kreditor, creditor	krewshul, crucial	kronacle, chronicle
kreduble, credible	krewsufix, crucifix	kronalogical, chronology(gical)
kreecher, creature	krewton, crouton	krone, crone / crony
kreel, creel	kri, cry	krones, crony(s)
kreen, careen	krib, crib	kronic, chronic
kreenkul, crinkle	kribage, cribbage	kronicle, chronicle
kreep, creep	krid, cried	kronilogical, chronology(gical)
kreepy, creep	kridecal, critical	kronlogical, chronology(gical)
kreer, career	kridenshul, credential	kronucle, chronicle
kreisote, creosote	krider, critter	kronulogikul, chronology(gical)
kreke, creak / creek	kridesize, criticize	krony, crony
krekit, cricket	krien, cry(ing)	krook, crook

kroose, cruise / crew(s)	krysus, crisis	kuldesac, cul-de-sac
krop, crop	ku, cue	kuleckshun, collection
kroshay, crochet	kuack, quack	kulecter, collect(or)
kross, cross	kuagmire, quagmire	kulejet, collegiate
krotch, crotch	kubby, cubby	kulekt, collect
krouch, crouch	kube, cubby / cube	kulenary, culinary
krout, kraut	kubek, cubic	kulendula, calendula
krow, crow	kubekle, cubicle	kuler, color / cooler / collar
krowch, crouch	kuberd, cupboard	kulesterol, cholesterol
krowd, crowd	kubic, cubic	kulid, collide
krown, crown	kubicul, cubicle	kulidescope, kaleidoscope
krows, crow(s) / carouse	kuburd, cupboard	kulijin, collision
krowshay, crochet	kubuse, caboose	kulishun, collision
krowt, kraut	kuchen, cushion	kulition, collision
kru, crew	kucky, cookie	kulmenate, culminate
kruch, crutch	kucumber, cucumber	kulminate, culminate
krude, crude	kud, cud / could / cue(d)	kuloge, collage
krudenshul, credential	kudaver, cadaver	kuloje, collage
krue, crew	kudel, cuddle	kulokweul, colloquial
kruke, crook	kudent, couldn't	kulon, cologne / colon
kruks, crux	kudet, cadet	kuloneal, colonial
krum, crumb	kudint, couldn't	kuloquial, colloquial
krumble, crumble / crumple	**kudos, BONUS, CREDIT**	kulor, color / cooler
krumple, crumble / crumple	kufer, cover	kulosel, colossal
krunch, crunch	kuferege, coverage	kulosil, colossal
krupt, corrupt	kuff, cuff	kulown, cologne / colon
krusade, crusade	kufredge, coverage	kulpret, culprit
kruse, cruise / crew(s)	kuger, cougar	kulsher, culture
krusefix, crucifix	kugole, cajole	kult, cult
krusendo, crescendo	kuhoot, cahoot	kultavashen, cultivate(tion)
krush, crush	kuhute, cahoot	kultivashen, cultivate(tion)
krushul, crucial	kuk, kook / cook	kultivate, cultivate
krusont, croissant	kuke, cook / cookie / kook	kultsher, culture
krust, crust	kukoon, cocoon	kulture, culture
krustashen, crustacean	kuku, cuckoo	kultuvashen, cultivate(tion)
krutch, crutch	kukumber, cucumber	kulvert, culvert
kruteke, critique	kukune, cocoon	kum, come / cum
kruton, crouton	kul, cool / cull	kumand, command
krux, crux	kulamity, calamity	kumander, commander
kry, cry	kulandur, colander	kumbarsome, cumber(some)
kryeng, cry(ing)	kulaps, collapse	kumber, cumber
kryptic, cryptic	kulapsebul, collapse(sible)	kumberbun, cummerbund
krystal, crystal	kulcher, culture	kumbine, combine

kumbirsome,cumber(some)
kumbur,cumber
kumbuschen,combustion
kumbustuble,combustible
kumedeun,comedian
kumemerate,commemorate
kumenduble,commendable
kumensirit,commensurate
kuments,commence
kumfert,comfort
kumferter,comfort(er)
kumfertible,comfortable
kuminduble,commendable
kumit,commit
kumitment,commitment
kumity,committee
kumlod,cum laude
kumodety,commodity
kumpar,compare
kumpareson,comparison
kumpartment,compartment
kumpashun,compassion
kumpashunate,compassionate
kumpeny,company
kumpile,compile
kumplane,complain
kumpleks,complex
kumplete,complete
kumplians,compliant(nce)
kumplient,compliant
kumply,comply
kumponint,component
kumposier,composure
kumposit,composite
kumpoze,compose
kumpozer,composure
kumpreshun,compression
kumpresor,compressor
kumpress,compress
kumpuder,computer
kumpulsery,compulsory
kumpulshun,compulsion
kumpuss,compass

kumpute,compute
kumputer,computer
kumulative,cumulative
kumunal,communal
kumuneon,communion
kumutable,commute(table)
kumutble,commute(table)
kumyewtable,commute(table)
kunal,canal
kuncideration,considerate(tion)
kunclusev,conclusive
kundem,condemn
kundinse,condense
kundishen,condition
kundition,condition
kundolense,condolence
kundone,condone
kundukt,conduct
kundukter,conductor
kunekshen,connection
kunekt,connect
kunfekshun,confection
kunferm,confirm
kunfermashun,confirmation
kunfes,confess
kunfeshun,confession
kunfety,confetti
kunfide,confide
kunfigerashun,configuration
kunfine,confine
kunfinment,confinement
kunflict,conflict
kunform,conform
kunfrunt,confront
kunfujen,confusion
kunfuze,confuse
kunglomurete,conglomerate
kungradulashun,congratulation
kungratshulate,congratulate
kungruedy,congruent(uity)
kungruint,congruent
kungruity,congruent(uity)
kungunctavitis,conjunction(ivitis)

kunikkunik,kinnikinnick
kuning,cunning
kunjest,congest
kunjested,congest(ed)
kunjunction,conjunction
kunklude,conclude
kunklujen,conclusion
kunklusef,conclusive
kunkokt,concoct
kunkushen,concussion
kunning,cunning
kunsecutive,consecutive
kunsedurashen,considerate(tion)
kunseed,concede
kunseel,conceal
kunseet,conceit
kunseevable,conceivable
kunseeve,conceive
kunsent,consent
kunsentric,concentric
kunsepshual,conceptual
kunsepshun,conception
kunsern,concern
kunservator,conservator
kunservatory,conservatory
kunserve,conserve
kunseshun,concession
kunsestently,consistent(ly)
kunsevable,conceivable
kunsider,consider
kunsinment,consignment
kunsirvator,conservator
kunsirvatory,conservatory
kunsirvutive,conservative
kunsise,concise
kunsist,consist
kunsistency,consistence(cy)
kunsiter,consider
kunsole,console
kunsoludate,consolidate
kunsoom,consume
kunsoul,console
kunspearucy,conspiracy

kunspikyus,conspicuous	kunvulgin,convulsion	kurin,curtain
kunstrict,constrict	kunvulshen,convulsion	kurinsy,currency
kunstrucshen,construction	kup,cup / coop	kurint,current
kunstruct,construct	kupasity,capacity	kuriosity,curiosity
kunsult,consult	kupcake,cupcake	kurisma,charisma
kunsume,consume	kupe,coop	kurl,curl
kunsumshen,consumption	kupil,couple	kurnel,colonel / kernel
kunsurvatory,conservatory	kupler,coupler	kuroburate,corroborate
kunsurve,conserve	kupon,coupon	kurode,corrode
kunsurvutive,conservative	kupoot,kaput	kuroky,karaoke
kunsuvator,conservator	kupul,couple	kurosef,corrode(osive)
kuntagus,contagious	kuput,kaput	kurote,karate
kuntain,contain	kurable,curable	kurotion,corrode(osion)
kuntamunate,contaminate	kurader,curator	kuroty,karate
kuntane,contain	kural,choral / coral / corral / chorale	kurowse,carouse
kunteguis,contiguous	kurb,curb	kursanthimum,chrysanthemum
kuntemporary,contemporary	kurd,curd	kursathimum,chrysanthemum
kuntemt,contempt	kurdesy,courtesy	kurse,curse
kuntend,contend	kurdeus,courteous	kursif,cursive
kuntent,content	kurdisy,courtesy	kursive,cursive
kuntenual,continue(ual)	kurdle,curdle	kursoge,corsage
kuntenuense,continuance	kure,cure	kurtale,curtail
kuntenule,continue(ual)	kurect,correct	kurten,curtain
kuntest,contest	kureen,careen	kurtesy,courtesy
kuntiguis,contiguous	kureer,career	kurteus,courteous
kuntimporary,contemporary	kurege,courage	kurtin,curtain
kuntorshenist,contortionist	kureje,courage	kurtle,curdle
kuntrakshen,contraction	kurekt,correct	kurtse,curtsy
kuntree,country	kurekulum,curriculum	kurupt,corrupt
kuntrery,contrary	kuren,careen / cure(ring)	kurvachure,curvature
kuntribute,contribute	kurensy,currency	kurve,curve
kuntrishen,contrition	kurent,currant / current	kury,curry
kuntrol,control	kureosety,curiosity	kus,cuss
kunveenyut,convenient	kureosudy,curiosity	kusen,cousin
kunvene,convene	kures,care(s) / caress / cure(s)	kuset,cassette
kunvense,convince	kureur,courier	kushen,cushion
kunvenshen,convention	kureus,curious	kusin,cousin
kunvenyant,convenient	kureusol,creosol	kusp,cusp
kunvergin,conversion	kurf,curve	kusped,cuspid
kunvershen,conversion	kurfew,curfew	kuss,cuss
kunvert,convert	kurfue,curfew	kustedy,custody
kunvertable,convertible	kurige,courage	kustem,custom
kunvict,convict	kuri,curry	kustemary,customary

kustemize, customize	kwant, quaint	kweer, queer, career
kusterd, custard	kwantefy, quantify	kwefir, quiver
kustimer, customer	kwantem, quanta(tum)	kwefur, quiver
kustodeun, custodian	kwantetative, quantitative	kwek, quick
kustomary, customary	kwantety, quantity	kwekest, quick(est)
kustomer, customer	kwantify, quantify	kwekly, quick(ly)
kustomize, customize	kwantifyer, quantify(fier)	kweky, quick(ie)
kut, cut / cat	kwantim, quanta(tum)	kwel, quill
kutastrufee, catastrophy / catastrophe	kwantity, quantity	kwelt, quilt
kute, cute	kwantry, quandary	kwench, quench
kutecle, cuticle	kwantum, quanta(tum)	kwentuplet, quintuplet
kuth, couth	kward, quart	kwer, queer, career
kutlury, cutlery	kwarder, quarter	kwerk, quirk
kutukle, cuticle	kwarderly, quarter(ly)	kwerky, quirk
kuvenant, covenant	kwards, quartz / quart(s)	kwery, query
kuver, cover	kwardur, quarter	kwes, quiz
kuvit, covet	kwardurly, quarter(ly)	kwesden, question
kuvridge, coverage	kwardz, quartz / quart(s)	kwesekal, quiz(zzical)
kuvunent, covenant	kware, quarry	kweshten, question
kuzn, cousin	kwarel, quarrel	kwest, quest
kwack, quack / quake	kwarentene, quarantine	kwestenair, question(nnaire)
kwad, quad	kwaril, quarrel	kwesteun, question
kwadrant, quadrant	kwarintene, quarantine	kwestshunar, question(nnaire)
kwagmire, quagmire	kwark, quark	kwestun, question
kwaik, quake	kwarol, quarrel	kwet, quit / quite
kwail, quail	kwart, quart	kweter, quit(tter) / quiet(er)
kwaint, quaint	kwarter, quarter	kwever, quiver
kwak, quack / quake	kwarterly, quarter(ly)	kwez, quiz
kwale, quail	kwarts, quartz / quart(s)	kwezekal, quiz(zzical)
kwaledy, quality	kwarul, quarrel	kwezene, cuisine
kwalefication, qualify(fication)	kwary, quarry / query	kwezt, quest
kwalefikashen, qualify(ficat on)	kwasar, quasar	kwiet, quiet
kwalefiuble, qualify(fiable)	kwasy, quasi	kwietly, quiet(ly)
kwalefiur, qualify(fier)	kwaundre, quandary	kwifir, quiver
kwaletatif, quality(tative)	kwaure, quarry	kwifor, quiver
kwalety, quality	kwawrel, quarrel	kwik, quick
kwalifekashen, qualify(ficat on)	kwawrul, quarrel	kwikest, quick(est)
kwalify, qualify	kwawry, quarry	kwikly, quick(ly)
kwalitatif, quality(tative)	kwaysar, quasar	kwiky, quick(ie)
kwalitee, quality	kwazar, quasar	kwil, quill
kwalm, qualm	kwazee, quasi	kwilt, quilt
kwandery, quandary	kwazene, cuisine	kwinch, quench
kwandree, quandary	kween, queen	kwintuplet, quintuplet

kwire,choir	kwontifyer,quantify(fier)	kwurintene,quarantine
kwirk,quirk	kwontim,quanta(tum)	kwurk,quirk
kwiry,query	kwontity,quantity	kwurky,quirk
kwisekal,quiz(zzical)	kwontre,quandary	kwyit,quiet
kwisine,cuisine	kwontum,quanta(tum)	kwyre,choir
kwit,quit / quite	kworam,quorum	kyak,kayak
kwiter,quit(tter) / quiet(er)	kword,quart	la,law / lay
kwiut,quiet	kworder,quarter	labarenth,labyrinth
kwiutly,quiet(ly)	kworderly,quarter(ly)	labedo,libido
kwiver,quiver	kwords,quartz / quart(s)	**label,*,**,led, ling,A WAY TO REMEMBER/ SAVE/ RETRIEVE/ CATEGORIZE THINGS "prefixes: un"
kwiyet,quiet	kwordur,quarter	laber,labor
kwiz,quiz	kwordurly,quarter(ly)	laberatory,laboratory
kwizekal,quiz(zzical)	kwordz,quartz / quart(s)	labeul,labial
kwochent,quotient	kwore,quarry	**labi**,PREFIX INDICATING "LIP" MOST OFTEN MODIFIES THE WORD
kwod,quad	kworel,quarrel	
kwoda,quota	kworem,quorum	**labial**,lly, lize, lization,SOUND, OF THE LIPS, ORGAN PIPE "prefixes: bi"
kwodabul,quote(table)	kworentene,quarantine	
kwodashen,quote(tation)	kworil,quarrel	labido,libido
kwode,quote	kworim,quorum	labil,label
kwodrent,quadrant	kworintene,quarantine	**labio**,PREFIX INDICATING "LIP" MOST OFTEN MODIFIES THE WORD
kwodu,quota	kwork,quark	
kwoledy,quality	kworol,quarrel	labiol,labial
kwolefikashen,qualify(fication)	kworom,quorum	labl,label
kwolefy,qualify	kwort,quart	lable,label
kwoletatif,quality(tative)	kworter,quarter	**labor,*,**,red, ring,rious, riously, riousness, rism,rist, rer, PHYSICALLY WORKING "prefixes: un"
kwoletative,quality(tative)	kworterly,quarter(ly)	
kwolety,quality	kwortir,quarter	**laboratory,**ries,PLACE FOR STUDY/ EXPERIMENTS AND OBSERVATION
kwolification,qualify(fication)	kworts,quartz / quart(s)	
kwolifikashen,qualify(fication)	kwortur,quarter	laborenth,labyrinth
kwolifiuble,qualify(fiable)	kworul,quarrel	labratory,laboratory
kwolifiur,qualify(fier)	kworum,quorum	labrinth,labyrinth
kwolitatif,quality(tative)	kworuntene,quarantine	labrutory,laboratory
kwolitative,quality(tative)	kwoshent,quotient	labul,label
kwolitee,quality	kwosy,quasi	labur,labor
kwolm,qualm	kwota,quota	**labyrinth,*,**,A MAZE, CHAOTIC CIRCUMSTANCES
kwolufy,qualify	kwotabul,quote(table)	**lace,*,**, ed, cing,cy, cier, ciest, ciness,SECURE SHOES WITH, WOVEN STRING "prefixes: en/ un"
kwondery,quandary	kwotashen,quote(tation)	
kwontefy,quantify	kwotation,quote(tation)	**lacerate,*,**,ed, ting,tion,GASH/ RIP SOMETHING BY PENETRATION
kwontefyer,quantify(fier)	kwote,quote	
kwontem,quanta(tum)	kwotu,quota	lacereit,lacerate
kwontetative,quantitative	kwozy,quasi	lach,latch / lodge / lash
kwontety,quantity	kwurentene,quarantine	lacireit,lacerate
kwontify,quantify		

lack,*,ked,king,BELIEF THA~ ONE DOES NOT HAVE ENOUGH OF SOMETHING (or see lake)
lackative,laxative
lacker,lacquer / lager
lacks,lax / lake(s) / lack(s)
lacktat,lactate
lacquer,*,VARNISH
lacrosse,ORIGINALLY A NATIVE AMERICAN SPORTS GAME
lacs,lax
lacsetive,laxative
lact,PREFIX INDICATING "MILK" MOST OFTEN MODIFIES THE WORD
lactate,*,ed,ting,tion,MILK BEING PRODUCED IN MAMMALS
lacteit,lactate
lacti,PREFIX INDICATING "MILK" MOST OFTEN MODIFIES THE WORD
lacto,PREFIX INDICATING "MILK" MOST OFTEN MODIFIES THE WORD
lactose,SUGAR FROM COW MILK
lad,*,YOUNG MEN (or see laid/ late)
ladder,*,TWO POLES WITH RUNGS FOR CLIMBING (or see later)
lade,laid / lady / late
ladel,ladle
laden,BURDENED DOWN,HEAVY LOAD
lader,ladder / later / latter
laderal,lateral
laderuly,laterall(ly)
ladery,lottery
lades,lattice / lady(dies) / lettuce
ladir,latter / ladder / later
ladis,lattice / lady(dies) / lettuce
laditude,latitude
ladle,*,ed,ling,LONG HANDLE SPOON TO SERVE FOOD
ladul,ladle
ladur,later / ladder / latter
ladural,lateral
ladutude,latitude
lady,dies,A WOMAN
lae,lay

laebial,labial
laed,laid / late
laeng,lay(ing)
laer,layer
laevo,PREFIX INDICATING "COUNTER-CLOCKWISE" MOST OFTEN MODIFIES THE WORD
laf,laugh
lafdur,laughter
lafender,lavender
lafter,laughter
lag,*,gged,gging,BE SLOWER THAN THE OTHERS,SHAPE OR CASING,DELAY (or see log/ lodge/ lack/ leg/ lake)
lager,BEER (or see logger/ lacquer)
lageslat,legislate
lagestics,logistic(s)
lagetamate,legitimate
lagicul,logic(al)
lagir,logger / lacquer
lagislat,legislate
lagistics,logistic(s)
lagitamate,legitimate
lagoon,*,ENCLOSED/ NEARLY ENCLOSED SMALL BODY OF WATER NEAR LARGER BODY OF WATER
lagor,logger / lacquer
lagoslat,legislate
lagur,lacquer / lager / logger
laguslat,legislate
lai,lay
laiabol,liable
laibreri,library
laicens,license
laicwais,likewise
laid,PAST TENSE FOR THE WORD "LAY" (or see late)
laier,liar
laif,life
laiion,lion
laik,like
laiken,liken
laiknes,likeness
laikwais,likewise
laim,lime
laimlait,limelight

lain,PAST TENSE FOR THE WORD "LAID" (or see lane/ line)
lainer,liner
laing,lay(ing) / lying
laingwege,language
laining,lining
laiqnes,likeness
laiquen,liken
laiqwais,likewise
lair,*,red,ring,ANIMALS DEN (or see lyre/ layer)
laisens,license
lait,light / lite
laitnes,lightness
laitning,lightening
laivleud,livelihood
laivliud,livelihood
laj,lodge
lajekul,logic(al)
lajeslat,legislate
lajislat,legislate
lajistics,logistic(s)
lajoslat,legislate
lajur,lacquer / lager / logger
lajuslat,legislate
lake,*,LARGE BODY OF WATER FED BY SPRINGS (or see lack)
laker,lacquer / lager / logger
lakross,lacrosse
laks,lax / lake(s) / lack(s)
laksetif,laxative
laksutef,laxative
laktate,lactate
lakteit,lactate
laktose,lactose
lam,RUNNING FROM TROUBLE (or see lamb/ lame)
lama,llama
lamb,*,YOUNG SHEEP (or see lam/ lame)
lame,ly,eness,PERMANENTLY INJURED LIMB/ LIMBS THAT DON'T WORK (or see lamb/ lam)
lamenate,laminate
lament,*,ted,ting,tingly,table,tably,tableness,tation,ter,MOURN THE LOSS OF SOMEONE,SPEND TIME IN THE PAST ON REGRETS

laminate, *, ed, ting, tion, tor, able, GLUE LAYERS TOGETHER "prefixes: inter/ multi/ non"
lamp, *, A LIGHT WITH A SHADE/ COVER OVER THE BULB
lamunate, laminate
lan, lawn
lance, *, ed, cing, er, MEDIEVAL WEAPON
lanch, launch
land, *, ded, ding, dless, EARTH, SETTLE ONTO, DIVIDING THE GROUND
landern, lantern
landers, launder(s)
landlord, *, OWNER WHO RENTS/ LEASES PROPERTY
landscape, *, ed, ping, er, FOLIAGE/ FAUNA/ TERRAIN OF WHAT THE EYE SEES
landskeip, landscape
landslaid, landslide
landslide, *, WHEN LAND BREAKS AWAY FROM OTHER LAND DUE TO WATER
lane, *, PASSAGEWAYS/ ROADS FOR VEHICLES, PATHS IN BOWLING (or see lain)
lanelin, lanolin
language, *, WORDS/ MEANS OF COMMUNICATION IN DIFFERENT REGIONS "prefixes: inter"
languich, language
languill, language
languweg, language
lankwij, language
lanky, kily, kiness, TALL AND THIN
lanlord, landlord
lanolin, OIL FROM WOOL
lanqueg, language
lanqui, lanky
lans, lance / lane(s) / land(s)
lanskap, landscape
lanskapur, landscape(r)
lanskeip, landscape
lanslaid, landslide
lansqueip, landscape
lant, land
lantern, *, FUELED FLAME WITHIN CONTAINER
lantlord, landlord
lantscape, landscape
lantslide, landslide

lanulin, lanolin
lap, *, pped, pping, TO GO AROUND, HOW ANIMALS DRINK, CREATED IN SITTING POSITION "prefixes: over"
lapadary, lapidary
lapel, *, COLLARS
lapidary, ries, rian, CUT/ POLISH/ ENGRAVE STONES
laprutory, laboratory
laps, lapse / lap(s)
lapse, *, ed, sing, SLIPPING INTO, LOOSE A MOMENT IN TIME, PAUSE (or see lap(s)) "prefixes: pro"
lapudary, lapidary
laqmineit, laminate
lar, lair / layer
larch, large
lard, FAT FROM DEAD PIGS (or see yard)
larel, laurel
larengitis, laryngitis
lareut, laureate
large, er, est, ely, eness, BIG "prefixes: en"
larges, largess / large(st)
largess, GENEROUS GIFT/ DONATION EXPECTING NOTHING IN RETURN
largist, large(st)
largly, large(ly)
lariet, laureate
lariette, laureate
larinex, larynx
larinllaidis, laryngitis
larj, large
larjes, largess
lark, *, BIRD, PRANT, ON AN IMPULSE FOR FUN
larniks, larynx
larol, laurel
larva, al, BABY INSECT THAT RESEMBLES A WORM BEFORE IT BECOMES AN ADULT
larying, PREFIX INDICATING "LARYNX/ VOCAL ORGAN" MOST OFTEN MODIFIES THE WORD
laryngitis, ic, THROAT INFLAMMATION
larynx, THROAT
lasarate, lacerate
lasd, last / lace(d)
lase, lace / lace / lazy

lasench, lozenge
laser, *, A LIGHT FREQUENCY
laserashen, lacerate(tion)
laserate, lacerate
laseration, lacerate(tion)
lasereit, lacerate
lash, hes, hed, hing, her, HAIRS ON THE EYE, USE SOMETHING SUCH AS ROPE TO STRIKE/ TIE UP SOMETHING, THRUST OUT WITH ILL INTENT "prefixes: un"
lasinch, lozenge
lasir, laser
lasirashen, lacerate(tion)
lasirate, lacerate
lasiration, lacerate(tion)
lasireit, lacerate
lass, ssie, GIRL
lasso, oes, SLIDING HOOP MADE OF ROPE
last, *, ted, ting, tly, NOT THE FIRST, WON'T GO AWAY FOR QUITE AWHILE (or see lace(d))
lasuit, lawsuit
lasur, laser
lasurashen, lacerate(tion)
lasurat, lacerate
lasuration, lacerate(tion)
lasut, lawsuit
lasute, lawsuit
latch, hes, hed, CLOSURE FOR A DOOR/ LID
late, er, ely, eness, tish, NOT ON TIME, OF A PARTICULAR TIME (or see lady/ ladder/ latter)
laten, laden
latent, tly, ncy, A TIME LAPSE BETWEEN WHEN IT HAPPENED AND THE REACTION
later, FURTHER ALONG IN TIME (or see late/ ladder/ latter)
lateral, lly, EXTENDS FROM THE SIDE, A MOVEMENT IN A SIDEWAYS DIRECTION "prefixes: bi/ contra/ multi/ uni"
latex, xes, tices, FORM OF MANMADE RUBBER/ PLASTIC USED FOR GLOVES, PAINT, ETC.
lath, *, NARROW STRIPS OF WOOD USED TO BUILD WITH (or see lathe)
lathargic, lethargic

lathe,* ,ed,hing,WOOD SHAPING MACHINE (or see lath)
lather,* ,red,ring,ry,rer,SCAPY/ FOAMY BUBBLES (or see leather)
latil,ladle
latincy,latent(ncy)
latise,lattice
latitude,* ,dinal,dinally,LINES THAT RUN NORTH/ SOUTH
latle,ladle
latrine,* ,MILITARY WORD FOR TOILET
latter,rly,MORE TOWARDS THE LAST (or see ladder)
lattice,ed,WOOD STRIPS CRISSCROSSED TOGETHER FOR DECORATION
latur,later / ladder / latter
latural,lateral
latury,lottery
laty,lady
lau,law
laud,loud
lauger,lager / logger
laugh,hes,hed,hing,hable,hably,hter,DISPLAY/ EXPRESS GLEE/ ENJOYMENT IN VOCAL BURSTS
laughter,VOCAL EXPRESSION OF HAPPINESS/ GLEE
lauk,lock / log
laukd,lock(ed)
laun,lawn
launch,hes,hed,hing,her,PROPEL/ SHOOT SOMETHING (or see lounge)
launder,* ,rer,ry,WASH AND IRON CLOTHING
laundry,CLEANING/ CARING OF CLOTHES
laung,lounge / long
laur,layer
laurch,large
laureate,eship,HONORED/ DISTINGUISHED POET
laurel,A TREE,REST ON PREVIOUS AWARDS
lausut,lawsuit
lauyer,lawyer
lava,MOLTEN ROCK
laven,leaven(ed)
lavender,A PLANT
lavesh,lavish
lavinder,lavender
lavish,hes,her,hly,hness,hment,TO BESTOW UPON SOMEONE GIFTS AND OTHER THINGS

lavun,leaven(ed)
lavunder,lavender
law,* ,wful,wfully,wfulness,wless,wlessly,RULES SUPPORTED BY A GOVERNMENT "prefixes: un"
lawn,* ,GRASSY AREAS
lawn mower,* ,MACHINE FOR MOWING GRASS
lawnch,launch
lawsuit,* ,A CASE BROUGHT BEFORE A JUDGE CONCERNING THE LAW
lawyer,* ,PAID PEOPLE TO HELP YOU WITH THE LAWS
lax,xly,xness,xity,xative,RELAXED,NO HURRY (or see lake(s)/ lack(s))
laxative,* ,PLANT/ CHEMICALS FOR RELAXING THE BOWELS
laxsutif,laxative
laxutif,laxative
lay,* ,aid,ying,yer,SET ASIDE/ DOWN AN OBJECT,TO INSTALL,SOMEONE WHO IS TRAINING TO BE AN UPPER RANK,RECLINE (or see lie) "prefixes: in/ mis/ over/ re-/ un/ under"
layabol,liable
laybreri,library
laycens,license
ayeng,lay(ing) / lying
layer,* ,red,ring,THICKNESS OF SOMETHING OVER TOP OF ANOTHER,ONE LEVEL OVER ANOTHER (or see lawyer) "prefixes: bi/ multi"
layon,lion
laytex,latex
layur,layer / lawyer
lazanya,lasagna
lazarashen,lacerate(tion)
laze,lazy
lazeng,lozenge
lazer,laser
lazeur,lazy(zier)
lazing,lozenge / laze(zing)
lazy,zier,ziest,zily,ziness,NO AMBITION TO DO ANYTHING (or see lace)
lbo,elbow
le,lay
leach,hes,hed,hing,SEEPING/ PERCOLATING LIQUID (or see leech)

lead,* ,ded,dless,der,derless,ding,den,denly,denness,A HEAVY METAL,SOMEONE WHO TAKES CHARGE OF A SITUATION "prefixes: mis/ un"
leader,* ,rless,rship,ONE WHO TAKES CHARGE (or see letter/ liter)
leaf,aves,fy,fier,fiest,finess,GROWS ON A TREE/ BUSH "prefixes: inter"
league,* ,er,GROUPS PARTICIPATING IN A SIMILAR ACTIVITY DIVIDED INTO REGIONS/ ABILITIES "prefixes: pro"
leak,* ,ked,king,kage,ky,kiness,WHEN LIQUID/ INFORMATION SEEPS OUT (or see leek)
lean,* ,nly,nness,ner,nest,VERY LITTLE FAT,VERTICAL POSITION LEANING TOWARDS A HORIZONTAL STATE (or see lien)
leap,* ,ped,ping,pt,TO BOUND/ JUMP
lear,leer
learn,* ,ned,ning,nable,ner,nedly,nedness,TAKE IN INFORMATION AS KNOWLEDGE "prefixes: un"
leary,leery
lease,* ,ed,sing,sable,ssee,er,BORROW/ USE FOR AWHILE IN EXCHANGE FOR MONEY (or see lees) "prefixes: re-/ sub"
leash,es,hed,hing,RESTRAINT FOR ANIMALS "prefixes: un"
leason,liaison
least,twise,SMALLEST AMOUNT,GREATER THAN "LESS" (or see lease(ed))
leasy,lessee
leather,* ,red,ring,DRIED SKIN FROM ANIMALS
leave,* ,ving,eft,TO GO AWAY,PAST TENSE FOR THE WORD "LEAF/ LEAVE" (or see leaf/ leaven) "prefixes: inter"
leaven,* ,ned,ning,USED TO FERMENT DOUGH,TO RAISE MOODS/ SPIRITS (or see leave(ving)) "prefixes: un"
leazon,liaison
lebarul,liberal
lebirate,liberate
lebrul,liberal
leburate,liberate
leburty,liberty
lecar,liquor / liqueur / lick(er)

lech,leech / leach / ledge
lechibol,legible
lecshur,lecture
lecture,*,ed,ring,er,TO SPEAK AT GREAT LENGTH ABOUT SOMETHING TO A GROUP OF PEOPLE
lecur,liquor / liqueur / lick(er)
led,PAST TENSE FOR THE WORD "LEAD" (or see lid/ lead/ let)
ledagation,litigate(tion)
ledal,little
ledaret,literate
leder,liter / litter / letter / leader
lederachure,literature
lederary,literary
lederul,literal
ledge,*,er,A FLAT LANDING ATOP A WALL / SECTION, A BOOK WHICH KEEPS ACCOUNTING RECORDS, AN OVERHANG
ledigation,litigate(tion)
ledir,leader / letter / liter / litter
ledis,lettuce
leds,let(s) / lead(s)
ledur,liter / litter/ letter / leader
ledurasy,literacy
ledus,lettuce
leech,hes,BLOOD SUCKING BUG (or see leach)
leed,lead
leef,leaf / leave
leeg,league
leek,A VEGETABLE (or see leak)
leen,lean / lien
leenyency,leniency
leep,leap
leer,*,red,ring,ry,A LONG GLANCE WITH MALICIOUS INTENT
leery,SUSPICIOUS/ WARY OF
lees,SEDIMENTS OF WINE/ LIQUOR (or see lease)
leese,lease
leesh,leash
leest,least / lease(d)
leet,lead
leeward,AWAY FROM THE WIND
lef,leaf / live / leave / left

lefd,lift / left / leaf(ed) / live(d)
lefee,levee / levy / leaf
lefol,level
left,*,ty,LEFT VS. RIGHT, PAST TENSE FOR THE WORD "LEAVE", APPEARS TO BE GONE (or see lift/ live(d))
leful,level
leg,*,gged,gging,ggings,EXTREMITY ON THE LOWER END OF THE TORSO, SUPPORT FOR TABLE/ CHAIRS, AN EXTENSION, COVER FOR LEGS (or see league/ ledge)
legacy,cies,SOMETHING HANDED DOWN FROM PREDECESSORS
legal,ly,lity,lities,lize,lization,lism,RULES AS DECIDED BY THE SUPREME COURT "prefixes: il"
legament,ligament
leganse,allegiance / elegance
legasy,legacy
lege,ledge / league
legebul,legible
legecy,legacy
legend,*,dary,daries,A STORY HANDED DOWN THROUGH HISTORY
leger,leisure / ledge(r)
legeslat,legislate
legesy,legacy
legible,ly,bility,WRITING CAPABLE OF BEING READ "prefixes: il"
legibul,legible
legido,libido
legind,legend
legion,*,nary,naries,LARGE GROUP ASSOCIATED WITH THE MILITARY
legislat,legislate
legislate,*,ed,ting,tion,tive,tor,ture,RELATED TO LAWMAKING
legislation,PASSING AND CREATING LAWS
legislative,ely,RELATED TO LAWMAKING
legislature,LAWMAKING BRANCH
legistics,logistic(s)
legisy,legacy
legitemet,legitimate

legitimate,*,ed,ting,ely,eness,tize,acy,tion,mist,mize, mized,mizing,mizer,azation,LEGALLY RECOGNIZED "prefixes: il"
legium,legume
legoslat,legislate
leguble,legible
legue,league
legul,legal
legulize,legal(ize)
legume,*,SPECIES OF PLANT
legun,lesion / legion
leguse,legacy
leguslashen,legislation
leguslat,legislate
legusletive,legislative
legusture,legislature
legusy,legacy
legzi,lazy
lei,lay
leibal,label
leiber,labor
leibol,label
leibor,labor
leic,lake
leid,laid
leidel,ladle
leider,later
leidi,lady
leidol,ladle
leier,layer
leif,leave / leaf
leik,lake
leim,lame
lein,lain / lane
leingt,length
leinguich,language
leinki,lanky
leinqui,lanky
leinth,length
leis,lace
leiser,laser
leisi,lazy / lace

leisure, ed, eless, ely, reliness, eness, RELAXED, UNHURRIED
leit, late
leitecs, latex
leiter, later
leitex, latex
leith, lathe
leizer, laser
leizi, lazy
lej, ledge / leech
lejable, legible
lejanse, allegiance
lejebul, legible
lejen, lesion / legion
lejend, legend
lejer, leisure / ledge(r)
lejeslat, legislate
lejibul, legible
lejin, legion / lesion
lejislashen, legislation
lejislat, legislate
lejislative, legislative
lejislature, legislature
lejitamet, legitimate
lejoslat, legislate
lejun, legion / lesion
lejuslat, legislate
lek, lick / leak / leek / league
leked, lick(ed) / leak(ed)
lekemia, leukemia
leker, liquor / liqueur / lick(er)
lekoresh, licorice
leksher, lecture
lekture, lecture
lekume, legume
lekur, liquor / liqueur / lick(er)
lekwefide, liquify(fied)
lekwid, liquid
lekwidate, liquid(ate)
lekwify, liquify
lellend, legend
lellidamet, legitimate
lellislachur, legislative

lellislelchon, legislation
lem, limb
lemazene, limousine
lemb, limb
lember, limber
lembo, limbo
lemet, limit
lemfatic, lymph(atic)
lemintation, lament(tation)
lemit, limit
lemitation, limit(ation)
lemon, *, ny, nade, CITRUS FRUIT, JUICE
lemp, limp
lemphatic, lymph(atic)
lemune, lemon
lemusine, limousine
lemutation, limit(ation)
lemuzene, limousine
len, lean / lien
lenament, liniment
lend, *, ding, nt, der, LET SOMEONE BORROW SOMETHING (or see lint/ lean(ed))
leneanse, leniency
lenear, linear
lenen, linen
leneuge, lineage
leneul, lineal
lenger, linger
lengo, lingo
length, *, hen, hener, hy, hiness, HOW LONG SOMETHING IS
lengual, lingual
lenguist, linguist
lenguistic, linguistic
lenguistics, linguistic(s)
lengwestic, linguistic
lengwist, linguist
lengwistics, linguistic(s)
lengwul, lingual
leniach, lineage
leniall, lineage
leniansy, leniency
leniency, cies, ce, nt, ntly, NOT RIGID OR TOO STRICT

lenin, linen / lean(ing)
leniuge, lineage
leniur, linear
lenk, link
lenkage, link(age)
lenker, linger
lenkth, length
lenkwol, lingual
lenoleum, linoleum
lenon, linen / lean(ing)
lens, PART OF THE EYE, USED IN GLASSES
lenseed, linseed
lent, PAST TENSE FOR THE WORD "LEND", LET SOMEONE BORROW, A RELIGIOUS EVENT (or see lint/ lend/ lean(ed))
lenth, length
lentil, *, PLANT IN THE LEGUME FAMILY
lentul, lentil
lenument, liniment
lenyensy, leniency
leotard, *, HEAVYWEIGHT PANTYHOSE
lep, lip / leap
lepel, lapel
leqer, liquor / liqueur
leqid, liquid
leqidate, liquid(ate)
leqifide, liquify(fied)
leqify, liquify
leranex, larynx
lerch, lurch
lere, leery
lerengitis, laryngitis
leric, lyric
lerinex, larynx
leringitis, laryngitis
lerinllaytis, laryngitis
lerk, lurk
lern, learn
lernicks, larynx
lery, leery
les, less / lease
lesard, lizard

lesbian, *, WOMAN WHO PREFERS INTIMATE COMPANIONSHIP WITH ANOTHER WOMAN
lese,lessee
lesee,lessee
lesen,lessen / lesson / listen
leser,lesser / lessor
lesh,leash
leshun,lesion
lesi,lessee
lesin,lessen / lesson / listen
lesion, *, AN INJURED SPOT ON HUMAN TISSUE
lesir,lesser / lessor
lesless,listless
leson,lessen / lesson / listen
lesp,lisp
less,sser,NOT AS MUCH AS BEFORE OR AS EXPECTED
lessee, *, ONE WHO IS LEASING
lessen,TAKE SOME AWAY, REMOVE SOME (or see lesson)
lesser,NOT AS MUCH AS BEFORE, LESS THAN (or see lessor)
lesson, *, A TEACHING/ LEARNING SECTION/ SESSION (or see lessen)
lessor, *, ONE WHO LEASES OUT PROPERTY TO OTHERS (or see lesser)
lest, list / least
lesten,listen
lestless,listless
lesun,lessen / lesson / listen
lesur,lesser / lessor
let, *, tting, PERMIT, ALLOW (or see led/lead)
let's, CONTRACTION OF THE WORDS "LET US"
leter,liter / litter / letter / leader
leteracy,literacy
leteral,literal
leterally,literal(ly)
leterary,literary
leterate,literate
leterature,literature
letes,lettuce
lethal,lly, lity, DEADLY "prefixes: non/ semi"
lethargic,cally, gy,SLEEPY, NO ENERGY,SLUMPED
lethargy,gic, SLEEPY, HARD TO MOVE, NO ENERGY

letharllic, lethargic
lether, leather
lethergy, lethargy
lethourgic, lethargic
lethul, lethal
letir,liter / litter / letter / leader
letiracher,literature
letis,lettuce
letmus,litmus
letrine,latrine
letter, *, red, ring, SYMBOLS OF THE ALPHABET, PAPER WITH WRITING TO SOMEONE, MAKE LETTER SHAPES (or see leader) "prefixes: un"
lettuce, AN EDIBLE PLANT
letur,liter / litter / letter / leader
leturacher,literature
letus,lettuce
leuc,PREFIX INDICATING 'WHITE/ COLORLESS' MOST OFTEN MODIFIES THE WORD
leuco,PREFIX INDICATING 'WHITE/ COLORLESS' MOST OFTEN MODIFIES THE WORD
leukemia, ic, A FATAL DISEASE
leuko,PREFIX INDICATING 'WHITE/ COLORLESS' MOST OFTEN MODIFIES THE WORD
leutard,leotard
lev, PREFIX INDICATING 'COUNTERCLOCKWISE' MOST OFTEN MODIFIES THE WORD
levabul,live(vable)
leval,level
levatate,levitate
leve, leave / levy / levee
levee, *, TRENCH/ EMBANKMENT FOR CONTROLLING WATER (or see levy)
level, *, led, ling, lly, lness, ler, STRAIGHT UP OR HORIZONTAL, TRUTHFUL WITH SOMEONE "prefixes: multi/ un"
leven,leaven(ed)
lever, *, rage, APPLY PHYSICS/ HARDWARE TO LIFT "prefixes: un"
levi,levee / levy
levid,livid
levil,level
levitate, *, ed, ting, tion, ty, DEFY GRAVITY

leviteit,levitate
levo,PREFIX INDICATING "COUNTERCLOCKWISE" MOST OFTEN MODIFIES THE WORD
levol,level
levor,lever / liver
levs,leave(s)
levuble,live(vable)
levul,level
levun,leaven(ed)
levur,liver / lever
levury,livery
levtate,levitate
levy, vies, vied, vying, viable, vier, USED TO COLLECT MONEY, WAGE WAR (or see levee)
lew,lieu
lewb,lube
lewbrecashen,lubricate(tion)
lewbrecate,lubricate
lewbrikate,lubricate
lewcid,lucid
lewcratef,lucrative
lewd,dly, dness, OBSCENE, GIVEN TO LUST AND INDECENCY (or see loot)
lewdakris,ludicrous
lewducris,ludicrous
lewkrative,lucrative
lewkwarm,lukewarm
lewlu,lulu
lewmenary,luminary
lewmenesense,luminescence
lewmenosity,luminosity
lewmenus,luminous
lewmin,lumen
lewner,lunar
leword,leeward
lewpine,lupine
lewse,loose / lose
lewsid,lucid
lewsun,loose(n)
lewt,loot / lute / lewd
leydi,lady
leyend,legend
leyidament,legitimate

leyisleishon, legislation
leyor, layer
leytex, latex
lezard, lizard
lezbeun, lesbian
li, lie / lye / lay
liabelity, liable(bility)
liable, bility, bilities, SOMEONE TO BE BLAMED
liaison,*, FORMATION OF DEEP CONNECTION BETWEEN PEOPLE FOR MANEUVERING, BONDING
liar,*, SOMEONE WHO DOESN'T TELL THE TRUTH (or see lyre)
liatard, leotard
libareit, liberate
libary, library
libel, llant, lee, lous, lously, WRITE MALICIOUS WORDS ABOUT SOMEONE ELSE FOR PUBLIC VIEWING (or see liable)
liberal,*, lly, lness, lism, lity, lities, listic, list, MODERATE, TOLERANT, PROVIDE FREELY "prefixes: neo"
liberate,*, ed, ting, tion, tor, TO SET FREE
liberde, liberty
libereit, liberate
liberty, ties, THE ACT OF FREEDOM
libery, liberty
libido, dinal, dinally, THOUGHTS WHICH DRIVE THE SEXUAL IMPULSES
lible, libel / liable
libol, libel
liborashun, liberate(tion)
liborate, liberate
liboration, liberate(tion)
liborte, liberty
liborul, liberal
library, ries, rian, A PLACE WHICH COLLECTS AND DISSEMINATES WRITTEN HISTORY "prefixes: inter"
librul, liberal
libul, libel / liable
libural, liberal
licd, lick(ed) / like(d)
lice, PLURAL WORD FOR LOUSE, PARASITIC INSECT (or see like/ lick/ lie(s)/ lay(s))

license,*, ed, sing, sable, see, er, A PERMIT TO OPERATE "prefixes: sub/ un"
lich, leach / leech
lichen,*, MOSS, A FORM OF PLANT WITH HEALING QUALITIES (or see liken)
lichon, legion / lesion / lichen
licinse, license
lick,*, ked, king, ker, USING THE TONGUE (or see like) "prefixes: un"
licorice, A PLANT EXTRACT, A CANDY
lict, lick(ed) / like(d)
lid,*, dded, dless, TOP FOR A CONTAINER, A COVERING (or see lie(d)/ light/ lit)
lidagachon, litigate(tion)
lidagation, litigate(tion)
lidagashen, litigate(tion)
lidegate, litigate
lidel, little
lider, liter / litter / light(er) / leader
liderachure, literature
lideral, literal
liderally, literal(lly)
liderary, literary
liderasy, literacy
liderate, literate
lidereture, literature
liderit, literate
lidigachen, litigate(tion)
lidigate, litigate
lidigation, litigate(tion)
lidirachure, literature
lidirary, literary
lidol, little
lidor, litter / leader / liter / letter
lidul, little
liduracher, literature
lidurally, literal(ly)
lidurare, literary
lie,*, ed, lying, TO NOT TELL THE TRUTH, BODY IN A RECLINED/ FLAT POSITION, INACTIVE POSITION (or see lay/ lye) "prefixes: under"
lieizan, liaison

lien,*, SOMEONE WHO TAKES AWAY PROPERTY FOR MONEY DUE (or see lion)
lieng, lying
lier, liar / lyre
lieu, INSTEAD OF, IN PLACE OF
lieutenant,*, A MILITARY OFFICER
lieysan, liaison
lif, life/ live/ leaf/ leave
lifd, lift / live(d)
life, er, ive, ANIMATE MATTER/ ORGANISM "prefixes: pro-"
lifeble, live(vable)
lifle, live(ly)
liflehood, livelihood
liflehud, livelihood
lift,*, ted, ting, ter, PICK/ HOIST UP (or see live(d)/ left) "prefixes: up"
lig, league
ligal, legal
ligale, legal(lly)
ligality, legal(ity)
ligament,*, tous, tal, tary, FIBROUS TISSUE IN THE BODY
ligan, legion / lesion / lichen
light,*, ted, ting, tly, it, ten, tens, tened, tening, tless, tness, VISIBLE WAVE/ PARTICLES, NOT HEAVY "prefixes: en"
lightening, ILLUMINATED ELECTRICAL BOLTS IN SKY
lightness, NOT HEAVY, FEATHER WEIGHT, DEGREE OF ILLUMINATION
ligol, legal
ligole, legal(lly)
ligoly, legal(lly)
ligon, legion / lesion / lichen
ligoon, lagoon
ligument, ligament
lik, lick/ like/ leak/ leek
likd, lick(ed)/ like(d)
like,*, ed, kable, eness, ely, elier, eliest, SIMILAR TO SOMETHING/ SOMEONE ELSE, ENJOY SOMETHING, ATTRACTED TO SOMETHING (or see lick) "prefixes: dis/ un"
liken,*, SIMILAR TO, RESEMBLING (or see lichen/ lick(ing))

likeness, SIMILAR TO, RESEMBLING
liker, liquor / liqueur / lick(er)
likerish, licorice

likewise, SIMILARLY, ALSO
likness, likeness
likor, liquor / liqueur
likoresh, licorice
likt, like(d) / lick(ed)
likuble, like(kable)
likued, liquid
likuefi, liquify
likun, liken
likwed, liquid
likwid, liquid
likwidate, liquid(ate)
likwifide, liquify(fied)
likwify, liquify
likwise, likewise

lilac, *, AROMATIC PLANT
lillon, legion
liluc, lilac
limasen, limousine
limazene, limousine

limb, *, bed, bing, BRANCHES OF TREES/ SHRUBS, TO REMOVE BRANCHES/ EXTRUSIONS FROM THE BODY TORSO

limber, *, red, ring, rly, rness, ABLE TO MOVE BODY SMOOTHLY, WITH DEXTERITY "prefixes: un"

limbo, PLACE BETWEEN HERE AND THERE, WITH UNCERTAINTY, A PHYSICAL GAME

lime, *, A CITRUS FRUIT, MINERAL FOR SETTING BRICKS/ STONE

limelight, *, BEING IN THE SPOTLIGHT
limen, lemon
limesine, limousine
limet, limit
limetation, limit(ation)
limfatic, lymph(atic)

limit, *, ted, ting, tation, tless, tative, ter, tary, ONLY GO SO FAR, A FIXED VALUE "prefixes: il/ sub/ un"
limlite, limelight
limon, lemon
limosen, limousine

limousine, *, LONG AUTOMOBILE FOR TRANSPORTING PEOPLE
limozen, limousine

limp, *, ped, ping, ply, per, NOT STIFF/ RIGID, LOSS OF FUNCTION, LACK OF WILLFUL CONTROL OVER THE BODY
limphatic, lymph(atic)
limpt, limp(ed)
limusine, limousine
limuzene, limousine
lin, line / lean / lend
linament, liniment
lind, lend / lint / line(d)

line, *, ed, ning, er, eless, eable, eal, ear, eate, BETWEEN TWO POINTS, FOR FISHING "prefixes: inter/ multi/ un/ under"

lineage, *, OUR ANCESTORS, FAMILY TREE, WHERE WE COME FROM

lineal, lly, HEREDITY FOLLOWING A DIRECT PATH "prefixes: bi/ inter/ multi/ uni"
lineansi, leniency

linear, rly, rize, rizes, rized, rizing, rization, rity, PATH STRAIGHT AHEAD WITH NO DEVIATION "prefixes: bi/ inter/ multi/ non/ uni"

linen, *, TAN COTTON FABRIC (or see linin/ lining) "prefixes: under"
lineng, lining

liner, *, COATING INSIDE A VESSEL FOR PROTECTION
lineur, linear

linger, *, red, ring, ringly, er, STAY AROUND LONGER, LOITER, WAITING

lingo, oes, WAY TO SAY SOMETHING, UNIQUE METHOD OF COMMUNICATION

lingual, lly, OF THE TONGUE/ LANGUAGE "prefixes: bi/ intra/ multi/ sub"

linguist, *, tic, ONE WHO SPECIALIZED IN LANGUAGES

linguistic, *, tical, tically, STUDY OF LANGUAGES AND SPEECH
lingwestic, linguistic
lingwist, linguist
lingwistics, linguistic(s)
lingwul, lingual
liniansi, leniency

liniment, *, HEALING OINTMENTS
linin, IN CELL NUCLEUS (or see linen/ lining)
lining, *, LAYER INSIDE OF EXTERIOR LINING (or see linin/ linen)
liniul, lineal

link, *, ked, king, kage, ker, TWO THINGS JOINED TOGETHER "prefixes: inter/ up"
links, lynx / link(s)
linkth, length
linkuge, link(age)
linkwol, lingual

linoleum, FLOOR COVERING
linouliom, linoleum
lins, lens / line(s)

linseed, OIL
linsid, linseed

lint, *, ty, tless, FUZZ FROM MATERIAL (or see lent/ line(d))
linth, length
lintul, lentil
linument, liniment
linur, liner
linx, lynx
linz, lens / line(s)

lion, *, ness, A WILD ANIMAL (or see lien)
lior, liar
liotard, leotard

lip, *, pped, pping, ppy, pless, PREFIX INDICATING "FATTY" MOST OFTEN MODIFIES THE WORD, FLESHY FOLDS WORKING TOGETHER, A RIM, PART OF THE MOUTH "prefixes: under"

lipo, PREFIX INDICATING "FATTY" MOST OFTEN MODIFIES THE WORD
liprul, liberal
liqer, liquor / liqueur
liqoresh, licorice

liqueur, *, A SWEETENED/ FLAVORED ALCOHOLIC LIQUID (or see liquor)

liquid, *, date, dated, dating, dation, dize, dity, ify, uefy, FLUID

liquify, fiable, fier, fies, fied, ȳing, faction, factive, fier, uifiable,uifier,uifies,uifies,uified,uifying,uifaction, uifactive, uifier, TURN TO LIQUID/ FLUID, ALSO SPELLED 'LIQUEFY"
liquerish,licorice
liquifying, liquify(ing)
liquor,*, FERMENTED ALCOHOLIC LIQUID (or see liqueur)
lir, leer / liar
lirch,lurch
lire, leery / leer
lirec,lyric
liric, lyric
lirn,learn
lis, lie(s) / lease / list / lice
lisard,lizard
lisen,listen
lisense,license
liserd,lizard
lish,leash
lishan,legion / lesion
lisher,leisure
lishor,leisure
lisles,listless
lison,listen
lisp,*, pingly,PRONUNCIATION IS CHALLENGED BY SHAPE OF TEETH/ JAW MUSCLE FORMATION
list,*, ted, ting, IDENTIFY OBJECTS BY ITEMIZING, ORGANIZING TECHNIQUE "prefixes: en/ un"
listen,*, ned,ning, TO HEAR AND PAY ATTENTION
listless,ssly, ssness,NO ENERGY, LACKS INTEREST
lisun,listen
lisuns,license
lisurt,lizard
lit,PAST TENSE FOR THE WORD "LIGHT" (or see lite/ lid/ light/ lie(d)) "prefixes: un"
lite, SHORT SPELLING OF "LIGHT", LOW IN SOMETHING (or see lid/ lit/ light/ lie(d))
litegation,litigate(tion)
litel,little
litening, lightening
liter,*, METRIC MEASUREMENT (or see litter,' light(er)) "prefixes: deca"

literacy,ABILITY TO WRITE AND READ "prefixes: il"
literal,lly, lity, lize, list, listic, lism, QUITE SO, PERFECT INTERPRETATION "prefixes: uni"
literale, literal(lly)
literary,rily, riness,ate,OF WRITTEN TEXT, LEARNED, EDUCATED "prefixes: sub"
literate, *, ely, acy, ture,EDUCATED,SKILLFUL "prefixes: il/ pre/ semi/ sub"
literature, WRITINGS ABOUT EVERYTHING, TEXT "prefixes: sub"
lithal,lethal
lithargic, lethargic
lithargy, lethargy
lithol, lethal
litigate, *, ed, ting, tor, tion, gious, giousness, BRING DISPUTE INTO LAWFUL JUDGMENT,TAKE TO COURT
litigation,*, A LAWSUIT
litle, little
litly, light(ly)
litmas, litmus
litmos, litmus
litmus,AN ACID TEST
litneng, lightening
litness, lightness
litning, lightening
litor, light(er) / litter / liter / leader
litr, light(er) / litter / liter / leader
litter, *, red, ring, TRASH/ GARBAGE WHERE IT DOESN'T BELONG, GROUP OF INFANT ANIMALS IN A CERTAIN SPECIES (or see liter/ light(er))
little, SMALL SIZE IN COMPARISON
litul, little
litur, litter / liter / light(er) / leader
liturally,literal(ly)
liu,lieu
liubility, liable(bility)
liur, liar / lyre
liuri,leery
liv, live / life / alive
livad, livid
livapul, live(vable)

live, *, ed, ving, ely, vable, vability, PLACE WHERE YOU DWELL, NOT DEAD, ACTIVE/ VITAL "prefixes: en/ re/ un"
liveable, live(vable)
livebul, live(vable)
livelihood, *, OCCUPATION
livelyhood, livelihood
liver, *, AN ORGAN IN THE BODY
livery,ries, UNIFORM, CARE OF HORSES
livid,dly, dness, dtity, FURIOUS, BRUISED FLESH COLOR
livle, live(ly)
livlihood, livelihood
livly, live(ly)
livur, liver
livury, livery
lizard,*, A REPTILE
llac,jack
llacas, jackass
llacs, jacks
llaib, jibe
llaif, jive
llaiv, jive
llacet, jacket
llaket, jacket
llam, jam
llama, *, A WOOLY MAMMAL
llandis, jaundice
llanitor, janitor
llanitor, janitor
llaniueri, January
llant, jaunt
llanueri, January
llaquet, jacket
llar, jar
llargon, jargon
llat, yacht
llau, jaw
llauns, jounce
llaust, joust
llava, java
llaw, jaw
lleivac, jaywalk
llel, jail / gel / jell

lleli,jelly	llincs,jinx	lloviaI,jovial
llelos,jealous	llingol,jingle	llubilent,jubilant
llelp,yelp	llini,genie	llubili,jubilee
llelutin,gelatin	llinller,ginger	lluc,juice
llem,gem / gym	llinom,genome	llucsta,juxta
llener,genre	llio,geo	lludishal,judicial
lleneraishen,generation	lliografi,geography	lludishos,judicious
llenereit,generate	lliololli,geology	lludo,judo
lleneros,generous	lliometri,geometry	lluis,juice
llenetic,genetic	llir,year	llul,jewel / joule
llenial,genial	llirbol,gerbil	lluli,July
lleniuain,genuine	llist,yeast	llun,June
llenius,genius	llit,jilt	llundis,jaundice
llenom,genome	lliter,jitter	llunior,junior
llenre,genre	llius,juice	llunity,unity
llenral,general	llob,job	lluri,jury
llental,gentle	lloc,jack	llurisdicshon,jurisdiction
llentl,gentle	lloch,judge	llurnal,journal
llentli,gentle(lly)	llochment,judge(gment)	llurnalist,journalist
llenus,genius / genus	llog,jug / jog	llurni,journey
llepordi,jeopardy	llogol,juggle	llurnol,journal
llerbil,gerbil	lloi,joy	lluror,juror
llerc,jerk	lloin,join	llus,juice
llerki,jerky	lloist,joist	llut,jute
llerm,germ	lloki,jockey	lluvenayol,juvenile
llermineit,germinate	lloli,jolly	lluxta,juxta
llern,yearn	llolt,jolt	lo,low
lleschur,gesture	llombol,jumble	load, * , ded, ding,der, BURDEN, WEIGHT, HEAP/ PILE INTO A VESSEL, ADD AMMUNITION "prefixes: un/ up"
llest,jest	llomp,jump / hump	loaf, * , fed, fing, fer, aves, OF BREAD, SOMEONE WHO LIES AROUND DOING NOTHING, A SHOE, FOOD SHAPE
llestur,gesture	llonchon,junction	loafer, * , SOMEONE WHO IS LAZY, A SHOE
lleti,jetty	lloncshon,junction	loam,my, A RICH/ ORGANIC SOIL
lletstrim,jetstream	lloncshur,juncture	loan, * , ned, ning,lent, ALLOW SOMEONE TO BORROW SOMETHING (or see lone)
llib,jib	llongol,jungle	loathe, * , ed, hing, er, hsome, hsomely, hsomeness, DESPISES, STRONGLY DISLIKES
lliber,jibber	llonki,junkie	lob, * , bbed, bbing, bber, A HIGH, ROUNDED ARCH BY A BALL IN A SPORT (or see lobe/ lop)
llider,jitter	llont,jaunt	lobby, bbies, bbied, ying, yist, yism, WAITING/ RESTING ROOM, TO COERCE POLITICAL LAWMAKERS FOR VOTES
llifi,jiffy	llost,just	
llig,jig	llostifai,justify	
lliger,jigger	llostifayabol,justifiable	
lligol,jiggle	llostis,justice	
lligsa,jigsaw	llot,jut	
llimi,jimmy	llouc,joke	
llimy,jimmy	lloul,jowl	
llin,gene / jean / gin	llouvial,jovial	lobd,lob(bbed)

lobe,,ed,bule,BULBOUS PART OF THE EAR/ A PLANT, ROUND SHAPE (or see lobby)
lobster,,,AN EDIBLE CRUSTACEAN
loby,lobby
loc,lock
locader,locate(tor)
local,,,lly,le,lism,lity,lities,lize,IN THE AREA, WITHIN DESIGNATED REGION
localety,local(ity)
localize,ed,zation,TO BE LOCATED IN A SPECIFIC REGION, IN THE AREA
locashen,locate(tion)
locate,,ed,ting,tion,tive,tor,TO IDENTIFY A SPECIFIC PLACE "prefixes: dis/ re"
locemoshen,locomotive
locer,locker
locest,locust
loch,lodge / lock
lock,,ked,king,kage,kable,kless,ker,MECHANISM WHICH REQUIRES A KEY, SECURE, BE INEXCUSABLY INVOLVED, EXCLUDED 'prefixes: inter/ un"
locker,,,A CONTAINER WITH A LOCK
locksmith,,,ONE WHO WORKS WITH LOCKS
loco,,CRAZY
locomotion,,THE ACT OF MOVING, LOCATING FROM ONE PLACE TO ANOTHER
locomotive,,,THE BODILY OR PHYSICAL ACT OF MOVEMENT FROM ONE PLACE TO ANOTHER
locsmith,locksmith
locul,local
loculizashen,localize(zation)
loculize,localize
loculy,local(ly)
locumoshen,locomotion
locumotive,locomotive
locur,locker
locust,,,A BUG ("T" IS SILENT)
lod,load
lodery,lottery
lodge,,ed,ging,gment,SOMETHING JAMMED INTO A TIGHT SPACE, HABITATION FOR VISITORS WHO OCCASIONALLY COME FOR THE NIGHT, BRING FORTH ACTION ("D" IS SILENT) "prefixes: dis"

lodis,lotus
lodury,lottery
lodus,lotus
loeder,loiter
loen,loin
loer,lower / lawyer
loest,low(est)
loeul,loyal
lof,loaf
lofa,lava
lofer,loafer
lofly,lovely
loft,,,ted,ting,ty,tily,SMALL LANDING ABOVE THE MAIN FLOOR, PROPEL SOMETHING INTO THE AIR
lofur,loafer
log,,,gged,gging,gger,MAKE A WRITTEN NOTE OF, REMOVED SECTION OF LIMB/ TREE, TO REMOVE TIMBER, MEASURE VELOCITY (or see lodge)
logarithm,,,mic,mically,A MATH FUNCTION "prefixes: semi"
loge,lodge
logec,logic
logecul,logic(al)
loger,logger
logestics,logistic(s)
logger,,,SOMEONE WHO CUTS TREES (or see lager)
logic,,,cal,cally,cality,calness,TO MAKE SENSE OF, BE REASONABLE "prefixes: il"
logicul,logic(al)
logir,logger
logistic,,,cal,cally,cian,ARRANGING ACTIONS TO BENEFIT AN ADDITIONAL ACTION, CALCULATING
logo,,,A THEME OR SYMBOL WHICH IDENTIFIES
logrethm,logarithm
logrythm,logarithm
logur,logger
loider,loiter
loier,lawyer / layer
loin,,,SECTION OF A BODY
loir,lower
loiter,,,red,ring,TO STAND AROUND, HANGING OUT
lojecul,logic(al)
lojek,logic

lojic,logic
lojical,logic(al)
lojik,logic
lojistic,logistic
lok,look / lock
lokality,local(ity)
lokashen,locate(tion)
lokate,locate
lokator,locate(tor)
lokel,local
lokelizashen,localize(zation)
lokelize,localize
lokely,local(ly)
lokemotive,locomotive
loker,locker / look(er) / logger
lokes,locust / look(s) / lock(s)
lokimoshen,locomotive
lokimotev,locomotive
lokir, locker / look(er) / logger
lokist,locust
loko,loco
loksmeth,locksmith
lokt,lock(ed) / look(ed)
lokul,local
lokule,local(ly)
lokulization,localize(zation)
lokulize,localize
lokumoshen,locomotion
lokumotef,locomotive
lokumotive,locomotive
lokur,locker / look(er) / logger
lokus,locust
lolegag,lollygag
lolepop,lollipop
loligag,lollygag
lollic,logic
lollipop,,,CANDY
lollistic,logistic
lollygag,,gged,gging,TO LOITER/ HANG AROUND DOING NOTHING
loly,low(ly)
lolypop,lollipop
lom,loam / loom

loma,llama
lomanesense,luminescence
lombur,lumber / lumbar
lome,loam
lomp,lump
lomunesense,luminescence
lomy,loam
lon,lone / loan / lawn
lon mower,lawn mower
lonch,launch / lunch
londer,launder
londry,laundry
londurer,launder(er)
lone,er,ely,eliness,esome,esomely,esomeness,BY ITSELF,SINGLED OUT,JUST ONE (or see loan)
long,ger,gest,THE LENGTH/ DURATION OF SOMETHING, MEASURE OF TIME
longatude,longitude
longetudenul,longitude(dinal)
longir,long(er)
longist,long(est)
longitude,*,dinal,dinally,INVISIBLE LINE ON EARTH THAT RUNS EAST, WEST
lonir,lone(r)
lonjatude,longitude
lonjetudenul,longitude(dinal)
lonjitude,longitude
lonk,long
lonker,long(er)
lonkist,long(est)
lonllitud,longitude
lonly,lone(ly)
lonmouer,lawn mower
lons,lawn(s) / loan(s)
lonsem,lone(some)
lonsum,lone(some)
lonter,launder
lontre,laundry
lonur,lone(r)
loob,lube
loobrucate,lubricate
lood,lewd / load
loodekres,ludicrous

look,*,ked,king,ker,TO VIEW WITH THE EYES
lookwarm,lukewarm
looloo,lulu
loom,*,med,ming,INTO THE FUTURE,LATER IN TIME,A MACHINE FOR WEAVING YARN/ THREAD (or see loam)
loomanocity,luminosity
loomenesent,luminescence(nt)
loomenocity,luminosity
loominesinse,luminescence
loominocity,luminosity
loominus,luminous
loomy,loam
loon,*,ny,A BIRD, BEHAVING GOOFY (or see lune)
looner,lunar
loop,*,ped,ping,py,A SEMI-CIRCULAR SHAPE,WRAP/ GO AROUND, BEHAVING ODDLY
loopen,lupine
loose,*,sing,en,ens,ened,ening,MISPLACE/ FORGET SOMETHING, RELAX HOLD ON, UN-TIGHTEN, SLOPPY, GET RID OF (or see lose) " prefixes: un"
loosid,lucid
loot,*,ted,ting,ter,MONEY/ GOODS,ONE WHO STEALS THINGS (or see lute/ lewd)
looze,loose / lose
lop,*,pped,pping,ACT OF REMOVING, ROUGHLY (or see lobe/ lope)
lope,*,er,ed,ping,EASY STRIDES WITH BOUNCE (or see lop)
lor,lore / low(er)
lorch,large
lord,*,ded,ding,MASTER,ONE WHO TAKES OWNERSHIP
lore,*,BELIEF IN THE FORM OF A STORY OF THE PAST
loreate,laureate
lorg,large
loriette,laureate
lorj,large
lort,lord
lorul,laurel
losd,lost
lose,*,er,sing,st,PAST TENSE FOR THE WORD "LOST", HAVING LOST (or see loose)
losenge,lozenge

losh,lush
loshen,lotion
loshin,lotion
losinge,lozenge
losinje,lozenge
losir,lose(r) / loose(r)
loss,ses,TAKEN AWAY, REMOVED
lost,PAST TENSE FOR THE WORD "LOOSE", CANNOT BE FOUND (or see lust)
loster,luster
losuit,lawsuit
losur,lose(r) / loose(r)
losute,lawsuit
lot,*,tted,tting,WHOLE BUNCH,A SPECIFIC SIZE OF SOMETHING,A SECTION AMONG MANY
lotery,lottery
lotes,lotus
lothe,loathe
lotion,*,CREAMY LIQUID TO APPLY TO THE BODY
lotis,lotus
lottery,ries,GAMBLING
lotury,lottery
lotus,A FLOWER,A POSITION,A PLANT
loub,lobe
loucal,local
loucalais,localize
loucol,local
loucomodif,locomotive
loucomoushon,locomotion
loucus,locust
loud,dly,dness,der,dest,SOUND THAT IS BEYOND A COMFORTABLE HEARING RANGE
loudus,lotus
louf,loaf
loufer,loafer
lougou,logo
loul,loyal
loum,loam
loun,loan / lone
lounch,lounge
lounge,*,ed,ging,er,TO LIE AROUND, RECLINED POSITION,ROOM WHERE PEOPLE REST/ RELAX
louqueit,locate

lour,lower
loushon,lotion
louth,loathe
loutus,lotus
louver, *, SHUTTERS
lova,lava
love, *, ed,ving,vable,vableness,vably,vability,er, eless,ely, A SPECIAL/DEEP AFFECTION FOR (or see lovely) "prefixes: un"
lovely,lier,liest,liness,PERFECTLY ATTRACTIVE "prefixes: un"
lovlie,lovely
lovte,loft
lovu,lava
low, wer,west,wly,CLOSE TO THE BOTTOM/ GROUND, LACK OF ENERGY
lowd,loud
lowder,loud(er)
lowdest,loud(est)
lowen,loin
lower, *, red,ring,ACT OF LETTING DOWN, CLOSE TO THE BOTTOM OR GROUND,LESSEN
lownch,lounge
lownge,lounge
lows,low(s) / loathe(s)
lowt,loud / load
lowtest,loud(est)
lowyer,lawyer
lowyul,loyal
loyal,list,lly,lty,lties,FAITHFUL "prefixes: dis"
loyer,lawyer / layer
loyn,join
loyulty,loyal(ty)
loyure,lawyer
lozenge, *, THROAT MEDICINE
lu,lieu
lub,lube
lube, *, ed,bing,bricate,GREASE
lubracashen,lubricate(tion)
lubracate,lubricate
lubrakeit,lubricate
lubraqeit,lubricate
lubricate, *, ed,ting,tion,ant,TO GREASE/ OIL UP

lubrikeit,lubricate
lubriqeit,lubricate
luc, look / luck / lug
lucen, loose(n)
luceng, look(ing) / lug(gging)
lucgireate,luxury(riate)
lucgiry,luxury
lucheus,luscious
luchious,luscious
luchness,lush(ness)
lucid,dity, dness,dly,A STATE OF BEING BETWEEN HERE AND THERE
lucin, loose(n)
lucing, look(ing) / lug(gging)
lucjireate,luxury(riate)
lucjiry,luxury
luck,ky,kily, kier, kiest, kless, GOOD FORTUNE (or see lug) "prefixes: un"
lucke,luck
luckgerious,luxurious
luckjiry,luxury
lucrative,ely,eness,COULD YIELD PROFIT OR GAIN
lucwarm,lukewarm
ludakris,ludicrous
lude,lewd / lute / loot
ludecris,ludicrous
luder,loot(er)
ludicrous,sly, sness, RIDICULOUS
luf,love
lufable,love(vable)
lufer,louver / love(r)
lufless,love(less)
lufly,lovely
lug, *, gged,gging,CARRY AROUND A HEAVY LOAD,ON A WHEEL,PULL (or see luck/ look)
lugach,luggage
lugd,lug(gged)
lugege,luggage
luggage, TRAVELING BAGS
lugich,luggage
lugije,luggage
lugjureus,luxurious
lugshureant,luxuriant

lugshureous,luxurious
lugshury,luxury
lugt,lug(gged)
luk,look / luck / lug
lukchury,luxury
luke,luck / luck / look
lukege,luggage
lukemea,leukemia
lukewarm,BETWEEN WARM AND HOT
lukgery,luxury
lukgureus,luxurious
lukiest,luck(iest)
lukige,luggage
lukjereus,luxurious
lukrative,lucrative
luks,look(s) / luck(s)
lukshereant,luxuriant
lukshury,luxury
luksuryant,luxuriant
lukwarm,lukewarm
luky,luck
lull, *, led,ling,A PAUSE,GENTLY COAX,CAUSE TO RELAX
lulu, *, REAL WINNER
lum,loom
lumanesense,luminescence
lumbar, *, AREA IN LOWER BACK (or see lumber)
lumber, rer,rman,ring,BOARDS CUT FROM TIMBER (or see lumbar)
lumbir,lumber / lumbar
lumbur,lumber / lumbar
lume,loom
lumen, *, mina,minal,minous,OF LIGHT, GIVING OFF LIGHT, UNIT OF MEASURE "prefixes: il"
lumenary,luminary
lumenesense,luminescence
lumenesent,luminescence(nt)
lumenosidty,luminosity
lument,lament
lumentation,lament(ation)
lumenus,luminous
lumenusly,luminous(ly)
luminary,ria,ries,GIVING OFF LIGHT
luminescence,nt,GIVING OFF LIGHT "prefixes: bio"

luminosity, ties, INTENSITY OF LIGHT
luminous, sly, sness, AMOUNT OF LIGHT, OF LIGHT
luminus, lumen(ous)
lump, *, ped, ping, py, MASS OR AGGREGATE OF SOMETHING
lumunesense, luminescence
lun, loon / lune
lunar, ate, rian, OF THE MOON "prefixes: inter/ semi/ sub"
lunch, hes, hed, hing, heon, AFTERNOON MEAL (or see lunge)
lune, nula, MOON WHEN IT'S NOT FULL (or see loon)
luney, loon / lune
lung, *, ORGAN OF THE BODY (or see lunge)
lunge, *, ed, ging, LEAP FORWARD TOWARDS SOMETHING, PULL QUICKLY/ HARD AGAINST RESTRAINTS
lunir, lunar
lunje, lunge
lunur, lunar
up, loop
lupe, loop / loop
lupel, lapel
lupen, lupine
lupine, *, A WOLF, A PLANT
luqimia, leukemia
lurch, hes, hed, hing, her, HANG ABOUT SUSPICIOUSLY, DRUNKEN STAGGER, LEAP INTO ACTION
lurk, *, ked, king, ker, STALK, SECRETLY WAIT TO AMBUSH
lus, loose / lose
luscious, sly, sness, GLORIOUS SENSORY EXPERIENCE OF SOMETHING USING TASTE/ SMELL/ SIGHT / TOUCH
lusd, lust
lusder, luster
lusdruss, lust(rous)
luse, loose / lose
used, lucid
lusen, loose(n)
lush, hly, hness, ABUNDANT, OPULENT FLORAL AND FAUNA, RICH IN FOLIAGE, AN ALCOHOLIC
lusheous, luscious
lushus, luscious
lusid, lucid

lusin, loose(n)
lusonya, lasagna
lust, *, ted, ting, tful, tfully, tfulness, trous, TEMPORARY INTENSE DESIRE
luster, *, red, ring, rless, GLISTENING, WAY LIGHT REFLECTS, AS IF GLOWING, SHINY REFLECTION
lustious, luscious
lusty, tily, tiness, HEARTY AND JOVIAL, ROBUST
lut, lute / loot / lewd
lute, *, A MUSICAL INSTRUMENT (or see loot/ lewd)
lutenant, lieutenant
luter, loot(er)
lutinant, lieutenant
lutrene, latrine
luv, love
luvabul, love(vable)
luver, louver / love(r)
luvle, lovely
luvless, love(less)
luxuriant, nce, ncy, tly, VERY HEALTHY, RICHLY ABUNDANT, PROFUSE
luxurious, sly, sness, EXPENSIVE COMFORT
luxury, ries, riate, riated, riating, rious, GREAT RICHNESS, OPULENT, OVERLY ABUNDANT
luz, loose / lose
luzonya, lasagna
ly, lye / lie
lye, WOOD ASH FOR SOAP (or see lie)
lying, NOT TELLING THE TRUTH, PAST TENSE FOR THE WORD "LIE" (or see lay(ing))
lymfatic, lymph(atic)
lymph, hatic, FLUID WITH WHITE BLOOD CELLS, OF THE BODY, PREFIX INDICATING "LYMPH/ YELLOWISH" MOST OFTEN MODIFIES THE WORD
lympho, PREFIX INDICATING "LYMPH/ YELLOWISH" MOST OFTEN MODIFIES THE WORD
lynx, xes, A WILD ANIMAL
lyo, PREFIX INDICATING "DISSOLVED/ DISPERSED" MOST OFTEN MODIFIES THE WORD
lyre, *, AN INSTRUMENT (or see liar)
lyric, *, cal, cally, cism, cist, WORDS SANG IN A SONG
lys, PREFIX INDICATING "DISSOLVED/ DISPERSED" MOST OFTEN MODIFIES THE WORD

lyso, PREFIX INDICATING "DISSOLVED/ DISPERSED" MOST OFTEN MODIFIES THE WORD
m, am
ma, may
mab, mob
mabe, maybe
mabilety, mobile(lity)
mac, mach / make / mock / mace
macaroni, ies, CHEESY NOODLES
macaroon, *, A COOKIE
macasen, moccasin
macasin, moccasin
macaw, *, A TROPICAL BIRD
mace, ed, SPICE, MEDIEVAL WEAPON, CHEMICAL SPRAY (or see make/ maize/ maze/ mach)
mach, AMOUNT OF SPEED (or see make/ match/ mock/ mash)
machenery, machine(ry)
macheng, match(ing) / mash(ing)
macherel, mackerel
macherly, mature(ly)
maches, match(es) / mash(es)
machestral, magistral
machestrate, magistrate
machete, *, A CHOPPING HAND TOOL
machine, *, nability, nable, nate, nation, nator, ery, eries, nist, DEVICE WITH MOVING PARTS THAT PERFORMS WORK
machis, match(es) / mash(es)
machistral, magistral
machistrate, magistrate
machurashen, mature(ration)
machure, mature
machuredy, mature(rity)
machuril, mackerel
machus, match(es) / mash(es)
mack, make / mach / mock
mackerel, *, EDIBLE FISH
macks, max / make(s)
macrame, LACED/ WOVEN ROPE
macreima, macrame
macro, PREFIX INDICATING "DISSOLVED/ DISPERSED" MOST OFTEN MODIFIES THE WORD

macrocosm, *, mic, mically, THE BIG PICTURE, INCORPORATES EVERYTHING BIG AND SMALL
macruma, macrame
macs, max / make(s)
macsemaiz, maximize
macsimais, maximize
macsimal, maximal
macsimul, maximal
macsimum, maximum
macuroni, macaroni
macuroon, macaroon
macusen, moccasin
mad, dder, ddest, dden, ddening, ddeningly, dness, NOT HAPPY, MORE THAN IRRITATED, ANGRY (or see made/ maid/ matte/ mat/ mate)
madch, match
made, PAST TENSE FOR THE WORD "MAKE" , HAVING CREATED (or see maid/ mate) "prefixes: re/ un"
madekulus, meticulous
madel, modal / model / mcttle
madena, matinee
mader, matter / mad(dder)
maderde, maitre d'
madereulise, materialize
madernize, modern(ize)
madernulistic, maternal(istic)
madesenul, medicine(nal)
madina, matinee
madir, mad(dder) / matter
madirde, maitre d'
madisenul, medicine(nal)
madist, mad(ddest)
madna, matinee
madnes, mad(dness)
mado, motto
madou, motto
madramony, matrimony
madreark, matriarch
madrearkul, matriarch(al)
madremony, matrimony
madren, matron
madress, mattress
madrexs, matrix
madricks, matrix
madrimony, matrimony
madris, mattress
madron, matron
madur, matter / mad(der)
madurde, maitre d'
mae, may
maer, mayor
maestro, *, MASTER OF ANY MEDIUM RELATED TO ART
mafe, mauve
maferick, maverick
mafrek, maverick
magacul, magic(al)
magazine, *, COMPILED PAGES OF WRITTEN ARTICLES, HAVING TO DO WITH WEAPONS
mager, major
magesine, magazine
magestral, magistral
magestrate, magistrate
magesty, majesty
maggot, *, LARVA OF AN INSECT
magic, cal, cally, cian, DIDN'T VISIBLY WITNESS THE CHANGE OF EVENTS WHICH LED TO AN EVENT
magir, major
magirete, major(ette)
magistral, lly, lity, ature, terial, terially, terialness, terium, ate, LOCAL OFFICIAL OFFICE
magistrate, *, acy, acies, ture, al, LOCAL OFFICIAL OFFICE
magisty, majesty
magit, maggot
magizene, magazine
magma, *, ata, atic, MOLTEN ROCK
magnate, *, PROMINENT INDUSTRIALIST (or see magnet))
magnatise, magnetize
magnatisum, magnet(ism)
magnatude, magnitude
magnedic, magnet(ic)
magnefecashen, magnify(fication)
magnefasent, magnificent
magnefesently, magnificent(ly)
magnefiable, magnify(iable)
magnefy, magnify

magnet, *, tic, tically, tism, tize, DRAWN TO, ORE FROM THE EARTH, TOWARD THE NORTH/ SOUTH ENDS, PREFIX INDICATING "MAGNET" MOST OFTEN MODIFIES THE WORD (or see magnate) "prefixes: bio"
magnetaize, magnetize
magnetize, *, ed, zing, zable, zation, zer, BE DRAWN TO, MAKE POLAR
magneto, PREFIX INDICATING "MAGNET" MOST OFTEN MODIFIES THE WORD
magnetude, magnitude
magnefesent, magnificent
magnificent, tly, nce, SPLENDID
magnify, fies, fied, ying, fiable, fier, fication, TO ENLARGE, GET CLOSER TO, MAKE BIGGER "prefixes: bio"
magnit, magnet / magnate
magnitise, magnetize
magnitude, *, dinous, THE SIZE OR EXTENT OF, THE DEGREE OF
magnufecashen, magnify(fication)
magnufy, magnify
magnutise, magnetize
magnutisum, magnet(ism)
magnutude, magnitude
magoredy, major(ity)
magorete, major(ette)
magority, major(ity)
magot, maggot
maguk, magic
magul, module
maguler, module(lar)
magur, major
magurete, major(ette)
magustrate, magistrate
maguzene, magazine
mahanaiz, mechanize
mahinaiz, mechanize
mai, may / my
maicron, micron
maicroub, microbe
maicroufoun, microphone
maicroumiter, micrometer
maicrow, micro

maicroweive, microwave
maicrowmiter, micrometer
maicrowscoup, microscope
maid,*,den, ONE WHO CLEANS BEHIND OTHERS FOR A LIVING (or see made/ mate)
maigrein, migraine
maigrent, migrant
mail,*,led,ling,ler, SEND A PHYSICAL THING AWAY TO SOMEONE (or see male/ mile)
maild, mild
maillor, major
maim,*,med,ming, TO MUTILATE/ DESTROY (or see mime)
main,*,nly, THE MOST IMPORTANT ONE, THE ONE THAT STANDS OUT (or see mane/ mine)
maind, mind
maineis, mayonnaise
maingy, mangy
mainor, minor
mainos, minus
maintain,*,,ned,ning,nable,tenance, UPKEEP, KEEP IN GOOD REPAIR
maintenance, TO KEEP IN WORKING ORDER, TO FIX, SUPPORT, UPKEEP
maiol, mile
maiold, mild
maiosis, meiosis
maiser, miser
maisuliom, mausoleum
mait, might / mite
maitoucondria, mitochondria
maitre d',*, HEADWAITER/ HOTEL MANAGER
maize,*, CORN (or see maze)
maizer, miser
maizoliam, mausoleum
maj, image
majek, magic
majen, imagine
majer, major
majestrat, magistral
majestrate, magistrate
majesty, tic, tically, OF AUTHORITY/ GRANDEUR, GREAT IMPRESSION

majewlate, modulate
majic, magic
majir, major
majistral, magistral
majistrate, magistrate
majistreit, magistrate
major,*,,red,ring,rity,rities,rette, GREATEST NUMBER OF, A MILITARY RANK, FEMALE MARCHER, HIGHEST NUMBER OF
majoredy, major(ity)
majul, module
majulate, modulate
majur, major
majustrate, magistrate
mak, mach / make / mock
makanek, mechanic
makanekul, mechanic(al)
makanize, mechanize
makaril, mackerel
makarony, macaroni
makaroon, macaroon
makaw, macaw
make,*,,ade,king,er, TO CREATE, BRING TO REALITY (or see mach/ mock) "prefixes: re/ un"
maked, made / mock(ed)
makerony, macaroni
makinate, machine(nate)
makir, make(r)
makirony, macaroni
makreima, macrame
makremay, macrame
makrocosim, macrocosm
makrumay, macrame
maks, max / make(s) / mock(s)
maksamis, maximize
maksemal, maximal
maksemize, maximize
maksimul, maximal
maksimum, maximum
maksumum, maximum
makuril, mackerel
makurone, macaroni
makusen, moccasin

makzemize, maximize
mal, PREFIX INDICATING "BAD" MOST OFTEN MODIFIES THE WORD (or see mall/ maul/ male/ mail/ mole)
malable, malleable
malachusted, maladjusted
maladek, melody(dic)
maladjusted, tment, NOT SITUATED AS SHOULD BE, IMPROPER ORIENTATION
malado, mulato
malady, dies, A DISORDER OR CONFLICT BETWEEN THE BODY AND MIND, ABNORMAL ARRANGEMENT
malajusted, maladjusted
malanosis, melanosis
malaria, DISEASE TRANSPORTED TO HUMANS BY SOME MOSQUITOES
malarkey, DOESN'T APPEAR TO BE THE TRUTH, CALLING A BLUFF
malas, malice
malases, molasses
mald, maul(ed) / mail(ed) / malt
male,*,eness, THE MASCULINE GENDER, THE INSERTION END (or see mail)
maleable, malleable
maleble, malleable
maledy, malady
malegnent, malignant
malegusted, maladjusted
malegustment, maladjusted(tment)
malejusted, maladjusted
malekule, molecule
malekuler, molecule(lar)
maleneum, millennium
malenoma, melanoma
malenosis, melanosis
malerd, mallard
malese, malice
malesha, militia
maleshes, malicious
malest, molest
malet, mallet
maleuble, malleable
malevolent, tly, nce, MALICIOUS, HATEFUL

malfunction, *, ned, ning, DOESN'T WORK AS IT WAS INTENDED
malfunkshen, malfunction
maliabol, malleable
malible, malleable
malice, cious, DIRECT HATE TOWARDS ANOTHER, EMOTION OF FEAR/ INSECURITY
malicious, ciously, ciousness, DIRECT HATE TOWARDS ANOTHER, EMOTION OF FEAR/ INSECURITY
malignant, tly, ncy, ACT OF BEING MALICIOUS, DANGEROUS GROWTH "prefixes: pre"
maligusted, maladjusted
malineum, millennium
malinoma, melanoma
malisha, militia
malishes, malicious
malit, mallet
malitia, militia
mality, malady
maliuble, malleable
mall, *, LARGE BUILDING WITH SMALL STORES INSIDE (or see mail/ male/ maul/ mole)
mallard, *, WILD DUCK
malleable, billity, eness, SEEMINGLY STIFF MATERIAL/ METAL THAT'S EASILY WORKED/ MOLDED
mallesti, majesty
mallet, *, HAMMER TYPE TOOL
mallic, magic
mallistreit, magistrate
malluble, malleable
malnerished, malnourished
malnewtrishen, malnutrition
malniutrishon, malnutrition
malnourished, NOT ENOUGH NUTRITIONAL FOOD
malnureshed, malnourished
malnutrition, SUFFERING LACK OF NUTRITIOUS FOOD
malodic, melody(dic)
malos, malice
malpractice, *, cioner, DR. WHO PRODUCED A FATAL/ SERIOUS INJURY WHILE PRACTICING MEDICINE
malpraktes, malpractice
malt, *, ted, ty, A FROTHY COLD DRINK (or see maul(ed)/ molt)

maluble, malleable
maludy, malady
malugusted, maladjusted
malujustment, maladjusted(tment)
malunosis, melanosis
malurd, mallard
malus, malice
malut, mallet
mam, maim
mama, A MOTHER (or see mamma)
mamal, mammal
mamalean, mammal(ian)
mamel, mammal
mamento, memento
mamery gland, mammary gland
mameth, mammoth
mamil, mammal
maminto, memento
mamiry gland, mammary gland
mamith, mammoth
mamma, MILK SECRETING BREASTS/ TEATS/ ORGAN
mammal, *, lian, WARM BLOODED ANIMAL THAT GIVES BIRTH TO ITS YOUNG
mammary gland, *, GLANDS IN THE BREAST THAT SECRETES MILK
mammoth, ICE AGE ELEPHANT
mamory gland, mammary gland
mamoth, mammoth
mamt, maim(ed)
mamul, mammal
mamury gland, mammary gland
man, ADULT MALE (or see mane/ main) "prefixes: un"
manacle, *, WRIST RESTRAINTS
manage, *, ed, ging, ement, eable, eably, eableness, er, erial, ABILITY TO DEAL WITH AND ORCHESTRATE AFFAIRS SMOOTHLY "prefixes: mis/ un"
manakin, *, BIRD (or see mannikin/ manikin/ mannequin)
manakiuler, monocular
manakure, manicure
manalage, monologue
manarc, monarch
manark, monarch
manarkeul, monarch(ial)

manarky, monarch
manase, mayonnaise
manchen, mansion
manchi, mangy
mandala, *, A SYMBOL OF SPIRITUAL SIGNIFICANCE
mandalin, mandolin
mandarin, *, FRUIT
mandate, *, ed, ting, tory, A COMMAND, RULE
mandatory, ries, rily, COMMANDE, ORDERED
mandeit, mandate
mandel, mantel / mantle
mandelin, mandolin
manderin, mandarin
mandetory, mandatory
manditory, mandatory
mandle, mantel / mantle
mandola, mandala
mandolin, *, A STRINGED INSTRUMENT
mandrake, AN HERB
mandrel, *, A DEVICE TO AID IN CUTTING A SOLID MATERIAL
mandril, mandrel
mandrul, mandrel
mandul, mantel / mantle
manduren, mandarin
mandutory, mandatory
mane, HAIR ABOUT THE NECK OF AN ANIMAL (or see main/ many)
manea, mania
maneac, maniac
manecure, manicure
manee, many
manefest, manifest
manefesto, manifest(o)
manefold, manifold
manege, manage
manegment, manage(ment)
maneje, manage
manekin, manikin / manakin / mannequin
manekul, manacle
manense, maintenance
maner, manner / manor / manure
manerism, manner(ism)

manerlee, manner(ly)
maneuver, *, red, ring, rable, rability, rer, SKILLFUL DISPLAY OF MOVEMENT
manevest, manifest
mang, mange
mange, A SKIN CONDITION
manger, TROUGH FOR ANIMALS
mangle, *, ed, ling, er, TO SHRED/ TEAR UP, A LARGE IRON
mango, *, A FRUIT
mangul, mangle
mangy, gily, giness, SHABBY, ILL-KEPT
mania, INTENSE EMOTION
maniac, *, cal, cally, SOMEONE UNCONTROLLABLE ON A CONTINUOUS BASIS
manicle, manacle
manicure, *, ed, ring, rist, CARING OF FINGERNAILS
manifest, *, ted, ting, ter, tly, tation, tant, ter, to, DESIRED RESULT ACHIEVED WITH LITTLE EFFORT
manifold, *, ded, ding, der, dly, dness, ON A MOTOR, A COPY, TO MULTIPLY
manige, manage
manigment, manage(ment)
manikin, A MOLD OF A BODY FOR CLOTHING DISPLAY (or see manakin/ mannequin)
manikiur, manicure
manila, BUFF-COLORED HEMP PAPER
manipuleit, manipulate
manipulate, *, ed, ting, tion, able, ability, table, tor, tory, tive, tively, tiveness, CONTROL ENVIRONMENT/ EVENTS
manir, manner / manor / manure
manirism, manner(ism)
manirlee, manner(ly)
maniual, manual
maniufacshur, manufacture
maniuscript, manuscript
manj, mange
manjur, manger
manle, main(ly) / man(ly)
mannequin, *, LITTLE/ DWARFED HUMAN, MODEL OF PART OF THE BODY OR ENTIRE TORSO, SOMEONE WHO MODELS CLOTHING, ALSO SPELLED 'MANNIKIN' OR MANIKIN' (or see manakin/ manikin)

manner, *, red, rless, rism, rist, ristic, rly, HANDLE ONESELF PROPERLY, TO BE POLITE (or see manor) "prefixes: un"
manofestation, manifest(ation)
manogumy, monogamy
manolith, monolith
manopuly, monopoly
manor, *, HOME OF MEDIEVAL TIMES (or see manure/ manner)
manotny, monotony
manotone, monotone
manotunus, monotony(nous)
manoutoun, monotone
manowreil, monorail
manshen, mansion
mansion, *, A VERY LARGE HOME
mantane, maintain
mantanuble, maintain(able)
mantel, *, FIREPLACE SHELF (or see mantle)
mantenanse, maintenance
mantil, mantel / mantle
mantle, *, A CLOAK, A CLOTH SLEEVE FOR A GAS LANTERN (or see mantel)
mantul, mantel / mantle
mantunense, maintenance
manual, *, lly, DIRECTIONS ON HOW TO USE SOMETHING, TO DO BY HAND
manucle, manacle
manuel, manual
manuely, manual(ly)
manufacture, *, ed, ring, rer, rable, ral, CREATE SOMETHING FROM RAW MATERIALS
manufaksher, manufacture
manufestation, manifest(ation)
manufold, manifold
manuge, manage
manugment, manage(ment)
manuil, manual
manukin, manakin
manul, mantel / mantle
manur, manner / manor / manure
manure, rial, er, WASTE FROM ANIMALS (or see manor/ manner)

manurism, manner(ism)
manurly, manner(ly)
manuscript, *, STORY SOMEONE WRITES THAT MAY BECOME A BOOK/ MOVIE
manuskrept, manuscript
manustery, monastery
manuver, maneuver
many, MORE THAN A FEW (or see mini)
manyewfaksher, manufacture
manyual, manual
manyuskrept, manuscript
maonase, mayonnaise
maoneis, mayonnaise
maor, mayor
map, *, pped, pping, DIRECTIONS/ GUIDE TO A SPECIFIC AREA (or see mop)
mapal, maple
mapd, map(pped) / mop(pped)
mape, maybe
mapel, maple
maple, *, A TREE, SYRUP FROM TREE
mapul, maple
mar, *, rred, rring, TO RUIN/ DETRACT FROM (or see mare/ mayor)
maraje, mirage
marakulus, miracle(culous)
maranade, marinade / marinate
maranate, marinade / marinate
marange, meringue
marathon, *, ner, A LONG DISTANCE EVENT
marbel, marble
marble, *, ed, ling, ly, er, A LITTLE GLASS BALL, TYPE OF ROCK, A VISUAL EFFECT
marbul, marble
marc, mark
marcetable, market(able)
march, hes, hed, hing, her, BRISK FORM OF WALKING, MONTH OF THE YEAR
marchel, martial / marshal
marchel law, martial law
marchen, martian / march(ing) / margin(s)
marchenulize, marginalize
marchin, margin

marchoram, marjoram
marchul, martial / marshal
marchul law, martial law
marden, martin
mardene, martini
mardengale, martingale
marder, martyr
mardin, martin
mardine, martini
mardingale, martingale
mardir, martyr
mardur, martyr
mare, *, FEMALE HORSE (or see marry/ mayor)
mared, married / mar(rred)
maredean, meridian
mareg, marriage
maregold, marigold
marej, marriage
marejuana, marijuana
marena, marina
marenad, marinade / marinate
marene, marine
mareonette, marionette
maret, merit
maretime, maritime
maretul, marital
mareunette, marionette
marewana, marijuana
marfilus, marvelous
margarine, A FAKE BUTTER
margen, margin
margenul, margin(al)
margenulize, marginalize
margerem, marjoram
margin, *, nal, nally, nality, nalize, nate, nates, rated, nating, nation, SPACE OUTSIDE OF THE TEXT/ BORDER AREA "prefixes: sub"
marginalize, *, ed, zing, zation, nate, BLOCK SOMEONE FROM SOMETHING THEY NEED/ WANT
margorem, marjoram
margurim, marjoram
mari, marry
marich, marriage

marid, married
meridian, meridian
marig, marriage
marigold, *, A FLOWER
marij, marriage
marijuana, ALSO MARIHUANA, MEDICINAL PLANT (or see hemp)
marill, marriage
marily, merry(rily)
marina, *, FOR BOAT MOORING
marinade, *, ate, SAUCE WITH SPICES THAT FISH/ MEAT IS SOAKED IN (or see marinate)
marinate, *, ted, ting, tion, ade, THE ACT OF SOAKING FISH/ MEAT IN A SAUCE (or see marinade)
marine, *, er, CONCERNED WITH THE OCEAN/ SEA
marineid, marinade
marineit, marinate
marit, merit
maritaim, maritime
marital, lly, INVOLVES MARRIAGE "prefixes: pre"
marithon, marathon
maritime, OF THE OCEAN OR SEA
mariwana, marijuana
marjaren, margarine
marjeren, margarine
marjin, margin
marjinul, margin(al)
marjinulize, marginalize
marjoram, *, HERBAL PLANT
mark, *, ked, king, ker, kedly, A GOUGE/ LINE/ SCRATCH/ IMPRESSION "prefixes: un"
markee, marquee / marquis
marker, *, A LINE OF DEMARCATION, A TOOL OR INSTRUMENT THAT MARKS
market, *, ted, ting, table, tability, ter, ABOUT SELLING GOODS "prefixes: sub"
marki, marquee / marquis
markit, market
markt, mark(ed)

markur, marker
marllarin, margarine
marllin, margin
marlloram, marjoram
marmalade, A FRUIT PRESERVE
marmileid, marmalade
marmulade, marmalade
marn, martin / marten
maroon, *, ned, ning, BE LEFT ABANDONED, STRANDED, A COLOR
marose, morose
marow, marrow
marquee, A BANNER, TENT, SIGN OVER ENTRANCEWAY (or see marquis)
marquet, market
marquis, ses, sate, BRITISH RANK(or see marquee)
marriage, *, eable, eability, eableness, TWO PEOPLE WHO LEGALLY BOND IN MATRIMONY "prefixes: inter"
married, PAST TENSE FOR THE WORD "MARRY"
marrow, INNER BONE, PARTNER, MATE
marry, ries, ried, ying, riage, TWO PEOPLE LEGALLY BONDING (or see merry) "prefixes: inter/ un"
marsh, hes, hy, WETLAND
marshal, *, led, ling, lcy, lship, EUROPEAN OFFICER, SIMILAR TO A SHERIFF, TO LEAD, USHER (or see martial)
marshal law, martial law
marshen, martian / march(ing)
marshil, marshal / martial
marshin, martian / march(ing)
marshmallow, A SUGAR SWEET, AN HERBAL PLANT
marshmelow, marshmallow
marshul, marshal / martial
marsoopeal, marsupial
marsupeul, marsupial
marsupial, AN ANIMAL THAT SLEEPS DURING THE DAY
martch, march
marten, MEMBER OF THE WEASEL FAMILY (or see martin)
martengale, martingale
martengeil, martingale
marteny, martini
marter, martyr

martial, lism, list, lly, lness, OF WAR (or see marshal)
martial law, PERMANENT MILITARY RULE IN THE U.S.
martian,*,, PLANET MARS INHABITANTS
martin,*, A BIRD
martingale,*, A BIRD
martini,*, ALCOHOLIC DRINK
martir, martyr
martur, martyr
martyr,*, red, ring, rize, rdom, SOMEONE WHO RISKS THEIR LIVES FOR A CAUSE OF THEIR CHOOSING
marune, maroon
marut, merit
marutime, maritime
marvel,*, led, ling, lous, lously, lousness, GREATLY IMPRESSIVE, ATTENTION GETTER
marvelous, lously, lousness, VERY IMPRESSIVE
marvelus, marvelous
marvil, marvel
marvilus, marvelous
marvul, marvel
mary, marry / merry
maryarin, margarine
maryonette, marionette
mas, mace / mass / moss / maize
masa, mesa
masach, massage
masacism, masochism
masacism, masochism
masacistic, masochism
masacur, massacre
masage, massage
masakistic, masochism(stic)
masakisum, masochism
masakur, massacre
masall, massage
masanine, mezzanine
masaquer, massacre
masc, mask
mascara, A DYE PUT ON EYELASHES
mascarade, masquerade
mascot,*, A THING OF LUCK
masculine, ely, eness, nity, nize, nized, nizing, MALE
mascureid, masquerade
masd, mast

masdebashen, masturbate(tion)
masdek, mastic
masder, master
masderbade, masturbate
masdereus, mysterious
masdides, mastitis
masdik, mastic
masdir, master
masditis, mastitis
masdurful, master(full)
mase, mace / maize / maze
masectame, mastectomy
masectome, mastectomy
masecur, massacre
masef, massive
masekur, massacre
masen, mason
masenger, messenger
masenry, mason(ry)
maseurse, masseuse
maseve, massive
masgot, mascot
mash, hes, hed, hing, her, TO SHRED/ PULVERIZE/ SQUISH, TURN TO PASTE (or see match)
mashene, machine
mashenery, machine(ry)
mashenest, machine(nist)
mashes, mash(es) / match(es)
mashety, machete
mashin, machine / mash(ing)
mashinury, machine(ry)
mashis, mash(es) / match(es)
mashus, mash(es) / match(es)
masif, massive
masiker, massacre
masin, mason
masive, massive
mask,*, ked, king, COVER UP "prefixes: un"
maskalen, masculine
maskarade, masquerade
maskarate, masquerade
maskeet, mesquite
maskera, mascara

maskerate, masquerade
maskereid, masquerade
masketo, mosquito
maskewlen, masculine
maskot, mascot
maskulin, masculine
maskurade, masquerade
maskurate, masquerade
masochism, st, PATHOLOGICAL SELF-DESTRUCTION
masochist, tic, tically, sm, PATHOLOGICAL SELF-DESTRUCTION
masof, massive
masoge, massage
masoje, massage
masokism, masochism
masokistic, masochism(stic)
masokizum, masochism
masol, muscle / mussel
mason,*, nry, nries, nic, WORKS WITH STONE
masoose, masseuse
masoqism, masochism
masoquer, massacre
masquera, mascara
masquerade,*, ed, ding, er, USE A MASK OR DISGUISE TO COVER IDENTITY
masquilin, masculine
masquite, mesquite
masqureid, masquerade
mass, ses, sed, sing, sive, MEASURE OF VOLUME, WEIGHT, ACCUMULATION OF SIGNIFICANT AMOUNT "prefixes: bio"
massacre,*, ed, ring, KILLING OF SIGNIFICANT AMOUNT AT ONCE
massage,*, ed, ging, MANIPULATE/ RUB SKIN TO AFFECT INTERNAL TISSUE (or see message)
masseur,*, use, MALE WHO GIVES MASSAGE
masseuse,*, ur, FEMALE WHO GIVES MASSAGE
massiuse, masseuse
massive, ely, eness, OF GREAT QUANTITY, SIZE
massuer, masseur
massuse, masseuse
mast, PART OF SAIL ON VESSEL, HOG FEED (or see mace(d))

mastectomy, mies, BREAST REMOVAL
mastek, mastic
master, *, red, ring, ry, rful, rfully, rfulness, rliness, rly, rhood, ONE WHO IS HIGHLY SKILLFUL/ WISE "prefixes: over/ re"
masterbashen, masturbate(tion)
masterbate, masturbate
mastereus, mysterious
mastic, *, RESIN OR SEALANT FOR PROTECTIVE COAT
mastidis, mastitis
mastique, mystique
mastir, master
mastirbashen, masturbate(tion)
mastirful, master(full)
mastitis, ic, INFLAMED BREAST OR UDDER
masturbate, *, ed, ting, tion, TO STIMULATE ONE'S OWN SEXUAL ORGANS TO AROUSAL/ ORGASM
masturly, master(ly)
mastytis, mastitis
masuese, masseuse
masukestik, masochism
masukism, masochism
masukistic, masochism(stic)
masuqism, masochism
masure, masseur
masuse, masseuse
mat, *, tted, tting, FLAT ITEM FOR DOORSTEPS, FOR DISPLAYING VISUAL IMAGES, A FLAT MESH OF SOME MATERIAL (or see mac/ made/ mate/ matte)
matabulism, metabolism
match, hes, hed, hing, PAIR JP, PLACE SUITABLE ITEMS TOGETHER, CHEMICALLY TREATED ITEM USED TO CREATE FLAME "prefixes: mis/ over/ re/ un"
matcherashen, mature(ration)
matchure, mature
mate, *, ed, ting, TO JOIN TOGETHER, METHOD OF PROPAGATION, A CALL IN THE GAME OF CHESS (or see made/ maid/ matte) "prefixes: un"
matekulus, meticulous
matena, matinee
matenens, maintenance
mater, matter / mad(dder)
materde, maitre d'

materealise, materialize
matereul, material
material, *, lly, lism, list, listic, listically, lity, lities, lness, lize, NON-VIRTUAL, OF THE PHYSICAL PLANE, OF MASS, OF THE PHYSICAL "prefixes: bio/ im/ non"
materialaiz, materialize
materialize, *, ed, zing, zation, er, TO PHYSICALLY APPEAR "prefixes: im"
maternal, lly, listic, lism, MOTHERING, NURTURING
maternity, ties, A HUMAN STATE OF BEING PREGNANT
mateure, mature
math, LANGUAGE OF NUMBERS
mathematic, *, cal, cally, cian, SCIENCE AND LANGUAGE DEALING WITH NUMBERS "prefixes: bio"
mathology, mythology
matikulus, meticulous
matina, matinee
matinee, *, SPECIFIC AREA OF TIME WHEN A MOVIE IS SHOWN IN A THEATER
matinei, matinee
matir, mad(dder) / matter
matirde, maitre d'
matireal, material
matirnol, maternal
matirnulistic, maternal(istic)
matist, mad(ddest)
matna, matinee
matne, matinee
matness, mad(ness)
mato, motto
matou, motto
matramony, matrimony
matrearch, matriarch
matrearchal, matriarch(al)
matreark, matriarch
matreks, matrix
matremony, matrimony
matren, matron
matress, mattress
matrex, matrix
matriarch, *, hal, halism, hate, hy, hies, MOTHER IS LEADING ROLE
matricks, matrix

matriculate, *, ed, ting, tion, REGISTERED/ ENROLLED
matrimony, nies, nial, nially, OF MARRIAGE
matrin, matron
matris, mattress
matrix, xes, ices, MYSTERY/ LABYRINTH/ RIDDLE
matron, *, nage, nly, nal, nage, nize, A FEMALE CHAPERONE/ GUARDIAN/ ATTENDANT
matropolis, metropolis
matte, METAL STYLE, NON-GLOSSY SURFACE
matter, *, red, OF IMPORTANCE/ SUBSTANCE/ PHYSICAL MATERIAL
mattress, ses, BED OF STUFFING FOR SLEEPING ON
matunei, matinee
matunens, maintenance
matur, matter / mad(der)
maturde, maitre d'
mature, *, ed, ring, rate, ration, rational, rative, ely, eness, rity, GROWN TO PHYSICAL PEAK "prefixes: im/ pre"
maturnedy, maternity
maturnity, maternity
mauf, mauve
maugul, module
maujul, module
maul, *, led, ling, A TOOL, TO PHYSICALLY BATTER, REDUCE TO LESSER STATE (or see mall/ mole)
mauld, maul(ed) / malt
maunaz, mayonnaise
maund, mound
maunt, mount
maunten, mountain
mauntenus, mountain(ous)
mauroon, maroon
mausoleum, GRANDIOSE TOMB
mauth, mouth
mauve, A COLOR
mave, mauve
maverick, *, RADICALS, ONE'S WHO DON'T FOLLOW TRADITIONAL BELIEFS/ VALUES
mavrik, maverick
mavurek, maverick
mawnd, mound
mawnt, mount
mawntin, mountain

mawten, mountain
mawth, mouth
max, xes, xed, xing, ximal, ximize, ximum, SHORT FOR MAXIMUM
maxi, moxie
maximal, lly, THE MOST POSSIBLE
maximize, *, ed, zing, er, mum, THE MOST POSSIBLE
maximum, *, THE MOST POSSIBLE
may, ALLOWED TO, A MONTH IN THE YEAR (ENGLISH)
maybe, PERHAPS
maydreark, matriarch
mayenase, mayonnaise
mayer, mayor
mayneis, mayonnaise
mayonnaise, SPREAD OR SALAD DRESSING FOR FOOD
mayor, *, ral, ralty, ralties, POLITICAL POSITION
mazanine, mezzanine
mazdek, mastic
mazderful, master(full)
mazdik, mastic
mazdur, master
maze, *, ed, zing, zy, INABILITY TO MOVE/ THINK ALONG A CONTINUOUS PATH (or see mace/ maize)
mazef, massive
mazeker, massacre
mazektomy, mastectomy
mazenine, mezzanine
mazif, massive
maziker, massacre
mazonry, mason(ry)
mazt, mast
mazturbate, masturbate
mazzanine, mezzanine
me, FIRST PERSON, SELF, YOUR SELF
meadow, *, A FIELD GENERALLY WITHOUT TREES
meager, rly, rness, SMALL PORTION/ AMOUNT
meal, *, ly, lier, liest, liness, FOOD, FOOD EATEN AT CERTAIN TIME
mean, *, ning, ningful, ningfully, ningfulness, ningless, nt, ILL INTENT, EXPRESS THOUGHTS OF HARMFUL INTENT, METHOD OF ACHIEVING A GOAL, INTENT TO REFER/ CONVEY SOMETHING "prefixes: un"

meant, PAST TENSE FOR THE WORD "MEAN", ATTEMPT TO EXPRESS THOUGHTS
mear, mere
measles, A VIRUS
measure, *, ed, ring, rable, rably, rability, rableness, ement, USE NUMBERS/ WORDS TO EXPLAIN SIZE/ AMOUNT/ DISTANCE "prefixes: un"
meat, *, ty, tier, tiest, tiness, MUSCLE FIBER IN LIVING THINGS, EDIBLE PARTS (or see meet)
mecaneks, mechanic(s)
mech, mesh
mechanic, *, cal, cally, calness, ist, istic, istically, ize, ism, WORKS WITH PARTS WHICH MAKES OBJECTS MOVE, SYSTEM OF APPROACH "prefixes: bio/ un"
mechanize, *, ed, zing, zation, ist, istic, istically, er, ism, USE MACHINE TO PERFORM A TASK
mechen, mission
mechenary, mission(ary)
mecher, measure
mechrow, metro
med, mid / meet
meda, meta
medabulism, metabolism
medacate, medicate
medafesic, metaphysic
medafisical, metaphysic(al)
medafore, metaphor
medagashen, mitigate(tion)
medagate, mitigate
medal, *, llic, llist, llion, A BADGE/ OBJECT FOR AWARD (or see metal/ mettle/ meddle/ middle)
medamorfasis, metamorphosis
medaphore, metaphor
medaphysic, metaphysic
medaphysical, metaphysic(al)
medasen, medicine
medatashen, meditate(tion)
meddle, *, ed, ling, er, esome, esomeness, INTERFERE WITH OTHER'S THINGS/ AFFAIRS, (or see medal/ metal/ mettle/ middle) "prefixes: inter"
medea, media
medeader, mediate(tor)
medean, median

medeashen, mediate(tion)
medeat, mediate
medeator, mediate(tor)
medec, medic
medecal, medical
medefisic, metaphysic
medefl, medieval
medefol, medieval
medefore, metaphor
medek, medic
medekal, medical
medekulus, meticulous
medel, medal / metal / mettle / meddle / middle
medemorfasis, metamorphosis
medeokrity, mediocre(rity)
medeokur, mediocre
medeor, meteor
medeorite, meteorite
medeorology, meteorology
medephore, metaphor
meder, meter
medernedy, maternity
mederology, meteorology
medesin, medicine
medetashen, meditate(tion)
medeum, medium
medeur, meteor
medevul, medieval
medget, midget
media, *, AUDIO/ VIDEO MEANS OF COMMUNICATION "prefixes: multi/ retro"
median, *, nly, OF THE MIDDLE, SEPARATION
mediate, *, ed, ting, tion, tive, tize, tor, tization, TO FACILITATE/ DIFFUSE BETWEEN TWO OPPOSING PARTIES OR OBJECTS
medic, *, ONE'S WHO WORK WITH INJURIES, MEDICINE
medicable, ly, RESPONSIVE TO MEDICAL TREATMENT "prefixes: im/ non/ un"
medical, *, lly, cine, ate, OF MEDICINE, EXAMINATION "prefixes: bio/ pre"
medicasion, medicate(tion)
medicate, *, ed, ting, tion, GIVE MAN- MADE DRUGS TO "prefixes: pre"

medicine, *, nal, nally, MAN-MADE CHEMICALS TAKEN INTO THE BODY "prefixes: bio"
medieval, lism, list, lly, OF THE MIDDLE AGES
medifral, medieval
medifiseks, metaphysic(s)
medifl, medieval
medik, medic
medikulus, meticulous
medil, medal / metal / mettle / meddle / middle
mediocre, rity, rities, BETWEEN POOR AND GOOD QUALITY, IN-BETWEEN
mediocur, mediocre(rity)
medir, meter
medirology, meteorology
medisine, medicine
meditate, *, ed, ting, tion, tative, tatively, tor, tiveness, BE SILENT/ STILL, ELIMINATE THOUGHT "prefixes: pre"
medium, *, mistic, COMMUNICATION USING THE VIRTUAL FIELD, TRANSLATE INFORMATION FROM ONE FORM OF MEDIA TO ANOTHER
medjet, midget
medl, medal / meddle / metal / mettle / middle
medle, medal / metal / mettle / meddle / middle
medo, meadow
medol, medal / metal / mettle / meddle / middle
medow, meadow
medrapolitan, metropolitan
medrek, metric
medric, metric
medropoletan, metropolitan
medst, midst
medtrik, metric
medufore, metaphor
medugation, mitigate(tion)
medukul, medical
medul, medal / metal / mettle / meddle / middle
medulsom, meddle(some)
medumorfasis, metamorphosis
medur, meter
medurology, meteorology
medusin, medicine
medutashen, meditate(tion)
medwife, midwife

meek, kly, kness, GENTLE/ MILD TEMPERAMENT
meel, meal
meen, mean
meet, *, met, ting, COME TOGETHER, ARRIVE AT SAME DESTINATION AND TIME (or see meat)
mega, PREFIX INDICATING "MILLION/ VERY LARGE" MOST OFTEN MODIFIES THE WORD
megalo, PREFIX INDICATING "MILLION/ VERY LARGE" MOST OFTEN MODIFIES THE WORD
meger, meager / measure
megir, measure / major
megu, mega
megur, measure / meager
mehanaiz, mechanize
mei, may
meibi, maybe
meic, make
meid, made / maid
meiga, mega
meijor, major
meik, make
meil, male / mail
mein, main / mane
meinch, mange
meineis, mayonnaise
meinens, maintenance
meinia, mania
meiniac, maniac
meinll, mange
meinller, manger
meinlly, mangy
meintein, maintain
meior, mayor
meiosis, CELLULAR PROCESS, UNDERSTATEMENT
meipol, maple
meis, maize / maze / mace
meison, mason
meit, mate
meitrex, matrix
meitriark, matriarch
meitrics, matrix
meitrimoni, matrimony
meitron, matron

meiz, maze / maize / mace
mejer, measure / major
mejur, measure / major
mejut, midget
mek, meek / make
mekanais, mechanize
mekanek, mechanic
mekanekul, mechanic(al)
mekanise, mechanize
mekcher, mixture
mekenize, mechanize
meker, meager
mekschur, mixture
mekster, mixture
mekunize, mechanize
mekur, meager
mel, meal / mail / male / mill
melado, mulato
meladramatic, melodrama(tic)
melady, melody
melameter, milli(meter)
melan, melon
melancholy, lies, lily, liness, lic, DESPONDENT, DEPRESSED, CONTEMPLATIVE
melancoli, melancholy
melanoma, *, ata, osis, nism, TUMOR, CELLS WITH DARK PIGMENT
melanosis, oma, nism, OVER PRODUCTION OF PIGMENT MELANIN IN SKIN/ TISSUE
melasecond, millisecond
melatent, militant
melateristic, military(ristic)
melato, mulato
melaturize, military(rize)
meld, *, ded, ding, AS IF TO MELT TOGETHER, BLEND INTO ONE (or see melt/ mill(ed))
meldoo, mildew
meldu, mildew
meledy, melody
melen, melon
melencholy, melancholy
melenium, millennium
melenkaly, melancholy

melenoma, melanoma
meleonaire, million(aire)
melet, millet
meletary, military
melin, melon
melincholy, melancholy
mellinium, millennium
melinkoly, melancholy
melinoma, melanoma
melinosis, melanosis
melisha, militia
melit, millet
melitia, militia
melk, milk
mell, meal / mail / male / mill
mellapede, millipede
mellinium, millennium
mellow, wly, wness, BECOME SOFTENED/ RELAXED WITHOUT FEAR
melnutrishen, malnutrition
melo, mellow
melodrama,*, atic, atically, atist, EXAGGERATED ACT/ EVENT, OVER EMPHASIS
melody, dies, dic, dically, dious, diousness, A SERIES OF SOUNDS/ FREQUENCY, TUNES IN HARMONY
melogram, milli(gram)
melon,*, EDIBLE FRUIT
melonkoly, melancholy
melow, mellow
melt,*, ted, ting, table, tability, ter, TO CHANGE FROM SOLID TO LIQUID, CHANGE FORM (or see meld)
meltary, military
meludrumatek, melodrama(tic)
melugram, milli(gram)
meluleter, milli(liter)
melun, melon
meluncholy, melancholy
melunoma, melanoma
melunosis, melanosis
melupete, millipede
melusekund, millisecond
melutare, military
melutint, militant

melyonaire, million(aire)
melyun, million
memacree, mimic(ry)
memakry, mimic(ry)
member,*, rship, PART/ PERSON WHICH BELONGS TO LARGER ORGANISM/ ORGANIZATION
membrane,*, nal, nous, LAYER OF THIN TISSUE "prefixes: non/ semi"
membrein, membrane
memek, mimic
memento,*, ARTICLE/ OBJECT REMINDER OF THE PAST
memerabelia, memorabilia
memerable, memorable
memerize, memorize
memic, mimic
memoir,*, rist, PRINTED REMINDER OF THE PAST
memok, mimic
memorabilia, REMINDERS OF THE PAST
memorable, ly, eness, bility, bilia, WORTHY OF REMEMBERING
memorais, memorize
memorial,*, list, lly, lize, lizes, lized, lizing, lization, lizer, AN OBJECT PLACED IN MEMORY OF THOSE WHO DIED "prefixes: im"
memorize,*, ed, zing, zable, er, STORE INTO MEMORY
memory, ries, rize, COLLECTION OF STORED INFORMATION
memrable, memorable
memrize, memorize
memruble, memorable
memry, memory
memuk, mimic
memurabilea, memorabilia
memurise, memorize
memwar, memoir
men,*, HUMAN ADULT MALE (or see mean)
menace,*, ced, cing, HARMFUL/ THREATENING, A NUISANCE
menacher, miniature
menamize, minimize
menamul, minimal
menamuly, minimal
menamum, minimum

menapos, menopause
menarolization, mineral(ization)
menarul, mineral
menarulize, mineral(ize)
menas, menace
menasher, miniature
menaskewul, minuscule
menastrony, minestrone
menastry, minister
mences, menses
menchen, mention
mend,*, ded, ding, dable, TO FIX/ REPAIR (or see mint/ meant)
mene, mean / mini / many
meneacher, miniature
menemize, minimize
menengidos, meningitis
menenjidus, meningitis
menerable, memorable
menerul, mineral
menes, menace
menestrony, minestrone
menestry, minister
menet, minute
meneteri, monetary
meneul, menial
mengul, mingle
meni, mini / many
menial, lly, REQUIRES LITTLE THOUGHT
meniature, miniature
menila, manila
meningitis, ic, VIRUS OF THE BODY
menipause, menopause
menipulate, manipulate
menis, menace
meniu, menu
menk, mink
menmerable, memorable
mennow, minnow
meno, minnow
menogamy, monogamy
menokside, monoxide

menopause, sal, STOP HAVING MONTHLY ESTRUS CYCLES, ESTROGEN CHANGES IN FEMALES
menopuly, monopoly
menoscule, minuscule
menotnus, monotony(nous)
menotny, monotony
menoxide, monoxide
menruble, memorable
mens, men(s) / mean(s) / mince
menses, MENSTRUATION
menshen, mention
menstearation, menstruation
menstral, menstrual / minstrel
menstrashen, menstruation
menstration, menstruation
menstrual, uous, ate, uum, ation, MENSTRUATION (or see minstrel) "prefixes: pre"
menstruation, FEMALE MONTHLY UTERUS LINING DISCHARGE, A PERIOD
ment, mint / mend / meant
mental, lly, lity, THOUGHT, OF THE MIND
menthol, OIL
mention, *, ned, ning, nable. ner, CALLING BRIEF ATTENTION TO SOMETHING "prefixes: un/ under"
mentle, mental
mentol, mental
mentor, *, A COACH, GUIDE
mentur, mentor
menu, *, LIST OF RESTAURANT MEALS
menuet, minuet
menumem, minimum
menumly, minimal
menupause, menopause
menure, manure
menus, menace
menustrony, minestrone
menyew, menu
menyewet, minuet
menyon, mignon
meol, meal
mer, mere / mirror / mare
meracle, miracle
meraculus, miracle(culous)

merage, mirage
meragolt, marigold
merahuana, marijuana
meraje, mirage
merakl, miracle
merakulus, miracle(culous)
meral, morale / mural
meraly, merry(rily)
meranad, marinade / marinate
merang, meringue
merathon, marathon
mercantile, lism, list, COMMERCE, TRADE
mercenary, ries, rily, riness, HIRED TO KILL
merch, merge
merchandise, ed, sing, er, sable, sability, ize, izes, ized, izing, izer, GOODS FOR RETAIL SALE
merchant, *, table, ndise, ONE WHO DEALS IN GOODS FOR RETAIL
merchendais, merchandise
mercury, rial, rialism, rialize, rializes, rialized, rializing, rialization, ric, A PLANET, METALLIC ELEMENT USED IN THE PLANET, METALLIC ELEMENT USED IN THERMOMETERS
mercy, cies, ciful, cifully, ciless, cilessly, cilessness, PROVIDE COMPASSION/ BENEVOLENCE AT A CRUCIAL TIME "prefixes: un"
merder, murder
merdurer, murder(er)
mere, ely, SIMPLY FOR THE REASON OF, SMALL IN MATTER (or see marry/ merry/ mirror)
merech, marriage
mered, married
meredian, meridian
mereg, marriage
meregold, marigold
mereinett, marionette
merej, marriage
merekul, miracle
merenat, marinade / marinate
meren, marine
mereod, myriad
mereonett, marionette
meret, merit

meretal, marital
merethon, marathon
meretime, maritime
meretul, marital
mereunett, marionette
merewana, marijuana
merg, merge
merge, *, ed, ging, er, ence, COME TOGETHER AS ONE "prefixes: sub/ un"
meri, marry / merry
meriad, myriad
merich, marriage
merid, married
meridg, marriage
meridian, *, nal, nally, INVISIBLE CIRCLE RUNNING AROUND EARTH THROUGH NORTH/ SOUTH POLES
merigold, marigold
merihuana, marijuana
merijuana, marijuana
merill, marriage
merily, merry(rily)
merin, marine
merina, marina
merinad, marinade / marinate
merinat, marinade / marinate
meringue, WHIPPED EGGS
merit, *, ted, tedly, tless, torious, WORTHY OF HONOR OR NOTE "prefixes: un"
meritaim, maritime
merital, marital
merithon, marathon
meritime, maritime
meritol, marital
meriwana, marijuana
merje, merge
merk, murky
merkanteel, mercantile
merki, murky
merkiuri, mercury
merkury, mercury
merky, murky
merlen, merlin
merlin, BIRD

merll,merge
mermaid,*,ILLUSIONARY FISH WOMAN
mermeid,mermaid
mermer,murmur
mermur,murmur
mero,marrow
meroge,mirage
meroj,mirage
meror,mirror
merose,morose
merow,marrow
merqui,murky
merry,rriment,rrily,rriness,CHEERY,HAPPY
mersenary,mercenary
mershandise,merchandise
mersinary,mercenary
mersy,mercy
merukul,miracle
merur,mirror
mery,marry / merry
mes,PREFIX INDICATING "MIDDLE" MOST OFTEN MODIFIES THE WORD
mesa,*,LAND PLATEAU
mesach,message / massage
mesage,message / massage
mesalaneus,miscellaneous
mesaleinios,miscellaneous
mesall,message
mesals,measles / missile(s)
mesanine,mezzanine
mesbahave,misbehave
mesbaleef,misbelief
mesbaleve,misbelieve
mesbok,misspell
mesbokin,misspoke(n)
mescalculate,miscalculate
meschef,mischief
mesconstrue,misconstrue
mesdake,mistake
mesdamener,misdemeanor
mesderius,mysterious
mesdress,mistress
mesdriul,mistrial

mesdufy,mystify
mesdur,mister
mesdury,mystery
meseg,message
mesej,message
mesel,missile
mesencher,messenger
meseness,mess(iness)
mesenger,messenger
mesenine,mezzanine
mesenller,messenger
mesenturpet,misinterpret
meseur,mess(ier) / masseur
meseust,mess(iest)
mesfet,misfit
mesfire,misfire
mesforshen,misfortune
mesfortune,misfortune
mesgeving,misgiving
mesguge,misjudge
mesh,hes,hed,hing,INTERWOVEN METAL STRANDS TO CREATE A BLANKET/ NET "prefixes: en"
meshandle,mishandle
meshap,mishap
meshen,mission
meshenary,mission(ary)
meshor,measure
meshur,measure
mesige,message
mesije,message
mesil,missile
mesils,measles / missile(s)
mesinene,mezzanine
mesinform,misinform
mesinger,messenger
mesinturpret,misinterpret
mesjef,mischief
mesjug,misjudge
meskalaneus,miscellaneous
meskarege,miscarriage
meskedo,mosquito
meskeet,mesquite
meskenstrew,misconstrue

meskownt,miscount
meskwote,misquote
mesled,misled
mesleed,mislead
mesmach,mismatch
mesmerize,*,ed,zing,ism,ic,ically,ist,er,zation, INTENSELY ATTENTIVE TO THE POINT OF EXCLUDING ALL OTHER THINGS
mesmurize,mesmerize
mesnomer,misnomer
meso,PREFIX INDICATING "MIDDLE" MOST OFTEN MODIFIES THE WORD
mesoje,massage
mesonderstand,misunderstand
mesonderstood,misunderstood
mesonine,mezzanine
mespell,misspell
mesplase,misplace
mespok,misspoke
mespokin,misspoke(n)
mesprent,misprint
mesprunounce,mispronounce
mesquite,LAND TYPE,A TREE,SHRUB
mesquote,misquote
mesred,misread
mesrepresent,misrepresent
mesrepricent,misrepresent
mesruble,miserable
mess,ses,sed,sing,sy,sily,siness,sier,siest,SLOPPY, DISHEVELED,DISARRAY
message,*,ed,ging,SHORT NOTE OF VOICE/ TEXT
messanine,mezzanine
messenger,*,red,ring,ONE WHO DELIVERS A NOTE
messusege,misuse(sage)
mest,mist / midst / miss(ed) / mess(ed)
mestake,mistake
mestakin,mistake(n)
mestamener,misdemeanor
meste,mist
mesteek,mystique
mestefy,mystify
mesteik,mystic / mystique / mistake
mester,mister

mestereus, mysterious
mestic, mystic
mestides, mastitis
mestify, mystify
mestikul, mystic(al)
mestireus, mysterious
mestook, mistook
mestreat, mistreat
mestress, mistress
mestrete, mistreat
mestris, mistress
mestrit, mistreat
mestriul, mistrial
mestufy, mystify
mestuk, mistook
mestumener, misdemeanor
mestury, mystery
mesuge, message
mesuje, message
mesulaneus, miscellaneous
mesuls, measles / missile(s)
mesultoe, mistletoe
mesunderstand, misunderstand
mesunine, mezzanine
mesure, measure
mesurible, miserable
mesuse, masseuse / misuse
mesuseje, misuse(sage)
mesuze, misuse / masseuse
mesyews, misuse

met, PAST TENSE FOR THE WORD "MEET", (or see mitt/ mite/ meet/ meat) "prefixes: un"

meta, PREFIX INDICATING "BEYOND/ CHANGE" MOST OFTEN MODIFIES THE WORD

metabolism,*,ize,ic,ically, THE CONVERSION OF ENERGY IN A LIVING ORGANISM, FUNCTION OF LIFE

metabolize,*,ed,zing,zable, CONCERNED WITH METABOLISM

metabulism, metabolism
metacate, medicate
metafisical, metaphysic(al)
metagate, mitigate

metal,*,led,ling,llic,llically,llurgy, CHEMICAL ELEMENTS FOUND IN THE EARTH (or see mettle/ meddle/ medal/ middle) "prefixes: bi/ non/ semi/ un"

metamorphosis, MAJOR TRANSFORMATION AS A CATERPILLAR TO A BUTTERFLY

metanol, methanol

metaphor,*,ric,rical,rically, EXPRESSING THOUGHT USING UNCONVENTIONAL COMPARISONS

metaphysic,*,cal,cally, STUDY OF THE SUPERNATURAL, INVISIBLE

metapolize, metabolize
metasen, medicine
metatashen, meditate(tion)
mete, meat
metea, media
metean, median
meteashen, mediate(tion)
meteate, mediate
meteator, mediate(tor)
metefisical, metaphysic(al)
metein, methane
metek, medic
metekal, medical
metekulus, meticulous
metel, medal / metal / mettle / meddle / middle
metemorfusis, metamorphosis
meten, mitten
meteokrety, mediocre(rity)
meteokur, mediocre

meteor,*,ric,rite, rology, COMPACTED SAND AND ICE TRAVELING AT HIGH VELOCITY THROUGH SPACE

meteorite,*, METEOR THAT SURVIVES ENTRY THROUGH EARTH'S ATMOSPHERE

meteorology, gic, gical, gically, gist, STUDY OF THE ATMOSPHERE SUCH AS WEATHER/ CLIMATE

metephysical, metaphysic(al)

meter,*,red,ring, FORM/ INSTRUMENT OF MEASUREMENT "prefixes: deca/ un"

metesen, medicine
metetashen, meditate(tion)
meteum, medium
meteurology, meteorology
metevul, medieval

meteyorite, meteorite

meth, SHORT FOR METHAMPHETAMINE
methad, method
methadolgy, methodolgy

methadone, MAN-MADE DRUG, DOWNER, HIGHLY ADDICTIVE

methakul, myth(ical)
methalogic, mythologic

methamphetamine,*, ABBREVIATION FOR METH, MANMADE CHEMICAL STIMULANT

methane, A GAS
methanfetamene, methamphetamine

methanol, TOXIC LIQUID
methanphetamine, methamphetamine
methasize, myth(icize)
methecul, myth(ical)
methed, method
methedology, methodology
methedone, methadone
methein, methane
methemfetamine, methamphetamine
methenphetamine, methamphetamine
methid, method
methidology, methodology

method,*,,dize,dizes,dized,dizing,dizer,dical,dically, dicalness, dology, A SYSTEM/ PROCEDURE/ TECHNIQUE

methodology, gies, gical, gically, gist, A SYSTEM/ PROCEDURE/ TECHNIQUE

methology, mythology
methonol, methanol
methud, method
methudology, methodology
methudone, methadone
methunol, methanol
metia, media
metic, medic
metical, medical

meticulous, sly, sness, EXCESSIVE ATTENTION TO DETAIL/ CLEANLINESS/ EXACTING

metigeit, mitigate
metikiulos, meticulous
metil, medal / metal / mettle / meddle / middle

metin, mitten
meting, meet(ing)
metiqiulos, meticulous
metir, meter
metirology, meteorology
metisine, medicine
metitate, meditate
metle, medal / metal / mettle / meddle / middle
meto, meadow
metod, method
metr, PREFIX INDICATING "WOMB/ MOTHER" MOST OFTEN MODIFIES THE WORD
metrapolitan, metropolitan
metric, *, cal, cally, cate, cates, cated, cating, cation, cist, cize, cizes, cized, cizing, A MEASUREMENT SYSTEM "prefixes: bio"
metro, REFERRING TO TRANSIT SYSTEM IN CITY, SHORT FOR "METROPOLITAN"
metropolis, ses, CENTRAL CITY
metropolitan, nism, HUB OF CITY AND THOSE WHO DWELL THERE "prefixes: non"
metruk, metric
metst, midst
mettle, *, ed, esome, COURAGEOUS, SPIRITED (or see medal/ metal/ mettle / meddle/middle)
metukul, medical
metul, medal / metal / mettle / meddle / middle
metur, meter
meturnedy, maternity
meturnul, maternal
meturology, meteorology
metutashen, meditate(tion)
meuchuel, mutual
meudilate, mutilate
meukus, mucus
meul, meal / mule
meurol, mural
meus, muse
meusikul, music(al)
meut, mute
meutashen, mutate(tion)
meutat, mutate
meutene, mutiny

meutilate, mutilate
meutulashen, mutilate(tation)
meuzeim, museum
meuzek, music
meuzeshen, musician
mewfee, movie
mewfuble, move(vable)
mewkus, mucus
mewl, mule
mewn, moon
mewnisapaledy, municipal(ity)
mewnisepal, municipal
mewral, mural
mewse, muse / moose / mousse
mewseum, museum
mewsik, music
mewt, moot / mute
mewtashen, mutate(tion)
mewtelate, mutilate
mewteny, mutiny
mewtint, mutate(ant)
mewvee, movie
mewvuble, move(vable)
mewzishen, musician
mexcher, mixture
mexter, mixture
meyor, mayor
mez, mess
mezandul, mishandle
mezanine, mezzanine
mezdamener, misdemeanor
mezder, mister
mezdery, mystery
mezdumener, misdemeanor
mezenine, mezzanine
mezfet, misfit
mezfire, misfire
mezforchen, misfortune
mezhap, mishap
mezinform, misinform
mezinine, mezzanine
mezkwote, misquote
mezled, misled

mezleet, mislead
mezmach, mismatch
mezmurize, mesmerize
meznomer, misnomer
mezonine, mezzanine
mezpell, misspell
mezplase, misplace
mezprent, misprint
mezred, misread
mezreprezent, misrepresent
mezruble, miserable
meztake, mistake
meztamener, misdemeanor
meztek, mystic
mezter, mister
meztereus, mysterious
meztreat, mistreat
meztress, mistress
meztriul, mistrial
mezuls, measles
mezunine, mezzanine
mezury, misery
mezzanine, *, LOW UPPER FLOOR OR THEATER BALCONY
mfusiz, emphasize
mi, my
mibuleve, misbelieve
mic, meek
mica, ORGANIC, SILICATE
michanek, mechanic
michanekul, mechanic(al)
michen, mission
michenary, mission(ary)
michet, midget
micks, mix
micrawave, microwave
micro, VERY SMALL, PREFIX INDICATING "SMALL" MOST OFTEN MODIFIES THE WORD
microbe, *, bial, bian, bic, ORGANISMS SEEN ONLY UNDER A MICROSCOPE
micrometer, SYSTEM OF MEASUREMENT
micron, *, ra, nation, MICROMETER "prefixes: sub"
microphone, *, TRANSMITS SOUND

microscope, *, pic, pically, py, pist, INSTRUMENT WHICH ENLARGES OBJECTS FOR VIEWING WITH THE EYES "prefixes: sub"
microwave, *, ELECTROMAGNETIC WAVELENGTH, AN APPLIANCE
micshur, mixture
micu, mica
mid, PREFIX INDICATING "HALF/ MIDDLE" MOST OFTEN MODIFIES THE WORD (or see mitt)
midachondria, mitochondria
midagashen, mitigate(tion)
midagate, mitigate
middle, IN BETWEEN (or see medal/ metal/ mettle/ meddle)
midegate, mitigate
midegation, mitigate(tion)
mider, miter
midevil, medieval
midget, *, UNUSUALLY SMALL PERSON
midia, media
midian, median
midieit, mediate
midigashen, mitigate(tion)
midioker, mediocre
midium, medium
midival, medieval
midjet, midget
midle, middle
midochondria, mitochondria
midokondrea, mitochondria
midol, middle
midoses, mitosis
midst, LOCATED IN THE MIDDLE, AMONG
miduchondria, mitochondria
midul, medal / metal / mettle / meddle / middle
midur, miter
midwaif, midwife
midwife, eves, ery, ASSISTS MOTHER THROUGH BIRTHING A CHILD
miff, *, fed, fing, fy, BE OFFENDED
miger, meager
miget, midget

might, ty, tier, tiest, tily, tiness, STRENGTH, POWER, PERHAPS, MAYBE (or see mite)
mignon, *, SMALL, DELICATE
migraine, *, A SERIOUS HEADACHE
migrant, *, ONE WHO IS CONTINUOUSLY MOVING
migrashen, migrate(tion)
migrate, *, ed, ting, tion, ant, tor, tory, TO MOVE LOCATION OF HOME BASED UPON THE SEASONS
migro, micro
migrunt, migrant
migrutory, migrate(tory)
mijet, midget
mika, mica
mikanek, mechanic
mikanekul, mechanic(al)
mikaw, macaw
mikcher, mixture
mikount, miscount
mikrafone, microphone
mikrascope, microscope
mikrawave, microwave
mikro, micro
mikrobe, microbe
mikrofone, microphone
mikrometer, micrometer
mikron, micron
mikrowave, microwave
mikshter, mixture
mikster, mixture
miku, mica
mil, meal / mile
milado, mulato
milage, mile(age)
milagram, milli(gram)
milaleter, milli(liter)
milameter, milli(meter)
milapede, millipede
milarea, malaria
milasecond, millisecond
milasus, molasses
milatent, militant
milato, mulato
milaturestic, military(ristic)

milaturise, military(rize)
mild, der, dest, dly, dness, PLEASANT (or see mill(ed))
mildew, *, wed, wing, wy, FUNGI
mildu, mildew
mile, *, eage, U.S. MEASUREMENT FOR DISTANCE
milegram, milli(gram)
milekuler, molecule(lar)
milemeder, milli(meter)
milenium, millennium
mileonaire, million(aire)
milepete, millipede
miler, mill(er)
milesekent, millisecond
milest, molest
milet, millet
miletary, military
mileturezation, military(rization)
milicecond, millisecond
miligram, milli(gram)
milileter, milli(liter)
milimeter, milli(meter)
miliniium, millennium
milion, million
milionair, million(aire)
milipede, millipede
milipid, millipede
militant, tly, tness, ncy, ORDERLY, BY STRICT RULES
military, ries, rily, rism, rist, rize, rizes, rized, rizing, rization, ristic, ristically, GROUP OF PEOPLE BEING LED WITH STRICT RULES, AN ORDERLY GROUP
militia, *, GROUP ORGANIZED/ TRAINED TO FIGHT
milk, ker, ky, kiness, WHITE LIFE-GIVING FLUID EXCRETED BY MOTHERS OF MAMMALS, ANY RESEMBLANCE TO MILK
mill, *, lled, lling, ller, GRINDS GRAIN/ REMOVAL OF HULL (or see mile)
millaliter, milli(liter)
millameter, milli(meter)
millenium, millennium
millennia, ial, ium, MEASUREMENT BY 1,000 "prefixes: pre"
millennium, *, ia, MEASUREMENT BY 1,000
millet, EDIBLE GRAIN, GRASS (or see midget)

milli, igram, iliter, imeter, LATIN THOUSAND/ THOUSANDTH, PREFIX INDICATING "ONE THOUSANDTH" MOST OFTEN MODIFIES THE WORD
millinium, millennium
million, *, naire, U.S. NUMBER TO IDENTIFY QUANTITY "prefixes: multi"
millipede, *, INSECT
millisecond, *, METRIC NUMBER
miltary, military
miluge, mile(age)
milugram, milli(gram)
milumeter, milli(meter)
milupede, millipede
milutant, militant
milutare, military
milyen, million
milyonaire, million(aire)
mimakry, mimic(ry)
mimbrane, membrane
mimbur, member
mime, *, ed, ming, ACTOR WHO USES THE BODY TO ACT, COMMUNICATE WITHOUT USING WORDS
mimic, *, cking, cry, cries, TO COPY, IMITATE ANOTHER PERSON
mimorabilia, memorabilia
mimorabul, memorable
mimorealzation, memorial(ization)
mimoreul, memorial
mimorise, memorize
mimory, memory
mimuck, mimic
mimurabilia, memorabilia
mimwar, memoir
min, mean / mine
minacher, miniature
minamais, minimize
minamize, minimize
minamul, minimal
minamum, minimum
minapos, menopause
minaralize, mineral(ize)
minarul, mineral
minasher, miniature

minaskule, minuscule
minaster, minister
minastrony, minestrone
minchen, mention
mince, *, ed, cing, CHOP SOMETHING INTO SMALL PIECES
mind, *, ded, ding, dful, dfully, dfulness, dless, dlessly, dlessness, TO OBEY, PLACE WHERE THOUGHTS ARE GENERATED (or see mend/ mint)
mine, *, ed, ning, er, PAST TENSE FOR THE WORD "MY", CLAIMING OWNERSHIP, A FORMED TUNNEL INTO THE GROUND WHICH BEARS PRECIOUS ROCKS/ METALS, SUBSURFACE BOMB (or see mind/ main)
mineature, miniature
minemal, minimal
minemize, minimize
minemum, minimum
minengidus, meningitis
mineon, mignon
miner, mine(r) / minor
mineral, *, lize, lizes, lized, lizing, lizable, lization, lizer, logy, ORGANIC SUBSTANCES "prefixes: bio"
mines, minus / mine(s) / mince / menace
mineskule, minuscule
minester, minister
minestrone, SOUP
minet, minute
mingle, *, ed, ling, TO BE AMONG, ASSOCIATE WITH "prefixes: inter"
mini, LATIN FOR SMALL, SHORT, BRIEF, PREFIX INDICATING "SMALL" MOST OFTEN MODIFIES THE WORD (or see many)
miniature, *, rist, rize, rizes, rized, rizing, rization, SMALL FORM OF ORIGINAL SIZE "prefixes: sub"
minimais, minimize
minimal, ly, lism, THE LEAST POSSIBLE
minimize, *, ed, zing, MAKE SMALLER, LESS
minimum, *, THE LEAST POSSIBLE "prefixes: sub"
miniscule, minuscule
minister, *, ry, ries, rial, rially, PREACHING ABOUT RELIGION
miniucher, miniature
miniuet, minuet
mink, *, A RODENT

minnow, *, wed, wing, A VERY SMALL FISH
mino, minnow
minogumy, monogamy
minokside, monoxide
minon, mignon
minopos, menopause
minopuly, monopoly
minor, *, BELOW MAJOR, SMALLER THAN, MUSICAL CHORD (or see miner)
minority, ties, SMALLER NUMBER WHEN COMPARED TO PREDOMINANT GROUP
minos, minus / minnow(s)
minotnus, monotony(nous)
minotny, monotony
minow, minnow
minoxite, monoxide
minse, mince
minses, menses
minshen, mention
minsteration, menstruation
minstral, menstrual / minstrel
minstrel, *, ted, ting, ONE WHO ENTERTAINS WITH POETRY/ SONG (or see menstrual)
mint, *, ted, ting, AN HERB, PLACE WHERE COINS ARE MADE (or see meant/ mend)
mintalety, mental(ity)
mintel, mental
minter, mentor
minthol, menthol
mintle, mental
mintor, mentor
mintul, mental
minu, menu
minuet, *, SLOW RYTHM IN MUSIC, DANCE
minural, mineral
minure, manure
minus, MATH EXPRESSION, TAKE AWAY/ SUBTRACT FROM (or see menace)
minuscule, OF LITTLE IMPORTANCE, TINY, ALSO SPELLED "MINISCULE"
minuskule, minuscule
minustrony, minestrone

minute,*,ely,MEASURE OF TIME, RECORD A MEETING, SLIGHT/ SMALL
minuver, maneuver
minyew, menu
minyewet, minuet
minyon, mignon
miol, meal
miosis, meiosis
mir, mere / mire
mirach, mirage
miracle,*,culous, culously, EVENT PRECEDED BY MYSTERIOUS ACTIONS, SEEMINGLY IMPOSSIBLE OCCURRENCE
miraculus, miracle(culous)
mirage,*, AN OPTICAL ILLUSION
mirakle, miracle
miral, morale / mural
mirall, mirage
mirange, meringue
mircantile, mercantile
mirchandise, merchandise
mirchant, merchant
mire,*,ed,ing,ry, DIFFICULT, MUDDY
miread, myriad
mirekul, miracle
mireod, myriad
mirer, mirror
miriad, myriad
mirje, merge
mirkanteel, mercantile
mirky, murky
mirlin, merlin
mirmur, murmur
miroge, mirage
miror, mirror
mirose, morose
mirquery, mercury
mirror,*,red, ring, REFLECTION
mirseful, mercy(ciful)
mirsy, mercy
mirukul, miracle
mirur, mirror
mirurd, mirror(ed)

mis, PREFIX INDICATING "BAD/ WRONG/ WRONGLY" MOST OFTEN MODIFIES THE WORD (or see miss/ mice)
misalaneus, miscellaneous
misaleinios, miscellaneous
misandul, mishandle
misap, mishap
misapprehension,*,NOT CORRECT UNDERSTANDING/ IMPRESSION
misbaleef, misbelief
misbaleve, misbelieve
misbehave,*,ed,ving,vior, TO NOT BEHAVE
misbehavior, NOT BEHAVE
misbelief, DO NOT BELIEVE
misbelieve,*,ed,ving, PAST TENSE FOR THE WORD "MISBELIEF"
misbijeif, misbehave
misbijeiv, misbehave
misbilif, misbelief
misbiliv, misbelieve
misbok, misspoke
misbokin, misspoke(n)
misbuleef, misbelief
miscalculate,*,ed,ting,tion, NOT PROPER CALCULATION
miscalkiuleit, miscalculate
miscarill, miscarriage
miscarriage,*,ed,ging, LOSS IN CARRYING A FETUS TO FULL TERM
miscaunt, miscount
miscellaneous, VARIETY OF ELEMENTS/ THINGS WHICH HAVE NO RELEVANCE TO ONE ANOTHER
mischef, mischief
mischief, evous, evously, evousness, ACTION/ BEHAVIOR THAT CREATES AGITATION FOR OTHERS
misconstrue,*,ed,uing, MISINTERPRET, INCORRECT UNDERSTANDING OF INFORMATION
miscount,*,ted,ting, COUNT DIDN'T COME OUT CORRECTLY
miscownt, miscount
miscuout, misquote
miscwowt, misquote
misd, miss(ed) / mist
misdacism, mystic(icism)

misdaken, mistake(n)
misdamener, misdemeanor
misdemeanor,*, CITED FOR NOT OBEYING SET RULES
misdereus, mysterious
misdirection,*, WRONG DIRECTIONS/ INFORMATION
misdireus, mysterious
misdress, mistress
misdriul, mistrial
misdrus, mistress
misdufy, mystify
misdur, mister
misdury, mystery
mised, miss(ed) / mist
misel, missile
miself, my(self)
miseltoe, mistletoe
misenform, misinform
misenterpret, misinterpret
miser,rly,rliness, ONE WHO IS OVERLY FEARFUL ABOUT USING, SPENDING THEIR MONEY
miserable,ly, eness, EXTREMELY UNCOMFORTABLE, FEELING BEYOND CAPACITY
misery,ries, DREADFUL EMOTIONAL OR PHYSICAL STATE OF BEING
misfaier, misfire
misfayer, misfire
misfire,*,ed,ring, DIDN'T HIT THE TARGET
misfit,*, DOESN'T QUITE FIT IN WITH THE OTHERS
misfortune,*, UNPLANNED DISTURBING EVENT
misgef, mischief
misgiving,*, GIVEN TO DOUBT OR APPREHENSION IN MAKING A JUDGMENT
misguge, misjudge
mishandle,*,ed,ling, TO NOT TREAT CAREFULLY
mishap,* EVENT WHICH RENDERS UNCONTROLLABLE REACTIONS
mishen, mission
mishenary, mission(ary)
misinform,*,,med,ming,mant,mer,mation, NOT CORRECT INFORMATION
misinterpret,*,,ted,ting,tation, DOESN'T REPRESENT THE FACTS
mision, mission

misionary,mission(ary)
misius,misuse
misjap,mishap
misjif,mischief
misjudge,*,ed,ging,ement,MAKE DECISION WITHOUT TAKING ALL FACTS INTO CONSIDERATION
misjuge,misjudge
miskalaneus,miscellaneous
miskalculate,miscalculate
miskarich,miscarriage
miskedo,mosquito
miskeet,mesquite
miskerage,miscarriage
miskeruge,miscarriage
miskonstrue,misconstrue
miskownt,miscount
miskunstrew,misconstrue
misle,missile
mislead,*,ed,ding,MANIPULATE INTO UNDESIRABLE DIRECTION
misled,PAST TENSE FOR THE WORD MISLEAD
misletoe,mistletoe
mislid,mislead
mislloll,misjudge
mislluch,misjudge
mismach,mismatch
mismatch,hes,hed,hing,DO NOT MATCH UP TOGETHER
misnomer,*,INCORRECT NAME FOR
misoge,massage
misoje,massage
misols,measles
misonderstand,misunderstand
misonderstood,misunderstood
mispell,misspell
misplace,*,ed,cing,ement,NOT PLACED WHERE IT NORMALLY BELONGS
misplais,misplace
mispleis,misplace
mispoke,misspoke
mispokin,misspoke(n)
mispranouns,mispronounce
misprint,*,ted,ting,PRINTED INCORRECT INFORMATION

mispronounce,*,ed,cing,nunciation,WORD NOT SPOKEN CORRECTLY
misprunownse,mispronounce
misquote,*,ed,ting,tation,DIDN'T ACCURATELY REFLECT WHAT WAS ACTUALLY SAID
misread,*,TO NOT READ CORRECTLY
misred,misread
misrepresent,*,ted,ting,tation,tative,ter,DOESN'T ACCURATELY REPRESENT
misrepricent,misrepresent
misrid,misread
misruble,miserable
miss,sses,ssed,ssing,NOT IN USUAL/ PREFERRED PLACE, IN REFERENCE TO YOUNG UNMARRIED WOMAN
missile,*,ery,A THROWN OR SHOT PROJECTILE WITH INTENT TO INJURE
mission,*,nary,naries,SET OUT TO COMPLETE A TASK AS IF WITH AUTHORITY
misslede,mislead
misspell,*,lled,lling,TO SPELL INCORRECTLY
misspoke,en,DID NOT SAY WHAT WAS MEANT TO BE SAID, SPOKEN INCORRECTLY
missusage,misuse(sage)
missuse,misuse
mist,*,ted,ting,ty,tily,tiness,VERY LIGHT SPRAY OF WATER, A HAZE (or see midst/ miss(ed))
mistacism,mystic(icism)
mistake,*,en,enly,enness,kable,THINK IT IS SOMETHING IT IS NOT, INCORRECT "prefixes: un"
mistakuble,mistake(kable)
mistamener,misdemeanor
misteek,mystique
mistefy,mystify
mistek,mystic / mystique / mistake
mistektamy,mastectomy
mister,MR.(ABBREVIATION),REFERENCE TO A MAN
mistereus,mysterious
mistic,mystic
misticul,mystic(cal)
mistifai,mystify
mistique,mystique
mistireus,mysterious
mistirios,mysterious

mistletoe,PARASITIC PLANT ON A TREE
mistook,PAST TENSE FOR THE WORD 'MISTAKE'
mistraiol,mistrial
mistreat,*,ted,ting,tment,TREAT SOMETHING/ SOMEONE IMPROPERLY
mistreil,mistrial
mistress,sses,WOMAN IN POSITION OF COMMAND/ RULE
mistret,mistreat
mistrial,*,UNABLE TO MAKE A JUDGMENT IN A TRIAL DUE TO VARIOUS REASONS
mistrit,mistreat
mistro,maestro
mistufy,mystify
mistuk,mistook
misul,missile
misulaneus,miscellaneous
misulf,my(self)
misultoe,mistletoe
misunderstand,*,ding,tood,NOT ABLE TO COMPREHEND/ UNDERSTAND
misunderstood,PAST TENSE FOR THE WORD "MISUNDERSTAND"
misur,miser
misuruble,miserable
misury,misery
misus,miss(es)
misuse,*,ed,sing,er,sage,NOT USING PROPERLY
misuze,misuse
misyus,misuse
mit,mitt / mite / might / meat / meet / met
mitabolize,metabolize
mitachondria,mitochondria
mitagashen,mitigate(tion)
mitagate,mitigate
mitapolize,metabolize
mite,*,TINY INSECT, ANIMAL, SOMETHING TINY (or see might/ mitt/ might)
mitegeit,mitigate
miten,mitten
miter,*,red,ring,REFERENCE TO ANGLES (or see meter)
mitereul,material
miteur,might(ier)

mitevul,medieval
mith,myth
mithakul,myth(ical)
mithalogic,mythologic
mithasize,myth(icize)
mithecul,myth(ical)
mitholagize,mythologic(ize)
mitholochi,mythology
mithology,mythology
mithololli,mythology
mitiest,might(iest)
mitigate,*,able,tion,tive,tor,tory,TO LESSEN A BURDEN OR SEVERITY "prefixes: un"
mitior,meteor
mitiorait,meteorite
mitiorolochi,meteorology
mitiorololli,meteorology
mitir,meter / miter
mitochondria,al,ion,ORGANELLES WITHIN A CELL WHICH ASSIST IN METABOLISM
mitoesis,mitosis
mitosis,ic,CELL DIVISION FROM ORIGINAL CELL "prefixes: endo"
mitropolis,metropolis
mitst,midst
mitt,*,ten,A COVERING FOR THE HAND (or see mite/ might)
mitten,*,HAND COVERING TO PROTECT SKIN FROM GREAT TEMPERATURE DIFFERENCES
mitul,medal / metal / mettle / meddle / middle
mityest,might(iest)
miuchual,mutual
miuciem,museum
miudileit,mutilate
miukes,mucus
miul,mule
miunicipol,municipal
miuques,mucus
miurol,mural
mius,muse
music,music
miusiom,museum

miusishan,musician
miut,mute
miuteid,mutate
miuteit,mutate
miuteni,mutiny
miutileit,mutilate
miutini,mutiny
miutual,mutual
miuzishan,musician
mix,xes,xed,xing,xer,TO BLEND/ STIR VARIOUS ELEMENTS/ ARTICLES/ INGREDIENTS TOGETHER ELIMINATING ORDER "prefixes: inter"
mixchur,mixture
mixture,*,COMBINE DIFFERENT THINGS TOGETHER TO CREATE SOMETHING ENTIRELY DIFFERENT "prefix: inter"
mizconstsrue,misconstrue
mizdakin,mistake(n)
mizdamener,misdemeanor
mizdereus,mysterious
mizdress,mistress
mizdrus,mistress
mizdur,mister
mizdury,mystery
mizenformation,misinform(ation)
mizenturpret,misinterpret
mizer,miser
mizeruble,miserable
mizfet,misfit
mizfire,misfire
mizforchen,misfortune
mizgeving,misgiving
mizhandul,mishandle
mizhap,mishap
mizinform,misinform
mizkunstrew,misconstrue
mizkwote,misquote
mizled,misled
mizleed,mislead
mizmach,mismatch
miznomer,misnomer
mizpell,misspell
mizplase,misplace

mizpronounce,mispronounce
mizread,misread
mizreprezent,misrepresent
miztake,mistake
miztakuble,mistake(kable)
miztamener,misdemeanor
mizteek,mystique
miztek,mystic
mizter,mister
miztereus,mysterious
miztress,mistress
miztret,mistreat
miztrial,mistrial
mizunderstand,misunderstand
mizur,miser
mizury,misery
mizuse,misuse
mo,mow
moan,*,ned,ning,A LOW, GUTTURAL SOUND COMING FROM THE THROAT
moat,*,DUG OUT TRENCH AROUND A STRUCTURE WHICH IS NORMALLY FILLED WITH WATER (or see mote)
mob,*,bbed,bbing,GATHERING OF LARGE GROUP OF PEOPLE
mobal,mobile
mobalezation,mobile(lization)
mobalize,mobile(lize)
mobelity,mobile(lity)
mobeluzation,mobile(lization)
mobile,lity,lize,lized,lizing,lizer,lization,ABILITY TO BE PHYSICALLY ON THE MOVE, TEMPORARY "prefixes: im"
moble,mobile
mobt,mop(ped) / mope(d)
mobul,mobile
mobulization,mobile(lization)
mobulize,mobile(lize)
moc,mach / make / mock
moca,mocha
mocasin,moccasin
moccasin,*,SOFT LEATHER SHOE/ BOOT
moch,much / mock

mocha, COLOR, TYPE OF COFFEE
mochen, motion
mochenist, machine(nist)
mochiul, module
mochuleit, modulate
mochure, mature
mock, *, ked, king, kery, keries, kingly, ker, DISRESPECTFULLY MIMIC/ IMITATE SOMEONE (or see mach)
mocksy, moxie
mocsj, moxie
mocusen, moccasin
mod, mode / mud / mood
modafekashen, modify(fication)
modafy, modify
modal, *, llly, lity, lities, OF MODE/ MANNER/ FORM "prefixes: bi/ inter"
modavashen, motive(vation)
modavate, motive(vate)
mode, *, POSITION/ TYPE/ USAGE/ WAY/ FORM
modeef, motif
modef, motive
modefekashen, modify(fication)
modefy, modify
model, *, led, ling, ler, ABOUT SHAPE/ STYLE/ FORM (or see modal/ mottle/ motel/ muddle)
moder, motor / mutter
moderate, *, ed, ting, tion, tor, BETWEEN EXTREMES OF HIGH/ LOW, IN BETWEEN "prefixes: im"
moderet, moderate
moderet, moderate
modern, nism, nist, nistic, nize, nizes, nized, nizing, nizer, nization, CURRENT IN STYLE/ FASHION, TRENDY
modest, tly, ty, ties, MODERATE IN DEMEANOR, NOT EXTREME "prefixes: im"
modevashen, motive(vation)
modevate, motive(vate)
modeve, motive
modewlashen, modulate(tion)
modgual, module
modgul, module
modi, mood / muddy

modify, fies, fied, fying, fication, ficative, ficatory, fiable, fier, CHANGE/ ALTER THE MODE/ CONFIGURATION OR OPERATION OF
modil, modal / model / mottle
modiol, module
modir, motor
modireit, moderate
modirn, modern
modisly, modest(lly)
modist, modest
modisty, modest
modiuleit, modulate
modivashen, motive(vation)
modivate, motive(vate)
modive, motive
modjual, module
modjulashen, modulate(tion)
modjule, module
modle, modal / model / mottle
modo, motto
moduf, motive
moduficashen, modify(fication)
modul, modal / model / module / mottle
modulate, *, ed, ting, tion, tor, tory, ABILITY TO ADJUST TO ACCEPTABLE FREQUENCY "prefixes: inter"
module, *, lar, larity, lus, li, A STANDARDIZED SIZE/ SHAPE/ DIMENSION, PRE-MADE
modur, motor
modurashen, moderate(tion)
moduret, moderate
modurise, motor(ize)
modurn, modern
modurnasation, modern(ization)
moduvashen, motive(vation)
moduvate, motive(vate)
mody, mood
moer, mow(er)
moest, moist
mof, mauve / move
mofin, muffin
mofment, move(ment)
mog, mug
mogi, muggy

mogma, magma
mogulate, modulate
mogule, module
moguler, module(lar)
mohair, *, HAIR OF ANGORA GOAT
mohare, mohair
moir, mow(er)
moist, ten, tens, tened, tening, ture, turize, turizes, turized, turizing, turizer, tness, BETWEEN DRY/ WET, MORE THAN DAMP
mojul, module
mojulate, modulate
mojulir, module(lar)
mok, mach / make / mock
moka, mocha
mokasen, moccasin
mokery, mock(ery)
mokesin, moccasin
moksy, moxie
moku, mocha
mol, mall / maul / mole
molakul, molecule
molakuler, molecule(lar)
molar, *, rity, A TOOTH, CHEMISTRY AMOUNT "prefixes: pre"
molarky, malarkey
molasis, molasses
molasses, RICH/ DARK SYRUP
molch, mulch
mold, *, ded, ding, dy, diness, dable, FUNGI, CONTAINER USED TO MAKE A FORM, USED FOR FRAMING/ FINISHING WORK (or see molt/ maul(ed)) "prefixes: un"
moldibul, mold(able)
molduble, mold(able)
mole, *, A CHEMISTRY MEASUREMENT OF WEIGHT, A RODENT, A BEAUTY MARK, GROWTH ON SKIN
molecule, *, lar, larly, larity, TINY PARTICLES SUSPECTED TO EXIST BUT CANNOT BE SEEN "prefixes: bi/ bio/ inter/ intra"
molekiul, molecule
molekuler, molecule(lar)
molejiul, molecule

moler, molar
moleshes, malicious
molest, *, ted, ting, ter, tation, TO PHYSICALLY FORCE SOMEONE INTO AN UNACCEPTABLE SITUATION
molicious, malicious
molikule, molecule
moll, mall / maul / mole
mollusk, *, INVERTEBRATE GENERALLY WITH SHELLS AND NO SEGMENTS
molt, *, ted, ting, ter, TO SHED OUTER LAYER SUCH AS SKIN (or see mold/ malt/ maul(ed))
molti, multi
moltiplai, multiply
molur, molar
molusk, mollusk
mom, *, mma, mmy, PARENT WHO PERFORMED THE BIRTHING
moma, mamma
mombol, mumble
momendus, moment(ous)
moment, *, tary, tarily, tariness, tly, tous, tously, tousness, tum, VERY BRIEF MEASURE/ AMOUNT OF TIME
momento, memento
momentus, moment(ous)
momi, mummy
mominshus, moment(ious)
momint, moment
mominterily, moment(arily)
mominto, memento
momintum, moment(um)
momintus, moment(ous)
mon, PREFIX INDICATING "ALONG/ ONLY/ SINGLE" MOST OFTEN MODIFIES THE WORD (or see moan/ moon)
monafilament, monofilament
monagram, monogram
monakiuler, monocular
monalith, monolith
monalithic, monolith(ic)
monalogue, monologue
monaniucleosis, mononucleosis
monanukleosis, mononucleosis
monarale, monorail

monarch, *, hal, hial, hally, hical, hically, hism, hist, histic, hy,hies, LARGE BUTTERFLY, POWERFUL POSITION, SOLE RULER
monark, monarch
monarkial, monarch(ial)
monastery, ries, rial, tic, tical, ticism, PLACE OF ISOLATION
monater, monitor
monatone, monotone
monaxaid, monoxide
mondane, mundane
monday, *, A DAY OF THE WEEK (ENGLISH)
mondei, Monday
mondein, mundane
mone, moan / money
monee, money
monegram, monogram
monelogue, monologue
monenukleosis, mononucleosis
monerale, monorail
monestasism, monastery(tacism)
monestery, monastery
monetary, rily, tize, tization, rist, OF MONEY
monetone, monotone
monetor, monitor
monewment, monument
money, nies, MINTED COIN AND PAPER USED FOR EXCHANGE OF ITEMS OR SERVICES
mongrel, *, ly, lism, lize, lizes, lized, lizing, lization, MIXED BREED OF DOG
mongril, mongrel
mongrul, mongrel
monie, money
monigram, monogram
monilogue, monologue
moninukleosis, mononucleosis
monirale, monorail
monistery, monastery
monitary, monetary
monitone, monotone
monitor, *, red, ring, ry, rship, ENFORCER OF RULES, A MACHINE THAT READS VITAL LIFE SIGNS "prefixes: bio"
moniument, monument

monk, *, khood, kish, kishly, kishness, kery, keries, ONE WHO PRACTICES TO OVERCOME EGO
monkey, kies, ying, ANIMAL, MAMMAL, TO ACT LIKE A MONKEY
mono, SHORT FOR MONONUCLEOSIS, PREFIX INDICATING "ALONG/ ONLY/ SINGLE" MOST OFTEN MODIFIES THE WORD
monocsaid, monoxide
monocular, *, ITEM WHERE ONE EYE CAN SEE MAGNIFICATION
monofilament, *, ONE FILAMENT IN A BULB
monogamy, mous, mic, mist, mistic, mously, mousness, ADULT WHO ACCEPTS ONLY ONE PARTNER
monogram, *, med, ming, matic, LETTER/ CHARACTER REPRESENTING A NAME
monolith, hic, hically, SINGLE SKIN, STONE
monologue, *, gic, gist, gize, ONE PERSON WHO SPEAKS
mononucleosis, ONE-NUCLEUS BLOOD CELLS RESULTANT FROM A VIRUS
monopoly, lies, ONE COMPANY DOMINATES LEAVING NO CHOICE
monorail, *, A SINGLE RAIL FOR TRAVEL
monotary, monetary
monotone, *, nosity, ONE TONE
monotony, nous, nously, nousness, REPETITION, SAME THING OVER AND OVER AGAIN
monoureil, monorail
monowtoun, monotone
monoxide, ONE OXYGEN ATOM IN A MOLECULE
monsoon, *, GREAT RUSH OF RAIN IN A CERTAIN SEASON WHICH LASTS FOR MONTHS
monster, *, red, ring, trance, trous, trosity, USED TO DESCRIBE SOMETHING UNUSUAL/ FRIGHTENING, RELIGIOUS VESSEL, DRUNK
monstrasute, monstrosity
monstrausete, monstrosity
monstres, monstrous
monstrocity, monstrosity
monstrosete, monstrosity
monstrosity, sities, ous, USED TO DESCRIBE SOMETHING UNUSUAL/ FRIGHTENING/ ABNORMAL
monstrous, sly, sness, osity, USED TO DESCRIBE SOMETHING UNUSUAL/ FRIGHTENING

monstrus, monstrous
monstur, monster
monsune, monsoon
monten, mountain
month, *, hly, hlies, A MEASURE OF TIME WHICH DIVIDES DAYS OF THE YEAR INTO SECTIONS "prefixes: bi/ semi"
montin, mountain
monuer, manure
monugram, monogram
monulithic, monolith(ic)
monulogue, monologue
monument, *, tal, tally, talize, A MARKER/ STONE/ ARTICLE/ STRUCTURE IN HONOR OF SOMEONE/ SOMETHING
monumint, monument
monurale, monorail
monure, manure
monustery, monastery
monutary, monetary
monutone, monotone
mony, money
monyument, monument
monzoon, monsoon
monzter, monster
mood, *, dy, dier, diest, dily, diness, AN EMOTIONAL STATE OF MIND (or see moot/ mute)
moodyness, mood(iness)
moof, move
moofuble, move(vable)
moon, *, ned, ning, nish, nishly, ny, LARGEST PLANET SEEN AT NIGHT, A PRANK
moor, *, red, ring, rage, A BOG, A PLACE TO DOCK A BOAT, ACT OF DOCKING A SHIP (or see more) "prefixes: un"
moose, A LARGE MEMBER OF THE DEER FAMILY (or see mouse/ mousse)
moot, tness, UP FOR DISCUSSION WITHOUT DECISION, ARGUABLE, DEBATABLE (or see mute/ mood)
mootiness, mood(iness)
mooty, mood
moove, move

mop, *, pped, pping, AN ITEM USED WET TO CLEAN FLOORS (or see mob/ map)
mope, *, ed, ping, per, pey, TO BE DISINTERESTED DUE TO SADNESS/ BEING BORED, TO HAVE LOW SPIRITS (or see mop)
moped, mop(ped) / mope(d)
mopt, mop(ped) / mope(d)
mor, mar / more / moor
moral, *, lly, lism, list, listic, lize, lizes, lized, lizing, lization, lizer, ABILITY TO JUDGE/ BEHAVE RIGHT FROM WRONG (or see morale/ morel) "prefixes: im/ un"
morale, *, lity, lities, CONDITION/ STATE OF ONE'S ABILITY TO JUDGE/ ACT ON THOSE JUDGMENT (or see mural/ moral/ morel)
moralestic, moral(istic)
moraly, moral(ly)
moratorium, *, ry, A PURPOSELY IMPOSED DELAY FOR AN UNDETERMINED AMOUNT OF TIME
morbed, morbid
morbedly, morbid(ly)
morbel, marble
morbet, morbid
morbid, dly, dness, dity, AKIN TO DEATH/ DARKNESS
morbidety, morbid(ity)
morbil, marble
morbit, morbid
morbul, marble
morc, mark
morch, march
morchin, margin
morchoery, mortuary
morchuery, mortuary
mordar, mortar
mordel, mortal
mordir, mortar
mordul, mortal
morduly, mortal(ly)
mordur, mortar
more, OF A GREATER NUMBER WHEN COMPARING, GREATER (or see moor/ mow(er))
morege, moor(age)
morel, *, EDIBLE MUSHROOM (or see moral/ morale)
morelise, moral(ize)

morelistic, moral(istic)
mores, SOCIAL ACCEPTANCE
moretoreum, moratorium
morgage, mortgage
morge, morgue
morgech, mortgage
morgedge, mortgage
morgeje, mortgage
morgen, margin
morgenulize, marginalize
morgerin, margarine
morgesh, mortgage
morgije, mortgage
morgue, *, PLACE WHERE BODIES WITHOUT SPIRITS ARE TEMPORARILY HELD
morige, moor(age)
moril, moral / morel
morily, moral(ly)
moritoreum, moratorium
morjaren, margarine
morjenulize, marginalize
mork, morgue
morlarin, margarine
morlin, margin
mormaleid, marmalade
mormuleid, marmalade
morn, mourn / morning
mornen, morning / mourn(ing)
morneng, mourn(ing) / morning
mornful, mourn(ful)
mornin, morning / mourn(ing)
morning, *, MORN, FIRST PART OF THE DAY BEFORE 12 NOON (or see mourn(ing))
moroon, maroon
morose, ely, eness, sity, GLOOMY OR DARK THOUGHTS, IDEAS, BEHAVIOR
morotoreum, moratorium
morph, PREFIX INDICATING "SHAPE/ FORM/ STRUCTURE" MOST OFTEN MODIFIES THE WORD
mors, mores
morshuery, mortuary
mortal, *, lly, lity, lities, RELATED TO DEATH/ KILLING/ DYING "prefixes: im"

mortaledy, mortal(ity)
mortalidy, mortal(ity)
mortar, *, MIXTURE USED FOR JOINTS TO HOLD BRICK, VESSEL SHAPE WITH A PESTLE
mortel, mortal
morter, mortar
mortgage, *, ed, ging, ger, gor, TITLE/ DEED OF PROPERTY HELD BY SOMEONE WHICH REQUIRES MONEY TO OWN/ HAVE
mortil, mortal
mortingeil, martingale
mortir, mortar
mortuary, ries, A FUNERAL HOME
mortul, mortal
mortur, mortar
morul, moral
morulesm, moral(ism)
morulestic, moral(istic)
morulise, moral(ize)
moruly, moral(ly)
moryarin, margarine
mos, moss / most
mosaic, *, cally, cist, MANY PIECES PLACED TOGETHER TO FORM A PICTURE
mosayic, mosaic
mosdereus, mysterious
mosdly, most(ly)
mose, moose / mousse
moseic, mosaic
moseik, mosaic
mosektimy, mastectomy
mosel, mussel / muscle
moshen, motion
moshenist, machine(nist)
moshrun, mushroom
mosk, mosque
moskeet, mesquite
mosketo, mosquito
moskewlur, muscle(cular)
moslin, muslin
mosly, most(ly)
mosol, muscle / mussel

mosoleum, mausoleum
mosoose, masseuse
mosque, *, A BUILDING WHERE MUSLIMS PRAY
mosquito, oes, oey, AN INSECT WHO SEEKS BLOOD
mosquler, muscle(cular)
moss, sses, ssy, ssier, ssiest, ssiness, A PLANT GROWTH
most, tly, PAST TENSE FOR THE WORD MORE, THE GREATEST AMOUNT IN COMPARISON TO ANOTHER AMOUNT (or see must) "prefixes: under/ up/ upper"
mostache, mustache / moustache
mostang, mustang
mostard, mustard
mostash, mustache / moustache
mostectemy, mastectomy
moster, monster / muster
mostereus, mysterious
mostique, mystique
mosuleum, mausoleum
mosuse, masseuse
mot, moat / mutt / mode / mote
metabolize, metabolize
motafikashen, modify(fication)
motapolize, metabolize
motavashen, motive(vation)
motchewlate, modulate
motchulashen, modulate(tion)
motchulate, modulate
mote, SPECK, PARTICLE (or see moat/ mode)
moteef, motif
motef, motif / motive
motel, *, LODGING WHERE YOU CAN PARK YOUR VEHICLE NEAR THE DOOR (or see mottle)
moter, motor / mutter
moterashen, moderate(tion)
moteret, moderate
motereul, material
moterise, motor(ize)
motern, modern
moternul, maternal
motevashen, motive(vation)
moth, *, A NOCTURNAL INSECT

mother, *, red, ring, rly, rless, rlessness, ONE WHO HAS GIVEN BIRTH, BACTERIAL COATING ON FERMENTING LIQUIDS, ORIGINATOR OF LIFE
motif, RECURRING THEME IN VISUAL PRESENTATION (or see motive)
motil, modal / mode / mottle
motion, *, nal, ned, ning, nless, nlessness, ACTIVITY, MOVEMENT
motir, motor
motirn, modern
motivashen, motive(vation)
motive, *, vate, vates, vated, vating, vation, vational, vative, vity, ENCOURAGE TO PERFORM ALONG IN A PLANNED DIRECTION (or see motif)
motle, mottle / modal / model
motled, mottle(d) / model(ed)
moto, motto
moton, mutton
motor, *, red, ring, rist, rize, rized, rizing, rization, AN ENGINE/ DEVICE USED TO CREATE MOTION
motour, motor
mottle, ed, er, ling, SPLOTCHY IN COLOR, PATCHES OF IRREGULAR SHAPES
motto, *, A CONCISE DESCRIPTION OF PRINCIPLE OR PURPOSE
motul, modal / model / mottle
motur, motor
moturashen, moderate(tion)
moturet, moderate
moturise, motor(ize)
moturn, modern
moturnize, modern(ize)
motuv, motive
motuvashen, motive(vation)
motuvate, motive(vate)
moubaiol, mobile
moubol, mobile
mouca, mocha
moucus, mucus
moud, mode / mood
mouder, motor
moueic, mosaic
moujeir, mohair

moujer, mohair
moul, mole / mold / mall
moular, molar
moun, moan
mound, *, ded, ding, A SMALL HILL/ PILE/ HEAP (or see mount)
mount, *, ted, ting, TO SIT ATOP OF, SHORT FOR MOUNTAIN, AFFIX SOMETHING, GET ON TOP OF "prefixes: dis/ re/ sur"
mountain, *, neer, nous, nously, nousness, GREAT HILLS OF ORGANIC MATTER, LARGE JUTTING EXTRUSIONS OF EARTH "prefixes: inter"
mounteneer, mountain(eer)
mountenus, mountain(ous)
mountin, mountain
moup, mope
mour, mow(er)
mourn, *, ned, ning, ningly, nful, nfully, nfulness, ner, EMOTIONALLY EXPERIENCE LOSS OF SOMETHING (or see morning)
mouse, er, sing, ey, mice, SMALL RODENT (or see moose/ mousse)
moushon, motion
mousse, DESSERT (or see mouse/ moose)
moust, most
moustache, FACIAL HAIR GROWING ABOVE THE LIP, ALSO SPELLED "MUSTACHE"
mout, moat / mote
moutel, motel
moutenus, mountain(ous)
mouth, *, hed, hing, her, hful, hfuls, hy, ORIFICE ON THE FACE WHICH MAKES SOUNDS/ INGESTS
moutif, motif
moutiv, motive
mov, mauve / move
movd, move(d)
move, *, ed, ving, vingly, er, vable, vableness, vably, vability, eless, elessly, elessness, ement, RELOCATE/ CHANGE FROM ONE PLACE/ LOCATION TO ANOTHER, BE IN MOTION "prefixes: im/ non/ re/ un"
movie, *, PICTURES IN MOTION
movment, move(ment)

mow, *, wed, wing, wer, CUT GRASS/ BRUSH WITH A TOOL/ MACHINE, REMOVE/ LOWER IN WIDE SWATHES
mowder, motor
mowenus, mountain(ous)
mownd, mound
mownden, mountain
mownt, mound / mount
mownten, mountain
mowse, mouse
mowten, mountain
mowteneer, mountain(eer)
mowtenus, mountain(ous)
mowth, mouth
mowtin, mountain
mowtinus, mountain(ous)
moxie, COURAGE, ASSERTIVE
moxy, moxie
moyeast, moist
moyster, moist(ure)
moysturize, moist(urize)
mozaek, mosaic
mozayic, mosaic
mozed, most
mozel, muzzle
mozly, most(ly)
mozoleum, mausoleum
mozt, most
mozuleim, mausoleum
mperical, empirical
mpethy, empathy
mpithy, empathy
mportant, important
mportens, important(nce)
mportent, important
mpress, impress
mpurfikt, imperfect
mputhy, empathy
mr, mister
mrk, mark
mt, empty
mubiledy, mobile(lity)
mubility, mobile(lity)

mucaw, macaw
mucel, muscle / mussel
much, AMOUNT OF SOMETHING, SIZABLE QUANTITY
muchanek, mechanic
muchanekul, mechanic(al))
muchene, machine
muchenist, machine(nist)
muchety, machete
muchual, mutual
muchure, mature
muchuredy, mature(rity)
muchurle, mature(ly)
muchyual, mutual
mucus, coid, citis, sity, cous, SLIPPERY SECRETED SUBSTANCE FOR PROTECTION OF SKIN
mud, *, dded, dding, ddy, DIRT MIXED WITH WATER (or see mood/ mutt)
mudalate, mutilate
muddle, *, ed, ling, TO CONFUSE, MAKE UNCLEAR, MAKE A MESS, CREATE DISORDER
muddy, ddies, ddier, ddiest, ddying, ddily, ddiness, WATER MIXED WITH DIRT
mude, mood / mute / muddy
mudel, muddle
mudelate, mutilate
muden, mutton
mudeness, mood(iness)
muder, mutter
mudereul, material
mudereulise, materialize
mudernol, maternal
mudiest, muddy(diest)
mudil, muddle
mudilate, mutilate
mudir, mutter
mudle, muddle
mudon, mutton
mudul, muddle
mudur, mutter
mudy, muddy / mood
mudyest, muddy(diest)
muer, moor
muerege, moor(age)

muf,move / muff
mufan,muffin / move(ving)
mufd,move(d) / muff(ed)
mufee,movie
mufen,muffin / move(ving)
muff,*,ffed,ffing,BE CLUMSY, BUNGLE SOMETHING, HAND WARMER, TUFT ON BIRDS/ FOWL
muffen,muffin
muffin,*,BAKED DESSERT
muffler,*,KEEPS LOUD NOISES QUIET
mufin,muffin
mufler,muffler
mufment,move(ment)
muft,move(d)
mufuble,move(vable)
mug,*,gged,gging,gger,ggy,DRINKING VESSEL, SOMEONE WHO ASSAULTS WITH INTENT TO ROB, A FACE, WARM/ DAMP/ STILL AIR
mugd,mug(gged)
muge,muggy
mugeness,muggy(giness)
mugestekal,majesty(tical)
mugestik,majesty(tic)
muggie,muggy
muggy,ggily,gginess,WARM AND HUMID
mugi,muggy
mugishen,magic(ian)
mugority,major(ity)
mugy,muggy
mugynes,muggy(giness)
muir,moor
muj,much
mujestical,majesty(tical)
mujishen,magic(ian)
mukanek,mechanic
mukanekul,mechanic(al)
mukaw,macaw
mukus,mucus
mul,mull / mule / mole / mall
mulado,mulato
muladou,mulato
mularea,malaria
mularky,malarkey

mulasis,molasses
mulato,oes,MIXTURE OF RACES OR BREEDS
mulch,hes,hed,hing,TO TILL UP GROUND, ADD ORGANIC MATERIAL TO SOIL
muldaplekashen,multiplication
muldapikation,multiplication
muldiply,multiply
mule,*,lish,HYBRID MAMMAL/ PLANT, STUBBORN PERSON, SHOE WITHOUT A BACK (or see mull)
mulecious,malicious
mulekuler,molecule(lar)
muleneum,millennium
muleshes,malicious
mulest,molest
mulevolens,malevolent(nce)
mulevolent,malevolent
mulicious,malicious
mulignant,malignant
mulinium,millennium
mulk,milk
mull,*,A FABRIC, TO STUDY/ THINK ABOUT, MUSLIN, HUMUS (or see mule)
mullenium,millennium
multaplekashen,multiplication
multaply,multiply
multch,mulch
multeply,multiply
multi,PREFIX INDICATING "MUCH/ MANY" MOST OFTEN MODIFIES THE WORD
multiplai,multiply
multiple,*,ly,lies,lied,lying,lier,licity,lication, DUPLICATES, A NUMBER THAT CAN BE DIVIDED WITH NO REMAINDERS "prefixes: sub"
multiplekashen,multiplication
multiplication,tive,tively,THE ACT OF WORKING NUMBERS TIMES NUMBERS
multiply,lies,lied,lying,lier,licity,TO INCREASE NUMBERS BY REPRODUCTION, ADDING NUMBERS TIMES NUMBERS, MATH
mumble,*,ed,ling,er,lingly,TO SPEAK WITHOUT ANNUNCIATING OR BE UNINTELLIGIBLE, SPOKEN WORDS NOT UNDERSTANDABLE
mumbul,mumble

mume,mummy
mummy,mmies,mmify,mmification,A DRIED UP CORPSE, WORD FOR MOM IN ENGLAND
mumps,A VIRUS WHICH ATTACKS THE THROAT
mumy,mummy
mun,moon
munarkikul,monarch(ical)
munarky,monarch
munda,monday
mundane,ely,eness,DULL ROUTINE
munday,monday
mundein,mundane
mune,moon / money
munepulate,manipulate
munesipality,municipal(ity)
munesipul,municipal
municipal,*,lity,lities,lly,lize,lization,TOWN/ CITY GOVERNED BY/ WITH ITS OWN LAWS
munie,money
munila,manila
manipulate,manipulate
munisepal,municipal
munisepality,municipal(ity)
munisipal,municipal
munk,monk
munkee,monkey
munky,monkey
munodnes,monotony(nous)
munogemy,monogamy
munogimy,monogamy
munokside,monoxide
munokuler,monocular
munopuly,monopoly
munorkeul,monarch(ial)
munotny,monotony
munotunus,monotony(nous)
munoxide,monoxide
munsoon,monsoon
munstrocity,monstrocity
munstrosedy,monstrocity
munsune,monsoon
munth,month
munthly,month(ly)

munure,manure
munuver,maneuver
muny,money
muraculus,miracle(culous)
muraje,mirage
murakulus,miracle(culous)
mural,*,LARGE PAINTING APPLIED ONTO A WALL
muralady,morale(lity)
murality,morale(lity)
murange,meringue
murchandise,merchandise
murchant,merchant
murder,*,red,ring,rer,rous,rousness,KILL SOMEONE UNLAWFULLY
murdir,murder
murdur,murder
murege,moor(age)
murel,mural
murena,marina
murene,marine
murge,merge
murgur,merge(r)
muridean,meridian
muril,mural
murina,marina
murine,marine
murje,merge
murk,murky
murkanteel,mercantile
murkery,mercury
murky,kily,kiness,DARK, SILTY OR THICK LIQUID/ AIR, GLOOMY
murlin,merlin
murmade,mermaid
murmer,murmur
murmir,murmur
murmur,*,rer,ring,ringly,rous,rously,A LOW STEADY STREAM OF SOUND, MUFFLED SOUND
muroge,mirage
muroje,mirage
murose,morose
mursenary,mercenary
mursinary,mercenary

mursy,mercy
mursyful,mercy(ciful)
murul,mural
murun,maroon
mus,mouse / mousse / moose
musal,mussel / muscle / muzzle
muscle,*,ed,ling,cular,cularity,cularly,THICK TISSUE WHICH MOVES BONES (or see mussel/ muzzle) "prefixes: intra/ non"
musdach,moustache
musdake,mistake
musdakin,mistake(n)
musderd,mustard
musdurd,mustard
muse,*,ed,sing,singly,er,WHAT INSPIRES AN ARTIST, A DEEP THINK/ CONTEMPLATION (or see mouse/ mousse)
musec,music
musecal,music(al)
musecian,musician
musecul,music(al)
musek,music
musektome,mastectomy
musekul,music(al)
musel,mussel / muscle / muzzle
museshen,musician
museum,*,A STRUCTURE FOR EXHIBITS OF INTERESTING ITEMS
mushedy,machete
mushene,machine
mushenest,machine(nist)
mushete,machete
mushinary,machine(ry)
mushroom,*,med,ming,FUNGI WITH BELL SHAPED HEAD ON A STEM
mushrum,mushroom
mushual,mutual
music,cal,cally,cality,calness,cian,TONES, SOUNDS PLAYED IN HARMONY ON INSTRUMENTS, PLEASING SOUND TO EARS "prefixes: un"
musician,*,nly,nship,PROFESSIONALLY INVOLVED IN CREATING MUSIC
musik,music

musil,mussel / muscle / muzzle
musishen,musician
muskedo,mosquito
muskeet,mesquite
muskera,mascara
musketo,mosquito
muskuler,muscle(cular)
musle,mussel / muscle / muzzle
muslen,muslin
muslin,*,MEDIUM WEIGHT COTTON CLOTH
musoge,massage
musoje,massage
musol,muscle / mussel / muzzle
musoose,masseuse
musquedo,mosquito
musquler,muscle(cular)
mussel,*,EDIBLE MARINE MOLLUSK WITH SHELL (or see muscle/ muzzle)
mussle,mussel / muscle / muzzle
must,HAS TO BE,IMPERATIVE
mustach,moustache
mustache,*,HAIR ON TOP OF THE UPPER LIP ON ADULT MALES, ALSO SPELLED "MOUSTACHE"
mustake,mistake
mustakin,mistake(n)
mustang,*,WILD HORSES
mustard,AN HERB USED AS A CONDIMENT
muster,*,red,ring,TO GATHER/ COLLECT/ ASSEMBLE
musterd,mustard
mustereus,mysterious
mustir,muster
mustird,mustard
mustireus,mysterious
musturd,mustard
musuese,masseuse
musul,muscle / mussel / muzzle
mususe,masseuse
mut,mutt / mute / mud / moot
mutabolize,metabolize
mutalate,mutilate
mutapolize,metabolize
mutashen,mutate(tion)

mutate,*,ed,ting,tive,tion,ant,ENDURED CHROMOSOME ALTERATION
mutch,much
mutchuel,mutual
mute,*,ed,ting,ely,eness,tism,NO SPEECH,UNABLE TO SPEAK (or see mutt/ moot)
mutelate,mutilate
muten,mutton / mutate(ant)
mutent,mutate(ant)
muteny,mutiny
muter,mutter
mutereolise,materialize
mutereul,material
muternedy,maternity
muternol,maternal
muternulistek,maternal(istic)
muther,mother
muthor,mother
mutil,muddle
mutilashen,mutilate(tation)
mutilate,*,ed,ting,tion,tor,TO SHRED,RIP,TEAR BEYOND RECOGNITION
mutin,mutton
mutint,mutate(ant)
mutiny,nous,RESISTANCE TO AUTHORITY BY MORE THAN ONE ENTITY
mutir,mutter
mutireul,material
mutirnil,maternal
mutle,muddle
muton,mutton
mutony,mutiny
mutt,*, MIXED BREED (or see mute)
mutter,*,red,ring,ringly, TO MURMUR, SPEAK LOW AND UNINTELLIGIBLY, UNDECIPHERABLE SPEECH
mutton,*, SHEEP MEAT
mutual,*,lly,lism,list,listic, ity,lize,lization,CONSENT TO SHARE/ AGREE
mutul,muddle
mutulashen,mutilate(tation)
mutune,mutiny
mutur,mature / mutter
muty,muddy / mood

muud,mood
muvd,move(d)
muve,move / movie
muvee,movie
muvi,movie
muvuble,move(vable)
muzdake,mistake
muzeim,museum
muzektame,mastectomy
muzekul,music(al)
muzel,muzzle
muzeshen,musician
muzeum,museum
muzik,music
muzikul,music(al)
muzishen,musician
muzlen,muslin
muzlin,muslin
muzt,must
muztake,mistake
muzter,muster
muztereus,mysterious
muzul,muzzle
muzzle,*,ed,ling,er, DEVICE TO RESTRAIN ANIMALS FROM BITING (or see muscle) "prefixes: un"
my, MYSELF, DENOTES OWNERSHIP, PREFIX INDICATING "MUSCLE" MOST OFTEN MODIFIES THE WORD
myc, PREFIX INDICATING "FUNGUS" MOST OFTEN MODIFIES THE WORD
mycrascope,microscope
mycrobeul,microbe(bial)
mycron,micron
mycrophone,microphone
myder,miter
mydokondrea,mitochondria
mydukondrea,mitochondria
mygrane,migraine
mygrashen,migrate(tion)
mygrate,migrate
mygratory,migrate(tory)
mykrafone,microphone
mykraskope,microscope
mykro,micro

mykrobe,microbe
mykrofone,microphone
mykrometer,micrometer
mykron,micron
mykrowave,microwave
myld,mild
myluge,mile(age)
myme,mime
myn,mine
mynd,mind / mend
myne,mine
myreod,myriad
myriad,MANY,MORE THAN TEN THOUSAND
mysdacism,mystic(icism)
mystecal,mystic(cal)
mysteek,mystique
mystek,mystique / mystic
mystereus,mysterious
mysterious,sly,sness,OF THE UNKNOWN, NOT ENOUGH FACTS TO UNDERSTAND
mystery,ries,rious,NOT ENOUGH FACTS TO UNDERSTAND,THE UNKNOWN
mystic,*,cal,cally,calness,cism,ify, A MYSTERY, THE UNSEEN/ UNEXPLAINED (or see mystique)
mystify,fies,fied,fying,fyingly,fication,PURPOSELY MISLEAD/ BE VAGUE
mystique,BELIEF/ AURA OF MYSTERIOUS POWER (or see mystic)
mystirious,mysterious
mystukul,mystic(cal)
mystury,mystery
mysulf,my(self)
myt,mitt / mite / might
myter,miter
myth,*, hic, hical, hically, hicize, hicizes, hicized, hicizing, hicization, hicizer, hography, hology,A STORY SURVIVING HISTORY THAT ISN'T SUPPORTED BY FACT
mythologic,cal,cally,OF MYTHS, LEGENDS, FOLKLORE
mythology,gies,gize,gizes,gized,gizing,gization,gize,gic, OF THE UNKNOWN,ATTEMPT TO EXPLAIN THE UNKNOWN
mytochondrea,mitochondria

mytokondrea, mitochondria
mytosis, mitosis
n, in / inn
nab,*, bbed, bbing, bber, TO GRAB/ SEIZE/ CATCH UNEXPECTEDLY
naber, neighbor
naberhood, neighbor (hood)
nabir, neighbor
nabken, napkin
nabkin, napkin
nabor, neighbor
naborhud, neighbor(hood)
nabt, nab(bed) / nap(ped)
nabur, neighbor
naburhood, neighbor (hood)
nacessity, necessity
nach, notch
nacheirpath, naturopath
nachen, nation
nachenaluty, nation(ality)
nachenul, nation(al)
nacher, nature
nacheralist, natural(ist)
nacheropethy, naturopath
nacherul, natural
nacheruly, natural(ly)
naches, nauseous
nachinal, nation(al)
nachir, nature
nachon, nation
nachrul, natural
nachur, nature
nachuril, natural
nachurily, natural(ly)
nachuropath, naturopath
nachuropathy, naturopath
nachus, nauseous
nadal, natal
nadef, native
nadefly, native(ly)
nadical, nautical
nadilus, nautilus
nadive, native

nadle, natal
nadol, natal
naduf, native
nady, naughty / knot(ty)
naefe, naive
naem, name
naevet, naive(te)
naevly, naive(ly)
nafee, navy
nafegashen, navigate(tion)
nafegubul, navigable
nafel, naval / navel / novel
nafigate, navigate
nafigubul, navigable
nafil, naval / navel / novel
nafol, naval / navel / novel
nafugate, navigate
nafuguble, navigable
naful, naval / navel / novel
nafulty, novelty
nafy, navy
nag,*, gged, gging, ggingly, AN ACT PERFORMED REPEATEDLY, IRRITATED BY REPETITION, YOUNG/ OLD HORSE
naglekt, neglect
nagosheate, negotiate
nagoshubul, negotiable
nagotiate, negotiate
nagutev, negative
naif, naive / knife
naighbor, neighbor
nail,*, led, ling, ler, SLENDER STEEL WITH POINT/ HEAD FOR HAMMERING, PROTECTIVE GROWTH ON FINGERS/ TOES
nailon, nylon
naim, name
nain, nine
nais, nice
nait, night / knight
naitragen, nitrogen
naitril, nitrile
naitrochen, nitrogen
naitrollen, nitrogen

naitrou, nitro
naive, ely, eness, ete, ety, LACKS INFORMATION, CLUELESS
nak, knack
naked, dly, dness, WITHOUT CLOTHES OR COVERING
nakit, naked
nale, nail
nalege, knowledge
namadik, pneumatic / nomad(ic)
name,*, ed, ming, ely, eless, elessly, elessness, LEGAL/ PROPER TITLE, WHAT TO CALL SOMETHING/ SOMEONE "prefixes: mis/ sur/ un"
namles, name(less)
namly, name(ly)
nane, nanny
nanny, nies, SOMEONE WHO IS HIRED BY A FAMILY TO TAKE CARE OF THE CHILDREN, A FEMALE GOAT
nano, PREFIX INDICATING "ONE BILLIONTH/ EXTREMELY SMALL" MOST OFTEN MODIFIES THE WORD
nany, nanny
nap,*, pped, pping, pper, SLEEP BRIEFLY, PILE/ CLOTH/ SUBSTANCE/ FUZZ (or see knap/ nape)
nape, BACK OF NECK (or see nap/ knap/ knap(ppy))
naped, nab(bed) / nap(pped)
napken, napkin
napkin,*, CLOTH/ PAPER USED AT MEALTIME FOR FACE/ HANDS
nappy, knap(ppy)
napquin, napkin
napt, nab(bed) / nap(ped)
narashen, narrate(tion)
narate, narrate
narative, narrate(tive)
narator, narrate(tor)
narcisim, narcissism
narcism, narcissism
narcissi, ssus, ssuses, ist, istic, istically, ism, EXCESSIVE SELF-LOVE
narcissism, st, stic, stically, EXCESSIVE SELF-LOVE
narcistic, narcissi(tic)
narcistik, narcissi(tic)
narco, PREFIX INDICATING "NARCOTIC/ STUPOR/ SLEEP" MOST OFTEN MODIFIES THE WORD

narcotic, *, cally, ize, izes, ized, izing, ization, CHEMICAL WHICH ALTERS BODY METABOLISM
nare, nary
nareit, narrate
narely, narrow(ly)
nari, nary
narkotek, narcotic
naro, narrow
naroly, narrow(ly)
narou, narrow
narowd, narrow(ed)
narrate, *, ed, ting, tion, tional, tive, tively, tor, TO RECOUNT/ TELL/ RELATE A STORY
narrow, *, wed, wing, wer, west, wly, wness, NOT AS WIDE AS USUAL/ NORMAL, THIN STRIP, MAKE SMALLER
narsesm, narcissism
narsistic, narcissi(tic)
nary, NEVER, NOT
nasal, lity, lism, lly, lize, lization, INVOLVING THE NOSE AND ITS PASSAGEWAYS "prefixes: intra"
nasdeor, nasty(tier)
nasdursheum, nasturtium
nasdy, nasty
nasel, nasal
nasely, nasal(ly)
nasesidy, necessity
nasesitate, necessitate
nashen, nation
nashenaledy, nation(ality)
nashenul, nation(al)
nashinality, nation(ality)
nashonul, nation(al)
nashos, nauseous
nashunaludy, nation(ality)
nashuropathy, naturopath
nasia, nausea
nasius, nauseous
nastee, nasty
nastershem, nasturtium
nastershum, nasturtium
nasti, nasty
nasturtium, *, A FLOWERING PLANT

nasty, tier, tiest, tily, tiness, UNDESIRABLE, OBJECTIONABLE, UNACCEPTABLE, NOT PROPER
nat, not / naught / knot / gnat
natal, OF/ RELATING TO BIRTH "prefixes: neo"
natcheropuchy, naturopath
natcherul, natural
natchural, natural
natchurely, natural(ly)
natecal, nautical
natef, native
nateuropath, naturopath
nateve, native
natical, nautical
natif, native
natilus, nautilus
natinuality, nation(ality)
nation, *, nal, nally, nalize, nalization, nhood, nless, nalism, nalist, nality, nalities, nalizer, DEVOTED/ LOYAL TO A PEOPLE/ COUNTRY "prefixes: bi/ inter/ intra/ multi"
native, *, ely, eness, vism, vist, vistic, vity, vities, BORN/ BELONG TO CERTAIN LAND/ AREA, RACE OF PEOPLES, NOT AN IMMIGRANT
natle, natal
natol, natal
natoreus, notorious
natorius, notorious
natsher, nature
natsheropethy, naturopath
natshur, nature
natuf, native
natufly, native(ly)
natul, natal
natural, *, lly, lness, lism, list, listic, listically, lize, lization, NOT REFINED/ MODIFIED/ REARRANGED/ CHANGED/ MOLDED OR MANIPULATED "prefixes: un"
naturapathy, naturopath
nature, *, ral, BASIC ESSENCE OF THINGS, CHARACTER, COMBINATION OF QUALITIES
naturel, natural
naturilist, natural(ist)
naturopath, *, hy, hic, TREATS ILLNES/ INJURIES WITH NATURAL REMEDIES

natuv, native
nau, gnaw / know / now
naude, naughty / knot(ty)
naudical, nautical
nauev, naive
naught, NOTHING, NOT, DON'T NEED ANYTHING (or see not/ knot)
naughty, tier, tiest, tily, tiness, IMPROPER BEHAVIOR, MISCHIEVOUS (or see knot(ty))
naumenol, nominal
nauminoly, nominal(lly)
naumune, nominee
naun, noun
nausdalgea, nostalgia
nausdalgik, nostalgic
nausdrel, nostril
nausea, ate, ating, atingly, FEELING ILL IN STOMACH
nauseous, sly, sness, STOMACH FEELING ILL
naushus, nauseous
nausious, nauseous
naustalgea, nostalgia
naustalgik, nostalgic
naustrel, nostril
naut, not / naught / knot
nautch, notch
nautical, ally, OCEAN NAVIGATION
nautilus, ses, li, SPIRAL OCEAN SHELL
nauves, novice
nauvulest, novel(ist)
nauvulte, novelty
navagate, navigate
navagation, navigate(tion)
naval, SHIPS, OF A NAVY (or see navel/ novel)
navee, navy
navegable, navigable
navegashen, navigate(tion)
navegate, navigate
navegation, navigate(tion)
navel, *, SPOT ON THE BELLY WHERE THE UMBILICAL CORD WAS SEVERED, MIDDLE/ CENTRAL PLACE (or see naval/ novel)
navember, november
navigable, bility, eness, ly, ABLE TO MANEUVER/ GUIDE

navigate, *, ed, ting, tion, tional, tionally, tor, STEER OR MANEUVER, ONE WHO STEERS/ MANEUVERS/ GUIDES
navil, naval / navel / novel
navimber, november
navol, naval / navel / novel
navugashen, navigate(tion)
navugate, navigate
navugation, navigate(tion)
navuguble, navigable
navul, naval / navel / novel
navuldy, novelty
navy, vies, val, COLLECTION OF SHIPS BELONGING TO A NATION
naw, gnaw / now
nawleg, knowledge
nawstrel, nostril
nayber, neighbor
nazdeur, nasty(tier)
nazdursheum, nasturtium
nazdy, nasty
nazel, nasal
nazely, nasal(ly)
nazil, nasal
nazily, nasal(ly)
naztersheum, nasturtium
nazty, nasty
ne, knee
near, *, rer, rest, rly, rness, CLOSE TO
neat, ter, test, tly, tness, ORDERLY/ ORGANIZED, APPEALING (or see need/ knead/ knee(d))
nebal, nibble
neber, neighbor
nebir, neighbor
neble, nibble
nebor, neighbor
nebul, nibble
nebur, neighbor
nec, niece / neck
necasery, necessary
necatene, nicotine
neccesary, necessary
neccessitate, necessitate

neccesity, necessity
neccessary, necessary
necdur, nectar
nece, niece
necesadi, necessity
necesary, necessary
necesitate, necessitate
necesite, necessity
necesiteit, necessitate
necessary, rily, riness, MUST BE/ HAVE, REQUIRED "prefixes: un"
necessatate, necessitate
necessitate, *, ed, ting, tion, tive, REQUIRED, ESSENTIAL
necessity, ties, tous, tously, tousness, REQUIRED, MUST HAVE
necesudi, necessity
neche, niche
nechel, nickel
necisary, necessary
neck, *, ked, king, PART OF THE BODY BETWEEN HEAD AND SHOULDERS, PART OF THE SPINE
necklace, *, ORNAMENT/ ADORNMENT FOR THE NECK
necklajay, negligee
neckleshay, negligee
neclas, necklace
neclasha, negligee
neclos, necklace
neclus, necklace
necotine, nicotine
necramancer, necromancer
necrimancer, necromancer
necromancer, *, cy, ntic, PERSON OR OCCURRENCE WHICH REFLECTS OUR GREATEST FEAR, THE DARK/ UNAPPEALING SIDE OF OUR NATURE
nectar, *, SWEET JUICE OF A FLOWER
nectarine, *, CROSS BETWEEN PEACH/ PLUM
necterene, nectarine
nectir, nectar
nectirene, nectarine
nectur, nectar
necturene, nectarine
ned, need / neat / knead / knee(d)
nede, need

neded, need(ed) / knead(ded)
nedel, needle / nettle
nedil, needle / nettle
nedle, needle / nettle
nedly, neat(ly)
nedul, needle / nettle
nedwurk, network
nedy, need
nee, knee
need, *, ded, ding, diness, dy, dful, dfully, dfulness, dless, dlessly, dlessness, REQUIRED, ESSENTIAL, MANDATORY (or see knead/ knee(d)/ neat)
needle, *, ed, ling, SLENDER METAL PIN WITH A SHARP POINT AT ONE END AND HOLE AT THE OTHER END, FOR SEWING (or see nettle)
needly, neat(ly)
neel, kneel
neer, near
neerer, near(er)
neerest, near(est)
neerly, near(ly)
nees, niece / knee(s)
nefew, nephew
nefir, never
nefiu, nephew
nefu, nephew
nefur, never
negative, *, ely, eness, vity, vism, vistic, MINUS, IN THE RED, OPPOSITE OF POSITIVE, FILM UNPROCESSED
negetiv, negative
neghbor, neighbor
neghborhood, neighbor(hood)
negitif, negative
negitive, negative
neglacha, negligee
neglagay, negligee
neglagense, negligence
neglagent, negligence(nt)
neglagible, negligence(gible)
neglagint, negligence(nt)
neglaja, negligee
neglect, *, ted, ting, tful, tfully, tfulness, tor, NOT BE RESPONSIBLE/ TAKE CARE OF

neglegable, negligence(gible)
neglegense, negligence
negligee, *, WOMEN'S UNDERGARMENTS
negligence, *, nt, ntly, gible, gibly, gibility, gible-ness, NOT TAKE CARE OF OR BE RESPONSIBLE FOR
neglijay, negligee
neglijents, negligence
neglillens, negligence
neglilli, negligee
neglisha, negligee
neglugense, negligence
negodev, negative
negosheate, negotiate
negosheuble, negotiable
negoshieit, negotiate
negoshubul, negotiable
negotef, negative
negotiable, bility, ABLE TO COME TO AGREEMENT
negotiate, *, ed, ting, tion, tcr, able, COME TO AGREEMENT BY COMMUNICATING
negoushieit, negotiate
negudev, negative
negutif, negative
negutive, negative
neibor, neighbor
neice, niece
neichor, nature
neichoroupath, naturopath
neidif, native
neighbor, *, rly, rhood, PEOPLE WHO DWELL NEAR YOU, THOSE WHO LIVE CLOSE TO YOU
neiked, naked
neil, nail
neim, name
neip, nape
neiqued, naked
neisal, nasal
neishon, nation
neisol, nasal
neither, NOT ONE OR THE OTHER, NOT THIS ONE OR THAT ONE
neitif, native
neival, naval / navel

neivol, naval / navel
nek, neck / nick
nekatene, nicotine
nekdur, nectar
nekil, nickel
neklagent, negligence(nt)
neklajense, negligence
neklegent, negligence(nt)
nekles, necklace
neklesha, negligee
neklijent, negligence(nt)
neklis, necklace
neklisha, negligee
neklus, necklace
nekotene, nicotine
nekrumanser, necromancer
nekst, next
nektarine, nectarine
nekter, nectar
nekturene, nectarine
nekul, nickel
nekzd, next
nel, nil / kneel / nail
nemf, nymph
nemfomanea, nymphomania
nemonia, pneumonia
nemph, nymph
nemphomanea, nymphomania
neo, PREFIX INDICATING "NEW" MOST OFTEN MODIFIES THE WORD
neol, nail
neon, A NOBLE/ INERT GAS, USED IN LAMPS
nep, nip
nepd, nip(pped)
nepe, nip(ppy)
nephew, *, FAMILY RELATION
nephu, nephew
nepil, nipple
nept, nip(pped)
nepul, nipple
nerador, narrate(tor)
nerashen, narrate(tion)
nerate, narrate

neratek, neurotic
nerative, narrate(tive)
nerator, narrate(tor)
nercher, nurture
nere, near / nary
nereit, narrate
neresh, nourish
nereshen, narrate(tion)
nerf, nerve
nerfona, nirvana
nerfus, nervous
neri, nary
nerly, near(ly)
nero, narrow
nerodic, neurotic
neroly, narrow(ly)
neron, neuron
nerosis, neurosis
nerotic, neurotic
nerow, narrow
nerreit, narrate
ners, nurse / near(s)
nerture, nurture
nerv, nerve
nervana, nirvana
nervas, nervous
nerve, *, ed, ving, eless, vous, SOFT TISSUE IN THE BODY WHICH RELATES BODY TO BRAIN BY ELECTRICAL IMPULSES, BODY'S FORM OF COMMUNICATION "prefixes: un"
nervous, sly, sness, UNGROUNDED, WORRIED, STRESSED, UNSURE, DOUBTFUL, FEARFUL
nervus, nervous
nery, nary
nes, knee(s) / niece
nesasary, necessary
nesd, nest
nesdalgik, nostalgic
nese, niece
nesesary, necessary
nesesitate, necessitate
nesesudy, necessity
nesil, nestle

nesisary, necessary
nesol, nestle
nesold, nestle(d)
nest, *, ted, ting, ter, A BIRD'S HOME
nestalgek, nostalgic
nestle, *, ed, ling, ler, COZY/ SNUGGLE UP AGAINST
nestursheum, nasturtium
nesul, nestle
net, *, tted, tting, table, tlike, A WEB, WEAVING OF SOMETHING, COLLECTION OF (or see neat/ knit) "prefixes: inter/ intra"
netal, needle / nettle
nete, neat / need
nethur, neither
netil, needle / nettle
netly, neat(ly)
netol, needle / nettle
netorius, notorious
netpiky, nitpick
netrishu, nutricious
netrishun, nutrition
netsh, niche
nettle, *, AN HERB (or see needle)
netul, needle / nettle
network, *, ked, king, ker, JOIN/ CONNECT TOGETHER "prefixes: inter"
netwurk, network
nety, need
neuder, neuter
neur, PREFIX INDICATING "NERVE" MOST OFTEN MODIFIES THE WORD
neural, lly, OF THE NERVOUS SYSTEM
neuresh, nourish
neurish, nourish
neurodic, neurotic
neuron, *, , nal, nally, osis, oses, OF THE NERVOUS SYSTEM "prefixes: inter"
neurosis, DISORDER OF NERVES/ EMOTIONS
neurotic, cally, cism, osis, DISORDER AFFECTING EMOTIONS AS IT RELATES TO THE NERVOUS SYSTEM
neuter, *, red, ring, A LIVING THING WITHOUT ABILITY TO REPRODUCE

neutral, lity, lly, lism, list, listic, lize, lizes, lized, lizing, lization, lizer, BETWEEN EXTREMES/ OPPOSITES, IN THE MIDDLE
neutreshen, nutrition
neutreshus, nutritious
neutretive, nutritive
neutricious, nutritious
neutrino, *, , TINY UNCHARGED PARTICLE
neutron, *, , nic, UNCHARGED PARTICLE IN ATOM
nevember, november
never, NOT EVER
nevimber, november
nevor, never
new, *, wer, west, wish, wly, wness, JUST CAME INTO BEING, JUST CREATED (or see knew) "prefixes: re"
newborn, *, JUST BORN
newcleate, nuclear(ate)
newcleur, nuclear
newdul, noodle
newdur, neuter
newkleate, nuclear(ate)
newkleus, nucleus
newlewed, newlywed
newlywed, *, COUPLES IN FIRST YEAR OF MARRIAGE
newmadik, pneumatic / nomad(ic)
newmarible, numerable
newmaril, numeral
newmatek, pneumatic
newmerology, numerology
newmerus, numerous
newmirary, numerary
newmonia, pneumonia
newmresy, numeracy
newmurable, numerable
newmurader, numerate(tor)
newmurary, numerary
newmurecy, numeracy
newmurology, numerology
newmurus, numerous
newron, neuron
newsans, nuisance
newspaper, *, PAPER WITH PRINTED TEXT CIRCULATED AS NEWS

newsuns, nuisance
newter, neuter
newtral, neutral
newtrative, nutritive
newtreant, nutrient
newtreno, neutrino
newtril, neutral
newtrishen, nutrition
newtrishus, nutritious
newtrol, neutral
newtron, neutron
next, FOLLOWS AFTER, COMING UP
nezt, nest
ngoy, enjoy
ni, knee
nibble, *, ed, ling, TINY BITE/ MORSEL TO EAT
nibul, nibble
nicatene, nicotine
nice, er, est, ely, ety, KIND, THOUGHTFUL, CONSIDERATE, APPEALING, PLEASANT
nicesiteit, necessitate
nicesity, necessity
niche, *, A CORNER OF, A LITTLE PLACE CARVED/ ETCHED OUT OF SOMETHING
nichel, nickel
nicity, nice(ty)
nick, *, ked, king, SHALLOW MARK/ CUT/ NOTCH, AT THE LAST MINUTE
nickel, *, led, U.S. COIN
nicotine, nic, nism, A CHEMICAL SUBSTANCE NATURALLY FOUND IN TOBACCO
nid, night / need / knead
nidal, needle
nider, neither
nidl, needle
nidol, needle
nidul, needle
niece, *, A RELATIVE BY BLOOD FAMILY
niese, niece
nif, knife
night, *, tly, tless, THE DARK PART OF A 24 HOUR PERIOD, WITHOUT THE SUN (or see knight) "prefixes: over"
niglekt, neglect

niglekted, neglect(ed)
nigosheate, negotiate
nigosheuble, negotiable
nigotiable, negotiable
nigotiate, negotiate
nik, nick
nikatene, nicotine
nikel, nickel
niknak, knick knack
nikotene, nicotine
nikul, nickel
nikutene, nicotine
nil, NOTHING, NONE (or see kneel)
nilon, nylon
nimf, nymph
nimfomanea, nymphomania
nimfomaneac, nymphomania(c)
ninfomania, nymphomania
nimonea, pneumonia
nimph, nymph
nimphomania, nymphomania
nindeith, nine(tieth)
nindes, nine(ties)
nindy, nine(ty)
nine,*, er, ety, eties, nth, ne=eenth, netieth, ENGLISH NUMBER BETWEEN EIGHT AND TEN
ninfomaneac, nymphomania(c)
ninphomania, nymphomania
nintenth, nine(teenth)
ninthe, nine(nth)
ninty, nine(ty)
nintys, nine(ties)
nio, neo
niol, kneel
nion, neon
nip,*, pped, pping, pper, ppy, TAKE A LITTLE BITE, TAKE IN JUST A LITTLE
niped, nip(pped)
niple, nipple
nipple,*, FORMED TIP EXTRUSIONS ON THE CHEST CAVITY, TIP WITH ORIFICE
nipul, nipple
nipy, nip(ppy)

niquel, nickel
nircher, nurture
nireshment, nourish(ment)
nirfona, nirvana
nirfus, nervous
niron, neuron
nirosis, neurosis
nirsaited, nearsighted
nirse, nurse
nirvana, A STATE OF BLISS WHERE ONE IS TRANSFORMED FROM THE MATERIAL PLANE
nirves, nervous / nerve(s)
nirvus, nervous
nis, nice / niece
nise, nice / niece
nisedy, nice(ty)
niser, nice(r)
nisesity, necessity
nisest, nice(st)
nistalgek, nostalgic
nit,*, PARASITIC LARVAE (or see night/ knit/ net/ knight)
nitch, niche
nite, night / knight / knit
nited, knit(tted) / knight(ed)
nither, neither
nitorius, notorious
nitpeky, nitpick
nitpick,*, ky, BE OVERLY CONCERNED ABOUT MINUSCULE/INSIGNIFICANT DETAILS
nitpiky, nitpick
nitr, PREFIX INDICATING "NITROGEN" MOST OFTEN MODIFIES THE WORD
nitragen, nitrogen
nitral, nitrile
nitregen, nitrogen
nitrel, nitrile
nitrigen, nitrogen
nitrile, CHEMICAL CLASSIFICATION
nitro, PREFIX INDICATING "NITROGEN" MOST OFTEN MODIFIES THE WORD
nitrogen, nous, A GAS
nitrul, nitrile
nitsh, niche

niu, new / knew
niuborn, newborn
niuder, neuter
niurodic, neurotic
niuron, neuron
niurosis, neurosis
niurousis, neurosis
niuspeiper, newspaper
niuter, neuter
niutral, neutral
niutrino, neutrino
niutrol, neutral
niutron, neutron
niw, new / knew
njoy, enjoy
no, NEGATORY (or see know)
nob,*, bby, BUMPS/ EXTRUSIONS (or see knob)
nobel, noble
nobelity, nobility
nobil, noble
nobility, ties, SUPERIOR, REPUTABLE, OF QUALITY
noble,*, er, est, esse, eman, bility, OF RANK/ REPUTATION, CHEMICALLY INERT "prefixes: en"
nobody, NO BODY, NO PERSON
noboty, nobody
nobul, noble
noc, nock / knock / nook
noch, notch / nudge
nochin, notion
nochus, nauseous
nock,*, ked, king, SETTING AN ARROW INTO PLACE ON BOW STRING, PART OF ARROW (or see knock)
nocol, knuckle
nocshos, noxious
noct, PREFIX INDICATING "NIGHT" MOST OFTEN MODIFIES THE WORD
nocturnal, lity, ne, ACTIVE AT NIGHT
nod,*, dded, dding, UP AND DOWN HEAD MOVEMENT (or see not/ node)
nodafekashen, notify(fication)
nodariety, notorius(iety)
nodary, notary
nodch, notch

Word	Definition/Forms
node,*,dal,dality,STUMP/ BULGE (too many definitions please see standard dictionary) (or see note/ naughty/ knot(tty)) prefixes: inter"	
nodefication, notify(fication)	
nodefy, notify	
nodekul, nautical	
nodelus, nautilus	
noderiety, notorius(iety)	
noderize, notary(rize)	
nodery, notary	
nodes, notice / node(s)	
nodical, nautical	
nodier, naughty(tier)	
nodiest, naughty(tiest)	
nodify, notify	
nodikal, nautical	
nodiriety, notorius(iety)	
nodirize, notary(rize)	
nodiry, notary	
nodis, notice	
nodle, noodle	
nodufikashen, notify(fication)	
nodufy, notify	
nodukul, nautical	
nodure, notary	
noduriety, notorius(iety)	
nodurise, notary(rize)	
nodus, notice	
nody, naughty / knot(ty)	
noefe, naive	
noese, noise / noise(sy) / nosy	
noeve, naive	
noevet, naive(te)	
nofa, nova	
nofel, novel	
nofelty, novelty	
nofember, november	
nofil, novel	
nofilty, novelty	
nofu, nova	
noget, nugget	
noglekted, neglect(ed)	
nois, noise	
noise,*, eless, elessly, elessness,sy, sily, siness, DISHARMONIC SOUND, AN ALARMING/ OFFENSIVE SOUND
noisey, noise
nok, nock / knock / nook
nokel, knuckle
nokshus, noxious
nokternul, nocturnal
nokturnal, nocturnal
nol, knoll / null
nole, knoll
nolech, knowledge
noleg, knowledge
nolige, knowledge
noll, knoll
nom, gnome / numb
nomad, *, dic, dically, dism, A WANDERER, WITHOUT A PERMANENT HOME (or see pneumatic) "prefixes: semi"
nomadek, pneumatic / nomad(ic)
nomanaded, nominate(d)
nomanate, nominate
nomanee, nominee
nomaneit, nominate
nomat, nomad
nomatic, nomad(ic) / pneumatic
nomenashen, nominate(tion)
nomenate, nominate
nomene, nominee
nomeneit, nominate
nomenoly, nominal(lly)
nominal,lly, lism, lize, lizes, lized, lizing, lization, LOW COST, OF A NAME, BANKING TERM, NOUN FORM "prefixes: pre/ pro"
nominate, *, ted, ting, tion, tive, tor, SELECT PEOPLE WHO WILL BE IN AN ELECTION "prefixes: de"
nominee, *, SOMEONE SELECTED TO BE VOTED FOR, ONE WHOM IS SELECTED FOR ELECTION
nomunashin, nominate(tion)
nomunate, nominate
nomunee, nominee
non, PREFIX INDICATING "NOT" MOST OFTEN MODIFIES THE WORD (or see known/ none/ nun/ noon)
noncense, nonsense
nonchalant, tly, nce, CASUAL, UNCONCERNED
nonchelot, nonchalant
nonchulot, nonchalant
none, WITHOUT ANY, ABSENT FROM (or see nun/ noun/ known)
nonfiction, nal, FACTUAL
nonsense, sical, sically, sicalness, ABSURB, GOOFY, NOT POSSIBLE, IRRATIONAL
nonsents, nonsense
nonshelont, nonchalant
nonshulot, nonchalant
nonsinse, nonsense
noo, new / knew
noocleate, nuclear(ate)
noodle, *, PASTA
noodul, noodle
nook, *, A CORNER/ CREVICE/ RECESSED AREA
noon, O'CLOCK P.M. (or see nun)
noos, noose / new(s)
noose, SLIPKNOT ROPE WITH A LOOPED END FOR HOLDING SOMETHING (or see new(s))
nooz, noose / new(s)
noozpaper, newspaper
nop, nob / knob / nope
nope, NO
nor, ANOTHER WORD FOR 'NEITHER'
norishment, nourish(ment)
norm, *, mal, SLANG FOR WHAT'S NORMAL
normal,lly, lity, lcy, lize, lizes, lized, lizing, lization, MIDDLE OF THE ROAD BEHAVIOR/ THOUGHT/ ACTION, IN BETWEEN, AVERAGE "prefixes: re/ sub/ un"
normul, normal
normuly, normal(lly)
nors, nurse
norsism, narcissism
norsistik, narcissi(tic)
north, hen, hener, hern, hernmost, her, herly, herlies, herliness, ONE OF FOUR COMPASS/ MAGNETIC DIRECTIONS
northirn, north(ern)
northurly, north(erly)
nos, nose / know(s)

nosdalgek, nostalgic
nosdalgia, nostalgia
nosdrul, nostril
nose, *, ed, sing, eless, sy, PROBOSCIS, FACIAL FEATURE REQUIRED FOR SMELLING AND BREATHING (or see know(s))
nosel, nozzle
noseus, nauseous
noshen, notion
noshes, nauseous
noshus, nauseous
nosil, nozzle
nosle, nozzle
nost, nose(d)
nostalgea, nostalgia
nostalgia, ic, REMINISCE/ REFER TO THE PAST
nostalgic, cally, REMINISCE, REFER TO THE PAST
nostalla, nostalgia
nostallic, nostalgic
nostrel, nostril
nostril, *, ORIFICES ON NOSE WHICH EMPLOYS AIR MOVEMENT
nostrul, nostril
nosul, nozzle
nosy, sier, siest, sily, siness, FOLLOW THE NOSE, PRY/ SNOOP AROUND IN ANOTHER'S BUSINESS, ALSO SPELLED 'NOSEY'
not, THIS ONE/ THAT ONE, NO (or see note/ knot/ naught)
notariety, notorius(iety)
notary, ries, rize, rizes, rized rizing, rization, AN OFFICIAL WHO PREPARES LEGAL DOCUMENTS
notch, hes, hed, hing, TO CUT/ KNOCK OUT A WEDGE IN SOMETHING, TO CARVE OUT OF
note, *, ed, ting, tice, WRITE TEXT ON PAPER, KEEP IN MIND, OBSERVE/ REMEMBER (or see node/ knot/ naught)
notee, naughty / knot(ty)
notefication, notify(fication)
notefikashen, notify(fication)
notefy, notify
notekul, nautical
notelus, nautilus

noterize, notary(rize)
notery, notary
notes, notice / note(s)
notheng, nothing
nothing, NOT A THING
notice, *, ed, cing, TAKE NOTE OF, OBSERVE A DISCREPANCY "prefixes: un"
notiest, naughty(tiest)
notifacation, notify(fication)
notify, fies, fied, fying, fication, TO INFORM, COMMUNICATE TO SOMEONE BY VARIOUS MEANS
notikal, nautical
notilus, nautilus
notion, *, AN INKLING/ VIEW/ OPINION "prefixes: pre"
notiriety, notorius(iety)
notiry, notary
notis, notice
notorious, sly, sness, iety, ieties, WIDELY KNOWN BUT WITHOUT POSITIVE REGARD
notufikashen, notify(fication)
notufy, notify
notukul, nautical
noturiety, notorius(iety)
noturize, notary(rize)
notury, notary
notus, notice
noty, naughty / knot(ty)
nou, know
noubadi, nobody
noubal, noble
noubeliti, nobility
noubilidi, nobility
nouble, noble
noubodi, nobody
noud, node
noudari, notary
noudifay, notify
noun, *, A WORD REFERRING TO PEOPLE PLACE/ THING/ TIME/ PROPER NAME (or see known)
noup, nope
nourish, hes, hed, hing, her, hment, TO PROVIDE NECESSARY NUTRIENTS "prefixes: under"
nous, noose / nose

nouse, noose
noushes, nauseous
noushon, notion
nousi, nosy
nout, note
noutari, notary
noutifai, notify
noutis, notice
noutorios, notorious
nouwer, nowhere
nova, *, STAR FLARE-UPS/ BURSTS, NEW STAR
novel, *, list, listic, ette, lize, lization, lla, lty, FICTITIOUS WRITING, IMAGINED PLOT AND CHARACTERS, A CREATIVE IDEA OR DESIGN
novela, novel(lla)
novelty, ties, UNUSUAL AND CREATIVE
november, A MONTH OF THE YEAR (ENGLISH)
noves, novice
novice, *, A BEGINNER
novil, novel
novildy, novelty
novimber, november
novis, novice
novle, novel
novlety, novelty
novu, nova
novul, novel
novulest, novel(list)
novulty, novelty
novuss, novice
now, IN THE MOMENT/ PRESENT
nowar, nowhere
noweesy, noise(sy)
nowere, nowhere
nowese, noise
nowhere, NO WHERE, NOT HERE NOW
nowleg, knowledge
nown, noun / known
noxious, sly, sness, HARMFUL TO HEALTH(or see nauseous)
noxus, noxious
noyse, noise
noze, nose / know(s)

nozeate,nausea(te)
nozel,nozzle
nozy,nosy
nozzle,*,AN APERTURE FOR SPRAYING
nu,new / knew
nuborn,newborn
nubshuel,nuptial
nuc,nook
nucle,PREFIX INDICATING "NUCLEUS/ NUCLEAR" MOST OFTEN MODIFIES THE WORD
nuclear,ate,ates,ated,ating,ation,HAVING TO DO WITH A NUCLEUS "prefixes: bi/ inter/ intra/ pro/ sub"
nucleus,ei,eic,ein,CENTRAL HUB, PRIMARY CONTROL "prefixes: pro"
nucliar,nuclear
nud,nude
nuddy,nut(ty) / nude(ies)
nude,*,ely,eness,dism,dity,dities,WITHOUT COVERINGS "prefixes: semi"
nudel,noodle
nuder,neuter
nudesm,nude(dism)
nudety,nude(dity)
nudge,*,ed,ging,GENTLY POKE/ PUSH
nudil,noodle
nudl,noodle
nudmeg,nutmeg
nudol,noodle
nudril,neutral
nudul,noodle
nudy,nut(ty)
nue,new / knew
nuendo,innuendo
nuer,new(er)
nufember,november
nuge,nudge
nuget,nugget
nugget,*,A SMALL CHUNK OF SOMETHING
nugit,nugget
nuglekt,neglect
nuglere,nuclear
nugleus,nucleus
nugosheate,negotiate

nugoshiable,negotiable
nugotiable,negotiable
nugotiate,negotiate
nuifai,nullify
nuindo,innuendo
nuisance,ANNOYING, OBNOXIOUS, CONTINUOUS IRRITATION
nuist,new(est)
nujt,nudge(d)
nuk,nook
nukle,knuckle
nukleate,nuclear(ate)
nukleir,nuclear
nukleus,nucleus
nukul,knuckle
nul,null
nulefy,nullify
nulewed,newlywed
nulify,nullify
null,llity,llities,llify,OF NO VALUE
nullify,fies,fied,fying,fier,fication,ity,RENDER NOT VALUABLE/ NECESSARY
nuly,new(l)
nulywed,newlywed
num,numb
numadik, pneumatic / nomad(ic)
numarader,numerate(tor)
numarery,numerary
numaril,numeral
numatic, pneumatic / nomad(ic)
numb,*,bed,bing,bness,VOID OF FEELING, INABILITY TO FEEL ANYTHING
number,*,red,ring,ral,A UNIT/ SYMBOL WHICH REPRESENTS AN AMOUNT "prefixes: un"
numberible,numerable
numbroble,numerable
numerable,CAN BE COUNTED, COUNTABLE "prefixes: in"
numeracy,COMMON MATH "prefixes: in"
numeral,*,lly,ate,ary,ric,ator,ONE NUMBER/ DIGIT, OF A DIGIT ,ADD/ SUBTRACT
numerary,ABOUT NUMBERS/ NUMBERING, NAME FOR POSITION "prefixes: super"

numerate,*,ed,ting,tion,tor,tors,BASIC MATH "prefixes: en/ in"
numeric,*,rical,rically,rous,USE OF NUMBERS
numerology,SCIENCE OF NUMBERS/ FREQUENCY
numeros,numerous
numerous,sly,sness,MANY IN NUMBER "prefixes: in"
numirator,numerate(tor)
numirology,numerology
numirus,numerous
numonia,pneumonia
numorator,numerate(tor)
numper,number
numpir,number
numral,numeral
numrecy,numeracy
numrisy,numeracy
numrul,numeral
numurery,numerary
numurologe,numerology
numurus,numerous
nun,*,RELIGIOUS WOMAN WHO VOWS TO OBEY RULES AS A NUN (or see non/ none/ known/ noun/ noon)
nundo,innuendo
nune,noon
nupshuel,nuptial
nuptial,lly,CONCERNS WEDDING/ RITUAL
nuradic,neurotic
nurcher,nurture
nuresh,nourish
nurfus,nervous
nurish,nourish
nurishment,nourish(ment)
nurodic,neurotic
nuron,neuron
nurosis,neurosis
nurotic,neurotic
nurs,nurse
nurse,*,ed,sing,er,ery,eries,TO NURTURE AND/ OR PROTECT VULNERABLE THINGS/ PEOPLE
nurture,*,PROVIDE NECESSARY NOURISHMENT TO
nurve,nerve
nurvis,nervous
nurvus,nervous

nus, new(s) / noose
nusans, nuisance
nusdalgik, nostalgic
nuse, noose / new(s)
nusel, nuzzle
nusense, nuisance
nusesidy, necessity
nusesitate, necessitate
nusil, nuzzle
nusinse, nuisance
nusle, nuzzle
nuspaper, newspaper
nustalgek, nostalgic
nusul, nuzzle
nut,*,tty, HIGH PROTEIN WOODY FRUIT, SOMEONE WHO DOESN'T BEHAVE LOGICALLY
nute, nude
nutedy, nude(dity)
nutel, noodle
nuter, neuter
nutesm, nude(dism)
nuthen, nothing
nuthing, nothing
nutil, noodle
nutle, noodle
nutmeg, A SPICE
nutoreus, notorious
nutral, neutral
nutrality, neutral(ity)
nutralize, neutral(ize)
nutreant, nutrient
nutreno, neutrino
nutreshen, nutrition
nutreshus, nutritious
nutrichas, nutritious
nutrient, FOOD THAT NOURISHES LIVING THINGS
nutril, neutral
nutrino, neutrino
nutrishen, nutrition
nutrishenal, nutrition(al)
nutrition,nal,nally,nist,ous,ive, GIVES/ PROVIDES NOURISHMENT
nutritious, sly, sness, PROVIDES NOURISHMENT

nutritive, ely, eness, PROVIDES NOURISHMENT
nutron, neutron
nuty, nut(ty)
nuvember, november
nuvimber, november
nuwkleus, nucleus
nuwlewed, newlywed
nuz, new(s)
nuzle, nuzzle
nuzpaper, newspaper
nuzzle,*,ed,ling, TO SNUGGLE/ DIG IN/ THRUST GENTLY INTO
nve, envy
nylon, A MANMADE CHEMICAL FIBER
nymph,*, ENTITIES, DEITIES, A STAGE IN THE DEVELOPMENT OF AN INSECT
nymphomania,ac, CONTINUAL/ INTENSE FOCUS ON SEXUAL ACTIVITY
nyn, nine
nyte, night / knight / knit
nzime, enzyme
o, oh
o'clock, SHORT FOR "ON THE CLOCK"
oak,*, A DECIDUOUS TREE WITH ACORNS
oar,*,red, USED TO ROW A BOAT (or see or)
oarthodox, orthodox
oases, oasis
oasis, SPOT OF TREES/ WATER IN THE DESERT, COMFORT AMIDST AN UNCOMFORTABLE ENVIRONMENT
oat,*, A GRAIN (or see ode)
oath,*, PLEDGE/ OBLIGATE TO CERTAIN RULES/ LAWS
oatmeal, EDIBLE OAT GRAIN
ob, PREFIX INDICATING "AGAINST/ TOWARDS/ IN THE WAY OF" MOST OFTEN MODIFIES THE WORD
obal, opal
obay, obey
obazit, opposite
obecity, obese(sity)
obedeinse, obedience
obedeint, obedient
obedience,*,nt, TO COMPLY/ OBEY "prefixes: dis"
obedient, ly, nce, TO COMPLY/ OBEY "prefixes: dis"
obees, obese

obel, opal
obese, ely, seness, sity, OVERLY HEAVY, EXCESSIVELY OVERWEIGHT
obetchuery, obituary
obeteinse, obedience
obey,*,yed,ying,edient, COMPLY, FOLLOW RULES AND LAWS "prefixes: dis"
obfeus, obvious
obgectif, object(ive)
obgectivity, object(ivity)
obgekshen, object(ion)
obgektif, object(ive)
obichuery, obituary
obideinse, obedience
obil, opal
obituary,ries, LIST OF PEOPLE WHO HAVE TRANSPIRED FROM THIS PHYSICAL PLANE
object,*,ted,ting,tion,tive,tively,tivism,tion,tionable, tionably,tionability, PHYSICAL/ TANGIBLE THINGS, ARGUE IN DEFENSE OF, NEUTRAL POSITION
oblagation, obligate(tion)
oblederate, obliterate
oblefeus, oblivious
oblegate, obligate
obleterate, obliterate
obleveus, oblivious
oblevion, oblivion
oblibion, oblivion
oblifeus, oblivious
oblig, oblige(d)
obligate,*,ed,ting,tion,tory,torily,toriness, ACCEPT TERMS/ RESPONSIBILITY TO PERFORM
oblige,*,ed,ging,gingly, WILLING TO HELP "prefixes: dis"
obligeit, obligate
oblij, oblige(d)
obliterate,*,ed,ting,tion,tive,tor, TO DESTROY COMPLETELY
oblivion,ous, COMPLETELY FORGET
oblivious,ously,ousness,on, COMPLETELY FORGET
obllect, object
oblong, LONGER LENGTH THAN SIDES, LONG/ ROUND
oblugashen, obligate(tion)
oblugate, obligate

obnoksheus, obnoxious
obnoxious, sly, sness, OFFENSIVE, ROUGH FREQUENCY, DISHARMONIC IN NATURE
obol, opal
obozit, opposite
obreble, operable
obruble, operable
obsalesens, obsolescent(nce)
obsalesent, obsolescent
obscene, ely, eness, nity, nities, VERY UNDESIRABLE, INDECENT
obscure, *, ed, ring, ely, eness, ration, er, est, rity, rities, VAGUE, UNFOCUSED, DIFFICULT TO EXPLAIN/ UNDERSTAND
obselesens, obsolescent(nce)
obselesent, obsolescent
obselete, obsolete
obsene, obscene
observe, *, ed, ving, vingly, vance, vant, vantly, TO WATCH/ SEE AND STUDY "prefixes: in"
obseshen, obsess(ion)
obsesive, obsess(ive)
obsess, sses, ssed, ssive, ssively, ssion, ssional, ssionally, TO BECOME OVERWHELMED WITH THOUGHT ABOUT ONE THING, COMPULSIVE
obshen, option
obsilesens, obsolescent(nce)
obsilete, obsolete
obsin, obscene
obsinety, obscene(nity)
obskior, obscure
obsolescent, nce, tly, NOT MODERN, OUT OF DATE
obsolesens, obsolescent(nce)
obsolete, ely, eness, NO LONGER MODERN
obsquire, obscure
obsquiur, obscure
obssesed, obsess(ed)
obssesion, obsess(ion)
obstacle, *, OBSTRUCTION, SOMETHING IN THE PATH
obstatrician, obstetrician
obstatrishen, obstetrician
obstetric, *, cal, cally, cian, SCIENCE INVOLVING WOMEN IN CHILDBEARING PROCESS (or see obstetrician)

obstetrician, *, PERSON PRACTICING MEDICINE ON WOMEN IN THE CHILDBEARING PROCESS
obstikul, obstacle
obstinate, ely, eness, acy, acies, RESOLVED IN PURPOSE/ OPINION, UNABLE TO ARGUE WITH, STUBBORN
obstineit, obstinate
obstruct, *, ted, ting, tion, tionist, tive, tively, tiveness, tor, GET INTO THE PATH OF, PREVENT FROM TRAVELING FURTHER
obstukel, obstacle
obstunint, obstinate
obsulesens, obsolescent(nce)
obsulesense, obsolescent
obsulete, obsolete
obsurvashen, observe(vation)
obt, opt
obtain, *, ned, ning, nment, nable, ACQUIRE, COME INTO POSSESSION OF
obtametry, optometry
obtamist, optimist
obtamize, optimize
obtane, obtain
obtein, obtain
obtek, optic
obtekul, optic(al)
obtemal, optimal
obtemist, optimist
obtemize, optimize
obtemum, optimum
obteshen, optician
obtience, obedience
obtik, optic
obtikul, optic(al)
obtimesum, optimism
obtimum, optimum
obtishen, optician
obtometrist, optometry(rist)
obtometry, optometry
obtomitrist, optometry(rist)
obtreshen, optician
obtroosive, obtrusive
obtrude, *, ed, ding, usion, usive, er, STICKS OUT, FORCED PRESENCE IN UNWELCOME WAY

obtrusive, ely, eness, ion, INTRUDES ON OTHERS, NOT WELCOME, THRUSTS OUT "prefixes: un"
obtumal, optimal
obtumem, optimum
obtumist, optimist
obtumistek, optimist(ic)
obtumize, optimize
obtumizum, optimism
obul, opal
obulent, opulent
obulint, opulent
obusev, abuse(sive)
obusif, abuse(sive)
obuzit, opposite
obveus, obvious
obvious, sly, sness, MOST APPARENT, PLAIN TO SEE/ INTERPRET
obzurvashen, observe(vation)
oc, PREFIX INDICATING "AGAINST/ TOWARDS/ IN THE WAY OF" MOST OFTEN MODIFIES THE WORD
ocashen, occasion
ocasional, occasion(al)
occasion, *, ned, nal, nally, nalism, NOT FREQUENT/ OFTEN
ocularist, ocular(ist)
occult, *, tism, A SCHOOL OF THOUGHT OUTSIDE OF SOCIETAL NORMS, KNOWLEDGE CONCERNING THE ESOTERIC SCIENCES
occupancy, cies, SPECIFIC NUMBER OF SPACES SET ASIDE FOR PEOPLE TO OCCUPY
occupation, *, nal, JOB/ ACTIVITY, BE IN A CERTAIN SPACE IN TIME "prefixes: non/ pre"
occupy, pies, pied, pying, pation, piable, pier, TO FILL A SPACE "prefixes: pre/ un"
occur, *, rred, rring, rrence, rrences, rrent, TO TAKE PLACE/ HAPPEN
occurinse, occur(rrence)
ocean, *, nic, LARGEST BODIES OF WATER "prefixes: inter/ sub"
ocen, ocean
ocerents, occur(rrence)
ockleit, osculate / oscillate
ocksadate, oxidate

Term	Definition/Related
ocksidate	oxidate
ocksudate	oxidate
ocksudation	oxidate(ticn)
ocra	A PALE YELLOW COLOR (or see okra)
ocru	ocra / okra
ocs	ox
ocsaid	oxide
ocsidant	oxidant
ocsileit	osculate / oscillate
ocsillen	oxygen
oct, PREFIX INDICATING "EIGHT" MOST OFTEN MODIFIES THE WORD	
octa, PREFIX INDICATING "EIGHT" MOST OFTEN MODIFIES THE WORD	
octagon	SIDED SHAPE WITH ANGLES
octahedron, * , ra, ral, FACED SOLID	
octajidron	octahedron
octane, *, METHANE HYDROCARBON	
octave, *, SECTION OF 8 TONES	
octein	octave
octif	octave
octihedron	octahedron
octo, PREFIX INDICATING "EIGHT" MOST OFTEN MODIFIES THE WORD	
october, A MONTH OF THE YEAR (ENGLISH)	
octopus, pi, SEA CREATURE WITH 8 ARMS	
octouber	october
octuf	octave
octugon	octagon
octuhedron	octahedron
octupus	octopus
ocular, rist, rly, ulist, OF THE EYE AND EYESIGHT "prefixes: intra"	
ocult	occult
ocupancy	occupancy
ocupashen	occupation
ocupation	occupation
ocupied	occupy(pied)
ocupy	occupy
ocurence	occur(rrence)
ocurinse	occur(rrence)
od, odd	ode / ought
odamin	ottoman
odamotive	automotive
odd, *, ddly, ddish, ddness, ddity, NOT EVEN/ NORMAL (or see ode/ ought)	
oddesy	odyssey
ode, POEM (or see odd/ ought)	
odeanse	audience
odeble	audible
odeinse	audience
odem	autumn
odeo	audio
oder	odor / otter / outer / utter / udder / other / odd(er)
odeshen	audition
odesy	odyssey
odet	audit
odete	odd(ity)
odetion	audition
odetoreum	auditorium
odety	odd(ity)
odible	audible
odim	autumn
odio	audio
odir	odor / otter/ outer / utter / udder / other / odd(er)
odishun	audition
odisi	odyssey
odissy	odyssey
odisy	odyssey
odit	audit
odite	odd(ity)
odition	audition
oditorium	auditorium
odity	odd(ity)
odle	odd(ly)
odly	odd(ly)
odmeal	oatmeal
odnes	odd(ness)
odobiaugrufe	autobiography
odograf	autograph
odomashen	automatic(ion)
odomatik	automatic
odomen	ottoman
odometer, *, INSTRUMENT THAT MEASURES NUMBER OF REVOLUTIONS OF A WHEEL AND DISTANCE	
odomobeel	automobile
odomotive	automotive
odor, *, rous, rless, SMELL (or see otter/ udder) "prefixes: in"	
oduble	audible
odum	autumn
odumin	ottoman
odur	odor / otter / outer / utter / udder / other / odd(er)
odyssey, *, A JOURNEY	
oel	oil
oeng	owe(wing)
oer	or / oar / over
oestur	oyster
oeul	oil
oeuly	oil
of, A WORD WHICH HELPS TO PULL SENTENCE STRUCTURE TOGETHER (or see off)	
ofarall	overall
ofary	ovary
ofashen	ovation
ofation	ovation
ofecial	official
ofel	awful / oval
ofem	ovum
ofen	oven / often
ofend	offend
ofense	offense
ofensive	offense(sive)
ofer	offer / over
oferbering	overbearing
ofercast	overcast
ofercot	overcoat
ofercout	overcoat
ofercum	overcome
oferien	ovary(rian)
oferkame	overcame
oferkast	overcast
oferkot	overcoat
oferkum	overcome
oferlay	overlay
oferly	over(ly) / overly
oferot	overwrought
ofert	overt / avert
oferture	overture

oferwelming,overwhelm(ing)
ofery,ovary
ofes,office
ofeser,office(r)
ofeshul,official
ofewlate,ovulate
off, NOT OPERATING, NOT ON (or see of)
offend, *, ded, ding, nse, TO IRRITATE/ ANNOY, BREAK RULES
offense, *, eless, sive, sively, siveness, INITIATE, MAKE THE FIRST MOVE "prefixes: in"
offer, *, red, ring, TO GRANT/ GIVE
offes,office
office, *, er, A PLACE/ PERSON CONDUCTING BUSINESS "prefixes: inter"
official, *, lly, lism, ASSIGNED BY DUTY, CONFIRMED BY AUTHORITY "prefixes: semi/ un"
offurt,overt / avert
ofice,office
oficer,office(r)
oficial,official
ofil,awful / oval
ofim,ovum
ofin,oven / often
ofind,offend
ofinse,offense
ofinsuf,offense(sive)
ofir,offer / over
ofirbering,overbearing
ofircame,overcame
ofircast,overcast
ofircot,overcoat
ofircum,overcome
ofirkame,overcame
ofirkast,overcast
ofirkot,overcoat
ofirkum,overcome
ofirly,over(ly)
ofirot,overwrought
ofirwelming,overwhelm(ing)
ofiry,ovary
ofis,office
ofiser,office(r)

ofishul,official
ofishuly,official(lly)
ofol,oval
often, FREQUENTLY, DO SOMETHING MORE THAN NOT
oftin,often
oful,awful / oval
ofulashen,ovulate(tion)
ofulate,ovulate
ofulation,ovulate(tion)
ofum,ovum
ofur,offer / over
ofurall,overall
ofurbering,overbearing
ofurcame,overcame
ofurcast,overcast
ofurla,overlay
ofurly,over(ly) / overly
ofurot,overwrought
ofurt,overt / avert
ofurture,overture
ofurwelming,overwhelm(ing)
ofury,ovary
ofus,office
ofuser,office(r)
ofvir,over
ofvur,over
ogast,august
oger,auger / ogre
ogern,adjourn
ogest,august
ogir,ogre / auger
ogirn,adjourn
ogist,august
ogli,ugly
ogly,ugly
ogment,augment
ogmint,augment
ogorn,adjourn
ogre, *, UGLY AND MEAN (or see auger)
ogua,aqua
ogur,ogre / auger
ogust,august
ogwa,aqua

ogwu,aqua
ogzelery,auxiliary
ogzilery,auxiliary
oh, AN EXCLAMATION OF SURPRISE OR SUDDENNESS
oil, *, led, ler, ling, ly, lier, liest, SLIPPERY/ LUBRICATING SUBSTANCE
oing,owe(wing)
ointment, *, A SALVE/ LOTION APPLIED TO THE SKIN FOR HEALING
oiol,oil
oister,oyster
ojern,adjourn
ojorn,adjourn
ok,okay / oak
okashenul,occasion(al)
okashiun,occasion
okay,O.K./ YES/ FINE
okeishon,occasion
okerinse,occur(rrence)
okest,august
okewpansy,occupancy
okewpie,occupy
okist,august
okiular,ocular
okiupansi,occupancy
okiupay,occupy
oklok,o'clock
okra,A VEGETABLE (or see ocra)
oks,ox
oksadashen, oxidate(tion)
oksadate, oxidate
oksagen,oxygen
oksedate, oxidate
oksedation, oxidate(tion)
oksejin,oxygen
oksen,ox(en)
okshin, auction
oksid,oxide
oksidashen, oxidate(tion)
oksidate, oxidate
oksidation, oxidate(tion)
oksigen,oxygen
oksijen,oxygen

oksilery,auxiliary
oksudashen,oxidate(tion)
oksudate,oxidate
oksin,ox(en)
oksudation,oxidate(tion)
oksugen,oxygen
oktahedron,octahedron
oktane,octane
oktegon,octagon
oktehedron,octahedron
oktev,octave
oktif,octave
oktihedron,octahedron
oktober,october
oktopus,octopus
oktuf,octave
oktugon,octagon
okularest,ocular(ist)
okult,occult
okupashen,occupation
okupensy,occupancy
okupit,occupy(pied)
okupy,occupy
okur,occur
okurinse,occur(rrence)
okust,august
okwa,aqua
okwadukt,aqueduct
okwafer,aquifer
okward,awkward
okwefer,aquifer
okword,awkward
okwu,aqua
okwurd,awkward
okzilary,auxiliary
ol,owl / all / awl / old
olastick,elastic
olau,allow
olaw,allow
olcer,ulcer
old,der,dest,PAST ITS PRIME,OF THE PAST
ole,old / all / awl
olef,olive

olempek,olympic
olempic,olympic
olesit,elicit / illicit
oleve,olive
olfebet,alphabet
olif,olive
olimpic,olympic
olisit,elicit / illicit
olive,*,A FRUIT FROM A TREE
oll,all
olmenak,almanac
olmost,almost
olone,alone
olser,ulcer
olso,also
olt,old
oltegether,altogether
olter,altar / alder / alter
olternativ,alternative
olternutev,alternative
oltigether,altogether
oltiriar,ulterior
oltirnutev,alternative
oltra,ultra
oltugethur,altogether
oltur,altar / alder / alter
olturnativ,alternative
olturnutev,alternative
oluf,aloof / olive
oluv,olive
olwaz,always
olympic,*,RELATING TO GAMES/ COUNTRY/ MOUNTAIN
om,home / them
omaga,omega
omed,omit / emit
omeded,omit(tted) / emit(tted)
omega,LAST,AT THE END
omeka,omega
omenus,ominous
omesable,omit(issible)
omeshin,omission / emission
omet,omit / emit
ometion,omission / emission

ominous,sly,sness,A SIGN,THREATENING DUE TO LACK OF UNDERSTANDING,FOREBODING
ominus,ominous
omishen,omission / emission
omissible,LEAVE SOMETHING OUT
omission,*,ible,THE ACT OF LEAVING SOMETHING OUT (or see emission)
omit,*,tted,tting,issible,ission,LEAVE SOMETHING OUT (or see emit)
omition,omission / emission
omne,omni
omnefurus,omnivore(ous)
omnevore,omnivore
omnevorus,omnivore(ous)
omni,ALL AS ONE,HAVING IT ALL,ALL OF IT,PREFIX INDICATING "ALL" MOST OFTEN MODIFIES THE WORD
omniferus,omnivore(ous)
omniverus,omnivore(ous)
omnivore,*,rous,rously,EATS ANYTHING DIGESTIBLE
omnuvore,omnivore
on,OPERATING,FUNCTIONING,PERFORMING (or see own/ one)
onabrichd,unabridged
onabrilld,unabridged
onarary,honorary
onbinown,unbeknown
once,ONLY ONE TIME,FORMER (or see want(s)/ ounce)
oncol,uncle
oncore,encore
ond,own(ed)
onder,under
onderhand,underhand
ondermain,undermine
ondernith,underneath
onderstand,understand
onderwei,underwear
onderwer,underwear
onderwey,underway
ondis,undies
ondiuleit,undulate
one,*,eness,SINGLE,NUMERAL MEANING LESS THAN TWO BUT MORE THAN ZERO(or see won/ own)

onebreated, inebriate(d)
oneng, awning / own(ing)
oner, honor / owner
onerable, honor(able)
onerd, unearth
onerth, unearth
onest, honest
onibreated, inebriate(d)
oning, awning / own(ing)
onion, *, A VEGETABLE
onir, honor / owner
onirable, honor(able)
onist, honest
onkore, encore
onle, only
onles, unless
onli, only
only, NO EXCEPTIONS, EXCLUSIVELY, MERELY
onomaly, anomaly
onor, honor / owner
onoruble, honor(able)
onruli, unruly
onry, ornery / honorary
ons, own(s) / ounce
onsbekable, unspeakable
onsboken, unspoken
onse, once / one(s) / own(s) / ounce
ont, own(ed)
ontel, until
ontil, until
onto, ON/ TO, ABOUT/ TOWARDS (or see unto)
ontra, entree
ontrapreneur, entrepreneur
ontre, entree
ontrupreneur, entrepreneur
ontu, onto
ontueprenuer, entrepreneur
onuiting, unwitting
onurary, honorary
onvasef, invasive
onward, *, FORWARD
onword, onward
onwry, ornery / honorary

onwurd, onward
onyen, onion
onyun, onion
oos, ooze
ooserp, usurp
oosurp, usurp
ooze, *, ed, zing, GENTLE FLOW, GENERAL OVERALL APPEARANCE OF EXCESSIVE, HEAVY MOISTURE
op, PREFIX INDICATING "AGAINST/ TOWARDS/ IN THE WAY OF" MOST OFTEN MODIFIES THE WORD (or see up)
opacalips, apocalypse
opaculips, apocalypse
opake, opaque
opakulips, apocalypse
opal, *, AN IRIDESCENT STONE
opalescence, nt, HAVING A COATING/ APPEARANCE OF RAINBOW COLORED/ IRIDESCENT LIGHT, FILMY/ COLORFUL
opaque, *, ely, NON-TRANSPARENT, DULL, DENSE
oparade, operate
oparate, operate
opaset, opposite
opasit, opposite
opaukalips, apocalypse
opaukolips, apocalypse
opazeshen, oppose(sition)
opazit, opposite
opbit, upbeat
opcion, option
opdemais, optimize
opdemom, optimum
opdimom, optimum
opeate, opiate
opeic, opaque
opel, opal
open, *, ned, ning, nness, ner, INVITING, ALLOWING, PENETRABLE, ACCEPTING "prefixes: re"
openeun, opinion
openyun, opinion
oper, upper
opera, *, retta, PLAY/ DRAMA WITH MUSIC/ SINGING

operable, bility, ly, CAN BE OPERATED ON "prefixes: in/ inter"
oparade, operate
oparader, operate(tor)
operashen, operate(tion)
operate, *, ed, ting, tion, tional, tive, tivity, tively, tor, MAKE FUNCTIONAL, PUT INTO EFFECT, MAKE ACTIVE, REMEDY WITH ACTION "prefixes: in/ post/ pre"
operative, *, ely, MAKE FUNCTIONAL/ ACTIVE, PUT INTO EFFECT, REMEDY, ENGAGE/EMPLOY "prefixes: in"
operater, operate(tor)
opereit, operate
opertune, opportune
opertunedy, opportune(nity)
opertunest, opportune(st)
opertunity, opportune(nity)
opesishen, oppose(sition)
opesit, opposite
opeum, opium
opeute, opiate
opewlent, opulent
opezit, opposite
opfeis, obvious
opfeus, obvious
ophil, awful
ophul, awful
opiate, *, DRUG/ NARCOTIC USED TO DULL PAIN AND INDUCE SLEEP
opil, opal
opilesent, opalescence(nt)
opilesinse, opalescence
opilessence, opalescence
opin, open
opinion, *, ned, nated, A JUDGMENT/ THOUGHT
opirashen, operate(tion)
opirate, operate
opirtune, opportune
opirtunedy, opportune(nity)
opirtunist, opportune(st)
opirtunity, opportune(nity)
opiruble, operable
opisit, opposite

opium, JUICE FROM FLOWERING POPPY FRUIT
opizit, opposite
opjev, upheave
oplagashen, obligate(tion)
opland, upland
opleveus, oblivious
opligate, obligate
oplige, oblige(d)
oplij, oblige(d)
opliveus, oblivious
oplivion, oblivion
oplong, oblong
oplugashen, obligate(tion)
oplugate, obligate
opnokshes, obnoxious
opocalips, apocalypse
opokolips, apocalypse
opol, opal
opolstri, upholstery
opon, upon
oponent, opponent
oponit, opponent
oporashin, operate(tion)
oporate, operate
oportune, opportune
opose, oppose
oposet, opposite
opossum, A MARSUPIAL ANIMAL
opostrufe, apostrophe
opounent, opponent
opous, oppose
opozishen, oppose(sition)
opasite, opposite
oppezit, opposite
opponent, *, THE OTHER SIDE IN COMPETITION, ONE OF TWO SIDES COMPETING
opportune, ely, eness, nism, nist, nistic, nistically, nity, nities, FAVORABLE MOMENT TO ACT/ MAKE A CHANGE "prefixes: in"
oppose, *, ed, sing, site, sitely, siteness, sition, ADVERSE/ CONTRARY/ CONTRASTING "prefixes: ur"
opposishen, oppose(sition)

opposite, *, ely, eness, tion, ADVERSE/ CONTRARY/ CONTRASTING
opposum, opossum
oppreshen, oppress(ion)
oppress, sses, ssed, ssing, ssion, ssive, ssively, ssiveness, ssor, CONTROL OTHER'S FREEWILL BEYOND REASONABLE EXTENT, TYRANNIZE, CRUEL/ UNUSUAL PUNISHMENT
opptimism, optimism
opptomistic, optimist(ic)
oppusite, opposite
opra, opera
oprait, upright
oprasef, opress(ive) / abrasive
oprasuf, opress(ive) / abrasive
oprater, operate(tor)
opres, oppress
opreshen, oppress(ion)
opresif, opress(ive) / abrasive
opress, oppress
opror, uproar
opru, opera
oprut, uproot
opsalesens, obsolescent(nce)
opsalesent, obsolescent
opscure, obscure
opseen, obscene
opselesens, obsolescent(nce)
opselete, obsolete
opsenity, obscene(nity)
opserve, observe
opset, upset
opshin, option
opsilesens, obsolescent(nce)
opsilesent, obsolescent
opsilete, obsolete
opsion, option
opsirvashen, observe(vation)
opskure, obscure
opsolesens, obsolescent(nce)
opsolete, obsolete
opstatrishen, obstetrician
opsteich, upstage

opsteill, upstage
opstekul, obstacle
opstenit, obstinate
opsters, upstairs
opstikul, obstacle
opstinesy, obstinate(acy)
opstitrishen, obstetrician
opstrukshen, obstruct(ion)
opstrukt, obstruct
opstukel, obstacle
opstunint, obstinate
opstutrishen, obstetrician
opsulesens, obsolescent(nce)
opsulesense, obsolescent
opsulete, obsolete
opsurvashen, observe(vation)
opt, ted, ting, tion, THE ACT OF MAKING A CHOICE, PREFIX INDICATING "EYE/ VISION" MOST OFTEN MODIFIES THE WORD
optametry, optometry
optamism, optimism
optamist, optimist
optamistek, optimist(ic)
optamisum, optimism
optamize, optimize
optane, obtain
optek, optic
optemais, optimize
optemal, optimal
optemistic, optimist(ic)
optemisum, optimism
optemum, optimum
opteshen, optician
optic, *, cal, cally, CONCERNING THE EYE
optician, *, DOCTOR WHO WORKS WITH EYES
optico, PREFIX INDICATING "EYE/ VISION" MOST OFTEN MODIFIES THE WORD
optimal, lly, lity, BEST THAT CAN BE ACHIEVED
optimesm, optimism
optimism, stic, BELIEF BASED ON HOPE/ FAITH, LOOKS ON THE BRIGHT SIDE
optimist, tic, tically, sm, ize, ization, BASED ON HOPE/ FAITH, HOPE FOR A BRIGHTER FUTURE

optimize,*,ed,zing,zation,mum,TO MAXIMIZE, REAP GREATEST BENEFIT FROM
optimum,*,OPTIMAL, HOPE FOR THE BEST
option,*,ned,nal,nally,A CHOICE
optishen,optician
opto,PREFIX INDICATING "EYE/ VISION" MOST OFTEN MODIFIES THE WORD
optometry,rist,ric,rical,DOCTOR OF THE EYES
optrood,obtrude
optrude,obtrude
optrusive,obtrusive
optumem,optimum
optumist,optimist
optumistek,optimist(ic)
optumle,optimal
opuard,upward
opul,opal
opulent,tly,nce,OVER ACCUMULATION OF WEALTH AND/ OR POWER
opulesense,opalescence
opulesent,opalescence(nt)
opulessence,opalescence
opulint,opulent
opun,open
opura,opera
opurader,operate(tor)
opurashen,operate(tion)
opurate,operate
opurtune,opportune
opurtunedy,opportune(nity)
opurtunest,opportune(st)
opurtunity,opportune(nity)
opusishen,oppose(sition)
opusit,opposite
opuzet,opposite
opuzishen,oppose(sition)
opuzit,opposite
opveus,obvious
opward,upward
opzerve,observe
oqua,aqua
oquelarist,ocular(ist)
oquepy,occupy

oquir,occur
oquiular,ocular
oquiupai,occupy
oquiupansi,occupancy
oquiur,occur
oqupensy,occupancy
oqupied,occupy(pied)
oqupy,occupy
oqwa,aqua
or, WORD USED AS A CONJUNCTION, OTHERWISE (or see oar/ ore/ over/ are)
oracle,*,lar,larity,larly,PERSON/ THING WHO HOLDS GREAT/ SECRET WISDOM (or see auricle)
orador,orator
orafes,orifice
orafus,orifice
oragen,origin
orageno,oregano
oragin,origin
orajin,origin
orajinate,originate
orakul,oracle / auricle
oral,lly,OF/ FROM THE MOUTH
orange,*,COLOR, FRUIT
oranll,orange
orashen,orator(tion)
orator,tion,tor,torical,torically,ry,ries,SPOKEN FROM THE MOUTH, PUBLIC SPEAKING
orb,*,bit,bited,biting,bital,biter,bitary,bicular,bicularly,bicularity,biculate,biculately,biteer,biteering, SPHERE, GLOBE, CIRCULAR "prefixes: sub"
orbut,orb(it)
orbutrate,arbitrate
orcanek,organic
orcanekly,organic(ally)
orcasem,orgasm
orced,orchid
orcestra,orchestra
orchard,*,FIELD OF FRUIT TREES
orchart,orchard
orchastra,orchestra
orchen,organ
orcherd,orchard

orchestra,*,al,ally,ate,ated,ating,ator,ation,GROUPS OF PEOPLE WITH INSTRUMENTS PERFORMING MUSIC TOGETHER IN SYNCHRONICITY
orchid,*,A FLOWER
orchird,orchard
orchistra,orchestra
orchurt,orchard
orcid,orchid
ordain,*,ned,ning,ner,nment,APPOINT "prefixes: pre"
ordane,ordain
ordanery,ordinary
ordaninse,ordinance
ordeal,*,MORE DRAMA THAN NECESSARY
ordein,ordain
ordel,ordeal
ordenary,ordinary
ordenate,ordinate
ordenense,ordinance
order,*,red,ring,rly,rliness,ORGANIZED, PROPER PLACEMENT, FOLLOWING SET OF RULES/ LAWS "prefixes: dis/ sub"
ordervs,hors d'oevres
ordinance,*,A LAW
ordinary,*,COMMON, EVERYDAY, AVERAGE "prefixes: sub"
ordinate,*,VERTICAL PLACEMENT/ POSITION "prefixes: sub"
ordinence,ordinance
ordinery,ordinary
ordir,order
ordirves,hors d'oevres
ordninse,ordinance
ordunery,ordinary
ordur,order
ordurvs,hors d'oevres
ore,*,ROCK CONTAINING METAL (or see oar)
orefis,orifice
orefus,orifice
oregano,AN HERB/ SPICE
oregen,origin
oregenate,originate
oregeno,oregano
oregin,origin

orginate,originate
oregino,oregano
oreint,orient
oreintul,orient(al)
orejen,origin
orejenal,origin(al)
orejenashen,originate(tion)
orejenat,origin(ate)
orejin,origin
orejinul,origin(al)
orel,oral
orenge,orange
orenj,orange
oretor,orator
oreundashen,orient(ation)
oreunt,orient
oreuntashen,orient(ation)
orfan,orphan
orfun,orphan
organ,*,nist,MUSICAL INSTRUMENT, A MAJOR INTERNAL BODY PART
organais,organize
organek,organic
organic,*,cally,city,cism,ALL NATURAL SUBSTANCE, FROM THE EARTH "prefixes: bio/ in"
organiseishon,organization
organism,*,mic,mically,A LIFE FORM
organization,*,nal,nally,SYSTEM/ METHOD OF OPERATION WHICH KEEPS A BODY/ HOST ALIVE, COLLECTION OF WORKING PARTS WHICH MAKE UP THE WHOLE "prefixes: dis"
organize,*,ed,zing,zable,er,zation,TO CREATE/ USE A METHOD/ SYSTEM WHICH CREATES ORDER/ FUNCTION BETWEEN MOVING PARTS "prefixes: dis/ re/ un"
orgasm,*,mic,mically,THE ELEVATED POINT/ HEIGHT OF AN EMOTIONAL/ PHYSICAL EXPERIENCE/ EVENT
orgazem,orgasm
orge,orgy
orgen,organ
orgenise,organize
orgeniseishon,organization
orgenism,organism
orgenuzashen,organization
orgin,organ / origin
orginazation,organization
orginesm,organism
orginise,organize
orginuzashen,organization
orgon,organ
orgunise,organize
orgunism,organism
orgy,gies,COMBINING NUMBERS OF BODIES WHO EXCESSIVELY INDULGE THEMSELVES
oriendul,orient(al)
orient,*,ted,ting,tates,tation,tational,tive,DEFINITE POSITION/ BEARING IN REFERENCE TO SPECIFIC POINTS, OF THE EAST "prefixes: dis"
oriental,*,lly,lism,list,lize,EASTERN PLACE IN RELATION TO THE REST OF THE WORLD
orifice,*,OPENINGS
origen,origin
origin,*,nal,nally,nality,nalities,nate,BEGINNING OF CREATION, FIRST THOUGHT, THE BEGINNING
originate,*,ed,ting,tion,tive,tively,tion,FROM WHERE IT BEGAN, FIRST THOUGHT
origineit,originate
orijenal,origin(al)
orijenate,originate
orijinal,origin(al)
orijineit,originate
orikul,oracle / auricle
oril,oral
orillijn,origin
orillilleit,originate
oringe,orange
orinj,orange
orivul,arrive(val)
orjy,orgy
orkan,organ
orkanek,organic
orkanekly,organic(ally)
orkanik,organic
orkanism,organism
orkanize,organize
orkanusashen,organization
orkastra,orchestra
orkasum,orgasm
orked,orchid
orken,organ
orkenasashen,organization
orkenism,organism
orkenize,organize
orkenuzashen,organization
orkestra,orchestra
orkestrete,orchestra(ate)
orket,orchid
orkid,orchid
orkin,organ
orkinasation,organization
orkinazashen,organization
orkinism,organism
orkinize,organize
orkistra,orchestra
orkit,orchid
orkunise,organize
orkunism,organism
orkustra,orchestra
orlli,orgy
ormer,armor
ormur,armor
ornade,ornate
ornament,*,tal,tally,tation,DECORATIONS, ACCESSORIZE, BEAUTIFY
ornamintal,ornament(al)
ornate,ely,eness,ARTISTICALLY DETAILED, EMBELLISHED
ornement,ornament
ornemintal,ornament(al)
ornery,riness,STUBBORN/ ADVERSE DISPOSITION OR ATTITUDE
ornge,orange
ornry,ornery
ornument,ornament
ornumentul,ornament(al)
orocle,oracle
orofes,orifice
orp,orb
orpet,orb(it)

orphan,*,nage,nhood, ONE LEFT WITHOUT PARENTS, PLACE FOR THOSE WITHOUT PARENTS
orphen,orphan
orpit,orb(it)
orput,orb(it)
orquestra,orchestra
orquid,orchid
orsherd,orchard
orshurd,orchard
ortanery,ordinary
ortenanse,ordinance
ortenary,ordinary
orter,order
orth, PREFIX INDICATING "MAKE NORMAL/ CORRECTION" MOST OFTEN MODIFIES THE WORD
orthodontic,*, ia, ist, TEETH/ DENTISTRY
orthodox,xes,xly,xy,xies,OF SOCIAL CUSTOM/ PRACTICE "prefixes: un"
orthopedic,*, cally, ist, TEETH/ DENTISTRY
orthridus,arthritis
orthudox,orthodox
ortinanse,ordinance
ortinary,ordinary
ortir,order
ortnense,ordinance
ortunense,ordinance
ortur,order
orufis,orifice
orugin,origin
orujin,origin
orukle,oracle / auricle
orukul,oracle / auricle
orul,oral
orunj,orange
orupt,erupt / irrupt
oryent,orient
oryentashen,orient(ation)
oryentol,oriental
oryentul,orient(al)
oryindashen,orient(ation)
os, us / owe(s)
osalate,osculate / oscillate
osanefurus,ozone(niferous)

---

oscillate,*, ed,ting,tion,tor,tory, VOLUME OF MOVEMENT/ VIBRATION IN BETWEEN,MOVE TO/ FRO (or see osculate)
osculate,*, ed, ting,tion,tor,tory, KISS, COME IN CONTACT, TWO OR MORE COINCIDENT POINTS (or see oscillate) "prefixes: inter"
osdrege,ostrich
osdrich,ostrich
osdrije,ostrich
ose,owe(s)
oselate,osculate / oscillate
osheanic,ocean(ic)
osher,usher
oshin,ocean
osilate,osculate / oscillate
osmose,ed,sing,sis, otic, otically, PENETRATION OF A BARRIER WHERE TWO SHARE THE SAME AS ONE, SHARING OF INFORMATION BETWEEN TWO "prefixes: end"
osmoses,osmose(sis)
osone,ozone
osonic,ozone(nic)
osonusfere,ozone(nosphere)
ost, PREFIX INDICATING "BONE" MOST OFTEN MODIFIES THE WORD
ostracize,*, ed,zing,ism, TO EXPEL OR EXCLUDE FROM A GROUP
ostrech,ostrich
ostreje,ostrich
ostresize,ostracize
ostrich,hes,A LARGE BIRD
ostrisize,ostracize
ostrusize,ostracize
osulashen,oscillate(tion)
osulate,osculate / oscillate
osum,awesome / assume
osuniferus,ozone(niferous)
ot, PREFIX INDICATING "EAR" MOST OFTEN MODIFIES THE WORD (or see oat/ odd/ ought/ ode)
otamate,automate
otamotive,automotive
otej,outage
otem,autumn

---

otemin,ottoman
oteo,audio
oter,odor / otter / outer / utter / udder
otesm,autism
otest,attest
otesy,odyssey
otezum,autism
oth,oath
othentik,authentic
other,*, THAT ONE NOT THIS ONE, THE FURTHER ONE, THE ALTERNATIVE (or see author)
othintik,authentic
othir,author
othoretarean,authoritarian
othorety,authority
othoritarean,authoritarian
othority,authority
othoruterein,authoritarian
otim,autumn
otiman,ottoman
otimobil,automobile
otimotive,automotive
otir,odor / otter / outer / utter / udder
otism,autism
otisum,autism
otisy,odyssey
otitoreum,auditorium
otizum,autism
otle,odd(ly)
otluk,outlook
otmel,oatmeal
otmost,utmost
otmoust,utmost
oto, PREFIX INDICATING "EAR" MOST OFTEN MODIFIES THE WORD
otobiografe,autobiography
otograf,autograph
otomadik,automatic
otoman,ottoman
otomashen,automatic(ion)
otomate,automate
otomobel,automobile
otomotive,automotive

otoneme,autonomy
otonume,autonomy
otopse,autopsy
otor,odor / otter / outer / utter / udder
otter,*,WATER MAMMAL
ottoman,*,FOOTSTOOL/ COUCH WITHOUT BACK/ ARMS
otur,odor / otter / outer / utter / udder
ou,oh / owe
oubediens,obedience
oubes,obese
oubey,obey
oubichueri,obituary
oubidiens,obedience
oubiquiti,ubiquity
oubis,obese
oubledereit,obliterate
oublitereit,obliterate
ouch,SOUND ASSOCIATED WITH PAIN/ GETTING HURT
oucra,okra / ocra
oud,ode / out
oudacity,audacity
oudameter,odometer
oudasedy,audacity
ouder,outer / odor
ouding,outing
oudomater,odometer
oudor,odor
oudsmart,outsmart
oudstand,outstand
oudwerd,outward
oudwet,outwit
oueisis,oasis
oufari,ovary
oufercast,overcast
oufercoat,overcoat
oufory,ovary
ouger,ogre
oughn,own
ought,SHOULD/ WOULD/ COULD TAKE ACTION/ DO SOMETHING
ouk,oak
oukei,o.k. / okay
oukra,okra

ould,old
oumega,omega
oumichon,omission
oumishon,omission
oumit,omit
ounce,*,MEASUREMENT FOR DRY PRODUCTS (or see once)
ounli,only
ouns,ounce / own(s)
oupal,opal
oupeic,opaque
oupen,open
oupiet,opiate
oupiom,opium
oupiulent,opulent
oupium,opium
oupres,oppress
our,*,BELONGS IN THE GROUP, OWNERSHIP (or see hour/ oar)
ourb,orb
ourle,hour(ly)
oushan,ocean
ousoun,ozone
out,tting,tage,ter,NOT IN, EXIT, NOT THERE ANY LONGER, BEYOND THE MAIN/ OBJECT, DOESN'T EXIST AS IT ONCE DID (or see ought)
outag,outage
outage,*,QUIT WORKING, LACKING WITHOUT
outer,BEYOND THE MAIN AREA OR BODY, NOT PART OF THE WHOLE ANY LONGER, EXTERIOR
outfit,*,tted,tting,tter,EXTERNAL GEAR/ CLOTHING
outgo,oes,oing,AWAY FROM THE CENTER, LEAVING THE AREA, REMOVED FROM THE PREVIOUS PLACE
outh,oath
outij,outage
outing,*,TAKE A SMALL EXCURSION AWAY, GO AWAY BRIEFLY
outlaw,*,PEOPLE WHO PERFORM ACTS OUTSIDE OF THE LAW
outlet,*,A WAY TO GET OUT
outline,*,ed,ning,BOUNDARIES OF, DEFINING PRINCIPLES, SKETCH OR WORDS DESCRIBING THE INSIDE

outlook,PERSPECTIVE OF THE OBSERVER, WAY OF PERCEPTION
outluk,outlook
outlying,ON THE OUTSKIRTS, OUTSIDE OF, BEYOND
outmial,oatmeal
outmil,oatmeal
outpost,*,A STATION OR POST OUTSIDE OF THE MAIN CONFINES, A REMOTE SETTLEMENT
output,THE RESULT OF MANUFACTURING, WHAT IS PRODUCED
outrage,*,ed,ging,eous,eously,eousness,EXCESSIVE EMOTIONAL REACTION, SUDDEN OUTBURST
outright,WITHOUT CONCEALMENT OR RESTRAINT, OPEN, STRAIGHT OUT
outset,AT THE BEGINNING
outside,er,NOT IN THE MAIN PORTION, REMOTE FROM THE CENTER
outskirt,*,AT THE EDGES OF TOWN, BORDER DISTRICTS
outskurt,outskirt
outsmart,*,ted,ting,OUTWIT
outstand,ding,STANDS OUT, PROTRUDES, APART FROM THE REST, LEAVE PORT
outward,*,dly,dness,AWAY FROM CENTER, TOWARDS THE EXTERIOR, ON THE OUTSIDE
outwit,*,tted,tting,OUTSMART, THINK FASTER THAN
ouval,oval
ouvari,ovary
ouveishon,ovation
ouver,over
ouverbearing,overbearing
ouvercast,overcast
ouvercom,overcome
ouvercot,overcoat
ouverkeim,overcome
ouverquein,overcome
ouverraht,overwrought
ouvioleit,ovulate
ouvol,oval
oval,*,lly,lness,ELONGATED CIRCLE, SHAPE OF EGG
ovalable,available
ovart,overt / avert
ovarwelming,overwhelm(ing)

Word	Definition	Related
ovary, ries, rian, rial, ritis, riotomy, riectomy,	REPRODUCTIVE GLANDS	
ovashen		ovation
ovashin		ovation
ovation, *,	ENTHUSIASTIC APPLAUSE	
ovau		avow
ovekt		evict
ovel		oval
ovem		ovum
oven, *, nable,	CONTAINER BUILT FOR HIGH HEAT TO COOK/ BAKE THINGS	
ovent		event
oventful		eventful
over, rly,	ABOVE AND BEYOND, MORE THAN NORMAL, PREFIX INDICATING "EXCESSIVELY/ COMPLETELY/ UPPER/ ABOVE/ OUTER" MOST OFTEN MODIFIES THE WORD	
overall,	SUMMARY, WITH ALL THINGS TAKEN INTO ACCOUNT	
overbearing, gly,	DOMINATING, OPPRESSING, TYRANNICAL, FORCEFUL	
overbering		overbearing
overcame,	PAST TENSE FOR THE WORD "OVERCOME"	
overcast, ting,	SHADOWING, GLOOMS OVER, SEWING ROUGH EDGES	
overcoat, *,	TO APPLY A COAT OVER ANOTHER	
overcome, ming, came,	TO RISE ABOVE AN OBSTACLE, TO MANAGE THROUGH A PROBLEM, RISE ABOVE OPPOSITION	
overcum		overcome
overhang, *, ging,	LEDGE/ OUTCROP WHICH JUTS OUT/ OVER, OVER AN UNDERCUT, HANGS UNDER	
overien		ovary(rian)
overkame		overcame
overkast		overcast
overkot		overcoat
overkum		overcome
overlap, *, pped, pping,	LAYER THAT PARTIALLY COVERS/ LAPS THE EDGE OF ANOTHER LAYER	
overlay, *, aid, ain, ying,	A COAT/ COVER AS TOP FOR PROTECTION	
overly,	TOO MUCH, TOO EXTREME	
overot		overwrought
overt, tly, tness,	NO ATTEMPT TO CONCEAL/ HIDE (or see avert)	
overter		overture
overture, *,	INTRODUCTION/ BEGINNING TO	
overwelming		overwhelm(ing)
overwhelm, *, med, ming, mingly,	OVERLOAD, OVERPOWERING, RESISTANCE IS FUTILE	
overwrot		overwrought
overwrought,	EMOTIONAL DISTRESS, TOO MUCH TO HANDLE GRACEFULLY	
overy		ovary
oveulate		ovulate
ovewlate		ovulate
ovil		oval
ovim		ovum
ovin		oven
ovint		event
ovintful		eventful
ovios		obvious
ovir		over
ovirall		overall
ovirbering		overbearing
ovircast		overcast
ovircot		overcoat
ovircum		overcome
ovirkast		overcast
ovirkot		overcoat
ovirkum		overcome
ovirla		overlay
ovirle		overly
ovirly		over(ly)
ovirot		overwrought
ovirshur		overture
ovirture		overture
ovirwelming		overwhelm(ing)
oviry		ovary
ovow		avow
ovul		oval
ovulashen		ovulate(tion)
ovulate, *, ed, ting, tion,	TO RELEASE AN EGG (OVUM) FROM THE OVARY "prefixes: pre"	
ovum, *,	AN EGG	
ovur		over
ovurall		overall
ovurbering		overbearing
ovurcast		overcast
ovurcoat		overcoat
ovurcum		overcome
ovure		ovary
ovurkame		overcame
ovurkast		overcast
ovurkot		overcoat
ovurkum		overcome
ovurla		overlay
ovurly		over(ly)
ovurot		overwrought
ovurt, overt /	avert	
ovurwelming		overwhelm(ing)
ovury		ovary
ow		owe
owc		oak
owch		ouch
owd, out / ought /	owe(d)	
owdacity		audacity
owdamotive		automotive
owdasedyy		audacity
owdege		outage
owdemotive		automotive
owdeng		outing
owdfit		outfit
owdimotive		automotive
owdir		outer
owdishun		audition
owdition		audition
owdline		outline
owdpost		outpost
owdrage		outrage
owdrit		outright
owdskirt		outskirt
owdsmart		outsmart
owdstand		outstand
owe, *, ed, wing,	TO BE INDEBTED FOR	
oweisis		oasis
owfercast		overcast
owl, *,	NOCTURNAL BIRD (or see oil)	

own,*,ned,ning,ner,HAVE FULL RIGHTS TO TITLE/ PROPERTY (or see one/ on) "prefixes dis"
owner,*,ONE WHO HOLDS RIGHTS/ TITLE TO PROPERTY
owns,ounce/ own(s)
owperable,operable
owr,are / hour / our
owra,aura
owrie,awry
owrit,outright
owrle,hour(ly)
owry,awry
owsh,ouch
owson,ozone
owt, out / ought
owtege,outage
owtej,outage
owtell,outage
owtfit,outfit
owtige,outage
owting,outing
owtir,outer
owtlaw,outlaw
owtlet,outlet
owtlieng,outlying
owtline,outline
owtlook,outlook
owtluk,outlook
owtpost,outpost
owtput,output
owtragus,outrage(ous)
owtraj,outrage
owtrite,outright
owtset,outset
owtside,outside
owtskirt,outskirt
owtsmart,outsmart
owtstand,outstand
owtwet,outwit
owtwit,outwit
owtwurd,outward
owur, hour / our
owval,oval
owveision,ovation

owverbering,overbearing
owvercast,overcast
owvercom,overcome
owveri,ovary
owverkeim,overcome
owvervat,overwrought
owviuleit,ovulate
ox,xen,xes,TYPE OF BOVINE (CATTLE)
oxa,PREFIX INDICATING "OXYGEN/ ADDITIONAL OXYGEN" MOST OFTEN MODIFIES THE WORD
oxadashen, oxidate(tion)
oxadate, oxidate
oxaid,oxide
oxajen,oxygen
oxedaiton, oxidate(tion)
oxedate,oxidant
oxedation,oxidate(tion)
oxejen,oxygen
oxejin,oxygen
oxidant,*,ation,ative, OXYGEN ACTIVELY PARTICIPATING WITH OTHER ELEMENTS
oxidashen,oxidate(tion)
oxidate, *, ed,ting,tion,ant, COATING/ RESIDUE RESULTANT OF REACTION WITH OXYGEN/OXIDES "prefixes: non/un"
oxide, * , dic, dize, dizes, dized, dizing, dizer, dizable, dation, dant, INTERACTION BETWEEN OXYGEN AND OTHER ELEMENTS "prefixes: sub"
oxijen,oxygen
oxilery, auxiliary
oxillen, oxygen
oxin,ox(en)
oxo,PREFIX INDICATING "OXYGEN/ ADDITIONAL OXYGEN" MOST OFTEN MODIFIES THE WORD
oxodashen, oxidate(tion)
oxsadashen, oxidate(tion)
oxsagen,oxygen
oxsigen,oxygen
oxsudashen, oxidate(tion)
oxudashen, oxidate(tion)
oxudate, oxidate
oxudiz, oxide(dize)
oxugen,oxygen

oxujin,oxygen
oxy,PREFIX INDICATING "OXYGEN/ ADDITIONAL OXYGEN" MOST OFTEN MODIFIES THE WORD
oxydate,oxidant
oxygen,nic, nicity, nate, nation,A GAS,GAS USED FOR RESPIRATION OF ALL LIVING THINGS
oyle,oil
oyntment,ointment
oyster,*,MARINE SHELLFISH,MOLLUSK
oystur,oyster
ozilate, osculate / oscillate
ozmosis,osmose(sis)
ozone,*,nic, niferous, nous, nide, nize, nized, nizing, nizer, nosphere, PURE AIR, FORM OF OXYGEN, LAYER AROUND THE EARTH
p,pea
pa,paw / pay
paber, paper / papier mache'
pabreka,paprika
pabur, paper / papier mache'
pace, *, ed, cing, er, RATE OF PROGRESS/ MOVEMENT, A GAIT/ STEP
pach, patch
pachen, passion
pachendly, patient(ly)
pachense, patience / patient(s)
pachin, passion
pachindly, patient(ly)
pachints, patience / patient(s)
pacht, patch(ed)
pacific, PEACEFUL, THE PACIFIC OCEAN
pacify, fies, fied, fying, fication, ficatory, fier, fism, TO CODDLE/ APPEASE/ SETTLE/ SOOTHE
pack, * , ked, king, kage, kaged, kaging, ker, ket, PREPARE FOR TRANSPORT "prefixes: pre/ retro/ un"
packet, *, SMALL COLLECTION OF DATA/ MATERIAL PROVIDING INFORMATION
packit, packet
pact, *, AN AGREEMENT (or see pack(ed))
pacterul,pectoral
pad, *, dded,dding,ddy, LAYER OF MATERIAL OF VARYING THICKNESS FOR PROTECTION, A RESIDENCE, BOTTOM OF PAW (or see pat/ paid)

pada, pate'
paddle,*, ed, ling, er, TO USE OARS/ FEET FOR MOBILIZATION, ITEM USED FOR ROWING, A SPANKING
paddock,*, SMALL AREA TO CONFINE ANIMALS/ VEHICLES TEMPORARILY
paddy, dies, HAVING TO DO WITH RICE (or see patty)
pade, paid / pad / paddy / patty / pate'
paded, pad(dded) / pat(tted)
padel, paddle
paden, patent
padeo, patio
padern, pattern
padestrein, pedestrian
padid, pad(dded) / pat(tted)
padik, paddock
padil, paddle
padin, patent
padio, patio
padiou, patio
padirn, pattern
padled, paddle(d)
padlock,*, LOCK WITH KEY OR COMBINATION DIAL
padok, paddock
padreark, patriarch
padrearkul, patriarch(al)
padreit, patriot / patriate
padren, patron
padreodic, patriot(ic)
padreut, patriot / patriate
padriarch, patriarch
padrin, patron
padrinize, patron(ize)
padrenize, patron(ize)
padrun, patron
padrunize, patron(ize)
padryet, patriot / patriate
padsee, patsy
padthulogical, pathology(gical)
padtult, paddle(d)
paduk, paddock
paduled, paddle(d)
padurn, pattern

pady, paddy / patty
pae, pay / pay(ee)
pael, pail / pale
paer, pay(er)
paet, paid
paf, pave
pafd, pave(d)
pafeleon, pavilion
paferty, poverty
pafileon, pavilion
pafmint, pave(ment)
paft, pave(d)
pafurted, pervert(ed)
pagamus, pajamas
pagan,*, nish, nism, nize, nizes, nized, nizing, nizer, PEOPLE WHO SUPPORT NATURE AS THEIR DEITY
page,*, ed, ging, ginate, gination, er, SHEET IN A BOOK, TO CALL FOR "prefixes: un"
pageant,*, try, tries, A SHOWY DISPLAY
pagen, pagan
pagenashen, page(gination)
pagenate, page(ginate)
pagense, patience / patient(s)
pagent, pageant
pagentre, pageant(ry)
pagin, pagan
paginashen, page(gination)
pagint, pageant
pagonism, pagan(ism)
pagun, pagan
pai, pay / pie / pi
paibul, pay(yable)
paic, pike
paid, PAST TENSE FOR THE WORD "PAY" (or see pad) "prefixes: pre/ re/ un"
pail,*, BUCKET TYPE VESSEL (or see pal/ pale/ pall)
pailet, pilot
pailot, pilot
pain,*, ned, nful, nfully, nfulness, nless, nlessly, nlessness, ENDINGS SENSING HARM/ THREAT (or see pane/ pine)
painapol, pineapple

paint,*, ted, ting, table, ter, MANMADE OR NATURAL BASED COLORANT, VIVID DESCRIPTION "prefixes: re/ under"
paiol, pile
paionir, pioneer
paios, pious
paip, pipe
pair,*, red, ring, TWO IDENTICAL/ SIMILAR ITEMS TOGETHER (or see par/ parr/ pare/ pear) "prefixes: un"
pairadox, paradox
pairait, pyrite
pairalise, paralyze
pairet, pirate
pairou, pyro
pairudox, paradox
pait, paid
paj, page
pajamas, SLEEPING GARMENTS
pajenashen, page(gination)
pajenate, page(ginate)
pajense, patience / patient(s)
pajent, pageant
pajinashen, page(gination)
pajint, pageant
pakd, pact / pack(ed)
pakeg, pack(age)
paket, packet
pakij, pack(age)
pakt, pact / pack(ed)
pakut, packet
pal,*, lled, lling, A FRIEND, SOMEONE YOU ENJOY HANGING OUT WITH (or see pail/ pale/ pall)
palace,*, DWELLING OF ROYALTY
palas, palace
palate, table, tableness, tability, tably, tal, tally, tize, ROOF OF THE MOUTH AS A SENSOR (or see pallet/ palette/ pallid) "prefixes: un"
pale,*, ed, ling, lish, ely, eness, llid, llidly, llidity, DIM/ WAN, STAKE WITH SHARP END, SPACE WITHIN A FIXED BOUNDARY (or see pal/ pall)
paled, pale(d) / palate / palette / pallet / pallid
paleduble, palate(table)

paleintology, paleontology
palenate, pollinate
paleo, PREFIX INDICATING "EARLY/ ANCIENT/ PREHISTORIC" MOST OFTEN MODIFIES THE WORD
paleontology, gies, SCIENCE CONCERNED WITH ALL LIFE IN THE PAST
paleredy, polar(ity)
palerity, polar(ity)
pales, palace / police / pale(s)
palesh, polish
palesy, policy
palet, palate / palette / pallet / pallid
paletical, politic(al)
palette, *, PAINTER'S BOARD, VARIETY OF COLORS/ TECHNIQUES (or see pallet/ palate)
paleuntology, paleontology
palid, pallid / palate / pa ette / pallet
paliduble, palate(table)
paligamus, polygamy(mous)
paligemy, polygamy
paligine, polygyny
palin, pollen
palinize, pollen(ize)
palip, polyp
palise, palace
palish, polish
palisy, policy
palit, palate / palette / pallet / polite / pallid
palitasize, politic(ize)
palite, palate / palette / pallet / polite / pallid
palitecal, politic(al)
palituble, palate(table)
pall, *, EVOKES A DULL/ OPPRESSIVE ATMOSPHERE, COVERING FOR A COFFIN (or see pal/ pale/ pail)
pallet, *, tize, tized, tizing, PLATFORM TO HOLD GOODS, A TOOL, IN A CLOCK/ WATCH, POTTER'S TOOL (or see palette/ palate/ pallid)
pallid, dly, dness, LACKS COLOR (or see palette/ palate/ pallet)
pallor, *, PALE IN COLOR, UNNATURAL COLOR
palm, *, THE HAND, A PLANT
palpitate, *, ed, ting, tion, PULSATE, TREMBLE
palt, pale(d)

palud, pallid
paluduble, palate(table)
paluse, palace
palushen, pollute(tion)
palut, palate / palette / pallet / pollute
palutent, pollute(tant)
palutics, politic(s)
palution, pollute(tion)
palygamus, polygamy(mous)
palyginy, polygyny
palyintology, paleontology
pam, palm
pamendo, pimento
pament, pay(ment)
pamento, pimento
pamflet, pamphlet
pamint, pay(ment)
pamphlet, *, PUBLICATION CONSISTING OF FOLDED PIECES OF PAPER WITH TEXT
pamplet, pamphlet
pamunt, pay(ment)
pan, *, nned, nning, FLAT METAL WITH SIDES, A COOKING UTENSIL, PREFIX INDICATING 'ALL' MOST OFTEN MODIFIES THE WORD (or see pane/ pain)
pancho, poncho
pancreas, atic, atin, PART OF THE STOMACH
pancreus, pancreas
pand, pond / pant
panda, *, A BLACK/ WHITE BEAR
pandees, pant(ies)
pander, ponder
pandilunes, pantaloon(s)
pandre, pantry
pandulunes, pantaloon(s)
pane, *, FRAME TO PLACE GLASS/ PHOTOGRAPHS, DIAMOND FACE (or see pain)
panek, panic
panel, *, led, ling, list, FLAT SHEET USED FOR COVER/ DECORATION, PEOPLE WORKING AS A GROUP TO MAKE A DECISION
panemine, pantomime
panensula, peninsula
paneramic, panorama(mic)

panic, *, cked, cking, cky, SUDDEN OVERWHELMING FEAR WHICH CAUSES REACTION
panik, panic
panil, panel
panimine, pantomime
paninsula, peninsula
paniramic, panorama(mic)
pankreus, pancreas
panol, panel
panomine, pantomime
panorama, *, mic, mically, ABILITY TO VIEW/ OBSERVE ENTIRE EVENT/ SCENE WITHOUT OBSTRUCTION
panoramic, panorama(mic)
pant, *, ted, ting, ties, BREATH/ GASP HEAVILY, ARTICLE OF CLOTHING FOR LEGS/ LOWER TORSO, UNDERWEAR (or see paint/ pan(nned)) "prefixes: under"
pantaloon, *, LOOSE FITTING PANTS
pantees, pant(ies)
panteloons, pantaloon(s)
pantemine, pantomime
panther, *, LARGE WILD CAT
panthur, panther
pantilunes, pantaloon(s)
pantimime, pantomime
pantomime, *, ed, ming, mist, mic, COMMUNICATE WITH GESTURES, NON SPEAKING PERFORMANCE
pantre, pantry
pantry, ries, A FOOD STORAGE CLOSET / ROOM
pantu, panda
pantulunes, pantaloon(s)
pantumime, pantomime
pantys, pant(ies)
panul, panel
panulist, panel(ist)
panumine, pantomime
paode, peyote
paodur, powder
paond, pound
paonse, pounce
paont, pound
paote, peyote
papaya, *, A FRUIT
papcorn, popcorn

**paper,*,,red,ring,rer,riness,ry,rless,USABLE SHEET OF MATERIAL FOR INK/ PAINT, MADE OF WOOD/ HEMP PULP, TO APPLY PAPER (or see paper)
**papier mache',DIFFERENT TYPES OF PAPER PUT TOGETHER, COLLAGE OF PAPER (or see paper)
papir,paper / pauper / pop(pper)
papor,paper / pauper / pop(pper)
papreka,paprika
**paprika,*,A SPICE
papur,paper / pauper / pop(pper)
papyu,papaya
**par,rred,rring,rity,AN AVERAGE OR NORMAL, BALANCE EQUALLY, A PREFIX, SPORTS TERM (or see parr/ pear/ pair/ pare) "prefixes: sub"
**para,PREFIX INDICATING "BESIDE/ BEYOND" MOST OFTEN MODIFIES THE WORD
**parable,*,,list,SHORT STORY/ SENTENCES WHICH REFLECTS HUMAN EMOTIONAL WISDOMS (or see parabola)
**parabola,*,,lic,BOWL SHAPE (or see parable)
**parachute,*,,ed,ting,tist,DEVICE FOR DROPPING FROM GREAT HEIGHT/ PLANES
**parade,*,,ed,ding,AN ORGANIZED CEREMONIAL MARCH DOWN STREETS OF A CITY
**paradigm,*,,matic,MAKING RELATIVE COMPARISONS, CATEGORIZING INTO A DEFINED SET
**paradox,xes,xical,xically,A CONTRADICTION OF TERMS, WORDS/ ACTIONS WHICH CANCEL EACH OTHER OUT
**paraffin,nic,MELTABLE/ WAXY SUBSTANCE
**paragraph,*,,SEVERAL SENTENCES TOGETHER SUPPORTING A THEME
**parakeet,*,A TROPICAL BIRD
paralais,paralyze
paralasis,paralysis
paralel,parallel
**parallel,*,,led,ling,EACH GOING THE SAME DIRECTION, SIDE BY SIDE, BELONG TOGETHER "prefixes: un"
parallyzed,paralyze(d)
paralusis,paralysis
**paralysis,ytic,yze,LOOSE ABILITY TO MOVE VOLUNTARILY

**paralyze,*,,ed,zing,ysis,ytic,ytically,LOOSE ABILITY TO MOVE VOLUNTARILY
paramater,parameter / perimeter
**paramedic,,*,,cal,MEDICAL PROFESSIONAL WHO TRAVELS TO GATHER INJURED/ SICK PEOPLE
**parameter,*,,tric,trical,A DEFINED BOUNDARY WHICH BELONGS AS A UNIT, A MATH EXPRESSION
parametic,paramedic
paramiter,parameter / perimeter
**paramount,tly,tcy,UPMOST IN IMPORTANCE, AT THE TOP, SUPERIOR TO ANYTHING ELSE
**paranoia,id,ic,FEAR WITHOUT APPARENT REASON
paranoyd,paranoia(id)
**paraplegia,ic,PARALYSIS OF LOWER TORSO, LOWER HALF OF BODY CANNOT BE MOVED VOLUNTARILY
paraquit,parakeet
**parasite,*,,tic,tical,tically,ticide,ticidal,tism,tize,tology,tosis,TAKES NOURISHMENT FROM ANOTHER WITHOUT PERMISSION/ WILLINGNESS FROM HOST "prefixes: endo"
parate,parade
**paratrooper,*,,ONE WHO JUMPS FROM PLANE WITH A PARACHUTE
**parcel,*,,led,ling,A SMALL PACKAGE, BOXED ITEMS, SMALL SECTION OF LAND, TO SECTION OFF
**parch,hed,hment,DRY, NEEDS MOISTURE
parcht,parch(ed)
parcle,parcel
pard,part / pair(ed) / pare(d)
pardake,partake
parde,party
pardekul,particle
pardes,party(ties)
pardesapate,participate
pardesubate,participate
pardezan,partisan
pardikul,particle
pardisubant,participate(ant)
pardisupate,participate
pardizan,partisan
pardner,partner
pardnur,partner
**pardon,*,,ned,ning,nable,nably,FORGIVE "prefixes: un"

pardukle,particle
pardun,pardon
parduzen,partisan
pardy,party
**pare,*,,ed,ring,TRIM, CUT-OFF (or see par/ parr/ pair/ pear)
parebolic,parabola(lic) / parable(lic)
paredime,paradigm
paredoks,paradox
parefen,paraffin
pareferul,peripheral
paregraf,paragraph
paregraph,paragraph
pareid,parade
parekeet,parakeet
parel,peril
parelel,parallel
parelize,paralyze
paremedic,paramedic
paremeter,perimeter / parameter
paremider,perimeter / parameter
paremount,paramount
parend,parent
parendul,parent(al)
pareneul,perennial
parenial,perennial
parenoid,paranoia(id)
parense,parent(s)
**parent,*,,ted,ting,tal,tage,PROVIDER OF DNA TO BIRTHED OFFSPRING "prefixes: bi"
**parenthesis,es,etic,tical,tically,ize,izes,ized,izing,TWO MARKS (SHAPED LIKE CRESCENT MOONS) ON EITHER SIDE OF WORDS INSERTED INTO A SENTENCE
parepheral,peripheral
pareplegic,paraplegia(ic)
parescope,periscope
paresh,parish / perish
paretruper,paratrooper
parews,peruse
parfa,parfait
parfae,parfait
**parfait,DESSERT

pari, PREFIX INDICATING "EQUAL" MOST OFTEN MODIFIES THE WORD
paribolic, parabola(lic) / parable(lic)
paride, parity / parody / parrot
paridime, paradigm
paridokical, paradox(ical)
paridoks, paradox
parifen, paraffin
parifuril, peripheral
parigraf, paragraph
parikeet, parakeet
pariel, parallel
parilize, paralyze
parimiter, perimeter / parameter
parimount, paramount
parind, parent
parinoid, paranoia(id)
parinse, parent(s)
parint, parent
parintal, parent(al)
parinthases, parenthesis
paripheral, peripheral
pariplegic, paraplegia(ic)
pariscope, periscope
parish, hes, hioner, CHURCH CONGREGATION (or see perish)
parishute, parachute
parisite, parasite
paritrooper, paratrooper
parituper, paratrooper
parity, THE ACT OF CUTTING/ DIVIDING (or see parody/ parrot)
park, ked, king, ker, LAND FOR PUBLIC REST/ RECREATION, SITUATE A VEHICLE WHERE IT WILL BE IMMOBILE FOR A PERIOD OF TIME
parka, *, HEAVY COAT WITH FUR
parkay, parquet
parkeet, parakeet
parket, parquet
parkt, park(ed)
parku, parka
parodoks, paradox

parody, dies, died, dying, dic, dical, dically, dist, A STORY MAKING LIGHT OF A SERIOUS DRAMA/ SITUATION (or see parity/ parrot)
parogative, prerogative
parokside, peroxide
parole, ed, ling, UNDER COURT SUPERVISION
parona, piranha
paroose, peruse
parot, parrot
paroxside, peroxide
parportional, proportion(al)
parquet, *, try, TYPE OF WOOD FLOORING
parr, YOUNG FISH (or see par/ pare/ pear/ pair)
parrot, *, ted, ting, ter, ty, A TROPICAL BIRD, TO REPEAT LIKE THE BIRD (or see parody)
parsel, parcel
parsen, parson
parshal, partial
parshul, partial
parsil, parcel
parsin, parson
parsle, parcel
parsley, AN EDIBLE HERB
parsly, parsley
parsnip, *, VEGETABLE
parson, *, nage, nic, nical, IN CHARGE OF CHURCH PARISH
parsul, parcel
parsun, parson
part, *, ted, ting, tition, titioned, titioning, SELECT PART OF THE WHOLE, LET GO OF "prefixes: under"
partake, *, king, took, TAKE PART, BE INVOLVED IN AN ASPECT OF
parteik, partake
partekul, particle
partekularly, particular(ly)
parten, pardon
partequler, particular
partequlurly, particular(ly)
partesan, partisan
partesapate, participate
parteshen, partition
partial, *, led, lling, lly, lity, lities, lness, PORTION/ SECTION FROM THE WHOLE, FOCUS ON ONE

participate, *, ed, ting, tion, ant, tive, tor, tory, WORK/ PLAY WITH A GROUP, BE A PART OF
particle, *, OF SMALL PIECE/ FRAGMENT IN SCIENTIFIC TERMS, PERTAINS TO ENGLISH GRAMMAR
particular, rate, rity, rities, rism, rist, ristic, rize, rization, rly, ate, REFERRING SPECIFICALLY TO A SMALL PIECE/ FRAGMENT/ PART
pariel, partial
partikquler, particular
partikul, particle
partikularly, particular(ly)
partin, pardon
partiquler, particular
partisan, *, SUPPORTS A SPECIFIC POLITICAL DOGMA
partisapate, participate
partisapunt, participate(ant)
partishen, partition
partisupent, participate(ant)
partition, *, ned, ning, ner, nment, SEGMENT OFF, DIVIDE UP INTO PARTS "prefixes: re"
partner, *, red, ring, ASSOCIATE, RELATIONS BETWEEN TWO PEOPLE/ GROUPS, ONE OF TWO PEOPLE
partook, PAST TENSE FOR THE WORD "PARTAKE", BE INVOLVED IN
partreg, partridge
partridge, *, A GAME BIRD
partrij, partridge
partucle, particle
partuk, partook
partukle, particle
partun, pardon
partusen, partisan
party, ties, tied, tying, yer, PEOPLE GATHERING FOR FUN/ SPORT/ LAUGHTER/ SPECIFIC REASON "prefixes: intra"
paruchute, parachute
parudime, paradigm
parudoks, paradox
parugraf, paragraph
parukeet, parakeet
parul, peril
parulel, parallel
parulize, paralyze

paramount, paramount
parunt, parent
paruplegic, paraplegia(ic)
paruse, peruse
parushute, parachute
parusite, parasite
paruskope, periscope
parutruper, paratrooper
paruze, peruse
parzly, parsley
parznip, parsnip
pas, pass / pause / pase
pasable, pass(able)
pasage, passage
paschurais, pasteurize
pascripshen, prescript(ion)
pasd, past / paste / pass(ed)
pasdasheo, pistachio
pasdel, pastel
pasder, pastor / pasture
pasderize, pasteurize
pasdirize, pasteurize
pasdor, pastor / pasture
pasdrame, pastrami
pasdre, pastry
pasdree, pastry
pasdrome, pastrami
pasdur, pastor / pasture
pasduresashen, pasteurize(zation)
pasdurize, pasteurize
pase, pace
paseble, pass(able)
pasedge, passage
pasef, passive
pasefikashen, pacify(fication)
pasefy, pacify
paseg, passage
pasej, passage
pasenger, passenger
pases, possess / pass(es) / pause(s)
paseshen, position / possess(ion)
pasesuf, possess(ive)
pasev, passive

pashen, passion
pashendly, patient(ly)
pashenit, passion(ate)
pashens, patience / patient(s)
pashin, passion
pashindly, patient(ly)
pashins, patience / patient(s)
pashinute, passion(ate)
pashun, passion
pashunit, passion(ate)
pasif, passive
pasific, pacific
pasification, pacify(fication)
pasify, pacify
pasig, passage
pasij, passage
pasinger, passenger
pasinjur, passenger
pasion, passion
pasionate, passion(ate)
pasishen, position
pasition, position
pasive, passive
paskrepshen, prescript(ion)
paskripshen, prescript(ion)
paskription, prescript(ion)
pass, *, sses, ssed, ssing, ssable, ssably, SKIP FROM ONE TO THE NEXT, MOVE ALONG WITHOUT STOPPING, TO GO AROUND WITHOUT STOPPING "prefixes": over/ sur"
passage, *, ged, ging, eway, A NARROW WAY THROUGH, INTERCHANGE, CORRIDOR
passenger, *, PEOPLE RIDING ON/ IN A VEHICLE/ VESSEL TO SOME DESTINATION
passion, *, nate, nately, nal, nality, nless, DEEPLY DEVOTED DESIRE FOR SOMETHING "prefixes: dis"
passive, ely, eness, vity, HAS NO REACTION TO ACTION, DOESN'T GENERATE ACTION
past, PAST TENSE FOR THE WORD "PASS", YESTERDAY AND BEYOND, BACK THERE (or see pass(ed)/ paste)
pasta, PASTE USED TO MAKE NOODLES
pastachio, pistachio
pastasheo, pistachio

paste, *, ed, ting, ty, A THICK/ VISCOUS LIQUID TEXTURE MADE OF A VARIETY OF MATERIAL (or see past)
pastel, *, list, PALE IN COLOR, TYPE OF PAINTING
paster, pastor / pasture
pasteurize, *, ed, zing, zation, zer, HIGH TEMPERATURE OVER PERIOD OF TIME TO KILL BACTERIA
pastirize, pasteurize
pastor, *, rship, ONE IN CHARGE OF A CHURCH CONGREGATION (or see pasture)
pastrami, PICKLED BEEF
pastrome, pastrami
pastry, ries, DESSERT, BAKED GOODS
pasture, *, ed, ring, rage, rer, GRASS FIELD USED FOR GRAZING ANIMALS (or see pastor)
pasturesashen, pasteurize(zation)
pasturize, pasteurize
pasuble, pass(able)
pasuf, passive
pasufi, pacify
pasuges, passage(s)
pasuj, passage
pasuve, passive
pat, *, tted, tting, TO LIGHTLY/ GENTLY SLAP/ STROKE USING THE HANDS/ FEET (or see paid/ pate')
pata, pate'
patado, potato
pataseum, potassium
patato, potato
patch, hes, hed, hing, hy, COVER A HOLE WITH SOMETHING, PROTECTION FOR OPENING
pate', *, A PASTE (or see paid/ pat(tty))
pateet, petite
patel, paddle
paten, patent
patenchul, potential
patenshil, potential
patent, *, ted, ting, ncy, tly, tability, table, tor, LEGAL OWNERSHIP OF A PROPERTY/ IDEA/ INVENTION
patential, potential
pateo, patio
paterbed, perturb(ed)
patern, pattern
paternal, lly, lism, list, listic, nity, MALE PARENT

pateshen,petition
patet,petite
path,*,hway,A DEFINED TRAIL
pathalogical,pathology(gical)
pathetic,cally,MISERY,INHUMANE QUALITY, UNAGREEABLE CONDITION
patho,PREFIX INDICATING "DISEASE" MOST OFTEN MODIFIES THE WORD
pathology,gies,gic,gical,gically,SCIENCE FIELD WHICH STUDIES DISEASE
patience,RELAX AND ALLOW A NATURAL COURSE (or see patient(s))
patient,*,tly,PAST TENSE FOR THE WORD "PATIENCE", PERSON UNDERGOING MEDICAL CARE (or see patience) "prefixes: im/ in"
patil,paddle
patina,*,,CHEMICAL APPLICATION FOR METAL
patinchul,potential
patint,patent
patintial,potential
patio,*,OUTSIDE AREA NEAR DOOR INTO DWELLING
patirn,pattern
patirnal,paternal
patishen,petition
patite,petite
patition,petition
patle,paddle
patloc,potluck
patlok,padlock
patluc,potluck
patreark,patriarch
patrearkul,patriarch(al)
patreit,patriot / patriate
patren,patron
patrenize,patron(ize)
patreotic,patriot(ic)
patreut,patriot / patriate
patriarch,hal,hy,hies,MALE WHO IS HEAD OF HOUSEHOLD,DOMINANT MALE
patriate,*,ed,ting,TAKE CONTROL OF COUNTRY UNDER FORMER COLONIAL POWER (or see patriot)
patrinize,patron(ize)

patriot,*,tic,tically,tism,SOMEONE WITH STRONG EMOTIONAL TIES TO THEIR COUNTRY (or see patriate)
patrol,*,lled,lling,ONE WHO COVERS PRESCRIBED/ DESIGNATED AREA FOR SECURITY,TO PATROL
patroleum,petrol(eum)
patron,*,nal,nage,nize,nized,nizing,nizingly,SOMEONE WHO PROVIDES SUPPORT FOR GROUPS OF PEOPLE IN NEED,CLIENT
patronise,patron(ize)
patrude,protrude
patrun,patron
patrunize,patron(ize)
patrushen,protrude(usion)
patryarkle,patriarch(al)
patse,patsy
patsy,sies,THE SCAPEGOAT,TAKES THE BLAME
pattern,*,ned,ning,A SHAPE MADE TO REPRESENT AN ORIGINAL TO BE REPRODUCED,ORIGINAL TO BE REPRODUCED
patty,tties,FLAT/ ROUND SHAPE (or see paddy)
patunia,petunia
patunya,petunia
paturbed,perturb(ed)
paturn,pattern
paturnal,paternal
paty,patty / paddy
pauber, paper/pauper/pop(pper)
pauble, pay(yable)
paubur, paper/pauper/pop(pper)
pauch,pouch
pauder,powder
pauer,power
paulanize,pollen(ize)
paulen,pollen
paulenize,pollen(ize)
pauletics, politic(s)
paulip,polyp
paum,palm
paun,pawn
paund,pound / pawn(ed) / pond
paunder,pound(er)/ ponder
pauns,pounce / pound(s) / pawn(s)

paupar, paper/pauper/pop(pper)
pauper,*,rism,rage,BEING POOR, DESTITUTE (or see paper/ pop(pper))
paupur, paper/pauper/pop(pper)
paur, pay(er) / power
paus,pause / paw(s)
pauschur, posture
pausder, posture
pausdur, posture
pause,*,ed,sing,sal,A BRIEF MOMENT OF SILENCE BETWEEN,BRIEF HESITATION (or see paw(s))
paustr, posture
pausture, posture
paut, pout
pauvurde, poverty
pauwer, power
pauwr, power
pauzder, posture
pave,*,ed,ving,ement,TO LAY/ PREPARE A TRAIL/ ROAD/ PATH FOR SMOOTHER TRAVEL,APPLY A COMPOSITE ON TOP OF THE GROUND
paverdy,poverty
pavershen,pervert(rsion)
pavilion,*,SMALL ADDITION TO A LARGER BUILDING WHICH IS NORMALLY EXPOSED TO THE ELEMENTS
pavillion, pavilion
pavmint, pave(ment)
pavt,pave(d)
pavurted,pervert(ed)
paw,*,wed,wing,ANIMAL FOOT
pawer, power
pawir, power
pawlen, pollen
pawn,*,ned,ning,BORROW MONEY AGAINST AN ARTICLE FOR LATER RETRIEVAL,TO PLEDGE
pawur, power
paxs,pack(s)
pay,es,aid,ying,yment,yable,yee,yer,TO GIVE MONEY IN EXCHANGE FOR GOODS/ SERVICES (or see pad/ paid/ pie) "prefixes: pre/ re"
payd,paid
payl,pile
payleontology, paleontology

payn,pain / pane / pine
paynapol,pineapple
paynt,paint / pane(d) / pain(ed)
payode,peyote
payol,pile
payonir,pioneer
payos,pious
payote,peyote
payp,pipe
payst,paste
payt,paid
pazd,past / paste / pass(ed)
pazdel,pastel
pazdry,pastry
pazefy,pacify
pazenjer,passenger
pazinger,passenger
pazishen,position
pazt,past / paste / pass(ed)
pe,pee / pay
pea,*,LEGUME/ FOOD (or see pee/ peace/ piece)
peace,eful,efully,efulness,eable,eableness,eably, ATTITUDE/ AIRE OF CALM/ QUIET (or see piece)
peach,hes,hy,A FRUIT
peacock,*,A COLORFUL BIRD
peak,*,ked,king,kedness,THE CLIMAX/ HIGHEST POINT OF A WAVE/ OBJECT, MAXIMUM POINT (or see peek/ pique)
peakok,peacock
peal,SOUNDS/ RINGS (or see peel)
peano,piano
peanut,*,A LEGUME, SMALL NUT
pear,*,A FRUIT (or see pare/ pair)
pearl,*,ly,lized,PRODUCED BY OYSTER, HAVING THE QUALITIES OF A PEARL
peasant,*,try,SIMPLE PERSON WHO LIVES OFF THE LAND (or see pheasant)
peasful,peace(ful)
peat,ty,DRIED PLANTS PARTIALLY DECAYED (or see pit)
peave,peeve
pebble,*,TINY ROCKS/ STONES
pebel,pebble
peber,pepper

pebil,pebble
pebir,pepper
pebl,pebble
pebol,pebble
pebul,pebble
pebur,pepper
pec,peck / pick / pig / pique / peak / peek
pecalo,piccolo
pecan,*,AN EDIBLE NUT
pecd,pique(d) / peak(ed) / pick(ed) /peck(ed) / pike(d) / piece(d)
pecdorul,pectoral / pictorial
peced,pique(d) / peak(ed) / pick(ed) /peck(ed) / pike(d) / piece(d)
pech,peach / pitch
peched,pitch(ed)
pecher,pitcher / picture
pechr,pitcher / picture
peck,*,ked,king,ker,BIRDS USING THEIR BILLS TO STAB/ JAB, A MEASUREMENT OF WEIGHT (or see pick/ pig/ pique/ peak/ peek)
pecnic,picnic
pecok,peacock
pecon,pecan
pecs,SHORT FOR PECTORAL MUSCLES(or see peck(s))
pecsher,picture / pitcher
pect,pique(d) / peak(ed) / pick(ed) /peck(ed) / pike(d) / piece(d)
pecten,*,A SCIENTIFIC PROCESS (or see pectin)
pectin,WAXY SUBSTANCE COLLECTED FROM WALLS OF PLANTS, USED TO STIFFEN (or see pecten)
pecton,pectin / pecten
pectoral,*,OF THE CHEST/ BREAST, FINS ON FISH
pectorial,pectoral / pictorial
pectun,pectin / pecten
pecturul,pectoral
peculiar,rly,rity,rities,STRANGE, UNUSUAL
ped,PREFIX INDICATING "FOOT/ CHILD" MOST OFTEN MODIFIES THE WORD
pedagogy,gies,gogue,gic,gical,gically,gics,ART/ SCIENCE OF TEACHING, AN EDUCATOR
pedagree,pedigree
pedakure,pedicure

pedal,*,led,ling,USE FOOT/ LEVER TO CREATE MOVEMENT/ ACTION (or see petal/ peddle)
peddle,*,ed,ling,er,MOVING/GOING ABOUT SELLING WARES/ GOODS (or see petal/ pedal)
pede,petty / pity
pedeatrician,pediatrician
pedeatrics,pediatrics
pedeatrishen,pediatrician
pedecoat,petticoat
pedegogy,pedagogy
pedegree,pedigree
pedekote,petticoat
pedekure,pedicure
pedel,pedal / petal / peddle
peder,peter
pedestal,*,led,ling,A BASE/ STAND/ PODIUM
pedestle,pedestal
pedestrian,*,ONE WHO TRAVELS BY FOOT/ ON THEIR FEET, SOMEONE WHO IS WALKING
pedeutrishen,pediatrician
pedi,PREFIX INDICATING "FOOT/ CHILD" MOST OFTEN MODIFIES THE WORD
pediatrician,*,DOCTOR FOR CHILDREN
pediatrics,SCIENCE THAT WORKS WITH CHILDREN
pediatrishen,pediatrician
pedicoat,petticoat
pedicure,*,rist,WORKING WITH THE FEET
pedid,pet(tted)
pedigogy,pedagogy
pedigree,*,eed,HAS LEGAL PAPERS SHOWING ANCESTRY
pedikiur,pedicure
pedikote,petticoat
pedil,pedal / petal / peddle
pediqiur,pedicure
pedir,peter
pedistal,pedestal
pedle,pedal / petal / peddle
pedo,PREFIX INDICATING "FOOT/ CHILD" MOST OFTEN MODIFIES THE WORD
pedol,pedal / petal / peddle
pedrafication,petrify(fication)
pedrify,petrify

pedrol,petrol
pedroleim,petrol(eum)
pedrufy,petrify
peds,pet(s)
pedugogy,pedagogy
pedugree,pedigree
pedul,pedal / petal / peddle
pedur,peter
pedustal,pedestal
pedy,petty / pity
pee,*,eed,eeing,TO URINATE (or see pea)
peech,peach
peed,peat / pee(d)
peek,*,ked,king,ker,TO GET A QUICK GLIMPSE OF,TO LOOK QUICKLY (or see peak)
peekt,peek(ed)
peel,*,led,ling,ler,TO REMOVE OUTER LAYER/ SKIN
peenk,pink
peep,*,ped,ping,per,LOOK/ GLIMPSE INTO
peeple,people
peer,*,rless,rlessly,rlessness,OF THE SAME AGE/ RANK/ STATUS, TO FOCUS YOUR GAZE FARAWAY, LOOK INTO (or see pyre/ pierce/ pier(s))
peeroet,pirouette
peers,pier(s) / peer(s) / pierce
pees,pea(s) / peace / piece / pee(s)
peeve,*,vish,vishly,vishness,IRRITATE/ AGGRAVATE
pef,peeve
pefs,peeve(s)
peg,*,gged,gging,A SPIKE OF ANY MATERIAL USED TO HOLD UP/ DOWN SOMETHING "prefixes: un"
pegamus,pajamas
pegated,picket(ed)
pegen,pigeon
peget,picket
pegul,pickle
pegy,pig(ggy) / pick
peif,pave
pein,pain / pane
peiny,peony
peioudi,peyote
peiper,paper
peiper mache,paper mache

peir,pier / peer / pyre
peirce,pierce
peirse,pierce / pier(s) / peer(s)
peishens,patience
peishent,patient
peist,paste
peistri,pastry
peitriarc,patriarch
peitriot,patriot
peitron,patron
peiv,pave
pejamus,pajamas
pejen,pigeon
pek,peck / pick / pig / pique / peak / peek
pekalo,piccolo
pekan,pecan
pekd,pique(d) / peak(ed) / pick(ed) /peck(ed) / pike(d) / piece(d)
peked,pique(d) / peak(ed) / pick(ed) /peck(ed) / pike(d) / piece(d)
pekel,pickle
peker,pick(er) / peck(er)
pekewler,peculiar
pekit,picket
peknik,picnic
pekok,peacock
pekol,pickle
pekon,pecan
peksher,picture / pitcher
pekt,pique(d) / peak(ed) / pick(ed) /peck(ed) / pike(d) / piece(d)
pektin,pectin / pecten
pektoral,pectoral / pictorial
pektun,pectin / pecten
pekture,picture / pitcher
pekul,pickle
pekuler,peculiar
pekuleur,peculiar
pekur,pick(er) / peck(er)
peky,pick
pel,peel / peal / pill / pale
pelacan,pelican
pelaf,pilaf

pelage,pillage
pelakan,pelican
pelar,pillar
pelaredy,polar(ity)
pelej,pillage
pelekan,pelican
peler,pillar
pelese,police
pelet,pellet
peletical,politic(al)
pelgrem,pilgrim
pelgremege,pilgrim(age)
pelgrim,pilgrim
pelican,*,A LARGE BIRD WHO EATS FISH
peligamus,polygamy(mous)
peligamy,polygamy
peliquen,pelican
pelit,pellet / polite
pelitecal,politic(al)
pellet,*,ANYTHING SMALL/ ROUND/ HARD
pellouti,peyote
pellow,pillow
pelminary,pulmonary
pelof,pilaf
pelot,pellet
pelow,pillow
pelt,*,ted,ting,ANYTHING SMALL/ ROUND/ HARD HITTING SOMETHING, HIDE/ HAIR FROM SMALL ANIMAL
peluch,pillage
peludge,pillage
peluge,pillage
pelukin,pelican
pelushen,pollute(tion)
pelut,pellet / pollute
pelutent,pollute(tant)
pelution,pollute(tion)
pelvek,pelvic
pelves,pelvis
pelvic,LARGE BONE ON LOWER TORSO WHERE LEGS ARE ATTACHED
pelvis,es,ic,LARGE BONE ON LOWER TORSO WHERE LEGS ARE ATTACHED

pelygamus, polygamy, polygamy(mous)
pelygamy, polygamy
peminto, pimento
pemp, pimp
pempul, pimple
pemt, pimp(ed)
pen, *, nned, nning, INSTRUMENT WITH INK FOR WRITING, HAVING BEEN WRITTEN/ COMPOSED, FEMALE SWAN, CAGE FOR PIGS (or see pin/ pent)
penacle, pentacle / pinnacle
penada, pinata
penagon, pentagon
penagram, pentagram
penakle, pinnacle / pentacle
penal, lize, lizes, lized, lizing, lization, lly, lty, lties, PUNISHMENT
penasilen, penicillin
penatentiary, penitentiary
penatinchory, penitentiary
penatrable, penetrable
penatrashen, penetrate(tion)
penatrate, penetrate
penc, pink
pench, pinch
penchant, DESIRE MOSTLY, STRONG LIKING FOR, BIAS
penchers, pinch(ers) / pincers
pencil, *, led, ling, WOODEN/ GRAPHITE WRITING INSTRUMENT, TO USE TO WRITE
pendalum, pendulum
pendant, dent, *, ITEM HANGING FROM SOMETHING, SUSPENDED ITEM
pendelum, pendulum
pending, ACTION IN PROCESS AIMED FOR COMPLETION
pendlum, pendulum
pendo, pinto
pendulum, *, Jar, SUSPENDED FROM A FIXED POINT, ENDS FREE TO SEEK BALANCE/ EQUILIBRIUM
peneal gland, pineal gland
penechreit, penetrate
penecilin, penicillin
penecle, pinnacle / pentacle
penegram, pentagram
penensula, peninsula

peneol gland, pineal gland
penes, penis
penesilin, penicillin
penetrable, bility, eness, ly, EXPOSED, ACCEPT / EXPERIENCE INCOMING PENETRATION, BOUNDARIES ALLOWING FOR INFILTRATION
penetrate, *, ed, ting, tion, ant, tive, tively, tiveness, ENTER/ PIERCE / AFFECT "prefixes: inter"
penetreit, penetrate
pengalum, pendulum
pengilum, pendulum
penguin, *, BIRD OF THE ANTARCTIC
pengwen, penguin
peni, penny
penial gland, pineal gland
penicillin, ium, ia, ANTIBIOTIC DERIVED FROM A MOLD, USED FOR KILLING BACTERIA
penikul, pentacle / pinnacle
peninsula, *, ar, FINGER/ PORTION OF LAND JUTTING FROM THE MAINLAND, SURROUNDED BY WATER
penis, MALE ORGAN USED FOR COPULATION/ URINATION (or see penny(nies))
penitenchery, penitentiary
penitentiary, ries, PRISON, ROMAN CATHOLIC TERM
penitintiary, penitentiary
penjalum, pendulum
penjulem, pendulum
penk, pink
penkwen, penguin
penky, pink
pennicilin, penicillin
penny, nnies, A U.S. COIN
pennyul gland, pineal gland
pensel, pencil
pensers, pincers / pinch(ers)
penshen, pension
penshent, penchant
pensil, pencil
pension, *, nable, nary, naries, ner, A REGULARLY ALLOTTED ALLOWANCE
pensul, pencil
pent, CLOSED OFF, SHUT IN (or see pen(ned)/ pint)
pentacle, *, A FIVE POINT STAR

pentagon, nal, nally, U.S. OFFICE OF DEFENSE
pentagram, *, A PENTACLE, FIVE POINT STAR
pentalum, pendulum
pentegram, pentagram
pentigon, pentagon
pentilum, pendulum
penting, pending
pento, pinto
pentucle, pentacle / pinnacle
pentugon, pentagon
pentulem, pendulum
penud, peanut
penugon, pentagon
penugram, pentagram
penukel, pentacle / pinnacle
penulize, penal(ize)
penulty, penal(ty)
penus, penis
penusilen, penicillin
penut, peanut
penutrashen, penetrate(tion)
penutruble, penetrable
peny, penny
penyada, pinata
penyoda, pinata
peode, peyote
peol, pail / pale / peel
peony, nies, A FLOWER
people, *, HUMANS
peote, peyote
pep, *, pped, pping, ppy, VIGOR/ ENERGY, ENERGETIC (or see peep)
pepal, people
pepe, pep(ppy)
peper, pepper
pepil, people
pepir, pepper
pepiu, papaya
pepl, pebble / people
peple, people
peporshenal, proportion(al)
pepper, *, red, ring, ry, A SPICE/ VEGETABLE, TO BE SPRINKLED/ PELTED BY

pepul, people
pepur, pepper
pepy, pep(ppy)
pequleur, peculiar
per, BY/ THROUGH/ EACH, PREFIX INDICATING "COMPLETELY/ THOROUGHLY" MOST OFTEN MODIFIES THE WORD (or see peer/ purr/ pear/ pier/ pair/ pare)
perabolic, parabola(lic) / parable(lic)
perabul, parable
perade, parade
peradime, paradigm
peradox, paradox
perafen, paraffin
peragative, prerogative
peragraf, paragraph
perakeet, parakeet
peralais, paralyze
peralasis, paralysis
peralel, parallel
peralises, paralysis
peralusis, paralysis
peramaunt, paramount
peramedur, parameter / perimeter
perametic, paramedic
perametur, parameter / perimeter
peramid, pyramid
peramitur, parameter / perimeter
peramount, paramount
peranoid, paranoia(id)
peranoyd, paranoia(id)
perant, parent
peraplegic, paraplegia(ic)
peraplichia, paraplegia
perapillia, paraplegia
perasait, parasite
perascope, periscope
perashute, parachute
perasite, parasite
perate, parade
peratruper, paratrooper
peraty, parody / parity / parrot
perbendikuler, perpendicular

perbert, pervert
perceive, *, ,ed, ving, er, SEE/ UNDERSTAND/ KNOW
percent, *, ,tage, tages, tile, tum, PORTION OF THE WHOLE AMOUNT
percept, tion, tional, tive, tively, tiveness, tivity, tual, tually, TO KNOW/ PERCEIVE WITH THE SENSES
perceptible, bility, bly, KNOW/ PERCEIVE WITH SENSES
perceve, perceive
perch, hes, hed, hing, A FISH, WHERE BIRDS ROOST, TINY BUILDING OUTCROP (or see purge)
perchus, purchase / perch(es)
percieve, perceive
percintage, percent(age)
percipatation, precipitate(tion)
percivere, persevere
percrastination, procrastinate
percushen, percussion
percussion, *, ,nist, ive, ively, iveness, IMPACT BETWEEN TWO BODIES OF MATTER, MUSICAL INSTRUMENT GROUP
pereadontek, periodontic
pereadontist, periodontist
pereatic, periodic
pereaudic, periodic
perebolic, parabola(lic) / parable(lic)
perebul, parable
perechute, parachute
peredime, paradigm
peredox, paradox
peredy, parody / parity / parrot
pereferul, peripheral
perefin, paraffin
peregraf, paragraph
perekeet, parakeet
perel, peril
perelel, parallel
perelize, paralyze
peremedic, paramedic
peremont, paramount
peremownt, paramount
perend, parent
perenial, perennial
perennial, *, ,lly, EXISTS/ GROWS ALL YEAR LONG

perenoya, paranoia
perens, parent(s)
perent, parent
pereod, period
pereodic, periodic / periotic
pereot, period
pereotecul, periodic(al)
pereotic, periodic / periotic
pereotical, periodic(al)
perepheral, peripheral
pereple, parable
pereplegic, paraplegia(ic)
perescope, periscope
peresh, parish / perish
pereshute, parachute
peresite, parasite
peret, parrot
peretruper, paratrooper
pereud, period
pereudonteks, periodontic(s)
pereudontest, periodontist
perfect, *, ,ted, ting, tion, tness, tible, tionism, tionist, tive, tiveness, tivity, tly, to, GREAT AT THE MOMENT, SYNCHRONOUS, HARMONIC
perfekshen, perfect(ion)
perferted, pervert(ed)
perfeum, perfume
perfikt, perfect
perfium, perfume
perform, *, ,med, ming, mance, mances, mable, mer, ACT/ PLAY OUT/ MOTION/ FUNCTIONAL " prefixes: over/ under"
performence, perform(ance)
perfume, *, ,ed, ming, ery, eries, SCENT/ SMELL WHICH COMES NATURALLY OR IS APPLIED
pergatory, purgatory
perge, purge
perger, perjure
pergery, perjure(ry)
pergitory, purgatory
pergury, perjure(ry)
perguttory, purgatory
perhaps, COULD BE, LIKELY, POSSIBLE

peri, PREFIX INDICATING "AROUND/ ABOUT" MOST OFTEN MODIFIES THE WORD
periadontist, periodontist
peribolic, parabola(lic) / parable(lic)
peribul, parable
perichute, parachute
peridime, paradigm
peridox, paradox
peridy, parody / parity / parrot
perifen, paraffin
perifuril, peripheral
perigraf, paragraph
perikeet, parakeet
peril, *, led, ling, lous, lously, lousness, CAUTION, GREAT DANGER, HAZARDOUS (or see pearl)
perilel, parallel
perilize, paralyze
perimed, pyramid
perimedic, paramedic
perimeter, *, tric, trical, trically, try, AROUND A PARTICULAR AREA, CIRCUMFERENCE, BOUNDARY/ SIDES (or see parameter)
perimetic, paramedic
perimider, perimeter / parameter
perimiter, perimeter / parameter
perimount, paramount
perind, parent
perinoid, paranoia(id)
perinoya, paranoia
perinse, parent(s)
perint, parent
period, *, A PUNCTUATION MARK, SPAN OF TIME, MENSTRUATION
periodic, cal, cally, city, RECURRING, PREDICTABLE PATTERN (or see periotic)
periodontic, *, tal, ia, ium, SCIENCE/ STUDY OF TEETH/ GUMS
periodontist, DENTIST/ DOCTOR, OF TEETH
periotic, OF THE EAR (or see periodic)
perioudontic, periodontic
perioudontist, periodontist

peripheral, ric, rally, ry, ries, GENERAL EXTERIOR AREA AROUND A NUCLEUS/ CENTER/ TOWN, CIRCUMFERENCE
periple, parable
periplegic, paraplegia(ic)
periscope, *, pic, pical, USED IN SUBMARINES/ TANKS FOR VIEWING ABOVE THE VESSEL/ WATER
perish, hes, hed, hing, hable, hably, hability, hableness, STOP BEING ALIVE, END OF GROWING/ BREATHING, BEGIN TO ROT (or see parish)
perisite, parasite
perit, parrot
perituper, paratrooper
perity, parody / parity / parrot
perje, purge
perjure, *, ed, ring, er, ry, ries, rious, riously, KNOWINGLY MAKE A FALSE STATEMENT UNDER OATH
perkeet, parakeet
perkrastination, procrastinate
perkushen, percussion
perkusion, percussion
perl, pearl
perllor, perjure
permanence, cy, cies, nt, THE STATE OF BEING PERMANENT/ FIXED
permanent, tly, tness, nce, CHEMICAL TREATMENT TO HAIR, FIXED POSITION, NONMOVING "prefixes: semi"
permanins, permanence
permeable, ly, bility, FILTERS/ SPREADS/ ABSORBS, FILLS SPACE IN BETWEEN "prefixes: semi"
permeate, *, ed, ting, tion, tive, ance, able, ableness, ably, ability, FILTERS/ SPREADS/ ABSORBS, FILLS SPACE IN BETWEEN
permenant, permanent
permenence, permanence
permeuble, permeable
permiable, permeable
permiabol, permeable
permiate, permeate
permichen, permission
perminet, permanent
permisable, permissible
permisen, permission

permishen, permission
permisive, permissive
permissible, ly, bility, HAVE APPROVAL FOR/ OF, ALLOWABLE "prefixes: non"
permission, ible, ive, HAVE APPROVAL FOR/ OF
permissive, ely, eness, ion, ible, MORE ALLOWABLE THAN THE NORM
permisuble, permissible
permisuf, permissive
permit, *, tted, tting, tter, RECEIPT/ LICENSE/ ALLOWING APPROVAL (or see pyramid)
permited, permit(tted)
permition, permission
permunins, permanence
permunint, permanent
perocsaid, peroxide
perodox, paradox
perody, parody / parity / parrot
peroet, pirouette
perogative, prerogative
perograf, paragraph
perokside, peroxide
perole, parole
perona, piranha
peront, parent
peroose, peruse
perosity, porosity
peroty, parody / parity / parrot
peroxaid, peroxide
peroxide, ed, ding, A CHEMICAL
perpel, purple
perpendicular, rity, rly, RIGHT ANGLE TO A PLANE
perpes, purpose
perpesly, purpose(ly)
perpetrate, *, ed, ting, tion, tor, EXECUTE, COMMIT
perpetshuate, perpetual(ate)
perpetual, lly, ate, able, ation, ator, uity, ONGOING, FOREVER, CONTINUOUS
perpetuity, uties, FOREVER, ONGOING, CONTINUOUS
perpil, purple
perpindicular, perpendicular
perpis, purpose
perpisly, purpose(ly)

perpitrate, perpetrate
perpitreit, perpetrate
perpituity, perpetuity
perple, purple
perplex, xes, xed, xing, xingly, xity, xities, ION, UNDERSTANDING, CONFUSED
perpol, purple
perporshenal, proportion(al)
perportional, proportion(al)
perpos, purpose
perposly, purpose(ly)
perposterus, preposterous
perpul, purple
perpus, purpose
perpusle, purpose(ly)
perputrate, perpetrate
perennial, perennial
pers, pierce / purse / pier(s) / peer(s)
persacute, persecute
persafere, persevere
persanu, person(a)
persarverance, persevere(rance)
persavere, persevere
persbektif, perspective
persbiration, perspiration
persbire, perspire
perscripshen, prescript(icn)
perse, pierce / purse / pier(s) / peer(s)
persebduble, perceptible
persebtef, percept(ive)
persecute, *, ed, ting, tion, tive, tor, AGGRAVATE/ HARASS/ PUNISH (or see prosecute)
persede, precede / proceed
persef, perceive
persenality, personality
persenaly, personal(lly)
persenel, personnel
persent, percent
persentige, percent(age)
persentil, percent(ile)
persenuble, person(able)
persenulize, personal(ize)
persepatashen, precipitate(tion)

persepshen, percept(ion)
perseptable, perceptible
perseptef, percept(ive)
perseption, percept(ion)
perseptive, percept(ive)
persequit, persecute
perseverance, persevere(rance)
persevere, persevere
perseshen, precision / procession / precession
persest, persist
persestince, persist(ence)
persev, perceive
perseve, perceive
persevere, *, ed, ring, ringly, rance, TO PERSIST, CONTINUE ON DESPITE ODDS/ OBSTACLES
persh, perch / purge
pershis, purchase / perch(es)
persikute, persecute
persin, person
persinaledy, personality
persinel, personnel
persint, percent
persinuble, person(able)
persinul, personal
persinulize, personal(ize)
persinuly, personal(lly)
persipetashen, precipitate(tion)
persipitation, precipitate(tion)
persirverance, persevere(rance)
persishen, precision
persist, *, ted, ting, tence, tency, tent, tently, CONSISTENT IN FOCUS, TENACIOUS
persition, precision
persiv, perceive
persivere, persevere
persiverense, persevere(rance)
perskripshen, prescript(ion)
persokut, persecute
person, *, na, nable, nably, nability, nableness, nage, nal, nate, nality, nation, nator, nify, nnel, nhood, ONE HUMAN BEING "prefixes: un"

personal, *, ly, lism, lity, lize, AURA/ ESSENCE/ ATTITUDE/ BEHAVIOR OF A PERSON, CAN RELATE TO OTHERS "prefixes: im/ inter/ intra/ un/ uni"
personality, ties, A PERSON'S ATTITUDE/ BEHAVIOR
personefication, person(ification)
personel, personnel / personal
personify, fies, fied, fying, fication, fier, TO REPRESENT AS HUMAN, ACT LIKE, ACT AS IF
personnel, GROUP/ BODY OF PEOPLE, DEPARTMENT WHICH HANDLES EMPLOY OF PEOPLE
persoo, pursue
perspaier, perspire
perspective, *, ely, FROM A CERTAIN POINT OF VIEW
persperashen, perspiration
perspiration, TO SWEAT, RELEASE WATER FROM THE PORES TO COOL OFF
perspire, *, ed, ring, ration, ratory, TO SWEAT, RELEASE WATER FROM THE PORES TO COOL OFF
perspireishon, perspiration
persu, pursue
persuade, *, ed, ding, asion, dable, asive, asively, asiveness, asion, COERCE/ SWAY/ IMPRESS SOMEONE/ SOMETHING TO COMMIT TO YOUR IDEALS "prefixes: over"
persuasion, ive, COERCE/ SWAY/ IMPRESS SOMEONE
persude, pursue(d)
persueid, persuade
persun, person
persunal, personal
persunality, personality
persunaly, personal(lly)
persunel, personnel
persute, pursue(uit)
persuvere, persevere
perswade, persuade
perswaseve, persuade(asive)
perswashen, persuade(asion)
perswasif, persuade(asive)
pert, tly, tness, BRIGHT, LIVELY
pertain, *, ned, ning, ASSOCIATED WITH, BELONGS TO
pertane, pertain
pertein, pertain
pertishen, partition

pertrayal, portray(al)
pertrude, protrude
perturb, *, bed, bing, bable, bation, bational, BOTHERED BY, DISTURBED "prefixes: un"
peruble, parable
perudime, paradigm
perudox, paradox
perufin, paraffin
perugraf, paragraph
perukeet, parakeet
perul, peril
peruleI, parallel
perulised, paralyze(d)
perulize, paralyze
perumedic, paramedic
perumid, pyramid
perumount, paramount
perund, parent
perunoid, paranoia(id)
perunoya, paranoia
perunt, parent
peruphen, paraffin
peruplegic, paraplegia(ic)
perupul, parable
peruse, *, ed, sing, sal, TO READ/ EXAMINE CAREFULLY
perushute, parachute
perusite, parasite
peruskope, periscope
perut, parrot
perutruper, paratrooper
pervade, *, ed, ding, er, asion, asive, asively, asiveness, PERMEATE, SPREAD THROUGHOUT
pervashen, pervade(asion)
pervasif, pervade(asion)
perveid, pervade
perversef, pervert(rsive)
pervert, *, ted, tedly, tedness, ter, tible, rse, rsely, rseness, rsion, rsity, rsities, rsive, rsively, rsiveness, DEVIANT BY SOCIETAL NORMS
pervirsive, pervert(rsive)
perzakute, persecute
perzaverinse, persevere(rance)
pes, peace / piece / pee(s) / pea(s)

pesa, pizza
pesamist, pessimism(st)
pesamistic, pessimism(stic)
pesamisum, pessimism
pesant, peasant
pesd, pest
pesdalense, pestilence
pesdasheo, pistachio
pesdaside, pesticide
pesdrome, pastrami
pesdulinse, pestilence
pesebly, peace(ably)
pesel, pestle
pesemisum, pessimism
pesent, peasant
peses, possess
pesesuf, possess(ive)
pesful, peace(ful)
pesher, pitcher / picture
pesibly, peace(ably)
pesific, pacific
pesil, pestle
pesimesum, pessimism
pesimisom, pessimism
pesimist, pessimism(st)
pesimistic, pessimism(stic)
pesint, peasant
pesishen, position
pesition, position
peskripshen, prescript(ion)
pesol, pestle
pesont, peasant
pessimism, st, stic, CONTRARY TO, THE DOWNSIDE
pessimistic, cally, CONTRARY TO, THE DOWNSIDE
pest, *, ty, ANNOYANCE, BOTHERSOME
pestachio, pistachio
pestal, pestle / pistol / pistil
pestalinse, pestilence
pestasheo, pistachio
pestaside, pesticide
pestel, pistil / pistol / pestle
pestelinse, pestilence
pesten, piston

pesticide, *, dal, HARMFUL/ POISONOUS CHEMICALS USED TO KILL INSECTS/ ANIMALS/ PLANTS
pestil, pistil / pistol / pestle
pestilence, DISEASE WHICH SPREADS THROUGHOUT
pestin, piston
pestisaid, pesticide
pestle, *, ed, ling, GRIND/ PULVERIZE/ CRUSH/ SMASH AGAINST A SURFACE WITH THIS AS A TOOL, NORMALLY ASSOCIATED WITH MORTAR/ PESTLE
pestrome, pastrami
pestul, pistil / pistol / pestle
pestuled, pestle(d)
pestun, piston
pestuside, pesticide
pesuble, peace(able)
pesubly, peace(ably)
pesul, pestle
pesumisem, pessimism
pesumistic, pessimism(stic)
pesunt, peasant
pet, *, tted, tting, AN ANIMAL KEPT CONFINED AND FED BY HUMANS, TO STROKE (or see peat)
peta, PREFIX INDICATING "FIVE" MOST OFTEN MODIFIES THE WORD
petado, potato
petagogy, pedagogy
petagojik, pedagogy(gic)
petagree, pedigree
petakure, pedicure
petal, *, led, PART OF FLOWER (or see pedal/ peddle)
petaseum, potassium
petasium, potassium
petato, potato
petch, pitch
petcher, pitcher / picture
petchir, pitcher/ picture
pete, petty / pity
petatriks, pediatrics
peteatrishen, pediatrician
petecoat, petticoat
peted, pet(tted)
petegree, pedigree
petekote, petticoat

petekure,pedicure
petel,pedal / petal / peddle
petena,patina
peteness,petty(ttiness)
peter,*,red,ring,TO GET TIRED, RUN OUT OF ENERGY
petestul,pedestal
peteutrishen,pediatrician
pethetic,pathetic
peti,petty
petiatrics,pediatrics
peticoat,petticoat
peticure,pedicure
petier,petty(ttier)
petiest,petty(ttiest)
petigree,pedigree
petikote,petticoat
petikure,pedicure
petil,pedal / petal / peddle
petina,patina
petinchul,potential
petiness,petty(ttiness)
petinshul,potential
petir,peter
petistul,pedestal
petite,eness,SMALL WITH NORMAL PROPORTIONS
petition,*,ned,ning,SOLICIT/ APPROACH/ REQUEST SOMETHING
petle,pedal / petal / peddle
petnik,picnic
petr,PREFIX INDICATING "STONE/ PETROLEUM" MOST OFTEN MODIFIES THE WORD
petrafikashen,petrify(fication)
petrafy,petrify
petrefication,petrify(fication)
petrefy,petrify
petrewd,protrude
petrify,fies,fied,fying,fication,factive,faction,FROZEN WITH HORROR, TURNED TO STONE
petro,PREFIX INDICATING "STONE/ PETROLEUM" MOST OFTEN MODIFIES THE WORD
petrol,*,leum,HYDROCARBON/ OIL/ FUEL
petrolium,petrol(eum)
petrude,protrude

petrushen,protrude(usion)
petsa,pizza
petticoat,*, UNDERGARMENT, LAYERED SLIP
petty,ttier, ttiest, ttily, ttiness,SMALL/ RESTRICTIVE/ HABITUAL OUTLOOK LOOK FOR FLAWS
petugogy,pedagogy
petugree,pedigree
petul,pedal/ petal/ peddle
petunia,*, A FLOWER
petur,peter
peturbed,perturb(ed)
peturnol,paternal
petustel,pedestal
pety,petty / pity
peu,pew
peub,pube
peuberdy,puberty
peubesent,pubescent
peubik,pube(bic)
peuburdy,puberty
peuk,puke
peunatef,punitive
peune,peony / puny
peunutive,punitive
peuny,peony / puny
peupul,pupil
peur,pier / peer / pyre / pure
peuraficashen,purify(fication)
peure,puree'
peurefide,purify(fied)
peurefy,purify
peurly,pure(ly)
peury,puree'
peutrid,putrid
pev,peeve
pevurted,pervert(ed)
pew,*, BENCH SEATS IN CHURCH
pewbesent,pubescent
pewder,pewter
pewding,pudding / putt(ing)
pewdur,pewter
pewne,puny
pewpul,pupil

pewt,put
pewter,rer,SOFT/GRAY METAL MADE WITH LEAD, USED AS DISHES/ VESSELS
pewtrid,putrid
pex,pick(s) / peck(s)
peyer,pure
peyeree,puree'
peyerify,purify
peyerly,pure(ly)
peyir,pure
peyote,*, tle,CACTUS, PRODUCES MESCALINE
peyur,pure
peyuree,puree'
peyurefide,purify(fied)
peyurify,purify
peyurly,pure(ly)
pez,pea(s) / peace / piece
peza,pizza
pezamistic,pessimism(stic)
pezd,pest
pezdalense,pestilence
pezdaside,pesticide
pezent,peasant
pezes,possess
pezful,peace(ful)
pezt,pest
pezubly,peace(ably)
pezunt,peasant
phace,phase
phalanthropy,philanthropy
phalek,phalli(c)
phalicity,felicity
phalli,ic,icism,ism,icist,lluses,OF THE PENIS
phalosify,philosophy
phanetik,phonetic / fanatic
phanik,phonic
phanomena,phenomena
phanomenal,phenomenal
phantem,phantom
phantom,*, AN ILLUSIVE/ SURREAL APPARITION, NOT PHYSICAL
pharoah,*, onic,onical,EGYPTIAN KINGS

pharmac, PREFIX INDICATING "DRUGS/ MEDICINES" MOST OFTEN MODIFIES THE WORD
pharmaceutic, *, cal, cally, DISPENSING OF MANMADE CHEMICALS/ DRUGS "prefixes: bio"
pharmasutical, pharmaceutic(al)
pharmicist, pharmacist
pharmacist, *, ONE WHO DISPENSES MANMADE CHEMICALS/ DRUGS/ MEDICINE
pharmusutical, pharmaceutic(al)
pharoh, pharoah
phase, *, ed, sing, AN ASPECT/ PORTION OF AN OVERALL PROJECT/ DESIGN, CHANGES/ MOVEMENT (or see faze) "prefixes: in/ inter/ multi"
phasechan, physician
phasek, physique
phaselity, facility
phasetion, physician
phasic, physique
phasichan, physician
phasility, facility
phasishen, physician
phasphate, phosphate
phausfate, phosphate
phaze, phase / faze
phazechan, physician
phazition, physician
pheasant, *, GAME BIRD
pheladendron, philodendron
phelanthrapist, philanthropy(pist)
phelanthropek, philanthropy(pic)
phelarmonic, philharmonic
phelicity, felicity
phelodendron, philodendron
phelosofy, philosophy
pheludindron, philodendron
phenaminan, phenomenon
phenomena, al, OF THE INCREDIBLE, EXTRAORDINARY
phenomenal, ly, lism, list, listic, listically, INCREDIBLE, EXTRAORDINARy
phenomenon, *, STRANGE/ UNCHARACTERISTIC BEHAVIOR/ EVENT, GIVEN TO THE INVISIBLE
phenominon, phenomenon
pheroh, pharoah

phesant, pheasant
phesasist, physicist
phesek, physique / physic
pheselity, facility
phesent, pheasant
pheseology, physiology
pheseshan, physician
phesesist, physicist
phesetion, physician
phesic, physic / physique
phesility, facility
phesint, pheasant
phesishen, physician
phesition, physician
phesod, facade
phesunt, pheasant
phezeshen, physician
phezishen, physician
phezition, physician
phil, PREFIX INDICATING "LOVE" MOST OFTEN MODIFIES THE WORD
philadendron, philodendron
philanthrapist, philanthropy(pist)
philanthropek, philanthropy(pic)
philanthropy, pies, pic, pical, pically, pist, GIVE TO MANKIND VIA A KIND ACT/ MONEY, A BENEFACTOR
philarmonic, philharmonic
philasofical, philosophy(hical)
philasophical, philosophy(hical)
philermonic, philharmonic
philharmonic, *, LOVE OF HARMONICS, ENJOYMENT OF HARMONIC MUSICAL INSTRUMENTS
philodendron, *, A TROPICAL PLANT
philosofy, philosophy
philosophy, hies, her, hic, hical, hically, hize, hizer, ACQUISITION/ ACCUMULATION OF WISDOM WHETHER PHYSICAL OR METAPHYSICAL
philudindron, philodendron
philurmonic, philharmonic
phinaminan, phenomenon
phinaumena, phenomena
phinetik, phonetic / fanatic
phinite, finite

phinomenal, phenomenal
phinominan, phenomenon
phisasist, physicist
phisecal, physical
phisek, physique / physic
phiseks, physics
phiseologikul, physiology(gical)
phiseology, physiology
phisesist, physicist
phisetion, physician
phishen, fission
phisic, physic / physique
phisical, physical
phisiks, physics
phisiology, physiology
phisishen, physician
phisisist, physicist
phisition, physician
phisyological, physiology(gical)
phisyologist, physiology(gist)
phlabadumist, phlebotomy(mist)
phlezeshen, physician
phlizition, physician
phlabitis, phlebitis
phlabodumist, phlebotomy(mist)
phlabotomy, phlebotomy
phlebitis, ic, VEIN INFLAMMATION/ SWELLING
phlebodomist, phlebotomy(mist)
phlebotomy, mic, mist, mize, OPENING VEINS TO RELIEVE PRESSURE
phlegm, my, MUCUS
phlem, phlegm
philbites, phlebitis
philbodumist, phlebotomy(mist)
philbotomy, phlebotomy
phlim, phlegm
phlubotomy, phlebotomy
phnegraf, phonograph
phobea, phobia
phobia, *, bic, UNFOUNDED FEAR, NO APPARENT REASON FOR FEAR/ DREAD
phodagraf, photo(graph)
phodasinthesis, photosynthesis

phodegraf, photo(graph)
phodesinthesis, photosynthesis
phodo, photo
phodograf, photo(graph)
phodon, photon
phodosynthesis, photosynthesis
phodugraf, photo(graph)
phon, PREFIX INDICATING "SOUND" MOST OFTEN MODIFIES THE WORD (or see phone/ fawn)
phone, *, ed, ning, SPEAKING/ HEARING COMMUNICATION DEVICE "prefixes: inter"
phonegraph, phonograph
phoneme, *, mic, mics, DISTINCT SOUNDS OF LETTERS
phonetic, *, cal, cally, HOW WORDS ARE HEARD/ SPOKEN/ TRANSMITTED, THE SOUND; AUDIO CONCERNING WORDS "prefixes: un"
phonic, *, IDENTIFYING/ SPELLING WORDS ACCORDING TO THEIR SOUNDS
phonigraf, phonograph
phonimic, phoneme(mic)
phonograph, *, hic, hical, hically, RECORD PLAYER
phony, ney, nies, nier, niest, nily, niness, FAKE, NOT REAL, ALSO SPELLED "PHONEY"
phoseshen, physician
phosetion, physician
phosfade, phosphate
phosfate, phosphate
phosishen, physician
phosition, physician
phosphate, *, A CHEMICAL/ SALT
phot, PREFIX INDICATING "LIGHT" MOST OFTEN MODIFIES THE WORD
photagraf, photo(graph)
photasinthesis, photosynthesis
photigraf, photo(graph)
photo, *, ograph, ographable, ographer, ography, ographic, ogenic, ogerically, PICTURE CREATED IN A PROCESS USING LIGHT "prefixes: un"
photograf, photo(graph)
photon, *, nic, A QUANTUM PARTICLE WITH NO MASS/ CHARGE
photosinthesis, photosynthesis

photosynthesis, ize, etic, etically, PROCESS WHERE PLANTS TURN LIGHT INTO ENERGY
photugraf, photo(graph)
phozeshen, physician
phozetion, physician
phozishan, physician
phozition, physician
phsycist, physicist
phulanthrapy, philanthropy
phulicity, felicity
phulosefy, philosophy
phunamina, phenomenon
phunomenal, phenomenal
phuseshan, physician
phusetion, physician
phusility, facility
phusishen, physician
phusition, physician
phuzek, physique
phuzeshan, physician
phuzition, physician
phycisian, physician
phycisist, physicist
physasist, physicist
physecal, physical
physek, physique / physic
physeks, physics
physekul, physical
physeological, physiology(gical)
physeology, physiology
physeshan, physician
physesist, physicist
physi, PREFIX INDICATING "PHYSICAL/ NATURAL" MOST OFTEN MODIFIES THE WORD
physic, *, cist, OF NATURE (or see physique/ physics)
physical, *, lly, lities, CAN BE SEEN/ SENSED WITH THE EYE, AN EXAM
physician, *, LICENSED TO PRACTICE MEDICINE
physicist, *, ONE WHO STUDIES PHYSICS
physico, PREFIX INDICATING "PHYSICAL/ NATURAL" MOST OFTEN MODIFIES THE WORD
physics, cist, THE STUDY OF SUBATOMIC PARTICLES, A SCIENCE (or see physic/ physique) "prefixes: bio"

physik, physique / physic
physiology, gist, gical, gically, gist, CONCERNING PLANTS/ ANIMALS, SCIENCE OF NATURE
physique, PHYSICAL BODY/ STRUCTURE
physishen, physician
physisist, physicist
physition, physician
physition, physician
phyt, PREFIX INDICATING "PLANT" MOST OFTEN MODIFIES THE WORD
phyzechan, physician
phyzeshen, physician
phyzition, physician
pi, GREEK LETTER WHICH STANDS FOR MATHEMATICAL RATIO 3.141592 (or see pie/ pea/ pee)
pial, pile
pianeer, pioneer
piano, *, USING KEYS TO STRIKE STRINGS OF THIS INSTRUMENT HOUSED IN A LARGE WOODEN BOX
pibe, pipe
pic, *, SMALL/ TRIANGULAR/ FLAT/ RIGID ITEM USED TO STRUM STRINGS OF A MUSICAL INSTRUMENT (or see pick/ pig/ pique/ peak/ peek/ pike)
picalo, piccolo
piccolo, *, list, INSTRUMENT/ FLUTE
picd, pique(d) / peak(ed) / pick(ed) / peck(ed) / pike(d) / piece(d)
picdorul, pectoral / pictorial
pich, pitch / peach
pichen, pigeon
picher, pitcher / picture
pichon, pigeon
pichuiteri, pituitary
pichur, pitcher / picture
pichy, pitch
pick, *, ked, king, kier, kiest, ky, ker, CHOOSE/ SELECT FROM AMONGST OTHERS, ACQUIRE (or see pic/ pig/ pique/ peak/ peek/ pike) "prefixes: un"
pickalo, piccolo
picket, *, ter, ted, ting, WOODEN POST WITH SHARPENED END, BARRIER/ FENCE AS IN A UNION STRIKE, POST GUARD
pickle, *, ed, ling, TO SOAK/ MARINATE FOOD IN A BRINE/ SALT SOLUTION

picknic,picnic
pickul,pickle
picnic,*,A LUNCH OUTDOORS
picol,pickle
picon,pecan
picsher,picture / pitcher
pict,pick(ed) / pig(gged)
picter,picture / pitcher
pictorial,*,lly,lism,lness,VISION, ENVISIONED AS A PICTURE
picture,*,ed,ring,A VISUAL REPRESENTATION OF A SCENE
piculear,peculiar
pid,pit
pide,pity
pidestreun,pedestrian
pidi,pity
pidiatrics,pediatrics
pidiatrishan,pediatrician
pidy,pity
pie,*,FOOD ITEM INCORPORATING A CRUST AND FILLING (or see pi)
piece,*,ed,cing,er,ONE PART OF THE WHOLE, ONE AMONGST MANY (or see peace)
piel,pile
pieneer,pioneer
pieni,peony
pieno,piano
pier,*,MANMADE OUTCROP ON THE WATER FOR DOCKING BOATS/ FISHING (or see peer/ pierce/ pyre)
pierce,*,ed,cing,cingly,TO PENETRATE/ PUNCTURE (or see peer(s)/ pier(s))
pies,pious
piethon,python
pif,peeve
pig,*,gged,gging,ggish,ggy,DOMESTICATED SWINE/ BOAR (or see peg/ pick/ pic)
pigal,pickle
pigamus,pajamas
pigated,picket(ed)
pigen,pigeon
pigeon,*,A CITY BIRD,OF THE DOVE FAMILY

piget,picket
pigeted,picket(ed)
pigil,pickle
pigin,pigeon
pigit,picket
pigle,pickle
pigme,pygmy
pigmi,pygmy
pigul,pickle
pigy,pig(ggy)
pijamus,pajamas
pijen,pigeon
pik,pic / pick / pike / pig
pikal,pickle
pikalo,piccolo
pikcher,picture / pitcher
pikchor,picture / pitcher
pikchr,picture / pitcher
pikchur,picture / pitcher
pikd,pick(ed) / pique(d) / pike(d)
pike,*,ed,king,er, A FISH, STAFF WITH POINTED TIP USED AS WEAPON/ TOOL, A POINT, TURNPIKE, GYMNASTIC/DIVING FORM (or see peak/ peek/ pic/ pick/ pig/ pique)
pikel,pickle
piker,pick(er)
piket,picket
pikeust,pick(iest)
piki,pick
pikiest,pick(kiest)
pikir,pick(er)
pikit,picket
pikl,pickle
pikle,pickle
piknik,picnic
pikol,pickle
pikon,pecan
piksher,picture / pitcher
pikshr,picture / pitcher
pikt,pick(ed) / pique(d)
piktorul,pectoral / pictorial
pikture,picture / pitcher
pikul,pickle

pikuleur,peculiar
pikur,pick(er)
piky,pig(ggy) / pick
pil,pill / pile / peel
pilach,pillage
pilaf,ASIAN STYLE OF RICE
pilage,pillage
pilall,pillage
pilar,pillar
pilaredy,polar(ity)
pile,*,ed,ling,lings,MOUND/ ACCUMULATION OF SOMETHING,A POST/ TIMBER/ PILLAR WITH POINTED END,NAP OF FABRIC, HEMORRHOIDS (or see peel/ pill)
pilech,pillage
pileg,pillage
pilej,pillage
pilengs,pile(lings)
piler,pillar
pilerity,polar(ity)
pilese,police
pilet,pilot
pilgrim,*,mage,ORIGINAL SETTLERS IN AMERICA FROM EUROPE, THOSE WHO TRAVEL TO UNSEEN PLACES
pilich,pillage
pilig,pillage
pilij,pillage
pilite,polite / pilot
pill,*,TABLET/ CAPSULES
pillach,pillage
pillage,*,ed,ging,TO GO THROUGH OTHER PEOPLES STUFF,TO PLUNDER/ TAKE AWAY/ STEAL
pillar,*,A POST/ MONUMENT/ SUPPORT
pillon,pigeon
pillow,*,A CUSHION, HEAD SUPPORT WHEN LYING DOWN,CUSHION TO PROTECT FROM HARM
pilot,*,ted,ting,tage,tless,ONE WHO NAVIGATES/ OPERATES A VESSEL, ONE THAT STEERS,FLAME ON A GAS APPLIANCE
pilow,pillow
pils,pill(s) / pile(s) / peel(s)
piluch,pillage

piudge,pillage
piluge,pillage
pilur,pillar
pilushen,pollute(tion)
pilut,pilot / pollute
pilutent,pollute(tant)
pilution,pollute(tion)
pimento,*,A SWEET PEPPER
pimp,*,ped,ping,VIOLENT/ ABUSIVE PERSON WHO CAPITALIZES OFF OF WOMEN,INSIGNIFICANT, PETTY, COOL
pimpel,pimple
pimple,*,INFLAMED SKIN PORES
pimpul,pimple
pin,*, nned,nning,nner TO FASTEN,SHARP TIPPED THIN OBJECT (or see pen/ pent/ pine) "prefixes: un"
pinacle,pentacle / pinnacle
pinada,pinata
pinagon,pentagon
pinagram,pentagram
pinakle,pinnacle / pentacle
pinal,penal
pinalty,penal(ty)
pinaple,pineapple
pinapple,pineapple
pinasilun,penicillin
pinata,*,A PAPIER MACHE PARTY DECORATION FILLED WITH GOODIES FOR CHILDREN
pinatentiary,penitentiar/
pinatrate,penetrate
pinatruble,penetrable
pinc,pink
pincers,USED FOR GRIPPING, CLAWLIKE (or see pinch(ers)
pinch,hes,hed,hing,her,SQUEEZE TOGETHER FOR HOLDING SOMETHING, TWO SIDES COMING TOGETHER (or see pincers)
pinchent,penchant
pinchers,pinch(ers) / pincers
pind,pine(d) / pin(nned)
pindalem,pendulum
pindent,pendant / pendent
pinding,pending

pindlum,pendulum
pindo,pinto
pindulum,pendulum
pine,*, ed,ning,EVERGREEN TREE, PAINFULLY LONG FOR SOMEONE/ SOMETHING (or see pain/ pane)
pineal gland,PINE CONE SHAPED ORGAN IN THE BODY WHICH SECRETES MELATONIN
pineapple,*,A TROPICAL FRUIT
pinecillin,penicillin
pinecle,pinnacle / pentacle
pineer,pioneer
pinegon,pentagon
pineng,pine(ning) / pin(nning)
pines,pine(s) / penis
pinetentiary,penitentiary
pinetrate,penetrate
pingalum,pendulum
pinguin,penguin
pingwen,penguin
pinial gland,pineal gland
piniol gland,pineal gland
piniselin,penicillin
pinitenchery,penitentiary
pinjalum,pendulum
pinjulim,pendulum
pink,*, ky,A COLOR, THE LITTLE FINGER ON THE HAND
pinkwen,penguin
pinnacle,*, PEAK/ POINT/ CREST/ CONE (or see pentacle)
pinol,penal
pinos,penis
pinot,peanut
pinotrashen,penetrate(tion)
pinotrate,penetrate
pinsel,pencil
pinsers,pincers / pinch(ers)
pinshen,pension
pinshent,penchant
pinsil,pencil
pinsion,pension
pinsul,pencil
pint,*,A U.S. FORM OF MEASUREMENT FOR LIQUIDS (or see paint/ pine(d)/ pent/ pin(nned))
pintacle,pentacle / pinnacle

pintagon,pentagon
pintagram,pentagram
pintalum,pendulum
pintegon,pentagon
pinting,pending
pinto,*,SPOTTED HORSE/ BEAN
pintucle,pentacle / pinnacle
pintulem,pendulum
pinugram,pentagram
pinukle,pinnacle / pentacle
pinulize,penal(ize)
pinulty,penal(ty)
pinusilun,penicillin
pinut,peanut
pinutentiary,penitentiary
pinutrashen,penetrate(tion)
pinutrate,penetrate
pinutruble,penetrable
piny,penny / pine
pinyada,pinata
pioneer,*,red,ring,ONE WHO DISCOVERS NEW TERRITORY/ THE UNKNOWN
pious,sly,sness,HOLIER THAN THOU, INTENSELY MOTIVATED ABOUT THEIR GOD, REVERENCE FOR
pip,peep
pipe,*, ed,ping,TUBULAR/ HOLLOW FORM
pipol,people
piporshenal,proportion(al)
pique,*, ed,uing, HEIGHTEN/ STIMULATE, RIBBED/ RAISED EFFECT (or see peak/ peek)
piquleur,peculiar
pir, per / purr / peer / pier
pirade,parade / pirate
piraet,pirouette
piralusis,paralysis
piramid,pyramid
pirana,piranha
piranha,*,FLESH EATING FRESH WATER FISH (or see prana)
pirat,parade/ pirate
pirate,*, ed,ting,acy,ONE WHO TRAVERSES THE SEAS STEALING FROM OTHERS, TAKE FROM OTHERS WITHOUT PERMISSION "prefixes: bio"

Misspelling	Correct
pirbendikuler	perpendicular
perceive	perceive
pircent	percent
perceptible	perceptible
pirch	perch / purge
pirchus	purchase / perch(es)
pircushen	percussion
pircusion	percussion
pirdly	pert(ly)
piremid	pyramid
pireneal	perennial
pireod	period
pireodic	periodic / periotic
pireodontic	periodontic
pireodontist	periodontist
pireot	period
pireoticul	periodic(al)
piret	pirate
pireud	period
pireut	period
pirews	peruse
pirfect	perfect
pirfekd	perfect
pirferted	pervert(ed)
pirfeum	perfume
pirfikt	perfect
pirfium	perfume
pirform	perform
pirformence	perform(ance)
pirfume	perfume
pirgatory	purgatory
pirge	purge
pirger	perjure
pirgery	perjure(ry)
pirgetory	purgatory
pirgury	perjure(ry)
pirgutory	purgatory
pirhaps	perhaps
piright	pyrite
piriodontic	periodontic
piriodontist	periodontist
pirioudontic	periodontic
pirit	pirate / pyrite

Misspelling	Correct
pirje	purge
pirjury	perjure(ry)
pirkrastination	procrastinate
pirkushen	percussion
pirmanence	permanence
pirmanent	permanent
pirmeate	permeate
pirmenant	permanent
pirmesabul	permissible
pirmet	permit
pirmeuble	permeable
pirmishen	permission
pirmisive	permissive
pirmisuf	permissive
pirmit	permit
pirmition	permission
pirment	permanent
piro	pyro
piroet	pirouette
pirogative	prerogative
pirokside	peroxide
pirole	parole
pirona	piranha
pirosedy	porosity
pirosity	porosity
pirot	pirate
piroudontist	periodontist
pirouette, *, TO TWIRL ABOUT ON THE TIPS OF TOES	
piroxside	peroxide
pirpechuel	perpetual
pirpendicular	perpendicular
pirpendiqiuler	perpendicular
pirpes	purpose
pirpeshual	perpetual
pirpesly	purpose(ly)
pirpetrate	perpetrate
pirpetshuate	perpetual(ate)
pirpetual	perpetual
pirpetuate	perpetual(ate)
pirpetuity	perpetuity
pirpis	purpose
pirpisly	purpose(ly)
pirple	purple

Misspelling	Correct
pirpleksity	perplex(ity)
pirplexity	perplex(ity)
pirporshenal	proportion(al)
pirportional	proportion(al)
pirpos	purpose
pirposful	purpose(ful)
pirposly	purpose(ly)
pirpus	purpose
pirpusly	purpose(ly)
pirputrate	perpetrate
pirs	purse / pierce / peer(s) / pier(s)
pirsacute	persecute
pirsavere	persevere
pirsbektif	perspective
pirsbiration	perspiration
pirsbire	perspire
pirscripshen	prescript(ion)
pirscription	prescript(ion)
pirsebtef	percept(ive)
pirsecute	persecute
pirsen	person
pirsenal	personal
pirsenaledy	personality
pirsenality	personality
pirsenaly	personal(lly)
pirsenel	personnel
pirsent	percent
pirsentage	percent(age)
pirsenuble	person(able)
pirsenulize	personal(ize)
pirseptable	perceptible
pirseptive	percept(ive)
pirseshen	precision
pirsest	persist
pirsestans	persist(ence)
pirseve	perceive
pirseverense	persevere(rance)
pirsh	perch / purge
pirshes	purchase / perch(es)
pirsikute	persecute
pirsinuble	person(able)
pirsinulize	personal(ize)
pirsistence	persist(ence)

pirskripshen,prescription)
pirson,person
pirsona,person(a)
pirsonality,personality
pirsonefication,person(ification)
pirsonel,personnel / personal
pirsonification,person(ification)
pirsonifikashen,person(ification)
pirsonify,personify
pirsonuble,person(able)
pirsoo,pursue
pirspective,perspective
pirspektif,perspective
pirspiration,perspiration
pirspire,perspire
pirsu,pursue
pirsuade,persuade
pirsuasion,persuade(asion)
pirsuasive,persuade(asive)
pirsude,pursue(d)
pirsunal,personal / personnel
pirsunel,personnel / personal
pirsute,pursue(uit)
pirsuvere,persevere
pirswade,persuade
pirswashen,persuade(asion)
pirswasif,persuade(asive)
pirt,pert
pirtain,pertain
pirtane,pertain
pirtly,pert(ly)
pirtray,portray
pirtrayal,portray(al)
pirturb,perturb
pirumid,pyramid
piruse,peruse
pirut,pirate
pirvade,pervade
pirvashen,pervade(asion) / provision
pirvasif,pervade(asion)
pirvershen,pervert(rsion)
pirversive,pervert(rsive)
pirvert,pervert

pirvirsev,pervert(rsive)
piryte,pyrite
pirzukewt,persecute
pis,peace / piece / pie(s) / pea(s)
pisa,pizza
pisdachio,pistachio
pisdasheo,pistachio
pisdrome,pastrami
pises,possess
piseshen,position
pisesif,possess(ive)
pisher,pitcher / picture
piskrepshin,prescript(ion)
pistachio, *, AN EDIBLE NUT
pistasheo,pistachio
pisten,piston
pistil, *, ,llate,PART OF A FLOWER (or see pistol)
pistol, *, ,led,ling,HANDGUN/ FIREARM (or see pistil)
piston, *, PART OF AN ENGINE
pistrome,pastrami
pistul,pistil / pistol / pestle
pistun,piston
pit, *, tted,tting,THE SEED OF A FRUIT, A HOLLOWED DEPRESSION (or see pet/ peat)
pitado,potato
pitaseum,potassium
pitasium,potassium
pitato,potato
pitch,hes,hed,hing,hy,TAR, BASEBALL MANEUVER "prefixes: over/ un"
pitcher, *, POSITION IN THE GAME OF BASEBALL, A VESSEL FOR HOLDING LIQUIDS (or see picture)
pite,pity
pitena,patina
pitenchul,potential
pitenshil,potential
pithon,python
piti,pity
pitifol,pity(tiful)
pitina,patina
pitinshil,potential
pitnik,picnic
pitrol,patrol

pitroleum,petrol(eum)
pitrood,protrude
pitrude,protrude
pitrushen,protrude(usion)
pitsa,pizza
pituitary,ries,PERTAINING TO A GLAND PRODUCING HORMONES
pitunia,petunia
piturbed,perturb(ed)
pity,ties,tied,tying,tier,tiful,tifully,tifulness,tiless, tilessly,tilessness,ying,tiable,tiably,tiableness, FEEL SYMPATHY/ GRIEF/ COMPASSION FOR SOMEONE
pitza,pizza
piu,pew
piub,pube
piuberti,puberty
piuder,pewter
piul,pile
piuneer,pioneer
piuny,puny
pius,pious
piuter,pewter
piutrid,putrid
piv,peeve
pivurted,pervert(ed)
piwrite,pyrite
piwro,pyro
pix,pick(s) / pic(s)
piyuree,puree'
pizdromy,pastrami
pizes,possess
piztacheo,pistachio
pizza, *, A FLAT BREAD WITH OTHER FOODS COOKED ON TOP OF IT
pla,play
placard, *, FLAT CARD DISPLAYING INFORMATION
placate, *, ed,ting,er,tion,tive,tory,TO PACIFY/ APPEASE / LET THEM HAVE THEIR WAY
place, *, ed,cing,ement,POSITION/ AREA "prefixes: dis/ mis/ re/ un"
placebo, *, AN IMITATION/ FAKE, PRETENDING TO BE THE REAL THING
placed,placid / place(d)

placenta,*,al,ary,ation,LINING OF A MAMMALS WOMB/ UTERUS WHICH HOLDS THE FETUS
placerd,placard
placibo,placebo
placid,dity,dness,dly,CALM/ GENTLE/ QUIET
plack,plaque
placment,place(ment)
placurd,placard
plad,plaid / plait / played) / plate
pladenum,platinum
plader,platter
pladform,platform
pladinum,platinum
pladir,platter
pladnum,platinum
pladur,platter
plaeng,play(ing)
plag,plague
plagarism,plagiarism
plager,please(sure)
plagerism,plagiarism
plagiarism,st,stic,ize,izes,ized,izing,izer,COPY SOMEONE ELSES WORK WITHOUT PERMISSION
plagiresm,plagiarism
plague,*,ed,uing,A SPREADING DISEASE WHICH CAUSES HARM, A NUISANCE (or see plaque)
plagur,please(sure)
plagurism,plagiarism
plai,play / ply
plaiabol,pliable
plaid,*,ded,A CROSS WEAVING PATTERN (or see plait/ play(ed))
plaigerism,plagiarism
plain,*,nly,nness,WITHOUT ACCENTS/ ORNAMENTS, NO OUTSTANDING FEATURES (or see plane)
plait,*,ted,ting,ter,BRAID/ FOLD OVER/ INTERWOVEN (or see plate/ plaid / plight)
plaiwud,plywood
plajer,please(sure)
plajerism,plagiarism
plajir,please(sure)
plajur,please(sure)
plajurism,plagiarism

plak,plaque
plakard,placard
plakate,placate
plakurd,placard
plan,*,nned,nning,nner,TO CONTRIVE/ DREAM/ CONJURE/ DESIGN (or see plane / plain) "prefixes: un"
planaterium,planetary(rium)
plancton,plankton
plane,*,ed,ning,er,nar,narity,FLAT/ LEVEL SURFACE, A FLYING VESSEL (or see plan/ plain) "prefixes: bi/ de/ en/ uni"
planet,*,A SPHERICAL BODY IN SPACE
planetary,rium,riums,OF/ CONCERNING BODIES OF MATTER IN SPACE
planit,planet
planitareum,planetary(rium)
plank,*,ked,king,FLAT/ WIDE BOARD
plankton,nic,TINY WATER ORGANISMS
plant,*,ted,ting,ter,ORGANISM WHICH TRANSFORMS LIGHT ENERGY AND HAS NO NERVOUS SYSTEM, TO TAKE A STAND, TAKE ROOT "prefixes: re"
plantain,*,ANTI- BACTERIAL/ INFLAMMATORY/ VIRAL/ HEALING PLANT
plantane,plantain
plantashen,plantation
plantation,*,ESTATE WHICH GROWS LARGE FIELDS OF CROPS
planter,*,VESSEL/ CONTAINER WHICH HOLDS PLANTS/ DIRT
planut,planet
plaque,*,A COATING OF SOMETHING, A FLAT BOARD WITH TEXT COMMEMORATING SOMEONE
plasa,plaza
plasdur,plaster
plasebo,placebo
plased,placid
plashur,please(sure)
plasible,plausible
plasinta,placenta
plasit,placid
plasma,mic,CONCERNS THE BLOOD "prefixes: endo"
plasment,place(ment)

plastek,plastic
plaster,*,red,ring,ry,A GYSUM OR OTHER PASTE MATERIAL THAT SPREADS, TO COAT WITH
plastic,*,MOLDABLE/ VERSATILE SUBSTANCE
plasu,plaza
plasuble,plausible
plat,*,tted,tting,MAP/ CHART/ PLOT, A BRAID (or see plate/ plait/ played))
platau,plateau
plate,*,ed,ting,FLAT/ ROUND VESSEL (or see plat/ plait/ play(ed)) "prefixes: retro"
plateau,*,ELEVATED AREA OF LAND WITH A FLAT TOP
platepus,platypus
plater,platter
platform,*,ELEVATED FORM WITH A FLAT TOP/ AREA
platibus,platypus
platinum,*,A METAL
platipus,platypus
platir,platter
platnum,platinum
plato,plateau
platonic,ism,ist,istic,ize,LOVE/ FRIENDSHIP WITHOUT SEX, SPIRITUAL, OF PLATO
platoon,*,A GROUP/ UNIT IN MILITARY
platter,*,A FLAT PLATE/ VESSEL
platur,platter
platypus,ses,pi,UNDERWATER MAMMAL WITH BIRD-LIKE QUALITIES
plau,plow
plauding,plod(dding) / plot(tting)
plausible,bility,eness,ly,ive,POSSIBLE/ CONVINCING
plauteng,plod(dding) / plot(tting)
plaw,plow
play,*,yed,ying,yer,yful,yfully,yfulness,BEHAVE CHEERFULLY/ JOYFULLY/ HAPPY "prefixes: inter/ over/ re/ under"
playkate,placate
playkeit,placate
playwud,plywood
plaza,A SQUARE CITY CENTER/ TOWN
plazma,plasma
plaztek,plastic
plea,*,ad,BEG/ DECLARE/ ARGUE FOR (or see pleat)

plead, *, ded, ding, dab e, der, BEG/ DECLARE/ ARGUE FOR (or see pleat) "prefixes: inter/ mis"
pleasant, try, tly, tness, try, tries, AMIABLE/ ENJOYABLE/ UNDRAMATIC EXPERIENCE "prefixes: un"
please, *, ed, sing, singly, singness, surable, surableness, surably, sure, sures, sured, SATISFY/ QUENCH/ APPEASE/ PROVIDE COMFORT "prefixes: dis"
pleat, *, ted, ter, FOLDS; CREASES (or see plead)

placebo, placebo
placent, pleasant
placenta, placenta
plech, pledge
plecher, please(sure)
plecht, pledge(d)
plechur, please(sure)
plecksiglass, plexiglass
plecseglas, plexiglass
plecsiglas, plexiglass
pleded, plea(ded)
pledge, *, ed, ging, ger, OFFER A PROMISE/ GUARANTEE
pledonic, platonic
pleduble, plea(dble)
pleed, plead
plees, please / plea(s)
pleet, pleat / plead
plege, pledge
pleger, please(sure)
plegeurism, plagiarism
plegir, please(sure)
plegt, pledge(d)
plegur, please(sure)
pleicharisom, plagiarism
pleichorisem, plagiarism
pleig, plague
pleikeit, placate
plein, plain / plane
pleiqueit, placate
pleis, place / play(s)
pleit, plait / plate
pleje, pledge
plejer, please(sure)
plejir, please(sure)
plejur, please(sure)

pleksaglass, plexiglass
pleksiglass, plexiglass
plell, pledge
plendiful, plenty(tiful)
plendy, plenty
plentaful, plenty(tiful)
plenty, tiful, tifully, tifulness, teous, teously, teousness, ENOUGH/ AMPLE AMOUNT
pleral, plural
pleril, plural
ples, please / plea(s)
plesant, pleasant
plesebo, placebo
plesent, pleasant
pleser, pleas(sure) / please(r)
plesher, please(sure)
pleshur, please(sure)
plesinta, placenta
plesunt, pleasant
plesure, please(r)
plet, pleat / plead
pleted, plea(ded)
pleto, plateau
pletonic, platonic
pletoon, platoon
pletune, platoon
plewm, plume
plewrel, plural
plewtonium, plutonium
plexaglass, plexiglass
plexiglass, CLEAR SHEET OF PLASTIC
pley, play
plez, please / plea(s)
plezent, pleasant
plezint, pleasant
pli, ply / plea
pliable, bility, eness, ly, BENDABLE/ FLEXIBLE
plicebo, placebo
plieble, pliable
plight, *, SITUATION/ CONDITION (or see polite)
plintaful, plenty(tiful)
plinty, plenty
plirul, plural

plis, please / ply(lies)
plisebo, placebo
plisenta, placenta
plit, plight/ polite/ pleat
plito, plateau
plitonic, platonic
plitune, platoon
pliuble, pliable
pliwood, plywood
pliwute, plywood
ploc, pluck
plod, *, dded, dding, ddingly, dder, MOVE ABOUT WITHOUT ENTHUSIASM, IN THE DOLDRUMS, HEAVY/ SLOW WALKING (or see plot)
ploded, plod(dded) / plot(tted)
ploding, plod(dding) / plot(tting)
ploe, ploy
plog, plug
ploi, ploy
plom, plum / plumb / plume / plump
plomber, plumb(er)
plomer, plumb(er)
plomet, plummet
plomp, plump
plomr, plumb(er)
plonch, plunge
plonll, plunge
ploom, plume
plop, *, pped, pping, SOUND/ MOVEMENT RESEMBLING DROPPING SOMETHING HEAVY/ FLAT
ploped, plop(pped)
plopt, plop(pped)
plos, plus
ploseble, plausible
plosh, plush
plosible, plausible
plot, *, tted, tting, tter, ttage, MAP/ PLAN/ CHART OUT (or see plod) "prefixes: sub/ under"
ploted, plot(tted)
ploteng, plod(dding)/ plot(tting)
ploter, plot(tter)
plotoon, platoon
plotune, platoon

plow, *, wed, wing, wable, wer, PHYSICALLY CAUSE TO TURN OVER/ ROLL/ REARRANGE "prefixes: un"
plowee, ploy
ploy, *, A TRICK
plozible, plausible
pluc, pluck
placenta, placenta
pluck, *, ked, ker, king, ky, kily, kiness, PULL STRINGS ON INSTRUMENT, REMOVE FEATHERS
pludonic, Platonic
plug, *, gged, gging, AN OBJECT WHICH FILLS/ FITS INTO HOLES, SHOOT, BULLET (or see pluck) "prefixes: un"
pluk, pluck / plug
plum, *, A FRUIT (or see plumb/ plume)
plumb, *, bed, ber, bing, USE PIPES TO TRANSPORT LIQUIDS/ GAS, TO SQUARE/ MAKE LEVEL (or see plum) "prefixes: un"
plume, *, ed, ming, my, BILLOWY CLOUD OF MATTER FROM VOLCANO, BIRD'S FEATHERS (or see plum/ plumb)
plumer, plumb(er)
plumit, plummet
plummet, *, ted, ting, FALL STRAIGHT DOWN, USED TO TEST FOR PERPENDICULAR LEVEL
plump, ply, pish, ROUND/ FULL/ CHUBBY, HEAVY FALLING SOUND (or see plumb)
plunch, plunge
plunder, *, red, ring, rer, rable, rous, rage, TO FORCIBLY ROB
plunje, plunge
plunter, plunder
plunge, *, ed, ging, er, DIVE/ DELVE/ THRUST INTO
plural, lly, lism, list, listic, lity, lities, lize, lized, lizing, lization, MORE THAN ONE
plus, ses, TO ADD/ GAIN/ POSITIVE "prefixes: non"
plusebo, placebo
plusenta, placenta
plush, hy, hier, hiest, hly, THICK/ SOFT/ LUXURIOUS
plusinta, placenta
pluto, plateau
plutonic, platonic
plutonium, A CHEMICAL ELEMENT
plutoon, platoon

plutune, platoon
pluwrel, plural
ply, lies, lied, ying, liable, TO DO/ FURNISH/ WORK AT, OF LAYERS
plyible, pliable
plys, ply(lies) / please
plyt, plight / polite
plyuble, pliable
plywood, FORMED SHEET CONSISTING OF LAYERS OF WOOD/ COMPOSITE
plywude, plywood
plywute, plywood
pneumatic, *, cally, USING COMPRESSION TO OPERATE TOOLS, AIR/ GAS SCIENCE
pneumonia, ic, LUNG INFLAMMATION
pnewmatic, pneumatic
pnumatic, pneumatic
pnumonia, pneumonia
po, poor / pour
poach, hes, hed, hing, her, WAY TO COOK EGGS, UNLAWFULLY TAKE/ KILL ANIMALS/ FISH (or see pouch)
poatry, poetry
pob, pub
pober, paper/ pauper/ pop(pper)
pobir, paper/ pauper/ pop(pper)
poblec, public
poblecher, publish(er)
poblecis, publicize
poblecist, publicist
poblek, public
poblesh, publish
poblesist, publicist
poblesiz, publicize
public, public
publicis, publicize
publicist, publicist
poblisest, publicist
poblisher, publish(er)
poblisist, publicist
poblisiz, publicize
pobur, paper/ pauper/ pop(pper)
poc, poke / pock

pocediv, positive
poces, possess
poceshen, possess(ion)
pocetion, possess(ion)
pocetiv, positive
poch, poach
pocht, poach(ed)
pock, SCAR/ PIT/ ERUPTION ON THE SKIN (or see poke)
pocker, poker
pocket, *, ted, ting, tful, A FOLD IN CLOTHING WHICH HOLDS THINGS, STORAGE PLACE IN CLOTHING
pocks, pox
procreate, procreate
pod, *, dded, dding, THAT WHICH ENVELOPES SOME OF MANY (or see pot) "prefixes: uni"
podable, potable
podary, potter
pode, potty
podebul, potable
poded, pot(tted) / pod(dded)
podel, puddle / poodle
podend, potent
podeng, pudding
podensy, potent(ncy)
podent, potent
poder, potter
podery, potter
podestrein, pedestrian
podeum, podium
podibul, potable
podid, pot(tted) / pod(dded)
podind, potent
poding, pudding
podinsy, potent(ncy)
podir, potter
podiry, potter
podium, *, A PLATFORM FOR SPEAKERS, PEDESTAL
podl, puddle
podlach, potlatch
podlage, potlatch
podluk, potluck
podol, puddle
podpory, potpourri

poduble, potable
podunsy, potent(ncy)
podur, potter
podury, potter
pody, potty
poed, poet
poedik, poet(ic)
poem, *, , TEXT/ WRITINGS WHICH DEPICT A STORY/ THOUGHT/ EMOTION
poenseda, poinsettia
poenseta, poinsettia
poent, point
poenyent, poignant
poenzeda, poinsettia
poes, poise / pose
poesin, poison
poet, *, , tic, tical, tically, ticize, ticized, ticizing, SOMEONE WHO WRITES/ IS GIVEN TO POETRY
poetry, LITERARY VERSE PROJECTING EMOTIONS/ EVENT/ IDEA
poez, poise
poezun, poison
pof, puff
poferdy, poverty
pofirty, poverty
pofurdee, poverty
poger, poker
poid, poet
poignant, tly, ncy, TO THE POINT, PRECISE, EXACT
poim, poem
poinant, poignant
poinedia, poinsettia
poinseda, poinsettia
poinsettia, *, A SEASONAL FLOWERING PLANT
point, *, ted, ter, ting, ty, tless, tlessly, tlessness, THE TIP, DIRECT, AIM, SHOW, PRIMARY THEME/ ISSUE
poinyent, poignant
poinzeta, poinsettia
poise, ed, IN POSITION TO, SUSPENDED ACT ON, IN EQUILIBRIUM
poison, *, , ned, ning, nous, nously, TOO HIGH A DOSE OF THIS WILL KILL, ABILITY TO HARM
poit, poet

poitry, poetry
poizen, poison
pok, poke / pock
pokd, poke(d)
poke, *, ed, king, ey, USE SOMETHING TO PRY/ PUSH/ MOVE, TO BE SLOW (or see pock)
poker, A CARD GAME, A TOOL
poket, pocket
pokit, pocket
pokreate, procreate
poks, pox
pokut, pocket
poky, poke
polait, polite
pol, pole / poll / pool / pall
polar, rity, rities, rize, rization, OPPOSITE ELECTRICAL IMPULSE/ STREAM "prefixes: bi/ de/ re/ sub/ uni"
polaredy, polar(ity)
polarization, OF CELL ELECTRICAL SIGNALS "prefixes: re"
polarize, *, ed, zing, zation, zable, er, OPPOSITE FREQUENCY/ PULSE/ POLES
polatics, politic(s)
pold, poll(ed)
poldes, poultice
poldis, poultice
poldre, poultry
poldus, poultice
pole, *, ROD, STAFF, (too many definitions please see standard dictionary) (or see poll)
polegimy, polygamy
polegon, polygon
polegraf, polygraph
polegraph, polygraph
polehedron, polyhedron
polemur, polymer
polen, pollen
polenade, pollinate
polenate, pollinate
polenation, pollinate(tion)
polenize, pollen(ize)
poleo, polio
polep, polyp
poler, polar

polerize, polarize
polese, police
polesh, polish
polester, polyester
polesy, policy
polet, pullet
poletics, politic(s)
poleticul, politic(al)
poletishen, politic(ian)
poley, pulley
poli, pulley
police, *, ed, cing, KEEP WATCH OVER A DESIGNATED AREA, ONE WHO KEEPS WATCH
policy, cies, RULES ESTABLISHED BY PRINCIPLES WHICH GUIDE BUSINESS AFFAIRS
polie, pulley
poliester, polyester
poligamus, polygamy(mous)
poligamy, polygamy
poligine, polygyny
poligon, polygon
poligraf, polygraph
poligraph, polygraph
polihedren, polyhedron
polijidron, polyhedron
polimer, polymer
polin, pollen
polinate, pollinate
polination, pollinate(tion)
polinize, pollen(ize)
polio, POLIOMYELITIS, A CRIPPLING DISEASE
polip, polyp
polir, polar
polirize, polarize
polis, police
polish, hes, hed, hing, her, USE CHEMICAL/ FRICTION TO REMOVE OXYDATION, A NATIONALITY
polit, pullet
polite, ely, eness, CONSIDERATE, RESPECTFUL
politecal, politic(al)
politecize, politic(ize)
politeshen, politic(ian)

politic, *, cal, cally, cian, cize, cized, cizing, CONCERNING GOVERNMENT "prefixes: de"

politicize, *, ed, zing, zation, MAKE AWARE OF/ ABOUT POLITICS "prefixes: de"

poll, *, lled, lling, ller, USED TO TAX/ SURVEY/ VOTE, PART OF HEAD WITH HAIR (or see pole) "prefixes: un"

pollen, *, nize, nizes, nized, nizer, nizing, nate, nia, nium, MICROSCOPIC SPORES PRODUCED BY PLANTS

pollenate, pollinate

pollinate, *, ed, ting, tion, tor, niferous, nize, nizes, nizer, nizing, POLLEN TRANSMITTED FROM ONE PLANT TO ANOTHER

pollute, *, ed, er, tant, ting, tion, HARMFUL (BYPRODUCTS) RELEASED INTO THE ENVIRONMENT "prefixes: de"

polm, palm
polomer, polymer
polre, polar
pols, poll(s) / pole(s) / pulse
polt, poll(ed)
poltes, poultice
poltice, poultice
poltis, poultice
poltree, poultry
poltry, poultry
poltus, poultice
polun, pollen
polunize, pollen(ize)
polup, polyp
polur, polar
polurize, polarize
polusee, policy
polushen, pollute(tion)
polusy, policy
polut, pullet / pollute
polutent, pollute(tant)
poluteshen, politic(ian)
polutics, politic(s)
polution, pollute(tion)

poly, PREFIX INDICATING "MANY" MOST OFTEN MODIFIES THE WORD

polyester, rification, CHEMICAL CHAIN WHICH IS USED TO MAKE PRODUCTS

polygamus, polygamy(mous)

polygamy, mist, mous, MAN/ WOMAN HAVING MORE THAN ONE LEGAL PARTNER/ SPOUSE AT A TIME (or see polygyny)

polyginy, polygyny

polygon, *, nal, nally, THREE OR MORE STRAIGHT SIDES

polygraph, *, hic, VERSATILE INSTRUMENT FOR REPLICATING/ RECORDING

polygyny, nous, HAVING MORE THAN ONE WIFE AT A TIME (or see polygamy)

polyhedren, polyhedron

polyhedron, *, ra, ral, A SOLID SURROUNDED BY MANY PLANED SURFACES

polymer, *, ric, rism, rization, rize, COMPOUNDS OF TWO OR MORE WITH A SIMILAR RELATIONSHIP

polymir, polymer

polyp, *, pous, pary, MANY GROWTHS/ TUMORS

pom, palm / poem
pomagranate, pomegranate
pombus, pompous

pomegranate, *, A FRUIT

pomel, pummel
pomigranate, pomegranate
pomil, pummel
pomkin, pumpkin
pomp, pump
pompis, pompous

pompous, sly, sness, EXAGGERATED EXPRESSION TO SHOW SELF-IMPORTANCE

pompus, pompous
pomugranate, pomegranate
pomul, pummel
pon, pawn
ponc, punk
ponchent, pungent

poncho, *, BLANKET/ COAT

poncsher, puncture
poncshual, punctual
poncshuate, punctuate
ponctshur, puncture

pond, *, SMALL BODY OF WATER (or see pawn(ed))

ponder, *, rance, red, ring, rable, rer, rous, rously, rousness, TAKE TIME TO CONTEMPLATE SOMETHING "prefixes: pre"

pondificate, pontificate
pondir, ponder
pondoon, pontoon
pondune, pontoon
pondur, ponder
pone, pony
ponk, punk
ponsho, poncho
pont, pond / pawn(ed) / punt
pontcho, poncho
ponteficate, pontificate
ponter, ponder

pontificate, *, ed, ting, tion, tor, HAVE DOGMATIC CHARACTERISTICS, RELIGIOUS EXPRESSION

pontifikeit, pontificate
pontifiqueit, pontificate

pontoon, *, FLOATS ON A PLANE IN PLACE OF WHEELS, A TYPE OF BOAT

pontune, pontoon
pontur, ponder

pony, nies, YOUNG/ SMALL HORSE

pooch, hes, DOG

pood, put
pooding, pudding / putt(ing)

poodle, *, A BREED OF DOG (or see puddle)

pool, *, led, ling, PLACE TO SWIM, GAME USING BALLS/ STICKS, COLLECTION/ ACCUMULATION OF LIQUID

poold, pull(ed) / pool(ed)
poolt, pull(ed) / pool(ed)

poor, rish, rly, rness, LACKING BASIC NECESSITIES (or see pore/ pour)

poos, puss
poosh, push
pooshis, push(es)
pooshy, push
poosy, puss
poot, put
pootal, poodle
pooting, pudding / putt(ing)
pootle, poodle

pop, *, pped, pping, pper, A SOUND, A SOFT DRINK, SOMETHING BURSTING (or see pup)
popalashen, populate(tion)
popaler, popular
popcorn, *, COOKED CORN KERNEL
pope, pup(ppy) / poppy
poped, popped
popelashen, populate(tion)
popelur, popular
poper, paper/pauper/pop(pper)
popery, potpourri
popet, puppet
popewlashen, populate(tion)
popewler, popular
popi, pup(ppy) / poppy
popilashen, populate(tion)
popiler, popular
poping, pop(pping)
popir, paper/pauper/pcp(pper)
popiry, potpourri
popit, puppet
popiuleit, populate
popkorn, popcorn
popt, pop(pped)
populachen, populate(ticn)
popular, ly, rity, rize, rization, rizer, DESIRABLE BY MANY (or see poplar) "prefixes: un"
populashen, populate(tion)
populate, *, ed, ting, tion, list, lous, lously, lousness, TWO OR MORE THINGS TH-RIVING TOGETHER "prefixes: de/ over/ sub"
populus, populate(lous)
popur, paper/pauper/pop(pper)
popury, potpourri
popy, poppy
popya, papaya
poquet, pocket

por, poor / pour / pore
porc, pork / park
porcalin, porcelain
porcelain, FINE/ TRANSLUCENT CERAMIC "prefixes: semi"
porcepine, porcupine
porch, hes, A PLATFORM/ STOOP/ LANDING ADDED TO THE OUTSIDE OF A STRUCTURE
porchen, portion
porchun, portion
porcipine, porcupine
porcupine, *, LARGE RODENT WITH EXTERIOR QUILLS
pord, port / pour(ed)
pordable, portable
pordal, portal
pordeble, portable
pordel, portal
porder, porter
pordfolio, portfolio
pordible, portable
pordol, portal
porduble, portable
pordul, portal
pordur, porter
pore, *, ed, ring, rous, ONE OF MANY LOCATION ON THE SKIN/ SURFACE FOR RESPIRATION, LOOK/ EXAMINE WITH PERSEVERANCE (or see poor/ pour)
pores, porous / pore(s)
porform, perform
poris, porous
pork, ky, ker, MEAT/ OF PIGS/ BOAR
porkepine, porcupine
porkewpine, porcupine
porkipine, porcupine
porkiupain, porcupine
porkupine, porcupine
porogative, prerogative
porole, parole
porosity, sities, NUMBER/ AMOUNT OF OPENINGS/ PORES
porous, sly, sness, MANY OPENINGS/ PORES
porpis, porpoise

porpoise, *, LARGE FISH THAT LOOKS LIKE A DOLPHIN, A CETACEAN
porpus, porpoise
porquine, porcupine
porsalin, porcelain
porselan, porcelain
porsh, porch
porshin, portion
porsilan, porcelain
porsion, portion
porslin, porcelain
port, *, ted, ting, tly, table, A PLACE ON LAND WHERE VESSELS DOCK, TYPE OF WINE
portable, *, bility, bly, ABLE TO BE MOVED ABOUT EASILY
portal, *, OPENING ALLOWING ABILITY TO MOVE FROM ONE PLACE TO ANOTHER, PART OF THE LIVER
portch, porch
porteble, portable
porteon, portion
porter, *, AN ATTENDANT ON RAILCARS
portfolio, *, A DELIBERATE COLLECTION OF SPECIFIC PAPERS FOR PRESENTATION
portible, portable
portil, portal
portion, *, ned, ning, PART OF THE WHOLE "prefixes: pro"
portir, porter
portle, portal
portrait, *, tist, PAINTING/ PHOTO OF A PERSON
portrat, portrait
portray, *, yed, ying, yal, yer, ATTEMPT TO PERSONIFY/ DESCRIBE
portret, portrait
portuble, portable
portul, portal
portur, porter
porus, porous / peruse
porusness, porous(ness)
pos, pause / paw(s) / pose
posabiledy, possible(bility)
posability, possible(bility)
posative, positive
posatron, positron
posbone, postpone

poscher, posture
poschuleit, postulate
posd, post / pose(d)
posda, pasta
posdal, postal
posdchur, posture
posdel, postal
posder, poster / posture
posderety, posterior(ity)
posderior, posterior
posderity, posterior(ity)
posdil, postal
posdir, poster / posture
posdireor, posterior
posdle, postal
posdmark, postmark
posdpardum, postpardum, postpartum
posdr, posture / poster
posdu, pasta
posdul, postal
posdulate, postulate
posdur, poster / posture
pose, *, ed, sing, er, STRIKE/ HOLD AN ATTITUDE/ POSTURE (or see posse/ posy)
posebiledy, possible(bility)
posebly, possible(ly)
posebul, possible
posechon, position
posee, posy / posse
posem, opossum
poses, possess / pose(s) / posy / posse
poseshon, position
posesuf, possess(ive)
posetef, positive
posetive, positive
posetron, positron
posey, posse / posy
poshin, potion
poshon, potion
posibiledy, possible(ly)
posibly, possible(ly)
posibul, possible
posichen, position

posichon, position
posie, posse / posy
posim, opossum
posishen, position
positef, positive
position, *, ned, ning, nal, ner, POSTURE/ ATTITUDE/ STANCE/ PLACEMENT "prefixes: contra/ dis/ inter/ pre/ pro"
positive, *, ely, eness, vism, vist, vistic, TYPE OF CHARGE, ON THE UP SIDE, OPTIMISTIC "prefixes: contra/ dis/ pre"
positron, *, PARTICLE OF POSITIVE CHARGE
posl, puzzle
posmordum, postmortem
posmortem, postmortem
posol, puzzle
posom, opossum
posotive, positive
pospartum, postpartum
pospone, postpone
posse, A GROUP OUT TO COLLECT JUSTICE
possess, sses, ssed, ssing, ssion, ssive, ssively, ssiveness, OWN/ HAVE "prefixes: dis/ pre"
possesuf, possess(ive)
possible, bility, bilities, ly, MOST LIKELY COULD BE DONE/ PERFORMED "prefixes: im"
possum, opossum
post, *, ted, ting, ter, terize, MAKE INFORMATION PUBLIC, VERTICAL SUPPORT TO ATTACH SOMETHING TO (or see pose(d))
posta, pasta
postage, al, PRICE TO SHIP/ FREIGHT SOMETHING TO A MAILBOX/ LOCATION
postaj, postage
postal, age, MAIL BY POST, PAY TO MAIL "prefixes: semi"
postasheo, pistachio
postcher, posture
postege, postage
postej, postage
postel, postal
poster, *, LARGE/ BLOWN-UP PICTURE/ DIGITAL IMAGE (or see posture)
posterety, posterior(ity)

posterior, rly, THE REAR, FOLLOWS
posterity, CONCERNING THE FUTURE
postige, postage
postij, postage
postil, postal
postir, poster / posture
postireor, posterior
postiuleit, postulate
postle, postal
postmark, *, ked, king, AN INKED STAMP SHOWING DATE SOMETHING WAS MAILED
postmordem, postmortem
postmortem, A BODY ONCE THE SPIRIT IS REMOVED, AFTER DEATH
postpartum, AFTER GIVING BIRTH
postpone, *, ed, ning, nable, ement, er, PUT OFF UNTIL ANOTHER TIME
postr, posture / poster
postu, pasta
postuge, postage
postulate, *, ed, ting, tion, tor, TO CLAIM/ PETITION, ASSUME WITHOUT TRUTH
postur, poster / posture
posture, *, ed, ring, STANCE/ PHYSICAL ATTITUDE
posubel, possible
posubility, possible(bility)
posubly, possible(ly)
posum, opossum
posutron, positron
posy, sies, A FLOWER (or see posse)
pot, *, tted, tting, table, tability, tableness, FLAT BOTTOM CONTAINER FOR COOKING/ PLANTS (or see pod)
potable, bility, eness, WATER YOU CAN DRINK
potary, potter
potaseum, potassium
potassium, ic, METALLIC CHEMICAL ELEMENT
potato, oes, A STARCHY VEGETABLE
pote, putty / potty
poteble, potable
poted, pot(tted) / pod(dded)
potee, potty
poteido, potato
poteitou, potato

poten,potent
potenchul,potential
potend,potent
potenshul,potential
potensy,potent(ncy)
potent,ncy,ncies,tly,AMOUNT/ DEGREE OF STRENGTH "prefixes: pre/ sub/ uni"
potential,*,lly,lity,lities,STRONG POSSIBILITY "prefixes: bi"
poter,potter
potery,pottery
poteum,podium
poti,putty / potty
potible,potable
potid,pot(tted) / pod(dded)
potin,potent
potinchul,potential
potind,potent
potinshul,potential
potinsy,potent(ncy)
potint,potent
potintial,potential
potintiale,potential(lly)
potion,*,LIQUID WITH SPIRITUAL POWERS
potir,potter
potiry,pottery
potium,podium
potlach,potlatch
potlatch,hes,FESTIVAL/ PARTY EXCHANGING GIFTS/ GOODS
potlege,potlatch
potloc,potluck
potluck,*,A GATHERING OF PEOPLE WHERE EACH BRINGS A DISH OF FOOD TO SHARE
potluk,potluck
potpery,potpourri
potpourri,*,DRIED PLANTS COMBINED FOR THEIR AROMATHERAPY
potrude,protrude
potrushen,protrude(usion)
potter,*,ONE WHO WORKS WITH CLAY
pottery,ries,THINGS MADE OF CLAY THEN FIRED IN A KILN

potty,tties,A TOILET
potuble,potable
potun,potent
potunsy,potent(ncy)
potury,potter
poty,potty
pouc,poke
pouch,hes,hed,BAG/ SACK/ CAVITY FOR HOLDING THINGS (or see poach)
poud,pout
poudent,potent
pouder,powder
poudiom,podium
poudir,powder
pouem,poem
pouer,power
pouet,poet
pouetri,poetry
pouker,poker
poular,polar
poultes,poultice
poultice,*,ed,cing,CRUSHED PLANTS/ HERBS MIXED WITH A BASE FOR APPLICATION
poultry,ries,EDIBLE BIRDS/ FOWL
poum,poem
pounce,*,ed,cing,JUMP/ LEAP TOWARDS AS IF TO GRAB/ ATTACK, A POWDER
pound,*,ded,ding,U.S. MEASUREMENT FOR SOLIDS, TO HAMMER/ STRIKE, BRITISH MONEY, AN AREA OF CONFINEMENT/ HOLDING
pouni,pony
pounse,pounce
pount,pound
pouperi,potpourri
pouquer,poker
pour,*,red,ring, WHEN TRANSFERRING LIQUID, A STREAMING FROM ONE PLACE TO ANOTHER (or see pore/ poor/ power) "prefixes: in"
pourus,porous
pous,pose
poushen,potion
pousi,posy
poustmark,postmark

poustmortem,postmortem
poustpartom,postpartum
poustpoun,postpone
pout,*,ted,ting,ter,TO SULK, BE SULLEN, A FISH (or see poet)
pouten,potent
poutenshal,potential
poutinshol,potential
pouwir,power
pouwur,power
poverdy,poverty
poverty,WITHOUT BASIC NEEDS BEING FULFILLED
povileon,pavilion
povirty,poverty
povurty,poverty
powar,power
powc,poke
powch,pouch
powd,pout
powder,*,red,ring,rer,ry,FINELY CRUSHED MINERAL/ PLANT, PULVERIZED
powdir,powder
powdur,powder
power,*,red,ring,rful,rfully,rfulness,rless,rlessly,rlessness,A CHARGE, RAISING FREQUENCY, EUPHORIC SENSE OF SUPREMACY/ MASTERY (or see poor/ pour) "prefixes: over"
powir,power
powker,poker
powlar,polar
powler,polar
powlur,polar
pownd,pound
pownse,pounce
pownt,pound
powr,power
powshon,potion
powt,pout
powtch,pouch
powtur,powder
powur,power
pox,INDICATION THAT ONE IS DISTURBED BY A VIRUS IN THE BODY

poynt	point
poynyent	poignant
poyse	poise
poysin	poison
poz,pause / paw(s) / pose	
pozd,pose(d) / pause(d)	
pozda	pasta
pozdal	postal
pozderedy	posterior(ity)
pozdmark	postmark
pozdmordum	postmortem
pozdr	posture
pozdu	pasta
pozdul	postal
poze,pose / pause / posy / paw(s)	
pozeble	possible
pozebly	possible(ly)
pozee	posy
pozetron	positron
pozible	possible
pozishen	position
pozitef	positive
pozol	puzzle
pozpardum	postpartum
pozpone	postpone
pozt,post / pose(d) / pause(d)	
pozta	pasta
poztaj	postage
poztal	postal
poztej	postage
poztel	postal
pozter,poster / posture	
poztereur	posterior
pozterior	posterior
poztij	postage
poztir,poster / posture	
poztmordum	postmortem
poztpardim	postpartum
poztu	pasta
poztul	postal
poztur,poster / posture	
pozuble	possible
pozubly	possible(ly)

pozutif	positive
pozy	posy
pra,pray / prey	
prabability	probable(bility)
prabable,probable / probable(ly)	
prabared	prepare(d)
prabebly	probably
praberty	property
prabibly	probably
prabirty	property
prablem	problem
prablum	problem
prabobelity	probable(bility)
prabozkus	proboscis
prabubilety	probable(bility)
prabubly	probably
prabugate	propagate
prabur	proper
praburly	proper(ly)
praburty	property
pracareus	precarious
pracaushen	precaution
pracawshen	precaution
pracedure	procedure
praceedure	procedure
pracepitous	precipitous
praces	process
pracess	process
pracipitashen	precipitate(tion)
pracipitous	precipitous
pracise	precise
pracisly	precise(ly)
pracktus	practice
praclame	proclaim
praclemashen	proclamation
praclevity	proclivity
praclimation	proclamation
praclivedy	proclivity
praclivity	proclivity
praclution	preclusion
pracoshus	precocious
pracrastination	procrastinate(tion)
pracrastunate	procrastinate

practekul	practical
practes	practice
practeshener	practitioner
practical	lly,lity,lness,BEING LOGICAL, EASE OF USE/ OPERATION/ FUNCTION "prefixes: im/ un"
practice,*	ed,cing,cal, PERFORM REPEATEDLY TO ACHIEVE MASTERY "prefixes: un"
practishener	practitioner
practitioner,*	ONE WHO PRACTICES
practus	practice
prad,parade / prod / pray(ed) / prey(ed)	
pradasheus	predacious
pradatious	predacious
pradecament	predicament
pradector	predict(or)
pradegul	prodigal
pradegy	prodigy
pradekament	predicament
pradekshen	predict(ion)
pradekt	predict
pradektability	predict(ability)
pradektable	predict(able)
pradicament	predicament
pradict	predict
pradiction	predict(ion)
pradictor	predict(or)
pradigul	prodigal
pradigy	prodigy
pradikament	predicament
pradikshen	predict(ion)
pradiktability	predict(ability)
pradiktable	predict(able)
pradomenate	predominate
pradomenatly	predominate(ly)
pradominate	predominate
pradukshen	product(ion)
praduktion	product(ion)
prae,pray / prey	
praer,pray(er)	
prafale	prevail
prafanedy	profane(nity)
prafanity	profane(nity)
prafedik	prophet(ic)

prafes, profess
prafeser, professor
prafeshenul, profession(al)
prafeshinul, profession(al)
prafesy, prophecy / prophesy
prafet, profit / prophet
prafetable, profit(able)
prafetek, prophet(ic)
prafetible, profit(able)
prafetik, prophet(ic)
prafide, provide
prafiduble, provide(dable)
prafishent, proficient
prafit, profit / prophet
prafiteer, profit(eer)
prafoundly, profound(ly)
prafusy, prophecy / prophesy
prageks, project(s)
pragekshin, project(ion)
pragektile, project(ile)
pragektor, project(or)
pragesterone, progesterone
pragmadik, pragmatic
pragmatic, *, cal, cally, ism, ist, istic, BUSINESSLIKE, OFFICIAL ACTIVITY, OF PRACTICALITY/ TRUTH
pragmatism, pragmatic(ism)
pragmitist, pragmatic(ist)
pragmutism, pragmatic(ism)
pragmutist, pragmatic(ist)
pragreshen, progress(ion)
pragresive, progress(ive)
pragress, progress
pragretion, progress(ion)
prahebatif, prohibit(ive)
prahebit, prohibit
prahibative, prohibit(ive)
prahibitory, prohibit(ory)
prahibit, prohibit
praid, parade / pride
prailin, praline
praim, prime
praimal, primal
praimeit, primate

praimeri, primary
praink, prank
praior, prior
prair, pray(er)
prairie, *, LARGE AREA OF LAND MOSTLY VOID OF TREES
prais, prize
praise, *, ed, sing, TO CONDONE/ COMPLIMENT SOMEONE/ SOMETHING (or see price) "prefixes: dis"
praivet, private
praivi, privy
prajection, project(ion)
prajeks, project(s)
prajekshun, project(ion)
prajektile, project(ile)
prajektor, project(or)
prajesterone, progesterone
prakawshen, precaution
praklaim, proclaim
praklemashen, proclamation
praklemation, proclamation
praklevity, proclivity
praklimation, proclamation
praklivity, proclivity
praklude, preclude
praklumation, proclamation
praklusion, preclusion
praklusive, preclusive
prakoshen, precaution
prakoshious, precocious
prakotius, precocious
prakrastenate, procrastinate
prakrastination, procrastinate(tion)
praktekul, practical
praktes, practice
prakteshener, practitioner
praktetioner, practitioner
praktical, practical
praktikul, practical
praktis, practice
praktishener, practitioner
praktitioner, practitioner
praktus, practice

praleminary, preliminary
pralene, praline
pralimenary, preliminary
praline, *, CANDY
pralong, prolong
pralongate, prolong(ate)
pralood, prelude
pralude, prelude
pramenant, prominent
pramenit, prominent
pramere, premier
prames, promise
prameskuis, promiscuity(uous)
pramesuble, permissible
praminade, prom(enade)
praminent, prominent
pramis, promise
pramisable, permissible
pramiskuis, promiscuity(uous)
pramisquety, promiscuity
pramisquos, promiscuity(uous)
pramoder, promote(r)
pramonishen, premonition
pramoshen, promote(tion)
pramoter, promote(r)
pramotion, promote(tion)
prana, LIFE/ ENERGY OF THE BREATH (or see piranha)
pranaunse, pronounce
prance, *, ed, cing, er, TO LIGHTLY DANCE ABOUT, TO WALK A GAIT WITH A PROUD/ BOLD POSTURE
prank, *, kish, kster, TO PULL A TRICK ON SOMEONE, A SHOWFUL TRICK
pranounce, pronounce
pranownse, pronounce
pranse, prance / prawn(s)
pranunseashen, pronounciate(tion)
pranunsiate, pronounciate
pranunsiation, pronounciate(tion)
prapablee, probably
prapare, prepare
praparidness, prepare(dness)
prapegate, propagate
prapel, propel

prapeler, propel(ller)	prasedger, procedure	prasum, presume
prapelint, propel(llant)	praseet, precede	prasumptive, presume(mptive)
praper, proper / prepare	prasejur, procedure	prasumshen, presume(mption)
praperedness, prepare(ness)	prasekushen, prosecute(tion)	prasumtif, presume(mptive)
praperly, proper(ly)	prasekute, prosecute	prasumtion, presume(mption)
praperty, property	prasentuble, present(able)	prasumtuis, presume(mptuous)
praphat, prophet / profit	praserve, preserve	prasurve, preserve
praphisy, prophecy / prophesy	prases, process / precess	pratect, protect
praphut, prophet / profit	praseshen, precision / procession / precession	pratection, protect(ion)
prapigate, propagate	prasetchur, procedure	pratekshen, protect(ion)
prapir, proper	prasetion, precision / procession / precession	pratekt, protect
prapirty, property	prasetyur, procedure	pratektuf, protect(ive)
praplum, problem	prasicute, prosecute	pratend, pretend
prapogate, propagate	praside, preside	pratended, pretend(ed)
praponint, proponent	prasidger, procedure	pratind, pretend
praporshen, proportion	prasijer, procedure	pratrude, protrude
praportion, proportion	prasikushen, prosecute(tion)	pratrugin, protrude(usion)
praposal, propose(sal)	prasintable, present(able)	pratrusef, protrude(usive)
prapose, propose	prasipatate, precipitate	pratrusion, protrude(usion)
praposition, proposition	prasise, precise	praublem, problem
praposterus, preposterous	prasishen, precision / procession / precession	praud, proud
prapostoris, preposterous	prasisly, precise(ly)	praudly, proud(ly)
prapoze, propose	prasited, preside(d)	praufet, prophet / profit
prapozishen, proposition	praskrepshen, prescript(ion)	praufut, prophet / profit
praprietor, proprietor	praskribe, prescribe / proscribe	praukse, proxy
prapubly, probably	praskribshen, prescript(ion)	praul, prowl
prapuganda, propaganda	praskript, prescript / prescribe(d)	praun, prawn
prapugashen, propagate(tion)	prasomtif, presume(mptive)	prauphet, prophet / profit
prapugate, propagate	praspect, prospect	prauses, process
prapur, proper	praspective, prospect(ive)	praustat, prostate / prostrate
prapurty, property	praspekt, prospect	praut, proud
prare, prairie	praspektif, prospect(ive)	prautly, proud(ly)
prarogative, prerogative	prasperus, prosper(ous)	pravale, prevail
prary, prairie	praspur, prosper	pravalent, prevalent
prascribe, prescribe / proscribe	prastate, prostate / prostrate	pravelent, prevalent
prascription, prescript(ion)	prastegis, prestige(gious)	pravense, province
prascriptive, prescript(ive)	prasteje, prestige	pravenshen, prevent(ion)
prasdeje, prestige	prastejus, prestige(gious)	pravent, prevent
prasdrate, prostrate / prostate	prastetute, prostitute	praventable, prevent(able)
prase, praise	prasthesis, prosthesis	praventive, prevent(ive)
prasechen, precision / procession / precession	prasthesus, prosthesis	praverb, proverb
prasecute, prosecute	prastrate, prostrate / prostate	praverbeul, proverb(ial)
prasede, precede / proceed	prasukushen, prosecute(tion)	pravide, provide

praviduble, provide(dable)
pravilent, prevalent
pravinse, province
pravinshen, prevent(ion)
pravinshul, province(cial)
pravint, prevent
pravintable, prevent(able)
pravirb, proverb
pravirbeal, proverb(ial)
pravocative, provocative
pravock, provoke
pravokative, provocative
pravoke, provoke
pravulent, prevalent
pravurb, proverb
pravurbeul, proverb(ial)
prawdly, proud(ly)
prawess, prowess
prawl, prowl
prawn, *, LARGE SHRIMP
prawt, proud
prawtly, proud(ly)
pray, *, yed, ying, yer, TO FOCUS ON A THOUGHT OR A DESIRE YOU WISH TO PHYSICALLY MANIFEST IN THE MOMENT OR THE FUTURE (or see praise/prey)
praylene, praline
praym, prime
praymeri, primary
praymet, primate
praymol, primal
prayor, prior
prayr, pray(er)
prayree, prairie
prayvet, private
prayvi, privy
praze, praise / pray(s)
prazens, presence / present(s)
prazent, present
prazentuble, present(able)
prazerve, preserve
prazint, present
prazumtues, presume(mptuous)
prazurve, preserve

pre, PREFIX INDICATING "BEFORE" MOST OFTEN MODIFIES THE WORD
preach, hes, hed, hing, hingly, her, hy, hifty, hified, hifying, VOCALLY TEACH A LESSON
preamble, BRIEF INTRODUCTION, PREFACE
preample, preamble
preampt, preempt
prebozkus, proboscis
precadent, precedent / president
precarious, sly, sness, UNCERTAIN ABOUT STABILITY OR FIRM POSITION, NOT SECURE
precastinate, procrastinate
precaushen, precaution
precaution, *, nary, nal, ous, TAKE STEPS TO PREPARE TO AVERT DANGER/ HARM
precede, *, ed, ding, ence, ency, ent, GOING/ BEING BEFORE, SETS GUIDELINES FOR ALL THAT FOLLOWS (or see proceed)
precedent, *, tly, tial, tially, GOING/ BEING BEFORE, SETS GUIDELINES FOR ALL THAT FOLLOWS (or see proceed) "prefixes: un"
precens, presence / present(s)
precent, present
precentashen, presentation
precenteishon, presentation
precepitate, precipitate
precepitous, precipitous
precersory, precursor
precess, ssion, FIRST IN ORDER/ RANK/ TIME, BEHAVIOR OF PLANETS/ AXIS/ MOTION
precession, ssional, FIRST IN ORDER/ RANK/ TIME, BEHAVIOR OF PLANETS/ AXIS/ MOTION (or see procession/ precision)
prech, preach
precher, preach(er)
precidense, precede(nce) / president(s)
precident, precede(nt) / president / precedent
precinct, *, AREAS DIVIDED FOR VOTING/ CONTROL
precious, ly, ness, HIGHLY CHERISHED, VALUABLE "prefixes: semi"
precipitate, *, ed, ting, able, ely, eness, tive, tor, tion, ant, ancy, antly, FALLING MOISTURE, BRING ABOUT

precipitous, sly, sness, BRING ABOUT QUICKLY WITHOUT MUCH THOUGHT, STEEP HEIGHT
precise, ely, eness, sion, EXACT/ CLOSE TO PERFECT, CAREFUL ATTENTION TO DETAIL
precishen, precision / procession / precession
precision, nist, EXACT/ CLOSE TO PERFECT, CAREFUL ATTENTION TO DETAIL (or see procession/ precession)
precius, precious
preclame, proclaim
preclude, *, ed, ding, usion, usive, PREVENT/ EXCLUDE SOMEONE/ SOMETHING
preclushen, preclusion
preclusion, PREVENT/ EXCLUDE SOMEONE/ SOMETHING
preclusive, ely, ion, PREVENT/ EXCLUDE SOMEONE/ SOMETHING
preclution, preclusion
precochusly, precocious(ly)
precocious, sly, sness, sity, MATURING EARLY/ QUICKLY
precognative, precognitive
precognishen, precognition
precognition, ive, ABLE TO SENSE/ KNOW THE FUTURE
precognitive, ABILITY TO SENSE/ KNOW THE FUTURE
precoshen, precaution
precoshus, precocious
precotion, precaution
precotious, precocious
precrastination, procrastinate
precugnishen, precognition
precursor, ry, sive, COMES BEFORE
predacious, sness, sity, ation, PREDATORY/ PREYS, ATTACKING/ KILLING/ HUNTING
predacity, predacious(ity)
predasesor, predecessor
predasheus, predacious
predater, predator
predatious, predacious
predator, *, rial, rily, ry,   ATTACKING/ KILLING/ HUNTING
predatoreul, predator(ial)
prede, pretty
predecesor, predecessor
predecessor, *, WHO LIVED/ CAME BEFORE, ANCESTOR
predekshen, predict(ion)

predekt,predict
predesesor,predecessor
predespasition,predispose(sition)
predespazishen,predispose(sition)
predespose,predispose
predetor,predator
predetorial,predator(ial)
predeur,pretty(ttier)
prediar,pretty(ttier)
predicament,*,tal,TO BE IN AN AWKWARD/ CHALLENGING/ DIFFICULT POSITION
predicesor,predecessor
predict,*,ted,ting,table,tably,tability,tion,tive,tively, tiveness,tor,TO FORETELL THE FUTURE "prefixes: un"
predier,pretty(ttier)
prediest,pretty(ttiest)
predikament,predicament
prediktable,predict(able)
predisesor,predecessor
predispazishen,predispose(sition)
predispose,*,ed,sing,sition,TENDENCY TOWARDS BEFOREHAND
preditor,predator
preditorial,predator(ial)
predomenashen,predominate(tion)
predominate,ely,tion,nant,nantly,ance,ancy, DOMINATE/ AUTHORITY/ CONTROL OVER
predsul,pretzel
preduction,product(ion)
predukshen,product(ion)
predusesor,predecessor
predutor,predator
predutoreul,predator(ial)
predutory,predator
predy,pretty
predyest,pretty(ttiest)
preech,preach
preechy,preach
preempt,tor,ption,ptive,ptively,TO OCCUPY/ SEIZE/ ACQUIRE BEFORE ANYONE ELSE CAN ACQUIRE OWNERSHIP
preemshen,preempt(ion)

preemt,preempt
preface,ed,cing,REMARKS/ INTRODUCTION BEFORE A BOOK/ LITERARY WORK
prefale,prevail
prefanedy,profane(nity)
prefanity,profane(nity)
prefeks,prefix
prefer,*,rred,rring,rence,rences,rable,rableness, rability,rably,rential,rentialist,rentialism,rentiality, rentially,rment,CHOOSE OVER OTHERS, MOST DESIRABLE
preferinse,prefer(ence)
preferuble,prefer(able)
prefese,preface
prefeshenul,profession(al)
prefesur,professor
prefex,prefix
preficks,prefix
prefide,provide
prefiduble,provide(dable)
prefiks,prefix
prefir,prefer
prefirability,prefer(ability)
prefirable,prefer(able)
prefirense,prefer(ence)
prefirenshul,prefer(ential)
prefirential,prefer(ential)
prefis,preface
prefix,xes,xal,xally,xation,xion,LETTERS BEFORE A BASE WORD THAT MODIFIES IT'S MEANING, EXISTS PRIOR TO
preforenshul,prefer(ential)
prefound,profound
prefoundly,profound(ly)
prefur,prefer
prefurabiledy,prefer(ability)
prefurable,prefer(able)
prefurenshul,prefer(ential)
prefurential,prefer(ential)
prefurinse,prefer(ence)
prefuse,preface
prefy,privy
pregadis,prejudice

pregedis,prejudice
pregekshin,project(ion)
pregesterone,progesterone
pregidis,prejudice
pregnant,tly,ncy,ncies,able,ability,BODY CARRYING AN EMBRYO
pregnensy,pregnant(ncy)
pregnet,pregnant
pregnint,pregnant
pregnonsy,pregnant(ncy)
pregnunt,pregnant
pregnut,pregnant
pregodis,prejudice
pregreshen,progress(ion)
pregretion,progress(ion)
pregudis,prejudice
prei,prey / pray
preilud,prelude
preimshen,preempt(ion)
preimt,preempt
preimtif,preempt(ive)
preimtive,preempt(ive)
preis,prey(s) / pray(s) / praise
prejadis,prejudice
prejekshin,project(ion)
prejidis,prejudice
prejodis,prejudice
prejudice,*,ed,cing,cial,cially,AN OPINION/ ATTITUDE ABOUT SOMETHING/ SOMEONE WITHOUT BASIS OF FULL KNOWLEDGE
prek,prick
prekareus,precarious
prekarius,precarious
prekastinate,procrastinate
prekaution,precaution
prekawshen,precaution
preked,prick(ed)
prekersery,precursor
prekirsor,precursor
prekirsory,precursor
preklame,proclaim
preklewd,preclude
preklude,preclude

preklushen,preclusion
preklusive,preclusive
preklution,preclusion
preknet,pregnant
preknut,pregnant
prekognative,precognitive
prekognishen,precognition
prekognition,precognition
prekoshen,precaution
prekoshious,precocious
prekoshus,precocious
prekotius,precocious
prekrastination,procrastinate
prekursor,precursor
prekursory,precursor
preleminary,preliminary
prelene,praline
prelewt,prelude
preliminary,ries,rily,INTRODUCTION TO THE MAIN
prellidos,prejudice
prelong,prolong
prelongate,prolong(ate)
prelood,prelude
prelude, *, ded, ding, er, usive, usively, usorily, usory, LEADING UP/ INTRODUCTORY TO
prelute,prelude
prem,prim
premachure,premature
premanishen,premoniticn
premanition,premonition
prematif,primitive
prematively,primitive(ly)
premature,ely,eness,rity,BEFORE RIPE/ MATURE/ FULLY FORMED
premear,premier
premechure,premature
premedatate,premeditate
premeditate, *, ed, ting, tion, tive, PLAN OUT BEFORE THE ACT OF "prefixes: un"
premeim,premium
premeneshen,premonition
premenishen,premonition
premenstrual,lly,PRIOR TO/ BEFORE MENS˜RUATION

premenzdrul,premenstrual
premere,premier
premese,premise
premetetate,premeditate
premetitate,premeditate
premeum,premium
premichure,premature
premier, *, PLAY/ OPERA/ MOVIE FIRST PUBLIC EXPOSURE
preminishen,premonition
preministrul,premenstrual
premiom,premium
premir,premier
premisabul,permissible
premise, *, ASSUMPTION, BEFOREHAND, LAND WITH TENANTS, BEGINNING OF, PROPOSITION
premiskues,promiscuity(uous)
premitive,primitive
premiture,premature
premium, *, BONUS, ADDITIONALLY
premoder,promote(r)
premoneshen,premonition
premonition, *, SENSE/ FEELING BEFORE AN EVENT
premose,premise
premoshen,promote(tion)
premote,promote
premotion,promote(tion)
premoture,premature
premp,primp
prempt,primp(ed)
premuchure,premature
premunishen,premonition
premunition,premonition
premuse,premise
premutif,primitive
premuture,premature
prenauns,pronounce
prence,prince / print(s)
prenceses,princess(es)
princess,princess
principle,principle / principal
prend,print
prendable,print(able)

prender,print(er)
prendible,print(able)
prenduble,print(able)
prenoense,pronounce
prenounce,pronounce
prensabul,principle / principal
prensaple,principle / principal
prense,prince / print(s)
prenses,princess / prince(s)
prensibul,principle / principal
prensipul,principle / principal
prensis,princess / prince(s)
prensuple,principle / principal
prent,print
prentabul,print(able)
prenter,print(er)
prentible,print(able)
prentr,print(er)
prentur,print(er)
prenunseate,pronounciate
prenunsiation,pronounciate(tion)
prenus,apprentice
prep, *, pped, pping, pper, ppy, PREPARE/ MAKE READY FOR
prepare, *, ed, edness, ring, ration, rative, ratively, rator, ratory, rer, EQUIP/ COMPOSE/ ASSEMBLE/ MANUFACTURE/ CONDITION SOMETHING/ SOMEONE FOR ACTIVITY/ EVENT "prefixes: un"
prepaseshen,preposition / proposition / prepossess(ion)
prepazishen,preposition / proposition / prepossess(ion)
preperashen,prepare(ration)
preperatory,prepare(ratory)
preperidness,prepare(ness)
prepiration,prepare(ration)
prepiratory,prepare(ratory)
prepiseshen,preposition / proposition / prepossess(ion)
preponent,proponent
preporashen,prepare(ration)
preporshen,proportion
preportion,proportion
preposal,propose(sal)
prepose,propose
preposeshun,prepossess

preposesing, prepossessing
preposishen, preposition / proposition / prepossess(ion)
preposition, *, ned, ning, nal, nally, ENGLISH LANGUAGE TERM (or see proposition)
prepossess, ssing, ssion, POSSESS BEFORE SOMEONE ELSE DOES, TO IMPRESS
prepossessing, gly, gness, ion, TO IMPRESS/ CHARM FAVORABLY "prefixes: un"
preposterous, sly, sness, BEYOND RATIONAL, GOES AGAINST COMMON SENSE
preposturis, preposterous
prepoze, propose
prepozes, prepossess
prepozishen, preposition / proposition / prepossess(ion)
prepozle, propose(sal)
prepriator, proprietor
prepurashen, prepare(ration)
prepuration, prepare(ration)
prepusition, proposition
prepuzishen, preposition / proposition / prepossess(ion)
prer, pray(er)
prere, prairie
prerogative, *, PRIVILEGED
prery, prairie
pres, press
presadense, precede(nce) / president(s)
presadenshul, president(ial)
presadent, precedent/ president
presadinse, precede(nce) / president(s)
presadint, precede(nt) / president
prescrebshin, prescript(ion)
prescribe, *, ed, bing, er, RULE/ COURSE/ ACTION TO BE FOLLOWED (or see prescript/ proscribe)
prescripshen, prescript(ion)
prescript, tible, tion, tive, tively, tiveness, tivism, CLAIM/ CUSTOM/ RULE/ RIGHT/ TITLE TO (or see prescribe)
prescrishen, prescript(ion)
presd, press(ed)
presdeje, prestige
presdo, presto
presede, precede / proceed
presedent, precede(nt) / president
presedential, president(ial)

presedger, procedure
presedintial, president(ial)
presedyur, procedure
presee, prissy
preseet, precede
preseger, procedure
presejur, procedure
presence, OF BEING PRESENT, IN IMMEDIATE VICINITY OF (or see present)
presenked, precinct
presenkt, precinct
presens, presence / present(s)
present, *, ted, ter, ting, tly, tness, table, tableness, tability, tably, tment, tation, nce, GIVEN FREELY, ACCEPTABLE, TO OFFER SOMETHING, IN IMMEDIATE VICINITY OF, MAKE VISIBLE (or see presence) "prefexis: re"
presentation, *, nal, ive, OFFER/ EXHIBIT/ PRESENT SOMETHING "prefixes: re"
prespitous, precipitous
preser, pressure / press(er)
preservashen, preserve(vation)
preserve, *, ed, er, vable, vation, ving, PROTECT FROM, PREVENT CONDITION FROM BEING ALTERED/ EXPLOITED/ CHANGED
preses, precess
preseshen, precede(nce) / president(s) / precession
presetgur, procedure
presetion, precision / procession / precession
presh, preach
presher, pressure
presherize, pressure(rize)
preshes, precious
preshir, pressure
preshis, precious
preshorize, pressure(rize)
preshur, pressure
preshurize, pressure(rize)
preshus, precious
preside, *, ed, ding, er, ONE IN A HIERARCHAL POSITION OVER, THE AUTHORITY OF THE GROUP, OVERSEEING
presidense, precede(nce) / president(s)
presidenshul, president(ial)

president, *, ncy, ncies, tial, LEADERSHIP POSITION (or see precedent)
presiger, procedure
presijur, procedure
presim, prism
presin, prison
presinct, precinct
presiner, prison(er)
presinked, precinct
presinkt, precinct
presinse, presence
presint, present
presintable, present(able)
presintashen, presentation
presintation, presentation
presintly, present(ly)
presints, present(s) / presence
presipatate, precipitate
presipatation, precipitate(tion)
presipitate, precipitate
presipitous, precipitous
presiputashen, precipitate(tion)
presir, pressure / press(er)
presirvation, preserve(vation)
presis, precise / press(es)
presishen, precision / procession / precession
presisly, precise(ly)
presited, preside(d)
presition, precision/ procession
preskrepshen, prescript(ion)
preskribe, prescribe / proscribe
preskribshen, prescript(ion)
presm, prism
presmadik, prism(atic)
presodent, precede(nt) / president
presomtif, presume(mptive)
preson, prison
press, sses, ssed, ssing, sser, APPLY/ EXERT FORCE, SQUEEZE, COMPACT "prefixes: re"
pressure, *, ed, ring, rize, rizer, rizing, rization, THE APPLICATION/ EXERTION OF FORCE, SQUEEZE, COMPACT, REMOVE AIR "prefixes: over"
prest, priest / press(ed)

prestege, prestige
prestegus, prestige(gious)
prestej, prestige
prestene, pristine
prestess, priest(ess)
presthesus, prosthesis
presthood, priest(hood)
prestige, gious, giousness, giously, OF DISTINCTION RANK/ QUALITY
prestigous, prestige(gious)
prestill, prestige
prestine, pristine
prestish, prestige
prestly, priest(ly)
presto, INSTANT/ AUTOMATIC/ SUDDEN/ QUICK
presudent, precede(nt) / president / precedent
presum, prism / presume
presume, *, ed, ming, er, mption, mptive, mptively, tuous, tuously, tuousness, MOST PROBABLE WITHOUT PROOF, CONCLUSION/ SUPPOSING WITHOUT FACTS
presumshen, presume(mption)
presumtif, presume(mptive)
presumtion, presume(mption)
presumtuis, presume(mptuous)
presumtuous, presume(mrptuous)
presun, prison
presur, pressure / press(e-)
presurf, preserve
presurvashen, preserve(vation)
presurve, preserve
presus, press(es)
presy, prissy
prete, pretty
pretekt, protect
pretektif, protect(ive)
pretektive, protect(ive)
pretend, *, ded, ding, der, nse, ACT AS IF REAL, MAKE BELIEVE, DECEPTIVE "prefixes: un"
pretense, *, sion, sionless, sive, ntious, ACT AS IF REAL, MAKE BELIEVE, DECEPTIVE
pretenshen, pretense(sion)
pretentious, sly, sness, FIRMLY CONFIDENT, OVERSTEPS OTHERS' BOUNDARIES "prefixes: un"

preteur, pretty(ttier)
pretiest, pretty(ttiest)
pretind, pretend
pretinse, pretense
pretinshen, pretense(sion)
pretrude, protrude
pretrusion, protrude(usion)
pretsul, pretzel
pretty, ttier, ttiest, tties, ttiness, ttily, ttyish, ttify, ttifier, ttifying, ttification, ATTRACTIVE/ VISUALLY PLEASING
prety, pretty
pretzel, *, led, DOUGHY FOOD TWISTED INTO A KNOT
prevade, pervade
prevail, *, led, ling, WILL ENDURE, ONGOING, WILL NOT BE OVERCOME
prevale, prevail
prevaleg, privilege
prevalense, prevalent(nce)
prevalent, tly, nce, WILL PREVAIL, MOST COMMON/ POPULAR
prevalige, privilege
prevalijes, privilege(s)
prevalinse, prevalent(nce)
prevalint, prevalent
prevalt, prevail(ed)
preveis, previous
preveisly, previous(ly)
prevelent, prevalent
prevelinse, prevalent(nce)
prevelint, prevalent
prevenshen, prevent(ion)
prevent, *, ted, ting, tion, tability, table, ter, tive, tively, tiveness, tative, STOP/ PREPARE/ KEEP FROM HAPPENING
preveos, previous
preveosly, previous(ly)
preveus, previous
preveusly, previous(ly)
previde, provide
previduble, provide(dable)
previlege, privilege
previlense, prevalent(nce)
previlent, prevalent

previnshun, prevent(ion)
previntion, prevent(ion)
previntive, prevent(ive)
previous, sly, HAPPENED/ OCCURRED BEFORE
previus, previous
previusly, previous(ly)
prevlej, privilege
prevlig, privilege
prevocative, provocative
prevok, provoke
prevokative, provocative
prevokt, provoke
prevulense, prevalent(nce)
prevulent, prevalent
prevulinse, prevalent(nce)
prevy, privy
prey, *, yed, ying, yer, STALK/ HUNT DOWN SOMEONE/ SOMETHING FOR SATISFACTION/ NOURISHMENT (or see pray)
preylin, praline
prezadinshul, president(ial)
prezadint, precede(nt) / president
prezedinshul, president(ial)
prezedint, precede(nt) / president
prezent, present
prezentashen, presentation
prezents, presence / present(s)
prezervashen, preserve(vation)
prezerve, preserve
prezident, precede(nt) / president
preziner, prison(er)
prezint, present
prezintly, present(ly)
prezints, presence / present(s)
prezodent, precede(nt) / president
prezomtuis, presume(mptuous)
pret, priest
prezudenshul, president(ial)
prezudent, precede(nt) / president
prezum, prism
prezumtues, presume(mptuous)
prezunt, present
prhaps, perhaps

pri, pry / pre
priboskus, proboscis
pric, prick / price
pricarius, precarious
pricashen, precaution
pricastinate, procrastinate
pricaushen, precaution
pricaution, precaution
price, *, ed, cing, ey, eless, COST OF/ FOR SOMETHING (or see prick) "prefixes: under"
pricechen, precession / procession / precision
precede, precede / proceed
pricersor, precursor
prices, price(s) / precess
priceshen, precession / procession / precision
pricise, precise
pricisely, precise(ly)
pricishen, precession / procession / precision
pricishon, precision
pricision, precession / procession / procession / precision
prick, *, ked, king, kley, kliest, kliness, PIERCE/ PUNCTURE WITH SHARP POINT, SLANG FOR MALE ORGAN
priclame, proclaim
priclude, preclude
priclushen, preclusion
priclution, preclusion
pricochen, precaution
pricognative, precognitive
pricogneshen, precognition
pricognition, precognition
pricoshus, precocious
pricotion, precaution
pricotious, precocious
pricursor, precursor
pricy, price
pridachus, predacious
pridacity, predacious(ity)
pridashius, predacious
pridashius, predacious
pride, *, ded, ding, eful, efully, efulness, roud, EGO PROTECTING ITS SELF-ESTEEM, BOASTFUL, ARROGANT

pridear, pretty(ttier)
pridecament, predicament
pridect, predict
pridekter, predict(or)
pridespose, predispose
prideur, pretty(ttier)
pridful, pride(ful)
pridfulness, pride(fulness)
pridfuly, pride(fully)
pridi, pretty
pridicament, predicament
pridictable, predict(able)
pridiction, predict(ion)
pridiest, pretty(ttiest)
pridikament, predicament
pridikshen, predict(ion)
pridikt, predict
pridispose, predispose
pridominate, predominate
pridukshen, product(ion)
priduktion, product(ion)
pridy, pretty
pridyest, pretty(ttiest)
priempt, preempt
priemt, preempt
prieng, pry(ing)
prier, prior
prieredy, prior(ity)
priest, * , tly, tliness, thood, tess, ASSIGNED PERSON TO REPRESENT A RELIGIOUS BELIEF
prifale, prevail
prifasee, private(acy)
prifatize, private(tize)
prifatlee, private(ly)
prifee, privy
prifeis, preface
prifer, prefer
prifes, profess
prifeshen, profession
prifeshinol, profession(al)
prifesor, professor
prifesy, private(acy)
prifet, private

prifetize, private(tize)
prifetlee, private(ly)
prifex, prefix
prifide, provide
prifir, prefer
prifisee, private(acy)
prifit, private
prifitize, private(tize)
prifitlee, private(ly)
prifix, prefix
prifot, private
prifotize, private(tize)
prifound, profound
prifur, prefer
prifusy, private(acy)
prifut, private
prifutize, private(tize)
prifutlee, private(ly)
prify, privy
prigekshen, project(ion)
prignostik, prognostic
prigreshen, progress(ion)
prijekshen, project(ion)
prijektile, project(ile)
prijidus, prejudice
prik, prick
prikareus, precarious
prikashen, precaution
prikastinate, procrastinate
prikaushen, precaution
prikd, prick(ed)
priked, prick(ed)
prikereous, precarious
priklame, proclaim
prikle, prick(ly)
priklusion, preclusion
priklusive, preclusive
prikognishen, precognition
prikoshen, precaution
prikoshus, precocious
prikotion, precaution
prikotius, precocious
prikrastination, procrastinate

prikt, prick(ed)
prilemenary, preliminary
prilimineri, preliminary
prilong, prolong
prilongate, prolong(ate)
prim, mmer, mmest, mly, mness, FORMAL/ PROPER (or see prime)
primachur, premature
primade, primate
primais, premise
primal, PRIMITIVE, BASE, FUNDAMENTAL
primary, ries, rily, MAIN ONE, CENTRAL, MOST IMPORTANT, FUNDAMENTAL
primate, *, eship, tial, MAMMALS, MAN/ MONKEYS/ APES
primatif, primitive
primative, primitive
primativly, primitive(ly)
prime, ed, ming, eness, er, AT ITS PEAK, READY, PREPARED FOR AN EVENT, TYPE OF NUMBER "prefixes: un"
primechur, premature
primeditate, premeditate
primediteit, premeditate
primel, primal
primenstral, premenstrual
primer, premier / prime(r)
primerily, primary(rily)
primery, primary
primir, prime(r) / premier
primise, premise
primitive, *, ely, eness, vism, vist, vistic, SIMPLE, EARLIEST EXPRESSION, CRUDE, GEOMETRIC EXPRESSION
primium, premium
primle, primal
primly, prim(mmly) / prime(ly)
primoder, promote(r)
primol, primal
primoshen, promote(tion)
primote, promote
primoter, promote(r)
primotion, promote(tion)
primp, *, ped, ping, TO ADORN/ GROOM/ DRESS UP
primul, primal
primur, prime(r) / prim(mmer)

primutif, primitive
prinaunse, pronounce
princabol, principal/ principle
prince, *, edom, MALE POSITION OF ROYALTY
princepol, principal/ principle
princess, sses, FEMALE POSITION OF ROYALTY
principal, *, lly, lship, lity, lities, lly, PRIMARY/ FIRST IN POSITION/ IMPORTANCE, TERM HAVING TO DO WITH MONEY/ LAW (or see principle) "prefixes: sub"
principle, *, ed, MAIN POINT, GENERAL TRUTH, ADOPTED METHOD/ RULE/ LAW (or see principal) "prefixes: un"
principol, principal/ principle
prind, print
prinounce, pronounce
prinownse, pronounce
prins, prince / print(s)
prinsabul, principle / principal
prinse, prince / print(s)
prinsepul, principle / principal
prinses, princess / prince(s)
prinseses, princess(es)
prinsipul, principle / principal
prinsuple, principle / principal
print, *, ted, ting, table, tability, ter, tery, tless, USE OF TEXT TO COMMUNICATE "prefixes: mis/ over/ pre/ un"
printuble, print(able)
printur, print(er)
prinunseashen, pronounciate(tion)
prinunseate, pronounciate
prinunsiation, pronounciate(tion)
prior, rly, rship, rate, rity, rities, FIRST, BEFORE, EARLIER, RELIGIOUS RANK
priorety, prior(ity)
prioridy, prior(ity)
pripare, prepare
pripeler, propel(ller)
priper, prepare
pripocishon, preposition
priponent, proponent
priporshen, proportion
priportion, proportion

priposal, propose(sal)
pripose, propose
priposteros, preposterous
pripostirus, preposterous
pripozle, propose(sal)
pripriator, proprietor
prirogative, prerogative
pris, price / prize
prisaid, preside
prisais, precise
priscraib, prescribe
priscribe, prescribe / proscribe
priscript, prescript
prisdeje, prestige
prise, price / price / prize
prisechen, precision / procession / precession
prised, precede / proceed / price(d)
prisedger, procedure
prisee, prissy / price
priseet, precede / proceed
prisejur, procedure
prisem, prism
prisen, prison
prisener, prison(er)
presentable, present(able)
prisentashin, presentation
presentation, presentation
priserv, preserve
priservation, preservation
priserve, preserve
prises, price(s) / precess
priseshen, precision / procession / precession
prisetgur, procedure
prisetion, precision / procession / precession
priside, preside / precede
prisigur, procedure
prisim, prism
prisin, prison
prisipatate, precipitate
prisipatation, precipitate(tion)
prisise, precise
prisisly, precise(ly)
priskrepshen, prescript(ion)

priskribe, prescribe / proscribe
prisless, price(less)
prislis, price(less)
prism, *, matic, matically, GEOMETRICAL SHAPE, OPTICAL/ CRYSTAL/ RAINBOW EFFECT
prismadik, prism(atic)
prisom, prism
prisomtif, presume(mptive)
prison, *, ner, BUILDING USED TO CONFINE/ HOLD, A FEELING OF INVOLUNTARY RESTRAINT
prisontation, presentation
prissy, ssily, ssiness, ARROGANTLY PRIM, GIRLY GIRL
prist, priest / price(d)
pristege, prestige
pristegus, prestige(gious)
pristeje, prestige
pristene, pristine
pristine, ely, UNCONTAMINATED, PURE
prisum, prism / presume
prisumptive, presume(mptive)
prisumtion, presume(mption)
prisumtuis, presume(mptuous)
prisun, prison
prisuner, prison(er)
prisurf, preserve
prisurve, preserve
prisy, prissy / price
prit, pride
pritear, pretty(ttier)
pritect, protect
pritection, protect(ion)
prited, pride(d)
pritekshen, protect(ion)
pritekt, protect
pritektif, protect(ive)
pritenchus, pretentious
pritend, pretend
pritenshen, pretense(sion)
pritenshus, pretentious
pritetur, pretty(ttier)
pritful, pride(ful)
priti, pretty

pritiest, pretty(ttiest)
pritinchos, pretentious
pritinshus, pretentious
pritintious, pretentious
pritrude, protrude
pritrushen, protrude(usion)
pritrusion, protrude(usion)
prity, pretty
priur, prior
prival, prevail
privaledged, privilege(d)
privalent, prevalent
privalije, privilege
privalt, prevail(ed)
privasee, private(acy)
private, *, ely, acy, tness, tize, tized, tizing, tization, tion, tist, tism, MUST GAIN PERMISSION TO ACCESS, SECLUDED, U.S.MILITARY RANK, NON-GOVERNMENTAL "prefixes: semi"
privatisation, private(tization)
privatly, private(ly)
privecy, private(acy)
privee, privy
priveisly, previous(ly)
priveledged, privilege(d)
privelent, prevalent
privelige, privilege
privenshen, prevent(ion)
privent, prevent
priventable, prevent(able)
priventive, prevent(ive)
priverbeul, proverb(ial)
privese, private(acy)
privet, private
privetisation, private(tization)
privetly, private(ly)
priveus, previous
priveusly, previous(ly)
privicy, private(acy)
prividuble, provide(dable)
privilege, *, ed, ging, SPECIAL, HONORARY, FAVORED, CHOSEN "prefixes: under"
privilent, prevalent

privilige, privilege
privios, previous
privit, private
privitly, private(ly)
priviusly, previous(ly)
privlich, privilege
privlilil, privilege
privocative, provocative
privock, provoke
privokative, provocative
privoke, provoke
privokt, provoke(d)
privolent, prevalent
privulej, privilege
privusee, private(acy)
privut, private
privutization, private(tization)
privutly, private(ly)
privvy, privy
privy, vies, vier, viest, OUTDOOR TOILET, IN ON A PRIVATE MATTER/ SECRET
privyed, privy(vied)
prize, *, ed, zing, GIFT/ REWARD/ AWARD FOR ACCOMPLISHMENT/ WINNING (or see price/ pry(s))
prizen, prison
prizener, prison(er)
prizent, present
prizerve, preserve
prizin, prison
prizis, prize(s) / price(s)
prizm, prism
prizmadik, prism(atic)
prizmatic, prism(atic)
prizomtuis, presume(mptuous)
prizoner, prison(er)
prizum, prism
prizumshen, presume(mption)
prizumtues, presume(mptuous)
prizun, prison
prizuner, prison(er)
prizus, prize(s) / price(s)
pro, *, SHORT FOR PROFESSIONAL (or see prose) "prefixes: semi"

prob,prop / probe
probabil,probable
probable,ly,bilism,bilist,bilistic,bility,bilities,MOST LIKELY,CHANCE TO OCCUR/ HAPPEN "prefixes: im"
probably,MOST LIKELY TO OCCUR/ HAPPEN
probade,probate
probaganda,propaganda
probagashen,propagate(tion)
probagate,propagate
probagation,propagate(tion)
probane,propane
probashen,probate(tion)
probashinul,probate(tional)
probate,*,ed,ting,tion,tional,tionary,tionally,tioner,tive,tory,EXAMINATION/ INVESTIGATE THE TRUTH/ VALIDITY/ GENUINENESS/ AUTHENTICITY "prefixes: re"
probatid,probate(d)
probe,*,ed,bing,er,DEEPLY INVESTIGATE/ OBSERVE, INSTRUMENT/ ACT FOR RELAYING FACTUAL INFORMATION (or see prop)
probebly,probably
probebul,probable
probeganda,propaganda
probegashen,propagate(tion)
probegate,propagate
prober,proper
proberte,property
probibly,probably
probibul,probable
probiganda,propaganda
probigashen,propagate(tion)
probigate,propagate
probirty,property
problem,*,matic,matical,matically,CHALLENGING SITUATION/ INFORMATION WHICH REQUIRES RESOLUTION/ ANSWERS/ RESULTS
problum,problem
probobul,probable
proboganda,propaganda
probogation,propagate(tion)
proboscis,ses,ides,SNOUT/ NOSE/ TRUNK
probs,probe(s) / prop(s)

probubilety,probable(bility)
probuble,probable
probuganda,propaganda
probugashen,propagate(tion)
probugate,propagate
probur,proper
proburty,property
procede,proceed
procedure,*,ral,rally,NORMAL/ PROPER ACTION/ METHOD/ PROCESS
proceed,*,ded,ding,GO AHEAD/ VENTURE FORTH, PROFIT/ REVENUE FROM EVENT (or see precede)
proceedure,procedure
proces,process
procseshen,precision / procession / precession
procesion,precision / procession / precession
process,sses,ssed,ssing,ssor,ssion,ssional,ssionally, STEPS TO ACHIEVE A GOAL,INCREMENTAL/ GRADUAL CHANGES "prefixes: bio"
procession,nal,nally,MOVING ALONG AS A GROUP (or see precession/ precision)
procetion,precision / procession / precession
procilur,procedure
prockreashen,procreate(tion)
proclaim,*,med,ming,mer,MAKE VERBAL ANNOUNCEMENT WITH AUTHORITY
proclamashen,proclamation
proclamation,*,ANNOUNCE/ DECLARE TO THE PUBLIC
proclameishon,proclamation
proclimation,proclamation
proclumashen,proclamation
proclumation,proclamation
procram,program
proclivity,ties,A TENDENCY TOWARDS
procrastinate,*,ed,ting,tion,tor,REPEATEDLY PUT OFF UNTIL LATER
procreashen,procreate(tion)
procreate,*,ed,ting,tion,tive,tor,TO REPRODUCE/ PRODUCE
prod,*,dded,dding,dder,POKE/ JAB,POLE/ STICK WITH POINTED END
prodakol,protocol
prodashay,protege

prodatipe,prototype
prodegul,prodigal
prodegy,prodigy
prodekol,protocol
prodest,protest
prodetipe,prototype
prodews,produce
prodicol,protocol
prodigal,lity,lly,ONE WHO SPENDS/ WASTES TOO MUCH MONEY
prodigul,prodigal
prodigy,gies,YOUTH WITH REMARKABLE TALENTS/ SKILLS/ APTITUDE
prodikol,protocol
prodikt,predict
proditipe,prototype
prodoct,product
prodon,proton
prodotype,prototype
produce,*,ed,cing,cible,er,CREATE/ MANUFACTURE/ BRING FORTH,FRUIT/ VEGETABLE "prefixes: re"
producol,protocol
producshen,product(ion)
product,*,tion,tive,SOMETHING PRODUCED/ DEVELOPED/ MANUFACTURED AS MARKETABLE GOODS,ACT OF CREATING GOODS "prefixes: pre/ re"
productive,ely,eness,vity,ion,SOMETHING PRODUCED/ MANUFACTURED/ DEVELOPED AS MARKETABLE GOODS,ACT OF CREATING GOODS "prefixes: re/ un"
produgee,prodigy
produgil,prodigal
produkol,protocol
produkshen,product(ion)
produktion,product(ion)
produse,produce
produtipe,prototype
prof,proof / prove
profable,prove(vable)
profail,prevail / profile
profalaktik,prophylactic
profale,prevail

profane, ely, eness, er, nity, nities, TO MISUSE WORDS, VULGAR LANGUAGE
profanedy, profane(nity)
profat, profit / prophet
profedik, prophet(ic)
profelaktik, prophylactic
profeser, professor
profeshen, profession
profeshenul, profession(al)
profesional, profession(al)
profesor, professor
profess, sses, ssed, ssedly, ssing, TO VOW, CLAIM ALLEGIANCE/ ACCEPTANCE
profession, *, nal, nally, nalism, nalize, LOYAL TO A VOCATION, ADEPT IN THEIR FIELD "prefixes: semi/ sub/ un"
professor, *, rial, rially, rate, riate, rship, TEACHER ON COLLEGE/ UNIVERSITY STAFF
profesy, prophecy / prophesy
profet, profit / prophet
profetable, profit(able)
profeteer, profit(eer)
profetible, profit(able)
profetik, prophet(ic)
proficient, tly, ncy, SKILLED/ KNOWLEDGEABLE
profide, provide
profiduble, provide(dable)
profilaktik, prophylactic
profile, *, ed, ling, SIDE VIEW OF FACE, OUTLINE/ CONTOUR, BIOGRAPHICAL OUTLINE
profishent, proficient
profisy, prophecy / prophesy
profit, *, ted, ting, tless, table, tably, tability, tableness, teer, GAIN ON THE SALE OF SOMETHING (or see prophet) "prefixes: un"
profituble, profit(able)
profulaktik, prophylactic
profound, dly, dness, DEEP/ SIGNIFICANT IN KNOWLEDGE/ INSIGHT
profownd, profound
profowndly, profound(ly)
profownt, profound
profulaktik, prophylactic

profusy, prophecy / prophesy
progeks, project(s)
progekshin, project(ion)
progekt, project
progektile, project(ile)
progesterone, CHEMICAL PRODUCED BY FEMALES HUMANS/ MAMMALS
prognastic, prognostic
prognosis, ses, A MEDICAL OPINION
prognostic, *, cate, cative, cator, cation, PREDICT A MEDICAL CONDITION'S OUTCOME
prognousis, prognosis
program, *, mmed, mming, mmer, mmatic, mmatically, OUTLINE OF EVENTS/ ACTIONS/ SCHEDULES "prefixes: de/ pre/ sub"
programt, program(mmed)
progreshen, progress(ion)
progresive, progress(ive)
progress, sses, ssed, ssing, ssion, ssional, ssionist, ssive, FORWARD MOVEMENT, ADVANCEMENT, EVOLUTION
progressive, ely, eness, ADVANCEMENT/ EVOLUTION/ FORWARD MOVEMENT
progretion, progress(ion)
progris, progress
prohabeshin, prohibit(ion)
prohebatory, prohibit(ory)
prohebit, prohibit
prohebition, prohibit(ion)
prohibatif, prohibit(ive)
prohibetory, prohibit(ory)
prohibit, *, ted, ting, tive, tively, tion, tionist, tory, NOT ALLOWED TO DO, FORBID, PREVENT
project, *, ted, ting, table, tile, tion, tional, tionist, tive, tively, tivity, tor, PLAN/ OBJECTIVE/ UNDERTAKING TO BE CARRIED OUT, JUT OUT, PROTRUDE, PRESENT
projekshin, project(ion)
projeksion, project(ion)
projektile, project(ile)
projesterone, progesterone
projestirone, progesterone
prokastinate, procrastinate
proklaim, proclaim

proklame, proclaim
proklemashen, proclamation
proklevidy, proclivity
proklumation, proclamation
proklusion, preclusion
proklusive, preclusive
proknosis, prognosis
prokram, program
prokrastinate, procrastinate
prokrastination, procrastinate(tion)
prokreashen, procreate(tion)
prokreate, procreate
prokreation, procreate(tion)
prokriate, procreate
prokse, proxy
proksemate, proximate
proksimety, proximate(mity)
proksumit, proximate
proleminary, preliminary
prolimenary, preliminary
prollect, project
prollesteroun, progesterone
prolog, prologue
prologue, *, ed, uing, uize, uized, uizing, INTRO/ PREFACE/ SPEECH BEFORE A BOOK/ PLAY/ POEM/ NOVEL
prolok, prologue
prolong, *, ged, ging, gate, gates, gated, gating, gation, EXTEND/ LENGTHEN/ ELONGATE TIME
prolongade, prolong(ate)
prolonk, prolong
prom, *, menade, menaded, menading, menader, FORMAL DANCE
promanent, prominent
promanintly, prominent(ly)
promanitly, prominent(ly)
promd, prompt
promded, prompt(ed)
promdly, prompt(ly)
promenant, prominent
promenintly, prominent(ly)
promes, promise
promeskuis, promiscuity(uous)
promesquis, promiscuity(uous)

promesquity, promiscuity
prominade, prom(enade) / prominent
prominate, prom(enade) / prominent
prominent, tly, ncy, PRONOUNCED/ DISTINCT/ JUTS OUT/ STANDS OUT/ NOTICEABLE
prominet, prominent
promiscuity, uous, uously, uousness, GIVEN TO CONDUCTING SEXUAL/ RANDOM/ INDISCRIMINATE ACTIVITY WITH MANY
promise, *, ed, sing, ser, see, sor, sory, PLEDGE, AGREE, LOYALTY TO FOLLOW THROUGH AS STATED "prefixes: un"
promiskuis, promiscuity(uous)
promisquis, promiscuity(uous)
promisquity, promiscuity
promist, promise(d)
promote, *, ed, ting, tion, tional, tive, tiveness. er, ADVERTISE/ PRESENT/ ENGAGE TO FURTHER A PROJECT/ EVENT/ SALE
promout, promote
prompnes, prompt(ness)
prompt, *, ted, ting, tly, tness, ter, titude, TIMELY/ EXACT/ TO REMIND/ PUNCTUAL "prefixes: un"
promt, prompt
promted, prompt(ed)
promtlee, prompt(ly)
promunetly, prominent(ly)
promus, promise
prona, prana / piranha
pronaun, pronoun
pronauns, pronounce
pronaunse, pronounce
prondo, pronto
prone, eness, GIVEN/ INCL NED TO, HAVE AN AFFILIATION FOR
prones, prone(ness) / prawn(s)
pronnis, prone(ness)
pronoun, CLASS OF WORDS IN ENGLISH GRAMMAR
pronounce, *, ed, edly, cing, eable, er, ement, ARTICULATE, SPEAKING, DEFINE, SPEAK WITH CONFIDENCE/ AUTHORITY "prefixes: mis/ un"
pronown, pronoun
pronto, QUICKLY/ IMMEDIATELY

pronu, prana / piranha
pronounciate, *, ed, ting, tion, ARTICULATE, BE SPECIFIC IN SPEAKING, SPOKEN ALOUD AS PRONUNCIATE
pronunseashen, pronounciate(tion)
pronunseate, pronounciate
pronunsiation, pronounciate(tion)
prood, prude
proodish, prude(dish)
proof, *, fed, fing, fer, FACTUAL EVIDENCE, SUPPORT THE TRUTH, TESTED (or see prove) "prefixes: dis/ over/ re"
proon, prune
proot, prude
proove, prove
prop, *, pped, pping, THEATER STAGE SET TERM, A SUPPORT, AIRPLANE PROPELLER (or see probe) "prefixes: under"
propabel, probable
propabelity, probable(bility)
propable, probable / probably
propabul, probable
propagade, propagate
propaganda, dist, distic, distically, dism, dize, MISINFORMATION, PURPOSEFUL HALF-TRUTHS
propagashen, propagate(tion)
propagate, *, ed, ting, tion, tional, tive, tor, BREED/ REPRODUCE/ MAKE MORE OF
propain, propane
propane, A GAS
propasishen, preposition / proposition / prepossess(ion)
propasterus, preposterous
propazishen, preposition / proposition / prepossess(ion)
propd, prop(pped) / robe(d)
propebly, probably
proped, prop(pped) / probe(d)
propeganda, propaganda
propegashen, propagate(tion)
propegate, propagate
propegation, propagate(tion)
propein, propane

propel, *, lled, lling, llant, ller, EXERT/ GIVE MOMENTUM/ START INTO ACTION, MOVING PART ON A PLANE, ELEMENT USED TO CREATE MOVEMENT "prefixes: bi"
propeler, propel(ller)
propelint, propel(llant)
proper, rly, rness, CORRECT/ ACCURATE
properedness, prepare(dness)
properidness, prepare(dness)
property, ties, tied, tyless, SOMETHING TANGIBLE/ PHYSICAL TO BE OWNED BY SOMEONE
prophalaktik, prophylactic
prophecy, cies, PREDICTION OF A DIRE/ UNDESIRABLE FUTURE (or see prophesy)
prophelaktik, prophylactic
prophesy, sies, sied, sying, siable, sier, PREDICTION OF THE FUTURE (or see prophecy)
prophet, *, tic, ecy, esy, ONE WHO IS BELIEVED TO HAVE CONNECTION TO THE UNKNOWN SOURCE FOR PREDICTIONS/ ANSWERS (or see profit)
prophilaktik, prophylactic
prophile, profile
prophisy, prophecy / prophesy
prophit, prophet / profit
propholaktik, prophylactic
prophylactic, *, cally, ITEM USED FOR CONTRACEPTION
propibly, probably
propigade, propagate
propiganda, propaganda
propigashen, propagate(tion)
propigate, propagate
propigation, propagate(tion)
propiseshen, preposition / proposition / prepossess(ion)
proplem, problem
proplum, problem
propogade, propagate
proponent, *, ONE WHO MAKES A PROPOSAL
proporshen, proportion
proportion, *, ned, ning, nal, nally, nable, nality, nate, nately, nateness, PARTS EQUAL/ RELATIVE IN PERSPECTIVE/ SIZE "prefixes: dis/ over"
propose, *, ed, er, sing, sal, sition, OFFER/ PRESENT AN IDEA (or see preposition)

proposishen,preposition / proposition / prepossess(ion)
proposition,,nal,nally,OFFER/ PRESENT AN IDEA/ SUGGESTION
proposterus,preposterous
propozishen,preposition / proposition / prepossess(ion)
propriater,proprietor
proprietor,,rship,ty,ties,tary,LEGAL OWNER/ TITLEHOLDER
propriuter,proprietor
propseshen,preposition / proposition / prepossess(ion)
propt,prop(pped) / probe(d)
propubil,probable
propubiledy,probable(bility)
propubly,probably
propuganda,propaganda
propugashen,propagate(tion)
propugate,propagate
propugation,propagate(tion)
propur,proper
propurle,proper(ly)
propuzishen,preposition / proposition / prepossess(ion)
pros,prose / pro(s)
prosberity,prosper(ity)
proscraib,proscribe
proscribe,*,ed,bing,er,OUTLAW/ PROHIBIT (or see prescribe)
prosdatoot,prostitute
prosdetushen,prostitute(tion)
prosditute,prostitute
prosdition,prostitute(tion)
prosdrate,prostrate / prostate
prose,MORE LIKE NORMAL WRITTEN LANGUAGE THAN POETRY (or see pro(s))
prosechin,precision / procession / precession
prosecute,*,ed,ting,tion,tor,FOLLOW THROUGH, FINAL DETERMINATION,ENFORCE THE LAW, INITIATE A LAWSUIT (or see persecute)
prosed,proceed
proseds,proceed(s)
proseets,proceed(s)
proseetsher,procedure
proseger,procedure
prosejur,procedure

prosekewt,prosecute
prosekiut,prosecute
prosekushen,prosecute(tion)
prosekution,prosecute(tion)
proses,process
proseshen,precision / procession / precession
prosetion,precision / procession / precession
prosichor,procedure
prosicute,prosecute
prosidger,procedure
prosijur,procedure
prosikushen,prosecute(tion)
prosikute,prosecute
prosis,process
prosparidy,prosper(ity)
prospect,*,ted,ting,tor,tive,tively,tus,EXPECTING/ FUTURE/ POSSIBLE EVENT/ SITUATION, MINING FOR SOMETHING "prefixes: bio"
prospectif,prospect(ive)
prospekt,prospect
prospektif,prospect(ive)
prosper,*,red,ring,rity,rities,rous,rously,rousness, BENEFIT GREATLY, BE SUCCESSFUL
prosperidy,prosper(ity)
prospir,prosper
prospirus,prosper(ous)
prospures,prosper(s) / prosper(ous)
prostate,ectomy,ectomies,tism,PERTAINS TO A GLAND AROUND THE MALE URETHRA (or see prostrate)
prostatution,prostitute(tion)
prosteit,prostate / prostrate
prostetute,prostitute
prostetution,prostitute(tion)
prosthesis,etic,etically,ARTIFICIAL REPLACEMENT OF A BODY PART
prosthesus,prosthesis
prostitute,*,,tion,tor,PERSON WHO TRADES SEXUAL FAVORS FOR MONEY/ GOODS
prostrade,prostrate / prostate
prostrate,*,ed,ting,tion,tor,TO PLACE ONE'S BODY INTO A SUBMISSIVE POSITION/ POSTURE, ASSUME A HUMILIATED/ HELPLESS/ POWERLESS POSITION (or see prostate)

prosukushen,prosecute(tion)
prot,prod
protacol,protocol
protaga,protege'
protagenist,protagonist
protagonist,*,,LEADING/ PRINCIPAL CHARACTER
protajay,protege'
protakol,protocol
protatype,prototype
protean,protein
protecol,protocol
protect,*,ted,ting,tion,tionism,tionist,tive,tor,GUARD/ SHIELD/ PREVENT FROM DANGER/ HARM/ DESTRUCTION "prefixes: un"
protectif,protect(ive)
protega,protege'
protege',,YOUNG PERSON UNDER CARE/ PROTECTION OF AN ELDER/ MASTER (or see prodigy)
protein,*,,CHEMICAL COMPOUNDS
protejay,protege'
protekol,protocol
protekshen,protect(ion)
protekt,protect
protektuf,protect(ive)
protene,protein
protes,protest
protest,*,ted,ting,ter,TAKE ACTION AGAINST A PERCEIVED INJUSTICE TO AFFECT CHANGE
protestur,protest(er)
protetipe,prototype
protetype,prototype
protexei,protege
proticol,protocol
protiga,protege'
protijay,protege'
protikol,protocol
protitype,prototype
protocol,*,,led,ling,GENERAL RULE WHETHER FORMALIZED OR NOT
proton,*,,nic,A MOLECULAR PARTICLE OF POSITIVE CHARGE
protonek,proton(ic)
prototipe,prototype

prototype, *,pal,pic,A MODEL/ REPLICATE OF ORIGINAL, FIRST MODEL

protract, tion,tive,ted,tor,DRAW OUT/ LENGTHEN TIME/ SPACE/ DISTANCE,A TOOL FOR DRAWING
protrakt,protract
protrakter,protract(or)

protrude, *,ed,ding,ent,usible,usion,usile,usive,usively, usiveness,EXTENDS/ PROJECTS OUT
protrugin,protrude(usion)
protrushen,protrude(usion)
protrusuf,protrude(usive)
protukol,protocol
protutipe,prototype
proub,probe
proubeit,probate
prouboskus,proboscis
proucid,proceed
proucleim,proclaim
prouclivedi,proclivity
proucrastineit,procrastinate
proucrieit,procreate

proud, dly,dness,PAST TENSE FOR THE WORD "PRIDE", HAPPY ABOUT AN ACCOMPLISHMENT
proues,prowess
proufaund,profound
proufein,profane
prougram,program
prouhibit,prohibit
prouis,prowess
proukrieit,procreate
proul,prowl
proulog,prologue
proulong,prolong
proun,prone
prounaun,pronoun
proupraietor,proprietor
prous,prose
prousid,proceed
proutagonist,protagonist
prouteshey,protege
proutin,protein
provacation,provocative(ion)
provakashen,provocativeion)

prove, *,ed,ving,vable,vably,BRING FORTH FACTS, MAKE TRUTH KNOWN (or see proof) "prefixes: dis/ re"
proveable,prove(vable)
proveble,prove(vable)
provecation,provocative(ion)
provekation,provocative(ion)
provence,province
provencial,province(cial)
provensial,province(cial)
provent,prevent
provents,province / prevent(s)

proverb, *, bial,bially,POPULAR/ WISE SAYING
proverbeil,proverb(ial)
proverbeul,proverb(ial)
proveshen,provision
provible,prove(vable)
provication,provocative(ion)

provide, *, ed,ding,er,dable, MAKE AVAILABLE/ GIVE/ EXPOSE "prefixes: un"
provikation,provocative(ion)

province, *,,cial,cially,ciality,cialize,cialities,cialist,cialize, cialism, DESIGNATED AREA OUTSIDE OF MAINSTREAM GIVEN TO A SPECIFIC ORDER/ RULE
provinshul,province(cial)
provint,prevent
provints,province
provirb,proverb
provirbeul,proverb(ial)

provision, *, ned,ning,ner,SUPPLIES,ALLOWANCES, PROVIDE FOR

provocative,ely,eness,ion,STIMULATE/ ENTICE TO REACT
provokative, provocative

provoke, *, ed,king,kingly,ocation,ENTICE/ LURE/ MANIPULATE TO REACT

provost, tship,CHURCH/ EDUCATIONAL SUPERIOR
provuble, prove(vable)
provukashen,provocative(ion)
provukation,provocative(ion)
provurb,proverb
provurbeul,proverb(ial)
provurbial,proverb(ial)
prowb,probe

prowclivedi,proclivity
prowd,proud
prowdly,proud(ly)
prowess, EXCEPTIONAL BRAVERY/ SKILL
prowis,prowess
prowl, *, led,ling,ler,SOMEONE SNEAKING AROUND IN SEARCH OF SOMETHING/ SOMEONE
prowt,proud
prowtly,proud(ly)
proxamit, proximate
proxemidy,proximate(mity)
proximate,ely, eness,mity,al,NEXT/ NEAR IN TIME/ SPACE, CLOSE TO (or see approximate)
proxsemity,proximate(mity)
proxumit, proximate
proxy,xies,AUTHORIZED/ LEGAL TO SUBSTITUTE FOR
proyect, project
prozdatute, prostitute
prozdetushen,prostitute(tion)
prozditushin,prostitute(tion)
prozdrate, prostrate / prostate
proztate,prostate / prostrate
prubaskis, proboscis
prubozkis, proboscis
prucede, precede / proceed
prucedure,procedure
prucepitous, precipitous
pruclivity,proclivity
pruclusion, preclusion
pruclusive, preclusive
prude, ery,eries,dish,dishness,SOMEONE UNCOMFORTABLE WITH SEX RELATED ISSUES
prudence,nt,ntly,ntial,ntially,PRACTICING CAUTION/ GOOD JUDGMENT
prudense, prudence
prudesh, prude(dish)
prudikament, predicament
prudinse, prudence
prudunt, prudence(nt)
pruf, proof / prove
prufanedy, profane(nity)
prufanity, profane(nity)
prufedik, prophet(ic)

prufeshen, profession
prufeshinul, profession(al)
prufesional, profession
prufible, prove(vable)
prufide, provide
prufiduble, provide(dable)
prufuble, prove(vable)
prugektile, project(ile)
prugnostik, prognostic
prugnoztek, prognostic
prugreshen, progress(ion)
prugresif, progress(ive)
prugresive, progress(ive)
prugretion, progress(ion)
pruhebit, prohibit
pruhibatif, prohibit(ive)
pruhibet, prohibit
prujektile, project(ile)
prukivedy, proclivity
prukivity, proclivity
pruklusion, preclusion
pruklusive, preclusive
pruleminary, preliminary
prulimenary, preliminary
prumere, premier
prumiskues, promiscuity(uous)
prumoder, promote(r)
prumoshen, promote(tion)
prumote, promote
prumoter, promote(r)
prumotion, promote(tion)
prune, *, ed, ning, DRIED PLUM, TRIM A SHRUB/ TREE
prunownse, pronounce
prupare, prepare
prupel, propel
prupeler, propel(ller)
prupelint, propel(llant)
prupelir, propel(ller)
prupelt, propel(lled)
pruponent, proponent
pruporshen, proportion
pruporshenate, proportion(al)
pruportion, proportion

prupose, propose
pruposition, proposition
pruposle, propose(sal)
prupoze, propose
prupozel, propose(sal)
prupozishen, proposition
prupriater, proprietor
pruprietor, proprietor
prusdej, prestige
prusdejus, prestige(gious)
prusechen, precision / procession / precession
prusede, precede / proceed
prusejur, procedure
prusepitous, precipitous
pruseshin, precision / procession / precession
prusetgur, procedure
prusetion, precision / procession / precession
prusipitous, precipitous
prusiputashen, precipitate(tion)
prusishen, precision
prusisly, precise(ly)
prusition, precision / procession / precession
pruskribe, prescribe / proscribe
prusteg, prestige
prustegis, prestige(gious)
prustejus, prestige(gious)
prute, prude
prutective, protect(ive)
prutekshen, protect(ion)
prutektuf, protect(ive)
prutish, prude(dish)
protrude, protrude
prutrushen, protrude(usion)
prutrusion, protrude(usion)
pruv, prove
pruvale, prevail
pruvencial, province(cial)
pruvenshen, prevent(ion)
pruvenshul, province(cial)
pruvent, prevent
pruventable, prevent(able)
pruventive, prevent(ive)
pruverbeul, proverb(ial)

pruvide, provide
pruviduble, provide(dable)
pruvinshul, province(cial)
pruvint, prevent
pruvintable, prevent(able)
pruvokative, provocative
pruzentuble, present(able)
pruzumshen, presume(mption)
pry, ries, ried, ying, yingly, rier, PEEP IN, METHOD OF OPENING SOMETHING THAT'S TIGHTLY CLOSED
pryer, prior
prymate, primate
psalm, *, BIBLICAL SONG
psariasis, psoriasis
pseudo, PREFIX INDICATING 'FALSE/ PRETEND/ IMITATION' MOST OFTEN MODIFIES THE WORD
pseudonym, *, USING ANOTHER NAME
psicheatric, psychiatric
psichopathologist, psychopath(ologist)
psikeatric, psychiatric
psikik, psychic
psikilegekul, psychology(gical)
psikilegy, psychology
psikogekul, psychology(gical)
psikologest, psychology(gist)
psikology, psychology
psikopath, psychopath
psikopathic, psychopath(ic)
psikopathologist, psychopath(ologist)
psikosis, psychosis
psikotic, psychotic
psoriasis, atic, SKIN PROBLEM
psudo, pseudo
psuriesis, psoriasis
psych, PREFIX INDICATING 'MIND/ MENTAL' MOST OFTEN MODIFIES THE WORD
psychadelic, psychedelic
psyche, edelic, OVERALL ESSENCE OF THE HUMAN BEING, SOUL/ BODY/ MIND/ SPIRIT (or see sic/ sick)
psycheatric, psychiatric
psychedelic, *, HALLUCINATION/ DELUSION/ MIND ALTERING

psychiatric,*,cally,FIELD OF SCIENCE WHICH STUDIES THE MIND/ EMOTIONS
psychiatric,psychiatry
psychiatry,rist,PHYSICIAN WHO STUDIES THE MIND, STUDY OF THE MIND/ EMOTIONS
psykiutry,psychiatry
psyko,psycho
psychic,*,cal,cally,USE OF THE MORPHOGENIC FIELD TO SEE PAST/ PRESENT/ FUTURE EVENTS, EXTRA-SENSORY PERCEPTION "prefixes: intra"
psykolegy,psychology
psykoligekul,psychology(gical)
psykoligy,psychology
psychidelic,psychedelic
psykologekul,psychology(gical)
psychietrist,psychiatry(rist)
psykologest,psychology(gist)
psychietry,psychiatry
psykology,psychology
psychiotrist,psychiatry(rist)
psykopath,psychopath
psycho,*,SLANG FOR SOMEONE WHO IS BEING LUDICROUS/ CRAZY
psykopathic,psychopath(ic)
psykopatholagist,psychopath(ologist)
psychodelic,psychedelic
psykosis,psychosis
psycholagy,psychology
psykotic,psychotic
psycholgekul,psychology(gical)
psykudelic,psychedelic
psychology,gies,gical,gical y,gism,gist,gize,FIELD OF SCIENCE RELATED TO STUDYING THE MIND/ MENTAL "prefixes: bio"
psykyatric,psychiatric
pu,pew
pub,*,A TAVERN (or see pube)
psychopath,*,hic,hically,hw,hology,hylogical,hologist, SOMEONE WHO HAS OR WORKS WITH A PERSONALITY DISORDER
pube,*,bic,escent,escence,escency,HAIR ON GENITALS WHICH APPEAR DURING PUBERTY, THE DOWN ON PLANTS
pubek,pube(bic)
psychopathic,psychopath(ic)
puberdy,puberty
psychopatholagist,psychopath(ologist)
puberty,BECOMING OF AGE FOR REPRODUCTION
psychosis,A MENTAL DISORDER WHICH RENDERS A PERSON UNATTACHED FROM NORMAL REALITY
pubescent,nce,ncy,GOING THROUGH PUBERTY "prefixes: pre"
pubirty,puberty
psychotic,cally,MENTAL DISORDER THAT RENDERS A PERSON UNATTACHED FROM NORMAL REALITY "prefixes: non"
publacation,publication
publacist,publicist
publakashen,publication
publakation,publication
psychudelic,psychedelic
publash,publish
psycik,psychic
publasher,publish(er)
psykadelic,psychedelic
publasist,publicist
psykapathic,psychopath(ic)
publasize,publicity(ize)
psykeatric,psychiatric
publecation,publication
psykedelic,psychedelic
publecist,publicist
psykek,psychic
publecity,publicity(ity)
psykepathic,psychopath(ic)
publek,public
psykiatric,psychiatric
publekashin,publication
psykiatrist,psychiatry(rist)
publekation,publication
psykiatry,psychiatry
publesher,publish(er)
psykidelic,psychedelic
publeshuble,publish(able)
psykik,psychic
publesist,publicist
psykipathic,psychopath(ic)

publesity,publicity(ity)
publesize,publicity(ize)
public,cly,cness,NOT PRIVATE
publicashen,publication
publication,*,ISSUE PRINTED MATERIAL FOR PUBLIC
publicist,ity,ize,cation,INVOLVED IN THE PRODUCTION/ DISSEMINATION OF WRITTEN TEXT
publicity,USING MEDIA TO GAIN PUBLIC ATTENTION
publicize,*,ed,zing,ADVERTISE,MAKE PUBLICLY KNOWN
publikashen,publication
publikation,publication
publikeishon,publication
publisaty,publicist(ity)
publisety,publicity(ity)
publish,hes,hed,hing,hable,her,INVOLVED IN PRODUCTION/ DISSEMINATION OF WRITTEN TEXT/ INFORMATION "prefixes: un"
publishuble,publish(able)
publisist,publicist
publisity,publicist(ity)
publisize,publicity(ize)
publokashen,publication
publosher,publish(er)
publosist,publicist
publosize,publicity(ize)
publucation,publication
publucist,publicist
publukation,publication
publush,publish
publushable,publish(able)
publusher,publish(er)
publusist,publicist
publusize,publicity(ize)
puburdy,puberty
puc,puck / puke
puch,pooch / push
puck,*,A DISC USED IN HOCKEY (or see puke)
pud,put
pudado,potato
pudal,puddle / poodle
puddil,puddle / poodle
pudding,A CREAMY DESSERT (or see putt(ing))

puddle, *, ed, ing, SMALL POOL OF LIQUID (or see poodle)
puddul, puddle / poodle
pude, put / putty
pudel, puddle / poodle
pudeng, pudding / putt(ing)
puder, pewter / putt(er)
pudestrein, pedestrian
pudgie, pudgy
pudgy, A BIT OVERWEIGHT
pudil, puddle / poodle
puding, pudding / putt(ing)
pudir, pewter / putt(er)
pudje, pudgy
pudl, puddle/ poodle
pudul, puddle / poodle
pudur, pewter / putt(er)
pudy, putty
puer, poor / pour / pore
puf, puff
pufeleon, pavilion
pufer, puff(er)
puff, *, ffed, ffing, ffer, SHORT/ SUDDEN BURST OF AIR/ SMOKE, TO INHALE/ EXHALE SMOKE
pufileon, pavilion
pufs, puff(s)
puft, puff(ed)
pugamus, pajamas
puge, pudgy
puir, poor / pour / pore
puit, put
pujamus, pajamas
puje, pudgy
pujomus, pajamas
puk, puck / puke
puke, *, ed, king, TO VOMIT/ THROW-UP (or see puck)
pukon, pecan
pukuleur, peculiar
pul, pull / pool
pularity, polar(ity)
puld, pull(ed) / pool(ed)
pule, pool / pulley
puled, pull(ed) / pool(ed)

pulegimy, polygamy
puleridy, polar(ity)
pules, police / pulley(s)
pulet, pullet
pulewshen, pollute(tion)
puley, pulley
pulferise, pulverize
pulfurise, pulverize
puli, pulley
pulies, pulley(s)
puligamus, polygamy(mous)
puligemy, polygamy
puligine, polygyny
puling, pull(ing) / pool(ing)
pulit, pullet / polite
pull, *, lled, lling, ller, lley, TO DRAW/ BRING TOWARDS, TUG SOMETHING/ SOMEONE (or see pool)
pullet, *, YOUNG DOMESTICATED HEN
pulley, *, TOOL USED WITH ROPE FOR LIFTING/ PULLING
pullit, pullet
pulmanery, pulmonary
pulmonary, PERTAINING TO THE LUNGS
pulmunery, pulmonary
pulp, piness, py, FIBROUS/ THICK SUBSTANCE LEFT BEHIND WHEN VEGETABLE/ FRUIT/ PLANTS ARE COOKED/ SMASHED
pulpet, pulpit
pulpit, CHURCH PLATFORM
pulsashen, pulsate(tion)
pulsate, *, ed, ting, tile, tion, tor, tory, PULSE/ THROB
pulse, *, ed, sing, THROB/ BEAT RYTHMICALLY
pulseit, pulsate
pult, pull(ed) / pool(ed)
pulushen, pollute(tion)
pulut, pollute / pullet
pulutent, pollute(tant)
pulution, pollute(tion)
puverize, *, ed, zing, er, REDUCE TO POWDER/ PULP
pulvirise, pulverize
pulvorise, pulverize
puly, pulley
pulygamus, polygamy(mous)
pulygamy, polygamy

pulyginy, polygyny
pulzate, pulsate
pumal, pummel
pumas, pumice
pumb, pump
pumbt, pump(ed)
pumcan, pumpkin
pumel, pummel
pumes, pumice
pumice, eous, VOLCANIC STONE USED FOR SANDING
pumil, pummel
pumis, pumice
pumkan, pumpkin
pumle, pummel
pummel, *, led, ling, POMMEL/ HIT REPEATEDLY CAUSING DAMAGE
pumol, pummel
pumos, pumice
pump, *, ped, ping, per, FORCE LIQUID/ OBJECT TO MOVE INTO A DESIGNATED DIRECTION
pumpken, pumpkin
pumpkin, *, A LARGE SQUASH
pumpt, pump(ed)
pumul, pummel
pumus, pumice
pun, *, nned, nning, TO USE WORDS SIMILAR BUT DIFFERENT FOR HUMOROUS INTENT
punatef, punitive
punative, punitive
punch, hes, hed, hing, her, STRIKE AGAINST SOMETHING WITH FORCE, TO PIERCE, DRINK MIXTURE
puncherd, puncture(d)
puncht, punch(ed)
punchuate, punctuate
puncsher, puncture
punchshuate, punctuate
punchuel, punctual
punctewashen, punctuate(tion)
punctual, lity, lly, ARRIVE ON TIME
punctuashen, punctuate(tion)
punctuate, *, ed, ting, tion, tor, USE MARKS/ SYMBOLS IN TEXT FOR CLARIFICATION

puncture, *, ed, ring, rable, PIERCE/ PERFORATE/ PRICK THROUGH SOMETHING
pund, punt / pun(nned)
punech, punish
puneched, punish(ed)
punechmint, punish(ment)
punensula, peninsula
punesh, punish
puneshmint, punish(ment)
punesht, punish(ed)
punetive, punitive
pungensy, pungent(ncy)

pungent, tly, ncy, STRONG/ SHARP SMELL OR TASTE
punginsy, pungent(ncy)
pungunt, pungent
punich, punish
punichment, punish(ment)
puninsula, peninsula

punish, hes, hed, hing, her, hable, hment, APPLY MEASURES TO CORRECT INTOLERABLE ACT
punishmint, punish(ment)
punisht, punish(ed)

punitive, ely, eness, INFLICT/ IMPOSE PUNISHMENT
punjensy, pungent(ncy)
punjinsy, pungent(ncy)
punjunt, pungent

punk, *, ker, STICK USED FOR STARTING FIREWORKS, DEROGATORY WORD FOR BAD BEHAVIOR
punkchashen, punctuate(tion)
punkcher, puncture
punkchewashen, punctuate(tion)
punkchewate, punctuate
punkchir, puncture
punkchuate, punctuate
punkchuation, punctuate(-ion)
punkchur, puncture
punkir, punk(er)
punksher, puncture
punkshewal, punctual
punkshewashen, punctuate(tion)
punkshewate, punctuate
punkshewul, punctual
punkshir, puncture

punkshooate, punctuate
punkshoooation, punctuate(tion)
punkshooel, punctual
punkshor, puncture
punkshual, punctual
punkshuashen, punctuate(tion)
punkshuate, punctuate
punkshuation, punctuate(tion)
punkshuol, punctual
punkshur, puncture
punktual, punctual
punktuate, punctuate
punotif, punitive
punsh, punch
punshur, puncture / punch(er)

punt, *, ted, ting, ter, DROP/ KICK A BALL, PROPEL, OF A POINTED NATURE, GAMBLE (or see pun(ed))
punched, punish(ed)
punchment, punish(ment)
punudeve, punitive
punudive, punitive
punushed, punish(ed)
punushment, punish(ment)
punutive, punitive

puny, nier, niest, INSIGNIFICANT, SMALL, WEAK IN SIZE/ STRENGTH

pup, *, ppy, ppies, A NEWBORN DOG/ SEAL (or see pop)
pupal, pupil
pupater, puppet(eer)
pupatree, puppet(ry)
pupe, pup(ppy)
pupel, pupil
pupet, puppet
pupeteer, puppet(eer)
pupetry, puppet(ry)

pupil, *, llary, PART OF THE EYE, STUDENT UNDER TUTELAGE OF INSTRUCTOR/ GUARDIAN "prefixes: inter"
pupit, puppet
pupiteer, puppet(eer)
pupitry, puppet(ry)
pupiya, papaya
puplasher, publish(er)

puplasist, publicist
puplasize, publicity(ize)
puple, pupil
puplek, public
puplekashin, publication
puplesh, publish
puplesist, publicist
puplik, public
puplikashen, publication
puplish, publish
puplisher, publish(er)
puplisist, publicist
puplisize, publicity(ize)
puplosher, publish(er)
puplosist, publicist
puplukashin, publication
puplusher, publish(er)
puplusize, publicity(ize)
pupol, pupil
puporshenal, proportion(al)
puportion, proportion
puppateer, puppet(eer)

puppet, *, try, teer, A DOLL/ FIGURE/ MARIONETTE RESEMBLING ANIMAL/ HUMAN
puppiteer, puppet(eer)
pupput, puppet
puppuiteer, puppet(eer)
pupul, pupil
puput, puppet
puputer, puppet(eer)
puputry, puppet(ry)
pupy, pup(ppy)
pupyu, papaya
pur, purr / per / pure / pour / poor
purabula, parabola
purade, parade
purafecashen, purify(fication)
purafication, purify(fication)
puragative, prerogative
puralasis, paralysis
puralises, paralysis
puramedur, parameter / perimeter
puramiter, parameter / perimeter

purapula, parable
purate, parade
purbendikuler, perpendicular
perceptible, perceptible
purch, perch / purge
purchase, *, ed, sing, er, sable, ACQUIRE/ SECURE OWNERSHIP OF
purchis, purchase / perch(es)
purcivere, persevere
purdly, pert(ly)
pure, ely, er, est, eness, NOT MIXED, FREE OF IMPURITIES/ CONTAMINANTS
puree', FOOD BOILED INTO A PULP AND RUN THROUGH A STRAINER/ SIEVE
purefacation, purify(fication)
pureferul, peripheral
pureficashen, purify(fication)
purefide, purify(fied)
purendal, parent(al)
pureneul, perennial
purental, parent(al)
purenthases, parenthesis
purfect, perfect
purfekshen, perfect(ion)
purfektion, perfect(ion)
purfert, pervert
purferted, pervert(ed)
purfikt, perfect
purform, perform
purformence, perform(ance)
purfume, perfume
purgatory, ries, tive, THEORETICAL PLACE WHERE A PERSON MAY SPEND TIME AFTER DEATH
purge, *, ed, ging, ger, PURIFY/ CLEANSE/ GET RID OF/ FREE/ REMOVE
purger, perjure
purgery, perjure(ry)
purgetory, purgatory
purgury, perjure(ry)
purgutory, purgatory
purhaps, perhaps
purifecation, purify(fication)
puriferul, peripheral

purificashen, purify(fication)
purifide, purify(fied)
purify, fies, fied, ying, ficator, fication, ACT OF CLEANSING/ RIDDING/ FREEING/ REMOVING
purineal, perennial
purintal, parent(al)
purinthusees, parenthesis
purje, purge
purjury, perjure(ry)
purkushen, percussion
purl, pearl
purly, pure(ly)
purmanence, permanence
purmanent, permanent
purmanins, permanence
purmeate, permeate
purmenint, permanent
purmeuble, permeable
purmishen, permission
purmisive, permissive
purmit, permit
purmited, permit(ted)
purmition, permission
purmnent, permanent
purogative, prerogative
purokside, peroxide
purole, parole
purona, piranha
purooze, peruse
purosedy, porosity
purosity, porosity
puroxside, peroxide
purpel, purple
purpendicular, perpendicular
purpes, purpose
purpeshual, perpetual
purpesly, purpose(ly)
purpetrate, perpetrate
purpetshual, perpetual
purpetshuate, perpetual(ate)
purpetual, perpetual
purpetuate, perpetual(ate)
purpetuity, perpetuity

purpil, purple
purpindicular, perpendicular
purpis, purpose
purpisly, purpose(ly)
purpitrate, perpetrate
purple, lish, A COLOR
purpleksity, perplex(ity)
purplex, perplex
purplexity, perplex(ity)
purporshenal, proportion(al)
purportional, proportion(al)
purpose, *, ed, sing, eful, efully, efulness, eless, ely, sive, sively, siveness, elessness, REASON FOR/ MISSION/ GOAL, DESIGN FOR "prefixes: multi"
purposly, purpose(ly)
purpul, purple
purpus, purpose
purpusly, purpose(ly)
purr, *, rred, rring, GUTTURAL SOUND COMING FROM A CATS THROAT WHEN PLEASED
pursacute, persecute
pursavere, persevere
pursbektif, perspective
pursbiration, perspiration
pursbire, perspire
purscription, prescript(ion)
purse, *, ed, sing, HAND BAG, PRIZE MONEY, SQUEEZE TIGHTLY TOGETHER
pursebduble, perceptible
pursebtef, percept(ive)
pursecute, persecute
pursen, person
pursenality, personality
pursenaly, personal(lly)
pursenel, personnel
pursent, percent
pursentige, percent(age)
pursentil, percent(ile)
pursenuble, person(able)
pursenul, personal
pursenulize, personal(ize)
pursepdable, perceptible
pursepshen, percept(ion)

purseptef, percept(ive)
purseption, percept(ion)
purseptive, percept(ive)
purseshen, precision
pursest, persist
purseve, perceive
purseverense, persevere(rance)
purshis, purchase / perch(es)
pursikute, persecute
pursin, person
pursinaledy, personality
pursinel, personnel
pursint, percent
pursinuble, person(able)
pursinulize, personal(ize)
pursinuly, personal(lly)
purspatation, precipitate(tion)
pursishen, precision
pursist, persist
pursistence, persist(ence)
purskripshen, prescript(ion)
purson, person
pursona, person(a)
pursonality, personality
pursonefication, person(ification)
pursonifekashen, person(ification)
pursonify, personify
pursoo, pursue
pursparashen, perspiration
purspective, perspective
pursperashen, perspiration
purspiration, perspiration
purspire, perspire
pursuade, persuade
pursuasion, persuade(asion)
pursuasive, persuade(asive)
pursude, pursue(d)
pursue, *, ed, uing, er, uant, uit, SEEKING/ STRIVING TO OVERCOME/ OVERTAKE
pursute, pursue(uit)
pursuvere, persevere
purswade, persuade
purswashen, persuade(asion)

purswasif, persuade(asive)
purt, pert
purtain, pertain
purtane, pertain
purterb, perturb
purterbt, perturb(ed)
purteshen, partition
purtishen, partition
purtrayal, portray(al)
purtrayed, portray(ed)
puruficashun, purify(fication)
purufied, purify(fied)
puruse, peruse
purvade, pervade
purvashen, pervade(asion)/ provision
purvasif, pervade(asion)
purversev, pervert(rsive)
purvert, pervert
purvirsev, pervert(rsive)
purvurshen, pervert(rsion)
pury, puree'
purzakute, persecute
pus, FLUID/ INFLAMMATION PRESENT AS THE RESULT OF AN INFECTION (or see puss)
pusdasheo, pistachio
pusdromy, pastrami
pusefic, pacific
pusel, puzzle
puseld, puzzle(d)
puses, possess
push, hes, hed, hing, hier, hiest, her, hy, hily, hiness, FORCE/ EXERT MOVEMENT
pushenis, push(iness)
pushir, push(er)
pusie, puss
pusific, pacific
pusil, puzzle
pusiled, puzzle(d)
pusishen, position
puskrepshen, prescript(ion)
pusl, puzzle
puss, ssy, ssies, A CAT, THE FACE WHERE THE MOUTH IS, SLANDER FOR A WHIMP (or see pus)

pustasheo, pistachio
pustrome, pastrami
pusul, puzzle
pusy, puss
put, *, tted, tting, tter, TO PLACE (or see putt)
putado, potato
putal, puddle / poodle
putato, potato
pute, putty / putt
putees, putty(tties)
putel, puddle / poodle
putena, patina
putenchul, potential
puteng, pudding / putt(ing) / put(tting)
putenshul, potential
potential, potential
puter, pewter / putt(er)
puterbd, perturb(ed)
puternol, paternal
putestrein, pedestrian
puthetic, pathetic
putil, puddle / poodle
putina, patina
putinchul, potential
puting, pudding / putt(ing) / put(tting)
putintial, potential
putir, pewter / putt(er)
putishen, petition / beautician
putition, petition
putle, puddle / poodle
putol, puddle / poodle
putoto, potato
putrid, dity, dness, dly, ROTTEN, CORRUPT, VILE
putrol, patrol
putrood, protrude
putrude, protrude
putt, *, tting, tter, A GOLF STROKE (or see put)
puttle, puddle / poodle
putty, tties, ttied, ttying, TACKY/ PASTY SUBSTANCE
putul, puddle / poodle
puty, putty
puveleon, pavilion
puvileon, pavilion

puvirted,pervert(ed)
puwding,pudding / putt(ing) / put(tting)
puzel,puzzle
puzeld,puzzle(d)
puzes,possess
puzil,puzzle
puzl,puzzle
puzled,puzzle(d)
puzzle,*,ed,ling,er,ement,PROBLEM WITH ONLY ONE SOLUTION, MANY PARTS MAKE UP THE BIG PICTURE
pyeni,peony
pygme,pygmy
pygmy,mies,VERY SMALL/ DWARFED IN COMPARISON TO OTHERS IN ITS SPECIES
pyis,pious
pyke,pike
pyle,pile
pype,pipe
pyramid,*,FOUR-SIDED/ TRIANGULAR STRUCTURE
pyrana,piranha
pyranna,piranha
pyre,*,MOUND OF COMBUSTIBLE MATERIAL WHERE AN EXPIRED BODY IS PLACED FOR CEREMONIAL CREMATION (or see pier/ peer/ pierce)
pyrite,*,tic,YELLOW COLORED METAL
pyro,*,SLANG FOR SOMEONE WHO PLAYS WITH FIRE, PREFIX INDICATING "FIRE/ HEAT" MOST OFTEN MODIFIES THE WORD
pyrona,piranha
python,*,A VENOMOUS SNAKE
q,cue
qiub,cube
qiubic,cubic
qiubicol,cubicle
qiucomber,cucumber
qiumulativ,cumulative
qiur,cure
qiurabol,curable
qiuredor,curator
qiurios,curious
qiuriositi,curiosity
qiut,cute
qiuticol,cuticle

qkumber,cucumber
qkwant,quaint
qords,quartz / quart(s)
qork,quark / cork
qorts,quartz / quart(s)
qu,cue
quack,*,ked,king,SOUND A DUCK MAKES, SLANG FOR A 'NO GOOD DOCTOR' (or see quake)
quad,*,SHORT FOR QUADRANT, FOUR, QUADRANGLE, QUADRUPLET
quadrant,*,tal,ONE QUARTER OF A CIRCLE
quadrint,quadrant
quael,quail
quaent,quaint
quagmire,*,BOG,SOFT EARTH HEAVY WITH MOISTURE
quail,*,A GAME BIRD
quaint,tly,tness,PLEASING/ COMFORTABLE/ PICTURESQUE
quak,quack
quake,*,ed,king,A TREMBLING/ SHAKING (or see quack)
quakmire,quagmire
qual,quail
qualedy,quality
qualefy,qualify
qualefyable,qualify(fiable)
qualetatif,quality(tative)
qualetative,quality(tative)
qualety,quality
qualidy,quality
qualify,fies,fied,fying,fiedly,fier,fiable,fying,fication,IS ELIGIBLE/ CAPABLE/ SKILLFUL ENOUGH "prefixes: dis/ over/ un"
qualifyable,qualify(fiable)
qualifyer,qualify(fier)
qualitatif,quality(tative)
quality,ties,tative,tatively,A MEASURE/ GUAGE OF RESULTS IN THE OUTCOME OF AN EFFORT, A SCALE WHICH RATES THE BEST/ WORST
qualm,*,mish,mishly,mishness,FEELING OF DOUBT/ TWINGE/ UNEASINESS
qualufecashen,qualify(fication)
qualufi,qualify
quam,qualm

quandary,ries,DIFFICULTY/ HESITANCY/ PERPLEXING
quandery,quandary
quandre,quandary
quanetative,quantitative
quanotative,quantitative
quant,quaint
quanta,tum,SMALLEST AMOUNT OF ENERGY CAPABLE OF EXISTING ON ITS OWN, QUALITY/ EXTENT
quantefy,quantify
quantefyer,quantify(fier)
quantem,quanta(tum)
quantery,quandary
quantetative,quantitative
quantety,quantity
quantify,fies,fied,fying,fiable,fication,fier,MEASURE/ DETERMINE THE AMOUNT OF
quantim,quanta(tum)
quantitative,ely,MEASURE BY QUALITY RATHER THAN QUANTITY
quantity,ties,MEASURE OF THE AMOUNT/ FREQUENCY OF OCCURRENCE
quantom,quanta(tum)
quantry,quandary
quarantine,*,ed,ning,nable,SECTION OFF/ ISOLATE FROM EVERYTHING ELSE
quarc,quark
quarder,quarter
quarderly,quarter(ly)
quardur,quarter
quardurly,quarter(ly)
quare,quarry / query
quarel,quarrel
quarentene,quarantine
quari,query
quaril,quarrel
quarinteen,quarantine
quark,*,BASIC/ ELEMENTARY PARTICLE (or see cork)
quarol,quarrel
quarontene,quarantine
quarrel,*,led,ling,lsome,lsomely,lsomeness,BICKER, ARGUE, BE AT ODDS WITH, ENHARMONIC, SQUARE SHAPED HEAD, A TOOL

quarry, rries, rried, ying, rrier, DIG A PIT INTO THE EARTH FOR STONE/ DIRT, PURSUED GAME
quart, *, U.S. MEASUREMENT OF LIQUID (or see quartz)
quarter, *, red, ring, rage, rly, ries, ONE-FOURTH OF THE WHOLE, U.S. COIN
quartirly,quarter(ly)
quartur,quarter
quarturly,quarter(ly)
quartz, zite, zose, zous, MINERAL/ ROCK (or see quart(s))
quarunteen,quarantine
quasadilla,quesadilla
quasar, *, ASTRONOMICAL OBJECT WITH HIGH ENERGY OUTPUT
quasi, SORT OF, SIMILAR, NOT CERTAIN
quawry,quarry
quayer,choir
quayet,quiet
quayt,quite
quazar,quasar
qucumber,cucumber
quean,queen
quechup,ketchup
queck,quick
queckest,quick(est)
queen, *, ned, nliness, nly, A FEMALE OF ROYALTY
queer, *, rly, rness, STRANGE/ ODD, HOMOSEXUAL
quefer,quiver
queias,chaos
queibol,cable
queik,quick
quein,cane
queint,quaint
queios,chaos
quek,quick
queke,quick(ie)
quekest,quick(est)
quekly,quick(ly)
quel,quill / quail / kale / owl
quelp,kelp
quelt,quilt
quemecol,chemical
quemical,chemical
quemistri,chemistry

quemulutive,cumulative
quench, hes, hed, hing, hable, her, hless, TO SATISFY, PUT AWAY, EXTINGUISH
quenel,kennel
quentuplet,quintuplet
querable,curable
querat,karat / carat / caret / carrot
querati,karate
queret,karat / carat / caret / carrot
querfiu,curfew
queri,query
queriouqui,karaoke
querk,quirk
querky,quirky
quernol,kernel
querosin,kerosene
query, ries, ried, rying, rist, ASK OF, QUESTION, INQUIRE
quesadilla, *, FLOUR TORTILLAS WITH FILLING
quesdun,question
quest, *, ted, ting, ter, ON A JOURNEY/ ADVENTURE SEEKING SOMETHING "prefixes: in"
questen,question
question, *, ned, ning, nable, nably, nability, nary, naries, nnaire, ASK/ INQUIRE, HAVE DOUBT, NEED INFORMATION ON MATTER/ SUBJECT "prefixes: un"
questshunar,question(nnaire)
questun,question
quet,quit / quite
queter,quit(tter) / quiet(er)
quetol,kettle
quevor,quiver
quevur,quiver
queyas,chaos
queyzar,quasar
quez,quiz
quezene,cuisine
quezt,quest
qui,key
quick, kly, ker, kest, kness, ken, kie, kener, FAST, WITHOUT DELAY, BRIEF, SKIN UNDER NAILS
quiet, ter, test, tly, tness, tism, tude, SILENT, CALM, STILL, TRANQUIL (or see quit/ quite) "prefixes: dis/ un"
quifur,quiver

quik,quick
quikest,quick(est)
quikly,quick(ly)
quiky,quick(ie)
quil,quill / kill / keel
quill, *, WING/ TAIL FEATHER OF LARGE BIRD
quilt, *, ted, ting, ter, HANDMADE/ STITCHED BLANKET, THICKLY BLANKETED (or see kilt)
quimotharopi,chemotherapy
quimoutherapi,chemotherapy
quin,keen / kin / queen
quinch,quench
quinsh,quench
quintuplet, *, FIVE OF ANYTHING
quirk, *, ky, kily, kiness, GIVEN TO ERRATIC MOVEMENT, JERKING, SUDDEN CHANGES
quiry,query
quisadilla,quesadilla
quisen,cuisine
quisine,cuisine
quit, *, tted, tting, tter, STOP (or see quite)
quite, COMPLETELY CERTAIN/ CLEAR (or see quit/ quiet)
quiut,quiet
quiutly,quiet(ly)
quiver, *, red, ring, CASE TO CARRY ARROWS, TREMBLE/ SHAKE/ TREMOR
quivor,quiver
quiz, zzes, zzed, zzing, zzical, zzically, zzicality, zzer, TO TEST/ WONDER, BE CONFUSED
qukumber,cucumber
qumulotive,cumulative
quochent,quotient
quochiunt,quotient
quoda,quota
quode,quote
quodrant,quadrant
quodrunt,quadrant
quodu,quota
quoledy,quality
quolm,qualm
quondery,quandary
quondry,quandary
quontefy,quantify

quotefyer,quantify(fier)	**quote,***,ted,ting,tation,table,tability,ta,tient,IDENTIFY/ CITE/ REPEAT EXACTLY WHAT WAS HEARD, STATE FACTS, USE MARKS AROUND WORDS SPOKEN "prefixes: un/ under"
quontem,quanta(tum)	
quontery,quandary	
quonety,quantity	
quontify,quantify	
quontim,quanta(tum)	**quotient,***, A MATHEMATICAL RESULT
quontity,quantity	quowry,quarry
quontre,quandary	qupon,coupon
quontum,quanta(tum)	qurader, curator
quord,quart	qureus,curious
quorderly,quarter(ly)	qutikle,cuticle
quordir,quarter	qwack,quack
quordorly,quarter(ly)	qwad,quad
quords,quartz / quart(s)	qwadrent,quadrant
quordurly,quarter(ly)	qwagmire,quagmire
quodz,quartz / quart(s)	qwaint,quaint
quore,quarry	qwak,quack / quake
quorel,quarrel	qwakmire,quagmire
quorem,quorum	qwale,quail
quorentene,quarantine	qwaledy,quality
quoril,quarrel	qwalefieur,qualify(fier)
quorim,quorum	qwalefiuble,qualify(fiable)
quorintene,quarantine	qwaletatif,quality(tative)
quork,quark	qwalety,quality
quorol,quarrel	qwalidy,quality
quorom,quorum	qwalifecation,qualify(fication)
quort,quart	qwalifikashen,qualify(fication)
quorter,quarter	qwalitative,quality(tative)
quorterly,quarter(ly)	qwalitee,quality
quortir,quarter	qwalm,qualm
quortirly,quarter(ly)	qwant,quaint
quorts,quartz / quart(s)	qwantefy,quantify
quorturly,quarter(ly)	qwantefyer,quantify(fier)
quortz,quartz / quart(s)	qwantem,quanta(tum)
quorum, THE MAJORITY OF A SELECTED GROUP	qwantety,quantity
quoruntene,quarantine	qwantify,quantify
quory,quarry	qwantifyer,quantify(fier)
quoshent,quotient	qwantim,quanta(tum)
quota,*, A PERMITTED NUMBER/ QUANTITY	qwantity,quantity
quotashen,quote(tation)	qwantum,quanta(tum)
	qwarder,quarter
	qwards,quartz / quart(s)
	qwardur,quarter
	qwarel,quarrel

qwarentene,quarantine	
qwaril,quarrel	
qwarintene,quarantine	
qwark,quark	
qwarol,quarrel	
qwarter,quarter	
qwarts,quartz / quart(s)	
qwartur,quarter	
qwarul,quarrel	
qwary,query	
qwasar,quasar	
qwasy,quasi	
qwazar,quasar	
qwazy,quasi	
qwear,queer	
qween,queen	
qweer,queer	
qwek,quick	
qwekest,quick(est)	
qwekly,quick(ly)	
qweky,quick(ie)	
qwel,quill	
qwelt,quilt	
qwench,quench	
qwensh,quench	
qwentuplet,quintuplet	
qwerk,quirk	
qwerky,quirk	
qwery,query	
qwes,quiz	
qwesden,question	
qwesekal,quiz(zzical)	
qweshten,question	
qwest,quest	
qwestchenair,question(nnaire)	
qwestshun,question	
qwestunair,question(nnaire)	
qwet,quit / quite	
qweter,quit(tter) / quiet(er)	
qwevir,quiver	
qwevur,quiver	
qwez,quiz	
qwezekal,quiz(zzical)	

qwik,quick	qwontify,quantify	rabeleon,rebel(llion)
qwikest,quick(est)	qwontifyer,quantifyer,quantify(fier)	rabeleus,rebel(llious)
qwikly,quick(ly)	qwontim,quanta(tum)	rabelius,rebel(llious)
qwiky,quick(ie)	qwontity,quantity	rabet,rabbit/ rabid/ rapid
qwil,quill	qworam,quorum	rabi,rabbi
qwilt,quilt	qworder,quarter	**rabid**,dity,dly,dness,ies,MADNESS/ FURIOUSNESS/ UNREASONABLE, DISEASE (or see rapid)
qwinch,quench	qwords,quartz / quart(s)	
qwinsh,quench	qwordur,quarter	rabit,rabbit / rabid / rapid
qwintuplet, quintuplet	qworel,quarrel	rablie,reply
qwirk,quirk	qworem,quorum	rabodek,robot(ic)
qwirky,quirk	qworentene,quarantine	rabot,rabbit / rabid / rapid
qwiry,query	qworil,quarrel	rabotik,robot(ic)
qwis,quiz	qworim,quorum	rabsady,rhapsody
qwit, quit / quite	qworintene,quarantine	rabsudy,rhapsody
qwiter,quit(tter) / quiet(er)	qwork,quark	rabt,rape(d) / wrap(pped) / rap(pped)
qwiver,quiver	qworol,quarrel	rabud,rabbit / rabid / rapid
qwiz,quiz	qworom,quorum	rabut,rabbit / rabid / rapid / rebut
qwizekal,quiz(zzical)	qworter,quarter	rabutal,rebut(ttal)
qwochent,quotient	qworts,quartz / quart(s)	rac,rack / rake / wrack / rock
qwod,quad	qwortur,quarter	racat,racket / racquet
qwoda,quota	qworul,quarrel	racateer,racketeer
qwodashen,quote(tation)	qworum,quorum	**raccoon**,*,PLANTIGRADE CARNIVOROUS MAMMAL
qwodation,quote(tation)	qwoshent,quotient	raccune,raccoon
qwode,quote	qwosy,quasi	**race**,*,ed,cing,er,cy,COMPETITION WITH MORE THAN ONE,GAME WITH A BEGINNING/ END,CATEGORY FOR HUMAN TYPES (or see raise) "prefixes: de"
qwodrent,quadrant	qwota,quota	
qwodrunt,quadrant	qwotashen,quote(tation)	
qwodu,quota	qwotation,quote(tation)	racede,recede
qwoduble,quote(table)	qwote,quote	raceptecle,receptacle
qwoledy,quality	qwotuble,quote(table)	racepter,receptor
qwolefikashen,qualify(fication)	qwozy,quasi	racepticle,receptacle
qwolefiuble,qualify(fiable)	qwurentene,quarantine	raception,reception
qwolefiur,qualify(fier)	qwurintene,quarantine	raceptucle,receptacle
qwoletatif,quality(tative)	qwurk,quirk	racet,racket / racquet
qwolety,quality	qwurky,quirk	raceteer,racketeer
qwolifekation,qualify(fication)	r,are	rach,rash
qwolm,qualm	ra,ray / raw	rachal,racial
qwomtum,quanta(tum)	rabay,rabbi	rachen,ration
qwondry,quandary	**rabbi**,*,JEWISH RELIGIOUS TITLE	racheo,ratio
qwontefy,quantify	**rabbit**,*,LONG-EARED RODENT	rachet,ratchet
qwontefyer,quantifyer,quantify(fier)	rabcity,rhapsody	rachil,racial
qwontem,quanta(tum)	rabed,rabbit / rabid / rapid	rachin,ration
qwontery,quandary	rabees,rabid(ies)	rachio,ratio
qwontety,quantity	rabel,rebel	rachit,ratchet

rachon,ration
rachul,racial
rachun,ration
rachunil,rational
rachut,ratchet
racial,lly,lism,list,listic,ism,ist,CHARACTERISTICS/ DIFFERENCES IN RACES/ PEOPLE "prefixes: bi/ inter"
racipeint,recipient
raciprocation,reciprocate(tion)
racism,*,HUMAN FEAR/ IGNORANCE TOWARDS PEOPLE OF A DIFFERENT COLOR/ RACE
racist,*,HUMAN FEAR/ IGNORANCE TOWARDS PEOPLE OF A DIFFERENT COLOR/ RACE
racit,racket / racquet / recite
raciteer,racketeer
rack,*,ked,king,ker,ket,APPARATUS USED FOR HANGING/ STRETCHING THINGS (or see rake/ wrack/ rock)
racket,*,teer,NOISY SOUND, USED IN SPORTS TO HIT A BALL (or see racquet)
racketeer,*,ring,SLANG FOR SOMEONE ENGAGED IN ILLEGAL ACTIVITY
rackit,racket / racquet
rackiteer,racketeer
rackoteer,racketeer
rackut,racket / racquet
rackuteer,racketeer
raconasinse,reconnaissance
raconstitushen,reconstitute(tion)
raconstitute,reconstitute
racoon,raccoon
racquet,*,STRINGED TOOL FOR SPORT (or see racket)
racrute,recruit
racruter,recruit(er)
racumbent,recumbent
racut,racket / racquet
racuteer,racketeer
rad,raid / rate
radar,*,A RADIO WAVE FREQUENCY
raddle,rattle
rade,raid
radeal,radial
radeans,radiance

radeant,radiant
radeashen,radiate(tion)
radeate,radiate
radeater,radiate(tor)
radeation,radiate(tion)
radecal,radical
radech,radish
radechulus,ridiculous
radeemible,redeem(able)
radefy,ratify
radeil,radial
radeim,radium
radeinse,radiance
radeint,radiant
radeints,radiance
radekly,radical(lly)
radekul,radical
radel,rattle
rademe,redeem
rademption,redemption
rademshin,redemption
rademtif,redemption(ive)
rademtion,redemption
rademtive,redemption(ive)
rademuble,redeem(able)
radeo,radio
radeol,radial
radeom,radium
radeos,radius / radio(es)
radequelus,ridiculous
radesh,radish
radeul,radial
radeum,radium
radeunse,radiance
radeunt,radiant
radeus,radius
radial,*,lly,CENTER WITH SPOKES/ RAYS GOING OUT FROM THE CENTER, TYPE OF TIRE "prefixes: bi/ inter"
radiance,cy,cies,nt,ntly,BRIGHT/ SHINING LIKE A STAR, GLOWING BRIGHT
radians,radiance

radiant,ntly,nce,TYPE OF HEAT/ WAVE/ LIGHT, TO GLOW "prefixes: ir"
radiashen,radiate(tion)
radiate,*,ed,ting,tion,tional,tive,tor,EMIT/ GIVE FORTH/ EXUDE "prefixes: ir/ re"
radiater,radiate(tor)
radical,*,lly,lness,lism,FAR-SWEEPING CHANGE/ ACT/ ATTITUDE FROM THE EXISTING IDEALISM
radicaly,radical(lly)
radich,radish
radicle,radical
radicly,radical(lly)
radiel,radial
radiem,radium
radient,radiant
radify,ratify
radikle,radical
radikly,radical(lly)
radikul,radical
radil,rattle
radio,*,oed,oing,WIRELESS AUDIO TRANSMITTING/ RECEIVING DEVICE, PREFIX INDICATING "RADIO/ RADIATION" MOST OFTEN MODIFIES THE WORD, FROM ANCIENT WORD "RADIUS" (RAY)
radiol,radial
radiquelus,ridiculous
radish,hes,A VEGETABLE
radiul,radial
radium,A METALLIC ELEMENT WHICH IS RADIOACTIVE
radiunse,radiance
radius,ii,ses,AREA WITHIN A CIRCLE,RAY EXTENDING FROM CENTER OF CIRCLE, BONE DESCRIPTIONS
radol,rattle
radon,A CHEMICAL ELEMENT
rador,radar
raduction,reduce(ction)
radufy,ratify
radukle,radical
radukly,radical(lly)
radukshen,reduce(ction)
radul,rattle
radundense,redundant(ncy)
radundent,redundant

radundunse,redundant(ncy)
radusable,reduce(cible)
raduse,reduce
radush,radish
raelm,realm
raelrod,railroad
raen,rain / reign / rein
raenbo,rainbow
raenj,range
raer,rare
raesesem,racism
raf,rave
rafal,raffle / ravel
rafalee,reveille
rafan,raven
rafash,ravish
rafd,raft / waft
rafded,raft(ed)
rafdur,raft(er)
rafe,rave
rafel,raffle / ravel / reveal
rafelashen,revelation
rafen,raven / ravine
rafenge,revenge
rafenje,revenge
rafenus,raven(ous)
rafeole,ravioli
rafer,revere / refer
rafers,reverse / refer(s)
rafesh,ravish
rafeusil,refuse(sal)
rafewsel,refuse(sal)
raffle,*,ed,ling,A GAME
rafiew,review / revue
rafif,revive
rafiful,revival
rafil,raffle / ravel
rafilee,reveille
rafin,raven / refine
rafinable,refine(nable)
rafinery,refine(ry)
rafinje,revenge
rafinment,refine(ment)

rafinuble,refine(nable)
rafinury,refine(ry)
rafinus,raven(ous)
rafioly,ravioli
rafirse,reverse
rafish,ravish
raflashen,revelation
rafle,raffle / ravel
raflect,reflect
raflection,reflect(ion)
raflective,reflect(ive)
raflekshen,reflect(ion)
raflektor,reflect(or)
rafol,raffle
rafolee,reveille
raformutory,reform(atory)
rafractory,refract(ory)
rafrain,refrain
rafraktory,refract(ory)
rafrane,refrain
rafregirant,refrigerate(ant)
rafregirator,refrigerate(tor)
rafresh,refresh
rafreshment,refresh(ment)
rafrigerant,refrigerate(ant)
rafrigerator,refrigerate(tor)
raft,*,ted,ting,ter,A SMALL BOAT MADE WITH A MATERIAL FILLED WITH AIR (or see rave(d))
raftur,raft(er) / waft(er)
rafue,review / revue
raful,raffle / ravel
rafulashen,revelation
rafulation,revelation
rafulee,reveille
rafun,raven
rafunus,raven(ous)
rafurbish,refurbish
rafurse,reverse
rafusel,refuse(sal)
rafute,refute
rag,*,gged,ggedness,ggedly,ggedy,TATTERED/ TORN/ WORN OUT MATERIAL/ CLOTH (or see rack/ rage)
ragalia,regal(ia)

ragardless,regard(less)
ragd,rage(d) / rag(gged)
rage,*,ed,ging,gingly,INTENSE/ VIOLENT ANGER, OF INTENSE/ GREAT FORCE "prefixes: en"
raged,rag(gged) / racket
ragedy,rag(ggedy)
ragektion,reject(ion)
rager,roger
raget,rag(gged) / racket
ragid,rag(gged) / racket
ragidy,rag(ggedy)
ragir,roger
ragit,rag(gged) / racket
ragity,rag(ggedy)
ragret,regret
ragreted,regret(tted)
ragretful,regret(ful)
ragretfuly,regret(fully)
ragt,rage(d) / rake(d) / rack(ed) / wrack(ed)
ragud,rag(gged) / racket
ragudy,rag(ggedy)
ragut,rag(gged) / racket
rai,wry
raid,*,ded,ding,der,A SUDDEN ENTRY/ ATTACK/ SALE (or see rate/ ride)
raifol,rifle
rail,*,led,ling,ler,METAL/ WOOD BARS/ POSTS/ TO PUNISH/ SCOLD,A BIRD (or see rale) "prefixes: de"
railroad,*,ded,ding,der,ROAD MADE OF RAILS, BRING A FALSE CHARGE AGAINST SOMEONE,OF LOCOMOTIVES
raim,rhyme
rain,*,ned,ning,ny,WATER RELEASED FROM CLOUDS (or see reign/ rein)
rainbow,*,AN ARC/ BOW OF COLORS NORMALLY CAUSED BY RAIN
raind,rind
rainder,reindeer
raing,range
raino,rhino
rainoceros,rhinoceros
rainstoun,rhinestone
raiol,rifle

raip,ripe
rair,rare
rairly,rare(ly)
rais,rise / raise / ray(s)
raise,es,ed,sing,er,TO LIFT/ BRING/ TAKE UP (or see ray(s)/ razor) "prefixes: un/ up"
raisin,*,A DRIED PLUM
raisom,rhizome
rait,rate / right / rite / write / wright
raith,writhe
raive,rave
raivol,rival
raizoum,rhizome
raj,rage
rajd,rage(d)
rajekshen,reject(ion)
rajekt,reject
rajektion,reject(ion)
rajer,roger
rajur,roger
rak,rack / rake / wrack / rag
rakat,racket / racquet
rakateer,racketeer
rake,*,ed,king,TOOL/ IMPLEMENT TO MOVE ORGANIC MATERIAL AROUND (or see rack/ wrack)
raket,racket / racquet
raketeer,racketeer
rakit,racket / racquet
rakiteer,racketeer
rakonesinse,reconnaissance
rakonstitute,reconstitute
rakonusents,reconnaissance
rakoon,raccoon
rakord,record
rakorder,record(er)
rakot,racket / racquet
rakoteer,racketeer
rakrute,recruit
rakruter,recruit(er)
rakt,rake(d) / rack(ed) / wrack(ed)
rakumbent,recumbent
rakune,raccoon
rakut,racket / racquet

rakuteer,racketeer
rakwest,request
rakwire,require
rakwirment,require(ment)
rakwit,requite
rakwitable,requite(table)
rakwrute,recruit
ralaks,relax
ralax,relax
rale,ABNORMAL BREATHING SOUND (or see rail/ rally)
raleenkwish,relinquish
ralef,relief
ralejis,religion(ous)
ralek,rollick
ralenkwish,relinquish
ralenqwish,relinquish
ralent,relent
ralentless,relentless
ralerode,railroad
ralese,release
raleve,relieve
ralevens,relevant(nce)
ralevent,relevant
ralevir,relieve(r)
rali,rely / rally
raliable,reliable
raliant,reliance(nt)
ralick,rollick
ralie,rally
raliense,reliance
raligeon,religion
raligis,religion(ous)
ralijus,religion(ous)
ralik,rollick
ralinkwish,relinquish
ralinquish,relinquish
ralintless,relentless
ralish,relish
raliubility,reliable(bility)
raluble,reliable
raliunts,reliance
ralivens,relevant(nce)
ralivent,relevant

rally,llies,llied,ying,llier,BRING/ CALL SUMMON FORTH SPIRIT/ ACTION/ ENTHUSIASM
ralm,realm
ralrod,railroad
ralrot,railroad
ralrus,walrus
raluctant,reluctant
raluctinse,reluctant(nce)
raluktint,reluctant
raluvence,relevant(nce)
raluvent,relevant
ralwrod,railroad
raly,rally / rely
ram,*,mmed,mming,mmer,MALE SHEEP, DEVICE USED TO STRIKE/ FORCE/ CRUSH/ POUND
ramadik,rheumatic
ramafication,ramification
ramafikashen,ramification
ramain,remain / romaine
ramander,remain(der)
ramane,remain / romaine
ramantek,romantic
ramantic,romantic
ramantisize,romantic(ize)
ramarkible,remark(able)
ramatik,rheumatic
rambal,ramble
rambant,rampant
rambint,rampant
ramble,*,ed,ling,er,WANDER/ MEANDER,STYLE OF HOME
rambul,ramble
rambunctious,sly,sness,NOISY/ BOISTEROUS/ LOUD
rambunktious,rambunctious
rambunt,rampant
ramd,ram(mmed)
ramedeul,remedy(dial)
ramediashen,remedy(diation)
ramediation,remedy(diation)
ramefekashen,ramification
ramefekation,ramification
ramember,remember
ramembranxe,remember(ance)

ramesable,remissible
rameshen,remission
ramet,remit
rameteul,remedy(dial)
ramidal,remit(ttal)
ramifekashen,ramification
ramification,*, THE RESULT/ RESPONSE OF AN ACTION
ramifikation,ramification
ramindur,remind(er)
ramint,remind
ramintur,remind(er)
ramishen,remission
ramisible,remissible
ramision,remission
ramit,remit
ramital,remit(ttal)
ramition,remission
ramituble,remit(ttable)
ramofer,remove(r)
ramorse,remorse
ramorsless,remorse(less)
ramote,remote
ramotly,remote(ly)
ramover,remove(r)
ramp,*,ped,ping,part, DEVICE TO CREATE INCLINE/ SLOPE FOR MOVING/ RAISING FROM ONE LEVEL TO ANOTHER
rampage,*, ed,ging, eous, eously, BOISTEROUS/ VIOLENT/ PASSIONATE BEHAVIOR
rampaje,rampage
rampant,tly,ncy,RUN AMUCK/ WILD/ UNPREDICTABLY
rampeich,rampage
rampeill,rampage
rampel,ramble
rampent,rampant
rampint,rampant
rample,ramble
rampt,ramp(ed)
rampunkshes,rambuncticus
rampunt,rampant
ramsum,ransom
ramt,ram(mmed)
ramuf,remove

ramufecation,ramification
ramufekashen,ramification
ramufel,remove(val)
ramufible,remove(vable)
ramufication,ramification
ramufikashen,ramification
ramufil,remove(val)
ramufucation,ramification
ramuneration,remunerate(tion)
ramuvable,remove(vable)
ramuval,remove(val)
ran,PAST TENSE FOR THE WORD "RUN" (or see rain/ rein/ reign) "prefixes: re"
ranbo,rainbow
ranbow,rainbow
ranced,rancid
ranch,hes, hed, hing, her, WHERE HORSES/ CATTLE ARE RAISED/ BOARDED,A TYPE OF DRESSING
ranchi,raunch
ranchur,ranch(er)
rancid,dity,dness,SMELL/ TASTE OF FOOD THAT IS SPOILED/ ROTTEN
rancud,rancid
rand,rant / rain(ed)
randam,random
rander,reindeer
randim,random
random,mly,mness,WITHOUT AN APPARENT/ RECOGNIZABLE ORDER "prefixes: non/ un"
rane,rain / reign / rein
renege,renege
range,*, ed,ging,er, DEFINED/ SPECIFIC AREA WHICH HOLDS DATA/ INFORMATION/ ANIMALS (or see ranch) "prefixes: de"
rangel,wrangle
ranglur,wrangle(r)
rangt,range(d)
rangul,wrangle
rangur,range(r)
ranige,renege
ranik,renege
ranj,range / ranch

rank,*, ked, king, ker, kest, kly, kness, CHRONOLOGICAL/ LINEAR ORDER,A BAD/ OFFENSIVE SMELL/ ODOR
ranone,renown
ranoserus,rhinoceros
ranosirus,rhinoceros
ranouncement,renounce(ment)
ranounse,renounce
ranown,renown
ranownsment,renounce(ment)
ransack,*, ked, king, ker, PLUNDER/ SEARCH THROUGH PEOPLE'S BELONGINGS
ransak,ransack
ransam,ransom
ransed,rancid
ransem,ransom
ransh,ranch
ransher,ranch(er)
ransid,rancid
ransim,ransom
ransit,rancid
ransom,*,mer, FORCE SOMEONE TO PAY FOR THE RETURN OF GOODS/ PEOPLE
ransud,rancid
ransum,ransom
ransut,rancid
rant,*, ted, ting, tingly, ter, TALK/ UTTER LOUD AGITATED OR AGGRESSIVE WORDS
rantsum,ransom
rantum,random
ranumerate,remunerate
ranzak,ransack
ranzum,ransom
raon,rayon
rap,*, pped,pping,pper, TYPE OF MUSIC AND THAT ASSOCIATED WITH IT, TYPE OF SOUND, BLAME/ PUNISHMENT/ FOR AN ILLEGAL ACT NOT RESPONSIBLE FOR (or see wrap/ rape)
rapad,rapid
rapar,repair
rapcher,rapture
rapcherus,rapture(rous)
rapchur,rapture
rapcity,rhapsody

rape, *, ed,ping,pist, VIOLENTLY/ FORCEFULLY/ PHYSICALLY PENETRATE A PERSON AGAINST THEIR WILL (or see rap/ wrap)
rapeal,repeal
rapeat,repeat
raped,rape(d) / rapid / rabid
rapededly,repeat(edly)
rapedly,rapid(ly)
rapedutif,repetitive
rapeel,repeal
rapel,rappel / repeal / repel
rapelein,rebel(llion)
rapelent,repellent
rapeleon,rebel(llion)
rapelinsy,repellent(ncy)
rapelint,repellent
rapenins,repent(ance)
rapent,repent
rapentinse,repent(ance)
raper,rap(pper) / rape(r) / wrap(pper)
rapest,rape(pist)
rapete,repeat
rapetedly,repeat(edly)
rapid, *, dly,dness,dity, QUICK (or see rabid)
rapinens,repent(ance)
rapint,repent
rapintense,repent(ance)
rapir,rap(pper) / rape(r) / wrap(pper)
raplacment,replace(ment)
raplase,replace
raplasmint,replace(ment)
raplenish,replenish
raplenishment,replenish(ment)
raplid,reply(lied)
raplinesh,replenish
rapor,rapport
raporder,report(er)
raport,rapport / report
raporter,report(er)
rapository,repository
rapour,rapport
rapozitory,repository

rappel, *, lled,lling, DESCEND FROM A HEIGHT WITH A ROPE (or see repel)
rapport, HARMONY/ AFFILIATION WITH
rapreshen,repress(ion)
rapresion,repress(ion)
rapress,repress
rapresuve,repress(ive)
raproch,reproach
raprochuble,reproach(able)
rapsety,rhapsody
rapshur,rapture
rapsuty,rhapsody
rapt, rape(d) / wrap(pped) / rap(pped)
raptcher, rapture
raptor, *, BIRD OF PREY (or see rapture)
raptur,raptor / rapture
rapture, *, ed, ring, rous, rously, rousness, EXTREME DELIGHT/ JOY/ PLEASURE (or see raptor) "prefixes: en"
rapublek,republic
rapublekan,republic(an)
rapublikan,republic(an)
rapud,rapid
rapugnense,repugnant(nce)
rapugnent,repugnant
rapulshen,repulse(sion)
rapulsif,repulse(sive)
rapulsion,repulse(sion)
rapuplekan,republic(an)
rapur,rap(pper) / rap(er) / wrap(pper)
rapust,rape(pist)
rapute,repute
raqet,racket / racquet
raqeteer,racketeer
raqrute,recruit
raquire,require
raquirment,require(ment)
raquitable,requite(table)
raquite,requite
raqut,racket / racquet
raquteer,racketeer
raqwest,request
raqwire,require

raqwirment,require(ment)
rar,rare
rare,ely, er, est, eness, rity, rities, efy, efies, efied, efying, efiable, MOST UNCOMMON, UNUSUAL, SCARCE, MEAT BARELY COOKED
rarety, rare(rity)
rarist, rare(rist)
rarity, rare(rity)
rarly, rare(ly)
rarudy,rare(rity)
raruty, rare(rity)
ras,race / raise / ray(s)
rasbery,raspberry
rascal, *, lly, lity, lities, MISCHIEVOUS/ PLAYFUL/ ROGUISH BEHAVIOR
rascul,rascal
rasd,race(d) / raise(d)
raseat, receipt
rasebshenist,receptionist
rasebshin,reception
rasebter,receptor
rasebtif,receptive
rasebtive, receptive
raseed,recede
rasefe, receive
rasefible, receive(vable)
rasemblinse, resemble(lance)
rasembul,resemble
rasen,raisin / race(cing) / raise(sing)
rasenful,resent(ful)
rasentment,resent(ment)
rasepdekle, receptacle
rasepe,recipe
rasepeunt,recipient
raseprikul,reciprocal
raseprocation,reciprocate(tion)
raseprokashen,reciprocate(tion)
raseprokate,reciprocate
rasepshenist,receptionist
rasepshun,reception
raseptacle, receptacle
raseptef, receptive
raseptikle, receptacle

raseptionest, receptionist	rashinul, rational	rasister, resist(or)
raseptive, receptive	rashinulization, rational(ization)	rasistive, resist(ive)
raseptor, receptor	rashio, ratio	rasisum, racism
raseptukle, receptacle	rashon, ration	rasite, recite
raser, razor / raise(r) / race(r)	rashonality, rational(ity)	rasitul, recite(tal)
raserekshen, resurrect(ion)	rashonalization, rational(ization)	rasizm, racism
raservation, reservation	rashonel, rational	rasizum, racism
raservist, reserve(vist)	rashs, rash(es)	raskle, rascal
rasesem, racism	rashul, racial	rasn, raisin / raise(sing) / race(cing)
raseshun, recess(ion)	rashun, ration	rasodo, risotto
raseif, recess(ive)	rashunal, ration(al)	rasolve, resolve
rasesion, recess(ion)	rashunaledy, rational(ity)	rasolvuble, resolve(vable)
rasesive, recess(ive)	rashunality, rational(ity)	rasor, razor / raise(r) / race(r)
rasesion, recess(ion)	rashunalization, rational(ization)	rasort, resort
rasest, racist	rashund, ration(ed)	rasoto, risotto
rasestef, resist(ive)	rashunil, rational	rasotto, risotto
rasestif, resist(ive)	raside, reside	**rasp**, *, per, pingly, py, A TOOL THAT ROUGHS/ SCRAPES/ SANDS, A ROUGH SOUND
rasestinse, resist(ance)	rasiduel, residue(ual)	**raspberry**, rries, AN EDIBLE BERRY
rasestint, resist(ant)	rasign, resign	raspect, respect
rasestive, resist(ive)	rasiliency, resilient(ncy)	raspectful, respect(ful)
rasesum, racism	rasilient, resilient	raspective, respect(ive)
rasete, receipt	rasimblanse, resemble(lance)	raspectuble, respect(able)
rasetion, recess(ion)	rasimble, resemble	raspekt, respect
raseve, receive	rasin, raisin / race(cing) / raise(sing)	raspektful, respect(ful)
rasevuble, receive(vable)	rasinful, resent(ful)	raspektif, respect(ive)
rash, hes, A SKIN FORMATION	rasipeant, recipient	raspektuble, respect(able)
rashal, racial	rasipeint, recipient	raspite, respite
rashel, racial	rasiprikul, reciprocal	raspond, respond
rashen, ration	rasiprocation, reciprocate(tion)	rasponder, respond(er)
rashenaledy, rational(ity)	rasiprokashen, reciprocate(tion)	rasponse, response
rashenality, rational(ity)	rasiprokate, reciprocate	rasponsef, response(sive)
rashenalization, rational(ization)	rasiprokul, reciprocal	rasponsive, response(sive)
rashent, ration(ed)	rasir, razor / raise(r) / race(r)	rasponsuble, response(sible)
rashenul, rational	rasirekshen, resurrect(ion)	rast, race(d) / raise(d)
rasheo, ratio	rasirvation, reservation	rastore, restore
rasheonalization, rational(ization)	rasirvist, reserve(vist)	rastrant, restrain(t)
rasheunolezashen, rational(ization)	rasis, race(s) / raise(s) / racist	rastrektif, restrict(ive)
rashil, racial	rasisem, racism	rastrektion, restrict(ion)
rashin, ration	rasism, racism	rastrikshen, restrict(ion)
rashinal, rational	rasist, racist / resist	rastrikt, restrict
rashinaledy, rational(ity)	rasistef, resist(ive)	rastriktive, restrict(ive)
rashinality, rational(ity)	rasistense, resist(ance)	rasume, resume
rashint, ration(ed)	rasistent, resist(ant)	

rasun, raisin / raise(sing) / race(cing)
rasur, razor / raise(r) / race(r)
rasurekshen, resurrect(ion)
rasus, racist / race(s)
rasusatate, resuscitate
rasuscitate, resuscitate
rasusitashen, resuscitate(tion)
rasusitate, resuscitate
rasusitator, resuscitate(tor)
rasust, racist
rasy, race
rat, * , tted, tting, tty, RODENT, SOMEONE WHO REVEALS OTHERS PRIVATE INFORMATION WITHOUT PERMISSION, TANGLED HAIR (or see rate/ raid)
ratainer, retain(er)
rataleashen, retaliate(tion)
rataleate, retaliate
rataleation, retaliate(tion)
ratane, retain
rataner, retain(er)
ratar, radar
ratash, radish
ratchat, ratchet
ratchet, * , ted, ting, A DEVICE/ TOOL
ratchut, ratchet
rate, * , ed, ting, table, RANK, QUALIFY, QUANTIFY, PROVIDE A VALUE FOR (or see raid) "prefixes: de/ over/ pro/ under"
rateal, radial
rateant, radiant
rateashen, radiate(tion)
rateate, radiate
rateater, radiate(tor)
rateation, radiate(tion)
ratecal, radical
ratech, radish
rated, rate(d) / rat(tted) / rot(tted)
ratefy, ratify
rateil, radial
rateim, radium
rateinse, radiance
rateint, radiant
rateints, radiance

rateis, radius
rately, radical(lly)
ratekul, radical
ratel, rattle
ratenshun, retention
ratentif, retentive
ratention, retention
ratentive, retentive
rateo, ratio / radio
rateod, radio(ed)
rateol, radial
rateom, radium
ratesh, radish
rateul, radial
rateum, radium
rateunse, radiance
rateunt, radiant
rateus, radius
rath, wrath
rather, THIS OVER THAT, PREFERENCE
rathful, wrath(ful)
rathur, rather
ratiate, radiate
ratiater, radiate(tor)
ratical, radical
ratich, radish
raticly, radical(lly)
ratid, rat(tted) / rate(d)
ratiel, radial
ratiem, radium
ratient, radiant
ratify, fies, fied, fying, fication, fier, APPROVE/ CONFIRM/ MAKE FORMAL
ratikly, radical(lly)
ratikul, radical
ratikuly, radical(lly)
ratil, rattle
ratinshun, retention
ratintion, retention
ratio, * , COMPARISON OF AMOUNTS
ratiol, radial
ration, * , ned, ning, A SPECIFIC/ LIMITED AMOUNT

rational, le, lly, lness, lism, list, listic, listically, lity, lities, lize, lizer, lization, FACTUAL/ LEVEL-HEADED/ NON EMOTIONAL THOUGHT "prefixes: ir"
rationalezation, rational(ization)
rationulization, rational(ization)
ratire, retire
ratirment, retire(ment)
ratisery, rotisserie
ratish, radish
ratisury, rotisserie
ratiul, radial
ratium, radium
ratiunse, radiance
ratius, radius
ratl, rattle
ratol, rattle
raton, radon
ratorical, rhetoric(al)
ratrakshen, retract(ion)
ratrakted, retract(ed)
ratrefe, retrieve
ratrefer, retrieve(r)
ratreful, retrieve(val)
ratreve, retrieve
ratrevul, retrieve(val)
ratrevur, retrieve(r)
rattle, * , ed, ling, er, ly, lier, liest, INSTRUMENT/ TOY WITH BEADS INSIDE TO CREATE SOUND
ratufy, ratify
ratukle, radical
ratukly, radical(lly)
ratul, rattle
ratush, radish
raty, rat(tty)
raudy, rowdy
rauk, rock
raunch, hy,hier, hiest, INDECENT/ FOUL
raund, round
raunyin, reunion
raunyun, reunion
raust, roust
raut, wrought / route
rauty, rowdy

rav,rave
ravage,*,ed,ging,TO VIOLENTLY DAMAGE/ DESTROY/ DEVASTATE
ravaje,ravage
raval,ravel
ravalashen,revelation
ravalee,reveille
ravalve,revolve
ravan,raven
ravash,ravish / ravage
rave,*,ed,ving,er,DELIRIOUS/ WILD/ EXCESSIVE, CARRYING ON,INCESSANT ABOUT
ravech,ravish / ravage
raveel,reveal
raveer,revere
ravege,ravage
ravegen,revise(sion)
raveje,ravage
ravejen,revise(sion)
ravel,*,led,ling,ler,lment,BECOME FRAYED/ ENTANGLED (or see reveal) "prefixes: un"
ravelation,revelation
ravelee,reveille
ravelt,reveal(ed)
raven,*,ner,ning,ningly,nous,nously,nousness,ner, BIRD,PLUNDER/ DEVOUR GREEDILY, VORACIOUS APPETITE (or see ravine/ rave(ving))
ravench,revenge
ravene,ravine
ravenge,revenge
ravengful,revenge(ful)
ravenje,revenge
ravenjful,revenge(ful)
ravenus,raven(ous)
raveoly,ravioli
raverberate,reverberate
raverbirate,reverberate
ravere,revere
raversuble,reverse(sible)
ravert,revert
ravesh,ravish / ravage
raveshen,revise(sion)
ravesion,revise(sion)

raview,review / revue
ravige,ravage
ravigen,revise(sion)
ravije,ravage
ravijen,revise(sion)
ravil,ravel
ravilashen,revelation
ravilation,revelation
ravilee,reveille / ravel
ravin,raven / ravine
ravinch,revenge
ravine,*,A DEEP GORGE/ DRIED RIVER BED WORN AWAY BY WATER (or see raven)
ravinge,revenge
ravingful,revenge(ful)
ravinje,revenge
ravinjful,revenge(ful)
ravinous,raven(ous)
ravinus,raven(ous)
ravioli,*,STUFFED PASTA/ NOODLE
ravirberate,reverberate
ravirse,reverse
ravirsuble,reverse(sible)
ravirt,revert
ravise,revise
ravish,hes,hed,hing,her,hment,CARRY AWAY/ TRANSPORT/ TAKE BY FORCE, OVERWHELM EMOTIONALLY
ravishen,revise(sion)
ravision,revise(sion)
ravival,revival
ravive,revive
ravivle,revival
ravivuble,revive(vable)
ravize,revise
ravl,ravel
ravocable,revocable
ravokable,revocable
ravoke,revoke
ravokt,revoke(d)
ravol,ravel
ravolashen,revelation
ravolation,revelation

ravolee,reveille
ravolfe,revolve
ravolfer,revolve(r)
ravolt,revolt
ravolushen,revolution
ravolutioniz,revolution(ize)
ravolve,revolve
ravolver,revolve(r)
ravon,raven / rave(ving)
ravonous,raven(ous)
ravu,review / revue
ravuge,ravage
ravuje,ravage
ravul,ravel
ravulashen,revelation
ravulation,revelation
ravulee,reveille
ravurbarate,reverberate
ravurse,reverse
ravurt,revert
raw,wly,wness,wish,UNFINISHED, UNCOOKED, UNADULTERATED,IN ITS NATURAL STATE
raward,reward
rawdy,rowdy
rawlik,rollick
rawnd,round
rawnt,round
raword,reward
rawst,roust
rawty,rowdy
ray,*,STREAM OF LIGHT/ HOPE/ ENERGY (or see rye)
raybees,rabid(ies)
raydar,radar
raydeans,radiance
raydon,radon
rayl,rail / rale
rayn,rain / reign / rein
raynbo,rainbow
rayol,rile
rayon,SYNTHETIC FIBER
rayot,riot
raysd,raise(d) / race(d)
rayunyon,reunion

Word	Definition / Forms
razberee	raspberry
razd,race(d) / raise(d)	
raze,raise / ray(s) / race	
razeleant,resilient	
razemble,resemble	
razemblinse,resemble(lance)	
razen,raisin / raise(sing) / race(cing)	
razent,resent	
razentment,resent(ment)	
razer,razor	
razervation,reservation	
razervist,reserve(vist)	
razesd,racist	
razesm,racism	
razest,racist / resist	
razide,reside	
raziduel,residue(ual)	
razilyent,resilient	
razimble,resemble	
razimbul,resemble	
razin,raisin / raise(sing) / race(cing) / resign	
razir,razor	
razirvation,reservation	
razisd,racist	
razism,racism	
razist,racist / resist	
razistef,resist(ive)	
razistense,resist(ance)	
razistent,resist(ant)	
razistur,resist(or)	
razite,recite	
razizum,racism	
razkel,rascal	
razkul,rascal	
razodo,risotto	
razolve,resolve	
razon,raisin / raise(sing) / race(cing)	
razoom,resume	
razor,*, SHARP BLADE INSTRUMENT FOR CUTTING HAIR	
razort,resort	
razoto,risotto	
razt,raise(d) / race(d)	
razume,resume	
razun,raisin / raise(sing) / race(cing)	
razur,razor	
razust,racist	
rchin,urchin	
re,PREFIX INDICATING "BACK/ AGAIN/ IN RESPONSE" MOST OFTEN MODIFIES THE WORD	
reach,hes, hed, hing, STRETCH FURTHER THAN NORMAL TO ACHIEVE/ GRASP/ ACQUIRE "prefixes: over"	
reacshen,react(ion)	
react,*, ted, ting, tion, tional, tionaries, tionist, tive, tance, tor, RESPOND/ ACT/ MOVE IN RESPONSE TO STIMULUS "prefixes: bio/ over/ un"	
reacter,react(or)	
reactur,react(or)	
read,*, ding, dable, dability, dableness, dably, der, ABLE TO VIEW/ SEE/ DECIPHER TEXT/ LETTERS/ NUMBERS/ SYMBOLS (or see red) "prefixes: mis/ un"	
ready,died, dying, dily, diness, PREPARED TO ACT/ PERFORM/ RESPOND (or see read) "prefixes: un"	
reaf,reef	
reak,wreak / reek / wreck	
reaked,wreck(ed) / wreak(ed) / reek(ed)	
reaks,react(s) / reek(s) / wreak(s)	
reakshen,react(ion)	
reakshun,react(ion)	
reakt,react	
reakted,react(ed)	
reaktef,react(ive)	
reakter,react(or)	
reaktif,react(ive)	
reaktion,react(ion)	
reaktir,react(or)	
reaktive,react(ive)	
reaktor,react(or)	
reaktuf,react(ive)	
reaktur,react(or)	
real,lness, lism, list, listic, listically, lly, lize, lizes, lized, lizing, lity, PHYSICAL/ TRUTHFUL/ FACTUAL (or see reel/ realty) "prefixes: ir/ neo/ sur"	
realdy,realty	
realedy,reality	
realestic,real(istic)	
realety,reality	
realidy,reality	
reality,ties, PHYSICAL, TRUTHFUL, FACTUAL (or see reel/ realty) "prefixes: un"	
really,TRULY, ACTUALLY, INDEED	
realm,*, AREA OF SCOPE/ INTEREST	
realty,ties, tor, OF REAL ESTATE/ PROPERTY	
ream,*, med, ming, mer, BUNDLED PAPER, ENLARGE/ BORE/ BEVEL/ ENLARGE/ SQUEEZE WITH A TOOL	
reanlistment,reenlist(ment)	
reap,*, ped, ping, per, ACCEPT, RECEIVE, HARVEST FOR YOUR EFFORTS	
rear,*, red, ring, THE END/ LAST/ BOTTOM OF SOMETHING, TO RISE UP ON HINDQUARTERS "prefixes: up"	
reary,weary	
reason,*, ned, ning, nable, nably, nableness, WEIGH LOGIC AGAINST EMOTIONS IN MAKING DECISIONS, USE MODERATE JUDGMENT "prefixes: un"	
reastat,rheostat	
reath,wreath / wreathe	
reatret,retreat	
reaultee,realty	
reax,react(s)	
reb,rib	
rebade,rebate	
rebaflavin,riboflavin	
rebal,rebel	
reban,ribbon	
rebate,*, er, TO RETURN BACK	
rebatishen,repetition	
rebeit,rebate	
rebel,*, lled, lling, llion, llious, lliously, lliousness, RISE UP/ GO AGAINST THE MAINSTREAM OF RULE/ THOUGHT	
rebelion,rebel(llion)	
rebelyus,rebel(llious)	
reben,ribbon	
reberkushen,repercussion	
reberkution,repercussion	
rebertwa,repertoire	
rebertwor,repertoire	
rebetishen,repetition	
rebeut,rebut / reboot	
rebeutashen,repute(tation)

rebeutel,rebut(ttal)
rebewk,rebuke
rebewt,rebut / reboot
rebewtel,rebut(ttal)
rebil,rebel
rebin,ribbon
rebirkushen,repercussion
rebirkution,repercussion
rebirtwa,repertoire
rebirtwor,repertoire
reble,rebel
rebled,rebel(lled)
rebleka,replica
reblekashen,replica(tion)
reblika,replica
reblikate,replica(te)
reblikation,replica(tion)
rebluka,replica
reblukashen,replica(tion)
reblukate,replica(te)
reblukation,replica(tion)
rebof,rebuff
reboflavin,riboflavin
rebol,rebel
rebon,ribbon
reboot,*,ted,ting, RESTART A COMPUTER/ MEMORY/ ACTION (or see rebut)
reborkushen,repercussion
rebotek,robot(ic)
rebound,ded,ding, REPERCUSSION/ REACTION TO A COLLISION WITH EMOTIONS/ ATTITUDES/ SOMETHING PHYSICAL
rebownd,rebound
rebownt,rebound
rebrahensible,reprehensible
rebrkushen,repercussion
rebt,rib(bbed) / rip(pped)
rebtile,reptile
rebtileun,reptile(lian)
rebudal,rebut(ttal)
rebudle,rebut(ttal)
rebuf,rebuff
rebuff,*,ffed,ffing, REFUSE/ REJECT

rebuflavin,riboflavin
rebuke,*,ed,king,er, SEVERE/ SHARP REJECT/ REFUSE
rebul,rebel
rebuled,rebel(lled)
rebun,ribbon
reburkushen,repercussion
reburkution,repercussion
reburtwa,repertoire
reburtwor,repertoire
rebut,*,tted,tting,ttable,ttal, ARGUE/ REFUTE/ OPPOSE/ THRUST BACK (or see reboot) "prefixes: sur"
rebutal,rebut(ttal)
rebutashen,repute(tation)
rebute,reboot
rebutishen,repetition
rebutle,rebut(ttal)
rec,wreck
recal,recall
recall,*,lled,lling,llable, CALL/ SOLICIT SOMETHING BACK TO THE SOURCE/ CREATOR
recamend,recommend
recansile,reconcile
recant,*,ted,ting, CONTRADICT/ RETRACT WHAT WAS JUST SAID
recap,*,pped,pping, SUMMARIZE/ RECOAT/ RESURFACE
recaul,recall
reccomend,recommend
reccomendable,recommend(able)
reccomendation,recommend(ation)
reccomended,recommend(ed)
reccomenduble,recommend(able)
recd,wreck(ed) / wreak(ed) / reek(ed)
recede,*,ed,ding, RETREAT/ WITHDRAW/ YIELD TO PREVIOUS/ PRIOR
receipt,*, ACKNOWLEDGEMENT/ INVOICE FOR HAVING RECEIVED SERVICES/ GOODS
receive,*,ed,ving,vable,vables,er,ership, ACCEPT/ ACQUIRE/ ACCUMULATE
recensile,reconcile
recent,tly,tness,ncy, HAVING OCCURRED NEAR/ CLOSE TO THE PRESENT TIME (or see resent)
recepe,recipe
receprocate,reciprocate

receprokul,reciprocal
recepshen,reception
recepshenist,receptionist
recepshin,reception
receptacle,*, A PLACE TO DELIVER, A RECEIVING PLACE, ELECTRICAL SOURCE
recepticle,receptacle
reception,*, AN EVENT/ CEREMONY/ DEVICE WHICH RECEIVES/ ACKNOWLEDGE/ ACCEPTS INCOMING
receptionist,*, SOMEONE WHO ACCEPTS INCOMING CALLS/ VISITORS/ CUSTOMERS
receptive,ely,eness,vity,tor, ABLE TO TAKE IN/ RECEIVE
receptor,*, THAT WHICH RECEIVES
receptucle,receptacle
recer,recur
reces,recess
recess,sses,ssed,ssing,ssion,ssional,ssionary,sive,sively, siveness, TO TAKE A BREAK, RECEDE
receve,receive
rech,wreck / wreak / reek / reach / wretch / rich
rechd,wreck(ed) / wreak(ed) / reek(ed) / reach(ed)
reched,reach(ed) / wreck(ed) / wreak(ed) / reek(ed)
rechem,regime
rechim,regime
rechis,reach(es) / rich(es)
rechister,register
rechistrashen,registration
rechly,rich(ly)
recht,wreck(ed) / wreak(ed) / reek(ed) / reach(ed)
rechual,ritual
rechuol,ritual
recicle,recycle
recieve,receive
recipe,*, DIRECTIONS FOR COOKING
recipient,*, THOSE WHO RECEIVE/ IN RECEIPT OF
recipracate,reciprocate
reciprocal,lity,lly, GIVE AND TAKE, BACK AND FORTH, MUTUALLY RESPONSIVE
reciprocate,*,ted,ting,tion,tive,tor, MOVES BACK AND FORTH, MUTUALLY RESPONSIVE
reciproqueit,reciprocate
recir,recur

recite, *, ed,ting,tal,tation,tative, REPEAT/ RELATE/ GIVE ACCOUNT FROM MEMORY
reck, wreck / wreak / reek
reckamendation, recommend(ation)
recken, wreck(ing) / reek(ing)
reckensile, reconcile
reckety, rickety
reckin, wreck(ing) / reek(ing)
reckinsile, reconcile
reckits, rickets
recklaim, reclaim / reclame
recklamashen, reclamation
recklame, reclaim / reclame
reckless, ssly, ssness, BE UNAWARE/ CARELESS OF SURROUNDING ENVIRONMENT POSING POTENTIAL DANGER/ PAIN
reckline, recline
recklus, recluse / reckless
reckognition, recognition
reckomend, recommend
reckomendation, recommend(ation)
reckon, *, ned,ning, SUPPOSE, TO BE CONSIDERED "prefixes: un"
reckonsile, reconcile
reckumend, recommend
reckumendation, recommend(ation)
reckun, reckon
reckunsile, reconcile
reclaim, *, med,ming,mer,mable,mant,mation, TAKE BACK, MAKE PURE/ USABLE AGAIN (or see reclame) "prefixes: ir"
reclaimable, *, bility, TAKE BACK, MAKE PURE/ USABLE AGAIN "prefixes: ir"
reclaimabol, reclaimable
reclaimashen, reclamation
reclamation, *, TAKE BACK, MAKE PURE/ USABLE
reclame, *, ADVERTISE ONESELF, PUBLIC ATTENTION/ NOTORIETY (or see reclaim)
reclameishon, reclamation
reclamer, reclaim(er)
recleim, reclaim / reclame
recles, reckless
recline, *, ed,ning,er, RECUMBENT POSITION/ LIE BACK
reclumashen, reclamation
reclumation, reclamation
recluse, *, sion,sive,sively,siveness, SHUT ONESELF OFF/ AWAY FROM SOCIETY/ SOCIAL ENVIRONMENT
reclushen, recluse(sion)
recochet, ricochet
recogneshen, recognition
recognetion, recognition
recognition, ive,tory, TO FIND FAMILIAR, FRIENDLY ATTENTION "prefixes: non"
recognize, *, ed,zing,zable,zability,zance, FIND FAMILIAR, KNOW, ACKNOWLEDGE "prefixes: de"
recognizuble, recognize(zable)
recoil, *, led,ling,lless, SUDDEN JERK/ DRAW BACK/ SHRINKING FROM
recol, recoil / recall
recold, recall(ed)
recolt, recall(ed)
recomendable, recommend(able)
recomendashen, recommend(ation)
recomindation, recommend(ation)
recommend, *, ded,ding,dation,dable,datory, ADVISE/ SUGGEST FAVORABLY
recommendashen, recommend(ation)
reconaisanse, reconnaissance
reconasinse, reconnaissance
reconcile, *, ed,ling,lable,lability,lableness,lably,ement,liation,liatory, REBUILD FRIENDSHIP, RESTORE UNION, ADJUST TO DIFFERENCES "prefixes: ir"
reconnaissance, EXAMINE PARAMETER/ TERRITORY
reconsile, reconcile
reconsileashen, reconcile(liation)
reconsileation, reconcile(liation)
reconstatute, reconstitute
reconstetushen, reconstitute(tion)
reconstitute, *, ed,ting,tion, RECONSTRUCT FROM A CONDENSED/ DRIED STATE
reconstetute, reconstitute
reconstruct, *, ted,ting,tion,tive,tible,tor, TO CONSTRUCT AGAIN, RESTORE "prefixes: un"
recoop, recoup
recooped, recoup(ed)
recooperashen, recuperate(tion)
recooperate, recuperate
record, *, ded,ding,dable,der, DOCUMENT/ TAPE/ WRITE/ DEFINE AN EVENT FOR POSTERITY, PRESERVE EVIDENCE "prefixes: pre"
recorse, recourse
recoup, *, ped,ping,pable,pment, TO REGAIN, BE COMPENSATED
recourse, RETURN FOR BACK-UP HELP, ONLY OPTION
recover, *, red,ring,rable,ry, TO GET BACK TO NORMAL/ HEALTHY, BECOME OPERABLE AGAIN "prefixes: ir"
recreashen, recreation
recreate, *, ed,ting,tion,tive,tor, AMUSEMENT/ DIVERSION/ PLAY
recreation, nal,ive, AMUSEMENT/ DIVERSION/ PLAY
recreminate, recriminate
recrieishon, recreation
recriminate, *, ed,ting,tion,tive,tor,tory, TO ACCUSE THE ONE WHO ACCUSED ORIGINALLY
recruit, *, ted,ting,ter,tment, ORGANIZE/ ENLIST/ ENTICE PEOPLE TO JOIN
recrut, recruit
recruter, recruit(er)
rect, wreck(ed) / wreak(ed) / reek(ed)
rectafy, rectify
rectal, lly,tum,ta, INVOLVES/ PERTAINING TO THE RECTUM
rectatude, rectitude
rectem, rectum
rectifie, rectify
rectify, fies,fied,fying,fiable,fication,itude, AMEND/ CORRECT/ MAKE RIGHT
rectil, rectal
rectitude, dinous, RIGHTEOUS IN FORM/ INTEGRITY
rectol, rectal
rectom, rectum
rectul, rectal
rectum, *, ta, THE LOWER LARGE INTESTINE
rectutude, rectitude
recufer, recover
recufry, recover(y)
recuisit, requisite
recumbent, tly,ncy, RECLINING/ LYING POSITION
recumendashen, recommend(ation)
recundrucdev, reconstruct(ive)

recunsile,reconcile
reconstruct,reconstruct
recupe,recoup
recuped,recoup(ed)
recuperashen,recuperate(tion)
recuperate, *, ed, ting, tior, tive, tory,RECOVER/ REGAIN FROM ILLNESS/ FINANCIAL STRESS
recur, *, rred, rring, rrent, r~ently, rrence, REPEATEDLY HAPPENING
recurd,record
recuver,recover
recuvry,recover(y)
recwuzit,requisite
recycle, *, ed, ling, er, lable, lables, lability, REUSE, USE AGAIN
red, *, dder, ddest, dding, dness, dden, A COLOR, PERTAINING TO THE COLOR (or see read)
redabel,read(able)
redabul,read(able)
redal,riddle
redard,retard
redasent,reticent
redasint,reticent
rede,ready
redeam,redeem
redeble,read(able)
reded,ready(died) / read
redeem, *, med, ming, mer, mable, CLEAR PAYMENT, RECOVER, FULFILL PLEDGE "prefixes: ir"
redeemible,redeem(able)
redempshun,redemption
redemption, *, nal, ner, ive, tory,TO BE/ ACT OF BEING REDEEMED
redemtion,redemption
redemtive,redemption(ive)
redemuble,redeem(able)
redents,rid(ddance)
reder,red(dder) / read(er)
redern,return
redge,ridge
redi,ready
redible,read(able)
redicint,reticent

redicule,ridicule
rediculus,ridiculous
redimtive,redemption(ive)
redin,red(dden)
redio,radio
redir,red(dder) / read(er)
redisent,reticent
redium,radium
redle,riddle
redna,retina
redniss,red(ness)
redo, oes, did, oing, one, DO AGAIN/ OVER
redoo,redo
redoose,reduce
redor,read(er) / red(dder)
redroactive, retroactive
redroaktif,retroactive
redrograte,retrograde
redrospection, retrospect(ion)
redrospekshin, retrospect(ion)
redubel,read(able)
redubol,read(able)
reduce, *, ed, cing, er, cible, cibly, cibility, ction, ctional, ctive,TO LOWER/ DIMUTION/ DIVIDE "prefixes: ir"
reducshen,reduce(ction)
reduing,redo(ing)
redukshen,reduce(ction)
reduktion,reduce(ction)
redul,riddle
redun,red(dden)
redundant, tly, ncy, ncies, OVER AND OVER, REPEATEDLY/ REPETITION/ UNNECESSARY
redundensy,redundant(ncy)
redur,red(dder) / read(er)
redurn,return
redusable,reduce(cible)
reduse,reduce
redusent,reticent
redusint,reticent
redy,ready
reech,reach
reed, *, ding, dy,A PLANT, CONVEX MOLDING, RIDGES (or see read)

reederate,reiterate
reef, *, fer,OCEAN LEDGE, PART OF A SAIL,SLANG FOR ROLLED MARIJUANA, REFRIGERATOR
reek, *, ked, king, ker, kingly, ky, OFFENSIVE/ STRONG/ AWFUL ODOR (or see wreak/ wreck)
reel, *, led, ling, ler, lable,TO WIND/ PULL IN,A DANCE, WOUND UP,REVOLVING TOOL (or see real) "prefixes: un"
reem,ream
reemberse,reimburse
reembersment,reimburse(ment)
reemburse,reimburse
reembursment,reimburse(ment)
reenact, *, ted, ting, tment, REPLICATE A PERFORMANCE/ EVENT
reenaktment,reenact(ment)
reenforse,reinforce
reenforsment,reinforce(ment)
reenlestment,reenlist(ment)
reenlist, *, ted, ting, tment, TO ENLIST AGAIN
reep,reap
reept,reap(ed)
reer,rear
reeth,wreath / wreathe
returate,reiterate
ref, reef / referee
refal,revel
refalashen,revelation
refalation,revelation
refald,revel(lled)
refalee,reveille
refar,river
refarmashen,reform(ation)
refarmation,reform(ation)
refeel,reveal
refel, revel / refill
refelable, refill(able)
refelashen, revelation
refelation, revelation
refeld, revel(lled) / refill(ed)
refelee, reveille
refeloble, refill(able)

refer, *, rred, rring, rable, rral, RECOMMEND/ HAND OVER/ REQUEST/ ASSIGN SOMEONE ELSE, SLANG FOR REFRIGERATOR (or see reef(er)/ river)
referal, refer(rral)
referbash, refurbish
referbish, refurbish
referbishment, refurbish(ment)
referd, refer(rred)
refere, referee
referee, *, eed, eeing, ASSIGNED TO SETTLE DISPUTES/ MAKE JUDGMENT CALLS
reference, *, ed, cing, DIRECTION, ALLUSION, GUIDE
referendum, *, da, MEASURE PUT BEFORE PUBLIC FOR VOTE
referil, refer(rral)
referindum, referendum
referinse, reference
refermashen, reformation
refermation, reformation
referse, reverse
refeuge, refuge
refeugy, refugee
refeuje, refuge
refeuse, refuse
refeusil, refuse(sal)
refeuze, refuse
refewge, refuge / refugee
refewje, refuge
refews, refuse
refewsel, refuse(sal)
refiew, review / revue
refiful, revival
refil, refill
refill, *, lled, lling, llable, FILL AGAIN
refilable, refill(able)
reflashen, revelation
reflation, revelation
refild, revel(lled)
refilee, reveille
refine, *, ed, ning, ery, nable, ement, REMOVE IMPURITIES/ ALLOYS, MAKE FINE "prefixes: un"
refinment, refine(ment)
refinury, refine(ry)

refir, refer / reef(er) / river
refiral, refer(rral)
refirans, reference
refirbash, refurbish
refirbish, refurbish
refird, refer(rred)
refired, refer(rred)
refiree, referee
refirence, reference
refirendum, referendum
refirense, reference
refirmashen, reformation
refirmation, reformation
refirse, reverse
refiuchi, refugee
refiull, refuge
refiulli, refugee
reflashen, revelation
reflecks, reflex / reflect(s)
reflecksef, reflex(ive)
reflect, *, ted, ting, tion, tive, tively, tiveness, tor, torize, MIRROR/ CAST BACK/ REPRODUCE AN IMAGE (or see reflex) "prefixes: retro/ un"
reflectif, reflect(ive)
refleks, reflex / reflect(s)
reflekshen, reflect(ion)
refleksif, reflex(ive)
reflekt, reflect / reflex(ed)
reflektif, reflect(ive)
reflektion, reflect(ion)
reflektor, reflect(or)
reflex, xes, xed, xing, xly, xive, xively, xiveness, xivity, REACTION/ RESPONSE (or see reflect) "prefixes: ir"
reflexsif, reflex(ive)
reflext, reflex(ed)
refol, revel
refolashen, revelation
refolation, revelation
refold, revel(lled)
refolee, reveille
refor, river / refer / reef(er)

reform, *, *, med, ming, mer, mation, mable, matory, matories, mative, CHANGE/ MODIFY/ RETRAIN/ REARRANGE/ RESTORE "prefixes: ir"
reformashen, reform(ation)
reformd, reform(ed)
reformitory, reform(atory)
reformutory, reform(atory)
refract, *, ted, ting, tion, tive, tory, DEFLECT/ REFLECT INTO A DIFFERENT DIRECTION/ DENSITY
refrain, *, ned, ning, nment, REPETITIVE BREAK/ INTERRUPTION, TO REPRESS/ ABSTAIN
refrakt, refract
refraktory, refract(ory)
refrane, refrain
refrans, reference / refrain(s)
refred, referee(d)
refree, referee
refregirant, refrigerate(ant)
refregirator, refrigerate(tor)
refrein, refrain
refrendum, referendum
refrense, reference
refresh, hes, hed, hing, her, hment, TO MAKE FRESH AGAIN/ INVIGORATE
refrichereit, refrigerate
refrichoreichon, refrigerate(tion)
refrigerate, *, ed, ting, tion, ant, USED TO KEEP THINGS COOL/ COLD
refrigerator, refrigerate(tor)
refrigerent, refrigerate(ant)
refrillereichon, refrigerate(tion)
refrillereit, refrigerate
refrindum, referendum
refrinse, reference
refry, referee
reft, rift
refuch, refuge
refuchi, refugee
refuge, *, review / revue
refuge, *, SANCTUARY/ SHELTER, SAFE PROTECTION
refugee, *, ONE ESCAPING PERSECUTION FROM A FOREIGN COUNTRY
refugy, refugee

refuiuch,refuge
refuje,refuge
reful,revel
refulashen,revelation
refulation,revelation
refulee,reveille
refund, *, ded,ding,dable, RETURN/ COMPENSATE/ GIVE BACK
refundible,refund(able)
refunduble,refund(able)
refunt,refund
refur,refer / reef(er) / rive⁻
refurbeshment,refurbish(ment)
refurbish, hes, hed, hing, hment, RENOVATE/ MAKE FRESH AGAIN
refurd,refer(rred)
refured,refer(rred)
refuree,referee
refurendum,referendum
refurense,reference
refuril,refer(rral)
refurindum,referendum
refurmashen,reform(ation)
refurse,reverse
refus,raffle / refuse
refuse, *, ed, sing, sal, er, NOT ACCEPT, DENY/ REJECT, TO DISCARD UNUSABLES/ TRASH
refusel,refuse(sal)
refute, *, ed, ting, tability, table, tably, tation, CHANGE/ MODIFY/ RETRAIN/ REARRANGE/ RESTCRE "prefixes: ir"
refuze,refuse
reg, rig / ridge
regal,llly, lia, lie, led, ling, lity, lities, PERTAINING TO LAVISH FEASTS/ ROYALTY
regalea,regal(ia)
regaledy,regal(ity)
regamen,regime(n)
regamentashen,regime(ntation)
regamentation,regime(ntation)
regamin,regime(n)
regamint,regime(nt)
regan,region

regard, *, ded,ding,dful,dfully,dfullness,dless,dlessly, dlessness,TO CONSIDER, SHOW CONCERN/ ATTENTION/ RESPECT "prefixes: dis/ ir"
regart, regard
regaster, register
regastrashen, registration
regastration, registration
regect, reject
regekshen, reject(ion)
regekt, reject
regektion, reject(ion)
regel, regal
regementation, regime(ntation)
regemin, regime(n)
regemint, regime(nt)
regemintation, regime(ntation)
regen, region
regenal, regional(al)
regenerate, *, ed, ting, able, acy, tely, tion, tive, tively, tor, RENEW, RESTORE, REPLACE, REVITALIZE "prefixes: un"
regenuradive, regenerate(tive)
reger, rigor
regergetate, regurgitate
regerjutate, regurgitate
regestir, register
regestrashen, registration
regestration, registration
reget, rigid
reguler, regular
regeulerly, regular(ly)
regewlashen, regulate(tion)
regewlate, regulate
regewlation, regulate(tion)
regewlerly, regular(ly)
regewvinate, rejuvenate
regid, rigid
regil, regal
regime, *, en, ent, ental, entally, entation, MODE/ SYSTEM OF RULE/ MANAGEMENT
regimentashen, regime(ntation)
regimin, regime(min)
regimint, regime(nt)

regimintation,regime(ntation)
regin,region
reginal,region(al)
reginuradive,regenerate(tive)
reginurate,regenerate
reginurative,regenerate(tive)
region, *, nal, nally, nalism, nalist, nalistic, AN AREA/ PART/ SECTION OF "prefixes: inter/ sub"
regirus,rigor(ous)
register, *, red, ring, tration, SIGN UP/ ENROLL TO PARTICIPATE "prefixes: de"
registrashen,registration
registration, *, SIGN UP/ ENROLL TO PARTICIPATE
regit,rigid
regiular, regular
reglar, regular
reglate, regulate
regle, regal
reglerly,regular(ly)
reglir,regular
reglurly,regular(ly)
regoise,rejoice
regon,region
regonal,region(al)
regoyse,rejoice
regres,regress
regresif,regress(ive)
regresive,regress(ive)
regress, sses, ssed, ssing, ssion, ssive, ssively, ssiveness, ssor, GOING BACK/ REVERSION
regresuf,regress(ive)
regret, *, tted, tting, tful, tfully, tfulness, ttable, ttably, tter, SENSE OF LOSS/ SORROW, SORRY
regreted,regret(tted)
regretfuly,regret(fully)
reguard,regard
reguardless,regard(less)
regul,regal
regular, *, rly, rity, rize, NORMAL/ AVERAGE/ TYPICAL "prefixes: ir"
regulashen,regulate(tion)
regulate, *, ed, ting, tion, tive, tor, tory, NORMALIZE, KEEP WITHIN LIMITS/ STANDARDS "prefixes: de"

reguler,regular
regulerly,regular(ly)
regulur,regular
regument,regime(nt)
regumentashen,regimentation,regime(ntation)
regumentation,regimentation,regime(ntation)
regumin,regime(n)
regumint,regime(nt)
regunal,region(al)
regurgitate,*,ed,ting,tion,RUSH/ SURGE BACK AND FORTH
regurjitate,regurgitate
regurs,rigor(s)
regurus,rigor(ous)
regustir,register
regustrashen,registration
regustration,registration
reguvanashen,rejuvenate(tion)
reguvanate,rejuvenate
reguvanation,rejuvenate(tion)
reguvinate,rejuvenate
reguvination,rejuvenate(tion)
reguvunate,rejuvenate
regwasit,requisite
regwazit,requisite
rehab,*,bber,bilitate,SLANG FOR REHABILITATION
rehabeletashen,rehabilitate(tion)
rehabeletate,rehabilitate
rehabilitate,*,ed,ting,tion,tive,RESTORE/ REINSTATE/ REESTABLISH
rehap,rehab
rehearse,*,ed,sing,sal,TO PRACTICE REPEATEDLY FOR A PERFORMANCE
rehebilatation,rehabilitate(tion)
rehersal,rehearse(sal)
reherse,rehearse
rehersul,rehearse(sal)
rehirsul,rehearse(sal)
rehubelatashen,rehabilitate(tion)
rehubilatate,rehabilitate
rehubiletation,rehabilitate(tion)
rehurse,rehearse
rehursil,rehearse(sal)

reibid,rabid
reich,rage
reicist,racist
reid,raid
reidar,radar
reiderate,reiterate
reidial,radial
reidians,radiance
reidieit,radiate
reidiom,radium
reidios,radius
reidiou,radio
reidon,radon
reidurate,reiterate
reign,*,ned,ning,HAVE RULE/ POWER/ SOVEREIGNTY (or see rain/ rein)
reik,rake
reil,real / reel / rale / rail
reilistec,real(istic)
reill,rage
reilroud,railroad
reiltee,realty
reilty,realty
reimberse,reimburse
reimbirsment,reimburse(ment)
reimburse,*,ed,sing,sable,ement,er,PAY BACK/ REFUND/ COMPENSATE
rein,*,ned,ning,nless,RESTRAINT/ CURB/ CONTROL (or see rain/ reign)
reinacment,reenact(ment)
reinacted,reenact(ed)
reinakt,reenact
reinaktment,reenact(ment)
reinbou,rainbow
reinch,range
reindeer,*,IN THE DEER FAMILY
reinforce,*,ed,cing,ement,INCREASE/ STRENGTHEN
reinforse,reinforce
reinforsment,reinforce(ment)
reinlest,reenlist
reinlismen,reenlist(men)
reinlist,reenlist
reinlistment,reenlist(ment)

reinll,range
reion,rayon
reip,rape / ripe / reap
reis,race / rise / raise
reishio,ratio
reishiou,ratio
reishol,racial
reisin,raisin
reisism,racism
reisisom,racism
reisist,racist
reit,rate
reiterate,*,ed,ting,tion,tive,tively,TO REPEAT/ SAY AGAIN
reiturate,reiterate
reiv,rave
reiven,raven/ ravine
rej,ridge / reach
rejament,regime(nt)
rejamin,regime(n)
rejamintashen,regime(ntation)
rejamintation,regime(ntation)
rejan,region
rejaster,register
reject,*,ted,ting,tion,ter,tive,REFUSE TO RECEIVE/ RECOGNIZE/ ACKNOWLEDGE/ ACCEPT
rejekshen,reject(ion)
rejekt,reject
rejektion,reject(ion)
rejen,region
rejenaradive,regenerate(tive)
rejenarative,regenerate(tive)
rejenul,region(al)
rejenurate,regenerate
rejestir,register
rejestrashen,registration
rejestration,registration
rejet,rigid
rejewvinate,rejuvenate
rejid,rigid
rejimen,regime(n)
rejiment,regime(nt)
rejin,region

rejinarate, regenerate
rejinul, region(al)
rejinuradive, regenerate(tive)
rejister, register
rejistrashen, registration
rejistration, registration
rejit, rigid
rejoese, rejoice
rejoice, *, ed, cing, er, cingly, TO DISPLAY JOY / GLADNESS
rejon, region
rejonal, region(al)
rejoyse, rejoice
rejumen, regime(n)
rejument, regime(nt)
rejumentashen, regime(ntation)
rejumin, regime(n)
rejumint, regime(nt)
rejumintashen, regime(ntation)
rejumintation, regime(ntation)
rejun, region
rejunal, region(al)
rejustir, register
rejustrashen, registration
rejustration, registration
rejuvanashen, rejuvenate(tion)
rejuvenate, *, ed, ting, tion. tor, nize, nescence, MAKE YOUTHFUL AGAIN
rejuvinashen, rejuvenate(tion)
rejuvinate, rejuvenate
rejuvination, rejuvenate(tion)
rek, wreck / wreak / reek
rekal, recall
rekamend, recommend
rekamendation, recommend(ation)
rekamenduble, recommend(able)
rekamented, recommend(ed)
rekanize, recognize
rekansile, reconcile
rekansileashun, reconcile(liation)
rekant, recant
rekap, recap
rekapt, recap(pped)
rekashay, ricochet

rekd, reek(ed) / wreck(ed) / wreak(ed)
rekedy, rickety
rekegnise, recognize
reken, reckon
rekendul, rekindle
rekenize, recognize
rekensile, reconcile
rekensileashun, reconcile(liation)
reker, recur / wrecker
rekerd, record
rekety, rickety
rekeulir, regular
rekewlashen, regulate(tion)
rekewpt, recoup(ed)
rekewpurate, recuperate
rekidy, rickety
rekimented, recommend(ed)
rekin, reckon
rekindle, *, ed, ling, RENEW
rekindul, rekindle
rekinise, recognize
rekinsile, reconcile
rekir, recur / wrecker
rekird, record
rekits, rickets
rekity, rickety
reklaimuble, reclaimable
reklamashen, reclamation
rekalme, reclaim / reclame
reklamshen, reclamation
reklamuble, reclaimable
reklas, reckless
reklemashen, reclamation
rekless, reckless
reklimashen, reclamation
reklimation, reclamation
rekline, recline
reklinur, recline(r)
reklir, regular
reklis, reckless
rekloos, recluse
reklumation, reclamation

reklus, reckless
rekluse, recluse
rekochet, ricochet
rekofry, recover
rekogneshen, recognition
rekognise, recognize
rekognition, recognition
rekognize, recognize
rekognizuble, recognize(zable)
rekoil, recoil
rekol, recall
rekold, recall(ed)
rekole, recoil / recall
rekolt, recall(ed)
rekomend, recommend
rekomendashen, recommend(ation)
rekomented, recommend(ed)
rekon, reckon
rekonasents, reconnaissance
rekonisense, reconnaissance
rekonize, recognize
rekonsdructive, reconstruct(ive)
rekonsile, reconcile
rekonsileat, reconcile(ate)
rekonsileation, reconcile(liation)
rekonstatute, reconstitute
rekonstetushen, reconstitute(tion)
rekonstetute, reconstitute
rekonstitution, reconstitute(tion)
rekonstruct, reconstruct
rekonusinse, reconnaissance
rekoop, recoup
rekooperate, recuperate
rekor, wrecker
rekord, record
rekorder, record(er)
rekorse, recourse
rekover, recover
rekoyl, recoil
rekreashen, recreation
rekreate, recreate
rekreation, recreation
rekreative, recreate(tive)

rekreminate, recriminate	rekunstrukdive, reconstruct(ive)
rekrimenate, recriminate	rekupe, recoup
rekroot, recruit	rekuperate, recuperate
rekrute, recruit	rekuperation, recuperate(tion)
rekruter, recruit(er)	rekupirate, recuperate
reks, reek(s) / wreck(s) / wreak(s)	rekupt, recoup(ed)
rekt, reek(ed) / wreck(ed) / wreak(ed)	rekupurashen, recuperate(tion)
rektafy, rectify	rekur, recur / wrecker
rektal, rectal	rekurd, record
rektatude, rectitude	rekushet, ricochet
rektel, rectal	rekuver, recover
rektem, rectum	rekuvry, recover(y)
rektify, rectify	rekwasit, requisite
rektitude, rectitude	rekwest, request
rektol, rectal	rekwire, require
rektom, rectum	rekwirment, require(ment)
rektufy, rectify	rekwrute, recruit
rektul, rectal	rekwuzit, requisite
rektum, rectum	rel, real / reel / rill / rail / rale
rekusit, requisite	rela, relay
rekufer, recover	relabs, relapse
rekufry, recover	relagashen, relegate(tion)
rekugnise, recognize	relagate, relegate
rekugnishen, recognition	relagation, relegate(tion)
rekugnize, recognize	relaks, relax
rekugnizuble, recognize(zable)	relantless, relent(less)
rekulade, regulate	relaps, relapse
rekular, regular	**relapse**, *, ed, sing, er, TO BACKSLIDE/ FALL BACK
rekulashen, regulate(tion)	relashen, relate(tion)
rekulate, regulate	relashunship, relate(tionship)
rekulation, regulate(tion)	**relate**, *, ed, ting, tion, tional, table, tionship, edness, BE ALLIED/ ASSOCIATED/ CONNECTED WITH, TO TELL/ NARRATE "prefixes: inter"
rekumbent, recumbent	
rekumend, recommend	
rekumendashen, recommend(ation)	relatevity, relativity
rekumenduble, recommend(able)	relatif, relative
rekumented, recommend(ed)	**relative**, *, ely, eness, vism, vist, vistic, vity, ASSOCIATED/ SIMILAR/ CLOSE/ CONNECTION "prefixes: ir"
rekumind, recommend	**relativity**, vities, THAT WHICH IS RELATIVE
rekun, reckon	relativly, relative(ly)
rekunize, recognize	relavance, relevant(nce)
rekunsile, reconcile	relavant, relevant
rekunsileashen, reconcile(liation)	relavence, relevant(nce)
rekunsileation, reconcile(liation)	relavent, relevant
rekunstruct, reconstruct	

relax, xes, xed, xing, xation, xedly, xedness, xer, xant, BECOME CALM/ LOOSE/ SLACK "prefixes: un"	
relay, *, yed, ying, USE OF MACHINERY/ ELECTRICITY/ PEOPLE/ TECHNOLOGY/ ANIMALS TO SEND/ TRANSMIT/ RETRIEVE	
rele, really / reel / real	
release, *, ed, sing, er, sable, TO FREE	
relef, relief	
relegate, *, ed, ting, tion, SEND AWAY	
releve, relieve	
relek, relic	
relent, *, ted, ting, tless, INTENSELY PERSISTENT/ DEMANDING/ PUNISHING "prefixes: un"	
relentless, ssly, ssness, MERCILESS/ HARSH	
relese, release	
relesh, relish	
retetif, relative	
retetivity, relativity	
retetivly, relative(ly)	
relevant, tly, nce, ncy, PERTAINS/ APPLICABLE TO, SUPPORTIVE/ IMPORTANT "prefixes: ir"	
relev, relieve / relief	
relevence, relevant(nce)	
relevent, relevant	
relever, relieve(r)	
relevur, relieve(r)	
reli, really / rely	
reliable, bility, leness, ly, CONFIDENCE/ TRUST IN, DEPEND ON "prefixes: un"	
reliance, cy, nt, ntly, CONFIDENCE/ TRUST/ DEPENDENT	
reliaple, reliable	
relic, *, MEMENTOS/ PRESERVED/ KEEP SAKES	
relichon, religion	
relidy, reality	
relief, eve, EASE/ REMOVAL/ ALLEVIATION FROM PAIN	
relieve, *, ed, ving, er, vable, EASED/ REMOVED/ ALLEVIATED FROM PAIN (or see relief)	
religashen, relegate(tion)	
religate, relegate	
religation, relegate(tion)	
religeon, religion	
religion, *, ous, ously, ousness, BELIEF IN A GOD IN A SPECIFIC/ ARTICULAR WAY "prefixes: inter/ ir"	

religon,religion
religus,religion(ous)
relik,relic
relillon,religion
relinkwish,relinquish
relinquish,hes,hed,hing,hment,her,GIVE UP POSSESSION OF
relintless,relent(less) / relentless
relish,hes,hed,hing,hable,APPETIZER, PICKLED CONDIMENT, BE GRATIFIED/ PLEASED/ LIKE/ SAVOR SOMETHING
relity,reality
reliubility,reliable(bility)
reliuble,reliable
reliunse,reliance
reliunt,reliance(nt)
relivance,relevant(nce)
relivant,relevant
relivence,relevant(nce)
relivent,relevant
reliver,relieve(r)
rellim,regime
rellister,register
rellistreishon,registration
relm,realm
reloctant,reluctant
relogate,relegate
relogation,relegate(tion)
reltifly,relative(ly)
relty,realty
reluctant,tly,nce,APPREHENSIVE/ RESISTANT/ UNWILLING
reluctinse,reluctant(nce)
reluctint,reluctant
relugashen,relegate(tion)
relugate,relegate
relugation,relegate(tion)
reluktant,reluctant
reluktense,reluctant(nce)
reluktint,reluctant
relur,regular
relush,relish
relutif,relative

relutivly,relative(ly)
reluvence,relevant(nce)
reluvent,relevant
rely,lies,lied,lying,liable,liability,liableness,liably, TRUSTWORTHY/ SUPPORTIVE/ DEPENDABLE (or see really)
rem,ream / realm / rim
remade,remedy
remadik,rheumatic
remain,*,ned,ning,nder,STAY BEHIND/ LEFT OVER (or see romaine)
remaind,remind
reman,remain / romaine
remanis,reminisce
remanisent,reminisce(nt)
remantisize,romantic(ize)
remar,ream(er)
remark,*,ked,king,kable,kably,kableness,WORTHY OF COMMENT/ OBSERVATION/ NOTICE "prefixes: un"
remarkuble,remark(able)
rematik,rheumatic
rematy,remedy
rembunctious,rambunctious
rembunkshes,rambunctious
reme,ream
remede,remedy
remediashen,remedy(diation)
remedy,dies,died,dying,diable,diableness,diably,diless, dial,diation,FIX/ IMPROVE DAMAGE, RELIEVE DISORDER "prefixes: ir"
remember,*,red,ring,brance,brancer,ACKNOWLEDGE/ THINK OF/ RECOLLECT THE PAST "prefixes: dis"
remembrinse,remember(ance)
remembur,remember
remenis,reminisce
remenisent,reminisce(nt)
remer,ream(er)
remeshen,remission
remet,remit
remety,remedy
remidal,remit(ttal)
remidy,remedy

remind,*,ded,ding,der,dful,CAUSE TO RECOLLECT/ REMEMBER
remindur,remind(er)
reminis,reminisce
reminisce,*,ed,cing,ent,ently,LONGINGLY REMEMBER/ THINK OF THE PAST
reminisent,reminisce(nt)
reminitur,remind(er)
remir,ream(er)
remishen,remission
remision,remission
remissible,bility,CAN BE FORGIVEN "prefixes: ir"
remission,ABATEMENT, TEMPORARY REDUCTION/ DISAPPEARANCE
remit,*,tted,tting,tment,ttable,tter,ttance,ttent, ttently,ttal,TRANSMIT/ SEND/ GIVE BACK "prefixes: un"
remital,remit(ttal)
remited,remit(tted)
remition,remission
remituble,remit(ttable)
remity,remedy
remnant,*,LEFT OVERS/ REMAINS/ SCRAPS
remnet,remnant
remnint,remnant
remofer,remove(r)
remonis,reminisce
remoof,remove
remooval,remove(val)
remoovil,remove(val)
remorse,eful,efully,efulness,eless, elessly,elessness, PAIN/ GUILT WHEN LOOKING TO SOMETHING IN THE PAST
remorsful,remorse(ful)
remorsless,remorse(ful)
remote,*,ely,eness,REMOVED FROM SOCIAL CENTERS, FAR OFF IN DISTANCE/ TIME
remotly,remote(ly)
remove,*,ed,ving,vable,vability,vableness,vably,val,ver, TAKE AWAY/ ERASE "prefixes: ir"
remudy,remedy
remufe,remove
remufer,remove(r)

remufible, remove(vable)
remufil, remove(val)
remunerashen, remunerate(tion)
remunerate, *, ed, ting, able, ability, tion, tive, tively, PAY FOR LOSS/ REPAY/ COMPENSATE/ REWARD
remuneration, remunerate(tion)
remunirate, remunerate
remuniration, remunerate(tion)
remunis, reminisce
remur, ream(er)
remutoed, rheumatic(toid)
remuty, remedy
remuvable, remove(vable)
remuve, remove
remuvel, remove(val)
remuvul, remove(val)
ren, wren
renagade, renegade
renaisance, renaissance
renaissance, PERIOD OF TIME IN EUROPE
renasons, renaissance
renauserus, rhinoceros
renavashen, renovate(tion)
renavate, renovate
renavation, renovate(tion)
renawserus, rhinoceros
rench, wrench
rendal, rent(al)
render, *, ed, ring, rable, rer, RETURN/ GIVE IN/ SUBMIT/ FURNISH/ SURRENDER/ CAUSE (or see rent(er)
rendezvous, ARRANGE TO MEET, MEET UP WITH
rendur, render
renegade, *, do, ONE WHO DESERTS, A TRAITOR
renege, *, ed, ging, er, TO FAIL/ GO BACK ON WORD, VIOLATE CARD GAME RULE
renegeid, renegade
renevashen, renovate(tion)
renevate, renovate
renevation, renovate(tion)
renew, *, wed, wing, wable, wably, wability, wal, wer, REFRESH/ MAKE LIKE NEW/ REFURBISH/ UPDATE
reng, ring / rink / wring
renger, ring(er) / ranger

renig, renege
renigade, renegade
renigeid, renegade
renik, renege
renisance, renaissance
renissance, renaissance
reniu, renew
renk, ring / rink / wring
renkle, wrinkle
renkul, wrinkle
renlistment, reenlist(ment)
renone, renown
renoserus, rhinoceros
renosirus, rhinoceros
renosonse, renaissance
renounce, *, ed, cing, eable, ement, er, DISOWN/ REJECT/ CAST OFF
renounse, renounce
renounsment, renounce(ment)
renovaded, renovate(d)
renovashen, renovate(tion)
renovate, *, ed, ting, tion, tor, REPAIR TO LIKE NEW CONDITION
renown, ned, ACHIEVEMENTS/ REPUTATION KNOWN FAR AND WIDE
renownse, renounce
renownsment, renounce(ment)
rens, rinse / wren(s) / rent(s)
rensd, rinse(d)
rensur, rinse(r)
rent, *, tal, ted, ting, table, ter, tor, PAY SOMEONE TO BORROW THE USE OF PROPERTY
rentel, rent(al)
renter, render / rent(er)
rentible, rent(able)
rentil, rent(al)
rentuble, rent(able)
rentul, rent(al)
renu, renew
renuable, renew(able)
renuel, renew(al)
renugade, renegade
renuil, renew(al)

renumerate, remunerate
renumeration, remunerate(tion)
renusans, renaissance
renusons, renaissance
renussance, renaissance
renuvadid, renovate(d)
renuvashen, renovate(tion)
renuvate, renovate
renuvation, renovate(tion)
renuzons, renaissance
reol, real / reel / rail / rale
reolistic, real(istic)
reoltee, realty
reoly, realty
reostat, rheostat
rep, rip / ripe / reep
repair, *, red, ring, rer, arable, aration, TO FIX/ RESTORE TO A USABLE CONDITION "prefixes: dis"
repal, rebel / ripple
reparable, ly, bility, ative, ation, ABLE TO BE REPAIRED "prefixes: ir"
reparashen, reparation
reparation, *, ABLE TO BE REPAIRED
reparcushen, repercussion
repare, repair
repareishon, reparation
reparkushen, repercussion
repateshen, repetition
repatishus, repetition(ous)
repatition, repetition
repatitious, repetition(ous)
repd, rip(pped) / reep(ed)
repeal, *, led, ling, lable, TO END/ ABOLISH A LAW (or see repel/ rappel) "prefixes: ir"
repeat, *, ted, ting, ter, tedly, table, tability, TO SAY/ DO/ HAPPEN AGAIN, MORE THAN ONCE "prefixes: un"
reped, rip(pped) / reep(ed)
repedatif, repetitive
repededly, repeat(edly)
repedutif, repetitive
repeel, repeal
repeet, repeat

repel, *, lled, lling, ller, llency, llent, KEEP SOMETHING AWAY/ OFF OF, REJECTS/ RESISTS (or see rappel/ repeal/ ripple)
repelent, repellent
repelinsy, repellent(ncy)
repellent, *, tly, ncy, REJECT/ RESIST, KEEP OFF OF
repellinsy, repellent(ncy)
repense, repent(s)
repent, *, ted, ting, tance, tant, ter, REALIZE/ REMEDY WRONGDOING
repentinse, repent(ance)
reperable, reparable
reperashen, reparation
reperation, reparation
repercushen, repercussion
repercussion, *, ive, THE EFFECTS/ DEVELOPMENT ACHIEVED/ RESULTING FROM AN ACTION
reperkushen, repercussion
reperkution, repercussion
repertoire, *, LIST OF DRAMAS/ PERFORMANCES/ TALENTS/ AVAILABLE RESOURCES
repertor, repertoire
repertwa, repertoire
repertwor, repertoire
repete, repeat
repetedly, repeat(edly)
repetishen, repetition
repetishus, repetition(ous)
repetition, *, ous, ously, ousness, ive, REPEAT/ SAY/ DO SOMETHING OVER AND OVER, ROUTINE
repetitive, ely, eness, ion, REPEAT OVER AND OVER
repetitous, repetition(ous)
repeutashen, reputation
reputation, repute(tation)
reputable, repute(table)
rephund, refund
repil, rebel / ripple
repint, repent
repintense, repent(ance)
repirable, reparable
repirashen, reparation
repiration, reparation
repircushen, repercussion
repirkution, repercussion
repirtoire, repertoire
repirtwor, repertoire
repitishen, repetition
repitishus, repetition(ous)
repitition, repetition
repititious, repetition(ous)
repl, repel / ripple / rebel
replacation, replica(tion)
replace, *, ed, cing, ement, eable, er, PUT SOMETHING IN PLACE OF SOMETHING ELSE "prefixes: ir"
replacment, replace(ment)
replakation, replica(tion)
replasmint, replace(ment)
reple, rebel / ripple
repleca, replica
replecation, replica(tion)
repleka, replica
replekate, replica(te)
replekation, replica(tion)
repleneshment, replenish(ment)
replenish, hes, hed, hing, her, hment, TO RESTOCK/ REFILL
replica, *, ate, ated, ating, ation, MAKE AN EXACT COPY OF
replikate, replica(te)
replucation, replica(tion)
repluka, replica
replukate, replica(te)
replukation, replica(tion)
reply, lies, lied, lying, lier, TO ANSWER BACK/ RESPOND
repoflavin, riboflavin
repoire, rapport
repol, rebel / ripple
repor, rapport
reporashen, reparation
reporation, reparation
reporder, report(er)
reporkushen, repercussion
report, *, ted, tedly, ting, ter, table, tage, torial, torially, GIVE ACCOUNT OF AN EVENT/ OCCURRENCE "prefixes: mis/ under"
repository, ries, A PLACE/ SHELTER/ DWELLING WHICH STORES/ PRESERVES
reposutory, repository
repoteshen, repetition
repour, rapport
repozitory, repository
reprable, reparable
repraduction, reproduce(ction)
repradukshen, reproduce(ction)
repraduse, reproduce
reprahensible, reprehensible
repramand, reprimand
reprasent, represent
reprazintation, represent(ation)
repreble, reparable
repreduction, reproduce(ction)
reprehensible, bility, bly, UNACCEPTABLE/ TO BE CENSURED, SUPPORTIVE/ IMPORTANT "prefixes: ir"
reprehinsible, reprehensible
repremand, reprimand
represent, *, ted, ting, table, ter, tation, tational, tative, tatively, tativeness, TO ACT ON BEHALF OF SOMEONE/ SOMETHING ELSE "prefixes: mis/ under"
represhin, repress(ion)
represif, repress(ive)
represion, repress(ion)
represive, repress(ive)
repress, sses, ssed, ssing, ssion, sser, PREVENT/ SUPPRESS/ BLOCK NATURAL EXPRESSION (or see oppress) "prefixes: de/ ir"
represuve, repress(ive)
reprible, reparable
reprimand, *, ded, ding, TO BE REPRESSED/ REPROVED/ FORMALLY REBUKED
reprisent, represent
reprkushen, repercussion
reproach, hes, hed, hing, hingly, hable, hableness, hably, her, BLAMED/ CRITICIZED FOR WRONGDOING "prefixes: ir"
reproch, reproach
reprochuble, reproach(able)
reproduce, *, ed, cing, cible, cibility, er, ction, ctive, ctively, ctiveness, PRODUCE ANEW, DUPLICATE/ REPEAT/ REMEMBER "prefixes: ir"
reprodukshen, reproduce(ction)
reproduse, reproduce

repruble, reparable
reproduction, reproduce(ction)
reprudukshen, reproduce(ction)
reprumand, reprimand
reprusent, represent
repruzentation, represent(ation)
rept, reap(ed) / rip(pped) / reep(ed)
reptail, reptile
reptayol, reptile
repteleun, reptile(lian)
reptile, *, lian, COLD BLOODED VERTEBRATE
reptilein, reptile(lian)
reptishus, repetition(ous)
republek, republic
republekin, republic(an)
republic, *, can, A TYPE OF POLITICAL SYSTEM "prefixes: pre"
republikan, republic(an)
repugnant, tly, nce, ncy, STRONG OPPOSITION/ DISLIKE/ AVERSION
repugnense, repugnant(nce)
repugnent, repugnant
repul, ripple / rebel
repuld, ripple(d)
repulse, *, ed, sing, sion, sive, sively, siveness, REPEL/ AVERT/ REBUFF/ FORBID
repulshen, repulse(sion)
repulsif, repulse(sive)
repult, ripple(d)
repurable, reparable
repurashen, reparation
repuration, reparation
repurcushen, repercussion
repurkution, repercussion
repurtoire, repertoire
repurtwa, repertoire
repurtwor, repertoire
reputashen, repute(tation)
repute, ed, edly, table, tably, tability, tation, TYPE OF CHARACTER "prefixes: dis"
reputeshen, repetition
reputishus, repetition(ous)
reputition, repetition

reputitious, repetition(ous)
reqrute, recruit
request, *, ted, ting, ASK/ PETITION/ SOLICIT FOR
require, *, ed, ring, ement, ESSENTIAL/ NECESSARY
requisite, *, ely, eness, REQUIRED/ NECESSARY "prefixes: de/ pre"
requisition, *, ned, ning, nary, REQUEST TO OBTAIN, FORMAL DEMAND "prefixes: de"
requite, *, ed, ting, table, tably, tal, ement, er, ASK/ PETITION/ SOLICIT FOR "prefixes: un"
requpe, recoup
reqwasit, requisite
reqwest, request
reqwire, require
reqwirement, require(ment)
rer, rear / rare
rerd, rear(ed)
rere, weary
reridy, rare(rity)
rerity, rare(rity)
resadenshul, reside(ntial)
resadensy, reside(ncy)
resadential, reside(ntial)
resadinshul, reside(ntial)
resadinsy, reside(ncy)
resadue, residue
resal, wrestle
resalushen, resolute(tion)
resan, reason / resin / rise(n)
resanate, resonate / resinate
resandly, recent(ly)
resanense, resonance
resanent, resonance(nt)
resaninse, resonance
resanuble, reason(able)
resape, recipe
resarektion, resurrect(ion)
resatashen, recite(tion)
resauluble, resoluble
rescue, *, ed, uing, er, SAVE/ SPARE FROM DANGER/ HARM
resdrane, restrain

research, hes, hed, hing, her, TO STUDY/ OBSERVE/ DERIVE FROM FACTS
resebshen, reception
resebshinist, receptionist
resebter, receptor
resebtif, receptive
resebtive, receptive
resede, recede
reseded, recede(d)
resedenshul, reside(ntial)
resedential, reside(ntial)
resedinse, reside(ncy)
resedue, residue
reseed, recede
reseef, receive
reseet, receipt
reseeve, receive
resefe, receive
resefuble, receive(vable)
resegnation, resign(ation)
reselute, resolute
resemble, *, ed, ling, lance, SIMILAR/ LIKENESS
resemblinse, resemble(lance)
resen, reason / resin / rise(n)
resenate, resonate / resinate
resenation, resonate(tion)
resenator, resonate(tor)
resendly, recent(ly)
reseninse, resonance
resent, *, ted, ting, tful, tfully, tfulness, tment, FEEL SORRY FOR ONESELF, DOESN'T FEEL APPRECIATED FOR A DEED DONE (or see recent)
resenuble, reason(able)
resepdekle, receptacle
resepe, recipe
resepeunt, recipient
reseprocal, reciprocal
reseprocation, reciprocate(tion)
reseprokashen, reciprocate(tion)
resepshen, reception
resepshenist, receptionist
resepshun, reception
reseptacle, receptacle

resepticle, receptacle
reseptif, receptive
reseption, reception
reseptionest, receptionist
reseptive, receptive
reseptor, receptor
reseptukle, receptacle
reserch, research
reserect, resurrect
reserection, resurrect(ion)
reserf, reserve
reserfd, reserve(d)
reserginse, resurge(nce)
resergint, resurgent
reservation, *, nist, RESERVE SOMETHING, KEEP BACK/ WITHHOLD, TERRITORY MANAGED BY NATIVE TRIBES
reserve, *, ed, ving, edly, edness, vist, vation, HAVE EXTRA/ SPARE/ STORED UP "prefixes: un"
reservoir, *, WHERE WATER IS COLLECTED/ STORED
reservor, reservoir
reses, recess
reseshun, recess(ion)
resesif, recess(ive)
resesion, recess(ion)
resesive, recess(ive)
resession, recess(ion)
reset, receipt
resetion, recess(ion)
reseve, receive
resevuble, receive(vable)
reside, *, ed, ding, er, ence, ency, encies, ent, ential, entially, entiary, entiaries, PLACE/ AREA WHERE PEOPLE DWELL/ LIVE/ OCCUPY "prefixes: non"
residenshul, reside(ntial)
residensy, reside(ncy)
residinsy, reside(ncy)
residue, *, ual, ually, uary, WHAT'S LEFT OVER/ REMAINING AFTER A SEPARATION PROCESS
residuel, residue(ual)
resign, *, ned, ning, nation, nedness, ner, GIVE UP/ RELINQUISH A POSITION/ AUTHORITY
resignashin, resign(ation)

resikle, recycle
resil, wrestle
resiliensy, resilient(ncy)
resilient, tly, nce, ncy, ABILITY TO SPRING BACK/ BE FLEXIBLE/ ELASTIC
resilute, resolute
resimblanse, resemble(lance)
resimble, resemble
resin, *, nous, nate, ORGANIC/ INORGANIC CHEMICAL USED FOR VARNISH/ PLASTIC/ MANY USES (or see reason/ rise(n))
resinate, *, ed, ting, TO IMMERSE IN RESIN (or see resonate)
resination, resonate(tion)
resinator, resonate(tor)
resindly, recent(ly)
resinense, resonance
resinent, resonance(nt)
resint, recent
resintly, recent(ly)
resinuble, reason(able)
resipe, recipe
resipeant, recipient
resipeint, recipient
resipient, recipient
resiprekul, reciprocal
resiprocal, reciprocal
resiprocation, reciprocate(tion)
resiprokashen, reciprocate(tion)
resiprokate, reciprocate
resirch, research
resirect, resurrect
resirection, resurrect(ion)
resirf, reserve
resirgense, resurge(nce)
resirgent, resurgent
resirgint, resurgent
resirvation, reservation
resirvd, reserve(d)
resirve, reserve
resirvist, reserve(vist)
resirvor, reservoir

resist, *, ted, ting, tance, tant, ter, tible, tibility, tibly, tive, tively, tivity, tless, tor, DEFEND/ PROTECT AGAINST "prefixes: ir"
resitashen, recite(tion)
resitation, recite(tion)
resite, recite
resitle, recite(tal)
resitul, recite(tal)
resk, risk
resked, risk(ed)
reskeu, rescue
reskiu, rescue
reskt, risk(ed)
resku, rescue
reskud, rescue(d)
resl, wrestle
resnibul, reason(able)
resnuble, reason(able)
resodo, risotto
resol, wrestle
resoluble, bility, eness, CAN BE SOLVED/ RESOLVED, DISSOLVED TWICE "prefixes: ir"
resolushin, resolute(tion)
resolute, *, ely, eness, tion, HAVING FIRM RESOLVE/ DETERMINATION, FIXED PURPOSE/ DECISION "prefixes: ir"
resolve, *, ed, ving, vable, er, ent, FINAL DETERMINATION/ SETTLEMENT "prefixes: ir/ un"
resolvuble, resolve(vable)
reson, reason / resin / rise(n)
resonance, nt, ntly, A SYMPATHETIC VIBRATION/ SYNCHRONIZED WAVES
resonate, *, ed, ting, tion, tor, RESOUND/ ECHO/ EXTENDED EFFECT/ BE FAMILIAR (or see resinate)
resondly, recent(ly)
resonense, resonance
resonent, resonance(nt)
resoninse, resonance
resontly, recent(ly)
resope, recipe
resorse, resource
resorsful, resource(ful)

resort, *, ted, ting, ter, RECOURSE/ REVERBERATE, PLACE TO RELAX, FALL BACK ON
resorvor, reservoir
resoto, risotto
resotto, risotto
resource, *, eful, efully, efulness, AVAILABLE MEANS/ MEASURE/ PROPERTY/ SOURCES
resparater, respiration(tor)
respect, *, ted, ting, tful, tfully, tfulness, ter, table, tably, tableness, tability, tabilities, tive, tively, tiveness, TO HONOR/ PAY TRIBUTE/ RELATE/ REGARD/ HOLD IN HIGH ESTEEM "prefixes: dis/ ir"
respectif, respect(ive)
respektful, respect(ful)
respektif, respect(ive)
resperashen, respiration
resperater, respiration(tor)
resperation, respiration
respirashen, respiration
respirater, respiration(tor)
respiration, nal, tor, tory, INHALE/ EXHALE OF THE BREATH IN PLANTS/ ANIMALS
respite, REST/ RELIEF FROM LABOR/ SUFFERING/ FEAR
respond, *, ded, ding, dent, der, ANSWER/ REPLY/ CORRESPOND
respondint, respond(ent)
response, *, sible, sibility, sibilities, sibleness, sibly, sive, sively, siveness, ANSWER/ REPLY/ CORRESPOND "prefixes: ir/ non/ un"
responsef, response(sive)
responsive, response(sive)
responsuble, response(sible)
respont, respond
respurashen, respiration
respurater, respiration(tor)
respuration, respiration
resque, rescue
resrektion, resurrect(ion)
rest, *, ted, ting, tful, tfully, tfulness, TIME/ TRANQUILITY/ PEACE BETWEEN MOMENTS OF MENTAL/ PHYSICAL EXERTION (or see wrest/ wrist) "prefixes: un"
restaraunt, restaurant
restaront, restaurant

restatushen, restitution
restatution, restitution
restatutive, restitution(ive)
restaurant, *, A PUBLIC EATERY
resterashen, restore(ration)
resteration, restore(ration)
restetushen, restitution
restetution, restitutions
restfuly, rest(fully)
restid, rest(ed) / wrest(ed)
restirashen, restore(ration)
restiration, restore(ration)
restitushen, restitution
restitution, *, tive, itory, COMPENSATING/ GIVING BACK FOR A LOSS
restorant, restaurant
restorashen, restore(ration)
restoraunt, restaurant
restore, *, ed, ring, er, ration, rative, REFURBISH/ REFINISH BACK TO NEAR ORIGINAL
restrain, *, ned, ning, nt, nable, STOP/ CONTROL SOMETHING/ SOMEONE FROM DOING SOMETHING "prefixes: un"
restrane, restrain
restrant, restaurant / restrain(t)
restrein, restrain
restrektif, restrict(ive)
restrict, *, ted, ting, tion, tive, tively, tiveness, CONTROL/ LIMIT THE FLOW OF "prefixes: de/ un"
restrikshen, restrict(ion)
restrikt, restrict
restriktion, restrict(ion)
restriktive, restrict(ive)
restront, restaurant
resturashen, restore(ration)
resturation, restore(ration)
restutushen, restitution
restutution, restitution
resucitate, resuscitate
resudenshul, reside(ntial)
resudensy, reside(ncy)
resudent, reside(nt)
resudential, reside(ntial)

resudinshul, reside(ntial)
resudinsy, reside(ncy)
resdue, residue
resugnashin, resign(ation)
resugnation, resign(ation)
resul, wrestle
result, *, ted, ting, tant, THE OUTCOME/ REACTION/ CONDITION OF AN ACTION
resulushin, resolute(tion)
resulute, resolute
resuma, resume
resume, *, ed, ming, mable, CONTINUE/ CARRY ON, SUMMARY OF SOMEONE'S WORK HISTORY
resun, reason / resin / rise(n)
resunate, resonate / resinate
resunation, resonate(tion)
resunator, resonate(tor)
resundly, recent(ly)
resunense, resonance
resunent, resonance(nt)
resuninse, resonance
resuntly, recent(ly)
resunuble, reason(able)
resupe, recipe
resurch, research
resurect, resurrect
resurection, resurrect(ion)
resurfs, reserve(s)
resurge, *, ed, ging, ent, ence, RISE UP/ STRENGTHEN AGAIN
resurgense, resurge(nce)
resurgent, *, nce, RISE UP/ STRENGTHEN AGAIN
resurginse, resurge(nce)
resurgint, resurgent
resurrect, *, ted, ting, tion, tional, tionist, tionism, RAISE FROM THE DEAD, TO REINSTATE/ RESTORE
resurvd, reserve(d)
resurve, reserve
resurvor, reservoir
resusatashen, resuscitate(tion)
resusatator, resuscitate(tor)
resuscitate, *, ed, ting, tion, tive, tor, RESTORE LIFE TO BREATHING AGAIN

resusitate,resuscitate
resusitator,resuscitate(tor)
resycle,recycle
ret,red / read
retabul,read(able)
retail,*,led,ling,ler,SALE OF GOODS IN SMALL QUANTITIES TO CONSUMERS
retain,*,ned,ning,ner,nable,nability,nmert,TO CONTINUE/ HOLD/ KEEP IN POSESSION
retal,retail
retaleashen,retaliate(tion)
retaleate,retaliate
retaleation,retaliate(tion)
retaler,retail(er)
retaliate,*,ed,ting,tion,TO RETURN A PUNISHMENT, DELIBERATE HARM IN REVENGE
retan,retain
retaner,retain(er)
retanse,rid(ddance)
retard,*,ded,ding,dant,cation,dative,date,der, DEVELOPMENT/ GROWTH IS SLOWED DOWN/ CURBED/ DELAYED
retardashen,retard(ation)
retardat,retard(ate)
retardint,retard(ant)
retardir,retard(er)
retardunt,retard(ant)
retaric,rhetoric
retasense,reticent(nce)
retasent,reticent
retashin,rotate(tion)
retasint,reticent
retch,rich / wretch
reted,ready(died) / read
retee,ready
retenshun,retention
retentif,retentive
retention,ive,ivity,ABLE TO HOLD/ MAINTAIN/ REMEMBER
retentive,vity,vities,ABLE TO HOLD/ MAINTAIN/ REMEMBER
reter,red(dder) / read(er)
retern,return

reternd,return(ed)
reth,wreath / wreathe
rethem,rhythm
rethum,rhythm
reti,ready
reticent,tly,nce,RESERVED/ APPREHENSIVE IN SPEAKING FREELY
reticint,reticent
retina,*,al,nitis,ASSOCIATED WITH THE EYE
retinse,rid(ddance)
retinshun,retention
retintion,retention
retir,read(er) / retire
retire,*,ed,ring,ringly,ringness,rement,REMOVE/ RETREAT/ WITHDRAW FROM SOME FORM OF ACTIVITY/ CIRCULATION/ WORK "prefixes: semi"
retirec,rhetoric
retirment,retire(ment)
retirn,return
retirndt,return(ed)
retisense,reticent(nce)
retisent,reticent
retisint,reticent
retna,retina
retnu,retina
retor,read(er)
retorec,rhetoric
retoric,rhetoric
retorical,rhetoric(al)
retract,*,ted,ting,tion,tability,table,tation,tile,tive, WITHDRAW/ REMOVE/ TAKE BACK "prefixes: un"
retraction,retract(ion)
retrad,retread
retrakshen,retract(ion)
retrakted,retract(ed)
retread,*,ded,ding,RESURFACE/ RECAP/ GO OVER AGAIN
retreat,*,ted,ting,ter,tal,tive,tful,tant,tism,tist, WITHDRAW/ FALL BACK/ REFUGE/ ASYLUM/ DO AGAIN
retred,retread
retreded,retreat(ed)
retredid,retread(ed)

retrefe,retrieve
retrefer,retrieve(r)
retreful,retrieve(val)
retret,retreat
retreted,retreat(ed)
retrevul,retrieve(val)
retrevur,retrieve(r)
retrieve,*,ed,ving,val,er,RESTORE/ REMEDY/ SAVE/ GET SOMETHING BACK,A TYPE OF DOG "prefixes: ir"
retrive,retrieve
retro,PREFIX INDICATING "BACKWARDS" MOST OFTEN MODIFIES THE WORD
retroactif,retroactive
retroactive,ely,BACK TO SOME POINT IN THE PAST
retroaktif,retroactive
retroaktive,retroactive
retrograde,*,ed,ding,dation,ely,MOVING CONTRARY/ BACKWARDS/ REVERSE/ INVERSE
retrogratashen,retrograde(dation)
retrogreat,retrograde
retrosbekt,retrospect
retrospect,tion,tive,tives,tively,RECOLLECTION/ REVIEW OF THE PAST
retrospekt,retrospect
retrospektion,retrospect(ion)
retsee,ritzy
retsy,ritzy
retual,ritual
retubil,read(able)
retuble,read(able)
retul,riddle
retur,red(dder) / read(er)
returec,rhetoric
returic,rhetoric
return,*,ned,ning,ner,nable,GO BACK TO THE PLACE OF THE ORIGINATION/ BEGINNING/ MOMENT
returndt,return(ed)
retusense,reticent(nce)
retusent,reticent
retusint,reticent
rety,ready
retzy,ritzy
reuiuleit,regulate

reul, real / reel
reuldee, realty
reuldy, realty
reulestic, real(istic)
reulistic, real(istic)
reulty, realty
reum, realm
reunacment, reenact(ment)
reunactment, reenact(ment)
reunakt, reenact
reunaktment, reenact(ment)
reunforse, reinforce
reunforsment, reinforce(ment)
reunion, *, GATHERING, COMING TOGETHER
reunyun, reunion
reustat, rheostat
reval, revel
revalation, revelation
revalee, reveille
revaleishon, revelation
revaler, revel(er)
revalushen, revelation
revalution, revolution
revalutioniz, revolution(ize)
revalve, revolve
revaly, reveille
revar, river
revarent, reverent
reveal, *, led, ling, ler, lingly, EXPOSE/ MAKE KNOWN/ UNCOVER, BE FRANK (or see revel)
reveelt, reveal(ed)
reveer, revere
reveille, *, MILITARY WAKE-UP CALL/ SIGNAL
revejen, revise(sion)
revel, *, led, ling, ler, PLEASURE/ ENJOYMENT IN SOMETHING (or see reveal/ reveille)
revelashen, revelation
revelation, *, nal, tory, SUDDEN REALIZATION/ UNDERSTANDING OF VALUABLE/ SURPRISING INFORMATION
reveld, revel(lled) / reveal(ed)
revelee, reveille
revelir, revel(er)

revelushen, revolution
revelutioniz, revolution(ize)
revely, reveille
revench, revenge
revene, ravine / raven
revenge, eful, efully, er, BE RETALIATORY/ HARMFUL WITH INTENT
revengful, revenge(ful)
rever, revere / river
reverberate, *, ed, ting, ant, tion, tive, tor, AN ECHO, REFLECTION OF WAVES OFF A SURFACE
reverbirate, reverberate
revere, *, ed, ring, DEEPLY ADMIRE/ RESPECT SOMEONE
reverent, tly, nce, tial, tially, EXPRESS AWE/ RESPECT "prefixes: ir"
reverse, *, ed, sing, sal, sely, er, sible, sibly, sibility, CHANGE TO OPPOSITE, INSIDE OUT/ BACKWARD "prefixes: ir"
reversuble, reverse(sible)
revert, *, ted, ting, ter, tible, GO BACK TO PREVIOUS/ FORMER/ ORIGINAL
reveshen, revise(sion)
revesion, revise(sion)
revew, review / revue
review, *, wed, wing, wable, wer, EXAMINE/ INSPECT/ CRITIQUE/ SURVEY/ ASSESS (or see revue)
revigen, revise(sion)
revil, revel / reveal
revilashen, revelation
reviliation, revelation
revild, revel(lled)
revilee, reveille
reviler, revel(er)
revilushen, revolution
revilutioniz, revolution(ize)
revily, reveille
revinch, revenge
revine, ravine
revingful, revenge(ful)
revir, river
revirberate, reverberate
revirent, reverent
revirse, reverse
revirsuble, reverse(sible)

revirt, revert
revise, *, ed, sing, sion, sable, er, sory, ADJUST/ UPDATE/ ALTER/ IMPROVE UPON
revishen, revise(sion)
revision, revise(sion)
revival, *, RENEWAL/ RECOVERY/ REESTABLISHMENT OF FLOURISH/ VIGOROUS AGAIN
revive, *, ed, ving, vable, er, val, BECOME CONSCIOUS/ REVIVLE, REVIVAL
revivle, revival
revivuble, revive(vable)
revlashen, revelation
revocable, ly, bility, ABILITY TO BE CANCELLED/ CALLED BACK IN "prefixes: ir"
revokability, revocable(bility)
revokable, revocable
revoke, *, ed, king, er, ocable, MAKE NULL AND VOID, CANCEL, SUMMON SOMEONE/ SOMETHING BACK
revol, revel
revolashen, revelation
revolation, revelation
revold, revolt / revel(lled)
revolee, reveille
revolfe, revolve
revolt, *, ted, ting, REBEL/ DEFY AUTHORITY, REPULSED
revoltid, revolt(ed)
revolution, *, nary, naries, nize, nizes, nized, nizing, nism, nist, nists, REBEL/ DEFY POWERS THAT BE, OF CIRCULAR SHAPE/ MOTION
revolve, *, ed, ving, er, vable, RECURRING CIRCULAR MOVEMENT, A TYPE OF GUN
revorent, reverent
revue, *, MUSICAL EVENT (or see review)
revul, revel
revulashen, revelation
revulation, revelation
revuled, revel(lled)
revulee, reveille
revuler, revel(er)
revulushen, revolution
revulutioniz, revolution(ize)
revuly, reveille
revur, river
revurbarate, reverberate

revurent,reverent
revurse,reverse
revursuble,reverse(sible)
revurt,revert
rew,rue / roux
reward,*,ded,ding,SOMETHING RECEIVED FOR HAVING DONE SOMETHING COMMENDABLE
rewbe,ruby
rewd,rude
rewdest,rude(st)
rewf,roof
rewge,rouge
rewje,rouge
rewl,rule
rewlet,roulette
rewm,room
rewmer,rumor
rewmur,rumor
reword,reward
rewral,rural
rewralee,rural(lly)
rewrul,rural
rewrulee,rural(lly)
rewsdir,rooster
rewsdur,rooster
rewse,ruse
rewstur,rooster
rewt,route / root / rude
rewteen,routine
rewthles,ruthless
rewtlee,rude(ly)
rey,ray
reyd,raid
reydiol,radial
reyewnyin,reunion
reyon,rayon
reyshal,racial
reyunyon,reunion
reyven,raven / ravine
reyzor,razor
rezadenshul,reside(ntial)
rezadensy,reside(ncy)
rezadinsy,reside(ncy)

rezadue,residue
rezalushen,resolute(tion)
rezalute,resolute
rezalution,resolute(tion)
rezan,reason / resin / rise(n)
rezand,recent
rezandly,recent(ly)
rezanense,resonance
rezanent,resonance(nt)
rezant,recent
rezanuble,reason(able)
rezarection,resurrect(ion)
rezarektion,resurrect(ion)
rezedue,residue
rezegnation,resign(ation)
rezelute,resolute
rezen,reason / resin / rise(n)
rezenate,resinate/ resonate
rezenator,resonate(tor)
rezend,recent
rezendly,recent(ly)
rezent,recent / resent
rezenuble,reason(able)
rezerect,resurrect
rezerf,reserve
rezervation,reservation
rezervor,reservoir
rezide,reside
rezidensy,reside(ncy)
rezidinsy,reside(ncy)
rezidual,residue(ual)
rezidue,residue
rezignashin,resign(ation)
rezilute,resolute
rezin,reason / resin / rise(n)
rezinate,resonate / resinate
rezinator,resonate(tor)
rezind,recent
rezindly,recent(ly)
rezine,resign
rezint,resonance(nt)
rezint,recent / resent
rezinuble,reason(able)

rezirect,resurrect
rezirvation,reservation
rezirvor,reservoir
rezist,resist
rezistense,resist(ance)
rezistent,resist(ant)
rezistif,resist(ive)
rezistor,resist(or)
reznuble,reason(able)
rezodo,risotto
rezolushin,resolute(tion)
rezolute,resolute
rezolve,resolve
rezom,resume
rezon,reason / resin / rise(n)
rezonate,resonate / resinate
rezondly,recent(ly)
rezonense,resonance
rezontle,recent(ly)
rezoom,resume
rezort,resort
rezorvor,reservoir
rezoto,risotto
rezrekshen,resurrect(ion)
rezt,rest / wrist / wrest
rezudensy,reside(ncy)
rezudinsy,reside(ncy)
rezudue,residue
rezult,result
rezultent,result(ant)
rezultunt,result(ant)
rezulushen,resolute(tion)
rezulute,resolute
rezulution,resolute(tion)
rezume,resume
rezun,reason / resin / rise(n)
rezunate,resonate / resinate
rezunation,resonate(tion)
rezund,recent
rezundly,recent(ly)
rezunense,resonance
rezunent,resonance(nt)
rezunt,recent

rezunuble,reason(able)
rezurect,resurrect
rezurection,resurrect(ion)
rezurekshen,resurrect(ion)
rezurf,reserve
rezurve,reserve
rezurvor,reservoir
rezuvor,reservoir
rhain,rain / reign / rein
rhanoceros,rhinoceros
rhanosirus,rhinoceros
rhapsady,rhapsody
rhapsedy,rhapsody
rhapsody,dies,IRREGULAR/ INTENSE IMPROVISATION IN REGARD TO MUSIC/ EXPRESSION/ LITERATURE
rhapsuty,rhapsody
rhatorecal,rhetoric(al)
rhatorical,rhetoric(al)
rhedaric,rhetoric
rheduric,rhetoric
rhein,rain / reign / rein
rheindeer,reindeer
rhen,rain / reign / rein
rhenoceros,rhinoceros
rhenosirus,rhinoceros
rheostat,*,tic,ELECTRONIC DEVICE
rhetarec,rhetoric
rheteric,rhetoric
rhethm,rhythm
rhethym,rhythm
rhetoric,*,cal,cally,THE ART OF SPEAKING/ WRITING EFFECTIVELY/ PERSUASIVELY
rheturec,rhetoric
rheumatic,*,ism,toid,toidal,ASSOCIATED WITH STIFF JOINTS/ MUSCLES IN THE BODY
rhime,rhyme
rhinasurus,rhinoceros
rhinauserus,rhinoceros
rhinestone,*,FAKE GEMS
rhino,*,SHORT FOR RHINOCEROS
rhinoceros,ses,A MAMMAL/ ANIMAL
rhinosurus,rhinoceros
rhinstone,rhinestone

rhisome,rhizome
rhithm,rhythm
rhithum,rhythm
rhitorecal,rhetoric(al)
rhitorical,rhetoric(al)
rhiz,PREFIX INDICATING "ROOT" MOST OFTEN MODIFIES THE WORD
rhizome,*,TYPE OF PLANT ROOT
rhod,PREFIX INDICATING "RED" MOST OFTEN MODIFIES THE WORD
rhodadendron,rhododendron
rhodidendron,rhododendron
rhodo,PREFIX INDICATING "RED" MOST OFTEN MODIFIES THE WORD
rhododendron,*,rum,CAN BE SPELLED EITHER WAY, FLOWERING PLANT/ BUSH
rhodudindron,rhododendron
rhotorecal,rhetoric(al)
rhotorical,rhetoric(al)
rhubarb,AN EDIBLE PLANT
rhunoceros,rhinoceros
rhunosirus,rhinoceros
rhutorecal,rhetoric(al)
rhutorical,rhetoric(al)
rhyme,*,ed,ming,er,PUT WORDS TOGETHER IN SPEECH WHICH SOUND LIKE EACH OTHER
rhysome,rhizome
rhythm,*,mic,mical,mically,REPETITIOUS BEAT/ FREQUENCY/ PATTERN "prefixes: bio"
rhyzome,rhizome
ri,rye / wry
riact,react
rial,real / rile
rib,*,bbed,bbing,BONES IN TORSO
ribaflavin,riboflavin
riban,ribbon
ribaund,rebound
ribbin,ribbon
ribbon,*,ny,THIN STRIP OF SOMETHING, A DECORATION USED AS AN AWARD
ribbun,ribbon
ribeled,rebel(lled)
ribeleon,rebel(llion)
ribeleus,rebel(llious)

riben,ribbon
ribin,ribbon
riblase,replace
riblie,reply
ribodek,robot(ic)
ribof,rebuff
riboflavin,*,A CHEMICAL COMPOUND/ VITAMIN
ribon,ribbon / rib(bbing)
ribt,rib(bbed) / rip(pped)
ribun,ribbon / rib(bbing)
ribut,rebut / reboot
ributle,rebut(ttal)
ric,reek / rice
ricachet,ricochet
ricant,recant
ricap,recap
ricashay,ricochet
rice,A GRAIN (or see rise)
ricebder,receptor
ricebdif,receptive
riced,recede
ricent,recent
ricepter,receptor
ricerch,research
rices,recess
rich,hes,her,hest,hly,hness,ABUNDANT/ FERTILE/ PRODUCTIVE (or see reach/ ridge/ wretch) "prefixes: en"
richas,right(eous) / rich(es)
richecshen,reject(ion)
richect,reject
riched,rigid
richem,regime
riches,right(eous) / rich(es)
richewul,ritual
richid,rigid
richoal,ritual
richon,region
richos,right(eous) / rich(es)
richuol,ritual
richus,right(eous) / rich(es)

ricid,reside / recede
ricipient,recipient
ricis,recess
ricit,receipt / recite
riciv,receive
rickets,VITAMIN DEFICIENCY DISEASE
rickety,UNSTABLE CONDITION
rickidy,rickety
rickits,rickets
rickity,rickety
rickliner,recline(r)
rickonusinse,reconnaissance
riclain,recline
ricleim,reclaim / reclame
ricleimabol,reclaimable
riclusion,recluse(sion)
ricochet,*,ted,ting,THE ACTION OF REBOUNDING/ BOUNCING OFF AN OBJECT
ricoil,recoil
ricomben,recumbent
riconisans,reconnaissance
riconsile,reconcile
riconstitushen,reconstitute(tion)
riconstitute,reconstitute
ricord,record
ricors,recourse
ricoshay,ricochet
ricover,recover
ricrut,recruit
ricuayer,require
ricuest,request
ricumbent,recumbent
ricup,recoop
ricuperate,recuperate
ricushay,ricochet
rid,*,dded,dding,ddance,BE DISPOSED OF/ DONE AWAY WITH (or see ride/ red/ read/ reed/ right)
ridakeul,ridicule
ridakule,ridicule
ridal,riddle
ridanse,rid(ddance)
ridar,ride(r) / write(r)
ridch,ridge

riddle,*,ed,ling,er,PUZZLE OF WORDS "prefixes: un"
ride,*,ding,rode,er,BE CARRIED/ MOVED ALONG IN/ ON SOMETHING (or see write/ right) "prefixes: over"
ridecule,ridicule
rideculus,ridiculous
rideemible,redeem(able)
ridekule,ridicule
ridekulus,ridiculous
ridem,redeem
ridempshun,redemption
ridemtion,redemption
ridemuble,redeem(able)
ridense,rid(ddance)
ridents,rid(ddance)
rider,ride(r) / write(r) / retire
ridge,*,ed,RAISED AREA
ridicule,*,ed,ling,er,lous,TO MAKE FUN OF
ridiculous,sly,sness,NOT POSSIBLE/ ACCEPTABLE
ridikule,ridicule
ridikulus,ridiculous
ridim,redeem
ridinse,rid(ddance)
ridle,riddle
ridol,riddle
ridondent,redundant
ridoose,reduce
ridu,redo
riduction,reduce(ction)
ridukeul,ridicule
ridukshen,reduce(ction)
riduktion,reduce(ction)
ridul,riddle
ridundensy,redundant(ncy)
ridundent,redundant
ridundinsy,redundant(ncy)
ridundint,redundant
ridus,reduce
ridusable,reduce(cible)
rie,rye / wry
riel,rile
riemburs,reimburse
rienact,reenact
rienlist,reenlist

riestat,rheostat
riet,riot
rieterate,reiterate
rif,reef / rift
rifal,rifle
rifar,river / refer
rifeel,reveal
rifeelt,reveal(ed)
rifel,rival / rifle
rifenge,revenge
rifenje,revenge
rifer,river / refer
riferbishment,refurbish(ment)
riferse,reverse
rifeusil,refuse(sal)
rifewsel,refuse(sal)
rififul,revival
rifil,rival / rifle
rifin,refine
rifinable,refine(nable)
rifine,refine
rifinery,refine(ry)
rifinje,revenge
rifinment,refine(ment)
rifinury,refine(ry)
rifius,refuse
rifle,*,ed,ling,A GUN,SWIFTLY GO THROUGH,LOOK THROUGH STUFF TO STEAL "prefixes: un"
riflecs,reflect(s) / reflex
riflect,reflect
riflection,reflect(ion)
rifletive,reflect(ive)
riflector,reflect(or)
riflekshen,reflect(ion)
riflekt,reflect
riflektif,reflect(ive)
riflektor,reflect(or)
rifletive,reflect(ive)
rifol,rifle
rifond,refund
rifor,river / refer
riformitory,reform(atory)
rifract,refract

rifractory, refract(ory)
rifrain, refrain
rifrakt, refract
rifraktory, refract(ory)
rifrane, refrain
rifrein, refrain
rifresh, refresh
rifresher, refresh(er)
rifreshment, refresh(ment)
rifrigerator, refrigerate(tor)
rift, *, ted, ting, SLOWLY SPREAD APART, GROWING CHASM
riful, rival / rifle
rifur, river / refer
rifural, refer(rral)
rifurbishment, refurbish(ment)
rifurse, reverse
rifusel, refuse(sal)
rig, *, gged, gging, gger, ASSEMBLE DEVICES TOGETHER (or see ridge)
rigal, wriggle / regal
rigaledy, regal(ity)
rigalia, regal(ia)
rigality, regal(ity)
rigard, regard
rigardless, regard(less)
rige, ridge
rigect, reject
riged, rigid
rigekshen, reject(ion)
rigekt, reject
rigektion, reject(ion)
riger, rigor
riget, rigid
right, *, ted, ting, table, ter, tness, teous, teously, teousness, tful, tfulness, tism, tist, tly, ty, BE CORRECT, SPECIFIC DIRECTION/ ORIENTATION, OTHER SIDE OF LEFT (or see rite/ write/ wright/ writ) "prefixes: un/ up"
rigid, dly, dness, dity, dizer, dify, ification, STIFF/ UNYIELDING "prefixes: semi"
rigirs, rigor(s)
rigit, rigid

rigle, wriggle
rigol, wriggle
rigor, *, rous, rously, rousness, CONDITIONS INVOLVING HARDSHIP/ SEVERITY/ TOUGH DEMANDS
rigres, rigor(ous) / regress
rigreshen, regress(ssion)
rigresif, regress(ive)
rigresive, regress(ive)
rigress, regress
rigret, regret
rigreted, regret(tted)
rigretful, regret(ful)
rigretfuly, regret(fully)
rigrus, rigor(ous)
rigul, wriggle
rigurchiteit, regurgitate
rigurlliteit, regurgitate
rigurs, rigor(s)
rigurus, rigor(ous)
rij, ridge
rijab, rehab
rijabiliteit, rehabilitate
rijed, rigid
rijekshen, reject(ion)
rijekt, reject
rijektion, reject(ion)
rijers, rehearse
rijet, rigid
rijid, rigid
rijit, rigid
rikachet, ricochet
rikashay, ricochet
rikedy, rickety
rikendal, rekindle
rikerus, rigor(ous)
rikeshay, ricochet
rikete, rickety
rikets, rickets
rikidy, rickety
rikishay, ricochet
rikity, rickety
riklain, recline
rikliner, recline(r)

rikochet, ricochet
rikonasinse, reconnaissance
rikonstitute, reconstitute
rikonusins, reconnaissance
rikord, record
rikorder, record(er)
rikrute, recruit
rikruter, recruit(er)
rikumbent, recumbent
rikurus, rigor(ous)
rikwest, request
rikwire, require
rikwirment, require(ment)
ril, real / reel / rile / rill
rilacs, relax
rilai, rely
rilaps, relapse
rilat, relate
rilax, relax
rilay, rely
rile, *, ed, ling, PROVOKE INTO ACTION (or see rill/ really)
rilef, relief
rilegeon, religion
rilegon, religion
rilegous, religion(ous)
rileit, relate
rilenquish, relinquish
rilentles, relentless
rilese, release
rilevar, relieve(r)
rileve, relieve
rilevir, relieve(r)
rili, rely / really
rilians, reliance
riliaple, reliable
rilichon, religion
rilients, reliance
rilif, relief
riligen, religion
rilis, release
riliubility, reliable(bility)
riliuble, reliable
riliunse, reliance

riiunt,reliance(nt)
riiv,relieve
rill,*, NARROW VALLEY/ CHANNEL (or see real/ reel/ rile)
rillecshon,reject(ion)
rillect,reject
rillim,regime
rillois,rejoice
rillon,region
rillureniechon,rejuvenate(tion)
rillureniet,rejuvenate
rilly,really
rilm,realm
rilte,realty
riluctanse,reluctant(nce)
riluctant,reluctant
riluktense,reluctant(nce)
riluktint,reluctant
rily,really / rely
rim,*, mmed,mming,CURVED/ CIRCULAR OUTER EDGE (or see ream/ rhyme)
rimadik,rheumatic
rimander,remain(der)
rimane,remain / romaine
rimanis,reminisce
rimanisent,reminisce(nt)
rimantek,romantic
rimantisize,romantic(ize)
rimark,remark
rimarkible,remark(able)
rimarkt,remark(ed)
rimarkuble,remark(able)
rimatik,rheumatic
rimaty,remedy
rimbunctious,rambunctious
rimbunkshes,rambuncticus
rime,rhyme
rimedeul,remedy(dial)
rimedial,remedy(dial)
rimediashen,remedy(diation)
rimediation,remedy(diation)
rimein,remain
rimembranse,remember('ance)
rimembur,remember

rimeng,rhyme(ming)
rimenis,reminisce
rimenisent,reminisce(nt)
rimet,remit
rimeted,remit(tted)
rimetuble,remit(ttable)
rimety,remedy
rimidy,remedy
rimind,remind
rimindur,remind(er)
riming,rhyme(ming)
rimintur,remind(er)
rimishen,remission
rimission,remission
rimit,remit
rimital,remit(ttal)
rimition,remission
rimity,remedy
rimnent,remnant
rimnet,remnant
rimnint,remnant
rimofer,remove(r)
rimonis,reminisce
rimonisent,reminisce(nt)
rimors,remorse
rimorsful,remorse(ful)
rimorsless,remorse(less)
rimot,remote
rimotly,remote(ly)
rimout,remote
rimover,remove(r)
rimudy,remedy
rimufel,remove(val)
rimufer,remove(r)
rimufible,remove(vable)
rimunerashen,remunerate(tion)
rimunerate,remunerate
rimunirate,remunerate
rimuniration,remunerate(tion)
rimunis,reminisce
rimunisent,reminisce(nt)
rimuty,remedy
rimuv,remove

rimuvable,remove(vable)
rin,wren
rinagade,renegade
rinasonse,renaissance
rinasurus,rhinoceros
rinaun,renown
rinauns,renounce
rinauserus,rhinoceros
rinavashen,renovate(tion)
rinavate,renovate
rinavation,renovate(tion)
rinawserus,rhinoceros
rinch,wrench
rincol,wrinkle
rind,*, THE EXTERIOR COVERING/ SKIN OF SOME FRUIT/ TREES/ CHEESE
rinder,render
rindur,render
rineg,renege
rinegade,renegade
rinesonse,renaissance
rinestone,rhinestone
rinevashen,renovate(tion)
rinevate,renovate
rinevation,renovate(tion)
ring,*, ged,ging,ger,rung,A SOUND,ARTICLE OF JEWELRY,CIRCULAR SHAPE (or see wring/ rink)
ringur,ring(er) / ranger
rinige,renege
riniu,renew
rink,*, PLACE FOR SKATING (or see ring)
rinkle,wrinkle
rinkul,wrinkle
rino,rhino
rinone,renown
rinoserus,rhinoceros
rinosonse,renaissance
rinosurus,rhinoceros
rinounce,renounce
rinouncement,renounce(ment)
rinovadid,renovate(d)
rinovashen,renovate(tion)
rinovate,renovate

rinovation, renovate(tion)
rinoveit, renovate
rinown, renown
rinownse, renounce
rinownsment, renounce(ment)
rinoz, rhino(s)
rins, rinse / rind(s) / wren(s)
rinsd, rinse(d)
rinse, *, ed, sing, er, TO WASH/ CLEAN WITH A LIQUID
rinstone, rhinestone
rinsur, rinse(r)
rint, rind / rent
rinter, render / rent(er)
rintible, rent(able)
rintuble, rent(able)
rinu, renew
rinuable, renew(able)
rinuel, renew(al)
rinugade, renegade
rinumerate, remunerate
rinusonts, renaissance
rinuvadid, renovate(d)
rinuvashen, renovate(tion)
rinuvat, renovate
rinztone, rhinestone
riol, rile / real / reel
riole, really
riolm, realm
riolti, realty
riostat, rheostat
riot, *, ted, ting, ter, ANGRY CROWD/ MOB OF PEOPLE WHO MAY OR MAY NOT BE VIOLENT
rioustat, rheostat
rip, *, pped, pping, pper, TO TEAR/ SLICE SOMETHING OPEN/ APART (or see ripe/ reap) "prefixes: un"
ripaflavin, riboflavin
ripair, repair
ripal, ripple
ripar, repair
ripd, rip(pped)
ripe, en, ened, er, est, ening, eness, FULLY MATURE/ PRIME IN DEVELOPMENT (or see rip) "prefixes: over/ un"
ripeal, repeal

ripeat, repeat
riped, rip(pped)
ripededly, repeat(edly)
ripeel, repeal
ripeet, repeat
ripeir, repair
ripel, rappel / repeal / repel
ripelent, repellent
ripeleon, rebel(llion)
ripelinsy, repellent(ncy)
ripelint, repellent
ripellinsy, repellent(ncy)
ripend, ripe(ned)
ripenins, repent(ance)
ripense, repent(s)
ripent, repent
riper, repair / rip(pper)
ripercoshon, repercussion
ripetative, repetitive
ripete, repeat
ripetedly, repeat(edly)
ripil, repeal
ripin, ripe(n) / rip(pping)
ripit, repeat
ripiut, repute
riplace, replace
riplacement, replace(ment)
riplai, reply
riplase, replace
riplasmint, replace(ment)
riple, ripple
ripleis, replace
riplenesh, replenish
riplenish, replenish
riplenishment, replenish(ment)
riplid, reply(lied)
riplied, reply(lied)
riply, reply
ripnes, ripe(ness)
ripoblic, republic
ripoflavin, riboflavin
ripognant, repugnant
ripoire, rapport

ripol, ripple
ripold, ripple(d)
ripols, repulse
ripolsev, repulse(sive)
ripon, ribbon / ripe(n)
ripor, rapport / rip(pper)
riporder, report(er)
riport, report
riporter, report(er)
ripository, repository
riposutory, repository
ripozitory, repository
ripple, *, ed, ling, A SMALL WAVE
ripreshen, repress(ion)
ripresif, repress(ive)
ripresion, repress(ion)
ripresive, repress(ive)
ripress, repress
ripresuve, repress(ive)
riproch, reproach
riprochuble, reproach(able)
riproductive, reproduce(ctive)
riprodus, reproduce
riprouch, reproach
ripublek, republic
ripublekan, republic(an)
ripublic, republic
ripublican, republic(an)
ripugnense, repugnant(nce)
ripugnent, repugnant
ripul, ripple / rebel
ripuld, ripple(d)
ripuls, repulse
ripulshen, repulse(sion)
ripulsif, repulse(sive)
ripulsion, repulse(sion)
ripult, ripple(d)
ripun, ripe(n)
ripund, ripe(ned)
ripunt, ripe(ned)
ripuplecan, republic(an)
ripuplican, republic(an)
ripur, ripe(r)

ripust,ripe(st)	rispectful,respect(ful)
riqrute,recruit	rispective,respect(ive)
riquair,require	rispectuble,respect(able)
riquest,request	rispekt,respect
riqueti,rickety	rispektful,respect(ful)
riquire,require	rispektif,respect(ive)
riquirment,require(ment)	rispektuble,respect(able)
riquite,requite	rispite,respite
riqwire,require	rispond,respond
riqwirment,require(ment)	rispondent,respond(ent)
rir, rear / we're / were / whirr	risponder,respond(er)
risaid,reside	response,response
risain,resign	risponsive,response(sive)
risait,recite	risponsuble,response(sible)
risbond,respond	rispont,respond
risbons,response	rist,wrist
risdrane,restrain	ristor,restore
rise,*, sing, en, er, rose, ASSOCIATED WITH UPWARDS/ MOVING UP/ UPWARD BOUND (or see rice) "prefixes: up"	ristrain,restrain
	ristraint,restrain(t)
	ristrane,restrain
	ristrant,restrain(t)
riseat,receipt	ristrect,restrict
risebdef,receptive	ristrikt,restrict
risebtif,receptive	ristriktive,restrict(ive)
riseed,recede	risuma,resume
riseef,receive	risume,resume
riseet,receipt	risurgent,resurgent
risefe,receive	risurllent,resurgent
risileant,resilient	risurs,rise(rs)
risemblance,resemble(lance)	risurve,reserve
risent,recent / resent	risuryent,resurgent
risentful,resent(ful)	risusatator,resuscitate(tor)
risentment,resent(ment)	risusetate,resuscitate
risepdekle,receptacle	risusitashen,resuscitate(tion)
risepdikul,receptacle	rit,rite / write / wright / writ / right / rid / ride
risepeant,recipient	ritacule,ridicule
risepeunt,recipient	ritainer,retain(er)
risepshun,reception	ritakule,ridicule
riseptacle,receptacle	rital,riddle / retail
riseptef,receptive	ritaleashen,retaliate(tion)
riseptekle,receptacle	ritaleate,retaliate
risepter,receptor	ritaleation,retaliate(tion)
riseption,reception	ritaliation,retaliate(tion)

riseptive,receptive	
riseptukle,receptacle	
riserch,research	
riserv,reserve	
riservist,reserve(vist)	
riseshun,recess(ion)	
risesif,recess(ive)	
risesion,recess(ion)	
risesive,recess(ive)	
risession,recess(ion)	
risestanse,resist(ance)	
risestor,resist(or)	
risete,receipt	
risetion,recess(ion)	
risevuble,receive(vable)	
rishis,right(eous) / rich(es)	
rishuel,ritual	
rishus,right(eous) / rich(es)	
riside,reside / recede	
risign,resign	
risileant,resilient	
risilyent,resilient	
risipeunt,recipient	
risir,rise(r)	
risit,receipt / recite	
risitle,recite(tal)	
risitul,recite(tal)	
risiv,receive	
risk,*, ked,king,ky,TAKE A CHANCE / GAMBLE	
riskt,risk(ed)	
risodo,risotto	
risolt,result	
risoltant,result(ant)	
risolv,resolve	
risolvuble,resolve(vable)	
risome,rhizome	
rison,reason / rise(n) / rhizome	
risor,rise(r)	
risors,resource	
risort,resort	
risoto,risotto	
risotto, TYPE OF EDIBLE DISH/ FOOD	
rispect,respect	

ritane,retain
ritaner,retain(er)
ritanse,rid(ddance)
ritard,retard
ritashen,rotate(tion)
ritayer,retire
ritch,rich / wretch
ritches,right(eous) / rich(es)
ritchly,rich(ly)
ritchuil,ritual
ritchus,right(eous) / rich(es)
rite,*,A CEREMONY/ OBSERVANCE (or see ride / right/ write/ white/ writ/ wright)
ritein,retain
ritel,retail / riddle
ritense,rid(ddance)
ritenshun,retention
ritentif,retentive
riter,ride(r) / write(r) / retire
rith,writhe
rithem,rhythm
rithm,rhythm
rithum,rhythm
ritinshun,retention
ritire,retire
ritirment,retire(ment)
ritle,riddle
ritorical,rhetoric(al)
ritous,right(eous) / rich(es)
ritracted,retract(ed)
ritraction,retract(ion)
ritrakshen,retract(ion)
ritrakted,retract(ed)
ritrefe,retrieve
ritrefer,retrieve(r)
ritreful,retrieve(val)
ritreve,retrieve
ritrevul,retrieve(val)
ritrevur,retrieve(r)
ritsee,ritzy
ritsy,ritzy
ritual,*,lly,lism,list,listic,listicallly,lize,lization, CEREMONY

rituil,ritual
ritukeul,ridicule
ritul,riddle
riturn,return
ritzy,zier,ziest,SWANKY/ ELEGANT
riul,rile
riunyen,reunion
riunyun,reunion
riuse,ruse
riut,riot
riuted,riot(ed)
riuter,riot(er)
rivais,revise
rivaiv,revive
rivaivol,revival
rival,*,led,ling,lry,lries,COMPETITOR "prefixes: un"
rivalfe,revolve
rivalree,rival(ry)
rivalve,revolve
riveel,reveal
riveelt,reveal(ed)
riveer,revere
rivegen,revise(sion)
rivejen,revise(sion)
rivel,rival / arrival
rivench,revenge
rivenge,revenge
rivengful,revenge(ful)
rivenje,revenge
river,*,TRIBUTARY/ CHANNEL OF WATER, SOMETHING FLOWING "prefixes: up"
riverberate,reverberate
rivere,revere
rivers,river(s) / reverse
riversuble,reverse(sible)
rivert,revert
riveubereit,reverberate
riview,review / revue
rivigen,revise(sion)
rivijen,revise(sion)
rivil,revel
riving,revenge
rivingful,revenge(ful)

rivinje,revenge
rivir,revere
rivirbarate,reverberate
rivirs,reverse
rivirt,revert
rivise,revise
rivishen,revise(sion)
rivision,revise(sion)
riviu,review
rivival,revival
rivive,revive
rivivuble,revive(vable)
rivivul,revive(val)
rivize,revise
rivlree,rival(ry)
rivocability,revocable(bility)
rivocable,revocable
rivokability,revocable(bility)
rivokable,revocable
rivoke,revoke
rivokt,revoke(d)
rivol,rival / arrival
rivolfe,revolve
rivolfer,revolve(r)
rivolree,rival(ry)
rivolt,revolt
rivolv,revolve
rivolver,revolve(r)
rivouc,revoke
rivoucabol,revocable
rivul,rival / arrival
rivulree,rival(ry)
rivurbarate,reverberate
rivurse,reverse
rivurt,revert
riward,reward
riword,reward
riyewnyen,reunion
riyois,rejoice
riyunion,reunion
riyunyun,reunion
riyuveneishon,rejuvenate(tion)
riyuveneit,rejuvenate

rizain, resign
rizalfe, resolve
rize, rise / rice
rizelyent, resilient
rizemblanse, resemble(lance)
rizemble, resemble
rizent, resent
rizentful, resent(ful)
rizentment, resent(men:-)
rizer, rise(r)
rizid, reside
rizilyent, resilient
rizine, resign
rizist, resist
rizite, recite
rizodo, risotto
rizolve, resolve
rizolvuble, resolve(vable)
rizom, resume
rizome, rhizome
rizoom, resume
rizort, resort
rizoto, risotto
rizultent, result(ant)
rizultunt, result(ant)
rizum, resume
rizuma, resume / resume'
rizume, resume / resume'
rizur, rise(r)
ro, row / raw
roach, hes, AN INSECT, BUTT END OF HERB CIGARETTE
road, *, dy, A PATH/ PASSAGE/ WIDE TRAIL TO TRAVEL ON (or see rode/ wrote) "prefixes: in"
roam, *, med, ming, mer, TO WANDER/ MOVE ABOUT AIMLESSLY (or see room)
roar, *, red, ring, LOUD/ DEEP SOUND/ EXPRESSION COMING FROM THE THROAT (or see row(er)) "prefixes: up"
roast, *, ted, ting, ter, SLOWLY COOK IN AN OVEN, BAKE WITHOUT A FLAME
rob, *, bbed, bbing, bber, STEAL/ TAKE AWAY FROM WITHOUT PERMISSION (or see robe/ rope)
robd, robe(d) / rob(bbed) / rope(d)

robe, *, ed, bing, LONG/ LOOSE SLEEVED GARMENT (or see rob/ rope) "prefixes: dis/ en"
robed, robe(d) / rob(bbed) / rope(d)
robeled, rebel(lled)
robeleus, rebel(llious)
roben, robin / rob(bbing)
rober, rob(bber)
robin, *, A TYPE OF BIRD (or see rob(bbing))
robodezashen, robot(ization)
robodik, robot(ic)
robost, robust
robot, *, tic, tism, tize, tization, A MACHINE WHICH WORKS FOR PEOPLE
robotisashen, robot(ization)
robotizashen, robot(ization)
robt, rob(bbed) / rope(d) / robe(d)
robudezashin, robot(ization)
robun, robin / rob(bbing)
robushus, robust(ious)
robust, tly, tness, tious, tiously, tiousness, FULL/ HEALTHY/ STRONG
robustus, robust(ious)
robutesation, robot(eer)
robuzd, robust
roch, roach
rocher, roger
roches, roach(es)
rochir, roger
rochur, roger
rock, *, ked, king, ker, ky, HARD MINERAL, BACK AND FORTH MOTION
rockateer, rocket(eer)
rocket, *, try, teer, A FUELED CYLINDER WITH POINTED TIP
rod, *, dded, dding, dless, THIN ROUND/ CYLINDRICAL STAFF/ POLE/ STICK SHAPE (or see rotor/ road/ rode/ wrote)
rodadendron, rhododendron
rodadindron, rhododendron
rodant, rodent
rodar, rotor
rodaree, rotary
rodary, rotary

rodatelir, rototiller
rodatilur, rototiller
rode, PAST TENSE FOR THE WORD "RIDE" (or see road/ wrote) "prefixes: over"
rodedendron, rhododendron
rodedindron, rhododendron
rodent, *, A SMALL MAMMAL
rodeo, *, oed, oing, GAME IN ARENA USING HORSES/ COWS/ ROPES
roder, rotor
rodery, rotary
rodetilur, rototiller
rodidendron, rhododendron
rodidindron, rhododendron
rodint, rodent
rodio, rodeo
rodiquelus, ridiculous
rodir, rotor
roditelur, rototiller
rododendrem, rhododendron
rodotiler, rototiller
rodudindron, rhododendron
rodunt, rodent
rodur, rotor
roduree, rotary
rodury, rotary
rodutiler, rototiller
roeal, royal
roeul, royal
roeyul, royal
rof, rove / rough
rofeelt, reveal(ed)
rofer, revere / refer / rove(r)
roferse, reverse
rofeusil, refuse(sal)
rofiew, review / revue
rofifful, revival
rofir, rove(r) / rough(er)
rofirst, reverse
rofol, ruffle
rofue, review / revue
rofur, rove(r) / rough(er)
rofurse, reverse

rofute,refute
rog,rogue / rouge
roged,rugged
roger,RADIO COMMUNICATION WHICH MEANS "OKAY", SOMEONE'S NAME
rogir,roger
rogue,*,uish,uishly,uishness,ery,eries,SWINDLER/ TRICKY/ DEVIANT BEHAVIOR (or see rouge)
rogur,roger
roiel,royal
roiul,royal
rojer,roger
rojur,roger
rok,rock / rogue
rokateer,rocket(eer)
roket,rocket
roketeer,rocket(eer)
rokut,rocket
rokuteer,rocket(eer)
rokwit,requite
rokwitable,requite(table)
rol,roll / role
rolar,roll(er)
role,*,,A PART/ CHARACTER IN A PLAY (or see roll)
rolec,rollick
roled,roll(ed)
rolek,rollick
rolent,relent
roler,roll(er)
rolic,rollick
rolik,rollick
rolir,roll(er)
roll,*,,lled,lling,ller,A BREAD SHAPE,MOVES/ GOES AROUND IN CIRCULAR FASHION (or see role) "prefixes: un"
roller,roll(er) / roger
rollick,*,ked,king,TO PLAYFULLY ROLL/ TUMBLE/ JUMP/ SKIP AROUND
rolor,roll(er)
rolres,walrus
rolrus,walrus
rolur,roll(er)
rom,roam / room / rum

romach,rummage
romadik,rheumatic
romaine,TYPE OF LETTUCE (or see remain)
romance,*,ed,cing,er,ntic,FANCIFUL/ WHIMSICAL/ EXTRAVAGANT EXPERIENCE WITH INFATUATION/ LOVE BETWEEN TWO PEOPLE
romane,romaine / remain
romanek,romantic
romanse,romance
romantic,cally,cism,cist,cize,cization,INVOLVES ROMANCE
romantisize,romantic(ize)
romark,remark
romatik,rheumatic
romatoyd,rheumatic(toid)
romb,romp
rombed,romp(ed) / roam(ed)
rombl,rumble / rumple
rombol,rumble / rumple
romediashen,remedy(diation)
romediation,remedy(diation)
romeshen,remission
rometeul,remedy(dial)
romidal,remit(ttal)
romind,remind
romindur,remind(er)
romintur,remind(er)
romishen,remission
romision,remission
romission,remission
romital,remit(ttal)
romited,remit(tted)
romition,remission
romituble,remit(ttable)
romp,*,ped,ping,per,PLAYFULLY FROLIC/ JUMP/ BOUNCE AROUND (or see rump)
rompt,romp(ed)
roms,room(s) / roam(s)
romufel,remove(val)
romufible,remove(vable)
romufil,remove(val)
romunerate,remunerate
romunirashen,remunerate(tion)

romunirate,remunerate
romuvable,remove(vable)
romuver,remove(r)
romy,room
ron,run
ronchee,raunch
ronchy,raunch
rondavous,rendezvous
rondavu,rendezvous
ronduvu,rendezvous
ronege,renege
rong,wrong / rung / wrung
rongle,wrong(ly)
ronige,renege
ronk,wrong
ronouncement,renounce(ment)
ronounse,renounce
ronownse,renounce
ronownsment,renounce(ment)
ronshy,raunch
ront,runt
rontavu,rendezvous
rontchy,raunch
rontivu,rendezvous
roobarb,rhubarb
rood,rude / root
roodly,rude(ly)
rooen,ruin
rooenus,ruin(ous)
roof,*,fed,fing,fer,TOP/ COVER OF A DWELLING/ STRUCTURE
rooin,ruin
rooinus,ruin(ous)
rook,*,,A BIRD,CHEAT MONEY OUT OF SOMEONE,GAME PIECE IN CHESS
roold,rule(d)
rooler,rule(r)
roolet,roulette
roolir,rule(r)
roolt,rule(d)
roolur,rule(r)

room, *, med, ming, mer, mful, my, miness, mily, CUBICLE/ SPACE/ PLACE WITH WALLS WITHIN A LARGER DWELLING/ STRUCTURE (or see roam)
rooman, rumen
roomanu, rumina
roomatoyd, rheumatic(toid)
roomen, rumen
roomena, rumina
roomenate, rumina(te)
roomenator, rumina(tor)
roomin, rumen
roominate, rumina(te)
roominator, rumina(tor)
roomon, rumen
roon, rune
roonashen, ruin(ation)
roonation, ruin(ation)
roose, ruse
roost, *, ted, ting, ter, SIT ATOP SOMETHING TO REST/ SLEEP, NORMALLY HOW BIRDS SLEEP (or see roast/ rust/ roust)
rooster, *, A MALE CHICKEN
root, *, ted, ting, ter, tage, -less, ty, PART OF PLANT THAT'S UNDERGROUND "prefixes: up"
rop, rope / rob
ropair, repair
ropare, repair
ropcher, rupture
rope, *, ed, ping, er, MANY STRANDS WOVEN TOGETHER INTO ONE (or see robe)
ropeel, repeal
ropeet, repeat
ropel, rappel / repeal / repel
ropelinsy, repellent(ncy)
ropent, repent
ropete, repeat
roplenish, replenish
roposutory, repository
roquitable, requite(table)
roquite, requite
ror, roar / row(er)
ros, rose / row(s)
rosaree, rosary

rosary, ries, STRAND OF BEADS WITH A CROSS ON IT
rosdrane, restrain
rose, *, eate, eately, ette, etta, A FLOWER, COLOR, PAST TENSE FOR "RISE" (or see row(s))
rosebshin, reception
rosebshinist, receptionist
rosebtif, receptive
rosefe, receive
rosefible, receive(vable)
rosen, rosin
rosepdekle, receptacle
rosepdikul, receptacle
rosepeunt, recipient
roseprikul, reciprocal
rosepshen, reception
rosepshenist, receptionist
roseptekle, receptacle
roseptif, receptive
roseptionest, receptionist
roseptive, receptive
roseree, rosary
roseshun, recess(ion)
rosesive, recess(ive)
rosetion, recess(ion)
roseve, receive
rosevuble, receive(vable)
rosh, rush
rosin, *, ned, ny, OIL FROM TURPENTINE
rosipeant, recipient
rosipeint, recipient
rosiprekul, reciprocal
rosiree, rosary
rosodo, risotto
rosoto, risotto
rospective, respect(ive)
rospektif, respect(ive)
rost, roast / rust
rostar, roster / roast(er) / rooster
roster, *, LIST OF NAMES/ EVENTS (or see roast(er)/ rooster)
rostic, rustic
rostir, roster / roast(er) / rooster
rostore, restore

rostrain, restrain
rostrane, restrain
rostrektif, restrict(ive)
rostrikshen, restrict(ion)
rostrikt, restrict
rostriktion, restrict(ion)
rostriktive, restrict(ive)
rostur, roster / roast(er) / rooster
rosun, rosin
rosuree, rosary
rot, *, tted, tting, DETERIORATE/ DISINTEGRATE (or see rod/ rode/ wrote/ rote/ wrought)
rotade, rotate
rotaleation, retaliate(tion)
rotaliation, retaliate(tion)
rotan, rotten
rotaree, rotary
rotary, ries, A SPINNING/ ROTATION ON AN AXIS/ HUB
rotashen, rotate(tion)
rotashenul, rotate(tional)
rotashun, rotate(tion)
rotate, *, ed, ting, table, tion, tional, tive, tor, tory, TAKE TURNS, REVOLVE/ ALTERNATE
rotatelur, rototiller
rotatiller, rototiller
rote, REPETITION, OVER AND OVER (or see wrote/ rotor/ road/ rode)
roten, rotten
roteo, rodeo
roter, rotor
rotery, rotary
rotesaree, rotisserie
rotesuree, rotisserie
rotetiller, rototiller
rotin, rotten
rotio, rodeo
rotir, rotor / retire
rotiry, rotary
rotisaree, rotisserie
rotisserie, *, A FOOD COOKER
rotisuree, rotisserie
rotitelir, rototiller
rotor, *, TO DO WITH ROTATION/ HUB

rototiler, rototiller
rototiller,*, MACHINE TO TILL GROUND
rotten, PAST TENSE FOR "ROT"
rotun, rotten
rotur, rotor
rotury, rotary
rou, row
roub, robe
roubat, robot
roubost, robust
roubot, robot
rouch, roach
roud, road / rode
roudent, rodent
roudiou, rodeo
roudoudendren, rhododendron
roudoutiler, rototiller
roudy, rowdy
rouf, rough / roof
roug, rogue / rouge
rouge, RED MAKE-UP FOR FACE (or see rogue)
rough,*, hed, hing, hen, her, hest, hly, hness, hage, hen, hish, ABRASIVE/ FIBROUS/ UNREFINED/ UNEVEN
roulette, GAME WITH SPINNING DISK/ BALL
roum, roam
roumans, romance
roumein, romaine
rounation, ruin(ation)
round,*, ded, ding, der, dest, dish, dly, dness, CIRCULAR SHAPE, AROUND, MAKE MORE EVEN/ SMOOTH TO SHAPE "prefixes: un"
rount, round
roup, rope
rous, rose
rouseri, rosary
roust,*, ted, ting, WAKEN/ AROUSE, FORCE TO ACTION (or see roost)
rout, route / rote / wrote
routari, rotary
route,*, ed, ting, er, SPECIFIC/ PARTICULAR PATH/ NETWORK/ LINES (or see root)
routeen, routine
routeit, rotate

routine,*, ely, nize, nized, nizing, PERFORM SPECIFIC FUNCTION ON CONTINUOUS BASIS "prefixes: sub"
routiseri, rotisserie
routy, rowdy
roux, A PASTE FOR SAUCE/ GRAVY (or see rue)
rovalfe, revolve
rove,*, ed, ving, er, TO WANDER/ MOVE AIMLESSLY SEEKING FOR SOMETHING "prefixes: un"
roveel, reveal
roveelt, reveal(ed)
rovegen, revise(sion)
rovejen, revise(sion)
rovench, revenge
rovene, ravine
rovenge, revenge
rovengful, revenge(ful)
rovenjful, revenge(ful)
roverberate, reverberate
roverbirate, reverberate
rovere, revere
roverse, reverse
rovert, revert
roveshen, revise(sion)
rovesion, revise(sion)
roview, review / revue
rovigen, revise(sion)
rovijen, revise(sion)
rovinch, revenge
rovinjful, revenge(ful)
rovir, rove(r)
rovirbarate, reverberate
rovirberate, reverberate
rovirse, reverse
rovirsuble, reverse(sible)
rovirt, revert
rovise, revise
rovishen, revise(sion)
rovision, revise(sion)
rovival, revival
rovive, revive
rovivle, revival
rovivuble, revive(vable)
rovize, revise

rovocability, revocable(bility)
rovolfe, revolve
rovolfer, revolve(r)
rovolve, revolve
rovue, review / revue
rovur, rove(r)
rovurse, reverse
rovurt, revert
row, wed, wer, wing, USE OF OARS/ PADDLES TO NAVIGATE THROUGH WATER
roward, reward
rowbot, robot
rowch, roach
rowdy, dier, diest, TALK LOUD, BE ROUGH/ RAMBUNCTIOUS
rowmane, romaine
rowmanse, romance
rownd, round
rownt, round
roword, reward
rowp, rope
rowr, row(er) / roar
rowst, roust
rowtee, rowdy
rowty, rowdy
royal, lty, lties, lly, lism, list, OF KINGS/ QUEENS, A SOVEREIGN POWER/ RIGHT, PERCENTAGE AS GAIN
royel, royal
royer, roger
royul, royal
roz, rose / row(s)
rozaree, rosary
roze, rose / row(s)
rozen, rosin
rozeree, rosary
rozin, rosin
roziree, rosary
rozodo, risotto
rozt, roast
rozter, roster
roztur, roster
rozun, rosin
rozuree, rosary

ru,rue
rub,*,bbed,bbing,bber,USE MOTION/ MASSAGE TO WORK AN AREA
rubal,rubble
rubar,rubber
rubarb,rhubarb
rubash,rubbish
rubber,*,rize,rizes,rized,rizing,ry,MATERIAL DERIVED FROM PETROLEUM/ TREES
rubbish,GARBAGE/ TRASH, WORTH REJECTING/ ELIMINATING
rubble,ROCKS/ DEBRIS LAYING AROUND
rube,ruby
rubed,rub(bbed)
rubee,ruby
rubel,rubble
rubeled,rebel(lled)
rubelein,rebel(llion)
rubeleus,rebel(llious)
rubelyon,rebel(llion)
ruber,rubber
ruberize,rubber(ize)
rubesh,rubbish
rubil,rubble
rubir,rubber
rubirize,rubber(ize)
rubish,rubbish
rublase,replace
ruble,rubble
rublie,reply
rubodek,robot(ic)
rubodizashen,robot(ization)
ruborb,rhubarb
rubotek,robot(ic)
rubotiks,robot(ics)
rubt,rub(bbed)
rubul,rubble
rubur,rubber
ruby,bies,A GEMSTONE
rucede,recede
rucepter,receptor
ruch,rush
ruciprocation,reciprocate(tion)

ruck,rug
ruclaimuble,reclaimable
rucumbent,recumbent
rudder,*,rless,A BLADE ON A BOAT WHICH STEERS
rude,er, est,dly, eness,TO OFFEND SOMEONE WITH BEHAVIOR/ WORDS, UNREFINED/ RAW
rudeculus,ridiculous
rudeemible, redeem(able)
rudeme,redeem
rudemption, redemption
rudemshen, redemption
ruder,rudder
rudikulus, ridiculous
rudir, rudder
rudist, rude(st)
rudur, rudder
ruduse,reduce
rudusible, reduce(cible)
rue,*,AN HERB (or see roux)
ruebarb,rhubarb
ruel, rule
ruelur,rule(r)
ruen,ruin
ruenashen, ruin(ation)
ruenation, ruin(ation)
ruenus, ruin(ous)
ruf, roof / rough / ruff
rufag, rough(age)
rufal, ruffle
rufeel, reveal
rufeelt, reveal(ed)
rufeer, revere
rufeg, rough(age)
rufej, rough(age)
rufel, ruffle
rufen, ravine / rough(en)
rufenge, revenge
rufenje, revenge
rufer, roof(er) / rough(er) / refer
rufere, revere / refer
ruferse, reverse / refer(s)
rufest, rough(est)

ruff,*,ffed,ELABORATE COLLAR,CARD GAME TERM (or see rough/ roof)
ruffle,*,ed,ling,TO MESS UP/ DISTURB "prefixes: un"
rufiew, review revue
rufiful, revival
rufig, rough(age)
rufij, rough(age)
rufil, ruffle
rufinable, refine(nable)
rufine, refine
rufinery, refine(ry)
rufinje, revenge
rufinment, refine(ment)
rufinuble, refine(nable)
rufinury, refine(ry)
rufir, rough(er) / roof(er) / refer
rufirse, reverse
rufist, rough(est)
rufle, ruffle
ruflection, reflect(ion)
ruflee, rough(ly)
ruflekshen, reflect(ion)
ruflekt, reflect
ruflektion, reflect(ion)
ruflektor, reflect(or)
rufly, rough(ly)
rufol, ruffle
rufor, rough(er) / roof(er) / refer
rufractory, refract(ory)
rufrain, refrain
rufraktory, refract(ory)
rufrane, refrain
rufregirant, refrigerate(ant)
rufregirator, refrigerate(tor)
rufresher, refresh(er)
rufreshment, refresh(ment)
rufrigirant, refrigerate(ant)
rufrigirator, refrigerate(tor)
rufs, roof(s) / ruff(s)
ruft, roof(ed) / rough(ed)
rufue, review / revue
ruful, ruffle
rufur, rough(er) / roof(er) / refer

rufurse,reverse
rufursuble,reverse(sible)
rufust,rough(est)
rufute,refute
rug,*,REMOVABLE FLOOR COVERING
rugard,regard
ruge,rouge
ruged,rugged
rugged,dly,dness,ROUGH/ COARSE/ UNREFINED/ IRREGULAR "prefixes: semi"
rugit,rugged
rugresif,regress(ive)
rugresive,regress(ive)
rugret,regret
rugreted,regret(tted)
rugretful,regret(full)
rugretfully,regret(fully)
rugud,rugged
rugut,rugged
ruil,rule
ruin,*,ned,ning,nation,nous,BREAK/ DESTROY, COMPLETE FAILURE/ DECAY
ruj,rouge
ruk,rug / rook
ruklamuble,reclaimable
rukliner,recline(r)
rukord,record
rukorder,record(er)
rukumbent,recumbent
rukwest,request
rukwire,require
rukwirment,require(ment)
rukwit,requite
rul,rule
rulaks,relax
rular,rule(r)
rulax,relax
ruld,rule(d)
rule,*,ed,ling,er,LAW/ COMMAND/ METHOD,PERIOD OF GOVERNING,DEVICE TO MEASURE "prefixes: mis/ over"
rulegis,religion(ous)
rulejis,religion(ous)

rulenquish,relinquish
rulent,relent
rulentless,relentless
rulese,release
rulet,roulette
rulette,roulette
ruleve,relieve
rulever,relieve(r)
ruli,rely
ruliability,reliable(bility)
rulianse,reliance
ruliense,reliance
ruligeon,religion
ruligous,religion(ous)
rulijes,religion(ous)
rulinkwish,relinquish
rulinqish,relinquish
rulintless,relentless
rulir,rule(r)
rult,rule(d)
ruluktense,reluctant(nce)
ruluktint,reluctant
rulur,rule(r)
ruly,rely
rum,*,mmer,mmy,LIQUOR,UNUSUAL
rumach,rummage
rumadik,rheumatic
rumadoed,rheumatic(toid)
rumage,rummage
rumain,remain / romaine
rumaje,rummage
rumanater,rumina(tor)
rumander,remain(der)
rumane,remain / romaine
rumanek,romantic
rumantek,romantic
rumanticize,romantic(ize)
rumantisize,romantic(ize)
rumanu,rumina
rumar,rumor
rumared,rumor(ed)
rumark,remark
rumarkt,remark(ed)

rumarkuble,remark(able)
rumatezum,rheumatic(ism)
rumatik,rheumatic
rumatism,rheumatic(ism)
rumatizum,rheumatic(ism)
rumatoed,rheumatic(toid)
rumb,rump
rumbal,rumble / rumple
rumble,*,ed,ling,er,ly,DEEP/ ROLLING SOUND,A FIGHT (or see rumple)
rumbul,rumble / rumple
rume,room
rumech,rummage
rumedeal,remedy(dial)
rumedge,rummage
rumedial,remedy(dial)
rumediashen,remedy(diation)
rumediation,remedy(diation)
rumedoed,rheumatic(toid)
rumege,rummage
rumeje,rummage
rumember,remember
rumen,*,mina,STOMACH IN RUMINANT ANIMALS (many stomachs)
rumena,rumina
rumenate,rumina(te)
rumenator,rumina(tor)
rumer,rumor / room(er)
rumered,rumor(ed)
rumert,rumor(ed)
rumes,room(s)
rumeshen,remission
rumet,remit
rumetisem,rheumatic(ism)
rumetism,rheumatic(ism)
rumetoid,rheumatic(toid)
rumich,rummage
rumidal,remit(ttal)
rumidoed,rheumatic(toid)
rumige,rummage
rumije,rummage
rumina,al,ant,antly,ate,ation,ative,atively,ator, PERTAINING TO CHEWING OF CUD,FIRST STOMACH

rumind,remind
rumindur,remind(er)
rumintur,remind(er)
rumir,rumor / room(er)
rumired,rumor(ed)
rumishen,remission
rumission,remission
rumit,remit
rumitable,remit(ttable)
rumited,remit(tted)
rumitezum,rheumatic(ism)
rumition,remission
rumitizum,rheumatic(ism)
rumitoed,rheumatic(toid)
rumitoid,rheumatic(toid)
rummage, *,ed,ging,GO THROUGH/ SEARCH/ RANSACK
rummige,rummage
rumofer,remove(r)
rumor, *,red,GOSSIP/ HEARSAY/ GENERAL TALK
rumorse,remorse
rumorsful,remorse(ful)
rumorsless,remorse(ful)
rumote,remote
rumotisem,rheumatic(ism)
rumotism,rheumatic(ism)
rumotly,remote(ly)
rumovable,remove(vable)
rumover,remove(r)
rump, *,REAR/ TAIL END,BUTTOCKS
rumple, *,ed,ling,CREASE/ FOLD/ WRINKLE (or see rumble)
rums,room(s)
rumuch,rummage
rumufer,remove(r)
rumufible,remove(vable)
rumuge,rummage
rumun,rumen
rumunerashen,remunerate(tion)
rumunerate,remunerate
rumuneration,remunerate(tion)
rumunirashen,remunerate(tion)
rumunirate,remunerate
rumur,rumor

rumurt,rumor(ed)
rumutezim,rheumatic(ism)
rumutizem,rheumatic(ism)
rumy,room
run, *,nning,nner,nny,ran,MOVE QUICKLY USING LEGS, MOVING LIQUID (or see rune) "prefixes: over/ re/ under"
runar,run(nner)
rund,runt
rune, *,nic,SYMBOLS/ ALPHABET (or see run/ ruin/ run(nny))
runege,renege
runer,run(nner)
rung, *,PAST TENSE FOR THE WORD "RING", STEPS/ LEVELS OF A LADDER,STEERING FOR SHIP (or see wrung)
runige,renege
runik,renege
runir,run(nner)
runone,renown
runoserus,rhinoceros
runosirus,rhinoceros
runounsment,renounce(ment)
runown,renown
runownse,renounce
runownsment,renounce(ment)
runre,run(nner)
runt, *,tier,tiest,tiness,ty,SMALLEST OF A GROUP/ LITTER/ SPECIES
runumerate,remunerate
runur,run(nner)
rup,rip / ripe / rub
rupair,repair
rupal,rubble
rupare,repair
rupcher,rupture
rupchur,rupture
rupeal,repeal
rupeat,repeat
rupedidly,repeat(edly)
rupedutif,repetitive
rupee,ruby
rupeel,repeal

rupeet,repeat
rupel,rappel / repeal / repel / rubble
rupelein,rebel(llion)
rupelent,repellent
rupelinsy,repellent(ncy)
rupelint,repellent
rupense,repent(s)
rupent,repent
rupentinse,repent(ance)
ruper,rubber
rupesh,rubbish
rupete,repeat
rupetedly,repeat(edly)
rupil,rubble
rupinens,repent(ance)
rupint,repent
rupintense,repent(ance)
rupir,rubber
rupish,rubbish
ruplace,replace
ruplasmint,replace(ment)
ruple,rubble
ruplenesh,replenish
ruplenish,replenish
ruplid,reply(lied)
ruplied,reply(lied)
ruply,reply
rupor,rapport
ruporder,report(er)
ruport,report
ruporter,report(er)
rupository,repository
rupozitory,repository
rupreshen,repress(ion)
rupresif,repress(ive)
rupress,repress
rupresuve,repress(ive)
ruproch,reproach
ruprochuble,reproach(able)
rupshar,rupture
rupsheruble,rupture(rable)
rupshir,rupture
rupshiruble,rupture(rable)

rupshur, rupture
rupshuruble, rupture(rable)
rupt, rub(bbed)
rupture, *, ed, ring, rable, BURST/ BREACH CONTAINER
rublekan, republic(an)
rupublican, republic(an)
rupugnenst, repugnant(nce)
rupugnint, repugnant
rupul, rubble
rupulshin, repulse(sion)
rupulsion, repulse(sion)
rupur, rubber
ruquire, require
ruquirment, require(ment)
ruquitable, requite(table)
ruquite, requite
ruqwest, request
ruqwire, require
ruqwirment, require(ment)
rur, roar
rural, lly, lity, lism, list, lize, lization, CITY OUTSKIRTS
 "prefixes: semi"
ruril, rural
rurilee, rural(lly)
rurul, rural
rurulee, rural(lly)
rus, ruse
rusde, rust
rusder, rooster
rusdrane, restrain
rusdur, rooster
ruse, A TRICK
ruseat, receipt
rusebshin, reception
rusebshinist, receptionist
rusebtif, receptive
rusebtive, receptive
ruseed, recede
ruseef, receive
ruseet, receipt
rusefible, receive(vable)
ruseliensy, resilient(ncy)
rusemblinse, resemble(lance)

rusentful, resent(ful)
rusentment, resent(ment)
rusepdekle, receptacle
rusepdikul, receptacle
rusepeunt, recipient
ruseprocation, reciprocate(tion)
ruseprocul, reciprocal
rusepshen, reception
rusepshenist, receptionist
rusepterf, receptive
ruseptekle, receptacle
rusepter, receptor
rusepticke, receptacle
ruseption, reception
ruseptionest, receptionist
ruseptive, receptive
ruserved, reserve(d)
ruseshun, recess(ion)
rusesif, recess(ive)
rusesion, recess(ion)
rusesive, recess(ive)
rusession, recess(ion)
rusestinse, resist(ance)
rusestive, resist(ive)
rusete, receipt
rusetion, recess(ion)
ruseve, receive
rusevuble, receive(vable)
rush, hes, hed, hing, hy, UNEXPECTEDLY/ FORCEFULLY
 MOVE FORWARD, HURRY ALONG "prefixes: in"
rushd, rush(ed)
ruside, reside
rusiduil, residue(ual)
rusileant, resilient
rusilient, resilient
rusimblense, resemble(lance)
rusimbul, resemble
rusine, resign
rusintment, resent(ment)
rusipeint, recipient
rusiprocation, reciprocate(tion)
rusiprocul, reciprocal
rusiprokate, reciprocate

rusiprokle, reciprocal
rusirfed, reserve(d)
rusist, resist
rusistanse, resist(ance)
rusistense, resist(ance)
rusistent, resist(ant)
rusister, resist(or)
rusistive, resist(ive)
rusitil, recite(tal)
rusitle, recite(tal)
rusodo, risotto
rusolve, resolve
rusort, resort
rusoto, risotto
rusotto, risotto
ruspect, respect
ruspectful, respect(ful)
ruspective, respect(ive)
ruspectuble, respect(able)
ruspekt, respect
ruspektful, respect(ful)
ruspektif, respect(ive)
ruspektuble, respect(able)
ruspite, respite
ruspond, respond
ruspondent, respond(ent)
rusponder, respond(er)
rusponse, response
rusponsef, response(sive)
rusponsive, response(sive)
rusponsuble, response(sible)
ruspont, respond
rust, *, ted, ting, ty, tier, tiest, OXIDATION OF METAL (or
 see roost)
rustek, rustic
ruster, rooster
rustic, *, cally, cate, cates, cated, cating, cation, cator, city,
 cities, COUNTRY STYLE, SIMPLE
rustid, roost(ed)
rustik, rustic
rustir, rooster
rustore, restore
rustrain, restrain

rustraint,restrain(t)
rustrane,restrain
rustrant,restrain(t)
rustrekt,restrict
rustrektif,restrict(ive)
rustrikshen,restrict(ion)
rustrikt,restrict
rustriktion,restrict(ion)
rustriktive,restrict(ive)
rustuk,rustic
rustur,rooster
rusurfed,reserve(d)
rususitate,resuscitate
rususetate,resuscitate
rususitashen,resuscitate(tion)
rususitate,resuscitate
rususitator,resuscitate(tor)
rut, *, tted, tting, NOISE DEER MAKES, A TRENCH/ GROOVE/ FURROW (cr see route/ root/ rude/ wrought)
rutainer,retain(er)
rutaleashen,retaliate(tion)
rutaleate,retaliate
rutaleation,retaliate(tion)
rutaliation,retaliate(tion)
rutane,retain
rutaner,retain(er)
rutashen,rotate(tion)
rute,rude / root / route
ruted,rut(tted)
ruteen,routine
rutenshun,retention
rutentif,retentive
rutention,retention
rutentive,retentive
ruter, rudder
rutesary,rotisserie
rutest,rude(st)
ruthlesnes,ruthless(ness)
ruthless,ssly, ssness, SPEAKING/ ACTING WITHOUT MERCY
ruthlis,ruthless
rutine,routine

rutinshun,retention
rutintion,retention
rutir, rudder
rutire,retire
rutirment,retire(ment)
rutisary,rotisserie
rutisury,rotisserie
rutlee,rude(ly)
rutorekle,rhetoric(al)
rutorikle,rhetoric(al)
rutracted,retract(ed)
rutraction,retract(ion)
rutrakshen,retract(ion)
rutrakted,retract(ed)
rutre, rudder
rutref,retrieve
rutrefer,retrieve(r)
rutreful,retrieve(val)
rutreve,retrieve
rutrevur,retrieve(r)
rutur, rudder
ruvalfe,revolve
ruvalve,revolve
ruveel,reveal
ruveelingly,reveal(ingly)
ruveelt,reveal(ed)
ruveer,revere
ruvegen,revise(sion)
ruvejen,revise(sion)
ruvench,revenge
ruvene,ravine
ruvenge,revenge
ruvengful,revenge(ful)
ruvenje,revenge
ruvenjful,revenge(ful)
ruverbarate,reverberate
ruverbirate,reverberate
ruvere,revere
ruversuble,reverse(sible)
ruvert,revert
ruveshen,revise(sion)
ruvesion,revise(sion)
ruview,review / revue

ruvigen,revise(sion)
ruvijen,revise(sion)
ruvinch,revenge
ruvine,ravine
ruving,revenge
ruvingful,revenge(ful)
ruvinje,revenge
ruvinjful,revenge(ful)
ruvirberate,reverberate
ruvirse,reverse
ruvirsuble,reverse(sible)
ruvirt,revert
ruvise,revise
ruvishen,revise(sion)
ruvision,revise(sion)
ruvival,revival
ruvive,revive
ruvivle,revival
ruvivuble,revive(vable)
ruvize,revise
ruvocability,revocable(bility)
ruvocable,revocable
ruvokability,revocable(bility)
ruvokable,revocable
ruvoke,revoke
ruvokt,revoke(d)
ruvolfe,revolve
ruvolfer,revolve(r)
ruvolt,revolt
ruvoltid,revolt(ed)
ruvolve,revolve
ruvolver,revolve(r)
ruvue,review / revue
ruvurse,reverse
ruvurt,revert
ruward,reward
ruwidable,requite(table)
ruword,reward
ruwul,rural
ruzemblinse,resemble(lance)
ruzentful,resent(ful)
ruzentment,resent(ment)
ruzerved,reserve(d)

ruzestif, resist(ive)
ruzestir, resist(or)
ruzide, reside
ruziduil, residue(ual)
ruzileant, resilient
ruzilient, resilient
ruzimble, resemble
ruzimblense, resemble(lance)
ruzine, resign
ruzintful, resent(ful)
ruzintment, resent(ment)
ruzist, resist
ruzistanse, resist(ance)
ruzistant, resist(ant)
ruzistef, resist(ive)
ruzistense, resist(ance)
ruzistent, resist(ant)
ruzister, resist(or)
ruzodo, risotto
ruzolfe, resolve
ruzolve, resolve
ruzort, resort
ruzoto, risotto
ruzt, rust / roost
ruztek, rustic
ruztid, rust(ed)
ruztuk, rustic
ruzty, rust
ruzurfs, reserve(s)
ry, rye / wry
rye, A GRAIN (or see wry)
ryle, rile
ryme, rhyme
ryno, rhino
rynstone, rhinestone
rysome, rhizome
ryth, writhe
rythem, rhythm
rythom, rhythm
ryut, riot
ryzome, rhizome
sa, saw / say
sabal, sable

sabateur, saboteur
sabatoj, sabotage
sabature, saboteur
sabdu, subdue
saber, *, red, ring, BROADSWORD, LIGHTWEIGHT SWORD WITH BLUNT TIP
sabereoredy, superior(ity)
sabereority, superior(ity)
sabereur, superior
sabetaje, sabotage
sabetoge, sabotage
sabeture, saboteur
sabil, sable
sabir, saber
sabitaje, sabotage
sabiteur, saboteur
sabitoge, sabotage
sabitoj, sabotage
sabiture, saboteur
sable, *, CARNIVOROUS ANIMAL
sableng, sapling
sabling, sapling
sabol, sable
sabor, saber
sabotach, sabotage
sabotage, *, ed, ging, teur, HINDER/ DAMAGE SOMEONE'S ATTEMPTS/ POSSESSIONS/ EFFORTS
sabotaj, sabotage
sabotaje, sabotage
sabotall, sabotage
saboteur, *, ONE WHO COMMITS SABOTAGE
saboture, saboteur
sabre, saber
sabul, sable
sabur, saber
sabutaje, sabotage
sabuteur, saboteur
sabutoge, sabotage
sabutoj, sabotage
saccaren, saccharin
saccerin, saccharin
saccharin, ne, nely, nity, MANMADE SUGAR
saccuren, saccharin

sacede, secede
sacha, sachet
sachal, satchel
sacharate, saturate
sacharation, saturate(tion)
sachatory, statutory
sachay, sashay / sachet
sache, sachet
sacheable, sate(tiable)
sacheatid, sate(tiated)
sachel, satchel
sacherashen, saturate(tion)
sacherate, saturate
sacheration, saturate(tion)
sacherin, saccharin
sachet, *, SMALL/ AROMATIC BAG (or see sashay)
sachetory, statutory
sacheuble, sate(tiable)
sachil, satchel
sachirashen, saturate(tion)
sachirate, saturate
sachiration, saturate(tion)
sachiren, saccharin
sachol, satchel
sachul, satchel
sachurate, saturate
sachuration, saturate(tion)
sachureit, saturate
sachutory, statutory
sack, *, ked, king, ker, kful, BAG MADE OF VARIOUS MATERIALS USED TO CONTAIN/ HOLD SOMETHING, TO BAG/ TACKLE (or see sax)
sackarin, saccharin
sackralegus, sacrilege(gious)
sackralijes, sacrilege(gious)
sackrament, sacrament
sackrul, sacral
sackrument, sacrament
sackuren, saccharin
saclusion, seclusion
saclusive, seclusive
sacrafais, sacrifice
sacrafise, sacrifice

sacral, ASSOCIATED WITH RITES "prefixes: de"
sacraleje, sacrilege
sacraligous, sacrilege(gious)
sacrament, *, tal, tally, tality, talism, talist, tarian, tarianism, THAT WHICH IS SACRED
sacrasankt, sacrosanct
sacred, dly, dness, OF REVERENCE/ WORSHIPPED
sacrefise, sacrifice
sacrel, sacrum(ral)
sacreleje, sacrilege
sacreligous, sacrilege(gious)
sacrem, sacrum
sacremint, sacrament
sacresanct, sacrosanct
sacresant, sacrosanct
sacreshen, secrete(tion)
sacresion, secrete(tion)
sacrete, secrete / sacred
sacretion, secrete(tion)
sacrid, sacred
sacrifais, sacrifice
sacrifice, *, ed, cing, er, cial, cially, GIVE UP WITHOUT PROFIT/ RETURN, DENY ONESELF
sacril, sacrum(ral)
sacrilege, gious, giously, giousness, VIOLATION OF SACRED
sacrim, sacrum
sacrosanct, tity, tness, TOO HOLY TO BE CRITICIZED/ SLANDERED
sacrud, sacred
sacrufise, sacrifice
sacrul, sacrum(ral)
sacruleje, sacrilege
sacruligus, sacrilege(gious)
sacrum, ral, LUMBAR VERTEBRAE ON THE SPINE
sacrument, sacrament
sacsafoun, saxophone
sacumb, succumb
sacure, secure
sad, dly, dness, dden, dder, ddest, SORROWFUL/ MOURNFUL, UNHAPPY WITH RESULTS (or see sat)
sadalight, satellite
sadalite, satellite

sadami, sodomy
sadarday, saturday
sadasfaction, satisfy(faction)
sadasfakshen, satisfy(faction)
sadasfy, satisfy
sadashen, sedate(tion)
sadasion, sedate(tion)
sadate, sedate
sadation, sedate(tion)
saddle, *, ed, ling, er, DEVICE/ SEAT USED TO RIDE ON A FOUR LEGGED ANIMAL "prefixes: un"
sadel, saddle
sadelite, satellite
sademize, sodomy(mize)
saden, sad(dden) / satin
sadentary, sedentary
sadeny, satin
saderday, saturday
sadesfaction, satisfy(faction)
sadesfakshen, satisfy(faction)
sadesfy, satisfy
sadesum, sadism
sadews, seduce
sadil, saddle
sadilight, satellite
sadilite, satellite
sadimize, sodomy(mize)
sadin, sad(dden) / satin
sadintary, sedentary
sadiny, satin
sadirday, saturday
sadisfaction, satisfy(faction)
sadisfaksen, satisfy(faction)
sadisfy, satisfy
sadism, stic, st, stically, SEXUALLY AROUSED BY PAIN/ TORTURE
sadisum, sadism
sadle, saddle
sadnes, sad(ness)
sadnis, sad(ness)
sadolait, satellite
sadolite, satellite
sadomasakisum, sadomasochism

sadomasochism, st, stic, ASSOCIATED WITH SADISM
sadomasukezim, sadomasochism
sadoose, seduce
sadosfaction, satisfy(faction)
sadosfaksen, satisfy(faction)
saducshen, seduce(ction)
saductive, seduce(ctive)
saduktion, seduce(ction)
saduktive, seduce(ctive)
sadul, saddle
saduld, saddle(d)
sadulite, satellite
sadun, sad(dden) / satin
sadurday, saturday
sadurdei, Saturday
saduse, seduce
sadusfaksen, satisfy(faction)
sadusfy, satisfy
sae, say
saed, said / set
saen, sane / sain
saend, sound
saent, saint
safaier, sapphire
safari, *, HUNTING EXPEDITION
safd, save(d)
safe, ely, er, est, eness, ety, PROTECT FROM HARM (or see salve)
safekate, suffocate
safekation, suffocate(tion)
safeks, suffix
safestikashen, sophisticate(tion)
safestikated, sophisticate(d)
safestikation, sophisticate(tion)
safex, suffix
safflower, FLOWERS WHICH PRODUCED OIL
saffron, A FLOWER/ COLOR
saficashen, suffocate(tion)
saficate, suffocate
safication, suffocate(tion)
saficient, sufficient
saficient, sufficient
safikashen, suffocate(tion)

safikate,suffocate
safikation,suffocate(tion)
safiks,suffix
safinth,seventh
safir,safe(r) / savor / sapphire
safire,sapphire
safise,suffice
safishent,sufficient
safishently,sufficient(ly)
safishunt,sufficient
safist,safe(st)
safistakashen,sophisticate(tion)
safistakated,sophisticate(d)
safistakation,sophisticate(tion)
safix,suffix
saflawur,safflower
saflee,safe(ly)
saflour,safflower
saflower,safflower
safly,safe(ly)
safmor,sophomore
safmore,sophomore
safocashen,suffocate(tion)
safocate,suffocate
safocation,suffocate(tion)
safron,saffron
safrun,saffron / sovereign
saftee,safe(ty)
safucashen,suffocate(tion)
safucate,suffocate
safucation,suffocate(tion)
safukashen,suffocate(tion)
safukate,suffocate
safur,safe(r) / savor
safy,savvy
safyur,savior
sag, *, gged,gging,ggy, TO BOW/ BEND IN A CERTAIN AREA (or see sack/ sage)
sagd,sag(ged) / sage(d)
sage, *, ed,ging,ely,eness, AN HERB/ PLANT, SOMEONE WISE
saged,sag(ged) / sage(d)
sagee,sag(ggy)

sagi,soggy
sagis,sage(s)
saguaro, *, A CACTUS
sagus,sage(s)
sagy,sag(ggy)
saibernetics,cybernetics
saiborg,cyborg
saicol,cycle
saicolochi,psychology
saicololli,psychology
saicopath,psychopath
saicotic,psychotic
saicou,psycho
saicoupath,psychopath
saicousis,psychosis
said, PAST TENSE FOR THE WORD "SAY" (or see set "prefixes: un"
saider,cider
saigou,zygo
saikaietri,psychiatry
saikiatric,psychiatric
saikic,psychic
sail, *, led,ling,lor,OF/ GIVEN TO A BOAT WITH SAILS, USE OF WIND TO NAVIGATE BOAT/ VESSEL (or see sale/ sailor))
sailin,xylene / sailing
sailofoun,xylophone
sailograf,xylograph
sailom,xylem
sailor, *, PEOPLE WHO OPERATE SEAGOING VESSELS (or see sail(er))
sailotomi,xylotomy
sailous,xylose
saim,same
saimololli,zymology
saimou,zymo
saimurchi,zymurgy
sain, MAKE THE SIGN OF THE CROSS (or see sane/ say(ing))
sainkshuary,sanctuary
saint, *, ted,ting,tly,tdom,thood, OFFICALLY RECOGNIZED IN DYING FOR A HOLY CAUSE, A VERY KIND PERSON

saionaide,cyanide
sairus,cirrus
sait,cite
saiteishon,citation
saje,sage
sajed,sage(d)
sak,sack / sake / sag / sax
sakaren,saccharin
sakarin,saccharin
sakd,sack(ed)
sake, PURPOSE/ BENEFIT OF, JAPANESE ALCOHOL BEVERAGE (or see sack)
saker,soccer / sack(er)
sakeren,saccharin
sakerin,saccharin
sakeuridy,secure(rity)
sakewr,secure
sakewrity,secure(rity)
sakful,sack(ful)
sakir,soccer / sack(er)
sakiuredy,secure(rity)
sakiutrest,psychiatry(rist)
saklooded,seclude(d)
saklude,seclude
sakluded,seclude(d)
saklusive,seclusive
saklution,seclusion
sakrafise,sacrifice
sakraleje,sacrilege
sakralige,sacrilege
sakraligus,sacrilege(gious)
sakrament,sacrament
sakramintal,sacrament(al)
sakrasinkt,sacrosanct
sakred,sacred
sakrefise,sacrifice
sakrel,sacral
sakrem,sacrum
sakrement,sacrament
sakren,saccharin
sakreshen,secrete(tion)
sakresion,secrete(tion)
sakret,sacred

salfent, solvent
salfint, solvent
salicit, solicit
salicitation, solicit(ation)
saliciter, solicit(er)
salid, salad / solid
salidarity, solidarity
salidefy, solid(ify)
salidness, solid(ness)
salilakwy, soliloquy
salilaqwy, soliloquy
salim, solemn
salimandur, salamander
salimly, solemn(ly)
saline, na, nity, nization, PERTAINS TO SALT "prefixes: de"
salinidy, saline(nity)
salinoid, solenoid
salir, sail(er) / sailor
saliry, salary / celery
salis, solace
saliset, solicit
saliseter, solicit(er)
salsit, solicit
salsitation, solicit(ation)
salsiter, solicit(er)
salit, salad
salitefy, solid(ify)
saliva, ary, ate, ation, FLUID SECRETED BY GLANDS IN THE MOUTH "prefixes: in"
salm, psalm
salmin, salmon
salmon, a fish
salmonela, salmonella
salmonella, BACTERIA WHICH POISONS FOOD
salmun, salmon
salod, salad
salomander, salamander
salomantur, salamander
salomee, salami
salon, *, CUTS/ STYLES HAIR
saloon, *, TYPE OF DRINKING ESTABLISHMENT
saloot, salute

---

sakrete, secrete
sakrid, sacred
sakrifice, sacrifice
sakril, sacral
sakrilege, sacrilege
sakrim, sacrum
sakriment, sacrament
sakrimental, sacrament(al)
sakrin, saccharin
sakrit, sacred
sakrom, sacrum
sakrosankt, sacrosanct
sakrud, sacred
sakrufise, sacrifice
sakrufishul, sacrifice(cial)
sakrul, sacral
sakruleje, sacrilege
sakruligus, sacrilege(gious)
sakrum, sacrum
sakrument, sacrament
sakrun, saccharin
sakrusankt, sacrosanct
sakrut, sacred
saks, sack(s) / sag(s) / sax
saksafone, saxophone
saksaphone, saxophone
saksufone, saxophone
saksuphone, saxophone
sakt, sack(ed)
sakum, succumb
sakur, soccer / sack(er)
sakure, secure
sakuren, saccharin
sakurin, saccharin
sakurity, secure(rity)
sakwenshul, sequence(ntial)
sakwential, sequence(ntial)
sakwoia, sequoia
sal, sale / sail / saw
salad, *, COLD MIXED FOOD DISH, TOSSED GREENS
saladerity, solidarity
salaiva, saliva
salal, plant

salamander, *, AMPHIBIOUS LIZARD
salami, A SAUSAGE
salan, salon
salar, sail(er) / sailor
salaree, salary / celery
salary, ries, ried, STEADY PAY IN COMPENSATION FOR WORK PERFORMED
salatood, solitude
salatude, solitude
sald, salt / sail(ed)
salder, solder
saldered, solder(ed)
sale, *, eable, sell, SELL GOODS/ SERVICES (or see sail) "prefixes: pre/ re"
salebrity, celebrity
salective, select(ive)
saled, sail(ed) / salad
saledarity, solidarity
saledify, solid(ify)
saleen, saline
saleks, select(s)
salekshen, select(ion)
salekt, select
salektif, select(ive)
salektion, select(ion)
salektive, select(ive)
salelaquy, soliloquy
salem, solemn
salemandur, salamander
salemantur, salamander
salemly, solemn(ly)
salen, saline
salenity, saline(nity)
salenium, selenium
salenoid, solenoid
saler, sail(er) / sailor
saleree, salary celery
salesteal, celestial
salet, salad
saleutation, salute(tation)
salevate, saliva(te)
salewtashen, salute(tation)
salf, solve

salt,* ted,ting,ty,tier,tiest,ter, SODIUM/ CHEMICAL COMPOUND (or see sail(ed)) "prefixes: de"
salud, salad
saludid, salute(d)
saludness, solid(ness)
salum, solemn
salumandur, salamander
salumly, solemn(ly)
salune, saloon
salunization, saline(nization)
salunoid, solenoid
salur, sail(er) / sailor
saluree, salary / celery
salus, solace
salushen, solution
salut, salad
salutashen, salute(tation)
salute,* ed,ting,tary,tarily,tariness,tation,tational, tatorian,tor,tories,ter, METHOD OF GREETING
salutid, salute(d)
salution, solution
saluvate, saliva(te)
salv, solve
salvach, salvage
salvage,* ed,ging,eable,er, THOUGH DAMAGED, IS STILL WORTHY OF SAVING
salvall, salvage
salvashen, salvation
salvation, nal,nism, PRESERVE/ PROTECT FROM DANGER/ HARM
salve,* ed,ving, AN OINTMENT/ BALM USED FOR HEALING SORES (or see solve)
salvech, salvage
salved, solve(d)
salveishon, salvation
salvent, solvent
salvige, salvage
salvije, salvage
salvuble, solve(vable)
salvug, salvage
salyewble, soluble(ize)
salyutashen, salute(tation)
saman, salmon

samanela, salmonella
samantics, semantics
samber, somber
same, eness, ALIKE/ SIMILAR
samen, salmon
samenela, salmonella
samesdur, semester
samester, semester
sametrek, symmetry(ric)
sametric, symmetry(ric)
samin, salmon
saminela, salmonella
samonela, salmonella
sampal, sample
sample,* ed,ling,er, A SMALL AMOUNT/ TASTE OF SOMETHING "prefixes: re/ sub"
samplir, sample(r)
sampul, sample
samun, salmon
samunela, salmonella
san, sane / sain / sand
sanada, sonata
sanareo, scenario
sanatarium, sanitorium
sanatate, sanitate
sanatesation, sanitize(zation)
sanatezashen, sanitize(zation)
sanatization, sanitize(zation)
sanatize, sanitize
sanatoreum, sanitorium
sanatu, sonata
sanchuery, sanctuary
sancshen, sanction
sancshin, sanction
sancshuary, sanctuary
sancshun, sanction
sanctafie, sanctify
sanctify, fies,fied,fying,fication,fier, MAKE HOLY
sanction,* ,ned,ning,ner,nable, FORMAL/ BINDING PERMISSION
sanctofie, sanctify
sanctuary, ries, REPRIEVE FROM PROBLEMS, PLACE OF IMMUNITY

sanctuery, sanctuary
sanctufy, sanctify
sand,* ,ded,ding,dy,der, TINY ROCKS, SMOOTH A SURFACE BY SANDING
sandal,* , TYPE OF SHOE
sandee, sand
sandel, sandal
sandul, sandal
sandur, sand(er)
sandwech, sandwich
sandwich, hes,hed,hing, MEAT/ VEGETABLES BETWEEN TWO PIECES OF BREAD, PHYSICALLY BE BETWEEN TWO THINGS
sandwitch, sandwich
sane, ely,eness,nity,nities, OF SOUND MIND/ JUDGMENT (or see sain/ sand)
sanedy, sanity
sanek, sonic
sanelity, senile(lity)
sanereo, scenario
sanerist, scenario(ist)
sanetais, sanitize
sanetareum, sanitorium
sanetary, sanitary
sanetate, sanitate
saneteit, sanitate
sanetery, sanitary
sanetize, sanitize
sanetoreum, sanitorium
sanetorium, sanitorium
sanety, sanity
sanic, sonic
sanidy, sanity
sanility, senile(lity)
sanitais, sanitize
sanitareum, sanitorium
sanitarium, sanitorium
sanitary, rian,rily,riness, CLEAN/ FREE OF MOST HARMFUL BACTERIA "prefixes: in"
sanitate,* , ed,ting,tion, CLEAN/ RID OF HARMFUL BACTERIA
saniteit, sanitate
sanitery, sanitary

sanitezation,sanitize(zation)
sanitised,sanitize(d)
sanitize,*,ed,zing,zation,er,CLEAN/ RID OF HARMFUL BACTERIA
sanitizer,sanitize(r)
sanitorium,*,RESORT/ FACILITY FOR LONG-TERM CARE OF ILLNESS/ HEALTH
sanity,ties,RELATED TO A SOUND MIND/ JUDGMENT
sankchuery,sanctuary
sankdefide,sanctify(fied)
sankdefy,sanctify
sankdify,sanctify
sankdufide,sanctify(fied)
sankdufy,sanctify
sankshen,sanction
sankshin,sanction
sankshuery,sanctuary
sankshun,sanction
sanktafi,sanctify
sanktify,sanctify
sanktion,sanction
sanktofie,sanctify
sanktuary,sanctuary
sanktuery,sanctuary
sanktufie,sanctify
sanoda,sonata
sanografee,scenography
sanopsis,synopsis
sanota,sonata
sanquich,sandwich
sant,saint
sante,sand
santels,sandal(s)
santly,saint(ly)
santuls,sandal(s)
santur,sand(er)
santwech,sandwich
santwitch,sandwich
sanuc,sonic
sanudy,sanity
sanuk,sonic
sanut,sonnet
sanutareum,sanitorium

sanutary,sanitary
sanutate,sanitate
sanutery,sanitary
sanutezashen,sanitize(zation)
sanutisation,sanitize(zation)
sanutised,sanitize(d)
sanutize,sanitize
sanutizer,sanitize(r)
sanuty,sanity
sanwech,sandwich
saons,se'ance
sap,*,pped,pping,ppy,THE LIFEBLOOD OF PLANTS
saped,sap(pped)
sapena,subpoena
sapenid,subpoena(ed)
sapenud,subpoena(ed)
saperb,superb
saperblee,superb(ly)
sapereor,superior
sapereoredy,superior(ity)
sapereority,superior(ity)
saperlative,superlative
saperlutif,superlative
saphire,sapphire
saphmore,sophomore
sapinud,subpoena(ed)
sapirb,superb
sapirblee,superb(ly)
sapireor,superior
sapireority,superior(ity)
sapirlutif,superlative
sapleminul,subliminal
sapleng,sapling
sapli,supply
saplier,supply(lier)
sapling,*,YOUNG TREES
sapliur,supply(lier)
saply,supply
saport,support
saportef,support(ive)
saportive,support(ive)
sapose,suppose
sapository,suppository

saposubly,suppose(dly)
sapoze,suppose
sapozetory,suppository
sapozitory,suppository
sapozubly,suppose(dly)
sapphire,*,A GEM STONE
sappresion,suppress(ion)
saprechen,suppress(ion)
sapreem,supreme
sapremacy,supremacy
sapreme,supreme
sapremusist,supremacy(cist)
sapremusy,supremacy
sapreno,soprano
sapres,suppress
sapreshen,suppress(ion)
sapretion,suppress(ion)
saprimosy,supremacy
saprino,soprano
sapt,sap(pped)
sapurb,superb
sapurblee,superb(ly)
sapurlative,superlative
sapurlitef,superlative
sapurlutif,superlative
sapy,sap(ppy)
saquential,sequence(ntial)
saquer,secure
saquerin,saccharin
saquir,secure
saquoia,sequoia
sar,czar
saran,A THIN PLASTIC
sarandipity,serendipity
sarape,serape
sarcafagus,sarcophagus
sarcasm,*,stic,REMARKS MEANT TO BE DEMEANING/ MOCKERY TO ANOTHER
sarcastecly,sarcastic(ally)
sarcastek,sarcastic
sarcastic,cally,REMARKS MEANT TO BE DEMEANING/ MOCKERY TO ANOTHER

sarcastikly,sarcastic(ally)
sarcastuk,sarcastic
sarcazum,sarcasm
sarcophagus, ses, gi, STONE COFFIN
sardeen,sardine
sardene,sardine
sardine, *, TINY EDIBLE FISH
sardo,sourdough
sarebrul,cerebral
sarel,sorrel / surreal
sarench,syringe
sarender,surrender
sarendipity,serendipity
sarene,serene
sarenge,syringe
sarenity,serene(nity)
sarenje,syringe
sarenk,saw(ing)
sargeant,sergeant / surgent
sargent,sergeant / surgent
sargint,sergeant / surgent
sari,sorry / saury
saribrol,cerebral
sarinch,syringe
sarinder,surrender
sarindipity,serendipity
saring,saw(ing)
saringe,syringe
sarinje,syringe
sarink,saw(ing)
sariosis,psoriasis
sariusis,psoriasis
sarjent,sergeant
sarjint,sergeant
sarkafigus,sarcophagus
sarkasem,sarcasm
sarkasim,sarcasm
sarkastek,sarcastic
sarkastiklee,sarcastic(ally)
sarkastuk,sarcastic
sarkawfegus,sarcophagus
sarkazum,sarcasm
sarkofigus,sarcophagus

sarkofugus,sarcophagus
sarkophagus,sarcophagus
sarkrowt,sauerkraut
sarllent,sergeant
saro,sorrow
saroful,sorrow(ful)
sarong, *, MATERIAL/ CLOTH USED TO WRAP AROUND THE LOWER TORSO
sarope,serape
saroredy,sorority
sarority,sorority
saround,surround
sarow,sorrow
sarowful,sorrow(ful)
sarownd,surround
sarrated,serrate(d)
sarration,serrate(tion)
sarro,sorrow
sarundipity,serendipity
sarundipudy,serendipity
sary,saury / sorry
sas,sass / say(s)
sasafras,sassafras
sascha,sashay / sachet
sased,sass(ed) / secede
sasede,secede
sasefras,sassafras
saseg,sausage
sasej,sausage
sasenked,succinct
sasenkt,succinct
sasenktly,succinct(ly)
saseptible,susceptible
saseptif,susceptive
saseptive,susceptive
saseptuble,susceptible
saseptuf,susceptive
saser,saucer
saseshen,secession
sasesion,secession
saset,secede
sasetion,secession
sasha,sachet

sashay, *, WISPILY WALK AS IF DANCING (or see sachet)
sasheable,sate(tiable)
sasheated,sate(tiated)
sashet,sashay / sachet
sasheuble,sate(tiable)
sasifras,sassafras
sasig,sausage
sasij,sausage
sasinked,succinct
sasinkt,succinct
sasinktly,succinct(ly)
sasir,saucer
sasofras,sassafras
sasor,saucer
saspekt,suspect
saspend,suspend
saspender,suspender
saspeshus,suspicious
saspishus,suspicious
sass,sses,ssing,ssy,SPEAK IMPUDENTLY,SMART BACK AT
sassafras, USEFUL TREE ROOT BARK
sasufras,sassafras
sasur,saucer
sasy,saucy / sass
sat,PAST TENSE WORD FOR 'SIT' (or see sate/ sad)
sata,saute / sate
sataier,satyr
satalait,satellite
satalite,satellite
satanek,satanic
satanic, cal,cally,ism,ist, MOCKERY OF CHRISTIAN RITUAL
satanuk,satanic
satanukel,satanic(al)
satarate,saturate
satarday,saturday
satasfaction,satisfy(faction)
satasfakshen,satisfy(faction)
satasfy,satisfy
satay,saute / sate
satchal,satchel
satcharashen,saturate(tion)
satcharate,saturate
satchatory,statutory

satchel,*, BAG/ CARRYING CASE
satcherashen,satcherate(tion)
satcherate,satcherate
satchetory,statutory
satchil,satchel
satchirashen,satcherate(tion)
satchirate,satcherate
satchitory,statutory
satchul,satchel
satchurashen,satcherate(tion)
satchurate,satcherate
satchutory,statutory
sate, ed, ting, tiable, tiably, tiability, tiate, tiates, tiated, tiating,tiation,tiety,TO BE COMPLETELY SATISFIED (or see saute) "prefixes : in"
sateable,sate(tiable)
satei,saute
satel,saddle
satelite,satellite
satellite,*, A PLANET OR MANMADE DEVICE WHICH ORBITS THE EARTH "prefixes: bio"
satemize,sodomy(mize)
saten,sad(dden) / satin
satentary,sedentary
sateny,satin
saterate,saturate
saterday,saturday
saterikul,satire(rical)
satesfaction,satisfy(faction)
satesfakshen,satisfy(faction)
satesfy,satisfy
satesm,sadism
satiaty,sate(tiety)
satilite,satellite
satimize,sodomy(mize)
satin,ny,A SOFT FABRIC
satintary,sedentary
satirate,saturate
satirday,saturday
satire,*, ric, rical, rically, rist, rize, rizes, rized, rizing, rization, rizer,EMPLOY IRONY/ WIT/ SARCASM (or see satyr)
satirest,satire(rist)

satisfakshen,satisfy(faction)
satisfy,fies, fied, fying, fiable, fier, fyingly, faction, factorily, NEEDS/ DEMANDS/ EXPECTATIONS FULFILLED "prefixes: dis/ un"
satisum,sadism
satle,saddle
satlee,sad(ly)
satnis,sad(ness)
satolite,satellite
satomasakisum,sadomasochism
satomasochism,sadomasochism
satosfaction,satisfy(faction)
satosfakshen,satisfy(faction)
satshetory,statutory
satul,saddle
satulite,satellite
saturate,*, ed, ting, tion, tor, UNABLE TO ABSORB ANYMORE LIQUID "prefixes: de/ un/ under"
saturday,*, A DAY OF THE WEEK (ENGLISH)
satusfakshen,satisfy(faction)
satusfy,satisfy
satutory,statutory
satyerashen,saturate(tion)
satyirate,saturate
satyr,*, ric, rical,MYTHOLOGICAL CREATURE (or see satire)
satyurate,saturate
satyuration,saturate(tion)
sau,saw
sauble,say(able)
sauce,*, ed, cing, cy,A THICK LIQUID WITH SPICES/ HERBS/ FLAVORINGS ADDED
saucer,*, A SMALL PLATE, SHAPE OF A PLATE
sauciur,saucy(cier)
saucy,cier, ciest, cily, ciness, BEING IMPUDENT/ FLIPPANT TOWARD SUPERIORS
saud,sod / sold / saw
sauder,solder
sauderd,solder(ed)
saudumize,sodomy(mize)
saudumy,sodomy
sauer,sour
sauercrat,sauerkraut

sauerdo,sourdough
sauerkraut, FERMENTED CABBAGE
saufari,safari
saufen,soft(en)
saufet,soffit
saufiner,soft(ener)
saufit,soffit
saufmore,sophomore
saufunir,soft(ener)
saugee,soggy
saught,saute / sought
sauir,sour
sauirdo,sourdough
sauirkrowt,sauerkraut
saulanoid,solenoid
saulder,solder
saulesmint,solace(ment)
saulid,solid
saulis,solace
saulisment,solace(ment)
saulitare,solitaire / solitary
saulderity,solidarity
saulus,solace
saulutare,solitaire / solitary
saulutude,solitude
saulyewble,soluble(ize)
sauna,*, ROOM WITH MOIST HEAT/ STEAM
saund,sound
saunek,sonic
saunet,sonnet
saunik,sonic
saunit,sonnet
saunt,sound
saunter,*, red, ring,A LEISURLEY WALK/ STROLL
saunu,sauna
saunut,sonnet
saur,sour
saurdo,sourdough
sauree,sorry / saury
sauro,sorrow
saury,ries,A FISH (or see sorry)
saus,sauce
sausage,*, MINCED MEAT WITH FLAVORINGS

sauseur,saucy(cier)	savinth,seventh
sausier,saucy(cier)	**savior,***,ONE CHOSEN BY PEOPLE TO LEAD THEM FROM IGNORANCE INTO ENLIGHTENMENT
saut,sought	
saute,*,eed,eing,QUICKLY FRY IN A PAN/ WOK (or see sate)	savir,savor / save(r) / savior
sauter,solder	savird,savor(ed)
sautered,solder(ed)	saviren,sovereign
sauvren,sovereign	savlawur,safflower
sauvter,soft(er)	savlee,safe(ly)
sauvuble,solve(vable)	savont,savant
sauyubil,soluble	**savor,***,red,ring,rer,ry,FOOD WITH MOST PALATABLE FLAVOR/ SMELL/ TASTE (or see savior) "prefixes: un"
sav,save / salve / solve	
savach,savage	savree,savor
savage,*,ely,eness,ery,eries,BEASTLY/ RUDE/ BARBARIAN	savren,sovereign
	savron,saffron / sovereign
savagly,savage(ly)	savrun,sovereign
savall,savage	savry,savor
savana,savanna	savtee,safe(ty)
savanna,MEADOW/ PLAIN WITH SHRUBS/ TREES	savuch,savage
savant,* , A WISE/ LEARNED PERSON	savugly,savage(ly)
savar,savor / save(r)	savugry,savage(ry)
savaren,sovereign	savuje,savage
savd,save(d)	savur,savor / save(r) / savior
save,* , ed,ving, er,RESCUE FROM DANGER/ HARM/ ALTERCATION (or see safe/ savvy/ salve)	savurd,savor(ed)
	savuren,sovereign
	savurin,sovereign
savech,savage	**savvy,vvies,vvied,vvying,vviest,INTELLIGENT/ SHREWD UNDERSTANDING**
savechry,savage(ry)	
savee,savvy	savy,savvy
savege,savage	sayer,savior
savegly,savage(ly)	sayur,savior
savegry,savage(ry)	**saw,*** , wed,wing,wer,PAST TENSE FOR THE WORD "SEE" ,BLADE WITH TEETH THAT CUTS (or see sauce) "prefixes: over"
saveje,savage	
savell,savage	
saver,save(r) / savor	sawardo,sourdough
saveridy,severe(rity)	sawarkrowt,sauerkraut
saverin,sovereign	sawaro,saguaro
saverity,severe(rity)	sawdemise,sodomy(mize)
savich,savage	sawdemy,sodomy
savichry,savage(ry)	sawder,solder
savier,savvy(vvier) / savior	sawdered,solder(ed)
savigly,savage(ly)	sawdimy,sodomy
savigry,savage(ry)	sawdumize,sodomy(mize)
savije,savage	sawdur,solder

	sawer,sour
	sawerdo,sourdough
	sawerkraut,sauerkraut
	sawfenir,soft(ener)
	sawfet,soffit
	sawfin,soft(en)
	sawfinur,soft(ener)
	sawfit,soffit
	sawfmore,sophomore
	sawfun,soft(en)
	sawfuner,soft(ener)
	sawgee,soggy
	sawir,sour
	sawirdo,sourdough
	sawirkraut,sauerkraut
	sawirkrowt,sauerkraut
	sawker,soccer
	sawled,solid
	sawlesmint,solace(ment)
	sawletare,solitaire / solitary
	sawlf,solve
	sawlid,solid
	sawlidness,solid(ness)
	sawlis,solace
	sawlisment,solace(ment)
	sawlitness,solid(ness)
	sawlud,solid
	sawludness,solid(ness)
	sawlutare,solitaire / solitary
	sawlutude,solitude
	sawnd,sound
	sawnek,sonic
	sawnet,sonnet
	sawnik,sonic
	sawnut,sonnet
	sawor,sour
	saworo,saguaro
	sawp,sop / sob
	sawpee,sop(ppy)
	sawree,saury / sorry
	sawrely,sorry(rily)
	sawrench,syringe
	sawrij,sorry / saury

sawro,saguaro / sorrow
sawrong,sarong
sawry,sorry / saury
saws,saw(s) / sauce / souse
sawsege,sausage
sawseje,sausage
sawser,saucer
sawsige,sausage
sawsor,saucer
sawst,souse(d)
sawsuge,sausage
sawsuje,sausage
sawsur,saucer
sawsy,saucy
sawt,saw(ed)
sawtay,saute / sate
sawte,saute / sate
sawtemy,sodomy
sawtered,solder(ed)
sawtimise,sodomy(mize)
sawtumy,sodomy
sawuble,soluble(ize)
sawur,sour
sawurdo,sourdough
sawurkraut,sauerkraut
sawurkrowt,sauerkraut
sawvuble,solve(vable)
sawyebul,soluble
sawyubil,soluble
sawzy,saucy
sax,SLANG FOR SAXOPHCNE (or see sack(s))
saxophone,*,,nic,nist,HORN INSTRUMENT
saxsifone,saxophone
saxsiphone,saxophone
say,*,,yer,ying,aid,WHAT HAS BEEN SPOKEN,TO SPEAK VERBALLY "prefixes: ,n"
sayabil,soluble
sayans,se'ance
saybernetics,cybernetics
sayborg,cyborg
sayclist,cyclist
saycloun,cyclone
saycol,cycle

sayder,cider
sayn,sain / sane / say(ing)
sayonaid,cyanide
sayons,se'ance
sayros,cirrus
sayulose,cellulose
sbase,space / space
sbaser,space(r)
sbast,space(d)
sbasur,space(r)
sbasy,space
sbegut,spigot
sbekit,spigot
sbekot,spigot
sbidel,spittle
sbidul,spittle
sbiget,spigot
sbikit,spigot
sbikot,spigot
sbital,spittle
sbitul,spittle
sblash,splash
sblat,splat
sblendur,splinter / splendor
sblent,splint
sblerge,splurge
sblerje,splurge
sblet,split
sbletur,split(tter)
sblices,splice(s)
sblin,spline / spleen
sbra spray
sblindur,splinter / splendor
sblint,splint
sblirge,splurge
sblirje,splurge
sblis,splice
sbliser,splice(r)
sblist,splice(d)
sblisur,splice(r)
sblit,split
sbliter,split(tter)
sblitur,split(tter)

sbloch,splotch
sblochy,splotch
sblotch,splotch
sblotchee,splotch
sblurje,splurge
sboel,spoil
sboeld,spoil(ed) / spoilt
sboeleg,spoil(age)
sboil,spoil
sboild,spoil(ed) / spoilt
sboiled,spoil(ed) / spoilt
sboileg,spoil(age)
sboke,spoke
sbon,spoon
sboon,spoon
sbore,spore
sboyl,spoil
sbra, spray
sbraket,sprocket
sbran,sprain
sbrauket,sprocket
sbraul,sprawl
sbre,spree
sbreg,sprig
sbrews,spruce
sbrig,sprig
sbrocket,sprocket
sbroket,sprocket
sbroose,spruce
sbruse,spruce
sbun,spun / spoon
sburd,spur(rred)
sburt,spur(rred)
scab,*,,bbed,bbing,bby,CRUST FORMED ON SKIN OVER OPEN WOUND,TERM FOR STRIKE WORKERS
scabard,scabbard
scabbard,*,,SWORD SHEATH/ SHEATHE
scabburd,scabbard
scabed,scab(bbed)
scabees,scabies
scaberd,scabbard
scabies,etic,ious,SKIN DISEASE
scaburd,scabbard

scaby,scab(bby)
scad,*,EDIBLE FISH,LARGE NUMBER/ QUANTITY
scader,skate(r) / scatter
scadered,scatter(ed)
scadir,skate(r) / scatter
scadured,scatter(ed)
scaffold,*,ding,TEMPORARY FRAMEWORK WITH PLANKS USED TO BUILD
scafold,scaffold
scai,sky
scair,scare
scairslee,scarce(ly)
scairsness,scarce(ness)
scalar,A PHYSICS EXPRESSION,OF MASS AND TIME
scald,*,ded,ding,SURFACE BURN
scale,*,ed,ling,eless,eliness,lable,ly,INSTRUMENT FOR MEASURING WEIGHT,MUSICAL LADDER,TO CLIMB (or see scaly) "prefixes: de/ over/ re/ up"
scaleness,scaly(liness)
scaleon,scallion
scalep,scallop
scaleun,scallion
scaley,scaly
scalion,scallion
scalip,scallop
scallion,*,TYPE OF ONION
scallop,*,per,SHELLFISH,TYPE OF DISH/ SHAPE
scalop,scallop
scalor,scalar
scalp,*,ped,ping,SKIN ON HUMAN SKULL,WAY OF SELLING TICKETS (or see scallop)
scalpal,scalpel
scalpel,*,A SURGICAL KNIFE
scalpul,scalpel
scalup,scallop
scaly,liness,leless,SIMILAR/ SAME AS SCALES ON A FISH
scalyin,scallion
scalyun,scallion
scamatic,scheme(matic)
scan,*,nned,nning,nner,A MACHINE WHICH COPIES/ TAKES DIGITAL IMAGES "prefixes: over"
scandal,*,lize,lous,lously,lousness,EVENT WHICH DEGRADES/ OFFENDS A SOCIAL VALUE/ IDEA

scandel,scandal
scandelus,scandal(ous)
scandil,scandal
scandolus,scandal(ous)
scandul,scandal
scandulus,scandal(ous)
scaner,scan(nner)
scanerio,scenario
scanir,scan(nner)
scanography,scenography
scant,tily,tness,LIMITED RESOURCE
scantuly,scant(ily)
scanur,scan(nner)
scapala,scapula
scapel,scalpel
scapeula,scapula
scapewla,scapula
scapil,scalpel
scapila,scapula
scapul,scalpel
scapula,*,SHOULDER BLADE
scar,*,rred,rring,A PHYSICAL MARK LEFT AFTER A BODILY INJURY HAS HEALED (or see scare)
scarce,ely,city,eness,IN DEMAND, RARE
scarcedy,scarce(city)
scare,*,ed,ring,ry,FRIGHTEN/ ALARM
scared,scare(d) / scar(rred)
scarf,fes,fed,fing,rves,A LIGHTWEIGHT MATERIAL WORN ON THE HEAD,TO WOLF DOWN FOOD/ DRINK
scarfd,scarf(ed)
scarfs,scarf(rves)
scarft,scarf(ed)
scarlet,A COLOR
scarlut,scarlet
scarse,scarce
scarsedy,scarce(city)
scarsity,scarce(city)
scarsly,scarce(ly)
scarsness,scarce(ness)
scarsudy,scarce(city)
scart,scar(rred) / scare(d)
scary,scare

scat,*,tted,tting,SINGING IMPROVISATION,TO HURRY AWAY,FISH,ANIMAL FECAL (or see skat/ skate)
scater,scatter
scathe,*,ed,hing,hingly,TO INJURE/ HARM "prefixes: un"
scatir,scatter
scatter,*,red,ring,rable,DISPERSED ABOUT IRREGULARLY (or see skate(r))
scatur,scatter
scauler,scholar
scaulerly,scholar(ly)
scavage,scavenge
scavager,scavenge(r)
scavenge,*,ed,ging,er,SEARCH/ SEEK FOR USABLE ITEMS
scavuge,scavenge
scavunjer,scavenge(r)
scawler,scholar
scawlerly,scholar(ly)
scem,scheme / skim
scenac,scene(nic)
scenario,*,ist,TO OUTLINE SCENES/ CHARACTERS FOR PLAY/ MOVIE
scenary,scene(ry)
scene,*,ery,eries,nic,nerio,nography,VISUAL PRESENTATION OF A PLACE/ EVENT
scenic,scene(nic)
sceniry,scene(ry)
scenography,hic,her,RULES IN CREATING PERSPECTIVE
scent,*,ted,tless,tlessness,ODOR/ FRAGRANCE
scenur,skinner
sceptacism,skeptic(ism)
sceptasisum,skeptic(ism)
sceptasium,skeptic(ism)
scepter,*,red,ring,ROD OF AUTHORITY/ ROYALTY
scepticism,skeptic(ism)
sceptik,skeptic
sceptir,scepter
sceptisitum,skeptic(ism)
sceptor,scepter
sceptuk,skeptic
sceptur,scepter
sceptusisum,skeptic(ism)
scer,scare

scerfy,scurvy
sceris,scirrhus / cirrus
scersity,scarce(city)
scersly,scarce(ly)
scersudy,scarce(city)
scerus,scirrhus / cirrus
scery,scurry
scesurs,scissor(s)
scewbu,scuba
scewp,scoop
scewper,scoop(er)
schalastic,scholastic
schaler,scholar
schalerly,scholar(ly)
schamatic,scheme(matic)
schaulerly,scholar(ly)
schedewl,schedule
schedule,*,ed,ling,AN ITEMIZED LIST CONCERNING TIME AND APPOINTMENTS "prefixes: re"
scheem,scheme
schelastic,scholastic
scheme,*,ed,ming,er,ma,mata,matic,matically,matism, matist,matize,matization,matizer,PLAN/ PLOT/ PROJECT
schemir,skim(mmer) / scheme(r)
schemur,skim(mmer) / scheme(r)
schilastic,scholastic
schimatic,scheme(matic)
schist,tose,tous,ROCK TYPE DETERMINED BY THE WAY IT EXFOLIATES
schitzophrenia,schizophrenia
schizofrenia,schizophrenia
schizoid,PERTAINING TO SCHIZOPHRENIA
schizophrenia,ic,MENTAL PROBLEM
schizoyd,schizoid
scholar,*,rly,rliness,ONE WHO HAS STUDIED/ LEARNED A GREAT DEAL
scholastic,*,cal,cally,cate,cism,RELATED/ CONCERNING SCHOOL "prefixes: irter"
scholer,scholar
scholerly,scholar(ly)
school,*,led,ling,ler,A PLACE TO LEARN "prefixes: pre/ un"

schooner,*,TYPE OF SAILING VESSEL
schuel,school
schulastic,scholastic
schule,school
schumatic,scheme(matic)
schuner,schooner
sciadeca,sciatic(a)
sciadica,sciatic(a)
scianse,science
sciantifek,scientific
sciantifekaly,scientific(ally)
sciantificly,scientific(ally)
sciatek,sciatic
sciatic,ca,cally,MAJOR NERVES IN THE BODY NEAR THE HIPS
sciatik,sciatic
science,*,ntific,ntist,FIELDS OF GENERAL LAWS CONCERNING EVERYTHING IN OUR REALITY "prefixes: bio"
scientest,scientist
scientifek,scientific
scientific,cally,OF FIELDS OF SCIENCE "prefixes: un"
scientifik,scientific
scientifikaly,scientific(ally)
scientist,*,sm,MAJORS IN THE FIELD OF SCIENCE "prefixes: bio"
scif,skiff
scikyatrus,psychiatry(rist)
scimatic,scheme(matic)
scinario,scenario
scinerio,scenario
scinography,scenography
scint,scent
scinur,skinner
scirfy,scurvy
scirhus,scirrhus / cirrus
scirrhus,hoid,hous,CONCERNING TUMORS IN THE BODY (or see cirrus)
scirus,scirrhus / cirrus
sciry,scurry
scisers,scissor(s)
scissor,*,TOOL TO CUT/ SEVER
scisurs,scissor(s)

scith,scythe
sciuntefikaly,scientific(ally)
sciuntist,scientist
scizurs,scissor(s)
scof,scoff
scofed,scoff(ed)
scoff,*,ffed,ffing,ffingly,ffer,SHOW MOCKERY/ DISTASTE,RIDICULE
scold,*,ded,ding,TO FIND FAULT/ REPRIMAND SOMEONE FOR THEIR BEHAVIOR (or see scald)
scoleosis,scoliosis
scoliosis,ic,CURVATURE OF THE SPINE
scolt,scold / scald
sconc,skunk
sconce,*,ed,cing,LIGHTS ON THE WALL,FORT, SKULL
scone,*,A BREAD CAKE
scons,scone(s) / sconce
sconts,sconce
scooba,scuba
scooder,scoot(er)
scoop,*,ped,ping,per,pful,GATHER UP QUANTITY OF SOMETHING ALL AT ONCE
scoopir,scoop(er)
scoot,*,ted,ting,ter,GO/ SEND HASTILY ALONG, SLIDE OVER (or see scute)
scorch,hes,hed,hing,her,LIGHTLY BURN
score,*,ed,ring,er,eless,MARK BY GOUGING/ SCRATCHING,POINTS IN COMPETITION "prefixes: over/ re/ under"
scorlis,score(less)
scorn,*,ned,ning,ningly,nful,nfully,nfulness,EXPRESS DISTATE/ CONTEMPT
scornfuly,scorn(fully)
scorpeon,scorpion
scorpion,*,AN ARACHNOID
scoul,scowl
scouled,scowl(ed)
scoundrel,*,lly,MEAN PERSON WHO HAS NO HONOR FOR OTHERS
scoundril,scoundrel
scoundrle,scoundrel
scour,*,red,ring,rer,SCRUB CLEAN,GO OVER, PURGE
scourd,scour(ed)

scourge, *, ed, ging, er, TORMENT/ TORTURE/ SEVERLY PUNISH
scout, *, ted, ting, ter, TO HUNT/ SEARCH FOR
scouwl, scowl
scower, scour
scowl, *, led, ling, WEARING A LOOK OF ANGER
scowndrel, scoundrel
scowr, scour
scowt, scout
scowurd, scour(ed)
scrach, scratch
scrag, *, gged, gging, ggy, gily, gginess, ggly, JAGGED/ SKINNY/ DISHEVELED/ BONEY/ SCRAWNY/ LEAN
scraggly, lies, lier, liest, ggily, gginess, UNEVEN/ IRREGULAR/ DISHEVELED/ MESSY
scragleur, scraggly(lier)
scragliest, scraggly(liest)
scragly, scrag(ily) / scraggly
scrakly, scrag(ily) / scraggly
scram, *, mmed, mming, GO AWAY QUICKLY
scrambal, scramble
scrambil, scramble
scramble, *, ed, ling, er, MIX UP TOGETHER, CLUMSILY TAKE ACTION "prefixes: de/ un"
scrambul, scramble
scrap, *, pped, pping, pper, ppage, SMALL PARTICLE/ PIECE/ FRAGMENT, LEFTOVERS, PICK A FIGHT (or see scrape)
scrapt, scrap(pped) / scrape(d)
scrapuble, scrap(able)
scrape, *, ed, ping, er, pable, RASP/ GRATE/ DAMAGE, NOISE BY DRAGGING SOMETHING/ MARKS (or see scrap)
scratch, hes, hed, hing, her, hy, MARK/ CUT/ CROSS OUT
scrawl, *, led, ling, ly, ler, AWKWARD/ IRREGULAR MARKS AS IF DONE HASTILY
screach, screech
scream, *, med, ming, mer, mingly, A LOUD/ SHRILL OUTCRY FROM THE THROAT
screan, screen
screanable, screen(able)
screbul, scribble
screch, screech

scred, screed
screech, hes, hed, hing, SHARP/ SHRILL/ LOUD SOUND
screed, *, ded, ding, SEPARATE PARTICLES FROM ONE ANOTHER, PLASTER/ MORTAR TECHNIQUE
screem, scream
screen, *, ned, ning, ner, nable, MATERIAL FOR WINDOWS, TO SORT/ SIFT THROUGH
scremp, scrimp
scremshaw, scrimshaw
scren, screen
screped, script
screpsher, scripture
scrept, script
screpture, scripture
screw, *, wed, wing, wer, wy, SMALL CYLINDRICAL OBJECT WITH POINTED TIP/ SLOTTED HEAD "prefixes: un"
screwdnee, scrutiny
screwge, scrooge
screwje, scrooge
screwpul, scruple
screwpulus, scrupulous
screwtney, scrutiny
scribble, *, ed, ling, er, SCRAWL, UNDECIPHERABLE MARKS
scribd, scribe(d) / script
scribe, *, ed, bing, er, bal, A WRITER
scrible, scribble
scribul, scribble
scrimage, scrimmage
scrimmage, *, ed, ging, PHYSICAL ROUGH ABOUT WITH OTHERS IN A GAME
scrimp, *, ped, ping, py, TIGHT BUDGET/ SPENDING HABIT
scrimshaw, IVORY CARVING
scrimuge, scrimmage
scrimuje, scrimmage
scripshur, scripture
script, *, ted, ting, THE CHARACTERS/ TEXT OF A PLAY/ MOVIE/ BROADCAST/ PROGRAM "prefixes: re/ un"
scripture, *, ral, rally, ralness, RELIGIOUS WRITING "prefixes: un"
scroge, scrooge
scroje, scrooge
scrol, scrawl / scroll
scroll, *, lled, lling, PARCHMENT/ PAPER ROLLED UP

scrooge, A MISER, TIGHTWAD
scrooje, scrooge
scrooteny, scrutiny
scrounge, *, ed, ging, gy, gier, giest, FORAGE AROUND, A DISHEVELED/ UNKEPT LOOK
scroungy, scrounge
scrowl, scrawl
scrowngy, scrounge
scrownje, scrounge / scrounge
scru, screw
scrub, *, bbed, bbing, bber, bby, RUB/ SCOURGE BRISKLY, LOW GROWTH TREE/ SHRUBS
scrudnee, scrutiny
scruf, scruff
scruff, ffy, BACK/ NAPE OF NECK
scrufy, scruff
scruge, scrooge
scruje, scrooge
scruny, scrutiny
scrup, scrub
scrupel, scruple
scrupewlus, scrupulous
scruple, *, ed, ling, REMAIN CONSCIOUSLY AWARE/ ALERT CONCERNING WHAT IS RIGHT/ PROPER "prefixes: un"
scrupol, scruple
scrupulous, osity, sness, sly, BEING CAREFUL
scrut, screw(ed)
scruteny, scrutiny
scrutiny, nize, nizes, nized, nizing, nization, nizer, CLOSELY EXAMINE/ EVALUATE
scruwy, screw
scruy, screw
scuabol, squabble
scuach, squash
scuad, squad
scuadron, squadron
scual, squall
scualid, squalid
scualor, squalor
scuander, squander
scuat, squat
scuba, *, UNDERWATER DEVICE FOR BREATHING

scuder, scoot(er)
scuelch, squelch
scuer, square
scuert, squirt
scuf, scuff
scufel, scuffle
scuff, *, ffed, ffing, LEAVE MARKS BY WEARING/ USAGE/ WALKING
scuffle, *, ed, ling, DISORDERLY PHYSICAL STRUGGLE/ FIGHT
scufil, scuffle
scuful, scuffle
scuid, squid
scuigol, squiggle
scuik, squeak
scuill, squeal
scuilli, squeegee
scuimish, squeamish
scuint, squint
scuis, squeeze
scuish, squish
scuiz, squeeze
scul, skull / school
sculbed, sculpt
sculbshir, sculpt(ure)
sculpshir, sculpt(ure)
sculpt, *, ted, ting, tor, ture, tural, turally, FORM BY HUMAN/ NATURAL PROCESS TO CREATE 3D IMAGES
sculpter, sculpt(ure)
scum, *, mmed, mming, mmy, NASTY/ VILE/ WORTHLESS, RESIDUE LEFT BEHIND
scumatic, scheme(matic)
scumy, scum(mmy)
scunario, scenario
scuner, schooner
scup, scoop
scupd, scoop(ed)
scupt, scoop(ed)
scufty, scurvy
scurry, rries, rried, rrying, TO SCAMPER/ HURRY
scurvy, vies, vier, viest, vily, viness, A DISEASE
scury, scurry
scute, *, BONY PLATE/ SHIELD (or see scoot)

scuter, scoot(er)
scwaled, squalid
scwolid, squalid
scythe, *, ed, hing, A TOOL WITH LONG BLADE USED IN SWEEPING MOTIONS TO CUT GRASS/ GRAIN
sdabul, stable
sdaleto, stiletto
sdaroyd, steroid
sdash, stash
sdeledo, stiletto
sdemulashen, stimulate(tion)
sdemulate, stimulate
sdemulation, stimulate(tion)
sderdy, sturdy
sdergen, sturgeon
sderjon, sturgeon
sderoed, steroid
sderoet, steroid
sderoyd, steroid
sderty, sturdy
sdewdeo, studio
sdewdeus, studious
sdewpendus, stupendous
sdewper, stupor
sdewpid, stupid
sdewpir, stupor
sdewpur, stupor
sdifel, stifle
sdiful, stifle
sdil, style / still
sdilesh, style(lish)
sdilest, style(list)
sdileto, stiletto
sdilist, style(list)
sdilush, style(lish)
sdime, stymie
sdimulashen, stimulate(tion)
sdimulate, stimulate
sdimulation, stimulate(tion)
sdirafom, styrofoam
sdirdy, sturdy
sdirefom, styrofoam
sdirty, sturdy

sdirufom, styrofoam
sdo, stow / store
sdoe, stow
sdoek, stoic
sdogee, stogy
sdogy, stogy
sdoik, stoic
sdok, stuck
sdol, stole
sdoledo, stiletto
sdolen, stole(n)
sdolun, stole(n)
sdon, stun
sdools, stool(s)
sdooped, stupid
sdoopid, stupid
sdoopiduudy, stupid(ity)
sdoopiduty, stupid(ity)
sdoopir, stupor
sdoopufid, stupefy(fied)
sdoopur, stupor
sdopid, stupid
sdored, story(ried)
sdoree, story
sdoreg, storage
sdorej, storage
sdores, story(ries)
sdorig, storage
sdorij, storage
sdorm, storm
sdormee, storm
sdow, stow
sdowek, stoic
sdowik, stoic
sdra, straw / stray
sdradagee, strategy
sdradajist, strategy(gist)
sdrade, stray(ed) / straight
sdrades, stratus
sdradis, stratus
sdradugee, strategy
sdradugist, strategy(gist)
sdradus, stratus

sdrae,stray
sdrain,strain
sdrand,strain(ed) / strand
sdrane,strain
sdrap,strap
sdras,stress
sdratagee,strategy
sdrategek,strategic
sdrategekly,strategic(ally)
sdrategist,strategy(gist)
sdrategy,strategy
sdratejik,strategic
sdratejikly,strategic(ally)
sdratejist,strategy(gist)
sdrates,stratus
sdratesfere,stratosphere
sdratesphere,stratosphere
sdratigek,strategic
sdratigekly,strategic(ally)
sdratis,stratus
sdratosfere,stratosphere
sdratosphere,stratosphere
sdratugee,strategy
sdratugist,strategy(gist)
sdratus,stratus
sdratusfere,stratosphere
sdratusphere,stratosphere
sdraw,straw
sdrayd,stray(ed) / straight
sdreakee,streak
sdrech,stretch
sdrecher,stretch(er)
sdrechr,stretch(er)
sdrechur,stretch(er)
sdreek,streak
sdreem,stream
sdreet,street
sdrek,streak
sdrekd,strict / streak(ed)
sdreke,streak
sdreknine,strychnine
sdrekun,stricken
sdreky,streak

sdrem,stream
sdremer,stream(er)
sdremur,stream(er)
sdreneus,strenuous
sdrenewus,strenuous
sdreng,string
sdrengee,string
sdrengint,stringent
sdrenjint,stringent
sdrenkth,strength
sdrenth,strength
sdrenues,strenuous
sdrep,strep/ strip / stripe
sdrepd,stripe(d) / strip(pped)
sdreped,stripe(d) / strip(pped)
sdreper,stripe(r) / strip(pper)
sdrepur,stripe(r) / strip(pper)
sdres,stress
sdresh,stretch
sdret,street
sdreun,strewn
sdrew,strew
sdriashen,striate(tion)
sdriate,striate
sdriation,striate(tion)
sdrife,strife / strive
sdrik,strike
sdrikd,strict
sdriked,strict
sdriken,stricken
sdriknin,strychnine
sdrikun,stricken
sdrinewus,strenuous
sdring,string
sdringee,string
sdrinjint,stringent
sdrinkth,strength
sdrinth,strength
sdrinues,strenuous
sdrip,strep/ strip / stripe
sdriped,stripe(d) / strip(pped)
sdripur,stripe(r) / strip(pper)
sdrivd,strive(d)

sdrive,strive / strife
sdro,straw
sdrobe,strobe
sdroganoff,stroganoff
sdroginof,stroganoff
sdroke,stroke
sdrol,stroll
sdroler,stroll(er)
sdrolur,stroll(er)
sdrong,strong
sdrongist,strong(est)
sdrongur,strong(er)
sdroodel,strudel
sdroodul,strudel
sdroon,strewn
sdrope,strobe
sdru,strew
sdruc,struck
sdrud,stood / stud
sdrudel,strudel
sdrudid,strut(tted)
sdrudil,strudel
sdrudul,strudel
sdrueng,strew(ing)
sdrugel,struggle
sdrugul,struggle
sdruk,struck
sdrukchur,structure
sdrukshur,structure
sdrukul,struggle
sdrum,strum
sdrumer,strum(mmer)
sdrun,strewn
sdrung,strung
sdrut,strut
sdrutegek,strategic
sdrutegekly,strategic(ally)
sdrutejik,strategic
sdrutigekly,strategic(ally)
sdruz,strew(s)
sdryate,striate
sdubee,stub(bby)
sdubel,stubble

sdubern,stubborn
sduble,stubble
sduborn,stubborn
sdubul,stubble
sduburn,stubborn
sduby,stub(bby)
sduded,study(died) / stud(dded)
sdudee,study
sdudeo,studio
sduder,stutter
sdudes,study(dies)
sdudeus,studious
sdudio,studio
sdudir,stutter
sdudius,studious
sdudur,stutter
sdudy,study
sduel,stool
sdufee,stuff
sduil,stool
sduk,stuck
sduko,stucco
sdule,stool
sduledo,stiletto
sdump,stump
sdumpee,stump
sdun,stun
sdunk,stunk
sdunt,stunt / stun(nned)
sduol,stool
sdupafid,stupefy(fied)
sduped,stub(bbed) / stupid
sdupeduedy,stupid(ity)
sdupeduty,stupid(ity)
sdupefy,stupefy
sdupel,stubble
sdupendus,stupendous
sduper,stupor
sdupidudy,stupid(ity)
sdupiduty,stupid(ity)
sdupify,stupefy
sdupil,stubble
sdupindus,stupendous

sdupir,stupor
sduple,stubble
sdupt,stub(bbed)
sdupud,stupid
sdupufie,stupefy
sdupul,stubble
sdupur,stupor
sdurdy,sturdy
sdurgen,sturgeon
sdurjon,sturgeon
sduter,stutter
sduty,study
sdwaple,squabble
sdylesh,style(lish)
sdyme,stymie
sdyrafom,styrofoam
se,see / sea

se'ance,A COMMUNICATION WITH SPIRITS BEYOND THE PHYSICAL PLANE
sea,*,LARGE SALTWATER BODY/ OCEAN (or see see) "prefixes: over/ under"
seable,see(able)
seabul,see(able)
sead,seed / said
seaesta,siesta
seafood,*,EDIBLE SHELLFISH/ AQUATIC ANIMALS
seal,*,led,ling,ler,lery,leries,AQUATIC MAMMAL, CLOSE SOMETHING TIGHTLY "prefixes: un/ under"
sealeng,seal(ing) / ceiling
seam,*,med,ming,mer,mless,mlessly,mlessness,my,A LINE/ PLACE WHERE TWO PIECES OF MATERIAL ARE JOINED (or see seem) "prefixes: in/ un"
seamen,semen
seamin,semen
seamly,seem(ly)
seamstress,ter,ONE WHO SEWS
sean,scene / seen
sear,*,red,ring,SCORCH/ BURN/ GRAZE A SURFACE (or see seer)
seara,sierra
search,hes,hed,hing,her,hable,hingly,hingness,TO LOOK/ SEEK FOR SOMETHING "prefixes: un"

searchuble,search(able)
searus,scirrhus / cirrus
seas,cease / sea(s) / see(s) / seize
seasan,season
seashell,*,SHELL OF A MOLLUSK
seasin,season
season,*,ned,ning,nal,nally,ner,nable,nably,nableness,TIME OF THE YEAR, MIXTURE OF HERBS/ SPICES FOR FOOD, EXPERIENCED/ SKILLED "prefixes: un"
seasun,season
seat,*,ted,ting,ter,A PLACE/ CHAIR/ BENCH TO SIT, SOMETHING FIRMLY FIT INTO PLACE, VACANCY FOR A PERSON "prefixes: re/ un"
seath,seethe
seaz,seize
sebconchus,subconscious
sebkonshes,subconscious
sebkontrakt,subcontract
sebling,sibling
sebtek,septic
sebtember,september
sebtik,septic
sebtimbur,september
seburat,separate
sec,sic / sick
secandery,second(ary)
secandly,second(ly)
secant,*,MATHEMATICAL EXPRESSION, DIVIDE INTO TWO PARTS (or see second/ secund)
secede,*,ed,ding,er,POLITICAL WITHDRAWAL
secendly,second(ly)
secesion,secession
secession,nal,nism,nist,TO SECEDE/ WITHDRAW
secewler,secular
sech,sedge
sechewashen,situate(tion)
sechewation,situate(tion)
sechuate,situate
sechuation,situate(tion)
secindery,second(ary)
seckal,sickle
secks,sex
seckstee,sixty

seclude, ed, ding, usion, usive, BECOME PRIVATE/ ISOLATED/ SHELTERED FROM
seclushen, seclusion
seclusion, ive, BECOME SECLUDED
seclusive, ely, eness, BECOME SECLUDED
seclution, seclusion
secolla, sequoia
second, *, ded, dly, dary, darily, der, AFTER THE FIRST, NOT PRIMARY, MEASURE OF TIME (or see secant/ secund)
secondery, second(ary)
secoority, secure(rity)
secragate, segregate
secrat, secret
secratary, secretary
secratereul, secretary(rial)
secratery, secretary
secrative, secret(ive)
secreshen, secrete(tion)
secret, *, tly, tness, ecy, tive, tively, tiveness, PRIVATE KNOWLEDGE ONLY FEW SHARE, HIDE FROM OTHERS (or see secrete) "prefixes: post/ semi"
secretareul, secretary(rial)
secretary, ries, rial, ONE WHO MAINTAINS PRIMARY OPERATIONS OF AN OFFICE "prefixes: under"
secrete, *, ed, ting, tion, tionary, tor, tory, FLUIDS THAT EXCRETE/ DISCHARGE FROM ANIMALS/ PLANTS/ HUMANS
secretion, secrete(tion)
secrit, secret
secritary, secretary
secritereul, secretary(rial)
secritery, secretary
secritive, secret(ive)
secrutly, secret(ly)
secrut, secret
secrutary, secretary
secrutereul, secretary(rial)
secrutery, secretary
secrutive, secret(ive)
secshen, section
secshenul, section(al)

secshual, sexual
secshun, section
secshunal, section(al)
secstaiol, sextile
secstillion, sextillion
secstopol, sextuple
secstuplet, sextuplet
sect, *, tarian, tarianism, tarianize, tarianizes, tarianized, tarianizing, tary, tile, tility, tion, SEGMENT/ SECTION OF SOMETHING "prefixes: bi"
secter, sector
sectet, sextet
section, *, ned, ning, nal, nally, nalize, nalizes, nalized, nalizing, nalization, nalism, ONE PART OF THE WHOLE "prefixes: inter/ re/ sub"
sectir, sector
sector, *, rial, A PART/ DIVISION OF THE WHOLE "prefixes: bi"
sectur, sector
secuin, sequin
secular, rly, rism, rist, ristic, rity, rities, rize, rizer, UNBIND FROM RELIGIOUS BELIEF
seculir, secular
secumb, succumb
secund, dly, BOTANICAL TERM (or see second/ secant)
secundery, second(ary)
secundly, second(ly)
secure, *, ed, ring, rable, ely, eness, ement, er, rity, rities, PROTECT FROM CERTAIN ELEMENTS, KEEP FIRMLY IN PLACE "prefixes: bio/ in/ un"
securety, secure(rity)
securidy, secure(rity)
sed, said / set / seed
sedalment, settle(ment)
sedam, sedum
sedamentary, sediment(ary)
sedamint, sediment
sedan, *, TYPE OF VEHICLE
sedantary, sedentary
sedashen, sedate(tion)
sedasion, sedate(tion)
sedate, *, ed, ting, ely, eness, tion, tive, APPEASE/ SUBSIDE/ CALM

sedeit, sedate
sedelment, settle(ment)
sedem, sedum
sedemint, sediment
sedentary, riness, NOT MUCH MOVEMENT/ STILL
sedews, seduce
sedge, *, gy, A SWAMP GRASS WITH EDGES
sedil, settle
sedilment, settle(ment)
sedim, sedum
sediment, *, tary, tal, tation, tology, tologic, tologist, ACCUMULATION OF MATTER CARRIED BY LIQUID
sedius, seduce
sedle, settle
sedlers, settle(rs)
sedling, seedling / settle(ling)
sediment, settle(ment)
sedol, settle
sedom, sedum
sedoose, seduce
seduce, *, ed, cing, er, cible, ction, ctive, ement, ctively, ctiveness, COERCED/ ENTICED AWAY FROM NORMAL PATTERN OF BEHAVIOR
seducshen, seduce(ction)
seductif, seduce(ctive)
seduktion, seduce(ction)
seduktive, seduce(ctive)
sedul, settle
sedulers, settle(rs)
sedulment, settle(ment)
sedum, *, A PLANT
sedumentary, sediment(ary)
sedumint, sediment
seduntary, sedentary
seduse, seduce
sedy, seed
see, *, eeable, eeing, een, eeing, eer, saw, USE OF THE EYES, VISUAL IMAGING (or see sea/ seize) "prefixes: over"
seed, *, ded, ding, dless, dful, der, dy, dling, PLANT POD THAT HOLDS THE FUTURE, DNA BLUEPRINTS "prefixes: re/ un"
seedling, *, GROWTH BURSTING FROM A SEED

seefood,seafood
seefud,seafood
seeg,siege
seej,siege
seek, *, ked,king,ker,TO SEARCH FOR
seekratif,secret(ive)
seekrutif,secret(ive)
seel,seal
seeld,seal(ed)
seem, *, med,ming,mingly,mingness,mly,mliness, APPEARS TO BE FACTUAL/ TRUTHFUL/ REAL, COULD BE (or see seam) "prefixes: un"
seemstras,seamstress
seemstrus,seamstress
seen,PAST TENSE FOR THE WORD "SEE" (or see scene/ seine) "prefixes: un"
seena,sienna
seengle,single
seengul,single
seengulerety,singular(ity)
seep, *, ped, ping, py, page, "THE OOZING OF LIQUID THROUGH A BARRIER (or see sipe/ sip)
seepige,seep(age)
seepuge,seep(age)
seer, *, ONE WHO SEES/ HAS SPIRITUAL INSIGHT/ PREDICTOR OF THE FUTURE (or see sear)
seera,sierra
sees,see(s) / sea(s) / seize / cease / say(s)
seesan,season
seeshell,seashell
seesin,season
seesta,siesta
seesun,season
seethe, *, ed,hing,hingly, STATE OF AGITATION/ EMOTION THAT IS BARELY CONTAINED
seety,seed
seez,seize / cease / sea(s) / seize / cease / see(s)
sef,sieve
sefal,civil
sefalezation,civil(ization)
sefalis,syphilis
sefan,seven
sefanteen,seventeen
sefanth,seventh
sefaree,safari
sefenteith,seventieth
sefestikashen,sophisticate(tion)
sefestikation,sophisticate(tion)
sefichent,sufficient
sefichunt,sufficient
sefil,civil
sefilezation,civil(ization)
sefin,seven
sefinteen,seventeen
sefinteith,seventieth
sefinth,seventh
sefise,suffice
sefishent,sufficient
sefishunt,sufficient
sefistukashen,sophisticate(tion)
sefistukation,sophisticate(tion)
seflus,syphilis
sefol,civil
sefolazation,civil(ization)
sefon,seven
sefonteen,seventeen
sefood,seafood
sefral,several
sefrense,severance
sefril,several
sefrinse,severance
sefrul,several
sefrunse,severance
sefud,seafood
seful,civil
sefules,syphilis
sefulezation,civil(ization)
sefulization,civil(ization)
sefun,seven
sefunteen,seventeen
sefunteith,seventieth
sefunth,seventh
seg,siege / sedge
segar,cigar
segaret,cigarette
sege,sedge / siege

seged,siege(d)
seger,seize(zure)
seges,sedge(s) / siege(s)
segir,seize(zure)
segis,sedge(s)
segiest,suggest
segiestion,suggest(ion)
segiestshen,suggest(ion)
segma,sigma
segment, *, ted,ting,tary,tal,tally,tation, ONE PORTION/ SECTION OF THE WHOLE
segmentul,segment(al)
segmintul,segment(al)
segmu,sigma
segnafiable,signify(fiable)
segnafier,signify(fier)
segnature,signature
segnifukent,significant
segnucher,signature
segnul,signal
segnushure,signature
segragashen,segregate(tion)
segragate,segregate
segregate, *, ed, ting, tion, tionist, tive, tor, able, ant, SET APART, SEPARATE/ DIVIDE FROM THE WHOLE
segregeit,segregate
segrigate,segregate
segrugashen,segregate(tion)
segrugate,segregate
segur,seize(zure)
seguret,cigarette
segus,sedge(s)
sehiur,secure
sei,say
seibel,sable
seiber,saber
seible,see(able)
seibol,sable
seich,sage
seicred,sacred
seicrol,sacral
seicrum,sacrum
seif,save / safe

seige, siege / sage	
seik, sake	
seikred, sacred	
seil, sail	
seilin, saline	
seilor, sailor	
seim, same	
sein, sane	
seinchon, sanction	
seinchueri, sanctuary	
seine, A NET (or see seen/ scene)	
seing, see(ing)	
seint, saint	
seiol, sale / sail	
seir, sear / seer	
seira, sierra	
seism, mic, mical, mically, micity, micities, mism, mogram, mograph, mology, mologist, FREQUENCY/ WAVES OF THE EARTH, EARTHQUAKE	
seista, siesta	
seit, sate	
seitanic, satanic	
seiv, save / safe	
seivant, savant	
seivent, savant	
seivior, savior	
seivor, savior	
seize, *, ed, zing, zure, zer, TO GRAB/ CONFISCATE QUICKLY/ FORCEFULLY (or see cease) "prefixes: dis"	
sej, sedge / siege	
sejd, siege(d)	
sejer, seize(zure)	
sejes, sedge(s)	
sejt, siege(d)	
sejur, seize(zure)	
sejus, sedge(s)	
sek, sic / sick / seek	
sekal, sickle	
sekamore, sycamore	
sekand, secant / second / secund	
sekandery, second(ary)	
sekandly, second(ly)	
sekendly, second(ly)	
sekent, secant / second / secund	sekregation, segregate(tion)
sekently, second(ly)	sekreshen, secrete(tion)
sekeuridy, secure(rity)	sekresion, secrete(tion)
sekewiir, secular	sekret, secret / secrete
sekewlur, secular	sekretive, secret(ive)
sekewr, secure	sekretly, secret(ly)
sekewrity, secure(rity)	sekrigashen, segregate(tion)
sekiatrist, psychiatry(rist)	sekrigate, segregate
sekiatry, psychiatry	sekrigation, segregate(tion)
sekil, sickle	sekrit, secret
sekind, secant / second / secund	sekritary, secretary
sekindery, second(ary)	sekritereul, secretary(rial)
sekindly, second(ly)	sekritery, secretary
sekintly, second(ly)	sekritive, secret(ive)
sekir, seek(er)	sekritly, secret(ly)
sekiular, secular	sekrogate, segregate
sekle, sickle	sekrtly, secret(ly)
seklushen, seclusion	sekrugashen, segregate(tion)
seklusion, seclusion	sekrugate, segregate
seklusive, seclusive	sekrugation, segregate(tion)
sekma, sigma	sekrut, secret
sekment, segment	sekrutary, secretary
sekmentul, segment(al)	sekrutef, secret(ive)
sekmint, segment	sekrutereul, secretary(rial)
seknafiur, signify(fier)	sekrutery, secretary
seknafy, signify	sekrutive, secret(ive)
seknashure, signature	sekrutly, secret(ly)
seknifukent, significant	seks, seek(s) / sex
seknishure, signature	sekshen, section
seknol, signal	sekshenul, section(al)
seknucher, signature	sekshin, section
seknul, signal	sekshinul, section(al)
sekol, sickle	sekshuel, sexual
sekondery, second(ary)	sekshuil, sexual
sekragashen, segregate(tion)	sekshun, section
sekragate, segregate	sekshunal, section(al)
sekragation, segregate(tion)	sekshwal, sexual
sekrat, secret	seksion, section
sekratary, secretary	seksis, sex(es)
sekratereul, secretary(rial)	seksless, sex(less)
sekratery, secretary	sekst, sex(ed)
sekratif, secret(ive)	sekstant, sextant
sekrative, secret(ive)	sekste, sixty

Word	Derivations/Definitions
selenic,ide,iferous,ious,ite,ium,CHEMICAL ELEMENT	
selenium,iferous,NONMETALLIC ELEMENT	
selenoid,solenoid	
seler,cellar / seal(er) / sell(er)	
selery,celery	
self,lves,flessly,flessness,fish,FIRST PERSON	
selfer,silver	
selferware,silverware	
selfesh,selfish	
selfeshly,selfish(ly)	
selfir,silver	
selfish,hly,hness,LESS THOUGHT FOR OTHERS THAN FOR SELF "prefixes: un"	
selfishlis,selfish(less)	
selflis,self(less)	
selflisness,self(lessness)	
selfs,self(lves)	
selfurware,silverware	
selfury,silver	
selfush,selfish	
seli,silly	
selibet,celibate	
selibrate,celebrate	
selibuse,celibate(acy)	
selicon,silicon / silicone	
selifane,cellophane	
selilaquy,soliloquy	
selines,silly(lliness)	
seling,ceiling / sell(ing) / seal(ing)	
selinoid,solenoid	
selir,cellar / seal(er) / sell(er)	
seliset,solicit	
selisetation,solicit(ation)	
seliseter,solicit(er)	
selivu,saliva	
selk,silk	
selkun,silk(en)	
selky,silk	
sell,*,lling,ller,sale,sold,TRADE GOODS/ SERVICES FOR MONEY (or see sail/ sale/ sill/ seal/ sedge) "prefixes: over/ un/ under"	
seller,cellar / sell(er)	
sellfish,selfish	

Word	Derivation
sekwents,sequence	
sekwil,sequel	
sekwin,sequin	
sekwinse,sequence	
sekwoia,sequoia	
sekwoya,sequoia	
sekwul,sequel	
sekwunts,sequence	
sel,seal / sell / sale / cell / sail	
selabet,celibate	
selabil,syllable	
selable,syllable	
selabrate,celebrate	
selabus,syllabus	
selafane,cellophane	
selakit,silica(te)	
selal,salal	
selamander,salamander	
selami,salami	
selanoid,solenoid	
selaphane,cellophane	
selar,cellar / sell(er) / seal(er)	
selareum,solarium	
selary,celery	
selawet,silhouette	
seld,seal(ed) / sold	
seldem,seldom	
seldemly,seldom(ly)	
seldom,mly,mness,RARELY/ INFREQUENTLY	
seldumly,seldom(ly)	
selebrety,celebrity	
selebusy,celibate(acy)	
select,*,ted,ting,tion,tionist,tness,tor,tee,tive,tively, tiveness,tivity,CHOOSE ONE AMONG MANY "prefixes: de"	
seled,salad	
selee,silly	
selekshen,select(ion)	
selekt,select	
selektif,select(ive)	
selektion,select(ion)	
selektive,select(ive)	
seleng,ceiling / seal(ing)	

Word	Derivation
seksteen,sixteen	
seksteenth,sixteen(th)	
sekstent,sextant	
sekstet,sextet	
seksteuth,sixtieth	
seksth,sixth	
sekstile,sextile	
sekstileon,sextillion	
sekstillion,sextillion	
sekstiuth,sixtieth	
sekstuple,sextuple	
sekstuplet,sextuplet	
sekstupul,sextuple	
seksty,sixty	
seksualedy,sexual(ity)	
seksuality,sexual(ity)	
seksus,sex(es)	
seksy,sex	
sekt,sect / seek(ed)	
sekter,sector	
sekth,sixth	
sektion,section	
sektional,section(al)	
sektir,sector	
sektur,sector	
sekul,sickle	
sekular,secular	
sekulir,secular	
sekum,succumb	
sekund,secant / second / secund	
sekundery,second(ary)	
sekundly,second(ly)	
sekuntly,second(ly)	
sekure,secure	
sekuredy,secure(rity)	
sekurity,secure(rity)	
sekurly,secure(ly)	
sekwal,sequel	
sekwel,sequel	
sekwen,sequin	
sekwense,sequence	
sekwenshul,sequence(ntial)	
sekwential,sequence(ntial)	

selluler,cellular
sellur,cellar / sell(er) / seal(er)
seloet,silhouette
selofane,cellophane
selofein,cellophane
selomee,salami
selon,salon
selonoid,solenoid
seloon,saloon
seloot,salute
selor, cellar/ seal(er) / sell(er)
sels, sell(s) / seal(s) / sail(s)
selseus,celsius
selt, seal(ed) / sold / silt / sail(ed)
seltashen,silt(ation)
seltation,silt(ation)
seltem,seldom
seltum,seldom
selty,silt
selubasy,celibate(acy)
selubel,syllable
selubet,celibate
selubrate,celebrate
selubus,syllabus
selufane,cellophane
selukon,silicon / silicone
selular,cellular
selulite,cellulite
selulose,cellulose
selune,saloon
selunoid,solenoid
selur, cellar / sell(er) / seal(er)
selure,celery
selushen,solution
selute,salute
selution,solution
selverware,silverware
selvir,silver
selvurware,silverware
selvury,silver
sely,silly
semaj,semi
semalarity,similar(ity)

semaler,similar
semalerly,similar(ly)
semanar,seminar
semantics,cal,cally,cist,STUDY OF LANGUAGE/ WORDS
semar, simmer
semashen,sum(mmation)
semation,sum(mmation)
sematry,symmetry
sembal,symbol
sembalism,symbol(ism)
sembathetik,sympathetic
sembathy,sympathy
sembeodik,symbiotic
sembeosis,symbiosis
sembeotek,symbiotic
sembilism,symbol(ism)
sembiosis,symbiosis
semblance,*,SIMILARITY/ RESEMBLANCE
semble,symbol
semblents,semblance
semblinse,semblance
sembolek,symbol(ic)
sembolik,symbol(ic)
sembul,cymbal / symbol
sembulism,symbol(ism)
sembuthetik,sympathetic
sembuthy,sympathy
semdum,symptom
semecolon,semicolon
semekolun,semicolon
semelur,similar
semelurly,similar(ly)
semen,miniferous,minal,SUBSTANCE CONTAINING MALE SPERM
semenal,seminal
semenar,seminar
sement,cement
semenul,seminal
semesder,semester
semester,*,tral,trial,SIX MONTH PERIOD OF TIME
semetary,cemetery
semetric,symmetry(ric)
semetry,symmetry

semeulate,simulate
semewlation,simulate(tion)
semfeny,symphony
semfonic,symphony(nic)
semfune,symphony
semi,PREFIX INDICATING "HALF/ PARTLY" MOST OFTEN MODIFIES THE WORD
semicolon,*,A PUNCTUATION MARK
semicoulon,semicolon
semikolin,semicolon
semilarity,similar(ity)
semiler,similar
semilerly,similar(ly)
semin,semen
seminal,lly,niferous,CAPABLE OF CREATING LIFE/ FUTURE DEVELOPMENT
seminar,*,rian,ries,ry,A GROUP OF PEOPLE CONVERGING TOGETHER TO LEARN ONE THING IN PARTICULAR
semingly,seem(ingly)
semir,simmer
semitary,cemetery
semliness,seem(liness)
semly,seem(ly)
semon,semen
semonal,seminal
semonar,seminar
semoolader,simulate(tor)
sempal,simple
sempalest, simple(st)
sempaly,simple(ly)
sempathee,sympathy
sempathetic,sympathetic
sempathize,sympathy(hize)
sempathy,sympathy
sempdum,symptom
sempel,simple
sempelist,simple(st)
sempethy,sympathy
semphonek,symphony(nic)
semphonic,symphony(nic)
semphuny,symphony
sempithize,sympathy(hize)

sempithy, sympathy
semple, simple
sempler, simple(r)
semplest, simple(st)
semplisity, simple(licity)
semplistec, simple(listic)
semply, simple(ly)
sempol, simple
sempoler, simple(r)
sempolest, simple(st)
semposeum, symposium
sempozeum, symposium
semptem, symptom
semptum, symptom
sempul, simple
sempuler, simple(r)
sempulest, simple(st)
sempuly, simple(ly)
semputhee, sympathy
semputhetic, sympathetic
semputhize, sympathy(hize)
semstras, seamstress
semstrus, seamstress
semtem, symptom
semtum, symptom
semulader, simulate(tor)
semularly, similar(ly)
semulashen, simulate(tion)
semulate, simulate
semulation, simulate(tion)
semulator, simulate(tor)
semuler, similar
semulerly, similar(ly)
semullarety, similar(ity)
semun, semen
semunal, seminal
semunar, seminar
semur, simmer
semutare, cemetery
semutree, symmetry
semwat, somewhat
semwere, somewhere
semwhat, somewhat

semwhere, somewhere
semwot, somewhat
sen, seen / scene / seine / sin
senada, sonata
senak, scene(nic)
senamon, cinnamon
senanem, synonym
senapse, synapse
senapsis, synapsis
senaptek, synaptic
senaptic, synaptic
senareo, scenario
senary, scene(ry)
senaster, sinister
senate, tor, A BODY/ HOUSE OF U.S. GOVERNMENT
senator, *, rial, rially, rship, ELECTED MEMBER OF THE U.S. GOVERNMENT
senatoriel, senator(ial)
senatu, sonata
senc, sync / sink / since
sench, cinch
senched, singe(d) / cinch(ed)
senchro, synchro
senchronus, synchrony(nous)
sencht, singe(d) / cinch(ed)
senchual, sensual
sencro, synchro
sencronize, synchrony(nize)
sencrony, synchrony
send, *, ding, der, nt, PUSH/ ENCOURAGE SOMETHING TO LEAVE YOUR VICINITY, HAVE DELIVERED
sendamental, sentiment(al)
sendamintal, sentiment(al)
sender, cinder / send(er)
sendicate, syndicate
sendication, syndicate(tion)
sendikation, syndicate(tion)
sendiket, syndicate
sendral, central
sendrem, syndrome
sendrum, syndrome
sendukit, syndicate
sendumentil, sentiment(al)

sendumeter, centimeter
sene, scene / seen
sened, sin(nned)
senek, scene(nic)
senema, cinema
seneority, senior(ity)
sener, sin(nner)
senerist, scenario(ist)
senery, scene(ry)
senete, senate
senetor, senator
senew, sinew
senful, sin(ful)
senfuly, sin(fully)
seng, sing / sink / singe / cinch
sengal, single
senge, singe / cinch
senged, singe(d) / cinch(ed)
sengel, single
senger, sing(er)
sengewler, singular
sengle, single
sengs, sing(s) / sink(s)
sengt, singe(d) / cinch(ed)
sengul, single
sengularedy, singular(ity)
sengularly, singular(ly)
senguled, single(d)
senguler, singular
senguleridy, singular(ity)
senguly, single(ly)
senical, cynical
senik, cynic / scene(nic)
senile, lity, WHEN THE MIND CEASES TO STAY SHARP/ ALERT DUE TO AGING
senilidy, senile(lity)
senior, *, rity, UPPER RANK, OLDER THAN MOST, HIGHER IN CLASS
senir, sin(nner)
senirgy, synergy
seniry, scene(ry)
senistur, sinister
senite, senate

Word	Forms / Definition
senitor	senator
senitoreul	senator(ial)
senj	singe / cinch
senjt	singe(d) / cinch(ed)
senk	sync / sink
senker	sink(er) / sing(er)
senkewler	singular
senkil	single
senkir	sink(er) / sing(er)
senkle	single(ly)
senkranes	synchrony(nous)
senkro	synchro
senkrone	synchrony
senkronize	synchrony(nize)
senkrunus	synchrony(nous)
senkt	sink(ed)
senkul	single
senkularedy	singular(ity)
senkularly	singular(ly)
senkuler	singular
senkur	sink(er) / sing(er)
senles	sin(less)
senoda	sonata
senodu	sonata
senografee	scenography
senography	scenography
senonemus	synonym(ous)
senonim	synonym
senonimus	synonym(ous)
senonym	synonym
senopsis	synopsis
senota	sonata
senotor	senator
sens	sense / since / cent(s) / sin(s) / scene(s)
sensability	sensible(bility)
sensable	sensible
sensaridy	sincere(rity)
sensarity	sincere(rity)
sensashen	sensation
sensation	*, nal, nally, nalism, nalist, nalistic, A FEELING/ SENSE/ KNOWINGNESS OF AN AFFECT
sensative	sensitive
sensatize	sensitize
sensd	sense(d)
sense	*, ed, sing, eless, sor, sors, sorial, sorially, sorium, sory, FEEL/ KNOW THE SIX SENSES; SOUND/ SIGHT/ SMELL/ TASTE/ TOUCH/ FEEL (or see sent/ cent(s)/ scene(s) "prefixes: non"
sensebility	sensible(bility)
senseble	sensible
senseishon	sensation
senser	sincere / censor
sensere	sincere / censor
senseredy	sincere(rity)
senserity	sincere(rity)
senserly	sincere(ly)
sensetize	sensitize
senshewality	sensual(ity)
senshewus	sensuous
senshual	sensual
senshuality	sensual(ity)
senshues	sensuous
senshuil	sensual
senshury	century
sensible	eness, ly, bility, bilities, BE NORMAL/ PREDICTABLE TO OTHERS "prefixes: in"
sensir	sensor / censor / censure
sensitive	ely, eness, vity, vities, ize, ization, izer, READILY RESPONDS TO STIMULUS "prefixes: de/ in/ pre"
sensitivity	sensitive(vity)
sensitize	*, ed, zing, zation, er, BECOME VERY SENSITIVE TO STIMULUS "prefixes: de"
sensless	sense(less)
sensor	*, red, ring, rial, rially, rium, ry, ABLE TO RESPOND TO A PARTICULAR STIMULUS/ IMPULSE (or see censor/ censure) "prefixes: bio"
sensoreal	sensor(ial)
sensual	lity, lly, lism, list, listic, lize, lization, uous, OPEN TO THE BODY'S EXPRESSION/ DESIRE/ FEELINGS, UNINHIBITED
sensuble	sensible
sensuous	sly, sness, OF BEING SENSUAL
sensur	sensor / censor / censure
sensus	census / sense(s)
sensutive	sensitive
sensutivity	sensitive(vity)

Word	Forms / Definition
sensutize	sensitize
sent	PAST TENSE FOR THE WORD 'SEND' (or see scent/ sin(nned))
sentaks	syntax
sentamental	sentiment(al)
sentax	syntax
sentchuous	sensuous
sented	scent(ed)
senteince	sentient(ncy)
senteint	sentient
sentekit	syndicate
sentement	sentiment
sentemental	sentiment(al)
sentence	*, ed, cing, ntial, ntially, COMPLETE THOUGHT GRAMMATICALLY, FORMAL JUDGMENT/ DECISION
senteneul	centennial
sentennial	centennial
sentense	sentence
senter	center
senthasis	synthesis
senthasize	synthesize
senthedik	synthetic
senthesis	synthesis
senthetic	synthetic
senthusis	synthesis
sentient	tly, nce, ncy, ABILITY/ FACULTY TO PERCEIVE CONSCIOUSLY "prefixes: in/ pre"
sentigrade	centigrade
sentiment	*, tal, tally, tality, talities, talism, talist, talize, talizes, talized, talizing, talization, EMOTIONALLY SWAYED BY THE PAST
sentimeter	centimeter
sentineol	centennial
sentinse	sentence
sentipede	centipede
sentles	scent(less)
sentrul	central
sentrulize	centralize
sentry	ries, A GUARD FOR GATE/ ENTRY
sents	since / sense / cent(s) / scent(s)
senttance	sentence
sentument	sentiment
sentumental	sentiment(al)

sentury,century
senu,sinew
senuee,sinew
senuk,scene(nic)
senunem,synonym
senupeded,centipede
senur,sin(nner)
senurgy,synergy
senury,scene(ry)
senuster,sinister
senute,senate
senutor,senator
senutoreul,senator(ial)
senutorial,senator(ial)
senuw,sinew
senuy,sinew
senwich,sandwich
senyer,senior
senyority,senior(ity)
senyuee,sinew
senyur,senior
seonse,se'ance
sep,seep / sip / sipe
sepage,seep(age)
sepal, *, led, lous, loid, PART OF A FLOWER
separable, bility, eness, bly, ABLE TO BE SEPARATED "prefixes: in"
separador,separator
separashen,separate(tion)
separate, *, ed, ting, tion, ely, eness, tist, tism, tistic, tive, tor, DIVIDE/ BREAK APART FROM THE WHOLE "prefixes: bio"
separator, *, THAT WHICH ENCOURAGES SEPARATION
separet,separate
separite,separate
sepausatory,suppository
sepd,sip(pped) / seep(ec)
sepea,sepia
sepege,seep(age)
sepej,seep(age)
sepena,subpoena
seperabul,separable
seperader,separator

seperashen,separate(tion)
seperate,separate
seperately,separate(tly)
seperation,separate(tion)
seperatly,separate(tly)
seperator,separator
seperible,separable
seperubil,separable
sepeu,sepia
sephelis,syphilis
sephules,syphilis
sepia, A COLOR/ PIGMENT, A FISH
sepige,seep(age)
sepij,seep(age)
sepil,sepal
sepirable,separable
sepirador,separator
sepirashen,separate(tion)
sepirate,separate
sepiration,separate(tion)
sepirator,separator
sepirlative,superlative
sepiruble,separable
sepkonshes,subconscious
sepkontrakt,subcontract
seplant,supplant
seple,sepal
sepli,supply
seplier,supply(lier)
sepling,sibling
sepliur,supply(lier)
seply,supply
sepol,sepal
seport,support
seportive,support(ive)
sepose,suppose
seposetory,suppository
seposubly,suppose(dly)
sepozatory,suppository
sepoze,suppose
sepozubly,suppose(dly)
seprabul,separable
seprashen,separate(tion)

seprat,separate
seprastism,separate(tism)
seprative,separate(tive)
sepratly,separate(tly)
seprator,separator
seprechen,suppress(ion)
sepreem,supreme
sepreme,supreme
sepres,suppress
sepreshen,suppress(ion)
sepret,separate
sepretion,suppress(ion)
sepretism,separate(tism)
sepretive,separate(tive)
sepretly,separate(tly)
sepribul,separable
seprino,soprano
seprit,separate
sepritesm,separate(tism)
sepritly,separate(tly)
sepruble,separable
seprut,separate
seprutly,separate(tly)
septar,scepter
septek,septic / styptic
september, A MONTH OF THE YEAR (ENGLISH)
septer,scepter
septic, *, cally, city, THAT WHICH CAUSES PUTREFACTION OR SEPSIS, OF BEING ROTTEN
septik,styptic
septimber,september
septir,scepter
septisity,septic(ity)
septor,scepter
septupil,septuple
septuple, *, ed, ling, SEVEN TIMES/ FOLD
septur,scepter
sepuge,seep(age)
sepuj,seep(age)
sepul,sepal
sepurabul,separable
sepurador,separator
sepurashen,separate(tion)

sepurate, separate
sepurately, separate(tly)
sepurater, separator
sepuration, separate(tion)
sepurb, superb
sepurblee, superb(ly)
sepurible, separable
sepurlative, superlative
sejiur, secure
sequel, *, litis, CONTINUATION ON THE STORY
sequence, *, ed, cing, cy, er, ntial, ntially, SERIES/ PARTS ALIGNED IN ORDER/ PATTERN
sequenshil, sequence(ntial)
sequer, secure
sequerity, secure(rity)
sequerly, secure(ly)
sequilar, secular
sequill, sequel
sequin, *, ned, SMALL REFLECTIVE DECORATIONS USED ON CLOTHING
sequir, secure
sequoia, *, TYPE OF TREE, A TRIBE
seqwen, sequin
ser, seer / sir / sear
seraget, surrogate
seran, saran
seranade, serenade
serandipity, serendipity
serandipudy, serendipity
serap, syrup
serape, *, OUTER GARMENT/ BLANKET/ SHAWL
serashen, serrate(tion)
serated, serrate(d)
seration, serrate(tion)
serbent, serpent
serafigus, sarcophagus
seramscribe, circumscribe
sercas, circus
sercemscribe, circumscribe
serch, search
sercharj, surcharge
serchuble, search(able)
sercit, circuit

sercle, circle
sercomscribe, circumscribe
sercophagus, sarcophagus
sercot, circuit
sercumfurens, circumference
sercumscribe, circumscribe
sercumsize, circumcise
sercumstans, circumstance
sercus, circus
sercut, circuit
serdafication, certificate(tion)
serdanly, certain(ly)
serdatude, certitude
serden, certain
serdenly, certain(ly)
serdifai, certify
serdufication, certificate(tion)
serdufy, certify
serdunly, certain(ly)
serdutude, certitude
sereal, serial / cereal / surreal
serealism, surrealism
serebral, cerebral
serebrul, cerebral
serees, series
sereit, serrate
serel, sorrel / surreal
serelism, surrealism
serenade, *, ed, ding, er, SOLITARY PERFORMANCE BY SOMEONE FOR SOMEONE IN PARTICULAR
serender, surrender
serendipity, tous, UNEXPECTED/ ACCIDENTAL HAPPY ENDING
serene, nly, eness, nity, nities, TRANQUIL/ PEACEFUL
sereneid, serenade
sereol, serial / cereal
serep, syrup
sereul, serial / cereal
sereulizum, surrealism
sereus, serious
sereusly, serious(ly)
serf, *, fage, fdom, fhood, fish, WORKER WHO BELONGED WITH THE LAND (or see surf/ serve)

serface, surface
serfdum, serf(dom)
serfee, surf
serfej, serf(age)
serfes, surface
serfis, surface / service
serfuge, serf(age)
serfunt, servant
serfur, surf(er)
serfus, surface / service
sergd, surge(d)
serge, A TWILLED FABRIC (or see surge)
sergeant, *, ncy, A RANK/ POSITION WITHIN THE U.S. MILITARY/ POLICE
sergen, surgeon
sergent, sergeant / surgent
sergeon, surgeon
sergery, surgery
sergikul, surgical
sergin, surgeon
sergiry, surgery
sergon, surgeon
sergree, surgery
sergukle, surgical
serguree, surgery
serial, lly, list, lize, lization, SUCCESSIVE NUMBER/ SERIES (or see cereal) "prefixes: uni"
seriasis, psoriasis
series, CORRESPONDING/ SUCCESSIVE EVENTS/ ITEMS
serim, serum
serimony, ceremony
serin, serene
serinade, serenade
serinder, surrender
serindipty, serendipity
serindipudy, serendipity
serious, sly, sness, EARNEST/ SOLEMN/ GRAVE
serip, syrup
seris, scirrhus / cirrus
seriulesm, surrealism
serius, serious
seriusis, psoriasis
serjakle, surgical

serjaree,survey(or)
serje,surge / serge
serjen,surgeon
serjent,sergeant / surgent
serjikul,surgical
serjint,sergeant / surgent
serjon,surgeon
serjree,surgery
serjukle,surgical
serkemscribe,circumscribe
serkemsize,circumcise
serkes,circus
serket,circuit
serkimscribe,circumscribe
serkimsize,circumcise
serkimstans,circumstance
serkis,circus
serkit,circuit
serkiuleit,circulate
serkiuler,circular
serkle,circle
serkofegus,sarcophagus
serkofigus,sarcophagus
serkomscribe,circumscribe
serkulate,circulate
serkuler,circular
serkumfurense,circumference
serkumsize,circumcise
serkumstans,circumstance
serkus,circus
serkut,circuit
serlee,surly
serloin,sirloin
serly,surly
sermais,surmise
serman,sermon
sermize,surmise
sermon,*,nic,nize,nizer,A RELIGIOUS DISCOURSE
sermun,sermon
serogate,surrogate
serondipity,serendipity
serong,sarong
serope,serape

seroredy,sorority
serority,sorority
seros,scirrhus / cirrus
seround,surround
serownd,surround
serpas,surpass
serpent,*,A SNAKE
serpentene,serpentine
serpentine,SHAPED/ MOVEMENT OF A SNAKE
serpint,serpent
serpintene,serpentine
serplus,surplus
serprize,surprise
serques,circus
serrate,*,ed,ting,tion,JAGGED/ TOOTHED OUTLINE LIKE A SAW
serrender,surrender
sersharge,surcharge
sertafy,certify
sertanle,certain(ly)
sertatude,certitude
sertefai,certify
sertefication,certificate(tion)
sertenly,certain(ly)
sertification,certificate(tion)
serticut,certificate
sertifikashen,certificate(tion)
sertifiquet,certificate
sertifucate,certificate
sertin,certain
sertinle,certain(ly)
sertinly,certain(ly)
sertufie,certify
sertunly,certain(ly)
seruget,surrogate
serum,*,A FLUID OF INOCULATION
serumony,ceremony
serunade,serenade
serundipety,serendipity
serundipudy,serendipity
serup,syrup
serus,cirrus / scirrhus
serva,survey

servaer,survey(or)
servailense,surveillance
servalinse,surveillance
servant,*,ONE EMPLOYED/ OWNED TO PERFORM DOMESTIC CHORES/ WORK
servatood,servitude
servatude,servitude
servaur,survey(or)
servayer,survey(or)
serve,*,ed,ving,er,vant,vice,vitude,ONE WHO PUTS A BALL INTO PLAY,PERFORM DUTIES FOR OTHERS "prefixes: sub"
serveilinse,surveillance
servent,servant
serveor,survey(or)
serves,service
serveyor,survey(or)
service,*,ed,cing,eable,eability,eableness,eably, PROVIDE OR ACCOMMODATE SOMEONE/ SOMETHING "prefixes: dis/ inter"
servics,cervix
servife,survive
serviks,cervix
servint,servant
servisuble,service(cable)
servitude,TO BE IN THE SERVICE OF OTHERS
servive,survive
serviver,survive(vor)
servivul,survive(val)
servunt,servant
servusable,service(cable)
servutude,servitude
ses,see(s) / sea(s) / seize / cease
sesal,sizzle
sesame,*,AN EDIBLE SEED
sesan,season
sesdamadik,system(atic)
sesdamatic,system(atic)
sesdan,sustain
sesdum,system
sesdumadik,system(atic)
sesdumatic,system(atic)
sesede,secede

sesee,sissy
sesel,sizzle
sesen,season
seseptability,susceptible(bility)
seseptif,susceptive
seseptive,susceptive
sesers,scissor(s)
seset,secede
sesetion,secession
seshell,seashell
seshon,session
sesid,secede
sesil,sizzle
sesime,sesame
sesin,season
sesion,session
sesirs,scissor(s)
sesle,sizzle
sesmek,seism(ic)
sesmic,seism(ic)
sesmical,seism(ical)
sesmik,seism(ic)
sesome,sesame
seson,season
sesors,scissor(s)
sespend,suspend
sespishus,suspicious
session,*,nal,A PERIOD/ COURSE/ SPECIFIC OF TIME "prefixes: inter"
sest,cyst / zest
sestain,sustain
sestane,sustain
sestanuble,sustain(able)
sester,sister
sestim,system
sestir,sister
sestum,system
sestumatic,system(atic)
sestur,sister
sesturly,sister(ly)
sesturn,cistern
sesul,sizzle
sesume,sesame

sesun,season
sesurs,scissor(s)
sesy,sissy
set,*,tting,ttee,tter,sat,COLLECTION OF SIMILAR ITEMS, PUT INTO PLACE (or see sit/ seat/ said) "prefixes: in/ over/ pre/ re/ sub/ un/ under"
setal,settle
setalment,settle(ment)
setament,sediment
setamentary,sediment(ary)
setamint,sediment
setanic,satanic
setanikul,satanic(al)
setantary,sedentary
setchuashen,situate(tion)
setee,set(ttee)
setel,settle
setelment,settle(ment)
setemint,sediment
setemintary,sediment(ary)
setentary,sedentary
seter,set(tter)
seterical,satire(rical)
seth,seethe / scythe
setibalais,stabilize
setidium,stadium
setil,settle
setillment,settle(ment)
setintary,sedentary
setion,session
setir,set(tter)
setle,settle
setling,seedling / settle(ling)
setlment,settle(ment)
settle,*,ed,ling,ement,er,FINAL AGREEMENT, BECOME STATIONARY "prefixes: re/ un"
setuashen,situate(tion)
setuation,situate(tion)
setul,settle
setulers,settle(rs)
setulment,settle(ment)
setumentary,sediment(ary)
setuntary,sedentary

setur,set(tter) / seat(er) / seed(er)
sety,city
seubil,see(able)
seuble,see(able)
seuler,cellular
seur,sear / seer
sev,sieve
sevan,seven
sevandy,seventy
sevant,savant
sevanteen,seventeen
sevanteith,seventieth
sevanth,seventh
sevanty,seventy
sevanu,savanna
sevarul,several
seven,*,,nteen,nth,ntieth,nty,A NUMBER
sevendeith,seventieth
sevendi,seventy
sevendy,seventy
seventeen,A DOUBLE DIGIT NUMBER
seventh,PLACE IN THE NUMBER SEQUENCE WHICH COMES AFTER THE 6TH
seventiet,seventieth
seventieth,COMES AFTER THE 69TH IN NUMBER SEQUENCE
seventin,seventeen
seventy,ties,COMES AFTER 69 IN NUMBER SEQUENCE
sever,*, red,ring,rable,ralty,rance,TO CUT OFF/ SEPARATE FROM THE HOST (or see severe)
several,lly,MORE THAN TWO
severance,SEPARATION/ SPLIT/ PARTING,FROM THE WORD "SEVER"
severe,ely, eness,rity,rities,EXTREME/ HARSH/ PUNISHING (or see sever)
severedy,severe(rity)
severinse,severance
severly,severe(ly)
severt,sever(ed)
severul,several
severunse,severance
sevik,civic
sevil,civil

Entry	Definition
sexshunol,section(al)	
sexshwal,sexual	
sextant,* , SIXTH PART OF A CIRCLE, AN INSTRUMENT	
sexteen,sixteen	
sextenth,sixteen(th)	
sextet,* , SIX IN A GROUP	
sexth,sixth	
sextile,llion,ASTRONOMICAL/ STATISTICAL EXPRESSION, 1/ 6TH OF ANYTHING	
sextileon,sextillion	
sextilion,sextillion	
sextillion,* ,nth,A NUMBER FOLLOWED BY 21 OR 36 ZEROS	
sextint,sextant	
sextion,section	
sextional,section(al)	
sextuple,* ,ed,ling,et, SIX FOLDS/ PARTS/ TIMES	
sextuplet,* , SIX EQUAL	
sexual,lly,llity,lize,lizes,lized,lizing, PERTAINING TO THE FIRST SEAL/ CHAKRA, FEATURE OF REPRODUCTION "prefixes: bi/ de/ inter/ intra/ non/ uni"	
sexuol,sexual	
sexuoly,sexual(lly)	
sexus,sex(es)	
sexyewality,sexual(ity)	
sexyewul,sexual	
sexyuality,sexual(ity)	
sexyuol,sexual	
sey,say	
seyer,sear / seer	
seyons,se'ance	
seyur,sear / seer	
sez,seize / cease / sea(s) / see(s)	
sezal,sizzle	
sezen,season	
sezil,sizzle	
sezin,season	
sezle,sizzle	
sezmek,seism(ic)	
sezmic,seism(ic)	
sezmical,seism(ical)	
sezors,scissor(s)	
sezul,sizzle	

Entry	Definition
sevur,sever	
sevural,several	
sevuranse,severance	
sevurd,sever(ed)	
sew,* ,wed,wing,wer,wn,TO JOIN/ UNITE PIECES WITH STITCHES (or see so/ sow) "prefixes: over"	
sewage,WASTE MATTER	
sewaro,saguaro	
sewd,sue(d) / sew(ed)	
sewdanim,pseudonym	
sewdo,pseudo	
sewdonim,pseudonym	
sewer,* ,wage,rage,A CHANNEL FOR WASTE/ WATER, SOMEONE WHO SEWS (or see sew(er))	
sewfaner,souvenir	
sewfineer,souvenir	
sewflay,soufflé'	
sewfuner,souvenir	
sewkrose,sucrose	
sewn,PAST TENSE FOR THE WORD "SEW" (or see son/ sown)	
seworo,saguaro	
sewpee,soup	
sewperb,superb	
sewpurb,superb	
sewpy,soup	
sewt,soot / suit	
sewtanim,pseudonym	
sewto,pseudo	
sewtonim,pseudonym	
sewture,suture	
sex,xes,xed,xing,xless,xv,xier,xiest,xily,xiness,xual, CONCERNING THE REPRODUCTIVE AREAS "prefixes: de/ inter/ over/ under/ uni"	
sexest,sexist	
sexis,sex(es)	
sexist,* ,A MAN WHO EXPLOITS/ DISCRIMINATES AGAINST WOMEN "prefixes: non"	
sexshen,section	
sexshin,section	
sexshinul,section(al)	
sexshualedy,sexual(ity)	
sexshuality,sexual(ity)	

Entry	Definition
sevilazation,civil(ization)	
sevilean,civilian	
sevin,seven	
sevindeith,seventieth	
sevindy,seventy	
sevinteen,seventeen	
sevinteith,seventieth	
sevinth,seventh	
sevinty,seventy	
sevir,severe	
seviral,several	
seviranse,severance	
sevird,severe(d)	
sevire,severe / sever	
sevirly,severe(ly)	
sevirt,sever(ed)	
sevirunse,severance	
sevlazation,civil(ization)	
sevlization,civil(ization)	
sevlozation,civil(ization)	
sevluzation,civil(ization)	
sevol,civil	
sevolazation,civil(ization)	
sevon,seven	
sevondeith,seventieth	
sevondy,seventy	
sevont,savant	
sevonteen,seventeen	
sevonteith,seventieth	
sevor,sever	
sevr,sever	
sevral,several	
sevrense,severance	
sevrul,several	
sevrunse,severance	
sevt,sift / sieve(d)	
sevun,seven	
sevundeith,seventieth	
sevundy,seventy	
sevunteen,seventeen	
sevunteith,seventieth	
sevunth,seventh	
sevunty,seventy	

sezun,season
sezurs,scissor(s)
sfarekil,sphere(rical)
sfeer,sphere
sfencks,sphinx
sfencter,sphincter
sfenktur,sphincter
sfenx,sphinx
sfer,sphere
sferakil,sphere(rical)
sfere,sphere
sferekul,sphere(rical)
sferical,sphere(rical)
sferukle,sphere(rical)
sfincs,sphinx
sfincter,sphincter
sfinks,sphinx
sfinktur,sphincter
sfinx,sphinx
sfir,sphere
sgoundrel,scoundrel
sgowndrul,scoundrel
sgragliest,scraggly(liest)
sgrakleur,scraggly(lier)
shabby,bbier,bbiest,bbily,bbiness,WORN,THREADBARE
shabely,shabby(bbily)
shabiness,shabby(bbiness)
shaby,shabby
shac,shack
shack,*,ked,king,SHANTY,PRIMITIVE HUT,CABIN (or see shag/ shake)
shackle,*,ed,ling,er,A FASTENER, CUFFS "prefixes: un"
shacol,shackle
shade,*,ed,ding,dy,eless,OVERHEAD PROTECTION FROM THE SUN
shader,shatter
shadey,shade(dy)
shadir,shatter
shado,shadow
shadow,*,wed,wing,wer,wy,AREA WHERE THE LIGHT DOESN'T PENETRATE,SCREEN/ PROTECT "prefixes: over"
shadur,shatter

shaem,shame
shaemful,shame(ful)
shaenk,shank
shafd,shaft / shave(d) / chafe(d)
shafe,shave / chafe
shafed,shaft / shave(d)
shaft,*,ted,ting,NARROW COLUMN/ CYLINDER (or see chafe(d)/ shave(d))
shag,gged,gging,ggy,ggier,ggiest,CARPET,TO RETRIEVE,LOOSE THREADS (or see shack)
shagier,shag(ggier)
shagiest,shag(ggiest) / shake(kiest)
shagy,shag(ggy)
shaim,shame
shaimless,shame(less)
shaink,shank
shak,shack / shake
shake,*,ed,king,er,ky,kier,kiest,hook,JUMBLE,JOSTLE,VIBRATE,MOVE UP/ DOWN,BUILDING MATERIAL (or see shack) "prefixes: un"
shaked,shack(ed) / shake(d)
shakel,shackle
shakul,shackle
shakult,shackle(d)
shakyest,shake(kiest)
shal,shall / shale / shawl
shall,COULD,ALLOWED/ ABLE TO (or see shawl)
shallot,*,PLANT BULBS USED IN COOKING
shallow,*,wly,wness,OF LITTLE DEPTH,SUPERFICIAL
shalo,shallow
shaloness,shallow(ness)
shalot,shallot
shalow,shallow
shalowness,shallow(ness)
shalut,shallot
sham,mmed,mming,mmer,COVER-UP FOR THE TRUTH (or see shame)
shaman,*,nic,nism,nist,nistic,WISE ONE WITH SPIRITUAL POWERS
shambal,shamble

shamble,*,ed,ling,UNSTEADY,DISORDER
shambul,shamble
shame,*,ed,ming,eful,efully,efulness,eless,DISGRACED, DISHONORED (or see sham)
shamed,shame(d) / sham(mmed)
shamen,shaman
shamer,sham(mmer)
shamful,shame(ful)
shamin,shaman
shaminesm,shaman(ism)
shamless,shame(less)
shamonek,shaman(ic)
shamonism,shaman(ism)
shampein,champagne
shample,shamble
shampoo,*,ooed,ooing,ooer,USE SOAP TO CLEAN HAIR/ CARPET/ UPHOLSTERY
shampoor,shampoo(er)
shampu,shampoo
shampuer,shampoo(er)
shampuir,shampoo(er)
shampul,shamble
shamrock,*,PLANT
shamrok,shamrock
shanal,channel
shanalize,channelize
shananigen,shenanigan
shananugin,shenanigan
shandalere,chandelier
shandulere,chandelier
shange,change
shanil,channel
shanilize,channelize
shank,*,PART OF THE BODY
shanty,ties,ROUGH/ FRONTIER STRUCTURE
shantys,shanty(ties)
shape,*,ed,ping,pable,eless,elessly,eliness,ely,er,OF FORM/ FIGURE "prefixes: re/ un"
shapeable,shape(pable)
shaperd,shepherd
shaplis,shape(less)
shaply,shape(ly)
shapuble,shape(pable)

shar,share / chair / char
sharade,charade
sharck,shark
shard,*,FRAGMENT
share,*,ed,ring,TO DIVIDE INTO PORTIONS "prefixes: over"
sharee,sherry
sharef,sheriff
shareid,charade
shari,sherry
sharif,sheriff
shark,*,MARINE FISH,LIKE A SHARK
sharp,ply,pness,pen,pens,pened,pening,pe ner,per, pest,pie,DISTINCT POINT/ TIP
sharpin,sharp(en)
sharpind,sharp(ened)
sharpinur,sharp(ener)
sharpnis,sharp(ness)
sharpuner,sharp(ener)
sharpy,sharp(ie)
sharry,sherry
sharuf,sheriff
shate,shade
shater,shatter
shatir,shatter
shato,shadow
shatord,shatter(ed)
shatoy,shadow
shatter,*,red,ring,REDUCE TO PIECES/ FRAGMENTS
shaturd,shatter(ed)
shauk,chalk / choke / shock / chock
shavar,shave(r)
shave,*,ed,ving,er,TO REDUCE THE SURFACE/ OUTCROP,SCRATCH, GRAZE THE SURFACE
shavir,shave(r)
shavur,shave(r)
shawer,shower
shawir,shower
shawl,*,EXTERIOR GARMENT FOR SHOULDERS
shawmen,shaman
shawmonism,shaman(ism)
shawur,shower
she,*,THAT FEMALE

she'd,CONTRACTION OF THE WORDS 'SHE HAD/ WOULD' (or see shed)
she'll,CONTRACTION OF THE WORDS 'SHE WILL' (or see shell)
sheaf,aves,BOUND STALKS,QUIVER OF ARROWS
shear,*,ed,ring,rer,horn,CUT WITH CLIPPERS (or see sheer)
sheath,hes,hed,hing,CLOSE FITTING CASE/ COVERING, ALSO SPELLED 'SHEATHE'
sheberd,shepherd
sheburd,shepherd
shechul,special
shed,*,dded,dding,SMALL STRUCTURE (or see she'd/ sheet)
sheef,sheaf
sheek,chic
sheeld,shield
sheen,*,,ned,ning,nier,niest,ny,RADIANT/ BRIGHT/ LIGHT (or see shin)
sheengul,shingle
sheep,pish,pishly,pishness,A RUMINANT ANIMAL
sheer,*,red,ring,rer,rly,rness,NAUTICAL TERM, OF LITTLE BODY/ SUBSTANCE,NEAR TRANSPARENT (or see shear)
sheet,*,ted,ting,THIN/ FLAT SUBSTANCE/ MATERIAL
sheeth,sheath
shef,chef / chief / sheaf
shefor,shiver
sheft,shift
shefur,shiver
sheic,shake
sheid,shade
sheif,shave
sheik,shake
sheild,shield
sheilt,shield
sheim,shame
sheiman,shaman
sheinc,shank
sheink,shank
sheip,shape
sheir,share
sheiv,shave

shel,she'll / shell / shale
shelak,shellac
sheld,shield / shell(ed)
sheldur,shelter
sheldurless,shelter(less)
shelf,Ives,HORIZONTAL LEDGE TO PLACE THINGS ON (or see shelve)
shelfs,shelve(s)
shell,*,lled,lling,ller,HOUSING/ PROTECTION FOR CREATURES,LAYERS OF ATOM,HAND OVER (or see she'll) "prefixes: sub"
shellac,*,ced,cing,A CHEMICAL SOLUTION, USED IN VARNISH
shelt,shell(ed)
shelter,*,red,ring,rless,COVER/ PROTECTION/ REFUGE
sheltired,shelter(ed)
sheltur,shelter
shelturd,shelter(ed)
shelturless,shelter(less)
shelve,*,ed,ving,er,PLURAL FOR SHELF,LEDGE TO PLACE ITEMS
shem,shim
shemed,shim(mmed) / shimmy(mmied)
shemee,shimmy
shemir,shimmer
shemmiry,shimmery
shemonic,shaman(ic)
shemur,shimmer
shemury,shimmery
shemy,shimmy
shen,sheen / shin / chin
shenanigan,*,NONSENSE TRICKERY
shengle,shingle
shengul,shingle
shep,sheep / ship / chip
shepard,shepherd
sheper,ship(pper) / chip(pper)
sheperd,shepherd
shepherd,*,THAT WHICH GUARDS/ PROTECTS
shepird,shepherd
shepish,sheep(ish)
sheprek,shipwreck
shept,ship(pped) / chip(pped)

shepur,ship(pper) / chip(pper)
shepurd,shepherd
shepwreck,shipwreck
sher,sure / share / chair / cheer
sherba,sherbet
sherbert,sherbet
sherbet,*,FRUIT FLAVORED ICE DESSERT
sherbirt,sherbet
sherburt,sherbet
sherd,shear(ed) / sheer(ed) / share(d)
sheered,shear(ed) / sheer(ed) / share(d)
sheredy,surety
sheri,sherry
sheridy,surety
sherif,sheriff
sheriff,*,LAW ENFORCEMENT OFFICIAL
sherir,shear(er)
sherity,surety
sherly,sure(ly)
sheror,shear(er)
sherrif,sheriff
sherry,ries,TYPE OF WINE
shert,shear(ed) / sheer(ed) / shirt
sheruf,sheriff
sherur,shear(er)
shery,sherry
shet,shed / sheet / she'd
shethd,sheath(ed)
sheult,shield
shevir,shiver
shevt,shift
shevtur,shift(er)
shevulry,chivalry
shevur,shiver
shew,shoe / chew
shewr,sure
shews,shoe(s)
shewt,chute / shoot / chew(ed)
shi,shy / she
shid,shy(hied) / she'd
shield,*,ded,ding,USED FOR DEFENSE/ PROTECTION
shier,shy(er)
shif,sheaf

shift,*,ted,ting,tingly,tingness,ter,tless,tlessly,tlessness,ty,tily,tiness,LEAVE ONE GEAR/ FOCUS/ PLACE/ POINT TO GO TO ANOTHER "prefixes: un/ up"
shiftur,shift(er)
shifur,shiver
shil,she'll / shell
shilak,shellac
shild,shield
shilee,shy(ly)
shily,shy(ly)
shim,*,mmed,mming,A THIN STRIP OF SOME MATERIAL USED TO FILL GAPS
shimanik,shaman(ic)
shimee,shimmy
shimer,shimmer
shimery,shimmer
shimes,shimmy(mmies) / shim(s)
shimmer,*,ry,LIGHT/ GLEAMING
shimmy,mmies,mmied,mmying,VIBRATION/ WOBBLING
shimonic,shaman(ic)
shimur,shimmer
shimury,shimmer
shimy,shimmy
shimyd,shimmy(mmied)
shimys,shimmy(mmies)
shin,*,nned,nning,PART OF THE LEG, SPLINT OF WOOD (or see shine/ chin)
shinanigan,shenanigan
shinanugan,shenanigan
shind,shine(d) / shin(nned)
shine,*,ed,ning,er,ny,nier,niest,niness,RADIANT/ REFLECTIVE (or see chin/ shin/ shiny)
shineist,shiny(niest)
shiness,shy(ness)
shineur,shiny(nier)
shingle,*,ed,ling,ROOF COVERING, PAINFUL VIRAL INFECTION
shingul,shingle
shinguled,shingle(d)
shinie,shiny
shiny,nier,niest,niness,RADIANT/ REFLECTIVE
shinyest,shiny(niest)

shinyness,shiny(niness)
ship,*,pped,pping,pper,WATER/ NAUTICAL VESSEL, SEND ITEM BY ROAD/ SEA/ AIR (or see chip) "prefixes: un"
shipd,ship(pped) / chip(pped)
shiper,ship(pper) / chip(pper)
shiprek,shipwreck
shipur,ship(pper) / chip(pper)
shipwreck,*,ked,BOAT WHICH WRECKS IN THE SEA
shipwrek,shipwreck
shir,sure / shy(er) / shear
shirbert,sherbet
shirbet,sherbet
shirburt,sherbet
shiredy,surety
shirety,surety
shirly,sure(ly)
shirt,*,UPPER TORSO GARMENT "prefixes: over/ under"
shister,shyster
shith,sheath
shiur,shy(er)
shivalry,chivalry
shiver,*,red,ring,SHAKE/ TREMBLE FROM COLD/ FEAR
shivt,shift
shivulry,chivalry
shivur,shiver
sho,show
shoal,*,SHALLOW AREA ASSOCIATED WITH A BODY OF WATER, SCHOOL OF FISH
shoar,shore / chore
shock,*,ked,king,ker,kingly,SUDDEN/ ABRUPT/ UNPREDICTABLE EVENT, JOLT OF ELECTRICITY, SUDDEN IMPACT
shod,*,ddy,TO SHOE A HORSE (or see show(ed)/ shoot/ shoe(d)/ should) "prefixes: un"
shoddy,ddier,ddiest,ddily,ddiness,INFERIOR PRODUCT/ SERVICE PRODUCED TO MOCK FINE QUALITY
shode,shoddy
shody,shoddy
shoe,*,ed,eing,er,FOOT/ HOOF COVERING
shofel,shovel
shofer,chauffeur
shok,chalk / choke / shock / chock

Word	Forms	Definition
shoked,shock(ed) / choke(d) / chock(ed)	shoty,shoddy	
shol,shawl / shoal	shoud,shout	
sholak,shellac	shoufur,chauffeur	
sholder,shoulder	shoul,shawl	
sholdur,shoulder	should,PAST TENSE FOR THE WORD 'SHALL'	
shole,shoal / shawl	should've,CONTRACTION OF THE WORDS 'SHOULD HAVE'	
sholtur,shoulder	shoulder,*,red,ring,BODY PART HOLDING THE ARM, TO USE THE SHOULDER	
shoman,shaman		
shomenism,shaman(ism)	shouldn't,CONTRACTION OF THE WORDS 'SHOULD NOT'	
shomin,shaman	shout,*,ted,ting,TO SPEAK/ VOICE WORDS LOUDLY	
shoo,shoe	shovanism,chauvinism	
shood,should / shoe(d)	shovanist,chauvinist	
shook,PAST TENSE FOR THE WORD "SHAKE",A SET OF PREFABRICATED PARTS (or see shuck)	shove,*,ed,ving,TO PUSH/ RAM AGAINST	
	shovel,*,led,ling,AN IMPLEMENT/ TOOL FOR DIGGING/ MOVING/ SCRAPING ORGANIC MATERIAL (or see shuffle)	
shoot,*,ting,ter,hot,AIM AT SOMETHING TO DISCHARGE INTO/ PIERCE/ CAPTURE AN IMAGE (or see shut/ should) "prefixes: over/ under"		
	shovenism,chauvinism	
shop,*,pped,pping,pper,SEEK TO PURCHASE GOODS ITEMS,PLACE TO MANUFACTURE/ PERFORM RETAIL ACTIVITIES (or see chop)	shovenist,chauvinist	
	shovinism,chauvinism	
	shovinist,chauvinist	
shoper,shop(pper)	shovonism,chauvinism	
shopur,shop(pper)	shovonist,chauvinist	
shor,shore / chore / sure	shovunism,chauvinism	
shord,shore(d) / short	shovunist,chauvinist	
shordist,short(est)	show,*,wed,wing,wn,wy,TO DISPLAY FOR SOMEONE	
shore,*,ed,ring,PLACE WHERE BODY OF WATER MEETS LAND (or see chore) ' prefixes: in"	shower,*,red,ring,ry,RAIN OR THE IMITATION OF	
	showfer,chauffeur	
shoreid,charade	showir,shower	
shork,shark	showl,shawl	
shorn,PAST TENSE FOR THE WORD "SHEAR"	showmin,shaman	
shorp,sharp	showt,shout / show(ed)	
shors,shore(s) / chore(s)	showur,shower	
short,*,ted,ter,test,BRIEF/ ABRUPT,SMALLER/ LESS THAN NORMAL (or see shore(d)/ shorts)	shoy,show	
	shrapnel,SHELL FRAGMENTS	
shortir,short(er)	shrapnul,shrapnel	
shortist,short(est)	shreak,shriek	
shorts,*, ,MEDIA LENGTH, PANTS TO THE KNEES (or see shore(d)) "prefixes: under"	shred,*,dded,dding,dder,TO TEAR/ CUT INTO SLIVERS/ THIN STRIPS/ PIECES	
shortur,short(er)	shredur,shred(dder)	
shos,shoe(s)	shreek,shriek	
shot,PAST TENSE FOR THE WORD 'SHOOT', TAKE A HIT OF/ FROM SOMETHING,TO FILM (or see shod) "prefixes: up"	shreful,shrivel	
	shrel,shrill	

Word	Forms	Definition
	shrelness,shrill(ness)	
	shremp,shrimp	
	shrempy,shrimp	
	shrenk,shrink	
	shrenkable,shrink(able)	
	shrevle,shrivel	
	shrevul,shrivel	
	shrew,*, ,wish,wishly,wishness,SMALL MAMMAL,TO BE ILL TEMPERED	
	shrewd,dly,dness,TO BE DISCERNING/ PRACTICAL	
	shrewtly,shrewd(ly)	
	shriek,*,ked,king,A SHRILL/ SHARP YELL OR SHOUT SOUNDED WHEN FRIGHTENED/ ANGRY	
	shrifle,shrivel	
	shril,shrill	
	shrill,lly,llness,PIERCING/ HIGH PITCHED SOUND	
	shrilness,shrill(ness)	
	shrimp,*, ,py,EDIBLE CRUSTACEANS,SMALL/ TINY	
	shrine, ,A STRUCTURE WITH RELIGIOUS IMPLICATIONS "prefixes: en"	
	shrink,*, ,runk,king,kable,BECOME SMALLER THAN ORIGINAL SIZE,SLANG FOR MENTAL DOCTOR	
	shrivel,*, ,led,ling,TO WRINKLE/ SHRINK	
	shrivle,shrivel	
	shronk,shrunk	
	shroo,shrew	
	shrood,shrewd	
	shroodly,shrewd(ly)	
	shrooish,shrew(ish)	
	shroot,shrewd	
	shroud,*, ,ded,ding,HIDE/ COVER/ CONCEAL "prefixes: en"	
	shrowd,shroud	
	shru,shrew	
	shrub,*, ,bbery,bby,LOW GROWING TREES/ BUSHES "prefixes: sub/ under"	
	shrubery,shrub(bbery)	
	shrubry,shrub(bbery)	
	shrud,shrewd	
	shrudly,shrewd(ly)	
	shrue,shrew	
	shrug,*, ,gged,gging,USE THE SHOULDERS FOR EMOTIONAL EXPRESSION	

shrunk, PAST TENSE FOR 'SHRINK' "prefixes: pre"
shrupree,shrub(bbery)
shrut,shrewd
shrutly,shrewd(ly)
shryn,shrine
shu,shoe
shuch,shush
shuck,*,ked,king,ker, REMOVE HULLS/ SHELLS/ OUTER HOUSING (or see shook)
shuckir,shuck(er)
shud,should / shut
shudal,shuttle
shudder,*,red,ring,ry, PHYSICAL/ EMOTIONAL RESPONSE TO SOMETHING GROTESQUE/ REPULSIVE (or see shutter)
shudel,shuttle
shuder,shutter / shudder / shoot(er)
shuderd,shudder(ed) / shutter
shudery,shudder
shudil,shuttle
shudir,shutter / shudder / shoot(er)
shudol,shuttle
shudur,shutter / shudder / shoot(er)
shuf,shove
shufal,shuffle / shovel
shuffle,*,ed,ling,ler, MOVE AROUND BY DRAGGING, AN ACT IN A CARD GAME, MOVE AS A CHESS PIECE ON GAMEBOARD (or see shovel) "prefixes: re"
shufil,shuffle / shovel
shuful,shovel / shuffle
shugar,sugar
shugur,sugar
shuk,shook / shuck
shukd,shuck(ed) / shook
shuker,sugar / shuck(er)
shukur,sugar / shuck(er)
shulak,shellac
shuld,should
shun,*,nned,nning, TO AVOID
shunanegin,shenanigan
shunanigen,shenanigan
shund,shun(nned) / shunt
shuner,shun(nner)

shunir,shun(nner)
shunt,*,ted,ter, SHIFT, RID OF, MOVE ASIDE (or see shun(nned))
shuntur,shunt(er)
shur,sure / shoe(r)
shurade,charade
shurba,sherbet
shurbert,sherbet
shurbet,sherbet
shurburt,sherbet
shuredy,surety
shureid,charade
shurity,surety
shurly,sure(ly)
shurt,shirt
shus,shoe(s)
shush, TO ENCOURAGE TO BE QUIET
shut,*,tter,tting, TO CLOSE/ STOP (or see should/ shoot/ chute)
shutal,shuttle
shute,chute / shoot
shuter,shutter / shudder / shoot(er)
shutir,shutter / shudder / shoot(er)
shutled,shuttle(d)
shutol,shuttle
shutter,*, A HINGED FLAP/ COVER OVER AN OPENING (or see shudder)
shuttle,*,ed,ling, CARRY/ TRANSPORT TO ANOTHER PLACE
shutur,shutter / shudder / shoot(er)
shuve,shove
shuvel,shovel
shuvul,shovel
shuw,shoe
shuz,shoe(s)
shy,hies,hied,ying,hier,hiest,yly,yness,yster, LESS THAN WILLING TO ACCEPT/ FACE HEAD-ON/ CONFRONT
shyster,*, ONE WHO IS UNETHICAL
shystur,shyster
si,sigh / see / sea
siadeka,sciatic(a)
siadika,sciatic(a)
sianide,cyanide

sianse,science
siantifek,scientific
siantist,scientist
siants,science
siatek,sciatic
siateka,sciatic(a)
siatic,sciatic
siatika,sciatic(a)
sibkonchus,subconscious
sibkontrakt,subcontract
siblengs,sibling(s)
sibling,*, LEGAL BROTHERS/ SISTERS
siborg,cyborg
sibra,zebra
siburnetiks,cybernetics
sic, WORD USED FOR REPLACEMENT IN TEXT, TO ENCOURAGE SOMETHING TO ATTACK (or see sick/ psyche)
sicede,secede
sicheatric,psychiatric
sichek,psychic
sichewashen,situate(tion)
sichewation,situate(tion)
sichiatric,psychiatric
sichic,psychic
sichologist,psychology(gist)
sichologekul,psychology(gical)
sichologest,psychology(gist)
sichology,psychology
sichopath,psychopath
sichopathologist,psychopath(ologist)
sichosis,psychosis
sichuaded,situate(d)
sichuashen,situate(tion)
sichuate,situate
sichuation,situate(tion)
sichudelic,psychedelic
sick, kish,kishness,kly,kliness,kness, PHYSICALLY/ MENTALLY ILL (or see psyche)
sickal,sickle / cycle
sickle,*, ed,ling, TOOL USED FOR CUTTING GRASS/ GRAIN, CRESCENT MOON SHAPE (or see cycle)
sicks,six

sickstee,sixty
sickteith,sixtieth
sickth,sixth
siclone,cyclone
sico,psycho
sicodek,psychotic
sicological,psychology(gical)
sicology,psychology
sicreshen,secrete(tion)
sicrete,secrete
sicretion,secrete(tion)
sicual,sequel
sicuens,sequence
sicuer,secure
sicuerity,secure(rity)
sicuerly,secure(ly)
sicumb,succumb
sid,sigh(ed) / side / sight / seed
sidan,sedan
sidar,sit(tter) / cider / side(r)
sidashen,sedate(tion)
sidasion,sedate(tion)
sidate,sedate
sidation,sedate(tion)
side, *, ed,ding,er, BE NEAR OR BESIDE BUT NOT ON, POSITION OFF FROM CENTER (or see s te/ sight) "prefixes: under/ up/ sub"
sideng,side(ding) / site(ting) / sight(ing)
sider, sit(tter) / cider / side(r)
sidewse,seduce
sidir, sit(tter) / cider / side(r)
sidling,seed(ling)
sidokshen,seduce(ction)
sidoose,seduce
sidor, sit(tter) / cider / side(r)
sids, sit(s) / set(s) / side(s)
siducshen,seduce(ction)
sidukshen,seduce(ction)
siduktion,seduce(ction)
siduktive,seduce(ctive)
sidur, sit(tter) / cider / side(r)
siduse,seduce
siduzen,citizen

siege, *, ed,ging, TAKE/ STEAL CONTROL OF FUNCTIONS
siegur,seize(zure)
siejur,seize(zure)
sienna, A COLOR/ PIGMENT
siense,science
sienses,science(s)
sientifekly,scientific(ally)
sientific,scientific
sientifikly,scientific(ally)
sientist,scientist
sier,sigh(er)
siera,sierra
sierra, SECTION OF HILLS/ RANGE, A FISH
siesta, *, AFTERNOON NAP
sieve, *, ed,ving, STRAINER/ NET FOR SOLIDS/ LIQUIDS
sieze,seize
sif,sieve
sifal,civil
sifalezation,civil(ization)
sifalis,syphilis
sifalization,civil(ization)
sifaree,safari
sifd, sieve(d) / sift
sifen,siphon
sifenul,siphon(al)
sifinal,siphon(al)
sifise,suffice
siflazation,civil(ization)
siflus,syphilis
sifol,civil
sifolezation,civil(ization)
sifon,siphon
sift, *, ted,ting,ter, SEPARATION OF VARIOUS GRAIN SIZES, SORT FOR A SPECIFIC THING (or see sieve(d))
siftur,sift(er)
sifules,syphilis
sifunil,siphon(al)
sigar,cigar
sigaret,cigarette
siger,seize(zure)
sigeret,cigarette
siggesdeve,suggest(ive)
siggestion,suggest(ion)

sigh, *, hed,hing,A DEEP/ RELEASING BREATH
sight, *, ted,ting,table,ter, tless,tlessly,tlessness,tly, tliness, VISUAL,ABLE TO SEE (or see site) "prefixes: in/ over/ un"
sigjesdeve,suggest(ive)
sigjestion,suggest(ion)
sigjestive,suggest(ive)
sigjestshen,suggest(ion)
sigma, GREEK ALPHABET LETTER
sigmu,sigma
sign, *, ned,ning,ner, WRITTEN TEXT,SYMBOL WITH MEANING,A PLACARD/ BOARD WITH WORDS/ SYMBOLS,A SIGNATURE (or see sine) "prefixes: con/ -re/ un/ under"
signacher,signature
signafiable,signify(fiable)
signafier,signify(fier)
signafy,signify
signal, *, led,ling,ler,llly,lize,lized,lizing,IMAGE/ GESTURE USED TO COMMUNICATE
signature, *, tory,tories, A PERSON'S NAME/ MARK,TO SIGN SOMETHING "prefixes: bio"
signefiable,signify(fiable)
signefukent,significant
signeture,signature
signifacantly,significant(ly)
significant,tly,nce,ation,ative,atively,OF IMPORTANCE, OUTSTANDING "prefixes: in"
signify,fied,fying,fiable,fier,INDICATE, POINT OUT
signuchur,signature
signufy,signify
signul,signal
signushure,signature
sigsag,zigzag
sigur,seize(zure)
siguret,cigarette
sijur,seize(zure)
sik,sick / psyche / seek
sikadelic,psychedelic
sikal,sickle / cycle
sikamore,sycamore
sike,psyche / sick / sic
sikeatree,psychiatry

sikeatric, psychiatric
sikedelic, psychedelic
sikek, psychic
sikel, sickle / cycle
sikepath, psychopath
sikeur, secure
sikeurety, secure(rity)
sikeurly, secure(ly)
sikewr, secure
silgest, suggest
sikgestion, suggest(ion)
sikiatree, psychiatry
sikiatrist, psychiatry(rist)
sikik, psychic
sikil, sickle / cycle
sikiotrist, psychiatry(rist)
sikiutrest, psychiatry(rist)
sikiutry, psychiatry
sikjest, suggest
sikjestion, suggest(ion)
sikjestshen, suggest(ion)
sikle, sickle
siklude, seclude
siklushen, seclusion
siklusive, seclusive
siklution, seclusion
sikma, sigma
siknacher, signature
siknafier, signify(fier)
siknashure, signature
siknature, signature
siknefakent, significant
siknefy, signify
sikneture, signature
siknifakent, significant
siknify, signify
siknishure, signature
siknol, signal
siknufy, signify
siknul, signal
siknuture, signature
siko, psycho
sikodelic, psychedelic

sikodik, psychotic
sikolegy, psychology
sikologekul, psychology(gical)
sikologest, psychology(gist)
sikology, psychology
sikopath, psychopath
sikopathic, psychopath(ic)
sikopatholagist, psychopath(ologist)
sikosis, psychosis
sikotic, psychotic
sikreshen, secrete(tion)
sikresion, secrete(tion)
sikrete, secrete
siks, six
sikstee, sixty
siksteen, sixteen
siksteenth, sixteen(th)
siksteith, sixtieth
sikstiuth, sixtieth
siksty, sixty
sikteith, sixtieth
sikth, sixth
sikudelic, psychedelic
sikul, sickle / cycle
sikulest, cyclist
sikum, succumb
sikumore, sycamore
sikure, secure
sikurity, secure(rity)
sikwenshul, sequence(ntial)
sikwential, sequence(ntial)
sikwoia, sequoia
sikwoya, sequoia
siky, psyche / sick
sil, zeal
silabes, syllabus
silabil, syllable
silacon, silicon / silicone
silakit, silica(te)
silakon, silicon / silicone
silal, salal
silami, salami
silanoid, solenoid

silanse, silence
silant, silent
silantly, silent(ly)
silantness, silent(ness)
silareum, solarium
silawet, silhouette
sild, silt
sildashen, silt(ation)
silebus, syllabus
sileca, silica
silecate, silica(te)
silective, select(ive)
silee, silly
sileka, silica
silekshen, select(ion)
silekt, select
silektif, select(ive)
silektion, select(ion)
silektive, select(ive)
silence, *, ed, cing, er, QUIET, NO SOUND
silendur, cylinder
sileness, silly(lliness)
sileng, ceiling / seal(ing)
silenium, selenium
silenoid, solenoid
silense, silence
silensur, silence(r)
silent, tly, tness, BEING QUIET, NO SOUND
silerium, solarium
silesit, solicit
silesitation, solicit(ation)
silesiter, solicit(er)
silesteul, celestial
sileur, silly(llier)
silewet, silhouette
silfer, silver
silferware, silverware
silfur, silver
silfurware, silverware
silfury, silver
silhouete, silhouette
silhouette, *, ed, ting, THE SHAPE/ OUTLINE OF SOMETHING

silica,ate,A NATURAL CHEMICAL COMPOUND
silicon,A NATURALLY OCCURRING ELEMENT (or see silicone)
silicone,*,A SILICON SUBSTITUTE, MANMADE CHEMICAL (or see silicon)
siliest,silly(lliest)
silinder,cylinder
siliness,silly(lliness)
siling,ceiling / seal(ing)
silinoid,solenoid
silins,silence
silinser,silence(r)
silion,zillion
silivu,saliva
silk,*,ken,ky,kily,kiness,THREAD/ FABRIC MADE FROM SILKWORMS
silkee,silk
silkeness,silk(iness)
silkun,silk(en)
sill,*,A HORIZONTAL SHELF (or see sell)
silly,llier,lliest,llies,lliness,GOOFY/ FUNNY, NOT SERIOUS
silo,*,oed,oing,A STRUCTURE/ HOUSING FOR GRAIN/ MISSILES/ ROCKETS
siloet,silhouette
silomee,salami
silon,salon
siloon,saloon
siloot,salute
silow,silo
silt,tation,ty,A VERY FINE DIRT/ SEDIMENT
siltashen,silt(ation)
siubel,syllable
silubes,syllabus
silubil,syllable
siluca,silica
silucone,silicon / silicone
siludid,salute(d)
siluet,silhouette
siluka,silica
siluket,silica(te)
silukon,silicon / silicone
silune,saloon
silunoid,solenoid

siluns,silence
silunsed,silence(d)
silunser,silence(r)
silunt,silent
siluntly,silent(ly)
siluntness,silent(ness)
silute,salute
silver,red,ry,riness,A TYPE OF SOFT METAL, THE COLOR OF SHINY GRAY
silverware,UTENSILS COATED IN SILVER
silvir,silver
silvur,silver
silvurware,silverware
silvury,silver
sily,silly
sim,seem / seam
simalarly,similar(ly)
simaler,similar
simalerety,similar(ity)
simalerly,similar(ly)
simaltaneus,simultaneous
simaltaneusly,simultaneous(ly)
siman,semen
simantics,semantics
simar,simmer
simashen,sum(mmation)
simation,sum(mmation)
simatry,symmetry
simbal,symbol
simbalism,symbol(ism)
simbathetik,sympathetic
simbathy,sympathy
simbeodek,symbiotic
simbeosis,symbiosis
simbeotek,symbiotic
simbethe,sympathy
simbethetic,sympathetic
simbiosis,symbiosis
simblanse,semblance
simblants,semblance
simble,symbol
simblense,semblance
simbol,cymbal / symbol

simbolek,symbol(ic)
simbolik,symbol(ic)
simbul,symbol
simbulism,symbol(ism)
simbuthe,sympathy
simbuthetic,sympathetic
simdum,symptom
simelarity,similar(ity)
simeltaneus,simultaneous
simeltaneusly,simultaneous(ly)
simelur,similar
simelurly,similar(ly)
simen,semen
siment,cement
simer,simmer
simesder,semester
simester,semester
simetrek,symmetry(ric)
simetric,symmetry(ric)
simetry,symmetry
simewlate,simulate
simfeny,symphony
simfonic,symphony(nic)
simfune,symphony
similar,rly,rity,rities,RESEMBLES SOMETHING ALMOST LIKE IT, NOT THE SAME BUT CLOSE, ALSO SPELLED "SIMULAR" prefixes: dis"
similur,similar
similurly,similar(ly)
simin,semen
simmer,*,red,ring,COOK GENTLY WITH LOW HEAT, TO CALM DOWN
simoltaneus,simultaneous
simoltaneus,simultaneous
simoltaneusly,simultaneous(ly)
simoolader,simulate(tor)
simpal,simple
simpalest,simple(st)
simpaly,simple(ly)
simpathee,sympathy
simpathetic,sympathetic
simpathize,sympathy(hize)
simpathy,sympathy

simpdum, symptom
simpel, simple
simpelest, simple(st)
simpely, simple(ly)
simpethize, sympathy(hize)
simpethy, sympathy
simphonek, symphony(nic)
simphonic, symphony(nic)
simphuny, symphony
simpithy, sympathy
simple, er, est, leness, ly, licity, licities, lify, lification, lifier, lism, listic, listically, NOT COMPLICATED, BASIC, UNDERSTANDABLE "prefixes: over"
simplisity, simple(licity)
simplistec, simple(listic)
simplur, simple(r)
simposeum, symposium
simpozeum, symposium
simptom, symptom
simptum, symptom
simpul, simple
simpuler, simple(r)
simpulest, simple(st)
simpuly, simple(ly)
simputhee, sympathy
simputhetic, sympathetic
simputhize, sympathy(hize)
simtem, symptom
simtum, symptom
simualtaneus, simultaneous
simuladur, simulate(tor)
simularity, similar(ity)
simularly, similar(ly)
simulashen, simulate(tion)
simulate, *, tive, tion, tor, REPRODUCTION OF ORIGINAL "prefixes: dis"
simuler, similar
simulerity, similar(ity)
simulerly, similar(ly)
simultaneous, sly, eity, HAPPENING AT SAME TIME
simultaneusly, simultaneous(ly)
simur, simmer
simurd, simmer(ed)

simurt, simmer(ed)
simutary, cemetery
simutree, symmetry
sin, *, nned, nning, nner, nful, nfully, nfulness, KNOWINGLY COMMIT AN IMMORAL ACT (or see seen/ sine/ seine/ sign)
sinada, sonata
sinail, senile
sinanem, synonym
sinapse, synapse
sinapsis, synapsis
sinaptek, synaptic
sinaptic, synaptic
sinareo, scenario
sinas, sinus
sinaster, sinister
sinata, sonata
sinatorial, senator(ial)
sinatur, senator
sinc, sync / sink
since, REFERRING TO THE PAST, FROM THEN UP UNTIL NOW, BECAUSE OF (or see sense/ cent(s)/ sin(s)/ scent(s))
sincere, ely, rity, eness, HONEST/ GENUINE "prefixes: in"
sincerly, sincere(ly)
sinch, cinch
sinched, singe(d) / cinch(ed)
sinchro, synchro
sinchronus, synchrony(nous)
sincht, singe(d) / cinch(ed)
sincronize, synchrony(nize)
sincrony, synchrony
sind, send / sign(ed) / sin(nned)
sinder, cinder / send(er)
sindicate, syndicate
sindication, syndicate(tion)
sindikation, syndicate(tion)
sindiket, syndicate
sindrem, syndrome
sindrulize, centralize
sindrum, syndrome
sindukit, syndicate
sindur, send(er)

sine, MATHEMATICAL FUNCTION (or see sign/ sin)
sined, sign(ed) / sin(nned)
sinegrade, centigrade
sinek, cynic
sinekal, cynical
sinema, cinema
sinemin, cinnamon
sineority, senior(ity)
sinepede, centipede
siner, sin(nner)
sinereo, scenario
sinergy, synergy
sinerist, scenario(ist)
sines, sign(s) / sin(s) / sinus
sinester, sinister
sineth, zenith
sinetor, senator
sinetorial, senator(ial)
sinew, w, TENDONS, TO STRENGTHEN
sinfuly, sin(fully)
sing, *, ging, ger, CREATE MELODIC NOTES/ SONGS WITH THE VOICE/ THROAT (or see singe/ sink)
singal, single
singar, sing(er)
singe, *, ed, ging, SCORCH/ SLIGHTLY BURN SOMETHING (or see sing/ cinch)
singel, single
singewlerety, singular(ity)
singil, single
singir, sing(er)
single, *, ed, ling, lism, ly, ONLY ONE, NOT WITH OTHERS
singul, single
singular, rly, rness, rize, rity, rities, OF BEING ONE/ ONCE, INDIVIDUAL "prefixes: non"
singuler, singular
singulerety, singular(ity)
singuleridy, singular(ity)
singulerly, singular(ly)
singuly, single(ly)
singur, sing(er)
singus, singe(s) / cinch(es)
sinia, zinnia
sinic, cynic

sinical,cynical
sinima,cinema
sinior,senior
sinir,sin(nner)
sinister,rous,rously,rly,rness,SOMETHING EVIL/ FOREBODING
sinj,singe / cinch
sinjd,singe(d) / cinch(ed)
sinjt,singe(d) / cinch(ed)
sink,*,sunk,king,ker,kage,kable,TO DESCEND/ LOWER/ RECLINE/ SUBMERGE,A BASIN (or see sync)
sinkd,sink(ed)
sinkewler,singular
sinkil,single
sinkir,sink(er) / sing(er)
sinkle,single
sinkly,single(ly)
sinkranes,synchrony(nous)
sinkrenus,synchrony(nous)
sinkro,synchro
sinkronee,synchrony
sinkronize,synchrony(nize)
sinkronus,synchrony(nous)
sinkrony,synchrony
sinkt,sink(ed)
sinkul,single
sinkularedy,singular(ity)
sinkularly,singular(ly)
sinkuler,singular
sinkur,sink(er) / sing(er)
sinles,sin(less)
sinnless,sin(less)
sinoda,sonata
sinodu,sonata
sinografee,scenography
sinography,scenography
sinome,tsunami
sinonemus,synonym(ous)
sinonim,synonym
sinonimus,synonym(ous)
sinonym,synonym
sinopsis,synopsis
sinota,sonata

sinoter,senator
sins,sign(s) / sin(s) / since / sense / cent(s)
sinsable,sensible
sinsaredy,sincere(rity)
sinsaridy,sincere(rity)
sinsashen,sensation
sinsation,sensation
sinsative,sensitive
sinsativity,sensitive(vity)
sinsatize,sensitize
sinse,since / sense / cent(s) / scent(s)
sinseer,sincere
sinseerly,sincere(ly)
sinsere,sincere
sinseredy,sincere(rity)
sinserity,sincere(rity)
sinserly,sincere(ly)
sinsery,sensor
sinsetive,sensitive
sinseur,sincere / censor / censure / sensor
sinshere,century
sinshewality,sensual(ity)
sinshewus,sensuous
sinshual,sensual
sinshuality,sensual(ity)
sinshuos,sensuous
sinshure,century
sinsiry,sensor
sinsless,sense(less)
sinsor,censor / censure
sinsoreal,sensor(ial)
sinsory,sensor
sinst,sense(d)
sinsual,sensual
sinsuble,sensible
sinsus,census / sense
sinsutive,sensitive
sinsutivity,sensitive(vity)
sinsutize,sensitize
sint,sent / cent / scent / sin(nned) / sign(ed)
sintaks,syntax
sintament,sentiment
sintamental,sentiment(al)

sintax,syntax
sintchuis,sensuous
sintekit,syndicate
sintement,sentiment
sinteneul,centennial
sintense,sentence
sinter,center
sinthasis,synthesis
sinthasize,synthesize
sinthedik,synthetic
sinthesis,synthesis
sinthetek,synthetic
sinthusis,synthesis
sinthusize,synthesize
sintimental,sentiment(al)
sintineul,centennial
sintinse,sentence
sintrie,sentry / centri
sintrul,central
sintrulize,centralize
sintry,sentry / centri
sintrys,sentry(ries)
sintugrade,centigrade
sintumental,sentiment(al)
sintury,century
sinu,sinew
sinuee,sinew
sinugrade,centigrade
sinumeter,centimeter
sinumon,cinnamon
sinunem,synonym
sinupede,centipede
sinur,sin(nner)
sinurgy,synergy
sinus,ses,sitis,RESPIRATORY CAVITIES/ PASSAGES IN THE FACE,BOTANICAL TERM
sinuster,sinister
sinutor,senator
sinutorial,senator(ial)
sinuy,sinew
sinyor,senior
sinyority,senior(ity)
sinyuee,sinew

siontefikly,scientific(ally)
siontest,scientist
siontifek,scientific
siontist,scientist
sip,*,pped,pping,pper,ppingly,TO PURSE THE LIPS TO DRINK,SMALL DRINKS (or see sipe/ seep)
sipasetory,suppository
sipausatory,suppository
sipe,*,ed,ping,SOAK/ DRIP THROUGH (or see sip/ seep)
siper,zipper
sipereor,superior
sipereority,superior(ity)
sipereur,superior
siperlitef,superlative
siphelis,syphilis
siphen,siphon
siphenul,siphon(al)
siphilis,syphilis
siphon,*,ned,ning,nal,nic,nless,USE PRESSURE/ SUCTION TO RELOCATE FLUIDS, ALSO SPELLED "SYPHON"
siphules,syphilis
sipkonchus,subconscious
siplant,supplant
sipli,supply
siplier,supply(lier)
sipling,sibling
sipliur,supply(lier)
siply,supply
siport,support
siportef,support(ive)
siportive,support(ive)
siposatory,suppository
sipose,suppose
siposubly,suppose(dly)
sipoze,suppose
sipozubly,suppose(dly)
sipreem,supreme
sipreno,soprano
sipres,suppress
sipreshun,suppress(ion)
siptek,styptic
siptik,styptic

sipur,sip(pper)
sipurb,superb
sipurblee,superb(ly)
sipurlitef,superlative
siq,seek / sick
siquel,sequel
siquential,sequence(ntial)
siquerly,secure(ly)
siquir,secure
siquirety,secure(rity)
siquoia,sequoia
sir,*,TITLE OF A MAN (or see sire/ seer)
siraded,serrate(d)
siraget,surrogate
siragit,surrogate
siramik,ceramic
siran,saran / siren
sirape,syrup / serape
sirashen,serrate(tion)
sirated,serrate(d)
siration,serrate(tion)
sircal,circle
sircas,circus
sircemscribe,circumscribe
sircharge,surcharge
sirchuble,search(able)
sircimscribe,circumscribe
sircit,circuit
sircle,circle
sircol,circle
sircomfurinse,circumference
sircomscribe,circumscribe
sircophagus,sarcophagus
sircot,circuit
sircul,circle
sircumferenc,circumference
sircumpherence,circumference
sircumsais,circumcise
sircumsize,circumcise
sircumstans,circumstance
sircus,circus
sircut,circuit
sirdify,certify

sire,*,ed,ring,MALE PARENT OF A MAMMAL (or see sir)
sireal,serial / cereal / surreal
sirealism,surrealism
sireilisum,surrealism
sirel,sorrel / surreal
sirelism,surrealism
sirem,serum
siren,*,LOUD/ PIERCING SOUNDS FROM A DEVICE,SEA NYMPHS
sirench,syringe
sirendur,surrender
sirene,serene
sireng,syringe
sirenidy,serene(nity)
sirenity,serene(nity)
sirenj,syringe
sireol,serial / cereal
sireous,serious
sirep,syrup
sires,series / sire(s) / cirrus / scirrhus
sireul,cereal / serial
sireulizum,surrealism
sireus,serious
sireusly,serious(ly)
sirf,surf / serf / serve
sirface,surface
sirfdum,serf(dom)
sirfege,serf(age)
sirfeje,serf(age)
sirfes,surface / service
sirfibul,surf(able)
sirfis,surface
sirfunt,servant
sirfur,surf(er)
sirg,surge / serge
sirgakle,surgical
sirgekul,surgical
sirgent,sergeant / surgent
sirgeon,surgeon
sirgon,surgeon
sirgree,surgery
sirgukle,surgical

sirguree,surgery
sirial,serial
siriasis,psoriasis
sirim,serum
sirin,siren
sirios,serious
siriosly,serious(ly)
siris,series
sirius,serious
sirjakle,surgical
sirje,surge / serge
sirjekul,surgical
sirjen,surgeon
sirjon,surgeon
sirjree,surgery
sirjukle,surgical
sirjuree,surgery
sirkawfigus,sarcophagus
sirkemscribe,circumscribe
sirkes,circus
sirkewler,circular
sirkis,circus
sirklar,circular
sirkofegus,sarcophagus
sirkomscribe,circumscribe
sirkulate,circulate
sirkumferinse,circumference
sirkumscribe,circumscribe
sirkumsize,circumcise
sirlee,surly
sirloin,*,A CUT OF BEEF
sirly,surly
sirman,sermon
sirmize,surmise
sirmon,sermon
sirogate,surrogate
sirom,serum
siron,siren
sirong,sarong
sirope,serape / syrup
siroredy,sorority
sirority,sorority
siros,scirrhus / cirrus

siround,surround
sirownd,surround
sirpas,surpass
sirpent,serpent
sirpentene,serpentine
sirpint,serpent
sirpintent,serpentine
sirplus,surplus
sirprize,surprise
sirrated,serrate(d)
sirrus,cirrus / scirrhus
sirtenly,certain(ly)
sirtin,certain
sirtunly,certain(ly)
sirum,serum
sirun,siren
sirup,syrup
sirus,cirrus / scirrhus
sirv,serve
sirva,survey
sirvailense,surveillance
sirvalense,surveillance
sirvatood,servitude
sirvatude,servitude
sirvaur,survey(or)
sirvayer,survey(or)
sirve,serve / survey
sirveilinse,surveillance
sirveor,survey(or)
sirves,service / survey(s) / serve(s)
sirvesable,service(cable)
sirveyor,survey(or)
sirvife,survive
sirvint,servant
sirvis,service
sirvitude,servitude
sirvive,survive
sirvivul,survive(val)
sirvont,servant
sirvunt,servant
sirvusable,service(cable)
sirvutude,servitude
sirys,series

sis,size / cease / seize
sisabul,size(zable)
sisal,sizzle
sisd,size(d) / cyst
sisdamadik,system(atic)
sisdamatic,system(atic)
sisdan,sustain
sisdem,system
sisdum,system
sisdumadik,system(atic)
sisdumatic,system(atic)
sise,size / sissy
siseble,size(zable)
sisede,secede
siseded,secede(d)
sisee,sissy
sisel,sizzle
siseptible,susceptible
siseptif,susceptive
siseptive,susceptive
siseptuble,susceptible
siseptuf,susceptive
sisers,scissor(s)
siseshen,secession
sisesion,secession
siset,secede
sisetion,secession
sisle,sizzle
sismec,seism(ic)
sismic,seism(ic)
sismical,seism(ical)
sismik,seism(ic)
sisors,scissor(s)
sispend,suspend
sissy,ssies,ssified,ssiness,yness,yish,BEHAVE LIKE A COWARD,UNMASCULINE
sist,cist / cyst
sistain,sustain
sistane,sustain
sistanuble,sustain(able)
sistem,system

sister,*,rly,hood,FEMALES WHO HAVE A STRONG AFFINITY/ RELATIONSHIP,FEMALE SIBLING BY LAW/ BLOOD
sistre,sister
sistum,system
sistumatic,system(atic)
sistur,sister
sisturly,sister(ly)
sisturn,cistern
sisubil,size(zable)
sisuble,size(zable)
sisul,sizzle
sisurs,scissor(s)
sisus,size(s)
sisy,sissy
sit,*,tting,tter,sat,POSITION RESTING ON THE BUTTOCKS, WHAT SOMETHING OCCUPYING SPACE/ POSITION DOES (or see set/ site/ side)
sitanic,satanic
sitanikul,satanic(al)
sitashun,citation
sitation,citation
sitchuashen,situate(tion)
sitchuate,situate
site,*,AREA OF SIGNIFICANCE (or see sight/ side)
siter,sit(tter) / cider / side(r)
siterical,satire(rical)
sitesin,citizen
sith,scythe / seeth
sither,zither
sitir,sit(tter) / cider / side(r)
sitor,sit(tter) / cider / side(r)
sitrek,citric
sitrik,citric
sitrus,citrus
situashen,situate(tion)
situate,*,ed,ting,tion,tional,tionally,LOCATION/ POSITION OF OBJECTS/ EVENTS
situatid,situate(d)
situr,sit(tter) / cider
situzin,citizen
sity,city
siunide,cyanide

siunse,science
siuntest,scientist
siuntifek,scientific
siuntifekaly,scientific(ally)
siuntist,scientist
siur,sigh(er)
siv,sieve
sival,civil
sivalezation,civil(ization)
sivana,savanna
sivant,savant
sivd,sieve(d) / sift
sivear,severe
sived,sieve(d) / sift
sivel,civil
sivelezation,civil(ization)
sivere,severe
siverity,severe(rity)
siverly,severe(ly)
sivic,civic
sivil,civil
sivilean,civilian
sivlazation,civil(ization)
sivol,civil
sivolazation,civil(ization)
sivont,savant
sivt,sift / sieve(d)
sivted,sift(ed)
sivter,sift(er)
sivul,civil
sivulization,civil(ization)
siworo,saguaro
six,xes,AN ENGLISH NUMBER AFTER FIVE
sixis,six(es)
sixstenth,sixteen(th)
sixtee,sixty
sixteen,nth,AN ENGLISH NUMBER AFTER FIFTEEN, 16 PARTS OF A WHOLE
sixteith,sixtieth
sixten,sixteen
sixth,*,AN ENGLISH NUMBER AFTER THE FIFTH,OF SIX EQUAL PARTS

sixtieth,ENGLISH NUMBER AFTER 59,OF 60 EQUAL PARTS
sixty,ties,AN ENGLISH NUMBER AFTER 59
sixtyn,sixteen
sixus,six(es)
siz,size / seize / sight(s) / see(s) / sea(s)
sizabil,size(zable)
sizal,sizzle
sizars,scissor(s)
sizd,size(d) / seize(d)
size,*,ed,zing,zable,zably,zableness eable,eably,eableness,AREA/ DIMENSION OF SOMETHING "prefixes: over/ under"
sizebul,size(zable)
sizel,sizzle
sizers,scissor(s)
sizible,size(zable)
sizis,size(s)
sizle,sizzle
sizmek,seism(ic)
sizmekul,seism(ical)
sizmik,seism(ic)
sizmikul,seism(ical)
sizold,sizzle(d)
sizors,scissor(s)
siztur,sister
sizuble,size(zable)
sizul,sizzle
sizurs,scissor(s)
sizus,size(s)
sizzle,*,ed,ling,er,A COOKING/ FRYING/ SIZZLING SOUND
skab,scab
skabard,scabbard
skabbard,scabbard
skabed,scab(bbed)
skabees,scabies
skaburd,scabbard
skabys,scabies
skad,scat / skate / skat / scad
skader,skate(r) / scatter
skaffold,scaffold

skafolding,scaffold(ing)	skapal,scalpel	skech,sketch
skai,sky	skapala,scapula	skechily,sketch(ily)
skair,scare	skapel,scalpel	skechis,sketch(es)
skairslee,scarce(ly)	skapela,scapula	skecht,sketch(ed)
skalar,scalar	skapeula,scapula	skechuly,sketch(ily)
skalastic,scholastic	skapil,scalpel	skechus,sketch(es)
skalb,scalp	skapila,scapula	skechwal,schedule
skalber,scalp(er)	skapul,scalpel	skechwul,schedule
skald,scald / scale(d)	skapula,scapula	sked,ski(ed) / scare(d) / skid
skale,scale	skar,scar / scare	skedchule,schedule
skalee,scaly	skarcedy,scarce(city)	skedule,schedule
skaleness,scaly(liness)	skarcity,scarce(city)	skeed,ski(ed) / skid
skaleon,scallion	skare,scare / scare	skeem,scheme
skalep,scallop	skarf,scarf	skeemer,skim(mmer) / scheme(r)
skaleun,scallion	skarlut,scarlet	skeen,skein / ski(iing)
skaley,scaly	skarse,scarce / scare(s)	**skeet**,TYPE OF TRAPSHOOTING
skalip,scallop	skarsedy,scarce(city)	skef,skiff
skaliun,scallion	skarsly,scarce(ly)	skeibis,scabies
skallion,scallion	skarsness,scarce(ness)	**skein**,FLOCK OF WILD BIRDS, BUNDLE OF THREAD/ YARN
skallop,scallop	skarves,scarf(rves)	(or see ski(iing)/ skin)
skalor,scalar	**skat**,A CARD GAME (or see scat/ skate)	skeing,ski(iing)
skalp,scalp	skatar,skate(r) / scatter	skeir,skier
skalpel,scalpel	**skate**,*,ed,ting, er, MOVE ABOUT WITH ROLLERS/	skel,skill / skull / school
skalper,scalp(er)	BLADES ATTACHED TO SHOES,TO MOVE IN GLIDING	skelastic,scholastic
skalpul,scalpel	MOTION (or see skat/ scat)	skelaten,skeleton
skalt,scald / scale(d)	skater,scatter / skate(r)	skelatul,skeletal
skalup,scallop	skathe,scathe	skelatun,skeleton
skaly,scaly	skator,skate(r) / scatter	skeld,skill(ed)
skalyin,scallion	skattur,scatter / skate(r)	skeled,skill(ed)
skalyun,scallion	skatur,skate(r) / scatter	**skeletal**,tally,BONES OF A BODY, BASIC FRAMEWORK
skamatek,scheme(matic)	skauler,scholar	"prefixes: exo/ endo"
skan,scan	skaulerly,scholar(ly)	skeletin,skeleton
skand,scan(nned)	skavage,scavenge	**skeleton**,*, ,tal,nize,nizer, BONES OF A BODY, BASIC
skandal,scandal	skavege,scavenge	FRAMEWORK "prefixes: endo/ exo"
skandelus,scandal(ous)	skaveger,scavenge(r)	skeletun,skeleton
skandul,scandal	skavenger,scavenge(r)	skelful,skill(ful)
skandulus,scandal(ous)	skavinger,scavenge(r)	skelit,skillet
skaner,scan(nner)	skavuge,scavenge	skeliton,skeleton
skanir,scan(nner)	skavunger,scavenge(r)	skelitul,skeletal
skant,scant / scan(nned)	skawler,scholar	skelitun,skeleton
skantily,scant(ily)	skawlerly,scholar(ly)	skelut,skillet
skantuly,scant(ily)	skeam,scheme	skelutin,skeleton
skanur,scan(nner)	skeat,skeet	skem,scheme / skim

skematik,scheme(matic)
skemd,skim(mmed) / scheme(d)
skeme,scheme
skemer,skim(mmer) / scheme(r)
skemur,skim(mmer) / scheme(r)
sken,skein / skin
skenee,skinny
skenir,skinner
skeniur,skinny(nier)
skeniust,skinny(niest)
skenlus,skin(lless)
skenur,skinner
skeny,skinny
skeor,skier
skep,skip
skepir,skipper
skeps,skip(s)
skept,skip(pped)
skeptacism,skeptic(ism)
skeptak,skeptic
skeptic, *, cal,cally,calness,cism,ONE WHO CHALLENGES/ DOUBTS DOCTRINATED BELIEFS, ALSO SPELLED "SCEPTIC"
skeptucism,skeptic(ism)
skeptuk,skeptic
skeptusisum,skeptic(ism)
sker,scare / skier
skerd,skirt / scare(d)
skere,scare
skerfy,scurvy
skerge,scourge
skerje,scourge
skers,skier(s) / scare(s) / scarce
skersedy,scarce(city)
skersity,scarce(city)
skersly,scarce(ly)
skersness,scarce(ness)
skersudy,scarce(city)
skert,skirt / scare(d)
skervy,scurvy
skery,scurry
skeryd,scurry(ried)
skes,ski(s) / sky(kies)

skeshily,sketch(ily)
sket,skeet / skit
sketch,hes,hed,hing,her,hily,hy,hiness,BRIEF/ ROUGH OUTLINE/ DRAWING/ IDEA
sketchewl,schedule
sketsh,sketch
skeu,skew
skeuer,skewer
skeuner,schooner
skeur,skier / skewer
skew,*,wed,wing,wness,SLANTED/ SLOPED/ DISTORTED/ OBLIQUE POSITION
skewbu,scuba
skewdur,scoot(er)
skewer,*,THIN/ LONG INSTRUMENT FOR HOLDING MEAT/ VEGETABLES FOR GRILLING
skewir,skewer
skewp,scoop
skewpur,scoop(er)
skewtur,scoot(er)
skewur,skewer
skezafrnea,schizophrenia
ski,*,ied,jing,ier,LONG DEVICES ATTACHED TO FEET TO ACHIEVE SPEED/ GLIDING ON VARIOUS SURFACES (or see sky)
skid,*,dded,dding,FRAMEWORK TO HELP SOMETHING SLIDE ALONG,SLIDE WHEN COMING TO A STOP (or see ski(ed)/ skit)
skidesh,skittish
skidush,skittish
skier,*,SOMEONE WHO SKIS
skif,skiff
skiff,*,SMALL BOAT
skiier,skier
skiir,skier
skiis,ski(s)
skil,skill
skilastic,scholastic
skilet,skillet
skilful,skill(ful)
skilfuly,skill(fully)

skill,*,led,lful,lfully,lfulness,less,GAIN APTITUDE/ EXPERIENCE PERFORMING A CRAFT/ TRADE/ ACT "prefixes: re/ semi/ un"
skillet,*,LONG HANDLED FRYING PAN
skilut,skillet
skim,*,mmed,mming,mmer,BE ON/ GLANCE OVER A SURFACE,REMOVE THE SURFACE (or see scheme)
skimatik,scheme(matic)
skimer,skim(mmer) / scheme(r)
skin,*,nned,nning,nner,nless,SURFACE ORGANISM THAT PROTECTS BODILY FLUIDS/ CONTENTS, REMOVE COVER/ LAYER OF PROTECTION FROM SOMETHING (or see skein)
skinee,skinny
skiner,skinner
skineust,skinny(niest)
sking,ski(iing)
skinles,skin(less)
skinner,*,ry,ONE WHO REMOVES SKIN
skinny,nnier,nniest,BONEY,NOT MUCH MUSCLE/ FAT ON THE BODY
skinur,skinner
skiny,skinny
skip,*,pped,pping,PASS OVER/ MISS A BEAT/ LEVEL
skiper,skipper
skipir,skipper
skipper,*,CAPTAIN OF A SHIP/ BOAT,AN INSECT,ONE WHO SKIPS
skipur,skipper
skir,skier
skireed,scurry(ried)
skirfy,scurvy
skirt,*,ted,ting,ter,A GARMENT WORN TO COVER/ PROTECT THE LOWER TORSO,TO EVADE/ PASS AROUND AND ISSUE/ EVENT "prefixes: under"
skirvy,scurvy
skiry,scurry
skisoed,schizoid
skisophrenea,schizophrenia
skit,*,A BRIEF/ SHORT PLAY
skitesh,skittish
skitish,skittish
skitsafrenea,schizophrenia

skitsophrenia,schizophrenia	skorsh,scorch	skremije,scrimmage
skittish,hly, EASILY FRIGHTENED	skorur,score(r)	skremp,scrimp
skitush,skittish	skoul,scowl	skremshaw,scrimshaw
skitzafrenea,schizophrenia	skour,scour	skremuge,scrimmage
skiur,skewer / squire	skout,scout	skremuje,scrimmage
skizoed,schizoid	skouter,scout(er)	skren,screen
skizofrenea,schizophrenia	skower,scour	skrenuble,screen(able)
skizoid,schizoid	skowir,scour	skreped,script
skizophrenia,schizophrenia	skowl,scowl	skrepshur,scripture
skof,scoff	skowndrel,scoundrel	skrept,script
skolar,scholar	skowr,scour	skrepture,scripture
skolarly,scholar(ly)	skowt,scout	skrew,screw
skolastic,scholastic	skowter,scout(er)	skrewge,scrooge
skold,scold / scald	skowurd,scour(ed)	skrewje,scrooge
skoleosis,scoliosis	skquer,skewer	skrewpal,scruple
skoler,scholar	skquir,skewer	skrewpel,scruple
skolerly,scholar(ly)	skrabs,scrap(s) / scrape(s)	skrewpewlis,scrupulous
skoliosis,scoliosis	skrach,scratch	skrewpils,scruple(s)
skolir,scholar	skrag,scrag	skrewpul,scruple
skolirly,scholar(ly)	skragliest,scraggly(liest)	skrewpules,scrupulous
skolt,scold / scald	skragly,scrag(ily) / scraggly	skrewpulisle,scrupulous(ly)
skolur,scholar	skrakleur,scraggly(lier)	skrewteny,scrutiny
skolurly,scholar(ly)	skrakly,scrag(ily) / scraggly	skrewtiney,scrutiny
skomatik,scheme(matic)	skram,scram	skrewy,screw
skone,scone	skrambul,scramble	skribe,scribe
skons,scone(s) / sconce	skrampul,scramble	skrible,scribble
skonts,sconce	skrap,scrap / scrape	skribler,scribble(r)
skoobu,scuba	skraper,scrape(r) / scrap(pper)	skribul,scribble
skooder,scoot(er)	skrapuble,scrap(able)	skrimage,scrimmage
skool,school	skratch,scratch	skrimije,scrimmage
skooner,schooner	skreach,screech	skrimp,scrimp
skoop,scoop	skream,scream	skrimshaw,scrimshaw
skooper,scoop(er)	skrean,screen	skrimuge,scrimmage
skoot,scoot / scute	skreblur,scribble(r)	skrimuje,scrimmage
skooter,scoot(er)	skrebul,scribble	skriped,script
skor,scar	skrech,screech	skripshur,scripture
skorch,scorch	skred,screed	skript,script
skore,score	skreech,screech	skripture,scripture
skorles,score(less)	skreed,screed	skripuld,scribble(d)
skorn,scorn	skreem,scream	skrol,scrawl / scroll
skornfully,scorn(fully)	skreen,screen	skroo,screw
skorpeon,scorpion	skreenuble,screen(able)	skrooge,scrooge
skorpeun,scorpion	skremage,scrimmage	skrooje,scrooge

skrooy,screw	skuid,squid	skwadron,squadron
skroul,scrawl	skuigul,squiggle	skwadur,squat(ttor)
skrounge,scrounge	skuir,skewer	skwair,square
skrowl,scrawl	skuish,squish	skwairly,square(ly)
skrownge,scrounge / scrounge	skuishy,squish	skwal,squall
skrowngy,scrounge	skul,school / skull	skwaled,squalid
skrownje,scrounge / scrounge	skulastic,scholastic	skwalid,squalid
skru,screw	skulbd,sculpt	skwalor,squalor
skrub,scrub	skulbsher,sculpt(ure)	skwander,squander
skrud,screw(ed)	skulbshir,sculpt(ure)	skwantur,squander
skrudnee,scrutiny	skulbt,sculpt	skwapel,squabble
skruel,squirrel	**skull**,*, BONE IN THE HEAD (or see school)	skwapul,squabble
skruf,scruff	skulpsher,sculpt(ure)	skward,square(d)
skrufy,scruff	skulpshur,sculpt(ure)	skware,square
skruge,scrooge	skulpt,sculpt	skwarlee,square(ly)
skruje,scrooge	skum,scum	skwart,square(d) / squirt
skrup,scrub	skumatek,scheme(matic)	skwash,squash
skrupel,scruple	skumy,scum(mmy)	skwat,squad / squat
skrupeulus,scrupulous	skuner,schooner	skwater,squat(ttor)
skrupul,scruple	**skunk**,*, OMNIVOROUS BLACK/ WHITE MAMMAL WITH STRONG SCENT GLANDS	skwatir,squat(ttor)
skrupules,scrupulous		skwatrin,squadron
skrupulous,scrupulous	skupe,scoop	skwaudren,squadron
skruteny,scrutiny	skuper,scoop(er)	skwauled,squalid
skrutiny,scrutiny	skurage,scourge	skwauiid,squalid
skruwe,screw	skuraje,scourge	skwaulir,squalor
skruy,screw	skured,scurry(ried) / skewer(ed)	skwaulur,squalor
sku,skew	skureed,scurry(ried)	skwaut,squad / squat
skual,squall	skurfy,scurvy	skwautrin,squadron
skuar,skewer	skurge,scourge	skwautron,squadron
skuba,scuba	skurige,scourge	skweak,squeak
skuder,scoot(er)	skurje,scourge	skwed,squid
skued,squid	skurt,skirt	skweegee,squeegee
skueel,squeal	skurvy,scurvy	skweeje,squeegee
skuegul,squiggle	skury,scurry	skweek,squeak
skuel,school	skuryd,scurry(ried)	skweel,squeal
skuelched,squelch(ed)	skut,skew(ed) / scoot / scute	skweemish,squeamish
skuelsh,squelch	skuter,scoot(er)	skwees,squeeze
skuer,skewer	skwabil,squabble	skweesir,squeeze(r)
skuesh,squish	skwabul,squabble	skweeze,squeeze
skueshy,squish	skwad,squad / squat	skwegal,squiggle
skuf,scuff	skwader,squat(ttor)	skwegee,squeegee
skufel,scuffle	skwadir,squat(ttor)	skwegul,squiggle
skuful,scuffle	skwadrin,squadron	skwegy,squeegee

skwejee,squeegee	skwod,squad / squat	slag hamer,sledge hammer
skwel,squeal	skwodir,squat(ttor)	slai,slay / sleigh
skwelch,squelch	skwodrin,squadron	slaid,slide
skweler,squeal(er)	skwodron,squadron	slaim,slime
skwelir,squeal(er)	skwodur,squat(ttor)	**slain**,PAST TENSE FOR THE WORD "SLAY", KILL VIOLENTLY
skwelsh,squelch	skwol,squall	slais,slice
skweltch,squelch	skwoled,squalid	slaisit,solicit
skwelur,squeal(er)	skwolid,squalid	slait,slight
skwemesh,squeamish	skwolor,squalor	slak,slack
skwemish,squeamish	skwondur,squander	slaker,slack(er)
skwent,squint	skwontur,squander	slakur,slack(er)
skweral,squirrel	skwopel,squabble	**slam,** *,mmed,mming,mmer,SHUT/ CLOSE/ STRIKE
skwerl,squirrel	skwopil,squabble	slamur,slam(mmer)
skwerly,squirrel	skwosh,squash	slan,slain
skwerm,squirm	skwot,squad / squat	**slander,** *,red,ring,rer,rous,rously,rousness,FALSE/ UNTRUE REMARKS/ WORDS
skwermy,squirm	skwoter,squat(ttor)	slanderus,slander(ous)
skwerol,squirrel	skwotir,squat(ttor)	slandured,slander(ed)
skwert,squirt	skwotrin,squadron	slanduris,slander(ous)
skwerul,squirrel	skwotron,squadron	**slang,** *,gily,giness,gy,NON-STANDARD USAGE OF WORDS,SHORT-LIVED WORDS
skwes,squeeze	skwotur,squat(ttor)	slank,slang
skweser,squeeze(r)	skwural,squirrel	**slant,** *,ted,ting,SLOPING/ OBLIQUE STANCE,NOT LEVEL, BIASED
skwesh,squish	skwurl,squirrel	slantur,slander
skweshy,squish	skwurly,squirrel	**slap,** *,pped,pping,pper,TO STRIKE WITH AN OPEN HAND,A CRISP/ SHORT BLOW
skwesir,squeeze(r)	skwurm,squirm	slapir,slap(pper)
skwesur,squeeze(r)	skwurmt,squirm(ed)	slapt,slap(pped) / slept
skwet,squid	skwurmy,squirm	slas,sleigh(s) / slay(s) / slaw(s)
skweze,squeeze	skwurt,squirt	**slash**,hes,hed,hing,her,TO DRIVE A SWEEPING STROKE/ BLOW,TO CUT/ OPEN WITH A BLADE
skwezur,squeeze(r)	**sky**, kies,FIRMAMENT/ FIELD ABOVE A PLANET (or see ski)	slashur,slash(er)
skwiarly,square(ly)	sla,slay / sleigh	**slat,** *,ted,ting,ty,THIN STRIPS OF WOOD/ METAL (or see slate/ slay(ed))
skwid,squid	**slab,** *, bbed, bbing,LARGE/ FLAT/ SOLID MATERIAL (or see slap)	**slate,** *, ed,ting,ty,CLAY/ SHALE/ COAL TYPES OF ROCK, AN APPOINTMENT (or see slat/ slay(ed))
skwigal,squiggle	slabt,slept / slap(pped)	slath,sloth
skwigul,squiggle	slac,slag	slau,slaw
skwint,squint	**slack,** *, ked,king,ker,ken,NOT TAUT/ TIGHT,PAIR OF DRESS PANTS,NOT SHARP/ ALERT (or see slag)	slaudir,slaughter
skwire,squire	slade,slay(ed) / slate	slaudur,slaughter
skwirl,squirrel	slader,slaughter	
skwirm,squirm	slae,slay / sleigh	
skwirmy,squirm	slafe,slave	
skwirt,squirt	slafree,slave(ry)	
skwirul,squirrel	slafry,slave(ry)	
skwish,squish	**slag**,WASTE REMNANTS FROM METALS (or see slack)	
skwishy,squish		
skwobil,squabble		
skwobul,squabble		

slaughter, *, red,ring,rer,rous,rously,VIOLENTLY KILL/ DESTROY
slauterus,slaughter(ous)
slave, *, ed,ving,ery,ONE WHO IS FORCED TO WORK FOR SOMEONE WITHOUT PAY, WORK HARDER THAN REASONABLE "prefixes: en"
slaven,sloven
slavenly,sloven(ly)
slavry,slave(ry)
slaw, *, COLD CABBAGE/ VEGETABLE DISH
slawb,slob
slawderus,slaughter(ous)
slawdur,slaughter
slawter,slaughter
slawterus,slaughter(ous)
slay, *, yed,ying,yer,slew,slain,KILL VIOLENTLY (or see sleigh)
sleak,sleek
sleaken,sleek(en)
sleaknes,sleek(ness)
sleat,sleet
sleave,sleeve
sleazy,zier,ziest,zily,ziness,OF CHEAP/ POOR CHARACTER/ QUALITY
sleber,sleep(er)
slebir,sleep(er)
slebry,slip(ppery)
slebt,slept
slebur,sleep(er)
slechjamer,sledgehammer
sleck,slick
slecker,slick(er)
sleckly,slick(ly)
sled, *, dded,dding,dder,TO SLIDE/ GLIDE SMOOTHLY ALONG THE GROUND (or see sleigh/ slid)
sledge hammer, LARGE/ HEAVY HAMMER
sledir,sled(dder)
sledur,sled(dder)
sleef,sleeve
sleek,ken,kens,kened,kening,ker,kly,kness,SHINY/ SMOOTH/ SOOTHING
sleeknis,sleek(ness)

sleep, *, ping,slept,per,pless,py,piness,pily,SLOW DOWN BASIC FUNCTIONS TO REST, BECOME UNCONSCIOUS, PLACE TO SLEEP "prefixes: over"
sleepee,sleep
sleeseist,sleazy(ziest)
sleesy,sleazy
sleet, *, ted,ting,ICY SNOW,FROZEN PRECIPITATION
sleeve, *, ed,ving,eless,COVER FOR MANY THINGS
sleezee,sleazy
sleezyest,sleazy(ziest)
slefs,sleeve(s)
slefur,sliver
sleg,slick
slege hamer,sledge hammer
slei,slay
sleif,slave
sleigh, *,hed,hing,A CONTRAPTION DESIGNED TO GLIDE/ SLIDE ALONG THE GROUND (or see sled)
sleight, *, ted,ting,ADROIT/ NIMBLE OF BODY/ MIND, SLEIGHT OF HAND (or see slight)
slein,slain
sleing,slang
sleit,slight / sleight / slate
sleiv,slave
sleje hamer,sledge hammer
slek,slick / sleek
sleker,slick(er) / sleek(er)
slekly,sleek(ly) / slick(ly)
sleknis, slick(ness) / sleek(ness)
slekur,slick(er) / sleek(er)
slelljamer,sledgehammer
slem,slim
slemd,slim(mmed) / slime(d)
slemest,slim(mmest)
slemir,slim(mmer)
slemt,slim(mmed) / slime(d)
slemur,slim(mmer)
slemust,slim(mmest)
slender, rly,rness, rize, SLIM
slendir,slender
slendirness,slender(ness)
slendur,slender
slendurness,slender(ness)

sleng,sling
slenger,sling(er)
slengur,sling(er)
slenk,sling / slink
slenky,slink
slenter,slender
slentur,slender
slep,sleep / slip / slept
slepd,slept / slip(pped)
sleper,sleep(er)
slepir,sleep(er)
slepless,sleep(less)
slepry,slip(ppery)
sleps,sleep(s) / slip(s)
slept,PAST TENSE FOR THE WORD 'SLEEP', TO TAKE A DEEP REST WITH EYES CLOSED
slepur,sleep(er)
slepy,sleep
sler,slur
sleried,slurry(ried)
slerp,slurp
slerpt,slurp(ed)
slert,slur(rred)
slery,slurry
sleryed,slurry(ried)
slesee,sleazy
sleseer,sleazy(zier)
sleseist,sleazy(ziest)
sleseur,sleazy(zier)
slesy,sleazy
slet,sled / slid
sleter,sled(dder)
sletir,sled(dder)
slets,sleet(s)
sletur,sled(dder)
sleuth, *, TRACK/ TRAIL/ DETECTIVE
sleve,sleeve
slever,sleeve(d)
slevir,sliver
slevs,sleeve(s)
slevur,sliver

slew, PAST TENSE FOR THE WORD "SLAY", LARGE AMOUNT/ NUMBER OF SOMETHING, TO PIVOT, ALSO "SLUE" (or see slue/ slough)
slewth,sleuth
sley,slay / sleigh
slezee,sleazy
slezeist,sleazy,sleazy(ziest)
slezeur,sleazy,sleazy(zier)
slezy,sleazy
sli,sly
slibree,slip(ppery)
slibry,slip(ppery)
sliburee,slip(ppery)
slice, *, ed, cing, er, TO CUT
slici,sleazy
slick, kly, kness, ker, kest, SLIPPERY/ SMOOTH
slid, PAST TENSE FOR THE WORD "SLIDE", GLIDE/ MOVE ALONG SMOOTHLY WITHOUT RESISTANCE (or see sled/ slide/ slit/ sleight/ slight)
slide, *, ding, er, slid, GLIDE/ MOVE ALONG SMOOTHLY WITHOUT RESISTANCE (or see slid/ slit/ slight/ sleight)
slided,slide(d) / slight(ed)
slider,slither
slidlee,slight(ly)
slif,sleave / sleeve
slifur,sliver
slig,slick
slight, *, ted, ted, test, ting, tingly, tly, tness, NEGLIGENT, PETTY, SLENDER, FRAIL, DISRESPECTFUL (or see sleight)
slightist,slight(est)
slik,slick / sleek
sliker,slick(er) / sleek(er)
slikness,slick(ness)
sliknis,slick(ness)
slikur,slick(er)
slily,sly(ly)
slim, *, mmer, mmest, mmed, mming, mly, UNDER PROPORTION, SMALL, UNSUBSTANTIAL (or see slime)
slimd,slim(mmed) / slime(d)

slime, *, ed, ming, my, mier, miest, mily, miness, VISCOUS/ MUCOUS/ OOZEY SECRETION (or see slim)
slimed,slim(mmed) / slime(d)
slimee,slime
slimely,slim(ly)
slimeness,slime(miness)
slimeur,slime(mier)
slimiest,slime(miest)
slimiur,slime(mier)
slimt,slim(mmed) / slime(d)
slimur,slim(mmer) / slim(er)
slimy,slime
slimyest,slime(miest)
slinder,slender
slindurness,slender(ness)
sliness,sly(ness)
sling, *, slung, ging, ger, DEVICE DESIGNED TO STRADDLE/ HOLD, TO FLING (or see slink) "prefixes: un/ under"
slingt,sling(ed) / slink(ed)
slingur,sling(er)
slink, *, ked, lunk, king, ky, MOVE/ CREEP/ WALK QUIETLY/ SECRETIVELY, BORN PREMATURELY
slinkd,slink(ed) / sling(ed)
slinkey,slink
slinkt,slink(ed) / sling(ed)
slinter,slender
slip, *, pped, pping, ppery, SLIDE/ GLIDE/ FALL AWAY, LOSS OF TRACTION/ FOOTING, AN UNDERGARMENT (or see sleep)
sliparee,slip(ppery)
slipry,slip(ppery)
slipt,slip(pped)
slipuree,slip(ppery)
slirp,slurp
sliry,slurry
slise,slice
sliser,slice(r)
slisi,sleazy
slit, *, tting, tter, CUT SLOTS/ OPENINGS INTO (or see slid/ slide/ slight/ sleight/ sleet)
slited,sleight(ed)/ slight(ed)/ slide(d)
slither, *, red, ring, ry, TO SNAKE/ SLIDE ALONG
slithry,slither

slithur,slither
slitly,slight(ly)
sliv,sleave / sleeve
sliver, *, red, ring, SMALL/ THIN PIECE OF MATTER WHICH SPLINTERS/ SEPARATES FROM LARGER OBJECT
slivir,sliver
slivur,sliver
slo,slaw / slow
slob, *, bbed, bbing, SOMEONE WHO IS UNKEPT/ UNCLEAN/ UNHEALTHY (or see slab/ slop)
slobber, *, red, ring, ry, DROOL/ WET SECRETION FROM THE MOUTH
slober,slobber
slobery,slobber
slobur,slobber
slobury,slobber
slod,slot / slow(ed)
slodder,slaughter
slode,slot / slow(ed)
sloder,slaughter
slods,slot(s)
slodur,slaughter
slodurus,slaughter(ous)
sloe,slough / slow
sloer,slow(er)
sloest,slow(est)
slof,slough
slofenly,sloven(ly)
slofun,sloven
slofunly,sloven(ly)
slogan, *, A CATCHWORD/ PHRASE/ MOTTO/ BATTLE CRY
slogun,slogan
sloir,slow(er)
sloist,slow(est)
sloken,slogan
slokun,slogan
slole,slow(ly)
sloly,slow(ly)
slonis,slow(ness)
sloo,slew / slue / slough
sloose,sluice
slooth,sleuth

slop,*,pped,pping,ppy,ppier,ppiest,ppily,ppiness, CARELESS, SPILLED LIQUID, NASTY FOOD, SLUSHY/ MUDDY (or see slob/ slope)
slopd,slope(d) / slop(pped)
slope,*,ed,ping,er,pingly,pingness,AN INCREASE/ DECREASE IN ANGLE ALONG A HORIZONTAL/ VERTICAL PLANE (or see slop) "prefixes: up"
slopee,slop(ppy)
slopeir,slop(ppier)
slopely,slop(ppily)
slopery,slobber
slopeur,slop(ppier)
slopily,slop(ppily)
slopiness,slop(ppiness)
slopry,slobber
slopt,slope(d) / slop(pped)
slopule,slop(ppily)
slopury,slobber
slopy,slop(ppy)
slopyer,slop(ppier)
slopyest,slop(ppiest)
slopyness,slop(ppiness)
slos,sloth(es)
slosh,hes,hed,hing,hy,LIQUID SPLASHING AROUND
sloshee,slosh
slot,*,tted,tting,NARROW OPENING/ CUT CREATED TO ALLOW INSERTION OF SOMETHING (or see slow(ed))
sloted,slot(tted)
sloter,slaughter
sloth,*,SLOW TREE-DWELLING MAMMAL (or see slough)
slouch,hes,hed,hing,her,hily,hiness,hier,hiest,DROOPS INTO A NON-ERECT POSITION
slougan,slogan
slough,*,hy,hiness,SHED/ CAST OFF, MARSHY/ SWAMPY AREA, CONDITION OF DEGRADATION (or see slew/ slue)
slour,slow(er)
sloutsh,slouch
sloutshed,slouch(ed)
sloven,nly,liness,nlier,nliest,UNTIDY/ CARELESSLY CLAD
slovin,sloven

slovinly,sloven(ly)
slovun,sloven
slovunliness,sloven(liness)
slovunly,sloven(ly)
slow,*,wed,wing,wer,west,wly,wish,wness,PERFORM AT LESS THAN NORMAL/ AVERAGE SPEED (or see slough)
slowb,slob
slowch,slouch
slowcheur,slouch(ier)
slowchily,slouch(ily)
slowgon,slogan
slowist,slow(est)
slowter,slaughter
slowur,slow(er)
slu,slew / slue / slough
sluce,sluice
slud,slue(d) / slough(ed) / slew(ed) / sleuth
sludch,sludge
sludchy,sludge(gy)
sludge,*,gier,giest,gy,A THICK/ VISCOUS LIQUID WITH HEAVY SEDIMENT
sludgeur,sludge(gier)
sludje,sludge
slue,*,ed,uing,TO PIVOT/ SWING AROUND, HAVING TO DO WITH SLEW (or see slew/ slough)
sluee,slough
slueness,slough(iness)
sluf,slough
slug,*,gged,gging,ggish,ggishly,ggishness,gger, REMNANT OF BULLET THAT'S BEEN SHOT, HIT/ LUG SOMETHING, GASTROPOD THAT EATS PLANTS
slugar,slugger
sluge,sludge
sluger,slugger
slugesh,slug(ggish)
slugeshness,slug(ggishness)
slugeur,sludge(gier)
slugger,*,ONE WHO HITS HARD/ HEAVY
slugir,slugger
slugish,slug(ggish)
slugishnes,slug(ggishenss)
slugt,slug(gged)

slugur,slugger
slugush,slug(ggish)
slugy,sludge(gy)
sluice,*,ed,cing,A CHANNEL/ CANAL OF WATER, ITEM USED TO PAN FOR GOLD
sluje,sludge
slujeir,sludge(gier)
slujy,sludge(gy)
sluk,slug
sluker,slugger
slukesh,slug(ggish)
slukir,slugger
slukishnes,slug(ggishness)
slukur,slugger
slum,*,mmed,mming,mmer,POOR/ HIGHLY POPULATED/ DIRTY AREA
slumber,*,red,ring,rer,rless,rous,ry,rously,rousness,TO SLEEP, BE QUITE INACTIVE, LIGHT SLEEP/ DOZE
slumbir,slumber
slumbrus,slumber(ous)
slumbrusly,slumber(ously)
slumbrusness,slumber(ousness)
slumbry,slumber
slumbur,slumber
slumd,slum(mmed)
slump,*,ped,ping,DIP IN PRODUCTION, A SURFACE/ VALUE
slumper,slumber
slumpur,slumber
slumur,slum(mmer)
slung,PAST TENSE FOR "SLING"
slunk,slung
slur,*,rred,rring,TO SMEAR/ SMUDGE WORDS/ SPEECH, INARTICULATE, CARELESS
slureng,slurry(ing) / slur(rring)
slurp,*,ped,ping,LOUD SIPPING SOUNDS WITH MOUTH
slurry,ried,ying,SOFT/ ORGANIC MATERIAL CHOPPED UP IN LIQUID
slury,slurry
sluryed,slurry(ried)
slurz,slur(s)
slus,sluice
sluse,sluice

slush, hes, hy, hiness, BETWEEN LIQUID AND SOLID
slushyness, slush(iness)
slutch, sludge
slutge, sludge
sluth, sleuth
slutje, sludge
sluy, slough
sly, yly, ylyness, SMOOTH/ DISCREET/ QUIET
slym, slim / slime
slynis, sly(ness)
slynke, slink
slyse, slice
slyt, slight / slide / slid
smack, *, ked, king, ker, TO DO WITH THE MOUTH, A SHARP BLOW, DIRECT, STRAIGHT, SAILING VESSEL
smak, smack
smaker, smack(er)
smal, small
smaler, small(er)
smalest, small(est)
smalist, small(est)
small, ller, llest, llness, NOT AS LARGE COMPARED TO NORMAL/ AVERAGE
smard alik,
smarden, smart(en)
smardest, smart(est)
smardin, smart(en)
smart, *, ted, ten, ter, test, ting, tly, tness, ty, SHARP/ QUICK/ ALERT/ PRACTICAL
smartie, smart
smartist, smart(est)
smash, hes, hed, hing, her, BLAST/ CRUSH/ DEMOLISH TO PIECES, DESTROY BY VIOLENT BLOWS
smashur, smash(er)
smear, *, red, ring, ry, TO SPREAD/ WIPE INTO, CAUSE TO RUN TOGETHER, SLANDER
smedin, smite(tten)
smeer, smear
smeery, smeer
smel, smell
smeld, smell(ed) / smelt
smelder, smelter
smeldur, smelter

smelee, smell
smell, *, led, ling, ly, lt, PERCEIVE WITH THE NOSE/ OLFACTORY
smelt, FISH (or see smell(ed))
smelter, *, METAL MELTING PROCESS
smely, smell
smer, smear
smerk, smirk
smerker, smirk(er)
smethureens, smithereens
smetin, smite(tten)
smiden, smite(tten)
smil, smile
smile, *, ed, ling, er, ey, lier, liest, FACIAL EXPRESSION STATING THAT ALL IS WELL, FRIENDLY EXPRESSION "prefixes: un"
smily, smile
smirk, *, ked, king, ker, kingly, SMUG SMILE EXPRESSING SUPERIORITY/ CONCEIT
smirkd, smirk(ed)
smit, smite
smite, *, ting, mote, tten, SERIOUSLY/ DEEPLY STRUCK/ AFFECTED, EXACT
smiten, smite(tten)
smithereens, BLOW/ SMASH TO PIECES/ BITS
smithureens, smithereens
smitin, smite(tten)
smiwree, smeer
smock, *, OUTER GARMENT LOOSELY COVERING MAIN TORSO (or see smoke)
smog, ggy, ggier, ggiest, gless, gginess, HEAVY AIRBORNE POLLUTION (or see smock/ smoke)
smogy, smog(ggy)
smok, smock / smog / smoke
smokd, smoke(d) / smog(gged)
smoke, *, ed, king, kier, kiest, kily, kiness, er, eless, ey, CLOUD OF GAS RESULTING FROM BURNED MATERIAL (or see smock)
smokir, smoke(r)
smokless, smoke(less)
smoklus, smoke(less)
smokt, smoke(d) / smog(ed)
smokur, smoke(r)

smoky, smoke / smog(ggy)
smol, small
smold, smolt
smolder, *, red, ring, SLOWLY COOK IN SMOKE WITHOUT FLAME
smoler, small(er)
smolir, small(er)
smolt, A STAGE IN SALMON/ FISH GROWTH
smolter, smolder
smoltur, smolder
smolur, small(er)
smooch, hes, hed, hing, TO HUG/ KISS
smooth, hes, hed, hing, her, hest, hly, hness, hen, hie, NOT ROUGH, PLEASANT TO THE SENSES
smoothie, *, A FRUIT SLUSH/ DRINK
smoothin, smooth(en)
smoothnis, smooth(ness)
smoothy, smoothie
smorgasboard, *, BUFFET WITH CONGLOMERATION/ SELECTION OF FOODS
smorgusboard, smorgasboard
smort, smart
smoth, smooth
smother, *, red, ring, COVER, PUT OUT, STIFLE, SUPPRESS, SUFFOCATE (or see smooth(er))
smuch, smooch / smudge
smuched, smooch(ed) / smudge(d)
smuches, smooch(es) / smudge(s)
smudeist, smut(ttiest)
smudeness, smut(ttiness)
smudeur, smut(ttier)
smudge, *, ed, ging, er, SMEAR/ STAIN, A SMOLDERING FIRE/ SMOKE FOR PROTECTION
smudy, smut(tty)
smug, gly, gness, SELF-SATISFIED/ CONCEITED (or see smooch)
smugal, smuggle
smugaler, smuggle(r)
smuge, smudge
smuggle, *, ed, ling, er, TRANSPORT SOMETHING ACROSS A LAWFUL BORDER WITHOUT PERMISSION
smuglir, smuggle(r)
smugul, smuggle

smuj,smudge
smuk,smug
smukil,smuggle
smuklee,smug(ly)
smukler,smuggle(r)
smukly,smug(ly)
smuknes,smug(ness)
smukul,smuggle
smukuler,smuggle(r)
smurk,smirk
smut,tted,tting,tty,ttier,ttiest,ttily,ttiness,SOOTY/ SMUDGED,INDECENT LANGUAGE,PLANT AFFECTED BY FUNGUS SPORES
smuteir,smut(ttier)
smuteist,smut(ttiest)
smuteness,smut(ttiness)
smuth,smooth
smuthen,smooth(en)
smuther,smooth(er) / smother
smuthie,smoothie
smuthir,smooth(er) / smother
smuthist,smooth(est)
smuthly,smooth(ly)
smuthness,smooth(ness)
smuthy,smoothie
smuty,smut(tty)
snabur,snap(pper)
snach,snatch
snachir,snatch(er)
snack,*,ked,king,BITS OF FOOD BETWEEN MEALS (or see snake/ snag)
snael,snail
snafoo,snafu
snafu,ued,uing,UNEXPECTED/ CHAOTIC TURN OF EVENTS
snag,*,gged,gging,ggy,ggier,ggiest,BE CAUGHT UP/ ENTANGLED (or see snack) "prefixes: un"
snageist,snag(ggiest)
snaggier,snag(ggier)
snail,*,GASTROPOD MOLLUSK WITH SHELL
snair,snare
snak,snack / snake / snag
snakd,snack(ed) / snake(d) / snag(gged)

snake,*,ed,king,ky,kily,REPTILE WITHOUT ARMS/ LEGS (or see snack)
snakey,snake(ky)
snaks,snack(s) / snake(s) / snag(s)
snakt,snack(ed) / snake(d) / snag(gged)
snale,snail
snap,*,pped,pping,pper,A QUICK/ BITING MOTION, CRISP BREAK, BRITTLE/ TENSE "prefixes: un"
snaper,snap(pper)
snapper,*,A FISH
snapur,snap(pper)
snard,snare(d)
snare,*,ed,ring,er,A TRAP/ NOOSE FOR CATCHING THINGS, USED FOR INSTRUMENT "prefixes: en"
snarl,*,led,ling,ler,ly,lingly,TO ENTANGLE/ COMPLICATE,A THREATENING SOUND "prefixes: en/ un"
snarlee,snarl
snart,snare(d)
snasee,snazzy
snaseur,snazzy(zier)
snasiest,snazzy(ziest)
snasy,snazzy
snatch,hes,hed,hing,her,SUDDEN/ SWIFT MOVE TO GRASP/ SEIZE SOMETHING
snaul,snail
snawt,snout
snazeir,snazzy(zier)
snazeist,snazzy(ziest)
snazeur,snazzy(zier)
snazy,snazzy
snazzy,zzier,zziest,FANCY
sneak,*,ked,king,kingly,kily,kiness,ky,ker,ENGAGE IN ACTIVITY IN A SECRETIVE MANNER
sneaker,*,TENNIS SHOES,SOMEONE WHO SNEAKS AROUND
sneakey,sneak
sneakuly,sneak(ily)
snear,sneer
sneaze,sneeze
sneazy,sneeze(zy)
snech,snitch
snechur,snitch(er)

sneek,sneak
sneeker,sneaker
sneeky,sneak
sneer,*,red,ring,rer,ringly,FACIAL EXPRESSION OF CONTEMPT/ SCORN
sneesy,sneeze(zy)
sneeze,*,ed,zing,zy,AN INVOLUNTARY GUST OF AIR FORCED THROUGH THE NASAL PASSAGES TO RELIEVE THEM OF AN IRRITANT
snef,sniff
snefdur,snifter
snefel,sniffle
snefer,sniff(er)
sneftur,snifter
sneful,sniffle
snefur,sniff(er)
snek,sneak
sneker,sneaker
snekily,sneak(ily)
snekir,sneaker
snekuly,sneak(ily)
snekur,sneaker / snicker
sneky,sneak
snep,snip
snepee,snip(ppy)
snepit,snippet
snept,snip(pped)
sner,snare / sneer
snert,snare(d) / sneer(ed)
snesy,sneeze(zy)
snetch,snitch
sneveler,snivel(ller)
snevil,snivel
snevlur,snivel(ller)
snevul,snivel
snevult,snivel(lled)
snewdy,snooty
snewp,snoop
snews,snooze
sneze,sneeze
snezy,sneeze(zy)
snibt,snip(pped) / snipe(d)
snich,snitch

snicher,snitch(er)
snicker,*,red,ring,EMOTE A NEGATIVE SNEERING LAUGH OUT OF DISRESPECT
snide,er,est,ely,INSINUATING/ SARCASTIC
snidly,snide(ly)
snif,sniff
snifal,sniffle
snifd,sniff(ed)
snifdur,snifter
snifer,sniff(er)
sniff,*,ffed,ffing,ffer,TO SMELL FOR, USE NOSE FOR DETECTION
sniffle,*,ed,ling,er,A NASAL SOUND
snifter,*,STYLE OF GLASS DRINKING VESSEL
sniftur,snifter
sniful,sniffle
snifur,sniff(er)
sniker,snicker
snikur,snicker
snip,*,pped,pping,ppy,CUT OFF A SMALL PORTION OF SOMETHING (or see snipe)
snipe,*,ed,ping,er,TYPE OF BIRD,TO SHOOT FROM A CAMOUFLAGED POSITION (or see snip)
sniped,snip(pped) / snipe(d)
snipee,snip(ppy)
snipet,snippet
snippet,*,SMALL BITS/ FRAGMENTS/ PARTS
snipur,snipe(r)
sniput,snippet
snitch,hes,hed,hing,her,FINK/ RAT ON SOMEONE, BE AN INFORMANT
snite,snide
snitly,snide(ly)
snivel,*,lled,lling,ller,WHINE/ CRY WHILE EXCREMENTING SNOT/ MUCOUS FROM NOSE
snivlur,snivel(ller)
snivul,snivel
sno,snow
snob,*,bby,bbery,bber es,bbish,bbishly,bbishness,SOMEONE APPEARING TO DISPLAY SUPERIORITY/ SMUGNESS/ SELF-RIGHTEOUSNESS
snobeshnis,snob(bbishness)
snobish,snob(bbish)

snoby,snob(bby)
snod,snow(ed) / snot
snody,snot(tty)
snoker,snooker
snoodeist,snooty(tiest)
snoody,snooty
snooker,*,GAME OF BILLIARDS
snoop,*,ped,ping,per,pier,piest,py,SOMEONE WHO IS NOSY/ PRYING/ PROWLING
snoose,snooze
snooty,tier,tiest,tily,tiness,SNOBBISH,BELIEVE THEY'RE EXCLUSIVE
snooze,*,ed,zing,er,SLEEP/ NAP
snop,snob
snopee,snob(bby)
snopy,snob(bby)
snore,*,ed,ring,er,EMIT LOUD BREATHING SOUND DURING SLEEP, TO SLEEP WITH THE MOUTH OPEN
snorkel,*,led,ling,UNDERWATER BREATHING APPARATUS
snorkul,snorkel
snorl,snarl
snorlingly,snarl(lingly)
snort,*,ted,ting,ty,LOUD/ QUICK BURST OF AIR FORCED FROM THE NOSE
snot,tty,MUCOUS IN THE SINUS CAVITIES, SOMEONE WHO HAS AN AIR OF SUPERIORITY/ CALLOUSNESS
snotee,snot(tty)
snoud,snout
snout,*,ted,THE NOSE/ MUZZLE OF ANIMALS
snow,*,wed,wing,wy,wless,WHITE/ LIGHT PRECIPITATION FALLING FROM CLOUDS, BURY/ COVER/ FOOL SOMEONE LIKE SNOW AS A BLANKET
snowd,snow(ed) / snout
snowee,snow
snowt,snout / snow(ed)
snub,*,bbed,bbing,bbness,bby,bbiness,TURNED UP NOSE WITH ATTITUDE, REBUKE/ REBUFF/ NEGLECT (or see snoop)
snube,snub(bby) / snoop
snubed,snoop(ed) / snub(bbed)
snubiness,snub(bbiness)
snubt,snoop(ed)

snuby,snub(bby)
snudy,snooty
snuf,snuff
snuff,*,ffer,ffy,ffier,ffiest,PAST TENSE FOR THE WORD "SNIFF", PUT OUT/ EXTINGUISH/ END, POWDERED TOBACCO
snuffely,snuffle(ly)
snuffle,*,ed,ling,ly,SNIFFLE/ NASAL CONGESTION
snufil,snuffle
snufir,snuff(er)
snufuly,snuffle(ly)
snufur,snuff(er)
snug,gger,ggest,gged,gging,gness,ggery,FIRMLY/ COMFORTABLY IN PLACE
snugelt,snuggle(d)
snuger,snug(gger)
snuggle,*,ed,ling,ly,COZY/ NESTLE UP COMFORTABLY AGAINST SOMETHING/ SOMEONE
snugle,snuggle
snugly,snuggle(ly)
snugnis,snug(ness)
snugul,snuggle
snuker,snooker
snukle,snuggle
snuklee,snuggle(ly)
snupe,snoop
snuper,snoop(er)
snupy,snoop
snuse,snooze
snuteir,snooty(tier)
snuteist,snooty(tiest)
snuty,snooty
snuze,snooze
snyd,snide
so,THAT WHICH IS APPROXIMATE (or see sew/ sow)
soak,*,ked,king,ker,EXPOSE TO MOISTURE UNTIL SATURATED
soap,*,ped,ping,py,piness,MANMADE COMPOUND USED FOR CLEANING (or see sop)
soar,*,red,ring,rer,RISE TO GREAT HEIGHTS EITHER LITERALLY/ FIGURATIVELY (or see sore)
soaside,suicide

sob, *, bbed, bbing, CRY WITH DEEP GASPS/ EMOTION (or see sop/ soap/ sub)
sobcity,subsidy
sobconshos,subconscious
sobcontract,subcontract
sobdue,subdue
sobed,sob(bbed) / soap(ed) / sop(pped)
sober, *, red, ring, ringly, rness, NOT INTOXICATED/ DRUNK, INFORMATION WHICH IS SERIOUS/ GRAVE IN NATURE
soberb,suburb
sobgekt,subject
sobir,sober
sobirnes,sober(ness)
sobject,subject
sobkonshus,subconscious
soblaim,sublime
sobleminal,subliminal
soblime,sublime
soblimenal,subliminal
sobmarine,submarine
sobmerge,submerge
sobmesev,submissive
sobmeshin,submission
sobmesiv,submissive
sobmet,submit
sobmirge,submerge
sobmisev,submissive
sobmishon,submission
sobmit,submit
sobmuren,submarine
sobordenate,subordinate
sobordenation,subordinate(tion)
sobort,support
sobpena,subpoena
sobpina,subpoena
sobragate,subrogate
sobregate,subrogate
sobriaty,sobriety
sobriety, BEING SOBER, FREE FROM EXCESS/ EXTRAVAGANCE, SERIOUS/ GRAVE "prefixes: in"
sobriudy,sobriety
sobrogate,subrogate

sobrugate,subrogate
sobsaid,subside
sobscraib,subscribe
sobsedy,subsidy
sobsequent,subsequent
sobsikwent,subsequent
sobstans,substance
sobstanshal,substantial
sobstins,substance
sobstreit,substrate
sobt,sop(pped) / sob(bbed)
sobtract,subtract
sobuei,subway
sobur,sober
soburnes,sober(ness)
sobvergin,subversion
sobvershen,subversion
sobversive,subversive
sobvert,subvert
sobvirgin,subversion
sobvirsev,subversive
sobvirshen,subversion
sobvirt,subvert
sobvurgin,subversion
sobvurshen,subversion
sobvursive,subversive
sobvurt,subvert
sobwei,subway
soccer, A TYPE OF FOOTBALL GAME
socebdubility,susceptible(bility)
socer,soccer
soch,such
sochably,sociable(ly)
sochalist,social(ist)
sochaly,social(lly)
sochealugist,sociology(gist)
sochebul,sociable
sochel,social
sochelize,social(ize)
sochely,social(lly)
socheelogy,sociology
socheolugist,sociology(gist)
socher,soldier

sochibly,sociable(ly)
sochibul,sociable
sochil,social
sochilest,social(ist)
sochilize,social(ize)
sochily,social(lly)
sochioligy,sociology
sochuble,sociable
sochubly,sociable(ly)
sochul,social
sochulee,social(lly)
sochulist,social(ist)
sochulize,social(ize)
sochur,soldier
sociable, bility, eness, ly, ABILITY TO INTERACT WITH OTHERS "prefixes: un"
social, *, lism, list, listic, listically, lite, lity, lize, lized, lizing, lization, lizer, lly, INTERACTION WITH OTHERS "prefixes: sub/ un"
socialest,social(ist)
socialigest,sociology(gist)
socialise,social(ize)
socialy,social(lly)
society, ties, tal, GROUPS OF PEOPLE WITH COMMONALITIES "prefixes: non"
socioligest,sociology(gist)
sociology, gical, gically, gist, SCIENCE OF STUDYING HOW SOCIAL INTERACTION IS CONDUCTED
socir,soccer
sociubly,sociable(ly)
sock, *, ked, king, A CLOTH FOOT COVERING, BE PUNCHED BY SOMEONE, WINDSOCK FOR WIND DIRECTION (or see soak)
socket, *, SOMETHING WITH THE SHAPE OF A HOLLOWED OUT/ SHORT CYLINDER WITH A BASE
sockit,socket
sockut,socket
socol,socket
socom,succumb
socseshan,succession
socsesion,succession
socshen,suction
socshun,suction

socur, soccer / secure
socurity, secure(rity)
socurly, secure(ly)
sod, dded, dding, ddy, TURF, GRASS WITH RCOTS (or see sold/ saw(ed)/ sought/ sew(ed))
soda, *, CARBONATED DR NK, COMPOUNDS OF SODIUM
sodame, sodomy
sodan, sedan
sodden, nly, nness, HEAVY WITH MOISTURE, SOGGY
soded, sod(dded) / sold
sodeim, sodium
sodemize, sodomy(mize)
sodemy, sodomy
soden, sodden
sodeum, sodium
sodimise, sodomy(mize)
sodimy, sodomy
sodin, sodden
sodinly, sodden(ly)
sodium, METALLIC/ NATURAL/ ACTIVE ELEMENT
sodl, subtle
sodn, sudden
sodol, subtle
sodomy, mize, mized, mizing, HATEFUL, SEL=CENTERED ACT OF ANAL PENETRATION FORCED ONTO ANOTHER
sods, suds
sodu, soda
sodumee, sodomy
sodumize, sodomy(mize)
sodun, sodden
sodunly, sodden(ly)
sody, sod(ddy)
soe, soy
soeal, soil
soebean, soybean
soee, soy
soeil, soil
soeled, soil(ed)
soem, psalm
soerdo, sourdough
soeul, soil
sofais, suffice

sofaree, safari
sofaren, sovereign
sofari, safari
sofecate, suffocate
sofekate, suffocate
sofeks, suffix
sofen, soft(en)
sofenir, soft(ener)
sofer, suffer
soferin, sovereign
sofeshent, sufficient
sofet, soffit
sofex, suffix
soffit, *, NECESSARY GEOMETRIC COMPONENT OF A STRUCTURE
soficate, suffocate
sofics, suffix
sofin, soft(en)
sofineer, souvenir
sofinur, soft(ener)
sofiren, sovereign
sofise, suffice
sofishent, sufficient
sofit, soffit
sofmore, sophomore
sofokeit, suffocate
sofomore, sophomore
sofoqeit, suffocate
sofr, suffer
sofrech, suffrage
sofren, sovereign
sofrenity, sovereign(ity)
sofrenudy, sovereign(ity)
sofrin, sovereign
sofrinedy, sovereign(ity)
sofrun, sovereign
soft, tly, tness, ten, tener, ty, SMOOTH/ COMFORTABLE "prefixes: semi"
softenur, soft(ener)
softur, soft(er)
sofun, soft(en)
sofuner, souvenir / soft(ener)
sofunir, soft(ener) / souvenir

sofuren, sovereign
sofut, soffit
sogee, soggy
sogenis, soggy(gginess)
soger, soldier
soggy, ggier, ggiest, ggily, gginess, THOROUGHLY SOAKED
sogir, soldier
sogiesgen, suggest(ion)
sogiest, suggest
soglleschun, suggest(ion)
sogllest, suggest
sogur, soldier
sogy, soggy
sogyness, soggy(gginess)
soht, sought/ sew(ed)
soi, soy
soibeen, soybean
soil, *, led, ling, lless, lage, DIRT, ORGANIC DECAYED MATTER "prefixes: sub"
soing, sew(ing) / sow(ing)
soiol, soil
soirdow, sourdough
sok, sock / soak
sokd, sock(ed) / soak(ed)
soked, sock(ed) / soak(ed)
sokee, soggy
sokenis, soggy(gginess)
soker, soccer / soak(er)
soket, socket
sokeulent, succulent
sokgeschen, suggest(ion)
sokir, soccer
sokit, socket
sokiulent, succulent
sokl, suckle
sokol, suckle
sokshen, suction
sokt, sock(ed) / soak(ed)
sokulent, succulent
sokur, soccer
sokut, socket
soky, soggy
sokynis, soggy(gginess)

sol, sole / soul / saw
solace, *, ed, cing, PROVIDE COMFORT, ALLEVIATION FROM WORRY/ SORROW/ GRIEF
salad, solid / salad
soladerity, solidarity
solami, salami
solanoyd, solenoid
solar, rize, rizes, rized, rizing, rization, rium, HEAT/ LIGHT PRODUCED BY SUN "prefixes: sub"
solarium, *, ENCLOSURE WHICH ALLOWS MAXIMUM PENETRATION OF THE SUNS RAYS
solas, solace / soul(ess) / sole(eless)
solatare, solitaire / solitary
solatarily, solitary(rily)
solatary, solitary
solatood, solitude
solatude, solitude
solcher, soldier
solchur, soldier
sold, PAST TENSE FOR THE WORD 'SELL' "prefixes: over/ un/ under"
solder, *, red, ring, rer, USE OF FLUX/ SOFT METAL TO MELD SEVERAL PIECES OF METAL TOGETHER
soldier, *, rly, rship, ry, ries, PEOPLE TRAINED TO PARTICIPATE IN WAR/ BATTLE
soldir, solder / soldier
soldired, solder(ed)
sole, *, ely, eness, eless, ONE AND ONLY, THE BOTTOM OF FEET/ SHOES (or see soul) "prefixes: in"
solective, select(ive)
soled, solid
soledarity, solidarity
soledify, solid(ify)
soledness, solid(ness)
solee, sole(ly)
solelukwy, soliloquy
solem, solemn
solemly, solemn(ly)
solemn, nly, nness, nity, nities, nize, nization, OBSERVANCE OF CELEBRATIONS/ RITES, OF A GRAVE/ SERIOUS ACTIVITY OR DISPOSITION
solen, sullen
solenium, selenium

solenoid, *, dal, dally, MAGNETICALLY CONTROLLED
soler, solar
solereum, solarium
solerize, solar(ize)
soles, solace / soul(ess) / sole(eless)
solesit, solicit
solesitation, solicit(ation)
solesiter, solicit(er)
solesment, solace(ment)
solet, solid
soletare, solitaire / solitary
soletarily, solitary(rily)
soletary, solitary
soletness, solid(ness)
soletood, solitude
soletude, solitude
solf, solve
solfaid, sulfide
solfeit, sulfate
solfely, soul(fully)
solfint, solvent
solfite, sulfite / sulfide
solfor, sulfur
solfuly, soul(fully)
solfunt, solvent
solger, soldier
solgur, soldier
solichud, solitude
solicit, *, ted, ting, tor, tation, tous, tously, tousness, REQUEST/ SEEK/ APPLY/ INFLUENCE/ PETITION FOR AN ACTION/ OPPORTUNITY/ FUNDING "prefixes: un"
solid, *, dly, dify, difiable, dification, dness, dity, dities, darity, GIVE THE IMPRESSION OF BEING HARD/ FIRM/ COMPACT/ THICK "prefixes: semi"
solidarity, ties, PEOPLE WHO FORM SOLID RELATIONSHIPS BASED ON COMMONALITIES
solidefy, solid(ify)
soliderity, solidarity
soliliaquy, soliloquy
soliloquy, uies, uist, uizer, TALK TO ONESELF, SHARE THOUGHTS OUT LOUD IN FRONT OF AN AUDIENCE
solim, solemn
solimly, solemn(ly)

solin, sullen
solinoid, solenoid
solir, solar
solirise, solar(ize)
solis, solace / soul(ess) / sole(eless)
soliset, solicit
solisetation, solicit(ation)
soliseter, solicit(er)
solisment, solace(ment)
solit, solid
solitaire, ry, CARD GAME PLAYED ALONE
solitary, ries, rily, riness, OF BEING COMPLETELY ALONE, SECLUDED
solitness, solid(ness)
solitude, ALONE/ REMOTE/ LONELY
soliubol, soluble
solivu, saliva
soljer, soldier
soljur, soldier
solking, sulk(ing)
soller, soldier
solm, psalm
solo, *, oed, oing, oist, TO PERFORM ALONE
solomi, salami
solon, salon
solonoid, solenoid
soloon, saloon
soloot, salute
solstes, solstice
solstice, *, itial, itially, TIME OF THE YEAR BASED UPON SUN'S POSITION
solstis, solstice
solt, sold / soil(ed)/ salt
soltri, sultry
soluble, eness, ly, bility, bilities, bilize, bilizes, bilized, bilizing, bilization, ABLE TO DISSOLVE IN WATER "prefixes: dis/ in/ re"
solud, solid
solum, solemn
solumly, solemn(ly)
solun, sullen
solune, saloon
solunoid, solenoid

solur,solar
solurize,solar(ize)
soluse,solace / soul(ess) / sole(eless)
solutare,solitaire / solitary
solutarily,solitary(rily)
solutary,solitary
solute,salute
solution, *, A COMBINATION OF CHEMICAL FORMS, THE ANSWER TO A PROBLEM, SETTLEMENT
solutood,solitude
solutude,solitude
solvant,solvent
solvashin,salvation
solve, *, ed, ving, vable, vability, vableness, er, REMEDY/ FIX/ UNDERSTAND (or see salve) "prefixes: in"
solvent, ency, ently, ABLE TO BE DISSOLVED
solvuble,solve(vable)
solvunt,solvent
soly,sole(ly)
solyewble,soluble(ize)
solyubel,soluble
som, psalm / sum / some
somber, rly, rness, MELANCHOLY/ GRAVE/ DEPRESSING IN MOOD/ ATTITUDE
sombi,zombie
sombir,somber
sombirly,somber(ly)
sombreo,sombrero
sombrero, *, A WIDE BRIM HAT
sombur,somber
somburly,somber(ly)
somchuos,sumptuous
some, PARTIAL, AN INDEFINITE AMOUNT, DISTANCE (or see sum)
somersait,somersault
somersault, *, ted, ting, AN ENTIRE BODY MANEUVER WITH HEELS GOING OVER HEAD
semester,semester
somet,summit
something, WANT FOR, INDETERMINABLE AMOUNT/ TYPE/ OBJECT OF, OPPOSITE OF NOTHING
sometime, *, UNSPECIFIED TIME
somewar,somewhere

somewat,somewhat
somewere,somewhere
somewhat,INDETERMINATE MEASURE
somewhere,UNSPECIFIED PLACE
somewot,somewhat
somewut,somewhat
somirsalt,somersault
somirsolt,somersault
somit,summit
somon,summon
somp,sump
sompchuos,sumptuous
somper,somber
somptuous,sumptuous
sompur,somber
somtaim,sometime
somtheng,something
somthing,something
somtime,sometime
somting,something
somuat,somewhat
somuer,somewhere
somwar,somewhere
somwat,somewhat
somwer,somewhere
somwhare,somewhere
somwhere,somewhere
somwot,somewhat
somwut,somewhat
son, *, nless, nny, PARENT'S MALE OFFSPRING (or see sun/ sown/ sewn)
sona,sauna
sonar, ACRONYM FOR SOUND NAVIGATION AND RANGING (or see soon(er))
sonata, A FORM FOR INSTRUMENTS IN MUSIC
sonareo,scenario
sonda,sunday
sondei,Sunday
sondree,sundry
sondrys,sundry(ries)
sonec,sonic
sonek,sonic
sonereo,scenario

sonet,sonnet
song, *, gful, gless, COLLECTION/ ARRANGEMENT OF MUSICAL NOTES AND/ OR ACCOMPANYING WORDS
sonic, cally, SOUNDWAVE/ FREQUENCY "prefixes: sub/ super"
sonik,sonic
sonit,sonnet
sonk,song
sonkles,song(less)
sonks,song(s)
sonnet, *, teer, tize, tization, A COMPLETE IDEA WRITTEN POETICALLY IN 14 LINES
sonor,sonar
sonseer,sincere
sonter,saunter
sontir,saunter
sontre,saunter
sontree,sundry
sontres,sundry(ries)
sontur,saunter
sonu,sauna
sonuk,sonic
sonut,sonnet
sooaside,suicide
soodar,suitor
soodir,suitor
soodo,pseudo
soodor,suitor
soody,soot
sooet,suet
soofaneer,souvenir
soofineer,souvenir
soofla,souffle'
sooflay,souffle'
soofuneer,souvenir
sooit,suet
sookrose,sucrose
soon, ner, nest, BEFORE IT'S TOO LATE, CLOSE TO NOW, READILY PREFER (or see sun/ son)
soopereur,superior
sooperfishul,superficial
sooperioredy,superior(ity)
soopireur,superior

soopirfishul,superficial
soopurb,superb
soopurfishul,superficial
soot,ty,BLACK CARBON RESULTANT OF BURNED MATERIAL (or see suit)
sooter,suitor
soothe,*,ed,hing,hingly,hingness,TO CALM, RELIEVE AGITATION
sootir,suitor
sootor,suitor
sooour,sewer
soovaneer,souvenir
soovuneer,souvenir
sop,*,pped,pping,ppy,ABSORB/ SATURATE SOMETHING WITH LIQUID (or see soap/ soup/ sob/ sap)
sopausetori,suppository
sopazeshan,supposition
sopd,sop(pped) / sob(bbed) / soap(ed)
sope,soap / sop / soap / sop(ppy)
soped,sop(pped) / sob(bbed) / soap(ed)
sopee,soap
soper,sober / sob(bber) / supper
superioredy,superior(ity)
superiority,superior(ity)
sophisticate,*,ed,edly,tion,IMPROVED QUALITY OF "prefixes: un"
sophmore,sophomore
sophomore,*,ric,rical,rically,STUDENT IN THE SECOND YEAR OF A FOUR-YEAR COURSE
soplai,supply
soplant,supplant
soport,support
sopos,suppose
soposetori,suppository
soposishon,supposition
soprano,*,HIGHEST OCTAVE ABLE TO BE OBTAINED BY VOICE OR INSTRUMENT
soprechen,suppress(ion)
sopremosy,supremacy
sopreno,soprano
sopres,suppress
sopreshen,suppress(ion)
sopretion,suppress(ion)

soprietee,sobriety
soprim,supreme
soprino,soprano
sopsaid,subside
sopscrepshon,subscription
sopsekwent,subsequent
sopsequent,subsequent
sopsid,subside
sopsikwent,subsequent
sopstans,substance
sopstanshal,substantial
sopt,sop(pped) / sob(bbed) / soap(ed)
sopy,soap / sop(ppy)
sopjulent,succulent
soquer,secure
soquerity,secure(rity)
soquerly,secure(ly)
sor,sore / soar
soran,saran
sorape,serape
soraund,surround
sorce,source
sorcerur,sorcery(rer)
sorcery,rer,rous,USING THE "SOURCE"/ INVISIBLE FIELD TO CREATE PHYSICAL THINGS/ ACTIONS
sord,soar(ed) / sword / sort
sorded,sordid / sort(ed)
sordedly,sordid(ly)
sordeen,sardine
sordene,sardine
sorder,sort(er)
sordid,dly,dness,OF BEING DIRTY/ MEAN (or see sort(ed))
sordir,sort(er)
sordud,sordid / sort(ed)
sordudly,sordid(ly)
sordur,sort(er)
sore,*, er, est, ely, eness, PAIN, INFLAMMATION, PERTURBED (or see soar/ sorry)
sored,soar(ed) / sword
soree,sorry / saury
sorel,sorrel / surreal
soren,serene

sorender,surrender
sorenidy,serene(nity)
sorenity,serene(nity)
soresury,sorcery
sorf,surf
sorfas,surface
sorfis,surface
sorgem,sorghum
sorgent,sergeant / surgent
sorghum,GRAIN USED FOR MANY PURPOSES
sorgint,sergeant / surgent
sorgum,sorghum
sori,sorry / saury
sorial,surreal
sorialism,surreal(ism)
soriasis,psoriasis
sorily,sorry(rily)
sorinder,surrender
soriol,surreal
soriolism,surreal(ism)
sorir,sore(r)
sorist,sore(st)
soriusis,psoriasis
sorkazem,sarcasm
sorkem,sorghum
sorkum,sorghum
sorly,sore(ly)
sormais,surmise
sorness,sore(ness)
sornis,sore(ness)
soro,sorrow
soroful,sorrow(ful)
sorority,ties,FEMALE COLLEGE ORGANIZATIONS
sorow,sorrow
sorowful,sorrow(ful)
sorples,surplus
sorplus,surplus
sorprais,surprise
sorpris,surprise
sorrel,AN EDIBLE PLANT (or see surreal)
sorro,sorrow
sorrow,*, wful,wfully,wfulness,GRIEF, SADNESS, REGRET

sorry, rrier, rriest, rrily, rr ness, APOLOGETIC, REGRETFUL, RESENTFUL (or see saury)
sors, source / sore(s) / czar(s)
sorseree, sorcery
sorserer, sorcery(rer)
sorsuree, sorcery
sorsurer, sorcery(rer)
sort,*, ted, ting, ter, table, CATEGORIZE/ COMPARTMENTALIZE/ ARRANGE BY ASSOCIATION (or see sword/ sord d) "prefixes: re-"
sortar, sort(er)
sorted, sordid / sort(ed)
sortedly, sordid(ly)
sortidly, sordid(ly)
sortir, sort(er)
sortud, sordid / sort(ed)
sortudly, sordid(ly)
sortur, sort(er)
sorur, sore(r)
sorva, survey
sorvaib, survive
sorvaif, survive
sory, saury / sorry
sorz, source / sore(s)
sos, sauce / saw(s) / sew(s)
sosach, sausage
sosbect, suspect
sosbenchen, suspension
sosbended, suspend(ed)
sosbenders, suspender(s)
sosbens, suspense
soscripshon, subscripticn
sose, saucy
sosege, sausage
soseje, sausage
sosell, sausage
soseptef, susceptive
soseptif, susceptive
soseptubility, susceptible(bility)
soser, saucer
soseshen, secession
sosetion, secession
soseur, saucy(cier)

soshable, sociable
soshaly, social(lly)
soshealegy, sociology
soshebul, sociable
soshel, social
soshelize, social(ize)
sosheolugest, sociology(gist)
sosheolugy, sociology
soshible, sociable
soshibly, sociable(ly)
soshibul, sociable
soshil, social
soshilist, social(ist)
soshilize, social(ize)
soshily, social(lly)
soshubil, sociable
soshubly, sociable(ly)
soshul, social
soshulist, social(ist)
soshulize, social(ize)
soshuly, social(lly)
sosiatal, society(tal)
sosiaty, society
sosiedle, society(tal)
sosier, saucy(cier)
sosietal, society(tal)
sosiety, society
sosige, sausage
sosije, sausage
sosiology, sociology
sosir, saucer
sosiudil, society(tal)
sosiudy, society
sosiutul, society(tal)
sosoge, sausage
sosoje, sausage
sospact, suspect
sosptef, suspect
sospenchen, suspension
sospens, suspense
sospeshen, suspicion
sospeshes, suspicious
sospinchen, suspension

sospinded, suspend(ed)
sospins, suspense
sospishon, suspicion
sospishus, suspicious
sosoge, sausage
sosuje, sausage
sosur, saucer
sosy, saucy
sot, sought / suite / soot
sota, soda
sotame, sodomy
sotanic, satanic
sotay, saute / sate
sote, saute / sate
soted, saute(d)
sotei, saute
soteim, sodium
sotemy, sodomy
soteum, sodium
sotiably, sociable(ly)
sotiabul, sociable
sotialy, social(lly)
sotu, soda
sotume, sodomy
sou, sew / sow
soudium, sodium
souerdow, sourdough
souffle', *, ed, A BAKED FLUFFY DISH
soufle', souffle'
sought, PAST TENSE FOR THE WORD "SEEK" "prefixes: un"
souirdow, sourdough
soul,*, lful, lfully, lfulness, lless, llessly, llessness, INVISIBLE FIELD/ DESTINY/ SPIRIT THOUGHT TO EXIST WITHIN THE BODY (or see sole/ sol) "prefixes: en/ in/ over"
soular, solar
soulenoid, solenoid
soules, solace
souliubol, soluble
soulou, solo
soun, sewn/ sown / zone
sounar, sonar

sound, *, ded, ding, der, dest, dly, dness, dless, dlessly, dlessness, AUDIBLE/ HEAR WITH EARS, RELIABLE, A FREQUENCY, LAND NEAR WATER "prefixes: un"
sounly, sound(ly)
soup, *, py, pier, piest, EDIBLE LIQUID BASE WITH BROTH AND/ OR VEGETABLES/ MEAT
sour, *, red, ring, rish, rly, rness, GONE BAD/ RANCID, TYPE OF TASTE REGISTERED ON A CERTAIN PLACE ON THE TONGUE
source, *, ed, cing, POINT OF ORIGINATION OF SOMETHING, BEGINNING/ PRIMARY "prefixes: in/ out"
sourcrowt, sauerkraut
sourdough, *, TYPE OF BREAD, NICKNAME FOR CANADIAN/ ALASKAN NATIVES
sourkraut, sauerkraut
sourkrowt, sauerkraut
souse, *, ed, sing, BE IMMERSED/ DRENCHED/ SATURATED IN, INTOXICATED
soust, souse(d)
sout, sought
souted, saute(d)
south, hern, herner, hernly, herly, herlies, NAVIGATIONAL DIRECTION
souvaneer, souvenir
souvenir, *, A TOKEN WHICH REMINDS/ SHOWS WHAT YOU HAVE DONE OR WHERE YOU HAVE BEEN
souvuneer, souvenir
sovana, savanna
sovant, savant
sovaren, sovereign
sovereign, nly, nty, nties, FREE FROM OUTSIDE CONTROL, SELF-SUFFICIENT
soverin, sovereign
soverity, severe(rity)
soviren, sovereign
sovont, savant
sovren, sovereign
sovrenedy, sovereign(ity)
sovrin, sovereign
sovrinedy, sovereign(ity)
sovrun, sovereign
sovt, soft

sovtur, soft(er)
sovurin, sovurin, sovereign
sow, *, wed, wing, wer, wn, TO PLANT/ IMPLANT/ PROPAGATE, FEMALE PIG (or see so/ sewn/ son/ sun/ souse)
sowarkraut, sauerkraut
sowd, sew(ed) / sow(ed)
sowded, sound(ded)
sowdiom, sodium
sower, sour
sowerdrow, sourdough
sowerkrowt, sauerkraut
sowir, sour
sowirdo, sourdough
sowirkraut, sauerkraut
sowlas, solace
sowler, solar
sowlitare, solitaire / solitary
sowliuble, soluble
sowlow, solo
sown, PAST TENSE FOR THE WORD "SOW" (or see sewn)
sownar, sonar
sownd, sound
sownded, sound(ded)
sowndlis, sound(less)
sowndly, sound(ly)
sownly, sound(ly)
sownt, sound
sownted, sound(ded)
sowpee, sop(ppy)
sowr, sour / sow(er)
sowree, saury / sorry
sows, sauce / sow(s) / souse / saw(s)
sowsd, souse(d) / sauce(d)
sowt, sew(ed) / sow(ed) / sought
sowth, south
sowuble, soluble(ize)
sowur, sour
sowurdo, sourdough
sowurkraut, sauerkraut
sowurkrowt, sauerkraut
soy, A SOYBEAN SAUCE/ CONDIMENT
soybean, *, A PLANT/ LEGUME

soybeen, soybean
soyible, soluble
soyl, soil
soyld, sold / soil(ed)
soyuble, soluble(ize)
soyul, soil
soz, sauce / saw(s)
sozy, saucy
spa, *, RETREAT/ RESORT/ HOT TUB/ MINERAL SPRINGS FACILITY (or see spay)
space, *, ed, cing, er, eless, ey, cious, PLACE WHERE NO APPARENT MATTER EXISTS, NOT OF THIS EARTH "prefixes: inter/ sub"
spachela, spatula
spachula, spatula
spacious, sly, sness, OPEN/ VAST/ BROAD AREA
spackel, spackle
spackle, *, ed, ling, er, PASTE FOR REPAIRING DAMAGE
spacol, spackle
spacy, space
spad, spade / spay(ed)
spadchewla, spatula
spadchula, spatula
spade, *, ed, ding, A SHOVEL/ SYMBOL/ SHAPE
spadshewlu, spatula
spadshula, spatula
spaenk, spank
spagedi, spaghetti
spagem, sphagnum
spageti, spaghetti
spaghetti, LONG/ SLENDER PASTA MADE OF FLOUR
spagnem, sphagnum
spagnum, sphagnum
spagol, spackle
spagum, sphagnum
spai, spy
spaider, spider
spaier, spire
spainel, spinal
spaingol, spangle
spaink, spank
spairal, spiral
spaircity, sparse(sity)

spairs,sparse / spare(s)
spairsly,sparse(ly)
spais,spice
spait,spite
spakel,spackle
spakil,spackle
spakul,spackle
span,*,nned,nning,nner,TOOL,MATCHED PAIR,SPACE/ DISTANCE BETWEEN
spangle,*,ed,ling,SPARKLING/ GLITTERY ORNAMENTS ON SOMETHING
spank,*,ked,king,OPEN HANDED SWATS ON BUTTOCKS, SPRITELY,LIVELY,NEW
spar,*,rred,rring,rry,PHYSICAL DISPUTE WITH, CRYSTAL-LINED MINERAL (or see spare)
sparadik,sporadic
sparadikly,sporadic(ally)
sparcity,sparse(sity)
sparckul,sparkle
sparcol,sparkle
spare,*,ed,ring,eable,ely,eness,ringly,LEFT OVER, EXTRA,TO SAVE,REFRAIN FROM,BOWLING EXPRESSION (or see spar) "prefixes: un"
sparengly,spare(ringly)
spark,*,ked,king,ky,RESULT BETWEEN TWO ELECTRICAL CHARGES COLLIDING,PARTICLES OF GLOWING MATTER
sparkal,sparkle
sparkil,sparkle
sparkle,*,ed,ling,er,GLITTERY/ FLASHING LIGHT
sparkul,sparkle
sparo,sparrow
sparrow,*,A BIRD
sparse,er,est,ely,eness sity,RARE,NOT MANY OF, MEAGER (or see spare(s)/ spar(s))
sparsedy,sparse(sity)
sparsidy,sparse(sity)
sparsly,sparse(ly)
sparsudy,sparse(sity)
spart,spare(d) / spar(rred)
spas,spa(s) / space / spay(s)
spasam,spasm
spasdek,spastic

spasdik,spastic
spase,space
spasee,space
spasefik,specific
spasefikly,specific(ally)
spasem,spasm
spaser,space(r)
spashel,spatial
spashely,spatial
spashes,spacious
spashesness,spacious(ness)
spasheus,spacious
spashewla,spatula
spashil,spatial
spashily,spatial(lly)
spashis,spacious
spashisnes,spacious(ness)
spashius,spacious
spashle,spatial
spashul,spatial
spashula,spatula
spashuly,spatial(lly)
spashus,spacious
spashusnes,spacious(ness)
spasifek,specific
spasifekly,specific(ally)
spasific,specific
spasim,spasm
spasiousness,spacious(ness)
spasir,space(r)
spasm,*,modic,modical,modically,MUSCLE CONTRACTION
spasom,spasm
spastek,spastic
spastic,cally,OCCURRENCE OF MUSCLE SPASMS
spastuk,spastic
spasum,spasm
spasur,space(r)
spasy,space
spat,PAST TENSE FOR THE WORD "SPIT" (or see spay(ed)/ spade)
spatchela,spatula
spatchula,spatula

spate,spade / spat / spay(ed)
spatial,lly,lity,SPACE WITH NO PHYSICAL MATTER APPARENT (or see special)
spatialy,spatial(lly)
spatious,spacious
spatiuly,spatial(lly)
spatshewla,spatula
spatshula,spatula
spatula,*,FLAT/ BROAD BLADE HAND IMPLEMENT/ TOOL
spatulu,spatula
spaun,spawn
spaus,spouse
spause,spouse
spaut,spout
spautles,spot(less)
spaw,spa
spawn,*,ned,ning,INCUBATE,GIVE BIRTH TO,PRODUCE OFFSPRING
spaws,spouse
spawt,spout
spawtles,spot(less)
spay,*,yed,ying,NEUTER TO PREVENT FROM CREATING OFFSPRING
spayer,spire
spazam,spasm
spazdek,spastic
spazduk,spastic
spazem,spasm
spazim,spasm
spaztek,spastic
spaztuk,spastic
spazum,spasm
speach,speech
speachless,speech(less)
spead,speed
speady,speed
speak,*,poke,ker,king,COMMUNICATE WITH VERBAL SOUNDS (or see speck) "prefixes: mis/ un"
speakible,speak(able)
speakuble,speak(able)
speal,spiel

spear,*,red,ring,LONG SHAFT WITH SHARP POINTED/ PIERCING INSTRUMENT ON ONE END
spec,speech / speak / speck
specafy,specify
specamen,specimen
specewlate,speculate
specewlum,speculum
spech,speech
spechal,special
spechalist,special(ist)
spechalize,special(ize)
spechelty,special(ity)
speches,speech(es)
spechil,special
spechilist,special(ist)
spechilize,special(ize)
spechis,speech(es)
spechle,special
spechles,speech(less)
spechlist,special(ist)
spechlize,special(ize)
spechlus,speech(less)
spechol,special / speck(le)
specholist,special(ist)
specholize,special(ize)
specholty,special(ity)
spechulist,special(ist)
spechulize,special(ize)
spechulty,special(ity)
special,*,lly,list,lty,tties,lism,list,listic,lization,lize,lizes, lized,lizing,lity,UNLIKE OTHERS,RARE,UNUSUAL, SPECIFIC CATEGORY "prefixes: sub/ un"
species,ORGANISMS GROUPED BY ABILITY TO BREED TOGETHER "prefixes: intra/ sub"
specific,*,cally,city,cation,CLEARLY AND DISTINCTLY STATE/ DEFINE/ MAKE KNOWN "prefixes: con/ inter/ intra/ non"
specifide,specify(fied)
specify,fies,fied,fying,fier,fiable,CLEARLY AND DISTINCTLY STATE/ DEFINE/ MAKE KNOWN/ REVEAL "prefixes: un"
specimen,*,SAMPLE/ EXAMPLE OF SOMETHING

speck,*,kle,kles,kled,kling,TINY FLECKS/ SPOTS (or see specs/ speak)
specktrum,spectrum
speckulashen,speculate(tion)
speckulation,speculate(tion)
specs,SHORT FOR SPECTACLES/ GLASSES/ DRAWINGS (or see speck)
spectacle,*,ed,GLASSES FOR THE EYES, FOR PUBLIC EXHIBITION/ VIEW "prefixes: be"
spectacul,spectacle
spectacular,rly,rity,rization,rism,rized,MOST IMPRESSIVE EVENT/ ACTIVITY/ OCCURRENCE "prefixes: un"
spectader,spectator
spectadur,spectator
spectakewler,spectacular
spectator,*,rial,rship,SOMEONE WATCHING AN EVENT WITHOUT PARTICIPATING
spectecul,spectacle
specteidor,spectator
specter,*,SPIRIT,GHOST APPEARANCE,APPARITION
specticle,spectacle
specticul,spectacle
spectir,specter
spector,specter
spectral,lity,lness,lly,GIVEN TO BE LIKE A SPIRIT/ GHOST
spectrim,spectrum
spectrol,spectral
spectrom,spectrum
spectrul,spectral
spectrum,*,RANGE OF SOMETHING BETWEEN TWO GIVEN POINTS
spectucle,spectacle
spectur,specter
specufy,specify
speculashen,speculate(tion)
speculate,*,ed,ting,tor,tion,tive,tiveness,tory, THEORIZE BASED UPON FACTS/ KNOWINGNESS
speculim,speculum
speculum,*,MEDICAL INSTRUMENT USED TO EXAMINE MORE CLOSELY
sped,PAST TENSE FOR THE WORD "SPEED"
spede,speed

spedeness,speed(iness)
speder,speed(er)
spedeur,speed(ier)
spedily,speed(ily)
spedir,speed(er)
spedul,spittle
speduly,speed(ily)
spedur,speed(er)
spedy,speed
speech,hes,hless,hlessness,VOCALLY EMPHASIZE SOUNDS/ WORDS
speed,*,ded,ding,dier,diest,der,dy,dily,diness,RATE/ VELOCITY OF MOVEMENT,TRAVEL FASTER THAN NORMAL
speedeness,speed(iness)
speeker,speak(er)
speekt,speak
speel,spiel
speer,sphere / spear
speget,spigot
spegit,spigot
spegot,spigot
spei,spay
speid,spade
speinc,spank
speingol,spangle
speis,space
speishol,spatial
speishos,spacious
speisos,spacious
spekabul,speak(able)
spekal,speck(le)
speker,speak(er)
spekeulate,speculate
spekeulatif,speculate(tive)
spekewlashen,speculate(tion)
spekewlate,speculate
spekewlation,speculate(tion)
spekewlative,speculate(tive)
spekewlem,speculum
spekible,speak(able)
spekil,speck(le)
spekir,speak(er)

spekiuleit,speculate
spekiulum,speculum
spekol,speck(le)
spekor,speak(er)
speks,specs / speak(s) / speck(s)
spekt,spoke
spektadur,spectator
spektakewler,spectacular
spektakle,spectacle
spektakul,spectacle
spektakuler,spectacular
spektar,specter
spektator,spectator
spektekul,spectacle
spekter,specter
spektikul,spectacle
spektir,specter
spektor,specter
spektrality,spectral(ity)
spektram,spectrum
spektrel,spectral
spektrem,spectrum
spektrul,spectral
spektrum,spectrum
spektukul,spectacle
spektur,specter
spekuble,speak(able)
spekul,speck(le)
spekulashen,speculate(tion)
spekulate,speculate
spekulation,speculate(tion)
spekulative,speculate(t:ve)
spekulem,speculum
spekulotif,speculate(tive)
spekulum,speculum
spekulutive,speculate(tive)
spekur,speak(er)
spekyewlem,speculum
spekyulate,speculate
spekyulatif,speculate(tive)
spel,spiel / spell / spill
spelar,spell(er)
speld,spill(ed) / spelt / spell(ed)
speler,spell(er)
spell,*,led,ling,ler,FORMULATE LETTERS INTO ACCEPTABLE FORMAT,BE SUBCONSCIOUSLY CONTROLLED "prefixes: mis"
spellur,spell(er)
spelor,spell(er)
spelt,PAST TENSE FOR THE WORD "SPELL",A TYPE OF WHEAT (or see spell(ed)/ spill(ed)/ spiel(ed))
spelur,spell(er)
spen,spin / spend
spenatch,spinach
spend,*,nt,ding,der,dy,TRADE OUTGOING FOR INCOMING (or see spent/ spin(nned)) "prefixes: mis/ over/ under"
spendal,spindle
spended,spent
spendir,spend(er)
spendle,spindle
spendly,spindle
spendul,spindle
spenech,spinach
spenich,spinach
spent,PAST TENSE FOR THE WORD "SPEND" (or see spend)
spentle,spindle
spentul,spindle
spenuch,spinach
spenur,spin(nner)
spenutch,spinach
speol,spiel
spejiuleit,speculate
spejiulom,speculum
sper,spare / spear / spur
speradik,sporadic
spercity,sparse(sity)
sperd,spear(ed) / spur(rred)
sperds,spurt(s)
sperichual,spiritual
sperichualidy,spiritual(ity)
speringly,spare(ringly)
sperit,spirit
speritshuality,spiritual(ity)
sperm,*,A METHOD OF CARRYING MALE DNA FOR PROCREATION,SEMEN "prefixes: endo"
spero,sparrow
sperow,sparrow
spers,sparse/ spare(s) / spear(s)/ spur(s)
spersity,sparse(sity)
sperslee,sparse(ly)
spersly,sparse(ly)
spersudy,sparse(sity)
spert,spurt / spare(d) / spear(ed)
spesaficashen,specify(fication)
spesafide,specify(fied)
spesafikation,specify(fication)
spesafy,specify
spesamen,specimen
spesamin,specimen
spesefakation,specify(fication)
spesefide,specify(fied)
spesefukation,specify(fication)
spesefy,specify
spesemin,specimen
speshal,special
speshalist,special(ist)
speshalize,special(ize)
speshelty,special(ity)
speshez,species
speshil,special
speshilest,special(ist)
speshilty,special(ity)
speshis,species
speshle,special
speshlist,special(ist)
speshlize,special(ize)
spesholty,special(ity)
speshul,special
speshulist,special(ist)
speshulize,special(ize)
speshulty,special(ity)
spesial,special
spesies,species
spesifakation,specify(fication)
spesifek,specific

spesificashen,specify(fication)
spesification,specify(fication)
spesifide,specify(fied)
spesifik,specific
spesifucashen,specify(fication)
spesifukation,specify(fication)
spesify,specify
spesimen,specimen
spesofecashen,specify(fication)
spesofecation,specify(fication)
spesofide,specify(fied)
spesufication,specify(fication)
spesufide,specify(fied)
spesufy,specify
spesumen,specimen
spesumin,specimen
spet,sped
spetil,spittle
spetle,spittle
spetoon,spittoon
spetul,spittle
spetune,spittoon
spetur,spit(tter)
speu,spew
speul,spiel / spill
spew,*,wed,wing,wn,RUN/ FLOW FORTH, EJECT FROM WITHIN, VOMIT
sphagnum,nous,VARIETY OF MOSS
spharikul,sphere(rical)
spharukil,sphere(rical)
sphenctur,sphincter
sphenktur,sphincter
spherakil,sphere(rical)
sphere,*,ed,ring,ral,rical,rics,ry,ricity,CIRCLE/ AREA EXTENDED AROUND THE CENTER WHERE DISTANCE IS EQUAL FROM THE CENTER "prefixes: bio/ en/ non"
spherekil,sphere(rical)
spherikul,sphere(rical)
sphincter,ral,rial,rate,ric,MUSCLE WHICH CONTRACTS THE ORIFICE ON THE LOWER TORSO
sphinkter,sphincter

sphinx,xes,xian,A FIGURE WITH THE HEAD OF ONE THING AND BODY OF SOMETHING DIFFERENT
sphire,sphere
spic,speak / spike / spice
spice,*,ed,cing,ery,cy,OF OR GIVEN TO SPICES, CULINARY PLANTS
spich,speech
spictacular,spectacular
spictakuler,spectacular
spid,spy(pied) / spite / speed / spit
spider,*,ry,EIGHT LEGGED ARACHNID
spidful,spite(ful)
spidul,spittle
spidur,spider
spidury,spider
spiel,*, TALK/ EXPLAIN AT LENGTH WITH PERSUASION
spiget,spigot
spigot,*,DEVICE/ FAUCET FOR ALLOWING/ STOPPING FLOW OF LIQUIDS
spigut,spigot
spike,*,ed,king,ker,ky,STIFF/ SHARP, USED TO IMPALE/ PIERCE,SHAPED LIKE A NAIL
spikt,spike(d)
spiktakewler,spectacular
spiktakuler,spectacular
spiky,spike(ky)
spil,spill
spill,*,lled,lling,llage,SOMETHING LOOSE/ LIQUID TO FLOW FROM CONTAINER/ SOURCE, TO DIVULGE (or see spiel/ spell) "prefixes: over"
spin,*,pun,nning,nner,TO WEAVE/ TWIST/ WRAP AROUND,TELL A STORY,PERFORM CIRCULAR MOTION (or see spine/ spend) "prefixes: under"
spinach,VEGETABLE/ PLANT
spinal,lly,ASSOCIATED WITH THE SPINE
spinall,spinach
spinatch,spinach
spind,spend / spin(nned)
spinded,spent
spinder,spend(er)
spindil,spindle
spindle,*,ed,ling,ly,A ROD/ PIN, TO WIND/ SPIN/ TWIST SOMETHING AROUND

spindly,spindle
spindul,spindle
spindur,spend(er)
spine,*,eless, elessly, elessness,ny,escent,escence, BACKBONE/ VERTEBRATE OF BODIES, A LONG CREST/ SET OF PEAKS
spinech,spinach
spinel,spinal
spiner,spin(nner)
spinlesness,spine(lessness)
spinless,spine(less)
spinol,spinal
spinor,spin(nner)
spint,spent
spinter,spend(er)
spintil,spindle
spintir,spend(er)
spintul,spindle
spintur,spend(er)
spinuch,spinach
spinul,spinal
spinur,spin(nner)
spinutch,spinach
spiny,spine
spiol,spiel
spir,spur / spire / spear
spiradek,sporadic
spiradik,sporadic
spiradikly,sporadic(ally)
spiral,*,led,ling,lly,REPEATED CIRCULAR CURVE WHOSE EVOLUTION AROUND CONSISTENTLY ASCENDS OR DESCENDS,CONTINUOUS CIRCULAR MOTION IN ONE DIRECTION OR ANOTHER
spiraly,spiral(lly)
spird,spire(d) / spur(rred) / spurt / spear(ed)
spire,ed,ring,ry,COMING TO A POINT,PYRAMID SHAPE
spirechualedy,spiritual(ity)
spirechuil,spiritual
spirel,spiral
spireshuil,spiritual
spiret,spirit
spiretshualety,spiritual(ity)
spirichual,spiritual

spirichualidy,spiritual(ity)
spirichuel,spiritual
spiril,spiral
spirit, *, ed, tism, tist, tistic, tual, CHARACTER/ DISPOSITION AND ESSENCE OF ENERGY, THAT WHICH ANIMATES/ MAKES THINGS LIFELIKE OR ALIVE, TYPE OF ALCOHOL "prefixes: di"
spiritchuel,spiritual
spiritual,lly,lness,lism,list,listic,lity,lities,lize,lized,lizing, IMMATERIAL ESSENCE/ SPIRIT/ LIFE, OF THE UNKNOWN, NOT PHYSICAL
spirm,sperm
spirt,spurt / spire(d)
spirul,spiral
spiruly,spiral(lly)
spisd,spice(d)
spise,spice / spice / spy(pies)
spised,spice(d)
spisis,species
spisury,spice(ry)
spisy,spice
spit, *, tted, tting, pat, tter, PROJECT/ FORCE SALIVA FROM THE MOUTH, ROD/ PIN FOR HOLDING MEAT WHILE COOKING, NARROW SLENDER EXTENSION OF LAND SURROUNDED BY WATER
spital,spittle
spite, ed, ting, eful, efully, efulness, OF MALICIOUS INTENT/ DISPOSITION
spitel,spittle
spiter,spider / spit(tter)
spitful,spite(ful)
spitle,spittle
spitoon,spittoon
spittle, SECRETION BY INSECTS
spittoon, *, VESSEL FOR SPIT
spittune,spittoon
spitul,spittle
spitune,spittoon
spitur,spider / spit(tter)
spiu,spew
spiz,spy(pies) / spice
spize,spice / spy(pies) / spice
spla,splay

splach,splotch / splash
splachy,splotch
splad,splat / splay(ed)
splader,splatter
spladur,splatter
splaer,splay(er)
splais,splice
splash, hes, hed, hing, her, hyhily, hiness, PARTICLES OF LIQUID SCATTERED INTO THE AIR
splat, BACK OF A CHAIR, A TYPE OF SOUND
splater,splatter
splator,splatter
splatter, *, red, ring, TO SPLASH A LIQUID
splatur,splatter
splaur,splay(er)
splay, *, yed, yer, SPREAD OUT/ FLARE/ FAN, CREATE CURVE
splean,spleen
spledur,split(tter)
spleen, *, nful, ny, AN ORGAN IN THE BODY, ILL HUMOR/ IRRITABLE
splei,splay
splen,spleen
splendant,splendent
splendedly,splendid(lly)
splendent, BRILLIANT/ RADIANT IN APPEARANCE
splender,splendor / splinter
splendid, dly, dness, GRAND/ MAGNIFICENT
splendint,splendent
splendir,splendor / splinter
splendit,splendid
splendor, *, rous, BRILLIANCE, LUSTER (or see splinter)
splendrus,splendor(ous)
splendunt,splendent
splendur,splendor / splinter
splene,spleen / spleen
splent,splint
splented,splendid
splentor,splendor / splinter
splentrus,splendor(ous)
splentur,splendor / splinter
spleny,spleen
splerge,splurge

splerje,splurge
splet,split
spletor,split(tter)
splice, *, ed, cing, er, GRAFT/ PIECE TOGETHER PERFECTLY, CUT TO JOIN
splider,split(tter)
splin,spline / spleen
splindant,splendent
splinded,splendid
splindedly,splendid(lly)
splindint,splendent
splindir,splendor / splinter
splindit,splendid
splindrus,splendor(ous)
splindud,splendid
splindunt,splendent
splindur,splendor / splinter
spline, *, ed, ning, INTERNAL PART OF A WHEEL, A SLAT, WAY TO SECURE A PART, MATHEMATICAL EXPRESSION (or see spleen)
splint, *, ter, USED TO REPAIR FRACTURES
splinted,splendid
splinter, *, red, ring, ry, A SMALL SLICE/ PIECE BROKEN/ CUT OFF LENGTHWISE, A SLIVER
splintird,splinter(ed)
splintor,splendor / splinter
splintrus,splendor(ous)
splintur,splendor / splinter
splirge,splurge
splirje,splurge
splisur,splice(r)
split, *, tting, tter, BROKEN/ TORN APART/ SEPARATED
splitor,split(tter)
sploch,splotch
sploche,splotch
splotch, hes, hed, hing, hy, hier, hiest, AN IRREGULAR SPOT/ SPLASH OF LIQUID/ COLOR/ STAIN
splurch,splurge
splurgd,splurge(d)
splurge, *, ed, ging, TO OVER SPEND
spo,spa
spock,spoke
spod,spot

spodable,spot(able)
spoded,spot(tted)
spodee,spot(tty)
spodible,spot(able)
spodid,spot(tted)
spodlis,spot(less)
spoduble,spot(able)
spoel,spoil
spoeld,spoil(ed) / spoilt
spoeleg,spoil(age)
spoelij,spoil(age)
spoelt,spoil(ed) / spoilt
spoeluj,spoil(age)
spogedi,spaghetti
spogeti,spaghetti
spoil,*,led,ling,lage,ler,lable,lt,TO GO BAD, DAMAGE, RENDER UNFIT "prefixes: un"
spoild,spoil(ed) / spoilt
spoileg,spoil(age)
spoilej,spoil(age)
spoilt,PAST TENSE FOR THE WORD "SPOIL" (or see spoil(ed))
spoiluje,spoil(age)
spointeinios,spontaneous
spoke,*,en,PAST TENSE FOR THE WORD "SPEAK", RODS/ WIRES RADIATING FROM THE HUB OF A WHEEL "prefixes: mis/ un"
spokun,spoke(n)
spon,spawn / spoon
sponch,sponge
sponge,*,ed,ging,gy,gier,giest,giness,er,SEA ANIMAL, SKELETON OF SEA ANIMALS USED TO CLEAN/ ABSORB LIQUIDS
sponser,sponsor
sponsor,*,red,ring,rial,rship,SOMEONE WHO PAYS/ SUPPORTS SOMEONE ELSE
sponsur,sponsor
spont,spawn(ed) / spoon(ed)
spontaineus,spontaneous
spontaneity,eities, eous, ABLE TO ACT QUICKLY ON IMPULSE WITHOUT CONSTRAINT
spontaneous,sly,sness,ACT QUICKLY ON IMPULSE WITHOUT CONSTRAINT

spontaneus,spontaneous
spontenaity,spontaneity
spontinaedy,spontaneity
spontunaity,spontaneity
sponzur,sponsor
spoof,*,TO TEASE/ DECEIVE WITH GOOD INTENT
spook,*,ked,king,ky,kish,GHOST, SPECTER, APPARITION
spool,*,led,ling,ler,ROUND/ CYLINDER SHAPE HOLDING LENGTHS OF SOMETHING WOUND AROUND IT
spoon,*,ned,ning,nful,UTENSIL WITH HANDLE AT ONE END AND A BOWL SHAPE ON THE OTHER
spor,spar / spore
sporadic,cal,cally,ERRATIC/ UNPREDICTABLE OCCURRENCES
sporadikly,sporadic(ally)
sporded,sport(ed)
spordee,sport
spordid,sport(ed)
spordy,sport
spore,*,red,ring,ral,roid,riferous,rulate,REPRODUCTIVE SEEDS OF BACTERIA AND SOME PLANTS
sporol,spore(ral)
sport,*,ted,ting,tive,tively,tiveness,ty,ATHLETIC/ OUTDOOR GAMES, TO CARRY, GOOD ATTITUDE
sportee,sport
sportef,sport(ive)
sportif,sport(ive)
sportud,sport(ed)
sporul,spore(ral)
spos,suppose
spot,*,tted,tting,tty,ttier,ttiest,tter,table,tless,tlessly, tlessness,FLAW/ MARK/ BLEMISH,A PARTICULAR/ SPECIFIC PLACE, TO SEE "prefixes: un"
spoted,spot(tted)
spotee,spot(tty)
spotible,spot(able)
spotid,spot(tted)
spotuble,spot(able)
spoty,spot(tty)
spouc,spoke
spouse,*,sal,ONE WHO IS ENGAGED/ VOWED/ MARRIED TO ANOTHER

spout,*,ted,ting,ter,PIPE/ NOZZLE PROJECTING FROM VESSEL FOR LIQUID
spown,spawn
spowse,spouse
spowsul,spouse(sal)
spowt,spout
spoyl,spoil
spoyleg,spoil(age)
spoylej,spoil(age)
spoyol,spoil
spra,spray
spraer,spray(er)
spraget,sprocket
spragit,sprocket
spraj,spry
sprain,*,ned,ning,TWIST/ WRENCH/ OVER STRETCH A MUSCLE IN THE BODY
spraket,sprocket
spral,sprawl
spran,sprain
spraoquet,sprocket
spraor,spray(er)
sprat,spray(ed)
spraukit,sprocket
spraul,sprawl
spraur,spray(er)
spraut,sprout
sprawl,*,led,ling,TO EXTEND/ SPREAD OUT IN IRREGULAR POSITION/ MANNER
sprawt,sprout
spray,*,yed,ying,yer,PARTICLES OF LIQUID RELEASED/ FORCED INTO THE AIR
spre,spree
spread,*,ding,der,FORCE/ EXTEND INTO A THIN LAYER OVER SUBSTANTIAL DISTANCE/ TIME/ SPACE
spred,spread
spredur,spread(er)
spree,*,TO FROLICK, HAVE A MERRY TIME
spreg,sprig / spray
sprein,sprain / spray(ing)
sprencol,sprinkle
spreng,spring
sprengee,spring

sprengy,spring
sprenk,spring
sprenkal,sprinkle
sprenkil,sprinkle
sprenkler,sprinkle(r)
sprenklor,sprinkle(r)
sprenkul,sprinkle
sprenkuler,sprinkle(r)
sprent,sprint
sprentur,sprint(er)
spret,spread
spreter,spread(er)
spretur,spread(er)
sprews,spruce
spri,spry / spree
sprig,*,SMALL BRANCH FROM PLANT
sprilee,spry(ly)
sprily,spry(ly)
sprincol,sprinkle
spring,*,,ging,rang,gy,gier,giest,gily,giness,A RIVULET OF WATER, COILED DEVICE "prefixes: up"
springey,spring
sprinis,spry(ness)
sprink,spring
sprinkel,sprinkle
sprinkle,*,,ed,ling,er,SHOOT/ RELEASE/ SPRAY HEAVY DROPS OF LIQUID
sprinklor,sprinkle(r)
sprinkul,sprinkle
sprinkuler,sprinkle(r)
sprint,*,,ted,ting,ter,RACE/ SPEED A SHORT DISTANCE
sprintor,sprint(er)
sprintur,sprint(er)
sprocket,*,,PART OF A WHEEL/ CHAIN
sprogit,sprocket
sprokut,sprocket
sprol,sprawl
sproose,spruce
sprout,*,,ted,ting,ter,TO GERMINATE, GROW INTO THE DAYLIGHT, SHOW GROWTH
sprowt,sprout
spruce,*,,ed,cing,ely,eness,er,est,TYPE OF TREE, GET DRESSED UP, GET FANCY

sprung,PAST TENSE FOR THE WORD SPRING "prefixes: un"
spruse,spruce
spry,yly,yness,LIVELY/ NIMBLE
sprynis,spry(ness)
spuc,spook
spud,*,,dded,dding,POTATOE,TOOL, TO WEED OUT
spuder,sputter
spudor,sputter
spue,spew
spufe,spoof
spugedi,spaghetti
spugeti,spaghetti
spuk,spook
spuky,spook
spule,spool
spun,PAST TENSE FOR THE WORD "SPIN" (or see spoon) "prefixes: over"
spunch,sponge
spune,spoon / spun
spunful,spoon(ful)
spung,sponge / spunk
spungee,sponge(gy)
spungenis,spunk(iness)
spungy,sponge(gy)
spunj,sponge
spunjy,sponge(gy)
spunk,ky,kily,kiness,kier,kiest,SPIRITED/ COURAGEOUS, TINDER FROM FUNGUS
spunkenis,spunk(iness)
spur,*,,rred,rring,rious,riously,riousness,STIMULATE/ ENCOURAGE TO GO ON, DEVICE FOR BOOTS/ RIDING (too many definitions, please see standard dictionary) (or see spurt)
spuradek,sporadic
spuradikly,sporadic(ally)
spurm,sperm
spurt,*,,ted,ting,SUDDEN JOLT/ GROWTH/ MOVEMENT, SHORT PERIOD OF TIME
spusefikly,specific(ally)
spusifikly,specific(ally)
sput,spud
sputer,sputter

sputter,*,,red,ring,rer,TO RAPIDLY/ INCOHERENTLY SPEAK, ERRATIC/ HALTING MOTION/ SOUND
sputur,sputter
spy,pies,pied,pying,SECRET SURVEILLANCE/ MONITORING
spyd,spy(pied)
spyder,spider
spydful,spite(ful)
spydur,spider
spyeng,spy(ing)
spyke,spike
spyse,spy(pies) / spice
spytur,spider
sqeek,squeak
sqit,skit
sqitish,skittish
sqrul,squirrel
squabble,*,,ed,ling,er,MINOR SCUFFLE/ DISPUTE
squad,*,,dron,SMALL GROUP OF SPECIFIC PEOPLE (or see squat)
squadir,squat(tter)
squadron,*,,SMALL MILITARY/ POLICE GROUP
squadur,squat(tter)
squaemish,squeamish
squaled,squalid
squalid,dly,dness,dity,NEGLECTED/ FOUL/ FILTHY
squall,*,,lled,lling,llier,lliest,lly,SUDDEN/ STRONG GUSTS OF WIND/ RAIN/ SLEET
squalor,NEGLECTED/ FOUL/ FILTHY
squander,*,,red,ring,RECKLESSLY LET GO OF/ USE/ WASTE
square,*,,ed,ring,ely,eness,rish,rishly,OF BEING FOUR EQUAL SIDES, TO BE PROPORTIONAL, SOMEONE DULL, A MATH OPERATION
squarly,square(ly)
squash,hes,hed,hing,A VEGETABLE, A GAME, TO SMASH/ CRUSH SOMETHING
squat,*,,tted,tting,tter,REST ON HAUNCHES, LOWER THE UPPER TORSO, TO SIT (or see squad)
squator,squat(tter)
squeak,*,,ked,king,kingly,ker,ky,A SHORT/ SHRILL SOUND

squeal, *, led, ling, ing, ler, LOUD/ SHRILL SOUND PRODUCED BY GLEE/ HAPPINESS, TELL A TRUTH ABOUT SOMEONE WITHOUT THEIR PERMISSION
squeamish, hly, hness, UNEASY/ UNSETTLING, DISGUSTED ABOUT SOMETHING
squed, squid
squeegee, *, eed, eeing, AN INSTRUMENT/ IMPLEMENT FOR REMOVING WATER/ LIQUID
squeejy, squeegee
squeek, squeak
squeel, squeal
squeelur, squeal(er)
squeemish, squeamish
squeese, squeeze
squeeze, *, ed, zing, er, zingly, zable, zably, TO FORCE BY TIGHTENING GRIP
squegy, squeegee
squeibis, scabies
squejy, squeegee
squel, squeal
squelch, hed, hing, her, SILENCE/ CRUSH/ SUPPRESS, A SOUND
squelur, squeal(er)
squemish, squeamish
squent, squint
squerl, squirrel
squerm, squirm
squermy, squirm
squert, squirt
squesh, squish
squeshy, squish
squesur, squeeze(r)
squeze, squeeze
squid, *, A CEPHALOPOD FOUND IN SALT WATER
squiggle, *, ed, ling, SQUIRM/ TWIST
squigy, squeegee
squil, squeal
squilli, squeegee
squint, *, ted, ting, TO CLOSE EYES TO A NARROW OPENING FOR PROTECTION
squire, *, ed, ring, MAN OF ARISTOCRATIC BIRTH, MAN WHO ESCORTS
squirel, squirrel

squirl, squirrel
squirm, *, med, ming, mer, my, mier, miest, WRITHE/ WRIGGLE LIKE A WORM
squirrel, *, lly, A RODENT, TO BEHAVE LIKE A SQUIRREL
squirt, *, ted, ting, NARROW STREAM OF LIQUID EMITTED FROM AN ORIFICE
squis, squeeze
squish, hes, hed, hing, hy, hier, hiest, SQUASH/ SMASH
squrt, squirt
sqwal, squall
sqwalid, squalid
sqwert, squirt
srgekul, surgical
sta, stay
stab, *, bbed, bbing, bber, TO POKE/ THRUST A BLADE WITH SHARP TIP INTO SOMETHING/ SOMEONE
stabalize, stabilize
stabelity, stability
stabilise, stabilize
stability, ties, ize, OF FIRM GROUND/ FORM/ FOUNDATION "prefixes: in"
stabilize, *, ed, zing, er, zation, TO PROVIDE/ ENSURE FIRM GROUND/ FORM "prefixes: de"
stabiludy, stability
stable, *, ed, ling, ly, eness, bilize, OF FIRM GROUND/ FORM, SHELTER FOR ANIMAL "prefixes: un"
stablize, stabilize
stabulize, stabilize
stac, stack / stake / steak / stalk / stock
stacado, staccato / stoccado
staccato, *, SHARP/ BRIEF MUSICAL NOTE (or see stoccado)
stachatory, statutory
stachur, stature
stachutory, statutory
stack, *, ked, king, ker, ORGANIZE/ PILE/ SET UP ITEMS ONE ON TOP OF ANOTHER (or see stake/ steak/ stalk)
stad, staid / stay(ed) / state
stadeim, stadium
stadek, static
stades, status
stadeum, stadium

stadiem, stadium
stadik, static
stadis, status
stadium, *, A LARGE ARENA FOR PEOPLE TO GATHER
stadus, status
staf, staff / staph / stave
stafed, staff(ed)
staff, *, ffed, ffing, GROUP OF HIRED PEOPLE, LONG POLE/ STICK TO BE CARRIED/ USED BY HAND (or see staph) "prefixes: over"
staft, staff(ed) / stave(d)
stag, *, gged, gging, gger, MALE IN THE DEER FAMILY, MALE UNACCOMPANIED AT A GATHERING (or see stage/ stack)
stagd, stag(gged) / stage(d)
stage, *, ed, ging, er, ey, PLATFORM DESIGNED FOR PLAYS/ THEATER, TO PERFORM (or see stag) "prefixes: sub"
staged, stag(gged) / stage(d)
stagee, stodgy
stager, stagger
stagger, *, red, ring, rer, ringly, TO SWAY/ WAVER/ WALK UNSTEADILY, SHOCKED, HORSE/ COW HIT BY A DISEASE
stagir, stagger
stagnade, stagnate
stagnait, stagnate
stagnant, tly, ncy, NO MOVEMENT/ MOTION
stagnashen, stagnate(tion)
stagnate, *, ed, ting, tion, QUIT MOVING, BECOME DULL/ QUIET
stagnatid, stagnate(d)
stagnit, stagnant
stagnunt, stagnant
stagnut, stagnant
stagred, stagger(ed)
stagt, stag(gged) / stage(d)
stagur, stagger
stagy, stodgy
stai, sty
staichutory, statutory
staid, dly, dness, IN PLACE OF, FIXED/ STEADY (or see stead/ stay(ed))
stail, style

stailos, stylus
staimi, stymie
stain, *, ned, ning, nable, r er, nless, nlessly, UNDESIRABLE MARK, PERMANENTLY PLACE/ AFFIX COLOR
staiol, style
stair, *, STEPS MAKING A RISE IN ELEVATION (or see stare)
stairafom, styrofoam
stairofom, styrofoam
stak, stack / stake / steak / stalk / stock
stakabul, stack(able)
stakado, staccato / stoccado
stakato, staccato / stoccado
stakd, stack(ed) / stake(c) / stalk(ed) / stock(ed)
stake, *, ed, king, LEVERAGE/ PLEDGE/ WAGER/ SUPPORT FOR SOMETHING, HAVE A VESTED INTEREST IN, BROAD POINTED POST FOR STRIKING/ DRIVING INTO GROUND (or see steak/ stack/ stalk/ stock)
staked, stack(ed) / staked) / stalk(ed) / stock(ed)
staker, stagger / stack(er) / stalk(er) / stock(er)
stakibel, stack(able)
stakibul, stack(able)
stakir, stagger / stack(er) / stalk(er) / stock(er)
staknade, stagnate
staknashen, stagnate(ticn)
staknate, stagnate
staknation, stagnate(tion)
staknunt, stagnant
stakodo, staccato / stoccado
stakoto, staccato / stoccado
stakt, stack(ed) / stake(c) / stalk(ed) / stock(ed)
stakubil, stack(able)
stakuble, stack(able)
stakur, stagger / stack(er) / stalk(er) / stoc<(er)
stal, stall / stale
stale, *, ed, ling, er, est, ely, eness, LOSS OF ACTION/ TASTE/ FLAVOR (or see stall)
staledo, stiletto
staleon, stallion
staleto, stiletto
staliun, stallion

stalk, *, ed, king, ker, FOLLOW SOMEONE/ SOMETHING WITH INTENT WITHOUT THEIR KNOWING, MAIN PORTION OF A POLE SHAPED PLANT
stall, *, lled, lling, A DWELLING FOR HORSES, TO HESITATE/ QUIT/ PAUSE (or see stale)
stalleto, stiletto
stallion, *, MALE HORSE CAPABLE OF BREEDING
stalwart, tly, tness, UNCOMPROMISING/ STRONG IN RESOLUTION
stalwort, stalwart
stalyun, stallion
stamen, *, nal, PLANT ORGAN
stamenu, stamina
stamer, stammer
stamin, stamen
stamina, LONGEVITY IN STRENGTH
stamir, stammer
stammer, *, red, ring, ringly, PAUSE/ HESITATE IN SPEECH
stamp, *, ped, ping, per, AFFIXED TO A POSTAL LETTER, A MARK LEFT BY PRESSING
stampede, *, ed, ding, A MAD/ SUDDEN RUSH IN ONE DIRECTION BY MANY
stampet, stampede
stampir, stamp(er)
stampur, stamp(er)
stamun, stamen
stamur, stammer
stan, stain
stance, A STAND/ ATTITUDE/ POSITION
stanchen, stanchion
stancheon, stanchion
stanchion, *, BEAM/ POST FOR SUPPORT
stand, *, ding, der, tood, PARTICULAR POSITION, BE UPRIGHT IN FOOTING "prefixes: up"
standard, *, dize, dized, dizing, dization, GENERAL CONSENSUS ON METHODOLOGY/ DIMENSIONS/ DEGREE OF MEASUREMENT "prefixes: non/ sub"
standerd, standard
standerdazation, standard(ization)
standurd, standard
standurdize, standard(ize)
stane, stain
staneble, stain(able)

stanible, stain(able)
stank, PAST TENSE FOR THE WORD "STINK"
stans, stance / stain(s) / stand(s)
stansa, stanza
stanshen, stanchion
stanshon, stanchion
stansu, stanza
stant, stand
stanuble, stain(able)
stanza, *, FOUR OR MORE IN A VERSE/ POEM
stap, stab
stapel, staple
staph, SHORT FOR STAPHYLOCOCCUS (or see staff)
staple, *, ed, ling, er, FASTENER MADE OF METAL, BASIC REQUIREMENTS FOR SURVIVAL
stapul, staple
star, *, rred, rring, rless, rry, CELESTIAL/ SHINING BODY IN SPACE, PERSON WHO ACHIEVES THE LIMELIGHT, GEOMETRIC SHAPE (or see stare/ stair/ store)
staralize, sterile(lize)
starc, stark
starch, hes, hed, hing, hy, hiness, NATURALLY OCCURRING CHEMICAL USED TO MAKE THINGS STIFF
starchenes, starch(iness)
stard, start / stare(d) / star(rred)
starder, starter
stardil, startle
stardul, startle
stardur, starter
stare, *, ed, ring, AFFIX EYES ONTO A SINGLE POINT WITHOUT MOVING (or see star/ stair/ star(rry))
stared, stare(d) / star(rred)
stareledy, sterile(lity)
starelidy, sterile(lity)
stareo, stereo
starf, starve
staril, sterile
starilety, sterile(lity)
starilize, sterile(lize)
stark, kly, kness, GRIM/ DESOLATE SCENE WITH LITTLE TO ENTERTAIN THE EYE
starling, *, A BIRD
staroed, steroid

staroid, steroid
stars, stair(s) / stare(s) / star(s)
start, *, ted, ting, ter, BEGIN, INITIAL ACTION (or see stare(d)) "prefixes: up"
starter, *, ELECTRIC MOTOR, BEGIN/ INITIATE ACTION
startil, startle
startir, starter
startle, *, ed, ling, BE ALARMED/ SURPRISED BY SUDDEN ACTION/ EVENT
startul, startle
startur, starter
starul, sterile
starulize, sterile(lize)
starvashen, starvation
starvation, SERIOUSLY LACK NOURISHMENT/ BASIC ESSENTIALS
starve, *, ed, ving, vation, SERIOUSLY LACK NOURISHMENT/ BASIC ESSENTIALS
starveishon, starvation
stas, stay(s)
stases, stasis
stash, hes, hed, hing, TO HIDE/ PUT SOMETHING AWAY
stashatory, statutory
stashen, station
stashenary, stationary / stationery
stasher, stature
stashetory, statutory
stashewesk, statue(sque)
stashewtory, statutory
stashin, station / stash(ing)
stashinary, stationary / stationery
stashir, stature
stashitory, statutory
stashonery, stationary / stationery
stashoot, statute
stashu, statue
stashuary, statuary
stashuery, statuary
stashuesk, statue(sque)
stashun, station
stashunery, stationary / stationery
stashur, stature
stashute, statute

stashutory, statutory
stasis, EQUILIBRIUM, FROZEN IN TIME/ MOVEMENT, INACTIVITY
stasos, stasis
stasus, stasis
stat, *, HOSPITAL EMERGENCY EXPRESSION, SHORT FOR STATISTICS (or see state/ stay(ed))
statchuesk, statue(sque)
state, *, ed, ting, ely, elier, eliest, eliness, LAND WITH SPECIFIC/ DIVISIVE BORDER, CURRENT CONDITION "prefixes: inter/ intra/ over/ re/ up"
statek, static
statement, *, SUMMARY/ REVIEW OF CONDITION/ STATUS
states, status / state(s)
stateur, stature
stateutory, statutory
static, *, cal, cally, NO MOVEMENT/ ACTION, AT REST
statik, static
station, *, PLACE TO MOMENTARILY REST/ RECEIVE SERVICES "prefixes: inter/ sub"
stationary, REST, STOP, BE STILL (or see stationery) "prefixes: non"
stationery, ENVELOPE/ PAPER FOR WRITING (or see stationary)
statis, status
statistic, *, cal, cally, A MATHEMATICAL ACCOUNT OF CURRENT SITUATION/ CONDITION
statiur, stature
statment, statement
statmunt, statement
stats, state(s) / stat(s)
statshu, statue
statshuery, statuary
statuary, ries, COLLECTION OF STATUES
statue, *, esque, ette, SOLID/ STATIONARY FORM CARVED/ MOLDED TO RESEMBLE SOMETHING/ SOMEONE
statuery, statuary
statuesk, statue(sque)
stature, PHYSICAL DIMENSIONS OF A LIVING THING
status, CURRENT POSITION/ STANDING
statute, *, tory, A FIXED PERMANENT LAW

statutory, rily, IMPOSED BY A STATUTE
stauk, stock
staunch, hly, hness, RIGID/ FIRM STRUCTURE/ FORM, LIQUID RESILIENT
staut, stout
stave, *, ed, ving, FIGHT OFF AN ATTACK, A ROD/ POLE/ STICK
stawgines, stodgy(giness)
stawk, stock / stalk
stawked, stock(ed) / stoke(d)
stawt, stout
stay, *, yed, ying, TO REMAIN BEHIND/ IN ONE PLACE, DON'T FOLLOW/ MOVE "prefixes: over"
staylos, stylus
stead, TO BE IN SOMEONE'S PLACE/ POSITION WHILE THEY'RE AWAY (or see steed/ staid)
steadeness, steady(diness)
steadfast, tly, tness, HOLDING FIXED / FIRM/ UNWAVERING (alternate spelling for 'stedfast')
steady, dies, died, dying, dier, diest, dily, diness, FIXED/ FIRM/ CONSTANT "prefixes: un"
steak, *, A CUT OF BEEF (or see stake)
steal, *, ling, tole, TAKE SOMETHING FROM SOMEONE WITHOUT THEIR PERMISSION (or see steel/ stile/ still)
stealth, hy, hily, hy, hiness, SECRECY
steam, *, med, ming, mer, mily, miness, my, HOT WATER TURNED TO GASEOUS STATE
stear, steer
stebel, steeple / stipple
stebul, steeple / stipple
stebulashen, stipulate(tion)
stebulation, stipulate(tion)
stebulatory, stipulate(tory)
stec, stick
steccado, staccato / stoccado
stech, stitch
sted, SHORT FOR "INSTEAD" (or see stead/ steed)
stede, steady
stedeness, steady(diness)
stedes, steady(dies)
stedfast, tly, tness, HOLDING FIXED/ FIRM/ UNWAVERING (alternate spelling for 'stedfast')

stedfastnes,steadfast(ness)
stedily,steady(dily)
stediness,steady(diness)
stedness,staid(ness) / stead(ness)
stedoscoup,stethoscope
steduly,steady(dily)
stedy,steady
steed,*, HORSE WITH SPIRIT, STALLION (or see stead)
steel,ly,lier,liest,liness, TYPE OF METAL (or see steal/ stile/ still)
steenkur,stink(er)
steenky,stink
steep,*, ped,ping,ply,press,per,pen, SHARP SLOPE, SOAK/ IMMERSE (or see step/ steppe)
steeple,*, TALL ROOF COMING TO A POINT AT THE TOP
steer,*, red,ring,rable,rer,rage, MANIPULATE/ CONTROL INTO PARTICULAR DIRECTION, CASTRATED BOVINE "prefixes: over/ under"
steerible,steer(able)
steeruble,steer(able)
stef,stiff
stefin,stiff(en)
stefnis,stiff(ness)
stegma,stigma
stegmadik,stigma(tic)
stegmatist,stigma(tist)
stei,stay
steic,stake / steak
steichutori,statutory
steid,staid / stay(ed)
steish,stage
steishon,statement
steishoneri,stationary / stationery
steit,state
steitment,statement
stek,stick / steak / stake
stekado,staccato / stoccado
stekato,staccato / stoccado
stekir,stick(er)
stekler,stickler

steklur,stickler
stekmu,stigma
stekodo,staccato / stoccado
stekor,stick(er)
stekoto,staccato / stoccado
stekur,stick(er)
steky,stick
stel,steel / steal / still / stile / stale
stelar,stellar
steledo, stiletto
steleto, stiletto
stelir,stellar
stellar,, OF THE STARS "prefixes: inter/ sub"
stelleto, stiletto
stelnis,still(ness)
stelnus,still(ness)
stelre,stellar
stels,still(s) / steal(s)
stelt, stilt / steal(ed) / still(ed)
stelth,stealth
stelur,stellar
stem,*, mmed,mming, BRANCH OF A WOODY PLANT, SUGGESTING OF A BRANCH, THE BASE/ BASIS OF SOMETHING
stemely,steam(ily)
stemer, steam(er)
stemewlasheon,stimulate(tion)
stemily,steam(ily)
stemir,steam(er)
stemulashen,stimulate(tion)
stemulate,stimulate
stemulation,stimulate(tion)
stemury,steam(ily)
stemur, steam(er)
stenaugrafer, stenograph(er)
stench, POWERFUL STINK
stenchee,stingy
stencil,*,led,ling,ler, A FORM/ OUTLINE/ TEMPLATE FOR REPRODUCING
steng,sting
stengd,sting(ed) / stink
stengee,stingy
stenger,sting(er) / stink(er)

stengles,sting(less)
stengt,sting(ed) / stink
stengur,sting(er) / stink(er)
stengyness,stingy(giness)
stenjee,stingy
stenjenes,stingy(giness)
stenk,stink
stenkee,stink
stenkenes,stink(iness)
stenkur,stink(er)
steno,SHORT FOR STENOGRAPHER
stenografir,stenograph(er)
stenograph,her, hers,hic, hical,hically,hy, USE OF SHORTHAND, A TYPE OF TYPEWRITER
stensh,stench
stenshee,stingy
stensil,stencil
stensul,stencil
stent,stint
step,*, pped,pping, RISE/ MOVE UP, RISER, UP IN INCREMENTS (or see steep/ steppe) "prefixes: mis/ over"
stepel,steeple / stipple
stepend,stipend
stepeulashen,stipulate(tion)
stepewlation,stipulate(tion)
stepil,steeple / stipple
stepind,stipend
steple,steeple / stipple
steppe,*, A PLAIN WITHOUT TREES (or see step)
stepul,steeple / stipple
stepulashen,stipulate(tion)
stepulation,stipulate(tion)
ster,stare / steer / stir
steral,sterile
steralize,sterile(lize)
sterchen,sturgeon
sterd,stare(d) / steer(ed) / stir(rred)
sterdy,sturdy
stered,stare(d) / steer(ed) / stir(rred)
stereledy,sterile(lity)

stereo, *, SOUND SYSTEM, PREFIX INDICATING "THREE DIMENSIONAL OR SOLID" MOST OFTEN MODIFIES THE WORD
stergen,sturgeon
stergon,sturgeon
sterib,stirrup
sterible,steer(able)
sterile,lity,lize,lizes,lized,lizing,lization,lizer,FREE FROM BACTERIA/ CONTAMINATION,UNPRODUCTIVE "prefixes: inter/ un"
sterilety,sterile(lity)
sterip,stirrup
sterjen,sturgeon
sterjon,sturgeon
sterleng,sterling
sterling,A STANDARD/ DEGREE OF SILVER
stern,ner, nest, nly, nness, HIND/ BACK END, BE HARSH/ RIGID
sternem,sternum
sternness,stern(ess)
sternum, *, PART OF THE SKELETON
steroed,steroid
steroet,steroid
steroid, *, dal, CHEMICAL COMPOUND
sterol,sterile
steror,stir(rrer)
steroyd,steroid
stert,steer(ed) / stir(rred)
sterty,sturdy
sterub,stirrup
steruble,steer(able)
sterul,sterile
sterulize,sterile(lize)
sterup,stirrup
stesh,stitch
stetch,stitch
stethaskope,stethoscope
stethiskopek,stethoscope(pic)
stethoscope, *, pic, pical, pically, py, INSTRUMENT A MEDICAL EXAMINER USES
stethuskope,stethoscope
stethuskopik,stethoscope(pic)
stetistiks,statistic(s)

steudeo,studio
steudint,student
steul,stool
steve,stiff
stew, *, wed, wing, A THICK SOUP
steward, *, dess, desses, ONE WHO MANAGES THE AFFAIRS OF OTHERS
stewardes,steward(ess)
stewbud,stupid
stewdeis,studious
stewdent,student
stewdeo,studio
stewdeus,studious
stewdio,studio
stewg,stooge
stewj,stooge
stewlee,stool(ie)
stewp,stoop
stewpendus,stupendous
stewper,stupor
stewpid,stupid
stewpidety,stupid(ity)
stewpir,stupor
stewpud,stupid
stewpur,stupor
stewul,stool
stewurd,steward
stey,stay
steybolaiz,stabilize
steydiom,stadium
steyshoneri,stationary / stationery
sti,sty
stibe,stipe
stible,stipple
stibul,stipple
stibulashen,stipulate(tion)
stibulation,stipulate(tion)
stibulatory,stipulate(tory)
sticado,staccato / stoccado
stich,stitch
stick, *, king, ky, ker, kier, kiest, kiness, kily, tuck, A BRANCH, SOMETHING TACKY, BE AFFIXED/ ADHERED TO "prefixes: un"

stickler, *, TO BE PARTICULAR, MYSTERIOUS/ PUZZLING
stid,steed
stif,stiff
stifal,stifle
stifel,stifle
stifen,stiff(en)
stifenur,stiff(ener)
stiff, *, ffed, ffing, ffer, ffest, ffish, ffly, ffness, ffen, ffener, RIGID/ TENSE/ UNBENDING/ SEVERE
stifle, *, ed, ling, er, lingly, DIFFICULT TO MOVE/ BREATH, OPPRESSIVE, MAMMAL'S JOINT
stifnes,stiff(ness)
stiful,stifle
stifun,stiff(en)
stifuner,stiff(ener)
stigma, *, ata, atist, atic, atically, atism, atize, atizes, atized, atizing, atization, atizer, BLEMISH/ MARK, TO BRAND
stigmadik,stigma(tic)
stigmutist,stigma(tist)
stik,stick
stikado,staccato / stoccado
stiker,stick(er)
stikir,stick(er)
stikler,stickler
stiklur,stickler
stikmu,stigma
stikodo,staccato / stoccado
stikor,stick(er)
stikoto,staccato / stoccado
stikur,stick(er)
stiky,stick
stil,still / stile / style
stild,still(ed) / stilt / style(d)
stile, *, FOR ASCENDING/ MOUNTING, A SHAPE (or see style/ still/ steal/ steel)
stiled,still(ed) / steal(ed) / style(d)
stiledo,stiletto
stiles,stylus / style(s)
stilesh,style(lish)
stilest,style(list)
stileto,stiletto
stiletto, *, A WOMANS SHOE, STYLE OF KNIFE/INSTRUMENT

stilis, stylus
stilish, style(lish)
stilishly, style(lishly)
stilize, style(lize)
still, *, lled, lling, llness, MOTIONLESS, DEVICE FOR DISTILLATION (or see stile/ style/ steal/ steel)
stilleto, stiletto
stillness, still(ness)
stilnus, still(ness)
stils, still(s) / steal(s) / style(s)
stilt, *, PAIR OF LONG MANMADE LEGS (or see still(ed)/ style(d))
stilus, stylus
stilush, style(lish)
stim, stem / steam
stime, stymie
stimed, stem(mmed) / stymie(d) / steam(ed)
stimee, stymie / steam
stimiuleit, stimulate
stimulashen, stimulate(tion)
stimulate, *, ed, ting, tion, ant, ants, tive, tor, lus, ENCOURAGE/ MOTIVATE TO MOVE/ PERFORM "prefixes: bio"
stimuleichon, stimulate(tion)
stimuleit, stimulate
stinaugrafur, stenograph(er)
stinch, stench
stinchee, stingy
stine, stein
sting, *, tung, ging, ger, gingly, gless, PAINFUL FEELING SENSATION, A COVERT OPERATION
stingd, sting(ed) / stink
stingee, stingy
stinglus, sting(less)
stingt, sting(ed) / stink
stingur, sting(er) / stink(er)
stingy, gier, giest, gily, giness, LACK GENEROSITY, TIGHT WITH RESOURCES (or see sting)
stingyness, stingy(giness)
stinjee, stingy
stinjenes, stingy(giness)
stink, *, king, ky, kiness, kingly, ker, tank, turk, FOUL/ OFFENSIVE SMELL

stinkee, stink
stinkur, stink(er)
stino, steno
stinografur, stenograph(er)
stinsel, stencil
stinsul, stencil
stint, *, ted, ter, tunt, LIMITED TIME/ AMOUNT, BRIEF ACTIVITY "prefixes: un"
stintud, stint(ed)
stiol, steal
stip, steep
stipe, RESEMBLES A STEM
stipend, *, diary, diaries, CONSISTENT/ STEADY PAYMENT/ COMPENSATION
stipeulate, stipulate
stipeulutory, stipulate(tory)
stipewlate, stipulate
stiplur, stipple(r)
stipol, steeple
stipple, ed, ling, er, MANY DOTS TO CREATE A SCENE/ PICTURE
stiptek, styptic
stiptik, styptic
stipulashen, stipulate(tion)
stipulate, *, ed, ting, tion, tive, tory, AGREEMENT WITH GUIDELINES
stir, *, rred, rring, rer, rringly, CREATE MOTION/ MOVEMENT
stirafom, styrofoam
stird, stir(rred)
stirdy, sturdy
stirefom, styrofoam
stirgen, sturgeon
stirgeon, sturgeon
stirjun, sturgeon
stirleng, sterling
stirn, stern
stirnem, sternum
stirnly, stern(ly)
stirnness, stern(ess)
stirnum, sternum
stirrup, *, PART ON A HORSE SADDLE
stirt, stir(rred)

stirty, sturdy
stirufom, styrofoam
stirup, stirrup
stish, stitch
stitch, hes, hed, hing, her, SEW TOGETHER, USE OF A NEEDLE
stiulize, style(lize)
stiuward, steward
stive, stiff
sto, stow / store
stoakul, stoic(al)
stob, stop
stobur, stop(pper)
stoc, stalk / stock / stoke
stocado, staccato / stoccado
stocato, staccato / stoccado
stoccado, TO STAB/ THRUST WITH A WEAPON (or se stocatta)
stoccato, staccato/ stoccado
stock, *, ked, king, ker, ky, TO COLLECT/ AMASS/ ACCUMULATE SOMETHING, HOLDING INTEREST IN A COMPANY (or see stalk/ stoke/ stocking) "prefixes: over"
stocking, *, MATERIAL FOR COVERING LEGS/ FEET
stodgeness, stodgy(giness)
stodgy, gily, giness, gier, giest, DULL/ NOT INTERESTING, HEAVY/ THICK (or see stogy)
stodgyest, stodgy(giest)
stoec, stoic
stoecul, stoic(al)
stoeg, stow(age)
stoej, stow(age)
stoek, stoic
stoekul, stoic(al)
stof, stove / stuff
stofs, stove(s) / stuff(s)
stoge, stogy / stodgy / stooge
stogeist, stodgy(giest)
stogenis, stodgy(giness)
stogey, stogy
stogiest, stodgy(giest)
stogines, stodgy(giness)
stogy, CIGAR, BOOT (or see stodgy)

stogyest,stodgy(giest)
stogyness,stodgy(giness)
stoic,*,cal,cally,cism,SECT WHO BELIEVES FREEDOM FROM PASSION/ GRIEF/ JOY IS A VIRTUE
stoicul,stoic(al)
stoig,stow(age)
stoij,stow(age)
stoikal,stoic(al)
stok,stock / stoke / stalk / stuck
stokada,staccato / stoccado
stokato,staccato / stoccado
stokd,stock(ed) / stoke(d)
stoke,*,ed,king,er,TO STIR/ FEED/ POKE (or see stock/ stalk)
stoked,stoke(d) / stack(ed) / stake(d) / stalk(ed) / stock(ed)
stokee,stock / stogy
stoker,stagger / stack(er) / stalk(er) / stock(er)
stokur,stagger / stack(er) / stalk(er) / stock(er)
stoky,stock / stogy
stol,stall
stolado, stiletto
stold,stall(ed)
stole,en,PAST TENSE FOR THE WORD "STEAL", FUR ACCESSORY FOR THE SHOULDERS
stolin,stole(n)
stolk,stalk / stock
stolker,stalk(er)
stolun,stole(n)
stolwart,stalwart
stolwort,stalwart
stomach,*,hic,hy,POUCH IN THE BODY WHICH HOLDS FOOD FOR DIGESTION
stomek,stomach
stomik,stomach
stomp,*,ped,ping,per,USING THE FOOT FOR FORCEFUL/ HEAVY STEPS (or see stump)
stompur,stomp(er)
stomuk,stomach
ston,stun / stone
stonch,staunch
stone,*,ed,ning,er,ny,nier,niest,nily,niness,ROCK UNDER HEAVY INFLUENCE OF SOMETHING

stoney,stone(ny)
stonsh,staunch
stonshly,staunch(ly)
stooart,steward
stoobid,stupid
stood,PAST TENSE FOR THE WORD 'STAND', UPRIGHT
stooerd,steward
stooge,*,TO BE TRICKED/ FOILED, A COMEDIAN
stool,*,lie,SMALL SEAT WITH NO BACK/ ARMS, FECES, AN INFORMER
stoole,stool(ie)
stoop,*,ed,ping,BEND OVER,LOWER IN STATUS,SMALL PORCH
stooped,stoop(ed) / stupid
stoopedity,stupid(ity)
stooper,stupor
stoopid,stupid
stoopufid,stupefy(fied)
stoopur,stupor
stop,*,pped,pping,ppage,pper,PUT AN END TO,HALT PROGRESS OF,BLOCK "prefixes: non/ un"
stopud,stupid
stopur,stop(pper)
stor,store / star
storach,storage
storage,*,KEEP/ STOCKPILE THINGS/ INFORMATION
storck,stork
stord,store(d) / star(rred)
store,*,ed,ring,er,eable,rage,PUT AWAY FOR SAFE KEEPING, RETAIL ESTABLISHMENT (or see story) "prefixes: over/ under"
storech,storage
storeg,storage
storij,storage
stork,*,A BIRD
storm,*,med,ming,my,CLASHING/ MEETING OF TWO DIFFERENT ENERGY FRONTS AND THE REPERCUSSIONS AS A RESULT
stormee,storm
stort,store(d) / star(rred)
storuch,storage
storug,storage

storuj,storage
story,ries,ried,A TALE/ EXPLANATION OF AN EVENT/ OCCURRENCE, VARIOUS FLOOR LEVELS WITHIN A BUILDING/ HOME
storyd,story(ried)
storys,story(ries)
stot,stow(ed) / stood
stoug,stow(age)
stouj,stow(age)
stout,*,SOLID/ HARDY/ ROBUST/ STRONG/ RESISTANT
stove,*,AN APPLIANCE/ APPARATUS FOR COOKING/ HEATING
stovs,stove(s) / stuff(s)
stow,*,wed,wing,wage,waway,PUT/ PLACE SOMETHING/ CARGO AWAY
stoweg,stow(age)
stowej,stow(age)
stowek,stoic
stowgee,stogy
stowic,stoic
stowig,stow(age)
stowij,stow(age)
stowik,stoic
stowt,stout / stow(ed)
stra,straw / stray
stradagee,strategy
stradajist,strategy(gist)
straddle,*,ed,ling,er,SIT ATOP OF SOMETHING, BE IN BETWEEN/ THE MIDDLE OF, BE ON BOTH SIDES OF SOMETHING AT THE SAME TIME
strade,stray(ed) / straight / strait
stradegist,strategy(gist)
stradejist,strategy(gist)
stradel,straddle
straden,straight(ened)
strades,stratus
stradigest,strategy(gist)
stradil,straddle
stradin,straight(ened)
stradis,stratus
stradle,straddle
strados,stratus
straduge,strategy

stradugist, strategy(gist)
stradujist, strategy(gist)
stradul, straddle
stradun, straight(ened)
stradus, stratus
strae, stray
stragel, straggle
strageler, straggle(r)
stragely, straggle(ly)

straggle, er, ly, lier, liest. WANDER OFF COURSE IN IRREGULAR PATTERN, DISORGANIZED/ DISHEVELED/ UNTIDY

straght, straight / strait
stragil, straggle
stragiler, straggle(r)
stragily, straggle(ly)
stragle, straggle
straglee, straggle(ly)
strageist, straggle(st)
straglur, straggle(r)
stragul, straggle
straguly, straggle(ly)

straight, ten, tens, tened, tening, tener, BE LINEAR/ LEVEL/ TRUE, WITHOUT DEVIATION BETWEEN POINT A AND B (or see strait)

strain, *, ned, ning, ner, STRETCH/ PUSH/ PULL TO MAXIMUM CAPACITY, SIFT/ SIEVE OUT LARGER PARTICLES, REMOVE PARTICULATE MATTER "prefixes: un"

strainly, strange(ly)
strainj, strange

strait, *, ten, tly, tness, NARROW PASSAGEWAY BETWEEN TWO BODIES OF WATER, DIFFICULT/ DESPERATE POSITION, CLOSE, STRICT, TIGHT (or see strait)

strakly, straggle(ly)
stran, strain
stranch, strange

strand, *, ded, ding, ONE ALL ALONE, BE SINGLED OUT AWAY FROM OTHERS

straner, strain(er)
strangal, strangle

strange, ely, er, est, eness, UNFAMILIAR/ ODD/ WEIRD

strangel, strangle

strangeulat, strangulate(tion)
strangir, strange(r)
strangist, strange(st)

strangle, *, ed, ling, er, gulate, CHOKE/ HINDER/ STOP/ CLOSE OFF

strangor, strange(r)
strangul, strangle
strangulashen, strangulate(tion)

strangulate, *, ed, ting, tion, CHOKE/ HINDER/ STOP/ CLOSE OFF

strangur, strange(r)
stranir, strain(er)
stranj, strange
stranjer, strange(r)
stranjest, strange(st)
stranjly, strange(ly)
stranjur, strange(r)
strankel, strangle
strankler, strangle(r)
strankul, strangle
strankulate, strangulate
stranor, strain(er)
stransh, strange
strant, strand
stranur, strain(er)

strap, *, pped, pping, NARROW/ THIN STRIP OF SOMETHING, TIE DOWN/ FASTEN/ SECURE WITH
strapeng, strap(pping)
stras, stray(s) / stress
strat, straight / strait / stray(ed)
stratagee, strategy
stratagist, strategy(gist)
strategek, strategic
strategekly, strategic(ally)

strategic, *, cal, cally, PERFORM ALONG A GUIDELINE/ METHODOLOGY, HAVE A PLAN "prefixes: un"

strategy, gies, gist, HAVE A METHOD/ PLAN TO PERFORM AN ACTION/ EVENT/ PLAY

stratejik, strategic
stratejikly, strategic(ally)
stratel, straddle
stratend, straight(en)
stratend, straight(ened)

strates, stratus
stratesfere, stratosphere
stratesphere, stratosphere
stratigek, strategic
stratigekly, strategic(ally)
stratigest, strategy(gist)
stratil, straddle
stratin, straight(en)
stratis, stratus
stratle, straddle
stratnur, straight(ener)
straton, straight(en)
stratoned, straight(ened)
stratos, stratus
stratosfere, stratosphere

stratosphere, ric, LAYER SEVEN MILES ABOVE EARTH "prefixes: sub"

stratugee, strategy
stratugist, strategy(gist)
stratugy, strategy
stratul, straddle

stratum, *, ta, tal, us, LAYER, LEVEL OF A SYSTEM/ FORMATION "prefixes: sub"

stratun, straight(ened)
stratuned, straight(ened)

stratus, UNIFORM/ WEAK LAYER OF CLOUDS

stratusfere, stratosphere
stratusphere, stratosphere

straw, *, STALK OF GRAIN, A TUBE TO SIP LIQUIDS

stray, *, yed, ying, yer, WANDER FROM THE GROUP/ CENTER

strayd, stray(ed) / straight

streak, *, ked, king, ky, kily, kiness, SMEARED AS IF WIPED, A BLURRED IMAGE

stream, *, med, ming, mer, GENTLE/ FLOWING/ CONSISTENT MOVEMENT "prefixes: un/ up"

strech, stretch
strecher, stretch(er)
strechnine, strychnine
strechur, stretch(er)
streekee, streak
streem, stream
streemer, stream(er)

streengy,string
street,*,A ROADWAY/ PATH WIDE ENOUGH FOR ALL TYPES OF TRAVEL
strek,streak
strekd,strict / streak(ed)
streke,streak
strekin,stricken
strekly,strict(ly)
streknine,strychnine
strekt,strict / streak(ed)
strekun,stricken
streky,streak
strem,stream
stremer,stream(er)
stremur,stream(er)
streneus,strenuous
strenewus,strenuous
streng,string
strengee,string
strengensees,stringent(ncies)
strengently,stringent(ly)
strengint,stringent
strength,*,hen,hened,hening,hener,STRONG ENOUGH, ENDURANCE "prefixes: under"
strenjint,stringent
strenkth,strength
strenth,strength
strenthin,strength(en)
strenues,strenuous
strenuous,sity,sness,STRAINING POINT/ CHALLENGE
step,ptococcal,ptococcus,STREPTOCOCCAL, BACTERIA AFFECTING THE THROAT (or see strip/ stripe)
strepdokokus,streptococcus
strepir,stripe(r) / strip(pper)
streptococcus,cal,BACTERIA AFFECTING THE THROAT
streptokokus,streptococcus
strepur,stripe(r) / strip(pper)
stres,stress
stresh,stretch

stress,sses,ssed,ssing,ssful,ssfully,ssless,sslessness, STRETCHED BEYOND NORMAL LIMIT OF ACCEPTANCE, CHALLENGE TO DEAL WITH "prefixes: pre/ un"
stret,street
stretch,hes,hed,hing,her,hability,hable,PULL AGAINST, EXTEND OUT/ BEYOND "prefixes: over/ up"
streu,strew
strew,*,wed,wing,wn,SCATTER/ SPREAD ABOUT
strewn,PAST TENSE FOR THE WORD "STREW", SCATTER/ THROW
striashen,striate(tion)
striate,*,ed,ting,tion,PARALLEL STREAKS/ SMEARS/ FURROWS "prefixes: un"
strichnine,strychnine
stricken,PAST TENSE FOR THE WORD "STRIKE", AFFLICTED WITH/ CHALLENGED, DEALT A BLOW (or see strike)
strict,ter,test,tly,tness,EXTREMELY FIRM/ GUARDED/ DISCIPLINED
stride,*,ed,rode,dden,ding,er,LARGE/ LONG STEPS, A TYPE OF GAIT WHEN WALKING "prefixes: over"
strife,eless,eful,OPPOSITION/ QUARREL/ CONFLICT (or see strive)
strikd,strict
strike,*,king,kingly,ruck,er,DEALT A SHARP/ FORCEFUL BLOW, TERM IN SPORTS, TO IGNITE (or see stricken) "prefixes: re"
striken,stricken
strikly,strict(ly)
striknine,strychnine
strikon,stricken
strikt,strict
strikun,stricken
strinewus,strenuous
string,*,ged,ging,ger,gy,THIN ROPE, LONG/ THIN/ TWISTED SUBSTANCE "prefixes: un"
stringensees,stringent(ncies)
stringent,tly,ncy,ncies,TO BE NARROW/ THIN/ BOUND/ TIGHT/ STRICT/ SEVERE
strength,strength
strinjint,stringent
strinkth,strength

strinth,strength
strinues,strenuous
strip,*,pped,pping,pper,TO REMOVE EXCESS/ EXTERNAL LAYER, REMOVE CLOTHES (or see stripe)
stripd,stripe(d) / strip(pped)
stripdokokus,streptococcus
stripe,*,ped,ping,per,py,pier,piest,THIN/ NARROW/ LONG UNIFORM SHAPE (or see strip)
stript,stripe(d) / strip(pped)
striptokokus,streptococcus
stripur,stripe(r) / strip(pper)
strite,stride
strive,*,ed,ving,WORK/ EXERT TO ACCOMPLISH A GOAL/ END RESULT (or see strife)
strivt,strive(d)
stro,straw
strobe,*,STROBOSCOPE, TYPE OF LIGHT
stroganoff,TYPE OF COOKED DISH WITH PASTA
stroginof,stroganoff
stroke,*,ed,king,er,FORCE/ BLOW TO MOVE SOMETHING, SWEEPING MOVEMENT, MEDICAL TERM "prefixes: up"
strol,stroll
stroler,stroll(er)
stroll,*,lled,lling,ller,A CASUAL GAIT IN WALKING, MOVE ABOUT WITH WHEELS
strolur,stroll(er)
strong,ger,gest,gly,gish,GREAT IN STRENGTH FORCE/ MASS/ POSITION/ MOVEMENT
strongist,strong(est)
strongur,strong(er)
stronkist,strong(est)
stronkur,strong(er)
stroodel,strudel
stroon,strewn
strope,strobe
strow,straw
stru,strew
struck,PAST TENSE FOR THE WORD "STRIKE", A SHARP/ FORCEFUL BLOW, TERM IN SPORTS, TO IGNITE
structure,*,ed,ring,reless,relessness,ral,rally,PLANNED/ SPECIFIC/ FORM/ SHAPE/ ARRANGEMENT, A DWELLING "prefixes: sub/ re/ un"

strudel, TYPE OF PASTRY
strudul, strudel
struen, strewn
strugel, struggle
struggle, *, ed, ling, er, TO RESIST/ FIGHT/ CONTEND WITH
strugle, struggle
strugul, struggle
struk, struck
strukcher, structure
strukel, struggle
strukle, struggle
struksher, structure
strukture, structure
strukul, struggle
strum, *, mmed, mming, mmer, USE FINGERS TO LIGHTLY TRAVEL OVER SEVERAL STRINGS OF AN INSTRUMENT
strumer, strum(mmer)
strun, strewn
strung, PAST TENSE FOR THE WORD STRING "prefixes: over/ un"
strut, *, tted, tting, A DEVICE USED TO BRACE/ SUPPORT, TO WALK WITH A PROUD GAIT
strutegek, strategic
strutejik, strategic
strutejikly, strategic(ally)
strutigekly, strategic(ally)
struz, strew(s)
stryate, striate
strychnine, POISON ORIGINATING FROM A PLANT
stryknine, strychnine
stu, stew
stualee, stool(ie)
stuardes, steward(ess)
stuart, steward
stuartes, steward(ess)
stub, *, bbed, bbing, bby, A KNOB/ STUMP, OF A THEATER TICKET, RECEIVE A STRIKING BLOW
stubble, *, ed, ly, SHORT STALKS THAT REMAIN AFTER CUTTING OFF TIP/ TOPS
stubborn, ner, nest, nly, ness, FIRMLY UNREASONABLE
stubed, stupid / stub(bbed)
stubee, stub(bby)

stubel, stubble
stubelidy, stability
stubelity, stability
stubern, stubborn
stubid, stupid
stubil, stubble
stubiledy, stability
stubility, stability
stubirn, stubborn
stuble, stubble
stuborn, stubborn
stubud, stupid
stubul, stubble
stuburn, stubborn
stucado, staccato / stoccado
stucato, staccato / stoccado
stucco, *, oed, oing, CEMENT/ PLASTER USED FOR WALL COVERING
stuch, stooge / stuck
stuck, PAST TENSE FOR THE WORD STICK "prefixes: un"
stuco, stucco
stucodo, staccato / stoccado
stucoto, staccato / stoccado
stud, *, dded, dding, STALLION, BREEDING MALE, BEAM/ POST/ BOARD IN WALLS/ ROOF OF A STRUCTURE (or see stew(ed)/ stood)
studar, stutter
stude, study
studed, study(died) / stud(dded)
studeis, studious
studens, student(s)
studeo, studio
studer, stutter
studes, study(dies)
studeus, studious
studid, study(died) / stud(dded)
studint, student
studio, *, SPACE/ ROOM FOR CREATING ARTWORK OF ANY MEDIUM
studious, sly, sness, DEVOTED TO GAINING KNOWLEDGE ABOUT SOMETHING "prefixes: un"

studir, stutter
studunt, student
studur, stutter
study, dies, died, ying, TAKE MENTAL NOTE OF, LEARN, READ UP ON, A ROOM TO READ/ WRITE "prefixes: un/ under"
stue, stew
stuel, stool
stuelee, stool(ie)
stuepiduty, stupid(ity)
stuerd, steward
stuerdes, steward(ess)
stuerdis, steward(ess)
stuf, stuff
stufee, stuff
stuff, *, ffed, ffing, ffy, ffier, ffiest, CRAM/ FORCE/ PACK SOMETHING INTO CONTAINMENT, REFERENCE TO A BUNCH OF THINGS, TIGHTLY CONFINED
stufy, stuff
stuge, stooge
stuil, stool
stuird, steward
stuirdes, steward(ess)
stuje, stooge
stuk, stuck
stukado, staccato / stoccado
stuko, stucco
stul, stool
stuledo, stiletto
stuleto, stiletto
stulie, stool(ie)
stulleto, stiletto
stumach, stomach
stumb, stump
stumbel, stumble
stumble, *, ed, ling, er, lingly, FAULTER/ TRIP/ BUMBLE/ FALL INTO
stumbul, stumble
stumek, stomach
stump, *, ed, ping, per, py, pier, piest, END OF SOMETHING WITH MAIN PART CUT OFF/ ELIMINATED/ REMOVED, TO BE AT A LOSS (or see stomp)

stumpee,stump
stumpul,stumble
stumuk,stomach
stun,*,nned,nning,nner,nningly,BE SURPRISED/ IMMOBILIZED EITHER PHYSICALLY/ MENTALLY/ PSYCHOLOGICALLY OR EMOTIONALLY
stund,stun(nned) / stunt
stunk,PAST TENSE FOR THE WORD "STINK", TO SMELL FOUL
stunt,*,ted,ting,tedness,A SHORT/ UNDEVELOPED/ QUICK ACT/ MOVEMENT, A STINT (or see stun(nned))
stuol,stool
stup,stoop
stupafid,stupefy(fied)
stupafie,stupefy
stuped,stupid / stub(bbed) / stoop(ed)
stupedity,stupid(ity)
stupee,stub(bby)
stupefy,fied,fying,fiedness,fyingly,faction,SHOCK/ OVERWHELM/ MAKE STUPID
stupendous,sly,sness,GREAT/ GRAND/ ASTONISHING
stupendus,stupendous
stuper,stupor
stupid,der,dest,dly,dness,dity,dities,BEHAVIOR GIVEN TO BE DULL/ BORING
stupify,stupefy
stupindus,stupendous
stupir,stupor
stupor,rous,MENTAL LACK OF STABILITY/ SENSIBILITY
stupt,stoop(ed) / stub(bbed)
stupufie,stupefy
stupy,stub(bby)
stur,stir
sturchan,sturgeon
sturdes,steward(ess) / steward(s)
sturdy,dier,diest,dily,diness,OF FIRM/ STABLE/ STRONG STATURE/ FORM
sturep,stirrup
sturgen,sturgeon
sturgeon,A FISH
sturgon,sturgeon
sturip,stirrup

sturjen,sturgeon
sturjun,sturgeon
sturling,sterling
sturn,stern
sturnem,sternum
sturnim,sternum
sturnly,stern(ly)
sturnness,stern(ess)
sturnum,sternum
sturor,stir(rrer)
sturty,sturdy
stuter,stutter
stutestiks,statistic(s)
stutir,stutter
stutistiks,statistic(s)
stutor,stutter
stutter,*,red,ring,rer,ringly,STAMMER/ REPEAT SECTIONS OF WORDS IN SPEAKING
stuwardes,steward(ess)
sty,ties,SWINE ENCLOSURE, EYE INFLAMMATION
style,*,ed,ling,er,eless,elessness,lish,lishly,lishness,list, listical,listically,lize,lization,lizer, MANNER OF FORM/ EXPRESSION OF THE ERA "prefixes: re"
styles,style(s) / stylus
stylest,style(list)
stylis,stylus
stylus,ses,POINTED INSTRUMENT FOR THE HAND TO USE FOR WRITING/ ENGRAVING/ DRAWING (or see style(list))
stymed,stymie(d)
stymie, *, ed, mying, A DIFFICULT SITUATION/ POSITION, BALL POSITION IN SPORTS
styn,stein
stype,stipe
styptic,cal,city,STOPS BLEEDING
styrafom,styrofoam
styrofoam,MANMADE SPONGEY MATERIAL WITH VARIOUS USES
styrufoam,styrofoam
su,sue / zoo
suad,suede / sway(ed) / swat
suade,suede / sway(ed)
suaf,suave

suafly,suave(ly)
suage,sewage
suaje,sewage
suar,sewer
suareje,sewer(age)
suaside,suicide
suasidul,suicide(dal)
suasite,suicide
suate,suede / sway(ed) / swat
suave,er,est,ely,eness,vity,SMOOTH, PLEASANT, SOPHISTICATED
suavidy,suave(vity)
suavly,suave(ly)
sub,*,SHORT FOR SUBSTITUTE/ SUBMARINE, TYPE OF SANDWICH, PREFIX INDICATING "BELOW/ UNDER/ NEAR/ IN PLACE OF SECONDARY" MOST OFTEN MODIFIES THE WORD
subchect,subject
subchugeit,subjugate
subcity,subsidy
subconchisly,subconscious(ly)
subconchus,subconscious
subconscious,sly,sness,NOT CONSCIOUS/ FULLY AWARE OF, UNDERLYING CONSCIOUSNESS
subconshes,subconscious
subconshus,subconscious
subcontract,*,ted,ting,tor,PERFORM UNDER ANOTHER PERSON'S CONTRACT
subdavaid,subdivide
subdavejen,subdivision
subdevaid,subdivide
subdevide,subdivide
subdevishen,subdivision
subdew,subdue
subdivide,*,ed,ding,dable,er,ision,TO DIVIDE UP INTO PARTS UNDER A CATEGORY
subdivision,*,HOUSING DEVELOPMENT
subdo,subdue
subdue,*,ed,uing,uer,ual,OVERCOME, OVERPOWER, INFLUENCE
subduvide,subdivide
subduvigun,subdivision
subduvishen,subdivision

subee, soup
suber, sup(pper) / super
superb, suburb / superb
suberbea, suburb(ia)
suberben, suburb(an)
superentendent, superintendent
supereur, superior
superfishul, superficial
superintendint, superintendent
subfert, subvert
subgegate, subjugate
subgekdif, subject(ive)
subgekt, subject
subgektive, subject(ive)
subgektivedy, subject(ivity)
subgigate, subjugate
subgugate, subjugate
subir, super / supper
subirb, suburb / superb
subirbea, suburb(ia)
subirben, suburb(an)
subirentendent, superintendent
subjagashen, subjugate(tion)
subjagate, subjugate
subjagation, subjugate(tion)
subject, *, ted, ting, tion, :ive, tively, tiveness, tivity, tivism, tivist, tivistic, UNDER RULE/ AUTHORITY/ SCRUTINY, OPEN TO CRITERIA
subjegate, subjugate
subjekt, subject
subjektef, subject(ive)
subjektivety, subject(ivity)
subjugate, *, ed, ting, tion, tor, tive, CONQUER/ DOMINATE/ ENSLAVE
subjugation, subjugate(tion)
subkonshus, subconscious
subkonshusly, subconscious(ly)
subkontrakt, subcontract
sublaim, sublime
sublamashen, sublime(mation)
sublamate, sublime(mate)
subleminaly, subliminal(ly)
subleminul, subliminal

sublimashen, sublime(mation)
sublime, er, est, ed, ming, ely, eness, er, mate, mation, mity, mities, minal, LOFTY/ ELEVATED/ SUPERIOR/ EXALTED/ HIGHER STATE OF BEING
sublimenaly, subliminal(lly)
sublimenul, subliminal
subliminal, lly, UNDERLYING, NOT FULLY AWARE OF
subllugeit, subjugate
sublumashen, sublime(mation)
sublyme, sublime
submareen, submarine
submaren, submarine
submarine, *, BULLET SHAPED OCEAN GOING VESSEL WHICH CAN SUBMERGE/ GO UNDER WATER
submechen, submission
submerge, *, ed, ging, gible, gence, rse, BE UNDER LIQUID
submerj, submerge
submerjebul, submerge(gable)
submerse, *, ed, sing, sible, sion, SURROUND WITH LIQUID "prefixes: semi"
submershen, submerse(sion)
submersible, submerse(sible)
submertion, submerse(sion)
submeshen, submission
submesif, submissive
submesive, submissive
submet, submit
submetid, submit(tted)
submetion, submission
submichen, submission
submirj, submerge
submirse, submerse
submirshen, submerse(sion)
submirtion, submerse(sion)
submisefly, submissive(ly)
submisevly, submissive(ly)
submishen, submission
submisive, submissive
submisivly, submissive(ly)
submission, *, RELINQUISH/ AGREE TO, ABIDE BY, UNDER THE AUTHORITY OF
submissive, ely, eness, ion, CAPABLE OF/ GIVEN TO SUBMIT/ COMPLY/ SURRENDER

submisuf, submissive
submit, *, tted, tting, ttal, ission, issive, TO COMPLY/ SURRENDER/ COMMIT/ YIELD
submitid, submit(tted)
submition, submission
submoren, submarine
submuren, submarine
submurg, submerge
submurj, submerge
submurjebul, submerge(gable)
submurs, submerse
submurshen, submerse(sion)
submurtion, submerse(sion)
subordenation, subordinate(tion)
subordenit, subordinate
subordinashen, subordinate(tion)
subordinate, *, ed, ting, ely, eness, tion, LESSER IN RANK/ ORDER/ SECONDARY/ DEPENDANT, BANKING TERM "prefixes: in"
subordnet, subordinate
subpenu, subpoena
subpoena, *, aed, aing, A LAWFUL PROCESS/ MANDATE TO CALL SOMEONE FORTH FOR INFORMATION
subregation, subrogate(tion)
subriedy, sobriety
subriety, sobriety
subrigate, subrogate
subrigation, subrogate(tion)
subriode, sobriety
subrogashen, subrogate(tion)
subrogate, *, ed, ting, tion, REPLACE/ SUBSTITUTE SOMEONE/ SOMETHING
subsadize, subsidy(dize)
subsaid, subside
subsaqwently, subsequent(ly)
subscraib, subscribe
subscrebshen, subscription
subscription, subscription
subscribe, *, ed, bing, er, iption, COMMIT PAYMENT TO RECEIVE SOMETHING, SIGNED STATEMENT "prefixes: over/ un"
subscribshen, subscription

subscription, *, AGREE TO COMMIT MONEY IN EXCHANGE FOR GOODS, SIGNATURE OF COMMITMENT
subsdanshul, substantial
subsdatushen, substitute(tion)
subsdents, substance
subsdratem, substrate(tum)
subsdutoot, substitute
subsdutushin, substitute(tion)
subsdutut, substitute
subsede, subsidy
subsedens, subsidy(dence)
subsediary, subsidiary
subsedize, subsidy(dize)
subsedy, subsidy
subsekwint, subsequent
subsekwintly, subsequent(ly)
subsequent, tly, nce, AFTER/ FOLLOWING IN A CERTAIN SEQUENCE/ ORDER
subseqwint, subsequent
subserveint, subservient
subserveintly, subservient(ly)
subserveints, subservient(nce)
subservient, tly, nce, FACILITATES PROMOTION OF/ ACT TO CREATE, TO SERVE
subsestense, subsistence
subsestinse, subsistence
subside, *, ed, ding, ence, TO SETTLE/ SINK/ FALL TO A LOWER LEVEL
subsidens, subsidy(dence)
subsidiary, ries, rily, AID/ ASSIST WITH A CONTRIBUTION
subsidy, dies, dize, dizes, dized, dizing, dization, dizer, ORGANIZATION/ GOVERNMENT WHO HELPS OTHERS BY PROVIDING MONEY/ SERVICES TOWARD OVERALL NEEDS OF SPECIFIC PEOPLE
subsikwent, subsequent
subsikwently, subsequent(ly)
subsirveins, subservient(nce)
subsirveint, subservient
subsistence, nt, BASIC FOUNDATION WHICH SUPPORTS LIFE
subsite, subside
subsitearee, subsidiary

subsitinse, subside(nce)
subsity, subsidy
subskrebshin, subscription
subskreption, subscription
subskrib, subscribe
subskripshen, subscription
subskription, subscription
substance, *, MATTER, FIRMNESS, REAL
substancheate, substantiate
substanchel, substantial
substanchely, substantial(lly)
substanchiative, substantiate(tive)
substanchil, substantial
substanchuly, substantial(lly)
substansheate, substantiate
substansheative, substantiate(tive)
substanshul, substantial
substantial, lly, lity, lness, OF ENOUGH, MORE THAN A LITTLE, REWARDING AMOUNT "prefixes: in/ un"
substantiate, *, ed, ting, tion, tive, OF SUBSTANCE, FACTUAL/ REAL "prefixes: un"
substashial, substantial
substatushen, substitute(tion)
substatute, substitute
substatution, substitute(tion)
substechuent, substituent
substense, substance
substetuent, substituent
substetute, substitute
substetution, substitute(tion)
substichuent, substituent
substinse, substance
substishuent, substituent
substitoot, substitute
substituent, *, REPLACE ONE PERSON FOR ANOTHER
substitushen, substitute(tion)
substitute, *, ed, ting, tion, table, tional, tionally, tionary, tive, tively, REPLACE ONE FOR ANOTHER
substrade, substrate
substradem, substrate(tum)
substrate, *, tum, tums, LAYER BELOW
substreit, substrate
substutushen, substitute(tion)

subsukwently, subsequent(ly)
subsuquently, subsequent(ly)
subsurveanse, subservient(nce)
subsurveint, subservient
subsurviently, subservient(ly)
subtavigen, subdivision
subtle, er, eness, ety, eties, ly, NOT OBVIOUS, SLIGHT HINT OF, SUGGESTIVE WITHOUT SPECIFICS
subtract, *, ted, ting, tion, ter, tive, TAKE AWAY FROM THE WHOLE/ ORIGINAL PART
subtrakshin, subtract(ion)
subtrakshun, subtract(ion)
subtrakt, subtract
subtraktion, subtract(ion)
subuei, subway
subur, super / supper
suburb, *, bia, ban, banite, banize, DISTRICT OUTSIDE OF MAJOR POPULATED AREA
suburbea, suburb(ia)
suburben, suburb(an)
suburintendent, superintendent
subversef, subversive
subvershen, subversion
subversion, sary, REMOVE THE BASIS/ FOUNDATION OF ANYTHING IN ORDER TO DESTROY IT
subversive, rsively, rsiveness, REMOVE THE BASIS/ FOUNDATION OF ANYTHING TO DESTROY IT
subvert, *, ted, ting, ter, rsive, REMOVE BASIS/ FOUNDATION OF ANYTHING IN ORDER TO DESTROY IT
subvertion, subversion
subvirsef, subversive
subvirshen, subversion
subvirsion, subversion
subvirt, subvert
subvursef, subversive
subvurshen, subversion
subvursive, subversive
subvurt, subvert
subvurtion, subversion
subwa, subway
subway, *, UNDERGROUND ELECTRIC TRAIN, A SANDWICH

subwei,subway
succeed,*,ded,ding,IMPROVE/ GAIN/ OVERCOME
succeses,success(es)
succesful,success(ful)
succesion,succession
success,es,ssful,ssfully,ssfulness,IMPROVING/ GAINING/ OVERCOMING/ ADVANCING "prefixes: un"
succession,nal,nally,SEQUENCE/ SERIES/ ONE AFTER THE OTHER OF SOMETHING/ SOMEONE
successive,ely,eness,FOLLOW IN ORDER WITHOUT INTERRUPTION
succinct,tly,tness,BRIEF/ SHORT/ SUMMARY
succor,rer,OFFER RELIEF/ SUPPORT/ AID IN TIME OF NEED (or see suck(er))
succsed,succeed
succulent,*,tly,nce,ncy,JUICY/ DELICIOUS TO THE PHYSICAL SENSES
succumb,*,bed,SURRENDER/ RETIRE TO,FALL FOR, YIELD/ GIVE WAY TO
sucdhen,suction
sucebdubility,susceptib e(bility)
sucede,secede
sucenct,succinct
suceptability,susceptible(bility)
suceptable,susceptible
sucer,succor / suck(er)
sucession,succession
such,USED TO MAKE A COMPARISON WITH SOMETHING IMPLIED BY CONTEXT
sucher,suture / suck(er)
suchur,suture / suck(er)
sucinct,succinct
sucjestion,suggest(ion)
suck,*,ked,king,ker,FORCEFULLY PULL/ DRAW SOMETHING AWAY FROM ITS SOURCE,A FISH, LOLLIPOP (or see succor)
suckle,*,ed,ling,THE ACT OF BREAST FEEDING
suckshun,suction
sucol,suckle
sucom,succumb
sucor,succor / suck(er)
sucour,succor / suck(er)
sucreshen,secrete(tion)

sucrete,secrete
sucretion,secrete(tion)
sucrose,SUGAR OBTAINED FROM PLANTS
sucsashen,succession
sucseed,succeed
succses,success
succsesful,success(ful)
sucseshon,succession
sucsesif,successive
sucsesiflee,successive(ly)
sucsetion,succession
sucsid,succeed
sucsinkt,succinct
suction,FORCEFULLY DRAW SOMETHING FROM ITS SOURCE, CREATE A VACUUM/ ADHERENCE
suculent,succulent
suculint,succulent
succumb,succumb
sucure,secure
sucurity,secure(rity)
sucurly,secure(ly)
sud,sue(d) / suds / suit
sudan,sedan
sudanem,pseudonym
sudanim,pseudonym
sudar,suitor
sudashen,sedate(tion)
sudasion,sedate(tion)
sudate,sedate
sudation,sedate(tion)
sudden,nly,nness,IMMEDIATELY,NO TIME LAPSE
sude,sue(d) / soot
suden,sudden
sudenim,pseudonym
sudenly,sudden(ly)
suder,suitor
sudews,seduce
sudin,sudden
sudinem,pseudonym
sudinly,sudden(ly)
sudir,suitor
sudn,sudden
sudo,pseudo

sudon,sudden
sudonem,pseudonym
sudonim,pseudonym
sudonly,sudden(ly)
sudoose,seduce
sudor,suitor
suds,sy,BUBBLES,FOAMY,LATHER,FROTH
suducshen,seduce(ction)
suductive,seduce(ctive)
suduktion,seduce(ction)
suduktive,seduce(ctive)
sudun,sudden
sudunly,sudden(ly)
suduse,seduce
sudy,soot
sue,*,ed,uing,LEGALLY ATTEMPT TO FORCE SOMEONE TO PAY MONEY FOR A WRONGDOING
suech,sewage
suecher,suture
suede,LEATHER (or see sway(ed))
suege,sewage
sueid,suede
sueje,sewage
suell,sewage
suenome,tsunami
suer,sewer
suereje,sewer(age)
sueside,suicide
suesidul,suicide(dal)
suesite,suicide
suet,PART OF ANIMALS WHICH YIELDS TALLOW (or see suit/ sweet)
sufais,suffice
sufait,zoophyte
sufaneer,souvenir
sufaree,safari
sufary,safari
sufecashen,suffocate(tion)
sufecate,suffocate
sufecation,suffocate(tion)
sufeer,severe
sufeerly,severe(ly)
sufekashen,suffocate(tion)

sufekate, suffocate
sufeks, suffix
sufeneer, souvenir
sufer, suffer / severe
suferd, suffer(ed)
sufere, severe
suferly, severe(ly)
sufestikashen, sophisticate(tion)
sufestikated, sophisticate(d)
sufestikation, sophisticate(tion)
sufex, suffix
suffais, suffice
suffer, *, red, ring, rable, rableness, rably, rer, rance, REACTION TO PAIN/ INFLICTION "prefixes: in"
suffice, ed, cing, cient, SUFFICIENT, ADEQUATE, SATISFIED
sufficent, sufficient
sufficient, tly, ncy, ENOUGH, ADEQUATE, SATISFIED "prefixes: in"
suffishent, sufficient
suffix, xes, xed, xal, xally, xion, xation, AN END ATTACHED TO A WORD/ SOMETHING
suffocate, *, ed, ting, tion, tive, tingly, SMOTHER, CHOKE OFF, REMOVE OXYGEN
suffrage, ette, gist, VOTING AND RIGHTS TO VOTE
suficashen, suffocate(tion)
suficate, suffocate
sufication, suffocate(tion)
sufice, suffice
suficent, sufficient
sufichent, sufficient
suficiently, sufficient(ly)
sufikashen, suffocate(tion)
sufikate, suffocate
sufikation, suffocate(tion)
sufiks, suffix
sufiksis, suffix(es)
sufir, suffer / severe
sufird, suffer(ed)
sufirly, severe(ly)
sufise, suffice
sufishent, sufficient
sufishintly, sufficient(ly)

sufishunt, sufficient
sufistakashen, sophisticate(tion)
sufistakation, sophisticate(tion)
sufix, suffix
sufixes, suffix(es)
sufla, souffle'
suflay, souffle
sufocashen, suffocate(tion)
sufocate, suffocate
sufocation, suffocate(tion)
sufokeit, suffocate
sufor, suffer
suford, suffer(ed)
suforeg, suffrage
sufr, suffer
sufrage, suffrage
sufragist, suffrage(gist)
sufraje, suffrage
sufranse, suffer(ance)
sufrech, suffrage
sufreje, suffrage
sufrige, suffrage
sufrigest, suffrage(gist)
sufrije, suffrage
sufrinse, suffer(ance)
sufrugist, suffrage(gist)
sufucashen, suffocate(tion)
sufukate, suffocate
sufukation, suffocate(tion)
sufuner, souvenir
sufuqeit, suffocate
sufur, suffer
sufurd, suffer(ed)
sugar, *, rless, red, ry, rless, SUCROSE, SUBSTANCE OBTAINED FROM PLANTS "prefixes: non"
sugchestshen, suggest(ion)
suger, sugar
sugest, suggest
suggesdiv, suggest(ive)
suggest, *, ted, ting, ter, tion, tive, tively, tiveness, tible, OFFER A FACT/ THEORY TO BE CONSIDERED
suggestshen, suggest(ion)
sugiesdiv, suggest(ive)

sugjesgen, suggest(ion)
sugjest, suggest
suggestion, suggest(ion)
suggestive, suggest(ive)
sugjieschen, suggest(ion)
sugllest, suggest
sugnefakent, significant
sugnifukent, significant
suicide, *, dal, dally, TAKE ONE'S OWN LIFE
suicidul, suicide(dal)
suige, sewage
suir, sewer
suireje, sewer(age)
suisaid, suicide
suiside, suicide
suisidul, suicide(dal)
suisite, suicide
suit, *, ted, ting, table, tability, tableness, tably, PANTS/ JACKET SET, IN A CARD GAME, PROPER/ AGREEABLE/ FITTING (or see suite/ sweet) "prefixes: un"
suite, *, TYPE OF ROOM (too many definitions, please consult standard dictionary) (or see suit/ sweet)
suitor, *, ONE WHO SUES, MAN COURTING A WOMAN
sujest, suggest
suk, suck
sukal, suckle
sukchen, suction
sukchest, suggest
sukchun, suction
sukel, suckle
suker, succor / suck(er)
sukeurly, secure(ly)
sukewlent, succulent
sukewlunt, succulent
sukewr, secure
sukewrity, secure(rity)
sukgeshin, suggest(ion)
sukgest, suggest
sukgestion, suggest(ion)
sukgestshen, suggest(ion)
sukiatrist, psychiatry(rist)
sukiatry, psychiatry
sukil, suckle

sukini,zuchinni	suleks,select(s)	sulitefy,solid(ify)
sukir,succor / suck(er)	sulekshen,select(ion)	sulivu,saliva
sukiulent,succulent	sulekt,select	**sulk**,*, ked,king,ky,kier,kiest,kily,kiness,UPSET AT NOT GETTING ENOUGH ATTENTION,REACTION TO BEING OFFENDED
sukiutrest,psychiatry(rist)	sulektion,select(ion)	
sukjesdev,suggest(ive)	sulektive,select(ive)	
sukjest,suggest	sulektof,select(ive)	sulkey,sulk
sukjestion,suggest(ion)	suleluquy,soliloquy	**sullen**,nly,nness,ALONE/ GLOOMY/ DISMAL
sukjestshen,suggest(ion)	sulen,sullen	sulomee,salami
sukle,suckle	sulenity,saline(nity)	sulon,salon
sukluded,seclude(d)	sulenium,selenium	suloon,saloon
suklusion,seclusion	sulerium,solarium	suloot,salute
suklusive,seclusive	sulesit,solicit	sulowl,salal
sukol,suckle	sulesitation,solicit(ation)	sulphade,sulfate
sukor,succor / suck(er)	sulesiter,solicit(er)	sulphate,sulfate
sukour,succor / secure ; suck(er)	sulesteul,celestial	sulpher,sulfur
sukqulent,succulent	sulewshen,solution	sulpherik,sulfur(ic)
sukreshen,secrete(tion)	sulewtion,solution	sulphide,sulfide
sukresion,secrete(tion)	sulfade,sulfate	sulphir,sulfur
sukrete,secrete	sulfaid,sulfide	sulphurek,sulfur(ic)
sukrose,sucrose	**sulfate**,*, ed,ting,ALSO SULPHATE,A SULFURIC ACID SALT "prefixes: bi"	**sultan**,*,nic,DOMESTICATED FOWL,DESPOT/ TYRANT
suksed,succeed		sultin,sultan
sukses,success	sulfats,sulfate(s)	sultree,sultry
suksesful,success(ful)	sulfer,sulfur	**sultry**,rily,riness,SWEATY/ HEAVY/ HOT, OVERPOWERING COMBINATION
sukseshen,succession	sulferik,sulfur(ic)	
suksesif,successive	**sulfide**,*, A SULFUR CHEMICAL COMPOUND "prefixes: bi"	sultun,sultan
suksesiflee,successive(lv)		sulun,sullen / saloon
sukshen,suction	sulfir,sulfur	sulushen,solution
sukshun,suction	sulfirek,sulfur(ic)	sulute,salute
sukul,suckle	**sulfite**,*, tic,A SULFUR CHEMICAL COMPOUND "prefixes: bi"	sulution,solution
sukulent,succulent		**sum**,*, mmed,mming,mmation,mmational,mmary, TOTAL OF,ALTOGETHER (or see zoom)
sukum,succumb	**sulfur**,ric,rize,rous,rously,ALSO SULPHUR, NONMETALLIC ELEMENT "prefixes: de"	
sukur,suck(er) / succor / secure		sumachin,sum(mmation)
sukurity,secure(rity)	sulfurik,sulfur(ic)	suman,summon
sukwenshul,sequence(ntial)	sulicit,solicit	sumantics,semantics
sukwential,sequence(ntial)	sulicitation,solicit(ation)	sumarely,summary(rily)
sukwoya,sequoia	suliciter,solicit(er)	sumarize,summary(rize)
sulal,salal	sulidefy,solid(ify)	sumaruly,summary(rily)
sulami,salami	sulilakwee,soliloquy	sumary,summary / summer
sulareum,solarium	sulin,sullen	sumashen,sum(mmation)
suldree,sultry	sulinidy,saline(nity)	sumation,sum(mmation)
sulebrity,celebrity	sulisetation,solicit(ation)	sumb,sump
sulective,select(ive)	sulisit,solicit	sumbreo,sombrero
suledify,solid(ify)	sulisiter,solicit(er)	sumbrero,sombrero

sumchewus,sumptuous
sumchuis,sumptuous
sumd,sum(mmed)
sumding,something
sumedul,summit(ttal)
sumen,summon
sumener,summon(er)
sument,cement
sumer,summer
sumerily,summary(rily)
sumerise,summary(rize)
sumersolt,somersault
sumeruly,summary(rily)
sumery,summary / summer
sumesder,semester
sumester,semester
sumet,summit / submit
sumetal,summit(ttal)
sumetrek,symmetry(ric)
sumetri,zoometry
sumetric,symmetry(ric)
sumfing,something
sumidul,summit(ttal)
sumin,summon
sumint,cement
sumir,summer
sumiry,summary / summer
sumit,summit / submit
sumitul,summit(ttal)
summary,ries,rize,rizes,rized,rizing,rizer,rist,rily,riness, CONCISE/ SIMPLIFIED SHORT VERSION
summen,summon
summer, *,red,ring,rly,ry,SEASON FROM JUNE THROUGH SEPTEMBER
summin,summon
summit, *, THE HIGHEST PART/ PEAK/ POINT/ RANK OF (or see submit)
summon, *,,ned,ning,ner,TO PETITION/ CALL/ SEND/ ORDER FOR ATTENDANCE
sumon,summon
sumoner,summon(er)
sumorfic,zoomorphic

sump,DEPRESSION WHERE POOL OF LIQUID CAN COLLECT
sumpchewus,sumptuous
sumpshues,sumptuous
sumptues,sumptuous
sumptuous,sly,sness,IMPRESSIVE,LUXURIOUS, MAGNIFICENT
sumshuis,sumptuous
sumt,sum(mmed)
sumtain,sometime
sumteng,something
sumthing,something
sumtime,sometime
sumting,something
sumur,summer
sumuree,summary / summer
sumurees,summary(ries)
sumurize,summary(rize)
sumursolt,somersault
sumury,summary / summer
sumut,summit / submit
sumware,somewhere
sumwat,somewhat
sumwer,somewhere
sumwhat,somewhat
sumwhere,somewhere
sumwot,somewhat
sumwut,somewhat
sun, *, nned,nning,nny,SOLAR PLANET THAT ALL PLANETS IN THE SYSTEM REVOLVE AROUND (or see son/ sunn/ soon)
sunada,sonata
suname,tsunami
sunapsis,synapsis
sunaptek,synaptic
sunaptic,synaptic
sunareo,scenario
sunatu,sonata
sunc,sung / sunk
sunda,sunday
sunday, *, A DAY OF THE WEEK (ENGLISH)
sundei,Sunday
sundiket,syndicate

sundree,sundry
sundres,sundry(ries)
sundry,ries,MANY SMALL THINGS
sundukit,syndicate
sune,sun(nny) / son
sunelity,senile(lity)
sunereo,scenario
sunerist,scenario(ist)
sung,PAST TENSE FOR THE WORD 'SING' "prefixes: un"
sunility,senile(lity)
sunk,PAST TENSE FOR THE WORD 'SINK'
sunn,A SHRUB (or see sun/ son)
sunoda,sonata
sunografee,scenography
sunome,tsunami
sunonimus,synonym(ous)
sunopsis,synopsis
sunota,sonata
sunseer,sincere
sunseerly,sincere(ly)
suntree,sundry
suny,sun(nny) / son
suoge,sewage
suografi,zoography
suor,sewer
suosidel,suicide(dal)
suove,suave
sup, *, pped,pping,pper,SHORT FOR HAVING SUPPER/ DINNER,TO SIP (or see sub/ soup)
supal,supple
suparlatif,superlative
suparstishus,superstitious
supasetory,suppository
supasition,supposition
supasitory,suppository
supausatory,suppository
supazeshen,supposition
supazishen,supposition
supcity,subsidy
supconchesly,subconscious(ly)
supconshus,subconscious
supcontrakt,subcontract
supdavide,subdivide

supdavijin,subdivision	supervishen,supervise(sion)	suple,supple
supdevid,subdivide	supervizury,supervise(sory)	suplement,supplement
supdevide,subdivide	supesition,supposition	suplementul,supplement(al)
supdew,subdue	supgekt,subject	suplemint,supplement
supdo,subdue	supgektif,subject(ive)	supleminul,subliminal
supdu,subdue	supil,supple	supli,supply
supduvide,subdivide	supina,subpoena	suplier,supply(lier)
supe,soup	supir,sup(pper) / super	suplime,sublime
supel,supple	supirb,suburb / superb	supliment,supplement
supenu,subpoena	supirblee,superb(ly)	suplimentul,supplement(al)
super,rable,rably,rableness,GREAT/ EXCESSIVE/ HIGH UP/ STRONG, PREFIX INDICATING "OVER/ ABOVE/ TO A VERY HIGH DEGREE" MOST OFTEN MODIFIES THE WORD (or see supper)	superintendent,superintendent	suplimenul,subliminal
	supireority,superior(ity)	suplument,supplement
	supireur,superior	suplumentul,supplement(al)
	supirfichul,superficial	suply,supply
	supirfishul,superficial	suplyer,supply(lier)
superb,bly,bness,GRAND/ SPLENDID (or see suburb)	supirflewus,superfluous	supmareen,submarine
superbea,suburb(ia)	supirfluis,superfluous	supmaren,submarine
superentendent,superintendent	supirlatif,superlative	supmerg,submerge
supereoredy,superior(ity)	supirlative,superlative	supmerjebul,submerge(gable)
supereority,superior(ity)	supirlutif,superlative	supmerse,submerse
supereur,superior	supirsdishen,superstition	supmersible,submerse(sible)
superfichul,superficial	supirsteshus,superstitious	supmet,submit
superficial,lity,lities,lly,lness,UNREAL/ ILLUSION/ FAUX/ FALSE LAYER	supirstition,superstition	supmeted,submit(tted)
	supireveshin,supervise(sion)	supmichen,submission
	supirvise,supervise	supmirj,submerge
superfishul,superficial	supirvisery,supervise(ry)	supmit,submit
superflewus,superfluous	supirvishen,supervise(sion)	supmited,submit(tted)
superflues,superfluous	supirvision,supervise(sion)	supmureen,submarine
superfluous,sly,sness,EXCESS	supizeshen,supposition	supmurg,submerge
superintendent,*,ONE WHO OVERSEES/ MANAGES	supjekt,subject	supmurjebul,submerge(gable)
superior,*,rity,rly,RANK/ AUTHORITY OVER ANOTHER, ELEVATED, BETTER QUALITY/ GRADE	supjektid,subject(ed)	supmurs,submerse
	supjektif,subject(ive)	supmursabul,submerse(sible)
superiordy,superior(ity)	supkonchisly,subconscious(ly)	supmurshen,submerse(sion)
superlatif,superlative	supkonchus,subconscious	supol,supple
superlative,*,ely,eness,SURPASSES ALL DEGREES/ RANK BY COMPARISON	supkonsheshly,subconscious(ly)	supor,super / supper
	supkonshus,subconscious	supordenate,subordinate
superlutif,superlative	supkontrakt,subcontract	supordinet,subordinate
supersdishen,superstition	suplai,supply	supordunet,subordinate
supersteshus,superstitious	suplamashen,sublime(mation)	suport,support
superstition,*,ous,ALLOW SOMETHING SEEMINGLY IRRATIONAL TO FORETELL FUTURE EVENTS	suplament,supplement	suportef,support(ive)
	suplamentul,supplement(al)	suportive,support(ive)
superstitious,sly,sness,ALLOW SOMETHING SEEMINGLY IRRATIONAL TO FORETELL FUTURE EVENTS	suplamint,supplement	supervise,supervise
	suplant,supplant	supose,suppose
supervise,*,ed,sing,sor,sory,sion,PROVIDE OVERSIGHT/ DIRECTION TO OTHERS		

Word	Spelling variants / definitions
suposetory, suppository	
suposidly, suppose(dly)	
suposition, supposition	
supository, suppository	
suposubly, suppose(dly)	
supozatory, suppository	
supoze, suppose	
supozeshin, supposition	
supozetory, suppository	
supozitory, suppository	
supozubly, suppose(dly)	
supper, DINNER, MEAL IN EVENING (or see super)	
supplament, supplement	
supplamentul, supplement(al)	
supplant, *, ted, ting, tation, ter, FORCEFUL/ UNDERHANDED REMOVAL OF SOMETHING/ SOMEONE	
supple, ely, ly, eness, FLEXIBLE/ GRACEFULLY CONFORMING (or see supply)	
supplement, *, ted, ting, tal, tary, tation, IN ADDITION TO THE BASIC	
supplimentul, supplement(al)	
supplument, supplement	
supplumentul, supplement(al)	
supply, lies, lied, lying, lier, SUPPORT/ PROVIDE GOODS/ SERVICES	
support, *, ted, ting, tive, tively, tiveness, ter, table, tably, TO ENABLE/ EMPOWER/ SUSTAIN/ ASSIST/ STRUCTURE SOMETHING OR SOMEONE "prefixes: in/un"	
suppose, *, ed, sing, edly, sable, sably, PROPOSE/ SUGGEST/ IMPLY AS TO THE WAY SOMETHING COULD BE "prefixes: pre"	
supposition, *, nal, nally, ous, ously, ive, HYPOTHESIS/ ASSUMPTION	
suppository, ries, PREPARATION FOR INSERTION INTO ORIFICE ON THE LOWER HALF OF THE BODY	
suppreshun, suppress(ion)	
suppresion, suppress(ion)	
suppress, sses, ssed, ssing, ssible, ssor, ssion, ssive, ssant, PREVENT/ RESTRAIN	
suprechen, suppress(ion)	
supreem, supreme	
supremacy, macist, BELIEVES THEY ARE SUPERIOR OVER OTHERS	
supremasist, supremacy(cist)	
supreme, ely, eness, HIGHEST OF QUALITY/ DEGREE	
supremusee, supremacy	
supremusist, supremacy(cist)	
supremusy, supremacy	
supreno, soprano	
supres, suppress	
supreshen, suppress(ion)	
supress, suppress	
supression, suppress(ion)	
supretion, suppress(ion)	
suprino, soprano	
suprogate, subrogate	
supriveshin, supervise(sion)	
suprvishen, supervise(sion)	
supsaid, subside	
supsakwently, subsequent(ly)	
supscrepshon, subscription	
supsdents, substance	
supsditushen, substitute(tion)	
supsedy, subsidy	
supsekwent, subsequent	
supsekwint, subsequent	
supsekwintly, subsequent(ly)	
supseqwint, subsequent	
supserveint, subservient	
supsestinse, subsistence	
supside, subside	
supsideary, subsidiary	
supsidinse, subside(nce)	
supsikwent, subsequent	
supsikwently, subsequent(ly)	
supsirveint, subservient	
supsistense, subsistence	
supsite, subside	
supskrepshen, subscription	
supskrib, subscribe	
supskription, subscription	
supstanchily, substantial(lly)	
supstans, substance	
supstansheate, substantiate	
supstanshol, substantial	
supstanshul, substantial	
supstanshulee, substantial(lly)	
supstantiate, substantiate	
supstatoot, substitute	
supstatushen, substitute(tion)	
supstense, substance	
supstetoot, substitute	
supstichuent, substituent	
supstinse, substance	
supstishuent, substituent	
supstitoot, substitute	
supstitushen, substitute(tion)	
supstitute, substitute	
supstradem, substrate(tum)	
supstrate, substrate	
supstratem, substrate(tum)	
supsurveint, subservient	
suptract, subtract	
suptrakchin, subtract(ion)	
suptrakshun, subtract(ion)	
suptrakt, subtract	
supul, supple	
supur, super / supper	
supurb, suburb / superb	
supurblee, superb(ly)	
supurfichul, superficial	
supurfishul, superficial	
suprintendent, superintendent	
supurlative, superlative	
supurlutif, superlative	
supurstishus, superstitious	
supurstition, superstition	
supurveshin, supervise(sion)	
supurvise, supervise	
supurvision, supervise(sion)	
supusition, supposition	
supuzishen, supposition	
supvert, subvert	
supvurt, subvert	
supwa, subway	
supy, soup	
suqiulent, succulent	

suquential,sequence(ntial)
suquir,secure
suquirity,secure(ly)
suquirly,secure(ly)
suqulent,succulent
sur, PREFIX INDICATING "OVER/ ABOVE/ TO A VERY HIGH DEGREE," MOST OFTEN MODIFIES THE WORD (or see sir/ sure)
suraget,surrogate
suragit,surrogate
suramik,ceramic
suran,saran
surape,serape
suratid,serrate(d)
suraund,surround
surbent,serpent
surcal,circle
surcas,circus
surcel,circle
surces,circus
surch,serge / surge / search
surchacol,surgical
surchan,surgeon
surcharge, *, ed, ging, AN EXCESS CHARGE, TAX OVER AND ABOVE THE NORM
surchari,surgery
surcharj,surcharge
surches,search(es) / surge(s)
surchon,surgeon
surchuble,search(able)
surcle,circle
surcol,circle
surcumcise,circumcise
surcumfirense,circumference
surcut,circuit
sure, er, est, ely, eness, MOST CERTAINLY, OF COURSE, INEVITABLE, CONFIDENTLY (or see surly) "prefixes: en/ un"
sureal,surreal
surealism,surrealism
suree,surrey
surej,surrey
sureilisum,surrealism

surel,sorrel / surreal
surelism,surrealism
surender,surrender
surene,serene
surenge,syringe
surenidy,serene(nity)
surenity,serene(nity)
surenje,syringe
sureolesum,surrealism
surety, ties, ONE WHO IS BOUND/ LIABLE/ RESPONSIBLE
sureulist,surrealism(st)
sureulizum,surrealism
surf, *, fed, fing, fable, fer, fy, WHERE OCEANS WAVES BREAK, CRUISE THE INTERNET/ TV (or see serf/ serve)
surface, *, ed, cing, eless, er, ficial, TOP/ EXTERNAL/ OUTSIDE PORTION OF (or see service) "prefixes: bio/ re/ sub/ under"
surfase,surface
surfd,surf(ed)
surfeje,serf(age)
surfent,servant
surfes,surface
surfibul,surf(able)
surfis,surface / service
surft,serve(d) / surf(ed)
surfunt,servant
surfur,surf(er)
surg,surge
surgakle,surgical
surgaree,surgery
surgarge,surcharge
surgd,surge(d)
surge, *, ed, ging, ENERGETIC SWELLING/ BURST/ FLUCTUATION OF SOMETHING (or see search(ed)) "prefixes: re/ up"
surgen,surgeon
surgent, UPRISING, SWELLING, STRONG FLUCTUATION
surgeon, *, ncy, ncies, DOCTOR WHO PERFORMS SURGICAL PROCEDURES (or see sergeant)
surgery, ries, PERFORM A MEDICAL OPERATION "prefixes: bio"

surgical, lly, ASSOCIATED WITH MEDICAL OPERATIONS
surgikul,surgical
surgin,surgeon
surgint,surgent / sergeant
surgis,surge(s)
surgon,surgeon
surgree,surgery
surgukle,surgical
suriasis,psoriasis
suringe,syringe
surinje,syringe
surjakle,surgical
surjaree,surgery
surje,surge
surjen,surgeon
surjent,surgent / sergeant
surjikul,surgical
surjon,surgeon
surjree,surgery
surjukle,surgical
surkawfigus,sarcophagus
surkewlate,circulate
surkofegus,sarcophagus
surkulir,circular
surkumfurens,circumference
surkumstans,circumstance
surkus,circus
surlee,surly
surlleri,surgery
surllical,surgical
surllon,surgeon
surloen,sirloin
surloin,sirloin
surly, lier, liest, liness, ROUGH/ RUDE (or see sure(lly))
surmais,surmise
surmin,sermon
surmise, *, ed, sing, ASSUME/ GUESS
surmize,surmise
surmon,sermon
surogate,surrogate
surogeit,surrogate
surong,sarong
surope,serape

suroredy, sorority
surority, sorority
suround, surround
surownd, surround
surpass, sses, ssed, ssing, ssable, ssingly, GO BEYOND EXPECTATIONS
surpent, serpent
surpentene, serpentine
surpint, serpent
surpintene, serpentine
surplus, ses, sage, MORE THAN NEEDED/ NECESSARY, OVERABUNDANCE
surprais, surprise
surprise, *, ed, sing, sal, ser, singly, UNEXPECTEDLY SHOWING UP/ APPEARING/ OCCURRING "prefixes: un"
surprize, surprise
surrated, serrate(d)
surreal, lism, list, listic, listically, lism, NOT OF THIS PLANE/ WORLD, UNREAL, TIME PERIOD IN ART
surrealism, NOT OF THIS PLANE/ WORLD, UNREAL, TIME PERIOD IN ART
surrender, *, red, ring, GIVE UP, RELINQUISH POWER
surrey, SMALL HORSE DRAWN CARRIAGE
surrogate, *, ed, ting, TO SUBSTITUTE SOMEONE AND THEIR DUTIES
surround, *, ded, ding, ENCOMPASS/ ENCIRCLE/ ENCLOSE AROUND
surry, surrey
surtatude, certitude
surten, certain
surthener, south(erner)
surtifecate, certificate
surtify, certify
surva, survey
survaiv, survive
survalinse, surveillance
survas, survey(s) / service
survatood, servitude
survatude, servitude
survaur, survey(or)
survayer, survey(or)
survd, serve(d)

surveilance, surveillance
surveillance, nt, OBSERVE/ WATCH OVER SOMEONE/ SOMETHING, SPYING
survent, servant
surveor, survey(or)
surves, service
survesable, service(cable)
survey, *, yed, ying, yor, TO CAPTURE FACTS/ VIEW/ DOCUMENT AN AREA/ SITUATION
survife, survive
surviks, cervix
survint, servant
survis, service
survisable, service(cable)
survive, *, ed, ving, val, vor, REMAIN ALIVE AFTER A TRAGIC/ SOLEMN EVENT
survivul, survive(val)
survont, servant
survunt, servant
survus, service
sury, surrey
suryical, surgical
suryon, surgeon
suryuri, surgery
susaptible, susceptible
susbect, suspect
susbend, suspend
susbenders, suspender(s)
susbind, suspend
susbinded, suspend(ed)
susbinders, suspender(s)
susceptible, eness, ly, bility, PRONE/ LIKELY/ GIVEN TO BE AFFECTED "prefixes: in"
susceptive, eness, vity, ible, ABLE/ LIKELY TO BE AFFECTED "prefixes: non/ un"
suscinkt, succinct
susdan, sustain
susdanuble, sustain(able)
susdeninse, sustenance
susdinense, sustenance
susede, secede
susenked, succinct
susenktly, succinct(ly)

susceptibility, susceptible(bility)
susceptible, susceptible
suseptif, susceptive
suseptive, susceptive
suseptuble, susceptible
suseptuf, susceptive
suseshen, secession
susesion, secession
susete, secede
sush, such
susiadul, society(tal)
susiete, society
susietul, society(tal)
susiety, society
susinkt, succinct
susinktly, succinct(ly)
susiudil, society(tal)
susiuty, society
suspect, *, ted, ting, LIKELY TO BE INVOLVED IN AN EVENT "prefixes: un"
suspekt, suspect
suspenchen, suspension
suspend, *, ded, ding, der, nsion, TEMPORARILY BAR/ RELIEVE/ REMOVE FROM DUTY, HANG IN THE AIR
suspender, *, SHOULDER HOLDERS FOR PANTS, ONE WHO SUSPENDS
suspense, eful, sive, sively, siveness, TO WAIT WITH UNCERTAINTY
suspensful, suspense(ful)
suspenshen, suspension
suspension, HANGING/ FLOATING IN LIQUID
suspent, suspend
suspention, suspension
suspeshen, suspicion
suspeshesly, suspicious(ly)
suspeshus, suspicious
suspicion, *, ous, SUSPECT TO/ OF, TO SUPPOSE WITHOUT CLEAR EVIDENCE
suspicious, sly, sness, SUSPECT, TO SUPPOSE WITHOUT CLEAR EVIDENCE
suspind, suspend
suspinder, suspender
suspinse, suspense

suspinsful,suspense(full)
suspinshen,suspension
suspintion,suspension
suspishes,suspicious
suspishesly,suspicious(ly)
suspishun,suspicion
suspitious,suspicious
sustain,*,ned,ning,nab e,ner,nment,tenance,ENDURE/ CONFIRM
sustane,sustain
sustanense,sustenance
sustanible,sustain(able)
sustanuble,sustain(able)
sustenance,BASIC PROVISIONS FOR SURVIVAL
susteninse,sustenance
sustunense,sustenance
sut,soot / suit / suite
sutal,subtle
sutaltee,subtle(ty)
sutanic,satanic
sutanikul,satanic(al)
sutar,suitor
sutcher,suture
sutchur,suture
sutel,subtle
suteltee,subtle(ty)
suten,sudden
sutenly,sudden(ly)
suter,suitor
suterical,satire(rical)
suth,soothe
sutherly,south(erly)
suthern,south(ern)
suthirnur,south(erner)
suthurn,south(ern)
sutil,subtle
sutiltee,subtle(ty)
sutin,sudden
sutinly,sudden(ly)
sutir,suitor
sutle,subtle
sutly,subtle(ly)
suto,pseudo

sutol,subtle
sutoltee,subtle(ty)
sutomi,zootomy
suton,sudden
sutonem,pseudonym
sutonim,pseudonym
sutor,suitor
suts,suds
sutultee,subtle(ty)
sutun,sudden
sutunly,sudden(ly)
suture,*,ed,ring,rally,USED TO STITCH A WOUND CLOSED
suty,soot
suvana,savanna
suvaner,souvenir
suvant,savant
suvear,severe
suvearly,severe(ly)
suveleun,civilian
suveneer,souvenir
suvere,severe
suverity,severe(rity)
suverly,severe(ly)
suviner,souvenir
suvire,severe
suvont,savant
suvuneer,souvenir
suvunir,souvenir
suwar,sewer
suwaro,saguaro
suwer,sewer
suwerige,sewer(age)
suwero,saguaro
suwir,sewer
suworo,saguaro
suwrench,syringe
suwurege,sewer(age)
svenks,sphinx
svenkter,sphincter
svenx,sphinx
svinks,sphinx
svinktur,sphincter

svinx,sphinx
swa,sway
swab,*,bbed,bbing,ABSORBENT MATERIAL TO DAB/ MOP/ CLEAN (or see swap)
swabed,swap(pped) / swab(bbed)
swabt,swap(pped) / swab(bbed)
swach,swatch
swad,suede / sway(ed)
swaddle,ed,ling,TO WRAP WITH STRIPS OF CLOTH
swade,suede / sway(ed)
swadul,swaddle
swae,sway
swaf,suave
swafly,suave(ly)
swag,*,gged,gging,HANG LOOSE (or see swage)
swage,ed,ging,BLACKSMITHS TOOL (or see swag)
swager,swagger
swagger,*,red,ring,rer,ringly,STRUT LIKE A BULLY/ DRUNK
swagur,swagger
swair,swear
swak,swag
swaker,swagger
swallow,*,wed,wing,TO TAKE DOWN THE THROAT, A BIRD
swalo,swallow
swalow,swallow
swam,PAST TENSE FOR THE WORD "SWIM"
swamp,*,ped,ping,py,pier,piest,piness,per,MARSHY/ WATERY LAND
swan,*,A LONG-NECKED BIRD
swang,PAST TENSE FOR THE WORD "SWING" (or see swank)
swank,ker,kily,kiness,ky,SOMEONE WHO MOVES WITH AN AIR OF DASHING SMARTNESS (or see swang)
swankee,swank
swap,*,pped,pping,TRADE/ BARTER (or see swab)
swaped,swap(pped) / swab(bbed)
swapt,swap(pped) / swab(bbed)
swar,swear
swarm,*,med,ming,mer,GROUP OF MANY BEES/ ZOOSPHORES/ PEOPLE
swarn,sworn

swasteka,swastika
swastika,* ,A SYMBOLIC SHAPE
swat,* ,tted,tting,tter,A STRIKING BLOW (or see sway(ed)/ suede)
swatch,hes,PIECE/ SAMPLE OF MATERIAL
swate,suede / sway(ed) / swat
swath,hes,TRAVEL IN LONG STRIPS GOING BACK AND FORTH IN SEQUENTIAL PARALLEL MOVEMENTS
swatul,swaddle
swave,suave
swavedy,suave(vity)
swavity,suave(vity)
swavly,suave(ly)
sway,* ,yed,ying,yable,yer,SWING BACK AND FORTH, SAG
swayd,suede / sway(ed)
sweap,sweep
swear,* ,ring,wore,worn,rer,TO USE PROFANITY, PLEDGE, PROMISE
sweat,* ,ted,ting,ty,ter,MOISTURE COMING THROUGH PORES OF SKIN TO COOL BODY DOWN, BE ANXIOUS, HEAT TO MELTING (or see sweet)
sweater,* ,A KNITTED ARTICLE OF CLOTHING
swebt,swept
swech,switch
sweder,sweater / sweet(er)
swedur,sweater / sweet(er)
swedy,sweat / sweet(ie)
sweep,* ,ped,ping,per,wept,REMOVE LOOSE DIRT FROM FLOOR/ GROUND, A GESTURE/ STROKE/ MOTION "prefixes: up"
sweet,* ,ter,test,tly,tness,tie,tish,PLEASANT TASTE, WITH SUGAR (or see sweat/ suit/ suite) "prefixes: semi"
sweft,swift
sweg,swig
swek,swig
swel,swell
sweld,swell(ed)
swelder,swelter
sweldur,swelter
swell,* ,lled,lling,wollen, TEMPORARILY BECOME
swelt,swell(ed)

swelter,* ,red,ring,ringly,AFFECTED BY OPPRESSIVE HEAT
sweltir,swelter
sweltur,swelter
swem,swim
swemur,swim(mmer)
swendul,swindle
sweng,swing
swengur,swing(er)
swep,sweep / swept
sweper,sweep(er)
swepur,sweep(er)
swerf,swerve
swerl,swirl
swerve,* ,ed,ving,SUDDENLY SWAY/ VEER DIRECTION "prefixes: un"
swesh,swish
swet,sweet / sweat
swetch,switch
swete,sweet(ie) / sweat
sweten,sweet(en)
sweter,sweater / sweet(er)
swetin,sweet(en) / sweat(ing)
swetir,sweater / sweet(er)
swetle,sweet(ly)
swetur,sweater / sweet(er)
swevel,swivel
swevul,swivel
swich,switch
swifd,swift
swifdly,swift(ly)
swifdnes,swift(ness)
swift,tly,tness,RAPID MOVEMENT
swig,* ,gged,gging,gger,TAKE LARGE DRINKS OF ALCOHOLIC LIQUID
swik,swig
swill,ller,FOOD FOR SWINE, TO GUZZLE
swim,* ,wam,mming,mmer,USE APPENDAGES OF BODY TO MOVE THROUGH WATER
swimd,swim(mmed)
swimt,swim(mmed)
swimur,swim(mmer)

swin,swine
swindal,swindle
swindle,* ,ed,ling,er,ONE WHO CHEATS/ SCHEME'S/ MANIPULATES MONEY FRAUDULENTLY
swindul,swindle
swine,* ,nish,nishly,nishness,DOMESTICATED PIG/ BOAR
swing,* ,ging,ger,wang,wung,GLIDE/ MOVE/ SWAY BACK AND FORTH, TYPE OF DANCE/ RELATIONSHIP "prefixes: in/ up"
swip,swipe
swipe,* ,ed,ping,TAKE/ STRIKE/ HIT, MOVE ACROSS A SCANNER
swirf,swerve
swirl,* ,led,ling,lly,lier,liest,MOVE IN CIRCULAR MOTION, TWIST/ CURL
swirve,swerve
swish,her,hy,hingly,A SOUND, A WISPY/ QUICK/ SWEEPING MOVEMENT
switch,hes,hed,hing,her,CHANGE/ FLIP/ DIVERT FROM ONE WAY/ SOURCE TO ANOTHER, STICK
swivel,* ,led,ling,ler,MOVEMENT CONSTRAINED TO A SINGLE PIVOT POINT
swivle,swivel
swivul,swivel
swob,swap / swab
swobed,swap(pped) / swab(bbed)
swobt,swap(pped) / swab(bbed)
swoch,swatch
swodel,swaddle
swodul,swaddle
swof,suave
swofly,suave(ly)
swolen,swollen
swollen,PAST TENSE FOR THE WORD "SWELL"
swolo,swallow
swolun,swollen
swomp,swamp
swompe,swamp
swomper,swamp(er)
swompy,swamp
swon,swan / swoon
swond,swoon(ed)

swoon,*,ned,ning,ner,n ngly,FAINT/ DIZZY FROM LACK OF OXYGEN OR FROM FEELINGS OF ELATION
swoop,*,ped,ping,DESCEND TO CAPTURE THEN ASCEND,BIRD'S MOVEMENT
swoosh,hed,hing,FAST/ RUSHING SOUND/ MOVEMENT
swop,swap / swab
swopt,swap(pped) / swab(bbed)
swor,swore
sword,*,A POINTED/ LONG/ SHARP DOUB_E-EDGED WEAPON
swore,PAST TENSE FOR THE WORD "SWEAR"
sworm,swarm
swormer,swarm(er)
sworn,PAST TENSE FOR THE WORD "SWEAR"
swosteku,swastika
swostiku,swastika
swot,swat
swotch,swatch
swoth,swath
swov,suave
swovity,suave(vity)
swovly,suave(ly)
swoztiku,swastika
swune,swoon
swung,PAST TENSE FOR THE WORD "SWING"
swup,swoop
swurf,swerve
swurl,swirl
swurve,swerve
swush,swoosh
sy,sigh
syanide,cyanide
sybernetics,cybernetics
syborg,cyborg
sycadelic,psychedelic
sycamore,*,A TREE/ FRUIT
sycek,psychic
sychadelic,psychedelic
syche, psyche / sick / sic
sychic,psychic
sycho, psycho
sychologekul,psychology/(gical)
sychology,psychology

sychopath, psychopath
sychosis, psychosis
sychotic, psychotic
syclone, cyclone
sycological, psychology(gical)
syfalis, syphilis
syfen,siphon
syflus, syphilis
syfules, syphilis
syfun,siphon
sykadelic, psychedelic
sykamore, sycamore
syke, psyche / sick / sic
sykeatric, psychiatric
sykek, psychic
sykiatrist,psychiatry(rist)
sykik, psychic
sykilogekul, psychology(gical)
sykle, cycle
syklist, cyclist
syko, psycho
sykodik, psychotic
sykologee, psychology
sykologest, psychology(gist)
sykopath, psychopath
sykopathic, psychopath(ic)
sykopathologist, psychopath(ologist)
sykosis, psychosis
sykotic, psychotic
syksteen, sixteen
syl, PREFIX INDICATING "TOGETHER/ UNITED/ ALIKE" MOST OFTEN MODIFIES THE WORD
sylable, syllable
sylabus, syllabus
syllable,*, ed, ling, WORD THAT CAN BE DIVIDED INTO PARTS BASED UPON PHONETIC SOUNDS "prefixes: deca/ dis"
syllabus, ses, AN OUTLINE/ SUMMARY OF LECTURES/ TEACHINGS
sym, PREFIX INDICATING "TOGETHER/ UNITED/ ALIKE" MOST OFTEN MODIFIES THE WORD
symatry, symmetry
symbal, symbol

symbalism, symbol(ism)
symbathe,sympathy
symbathetic, sympathetic
symbeotic, symbiotic
symbethe,sympathy
symbethetic, sympathetic
symbiosis,otic, TWO LIVE BODIES COEXISTING WITH MUTUAL BENEFITS "prefixes: endo"
symbiotic, cally, TWO LIVE BODIES COEXISTING WITH MUTUAL BENEFITS "prefixes: endo"
symbol,*, lic, lical, lically, lism, list, lize, lizes, lized, lizing, lization, lizer, logy, LETTER/ SHAPE WHICH HAS MEANING (or see cymbal)
symbolek, symbol(ic)
symbulism, symbol(ism)
symbuthe,sympathy
symbuthetic, sympathetic
symdum,symptom
symetrik, symmetry(ric)
symetry,symmetry
symfeny,symphony
symfonic, symphony(nic)
symfuny,symphony
symmetry, ries, ric, rical, rically, ricalness, rize, rization, MATHEMATICAL EXPRESSION, WHERE LINES ARE CONSISTENT WITHIN GUIDELINES "prefixes: dis"
sympathetic,cally, ABILITY TO RELATE/ REVERBERATE IN FREQUENCY/ FEELINGS
sympathy,hies, hetic, hize, hizes, hized, hizing, hizer, ABILITY TO RELATE/ REVERBERATE IN FREQUENCY/ FEELINGS
sympethy,sympathy
symphonek,symphony(nic)
symphony,nies, nic, nically, nious, HARMONIC WAVES/ FREQUENCY, ORCHESTRA
symphuny,symphony
sympl, simple / symbol
symposeum, symposium
symposium,*, CONFERENCE/ MEETING WHERE VIEWS ARE DISCUSSED
sympozeum, symposium
symptom,*, matic, matically, REACTION TO SOME UNSEEN AFFECTATION

symptum,symptom
symputhee,sympathy
sympuhize,sympathy(hize)
symtem,symptom
symtum,symptom
symutree,symmetry
syn,PREFIX INDICATING "TOGETHER/ UNITED/ ALIKE" MOST OFTEN MODIFIES THE WORD
synanem,synonym
synapse,*,ed,sing,ptic,WHERE TWO NERVE ENDINGS COMMUNICATE
synapsis,MEIOSIS PHASE WITH CHROMOSOMES (or see synapse)
synapsus,synapsis
synaptek,synaptic
synaptic,MEIOSIS PHASE WITH CHROMOSOMES (or see synapse)
sync,SHORT FOR SYNCHRONIZE (or see sink)
synchro,SHORT FOR SYNCHRONIZE
synchronus,synchrony(nous)
synchrony,nal,nic,nical,nically,nism,nistic,nistically,nize, nizes,nized,nizing,nous,nously,nousness,WHEN HARMONY BETWEEN THINGS/ PEOPLE/ WAVES/ FREQUENCY HAPPENS SIMULTANEOUSLY "prefixes: de/ un"
syncronize,synchrony(nize)
syncrony,synchrony
syndecate,syndicate
syndicashen,syndicate(tion)
syndicate,*,ed,tion,tor,COMPANIES/ CORPORATIONS BOUND FOR A FINANCIAL VENTURE
syndikation,syndicate(tion)
syndiket,syndicate
syndrem,syndrome
syndrome,*,,mic,COMBINATION OF CIRCUMSTANCES/ SYMPTOMS HAPPENING AT THE SAME TIME
syndrum,syndrome
synducate,syndicate
syndukit,syndicate
synergy,gies,getic,gism,gist,gistic,gistically,PARTS WORKING TOGETHER COOPERATIVELY
synik,cynic
synikal,cynical

synirgy,synergy
synkrenus,synchrony(nous)
synkronee,synchrony
synkronize,synchrony(nize)
synkrunus,synchrony(nous)
synonemus,synonym(ous)
synonim,synonym
synonimus,synonym(ous)
synonym,*,mic,mical,mity,mize,mized,mizing,mizer, mous,mously,ABOUT THE SAME/ SIMILAR CHARACTERISTICS
synopses,synopsis
synopsis,CONCENTRATED VERSION OF SOMETHING WRITTEN, SUMMARY
syntaks,syntax
syntax,xes,A GRAMMAR RULE
syntekit,syndicate
synthasis,synthesis
synthasize,synthesize
synthedik,synthetic
synthesis,sist,HUMAN MODIFICATION/ COMBINATION OF FREQUENCY/ ELEMENTS PRODUCING SOMETHING DIFFERENT "prefixes: bio"
synthesize,*,ed,zing,zation,HUMAN MODIFICATION/ COMBINATION OF FREQUENCY/ ELEMENTS PRODUCING SOMETHING DIFFERENT
synthetek,synthetic
synthetic,*,,cal,cally,HUMAN MADE CHEMICAL COMPOUNDS "prefixes: retro"
synthusis,synthesis
synumen,cinnamon
synunem,synonym
syphelis,syphilis
syphen,siphon
syphilis,itic,A VENEREAL DISEASE
syphin,siphon
syphon,siphon
syphules,syphilis
syrenge,syringe
syrinch,syringe
syringe,*,,TUBE WITH A PISTON FOR PULLING/ EXPELLING LIQUIDS
syrinje,syringe

syrip,syrup
syrup,*,,py,A VISCOUS/ THICK SUGAR BASED LIQUID
sysdamadik,system(atic)
sysdamatic,system(atic)
sysdem,system
sysdum,system
sysdumadik,system(atic)
sysdumatic,system(atic)
syst,cist / cyst
system,*,,mless,matic,matical,matically,maticness, matism,matist,matize,matization,matizer,mic, mically,mize,mization,mizer,OF/ PERTAINING TO A PLAN/ METHODOLOGY WITH PARTICULAR ORDER/ ARRANGEMENT,A CLASSIFICATION "prefixes: bio/ sub"
systumatic,system(atic)
syterical,satire(rical)
syth,scythe
t,tea / tee
t-shirt,*,,SHORT SLEEVE/ COLLARLESS SHIRT
tab,*,,bbed,bbing,bby,BILL FOR SERVICE PERFORMED,A SPACER (or see tap/ tape)
tabaco,tobacco
tabako,tobacco
tabal,table
tabby,bbies,bbied,ying,STYLE OF FUR ON A CAT
tabd,tab(bbed) / tap(pped)
tabe,tabby
tabel,table
tabernacle,*,ed,ling,cular,A NICHE/ DWELLING FOR SYMBOLIC STATUE,PART OF A BOAT
taberqulosis,tuberculosis
tabeulate,tabulate
tabew,taboo
tabewlashen,tabulate(tion)
tabewlate,tabulate
tabewlation,tabulate(tion)
tabewler,tabular
tabil,table
tabirnakle,tabernacle
tablau,tableau
table,*,ed,ling,GET RID OF, USABLE SURFACE TO SET ITEMS,PLATFORM OF INFORMATION "prefixes: re"

tableau,* , PRESENTATION/ ARRANGEMENT WITH PICTURES
tablet,* , BOUND COMPILATION OF PAPERS, PILL SHAPE, FLAT WRITING SURFACE
tablit, tablet
tablo, tableau
tabloed, tabloid
tabloid,* , GOSSIP NEWSPAPER WITH PICTURES
tabloyd, tabloid
tablut, tablet
tabogin, toboggan
taboo,* , ooed, ooing, PROHIBITED/ BANNED/ DISCRIMINATED AGAINST
tabt, tape(d) / tab(bbed) / tap(pped)
tabu, taboo
tabul, table
tabular, rly, RESEMBLING/ CAN BE USED AS A TABLE
tabulashen, tabulate(tion)
tabulate,* , ed, ting, tion, tor, ENTER/ LIST/ FORMULATE ONTO/ INTO A TABLE
tabuld, table(d)
tabuler, tabular
tabulir, tabular
taburnakle, tabernacle
taby, tabby
tacd, tact / tack(ed)
tacdil, tactile
tacdul, tactile
tacet, MUSICAL TERM/ ACTION (or see tacit)
tachometer, rically, ry, A DEVICE TO MEASURE LIQUID VELOCITY/ MOVEMENT
tachomitur, tachometer
tachy, PREFIX INDICATING "RAPID" MOST OFTEN MODIFIES THE WORD
tacit, tly, tness, IMPLIED WITHOUT SPEAKING IN WORDS (or see tacet)
tack,* , ked, king, ky, ker, ATTACH/ AFFIX TO, SAILING TERM, POINTED OBJECT WITH A BROAD HEAD FOR AFFIXING THINGS (or see take/ tact)
tackle,* , ed, ling, er, PURSUE/ OVERCOME/ ACCOMPLISH
tacksonamy, taxonomy
tacky, kiness, STICKY, DISORDERLY/ SHABBY (or see tachy)

taco,* , SHAPED CORN TORTILLA FILLED WITH FOODS
tacs, take(s)/ tax/ tack(s)
tacshoal, tactual
tacshuel, tactual
tacsidermi, taxidermy
tacsonomi, taxonomy
tact,* , tful, tfully, tfulness, tless, tlessly, tlessness, DIPLOMATIC/ APPROPRIATE IN PRESENTATION (or see tack/ take)
tactakul, tactic(al)
tactek, tactic
tactekil, tactic(al)
tactic,* , cal, cally, cian, STRATEGY/ PLAN TO PERFORM A MANEUVER/ EXPERIMENT/ ACTION
tactick, tactic
tactikel, tactic(al)
tactile, lity, PERTAINING TO THE SENSE OF TOUCH
taction, ACT OF TOUCHING
tactual, lly, PERTAINING/ GIVEN TO SENSE OF TOUCH
tactukil, tactic(al)
tada, today
tader, tater / tatter / potato
tadi, toddy
tador, tater / tatter / potato
tadpole,* , YOUNG FROG LARVAE
tadpowl, tadpole
tadur, tater / tatter / potato
tael, tail / tale / towel
taelur, tailor
taent, taint
tafe, taffy
tafedu, taffeta
tafee, taffy
tafeta, taffeta
taffeta, TYPE OF WOVEN FABRIC
taffy, A CANDY
tafy, taffy
tag,* , gged, gging, TO LABEL/ IDENTIFY SOMETHING, A GAME OF CHASE (or see tack/ take)
tagethur, together
tagle, toggle
tagol, toggle
taid, tide

taidal, tidal / title
taidi, tidy
taidings, tidings
taier, tire
taifun, typhoon
taifus, typhus
taiger, tiger
taigres, tigress
taik, tike
tail,* , led, ling, lless, APPENDAGE ON THE REAR OF SOMETHING, TO FOLLOW SOMEONE CLOSELY (or see tile/ tale/ tell/ tall/ towel)
tailor,* , red, ring, CUSTOM MAKES CLOTHING
taim, thyme / time / tame
taimos, thymus
tain, tine
taingo, tango
taini, tiny
taint,* , ted, ting, tless, DISTRACTING IMPREFECTION, CORRUPT/ POLLUTED
taiol, tile/ tail
taip, type
taipo, typo
taipoid, typhoid
tairani, tyranny
tairant, tyrant
tait, tight
taitol, tidal / title
taits, tights
tak, tack / take / tact
takal, tackle
takamidur, tachometer
takchen, taction
takchun, taction
takd, tact / talk(ed) / tack(ed)
takdel, tactile
take,* , took, king, en, ACQUIRE FOR ONE'S SELF, REMOVE FROM SOMETHING/ SOMEONE (too many definitions, please consult standard dictionary) (or see tack/ tag) "prefixes: over/ re/ under/ up"
taked, tact / tack(ed) / took
takee, tacky / take
takel, toggle

takela,tequila
taken,PAST TENSE FOR THE WORD "TAKE"
takil,tackle / toggle
takila, tequila
takin,taken / tack(ing)
takle, tackle / toggle
tako,taco
takol,tackle
takomeder,tachometer
takomitur,tachometer
taks, take(s) / tack(s)
taksachen,tax(ation)
taksation,tax(ation)
taksebul,tax(able)
taksed,taxi(ed)
taksedermy, taxidermy
taksee, taxi
takseng,taxi(ing) / tax(ing)
takshen, taction
takshuil, tactual
takshun, taction
taksibul, tax(able)
taksidermy, taxidermy
taksieng,taxi(ing)
taksobel,tax(able)
taksonimy, taxonomy
taksuble, tax(able)
taksudirmy, taxidermy
taksy, taxi
takt, tact / tack(ed)
taktakil, tactic(al)
taktek, tactic
taktekul, tactic(al)
taktik, tactic
taktikul, tactic(al)
taktil, tactile
taktion, taction
taktuk, tactic
taktukel, tactic(al)
taktul, tactile
takul, tackle / toggle
takun,taken / tack(ing)
taky,tacky / tachy

tal,tall / towel / tale / tail
talasman,talesman / talisman
talaspore,teliospore
talc,A CHEMICAL COMPOUND (or see talk)
tale, *, A STORY (or see tail/ tall/ towel)
talee, tally
talen, talon
talent, *, ted,HAVE NATURAL ABILITY FOR SOMETHING
taleology, teleology
talepathee, telepathy
taleputhee, telepathy
taler, tailor / tall(er)
talerible, tolerable
tales, tail(less)
talesman,SOMEONE PICKED FROM A COURTROOM TO SERVE ON A JURY (or see talisman)
talin, talon
talint, talent
talir, tailor / tall(er)
talirate, tolerate
talirense, tolerance
talisman,A CHARM/ FIGURINE FOR GOOD LUCK (or see talesman)
talk, *, ked,king, ker, kative, kativeness, kie, ky, USE THE MOUTH/ VOICE TO EXPRESS THOUGHT/ FEELING "prefixes: up"
talkatif, talk(ative)
tall, ller, llest, llish, llness, MORE THAN AVERAGE HEIGHT (or see tale/ tail/ towel)
tallow, wy, ANIMAL FAT "prefixes: un"
tally, llies, llied, llying, REGISTER/ RECORD/ LABEL, KEEP SCORE/ COUNT
talness, tall(ness)
talo, tallow
talon, *, ned, CLAWS OF A BIRD OF PREY
talor, tailor
talosman, talesman / talisman
talow, tallow
talr, tailor
talun, talon
talunt, talent
talur, tailor / tall(er)
talurashen, tolerate(tion)

talurate, tolerate
talurense, tolerance
talurent, tolerant
talurible, tolerable
talurint, tolerant
talusman, talesman / talisman
taly, tally
tambaren, tambourine
tambourine, *, A MUSICAL INSTRUMENT
tamburen, tambourine
tame, *, ed, ming, er, est, mable, mability, mableness, ely, eness, eless, TO DOMESTICATE/ CONTROL, CALM DOWN, MODIFY, ALTER
tamoro, tomorrow
tamp, *, ped, ping, per, pered, pering, perer, HAMMER/ STRIKE LIGHT BLOWS, DISRUPT/ CORRUPT
tampan, tampon
tampon, *, FEMININE HYGIENE PRODUCT
tampurd, tamp(ered)
tamulchuous, tumult(uous)
tamult, tumult
tan, *, nned, nning, nnish, nner, TO CHANGE/ MODIFY SKIN, PREFIX INDICATING "EXTEND/ EXPAND/ SPREAD/ CONTINUE/ SPIN OUT/ WEAVE/ PUT FORTH/ SHOW/ MANIFEST" MOST OFTEN MODIFIES THE WORD
tanage, tannage
tand, tan(nned)
tandem, ONE BEFORE THE OTHER
tandim, tandem
tandrem, tantrum
tandrum, tantrum
tandum, tandem
tanej, tannage
tanel, tunnel
taner, tan(nner)
tang, ged, gy, gier, giest, A SHARP SOUND/ TASTE, CHISEL STYLE TOOL
tangabul, tangible
tangarene, tangerine
tangebul, tangible
tangee, tang
tangel, tangle

tangent, *, ncy, tial, tially, tally, STRAIGHT LINE RADIATING/ DIVERGNG AWAY FROM A COMMON POINT "prefixes: sub"
tanger, tanker
tangerine, *, A CITRUS FRUIT
tangeur, tang(ier)
tangible, *, bility, eness, ly, ABLE TO BE FELT/ ACQUIRED/ ACCOMPLISHED PHYSICALLY "prefixes: in"
tangibul, tangible
tangil, tangle
tangint, tangent
tangirene, tangerine
tangle, *, ed, ling, er, ly, ement, TWISTED UP, PERPLEXING, CONFUSING "prefixes: en/ un"
tanglee, tangle(ly)
tanglmint, tangle(ment)
tango, *, oed, oing, A DANCE
tangol, tangle
tangubul, tangible
tangul, tangle
tangur, tanker
tangurene, tangerine
tanige, tannage
tanil, tunnel
tanir, tan(nner)
tanjable, tangible
tanjarene, tangerine
tanjebul, tangible
tanjent, tangent
tanjerine, tangerine
tanjibul, tangible
tanjint, tangent
tanjubul, tangible
tanjurene, tangerine
tank, *, ker, CONTAINER FOR LIQUIDS, A CONTAINER
tanker, CONTAINER WHICH TRANSPORTS LIQUIDS OVER A DISTANCE
tanko, tango
tankur, tanker
tannage, ACT/ RESULT OF TANNING HIDES
tanol, tunnel
tanpon, tampon
tansy, sies, A BITTER HERB

tant, taunt / taint / tan(nned)
tantalize, *, ed, zing, er, zingly, ENCOURAGE/ TEASE/ TORMENT WITHOUT HOPES OF RECEIVING AN END RESULT
tantamount, EQUIVALENT/ SIMILAR TO
tantelize, tantalize
tantem, tandem
tantilize, tantalize
tantim, tandem
tantimount, tantamount
tantra, rism, rist, RITUAL INVOLVING MOVEMENT OF FIRST LEVEL ENERGY
tantrem, tantrum
tantrest, tantra(rist)
tantrim, tantrum
tantru, tantra
tantrum, *, ANGRY/ EMOTIONAL OUTBURST
tantulise, tantalize
tantum, tandem
tantumownt, tantamount
tanuj, tannage
tanul, tunnel
tanur, tan(nner)
tap, *, pped, pping, pper, LIGHT BLOWS, A FAUCET/ VALVE USED TO ACCESS LIQUIDS FROM A CONTAINER (or see tape) "prefixes: un"
tapastre, tapestry
tape, *, ed, ping, er, STICKY PLASTIC USED TO SECURE/ WRAP/ MEND, LONG FLAT FLEXIBLE DEVICE/ MATERIAL (or see tap)
tapek, topic
tapekul, topical
tapeoka, tapioca
taper, *, red, ring, DESCRIPTION FOR SOMETHING LONG THAT DECREASES IN WIDTH AS IT REACHES THE END/ TIP/ POINT
tapestry, ries, LARGE WOVEN FABRIC/ THREADS ILLUSTRATING A DESIGN/ PICTURE
tapik, topic
tapioca, PUDDING DERIVED FROM STARCHY PLANT
tapiouca, tapioca
tapir, tater / tatter / potato
tapistre, tapestry

taploed, tabloid
taploid, tabloid
taployd, tabloid
taps, A MUSICAL SIGNAL USED FOR LIGHTS OUT IN MILITARY (or see tap(s)/ tape(s))
tapt, tape(d) / tap(pped)
tapuk, topic
tapur, taper / tap(pper)
tapustree, tapestry
taquela, tequila
taquila, tequila
tar, *, rred, rring, A WOOD/ COAL COMBINATION BY-PRODUCT (or see tare / tear)
tara, terra
tarafy, terrify
taragen, tarragon
taragon, tarragon
tarain, terrain / terrane
taranchula, tarantula
tarane, terrain / terrane
taranshula, tarantula
tarantula, *, A LARGE SPIDER
tararium, terrarium
taraso, terrazzo
tarazo, terrazzo
tard, tar(rred) / tart / tare(d) / tear(ed)
tardee, tardy
tardenes, tardy(diness)
tardur, tartar
tardy, dier, diest, dily, diness, LATE
tare, *, ed, ring, METHOD OF WEIGHING GOODS (or see tar/ tear/ tarry)
tarebly, terrible(ly)
tarebul, terrible
tared, tare(d) / tar(rred) / tear(ed) / tarry(ried)
taref, tariff
tarefic, terrific
tarefy, terrify
tarereim, terrarium
taresdreul, terrestrial
tarestreal, terrestrial
tarestrial, terrestrial
tareur, terrier

target,*,ted,ting,A POINT/ AREA TO AIM AT/ FOR
targit, target
targut, target
taribul, terrible
tarier, terrier
tarif, tariff
tarifek, terrific
tariff,*,A TAX
tarific, terrific
tarify, terrify
tarit, terret
tariur, terrier
tarlatan,*,LOOSELY WOVEN MATERIAL
tarletin, tarlatan
tarluten, tarlatan
tarmac,*,MATERIAL USED FOR ROADS/ LANDING PADS/ PARKING
tarmak, tarmac
tarnesh, tarnish
tarnish,hes, hed, hing, hable, OXIDATION WHICH DISCOLORS, CAUSE TO LOOSE LUSTER/ SHINE/ STATE OF BEING
tarnush, tarnish
tarp,*,ped,ping,A LARGE/ WOVEN MATERIAL FOR COVERING/ OVERHEAD PROTECTION
tarpalene, tarpaulin
tarpaulin,*,A WEATHERPROOF MATERIAL USED FOR A COVERING
tarpeline, tarpaulin
tarpin, tarpon
tarpon,*,LARGE OCEAN FISH
tarpulene, tarpaulin
tarpun, tarpon
tarragon,AN HERB/ PLANT
tarrazzo, terrazzo
terrestrial, terrestrial
tarrif, tariff
tarry,rries,rried,ying,rrier,LOITERING/ LINGERING/ NOT MOVING ALONG, COVERED IN TAR
tars,PREFIX INDICATING "EYELID/ ANKLE/ BONES" MOST OFTEN MODIFIES THE WORD
tart,*,tish,tishly,tly,tness,SOUR TASTE, PASTRY (or see tar(rred)/ tear(ed)/ tare(d)/ tort/ torte)

tartar,CALCIUM PHOSPHATE DEPOSIT, DEPOSIT FROM WINEMAKING, A SAUCE
tartir, tartar
tartoof, tartuffe
tartuffe,ery, COMIC DEPICTING A HYPOCRITE, ALSO SPELLED TARTUFE
tartur, tartar
taru, terra
taruf, tariff
tarufy, terrify
tarutoree, territory
tary, tarry
taryd, tarry(ried)
tas, that(s)
tasc, task
tasd, taste
tasde, taste(ty)
tasel, tassel
taset, tacet / tacit
tasil, tassel
tasit, tacet / tacit
task,*,ked,king,CHORE/ WORK TO BE DONE, CHALLENGE INVOLVING HARDSHIP
tasles, taste(less)
tasol, tassel
tassel,*,HANGING THREADED ORNAMENT
taste,*,ed,ting,er,eful,efully,efulness,eless,elessly, elessness,ty,tier,tiest,tily,tiness, SENSE/ FEELING WITHIN THE MOUTH "prefixes: dis"
tastee, taste(ty)
tasteir, taste(tier)
tastenes, taste(tiness)
tasteur, taste(tier)
tastful, taste(ful)
tastfule, taste(fully)
tastfully, taste(fully)
tastur, taste(r)
tasul, tassel
tat, taught / taut
tatel, tattle
tater,*,SHORT FOR POTATO (or see tatter)
tatewist, tattoo(ist)
tatil, tattle

tatir, tater / tatter
tatle, tattle
tatlur, tattle(r)
tatoist, tattoo(ist)
tatol, tattle
tatoo, tattoo
tator, tater / tatter
tatter,*,red,ring,WORN/ SHREDDED MATERIAL (or see tater)
tattle,*,ed,ling,er,TO RAT/ FINK/ TELL/ EXPOSE SOMEONE'S WORDS/ BEHAVIOR/ ACT
tattoo,*,ooed,ooing,ooer,ooist,TO APPLY PERMANENT INK INTO THE SKIN WITH A NEEDLE
tatuist, tattoo(ist)
tatul, tattle
tatur, tater / tatter
taturd, tatter(ed)
tauel, towel
tauer, tower
taught,PAST TENSE FOR THE WORD "TEACH" (or see taut/ tout) "prefixes: un"
taugt, taught / taut / tout
tauko, taco
tauksik, toxic
tauksufy, toxify(fication)
taul, towel / tall
tauler, tall(er)
taulir, tall(er)
taulk, talk / talc
taulky, talk
taulur, tall(er)
taulurinse, tolerance
taun, town
taunt,*,ted,ting,TEASE/ PROVOKE/ MANIPULATE SOMEONE TO REACT (or see tout)
taupe,A COLOR (or see toupee)
taupikul, topical
taut,ten,tly,tness,HOLD/ STRETCH TIGHT (or see taught/ taunt/ tout)
tauzel, tousle
tavern,*,ner,PLACE WHICH SELLS SPIRITS/ ALCOHOLIC BEVERAGES
tavurn, tavern

tawer,tower
tawir,tower
tawn,town
tawnt,taunt
tawp,taupe / top
tawsel,tousle
tawt,taught / taut / tout
tax,xes,xed,xing,xable,xability,xation,CHARGE ADDED ON TO GOODS/ RESOURCES/ SERVICE COLLECTED BY THE CITY/ STATE/ FEDERAL GOVERNMENTS, A CHALLENGE (or see taxi) "prefixes: over/ sur"
taxdermy,taxidermy
taxashen,tax(ation)
taxe,taxi
taxed,taxi(ed) / tax(ed)
taxdirmy,taxidermy
taxi,*,ied,iing,VEHICLE HIRED FOR TRANSPORTATION, NAVIGATE A PLANE/ BOAT AT SLOW SPEED, MEDICAL TERM (or see tax)
taxicolochi,toxicology
taxidermy,mies,mist,ONE WHO EMBALMS/ STUFFS ANIMALS
taxieng,taxi(iing)
taxonimy,taxonomy
taxonomy,mic,mical,mically,mist,METHOD TO CLASSIFY/ CATEGORIZE ANIMALS/ PLANTS
taxs,tax(es)
taxsachen,tax(ation)
taxsashen,tax(ation)
taxse,taxi
taxsedermy,taxidermy
taxsible,tax(able)
taxsuble,tax(able)
taxsudermy,taxidermy
taxudermy,taxidermy
taxus,tax(es)
tayler,tailor
taylur,tailor
taynt,taint
tayor,tire
te,tea / tee
tea,*,DRIED PLANTS STEEPED IN WATER (or see tee)

teach,hes,taught,hing,her,hable,hability,hableness,hably,TRAIN/ COACH/ INSTRUCT,INFORMATION/ KNOWLEDGE BEING PASSED ON TO OTHERS "prefixes: un"
teachs,teach(es)
teachuble,teach(able)
teachur,teach(er)
teak,A TREE
teal,A COLOR (or see teil)
team,*,med,ming,GROUP ATTEMPT TO WORK/ PLAY/ PERFORM TOGETHER (or see teem)
teanager,teenager
tear,*,red,ring,ry,rful,rfully,rfulness,rless,TO RIP, LIQUID COMING FROM THE EYES RELATED TO AN EMOTIONAL THOUGHT/ EVENT (or see tier)
tearu,tiara
tease,*,ed,sing,er,sable,singly,TAUNT/ PROVOKE/ ANNOY AS A DISTRACTION
teat,*,TIT/ NIPPLE/ UDDER
tebaco,tobacco
tebagen,toboggan
tebako,tobacco
tebea,tibia
tebogin,toboggan
tebse,tip(sy)
tech,*,SHORT FOR TECHNICAL (or see teach)
techable,teach(able)
techer,teach(er)
teches,teach(es)
techi,*,SHORT FOR TECHNICIAN
techible,teach(able)
techir,teach(er)
techis,teach(es)
technalogical,technology(gical)
technawlugee,technology
technecal,technical
technek,technique
techneque,technique
technical,lly,lness,lity,lities,DETAILED/ SPECIFIC, SPECIFIC TO THE LANGUAGE/ SCHOOL/ TRADE "prefixes: bio"
technikality,technical(ity)
technilogikul,technology(gical)

technique,*,METHOD OF PERFORMING SOMETHING FOR SPECIFIC END RESULTS
technology,gies,gist,gic,gical,gically,INDUSTRIAL SCIENCE/ ART "prefixes: bio"
technolugee,technology
technukality,technical(ity)
techololli,technology
techuble,teach(able)
techur,teach(er)
techus,teach(es)
tecnec,technique
tecnic,technique
tecshur,texture
tecst,text
tecstaiol,textile
tecstchur,texture
tectonic,*,cally,SCIENCE/ ART OF CONSTRUCTING/ STUDYING FORMS/ SHAPES
teda,today
tedbet,tidbit
tedbit,tidbit
teder,teeter
tedeus,tedious
tedeusly,tedious(lly)
tedious,sly,sness,DETAILED/ SLOW/ MONOTONOUS
tedir,teeter
tedius,tedious
tedur,teeter
tee,*,ed,eing,A TERM IN THE GAME OF GOLF, TO BE IRRITATED,SHAPE/ LETTER,ALL COMES TOGETHER SUITABLY/ PERFECTLY (or see tea)
teecher,teach(er)
teechuble,teach(able)
teechur,teach(er)
teek,teak
teel,teal / teil
teem,*,med,ming,OVERFLOWING/ ABUNDANT/ COMING FORTH (or see team)
teen,*,ny,nier,niest,nager,SHORT FOR TEENAGER, SOMETHING VERY SMALL
teenager,*,PRE-ADULT AGE (13-19 YEARS)
teeneur,teen(ier)
teenksher,tincture

teenkur, tinker	
teenyer, teen(ier)	
teepee, *, A CONICAL SHAPED DWELLING COMMON TO NATIVE AMERICANS	
teers, tear(s) / tier(s)	
teery, tear	
tees, tease / tea(s) / tee(s)	
teet, teat / tit	
teeter, *, red, ring, SHIFT WEIGHT BACK AND FORTH AS IN A ROCKING MOTION, HORIZONTAL BALANCING MOVEMENT / MANEUVER	
teeter-totter, *, SEESAW/ TOY, LONG BOARD ON A FULCRUM WHICH MOVES UP/ DOWN WITH SHIFTING OF WEIGHT	
teeth, hing, her, tooth, MORE THAN ONE TOOTH, ACT OF GROWING FIRST SET OF TEETH	
teetur, teeter	
tef, tiff	
teic, take	
teil, A LIME TREE (or see teal)	
teip, tape	
teiper, taper	
teipestri, tapestry	
teir, tier / tear	
teird, tier(ed) / tear(ed)	
teist, taste	
teiter, tater	
tek, teak / tech	
tekal, tickle	
tekdile, textile	
teke, tiki	
tekel, tickle	
tekela, tequila	
teket, ticket	
teki, techi / tiki	
tekil, tickle	
tekit, ticket	
tekle, tickle	
teklech, tickle(lish)	
teklish, tickle(lish)	
teknakaledy, technical(ity)	
teknalogical, technology(gical)	
teknalugee, technology	

teknek, technique	
teknekality, technical(ity)	
teknekul, technical	
tekneque, technique	
teknikul, technical	
teknilogikul, technology(gical)	
teknololli, technology	
teknolugee, technology	
teknukalety, technical(ity)	
teknukil, technical	
teknulogical, technology(gical)	
tekol, tickle	
tekot, ticket	
teksd, text	
teksdeur, texture	
teksdile, textile	
tekst, text	
tekster, texture	
tekstile, textile	
teksture, texture	
tekt, text / tick(ed)	
tektonek, tectonic	
tektonic, tectonic	
tekul, tickle	
tekut, ticket	
teky, tiki	
tel, PREFIX INDICATING "END/ FAR" MOST OFTEN MODIFIES THE WORD (or see teil/ teal)	
telacast, telecast	
telafase, telophase	
telafeis, telophase	
telafone, telephone	
telafoto, telephoto	
telagraf, telegraph	
telagram, telegram	
telagraph, telegraph	
telakanesis, telekinesis	
telakast, telecast	
telakinetic, telekinetic	
telakunesis, telekinesis	
telaphase, telophase	
telaphone, telephone	
telaphoto, telephoto	

telapromptur, teleprompter	
telar, teller	
telaskope, telescope	
telaskopic, telescope(pic)	
telathon, telethon	
telatipe, teletype	
telavais, televise	
telavichen, television	
telavision, television	
telavize, televise	
teld, tell / told / till(ed)	
tele, PREFIX INDICATING "DISTANCE" MOST OFTEN MODIFIES THE WORD	
telealogy, teleology	
teleaspore, teliospore	
telebais, televise	
telecast, *, ted, ting, ter, BROADCAST BY TELEVISION	
telefone, telephone	
telefoto, telephoto	
telefoudo, telephoto	
telefoun, telephone	
telegraf, telegraph	
telegram, *, SEND MESSAGE/ MONEY BY WIRE	
telegraph, her, hist, hic, hically, MESSAGE/ TRANSMISSION SENT BY USING AN INSTRUMENT, WIRE TRANSFER	
telekinesis, OBJECTS MOVING WHICH HAVE NO VISIBLE EXPLANATION AS TO CAUSE	
telekinetic, *, OBJECTS MOVING WHICH HAVE NO VISIBLE EXPLANATION AS TO CAUSE	
telekunesis, telekinesis	
telekunetic, telekinetic	
teleology, gism, gist, SCIENCE WHICH STUDIES ETHICS/ CAUSES/ ACTS IN NATURE	
telepathee, telepathy	
telepathy, hic, hically, hist, COMMUNICATE BY WAVELENGTH, MIND COMMUNICATION	
telephone, *, nic, nically, INSTRUMENT FOR VERBAL COMMUNICATION	
telephoto, ography, ographic, TAKING PHOTOS AT LONG DISTANCE	
teleprompter, *, A DEVICE WHICH ENLARGES TEXT FOR THOSE ON CAMERA TO READ FROM	
teleputhee, telepathy	

telequenises, telekinesis
telur, teller
telescope, *, ed, ping, pic, pically, INSTRUMENT THAT SEEMINGLY REDUCES DISTANCE BY USE OF LENSES (or see microscope)
teletaip, teletype
telethon, *, A TELEVISION BROADCAST WHICH LASTS A LONG TIME
teletipe, teletype
teletype, DEVICE USED TO TRANSMIT MESSAGES
telepromtur, teleprompter
teleuspore, teliospore
televais, televise
televigen, television
televijan, television
televise, *, ed, sing, sion, USING TELEVISION TO TRANSMIT/ BROADCAST
television, *, nary, VISUAL IMAGES SENT BY WAVES THROUGH DEVICE WHICH INTERPRETS THEM
teli, telly
telialegy, teleology
teliaulugy, teleology
telicast, telecast
telifone, telephone
telifoto, telephoto
telifoun, telephone
teligraf, telegraph
teligram, telegram
teligraph, telegraph
telikanesis, telekinesis
telikast, telecast
telikunesis, telekinesis
teliolochi, teleology
teliology, teleology
teliololli, teleology
teliospore, *, ric, METHOD OF FUNGI GERMINATION
teliphone, telephone
teliphoto, telephoto
telipromtur, teleprompter
telipromtur, teleprompter
telir, teller
teliskope, telescope
teliskopic, telescope(pic)

telithon, telethon
telitipe, teletype
teliuspore, teliospore
telivshen, television
telivision, television
telivize, televise
tell, *, ling, told, TO COMMUNICATE INFORMATION ALONG (or see teal/ teil) "prefixes: re"
teller, *, ONE WHO DEALS DIRECTLY WITH CUSTOMERS AT A BANK, NARRATOR, ONE WHO FACILITATES COMMUNICATION BETWEEN OTHERS
telltale, er, TATTLER, ONE WHO PASSES ALONG GOSSIP, A TOOL FOR NAVIGATION
telly, SHORT FOR TELEVISION
telo, PREFIX INDICATING "END/ FAR" MOST OFTEN MODIFIES THE WORD
telofase, telophase
telofeis, telophase
telokanesis, telekinesis
telokunesis, telekinesis
telophase, sic, BIOLOGICAL TERM
telor, teller
teloskope, telescope
teloskopic, telescope(pic)
telothon, telethon
telovishen, television
telt, till(ed) / told / tilt
teltail, telltale
teltale, telltale
telufase, telophase
telufone, telephone
telufoto, telephoto
telugraf, telegraph
telugram, telegram
telugraph, telegraph
telukanesis, telekinesis
telukast, telecast
telukenetick, telekinetic
telukinetik, telekinetic
telukunesis, telekinesis
teluphase, telophase
teluphone, telephone
teluphoto, telephoto

telupromtur, teleprompter
telur, teller
teluskope, telescope
teluskopic, telescope(pic)
teluthon, telethon
telutipe, teletype
teluvegun, television
teluvision, television
teluvize, televise
tem, team / teem
temaro, tomorrow
tembir, timber
tembrachure, temperature
tembrament, temperament
tembramentul, temper(mental)
tembrushure, temperature
tembur, timber
temd, team(ed) / teem(ed)
temed, timid
temidly, timid(ly)
temod, timid
temoro, tomorrow
tempal, temple
temparamint, temperament
tempararely, temporary(rily)
temparary, temporary
temparize, temporize
temperais, temporize
temper, *, red, ring, rament, ramently, ramentally, rance, rate, rabilty, rable, rer, rature, EMOTIONS WORKED INTO AN ANGRY STATE, HEATING UP CARBON MATERIAL TO FORCE MOLECULAR REALIGNMENT
tempera, tempura
temperais, temporize
temperament, *, tal, tally, OVERALL EMOTION/ PHYSICAL/ MENTAL TRAITS OF A PERSON/ LIVING THING "prefixes: non/ un"
temperarily, temporary(rily)
temperary, temporary
temperate, ely, eness, HEATING UP CARBON MATERIAL TO FORCE MOLECULAR REALIGNMENT, STABLE "prefixes: in/ sub"
temperature, *, MEASUREMENT OF HOT/ COLD VARIANCES

temperize,temporize
tempermint,temper(ment)
tempeshues,tempest(uous)
tempest,tuous,tuously,tuousness,BEING STORMY/ WINDY/ TURBULENT
tempil,temple
tempir,temper
tempirais,temporize
tempirament,temperament
tempirashure,temperature
tempirment,temper(ment)
templat,template
template,*,SOMETHING TO SUPPORT/ ALLOW THE FORM OF SOMETHING, FOR MAKING REPLICAS
temple,*,ed,RELIGIOUS STRUCTURE FOR WORSHIP, SPOT ON THE HEAD OF THE BODY
templeit,template
templut,template
tempo,*,THE RHYTHM OF A WAVE,RATE/ SPEED/ PACE OF MOVEMENT
tempol,temple
tempor,PREFIX INDICATING "TIME/ TEMPLES" MOST OFTEN MODIFIES THE WORD
temporal,lly,lness,lity,lities,OF OR GIVEN TO THIS TIME/ SPACE/ DISTANCE
temporarely,temporary(rily)
temporary,rarily,riness,SHORT DURATION IN TIME
temporely,temporal(lly)
temporize,*,ed,zing,zer,zation,zingly,GAIN/ DELAY/ YIELD/ MANIPULATE TIME
temporment,temper(ment)
temporo,PREFIX INDICATING "TIME/ TEMPLES" MOST OFTEN MODIFIES THE WORD
temporul,temporal
tempra,tempura
temprachure,temperature
tempral,temporal
tempramentul,temper(mental)
temprary,temporary
temprashure,temperature
temprature,temperature
tempremintul,temper(mental)
tempreruly,temporary(rily)

temprery,temporary
temprment,temperament
temprol,temporal
tempru,tempura
tempruminutl,temper(mental)
tempt,*,ted,ting,tingly,table,ter,tingness,tress,tation, TO ENTICE/ ALLURE/ SEDUCE/ INVITE
temptashen,temptation
temptation,*,APPREHENSION IN RESPONDING TO INVITATION/ ENTICEMENT/ SEDUCTION
tempteishon,temptation
tempul,temple
tempur,temper
tempura,BATTER DIPPED VEGETABLES/ FISH
tempurarily,temporary(rily)
tempurary,temporary
tempurely,temporal(lly)
tempureruly,temporary(rily)
tempurery,temporary
tempurize,temporize
tempurment,temper(ment)
tempust,tempest
temt,tempt / team(ed) / teem(ed)
temtashen,temptation
temtation,temptation
temted,tempt(ed)
temteishon,temptation
temtres,tempt(ress)
temulchuis,tumult(uous)
temulchuous,tumult(uous)
temult,tumult
temut,timid
ten,*,nth,ENGLISH NUMBER AFTER NINE/ BEFORE ELEVEN (or see tin/ teen)
tenabel,tenable
tenable,bility,eness,ly,CAN SURVIVE ATTEMPT AT BEING TAKEN/ CARRIED AWAY "prefixes: un"
tenachus,tenacious
tenacious,sly,sness,ity,PERSISTENT/ CONSISTENT, WITHOUT FALTER
tenacity,OF BEING TENACIOUS
tenacle,tentacle
tenager,teenager

tenakle,tentacle
tenament,tenement
tenansy,tenant(ncy)
tenant,*,tncy,tcies,try,BORROWER OF LAND/ STRUCTURE/ PROPERTY HELD/ OWNED BY ANOTHER "prefixes: sub"
tenasedy,tenacity
tenashus,tenacious
tenasity,tenacity
tenasuty,tenacity
tenat,tenet / tenant
tenatef,tentative
tenatious,tenacious
tenative,tentative
tencity,tense(sity)
tencol,tinkle
tend,*,ded,ding,der,dency,HAVE LEANING AFFINITY/ TENDENCY TOWARDS, TAKE CARE OF (or see tin(nned)/ tent/ tint)
tendatev,tentative
tendency,cies,ntious,ntiously,ntiousness,HAVE A LEANING/ INCLINATION TOWARDS, DISPOSITION/ CAPABILITY OF
tendenus,tendon(dinous)
tender,*,rly,rness,rer,rize,rizes,rized,rizing,rization, rizer,SOFTENED FIBERS,SOFT/ GENTLE IN NATURE/ TEMPERAMENT, OFFER TOWARDS DEBT (or see tinder)
tenderloin,*,CUT OF BEEF
tendid,tend(ed) / tint(ed)
tendin,tendon
tendinsy,tendency
tendir,tender / tinder
tendirloin,tenderloin
tendon,*,dinous,nitis,PART OF A MUSCLE
tendorize,tender(ize)
tendril,*,CURLING OF A PLANT/ HAIR
tendrul,tendril
tendun,tendon
tendunitus,tendon(itis)
tendunus,tendon(dinous)
tendur,tender / tinder
tendurize,tender(ize)

tendurloin,tenderloin
tendurly,tender(ly)
tendutif,tentative
tene,teen / tin(nny)
teneishos,tenacious
tenekle,tentacle
tenement,*,tary,DWELLING WHERE PEOPLE LIVE AS TENANTS, PERMANENT PROPERTY
tenen,tenon
tenensy,tenant(ncy)
tener,tenor
tenet,*,DOCTRINE/ BELIEF/ DOGMA HELD TO BE TRUE (or see tenant)
tenetif,tentative
tenetive,tentative
teneur,tenure / teen(ier)
teneust,teen(iest)
tenewus,tenuous
tenfold,TEN TIMES OVER/ GREATER
teng,ting / tinge
tenible,tenable
teniest,teen(iest)
tenikle,tentacle
teniment,tenement
tenin,tenon
tenios,tenuous
tenir,tenor
tenis,tennis
tenit,tenet / tenant
tenite,tonight
teniur,tenure
tenj,tinge
tenkchur,tincture
tenker,tinker
tenkil,tinkle
tenkir,tinker
tenkol,tinkle
tenkshir,tincture
tenkture,tincture
tenkul,tinkle
tenkur,tinker
tennis,A RACQUET GAME
tenon,A CARPENTRY TOOL

tenor,*,A PITCH/ LEVEL OF SOUND
tenos,tennis
tenpal,temple
tenparery,temporary
tenpermint,temperament
tenpest,tempest
tenpirery,temporary
tenpist,tempest
tenplit,template
tenpo,tempo
tenpol,temple
tenporal,temporal
tenporary,temporary
tenporat,temper(ate)
tenprachur,temperature
tenpral,temporal
tenprament,temperament
tenpret,temper(ate)
tenpriment,temperament
tenprit,temper(ate)
tenprochur,temperature
tenprot,temper(ate)
tens,ten(s) / tent(s) / tense / tint(s) / tend(s)
tense,*,ed,sing,ely,eness,sity,eless,sion,sional,sionless,sive,STRETCHED/ PUSHED/ STRAINED BEYOND A COMFORTABLE POSITION,TIGHT,INRELATION TO TIME (or see tent(s))
tensul,tinsel
tent,*,ted,ting,SHARP PEAK WITH TWO EQUAL SLOPES, TEMPORARY/ PORTABLE SHELTER, SURGICAL PROCEDURE (or see tint/ tend/ tin(nned))
tentacle,*,ed,cular,LONG/ FLEXIBLE APPENDAGES ON A LIVING THING
tentakle,tentacle
tentative,ely,eness,TEMPORARY PLAN/ TIME, NOT CERTAIN AS OF YET
tented,tint(ed) / tent(ed) / tend(ed)
tentekle,tentacle
tentetive,tentative
tenth,*,ONE PART OUT OF TEN
tentikle,tentacle
tentukle,tentacle
tentutive,tentative

tenuble,tenable
tenues,tenuous
tenukle,tentacle
tenument,tenement
tenunsy,tenant(ncy)
tenunt,tenant
tenuous,sly,sness,DELICATE/ WEAK/ FINE/ DILUTED
tenur,tenor
tenure,ed,rial,rially,HOLDING/ POSSESSING PROPERTY OR POSITION
tenus,tennis
tenutef,tentative
tenutive,tentative
teny,teen / tin(nny)
tenyewr,tenure
tenyewus,tenuous
tenyir,tenure
tenyur,tenure
tenzul,tinsel
tep,tip
tepakle,typical
tepd,tip(pped)
tepe,teepee
teped,tepid
tepekul,typical
teper,tip(pper)
tepid,dity,dness,dly,LUKEWARM,WARM TO TOUCH
tepikul,typical
tepod,tepid
tepor,tip(pper)
tepse,tip(sy)
tepud,tepid
tepufy,typify
tepukle,typical
tepur,tip(pper)
teqi,techi
teqnic,technique
teqnical,technical
teqnololli,technology
teqtonic,tectonic
tequila,A LIQUOR/ ALCOHOL
ter,PREFIX INDICATING "THREE" MOST OFTEN MODIFIES THE WORD (or see tare / tear / tier)

tera, PREFIX INDICATING "ONE TRILLION/ MONSTER" MOST OFTEN MODIFIES THE WORD	teret, turret / terret	**terminology**, gies, gical, gically, SPECIFIC WORDS/ LANGUAGE WITHIN A SCIENCE/ ART TO EXPLAIN PROCESSES
terable, terrible	tereur, tarry(rier) / terrier	terminololli, terminology
terace, terrace	terf, turf	terminul, terminal
terafy, terrify	terfil, tear(ful)	**termite**, *, WOOD EATING INSECT
teragen, tarragon	terful, tear(ful)	termoel, turmoil
teragin, tarragon	terible, terrible	termonel, terminal
terain, terrain / terrane	teribly, terrible(ly)	termunate, terminate
teranchula, tarantula	terif, tariff	termunolegy, terminology
terane, terrain / terrane / tyranny	terifai, terrify	**tern**, *, A BIRD (or see turn)
teranshulu, tarantula	terifek, terrific	ternament, tournament
terantula, tarantula	terify, terrify	ternd, turn(ed)
terareim, terrarium	teriny, tyranny	ternep, turnip
terarium, terrarium	terir, terror	terniment, tournament
teras, terrace	teris, terrace	ternip, turnip
terastrial, terrestrial	terism, tour(ism)	ternument, tournament
terat, terret	terist, tour(ist)	teror, terror
teratoreul, territory(rial)	terit, turret / terret	terpentin, turpentine
teratory, territory	teritoree, territory	terpewlent, turbulent
terazo, terrazzo	teritoreul, territory(rial)	terpulent, turbulent
terazzo, terrazzo	teriur, terrier	terpuntine, turpentine
terben, turban / turbine	terkoes, turquois	**terra**, PLANETS MOUNTAINOUS AREA
terbin, turban / turbine	terkois, turquois	**terrace**, *, ed, cing, VARIOUS LEVEL AREAS CUT INTO A SLOPE
terbiulent, turbulent	**term**, *, med, mless, INVOLVING A SPECIFIC PERIOD OF TIME, FIXED/ SPECIFIC QUANTITY/ VALUE	**terrain**, NATURALLY SHAPED LANDSCAPE (or see terrane)
terbo, turbo	termait, termite	**terrane**, GROUP OF NATURAL FORMATIONS PARTICULARLY ROCK (or see terrain) "prefixes: sub"
terbulens, turbulent(nce)	termarek, turmeric	**terrarium**, *, CONTAINER FOR PLANTS/ ANIMALS TO LIVE/ BE VIEWED
terbulent, turbulent	termd, term(ed)	**terrazzo**, MOSAIC PIECES OF STONE/ TILE
terbun, turban / turbine	termenal, terminal	**terrestrial**, *, lly, lness, BY/ OF LAND/ EARTH "prefixes: semi/ sub"
terd, tier(ed) / tear(ed) / tour(ed)	termenashen, terminate(tion)	**terret**, *, ON A SADDLE/ HARNESS (or see turret)
terdle, turtle	termenate, terminate	terreur, terrier
tere, tear	termenation, terminate(tion)	**terrible**, eness, ly, HORRIBLE/ AWFUL/ UNCOMFORTABLE/ STRESSFUL
tereble, terrible	termenator, terminate(tor)	**terrier**, *, BREED OF DOG
terefic, terrific	termenolegy, terminology	terrif, tariff
terefy, terrify	termenolochi, terminology	**terrific**, cally, EXCELLENT/ EXCITING/ WONDERFUL
terein, terrain	termenul, terminal	**terrify**, fies, fied, ying, yingly, STRICKEN WITH TERROR, HORRIFY/ FRIGHTEN
terene, tyranny	termerik, turmeric	
terer, terror	**terminal**, *, lly, able, ableness, ably, STATION/ CONDUIT/ CIRCUIT, TERMINATE, COME TO AN END "prefixes: sub"	
tereim, terrarium	terminashen, terminate(tion)	
teres, terrace	termineit, terminate	
teresdreul, terrestrial	**terminate**, *, ed, ting, tive, tively, tor, tion, tional, TO END	
teresm, tour(ism)		
terest, tour(ist)		
terestrial, terrestrial		

terrir,terror
territory,ries,rial,rially,:ialism,rialist,riality,lize,lized, lization,A SPECIFIC REGION/ AREA OF TURF/ LAND
terror,*,:rism,rist,ristic,:less,rize,rizes,rized,rizing, rization,rizer, EXTREME FEAR/ HORRCR "prefixes: bio"
terrur,terror
ters,tear(s) / tier(s)
terse,er,est,ely,eness, FREE OF FRIVOLTIES/ SUPERFICIALITY
tersheary,tertiary
tershury,tertiary
tert,tier(ed) / tear(ed)
tertiary,ries,ty, THREE/ TH RD/ THIRDS OF SOMETHING
tertil,turtle
tertul,turtle
teru,terra
terubil,terrible
terubly,terrible(ly)
teruf,tariff
terufy,terrify
terugen,tarragon
terugin,tarragon
terur,terror
terus,terrace
terut,turret
terutoree,territory
terutoreul,territory(riall)
terutory,territory
tery,tear / tarry
terz,tear(s) / tier(s)
tes,tease / test
tesabel,tease(sable)
tesdafai,testify
tesdamoneul,testimony(nial)
tesdee,testy
tesdekle,testicle
tesdi,testy
tesdukle,testicle
tesdumoneul,testimony(nial)
teseble,tease(sable)
tesh,teach
teshu,tissue

tesible,tease(sable)
test,*,ted,ting,ter,ty,TO CHALLENGE, EXPERIMENT FOR REACTION,A SHELL "prefixes: pre"
testafide,testify(fied)
testafy,testify
testament,*,tary,tal,WITNESS, CREATE A WILL "prefixes: inter"
testamint,testament
testamoneul,testimony(nial)
teste,testy
testefai,testify
testefide,testify(fied)
testefy,testify
testekle,testicle
testemint,testament
testemony,testimony
testicle,*,cular,culate,MALE REPRODUCTIVE GLANDS
testify,fies,fied,fying,fier,TO DECLARE UNDER OATH/ AS A WITNESS
testikle,testicle
testikuler,testicle(cular)
testiment,testament
testimony,nies,ial, PROVIDE WRITTEN/ VERBAL ACCOUNT AS A WITNESS
testir,test(er)
testufid,testify(fied)
testufy,testify
testukle,testicle
testument,testament
testumoneul,testimony(nial)
testumony,testimony
testur,test(er)
testy,tily,tiness, TOUCHY/ IRRITABLE
tesu,tissue
tesubil,tease(sable)
tesuble,tease(sable)
tesy,tizzy
tetanus,A BACTERIA WHICH ENTERS OPEN WOUNDS
tetbit,tidbit
teter,teeter
teth,teeth

tether,*,red,ring,CORD/ ROPE/ STRANDS TO SECURE SOMETHING FROM MOVING AWAY(or see teeth(er)" prefixes: un"
tethur,tether
tetir,teeter
tetnus,tetanus
tetra,*, FRESH WATER TROPICAL FISH, PREFIX INDICATING "FOUR" MOST OFTEN MODIFIES THE WORD
tetru,tetra
tetunes,testanus
tetur,teeter
teuburkwulosis,tuberculosis
teul,teal / tell / teil
teurd,tier(ed) / tear(ed)
teurism,tour(ism)
teusday,tuesday
tewb,tube
tewbles,tube(less)
tewbuler,tube(bular)
tewl,tool
tewm,tomb
tewnik,tunic
tewt,toot
tewth,tooth
tewthles,tooth(less)
texchur,texture
texder,texture
texdile,textile
texsdure,texture
text,*,ted,ting,tual,tually,tualism,tualist, PRINTED/ WRITTEN LETTERS TO FORM WORDS "prefixes: inter/ sub"
textail,textile
textile,*, ANY MATERIAL THAT CAN BE WOVEN
texture,*,ed,ring,ral,rally, ANY RAISED/ VARIANT PORTION OF A FLAT/ SMOOTH SURFACE "prefixes: inter"
tez,tease
tezzy,tizzy
tha,thaw / they
thad,they'd
thael,they'll

thai,thigh / thy
thaiamon,thiamine
thaim,thyme / time
thaimos,thymus
thain,thine
thair,there / their / they're
thairoid,thyroid
thaisain,thiazine
thaizain,thiazine
thal,they'll
thalamus,mi,mic,mically,PART OF A BRAIN/ FLOWER
thalas,thallus
thalimus,thalamus
thallus,NEW BUD OF A PLANT WITHOUT LEAVES, ETC.
thalmus,thalamus
thalumus,thalamus
thalus,thallus
thamadik,theme(matic)
than,WORD USED TO COMPARE/ CONTRAST
thanck,thank
thang,thong / thing
thank,*,ked,king,kful,kfully,kfulness,kless,klessly,klessness,APPRECIATION/ GRATITUDE
thanklis,thank(less)
thar,there / their / they're
tharbi,thereby
thare,there / their / they're
tharpist,therapy(pist)
tharpudik,therapy(peutic)
tharpy,therapy
tharfor,therefor / therefore
tharfour,therefor / therefore
tharipist,therapy(pist)
tharipudik,therapy(peutic)
tharipy,therapy
tharof,thereof
tharupist,therapy(pist)
tharupudik,therapy(peutic)
tharupy,therapy
thasoris,thesaurus
that,*,SOMEONE/ SOMETHING NOT IN THE IMMEDIATE AREA/ TIME FRAME, PREVIOUSLY MENTIONED, A PRONOUN (or see thought)

thatch,hes,hed,hing,her,MATTED/ LAYERED ORGANIC MATERIAL, SURFACE COVERING
thau,thaw / thou
thaud,thaw(ed) / thought
thaung,thong
thausand,thousand
thausend,thousand
thaut,thaw(ed) / thought
thaw,*,wed,wing,TEMPERATURE WARMING AWAY FROM FREEZING, UNFREEZING (or see thou)
thawt,thaw(ed) / thought
thayamen,thiamine
thayd,they'd
thayl,they'll
the,AN IDENTIFYING/ SPECIFYING WORD PRIOR TO A NOUN (or see thee)
theader,theater
theadir,theater
theadrekul,theatric(al)
theadrikal,theatric(al)
theadur,theater
thealegy,theology
theam,theme
theater,*,tre,A STRUCTURE FOR PERFORMING THE ARTS
theatir,theater
theatrek,theatric
theatrekul,theatric(al)
theatric,*,cal,calism,cality,calize,cally,THE ART OF PERFORMING, DRAMATIC "prefixes: non"
theatur,theater
thed,they'd
thee,REFERS TO A PERSON (or see the)
theef,thief / thieves
theem,theme
theesm,theism
thef,thief / they've
thefd,theft
theft,*,STEALING
thei,they
theid,they'd
theif,thief / they've
theifs,thief(s)

thei,they'll
theink,thank
their,*,REFERS TO PEOPLE, POSSESSIVE PLURAL PRONOUN (or see there/ they're)
theism,st,stic,stical,stically,BELIEF IN ONE DEITY
theiv,they've
theive,thief / thieves
thek,thick
thekin,thick(en)
thekinur,thick(ener)
thekist,thick(est)
thekit,thicket
theknur,thick(ener)
thekun,thick(en)
thekuner,thick(ener)
thekust,thick(est)
thekut,thicket
thel,they'll
them,mselves,PRONOUN REFERRING TO MORE THAN ONE (or see theme)
themadik,theme(matic)
themble,thimble
thembul,thimble
theme,*,matic,matically,A SPECIFIC TOPIC/ SUBJECT
themselves,PLURAL PRONOUN POSSESSIVE
then,SIGNIFIES TIME/ PLACE (or see thin/than)
thener,thin(nner)
theng,thing
thenir,thin(nner)
thenk,think
thenkar,think(er)
thenkur,think(er)
thenly,thin(ly)
thenur,thin(nner)
theo,PREFIX INDICATING "GOD" MOST OFTEN MODIFIES THE WORD (or see thio)
theology,gies,gian,gic,gical,gically,gize,gizer, PHILOSOPHY CONCERNING RELIGION
theolugy,theology
theory,ries,rize,rizes,rized,rizing,rem,rematic, rematically,retic,retical,retically,PRINCIPLES/ TECHNIQUES/ BELIEF IN AN ATTEMPT TO EXPLAIN/ UNDERSTAND EVENTS

ther,there / their / they're
therapudik,therapy(peutic)
therapy,pies, pist, peutic, peutics, peutically, peutist, TREATMENT TO REMEDY A MALADY "prefixes: bio/ sub"
therasik,thoracic
therbai,thereby
therbi,thereby
therd,third
therde,thirty
therdy,thirty
therdly,third(ly)
there,*,FOLLOWS NOUN/ PRONOUN TO DESCRIBE PLACE/ TIME/ EMPHASIS (or see their/ they're)
thereby,IN WHICH CASE/ INSTANCE
therefor,FOR IT/ THIS/ THAT (or see therefore)
therefore,IN REFERENCE TO THE BEFORE MENTIONED (or see therefor)
thereof,BECAUSE OF THAT
therepeudik,therapy(peutic)
therfor,therefor / therefore
therfour,therefor / therefore
therm,mic, mical, mal, CALORIES, PREFIX INDICATING "HEAT" MOST OFTEN MODIFIES THE WORD "prefixes: endo/exo"
thermal,*,lly, RELATED TO HEAT
thermamedur,thermometer
thermometer,*,tric, trical, trically, try, INSTRUMENT WHICH MEASURES HOT/ COLD VARIANCES
thermomuder,thermometer
thermul,thermal
thero,thorough
therof,thereof
therough,thorough
therow,thorough
thers,there(s) / their(s)
thersd,thirst
thersde,thursday / thirst
thersdy,thursday / thirst
therst,thirst
thersty,thursday / thirst
thert,third
therte,thirty

therty,thirty
theru,through / threw
theruf,thereof
therupist,therapy(pist)
therupudik,therapy(peutic)
therupy,therapy
thery,theory
thes,this / these
thesal,thistle
thesares,thesaurus
thesaurus,ses, BOOK OF SYNONYMS
thesbein,thespian
these,PLURAL TENSE OF "THIS" (or see this)
thesis,ses, SET/ PUT DOWN/ DOCUMENT/ PROVE
thesle,thistle
thesores,thesaurus
thespein,thespian
thespian,*,ACTOR/ ACTRESS
thesul,thistle
thesus,thesis
theury,theory
thev,thief / thieves
thevaree,thieves(ry)
thevury,thieves(ry)
thewre,theory
they,PLURAL OF "PERSONS IN GENERAL"
they'd,CONTRACTION OF OF THE WORDS 'THEY HAD/ WOULD'
they'll,CONTRACTION OF OF THE WORDS 'THEY SHALL/ WILL'
they're,CONTRACTION OF OF THE WORDS 'THEY ARE" (or see there/ their)
they've,CONTRACTION OF OF THE WORDS 'THEY HAVE"
theyl,they'll
thez,this
thi,PREFIX INDICATING "SULFUR" MOST OFTEN MODIFIES THE WORD (or see the/ thigh/ thy/ thee)
thiadur,theater
thiamen,thiamine
thiamine,VITAMIN COMPOUND
thiator,theater
thiatric,theatric
thiazine,CHEMICAL COMPOUND

thick,ken, kens, kened, kening, kener, ker, kest, kness, kly, kish, ket, HAVING NOTICEABLE DEPTH/ VISCOSITY/ DENSITY, EXCESSIVE
thicket,*,ted,ty, DENSE/ THICK SHRUBS
thief,*,eves,ONE WHO STEALS
thiemin,thiamine
thieves,ed, ving, ery, eries, vish, vishly, vishness, THOSE WHO STEAL
thiezene,thiazine
thigh,*,PORTION OF LEG ABOVE THE KNEE
thik,thick
thiken,thick(en)
thiket,thicket
thikist,thick(est)
thikit,thicket
thiknur,thick(ener)
thikuner,thick(ener)
thikust,thick(est)
thikut,thicket
thim,theme / them
thimadek,theme(matic)
thimadik,theme(matic)
thimas,thymus
thimatik,theme(matic)
thimble,*,DEVICE FOR PROTECTION OF FINGERTIPS
thimbul,thimble
thimes,thymus
thimomedur,thermometer
thimple,thimble
thimpul,thimble
thimselfs,themselves
thimselvs,themselves
thimus,thymus
thin,*,nned, nning, nner, nly, nness, nnish, LESS VISCOSITY/ WEIGHT/ THICKNESS/ DEPTH THAN PREFERRED/ NORMAL (or see then/ than/ thine)
thind,thin(nned)
thine,**hou,hy**,THIRD PERSON PRONOUN MEANING YOU/ YOURS (or see thin)
thiner,thin(nner)
thing,*,GENERIC TITLE FOR THAT WHICH IS NOT KNOWN/ UNDERSTOOD, WITHOUT A NAME (or see think)

think,*, king, ker, thought, kable, kingly, TO ENGAGE THE MIND, TO SUPPOSE/ CONTEMPLATE/ CONSIDER (or see thing) "prefixes: un"
thinkur, think(er)
thinur, thin(nner)
thio, PREFIX INDICATING "SULFUR" MOST OFTEN MODIFIES THE WORD (or see theo)
thiolochi, theology
thiololli, theology
thiqet, thicket
thirasik, thoracic
third,*, dly, NUMBER/ ONE MORE AFTER THE SECOND, 33.3% OF THE WHOLE
thirde, thirty
thirdy, thirty
thirdlee, third(ly)
thiri, theory
thirm, therm
thirmal, thermal
thirmamedur, thermometer
thirmamiter, thermometer
thirmek, therm(ic)
thirmel, thermal
thirmometur, thermometer
thirmul, thermal
thiro, thorough
thiroed, thyroid
thirogh, thorough
thiroid, thyroid
thirow, thorough
thiroyd, thyroid
thirsd, thirst
thirsde, thursday / thirst
thirst,*, ty, tier, tiest, tily, tiness, STRONG DESIRE FOR LIQUIDS, CRAVE SENSORY/ MENTAL INPUT
thirsty, thursday / thirst
thirt, third
thirty, ties, NUMBER AFTER 29
thiry, theory
this, PRONOUN/ POSSESSIVE PRESENT TIME (or see these)
thisal, thistle
thisares, thesaurus

thises, thesis
thisis, thesis
thisle, thistle
thisoris, thesaurus
thistle,*, A PLANT
thisul, thistle
thisus, thesis
thiumen, thiamine
thiuzene, thiazine
thiwroed, thyroid
thiz, this
tho, though / thou / thaw
thogh, though
thoght, thought
thoghtles, thought(less)
thom, thumb
thong,*, SHOES, UNDER GARMENT, LEATHER STRAP
thonk, thong
thoracic, cally, THE CHEST AREA
thoraks, thorax
thorasik, thoracic
thorax, xes, THE CHEST AREA
thorn,*, ny, nless, A SHARP/ PRICKLY POINT ON A PLANT/ TREE
thornee, thorn
thornlis, thorn(less)
thoro, thorough
thorough, hly, hness, COMPLETE/ DETAILED/ ACCURATE
thorow, thorough
thos, those / thus
those, PRONOUN FOR REMOTE
thosend, thousand
thosund, thousand
thot, thaw(ed) / thought
thotful, thought(ful)
thotles, thought(less)
thou,*, hine, THIRD PERSON PRONOUN MEANING YOU/ YOURS (or see though)
though, PLURAL ADJECTIVE MEANING THAT/ BUT/ HOWEVER
thought,*, tful, tfully, tfulness, tless, tlessly, tlessness, PAST TENSE FOR THE WORD "THINK/CONTEMPLATE" "prefixes: un"

thousand,*, dth, ENGLISH NUMBER AFTER 999
thousend, thousand
thousind, thousand
thousund, thousand
thow, thou / thaw / though
thowsand, thousand
thowsund, thousand
thowsunth, thousand(th)
thoz, those
thrab, throb
thrach, thrash
thrais, thrice
thraiv, thrive
thral, thrall
thrall, ENSLAVED/ SLAVE/ BONDAGE
thrang, throng
thrash, hes, hed, hing, her, FLAIL ABOUT VIOLENTLY, TO BEAT/ KICK/ TALK OVER AGAIN
thraul, thrall
thre, three
thread,*, ded, ding, der, dless, dy, diness, A THIN STRAND/ FILAMENT/ CORD "prefixes: un"
threat,*, ten, tens, tened, tening, teningly, CHALLENGE AGAINST SOMEONE/ SOMETHINGS IDEALS/ EXPECTATIONS
threch, thresh
threchold, threshold
thredold, threshold
thred, thread / threat
threden, threat(en)
thredined, threat(ened)
thredun, threat(en)
thredund, threat(ened)
three,*, rice, ENGLISH NUMBER AFTER TWO
threft, thrift
threfty, thrift
threl, thrill
threlur, thrill(er)
thresh, hes, hed, hing, her, BEAT GRAIN
threshold, threshold
threshold,*, A DOOR WAY/ SILL/ ENTRANCE "prefixes: sub"
thret, thread / threat

thretind,threat(ened)
thretund,threat(ened)
threw,PAST TENSE FOR THE WORD "THROW" (or see thru through)
thri,three
thrice,THREE TIMES
thrif,thrive
thrifd,thrift / thrive(d)
thrifde,thrift
thrifs,thrive(s)
thrift,ty,tily,tiness,MINDS/ WATCHES/ CONTROLS SPENDING/ USE OF RESOURCES (or see thrive(d))
thril,thrill
thriler,thrill(er)
thrill,*,lled,lling,ller,EMOTION EXAGGERRATED IN A POSITIVE FASHION,DELIGHT
thrilur,thrill(er)
thrise,thrice
thrive,*,ed,ving,vingly,er,TO EXIST SUCCESSFULLY
thro,throe / throw / through
throat,*,ted,ty,tily,tiness,CONICAL/ HOLLOW ENTRANCE/ PASSAGEWAY,FRONT PART OF NECK
throb,*,bbed,bbing,bber,PULSATE/ VIBRATE
throd,throat / throw(n)
throdul,throttle
throe,*,AMIDST STRONG PAIN/ AGONY/ EMOTIONAL TURMOIL (or see throw)
throl,thrall
throne,*,ed,ning,eless,SOVEREIGN/ AUTHORITATIVE PLACEMENT,A CHAIR (or see thrown) "prefixes: en"
throng,*,IN A CROWD/ MULTITUDE OF PEOPLE/ THINGS (or see thong)
thronk,throng
throsd,thrust
throst,thrust
throt,throat / throw(n)
throtal,throttle
throtil,throttle
throttle,*,ed,ling,er,CONTROL OF FLOW THROUGH AN ORIFICE/ OPENING/ THROAT
throtul,throttle
through,TO PENETRATE/ PASS/ MAKE IT TO THE END (or see threw)

throughout,PENETRATES/ EXISTS COMPLETELY
throun,throne / thrown
throut,throat
throw,*,wing,wn,TO TOSS/ ELIMINATE/ GET RID OF (or see throe/ throne) "prefixes: mis/ over/ up"
thrown,PAST TENSE FOR THE WORD "THROW" (or see throne)
throwt,throw(n) / throat
thru,TO PENETRATE/ PASS/ MAKE IT TO THE END (or see threw)
thruaut,throughout
thruch,thrush
thrusd,thrust
thrush,A BIRD,A CHILDREN'S DISEASE
thrust,*,ted,ting,ter,TO PLUNGE/ DRIVE/ FORCE FORWARD "prefixes: under/ up"
thruzd,thrust
thruart,thwart
thud,*,dded,dding,A SOLID/ HEAVY/ DROPPING/ FALLING SOUND
thug,*,ROBBERS/ IMMORAL PEOPLE
thuk,thug
thum,thumb
thumadik,theme(matic)
thumatik,theme(matic)
thumb,*,bed,bing,OPPOSABLE DIGIT ON THE HAND, USE OF THE THUMB (or see thump)
thumbt,thumb(ed) / thump(ed)
thump,*,ped,ping,FALLING/ HEAVY SOUND,SOUND OF HEARTBEAT (or see thumb)
thumpt,thumb(ed) / thump(ed)
thumselfs,themselves
thunder,*,red,ring,ringly,RUMBLING SOUND IN A RAIN STORM,SOUND MADE WHEN WEATHER FRONTS CONVERGE
thuntur,thunder
thurasik,thoracic
thurd,third
thurde,thirty
thurdy,thirty
thurdly,third(ly)
thurm,therm
thurmal,thermal

thurmamiter,thermometer
thurmic,therm(ic)
thurmil,thermal
thurmometer,thermometer
thurmomuder,thermometer
thuro,thorough
thurow,thorough
thursd,thirst
thursday,*,A DAY OF THE WEEK (ENGLISH)
thursde,thursday / thirst
thursdy,thursday / thirst
thurst,thirst
thurste,thursday / thirst
thursty,thursday / thirst
thurt,third
thurte,thirty
thurty,thirty
thurtly,third(ly)
thus,IN EFFECT,THEREFORE,AS A RESULT
thusares,thesaurus
thusores,thesaurus
thwart,*,ted,tedly,ting,TO INTERVENE/ WARD OFF/ DISTRACT A MISSION/ EVENT OR ACTION FROM IT'S GOAL/ ACCOMPLISHMENT
thwort,thwart
thy,hine,hou,THIRD PERSON PRONOUN MEANING YOU/ YOURS (or see thigh)
thyism,theism
thymas,thymus
thyme,AN HERBAL PLANT (or see time)
thymis,thymus
thymus,ses,mi,A GLAND IN THE BODY
thyroid,*,dless,GLAND/ CARTILAGE IN THE THROAT OF A BODY
thyuzene,thiazine
ti,tie / tea / tee
tiara,*,SMALL CROWN/ CORONET FOR HEAD
tibaco,tobacco
tibagen,toboggan
tibako,tobacco
tibea,tibia
tiberqulosis,tuberculosis
tibia,al,SHIN BONE IN LEG

tibogin,toboggan
tibse,tip(sy)
tic,A TWITCHING IN THE BODY/ FACE (or see tick)
tich,teach
tick, *, ked, king, ker, SMALL BLOOD SUCKING INSECT, RHYTHMIC CLOCK SOUND, A MARK ETCHED INTO SOMETHING, MATTRESS/ PILLOW COVERING, TELEGRAPH INSTRUMENT (or see tic)
ticol,tickle
tid,tide / tied / tight / teeth
tida,today
ticket, *, ted, ting, PIECE OF PAPER ISSUED WHICH BEARS INFORMATION SOLICITING YOUR PERSONAL APPEARANCE/ VISIT
tickle, *, ed, ling, er, lish, lishness, SENSATION TO SKIN/ EMOTIONS WHICH GENERATES SMILE/ LAUGHTER/ RESPONSE
tidal,lly, CONCERNING THE EBB AND FLOW OF THE SEA/ OCEAN (or see title) "prefixes: inter/ sub"
tiday,today
tidbet,tidbit
tidbit, *, A SNIPPET/ SMALL PORTION OF SOMETHING GREATER/ LARGER
tide, *, ed, ding, eful, eless, elessness, dings,dal, CONCERNING THE RISE/ FALL OF OCEAN/ SEA/ ECONOMICS (or see tight/ tied/ tidy)
tided,tidy / tide(d) / tied
tidel,tidal / title
tidle,tidal / title
tideness,tidy(diness)
tidil,tidal / title
tidon,tight(en)
tidond,tight(ened)
tidul,tidal / title
tidun,tight(en)
tidings, INFORMATION/ KNOWLEDGE SHARING
tidios,tedious
tidy,dies,died,dying,dily,diness, GET/ KEEP THINGS ORGANIZED/ IN ORDER "prefixes: un"

tie, *, ed,tying,ed,TO HOLD/ BUNDLE/ TIGHTEN THINGS TOGETHER USING TWINE/ STRING/ ROPE "prefixes: re/ un/ under"
tied,PAST TENSE FOR THE WORD "TIE" (or see tight/ tide)
tieng,tying
tier, *, red, ring, ELEVATE IN INCREMENTAL STEPS, RISERS, A LAYERED ARRANGEMENT OF ROWS (or see tear/ tire)
tiera,tiara
tif,tiff
tifes,typhus
tiff,small argument
tifis,typhus
tifoid,typhoid
tifoon,typhoon
tifun,typhoon
tifus,typhus
tig,thing
tigar,tiger
tiger, *, rish,LARGE WILD FELINE
tiget,ticket
tigethur,together
tight, *, tly, tness, ten, tened, tening, APPLY PRESSURE/ RESTRAINT/ SUPPRESSION "prefixes: up"
tights, SNUG FITTING OUTER WEAR
tigor,tiger
tigress,FEMALE WILD FELINE
tigur,tiger
tik,teak
tikal,tickle
tike, *, SMALL/ YOUNG CHILD (or see tiki)
tikel, tickle
tiker, tiger / tick(er)
tiket, ticket
tiki,A CARVED MYTHOLOGICAL FIGURE, OF POLYNESIAN CULTURE
tikil,tickle
tikir,tiger
tikit,ticket
tikle,tickle
tiklech,tickle(lish)
tiklush,tickle(lish)

tikol,tickle
tikor,tiger
tikot,ticket
tikres,tigress
tikt,tick(ed)
tikul,tickle
tikur,tiger
tikut,ticket
tiky,tiki
til,tile / till / teach / teal
tild,tile(d) / till(ed) / tilt
tile, *, ed,ling,er,FLAT/ THIN SLAB OF VARIOUS MATERIAL, TO STACK (or see till)
tilepathee,telepathy
tileputhee,telepathy
tilerean,telurian
till, *, lled, lling, ller, llage, PERFORM LABOR, PLACE FOR MONEY IN A BANK, ROTATING SOIL (too many definitions, please see standard dictionary) (or see tile/ teach)
tilt, *, ted, ting, ter, TO ROTATE OFF-CENTER, LEAN ONE WAY/ ANOTHER (or see till(ed)/ tile(d))
tilurean,telurian
tim,team / time
timado,tomato
timados,tomato(es)
timaro,tomorrow
timato,tomato
timber, *, rly, TREES VIEWED AS LUMBER (or see timbre)
timbrachure,temperature
timbre,A TONAL QUALITY (or see timber)
timbrushure,temperature
timbur, timber
timd, time(d)
time, *, ed, ming, er, ely, elier, eliest, eliness, eless, elessness, HUMAN CONSTRUCT TO DIFFERENTIATE BETWEEN PLACE/ SPACE, TO GUAGE HOW MANY SECONDS/ MINUTES/ HOURS/ DAYS/ MONTHS/ YEARS (or see thyme) "prefixes: over/ un/ under"
timed, timid / time(d)
timedly,timid(ly)
timet, timid
timid,dly,dity,dness,HESITANT/ CAUTIOUS

timly, time(ly)
timod, timid
timpal, temple
timparary, temporary
timparize, temporize
timparment, temperament
timper, temper
timperal, temporal
timperary, temporary
timperashure, temperature
timperize, temporize
timperol, temporal
timperushure, temperature
timpeshues, tempest(uous)
timpest, tempest
timpestuous, tempest(uous)
timpil, temple
timplat, template
timplut, template
timpo, tempo
timpol, temple
timporarely, temporary(rily)
timporul, temporal
timporachure, temperature
timpral, temporal
timpramentul, temper(mental)
timprary, temporary
timprashure, temperature
timprature, temperature
timprery, temporary
timpromintal, temper(mental)
timprumental, temper(mental)
timptashen, temptation
timptation, temptation
timptres, tempt(ress)
timpul, temple
timpur, temper
timpura, tempura
timpurarely, temporary(rily)
timpurary, temporary
timpurize, temporize
timpurment, temperament
timpust, tempest

timt, tempt
timtashen, temptation
timtation, temptation
timted, tempt(ed)
timtres, tempt(ress)
timud, timid
timulchuis, tumult(uous)
timulchuous, tumult(uous)
timult, tumult
timur, time(r)
timut, timid
tin,*, nned, nning, nnier, nniest, nny, nnilly, nniness, TYPE OF METAL, USE OF METAL, TINSMITH (or see tenor tine/ tint/ tiny/ tend/ teen)
tinable, tenable
tinachus, tenacious
tinacity, tenacity
tinakle, tentacle
tinament, tenement
tinamint, tenement
tinansy, tenant(ncy)
tinant, tenant
tinasedy, tenacity
tinashus, tenacious
tinasity, tenacity
tinatef, tentative
tinatif, tentative
tinatious, tenacious
tinative, tentative
tincchur, tincture
tinch, tinge
tinchd, tinge(d)
tinchur, tincture
tincity, tense(sity)
tincol, tinkle
tincture,*, PLANTS SUBMERGED IN ALCOHOL FOR MEDICINAL USE
tind, tin(nned) / tend
tindatev, tentative
tinded, tend(ed) / tint(ed)
tinden, tendon
tindensy, tendency
tindenus, tendon(dinous)

tinder, ry, USED FOR KINDLING (or see tender)
tinderize, tender(ize)
tinderloin, tenderloin
tinderly, tender(ly)
tindernes, tender(ness)
tindinsy, tendency
tindirloin, tenderloin
tindon, tendon
tindor, tinder / tender
tindorize, tender(ize)
tindrel, tendril
tindrul, tendril
tindun, tendon
tindur, tender / tinder
tindurize, tender(ize)
tindurloin, tenderloin
tindurly, tender(ly)
tindutif, tentative
tine,*, A POINT ON A TOOL/ INSTRUMENT/ HORN/ FORK (or see tin/ tiny)
tinekle, tentacle
tinemint, tenement
tinen, tenon
tinensy, tenant(ncy)
tinent, tenant
tiner, tenor
tines, tennis / tine(s) / time(s)
tinet, tenet / tenant
tineur, tenure
tinewus, tenuous
tinfold, tenfold
ting, A SOUND (or see tinge/thing)
tinge,*, ed, ging, A HINT/ TRACE/ SMALL BIT OF CHANGE IN COLOR/ QUALITY (or see ting)
tinible, tenable
tinikle, tentacle
tinir, tenor
tinit, tenet / tenant / tonight
tinj, tinge
tink, ting
tinkal, tinkle
tinkchur, tincture

tinker, *, red, ring, rer, TOY/ FONDLE/ MEND/ HANDLE SOMETHING

tinkle, *, ed, ling, ly, er, A FAINT LITTLE SOUND

tinkol, tinkle
tinksher, tincture
tinkture, tincture
tinkul, tinkle
tinkur, tinker
tinll, tinge
tinon, tenon
tinor, tenor
tinpal, temple
tinparery, temporary
tinpermint, temperament
tinpest, tempest
tinpirery, temporary
tinpist, tempest
tinplit, template
tinpo, tempo
tinpol, temple
tinporal, temporal
tinporary, temporary
tinporat, temper(ate)
tinprachur, temperature
tinpral, temporal
tinprament, temperament
tinpret, temper(ate)
tinpriment, temperament
tinprit, temper(ate)
tinprochur, temperature
tinprot, temper(ate)
tinquer, tinker
tins, tin(s) / tent(s) / tense / tint(s) / tend
tinse, tense / tent(s)

tinsel, *, led, ling, SHINY/ METALLIC STRIPS FOR DECORATION

tinsil, tinsel
tinsity, tense(sity)
tinsle, tinsel
tinsness, tense(ness)
tinsul, tinsel

tint, *, ted, ting, tless, CHANGE/ APPLY SHADE OF COLOR (or see tent/ tense/ tin(nned)/ tend) "prefixes: under"

tintakle, tentacle
tintative, tentative
tinted, tint(ed) / tent(ed) / tend(ed)
tintetive, tentative
tinth, tenth
tintid, tint(ed) / tent(ed) / tend(ed)
tintikle, tentacle
tintuckle, tentacle
tintud, tint(ed) / tent(ed) / tend(ed)
tintukle, tentacle
tintutive, tentative
tinuble, tenable
tinuis, tenuous
tinukle, tentacle
tinument, tenement
tinunsy, tenant(ncy)
tinunt, tenant
tinur, tenor
tinus, tennis
tinutef, tentative
tinutive, tentative

tiny, nier, niest, niness, LITTLE, VERY SMALL IN SCALE (or see tin(nny))

tinyewr, tenure
tinyewus, tenuous
tinyir, tenure
tinyur, tenure
tinzul, tinsel
tiol, teal

tip, *, pped, pping, pper, ppy, ppable, pless, psy, TO LEAN SOMETHING OFF-CENTER FROM ITS POINT OF GRAVITY (or see type)

tipakle, typical
tipd, tip(pped) / type(d)
tipe, type / tip(ppy)
tipekul, typical
tiper, tip(pper) / type(r)
tiphoon, typhoon
tiphune, typhoon
tipi, teepee / tip(ppy)
tipicol, typical
tipifai, typify
tipikul, typical
tipist, type(pist)
tipo, typo
tipography, topography
tipografe, topography
tipse, tip(sy)
tipt, tip(pped) / type(d)
tipufy, typify
tipukle, typical
tipur, tip(pper) / type(r)
tiqi, tiki
tiquila, tequila
tir, tire / tear

tirade, *, VERBAL/ VIOLENT OUTBURST

tiranchula, tarantula
tirane, terrain / terrane / tyranny
tiranekul, tyrannical
tiranikul, tyrannical
tiranshulu, tarantula
tirant, tyrant
tirantula, tarantula
tirate, tirade
tirazo, terrazzo
tirben, turban / turbine
tirbiulent, turbulent
tirbo, turbo
tirbulens, turbulent(nce)
tirbulent, turbulent
tirbun, turban / turbine
tird, tire(d)
tirdle, turtle

tire, *, ed, ring, eless, elessly, elessness, edly, edness, esome, esomely, esomeness, RUN OUT OF ENERGY, USED ON WHEELS "prefixes: un"

tireid, tirade
tirene, tyranny
tirent, tyrant
tireny, tyranny
tiresdreul, terrestrial
tirestrial, terrestrial
tirf, turf

tirit,turret	tisy,tizzy	tobaco,tobacco
tirkoes,turquois	**tit**,*,tty,tties,NIPPLE ON FEMALE OF SPECIES, TEAT (or see tied/ tight/ tights/ teat)	tobagen,toboggan
tirkoys,turquois	tital,title / tidal	tobako,tobacco
tirles,tire(less)	titan,tight(en)	toberkulosis,tuberculosis
tirlis,tire(less)	titbet,tidbit	tobogan,toboggan
tirm,term	titbit,tidbit	**toboggan**,*,ner,nist,TYPE OF SLED
tirmenashen,terminate(tion)	tite,tidy / tight / tied	tobogin,toboggan
tirmenate,terminate	titel,title / tidal	toch,touch
tirmenation,terminate(tion)	titen,tight(en)	tocsic,toxic
tirmenator,terminate(tor)	titend,tight(ened)	tocsicololli,toxicology
tirmenology,terminology	titenes,tidy(diness)	tocsufy,toxify(fication)
tirmenul,terminal	titer,teeter	tod,toad / toe(d) / tow(ed)
tirminate,terminate	titer-toder,teeter-totter	toda,today
tirmination,terminate(tion)	tith,teeth	todal,total
tirminator,terminate(tcr)	**tithe**,*,ed,hing,hable,A PERCENTAGE TO BE GIVEN AWAY TO SOMEONE/ SOMETHING	today,THE DAY WHICH IS PRESENT NOW
tirminolegy,terminology	titil,title / tidal	**toddler**,*,SMALL CHILD LEARNING TO WALK
tirminul,terminal	titind,tight(ened)	**toddy**,ddies,ALCOHOLIC MIXED DRINK (or see toady)
tirmite,termite	**title**,*,ed,ling,list,A NAME (or see tidal/ tight(ly)) "prefixes: inter/ re/ sub/ sur/ un "	tode,toad / toddy / toe(d) / toady
tirmoel,turmoil	titly,tight(ly)	todee,toddy / toady
tirmonel,terminal	titond,tight(ened)	todej,today
tirmunology,terminology	titul,title / tidal	todel,total
tirn,tern / turn	titun,tight(en)	todem,totem
tirnament,tournament	titund,tight(ened)	todil,total
tirnep,turnip	tity,tidy	todim,totem
tirnument,tournament	tiung,tying	todler,toddler
tirpentine,turpentine	tiusdei,Tuesday	todlur,toddler
tirpewlent,turbulent	**tizzy**,A FRENZIED STATE,A DITHER	todom,totem
tirpulent,turbulent	**to**,PREPOSITION IN THE ENGLISH LANGUAGE TO SHOW RELATIONSHIP BETWEEN PERSON/ PLACE/ THING (or see toe/ too/ tow)	todul,total
tirpuntine,turpentine	**toad**,*,AN AMPHIBIAN MOSTLY FOUND IN DRY TERRAIN (or see told/ toe(d)/ toady)	todum,totem
tirrazo,terrazzo	**toady**,dies,died,dying,dyish,dism,diness,TO GROVEL/ FLATTER OTHERS FOR SELF-SERVING REASONS	tody,toddy / toady
tirse,terse	toagrife,topography	**toe**,*,ed,eless,eing,INDEX ON A FOOT (or see to/ tow/ toy)
tirsheary,tertiary	**toast**,*,ted,ting,ter,TO BROWN FOOD WITH A HEAT SOURCE,HONORING SOMETHING/ SOMEONE BEFORE HAVING A DRINK	toel,toil
tirsnes,terse(ness)	tob,tub	toeld,toil(ed) / told
tirsum,tire(some)	**tobacco**,PLANT WHOSE LEAVES CONTAIN NICOTINE	toelet,toilet
tiritl,turtle		toeng,toe(ing) / toy(ing) / tow(ing)
tirtul,turtle		**tofu**,A SOYBEAN BASED FOOD
tirunt,tyrant		**toga**,*,A WRAP AS WORN BY ROMANS
tirut,turret		togal,toggle
tis,tense / this		togel,toggle
tise,tizzy		**together**,rness,BROUGHT/ COLLECTED/ ROUNDED UP INTO ONE PLACE
tishew,tissue		
tissue,*,A SMALL/ LIGHTWEIGHT PIECE OF PAPER		
tisue,tissue		

toggle, *, ed, ling, er, LEVER/ SWITCH FOR ALTERING ELECTRICAL CURRENT, A SYSTEM DEVISED TO FACILITATE MOVEMENT
toght, taught / taut / tout
togle, toggle
togu, toga
togul, toggle
toi, toy
toid, toy(ed)
toil, *, led, ling, ler, TO LABOR/ WORK VERY HARD
toild, toil(ed)
toilet, *, A FIXTURE FOR CAPTURING URING/ FECES
toiol, toil
tok, tuck / took
toka, toga
tokel, toggle
tokela, tequila
token, *, A SMALL DISK/ COIN/ PAPER RESEMBLING SOMETHING OF VALUE
tokik, toxic
tokil, toggle
tokila, tequila
tokin, token
tokle, toggle
toko, taco
toksakolegy, toxicology
toksek, toxic
toksen, toxin
toksikolegy, toxicology
toksufy, toxify(fication)
toksukolegy, toxicology
toksun, toxin
toku, toga
tokul, toggle
tokun, token
tol, tall / toll
tolarense, tolerance
tolarent, tolerant
tolarible, tolerable
tolarinse, tolerance
told, PAST TENSE FOR THE WORD "TELL" (or see toll(ed)) "prefixes: re/ un"
tole, toll

toler, tall(er)
tolerable, eness, bility, ly, BE PATIENT WITH DESPITE THE IRRITATION "prefixes: in"
tolerance, BE PATIENT WITH DESPITE THE IRRITATION "prefixes: in"
tolerant, ntly, BE PATIENT WITH DESPITE IRRITATION "prefixes: in"
tolerashen, tolerate(tion)
tolerate, *, ed, ting, able, ance, ant, ative, ation, BE PATIENT WITH DESPITE THE IRRITATION
tolereit, tolerate
tolerinse, tolerance
tolerint, tolerant
tolir, tall(er)
tolirashen, tolerate(tion)
tolirate, tolerate
tolirense, tolerance
toliruble, tolerable
tolk, talk / talc
toll, *, lled, lling, BELL RINGING, A REQUIRED FEE (or see tall)
tolness, tall(ness)
tolorinse, tolerance
tolrabol, tolerable
tolrant, tolerant
tolrens, tolerance
tolur, tall(er)
tolurashen, tolerate(tion)
tolurate, tolerate
toluration, tolerate(tion)
tolurense, tolerance
tolurent, tolerant
toluribel, tolerable
tolurinse, tolerance
tolurint, tolerant
tomado, tomato
tomaro, tomorrow
tomato, oes, A FRUIT/ VEGETABLE
tomb, *, STONE ENCLOSURE FOR A LIFELESS BODY "prefixes: en"
tombol, tumble
tomeitou, tomato
tomoro, tomorrow

tomorrow, THE DAY AFTER TODAY
ton, *, nnage, POUNDS (or see tone/ toon)
tonaledy, tone(nality)
tone, *, ed, ning, nal, nality, nally, ness, elessly, elessness, SOUND FREQUENCY, MAKE FIRM/ STRONG "prefixes: over/ semi/ under"
tonej, ton(nnage)
tonek, tonic
tong, *, TOOL USED FOR GRASPING/ PICKING THINGS UP (or see tongue)
tongue, *, ed, uing, MOVABLE ORGAN IN THE MOUTH, PART OF A HITCH, POINT ON LAND (or see tong)
tonic, *, cally, A MIXTURE, RELATED TO TONE "prefixes: sub"
tonight, THE NIGHT OF PRESENT TENSE
tonij, ton(nnage)
tonik, tonic
tonite, tonight
tonk, tong / tongue
tonles, tone(less)
tons, taunt(s) / ton(s) / tone(s)
tonsalodemy, tonsillotomy
tonsel, tonsil
tonselodemy, tonsillotomy
tonsil, *, llotomy, TISSUE HANGING IN THE THROAT
tonsillotomy, ACT OF REMOVING THE TONSILS
tonsilotomy, tonsillotomy
tonsul, tonsil
tonsulodemy, tonsillotomy
tont, taunt
tonul, tone(nal)
too, PREPOSITION MEANING ALSO/ MORE THAN ENOUGH (or see to/ toe/ tow/ two)
toob, tube
tooba, tuba
tooch, tush
toocha, touche'
took, PAST TENSE FOR THE WORD "TAKE", TO TAKE SOMETHING "prefixes: over/ re/ under"
tool, *, led, ling, lless, A DEVICE DESIGNED TO HELP WITH WORK "prefixes: re"
toolip, tulip
toom, tomb

toomer, tumor
toomur, tumor
toon, *, SHORT FOR CARTOON (or see tune)
toona, tuna
toonek, tunic
toonik, tunic
toonu, tuna
toopa, toupee
toopay, toupee
toosday, tuesday
toosh, tush
toot, *, ted, ting, A SOUND FROM A HORN
tooth, hless, hlessly, hyhi y, hiness, teeth, ENAMELED BONE PROJECTILES IN THE MOUTH, AN OUTCROP ON GEARS
tootoo, tutu
top, *, pped, pping, pper, oless, HEAD/ TIP/ UPPERMOST PART OF SOMETHING, A SPINNING TOY (or see taupe/ toupee)
topa, toupee
topagrafik, topography(hic)
topagraphical, topography(hical)
topagraphy, topography
topagrefi, topography
topal, topple
topalegy, topology
tope, toupee / taupe
topeary, topiary
topek, topic
topekul, topical
toper, top(pper)
tophu, tofu
topiary, ries, THE SCIENCE OF TRIMMING PLANTS
topic, *, SUBJECT/ TITLE/ THEME "prefixes : sub"
topical, lly, lity, lities, THE SURFACE, SHALLOW (or see tropical)
topiery, topiary
topigrafik, topography(hic)
topigrafikul, topography(hical)
topigraphic, topography(hic)
topigraphical, topography(hical)
topil, topple
tople, topple

toples, top(pless)
topo, *, PREFIX INDICATING "PLACE" MOST OFTEN MODIFIES THE WORD
topography, hies, hic, hical, hically, her, A SCIENCE WHICH IDENTIFIES ELEVATIONS/ DEPRESSION ON THE EARTH
topol, topple
topolegy, topology
topology, gic, gical, gically, gist, SCIENCE THAT CAN IDENTIFY ELEVATION/ DEPRESSION ON THE EARTH
topple, *, ed, ling, OVERTHROWN, COME DOWN, FALL OVER
topografik, topography(hic)
topografikul, topography(hical)
topographical, topography(hical)
topuk, topic
topukil, topical
topul, topple
tor, tar / tore
torc, torque
torch, hes, hed, hing, STAFF/ BRANCH WITH FIRE ON THE END
torcher, torture
torcherus, torture(rous)
torchuos, tortuous
torchur, torture
tord, toward / tour(ed) / tar(rred) / tore
tordis, tortoise
tordus, tortoise
tore, PAST TENSE FOR THE WORD "TEAR"
torenshul, torrent(ial)
torent, torrent
torential, torrent(ial)
tores, torus
torget, target
torgut, target
torifek, terrific
torinshul, torrent(ial)
torint, torrent
toris, torus
tork, torque
torment, *, ted, ting, ter, TO EXTEND/ APPLY CRUELTY/ PAIN TO SOMETHING/ SOMEONE

tormint, torment
tornado, oes, dic, A HIGH/ SWIRLING WIND WHICH BEGINS IN THE SKY THEN TOUCHES THE GROUND
tornados, tornado(es)
tornamet, tournament
tornato, tornado
torneidou, tornado
tornesh, tarnish
tornushd, tarnish(ed)
toros, torus
torp, tarp
torpedo, oes, oed, oing, A CONICAL/ BULLET-SHAPED MISSILE THAT PROPELS ITSELF THROUGH WATER
torpedod, torpedo(ed)
torque, AN EXERTED FORCE, AN ORNAMENT
torrent, *, tial, tially, A VIOLENT/ SUDDEN GUSH/ RUSH OF GREAT VOLUME
torsh, torch
torshen, torsion
torsher, torture
torshun, torsion
torshur, torture
torsion, nal, nally, TWIST AN OBJECT TO APPLY TORQUE
torso, *, si, THE MAIN PORTION/ TRUNK OF A BODY
tort, *, WRONG/ IMPROPER (or see torte/ tart)
torte, *, A HEAVILY MADE CAKE (or see tort/ tart)
tortelu, tortilla
tortes, tortoise
torteu, tortilla
torteus, tortuous
tortila, tortilla
tortilla, *, CORN BASED ROUND/ FLAT CAKE
tortis, tortoise
tortoise, A TURTLE LIVING ON LAND
tortuous, sly, sness, OF BEING TWISTED/ CROOKED/ BENT BY NATURE
torture, *, ed, ring, rable, edly, er, esome, ringly, rous, rously, PURPOSEFUL INFLICTION OF PAIN
tortus, tortoise
torus, RING SHAPED/ BULGE/ RIDGE
tos, toss / toe(s) / two(s) / tow(s)
tosc, tusk
tosd, toast / toss(ed)

tosday, tuesday
tosder, toast(er)
tosdur, toast(er)
toss, sses, ssed, ssing, GENTLY THROW WITH UPWARD MOTION (or see toe(s)) "prefixes: re"
tost, toast / toss(ed)
tostur, toast(er)
tot, *, tted, tting, A SMALL AMOUNT, WORD FOR YOUNG CHILD/ TODDLER, SHORT WORD FOR 'TOTAL' (or see taught/ taut/ tout/ tote)
total, *, led, ling, lly, lity, lizer, SUM OF ALL PARTS, COMPLETELY "prefixes: re/ sub"
totalitarian, *, nism, CENTRALIZED/ DICTATORIAL GOVERNMENT
tote, *, ed, ting, TO CARRY (or see tot/ taught/ taut/ tout)
totel, total
totem, *, mic, mism, mist, mistic, CARVED/ SYMBOLIC REPRESENTATION
toten, taut(en)
totil, total
totile, total(lly)
totim, totem
totin, taut(en)
totler, toddler
totlur, toddler
totnes, taut(ness)
totoletarian, totalitarian
totom, totem
totule, total(lly)
totum, totem
toty, toddy / toady
tou, toe / tow
toub, tube
touch, hes, hed, hing, hable, her, hy, hily, hiness, CONTACT/ PRESSURE/ EFFECT/ SENSATION AFFECTING SOME PART OF THE BODY (or see touche'/ tush) "prefixes: re/ un"
touche', FENCING/ SPORT EXPRESSION (or see touch/ tush)
toud, toad
toudem, totem
touerd, toward
touga, toga

tough, her, hest, hen, hener, hy, hly, hness, CHALLENGING/ DIFFICULT TO PENETRATE/ AFFECT/ CONVINCE/ ASSUME
tought, tuft
touken, token
toul, towel / tool
toun, town/ tune
toupalochi, topology
toupee, FALSE HAIR PIECE (or see taupe)
toupieri, topiary
toupogrefi, topography
toupologi, topology
tour, *, red, ring, rism, rist, PERUSE/ VISIT/ TRAVEL TO SITES WITHIN A SPECIFIC TIME FRAME
tournament, *, COMPETITION IN SPORTS
tousil, tousle
tousle, *, ed, ling, RUFFLE/ MESS UP
tout, *, ted, ting, TO SOLICIT FOR VOTES/ SALES/ INFORMATION (or see taut/ taught)
toutal, total
toutem, totem
tow, *, wed, wing, wer, TO HAUL/ PULL BEHIND (or see toe/ two/ too/ to/ toe(d)) "prefixes: under"
toward, *, dly, dliness, IN THE DIRECTION OF, EXPRESSING DIRECTION "prefixes: un"
towd, tow(ed) / toe(d) / toad
towel, *, led, ling, CLOTH/ MATERIAL FOR USE IN DEALING WITH LIQUID
tower, *, red, ring, VERTICAL RISE, STRUCTURE WITH GREAT HEIGHT
towir, tower
town, *, nie, DESIGNATED AREA WHERE PEOPLE LIVE/ COHABITATE/ CONDUCT BUSINESS "prefixes: up"
towp, taupe
towsil, tousle
towst, toast
towt, tout / taut / taught
towur, tower
tox, PREFIX INDICATING "POISON" MOST OFTEN MODIFIES THE WORD
toxakology, toxicology
toxek, toxic
toxen, toxin

toxi, PREFIX INDICATING "POISON" MOST OFTEN MODIFIES THE WORD
toxic, *, cally, cant, cation, city, cities, POISONOUS "prefixes: de/ endo"
toxico, PREFIX INDICATING "POISON" MOST OFTEN MODIFIES THE WORD
toxicolochi, toxicology
toxicology, gic, gical, gically, gist, cosis, SCIENCE/ STUDY OF POISONS
toxify, fies, fied, fying, fication, POISONED "prefixes: de"
toxik, toxic
toxikology, toxicology
toxin, *, POISON "prefixes: endo/ exo"
toxun, toxin
toy, *, yed, ying, PLAYTHING
toyl, toil
toylet, toilet
tozdur, toast(er)
tozt, toast
tra, PREFIX INDICATING "ACROSS/ OVER/ BEYOND" MOST OFTEN MODIFIES THE WORD (or see tray)
trabers, traverse
trac, track / trace
trace, *, ed, cing, er, eable, eableness, eably, eless, PATH/ LINE/ SCENT/ CLUES LEADING TO ORIGINATION/ BEGINNING POINT (or see tray(s)/ track) "prefixes: re"
trach, trash
trachea, al, ate, eitis, TUBE PLACED IN THE THROAT FOR AIR/ FOOD
trachedi, tragedy
trachekt, traject
trachic, tragic
trachoma, atous, EYELID INFLAMMATION/ INFECTION
track, *, ked, king, ker, kable, kless, klessness, PATH/ RAILS TO TRANSPORT/ NAVIGATE ALONG (or see tract)
trackshen, traction
tract, *, table, tion, A STRETCH/ AREA OF SPACE/ TIME/ DISTANCE (or see track(ed))
tractable, tability, tableness, tably, EASILY MANIPULATED/ FORMED (or see track(able))
tracter, tractor

traction,nal,ive,FIRM GRIP FOR MOMEN"UM,METHOD TO RELIEVE STRESS ON THE BODY "prefixes: re"
tractor,*,EQUIPMENT USED FOR WORK
tractur,tractor
tracuble,trace(able)
tracur,trace(r)
trade,*,ed,ding,er,dable,EXCHANGE ONE THING FOR ANOTHER (or see trait) "prefixes: over"
traden,trod(dden) / trot(tting)
tradeshenul,tradition(al)
tradeshin,tradition
tradetion,tradition
tradin,trod(dden) / trot;tting)
tradir,trade(r) / traitor
tradishenul,tradition(al)
tradition,*,nal,nally,na ism,nalist,nalistic,PRACTICED REPEATEDLY THROUGHOUT TIME
tradur,trade(r) / traitor
trae,tray
trael,trail
traf,trough
trafek,traffic
trafel,travel
traffic,cked,cking,MANY PEOPLE USING SAME ROADWAY/ PATH/ AVENUE/ METHOD ROUTINELY
trafik,traffic
trafil,travel
trafler,travel(er)
trafuk,traffic
traful,travel
tragedy,dies,gic,A GREAT CATASTROPHIC/ DISASTROUS EVENT
tragek,tragic
tragekle,tragic(ally)
tragekt,traject
tragektery,traject(ory)
tragety,tragedy
tragic,cally,A TRAGEDY
tragide,tragedy
tragik,tragic
tragude,tragedy
trai,try
traiad,triad

traiangiular,triangular
traiangol,triangle
traiangular,triangular
traib,tribe
traicicol,tricycle
traident,trident
traifel,trifle
traijidras,trihedras
traijidron,trihedron
trail,*,led,ling,ler,A PATH/ ROUTE "prefixes: en"
trailaderol,trilateral
trailateral,trilateral
trailer,*,CONTAINER ON WHEELS WITH HITCH, MOVIE PREVIEW (or see trail(er)) "prefixes: semi"
trailingual,trilingual
trailor,trawl(er) / trail(er) / trailer
train,*,ned,ning,ner,nable,LOCOMOTIVE/ RAILWAY CARS, DISCIPLINE TO FOLLOW DIRECTIONS AS COMMANDED/ INSTRUCTED (or see trine) "prefixes: de/ en/ re"
trainkwol,tranquil
trainqwil,tranquil
trainuble,train(able)
traiol,trial
traip,tripe
traipod,tripod
traipse,*,ed,sing,TO WALK AROUND WITHOUT PURPOSE
traiseps,triceps
traisicol,tricycle
trait,*,SPECIFIC QUALITIES/ FEATURES (or see trade)
traitor,*,rous,rously,ONE WHO BETRAYS ANOTHER
traiumf,triumph
traiumverent,triumvirate
traject,*,ted,ting,tion,tory,tories,THE CURVE/ ARC OF DIRECTION WHEN AIMING/ CASTING/ SHOOTING
trajectery,traject(ory)
trajek,tragic
trajekle,tragic(ally)
trajekt,traject
trajektery,traject(ory)
trajide,tragedy
trajik,tragic

trajude,tragedy
trak,track / tract
trakd,track(ed) / tract
trakea,trachea
traker,track(er)
trakia,trachea
trakible,track(able) / tract(able)
trakiu,trachea
traklis,track(less)
trakomu,trachoma
trakshen,traction
trakshun,traction
trakt,track(ed) / tract
traktor,tractor
trakuble,track(able) / tract(able)
trakur,track(er)
tral,trawl / troll / trowel
trale,trail / trolley
traler,trawl(er) / trail(er) / trailer
traley,trolley
trallect,traject
tralledi,tragedy
trallic,tragic
tralur,trawl(er) / trail(er) / trailer
tram,*,mmed,mming,MECHANICALLY ADJUST, TRANSPORTER ON RAILS,WOVEN SILK TECHNIQUE
trama,trauma
tramadik,trauma(tic)
tramatis,trauma(tize)
tramb,tramp
trambalen,trampoline
trambon,trombone
trambulen,trampoline
tramel,trommel
tramendus,tremendous
tramindusle,tremendous(lly)
tramol,trommel
tramp,*,STEP HEAVILY, TRAVEL ON FOOT FROM PLACE TO PLACE FOR SUBSISTENCE WITHOUT A HOME
trampalen,trampoline
trampil,trample
trample,*,ed,ling,STEP/ STOMP HEAVILY CAUSING HARM/ INJURY

tramplen, trampoline
trampol, trample
trampoline, *, er, nist, MATERIAL STRETCHED ACROSS A FRAME SUPPORTED BY SPRINGS TO JUMP ON
trampul, trample
trampulen, trampoline
tramu, trauma
tramul, trommel
tramutize, trauma(tize)
tran, PREFIX INDICATING "ACROSS/ OVER/ BEYOND" MOST OFTEN MODIFIES THE WORD (or see train) "prefixes: en"
trance, *, ed, cing, A SUBCONSCIOUS STATE OF MIND
trancefigurashen, transfigure(ration)
trancefushen, transfuse(sion)
trane, train
traneble, train(able)
tranes, train(s) / train(s) / trance
trangretion, transgress(ion)
tranible, train(able)
tranir, train(er)
trankuil, tranquil
trankwel, tranquil
tranquil, lly, lness, lize, lizes, lized, lizer, lizing, lity, PEACEFUL/ CALM/ RELAXING
tranqwul, tranquil
trans, trance / train(s) / tran(s)
transacshun, transact(ion)
transact, ted, ting, tion, tional, CARRY OUT/ MAKE EXCHANGE IN BUSINESS
transaktion, transact(ion)
transatif, transit(ive)
transbertashen, transport(ation)
transbir, transpire
transbirtashen, transport(ation)
transblant, transplant
transbonder, transponder
transbort, transport
transburtachen, transport(ation)
transcend, *, ded, ding, dent, dence, dency, dently, dental, dently, dentalism, dentalist, NOT OF THE MATERIAL/ PHYSICAL PLANE/ FREQUENCY
transcraib, transcribe

transcrepshen, transcription
transcribe, *, ed, bing, er, iption, PHYSICALLY/ LITERALLY MAKE NOTATION/ COPY, AVAILABLE FOR VIEWING
transcripshen, transcription
transcription, *, tional, tive, PHYSICALLY/ LITERALLY MAKE NOTATION/ COPY, AVAILABLE FOR VIEWING
transdews, transduce
transdewsur, transduce(r)
transduce, *, er, ction, CHANGE ONE TYPE OF FREQUENCY/ ENERGY INTO ANOTHER
transduction, *, nal, CHANGE TYPE OF FREQUENCY/ ENERGY INTO ANOTHER BIOLOGICALLY
transduse, transduce
transduxshin, transduction
transeant, transient
transechen, transit(ion)
transect, *, ted, ting, tion, DIVIDE/ SEVER/ CUT ACROSS
transekt, transect
transem, transom
transend, transcend
transendense, transcend(ence)
transendent, transcend(ent)
transendentul, transcend(ental)
transendul, transcend(ental)
transent, transcend
transeshenul, transit(ional)
transestur, transistor
transet, transit
transetif, transit(ive)
transetional, transit(ional)
transetory, transit(ory)
transeunt, transient
transexshen, transect(ion)
transfeks, transfix
transfer, *, rred, rring, rrer, rral, rrals, rable, rability, ree, rence, rential, MOVE/ SHIFT FROM ONE PLACE TO ANOTHER "prefixes: re"
transfermashen, transform(ation)
transfeugin, transfuse(sion)
transfews, transfix
transfex, transfix
transfigure, *, ed, ring, rement, ration, CHANGE APPEARANCE OF

transfirens, transfer(ence)
transfirmation, transform(ation)
transfiruble, transfer(able)
transfius, transfuse
transfix, xes, xed, xing, xion, HOLD/ FROZEN IN PLACE
transfor, transfer
transform, *, med, ming, mer, mation, mational, mationally, mative, mable, CHANGE FROM ONE TO ANOTHER, AN EVOLUTION "prefixes: inter/ re"
transformur, transform(er)
transfujen, transfuse(sion)
transfurd, transfer(rred)
transfurens, transfer(ence)
transfurmashen, transform(ation)
transfuruble, transfer(able)
transfuse, ed, sing, sable, sion, TRANSMISSION/ MOVEMENT OF LIQUID/ BLOOD
transgreshen, transgress(ion)
transgresif, transgress(ive)
transgress, sses, ssed, ssing, ssive, ssor, ssively, ssion, VIOLATING A LAW
transgretion, transgress(ion)
transichenul, transit(ional)
transient, *, tly, nce, ncy, PHYSICAL TEMPORARY/ PASSING
transim, transom
transind, transcend
transindense, transcend(ence)
transindentul, transcend(ental)
transishen, transit(ion)
transistor, *, rize, ELECTRONIC DEVICE
transit, *, ted, ting, tion, tionally, tive, tively, tiveness, tivity, tory, torily, toriness, PASSING OVER/ THROUGH/ ACROSS
transkribe, transcribe
translachen, translate(tion)
translade, translate
transladuble, translate(table)
transladur, translate(tor)
translate, *, ed, ting, tability, table, tor, tion, tional, tive, MOVE/ CONVEY INFORMATION/ ITEMS/ EFFECT, REPRODUCE WHILE RETAINING THE ORIGINAL
translatir, translate(tor)

translatuble, translate(table)
transleit, translate
translewsed, translucid
translewsins, translucent(nce)
translewsint, translucent
transloused, translucid
translucent, nce,ncy,ntly,cid, LIGHT CAN PENETRATE
translucid, LIGHT CAN PENETRATE
translusent, translucent
translusinse, translucent(nce)
translusit, translucid
transmechen, transmission
transmedable, transmit(ttable)
transmedal, transmit(ttal)
transmedur, transmit(tter)
transmesable, transmissible
transmeshen, transmission
transmetuble, transmit(ttable)
transmewt, transmute
transmewtuble, transmute(table)
transmichen, transmission
transmiduble, transmit(ttable)
transmidul, transmit(tta)
transmidur, transmit(tter)
transmisability, transmissible(bility)
transmision, transmission
transmissible, bility, PASSED ALONG, MOVEABLE, ABLE TO TRANSMIT
transmission,*, , GEARS WHICH ENCOURAGE MOVEMENT, EFFECTIVE COMMUNICATION
transmisuble, transmissible
transmit,*, ted,ting,ttable,ttal,ttance,ttancy,tter, ission,issible, PASS FROM ONE TO ANOTHER
transmitable, transmit(table)
transmiter, transmit(tter)
transmition, transmission
transmitle, transmit(ttal)
transmituble, transmit(ttable)
transmiut, transmute
transmutachen, transmute(tation)
transmute,*, ted,ting,ter,table,tableness, tability, tably, tation, tative, TRANSFORM/ CHANGE FROM ONE FORM TO ANOTHER

transmutible, transmute(table)
transmutuble, transmute(table)
transom,*, med, BEAM/ CROSSBOAR, VENTILATION WINDOW
transpair, transpire
transparensy, transparent(ncy)
transparent,*, tly, tness, ncy, ncies, CLEAR, ALLOWS VISUAL PENETRATION
transparint, transparent
transperinsy, transparent(ncy)
transperint, transparent
transpertashen, transport(ation)
transpire,*, ed,ring,rable,ratory, SWEAT/ PERSPIRE, TO HAPPEN, COME ABOUT
transpirtachen, transport(ation)
transpirtasion, transport(ation)
transplant,*, ted,ting,table,tation,ter, MOVE/ TRANSFER FROM ONE LOCATION TO ANOTHER
transplantuble, transplant(able)
transponder,*, A RADIO
transporduble, transport(able)
transport,*, ted,ting,tability,table,ter,tation,tive, CARRY/ RELOCATE
transportashen, transport(ation)
transportuble, transport(able)
transpose,*, ed,sing,sable,sition,sitional, MOVE
transpous, transpose
transpoz, transpose
transpurtachen, transport(ation)
transpuzishen, transpose(sition)
transum, transom
transutif, transit(ive)
transutory, transit(ory)
transverse,*, ely,sal,sally, LYING ACROSS THE SAME LINE TWICE, CROSSING
transvurs, transverse
tranuble, train(able)
tranur, train(er)
tranzacktion, transact(ion)
tranzakt, transact
tranzatef, transact(ive)
tranzbirtashen, transport(ation)
tranzblant, transplant

tranzbonder, transponder
tranzbort, transport
tranzbortuble, transport(able)
tranzdukshen, transduction
tranzdusir, transduce(r)
tranzeant, transient
tranzechen, transit(ion)
tranzekt, transect
tranzendentul, transcend(ental)
tranzeshenul, transit(ional)
tranzeshin, transit(ion)
tranzestur, transistor
tranzet, transit
tranzetory, transit(ory)
tranzfeks, transfix
tranzfermashen, transform(ation)
tranzfeugen, transfuse(sion)
tranzfewshen, transfuse(sion)
tranzfewz, transfuse
tranzfex, transfix
tranzfikyerashen, transfigure(ration)
tranzfir, transfer
tranzfix, transfix
tranzform, transform
tranzformashen, transform(ation)
tranzformur, transform(er)
tranzfujin, transfuse(sion)
tranzfur, transfer
tranzfuruble, transfer(able)
tranzgres, transgress
tranzgreshen, transgress(ion)
tranzgresif, transgress(ive)
tranzichen, transit(ion)
tranzishenul, transit(ional)
tranzit, transit
tranzitional, transit(ional)
tranzitory, transit(ory)
tranzkribe, transcribe
tranzlachen, translate(tion)
tranzlade, translate
tranzladuble, translate(table)
tranzladur, translate(tor)
tranzlate, translate

tranzlater,translate(tor)
tranzlatible,translate(table)
tranzlation,translate(tion)
tranzlewsed,translucid
tranzlewsense,translucent(nce)
tranzlewsint,translucent
tranzlousent,translucent
tranzlousid,translucid
tranzlused,translucid
tranzlusense,translucent(nce)
tranzlusent,translucent
tranzmedable,transmit(ttable)
tranzmedur,transmit(tter)
tranzmeshin,transmission
tranzmesuble,transmissible
tranzmet,transmit
tranzmetuble,transmit(ttable)
tranzmetur,transmit(tter)
tranzmeut,transmute
tranzmewtashen,transmute(tation)
tranzmichen,transmission
tranzmidul,transmit(ttal)
tranzmidur,transmit(tter)
tranzmishen,transmission
tranzmision,transmission
tranzmisuble,transmissible
tranzmit,transmit
tranzmition,transmission
tranzmitur,transmit(tter)
tranzmutachen,transmute(tation)
tranzmutasion,transmute(tation)
tranzmute,transmute
tranzmutuble,transmute(table)
tranzpazichen,transpose(sition)
tranzperint,transparent
tranzplant,transplant
tranzplantuble,transplant(able)
tranzponder,transponder
tranzporduble,transport(able)
tranzport,transport
transportashen,transport(ation)
tranzpoz,transpose
tranzutif,transit(ive)

tranzvurs,transverse
trap,*,,pped,pping,pper,CATCH/ HOLD/ PREVENT SOMETHING FROM ITS NORMAL MOVEMENT/ ACTION MUSICAL INSTRUMENT, DEVICE FOR TRAPPING "prefixes: en"
trapazoed,trapezoid
trapekul,tropic(al)
traper,trap(pper)
trapes,trapeze
trapeze,zist,A TYPE OF SWING
trapezoid,dal,A GEOMETRIC SHAPE
traphek,traffic
trapickul,tropic(al)
trapik,tropic
trapikul,tropic(al)
trapir,trap(pper)
trapis,trapeze
trapizoed,trapezoid
trapse,traipse
trapur,trap(pper)
trapuzoed,trapezoid
tras,tray(s) / trace
trasabul,trace(able)
trase,trace / tray(s)
trat,trade / trait
trater,trade(r) / traitor
trats,trait(s) / trade(s)
tratur,trade(r) / traitor
trau,trough / trowel
traudishen,tradition
traudition,tradition
traul,trough
traul,trawl/ troll/ trowel
traule,trolley
trauma,*,,tic,tically,tism,tize,tizes,tized,tizing,SUDDEN/ VIOLENT SHOCK TO THE SYSTEM

trausers,trousers
traut,trout
travail,*,,ENDURE A HARDSHIP
traveil,travail
travel,*,led,ling,ler,PHYSICALLY MOVE ABOUT/ AWAY (or see travail) "prefixes: un"
traverse,*,,ed,sing,sable,sal,ser,TO CROSS/ ACCOMPLISH A BARRIER/ BOUNDARY
travesty,ties,tied,tying,RIDICULE BY DISTORTING/ DEBASING/ MOCKING AN ACTUAL EXPERIENCE
travil,travel
travirs,traverse
travisty,travesty
travler,travel(er)
travoste,travesty
travul,travel
travusde,travesty
trawl,*,,led,ling,ler,BAITED HOOKS IN A LONG LINE/ NET FOR CATCHING FISH (or see troll/ trowel)
trawmu,trauma
trawpek,tropic
trawpekul,tropic(al)
trawpik,tropic
trawsers,trousers
trawt,trot / trout
tray,*,,SHALLOW PAN WITH SIDES FOR CARRYING/ HOLDING ITEMS "prefixes: under"
trayad,triad
trayedi,tragedy
trayic,tragic
traykoma,trachoma
tre,tree / tray
treacherous,sly,sness,DANGEROUS FOR VARIETY OF REASONS
treachery,ries,rous,RISKY, OF TREASON/ BETRAYAL/ TRICKERY
tread,*,,ded,ding,der,trod,trodden,HEAVY/ SLOW WALK,SWIM IN PLACE, TIRE IMPRINT (or see tree(d)) "prefixes: re"
tready,treaty
treason,nable,nous,nably,BEFRIEND THE ENEMY
treasure,*,,ed,ring,rable,er,ry,SOMETHING WORTHY/ VALUABLE

trash,hes,hed,hing,hy,hily,hiness,GARBAGE, DISPOSABLE/ DISCARDED ITEMS
trashd,trash(ed)
trashe,trash
trasible,trace(able)
traspas,trespass
trasuble,trace(able)

treasury,ries,MANAGES MONEY "prefixes: sub"
treat,*,ted,ting,ter,table,tability,ty,tment,TASTY MORSEL TO EAT,PAY THE CHARGE/ BILL FOR SOMEONE,TAKE FINANCIAL RESPONSIBILITY AS AN ACT OF KINDNESS "prefixes: en/ in/ mis/ pre/ re"
treaty,ties,tise,WRITTEN SETTLEMENT OF AGREEMENT BETWEEN TWO POWERS/ FACTIONS
treazen,treason
trebel,treble
trebeulashen,tribulation
trebun,tribune
trebut,tribute
trebutery,tributary
trebewlashen,tribulation
trebewn,tribune
trebil,treble
treble,ed,ling,TREBLE CLEF,MUSICAL PITCH/ NOTES, OF TRIPLE/ THREE, SYMBOL
trebul,treble
trebulashen,tribulation
trebun,tribune
trebute,tribute
trebutery,tributary
trechirus,treacherous
trechury,treachery
treck,trek
tred,tread / tree(d) / treat
trede,treaty
tredid,tread(ed) / treat(ed) / trade(d)
tredment,treat(ment)
treduble,treat(able)
tree,*,eed,eeing,eeless, eelessness,LARGE WOODY PLANT (or see treac)
treety,treaty
treezin,treason
trefea,trivia
treger,treasure / trigger
tregery,treasury
tregonometry,trigonometry
tregur,treasure / trigger
trei,tray
treid,trade
treikia,trachea

treil,trail
treilor,trailer
trein,train
treips,traipse
treiquia,trachea
treis,trace
treit,trait
treitor,traitor
trejere,treasury
trejur,treasure
trek,*, kked,kking,kker,kkie,TO JOURNEY/ TRAVEL/ MIGRATE SLOWLY
trekal,trickle
treked,trek(kked) / trick(ed)
trekil,trickle
trekinoses,trichinosis
trekir,trigger
trekol,trickle
trekoma,trachoma
trekt,trek(kked) / trick(ed)
trekul,trickle
trekur,trigger
trel,trill / trail
trelege,trilogy
treleim,trillium
treleon,trillion
treles,trellis
treleum,trillium
trelion,trillion
trelis,trellis
trellis,sed,DECORATIVE LATTICE
treluge,trilogy
trelus,trellis
trelyen,trillion
trem,trim
tremadik,trauma(tic)
tremar,tremor
trematik,trauma(tic)
trembil,tremble
tremble,*, ed,ling,er,lingly,VIBRATE/ SHAKE INVOLUNTARILY
trembul,tremble
tremd,trim(mmed)

tremendous,sly,sness,SUBSTANTIAL IN SIZE/ AMOUNT
tremendus,tremendous
tremer,trim(mmer) / tremor
tremindus,tremendous
tremor,*,rous,INVOLUNTARY VIBRATION/ SHAKING, RESULT OF EARTH CRUST MOVEMENT (or see trim(mmer))
trempul,tremble
tremur,trim(mmer) / tremor
trench,hes,hed,hing,her,hable,hment,hable, hment, DITCH/ FURROW DUG INTO A FLAT SURFACE "prefixes: en/ re/ un"
trend,*,dy,A TEMPORARY MOVEMENT IN DESIGN/ CLOTHING/ STYLE "prefixes: up"
trende,trend
trenedy,trinity
trenity,trinity
trenket,trinket
trenkit,trinket
trensh,trench
trent,trend
trente,trend
trenute,trinity
treo,trio
trep,trip
trepul,triple / treble
tresal,trestle
tresen,treason
treser,treasure
tresere,treasury
treshery,treachery / treasury
treshure,treachery / treasure
treshures,treacherous
tresil,trestle
tresin,treason
tresir,treasure
tresle,trestle
treson,treason
trespas,trespass
trespass,sses,ssed,ssing,sser,ENTER ONTO PROPERTY WITHOUT INVITATION/ PERMISSION
tresspas,trespass
trestle,*, ,SUPPORT FRAME/ BEAM

tresul, trestle
tresun, treason
tresure, treasure / treasury
tret, treat
trete, treaty
tretid, tread(ed) / treat(ed) / trade(d)
tretment, treat(ment)
tretuble, treat(able)
treuth, truth
trevail, travail
trevet, trivet
treveul, trivia(l)
trevia, trivia
trevit, trivet
treviul, trivia(l)
trew, drew / true
trewant, truant
trewbador, troubadour
trewent, truant
trewezm, true(uism)
trewint, truant
trewly, true(uly)
trewp, troop / troupe
trewpur, troop(er)
trews, truce
trewth, truth
trey, tray
trezen, treason
trezer, treasure
trezery, treasury
trezpas, trespass
trezun, treason
trezure, treasure / treasury
tri, PREFIX INDICATING "THREE" MOST OFTEN MODIFIES THE WORD (or see try)
triad, *, dic, dically, CONSISTING OF THREE PARTS/ ELEMENTS
trial, *, A MOMENT/ PERIOD/ PLACE OF CONSIDERATION/ REVIEW/ JUDGMENT "prefixes: mis/ re/ under"
triamverite, triumvirate
triangewlate, triangular(ate)
triangewlur, triangular

triangle, *, THREE SIDED GEOMETRIC SHAPE
triangul, triangle
triangular, rity, rly, ate, ates, ated, ating, ation, MAKE INTO THREE SIDES/ PARTS/ AREAS
triankl, triangle
triankulate, triangular(ate)
triankuler, triangular
triat, triad
trib, tribe
tribe, *, bal, bally, balism, balistic, PEOPLE OF A SOCIETY WHO SHARE COMMON BELIEFS/ VALUES/ MORALS "prefixes: de/ sub"
tribel, tribe(bal)
tribeun, tribune
tribeunul, tribune(nal)
tribeut, tribute
tribeutary, tributary
tribewlashen, tribulation
tribewn, tribune
tribewnul, tribune(nal)
tribewtery, tributary
tribiuleishon, tribe
tribiun, tribune
tribiuteri, tributary
tribul, tribe(bal)
tribulation, TRIAL/ STRESS/ TROUBLE
tribune, *, nal, eship, nate, THAT WHICH CHAMPIONS PEOPLES RIGHTS, COURT OF LAW, A PLATFORM
tribunel, tribune(nal)
tribunul, tribune(nal)
tributary, ries, rily, FLOWING/ STREAMING OF LIQUID/ WATER/ RESOURCES/ MONEY WHICH FEEDS/ MOVES INTO A LARGER BODY
tribute, *, ulation, TO OFFER/ SUPPLY GRATITUDE/ MONEY
triceps, ARM MUSCLES
trichanosis, trichinosis
trichinosis, DISEASE IN INTESTINES CAUSED BY WORMS
trichunosis, trichinosis
trick, *, ked, king, ker, kery, keries, ky, kiness, PRANK/ HOAX (or see trek)
trickle, *, ed, ling, TINY FLOWING STREAM
trickunosis, trichinosis

tricnousis, trichinosis
tricol, trickle
tricycle, *, ed, ling, THREE WHEELED BIKE
trid, tried / trite
trident, *, tate, tal, THREE PRONGED FORK/ BARB, BALLISTIC MISSILE SYSTEM
tridint, trident
tried, PAST TENSE FOR THE WORD "TRY", INCITED FOR A CRIME, TESTED (or see trite) "prefixes: un"
triel, trial
triemverat, triumvirate
triemverint, triumvirate
trieng, try(ing)
trifea, trivia
trifil, trifle
trifle, *, ed, ling, er, lingly, lingness, SMALL/ MINIMAL AMOUNT, NOT TAKE SERIOUSLY, IDLE TIME
triful, trifle
trigar, trigger
trigenometry, trigonometry
trigger, *, red, ring, rless, PART OF GUN WHICH RELEASES BULLET
trigonometry, MATH WITH SYMBOLS/ DESIGNS
trigur, trigger
trihedras, al, ron, OF THREE INTERSECTING LINES
trihedril, trihedron(ral)
trihedron, *, ras, ral, THREE INTERSECTING LINES
trihedrul, trihedron(ral)
trik, trick
trikal, trickle
trikanosis, trichinosis
trikel, trickle
trikenoses, trichinosis
trikery, trick(ery)
triknousis, trichinosis
trikol, trickle
trikul, trickle
trikure, trick(ery)
triky, trick
tril, trial / trill
trilabit, trilobite
triladerul, trilateral
trilateral, lity, lly, THREE SIDED

triaturil,trilateral
triebit,trilobite
triege,trilogy
triengwul,trilingual
trileon,trillion
trileum,trillium
trilingual,lly,THREE LANGUAGES
trilingwul,trilingual
trilion,trillion
trilium,trillium
tril,TYPE OF SOUND
trillion,*,nth,ONE MILLION TIMES ONE MILLION
trillium,A LAWFULLY PROTECTED PLANT
trilobait,trilobite
trilobite,*,tic,EXTINCT ARTHROPOD,THREE LOBES
trilochi,trilogy
trilogy,gies,THREE PARTS TOGETHER IN A MUSICAL/ LITERARY/ FILMED/ DRAMATIC WORK
trilolli,trilogy
triloyi,trilogy
trilubit,trilobite
triluge,trilogy
trilyun,trillion
trim,*,mmed,mming,mmer,TO REMOVE EXCESS, CREATE A CLEAN/ TIDY/ FINISHED APPEARANCE
trimer,trim(mmer) / tremor
trimur,trim(mmer) / tremor
trin,trine
trinch,trench
trind,trend
trine,*,nal,nity,OF THREE PARTS
trinedy,trinity
tring,try(ing)
trinity,ties,OF THREE PARTS
trinket,*,SMALL KNICK KNACK/ ORNAMENT
trinsh,trench
trint,trend
trio,*,THREE PARTS
triou,trio
trip,*,pped,pping,pper,ppingly,JOURNEY AWAY FROM, STUMBLE (too many definitions, please see standard dictionary) (or see tripe)
tripal,triple

tripd,trip(pped)
tripe,COW/ SHEEP STOMACH,POOR IN QUALITY
tripel,triple
tripewlashen,tribulation
triple,*,ed,ling,ly,let,licate,lication,THREE OF,THREE TIMES/ FOLD
tripod,*,THREE LEGGED
tripol,triple
tripot,tripod
tripul,triple
tripulashen,tribulation
tripuld,triple(d)
trisebs,triceps
trisekel,tricycle
triseps,triceps
trison,treason
trisycle,tricycle
trite,ely,eness,OF LITTLE INTEREST IN (or see tried)
triti,treaty
tritle,trite(ly)
tritly,trite(ly)
tritnes,trite(ness)
triul,trial
triumf,triumph
triumfent,triumph(ant)
triumph,*,hal,hant,hantly,A GAIN/ VICTORY/ SUCCESS
triumphent,triumph(ant)
triumvaret,triumvirate
triumvirate,GROUP OF THREE
triveal,trivia(l)
trivet,*,STAND WITH THREE LEGS
triveu,trivia
triveul,trivia(l)
trivia,al,alness,ality,alities,alization,alize,ally, INSIGNIFICANT/ UNIMPORTANT
trivit,trivet
trobol,trouble
troc,truck
trod,*,dden,PAST TENSE FOR THE WORD "TREAD", WALK HEAVILY/ SLOWLY WITH NO AMBITION (or see trot)
troden,trod(dden) / trot(tting)

trodeshinul,tradition(al)
trodin,trod(dden) / trot(tting)
trodition,tradition
troditional,tradition(al)
troe,troy
trof,trough / trove
trofe,trophy
trofl,truffle
trofy,trophy
trogectery,traject(ory)
troi,troy
trojektery,traject(ory)
trok,truck
trol,trawl / troll / trowel
trole,trolley / troll
troll,*,ller,TYPE OF SINGING, DRAGGING A HOOK, IMAGINARY CREATURE (or see trawl)
trolley,A CART/ VEHICLE WITH WHEELS ON RAILS
troly,trolley
troma,trauma
tromatizd,trauma(tized)
trombone,*,A MUSICAL INSTRUMENT
tromel,trommel
trommel,ROUND SCREEN FOR SEPARATING VARIOUS SIZES OF ORGANIC MATERIAL
tromp,*,ped,ping,BIG/ HEAVY FOOT STEPS, BEAT SOMEONE EXCESSIVELY (or see trump)
trompet,trumpet
tromu,trauma
tromul,trommel
tromutize,trauma(tize)
tronquet,truncate
troobudor,troubadour
troop,*,ped,ping,per,AN ASSEMBLY/ GROUP/ FLOCK (or see troupe)
troos,truce
tropeckul,tropic(al)
tropek,tropic
tropekul,tropic(al)
tropes,trapeze
trophe,trophy
trophy,hies,hic,MOUNTED HEAD OF ANIMAL, A COIN/ FIGURINE DESIGNED FOR AWARD/ ACHIEVEMENT

tropic, *, cal, cally, CONTINUOUS WARM WEATHER CLIMATE "prefixes: inter/ semi/ sub"
tropickul, tropic(al)
tropik, tropic
tropikul, tropic(al)
trost, trust
trot, *, tted, tting, tter, STYLE OF WALKING/ RUNNING (or see trout/ trod)
trotin, trod(dden) / trot(tting)
troubadour, POETS OF ANTIQUITY
trouble, *, ed, ling, esome, esomely, esomeness, lous, DIFFICULT/ CHALLENGING "prefixes: un"
trouel, trowel
trouf, trough / trove
troufi, trophy
trough, *, VESSEL FOR ANIMALS TO FEED/ DRINK, RECTANGULAR/ SHALLOW CHANNEL/ SHAPE
troul, trowel / troll
troup, troop
troupe, *, ped, ping, THEATER GROUP/ PERFORMERS (or see troop)
trousers, PANTS
trout, TYPE OF FISH
trouv, trove
trouwl, trowel
trove, *, A FIND/ DISCOVERY
trovers, traverse
trowel, *, led, ling, ler, HAND TOOL TO WORK PLASTER/ MUD/ MORTAR
trowsers, trousers
trowt, trout
trowzurs, trousers
troy, MEASUREMENT FOR WEIGHT OF PRECIOUS METALS
tru, true / through / thru / drew
truant, *, tly, ncy, NOT AT SCHOOL WITHOUT GOOD REASON
trubador, troubadour
trubel, trouble
trubidor, troubadour
trubudor, troubadour
trubul, trouble
truc, truck / truce

truce, COME TO AGREEMENT AFTER FIGHT/ ARGUMENT (or see truss)
truch, trudge
truck, *, ked, king, ker, VEHICLE FOR HAULING/ MOVING
trud, truth
trudeshin, tradition
trudeshinul, tradition(al)
trudge, *, ed, ging, WALK SLOWLY WITH HEAVY FEET
trudishenul, tradition(al)
tradition, tradition
traditional, tradition(al)
true, uly, uism, eness, uth, ACCURATE/ FACTUAL/ REAL/ STRAIGHT UP/ ON THE LEVEL "prefixes: un"
truel, twirl
truent, truant
truews, truce
truezm, true(uism)
trufal, truffle
truffle, *, ed, AN EDIBLE FUNGI, A CANDY
truful, truffle
trug, trudge
trugekt, traject
trugektery, traject(ory)
truint, truant
truizm, true(uism)
truj, trudge
trujd, trudge(d)
trujectery, traject(ory)
trujekt, traject
trujektery, traject(ory)
truk, truck
truker, truck(er)
trule, true(uly)
trull, trudge
trumadik, trauma(tic)
trumendus, tremendous
trumindus, tremendous
trump, *, ped, ping, per, pery, OVERRANK/ SURPASS/ DECEIVE (or see tromp)
trumpd, trump(ed) / tromp(ed)
trumpet, *, ter, BRASS HORNED INSTRUMENT
trumput, trumpet
trunc, trunk

truncate, *, ed, ting, tion, CUT OFF TIP/ END/ PART OF, CUT SHORT
trundel, trundle
trundle, er, CIRCLE/ WHEEL FOR ROTATION
trundul, trundle
trunk, *, MAIN BODY/ PART FROM WHICH ALL THINGS EXTEND BEYOND, CONTAINER FOR ITEMS, ELEPHANT NOSE
trunkate, truncate
truol, twirl
trupe, troop / troupe
trupel, trouble
truper, troop(er)
trupes, trapeze
trupir, troop(er)
trupl, trouble
trups, troop(s) / troupe(s)
trupul, trouble
trupur, troop(er)
trus, truce / truss
truse, truce / truss
truss, sses, sser, TO BOLSTER/ SECURE/ SUPPORT WITH BEAMS/ TIES/ ROPE (or see truce)
trust, *, ted, ting, tee, tful, tfully, tfulness, ty, tiness, PLACE HOPE/ FAITH/ BELIEF/ CONFIDENCE IN "prefixes: dis/ en/ mis"
truste, trust
truth, *, hless, hful, hfully, hfulness, ACCEPTED AS FACT/ CONSTANCY/ ACTUAL "prefixes: un"
truvale, travail
truvers, traverse
truwent, truant
truz, truce / truss
try, ries, ried, ying, yingly, PUT TO THE TEST, ATTEMPT, DIFFICULT/ CHALLENGE TO ACCOMPLISH "prefixes: re"
tryd, tried / trite
trydent, trident
tryeng, try(ing)
tryn, trine
tsunami, ic, GIGANTIC TIDAL WAVE
tsunome, tsunami
tu, two / to / too

tuailait,twilight
tuain,twine
tuais,twice
tub,*,bbable,bby,bbier,bbiest,bbiness,_ARGE VESSEL/ CONTAINER FOR LIQUID,ROUND LIKE A TUB (or see tube)
tuba,*,,HORNED INSTRUMENT
tubaco,tobacco
tubagen,toboggan
tubako,tobacco
tube,*,ed,bing,er,eless,erous,bular,bularity,bule,bulous,CYLINDER/ ROUND SHAPE (or see tub)
tubequlosis,tuberculosis
tuberculosis,ous,ously,DISEASE OF THE LUNGS
tuberquelosis,tubercu osis
tubeulur,tube(bular)
tubir,tube(ber)
tubirquelosis,tuberculosis
tubles,tube(less)
tubogin,toboggan
tubu,tuba
tubur,tube(ber)
tuby,tub(bby)
tuc,took / tuck
tuch,touch / tush
tucha,touche'
tuche,touch / touche'
tuchible,touch(able)
tuck,*,ked,king,ker,kered,TO PULL/ SECURE EDGES, PLACE AWAY SAFELY,WEARY/ TIRED FROM WORKING
tucsidou,tuxedo
tud,tooth
tuda,today
tudei,today
tuder,tutor
tudur,tutor
tuein,twain
tuel,tool
tuelf,twelve
tueni,twenty
tuente,twenty
tuentieth,twentieth

tuerl,twirl
tuerp,twerp / twirp
tuesday,*,,A DAY OF THE WEEK (ENGLISH)
tuf,tough
tufen,tough(en)
tufer,tough(er)
tufest,tough(est)
tuff,tough
tufin,tough(en)
tufir,tough(er)
tufist,tough(est)
tuft,*,ty,tier,tiest,CLUMP/ CLUSTER/ BUNCH OF THREADS/ HAIR/ MATERIAL/ FUR
tufun,tough(en)
tufur,tough(er)
tug,*,gged,gging,TO PULL/ DRAG/ HAUL
tugeder,together
tugethur,together
tugt,tug(gged)
tuic,tweak
tuid,tweed
tuidel,twiddle
tuidor,tweeter
tuig,twig
tuil,tool
tuin,twin
tuinch,twinge
tuincol,twinkle
tuinll,twinge
tuit,tweet
tuiter,tweeter
tuizer,tweezer
tuk,tuck / tug / took
tukd,tuck(ed) / tug(gged)
tuke,took
tukela,tequila
tukila,tequila
tuksedo,tuxedo
tuksido,tuxedo
tukt,tuck(ed) / tug
tukurd,tuck(ered)
tul,tool
tule,tool

tulep,tulip
tulepuhee,telepathy
tulip,*,,A FLOWER
tum,tomb
tumaro,tomorrow
tumato,tomato
tumauro,tomorrow
tumbel,tumble
tumble,*,,ed,ling,er,BE TOSSED ABOUT,A DRINKING VESSEL/ CAM/ LOCKING PART,BOLT ACTION, ACROBATICS
tumblir,tumble(r)
tumbul,tumble
tumer,tumor
tumerus,tumor(ous)
tumor,*,rous,A CLUMP/ MASS OF TISSUE
tumoro,tomorrow
tumulchewus,tumult(uous)
tumulchuis,tumult(uous)
tumult,tuary,tuous,tuously,tuousness,DISTURBANCE/ AGITATED/ DISORDER
tumures,tumor(ous)
tun,tune / toon / ton
tuna,*,,SALT WATER FISH
tunacity,tenacity
tunait,tonight
tunaledy,tone(nality)
tunasedy,tenacity
tunasity,tenacity
tundra,ARCTIC PLAINS AROUND NORTH/ SOUTH POLES
tundru,tundra
tune,*,ed,ning,er,eful,efully,efulness,eless,SET/ ADJUST HARMONY/ FREQUENCY (or see toon) "prefixes: de"
tuneg,ton(nnage)
tunej,ton(nnage)
tunek,tunic
tunel,tunnel
tungsten,nic,METAL ELEMENT,TYPE OF FILAMENT IN LIGHT BULBS
tungstin,tungsten
tunic,*,,LONG GARMENT,A COVERING
tunig,ton(nnage)

tunij, ton(nnage)
tunil, tunnel
tunir, tune(r)
tunite, tonight
tunl, tunnel
tunnel, *, led, ling, ler, TUBULAR SHAPED OPENING GOING INTO A SURFACE
tunor, tune(r)
tuns, tune(s) / ton(s) / toon(s)
tunsten, tungsten
tunstun, tungsten
tunt, tune(d)
tuntru, tundra
tunu, tuna
tunuk, tunic
tunul, tunnel
tunur, tune(r)
tup, tub
tupa, toupee
tupagrufe, topography
tupay, toupee
tupe, tube / tub(bby)
tupei, toupee
tupht, tuft
tupography, topography
tupogrufe, topography
tupuler, tube(bular)
tuquela, tequila
tuquila, tequila
tur, tour
turain, terrain / terrane
turanchula, tarantula
turane, terrain / terrane
turanshulu, tarantula
turantula, tarantula
turareum, terrarium
turazo, terrazzo
turbain, turbine
turban, *, LONG SCARF WRAPPED AS A HEADDRESS (or see turbine)
turben, turban / turbine
turbeulent, turbulent
turbin, turban / turbine

turbine, *, MOTOR WITH ROTORS SUPPLIED BY A CONSTANT FLOW (or see turban)
turbiulent, turbulent
turbo, *, POWERED BY/ AS IF BY A TURBINE MOTOR
turbon, turban / turbine
turbulens, turbulent(nce)
turbulent, tly, nce, ROUGH/ ERRATIC/ RANDOM FLOW
turcoys, turquois
turcucis, turquois
turd, tour(ed)
turdul, turtle
ture, tour
turefic, terrific
turein, terrain
turenshul, torrent(ial)
turereum, terrarium
turesdreul, terrestrial
turestrial, terrestrial
turet, turret
turf, *, fy, fier, fiest, GRASS/ ORGANIC MATERIAL FORMING A SURFACE BLANKET
turifek, terrific
turific, terrific
turist, tour(ist)
turisum, tour(ism)
turit, turret
turkes, turkey(s)
turkey, *, EDIBLE BIRD
turkie, turkey
turkois, turquois
turky, turkey
turm, term
turmait, termite
turmaric, turmeric
turmenashen, terminate(tion)
turmenate, terminate
turmenator, terminate(tor)
turmenology, terminology
turmenul, terminal
turmeric, SPICE FROM A PLANT
turmeruk, turmeric
turminashen, terminate(tion)
turminate, terminate

turmination, terminate(tion)
turminator, terminate(tor)
turminolegy, terminology
turminul, terminal
turmoel, turmoil
turmoil, STATE OF STRESS/ CONFUSION
turmoiol, turmoil
turmonel, terminal
turn, *, ned, ning, CHANGE DIRECTION, ROTATE/ CURVE/ BEND IN COURSE "prefixes: over/ up"
turnado, tornado
turnament, tournament
turnato, tornado
turnep, turnip
turniment, tournament
turnineit, terminate
turnip, *, A VEGETABLE
turnument, tournament
turpentine, MINERAL SPIRIT WITH VOLATILE OIL
turpewlent, turbulent
turpulent, turbulent
turpuntine, turpentine
turqui, turkey
turquois, BLUE/ GREEN GEMSTONE
turrestrial, terrestrial
turret, *, CYLINDRICAL OUTCROP AS SEEN ON CASTLES
tursdei, Thursday
turse, terse
tursheare, tertiary
turshieri, tertiary
turshury, tertiary
tursnes, terse(ness)
turtle, *, REPTILE WITH A SHELL
turut, turret
tusday, tuesday
tush, hes, REAR END, BUTTOCK (or see touch)
tusha, touche'
tushei, touche'
tusk, *, ked, LARGE EXTERIOR TOOTH
tusled, tousle(d)
tute, toot
tuter, tutor
tuth, tooth

tuthee,tooth
tuthles,tooth(less)
tutir,tutor
tutolatarian,totalitarian
tutor,*,red,ring,rage,rial,elage,TO MENTOR/ TEACH OR BE A GUARDIAN OF SOMEONE "prefixes: un"
tutu,*,OUTER GARMENT DANCERS WEAR
tutur,tutor
tuxedo,FORMAL ATTIRE FOR MEN
twailait,twilight
twain,RIVERBOAT TERM (or see twine)
twais,twice
twalth,twelfth
twan,twain
twang,gy,A VIBRATIONAL TONE
twank,twang
twead,tweed
tweak,*,ked,king,ker,ky,TO ADJUST
tweat,tweet
tweazer,tweezer
twed,tweed
twede,tweed
tweder,tweeter
twedul,twiddle
twedur,tweeter
tweed,*,dy,dier,diest,diness,TYPE OF WOOL/ WEAVE
tweek,tweak
tweenkul,twinkle
tweet,*,SOUND OF A BIRD
tweeter,TYPE OF SPEAKER FOR SOUND EQUIPMENT
tweezer,*,TOOL FOR PLUCKING/ PINCHING
tweg,twig
twein,twain
tweing,twang
twek,tweak / twig
tweke,tweak
twelf,twelve
twelfth,*,ONE OUT OF TWELVE
twelth,twelfth
twelve,*,ENGLISH NUMBER AFTER ELEVEN
twelvt,twelfth
twelvth,twelfth
twen,twin

twench,twinge
twende,twenty
tweng,twang
twenge,twinge
tweni,twenty
twenj,twinge
twenkul,twinkle
twenteith,twentieth
twentes,twenty(ties)
twentie,twenty
twentieth,ONE PART OF TWENTY PARTS
twenty,ties,tieth,ENGLISH NUMBER AFTER NINETEEN
twentys,twenty(ties)
twerl,twirl
twerp,A DEROGATORY SLANG
tweser,tweezer
twest,twist
twesur,tweezer
twet,tweet
twetur,tweeter
twezer,tweezer
twhirl,twirl
twic,tweak
twice,TWO TIMES
twid,tweed
twidal,twiddle
twiddle,*,ed,ding,er,TO ROTATE ONE AROUND ANOTHER,IDLY TOY WITH SOMETHING
twidul,twiddle
twig,*,ggy,PART OF A WOODY BRANCH
twik,twig
twilid,twilight
twilight,SUNSET/ SUNRISE
twilite,twilight
twin,*,TWO IDENTICAL/ SIMILAR (or see twine)
twinch,twinge
twincol,twinkle
twindy,twenty
twine,*,ed,ning,BRAIDED/ TWISTED ROPE/ THREAD (or see twin) "prefixes: en/ inter"
twinge,*,ed,ging,SHARP/ SUDDEN JERK RELATED TO PAINFUL SCENE/ EXPERIENCE
twinj,twinge

twinkal,twinkle
twinkle,*,ed,ling,er,SPARKLE/ GLEAM OF LIGHT
twintieth,twentieth
twinty,twenty
twirl,*,led,ling,ler,ly,SPIN/ WHIRL AROUND
twirp,*,DEROGATORY SLANG
twis,twice
twiser,tweezer
twist,*,ted,ting,ter,ty,COILED ROTATION IN ACTION "prefixes: en/ in/ inter/ re"
twit,tweet
two,*,ENGLISH NUMBER AFTER ONE (or see too/ to)
twoberkeuloses,tuberculosis
twobu,tuba
twobuler,tube(bular)
twocha,touche'
twonik,tunic
twonu,tuna
twopa,toupee
tworl,twirl
twotwo,tutu
twurl,twirl
twurp,twerp / twirp
ty,tie
tydengs,tidings
tyeng,tying
tyfoed,typhoid
tyfus,typhus
tying,PRESENT PARTICIPLE FOR THE WORD "TIE", TO FASTEN/ LOOP/ ATTACH STRING/ CORD, TO AFFIX "prefixes: re/ un/ under"
tyk,tike / tick
tynkshur,tincture
type,*,ed,ping,er,eable,eability,pist,USE OF A MACHINE TO CREATE TEXT (or see tip) "prefixes: mis/ pre/ re/ sub/ un"
typecul,typical
typefy,typify
typhis,typhus
typhoid,DISEASE OF THE INTESTINES
typhoon,*,HURRICANE
typhus,hous,A DISEASE CAUSED BY FLEAS
typical,lly,lness,lity,PREDICTABLE/ CHARACTERISTIC

typicul,typical
typify,fies,fied,fying,fication,SYMBOLIZES
typikul,typical
typo,*,TEXT ERROR
typukle,typical
tyrane,tyranny
tyranekal,tyrannical
tyranikul,tyrannical
tyrannical,lly,lness,OF BEING CRUEL/ PREDATORY
tyranny,nnies,nnous,nnously,nnousness,nnize,nnizes,
  nnized,nnizing,nnizer,nnic,nnical,nnically,
  nnicalness,nnicide,EVENT INVOLVING CRUEL/
  VICIOUS PREDATOR WHO EXPLOITS VICTIMS
tyrant,*,nny,CRUEL VICIOUS PREDATOR, ONE WHO
  EXPLOITS VICTIMS
tyreny,tyranny
u,you / yew / ewe
uabel,wobble
uabl,wobble
uac,walk / wok / whack
uacent,wasn't
uach,watch
uacs,wax
uad,wad
uader,water / wader
uadercres,watercress
uaderfol,waterfall
uaderpruf,waterproof
uadertait,watertight
uadever,whatever
uadol,waddle
uafol,waffle
uagen,wagon
uai,why
uaid,wide / wade
uaield,wild
uaier,wire
uaif,wife
uail,while / wail
uain,whine / wine / wane
uaini,whinny
uaiold,wild
uaip,wipe

uair,wire
uais,wise
uaish,wash
uait,wait / weight / white
uaivs,wives
uaiz,wise
uak,walk / wok / whack
uaker,walker
uaki,wacky
ual,wall
ualet,wallet
ualnut,walnut
ualop,wallop
ualou,wallow
ualrus,walrus
ualts,waltz
uan,won / one / wane
uance,once
uand,wand / want
uanderful,wonderful
uandor,wander
uans,once
uant,want / wand
uanton,wanton
uaqui,wacky
uar,war
uarant,warrant
uard,ward / word
uarm,warm/ worm
uarn,warn / worn
uas,was
uasent,wasn't
uasher,washer
uasp,wasp
uat,what / watt
uater,water / wader
uatercres,watercress
uaterpruf,waterproof
uatertait,watertight
uatever,whatever
uatich,watt(age)
uatl,what'll
uatol,what'll

ubart,apart
ubat,abate
ubatment,abate(ment)
ubedeins,obedience
ubedeint,obedient
ubeding,abet(tting)
ubedy,uppity
ubel,appeal
ubelaty,ability
ubelte,ability
ubet,abet
ubeting,abet(tting)
ubikwety,ubiquity
ubilde,ability
ubiledy,ability
ubilte,ability
ubiquity,tous,tary,tously,tousness,OMNIPRESENT,
  EXISTS EVERYWHERE
ubity,uppity
ubleveus,oblivious
ublij,apply
ublid,apply(lied)
ublig,oblige(d)
ublij,oblige(d)
ubliveus,oblivious
ubliz,apply(lies)
ubolesh,abolish
ubord,aboard / abort
uborded,abort(ed)
ubort,abort / aboard
ubprnetis,apprentice
ubropreat,appropriate
ubrenis,apprentice
ubresheate,appreciate
ubreshen,oppress(ion)
ubretiate,appreciate
ubreveashen,abbreviate(tion)
ubreveat,abbreviate
ubriged,abridged
ubroch,approach
ubrod,abroad
ubroof,approve
ubropreat,appropriate

ubrosh, approach
ubruf, approve
ubruv, approve
ubsakwently, subsequent(ly)
ubserd, absurd
ubsesd, obsess(ed)
ubseshen, obsess(ion)
ubset, upset
ubsolv, absolve
ubstane, abstain
ubstrakshen, obstruct(ion) / abstract(ion)
ubstrukt, obstruct
ubtane, obtain
ubtrude, obtrude
ubtrusive, obtrusive
ubzerd, absurd
ubzerve, observe
ubzolv, absolve
ubzorb, absorb
ubzurv, observe
uce, ooze
ucemble, assemble
ucend, ascend
ucenshen, ascension
uch, lush
uchamed, ashamed
ucher, assure
ucide, aside
ucimbul, assemble
ucinshen, ascension
ucompany, accompany
ucumpany, accompany
ucumulate, accumulate
udalize, utilize
udapt, adapt
udar, udder/ odor
udder, *, , TEATS ON A MILKING ANIMALS (or see utter)
udendum, addendum
uder, odor / otter / outer / utter / udder
uderus, uterus
udeshen, edition / add(ition)
udindum, addendum
udir, odor / otter / outer / utter / udder

udirens, utter(ance)
udirus, uterus
udishen, edition / add(ition)
udopt, adopt
udor, udder / utter / adore / odor/ otter
udrausety, atrocity
udroit, adroit
udrosity, atrocity
udulize, utilize
udur, odor / otter / outer / utter / udder
ueb, web
uebt, wept
uech, wedge / well
ued, wed
uedloc, wedlock
uei, way / weigh / whey
ueich, wage
ueid, wade
ueiders, waders
ueidor, waiter
ueif, wave / waive
ueifer, wafer / waiver
ueig, wage
ueik, wake
ueil, wail
uein, wain / wane
ueiol, wail
ueir, ware / where
ueist, waste/ waist
ueit, wait / weight / white
ueiter, waiter
ueiv, wave / waive
ueiver, wafer / waiver
ueivor, waiver
uel, we'll / wheel / wale / well
ueld, weld
uelfer, welfare
uell, wedge / well
uelt, welt
uelth, wealth
uen, when / win
uence, whence
uench, wench

uend, wend / wind
uenever, whenever
uens, whence / win(s)
uensdey, Wednesday
uent, went
ueo, wail
uepen, weapon / whip(pping)
uept, wept
uer, weir / we're / where / were / whirr / wear
ueras, whereas
uerd, where'd / weird
uere, ware / where
uerebol, warble
uerel, where'll
uerever, wherever
ueri, wary
uerl, whirl
uerlwind, whirlwind
uernt, weren't
uers, where's
ueruithal, wherewithal
uest, west
uet, wet / whet
uether, weather / wether / wither / whether
uey, way / weigh / whey
ufael, avail
ufermutif, affirm(ative)
ufeshent, efficient
ufileashen, affiliate(tion)
ufileate, affiliate
ufishent, efficient
ugilede, agile(ty)
ugilety, agile(ty)
ugle, ugly
ugleist, ugly(liest)
ugleur, ugly(lier)
ugly, lies, lier, liest, UNATTRACTIVE
ugre, agree
ugresev, aggressive
ugreshen, aggression
ugresuv, aggressive
ugretion, aggression
uhbart, apart

uhbli,apply	uhpel,appeal	uhprentis,apprentice
uhblid,apply(lied)	uhperense,appearance	uhpresheate,appreciate
uhbliz,apply(lies)	uhperent,apparent	uhpresheation,appreciate(tion)
uhbprnetis,apprentice	uhperinse,appearance	uhpreshete,appreciate
uhbpropreat,appropriate	uhperul,apparel	uhpreshetion,appreciate(tion)
uhbrenis,apprentice	uhpil,appeal	uhpretiate,appreciate
uhbresheate,appreciate	uhplaud,applaud	uhprintes,apprentice
uhbreshete,appreciate	uhplaus,applause	uhprisheate,appreciate
uhbretiate,appreciate	uhpli,apply	uhproach,approach
uhbroch,approach	uhplod,applaud	uhprobreat,appropriate
uhbroof,approve	uhplos,applause	uhproch,approach
uhbropreat,appropriate	uhpoent,appoint	uhproksamit,approximate
uhbrosh,approach	uhpoentment,appointment	uhproksamity,approximate(ly)
uhbruhf,approve	uhpoint,appoint	uhproksumit,approximate
uhcemble,assemble	uhpointment,appointment	uhproksumitly,approximate(ly)
uhcend,ascend	uhpoluge,apology	uhproof,approve
uhcenshen,ascension	uhpolugize,apology(gize)	uhproovul,approve(val)
uhchamed,ashamed	uhport,apart	uhpropreit,appropriate
uhcher,assure	uhportment,apartment	uhprosh,approach
uhcide,aside	uhpostrufe,apostrophe	uhproximate,approximate
uhcimbul,assemble	uhpotment,appointment	uhproximatly,approximate(ly)
uhcinshen,ascension	uhpoynt,appoint	uhpruhf,approve
uhdrausety,atrocity	uhpearanc,appearance	uhpruhval,approve(val)
uhdrosity,atrocity	uhpperinse,appearance	uhrain,arraign
uhod,ahold	uhpperul,apparel	uhraingment,arrange(ment)
uhold,ahold	uhpplaud,applaud	uhrainment,arraign(ment)
uhpairent,apparent	uhpplause,applause	uhrane,arraign
uhpairul,apparel	uhpplod,applaud	uhrangment,arrange(ment)
uhpalugize,apology(gize)	uhpply,apply	uhranjment,arrange(ment)
uhpalugy,apology(gize)	uhpprentis,apprentice	uhranment,arraign(ment)
uhparent,apparent	uhppreshiate,appreciate	uhrear,arrear
uhpart,apart	uhppropriate,appropriate	uhreighnment,arraign(ment)
uhpartment,apartment	uhpprove,approve	uhreinment,arraign(ment)
uhparul,apparel	uhpproximate,approximate	uhrena,arena
uhpastrufe,apostrophe	uhpproximately,approximate(ly)	uhrer,arrear
uhpauluge,apology	uhpraisul,appraisal	uhrest,arrest
uhpaulugize,apology(gize)	uhprased,appraise(d)	uhriful,arrival
uhpaurtment,apartment	uhpraz,appraise	uhrina,arena
uhpaustrufe,apostrophe	uhprazul,appraisal	uhrivul,arrival
uhpealing,appeal(ing)	uhpreceashun,appreciate(tion)	uhroma,aroma
uhpearanc,appearance	uhprecheat,appreciate	uhround,around
uhpearinse,appearance	uhpreciate,appreciate	uhrouz,arouse
uhpeel,appeal	uhprenis,apprentice	uhrownd,around

uhrows, arouse
uhrrear, arrear
uhrrest, arrest
uhrrivol, arrival
uhsacin, assassin
uhsail, assail
uhsal, assail
uhsalant, assail(ant)
uhsalt, assault
uhsasen, assassin
uhsault, assault
uhsberugus, asparagus
uhscend, ascend
uhscention, ascension
uhsdonesh, astonish
uhsdrawnumy, astronomy
uhsdronumy, astronomy
uhsemble, assemble
uhsemelate, assimilate
uhsemilate, assimilate
uhsemlate, assimilate
uhsend, ascend
uhsenshen, ascension
uhsent, assent
uhsention, ascension
uhsershen, assert(ion)
uhsert, assert
uhsertion, assert(ion)
uhses, assess / use(s)
uhsesment, assessment
uhsest, assist
uhsestens, assist(ance)
uhsestins, assist(ance)
uhseum, assume
uhsfekseate, asphyxiate
uhshamed, ashamed
uhside, aside
uhsign, assign
uhsilem, asylum
uhsimbul, assemble
uhsimelate, assimilate
uhsin, assign
uhsind, ascend

uhsinment, assignment
uhsinshen, ascension
uhsint, assent
uhsirshen, assert(ion)
uhsirt, assert
uhsirtion, assert(ion)
uhsist, assist
uhsistens, assist(ance)
uhsleep, asleep
uhslep, asleep
uhsocheat, associate
uhsocheation, associate(tion)
uhsociate, associate
uhsociation, associate(tion)
uhsolt, assault
uhsosheashun, associate(tion)
uhsosheut, associate
uhsoshiat, associate
uhsoshiation, associate(tion)
uhsparugus, asparagus
uhsperugus, asparagus
uhsphikseate, asphyxiate
uhspire, aspire
uhssal, assail
uhssasin, assassin
uhssenble, assemble
uhstonish, astonish
uhstraunume, astronomy
uhstronumy, astronomy
uhstrownumy, astronomy
uhsum, assume
uhsumpshen, assumption
uhsur, assure
uhsurt, assert
uhsylim, asylum
uhtach, attach
uhtachment, attach(ment)
uhtack, attack
uhtain, attain
uhtainable, attain(able) / obtain(able)
uhtak, attack
uhtanable, attain(able) / obtain(able)
uhtane, attain

uhtanmint, attain(ment)
uhtash, attach
uhtempt, attempt
uhtemt, attempt
uhtend, attend
uhtendens, attend(ance)
uhtending, attend(ing)
uhtenshen, attention
uhtentef, attentive
uhtentefness, attentive(ness)
uhtention, attention
uhtentive, attentive
uhtimt, attempt
uhtind, attend
uhtindens, attend(ance)
uhtinding, attend(ing)
uhtinshen, attention
uhtintef, attentive
uhtintion, attention
uhtintive, attentive
uhtintiveness, attentive(ness)
uhtire, attire
uhtrausety, atrocity
uhtrochus, atrocious
uhtroshes, atrocious
uhtrosity, atrocity
uhwrest, arrest
uhwround, around
uhwrous, arouse
ui, we / whee
uic, wick / weak / week
uich, which / witch / wish
uid, we'd / weed
uider, wither / wide(r)
uidheld, withheld
uidin, within / wide(n)
uidjold, withhold
uidol, wheedle / whittle / widow
uidow, widow
uidstand, withstand
uidstud, withstood
uidt, width / with / wit
uiel, whale

uield,wield / wheel(ed) / weld	uisp,wisp	ukresif,aggressive
uienscot,wainscot	uisper,whisper	ukulale,ukulele
uif,weave / we've	uisqui,whiskey	ukulayle,ukulele
uig,wig	uistiria,wisteria	**ukulele**, * ,SMALL FOUR STRING GUITAR
uigol,wiggle	uisurd,wizard	ukumpany,accompany
uii,wee	uit,width / with / wit / wheat	ukumplish,accomplish
uiin,ween / win	uitdra,withdraw	ukumulate,accumulate
uiip,weep	uith,wit / with / width	ukumulation,accumulate(tion)
uiird,weird	uithaut,without	ukustemed,accustom(ed)
uik,weak / week / wick	uithdra,withdraw	ukuz,accuse
uiked,wicked	uitheld,withheld	ukwire,acquire
uiker,wicker	uither,wither / wide(r)	ularm,alarm
uil,will	uithin,within / wide(n)	**ulcer**,*,red,rate,rated,rating,ration,rative,rous,
uild,weald / wild / wield / wheel(ed) / weld / wilt	uithjold,withhold	rousness,FESTERED SORES IN THE LINING OF THE
uildernes,wilderness	uithstand,withstand	STOMACH
uilow,willow	uithstud,withstood	ulceradid,ulcer(ated)
uilt,wilt / will(ed)	uitnes,witness	ulcir,ulcer
uim,whim	uitol,whittle	ulcirashen,ulcer(ation)
uimp,wimp	uiu,way / weigh / whey	ulcur,ulcer
uimper,whimper	uiv,weave / we've	uldamatum,ultimatum
uimsical,whimsical	uivol,weevil	uldamitle,ultimate(ly)
uin,wean / win	uiyu,way / weigh / whey	uldimatum,ultimatum
uince,wince	uiz,wheeze / whiz	uldimetle,ultimate(ly)
uinch,winch	uizard,wizard	uldrusonek,ultrasonic
uind,wind	uizdom,wisdom	uldumatum,ultimatum
uini,weeny / wiener	uizerd,wizard	uldumetle,ultimate(ly)
uinter,winter	ujar,ajar	ule,you'll / yule
uintry,wintry	ujaur,ajar	ulecit,elicit / illicit
uiol,we'll / wheel	ujiledy,agile(lity)	uliens,alliance
uip,whip	ujilety,agile(lity)	ulif,alive
uiperuil,whippoorwill	ujor,ajar	ulike,alike
uiperwil,whippoorwill	ukalale,ukulele	ulin,align
uiq,weak / week / wick	ukaumplish,accomplish	ulinment,align(ment)
uir,weir / we're / where / were / whirr	ukews,accuse	ulions,alliance
uirlwind,whirlwind	ukilale,ukulele	uliptic,elliptic
uirpul,whirlpool	ukle,ugly	uliset,elicit / illicit
uiry,weary	ukomplesh,accomplish	uliv,alive
uisdom,wisdom	ukomplis,accomplice	uloof,aloof
uish,wish	ukomplish,accomplish	ulope,elope
uisk,whisk	ukomudate,accommodate	ulostrious,illustrious
uisker,whisker	ukord,accord	ulow,allow
uiski,whiskey	ukordant,accord(ant)	ulowanse,allowance
uisol,weasel / whistle	ukount,account	ulser,ulcer

ulseradid, ulcer(ated)
ulserashen, ulcer(ation)
ulsirashen, ulcer(ation)
ulsur, ulcer
ulsurashen, ulcer(ation)
ulsurated, ulcer(ated)
ultamatem, ultimatum
ultament, ultimate
ultametle, ultimate(ly)
ultemit, ultimate
ultereur, ulterior
ulterior, rly, UNDERLYING, SECRETIVE, NOT UP FRONT (or see alterior)
ultimate, ely, eness, THE GREATEST OF ALL
ultimatum, ta, FINAL, DO THIS OR A PENALTY RESULTS
ultimetly, ultimate(ly)
ultireor, ulterior
ultirior, ulterior
ultra, THE GREATEST/ MOST/ BEST/ EXTREME
ultrasonic, *, ABOVE 20,000 VIBRATIONS PER SECOND
ultru, ultra
ultrusonek, ultrasonic
ultumetle, ultimate(ly)
ultumint, ultimate
ultumit, ultimate
uluf, aloof
ulustrious, illustrious
um, them
umaunt, amount
umbelikul, umbilical
umbilical, ate, ated, ation, RELATING TO THE NAVEL
umbrella, *, DOME-SHAPED COVER FOR PROTECTION "prefixes: sub"
umeba, amoeba
umend, amend
umindment, amend(ment)
umonea, ammonia
umount, amount
umpede, impede
un, PREFIX INDICATING THAT "NOT/ REVERSAL" MOST OFTEN MODIFIES THE WORD (or see prefix in/ en)
unable, NOT ABLE/ CAPABLE (or see enable/ inability)
unabridged, IN ITS FULL LENGTH

unabriged, unabridged
unacceptable, WILL NOT BE ALLOWED, NOT ACCEPTABLE
unacdev, enact(ive) / inactive
unacebtible, unacceptable
unacorn, unicorn
unacseptible, unacceptable
unactive, enact(ive) / inactive
unacurate, innacurate
unacycle, unicycle
unadime, anatomy
unafekachen, unification
unafi, unify
unafid, unify(fied)
unafiuble, unify(fiable)
unaform, uniform
unaformety, uniform(ity)
unaformly, uniform(ly)
unakdev, enact(ive) / inactive
unakorn, unicorn
unakseptible, unacceptable
unaktef, inactive / enact(ive)
unaktive, enact(ive) / inactive
unakuret, inaccurate
unamoly, anomaly
unanamus, unanimous
unanimous, sly, mity, AGREED TO BY TWO OR MORE PEOPLE
unanomus, unanimous
unapel, unable
unapl, unable
unappreciative, inappreciative
unapresheative, inappreciative
unapropreat, inappropriate
unasen, unison
unasikle, unicycle
unasycle, unicycle
unat, innate
unate, unity
unaterein, unitary(rian)
unatery, unitary
unathekol, (un)ethic(al)
unathical, (un)ethic(al)
unatize, unite(tize)

unaty, unity
unaumily, anomaly
unavers, universe
unaversal, universal
unaversity, university
unaversule, universal(lly)
unavirs, universe
unavirsity, university
unavirsul, universal
unavurs, universe
unavursal, universal
unavursity, university
unaxseptible, unacceptable
unbanone, unbeknown
unbanonst, unbeknown(st)
unbeknown, nst, NOT KNOWN
unbenon, unbeknown
unbenonst, unbeknown(st)
unbenownst, unbeknown(st)
unbinone, unbeknown
unbinonst, unbeknown(st)
unbinunst, unbeknown
unbunownst, unbeknown(st)
uncal, uncle
uncane, uncanny
uncanily, uncanny(nnily)
uncanines, uncanny(niness)
uncanny, nnier, nniest, nily, nniness, NOT FORESEEN/ ORDINARY
uncanuly, uncanny(nily)
uncany, uncanny
uncase, encase
uncased, encase(d)
uncel, uncle
unchues, unction(tuous)
uncil, uncle
uncle, *, THE BROTHER OF A FATHER/ MOTHER
uncoherent, incoherent
uncol, uncle
unconscionable, eness, ly, COMPLETELY UNACCEPTABLE
uncroach, encroach
uncrust, encrust
uncshen, unction

uncshuosity, unction(tuosity)
unction,*, tuous, tuosity, tuously, tousness, INSINCERE FLATTERY/ CHARM, VERY SOFT/ RICH, OILY/ SOOTHING SUBSTANCE
undemic, endemic
under, PREFIX INDICATING THAT "BELOW/ INCOMPLETE" MOST OFTEN MODIFIES THE WORD
undergerd, undergird
undergird,*, ded, ding, rt, SUPPORT/ SECURE FROM BELOW
underhand, ded, dedly, dedness, DISHONEST
underjand, underhand
undermain, undermine
undermine,*, ed, ning, er, REMOVE CREDIBILITY OF SOMEONE, ETCH AWAY AT THE FOUNDATION/ BASE/ FOOTING OF SOMETHING/ SOMEONE
underneath, BELOW/ UNDERSIDE/ LOWER, NOT VISIBLE
underneeth, underneath
underneth, underneath
undernith, underneath
underpass, sses, ROAD UNDER A BRIDGE
underpin,*, nned, nning, nnings, SUPPORT/ FOUNDATION FOR SOMETHING
understand,*, tood, ding, dability, dable, dably, dingly, KNOW/ COMPREHEND/ PERCEIVE " prefixes: mis"
understate,*, ed, ting, ement, ements, NOT FULLY RELEASING THE FACTS/ IMPORTANCE
understend, understand
understood, PAST TENSE FOR THE WORD "UNDERSTAND"
underuer, underwear
underway, ACTIVELY MOVING ALONG, IN THE PROCESS TOWARDS COMPLETION
underwear, UNDER CLOTHING
undes, undies
undeulate, undulate
undewlashen, undulate(tion)
undewlate, undulate
undewlated, undulate(d)
undewly, unduly
undies, SHORT FOR UNDERWEAR
undirhand, underhand
undirhandedly, underhand(edly)

undirhandid, underhand(ed)
undirmind, undermine(d)
undirmine, undermine
undirneth, underneath
undirstand, understand
undirstood, understood
undirstude, understood
undirwa, underway
undirwar, underwear
undole, unduly
undoli, unduly
undoly, unduly
undoole, unduly
undulashen, undulate(tion)
undulate,*, ed, ting, tion, tory, ant, WAVE MOTION
unduleit, undulate
unduly, BEYOND MODERATION, UNLAWFUL
undurhand, underhand
undurhandidly, underhand(edly)
undurmind, undermine(d)
undurmine, undermine
undurneth, underneath
undurstand, understand
undurstood, understood
undurstude, understood
undurwa, underway
uneak, unique
unearth,*, hed, hing, hly, hliness, REMOVE FROM THE EARTH/ DIRT, SOLVE A MYSTERY, NOT OF THIS PLANE/ REALITY
unebreated, inebriate(d)
unebriated, inebriate(d)
unebriged, unabridged
unecorn, unicorn
unecycle, unicycle
uneek, unique
uneekle, unique(ly)
uneeknes, unique(ness)
unefi, unify
unefid, unify(fied)
unefikashen, unification
uneform, uniform
uneformedy, uniform(ity)

uneformety, uniform(ity)
uneformly, uniform(ly)
unefy, unify
unegma, enigma / enema
uneibol, unable/ enable
unek, unique
unekle, unique(ly)
uneknes, unique(ness)
unekorn, unicorn
unekwitable, inequitable
unekwity, inequity
unekwul, inequal
uneladeral, unilateral
unelateral, unilateral
unema, enema / anemia
unemea, anemia / enema
unemek, anemic
uneonize, union(ize)
uneque, unique
unequitable, inequitable
unequity, inequity
unerd, unearth
unerth, unearth
unerthd, unearth(ed)
unesikul, unicycle
uneson, unison
unesunus, unison(ous)
unesycle, unicycle
unet, unit
unetarean, unitary(rian)
unetary, unitary
unete, unity
unethecal, (un)ethic(al)
unethical, (un)ethic(al)
unety, unity
uneversal, universal
unevursal, universal
unferl, unfurl
unflagging, gingly, TIRELESS, UNCHANGING
unflagingly, unflagging(ly)
unflapable, unflappable
unflappable, bility, ly, ABLE TO MAINTAIN CONSISTENT COMPOSURE NO MATTER WHAT

unfleched, unfledged
unfledged, INMATURE, LACKS ADULT FEATHERS
unflegd, unfledged
unflejd, unfledged
unfortunate, *, ely, eness, WILL/ DID NOT "URN OUT AS PLANNED
unfurl, *, led, ling, TO UNROLL OR SPREAD OUT
ungainly, liness, AWKWARD IN MOVEMENT/ APPEARANCE
unganly, ungainly
ungulate, *, ed, MAMMAL WITH HOOVES
unheini, uncanny
uni, PREFIX INDICATING THAT "ONE/ SINGLE" MOST OFTEN MODIFIES THE WORD
unibreated, inebriate(d)
unicorn, *, A MYTHOLOGICAL HORSE WITH A HORN COMING FROM IT'S FOREHEAD
unicycle, *, ling, ONE-WHEELED CYCLE (or monocycle)
unifekachen, unification
unifi, unify
unification, BROUGHT TOGETHER AS ONE/ UNIFIED PART
unifid, unify(fied)
unifikachen, unification
uniform, *, med, mly, mity, mness, mitariar, mitarianism, NEAR EXACT IN SHAPE/ FORM/ APPEARANCE/ CHARACTER
uniformedy, uniform(ity)
uniformety, uniform(ity)
unify, fies, fied, fier, fying, fiable, fication, ABILITY TO BE BROUGHT TOGETHER AS ONE/ UNIFIED PART "prefixes: non/ re/ un"
unifyable, unify(fiable)
unigma, enigma / enema
unikle, unique(ly)
unilateral, *, lly, lism, list, ONE UNIFIED/ LATERAL SIDE OF AN AXIS/ LINEAGE/ ORGANISM/ PART
unimea, anemia / enema
union, *, nism, nist, nize, nized, nizing, nizat on, nism, BRING/ FORM TOGETHER AS ONE, ALL PARTS WORKING AS ONE (or see onion) "prefixes: dis/ re"
unique, ely, eness, UNMATCHED, ONE OF A KIND
unirth, unearth

unirthd, unearth(ed)
unisen, unison
unisikul, unicycle
unison, nal, nous, ONE IN SOUND
unisycle, unicycle
unit, *, tage, ty, ONE PART/ COMPONENT OF THE WHOLE "prefixes: sub"
unitarein, unitary(rian)
unitary, rian, rianism, CHARACTER WITHIN A UNIT, AS A UNIT
unite, *, ed, ting, table, er, edly, tive, tize, tizes, tized, tizing, tization, ty, ALL PARTS/ SECTIONS/ FACTIONS COMING TOGETHER/ FUNCTIONING AS ONE/ WHOLE (or see unity) "prefixes: dis/ re"
uniterein, unitary(rian)
unituble, unite(table)
unity, ALL AS ONE, A JOINING (or see unite) "prefixes: dis"
universal, *, lly, lness, lism, list, lity, lities, lize, lization, APPLIES/ ACCEPTED/ RELATING TO EVERYWHERE/ EVERYONE/ EVERYTHING
universe, *, OF ONE, ALL TOGETHER
university, ties, A PLACE OF HIGHER EDUCATION
univurs, universe
univursal, universal
univursity, university
univursuly, universal(lly)
unjulate, ungulate
unkal, uncle
unkanely, uncanny(nily)
unkanenes, uncanny(niness)
unkany, uncanny
unkapacitated, incapacitate(d)
unkarnate, incarnate
unkase, encase
unkel, uncle
unkoherent, incoherent
unkonsheonable, unconscionable
unkroch, encroach
unkrust, encrust
unkshen, unction
unkshues, unction(tuous)
unkshuosedy, unction(tuosity)

unkshuosity, unction(tuosity)
unktion, unction
unkul, uncle
unles, unless
unless, OR, IN PLACE OF, AN EXCEPTION
unoculate, inoculate
ungeration, inaugurate(tion)
unoint, anoint
unokulate, inoculate
unomaly, anomaly
unoperable, inoperable
unoperate, inoperate
unoperative, inoperate(tive)
unovers, universe
unoversity, university
unowgeration, inaugurate(tion)
unoy, annoy
unqueini, uncanny
unquel, uncle
unroole, unruly
unruly, lier, liest, liness, NOT OBEDIENT/ CONFORMING
unsanitere, insanitary
unsbekable, unspeakable
unsboken, unspoken
unshuous, unction(tuous)
unspeakable, eness, ly, poken, NOT MAKE VERBAL SOUNDS, NOT MEANT TO BE SAID/ SPOKEN
unspoken, NOT MAKE VERBAL SOUNDS, NOT TO BE SAID/ SPOKEN
untel, until
until, TIME BETWEEN NOW AND THE FUTURE/ NEXT TIME
unto, SAME AS THE WORD 'UNTIL', SOMETHING ACCOMPLISHED (or see onto)
untoward, *, dly, dness, NOT APPROPRIATE/ PROPER, ADVERSE
untuord, untoward
untuosity, unction(tuosity)
untuword, untoward
untwo, unto / onto
untwoward, untoward
unubriged, unabridged
unucorn, unicorn

unufikachen, unification
unufikashen, unification
unuformady, uniform(ity)
unuiting, unwitting
unukorn, unicorn
unupropreat, inappropriate
unurth, unearth
unurthd, unearth(ed)
unusin, unison
unut, unit
unuvers, universe
unuversity, university
unuversule, universal(lly)
unuvirs, universe
unvasef, invasive
unvashen, invasion
unweting, unwitting
unwetingly, unwitting(ly)
unwitting, gly, NOT KNOWING/ AWARE
unwrule, unruly
unyen, union / onion
unyon, union / onion
unyunize, union(ize)
uoc, walk / wok / whack
uoch, watch
uok, walk / wok / whack
uol, wall
uoltz, waltz
uomp, whomp
uond, wand / want
uonder, wander
uonderful, wonderful
uop, whoop
uoper, whopper
uor, war
uorant, warrant
uorbler, warbler
uord, ward / word
uordon, warden
uoren, warren
uorm, warm / worm
uorn, warn / worn
uorp, warp

uos, was
uosh, wash / whoosh
uosp, wasp
uou, whoa
uouc, woke
uount, won't
uow, whoa
uowc, woke
uownt, won't

up, DIRECTION TOWARDS THE SKY, PREFIX INDICATING THAT "MOST RECENTLY/ HIGHER" MOST OFTEN MODIFIES THE WORD "prefixes: re"
upairent, apparent
upairul, apparel
upald, appall(lled)
upalugize, apology(gize)
upalugy, apology(gize)
upar, upper
uparent, apparent
upart, apart
upartment, apartment
uparul, apparel
upastrufe, apostrophe
upauld, appall(lled)
upauluge, apology
upaulugize, apology(gize)
upaurtment, apartment
upaustrufe, apostrophe
upbeat, HIGHER NOTE/ FREQUENCY/ ATTITUDE
upbet, upbeat
upbit, upbeat
upealing, appeal(ing)
upearanc, appearance
upearinse, appearance
upedy, uppity
upeel, appeal
upel, appeal
uper, upper
uperense, appearance
uperent, apparent
uperinse, appearance
uperul, apparel
upety, uppity

upheave, *, ed, ving, val, A LIFTING/ RISING OF
upheeve, upheave
uphev, upheave
uphevel, upheave(val)
uphevul, upheave(val)
uphold, *, , held, ding, SUPPORT/ MAINTAIN
upholestury, upholstery
upholsdure, upholstery
upholster, *, , red, ring, rer, ry, OF COVERING FURNITURE "prefixes: re"
upholstery, ries, rer, FABRICS FOR COVERING "prefixes: re"
upholsture, upholstery
upil, appeal
upir, upper
upity, uppity
upiv, upheave
upland, HIGHER REGION/ GROUND
uplaud, applaud
uplaus, applause
uplefeus, oblivious
uplend, upland
upleveus, oblivious
upli, apply
uplifeus, oblivious
uplige, oblige(d)
upliveus, oblivious
uplod, applaud
uplos, applause
upoent, appoint
upoentment, appointment
upoint, appoint
upointment, appointment
upold, appall(lled) / uphold
upolstri, upholstery
upoluge, apology
upolugize, apology(gize)
upon, VERY CLOSE TO, UP ON
upord, aboard
uport, apart
uportment, apartment
upostrufe, apostrophe
upotment, appointment

upov,above	upsters,upstairs
upoynt,appoint	upsurd,absurd
uppearanc,appearance	uptane,obtain
upper,THE HIGHER LEVEL	uptrood,obtrude
upperinse,appearance	uptroosiv,obtrusive
upperul,apparel	uptrude,obtrude
uppity,yness,SOMEONE BEHAVING STUCK-UP	upuard,upward
upplaud,applaud	upur,upper
upplause,applause	**upward**,*,MOVE UP
upplod,applaud	upwerd,upward
upply,apply	upwholstery,upholstery
upprentis,apprentice	upwird,upward
uppreshiate,appreciate	upwort,upward
uppropriate,appropriare	upwright,upright
upprove,approve	upwrite,upright
upproximate,approximate	upwror,uproar
upproximately,approximate(ly)	upwruted,uproot(ed)
upraisul,appraisal	upwurd,upward
uprait,upright	upzolv,absolve
uprased,appraise(d)	uqyni,whinny
uprasef,abrasive	uracer,eraser
uprasul,appraisal	uradiate,irradiate
uprayt,upright	uradik,erotic / erratic
upraz,appraise	urain,arraign
uprazel,appraisal	uraingment,arrange(ment)
uprazif,abrasive	urainment,arraign(ment)
upreceashun,appreciate(tion)	uralogy,urology
uprecheat,appreciate	uran,urine / arraign
upreciate,appreciate	uraneum,uranium
uprenis,apprentice	urangment,arrange(ment)
uprentis,apprentice	**uranium**,A METAL CHEMICAL
upresheat,appreciate	uranjment,arrange(ment)
upresheate,appreciate	uranment,arraign(ment)
upresheation,appreciate(tion)	uranologi,uranology
upreshen,oppress(ion)	**uranology**,gies,gical,STUDY OF ASTRONOMY/ THE HEAVENS
upreshetion,appreciate(tion)	
upress,oppress	urase,erase
upression,oppress(ion)	uraser,eraser
upretiate,appreciate	urater,ureter
upreveate,abbreviate	urathane,urethane
upright,tly,tness,BE VERTICAL,BE IN THE RIGHT	uraudik,erotic
uprintes,apprentice	

uprise,*,rose,sing,STAND UP FOR/ AGAINST/ WITH,RISE UP	
uprisheate,appreciate	
uprite,upright	
uproach,approach	
uproar,rious,riously,riousness,COMMOTION/ DISTURBANCE, ELEVATED EMOTIONAL STATE	
uprobreat,appropriate	
uproch,approach	
uproksamit,approximate	
uproksumit,approximate	
uproksumitly,approximate(ly)	
uproof,approve	
uproot,*,ted,ting,ter,REMOVE ROOTS FROM THE GROUND	
uproovul,approve(val)	
upropreit,appropriate	
upror,uproar	
uprose,PAST TENSE FOR THE WORD UPRISE	
uprosh,approach	
uproximate,approximate	
uproximatly,approximate(ly)	
upruf,approve	
uprut,uproot	
uprutid,uproot(ed)	
upruv,approve	
upruval,approve(val)	
upserd,absurd	
upsesed,obsess(ed)	
upseshion,obsess(ion)	
upset,*,,tting,A DISTURBANCE/ IMBALANCE	
upsolv,absolve	
upstag,upstage	
upstage,*,ed,ging,TO DISTRACT THE AUDIENCE FROM SOMEONE ELSE, BACK OF THE STAGE	
upstairs,GO TO UPPER LEVEL BY MEANS OF STAIRS	
upstaj,upstage	
upstajd,upstage(d)	
upstars,upstairs	
upsteich,upstage	
upsteig,upstage	
upsteill,upstage	
upsteirs,upstairs	

urban, nism, nist, nistic, nistically, nite, nity, nities, nize, nizes, nized, nizing, nization, LIFE ON THE OUTSKIRSTS OF CITY "prefixes: sub"
urben, urban
urbenite, urban(ite)
urbon, urban
urbonite, urban(ite)
urch, urge
urchen, urchin
urchin, *, A SEA CREATURE
urea, al, eic, CHEMICAL IN URINE
urear, arrear
uregenal, origin(al)
uregenate, originate
ureighnment, arraign(ment)
ureik, urea(eic)
ureinment, arraign(ment)
urejenate, originate
urejinal, origin(al)
urek, uric
uren, urine
urena, arena
urenaded, urinate(d)
urenary, urinary
urenate, urinate
urenology, uranology
urenul, urinal
urer, arrear
urest, arrest
ureter, ral, ric, CANAL FROM KIDNEY TO BLADDER CONTAINED WITHIN THE BODY
uretha, urethra
urethane, A MANMADE CHEMICAL
urethra, *, al, TUBE IN THE BODY WHICH FUNNELS URINE FOR DISCHARGE
urgd, urge(d)
urge, *, ed, ging, er, gingly, ency, ent, ently, OVERWHELMING DESIRE TO ACCOMPLISH/ FULFILL
urgint, urge(nt)
urgis, urge(s)
uri, awry
uria, urea
uric, OF THE URINE

urif, arrive
uriful, arrival
uriginal, origin(al)
uriginate, originate
urijenal, origin(al)
urik, uric
urin, urine
urina, arena
urinal, A DEVICE/ VESSEL FOR MALE'S TO URINATE INTO
urinary, OF THE URINE
urinate, *, ed, ting, tion, ACT OF RELEASING/ DISCHARGING URINE
urine, LIQUID WASTE SECRETION
urinery, urinary
urinology, uranology
urinul, urinal
uriter, ureter
urithane, urethane
urithra, urethra
uriv, arrive
urivul, arrival
urj, urge
urjd, urge(d)
urjent, urge(nt)
urjinse, urge(ncy)
urli, early
urll, urge
urn, *, VESSEL USED TO MAKE BUTTER, HOLD CONTENTS (or see earn/ yearn/ urine)
urodik, erotic
urolegy, urology
urology, gic, gical, gist, FIELD OF SCIENCE STUDYING THE URINARY TRACT
urologu, urology
urom, warm / worm
uroma, aroma
uron, urine
uround, around
urouz, arouse
urownd, around
urows, arouse
urrear, arrear
urrest, arrest

urrivol, arrival
urs, your(s)
urunal, urinal
urunate, urinate
urunery, urinary
urunology, uranology
us, PEOPLE INCLUDING SELF (or see ooze/ use/ yew(s))
usabil, usable
usable, *, bility, ly, eness, ABLE TO BE USED "prefixes: re/ un"
usacin, assassin
usage, *, ABILITY TO BE USED/ UTILIZED "prefixes: mis"
usail, assail
usal, assail
usalant, assail(ant)
usalt, assault
usary, usury
usasen, assassin
usault, assault
usberugus, asparagus
uscend, ascend
uscention, ascension
usd, use(d)
usdonesh, astonish
usdrawnumy, astronomy
usdronumy, astronomy
use, *, ed, sing, sable, sability, sage, sance, eful, efully, efulness, eless, elessly, elessness, er, sable, EMPLOY/ EXPLOIT/ UTILIZE TO ACCOMPLISH/ ACHIEVE SUCCESS, EXPLOIT RESOURCES (or see yew(s)) "prefixes: dis/ mis/ multi/ non/ over/ re/ un/ under"
useage, usage
usebil, usable
useble, usable
usech, usage
usedik, acetic / acidic / ascetic
useful, lly, lness, ABLE TO BE UTILIZED EASILY
useg, usage
usej, usage
useless, sly, sness, NOT ABLE TO BE UTILIZED EASILY
uselis, useless
usemble, assemble
usemelate, assimilate

usemilate, assimilate
usemlate, assimilate
usend, ascend
usenshen, ascension
usent, assent
usention, ascension
user, *, ONE WHO EXPLOITS OTHERS/ RESOURCES, THOSE WHO USE DRUGS (or see usury)
usere, usury
userp, usurp
userped, usurp(ed)
usershen, assert(ion)
usert, assert
usertev, assert(ive)
usertion, assert(ion)
usery, usury
uses, assess / use(s)
useshun, accession
usesment, assessment
usest, assist
usestens, assist(ance)
usestins, assist(ance)
useum, assume
usfekseat, asphyxiate
usfiksaet, asphyxiate
usfixeat, asphyxiate
usful, useful
ushamed, ashamed
usher, *, red, ring, TENDS TO GUESTS AT PUBLIC GATHERING, INDUCE/ ESCORT/ BRING ABOUT (or see assure)
ushir, usher / assure
ushwaly, usual(lly)
ushwule, usual(lly)
usibil, usable
usible, usable
usich, usage
uside, aside
usig, usage
usign, assign
usij, usage
usilem, asylum
usimbul, assemble

usimelate, assimilate
usin, assign
usind, ascend
usinment, assignment
usinshen, ascension
usint, assent
usir, user
usirshen, assert(ion)
usirt, assert
usirtif, assert(ive)
usirtion, assert(ion)
usiry, usury
usist, assist
usistens, assist(ance)
usitic, acetic / acidic / ascetic
usleep, asleep
uslep, asleep
uslis, useless
uslus, useless
usocheat, associate
usocheation, associate(tion)
usociate, associate
usociation, associate(tion)
usofegus, esophagus
usog, usage
usolt, assault
usordid, assorted
usortment, assortment
usosheashun, associate(tion)
usosheut, associate
usoshiat, associate
usoshiation, associate(tion)
usparugus, asparagus
usperugus, asparagus
usphikseate, asphyxiate
uspire, aspire
usry, usury
ussal, assail
ussasin, assassin
ussemble, assemble
ust, use(d)
ustonish, astonish
ustraunume, astronomy

ustronumy, astronomy
ustrownumy, astronomy
usual, lly, lness, MOST COMMON/ PREDICTABLE "prefixes: un"
usuch, usage
usug, usage
usuj, usage
usum, assume
usumpshen, assumption
usumshen, assumption
usur, user / assure
usure, usury
usurp, *, ped, ping, pation, per, TO UNLAWFULLY ASSUME POSSESSION OF
usurt, assert
usury, ries, rer, rious, riously, riousness, CHARGE EXORBITANT/ UNLAWFUL AMOUNT OF INTEREST FOR A LOAN
usylim, asylum
utachment, attach(ment)
utack, attack
utain, attain
utainable, attain(able) / obtain(able)
utak, attack
utanable, attain(able) / obtain(able)
utane, attain
utanmint, attain(ment)
utash, attach
uteludy, utility
utempt, attempt
utemt, attempt
utend, attend
utendens, attend(ance)
utending, attend(ing)
utenshen, attention
utensil, *, DEVICE/ INSTRUMENT/ TOOL FOR WORK
utensul, utensil
utentef, attentive
utentefness, attentive(ness)
utention, attention
utentive, attentive
uter, odor / otter / outer / utter / udder

uterus, ri, HOME FOR EMBRYO IN FEMALE MAMMALS "prefixes: intra"
utest, attest
uther, other
utilatarian, utilitarian
utilety, utility
utilitarian, *, nism, FOCUS ON USEFUL/ PRACTICALITY
utility, ties, ize, A USEFUL SERVICE FOR THE COMMON GOOD OF THE PEOPLE "prefixes: dis"
utilize, *, ed, zing, zable, zation, zer, MAKE USE OF "prefixes: mis/ re"
utilude, utility
utiluty, utility
utimt, attempt
utind, attend
utindens, attend(ance)
utinding, attend(ing)
utinsel, utensil
utinshen, attention
utinsul, utensil
utintef, attentive
utintion, attention
utintive, attentive
utintiveness, attentive(ness)
utir, odor / otter / outer / utter / udder / attire
utmost, BEST/ HIGHEST IN ORDER OF IMPORTANCE
utmoust, utmost
utopia, an, IDEAL SITUATION
utor, odor / otter / outer / utter / udder
utrausety, atrocity
utrochus, atrocious
utroshes, atrocious
utrosity, atrocity
utter, *, red, ring, rance, rable, rer, TO SPEAK (or see udder) "prefixes: un"
utur, odor / otter / outer / utter / udder
uturd, utter(ed)
uvale, avail
uvert, avert / advert / overt
uvou, avow
uvow, avow
uwa, away
uweic, awake
uwil, awhile
uwrest, arrest
uwround, around
uwrous, arouse
uzd, use(d)
uzing, use(sing) / ooze(zing)
uzre, usury / use(r)
vacabeulery, vocabulary
vacalate, vacillate
vacancy, ncies, UNOCCUPIED DWELLING
vacant, tly, tness, ncy, DWELLING NEEDING/ WITHOUT OCCUPANCY
vacashend, vacation(ed)
vacashun, vacation
vacate, *, ed, ting, TO LEAVE PERMANENTLY
vacation, *, ned, ning, nless, ner, nist, GO AWAY FOR A BRIEF VISIT/ EXCURSION WITH THE INTENT OF ENJOYMENT/ RELAXATION
vaccen, vaccine
vaccenate, vaccinate
vaccilate, vacillate
vaccinate, *, ned, tion, INOCULATE WITH A CHEMICAL/ MEDICINE TO AFFECT THE BODY
vaccine, *, nal, USED TO STIMULATE THE BODY TO PRODUCE ANTIBODIES, USED TO PROTECT AGAINST A VIRUS
vacculate, vacillate
vaccum, vacuum
vacelate, vacillate
vacenity, vicinity
vacensy, vacancy
vacent, vacant
vachaina, vagina
vacilate, vacillate
vacileit, vacillate
vacillate, *, ed, ting, tingly, tion, tor, tory, MOVE BACK AND FORTH, TO AND FRO, FLUCTUATE BETWEEN TWO POINTS
vacinate, vaccinate
vacine, vaccine
vacinity, vicinity
vacsenate, vaccinate
vacsinate, vaccinate
vacsination, vaccinate(tion)
vacsineit, vaccinate
vacum, vacuum
vacuole, *, lar, late, lates, lated, lating, lization, LACKING SUBSTANCE/ INTELLIGENCE/ AWARENESS
vacuous, sly, sness, LACKS SUBSTANCE/ INTELLIGENCE/ AWARENESS
vacuum, *, med, ming, MACHINE USED TO PULL/ SUCK/ PICK UP, SPACE CREATED BY REMOVING PARTICLES
vacuus, vacuous
vad, vat
vag, vague
vagabond, *, dish, dism, ONE WHO ROAMS WITHOUT A PERMANENT HOME/ SUSTENANCE
vagary, ried, rious, riously, WHIMSICAL, UNPREDICTABLE IN MOVEMENT/ BEHAVIOR
vage, vague
vagebond, vagabond
vagenul, vagina(l)
vagery, vagary
vagina, *, al, ally, TUBULAR SHAPED CANAL FOUND IN PLANTS/ FEMALE BODIES
vaginul, vagina(l)
vagiry, vagary
vagist, vague(st)
vagle, vague(ly)
vagly, vague(ly)
vagobond, vagabond
vagrant, *, tly, ncy, ncies, HOMELESS WHO WANDER/ ROAM
vagre, vagary
vagrense, vagrant(ncy)
vagrent, vagrant
vagrunse, vagrant(ncy)
vagry, vagary
vagubond, vagabond
vague, er, est, ely, eness, HAZY, UNCLEAR
vagury, vagary
vagust, vague(st)
vahement, vehemence(nt)
vahemins, vehemence
vaib, vibe
vaibrant, vibrant

word	definitions/forms
vaibreitor	vibrator
vaiking	viking
vail, *	TO LOWER/ REMOVE (or see vale/ veil/ vile)
vailent	violent
vailet	violet
vain, nly, nness	TO ATTEMPT WITHOUT SUCCESS, BE SELF-ABSORBED WITH ONE'S OWN SHALLOW VALUES (or see vane/ vein)
vainol	vinyl
vairal	viral
vairus	virus
vais	vice / vise
vaisor	visor
vaitamin	vitamin
vaitol	vital
vajenul	vagina(l)
vajina	vagina
vajinul	vagina(l)
vajunal	vagina(l)
vak	vague
vakabeulery	vocabulary
vakabulery	vocabulary
vakachend, vacation(ed)	
vakachun	vacation
vakadid, vacate(d)	
vakashen	vacation
vakashend, vacation(ed)	
vakashun	vacation
vakat	vacate
vakatid, vacate(d)	
vakchenashin, vaccinate(tion)	
vakchunashen, vaccinate(tion)	
vake	vague
vakeishon	vacation
vakense, vacant(ncy)	
vakent	vacant
vakently, vacant(ly)	
vakeum	vacuum
vakeuol	vacuole
vakinse, vacant(ncy)	
vakint	vacant
vakium	vaccum
vakiuol	vacuole
vakle, vague(ly)	
vakly, vague(ly)	
vakoum	vacuum
vakrent	vagrant
vakrint, **vagrant**	
vakseen, vaccine	
vaksen	vaccine
vaksenate	vaccinate
vakshenashin, vaccinate(tion)	
vaksinate	vaccinate
vaksination, vaccinate(tion)	
vaksine	vaccine
vaksunashen, vaccinate(tion)	
vakual	vacuole
vakum	vacuum
vakumd, vacuum(ed)	
vakunse, vacant(ncy)	
vakunt	vacant
vakuol	vacuole
vakuous	vacuous
vakuus	vacuous
vakyewm	vacuum
vakyewol	vacuole
vakyual	vacuole
vakyum	vacuum
val, vail / vale / veil	
vala	valet
valacity	velocity
valadectory	valedictory
valadiction	valediction
valadiktorean	valedictorian
valance, es, ed	SHORT CURTAIN (or see valence) "prefixes: uni"
valans	valance / valence
valantine	valentine
valatil	volatile
vale	A VALLEY (or see vail/ veil/ valley/ valet)
valeant	valiant
valed, valid / veil(ed)	
valediction	A VALEDICTORY
valedictorian	ONE WHO SPEAKS AT A SCHOOL COMMENCEMENT
valedictory, ries	SCHOOL FINAL/ FAREWELL CEREMONY
valediktorian	valedictorian
valediktory	valedictory
valedity, valid(ity)	
valei	valley
valeint	valiant
valence, cy, nt	A WAY TO MEASURE THE STRENGTH OF AN ATOM (or see valance) "prefixes: bi"
valens	valance / valence
valent, valence(nt) / valiant	
valentine, *	TO HONOR ONE WHOM YOU ARE ATTRACTED TO IN A ROMANTIC WAY
valer	valor
valerean	valerian
valerian	AN HERB
valerus, valor(ous)	
valet	ONE WHO PARKS CARS FOR GUESTS AT AN EVENT/ PUBLIC PLACE
valeubul, value(uable)	
valeunt	valiant
valeuntly, valiant(ly)	
valey	valley
valf	valve
valiant, tly, tness	OF COURAGE/ STRONG/ BRAVE
valid, dly, dness, date, dates, dating, dation, dity, dities, dness	REAL, FACTUAL, ACTUAL, TO ACKNOWLEDGE AUTHENTICITY "prefixes: in/ un"
validectory	valedictory
validete, valid(ity)	
validety, valid(ity)	
validiction	valediction
validictorian	valedictorian
validiktory	valedictory
valie	valley
valins	valance / valence
valint, valence(nt) / valiant	
valintine	valentine
valir	valor
valirus, valor(ous)	
valit	valid
valitel	volatile
valiu	value
valkano	volcano
vallaina	vagina

valley,*, AREA BETWEEN THE MOUNTAINS AT THE LOWEST POINTS
valor,velour / velure / valor
valor,rous, rously, rousness, QUALITY ATTRIBUTED TO MALE WHO DISPLAYS BRAVERY/ FIRM RESOLVE (or see velour/ velure)
valosedy,velocity
valosety,velocity
valotel,volatile
valu,value
valubel,value(uable)
valubul,value(uable)
valud,valid / value(d)
valudectory,valedictory
valudikshen,valediction
valudiktory,valedictory
value,*, ed,uing,eless,elessness,uable,uableness,uably, uate, uator, uation, uationally, WHAT SOMETHING IS WORTH "prefixes: de/ dis/ in/ un/ under"
values,value(less)
valum,volume
valuns,valance
valuntery,voluntary
valuntine,valentine
valupshuis,voluptuous
valuptuous,voluptuous
valur,velour / velure / valor
valut,valid
valutel,volatile
valv,valve
valve,*, eless,AN APETURE/ OPENING TO REGULATE FLOW OF AIR/ LIQUID/ MOLECULES "prefixes: bi/ un/ uni"
valy,valley
valyant,valiant
valyently,valiant(ly)
valyew,value
valyewbul,value(uable)
valyint,valiant
valyu,value
valyubil,value(uable)
valyuble,value(uable)

valyum,volume
valyunt,valiant
valyuntle,valiant(ly)
vamb,vamp
vambir,vampire
vamp,*, ed,ping,MOVE BITS/ PIECES AROUND TO CHANGE FLOW/ DIRECTION OF SOMETHING, IMPROVISE
vampayer,vampire
vampire,*, ric, rism, ONE THAT DWELLS IN THE NIGHT AND USES BLOOD FOR SUSTENANCE
van,*, nned,nning,TYPE OF VEHICLE (or see vane/ vain/ vein/ feign/ one) "prefixes: de"
vandal,*, lic, lism, listic, lize, lizes, lized, lizing,BREAK IN AND DESTROY ANOTHER'S PROPERTY
vandel,vandal
vandelism,vandal(ism)
vandelize,vandal(ize)
vandiktif,vindictive
vandil,vandal
vandilize,vandal(ize)
vandulism,vandal(ism)
vandulize,vandal(ize)
vane,*, ed, eless, DEVICE MOUNTED TO DISPLAY WIND DIRECTION, FEATHER ON AN ARROW (or see van/ vain/ vein/ feign)
vanech,vanish
vanedy,vanity
vaneer,veneer
vanela,vanilla
vaner,veneer
vanesh,vanish
vaneshd,vanish(ed)
vanesht,vanish(ed)
vanety,vanity
vangard,vanguard
vangart,vanguard
vanguard,THE FEW WHO ARE AHEAD OF THE GROUP
vanich,vanish
vanide,vanity
vanila,vanilla
vanilla, TYPE OF FRUIT/ BEAN
vanish,hes, hed, hing, TO DISAPPEAR

vanishd,vanish(ed)
vanity,ties,OF BEING VAIN,SELF-ABSORBED WITH SHALLOW VALUES
vankuesh,vanquish
vankwesh,vanquish
vankwish,vanquish
vankwishd,vanquish(ed)
vanquesh,vanquish
vanqueshd,vanquish(ed)
vanquish, hes, hed, hing, hable, OVERCOME/ SUBDUE/ DEFEAT
vanqwesh,vanquish
vanqweshd,vanquish(ed)
vanqwish,vanquish
vantage,*, A SUPERIOR POSITION/ LOCATION
vantech,vantage
vantej,vantage
vantich,vantage
vantig,vantage
vantuj,vantage
vanude,vanity
vanush,vanish
vanushd,vanish(ed)
vanute,vanity
vaper,vapor
vaperize,vapor(ize)
vapir,vapor
vapirize,vapor(ize)
vapor,*, rer,rish,rishness,rific, ring, rize, rizes, rized, rizing, rizable, rization, rizer, rous, rously, rousness, rosity, ry, FUMES/ CLOUD EMITTED/ GIVEN OFF BY SOMETHING WHEN EXPOSED TO THE AIR
vapur,vapor
vapurize,vapor(ize)
vaqium,vacuum
vaqiuol,vacuole
vaqum,vacuum
varashis,veracious / voracious
varayedi,variety
varayeti,variety
varcity,varsity
vare,vary / very
vareagashen,variegate(tion)

vareashen, variate(tion)
vareation, variate(tion)
vared, vary(ried)
varefication, verify(fication)
varefy, verify
vareins, variant(nce)
vareint, variant
vares, vary(ries)
vareuble, variable
vareuns, variant(nce)
vareunt, variant
vareus, vary(rious)
vari, vary / very
variable, *, bility, eness, y, CHANGE IN VALUE OF SOMETHING, THE GIVENS IN AN EQUATION, RATE OF SPEED/ FLOW/ FREQUENCY "prefixes: in"
variant, *, nce, RANGE CF SPEED/ FLOW/ FREQUENCY
variate, tion, tional, tionally, tive, tively, RATE OF CHANGE IN FLOW/ FREQUENCY/ DIRECTION" p refixes: bi"
variedy, variety
variegate, *, ed, ting, tion, OF A VARIETY
variety, ties, tal, tally, A RANGE OF CHOICES
varificashen, verify(fication)
varify, verify
varis, vary(ries)
variuble, variable
variugashen, variegate(tion)
variuns, variant(nce)
varius, vary(rious)
variuty, variety
varment, A TROUBLESOME ANIMAL
varmint, varment
varmun, varment
varnesh, varnish
varneshd, varnish(ed)
varnish, hes, hed, hing, her, hy, TRANSPARENT CHEMICAL COATING FOR PROTECTION "prefixes: un"
varnush, varnish
varsedy, varsity
varsety, varsity
varsity, ties, TYPE OF SCHOOL SPORTS TEAM
varsudes, varsity(ties)
varsuty, varsity

varufi, verify
vary, ries, ried, ying, yingly, rious, riously, riousness, MOVEABLE RANGE/ RATE OF CHANGE/ SELECTION (or see very)
varyd, vary(ried)
varys, vary(ries)
vas, vase
vasalashen, vacillate(tion)
vasalate, vacillate
vasalation, vacillate(tion)
vascular, rity, rly, FLOW WITHIN A SYSTEM "prefixes: intra/ non"
vasd, vast
vase, *, A CONTAINER
vasectomy, mies, SURGICAL PROCEDURE FOR MALES
vasektumy, vasectomy
vaselashen, vacillate(tion)
vaselate, vacillate
vaselation, vacillate(tion)
vasenedy, vicinity
vasenety, vicinity
vasilashen, vacillate(tion)
vasilate, vacillate
vasilation, vacillate(tion)
vasinedy, vicinity
vasinety, vicinity
vaskeuler, vascular
vaskewler, vascular
vaskiular, vascular
vaskuler, vascular
vasnes, vast(ness)
vasqiuler, vascular
vasqueler, vascular
vasquler, vascular
vast, tly, tness, ty, tier, tiest, titude, tity, GREAT AMOUNT IN RANGE/ DEGREES/ FREQUENCY/ AREA
vasul, vessel
vasulashen, vacillate(tion)
vasulate, vacillate
vasulation, vacillate(tion)
vat, *, tted, tting, A VESSEL FOR LIQUIDS
vau, vow
vauch, vouch

vaucher, vouch(er)
vaud, vow(ed)
vaudku, vodka
vaul, vowel
vaulatil, volatile
vaulcano, volcano
vaule, volley
vaulenteer, volunteer
vauli, volley
vaulinter, volunteer
vaulkano, volcano
vault, *, ted, ting, ter, HOLDING/ CONTAINER TO PROTECT VALUABLES, ARCHED HEIGHT WITHIN A DWELLING/ SPACE/ CONTAINER, LEAP HIGH (or see volt)
vaulum, volume
vauluntery, voluntary
vaulutil, volatile
vauly, volley
vaumet, vomit
vaumit, vomit
vaush, vouch
vausher, vouch(er)
vautku, vodka
vauz, vase
vaw, vow
vawch, vouch
vawcher, vouch(er)
vawd, vow(ed)
vawl, vowel
vawle, volley
vayabol, viable
vayaduct, viaduct
vayaina, vagina
vaygari, vagary
vayol, vail / vale / veil
vayoleit, violate
vayolin, violin
vayper, viper
vayrol, virile
vayrolent, virulent
vea, via
veakul, vehicle
veal, MEAT FROM THE CALF OF A BOVINE

vecenity, vicinity
vechen, vision
vechenary, vision(ary)
veches, vicious
vechetal, vegetal
vechetarian, vegetarian
vechetate,

vecheteit, vegetate
vechitarian, vegetarian
vechtable, vegetable
vechualize, visual(ize)
vechulante, vigil(ante)
vechun, vision
vechunary, vision(ary)
vechus, vicious
vechutarian, vegetarian
vecinity, vicinity
vecks, vex
vectomize, victim(ize)
vectumizashen, victim(ization)
vectumize, victim(ize)
vedeo, video
vederan, veteran
vedio, video
vedo, veto
vedod, veto(ed)
vedran, veteran
vedrify, vitrify
vedurin, veteran
veer,*, red, ring, ringly, SWERVE IN MOVEMENT, MOVE TOWARDS PARTICULAR DIRECTION
vegan,*, DOES NOT EAT/CONSUME MEAT/ANIMAL PRODUCTS "prefixes: non"
vegatashen, vegetate(tion)
vegatate, vegetate
vegatuble, vegetable
vegduble, vegetable
vegel, vigil
vegelante, vigil(ante)
vegen, vegan
veger, vigor
vegerus, vigor(ous)

vegetable,*, CATEGORY OF EDIBLE PLANTS
vegetal, OF BEING A VEGETABLE
vegetarian,*, nism, EATS PRIMARILY VEGETABLES "prefixes: non"
vegetate,*, ed, ting, tion, tional, tionless, tive, tively, tivness, SIT/ AGE/ RIPEN AS A VEGETABLE WITHOUT MOVEMENT "prefixes: re"
vegetuble, vegetable
vegetul, vegetal
vegil, vigil
vegilante, vigil(ante)
vegilent, vigil(ant)
vegin, vegan
veginu, vagina
vegir, vigor
vegirus, vigor(ous)
vegitashen, vegetate(tion)
vegitate, vegetate
vegiterean, vegetarian
vegituble, vegetable
vegitul, vegetal
vegolante, vigil(ante)
vegon, vegan
vegorus, vigor(ous)
vegtable, vegetable
vegtuble, vegetable
vegual, visual
vegulante, vigil(ante)
vegun, vegan
veguol, visual
veguolize, visual(ize)
vegur, vigor
vegurus, vigor(ous)
vegutarean, vegetarian
vegutashen, vegetate(tion)
vegutate, vegetate
vehecle, vehicle
vehekul, vehicle
vehemence, cy, nt, ntly, STRONG/ FORCEFUL FEELINGS BROUGHT ON BY AN EMOTIONAL STATE/ PASSION, STRONG/ FORCEFUL EVENT
vehemint, vehemence(nt)
vehicle,*, cular, MOVING/ POWERED VESSELS

vehicul, vehicle
vehikul, vehicle
veic, vague
veicanci, vacancy
veicant, vacant
veiceit, vacate
veig, vague
veigary, vagary
veigeit, vacate
veikle, vehicle
veil,*, led, ling, THIN/ TRANSPARENT/ REMOVABLE COVER (or see vail/ vale) "prefixes: un"
vein,*, ned, ning, nal, ny, nlet, TUBE/ CHANNEL THAT ALLOWS FLOW OF LIQUID (or see vane/ vain) "prefixes: de"
veipor, vapor
veiqaishon, vacation
veis, vase
veiwed, view(ed)
vejalante, vigil(ante)
vejalent, vigil(ant)
vejatashen, vegetate(tion)
vejatate, vegetate
vejaterean, vegetarian
vejdible, vegetable
vejduble, vegetable
vejetarean, vegetarian
vejetashen, vegetate(tion)
vejetul, vegetal
vejewelize, visual(ize)
vejinu, vagina
vejitarean, vegetarian
vejitashen, vegetate(tion)
vejitate, vegetate
vejitul, vegetal
vejolent, vigil(ant)
vejtuble, vegetable
vejual, visual
vejulante, vigil(ante)
vejulent, vigil(ant)
vejuolize, visual(ize)
vejutarean, vegetarian
vejutashen, vegetate(tion)

vejutate, vegetate
vekabeulery, vocabulary
vekabulery, vocabulary
vekan, vegan
veken, vegan
veker, vigor
vekin, vegan
vekir, vigor
vekon, vegan
vekor, vigor
veks, vex
veksashen, vex(ation)
veksation, vex(ation)
vektem, victim
vektemize, victim(ize)
vektumize, victim(ize)
vekun, vegan
vekur, vigor
vel, vale / vail / veil
vela, villa
velafy, vilify
velage, villa(ge)
velanus, villain(ous)
velarean, valerian
velcom, welcome
veledictore, valedictory
veledictorean, valedictorian
veledictori, valedictory
velefy, vilify
velege, villa(ge)
velej, villa(ge)
velen, villain
velenus, villain(ous)
velidety, valid(ity)
velin, villain
velletal, vegetarian
velltabol, vegetable
velocity, ties, tize, tizes, =ized, tizing, tization, RATE/ AMOUNT OF MOVEMENT/ SPEED
velon, villain
velour, *, red, ring, TYPE OF FABRIC/ VELVET (or see velure)
velu, villa

veluch, villa(ge)
velufy, vilify
velug, villa(ge)
veluj, villa(ge)
velun, villain
velunus, villain(ous)
velure, *, ed, ring, TYPE OF FABRIC (or see velour)
velutch, villa(ge)
velvet, *, ted, ting, teen, ty, THICK/ SILKY/ SOFT FABRIC
velvity, velvet
velvude, velvet
velvut, velvet
vem, vim
vemens, vehemence
venager, vinegar
venagrey, vinaigrette
venaker, vinegar
venam, venom
venamus, venom(ous)
venasin, venison
vench, venge
vencher, venture
venchful, venge(ful)
venchurd, venture(d)
vend, *, ded, ding, der, dition, TO SELL (or see vent)
vendacation, vindicate(tion)
vendalashen, ventilate(tion)
vendalate, ventilate
vendalation, ventilate(tion)
vendecate, vindicate
vendecation, vindicate(tion)
vendeda, vendetta
vendekduf, vindictive
vendektif, vindictive
vendetta, *, HAS A STRONG/ DEEP GRUDGE/ DISPUTE/ DISAGREEMENT WITH
vendicashen, vindicate(tion)
vendicate, vindicate
vendiktif, vindictive
venducation, vindicate(tion)
vendulashen, ventilate(tion)
veneer, *, red, ring, rer, rable, rability, rableness, THIN OVERLAYMENT USED FOR SURFACING

venegrey, vinaigrette
venela, vanilla
venem, venom
venemus, venom(ous)
venerate, *, ed, ting, tor, tion, able, ability, ableness, ably, CANONIZE/ WORSHIP/ PUT IN HIGH ESTEEM OVER ONESELF
venew, venue
venge, *, ed, ging, eance, eful, efully, efulness, SEEK AVENGE FOR A WRONG, BE VINDICTIVE/ RELENTLESS IN PURSUIT OF SATISFACTION
vengens, venge(ance)
vengful, venge(ful)
venguns, venge(ance)
veniger, vinegar
venigra, vinaigrette
venila, vanilla
venim, venom
venimus, venom(ous)
venir, veneer
venirate, venerate
venison, TERM FOR THE MEAT OF THE DEER FAMILY
veniu, venue
venj, venge
venjens, venge(ance)
venjful, venge(ful)
venjuns, venge(ance)
veno, vino
venom, *, mous, mously, mousness, POISON
venomus, venom(ous)
venorate, venerate
venosen, venison
vensable, vincible
vensher, venture
vensubul, vincible
vent, *, ted, ting, ALLOWS THE RELEASE OF AIR/ STEAM/ HEAT/ EMOTIONS (or see vend) "prefixes: bio"
ventag, vintage
ventalashen, ventilate(tion)
ventalate, ventilate
ventalation, ventilate(tion)
venteg, vintage
ventej, vintage

ventilashen, ventilate(tion)
ventilate, * , ed, ting, tion, tive, tor, tory, ENCOURAGE THE FLOW OF AIR
ventricle, * , cular, culus, culi, TUBES/ ARTERIES "prefixes: inter/ intra"
ventrikul, ventricle
ventriloquist, tic, sm, uy, ial, ially, ize, TO THROW/ PROJECT THE VOICE WITHOUT MOVING THE LIPS
ventrilukwist, ventriloquist
ventrukle, ventricle
ventuge, vintage
ventuj, vintage
venture, * , ed, ring, GO ON BRAVE/ DARING ADVENTURE, MOVE TOWARDS UNKNOWN TERRITORY
venu, venue
venue, * , WAYS/ PATHS, A LEGAL TERM
venuger, vinegar
venugray, vinaigrette
venuker, vinegar
venumus, venom(ous)
venurate, venerate
venusin, venison
venyou, venue
veol, vail / vale / veil / veal
ver, veer
veracious, sly, sness, TRUTHFUL/ UNERRING (or see voracious)
veracity, ties, EAGERNESS/ SUPPORT FOR THE TRUTH
verafecation, verify(fication)
verafikashen, verify(fication)
verafy, verify
verasedy, veracity / voracity
verashes, voracious / veracious
verasious, voracious / veracious
verasity, veracity / voracity
verb, * , bal, WORD WHICH DENOTES ACTION
verbadum, verbatim
verbal, lly, lism, list, listic, lize, lizes, lized, lizing, lization, lizer, VOICE/ SPEAK FROM THE MOUTH, MAKE THOUGHTS HEARD "prefixes: non"
verbatim, EXACT WORDS
verbatum, verbatim
verble, verbal / verbal(lly)

verblize, verbal(ize)
verboly, verbal(lly)
verbose, ely, eness, sity, TOO WORDY, USES TOO MANY WORDS TO DESCRIBE/ COMMUNICATE
verbosity, verbose(sity)
verbosudy, verbose(sity)
verbule, verbal / verbal(lly)
verbulize, verbal(ize)
verc, work
verch, verge
verchen, version / virgin
verchew, virtue
verchewul, virtual
verchoo, virtue
verchualedy, virtual(ity)
verchuality, virtual(ity)
verchuol, virtual
verd, veer(ed) / weird / word
verdabra, vertebra
verdacal, vertical
verdago, vertigo
verdekly, vertical(lly)
verdekt, verdict
verdekul, vertical
verdibra, vertebra
verdical, vertical
verdict, * , FINAL DECISION/ JUDGMENT
verdigo, vertigo
verdikly, vertical(lly)
verdikul, vertical
verdubra, vertebra
verdukol, vertical
vere, vary / very
vereability, variable(lity)
vereabl, variable
vereant, variant
vereas, vary(rious)
vereashen, variate(tion)
vereate, variate
vereation, variate(tion)
vered, vary(ried)
verefikashen, verify(fication)
verefukashen, verify(fication)

verefy, verify
veregate, variegate
vereishos, veracious/ voracious
veres, **vary**(ries)
vereuble, variable
vereugate, variegate
vereuns, variant(nce)
vereunt, variant
vereus, vary(rious)
verge, * , ed, ging, EDGE/ RIM/ PIVOT/ PEAK PRIOR TO
vergen, version / virgin
vergun, version / virgin
veri, vary / very
veriabol, variable
veriagashen, variegate(tion)
veriagate, variegate
veriant, variant
veriants, variant(nce)
veriate, variate
verient, variant
verietal, variety(tal)
veriety, variety
verifai, verify
verifikashen, verify(fication)
verifucation, verify(fication)
verify, fies, fied, fying, fication, ficative, ficatory, fiability, fiable, fiableness, fier, AUTHENTICATE/ RECOGNIZE ACKNOWLEDGE/ FOR TRUTH
verigate, variegate
veriubility, variable(lity)
veriuble, variable
veriugate, variegate
veriuns, variant(nce)
verius, vary(rious)
verj, verge
verjen, version / virgin
verk, work
verll, verge
verm, worm
vermakulite, vermiculite
vermekulite, vermiculite
vermen, vermin
vermiculite, TYPE OF ROCK

vermikewlite, vermiculite
vermin, nous, nously, ANNOYING CRITTERS IN GREAT QUANTITIES
vermiqulite, vermiculite
vermooth, vermouth
vermouth, ALCOHOLIC APERITIF
vermuth, vermouth
vernacular, rly, rism, WORD USED AS IT ORIGINATED, NATIVE USE OF WORD
vernakular, vernacular
verp, verb
verply, verbal(lly)
verpul, verbal
vers, verse / veer(s) / worse
versatile, ely, eness, lity, ABLE TO CONFORM TO MANY GIVEN SITUATIONS
versatilety, versatile(lity)
verse, *, ed, sing, sify, sifies, sified, sifying, sifier, sification, ONE PART / STANZA OF A GREATER PIECE/ STORY, TO MAKE VERSE (or see versus)
versetul, versatile
vershin, version
vership, worship
vershu, virtue
vershuality, virtual(ity)
vershun, version
version, *, ONE PART/ VIEW/ PERSPECTIVE OF A STORY/ EVENT
versis, verse(s) / versus
versital, versatile
versitilety, versatile(lity)
verson, worsen / version
verst, worst
versus, AGAINST, TWO PERSPECTIVES IN OPPOSITION (or see verse(s))
versutil, versatile
versutilety, versatile(lity)
vert, veer(ed)
vertabra, vertebra
vertebra, *, al, ally, ate, ation, A BONE IN THE SPINE "prefixes: inter"
vertego, vertigo
vertekul, vertical

verth, worth
vertibra, vertebra
vertical, lity, lness, lly, OPPOSED TO THE HORIZONTAL, AN UPRIGHT POSITION
verticly, vertical(lly)
vertigo, oes, DIZZY
vertikul, vertical
vertucly, vertical(lly)
vertue, virtue
vertugo, vertigo
verufecation, verify(fication)
verufikashen, verify(fication)
verufy, verify
verul, virile
very, MUCH/ LOTS, GREAT AMOUNT (or see vary/ worry)
veryus, vary(rious)
vesa, visa
vesabul, visible
vesatashen, visit(ation)
vesater, visit(or)
vesatir, visit(or)
vesatude, vicissitude
vescosedy, viscous(ity)
vescosity, viscous(ity)
vescosudy, viscous(ity)
vesdabule, vestibule
vesdubule, vestibule
vesectomy, vasectomy
vesel, vessel
vesenedy, vicinity
vesenety, vicinity
vesetashen, visit(ation)
veseter, visit(or)
veshen, vision
veshenary, vision(ary)
veshes, vicious
veshuel, visual
veshun, vision
veshunary, vision(ary)
veshus, vicious
vesil, vessel
vesinedy, vicinity
vesinety, vicinity

vesit, visit
vesitashen, visit(ation)
vesiter, visit(or)
vesitude, vicissitude
veskes, viscous
veskosedy, viscous(ity)
veskosity, viscous(ity)
veskus, viscous
vesle, vessel
vessel, *, A CONTAINER
vest, *, ted, ting, SLEEVELESS OUTER GARMENT, POSSESS POWER/ POSITION
vestabule, vestibule
vestibule, *, ed, ling, lar, late, A CHAMBER/ CAVITY
vestubule, vestibule
vesu, visa
vesubel, visible
vesubiledy, visibility
vesuble, visible / visible(ly)
vesul, vessel
vesut, visit
vesutashen, visit(ation)
vesuter, visit(or)
vesutude, vicissitude
vet, *, SHORT FOR VETERINARIAN AND VETERAN
vetaren, veteran
veteran, *, ONES WHO SURVIVED A WAR/ BATTLE OR GAINED WISDOM THOROUGH STUDY/ SERVICE
vetiren, veteran
veto, oes, oed, oing, oer, TO REJECT/ FORBID
vetod, veto(ed)
vetos, veto(es)
vetran, veteran
vetrefy, vitrify
vetrify, vitrify
veturen, veteran
veu, via / view
veud, view(ed)
veukle, vehicle
veva, viva
veved, vivid
vevidly, vivid(ly)
vevu, viva

Column 1	Column 2	Column 3
vew,view	vibratid,vibrate(d)	videmen,vitamin
vex,*,xes,xed,xing,xingly,xation,xatious,xatiously, xatiousness,xedly,xedness,TO PLAGUE/ IRRITATE/ CAUSE COMMOTION	**vibrator**,*,ry,MACHINE PRODUCING PULSES OF WAVES/ FREQUENCY	**video**,*,oed,oing,MOVING/ VISUAL FILM WITH MANY FRAMES/ PICTURES
vexashen,vex(ation)	vibrensy,vibrant(ncy)	vidio,video
veygari,vagary	vibrent,vibrant	vidl,vital
veyude,view(ed)	vibrently,vibrant(ly)	vidrefy,vitrify
vezabel,visible	vibrinsy,vibrant(ncy)	vidul,vital
vezabelity,visibility	vibrutory,vibrator	vidumen,vitamin
vezabiledy,visibility	vicabulary,vocabulary	vidumin,vitamin
vezatashen,visit(ation)	**vice**,*,REPLACING ONE INFERIOR WITH ANOTHER, INSTEAD OF (or see vise)	**vie**,ed,vying,COMPETITION/RIVALRY WITH ANOTHER
vezibiledy,visibility	vicenity,vicinity	vieble,viable
vezit,visit	vichen,vision	viebul,viable
vezitashen,visit(ation)	vichenary,vision(ary)	viecol,vehicle
vezubelity,visibility	viches,vicious	vieduk,viaduct
vezubiledy,visibility	vichol,vigil	vielashen,violate(tion)
vezutashen,visit(ation)	vichos,vicious	vielate,violate
vi,vie / bi / buy / by	vichualize,visual(ize)	**view**,*,wed,wing,wer,TO SEE WITH THE EYES "prefixes: over/ pre"
via,BY WAY/ MEANS OF	vichulante,vigil(ante)	vigalanty,vigil(ante)
viable,bility,ly,POSSIBLE/ CAPABLE "prefixes: non"	vichun,vision	vigalent,vigil(ant)
viabul,viable	vichunary,vision(ary)	vigel,vigil
viaduct,*,CHANNELS WHICH ALLOW FLOW/ TRANSPORT	vichus,vicious	vigelent,vigil(ant)
viaduk,viaduct	vichwal,visual	vigeng,viking
vial,*,led,ling,SMALL BOTTLE (or see vile)	vichwulize,visual(ize)	viger,vigor
vialashen,violate(tion)	**vicinity**,ties,WITHIN THE AREA	vigerus,vigor(ous)
vialate,violate	**vicious**,sly,sness,HATEFUL DISPOSITION,LASHING OUT WITH DARK/ NEGATIVE EMOTION	**vigil**,la,lance,lant,lantly,lante,lantism,TO WATCH OVER, PAY CAREFUL ATTENTION TO "prefixes: in"
vialation,violate(tion)	vicisitude,vicissitude	viging,viking
vialen,violin	**vicissitude**,dinary,dinous,TO MOVE FROM ONE FREQUENCY TO ANOTHER,A MUTATION	viginu,vagina
vialens,violent(nce)	victamize,victim(ize)	vigir,vigor
vialet,violet	victem,victim	vigirus,vigor(ous)
vialin,violin	**victim**,*,mize,mizes,mized,mizing,mization,mizer, RECEIVER OF ILL WILL,HELPLESS,INABILITY TO GAIN POWER IN A SITUATION	vigol,wriggle
vialint,violent		vigolante,vigil(ante)
vialunt,violent	victomizashen,victim(ization)	**vigor**,*,rous,roso,rously,rousness,OF VITALITY/ STRENGTH "prefixes: in"
vibd,vibe(d)	victomize,victim(ize)	
vibe,*,bing,SHORT FOR VIBRATION,A RHYTHMIC SYNCHRONICITY,RESOUNDS WELL TOGETHER	victum,victim	vigorus,vigor(ous)
vibrachun,vibrate(tion)	victumizashen,victim(ization)	vigual,visual
vibraded,vibrate(d)	victumize,victim(ize)	vigulante,vigil(ante)
vibrant,ncy,tly,PULSING WITH ENERGY/ LIFE	vidal,vital	vigulent,vigil(ant)
vibrashen,vibrate(tion)	vidamen,vitamin	viguol,visual
vibrate,*,ed,ting,tion,tor,ant,PULSATING RYTHM/ WAVES	videl,vital	vigur,vigor
		vigurus,vigor(ous)
		vijalante,vigil(ante)

vijalent, vigil(ant)
vijewelize, visual(ize)
vijicol, vehicle
vijinu, vagina
vijolent, vigil(ant)
vijual, visual
vijulante, vigil(ante)
vijulent, vigil(ant)
vijwel, visual
vijwul, visual
vijwulize, visual(ize)
vik, bike
vikabeulery, vocabulary
vikabulery, vocabulary
vikeng, viking
viker, vigor / bicker / bike(r)
viking, *, SCANDINAVIAN WARRIOR (or see bike(king))
vikini, bikini
vikir, vigor / bicker
vikor, vigor / bicker
viktem, victim
viktemizashen, victim(ization)
viktemize, victim(ize)
viktim, victim
viktumizashen, victim(ization)
viktumize, victim(ize)
vikur, vigor
vila, valet / villa
vilafy, vilify
vilage, villa(ge)
vilan, villain
vilanus, villain(ous)
vilarean, valerian
vile, *, ely, eness, DISGUSTING (or see vial,' villa/ valet)
viley, vilify
viiege, village)
vilej, village)
vilen, villain / violin
vilenus, villain(ous)
vileraen, valerian
vilet, valet
vilify, fies, fied, fier, vying, fication, TO DEFACE/ SLANDER/ DEGRADE

vilij, villa(ge)
vilin, villain / violin
vilinus, villain(ous)
villa, *, age, ager, agery, A RURAL/ COUNTRY TOWN (or see valet)
villain, *, nous, nously, nousness, ny, nies, THE BAD GUY/ ANTAGONIST, OF EVIL CHARACTER
villian, villain
villol, vigil
vilofi, vilify
vilon, villain
vilosedy, velocity
vilosety, velocity
vilu, villa
viluch, villa(ge)
vilufy, vilify
vilug, villa(ge)
viluj, villa(ge)
vilun, villain
vilunus, villain(ous)
vilur, velure / velour
vilutch, villa(ge)
vim, OF STRENGTH/ ENTHUSIASM
vin, vine
vinager, vinegar
vinagra, vinaigrette
vinagrette, vinaigrette
vinaigrette, SALAD DRESSING WITH MOSTLY VINEGAR
vinaker, vinegar
vinal, vinyl
vinamus, venom(ous)
vinasin, venison
vinch, venge
vincher, venture
vinchful, venge(ful)
vinchurd, venture(d)
vincible, lity, eness, CAN BE OVERCOME/ CONQUERED
vind, vend / vent
vindalashen, ventilate(tion)
vindalate, ventilate
vindecate, vindicate
vindedu, vendetta
vindekef, vindictive

vindektif, vindictive
vindeta, vendetta
vindetta, vendetta
vindicashen, vindicate(tion)
vindicate, *, ed, ting, able, ation, ative, ator, atory, ctive, TO BE LIBERATED BY AVENGING
vindictef, vindictive
vindictive, ely, eness, HAS A REVENGE
vindikduv, vindictive
vindiktif, vindictive
vinducation, vindicate(tion)
vindulashen, ventilate(tion)
vindulate, ventilate
vine, *, ey, A TRAILING PLANT SUCH AS IVY/ GRAPE
vineer, veneer
vinegar, *, ry, rish, RESULT OF FERMENTATION
vinegre, vinaigrette
vinegrette, vinaigrette
vinel, vinyl
vinemus, venom(ous)
viner, veneer
vinerate, venerate
vinew, venue
ving, venge
vingents, venge(ance)
vingful, venge(ful)
vinger, vinegar
vingre, vinaigrette
vingrette, vinaigrette
vinil, vinyl
vinila, vanilla
vinj, venge
vinjents, venge(ance)
vinjful, venge(ful)
vino, WINE
vinol, vinyl
vinosen, venison
vinsable, vincible
vinsher, venture
vinsuble, vincible
vint, vint / vend
vintage, RESULT OF A SUPERIOR CROP SEASON
vintalashen, ventilate(tion)

vintalate, ventilate
vintalation, ventilate(tion)
vinteg, vintage
vintelate, **ventilate**
vintilate, ventilate
vintrecal, ventricle
vintrecular, ventricle(cular)
vintrelukwist, ventriloquist
vintrical, ventricle
vintrikul, ventricle
vintrikuler, ventricle(cular)
vintrilukwist, ventriloquist
vintrukle, ventricle
vintuge, vintage
vintuj, vintage
vintulate, ventilate
vintur, venture
vintured, venture(d)
vinu, venue
vinuger, vinegar
vinugrey, vinaigrette
vinuker, vinegar
vinul, vinyl
vinumus, venom(ous)
vinurate, venerate
vinusen, venison
viny, vine
vinyl, TYPE OF PLASTIC
vinyou, venue
viola, STRINGED INSTRUMENT
violadid, violate(d)
violashen, violate(tion)
violate, *, ed, ting, tive, tor, tion, TO BASH BOUNDARIES/ LAWS SET FORTH BY PEOPLE/ NATURE "prefixes: in"
violen, violin
violens, violent(nce)
violent, tly, nce, USE OF AGGRESSIVE FORCE "prefixes: non"
violet, DARK COLOR OF RED/ BLUE
violin, *, STRINGED INSTRUMENT
violint, violent
violunt, violent
vioula, viola

vipe, vibe
viper, *, rish, rous, rously, POISONOUS SNAKE
vipir, viper
viporus, viper(ous)
viprus, viper(ous)
vipur, viper
vir, veer
viracedy, veracity / voracity
viracious, voracious / veracious
viracity, veracity / voracity
viral, lly, OF A VIRUS (or see virile) "prefixes: non/ retro"
viralent, virulent
viralint, virulent
virasedy, veracity / voracity
virashes, voracious / veracious
virasious, voracious / veracious
virasity, veracity
virb, verb
virbadum, verbatim
virbatum, verbatim
virble, verbal
virblize, verbal(ize)
virbly, verbal(lly)
virboly, verbal(lly)
virbos, verbose
virbosity, verbose(sity)
virbosudy, verbose(sity)
virbul, verbal
virbule, verbal(lly)
virbulize, verbal(ize)
virch, verge
virchen, version
virchew, virtue
virchewul, virtual
virchoo, virtue
virchual, virtual
virchualedy, virtual(ity)
virchuality, virtual(ity)
virchuil, virtual
virchuol, virtual
virdabra, vertebra
virdago, vertigo
virdego, vertigo

virdek, verdict
virdekly, vertical(lly)
virdekul, vertical
virdibra, vertebra
virdict, verdict
virdigo, vertigo
virdikly, vertical(lly)
virdikt, verdict
virdikul, vertical
virdubra, vertebra
virdugo, vertigo
virdukil, vertical
virdukly, vertical(lly)
virel, viral / virile
vires, virus
virge, verge
virgen, version / virgin
virgin, *, nal, PRISTINE/ NATURAL, HASN'T BEEN EXPLOITED/ ALTERED (or see version)
virgun, version / virgin
virile, lity, lism, HEALTHY MASCULINE QUALITIES (or see viral)
viris, virus
viriudy, variety
viriuty, variety
virje, verge
virjen, virgin
virjin, version / virgin
virllen, virgin
virmeculite, vermiculite
virmen, vermin
virmikewlite, vermiculite
virmikulite, vermiculite
virmin, vermin
virmiqulite, vermiculite
virmooth, vermouth
virmuth, vermouth
virnakuler, vernacular
virol, viral / virile
virolent, virulent
viros, virus
virp, verb
virply, verbal(lly)

virpul, verbal
virs, verse
virsatil, versatile
virsatilety, versatile(lity)
virsetal, versatile
virshen, version
virshuality, virtual(ity)
virsutil, versatile
virsutilety, versatile(lity)
virtebra, vertebra
virtego, vertigo
virtekul, vertical
virtibra, vertebra
virtigo, vertigo
virtikul, vertical
virtual, lity, lly, NOT PHYSICAL TO THE TOUCH
virtue, uosity, uosities, uoso, uous, uously, uousness, KNOWS OF EXCELLENCE, ONE WITH SUPRA KNOWLEDGE
virtugo, vertigo
virtukle, vertical(lly)
virul, viral / virile
virulent, VERY BITTER/ POISONOUS/ DANGEROUS
virulint, virulent
virus, ses, LIVING ORGANISM "prefixes: pro/ retro/ sub"
visa, aed, aing, A PASS/ PASSPORT
visabelity, visibility
visabil, visible
visabiledy, visibility
visabilety, visibility
visably, visible(ly)
visatashen, visit(ation)
visater, visit(or)
visatude, vicissitude
viscos, viscous
viscosedy, viscous(ity)
viscosity, viscous(ity)
viscous, sly, sness, osity, TEXTURE/ CONSISTENCY OF SYRUP "prefixes: non"
viscus, viscous
vise, *, ed, sing, A TOOL/ PRESS FOR GRIPING/ HOLDING ITEMS IN PLACE (or see vice)
visectomy, vasectomy

visekteme, vasectomy
visenedy, vicinity
visenety, vicinity
viser, visor
viset, visit
visetashen, visit(ation)
visetation, visit(ation)
viseter, visit(or)
visetude, vicissitude
vishen, vision
vishenary, vision(ary)
vishes, vicious
vishon, vision
vishos, vicious
vishuel, visual
vishun, vision
vishunary, vision(ary)
vishus, vicious
visibility, ties, THE DEGREE OF ABILITY TO SEE WITH THE NAKED EYE
visible, eness, ly, ABLE TO BE SEEN WITH THE EYE
visinedy, vicinity
visinety, vicinity
vision, *, nal, nally, nary, naries, nariness, nless, TO CONCEIVE/ VIEW THAT BEYOND OUR EYE'S ABILITY TO SEE "prefixes: en/ pre"
visir, visor
visit, *, ted, ting, table, tant, tation, tational, tatorial, tor, GO SEE SOMEONE/ SOMETHING BRIEFLY, RECEIVE GUESTS, BE A GUEST
visitashen, visit(ation)
visiter, visit(or)
visitude, vicissitude
viskes, viscous
viskosedy, viscous(ity)
viskosity, viscous(ity)
viskus, viscous
visor, *, GUARD/ SHIELD TO PROTECT SUN'S GLARES
vista, *, A LONG/ STRETCHING VIEW
visu, visa
visual, *, lly, lize, lization, lizer, USE OF EYES TO SEE, TO SEE AS IF WITH THE EYES "prefixes: non"
visubel, visible

visubelity, visibility
visubiledy, visibility
visuble, visible / visible(ly)
visur, visor
visut, visit
visutashen, visit(ation)
visutation, visit(ation)
visuter, visit(or)
visutude, vicissitude
vital, *, lly, lness, lism, listic, lity, lities, lize, lizes, lized, lizing, lization, LIFE ENERGY/ PROPERTIES, ESSENTIAL PROCESSES FOR CONTINUATION OF LIFE "prefixes: de/ intra"
vitaledy, vital(ity)
vitalidy, vital(ity)
vitamen, vitamin
vitamin, *, ORGANIC NUTRIENTS/ MINERALS
vitel, vital
vitemen, vitamin
vitl, vital
vito, veto
vitrify, fies, fied, fying, fiability, fiable, BECOME/ CHANGE INTO GLASS "prefixes: de"
vitul, vital
vitumen, vitamin
vitumin, vitamin
viu, view
viubil, viable
viuble, viable
viud, view(ed)
viuduk, viaduct
viuladid, violate(d)
viulashen, violate(tion)
viulation, violate(tion)
viulens, violent(nce)
viulet, violet
viva, acity, acities, LIFE
vivaches, vivacious
vivachusnes, vivacious(ness)
vivacious, sly, sness, ity, ities, BOUNDING WITH LIFE/ ENERGY/ SPIRIT
vivashes, vivacious
vivashous, vivacious

vivashusnes,vivacious(ness)
vived,vivid
vivedly,vivid(ly)
viveyshos,vivacious
vivid,dly,dness,BRIGHT/ DRAMATIC/ CLEAR
vivu,viva
viyudukt,viaduct
vizability,visibility
vizabil,visible
vizabiledy,visibility
vizably,visible(ly)
vizatashen,visit(ation)
vizater,visit(or)
vizer,visor
vizet,visit
vizetashen,visit(ation)
vizetur,visit(or)
vizibelity,visibility
vizibiledy,visibility
vizibul,visible
vizir,visor
vizit,visit
vizitashen,visit(ation)
viziter,visit(or)
vizivelity,visibility
vizor,visor
vizubel,visible
vizubelity,visibility
vizubiledy,visibility
vizuble,visible
vizubly,visible(ly)
vizur,visor
vizutashen,visit(ation)
vizuter,visit(or)
vocabeulery,vocabulary
vocabulary,ries,WORDS IN A PARTICULAR LANGUAGE USED FOR COMMUNICATION
vocal,*,lly,lness,lize,lizes,lized,lizing,lization,list,lism, lizer,USING THE VOICE "prefixes: de/ inter/ sub/ uni"
vocalise,vocal(ize)
vocashen,vocation
vocashenul,vocation(al)

vocation,*,nal,nally,AN ACQUIRED/ NATURAL SKILL/ PROFESSION USED TO EARN MONEY "prefixes: in"
vocel,vocal
vocul,vocal
voculize,vocal(ize)
voded,vote(d)
vodef,votive
voder,vote(r)
vodev,votive
vodid,vote(d)
vodif,votive
vodir,vote(r)
vodiv,votive
vodka,ALCOHOLIC SPIRITS
vodur,vote(r)
voed,void
voeg,voyage
voej,voyage
voes,voice
voezd,voice(d)
vog,vogue
vogue,IN FASHION
voice,*,ed,cing,eful,efulness,eless,elessly,elessness, SOUND COMING FROM THE MOUTH "prefixes: de/ un"
void,*,ded,ding,dable,dableness,der,dness,dance,ONE VAST NOTHING MATERIALLY ALL THINGS POTENTIALLY, RETURN TO NOTHING
voig,voyage
voij,voyage
vois,voice
voist,voice(d)
vok,vogue
vokabeulery,vocabulary
vokabulery,vocabulary
vokalize,vocal(ize)
vokashen,vocation
vokashenul,vocation(al)
vokation,vocation
vokationul,vocation(al)
vokeishon,vocation
vokel,vocal
vokelize,vocal(ize)

vokil,vocal
vokilize,vocal(ize)
vokul,vocal
vokulize,vocal(ize)
volanteer,volunteer
volanterd,volunteer(ed)
volatel,volatile
volatile,eness,lity,lize,lization,ABLE TO CHANGE SUDDENLY IN COMPOSITION,EXPLOSIVE "prefixes: de"
volcano,oes,nic,nicially,nism,nicity,nist,nize,nizes,nized, nizing,nization,MOUNTAIN ERUPTION FROM ITS CORE
volcher,vulture
vold,vault / volt
vole,volley
volee,volley
volenter,volunteer
volenterd,volunteer(ed)
volentery,voluntary
voleum,volume
volgar,vulgar
volj,volley
volinter,volunteer
volisity,velocity
volitel,volatile
volium,volume
volkano,volcano
volkeinou,volcano
volley,*,yed,ying,yer,TO GO BACK AND FORTH, DISCHARGE OF MANY THINGS AT ONCE
volly,volley
volnerable,vulnerable
volnirable,vulnerable
volnrable,vulnerable
volopchuis,voluptuous
volosedy,velocity
volqeino,volcano
volshur,vulture
volt,*,tage,taic,ELECTRICAL MEASUREMENT OF POWER (or see vault)
voltaec,voltaic
voltage,*,TYPE OF ELECTRICAL ACTION "prefixes: over"

voltaic,* , TYPE OF ELECTRICAL ACTION
voltauk,voltaic
voltshur,vulture
volume,* ,ed,ming,mincus,minously,minosity, LEVEL OF SOUND/ FREQUENCY, MANY THINGS BROUGHT TOGETHER, FORM OF MEASUREMENT
voluntary,rism,rist,ristic,ries,rily,riness,teer, FREELY OFFER SERVICE WITHOUT EXPECTING PAY/ MONEY/ EXCHANGE "prefixes: in"
volunteer,* ,red,ring, FREELY OFFER SERVICE WITHOUT EXPECTING PAY/ MONEY/ EXCHANGE
volunter,volunteer
volunterd,volunteer(ed)
voluntery,voluntary
voluptuous,sly,sness, OF SENSUALITY
volutel,volatile
volutil,volatile
volva,ate, FUNGI MEMBRANE (or see vulva)
voly,volley
volyewm,volume
vomet,vomit
vomit,* ,ted,ting,tous,tory,tories,turition,tus, THE ENERGETIC DISCHARGE OF CONTENTS OF THE STOMACH THROUGH THE MOUTH
vomut,vomit
voner,veneer
voodoo, FICTITIOUS PRACTICE OF SORCERY
voqeishon,vocation
vor,wore
voracious,sly,sness, DEVOUR WITH EXTREME GREED/ ENTHUSIASM (or see veracious)
voracity,ious, VORACIOUS/ EAGER/ RAVENOUS CONSUMPTION, GREAT APPETITE FOR (or see veracity)
vorashus,voracious / veracious
vorasity,voracity / voracity
vordes,vortex
vordex,vortex
voreishos,voracious / veracious
vorld,world
vorn,worn
vorteks,vortex
vortes,vortice

vortesis,vortex(es) / vortice(s)
vortex,xes,tices,tical,tically,ticose, A SWIRLING/ SPIRAL MOVEMENT
vortice,* ,cal,cally,cose, SWIRLING/ SPIRAL MOVEMENT AS IN A VORTEX
vortisus,vortex(es)
vos,vase
vosektumy,vasectomy
vot,vote
vote,* ,ed,ting,er,eless, TO MAKE A CHOICE/ DECISION BETWEEN TWO OR MORE THINGS
votef,votive
voteve,votive
votid,vote(d)
votif,votive
votive, DEDICATED WITH A VOW
votka,vodka
votku,vodka
votuve,votive
vouch,hes,hed,hing,her,hee, CONFIRM/ ATTEST/ UPHOLD THE LEGITIMACY/ VALIDITY OF SOMEONE/ SOMETHING
vouchd,vouch(ed)
voug,vogue / voyage
vouj,voyage
voul,vowel
vout,vote
vow,* ,wed,wing,wing, TAKE AN OATH, SWEAR TO UPHOLD
vowch,vouch
vowchur,vouch(er)
vowel,* , ONE OF SIX LETTERS OF THE ENGLISH ALPHABET WITH CERTAIN CHARACTERISTICS "prefixes: semi"
vowl,vowel
voyage,* ,ed,ging,er, A JOURNEY/ TRIP BY SEA
voyd,void
voyg,voyage
voyj,voyage
voys,voice
voyst,voice(d)
voz,vase
vrigol,wriggle
vucabeulery,vocabulary

vucinity,vicinity
vud,view(ed)
vudu,voodoo
vue,view
vugina,vagina
vuhemint,vahemence(nt)
vujina,vagina
vukabulery,vocabulary
vula,valet
vularean,valerian
vulchur,vulture
vuledity,valid(ity)
vulerean,valerian
vulerian,valerian
vulet,valet
vulfa,vulva / volva
vulgar,rly,rness,rian,rism,rity,rities,rize,rization,rizer, OFF COLOR IN BEHAVIOR/ LANGUAGE/ MANNERISM
vulgaredy,vulgar(ity)
vulger,vulgar
vulgeredy,vulgar(ity)
vulgurly,vulgar(ly)
vulidete,valid(ity)
vulnerable,bility,eness,bly, NOT WELL PROTECTED "prefixes: in"
vulnuruble,vulnerable
vulopchues,voluptuous
vulosedy,velocity
vulosety,velocity
vulsher,vulture
vulture,* , A LARGE SCAVENGER BIRD
vulupchuis,voluptuous
vuluptuis,voluptuous
vuluptuous,voluptuous
vulur,velour / velure
vulva, EXTERNAL FEMALE GENITALIA (or see volva)
vuneer,veneer
vunela,vanilla
vuner,veneer
vunila,vanilla
vuracious,voracious / veracious
vurashes,voracious / veracious
vurasity,veracity / voracity

vurb, verb
vurbadum, verbatim
vurbatum, verbatim
vurbelize, verbal(ize)
vurblize, verbal(ize)
vurbose, verbose
vurbuliz, verbal(ize)
vurchen, version / virgin
vurchew, virtue
vurchewul, virtual
vurchoo, virtue
vurchual, virtual
vurchuol, virtual
vurdabra, vertebra
vurdago, vertigo
vurdekly, vertical(lly)
vurdekt, verdict
vurdekul, vertical
vurdibra, vertebra
vurdigo, vertigo
vurdikly, vertical(lly)
vurdikt, verdict
vurdikul, vertical
vurdubra, vertebra
vurdukil, vertical
vurge, verge
vurgen, version / virgin
vurgun, version / virgin
vuriedy, variety
vurietal, variety(tal)
vuriety, variety
vurje, verge
vurjen, version / virgin
vurjun, version / virgin
vurmeculite, vermiculite
vurmikulite, vermiculite
vurmouth, vermouth
vurmuth, vermouth
vurnaculer, vernacular
vurnakuler, vernacular
vurp, verb
vurple, verbal / verbal(lly)
vurs, verse

vursatilety, versatile(lity)
vursitelity, versatile(lity)
vurtabra, vertebra
vurtego, vertigo
vurtekul, vertical
vurtibra, vertebra
vurtigo, vertigo
vurtikul, vertical
vurtue, virtue
vurtugo, vertigo
vusectemy, vasectomy
vusekteme, vasectomy
vusenedy, vicinity
vusinity, vicinity
vy, vie / bi / buy / by
vye, vie / bi / buy / by
vyle, vial / vile / bile
wa, way / weigh / whey
wabel, wobble
wabul, wobble
wac, wake / walk / wok / whack
wacent, wasn't
wach, wage / wash / watch / wake / wok / walk
wacher, washer / wage(r) / walk(er)
waches, wage(s) / watch(es)
wachir, washer / wage(r) / walk(er)
wachis, wage(s) / watch(es)
wachul, waggle
wachus, wage(s) / wash(es)
wack, wake / walk / wok / whack
wacks, wax / whack(s) / walk(s)
wacky, kily, kiness, SILLY, ERRATIC, CRAZY
wackyness, wacky(kiness)
wacs, wax / whack(s) / walk(s) / wake(s) / wok(s)
wad, *, dded, dding, CRUMPLE / CRINKLE / ROLL SOMETHING UP INTO A BALL SHAPE (or see wade/ what/ watt/ wait/ weight)
waddle, *, ed, ling, er, ly, MOVE BACK AND FORTH IN MOVEMENT SUCH AS A PENGUIN WALKING
wade, *, ed, ding, er, ers, WALK/ NAVIGATE THROUGH SHALLOW WATER/ LIQUID/ RESISTANT MATERIAL (or see wait/ wad/ weight)
wadel, waddle / what'll

wader, wader / water / waiter
wadercres, watercress
waderfol, waterfall
waderproof, waterproof
waderpruf, waterproof
waders, LONG RUBBER BOOTS FOR FEET TO PROTECT AGAINST DEEP WATER (or see waiters(s))
wadertait, watertight
wadertite, watertight
wadevr, whatever
wadid, wad(dded) / wait(ed) / wed(ed)
wadil, waddle / what'll
wadir, wader / water / waiter
wadirproof, waterproof
wadirpruf, waterproof
wadirs, waders / waiter(s) / water(s)
wadirtite, watertight
wadle, waddle / what'll
wadol, waddle / what'll
wador, wader / water / waiter
wadres, waitress
wadrus, waitress
wadud, wad(dded) / wait(ed) / wade(d)
wadul, waddle / what'll
wadur, wader / water / waiter
wadurd, water(ed)
wadurfol, waterfall
wadurproof, waterproof
wadurpruf, waterproof
wadurs, waders / waiter(s) / water(s)
wae, way / weigh / whey
wael, whale / wail / wale
waen, wain / wane
waest, waist / waste
waet, wait / weight
waf, wave
wafd, waft / raft / wave(d) / waive(d)
wafe, wave / wave(vy)
wafel, waffle
wafer, *, THIN SLICE OF SOMETHING (or see waiver)
waffle, *, ed, ing, BATTER COOKED IN A WAFFLE MAKER
wafil, waffle
wafir, wafer / waiver

wafle, waffle
waflis, wave(less)
wafor, wafer / waiver
waft, *, ted, ting, ty, tage, SMALL PENNANT SHAPED FLAG, BE CARRIED ALONG , FLOAT (or see raft/ wave(d)/ waive(d)
waful, waffle
wafur, wafer / waiver
wag,* gged, gging, gger, ggle, ggles, ggled, ggling, QUICKLY MOVE BACK AND FORTH SUCH AS A DOGS TAIL (or see wage)
wagd, wag(gged) / wage(d)
wage, *, ed, ging, eless, er, erer, MONEY EARNED BY WORKING, MAKE A BET, CREATE CONFLICT/ WAR (or see wag) "prefixes: un"
wagel, waggle
wagen, wagon
waggle, *, ed, ling, ly, ggingly, QUICKLY MOVE BACK AND FORTH SUCH AS A DOGS TAIL
wagil, waggle
wagin, wagon
wagir, wage(r)
wagle, waggle / waggle(ly)
wagly, waggle(ly)
wagon, *, ner, VESSEL WITH BOX SHAPED BASE AND FOUR WHEELS FOR CARRYING THINGS
waguen, wagon
wagul, waggle
wagun, wake(n) / wagon
wagur, wage(r)
wai, why
waid, wide/ wade
waield, wild
waier, wire
waif, wife
wail, *, led, ling, ler, lingly, lful, lfully, VERY HEAVY/ LOUD/ PAINFUL CRY (or see wale/ whale/ while)
wain, TYPE OF WAGON (or see wane/ whine/ wine)
waini, whinny
wainscot, ted, ting, WOOD/ SUBSTANCE ONLY COVERING LOWER HALF OF A WALL
wainskot, wainscot
waiold, wild

waip, wipe
wair, wire
wais, wise
waist, MIDDLE SECTION/ MIDRIFF OF A BODY BETWEEN RIBCAGE AND HIPS (or see waste)
wait, *, ted, ting, ter, TEMPORARILY PAUSE/ STOP MOMENTUM TO SERVICE ANOTHER'S NEEDS (or see wade/ weight)
waiter, *, ONE WHO SERVES PATRONS FOOD AT A RESTAURANT/ CAFE/ DINER (or see waders)
waitress, ses, FEMALES WHO SERVE PATRONS FOOD AT A RESTAURANT/ CAFE/ DINER
waive, *, ed, ving, er, RELINQUISH/ LET GO OF YOUR RIGHTS TO SOMETHING (or see wave/ wife)
waiver, *, A TEMPORARY PASS, TO GIVE UP RIGHTS
waivs, wives
waiz, wise
wajd, wage(d)
wajer, wage(r)
wajur, wage(r)
wak, walk / whack / wake / wok
wake, *, en, woke, eful, efully, efulness, eless, king, BE AWARE OF PHYSICAL REALITY AFTER BEING ASLEEP, WAVE CAUSED BY MOVEMENT, RITUAL PERFORMED FOR DECEASED (or see whack/ wok/ wacky)
wake up, TO BECOME ACTIVE/ AWARE, STOP SLEEPING
waken, wake(n) / wagon
wakenes, wacky(kiness)
waker, walker / wake(r) / whack(er)
wakin, wake(n) / wagon
wakle, waggle
wakon, wake(n) / wagon
waks, wax / whack(s) / walk(s) / wake(s) / wok(s)
wakse, wax
wakser, wax(er)
waksy, wax
wakul, waggle
wakun, wake(n) / wagon
waky, wacky
wakynes, wacky(kiness)
wal, wall / wail / whale
wald, wail(ed) / wale(d) / wall(ed)

wale, *, ed, ling, A WELT CAUSED BY A WHIPPING, SUPPORT FOR OUTSIDE PLANKING OF A BOAT (or see wail/ whale/ wall)
walep, wallop
walet, wallet
walip, wallop
walit, wallet
walk, *, ked, king, ker, MOVING/ TRAVELING ON FOOT
walker, *, A DEVICE TO HELP PEOPLE WALK (or see walk(er))
walkor, walk(er) / walker
wall, *, lled, lling, VERTICAL SECTION OF A DWELLING/ STRUCTURE (or see wail/ wale)
wallet, *, HOLDER FOR MONEY AND I.D.
wallit, wallet
wallop, *, ped, ping, THRASH/ STRIKE A BLOW TO
wallow, *, wed, wing, wer, LIKE A PIG SQUIRMING IN THE MUD, TO LIE/ BE DEEP INTO SOMETHING
wallut, wallet
walnut, *, A NUT
walo, wallow
walod, wallow(ed)
walop, wallop
waloped, wallop(ed)
walou, wallow
walow, wallow
walowed, wallow(ed)
walres, walrus
walrus, ses, A CARNIVOROUS/ MARINE MAMMAL
wals, waltz / wall(s) / wale(s) / wail(s)
walts, waltz
waltsd, waltz(ed)
waltz, zes, zed, zing, zer, DANCE TO 3/ 4 TIME MUSIC
walup, wallop
waluped, wallop(ed)
walupt, wallop(ed)
walut, wallet
walz, waltz
walzed, waltz(ed)
wamp, whomp
wan, *, WASHED OUT/ WEAK IN COLOR/ ENERGY/ MOTION (or see wain/ wane/ won/ one)

wand, *, SLENDER STICK USED FOR MANY PURPOSES (or see want/ won't)
wander, *, red,ring,ringly,rer, TO MOVE/ TRAVEL AIMLESSLY ABOUT (or see wonder)
wanderful, wonderful
wanderer, wander(er)
wane, *, ed,ning,ey,nier,niest, ON THE DOWNSIDE OF A PEAK/ WAVE, TO DIMINISH (or see wan/ wain)
wans, once
wanscoat, wainscoat
wanskot, wainscot
want, *, ted,ting, DESIRE SOMETHING (or see won't/ wand)
wanten, wanton
wanton, nly, nness, WANT FOR NOTHING, FREE/ UNBOUND/ UNRESTRAINED
wantun, wanton
wantunes, wanton(nness)
wantunle, wanton(ly)
wapen, weapon
wapun, weapon
war, *, rred,rring,rless, DISPLAY OF HOSTILITY/ OPPOSITION BETWEEN FORCES (or see wore/ wear/ where/ ware/ we're/ weir) "prefixes: pre"
warale, weary(rily)
warant, warrant
warante, warrant
waras, whereas
warbil, warble
warble, *, ed,ling,er, TYPE OF VIBRATION/ SOUND, A TUMOR/ SWELLING
warbler, *, A BIRD
warbul, warble
ward, *, ded,ding,den, TERRITORY/ AREA, FEND OFF, DEFEND AGAINST (or see word/ wart/ war(rred)/ where'd)
warden, *, A PAID OVERSEER IN A PRISON SYSTEM
wardon, warden
wardrobe, *, COLLECTION OF CLOTHING, PLACE WHERE CLOTHING IS KEPT
wardun, warden
ware, *, BE WATCHFUL OF, SPECIAL ITEMS OF USE/ VALUE (or see war/ wear/ where/ weary)

warefur, wherever
wareir, warrior
warele, weary(rily)
waren, warren
warent, warrant
warente, warrant
warenty, warrant
wareur, warrior
warevur, wherever
warf, wharf
warier, warrior
warily, weary(rily)
warin, warren
warint, warrant
warinte, warrant
warinted, warrant(ed)
warinty, warrant
warl, where'll
warm, *, med,ming,mer,mest,mth,mly,mish,mness, TEMPERATURE BETWEEN HOT/ COLD, BECOME COMFORTABLE WITH (or see worm)
warmist, warm(est)
warn, *, ned,ning,ningly, TO CAUTION SOMEONE AGAINST HARM/ PUNISHMENT (or see worn/ warren)
warp, *, ped,ping, BECOME TWISTED/ BENT/ BOWED IN SHAPE
warrant, *, ted,ting,ty,ties,ter, GUARANTEE/ CONTRACT/ AUTHORIZATION "prefixes: un"
warren, *, ENCLOSURE FOR BREEDING GAME
warrior, *, BRAVE FIGHTER IN WARFARE
warrun, warren
wars, war(s) / where(s) / wear(s) / was / worse / worst
warsh, wash
warshd, wash(ed)
wart, *, ted,ty, A BUMPY SKIN GROWTH FROM A VIRUS
wartrobe, wardrobe
warule, weary(rily)
warun, warren
warunt, warrant
warunte, warrant
warunted, warrant(ed)
warunty, warrant

warwithal, wherewithal
wary, rier,riest,rily,riness, BE CAUTIOUS/ CAREFUL OF (or see weary) "prefixes: un"
was, PAST TENSE FOR THE WORD "IS" (or see weigh(s)/ way(s))
wasd, waist / waste
wash, hes,hed,hing,her,hable,hy, TO CLEANSE WITH WATER/ LIQUID "prefixes: pre/ un"
washe, wash
washeble, wash(able)
washepl, wash(able)
washer, *, AN APPLIANCE TO WASH CLOTHES/ PARTS, SOMEONE WHO WASHES
washible, wash(able)
washipl, wash(able)
washir, washer
washt, wash(ed)
washuble, wash(able)
washur, washer
wasn't, CONTRACTION OF THE WORDS "WAS NOT", PAST TENSE FOR THE WORD "IS NOT"
wasp, *, A STINGING/ FLYING INSECT
wast, waist / waste
waste, *, ed,ting,er,tage,eness,tingly, MORE THAN NECESSARY, LEFTOVERS, REMAINS OF SOMETHING (or see waist)
wastid, waste(d)
wat, wait / weight / what / watt / wade / wad
watal, waddle / what'll
watch, hes,hed,hing,hful,hfully,hfulness, MONITOR/ LOOK AFTER, A DEVICE WORN ON THE WRIST "prefixes: un"
wated, wade(d) / wait(ed) / wad(dded)
watel, waddle / what'll
water, *, red,ring,ry,rless, CLEAR/ NATURAL SOLUTION THAT CONFORMS TO ICE/ LIQUID/ GAS "prefixes: un/ under"
watercress, AN EDIBLE PLANT
waterd, water(ed)
waterfall, A DOWNFLOWING OF WATER
waterfaul, waterfall
waterfol, waterfall
waterkres, watercress

waterproof,*,fed,fing,fer,WATER CANNOT PENETRATE
waterpruf,waterproof
waters,waders / waiter(s) / water(s)
watertait,watertight
watertight,tness,SEALS AGAINST WATER ENTERING
watertite,watertight
watever,whatever
watevur,whatever
watid,wade(d) / wait(ed) / wad(dded)
watil,waddle / what'll
watir,wader / water / wa:ter
watird,water(ed)
watirfal,waterfall
watirfol,waterfall
watirkres,watercress
watirproof,waterproof
watirpruf,waterproof
watirs,waders / waiter(s: / water(s)
watl,waddle / what'll
watle,waddle / what'll
watol,waddle / what'll
wator,wader / water / waiter
watres,waitress
watrus,waitress
watt,*,ttage,MEASURE OF ELECTRICITY (or see what/ wad)
watud,wade(d) / wait(ed) / wad(dded)
watul,waddle / what'll
watur,wader / water / waiter
waturcres,watercress
waturfal,waterfall
waturfol,waterfall
waturproof,waterproof
waturpruf,waterproof
waturs,waders / waiter(s) / water(s)
waubel,wobble
waubil,wobble
wauch,watch
wauchful,watch(ful)
wauded,wade(d) / wait(ed) / wad(dded)
waudel,waddle / what'll
wauder,water
waudertight,watertight

waudid,wade(d) / wait(ed) / wad(dded)
waudil,waddle / what'll
waudul,waddle / what'll
waufel,waffle
wauful,waffle
wauk,wok / walk
waul,whale / wail / wale / wall
waulep,wallop
waulet,wallet
waulk,walk
waulker,walk(er) / walker
waulkur,walk(er) / walker
waulnut,walnut
waulo,wallow
waulop,wallop
waulow,wallow
waults,waltz
waulup,wallop
waulut,wallet
waun,won / one
waund,wound
waunder,wander / wonder
waunt,want
wauper,whopper
waupur,whopper
waur,war(s) / where(s) / wear(s) / was / worse / worst
waurl,where'll
waurp,warp
waurs,war(s) / where(s) / wear(s) / was / worse / worst
waut,watt / what / wad
wautercres,watercress
wautertite,watertight
wavd,wave(d) / waive(d)
wave,*,ed,ving,eless,vy,vily,viness,er,SERPENTINE ACTION DISPLAYING UP/ DOWN/ BACK/ FORTH MOVEMENTS
wavenes,wave(viness)
waver,*,FLUCTUATE UP/ DOWN/ BACK/ FORTH (or see waiver/ wafer) "prefixes: un"
wavir,waiver / wafer
wavles,wave(less)
wavur,waiver / wafer
wavynes,wave(viness)

wax,xes,xed,xing,xer,xen,xy,xier,xiest,xiness,INCREASE IN INTENSITY/ SIZE/ STRENGTH,MATTER PRODUCED BY BEE/ PETROLEUM (or see whack(s)/ wake(s))
waxin,wax(en)
waxse,wax
way,*,,yless,METHOD,FASHION,STYLE,DIRECTION (or see weigh/ whey)
wayni,whinny
wayv,wave
waz,way(s) / weigh(s) / was
wazp,wasp
we,MORE THAN ONE WITH SELF INCLUDED (or see wee/ whee/ whey)
we'd,CONTRACTION OF THE WORDS "WE WOULD/ HAD" (or see wed/ weed/ wheat/ whet)
we'll,CONTRACTION OF THE WORDS "WE WILL" (or see well/ wheel)
we're,CONTRACTION OF THE WORDS "WE ARE" (or see were/ where/ weir/ whirr)
we've,CONTRACTION OF THE WORDS "WE HAVE" (or see weave)
weak,ker,kest,ken,kened,kening,kish,kishly,kishness, kener,kling,kly,kliness,kness,LACKING IN SKILL/ STRENGTH/ KNOWLEDGE (or see week)
weald,*,PRISTINE/ UNCULTIVATED FIELD AMIDST A FOREST (or see wield/ wheel(ed))
wealth,hy,hier,hiest,hily,hiness,AN OVER ABUNDANCE, MORE THAN ONE NEEDS
wean,*,ned,ning,ner,nling,SLOWLY REDUCE NEED FOR NOURISHMENT FROM THE MOTHER/ PRIMARY FOOD SOURCE (or see ween)
weane,weeny / wiener
weapan,weapon
weape,weep
weaped,weep(ed) / wept / reap(ed)
weapen,weapon
weapon,*,nry,nless,TOOL/ INSTRUMENT FOR PROTECTION OR TO HURT/ KILL "prefixes: bio"
weapun,weapon
weapy,weep
wear,*,ring,wore,worn,rable,USE SOMETHING UNTIL NO LONGER NEW,COVERING,CLOTHING (or see ware/ where/ we're/ weir)

weard, weird
weary, rier, riest, ried, rying, rily, riness, riful, rifully, rifulness, riless, risome, risomely, risomeness, TIRED/ EXHAUSTED/ FATIGUED (or see wary) "prefixes: un"
weasel, *, led, ling, CARNIVOROUS/ SLINKY/ RODENT/ MAMMAL
weather, *, red, ring, rability, rly, rliness, ELEMENTS/ ATMOSPHERE AROUND THE EARTH (or see whether/ wether/ wither)
weathur, weather / wether / wither / whether
weave, *, woven, ving, er, CRISS-CROSS PERPENDICULAR FIBERS ONE INTO/ THROUGH/ ACROSS THE OTHER (or see we've) "prefixes: in/ inter"
web, *, bbed, bbing, bby, INTERCONNECTING STRANDS CRISSCROSSING ONE ANOTHER, A NET, STRETCHED SKIN ON DUCK FEET (or see wept)
webd, web(bbed) / wept / weep(ed)
webt, web(bbed) / wept / weep(ed)
wech, which / witch / wedge
wechd, wedge(d)
wecht, wedge(d)
wed, *, dded, dding, GET MARRIED (or see wet/ we'd/ weed/ whet/ wheat)
weded, wed(dded) / weed(ed) / wet(tted)
wedeir, weed(er) / wet(tter)
wedel, whittle
weder, weed(er) / wet(tter) / weather
wedge, *, ed, ging, gie, gier, giest, A TRIANGULAR SHAPE, METHOD FOR RAISING/ LEVELING
wedible, wet(able)
wedid, wed(dded) / weed(ed) / wet(tted)
wediest, weed(iest)
wedil, wheedle / whittle
wedir, weed(er) / wet(tter) / weather
wedle, wheedle / whittle
wedlock, MARRIAGE
wedlok, wedlock
wednesday, *, A DAY OF THE WEEK (ENGLISH)
wedo, widow
wedol, wheedle / whittle
wedr, weed(er) / wet(tter) / weather
wedth, width
wedud, wed(dded) / weed(ed) / wet(tted)

wedul, wheedle / whittle
wedur, weed(er) / wet(tter) / weather
wee, TINY/ SMALL (or see we/ whee)
weed, *, ded, ding, dy, dier, diest, dless, der, dily, diness, PLANTS MISUNDERSTOOD/ UNDERAPPRECIATED FOR THEIR MEDICINAL QUALITIES (or see we'd)
week, *, kly, SEVEN DAYS IN A ROW (or see weak) "prefixes: bi/ semi"
weekle, week(ly)
weels, wheel(s) / wield(s)
ween, *, ned, ning, DESIRE/ EXPECT SOMETHING (or see wean)
weeny, nies, nier, niest, nsy, TINY/ SMALL, A TYPE OF HOTDOG/ WIENER
weep, *, ped, ping, py, pier, piest, PASSIONATE/ SAD/ INTENSE CRYING, AN OOZING/ LEAKING/ DRIPPING OF FLUIDS (or see wept/ reap)
weery, weary
weevil, *, led, ly, AN INSECT/ BEETLE WHICH BORES INTO PLANTS
wef, weave / we've
weful, weevil
weg, wedge / wig
wegal, wiggle
wegd, wedge(d)
wege, wedge / wedge(gy)
weged, wedge(d) / wig(gged)
wegis, wedge(s)
wegle, wiggle
wegul, wiggle
wegus, wedge(s)
wej, way / weigh / whey
weic, wake / whack
weicap, wake up
weich, wage
weid, wade
weiders, waders
weidor, waiter
weif, wave / waive
weifer, wafer / waiver
weig, wage

weigh, *, hed, hing, hable, her, ht, THE ACT OF MEASURING THE WEIGHT OF SOMETHING, TO FEEL WEIGHT (or see way/ whey)
weight, *, ted, ting, ty, tier, tiest, tless, tlessly, tlessness, ty, tier, tiest, tily, tiness, MEASUREMENT OF VOLUME/ DENSITY/ MASS (or see wait/ whet) "prefixes: over/ under"
weik, wake
weil, wail
weild, wield / weald / weld
wein, wain
weinscot, wainscot
weiol, wail / whale
weir, *, WALL/ DAM BUILT TO SLOW DOWN THE FLOW OF WATER (or see ware/ were/ we're/ wear/ where)
weird, der, dest, dly, dness, STRANGE/ UNCOMMON/ UNKNOWN/ UNLIKELY
weist, waste / waist
weit, wait / weight / white
weiter, waiter
weiv, wave / waive
weiver, wafer / waiver
weivor, waiver
wej, wedge
wejt, wedge(d)
wek, weak / week / wick
weked, wicked / wick(ed)
weker, wicker
wekle, week(ly)
wekur, wicker / weak(er)
wel, well / we'll / wheel
welcome, *, ed, ming, ely, eness, er, INVITE/ HONOR/ ENCOURAGE/ ACKNOWLEDGE THE ARRIVAL OF SOMETHING/ SOMEONE
welcomnes, welcome(ness)
welcum, welcome
weld, *, ded, ding, der, dability, dable, dment, FUSE TWO PIECES OF SUBSTANCE TOGETHER USING A FILLER, HERB (or see wheel(ed)/ wield/ weald)
weldid, weld(ed) / wield(ed)
weldir, weld(er) / wield(er)
weldmint, weld(ment)
welduble, weld(able) / wield(able)

weldur,weld(er) / wield(er)
weldurnes,wilderness
weler,wheel(er)
welfare,rism,ABLE TO FARE WELL AND FUNCTION NORMALLY/ PROPERLY
welfer,welfare
welkem,welcome
welkumd,welcome(d)
welkumt,welcome(d)
well,*,lled,lling,FIT,HEALTHY,STRUCTURE THAT HOLDS WATER SEEPING UP FROM A SPRING,WORD POSED AS A QUESTION,ALSO,IN ADDITION TO (or see will/ we'll/ wheel) "prefixes: un/ up"
wellth,wealth
welo,willow
wels,wheel(s) / wield(s)
welt,*,DISCOLORED/ RAISED AREA ON THE SKIN WHERE DAMAGE OCCURRED (or see weld/ wield/ wheel(ed)/ weald/ wilt)
welter,weld(er) / wield(er)
welth,wealth
welthe,wealth
weltheist,wealth(iest)
welthenes,wealth(iness)
weltheur,wealth(ier)
welur,wheel(er)
wem,whim
weman,women
wemin,women
wempe,wimp
wemped,wimp(ed)
wemper,whimper
wempur,whimper
wemsekul,whimsical
wemsukil,whimsical
wen,wean / ween / win / when
wenar,win(nner) / whire(r) / wiener
wence,wince
wench,hes,hing,DEROGATORY WORD FOR A WOMAN WHO IS FROM THE COUNTRY/ PROMISCUOUS (or see winch/ wrench)
wenchis,wench(es) / winch(es) / wrench(es)
wencht,wench(ed) / winch(ed) / wrench(ed)

wend,*,,ded,ding,TRAVELING ALONG A PATH/ ROUTE (or see wean(ed)/ ween(ed)/ wind)
wende,wind
wendeur,wind(ier)
wendy,wind
wene,weeny / whinny / wiener
wenefer,whenever
wenefur,whenever
wener,win(nner) / whine(r) / wiener / wean(er)
weng,wing / wink
wenging,wing(ing)
wenie,weeny / wiener / whinny
wenir,win(nner) / wiener
wenk,wing / wink
wenking,wing(ing)
wenor,win(nner) / whine(r) / wiener
wens,whence / win(s) / wince
wensda,wednesday
wensdei,Wednesday
wensh,wench / winch / wrench
wenshd,wench(ed) / winch(ed) / wrench(ed)
went,PAST TENSE FOR THE WORD "GO" (or see wind) "prefixes: under"
wenter,winter
wentre,winter
wentur,winter
wenur,win(nner) / whine(r) / wiener
weny,weeny / whinny / wiener
wenzda,wednesday
wep,web / weep / whip
wepd,web(bbed) / wept / weep(ed)
wepe,weep
weped,weep(ed) / wept / reap(ed)
wepen,whip(pping) / weapon
wepenre,weapon(ry)
weperwil,whippoorwill
wepeur,weep(ier)
wepin,whip(pping) / weapon
wepinre,weapon(ry)
wept,PAST TENSE FOR THE WORD 'WEEP',CRY (or see web(bbed)) "prefixes: un"
wepun,whip(pping) / weapon
wepunre,weapon(ry)

wepurwil,whippoorwill
wepy,weep
wepyer,weep(ier)
wer,wear/ ware / where / we're / were / weir
werable,wear(able)
werafir,wherever
weras,whereas
werd,word / weird / where'd
werder,weird(er)
werdest,weird(est)
werdist,weird(est)
werdly,weird(ly)
werdnes,weird(ness)
were,PAST TENSE FOR THE WORD "WAS/ IS" (or see where/ we're/ whirr/ weary/ wiry/ wire/ weir/ worry)
wereble,wear(able)
werefur,wherever
werel,where'll
weren't,CONTRACTION OF THE WORDS "WERE NOT"
werever,wherever
weri,wary / weary / worry
werible,wear(able)
werkd,work(ed)
werkt,work(ed)
werkuble,work(able)
werl,whirl / whorl / where'll
werld,whirl(ed) / world / whorl(ed)
werlpool,whirlpool
werlpul,whirlpool
werlwend,whirlwind
werlwind,whirlwind
werm,worm
wernd,weren't / warn(ed)
wernt,weren't
wers,where's / wear(s) / ware(s) / worse / worst
wersen,worsen / version
wershep,worship
wership,worship
wert,weird / word / where'd
werth,worth
werubel,wear(able)
weruble,wear(able)
werwithal,wherewithal

wery,weary / wary / worry / very
wes,wheeze
wesal,weasel
wesd,whiz(zzed)
wesdim,wisdom
wesdum,wisdom
wesdwurd,west(ward)
wesel,whistle
weseld,weasel(ed)
wesenes,wheeze(ziness)
weserd,wizard
weses,whiz(zzes)
wesh,wish
weshd,wish(ed)
wesil,weasel
wesk,whisk
weskd,whisk(ed)
weske,whiskey
wesker,whisker
weskur,whisker
wesky,whiskey
wesol,weasel / whistle
wesp,wisp
wespe,wisp
wesper,whisper
wesperd,whisper(ed)
wespur,whisper
wespurd,whisper(ed)
wespy,wisp
west,*, terly, tern, ternize, ternized, ting, tward, ONE OF THE FOUR DIRECTIONS ON THE EARTH
westirea,wisteria
westirly,west(erly)
westirn,west(ern)
westirnise,west(ernize)
westle,whistle
westorn,west(ern)
westornize,west(ernize)
westurle,west(erly)
westurly,west(erly)
westurn,west(ern)
westurnise,west(ernize)
westwerd,west(ward)

westwurd,west(ward)
wesul,weasel / whistle
wesuld,weasel(ed) / whistle(d)
wesuls,weasel(s) / whistle(s)
wesurd,wizard
wesus,whiz(zzes)
wet,*, tted, tting, tter, ttest, tly, tness, ttable, ttish, BATHED/ COATED/ AFFECTED BY A LIQUID (or see wheat/ wed/ whet/ we'd/ weed/ wit)
wetch,which / witch
wetel,whittle
weter,wet(tter) / whet(tter)
wetesh,wet(ish)
weth,with
wethar,weather / wether / wither / whether
wethaut,without
wethdrau,withdraw
wethdro,withdraw
wethdron,withdraw(n)
wethdroul,withdraw(al)
wetheld,withheld
wethen,within
wether,A RAM/ BUCK THAT HAS BEEN CASTRATED (or see weather/ wither/ whether)
wethhold,withhold
wethin,within
wethir,weather / wether / wither / whether
wethold,withhold
wethout,without
wethrdraul,withdraw(al)
wethstand,withstand
wethstood,withstood
wethstud,withstood
wethur,weather / wether / wither / whether
wethurle,weather(ly)
wetir,wet(tter) / whet(tter)
wetl,whittle
wetlok,wedlock
wetnes,witness / wet(ness)
wetnus,witness / wet(ness)
wetnusd,witness(ed)
weto,widow
wetuble,wet(able)

wetul,whittle
wetur,wet(tter) / whet(tter)
wety,wit(tty)
weuld,wield / weald / weld
weurd,weird
weurdest,weird(est)
weurl,where'll / whirl
wev,weave / we've
wevd,weave(d)
wevel,weevil
wevor,weave(r)
wevul,weevil
wevur,weave(r)
wewre,weary
wey,way / weigh / whey
wez,wheeze / whiz
wezard,wizard
wezd,whiz(zzed)
weze,wheeze(zy)
wezel,weasel
wezeld,weasel(ed)
wezil,weasel
wezines,wheeze(ziness)
wezt,west
wezul,weasel
wezuld,weasel(ed)
wezurd,wizard
whack,*, ked, king, ky, A SOUND, A SLAPPING ACTION
whad,wad / what / wade / wait
whaddle,waddle / what'll
whadul,waddle / what'll
whake,wacky / wake
whakiness,wacky(kiness)
whaky,wacky
whale,*, ed, ling, er, LARGE AQUATIC MAMMAL, CETACEAN, TO BEAT/ THRASH/ WHIP (or see wale/ wail)
whalep,wallop
whalup,wallop
whar,wear / ware / where / we're
wharas,whereas
whard,where'd
whare,where / ware / wear / were

wharevur, wherever
wharf,es,PLACE FOR BOATS TO DOCK AND UNLOAD/ LOAD ALONG A BODY OF WATER
whars,where's / ware(s) / wear(s)
wharwithal, wherewithal
what,*,A GENERAL WORD USED TO ASK A QUESTION OR LEARN MORE ABOUT SOMETHING (or see watt)
what'll,CONTRACTION OF THE WORDS "WHAT WILL/ SHALL" (or see waddle)
whatel, what'll / waddle
whatever,EITHER WAY, NOT THAT IMPORTANT
whatul, what'll / waddle
wheat,*,A GRAIN (or see weight/ weed/ we'd)
wheb,web
whech, which / witch
whed,wed / we'd / weed / wheat
whedil, wheedle / whittle
whedlok, wedlock
whedul, wheedle / whittle
whee,EXPRESSION OF JOY, SUDDEN EXCITEMENT (or see we/ wee)
wheedle,*,ed,ling,er,lingly,USE WORDS TO COAX/ ENTICE SOMEONE TO GIVE YOU SOMETHING (or see whittle)
wheel,*,ed,ling,ler,ROUND SHAPED DEVICE USED TO ROLL/ TRANSPORT (or see we'll/ well/ weld/ weald)
wheeze,*,ed,zing,zily,ziness,zy,ziness,RASPY BREATHING SOUND DUE TO LUNG IRRITATION
wheld, wheel(ed) / weld / wield / weald
whelm,*,med,ming,OVERTAKE, OVERPOWER, SUBMERGE "prefixes: over/ under"
whem,whim
when,REFERENCE TO TIME (or see win/ wean/ ween)
whence,REFERS TO "FROM/ ORIGIN/ WHEN" (or see wince)
whenever,NO SPECIFIC TIME
whenevur, whenever
whens, whence / wean(s) / wince
whent, went
whep, whip
whepurwil, whippoorwill
wher, where / were / we're / ware / weir
wheras, whereas

wherd, where'd / weird
where,*,IN REFERENCE TO PLACE (or see ware/ were/ we're/ whirr)
where'd,CONTRACTION OF THE WORDS "WHERE DID" (or see weird)
where'll,CONTRACTION OF THE WORDS "WHERE WILL"/ SLANG WORD (or see whirl)
where's,CONTRACTION OF THE WORDS "WHERE IS" (or see ware(s)/ wear(s))
whereas,ALTHOUGH, EXCEPT THAT, OTHER THAN
wherever,NO SPECIFIC PLACE
wherewithal,TO HAVE THE RESOURCES/ TIME
wherl, whirl / whorl / where'll
whirlpool, whirlpool
whirlwind, whirlwind
whers, where's / wear(s) / ware(s)
whert, where'd / weird
wherwithal, wherewithal
whesk, whisk
whesky, whiskey
whet,*,tted,tting,SMALL AMOUNT REMOVED/ ADDED/ CARVED OUT (or see wet/ wheat/ wit/ wed)
whether,WHEN ONE OF SEVERAL CHOICES HASN'T BEEN DECIDED, REFERRING TO CHOICE (or see weather/ wether/ wither)
whetle, whittle
whetlok, wedlock
whetul, whittle
whew,DEEP SIGH OF RELIEF AFTER A STRESSFUL MOMENT (or see woo/ hue/ who)
whey,INGREDIENT IN SOME ANIMALS MILK (or see way/ weigh)
whez, whiz / wheeze
wheze, wheeze(zy)
whezines, wheeze(ziness)
which,CHOICE BETWEEN, CHOOSE ONE (or see witch)
whid, wide / white
while,REFERENCE TO TIME, IN THE MEANTIME, DURING/ AT THE SAME TIME (or see will/ wile)
whim,msy,msies,msical,SPONTANEOUS, WITHOUT MUCH FORETHOUGHT
whimper,*,red,ring,rer,SOFT CRYING/ WHINING SOUND

whimsical,lly,lity,lness,WITH A FRIVOLOUS NATURE, ADVENTUROUS/ FANTASY
whine,*,ed,ning,ey,er,A NASAL/ NEEDY/ PLEADING/ WANTING SOUND (or see wine/ whinny)
whinefur, whenever
whinevur, whenever
whinny,nnies,nnied,nnying,SOUND A HORSE MAKES (or see whine)
whint, went
whiny, whine / whinny
whip,*,pped,pping,pper,BEAT/ WORK INTO A LATHER, LONG DEVICE MADE OF WOVEN LEATHER STRIPS (or see wipe)
whiperwil, whippoorwill
whippoorwill,A BIRD
whipurwil, whippoorwill
whirl,*,led,ling,ler,ly,SPIN AROUND (or see whorl)
whirlpool,*,A CIRCULAR/ SPIRAL MOTION IN THE WATER
whirlwind,*,CIRCULAR/ SPIRAL MOTION IN THE WIND
whirr,*,rred,rring,TYPE OF SOUND LIKE A MOTOR/ SPIRAL (or see were/ we're/ where/ whirl)
whisel, whistle
whisk,*,ked,king,BRUSH AWAY AS IF BY THE WIND
whisker,*,red,ry,LONG SENSITIVE/ SENSORY HAIRS AROUND ANIMALS NOSE/ SNOUT, FACIAL HAIR
whiskey,ALCOHOL FERMENTATION
whisky, whiskey
whisol, whistle
whisper,*,red,ring,rer,ry,SPEAK QUIETLY/ FAINTLY
whistle,*,ed,ling,er,FORCED AIR FROM BETWEEN PURSED LIPS PRODUCING SOUND
whisul, whistle
whit, white / wit / wide
white,*,ed,ting,er,est,en,ener,eness,ening,COLOR PRODUCED BY ALL COLORS OF THE LIGHT SPECTRUM, CALCIUM CARBONATE
whitle, whittle
whittle,*,ed,ling,er,SHAVE OFF SMALL PORTIONS/ SLIVERS OF WOOD
whitul, whittle
whity, wit(tty)

whiz,zzes,zzed,zzing,TO STREAK BY QUICKLY AS IF BLOWN BY A STRONG WIND
who,*,TO REFER TO "IN GENERAL" WITHOUT USING A NAME/ TITLE/ DESCRIPTION OF (or see whoa/ hue/ whew/ woo)
who'd,CONTRACTION OF THE WORDS "WHO HAD/ WOULD/ COULD"
who'll,CONTRACTION OF THE WORDS "WHO WILL/ SHALL"
who's,CONTRACTION OF THE WORDS "WHO IS/ HAS" (or see whose/ hose)
whoa,WORD TO GET A HORSE TO STOP (or see woo/ whew/ woe)
whodel,waddle / what'll
whodul,waddle / what'll
whoever,IN REFERENCE TO ANYBODY,SOMEONE WHOSE NAME/ TITLE IS NOT KNOWN AT THE TIME
whole,eness, esome,lly, ENTIRE THING, ALL OF IT, WELL-ROUNDED,COMPLETE (or see hole/ holy/ wholly)
wholesale,ling,er,SELL WITHOUT PRICE MARK-UP
wholesome,ely, eness, COMPLETE, WELL-ROUNDED "prefixes: un"
wholly,COMPLETE IN ITS ENTIRETY (or see holy/ hole/ whole)
wholsail, wholesale
wholsel, wholesale
wholsem, wholesome
wholsum, wholesome
wholupt, wallop(ed)
wholy, wholly / whole
whom, OBJECTIVE PRONOUN OF "WHO"
whomever, OBJECTIVE CASE OF "WHOEVER"
whomp,*, ped,ping,A SOUND, COMPLETE VICTORY
whoop,*, ped,ping,A TYPE OF SOUND USED IN WAR CRIES, GET A SPANKING/ BEATING
whoosh,hes,hed, hing,ACTION/ SOUND AS IF SWEPT UP BY THE WIND
whoper, whopper
whopper,*, GREAT/ GIANT/ HUGE
whore,*, ed,ring,DEROGATORY TERM FOR A PROMISCUOUS FEMALE
whorf, wharf

whorl,*, led, ling,LIKE A WHIRL/ SWIRL AS IF TURNED ABOUT BY THE WIND, SPIRAL (or see whirl)
whose,BELONGS TO SOMEONE/ SOMETHING IN PARTICULAR (or see who's)
whot, what / watt
whud, what / would
whudel, what'll / waddle
whudevur, whatever
whudul, what'll / waddle
whuever, whoever
whup, whoop
whurlwind, whirlwind
whut, what / would
whutel, what'll / waddle
whutever, whatever
whutul, what'll / waddle
wi, we / whee / why / wee
wic, witch / which / week / wick
wich, which / witch
wick,*, ked, king, ker, SLOWLY SOAK UP LIQUID, A WOVEN COTTON FOR LAMP OIL (or see wig)
wicked, dly, dness, EVIL/ MALICIOUSNESS INTENT (or see wick(ed))
wicker, FURNITURE BUILT OF WOODY/ WOVEN MATERIAL
wid, wide / ride / white / with / wit / weed / we'd
wide, er, est, en, eness, ener, dth, DIMENSION OF GIRTH/ BREADTH, EXTENT/ SPREAD OF (or see white/ width)
widel, whittle
wider, wither / wide(r) / white(r) / ride(r)
widheld, withheld
widin, within / wide(n)
widjold, withhold
widl, whittle
wido, widow
widol, wheedle / whittle
widow,*, wer, SPOUSE WHO LOST MATE TO DEATH
widstand, withstand
widstud, withstood
widt, width / with / wit
width,*, MEASUREMENT/ DISTANCE OF ONE SIDE OF SOMETHING

widul, whittle
wiel, while / will / well / wile
wield,*, ded, ding, dable, der, dy, USE/ GIVEN TO POWER/ COMMAND (or see weld/ wheel(ed)/ wealed/ wild) "prefixes: un"
wiener,*, A HOTDOG/ SMOKED SAUSAGE, ALSO SPELLED 'WEINER', SHORT FOR WIENER WURST VIENNESE SAUSAGE (or see wean(er))
wif, wife / weave / we've / with
wife, ely, ives, FEMALE LEGALLY BONDED IN MARRIAGE
wifes, wives
wifs, wives
wig,*, gged, gging, FALSE HAIR FOR THE HEAD, TO FREAK OUT/ ACT NUTS, BE UNCHARACTERISTICALLY UNPREDICTABLE (or see wick)
wiged, wig(gged)
wiggle,*, ed, ling, MOVE QUICKLY FROM SIDE TO SIDE (or see wriggle)
wigul, wiggle
wii, wee
wiin, ween / win
wiip, weep
wiird, weird
wik, weak / week / wick
wiked, wicked
wiker, wicker
wikur, wicker
wit, while / will / well / wile
wild, der, dest, dly, UNCONTROLLABLE, NO RESTRAINT IN ACTIONS (or see wile(d)/ will(ed))
wilderness, UNTAMED/ NATURAL FOREST
wildist, wild(est)
wildurnes, wilderness
wile, ed, LURE/ ENTICE AWAY FROM (or see while/ will)
will,*, lled, lling, llfully, llfulness, lfulness, lfulnesses, llingly, llingness, DESIRE/ INCLINATION TO MAKE HAPPEN, LEGAL DOCUMENT OUTLINING DIVISION OF PROPERTY AFTER DEATH (or see well/ wile/ while) "prefixes: un"
willdernes, wilderness
willow,*, wy,A TREE, LIKE THE TREE
wilo, willow
wilow, willow

wilt,*,ted,ting,DROOP FROM LACK OF NOURISHMENT AS A PLANT DOES (or see welt)
wim,whim
wiman,women
wimon,women
wimp,*,ped,ping,py,LACK OF COURAGE/ STRENGTH
wimpur,whimper
wimsecal,whimsical
wimsikul,whimsical
win,*,nning,nner,won,nnable,ADVANTAGE IN COMPETITION (or see when/ whine/ wine)
wince,*,ed,cing,TO FLINCH (or see whence)
winch,hes,hed,hing,PULL/ HOIST SOMETHING BY MEANS OF A DEVICE (or see wench/ wrench)
winchd,wench(ed) / winch(ed) / wrench(ed)
winchis,wench(es) / winch(es) / wrench(es)
wind,*,ded,ding,dy,dier,diest,wound,dless,AIR MOVING FASTER THAN A BREEZE, TURN SOMETHING UNTIL TIGHT/ TAUT (or see went) "prefixes: en/ in/ re/ un/ up"
wine,*,ning,FRUIT/ FLOWERS THAT HAVE BEEN CAREFULLY AGED/ FERMENTED (or see whine/ whinny)
wined,wine(d) / whine(d) / wind
winefer,whenever
winefur,whenever
winer,win(nner) / whine(r) / wiener
winey,whine / whinny
wing,*,ged,ging,gless, B RD/ INSECT/ PLANE ARMS, TO AD LIB "prefixes: under"
wini,weeny / whine / wiener / whinny
wink,*,ked,king,QUICK BLINK OF ONE EYE "prefixes: un"
winor,win(nner) / whine(r) / wiener / wean(er)
winsday,wednesday
winsh,wench / winch / wrench
winshd,wench(ed) / winch(ed) / wrench(ed)
wint,went / wend / whine(d) / wind
winter,*,red,ring,ry,SEASON BETWEEN FALL/ AUTUMN/ SPRING "prefixes: over"
wintre,winter / wintry
wintri,wintry
wintry,rier,riest,LIKE WINTER

wintur,winter
winur,win(nner) / whine(r) / wiener / wean(er)
winy,whine / whinny
wiol,we'll / wheel
wiold,weald / wild
wip,whip / wipe
wipd,whip(pped) / wipe(d)
wipe,*,ed,ping,er,REMOVE CONTAMINANT/ SURFACE DEBRIS/ MATERIAL TO CREATE SMOOTH PLANE/ SURFACE (or see whip)
wipen,whip(pping) / wipe(ping)
wiperwil,whippoorwill
wipon,whip(pping) / wipe(ping)
wipt,whip(pped) / wipe(d)
wipun,whip(pping) / wipe(ping)
wipurwil,whippoorwill
wiq,weak / week
wir,wire / were / wear / ware / where / we're / whirr / weir
wird,word / wire(d)
wire,*,ed,ring,eless,ry,METAL STRAND (or see were/ whirr/ weir) "prefixes: pre/ re/ un/ under"
wiri,worry / weary
wirk,work
wirkeble,work(able)
wirkt,work(ed)
wirkuble,work(able)
wirkur,work(er)
wirl,whirl / whorl
wirld,whirl(ed) / world / whorl(ed)
wirleng,whirl(ing)
wirles,wire(less)
wirlpul,whirlpool
wirlwind,whirlwind
wirm,worm
wirnt,weren't
wirpool,whirlpool
wirs,worse / worst
wirshep,worship
wirshup,worship
wirth,worth
wirthe,worth
wirthy,worth

wis,wise / whiz
wisd,whiz(zzed)
wisdem,wisdom
wisdom,KNOWLEDGE GAINED BY EXPERIENCE "prefixes: un"
wisdum,wisdom
wise,er, est, ely, eness, sdom,KNOWLEDGE GAINED BY EXPERIENCE "prefixes: un"
wisel,whistle
wiserd,wizard
wises,whiz(zzes) / wise(s)
wish,hes, hed, hing, hful, hfully, hfulness,HOPE/ IMAGINE FOR THE FUTURE "prefixes: un"
wishus,wish(es)
wisk,whisk
wiskd,whisk(ed)
wiske,whiskey
wisker,whisker
wiskur,whisker
wisky,whiskey
wisol,whistle / weasel
wisp,*,py,LIGHT, AIRY, OF LITTLE WEIGHT
wispe,wisp
wisper,whisper
wisperd,whisper(ed)
wispur,whisper
wispurer,whisper(er)
wisqui,whiskey
wisteria,A FLOWERING BUSH
wistle,whistle
wisul,whistle
wisurd,wizard
wisus,whiz(zzes)
wit,*,tted,tting,tty, ttier, ttiest,QUICK IN MIND/ RESPONSE (or see with/ wet/ white/ write/ wheat) "prefixes: un"
witch,hes, hing,hy, hery,hy,TERM FOR A FEMALE WHO GIVES IMPRESSION THEY HAVE SUPER POWER (or see which)
wite,wit(tty) / white
witel,whittle
with,PREFIX INDICATING 'BACK/ AWAY/ AGAINST' MOST OFTEN MODIFIES THE WORD (or see width)

Column 1	Column 2	Column 3
withaut,without	wizur,wise(r)	wokun,woken
withdrau,withdraw	wizurd,wizard	wol,wall / wool
withdraw,*,wing,wal,wn,hdrew,PULL/ MOVE BACK, RETREAT	wo,whoa / woo / woe / whew	wold,wall(ed)/ wail(ed) / would
withdro,withdraw	**wobble**,*,ed,ling,ly,LACKS STABILITY IN POSITION, NOT STEADY	wolen,wool(en)
withdron,withdraw(n)	wobul,wobble	wolep,wallop
witheld,withheld	woc,walk / woke / wok	wolet,wallet
withen,within	woch,wash / watch	**wolf**,lves,fing,OF THE WILD CANINE/ CANID FAMILY
wither,*,red,ring,SHRIVEL/ SHRINK FROM LACK OF NOURISHMENT/ MOISTURE, MEASUREMENT OF SOME QUADRUPED ANIMALS AT THE SHOULDER (or see weather/ wether/ whether)	wochd,watch(ed)	wolin,wool(en)
	woches,watch(es)	wolip,wallop
	wochful,watch(ful)	wolipd,wallop(ed)
	wocht,watch(ed)	woliped,wallop(ed)
withheld,PAST TENSE FOR THE WORD 'WITHHOLD', TO HOLD BACK	wochus,watch(es)	wolit,wallet
	wod,wad / wood / would / what / wait	wolk,walk / woke
withhold,*,ding,held,THE ACT OF HOLDING BACK, REFRAIN FROM MAKING VISIBLE/ APPARENT	wodent,wouldn't	wolken,walk(ing)
	woder,water	wolker,walk(er) / walker
within,CONTAINED, NOT VISIBLE/ APPARENT	wodercres,watercress	wolkur,walk(er) / walker
withjold,withhold	wodere,water	wolnut,walnut
withold,withhold	woderfol,waterfall	wolo,wallow
withor,wither	woderkres,watercress	wolod,wallow(ed)
without,LACKING, NOT HAVING	wodertite,watertight	wolop,wallop
withstand,*,ding,tood,TO STAND AGAINST,TOLERATE	wodery,water	wolopd,wallop(ed)
withstood,PAST TENSE FOR THE WORD 'WITHSTAND'	wodid,wad(dded) / wait(ed) / wade(d)	wolopt,wallop(ed)
withstud,withstood	wodil,waddle / what'll	wolres,walrus
withur,wither	wodint,wouldn't	wolrus,walrus
witle,whittle	wodir,water	wolsem,wholesome
witness,sses,ssed,ssing,HAVE KNOWINGNESS OF, HAVING SEEN	wodirfal,waterfall	wolst,waltz(ed)
	wodirkres,watercress	wolts,waltz
witnus,witness	wodirtite,watertight	woltsd,waltz(ed)
witol,whittle	wodul,waddle / what'll	woltz,waltz
witul,whittle	wodur,water	wolup,wallop
wity,wit(tty)	wodurkres,watercress	wolupt,wallop(ed)
wiv,weave / we've	wodurtite,watertight	wolut,wallet
wives,PLURAL WORD FOR 'WIFE', MORE THAN ONE WIFE	**woe**,*,eful,efully,efulness,SORROW/ LAMENT (or see woo/ whoa)	wolveren,wolverine
		wolverine,*, ANIMAL IN THE WEASEL FAMILY NOT RELATED TO WOLVES
wivol,weevil	wofal,waffle	
wiz,wise / whiz / wheeze	wofel,waffle	**wolves**,PLURAL FOR 'WOLF', IN THE CANID FAMILY
wizard,*,dry,A PERSON WHO PARTAKES IN ACTIONS INVOLVING MYSTICAL POWER	woful,waffle	wolwrus,walrus
	wok,*, VESSEL FOR COOKING (or see woke/ walk)	wolz,waltz
wizd,whiz(zzed)	**woke**,PAST TENSE FOR 'WAKE' (or see wok/ walk)	wom,womb
wizer,wise(r)	**woken**,PAST TENSE FOR 'WAKE', BRING TO CONSCIOUSNESS FROM A DEEP SLEEP	**woman**,men,nism,nless,nly,nliness,AN ADULT FEMALE
wizerd,wizard		**womanhood**,GROWING INTO ADULT FEMALE HUMAN
wizest,wise(st)	wokin,woken	**womanize**,*,ed,zing,er, MEN WHO DENIGRATE WOMEN

womb, *, FEMALE ORGAN THAT CREATES LIFE "prefixes: en"

women, PLURAL FOR 'WOMAN'
womin, woman / women
womp, whomp

won, PAST TENSE WORD FOR 'WIN' (or see one/wan)

won't, CONTRACTION OF THE WORDS 'WILL NOT' (or see want)
wond, wand / won / wane(d) / wan(ed)

wonder, *, red, ring, rful, QUESTION, PONDER MARVEL (or see wander)
wonderd, wander(ed) / wonder(ed)

wonderful, lly, lness, FULL OF AWE, IMPRESSED
wondurd, wander(ed) / wonder(ed)
wondurer, wander(er)
wons, once / want(s) / win(s)
wonten, wanton
wontenes, wanton(nness)
wonter, wander / wonder
wonton, wanton
wontunes, wanton(nness)
wontunle, wanton(ly)

woo, *, oed, oing, oingly, oer, PERFORM ACTS TO GAIN ATTENTION/ AFFECT ON/ APPROVAL FROM SOMEONE (or see whew/ woe/ whoa)

wood, *, ded, den, dy, dsy, dless, FIBROUS/ NATURAL MATERIAL, STEM/ BASE OF A TREE/ BUSH, HEAVILY TREED/ BUSHY AREA (or see would) "prefixes: under"

woofer, *, LOUDSPEAKER IN SOUND SYSTEM
woofur, woofer

wool, *, len, ly, HAIR FROM THE FLEECE OF ANIMALS
woolvs, wolves
woom, womb
woop, whoop
woose, woozy
woosh, whoosh
woosy, woozy

woozy, zily, ziness, zier, zies, FEELING OUT OF SORTS/ UNSTABLE/ SLIGHTLY DRUNK
wop, whoop
woper, whopper
wopur, whopper

wor, war / wore
worant, warrant
woracity, veracity / voracity
worbeld, warble(d)
worbild, warble(d)
worbler, warbler
worblur, warbler
worbuld, warble(d)
worchroub, wardrobe

word, *, ded, ding, dy, dily, diness, dless, dlessly, dlessness, LETTERS ARRANGED TOGETHER TO CREATE MEANING, USING TOO MANY WORDS TO DESCRIBE (or see war(rred)/ ward/ where'd/ wart) "prefixes: re"
worden, warden
wordn, warden
wordon, warden
wordrob, wardrobe
wordroub, wardrobe
wordun, warden

wore, PAST TENSE FOR THE WORD 'WEAR' (or see war)
woreir, warrior
woren, warren
worent, warrant
worented, warrant(ed)
worentes, warrant(ies)
worenty, warrant
woreur, warrior
worf, wharf
worier, warrior
worin, warren
worint, warrant
worinte, warrant
worinted, warrant(ed)
worinty, warrant

work, *, ked, king, ker, kable, kability, kableness, PERFORM ACTIONS/ TASKS TO ACCOMPLISH A DESIRED RESULT "prefixes: over/ re/ un"
workuble, work(able)
worl, whirl / whorl

world, *, dly, liness, OF/ BELONGS TO THIS PLANET "prefixes: un/ under"

worm, *, med, ming, mer, my, AN INVERTEBRATE WHICH LIVES MOSTLY CONCEALED FROM VIEW (or see warm)
wormd, warm(ed) / worm(ed)
wormer, warm(er) / worm(er)
wormest, warm(est)
wormle, warm(ly)
wormth, warm(th)
wormur, warm(er)
wormust, warm(est)

worn, PAST TENSE FOR THE WORD 'WEAR', USED MANY TIMES (or see warn) "prefixes: un"
wornd, warn(ed)
wornt, warn(ed) / weren't
worp, warp
worpd, warp(ed)

worry, rries, rried, rying, rrisome, yingly, rrier, BE CONCERNED/ FEARFUL ABOUT SOMETHING WHICH MAY/ MAY NOT HAPPEN

worse, st, en, MORE THAN BAD, MORE TROUBLE THAN EXPECTED/ ANTICIPATED (or see worst)

worsen, *, ned, ning, st, CONTINUES TO GET WORST/ DETERIORATE
worsh, wash
worshep, worship

worship, *, pped, pping, pper, ONE WHO IDOLIZES/ ADORES SOMEONE/ SOMETHING

worst, MORE EXTREME THAN WORSE, MORE TROUBLE THAN EXPECTED/ ANTICIPATED (or see worse)
wort, wart / word / ward

worth, hier, hiest, hiness, hless, hlessly, hily, hy, VALUE/ QUALITY OF SOMEONE /SOMETHING "prefixes: un"
worun, warren
worunt, warrant
worunty, warrant
wory, worry
wos, was / woe(s)
wosh, wash
woshd, wash(ed)
woshepl, wash(able)
wosher, washer
woshir, washer
wosht, wash(ed)

woshuble,wash(able)
woshur,washer
wosnt,wasn't
wosp,wasp
wosy,woozy
wot,watt / what / wad
wotch,watch
wotertite,watertight
woturd,water(ed)
wou,whoa
wouk,woke
would,PERHAPS WILL BE DONE/ ACCOMPLISHED, POSSIBLE (or see wood)
would've,CONTRACTION OF THE WORDS "WOULD HAVE"
wouldn't,CONTRACTION OF THE WORDS 'WOULD NOT', WILL NOT BE DONE/ ACCOMPLISHED
wound,*,ded,ding,dless,PHYSICALLY HARMED/ INJURED,PAST TENSE FOR THE WORD 'WIND' "prefixes: en/ un"
wount,won't
wove,en,PAST TENSE FOR THE WORD 'WEAVE' "prefixes: inter"
wownt,won't
woz,was
wozp,wasp
wozy,woozy
wra,ray / raw
wrack,*,ked,king,kful,WRECKED/ RUINED, PERTAINING TO CLOUDS (or see rack)
wraith,writhe
wrak,rack / rake / wrack / rag
wrangle,*,ed,ling,er,BE CONFRONTATIONAL/ ARGUMENTATIVE,TO ROUND UP CATTLE
wrangul,wrangle
wrap,*,pped,pping,pper,COVER/ SURROUND SOMETHING,TO PACKAGE UP (or see rap) "prefixes: en/ un"
wrased,raise(d) / race(d) / erase(d)
wrath,hful,hfully,EXTREMELY ANGRY/ PUNISHING/ REVENGEFUL

wreak,*,ked,king,CAUSE CONFUSION/ DAMAGE AS IF BY MEANS OF RAGE/ VENGEANCE (or see reek/ wreck)
wreath,*,hless,CIRCULAR GARLAND OF VARIOUS PLANT/ ORGANIC MATERIAL, CIRCULAR SHAPE, NOUN (or see wreathe)
wreathe,*,,hed,hing,THE ACTION OF CIRCLING/ ENCIRCLING, VERB (or see wreath) "prefixes: en"
wrech,wretch / reach
wreck,*,ked,king,ker,CRASH/ ALTER/ DESTROY (or see wreak)
wrecker,*,A TRUCK THAT TOWS VEHICLES
wreek,wreak / reak
wreeth,wreath / wreathe
wregul,wriggle
wreker,wrecker
wrekur,wrecker
wren,,A SMALL BIRD
wrench,hes,hed,hing,A HAND TOOL USED FOR TURNING/ TWISTING,TWIST SOMETHING AROUND (or see winch/ wench)
wrer,rear / rare / wear
wresil,wrestle
wrest,*,,ted,ting,TO FORCIBLY TWIST/ WRING/ REMOVE FROM GRASP/ POWER (or see wrist)
wrestle,*,,ed,ling,er,FORCIBLY ATTEMPT TO MANEUVER/ MANIPULATE
wresul,wrestle
wretch,hed,hedly, hedness,POOR/ MISERABLE/ UNHAPPY PERSON
wreth,wreath / wreathe
wriggle,*,,ed,ling,ly,TO SQUIRM/ WRITHE/ MOVE IN TWISTING/ TURNING MOTIONS (or see wiggle)
wright,PROFESSIONAL INVOLVED IN ART/ HAND WORK, AN ARTISAN(or see right/ rite/ writ)
wrigle,wriggle
wrigul,wriggle
wrin,wren
wrinch,wrench
wring,*,,ging,rung,TWIST SOMETHING AROUND TIGHTLY CREATING COMPRESSION (or see ring)
wrinkle,*,,ed,ling,ly,LINES, CREASES
wrist,A JOINT THE ARM (or see wrest)

writ,WRITTEN COURT ORDER (or see write/ right/ rite)
write,*,,tten,ting,rote,table,tability,PUT WORDS/ MUSIC INTO PHYSICAL/ VISIBLE FORM (or see writ/ right/ rite/ wright)" prefixes: over/ pre/ re/ under"
writer,*,,SOMEONE WHO WRITES (or see writ/ right/ rite/ wright)" prefixes: under"
writhe,*,,ed,hing,TWIST/ SQUIRM EMOTIONALLY AND/ OR PHYSICALLY
written,PAST TENSE FOR THE WORD WRITE "prefixes: un"
wrk,work
wrm,worm / warm
wrom,worm / warm
wron,worn / warn
wrong,*,,ged,ging,gly,gness,NOT SUITABLE/ CORRECT/ PROPER/ NORMAL
wrot,wrought / wrote / rote
wrote,PAST TENSE FOR THE WORD "WRITE" (or see rote/ wrought/ rot) "prefixes: under"
wrought,DECORATIVE METALWORK,PAST TENSE FOR THE WORD "WREAK", TWISTED WITH WORRY/ PAIN "prefixes: over"
wrout,wrought
wrudikulus,ridiculous
wrudiquelus,ridiculous
wrung,PAST TENSE FOR THE WORD "WRING" (or see rung)
wry,rier,riest,ylv,yness,TWISTEDLY IRONIC, OUT OF SHAPE (or see rye)
wryth,writhe
wu,whew / woo / what
wud,would / wood / what
wudal,what'll / waddle
wudent,wouldn't
wudever,whatever
wudil,what'll / waddle
wudint,wouldn't
wudnt,wouldn't
wudul,what'll / waddle
wue,whew / woo
wuf,wolf
wufer,woofer
wufir,woofer

wufor, woofer
wufs, wolves
wul, wool
wulen, wool(en)
wulf, wolf
wulferene, wolverine
wulin, wool(en)
wulveren, wolverine
wulviren, wolverine
wulvs, wolves
wum, womb
wumanjud, womanhood
wumen, woman / women
wumin, woman / women
wuminhud, womanhood
wuminizer, womanize(r)
wund, wound
wunderful, wonderful
wunefur, whenever
wunevur, whenever
wup, whoop
wur, were / whirr
wurd, word / where'd
wure, worry
wurj, worry
wurk, work
wurkd, work(ed)
wurkebul, work(able)
wurker, work(er)
wurkt, work(ed)
wurl, whirl / whorl
wurld, whirl(ed) / world / whorl(ed)
wurlpool, whirlpool
wurlpul, whirlpool
wurls, whirl(s) / whorl(s)
wurlt, whirl(ed) / world / whorl(ed)
wurlwend, whirlwind
wurlwind, whirlwind
wurm, worm
wurnt, weren't
wurs, worse / worst
wursen, worsen
wurshep, worship

wurshup, worship
wurst, worst
wurth, worth
wurthe, worth
wurthy, worth
wury, worry
wus, was / woo(s)
wuse, woozy
wush, whoosh
wusi, woozy
wusnt, wasn't
wut, what / would / wood
wutefer, whatever
wutel, what'll / waddle
wutever, whatever
wutil, what'll / waddle
wutul, what'll / waddle
wuus, wolves
wuz, was
wuznt, wasn't
wuzy, woozy
wy, why
x, ex
x-ray, *, yed, ying, RADIATION WHICH PENETRATES PHYSICAL MASS
xagurate, exaggerate
xajurate, exaggerate
xakut, execute
xam, exam
xamen, examine
xamin, examine
xampel, example
xampul, example
xamun, examine
xanth, PREFIX INDICATING 'YELLOW' MOST OFTEN MODIFIES THE WORD
xaspurate, exasperate
xaust, exhaust
xchang, exchange
xdra, extra
xdru, extra
xekute, execute
xemplify, exemplify

xempt, exempt
xen, PREFIX INDICATING 'STRANGE' MOST OFTEN MODIFIES THE WORD
xeno, PREFIX INDICATING 'STRANGE' MOST OFTEN MODIFIES THE WORD
xenon, A GAS
xenophobe, bia, bic, IRRATIONAL/ EXTREME HATRED/ CONTEMPT FOR FOREIGN PEOPLE
xer, PREFIX INDICATING 'DRY' MOST OFTEN MODIFIES THE WORD
xerafit, xerophyte
xeraphyte, xerophyte
xero, PREFIX INDICATING 'DRY' MOST OFTEN MODIFIES THE WORD
xerophily, lous, SURVIVES IN DRY/ HOT REGIONS
xerophyte, *, , tic, tically, tism, DROUGHT/ HEAT RESISTANT PLANT
xet, exit
xhale, exhale
xibit, exhibit
xil, exile
xilene, xylene
ximplify, exemplify
xiraphyte, xerophyte
xist, exist
xit, exit
xklud, exclude
xklumashen, exclamation
xkurshen, excursion
xkuse, excuse
xkuvate, excavate
xodik, exotic
xpand, expand
xpans, expanse / expense / expand(s)
xpekt, expect
xpel, expel
xpens, expense
xpereins, experience
xperumint, experiment
xpir, expire
xplan, explain
xplod, explode
xplor, explore

xployt,exploit
xport,export
xpoz,expose
xpres,express
xpudeshin,expedition
xpurt,expert
xsalint,excellent
xsed,exceed
xsel,excel / accel / axle
xsept,except
xses,excess
xsit,excite / exit
xsploshen,explosion
xsplosive,explosive
xsulent,excellent
xsurpt,excerpt
xsursiz,exercise / exorcise
xtend,extend
xtenshen,extension
xtenuate,extenuate
xtereur,exterior
xtinkt,extinct
xtra,extra
xtradite,extradite
xtrakt,extract
xtrem,extreme
xtrordenair,extraordinaire
xtrordinery,extraordinary
xtru,extra
xturnol,external
xukute,execute
xurt,exert
xyl,PREFIX INDICATING 'WOOD' MOST OFTEN MODIFIES THE WORD
xylafon,xylophone
xylagraf,xylograph
xylaphone,xylophone
xylatomy,xylotomy
xylaudomy,xylotomy
xylem,THAT WHICH FORMS WOODY FIBER/ TISSUE/ STEM IN PLANTS
xylene,* ,lol,A CHEMICAL

xylo,PREFIX INDICATING 'WOOD' MOST OFTEN MODIFIES THE WORD
xylofon,xylophone
xylograph,* ,her,hy,hic,hical,hically,WOOD CARVINGS USED TO EMBOSS SOMETHING ELSE
xylophone,* ,nist, MUSICAL INSTRUMENT
xylose,A CHEMICAL
xylotomy,mic,mical,mous,mist,THE ART OF CUTTING WOOD
xylum,xylem
y,why
y'all,CONTRACTION FOR THE WORDS 'YOU ALL' (or see yell)
ya,yaw / ye / yea / yeah
yac,jack
yacas,jackass
yacht,* ,ting,PLEASURE SHIP
yacs,jacks
yahoo,* ,EXPRESSION OF JOY, ROWDY PEOPLE
yaib,jibe
yaju,yahoo
yaket,jacket
yal,yawl / y'all / yowl / you'll
yam,* ,TYPE OF POTATO (or see jam)
yan,yawn
yandis,jaundice
yanidor,janitor
yanitor,janitor
yaniueri,January
yank,* ,ked,king,TO SWIFTLY JERK/ PULL
yant,jaunt
yaons,jounce
yaquet,jacket
var,jar
yard,* ,dage,ENGLISH MEASUREMENT OF DISTANCE/ LENGTH,THREE FEET,AREA FOR SPECIAL USE
yareu,urea
yareul,urea(l)
yargon,jargon
yarn,* ,SPUN THREADS
yarou,yarrow
yarrow,A WILD HERB
yart,yard

yat,yacht
yau,yaw / ye / yea / yeah
yaul,yawl / y'all / yowl / you'll
yaun,yawn
yaupon,SHRUB HOLLY
yaurd,yard
yaust,joust
yava,java
yaw,* ,wed,wing,VERTICAL ROLL/ TILT ON A SHIP/ VESSEL/ CRAFT (or see jaw)
yawl,* ,TYPE OF BOAT (or see y'all/ yowl)
yawn,* ,ned,ning,EXAGGERRATED STRETCHING OF JAW WHILE DEEPLY INHALING
ye,ANOTHER EXPRESSION OF "YOU"
yea,* ,VERBAL VOTE OF "YES" (or see yeah)
yeah,SAME MEANING AS "YES" (or see yea)
year,* ,rly, DAYS "prefixes: bi/ semi"
yearling,* ,AN ANIMAL IN ITS SECOND YEAR OF LIFE
yearn,* ,ned,ning,LONG FOR/ WANT SOMETHING
yeast,* ,ted,ting,ty,A FUNGUS THAT ACTIVATES FOOD TOWARD FERMENTATION
yeild,yield
yeivac,jaywalk
yel,jail / gel / jell / yell
yelatin,gelatin
yeld,yell(ed) / yield
yeli,jelly
yell,* ,lled,lling,TO VOICE/ VOCALIZE LOUDLY (or see yield)
yellow,* ,wed,wing,wer,west,A COLOR "prefixes: non"
yelo, yellow
yelos,jealous
yelp,* ,ped, ping, HIGH-PITCHED SOUND DOG MAKES ASSOCIATED WITH PAIN
yelt,yell(ed) / yield
yenc,yank
yental,gentle
yeol,jail / gel / jell
yeoman,* ,men,menly,A NAVAL TERM/ POSITION, ATTENDANT TO NOBILITY
yep,yip / yes
yepe,yippee
yeperdi,jeopardy

yer,your / you're
yeraneum,uranium
yerater,ureter
yerathan,urethane
yerc,jerk
yereik,urea(eic)
yerek,uric
yerethu,urethra
yerin,urine
yerinary,urinary
yerinate,urinate
yerolegy,urology
yerolugy,urology
yers,your(s)
yerun,urine
yerunal,urinal
yerunology,uranology
yes,ses,AFFIRMATIVE/ CONFIRM/ APPROVE
yeseg,usage
yest,yeast / jest
yesterday,THE DAY BEFORE TODAY
yet,EXCEPT/ BUT, IN REFERENCE TO TIME
yeti,jetty
yetstrim,jetstream
yeu,ewe / you / yew
yeuld,yield / yell(ed)
yew, *, A TREE (or see you/ ewe)
yewbikwite,ubiquity
yewcaliptus,eucalyptus
yewderis,uterus
yewdirus,uterus
yewdulize,utilize
yewjuale,usual(lly)
yewkalale,ukulele
yewkulale,ukulele
yewl,yule / you'll
yewnafid,unify(fied)
yewnaform,uniform
yewnaformedy,uniform(ity)
yewnasen,unison
yewnasikul,unicycle
yewnatery,unitary
yewnaversul,universal

yewnek,unique
yewnekorn,unicorn
yewneladeral,unilateral
yewnelateral,unilateral
yewnesikul,unicycle
yewnet,unit
yewnety,unity
yewnevers,universe
yewnikorn,unicorn
yewniladeral,unilateral
yewnilateral,unilateral
yewnit,unit
yewnitary,unitary
yewnite,unite
yewnufikashen,unification
yewnusen,unison
yewnusikul,unicycle
yewnutarean,unitary(rian)
yewnuversul,universal
yewnyun,union
yewsd,use(d)
yewshwul,usual
yewtensul,utensil
yewtilutarean,utilitarian
yewtilute,utility
yewtinsul,utensil
yewtopea,utopia
yewtulize,utilize
yewturis,uterus
yib,jib
yiber,jibber
yider,jitter
yield, *, ded, ding, GIVE WAY TO, GAIN/ PRODUCE
"prefixes: un"
yifi,jiffy
yig,jig
yiger,jigger
yigol,jiggle
yigsa,jigsaw
yiincs,jinx
yild,yield
yilt,jilt
yimi,jimmy

yimy,jimmy
yin,jean
yingol,jingle
yip, *, pped, pping, pper, ppee, SOUND/ BARK FROM A DOG (or see yep)
yipe,yippee
yippee,JUBILANT SOUND OF JOY
vipy,yippee
yir,your / you're / year
yiraneum,uranium
yirathan,urethane
yirek,uric
yiren,urine
yirenary,urinary
yirenate,urinate
yirenul,urinal
yirethu,urethra
yirling,yearling
yiruter,ureter
yius,juice
yiutilais,utilize
yo,yaw / ye / yea / yeah / jaw
yob,job
yoc,yoke / yolk / joke / jock
yocert,yogurt
yocurt,yogurt
yoch,judge
yochment,judge(gment)
yodel, *, led, ling, ler, FALSETTO SOUND COMING FROM THE THROAT
yoeman,yeoman
yog,jog / jug
yoga,FORM OF MEDITATIVE EXERCISE
yoge,yogi
yogi,ic,TEACHES/ PRACTICES THE ART OF YOGA
yogol,juggle
yogurt,FOOD WITH PUDDING TEXTURE/ CONSISTENCE(CY)
yohir,jog(gger)
yoh,jog
yoi,joy
yoin,join
yoist,joist

yok,yoke / yolk / joke / jock
yoke, *, ed, king, HARNESS (or see yolk) "prefixes: un"
yokel, *, A LOCAL/ COUNTRY TYPE PERSON
yokert,yogurt
yoki,jockey
yokir,joker / jog(gger)
yokirt,yogurt
yokurt,yogurt
yol,yawl / y'all / yowl / you'll
yoli,jolly
yolk, *, YELLOW PART OF EGG, EMBRYO (or see yoke)
yolt,jolt
yoman,yeoman
yombol,jumble
yomp,jump / hump
yonc,junk
yonchon,junction
yonder, WAY OVER THERE
yongol,jungle
yoni,FEMALE GENITALIA
yonitery,unitary
yonk,junk
yonscshur,juncture
yonster,youngsters
yont,jaunt
yor,your / you're
yord,yard
yoria,urea
yorithein,urethane
yorn,yarn
yosfol,useful
yost,just
yostifay,justify
yostifayabol,justifiable
yostis,justice
yot,jut / yacht
you, REFERRING TO A PERSON OTHER THAN SELF (or see yew/ ewe)
you'll,CONTRACTION FOR THE WORDS 'YOU WILL'
you're, CONTRACTION FOR THE WORDS 'YOU ARE' (or see your)
youbikwite, ubiquity
youc,joke / yoke

youdel,yodel
youdulize,utilize
youduris,uterus
youga,yoga
yougi,yogi
yougurt,yogurt
youl,yule / you'll
youman,yeoman
younanemus, unanimous
younaversul,universal
younavirsity,university
youneladeral,unilateral
younelateral,unilateral
younevirsul,universal
younevursity,university
young,ger,gest,gish,gster, YOUTHFUL, EARLIER YEARS
youngster, *, YOUNG PEOPLE/ CHILDREN
youni,yoni
youniversity,university
youniversul,universal
younivurs,universe
younuvers,universe
youpon,yaupon
your, *, IN REFERENCE TO SOMEONE ELSE'S POSSESSION (or see you're)
yourineril,urinal
yourneri,urinary
yourself, lves, MAKING REFERENCE TO SOMEONE ELSE
yous,use
yousd,use(d)
youseg,usage
youser,user
youserp,usurp
yousery,usury
yousful,useful
youshwule,usual(lly)
yousles,useless
youslus,useless
youtensul,utensil
youth, hful, YOUNG
youthful,lly,lness, OF BEING YOUNG
youtilady,utility
youtilutarean,utilitarian

youtilute,utility
youtopea,utopia
youtulize,utilize
youturis,uterus
youvial,jovial
youz,use
yovenail,juvenile
yovial,jovial
yowl, *, led, ling, ler, MOURNFUL CRY OF ANIMAL/ PERSON (or see jowl)
yu,you / yew / ewe
yubikwite,ubiquity
yubilent,jubilant
yubili,jubilee
yucsta,juxta
yuderus,uterus
yudishal,judicial
yudishos,judicious
yudo,judo
yuduris,uterus
yue, ewe / you / yew
yukaliptus, eucalyptus
yukulale, ukulele
yul,jewel / joule / yule / you'll
yule, PAGAN FESTIVAL AROUND CHRISTMAS (or see you'll/ jewel/ joule)
yuli,July
yun,June
yunait,unite
yunanemus, unanimous
yune,uni
yunecorn,unicorn
yunefai,unity
yuneform,uniform
yuneladeral,unilateral
yunelateral,unilateral
yunesaicol,unicycle
yuneversiti,university
yuni,uni
yunicorn,unicorn
yunifai,unity
yuniform,uniform
yunik,unique

yunion,union
yunior,junior
yunisaicaol,unicycle
yunison,unison
yunit,unit
yunitari,unitary
yuniti,unity
yuniversal,universal
yuniversiti,university
yup,yip / yes
yuraneum,uranium
yuranium,uranium
yuranology,uranology
yurathein,urethane
yurathen,urethane
yureik,urea(eic)
yureiniom,uranium
yurek,uric
yuren,urine
yurenal,urinal
yurenary,urinary
yurenat,urinate
yurenololli,uranology
yurethein,urethane
yurethu,urethra
yureu,urea
yureul,urea(l)
yuri,jury
yuric,uric
yurin,urine
yurinary,urinary
yurineit,urinate
yurinol,urinal
yurisdicshon,jurisdiction
yuriter,ureter
yurithra,urethra
yuritur,ureter
yurnal,journal
yurni,journey
yurnol,journal
yurolegy,urology
yurologi,urology
yurolugy,urology

yuron,urine
yuror,juror
yurs,your(s)
yurt,*,TENT/ DOME STRUCTURE/ DWELLING
yus,juice / use
yusary,usury
yusd,use(d)
yuseg,usage
yuser,user
yuseri,usury
yuserp,usurp
yusfol,useful
yusful,useful
yushual,usual
yushuel,usual
yushwul,usual
yusig,usage
yusir,user
yusirp,usurp
yusiry,usury
yusles,useless
yuslus,useless
yust,use(d) / just
yusurp,usurp
yut,you'd / jut / jute
yutensol,utensil
yuteros,uterus
yutilaiz,utilize
yutiliterian,utilitarian
yutility,utility
yutopea,utopia
yutopia,utopia
yutoupia,utopia
yutulize,utilize
yuturis,uterus
yuv,you've
yuwl,yawl / y'all / yowl / you'll
yuxta,juxta
yuze,use
yuzer,user
yuzir,user
yuzur,use
zafaier,zephyr

zafayer,zephyr
zail,xyl / sail
zailem,xylem
zailin,xylene / sailing
zailofoun,xylophone
zailograf,xylograph
zailotomi,xylotomy
zailou,xylo
zailous,xylose
zaimolochi,zymology
zaimololli,zymology
zaimurchi,zymurgy
zar,czar
zderty,sturdy
zdirdy,sturdy
zdurdee,sturdy
zdurty,sturdy
zeal,lous,lously,lousness,PASSIONATE/ EXUBERANT/ EAGER EMOTIONS
zealot,*,ONE WHO IS FANATICAL/ GETS CARRIED AWAY BY EMOTIONS
zebra,*,AFRICAN STRIPED HORSE
zebru,zebra
zefir,zephyr
zegzag,zigzag
zel,zeal
zeleon,zillion
zeles,zeal(ous)
zelet,zealot
zelis,zeal(ous)
zelit,zealot
zelus,zeal(ous)
zelut,zealot
zenafobia,xenophobe(bia)
zeneth,zenith
zeng,zing
zenge,zing
zenith,hal,HIGHEST/ FARTHEST PEAK/ POINT
zenk,zinc
zenofob,xenophobe
zenofobic,xenophobe(bic)
zenon,xenon
zenuth,zenith

zenya,zinnia
zep,zip
zephir,zephyr
zephyr,FRAGILE/ GENTLE WIND/ FABRIC
zepur,zipper
zerafit,xerophyte
zeraufilus,xerophily(lous)
zerconium,zirconium
zero,oes,oed,oing,NUMBER INDICATING NIL/ NOTHING, TARGET IN ON
zerofele,xerophily
zerofelus,xerophily(lous)
zerofit,xerophyte
zerofule,xerophily
zerofulus,xerophily(lous)
zest,ty,tful,tfrully,tfulness,WITH ENERGY/ SPICE/ GUSTO
zethur,zither
zibra,zebra
zigzag,*, GO BACK AND FORTH WHILE MOVING IN SPECIFIC DIRECTION
zil,zeal
zilafon,xylophone
zilagraf,xylograph
zilaudime,xylotomy
zilaugrafur,xylograph(er)
zilauteme,xylotomy
zilefon,xylophone
zilegraf,xylograph
zilem,xylem
zilen,xylene
zileon,zillion
zilion,zillion
ziliphone,xylophone
zillion,*, EXTREMELY HIGH NUMBER
zilodeme,xylotomy
zilograf,xylograph
zilom,xylem
zilos,xylose
zilot,zealot
ziloteme,xylotomy
zilufon,xylophone
zilugraf,xylograph
zilum,xylem

ziluphone,xylophone
zimerge,zymurgy
zimolege,zymology
zimurge,zymurgy
zinafobia,xenophobe(bia)
zinafobic,xenophobe(bic)
zineth,zenith
zinc,ced,cing,cic,coid,cous,cky,cy,cite,A METAL
zing,*, ged,ging,gy,A SPEEDY/ SHRILL SOUND/ ACTION WHICH HAPPENS VERY QUICKLY, FAST, SPEEDY
zinia,zinnia
zink,zinc
zinnia,*, A FLOWER
zinya,zinnia
ziol,zeal
zip,*, pped,pping,ppy,pper,FAST/ SWIFT "prefixes: un"
zipd,zip(pped)
zipe,zip(ppy)
ziped,zip(pped)
ziper,zipper
zipper,*, red,ring,A CLOSING DEVICE
zipur,zipper
zirafule,xerophily
zirconium,ON THE PERIODIC TABLE OF ELEMENTS
zircouniom,zirconium
zirkoneum,zirconium
zirofit,xerophyte
zirou,zero
ziruphyte,xerophyte
zither,*, AN INSTRUMENT
zithur,zither
zoademy,zootomy
zoagrafe,zoography
zodeak,zodiac
zodiac,cal,DEPICTION OF CONSTELLATIONS AND HOW THEY RELATE TO HUMANS
zoezu,zoysia
zoisa,zoysia
zombe,zombie
zombie,*, SOMEONE WHO IS ROBOTIC/ CONTROLLED BY A NON-HUMAN FORCE

zone,*, ed,ning,nal,nate,nated,nation,A SPECIFIC AREA DESIGNATED FOR SPECIFIC PURPOSES "prefixes: bi/ inter/ intra"
zoo,*, oography,oology,oometry,oomorphic,oophyte, ootomy,PLACE WHERE ANIMALS ARE AVAILABLE FOR VIEWING PUBLIC,PREFIX INDICATING "ANIMAL" MOST OFTEN MODIFIES THE WORD
zoodeme,zootomy
zoofit,zoophyte
zoography,her,hic,hical,hically,RELATED TO THE STUDY OF ANIMALS AND THEIR BEHAVIOR
zoogrufe,zoography
zoology,gical,gically,gist,SCIENCE OF STUDYING ANIMALS AND THEIR BEHAVIOR
zoom,*, med,ming,TO DECREASE DISTANCE BETWEEN OBSERVER AND THE OBSERVED
zoometry,ric,rical,rist,SCIENCE WHICH STUDIES ANIMALS AND THEIR SIZES/ PROPORTIONS
zoomorfik,zoomorphic
zoomorphic,ism,PORTRAY/ ASCRIBE ANIMALS AS IF HAVING HUMAN FEELINGS/ BEHAVIORS/ CHARACTERISTICS
zoophyte,*, tic,tical,ANIMALS THAT RESEMBLE PLANTS
zootomy,mic,mical,mist,STUDY/ DISSECTION OF THE ANATOMY OF ANIMALS
zorgem,sorghum
zorgum,sorghum
zorkum,sorghum
zoudiac,zodiac
zoysa,zoysia
zoysia,A GRASS
zu,zoo
zuamorfik,zoomorphic
zuchene,zuchinni
zuchinni,*, A VEGETABLE
zufait,zoophyte
zufit,zoophyte
zukene,zuchinni
zukine,zuchinni
zum,zoom
zumd,zoom(ed)
zumetri,zoometry
zuografe,zoography

zuografi, zoography
zuolege, zoology
zuolochi, zoology
zuologi, zoology
zuololli, zoology
zuometre, zoometry
zuquini, zuchinni
zurconium, zirconium
zurkoneum, zirconium
zyg, PREFIX INDICATING 'UNION/ PAIR' MOST OFTEN MODIFIES THE WORD
zygo, PREFIX INDICATING 'UNION/ PAIR' MOST OFTEN MODIFIES THE WORD
zym, PREFIX INDICATING 'UNION/ PAIR' MOST OFTEN MODIFIES THE WORD
zymerge, zymurgy
zymirgy, zymurgy
zymo, PREFIX INDICATING 'UNION/ PAIR' MOST OFTEN MODIFIES THE WORD
zymolege, zymology
zymology, gic, SCIENCE DEALING WITH FERMENTATION
zymurgy, STUDY OF THE PRINCIPLES OF FERMENTATION

www.ingramcontent.com/pod-product-compliance
Lightning Source LLC
Chambersburg PA
CBHW080116020526
44112CB00037B/2756